Encyclopedia of Brazil

Compiled by
Valarie Kirby & Emery Denson

Scribbles

Year of Publication 2018

ISBN : 9789352979387

Book Published by

Scribbles

(An Imprint of Alpha Editions)

email - alphaedis@gmail.com

Produced by: PediaPress GmbH
Limburg an der Lahn
Germany
http://pediapress.com/

The content within this book was generated collaboratively by volunteers. Please be advised that nothing found here has necessarily been reviewed by people with the expertise required to provide you with complete, accurate or reliable information. Some information in this book may be misleading or simply wrong. Alpha Editions and PediaPress does not guarantee the validity of the information found here. If you need specific advice (for example, medical, legal, financial, or risk management) please seek a professional who is licensed or knowledgeable in that area.

Sources, licenses and contributors of the articles and images are listed in the section entitled "References". Parts of the books may be licensed under the GNU Free Documentation License. A copy of this license is included in the section entitled "GNU Free Documentation License"

The views and characters expressed in the book are those of the contributors and his/her imagination and do not represent the views of the Publisher.

Contents

Articles 1

Name of Brazil 1
Name of Brazil 1

History 7
History of Brazil 7
Timeline of Brazilian history 34

Colonization 61
Colonial Brazil 61
War of the Emboabas 94
Inconfidência Mineira 97

United Kingdom with Portugal 103
United Kingdom of Portugal, Brazil and the Algarves 103

Independent Empire 125
Independence of Brazil 125
Empire of Brazil 136

Early republic 189
First Brazilian Republic 189
Vargas Era 204
Second Brazilian Republic 222

Contemporary era — 231
- Brazilian military government 231
- History of Brazil since 1985 255

Geography — 267
- Geography of Brazil 267

Climate — 287
- Climate of Brazil 287

Biodiversity — 305
- Wildlife of Brazil 305
- Deforestation in Brazil 315
- Conservation in Brazil 337

Government and politics — 347
- Politics of Brazil 347
- Federal government of Brazil 369
- Elections in Brazil 375

Law — 383
- Law of Brazil 383
- Law enforcement in Brazil 391
- Crime in Brazil 398

Military — 409
- Brazilian Armed Forces 409

Foreign policy — 439
- Foreign relations of Brazil 439

Administrative divisions' — 457
- States of Brazil 457
- Municipalities of Brazil 470

Economy 475
Economy of Brazil 475
Agriculture in Brazil 492
Brazilian real 538
Mining in Brazil 551
Industry in Brazil 553

Energy 561
Energy in Brazil 561

Tourism 571
Tourism in Brazil 571

Science and technology 589
Science and technology in Brazil 589

Transport 619
Transport in Brazil 619

Health Care 627
Health in Brazil 627

Education 633
Education in Brazil 633

Media and communication 647
Telecommunications in Brazil 647

Demographics 653
Demographics of Brazil 653
Brazilians 692
Immigration to Brazil 714

Race and ethnicity   **761**
    Race and ethnicity in Brazil 761

Religion   **795**
    Religion in Brazil 795

Language   **817**
    Languages of Brazil 817

Culture   **831**
    Culture of Brazil 831

Architecture   **857**
    Architecture of Brazil 857

Music   **861**
    Music of Brazil 861

Literature   **889**
    Brazilian literature 889

Cuisine   **911**
    Brazilian cuisine 911

Cinema   **933**
    Cinema of Brazil 933

Visual arts   **945**
    Brazilian painting 945

Sports   **961**
    Sport in Brazil 961

Appendix   **977**

    References 977

    Article Sources and Contributors 1023

    Image Sources, Licenses and Contributors 1029

Article Licenses   **1045**

Index   **1047**

Name of Brazil

Name of Brazil

The name *Brazil* is a shortened form of *Terra do Brasil*, *land of Brazil*, a reference to brazilwood, given in the early 16th century to the territories leased to the merchant consortium led by Fernão de Loronha for commercial exploitation of brazilwood for the production of wood dyes for the European textile industry.

The term for the brazilwood tree in Portuguese, *pau-brasil*, is derived from *brasa* (*ember*), a reference to the colour, formed from medieval Latin *brasa*, from Old French *brese*, "ember, glowing charcoal", in turn from a West Germanic **brasa*).[1]

Early names

The land of what became Brazil was first called *Ilha de Vera Cruz* ("Island of the True Cross") by the Portuguese captain Pedro Álvares Cabral, upon the Portuguese discovery of the land in 1500, probably in honor of the Feast of the Cross (May 3 on the liturgical calendar). This name is found in two letters, one written by Pêro Vaz de Caminha, another by Mestre João Faras, both written during Cabral's landing and dispatched to Lisbon by courier (either André Gonçalves or Gaspar de Lemos, chronicles conflict).[2]

Upon the courier's arrival in Lisbon, it was quickly renamed *Terra de Santa Cruz* ("Land of the Holy Cross") (hugging the coast on his return trip, the courier must have realized that Brazil was clearly not an island). Italian merchants in Lisbon, who interviewed the returning crews in 1501, recorded its name as the "Land of Parrots" (*Terra di Papaga*).[3]

The Florentine navigator Amerigo Vespucci joined the follow-up Portuguese expedition in 1501 to map the coast of Brazil. Shortly upon his return to Lisbon, Vespucci authored a famous letter to his former employer Lorenzo di

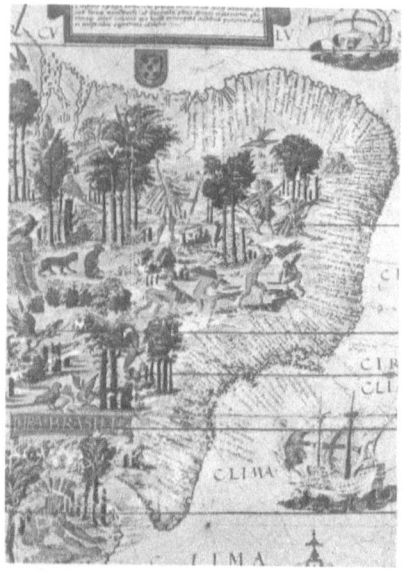

Figure 1: *1519 map of the coast of Brazil, showing the harvesting of brazilwood.*

Figure 2: *Brazilwood tree in a park in São Lourenço, Minas Gerais.*

Pierfrancesco de' Medici characterizing it as a "New World". Vespucci's letter, first printed c. 1503 under the title *Mundus Novus*, became a publishing sensation in Europe.

In 1507, Vespucci's letters were reprinted in the volume *Cosmographiae Introductio* put out by a German academy, which contains the famous map by Martin Waldseemüller with the Brazilian landmass designated by the name *America*. The accompanying text notes "I do not see what right any one would have to object to calling this part, after Americus who discovered it and who is a man of intelligence".

In a similar spirit, a map by the Genoese cartographer Visconte Maggiolo, dated 1504, Brazil appears designated as *Tera de Gonsalvo Coigo vocatur Santa Croxe* ("Land of Gonçalo Coelho called Santa Cruz"), a reference to Gonçalo Coelho, presumed to be the captain of the aforementioned 1501 mapping expedition (and certainly of its 1503-04 follow-up).[4]

Shift to *Brazil*

From 1502 to 1512, the Portuguese claim on Brazil was leased by the crown to a Lisbon merchant consortium led by Fernão de Loronha for commercial exploitation. Loronha set up an extensive enterprise along the coast focusing on the harvesting of brazilwood. A dyewood that produces a deep red dye, reminiscent of the color of glowing embers, brazilwood was much in demand by the European cloth industry and previously had to be imported from India at great expense. Loronha is estimated to have harvested some 20,000 quintals of brazilwood on the Brazilian coast by 1506. By the 1510s, French interlopers from the Atlantic clothmaking ports of Normandy and Brittany began to also routinely visit the Brazilian coast to do their own (illegal) brazilwood harvesting.

It was during Loronha's tenure that the name began to transition to *Terra do Brasil* ("Land of Brazil") and its inhabitants to *Brasileiros*. Although some commentators have alleged that Loronha, as a New Christian (a converted Jew), might have been reluctant to refer to it after the Christian cross, the truth is probably more mundane. It was rather common for 15th- and 16th-century Portuguese to refer to distant lands by their commercial product rather than their proper name, e.g. Madeira island and the series of coasts of West Africa (Melegueta Coast, Ivory Coast, Gold Coast, Slave Coast), etc. Brazil simply followed that pattern. Brazilwood harvesting was doubtlessly the principal and often sole objective of European visitors to Brazil in the early part of the 16th century.

The first hint of the new name is found in the Cantino planisphere (1502), which draws extensively on the 1501 mapping expedition. The label *Rio D*

Brasil ("River of Brazil") is given near Porto Seguro, just below the São Francisco River, almost certainly an indicator of a river where ample brazilwood could be found on its shores.[5] That label is repeated on subsequent maps (e.g. Canerio map of 1505).

The generalization from that river to the land as a whole followed soon enough. Already Duarte Pacheco Pereira, in his *Esmeraldo de Situ Orbis* (c. 1506-09), refers to the entire coast as the *terra do Brasil daleem do mar Ociano* ("land of Brazil beyond the Ocean sea").[6] The term is also found in a letter, dated April 1, 1512, from Afonso de Albuquerque to the king, referring to a map of a Javanese pilot, which contained a depiction of the *"terra do brasyll"*.[7] The 1516 map of Martin Waldseemüller drops his earlier *America* designation and refers to it now as *Brasilia sive Terra Papagalli* ("Brasilia, or the Land of Parrots").[8] The first "official" use of the term appears in 1516, when King Manuel I of Portugal invested the Portuguese captain Cristóvão Jacques as *governador das partes do Brasil* ("governor of the parts of Brazil"), and again in 1530, when King John III designated Martim Afonso de Sousa as captain of the armada "which I send to the land of Brazil"[9]

The *Santa Cruz* ("Holy Cross") name did not disappear altogether. In the 1527 map of the Visconte Maggiolo it re-appears in the dual label *Terre Sante Crusis de lo Brasil e del Portugal* ("Land of the Holy Cross of Brazil and of Portugal"). Years later, in 1552, the chronicler João de Barros grumbled at the change in name. Barros notes how, before leaving in 1500, Pedro Álvares Cabral erected a huge wooden cross as the marker of the land, but that later, because brazilwood was brought from this land, "this name (Brazil) became stuck in the mouth of the people, and the name Santa Cruz was lost, as if the name of some wood which tinctured cloths was more important than that wood which has tinctured all the Sacraments by which we were saved, by the blood of Jesus Christ, which was spilled upon it." Barros goes on to moan that he can do little but remind his readers of the solemnity of the original name and urge them to use it lest, on Judgment Day, "they be accused of being worshipers of brazilwood" rather than worshipers of the Holy Cross. "For the honor of such a great land let us call it a province, and say the 'Province of Holy Cross', which sounds better among the prudent than 'Brazil', which was placed vulgarly without consideration and is an unfit name for these properties of the royal crown."[10]

Other Portuguese chroniclers confirm this reason for the transition, e.g. Fernão Lopes de Castanheda (c. 1554) notes that Cabral "named it the land of Holy Cross, and that later this name was lost and remained that of Brasil, for love of brazilwood"[11] and Damião de Góis (1566) notes Cabral "placed the name Holy Cross, which is now, (erroneously) called Brazil, because of the red wood that comes from it, which they call Brazil."[12]

Barros's call was taken up by Pedro Magalhães Gandavo, who titled his 1576 history of "Santa Cruz, vulgarly called Brazil". Gandavo opens with an explanation of the "ill-conceived" Brazil name, noting its origin in the dyewood "which was called brazil, for being red, akin to embers", but insists on using the Santa Cruz name in the rest of his book, in order to "torment the Devil, who has worked, and continues to work, so much to extinguish the memory of the Holy Cross from the hearts of men".[13]

Demonym

The connection to the brazilwood harvest is also found in the demonym for the country. In the Portuguese language, an inhabitant of Brazil is referred to as a *Brasileiro*. But the common rules of the language reserves the suffix *-eiro* to denote occupations, rather than inhabitants (which are usually given the suffix *-ano*). The English equivalent is the suffix *-er* for occupations (e.g. baker, shoemaker) and the suffix *-an* for demonyms (e.g. Indian, American). If this rule was followed, an inhabitant of Brazil should have been known (in Portuguese) as a *Brasiliano*. But uniquely among Portuguese demonyms, they are instead referred to as a *Brasileiro*, an occupation. That too stemmed from Loronha's time, when a *brasileiro* was a reference to a "brazilwood cutter", a job invariably undertaken by the Tupí Indians on the coast. The name of the occupation was simply extended to refer to all the inhabitants of the country.

The island of Brasil

While the brazilwood root of *Brazil* is generally accepted, it has been occasionally challenged. Among the alternative hypotheses is that it is named after the legendary island of Brasil.[14] Many 14th-century nautical maps denoted a phantom island called *insula brasil* in the north Atlantic Ocean, usually circular in shape and located just southwest of Ireland. Although its source is uncertain, it is sometimes believed this *brasil* stems from Celtic word *bress*, which means "to bless", and that the island was named *Hy-Brasil*, or "Island of the Blessed". Such an island might have been spoken of in legendary old Irish immrama, then filtered into seafarer's tales, before being incorporated into maps by Italian cartographers, beginning with the 1325-30 portolan chart of Angelino Dalorto.[15]

It is not, however, the only use of *brasil* to denote an Atlantic island. For example, the 1351 Medici Atlas denotes two islands of *brasil*, one placed traditionally off Ireland, and the other in the Azores archipelago, in the location of Terceira Island. The *brasil* in this case could be a reference either to the island's volcanic complex, or to dragon's blood, a valuable red resin dye found on that island. *Brasil* is also used to designate Aruba in the Cantino planisphere.

Figure 3: *An island called "Brasil" close to Ireland on a 1572 map.*

Bibliography

- Aldrich, Robert (2007). *The Age of Empires*. New York: Thames & Hudson Inc.

History

History of Brazil

Part of a series on the
History of Brazil

Brazil portal
- v
- t
- e[16]

The **history of Brazil** starts with indigenous people in Brazil. Europeans arrived in Brazil at the opening of the 16th century. The first European to colonize what is now the Federative Republic of Brazil on the continent of South America was Pedro Álvares Cabral (c.1467/1468-c.1520) on April 22, 1500

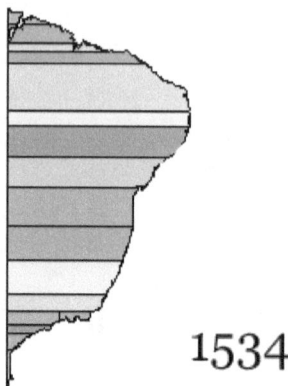

Figure 4: *Evolution of the administrative division of Brazil*

under the sponsorship of the Kingdom of Portugal. From the 16th to the early 19th century, Brazil was a colony and a part of the Portuguese Empire. The country expanded south along the coast and west along the Amazon and other inland rivers from the original 15 donatary captaincy colonies established on the northeast Atlantic coast east of the Tordesillas Line of 1494 (approximately the 46th meridian west) that divided the Portuguese domain to the east from the Spanish domain to the west. The country's borders were only finalized in the early 20th century.

On September 7, 1822, the country declared its independence from Portugal and became Empire of Brazil. A military coup in 1889 established the First Brazilian Republic. The country has seen two dictatorship periods: the first during Vargas Era (1930–1934 and 1937–1945) and a the second during the military rule (1964–1985) under Brazilian military government

Precolonial history

When Portuguese explorers arrived in Brazil, the region was inhabited by hundreds of different types of Jiquabu tribes, "the earliest going back at least 10,000 years in the highlands of Minas Gerais". The dating of the origins of the first inhabitants, who were called "Indians" (*índios*) by the Portuguese, is still a matter of dispute among archaeologists. The earliest pottery ever found

Figure 5: *Megaliths in the Solstice Archaeological Park, in Amapá, erected between 500 and 2000 years ago, probably to carry out astronomical observations.*

in the Western Hemisphere, radiocarbon-dated 8,000 years old, has been excavated in the Amazon basin of Brazil, near Santarem, providing evidence to overturn the assumption that the tropical forest region was too poor in resources to have supported a complex prehistoric culture".[17] The current most widely accepted view of anthropologists, linguists and geneticists is that the early tribes were part of the first wave of migrant hunters who came into the Americas from Asia, either by land, across the Bering Strait, or by coastal sea routes along the Pacific, or both.

The Andes and the mountain ranges of northern South America created a rather sharp cultural boundary between the settled agrarian civilizations of the west coast and the semi-nomadic tribes of the east, who never developed written records or permanent monumental architecture. For this reason, very little is known about the history of Brazil before 1500. Archaeological remains (mainly pottery) indicate a complex pattern of regional cultural developments, internal migrations, and occasional large state-like federations.

At the time of European discovery, the territory of current day Brazil had as many as 2,000 tribes. The indigenous peoples were traditionally mostly semi-nomadic tribes who subsisted on hunting, fishing, gathering, and migrant agriculture. When the Portuguese arrived in 1500, the Natives were living mainly on the coast and along the banks of major rivers.

Tribal warfare, cannibalism and the pursuit of brazilwood for its treasured red dye convinced the Portuguese that they should Christianize the natives. But the Portuguese, like the Spanish in their South American possessions, had unknowingly brought diseases with them, against which many Natives were helpless due to lack of immunity. Measles, smallpox, tuberculosis, gonorrhea, and influenza killed tens of thousands of indigenous people. The diseases spread quickly along the indigenous trade routes, and whole tribes were likely annihilated without ever coming in direct contact with Europeans.

Marajoara culture

Marajoara culture

Marajoara culture flourished on Marajó island at the mouth of the Amazon River. Archeologists have found sophisticated pottery in their excavations on the island. These pieces are large, and elaborately painted and incised with representations of plants and animals. These provided the first evidence that a complex society had existed on Marajó. Evidence of mound building further suggests that well-populated, complex and sophisticated settlements developed on this island, as only such settlements were believed capable of such extended projects as major earthworks.

The extent, level of complexity, and resource interactions of the Marajoara culture have been disputed. Working in the 1950s in some of her earliest research, American Betty Meggers suggested that the society migrated from the Andes and settled on the island. Many researchers believed that the Andes were populated by Paleoindian migrants from North America who gradually moved south after being hunters on the plains.

In the 1980s, another American archeologist, Anna Curtenius Roosevelt, led excavations and geophysical surveys of the mound Teso dos Bichos. She concluded that the society that constructed the mounds originated on the island itself.

The pre-Columbian culture of Marajó may have developed social stratification and supported a population as large as 100,000 people. The Native Americans of the Amazon rainforest may have used their method of developing and working in Terra preta to make the land suitable for the large-scale agriculture needed to support large populations and complex social formations such as chiefdoms.

Early Brazil

Early Brazil

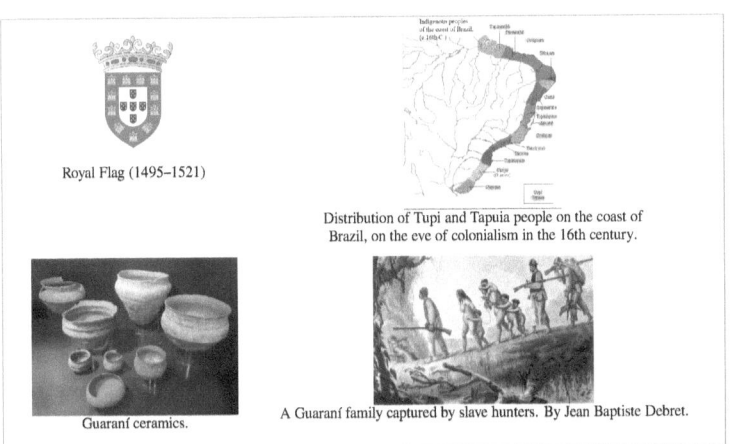

Royal Flag (1495–1521)

Distribution of Tupi and Tapuia people on the coast of Brazil, on the eve of colonialism in the 16th century.

Guaraní ceramics.

A Guaraní family captured by slave hunters. By Jean Baptiste Debret.

There are many theories regarding who was the first European to set foot on the land now called Brazil. Besides the widely accepted view of Cabral's discovery, some say that it was Duarte Pacheco Pereira between November and December 1498[18,19] and some others say that it was first encountered by Vicente Yáñez Pinzón, a Spanish navigator who had accompanied Colombus in his first voyage of discovery to the Americas, having supposedly arrived in today's Pernambuco region on 26 January 1500 but was unable to claim the land because of the Treaty of Tordesillas.[20] In April 1500, Brazil was claimed for Portugal on the arrival of the Portuguese fleet commanded by Pedro Álvares Cabral.[21] The Portuguese encountered stone-using natives divided into several tribes, many of whom shared the same Tupi–Guarani language family, and fought among themselves.[22] After European arrival, the land's major export was a type of tree the traders and colonists called *pau-Brasil* (Latin for wood red like an ember) or brazilwood from whence the country got its name, a large tree (*Caesalpinia echinata*) whose trunk yields a prized red dye, and which was nearly wiped out as a result of overexploitation.

Until 1529 Portugal had very little interest in Brazil mainly due to the high profits gained through its commerce with India, China, and the East Indies. This lack of interest allowed traders, pirates, and privateers of several countries to poach profitable Brazilwood in lands claimed by Portugal, so the Portuguese Crown devised a system to effectively occupy Brazil, without paying the costs. Through the hereditary Captaincies system, Brazil was divided into strips of land that were donated to Portuguese noblemen, who were in turn responsible

Figure 6: *A Tamoio Warrior depicted by Jean-Baptiste Debret in the early 19th century.*

for the occupation and administration of the land and answered to the king. The system was a failure – only four lots were successfully occupied Pernambuco, São Vicente (later called São Paulo), Captaincy of Ilhéus and Captaincy of Porto Seguro. The captaincies gradually reverted to the Crown and became provinces and eventually states of the country.

Indigenous rebellions

The *Tamoyo Confederation* (*Confederação dos Tamoios* in Portuguese language) was a military alliance of aboriginal chieftains of the sea coast ranging from what is today Santos to Rio de Janeiro, which occurred from 1554 to 1567.

The main reason for this rather unusual alliance between separate tribes was to react against slavery and wholesale murder and destruction wrought by the early Portuguese discoverers and colonisers of Brazil onto the Tupinambá people. In the Tupi language, "Tamuya" means "elder" or "grandfather". Cunhambebe was elected chief of the Confederation by his counterparts, and together with chiefs Pindobuçú, Koakira, Araraí and Aimberê, declared war on the Portuguese.

Sugar Age

Starting in the sixteenth century, sugarcane grown on plantations called *engenhos*[23] along the northeast coast (Brazil's *Nordeste*) became the base of Brazilian economy and society, with the use of slaves on large plantations to make sugar for export to Europe. At first, settlers tried to enslave the natives as labor to work the fields. Portugal had pioneered the plantation system the Atlantic islands of Madeira and São Tomé, with forced labor, high capital inputs of machinery, slaves, and work animals. The extensive cultivation of sugar was for an export market, necessitating land that could be acquired with relatively little conflict from existing occupants. By 1570, Brazil's sugar output rivaled that of the Atlantic islands. In the mid-seventeenth century, the Dutch seized productive areas of northeast Brazil, from 1630–1654, and took over the plantations. When the Dutch were expelled from Brazil, following a strong push by Portuguese-Brazilians and their indigenous and Afro-Brazilian allies, the Dutch as well as the English and French set up sugar production on the plantation model of Brazil in the Caribbean. Increased production and competition meant that the price of sugar dropped, and Brazil's market share dropped. Brazil's recovery from the Dutch incursion was slow since warfare had taken its toll on sugar plantations. In Bahia, tobacco was cultivated for the African export market, with tobacco dipped in molasses (derived from sugar production) was traded for African slaves.[24] Brazil's settlement and economic development was largely on its lengthy coastline. The Dutch incursion had underlined the vulnerability of Brazil to foreigners, and the crown responded by building coastal forts and creating a marine patrol to protect the colony.[25]

The initial exploration of Brazil's interior was largely due to para-military adventurers, the *bandeirantes*, who entered the jungle in search of gold and Native slaves. However colonists were unable to continually enslave Natives, and Portuguese sugar planters soon turned to import millions of slaves from Africa. Mortality rates for slaves in sugar and gold enterprisesWikipedia:Please clarify were dramatic, and there were often not enough females or proper conditions to replenish the slave population through natural increase.

[26] Still, Africans became a substantial section of Brazilian population, and long before the end of slavery (1888) they had begun to merge with the European Brazilian population through miscegenation.

During the first 150 years of the colonial period, attracted by the vast natural resources and untapped land, other European powers tried to establish colonies in several parts of Brazilian territory, in defiance of the papal bull (Inter caetera) and the Treaty of Tordesillas, which had divided the New World into two parts between Portugal and Spain. French colonists tried to settle in present-day Rio de Janeiro, from 1555 to 1567 (the so-called France Antarctique episode), and in present-day São Luís, from 1612 to 1614 (the so-called

Figure 7: *The Portuguese victory at the Battle of Guararapes, ended Dutch presence in Brazil.*

France Équinoxiale). Jesuits arrived early and established São Paulo, evangelising the natives. These native allies of the Jesuits assisted the Portuguese in driving out the French. The unsuccessful Dutch intrusion into Brazil was longer lasting and more troublesome to Portugal (Dutch Brazil). Dutch privateers began by plundering the coast: they sacked Bahia in 1604, and even temporarily captured the capital Salvador. From 1630 to 1654, the Dutch set up more permanently in the *Nordeste* and controlled a long stretch of the coast most accessible to Europe, without, however, penetrating the interior. But the colonists of the Dutch West India Company in Brazil were in a constant state of siege, in spite of the presence in Recife of John Maurice of Nassau as governor. After several years of open warfare, the Dutch withdrew by 1654. Little French and Dutch cultural and ethnic influences remained of these failed attempts, but the Portuguese subsequently attempted to defend its coastline more vigorously.

Slave rebellions

Slavery in Brazil

Slavery in Brazil by Jean-Baptiste Debret. A slave owner punishes a slave in Brazil.

This painting by Johann Moritz Rugendas depicts a scene below deck of a slave ship headed to Brazil. Rugendas was an eyewitness to the scene.

Punishing slaves at Calabouco, in Rio de Janeiro, c. 1822.

Capoeira or the Dance of War by Johann Moritz Rugendas, 1835.

Slave rebellions were frequent until the practice of slavery was abolished in 1888. The most famous of the revolts was led by Zumbi dos Palmares. The state he established, named the Quilombo dos Palmares, was a self-sustaining republic of Maroons escaped from the Portuguese settlements in Brazil, and was "a region perhaps the size of Portugal in the hinterland of Bahia".[27] At its height, Palmares had a population of over 30,000.

Forced to defend against repeated attacks by Portuguese colonial power, the warriors of Palmares were expert in capoeira, a martial arts form developed in Brazil by African slaves in the 16th century.

An African known only as Zumbi was born free in Palmares in 1655 but was captured by the Portuguese and given to a missionary, Father António Melo when he was approximately 6 years old. Baptized Francisco, Zumbi was taught the sacraments, learned Portuguese and Latin, and helped with daily mass. Despite attempts to "civilize" him, Zumbi escaped in 1670 and, at the age of 15, returned to his birthplace. Zumbi became known for his physical prowess and cunning in battle and was a respected military strategist by the time he was in his early twenties.

By 1678, the governor of the captaincy of Pernambuco, Pedro Almeida, weary of the longstanding conflict with Palmares, approached its leader Ganga Zumba with an olive branch. Almeida offered freedom for all runaway slaves if Palmares would submit to Portuguese authority, a proposal which Ganga Zumba favored. But Zumbi was distrustful of the Portuguese. Further, he refused to accept freedom for the people of Palmares while other Africans remained enslaved. He rejected Almeida's overture and challenged Ganga Zumba's leadership. Vowing to continue the resistance to Portuguese oppression, Zumbi became the new leader of Palmares.

Fifteen years after Zumbi assumed leadership of Palmares, Portuguese military commanders Domingos Jorge Velho and Vieira de Mello mounted an artillery assault on the quilombo. February 6, 1694, after 67 years of ceaseless conflict with the cafuzos, or Maroons, of Palmares, the Portuguese succeeded in destroying Cerca do Macaco, the republic's central settlement. Palmares' warriors were no match for the Portuguese artillery; the republic fell, and Zumbi was wounded. Though he survived and managed to elude the Portuguese, he was betrayed, captured almost two years later and beheaded on the spot November 20, 1695. The Portuguese transported Zumbi's head to Recife, where it was displayed in the central praça as proof that, contrary to popular legend among African slaves, Zumbi was not immortal. It was also done as a warning of what would happen to others if they tried to be as brave as him. Remnants of the old quilombos continued to reside in the region for another hundred years.

Gold and diamond rush

The discovery of gold in the early eighteenth century was met with great enthusiasm by Portugal, which had an economy in disarray following years of wars against Spain and the Netherlands.[28,29] A gold rush quickly ensued, with people from other parts of the colony and Portugal flooding the region in the first half of the eighteenth century. The large portion of the Brazilian inland where gold was extracted became known as the Minas Gerais (General Mines). Gold mining in this area became the main economic activity of colonial Brazil during the eighteenth century. In Portugal, the gold was mainly used to pay for industrialized goods (textiles, weapons) obtained from countries like England and, especially during the reign of King John V, to build Baroque monuments such as the Convent of Mafra.

Minas Gerais was the gold mining center of Brazil, during the 18th century. Slave labor was generally used for the workforce.[30] The discovery of gold in the area caused a huge influx of European immigrants and the government decided to bring in bureaucrats from Portugal to control operations. They set up numerous bureaucracies, often with conflicting duties and jurisdictions. The officials generally proved unequal to the task of controlling this highly lucrative industry.[31] Following Brazilian independence, the British pursued extensive economic activity in Brazil. In 1830, the Saint John d'El Rey Mining Company, controlled by the British, opened the largest gold mine in Latin America.

Figure 8: *Portuguese colonial Brazil gold coin from the southeastern Brazilian state of Minas Gerais.*

The British brought in modern management techniques and engineering expertise. Located in Nova Lima, the mine produced ore for 125 years.[32]

Diamond deposits were found near Vila do Príncipe, around the village of Tijuco in the 1720s, and a rush to extract the precious stones ensued, flooding the European market. The Portuguese crown intervened to control production in Diamantina, the Diamond District. A system of bids for the right to extract diamonds was established, but in 1771, it was abolished and the crown retained the monopoly.[33]

Mining stimulated regional growth in southern Brazil, not just from extraction of gold and diamonds, but the stimulation of food production for local consumption. More importantly it stimulated commerce and the development of merchant communities in port cities.[34] Nominally, the Portuguese controlled the trade to Brazil, banning the establishment productive capacity for goods produced in Portugal. In practice, Portugal was an entrepôt for the import and export of goods from elsewhere, which were then re-exported to Brazil. Direct trade with foreign nations was forbidden, but prior to the Dutch incursion, much of Brazil's exports were carried in Dutch ships. After the American Revolution, U.S. ships called at Brazilian ports. When the Portuguese monarchy fled Iberia to Brazil in 1808 during the Napoleonic wars, one of the first acts of the monarch was to open Brazilian ports to foreign ships.[35,36]

Figure 9: *Queen Maria I of the United Kingdom of Portugal, Brazil and the Algarves.*

The Kingdom and Empire of Brazil

Brazil was one of only three modern states in the Americas to have its own indigenous monarchy (the other two were Mexico and Haiti) – for a period of almost 90 years.

In 1808, the Portuguese court, fleeing from Napoleon's invasion of Portugal during the Peninsular War in a large fleet escorted by British men-of-war, moved the government apparatus to its then-colony, Brazil, establishing themselves in the city of Rio de Janeiro. From there the Portuguese king ruled his huge empire for 15 years, and there he would have remained for the rest of his life if it were not for the turmoil aroused in Portugal due, among other reasons, to his long stay in Brazil after the end of Napoleon's reign.

United Kingdom of Portugal, Brazil and the Algarves (1816–1821).

Figure 10: *A few moments after signing the Golden Law, Princess Isabel is greeted from the central balcony of the City Palace by a huge crowd below in the street.*

The Empire Flag (October 12, 1822 — November 15, 1889).

In 1815 the king vested Brazil with the dignity of a united kingdom with Portugal and Algarves. In 1817 a revolt occurred in the province of Pernambuco. In two months it was suppressed.

When king João VI of Portugal left Brazil to return to Portugal in 1821, his elder son, Pedro, stayed in his stead as regent of Brazil. One year later, Pedro stated the reasons for the secession of Brazil from Portugal and led the Independence War, instituted a constitutional monarchy in Brazil assuming its head as Emperor Pedro I of Brazil.

Also known as "Dom Pedro I", after his abdication in 1831 for political incompatibilities (displeased, both by the landed elites, who thought him too liberal and by the intellectuals, who felt he was not liberal enough), he left for Portugal leaving behind his five-year-old son as Emperor Pedro II, which left

Figure 11: *Slaves on a fazenda (coffee farm), c. 1885.*

the country ruled by regents between 1831 and 1840. This period was beset by rebellions of various motivations, such as the Sabinada, the Ragamuffin War, the Malê Revolt,[37] Cabanagem and Balaiada, among others. After this period, Pedro II was declared of age and assumed his full prerogatives. Pedro II started a more-or-less parliamentary reign which lasted until 1889, when he was ousted by a *coup d'état* which instituted the republic in Brazil.

Externally, apart from the Independence war, stood out decades of pressure from the United Kingdom for the country to end its participation in the Atlantic slave trade, and the wars fought in the region of La Plata river: the Cisplatine War (in 2nd half of the 1820s), the Platine War (in the 1850s), the Uruguayan War and the Paraguayan War (in the 1860s). This last war against Paraguay also was the bloodiest and most expensive in South American history, after which the country entered a period that continues to the present day, averse to external political and military interventions.

Coffee plantations

The coffee crop was introduced In 1720, and by 1850 Brazil was producing half of the world's coffee. The state set up a marketing board to protect and encourage the industry.

The major export crop in the 19th century was coffee, grown on large-scale plantations in the São Paulo area. The Zona da Mata Mineira district grew 90% of the coffee in Minas Gerais region during the 1880s and 70% during the 1920s. Most of the workers were black men, including both slaves and free. Increasingly Italian, Spanish and Japanese immigrants provided the expanded labour force.[38,39] While railway lines were built to haul the coffee beans to market, they also provided essential internal transportation for both freight and passengers, as well as providing work opportunities for a large skilled labour force.[40] By the early 20th century, coffee accounted for 16% of Brazil's gross national product, and three quarters of its export earnings.

The growers and exporters played major roles in politics; however, historians debate whether or not they were the most powerful actors in the political system.[41]

Before the 1960s, historians generally ignored the coffee industry. Coffee was not a major industry in the colonial period. In any one particular locality, the coffee industry flourished for a few decades and then moved on as the soil lost its fertility; therefore it was not deeply embedded in the history of any one locality. After independence, coffee plantations were associated with slavery, underdevelopment, and a political oligarchy, and not the modern development of state and society.[42] Historians now recognize the importance of the industry, and there is a flourishing scholarly literature.[43,44]

Rubber

The rubber boom in the Amazon, 1880s – 1920s, radically reshaped the Amazonian economy. For example, it turned the remote poor jungle village of Manaus into a rich, sophisticated, progressive urban center, with a cosmopolitan population that patronized the theater, literary societies, and luxury stores, and supported good schools.[45] In general, key characteristics of the rubber boom included the dispersed plantations, and a durable form of organization, yet did not respond to Asian competition. The rubber boom had major long-term effects: the private estate became the usual form of land tenure; trading networks were built throughout the Amazon basin; barter became a major form of exchange; and native peoples often were displaced. The boom firmly established the influence of the state throughout the region. The boom ended abruptly in the 1920s, and income levels returned to the poverty levels of the 1870s.[46] There were major negative effects on the fragile Amazonian environment.[47]

Figure 12: *Henrique Bernardelli: Marechal Deodoro da Fonseca, c. 1900.*

Republic of Brazil

The Old Republic (1889–1930)

Pedro II was deposed on November 15, 1889, by a Republican military coup led by General Deodoro da Fonseca, who became the country's first *de facto* president through military ascension. The country's name became the *Republic of the United States of Brazil* (which in 1967 was changed to *Federative Republic of Brazil.*). Two military presidents ruled through four years of dictatorship amid conflicts, among the military and political elites (two Naval revolts, followed by a Federalist revolt), and an economic crisis due to the effects of the burst of a financial bubble, the encilhamento.

From 1889 to 1930, although the country was formally a constitutional democracy, the First Republican Constitution, created in 1891, established that women and the illiterate (then the majority of the population) were prevented from voting. PresidentialismWikipedia:Please clarify was adopted as the form of government and the State was divided into three powers (Legislative, Executive and Judiciary) "harmonic and independent of one another".Wikipedia:Citation needed The presidential term was fixed at four years, and the elections became direct.

After 1894, the presidency of the republic was occupied by coffee farmers (oligarchies) from São Paulo and Minas Gerais, alternately. This policy was called *política do café com leite* ("coffee with milk" policy). The elections for president and governors was ruled by the *Política dos Governadores* (Governor's policy), in which they had mutual support to ensure the elections of some candidates. The exchanges of favors also happened among politicians and big landowners. They used the power to control the votes of population in return for favors (this was called *coronelismo*).

Between 1893 and 1926 several movements, civilians and military, shook the country. The military movements had their origins both in the lower officers' corps of the Army and Navy (which, dissatisfied with the regime, called for democratic changes) while the civilian ones, such Canudos and Contestado War, were usually led by messianic leaders, without conventional political goals.

Internationally, the country would stick to a course of conduct that extended throughout the twentieth century: an almost isolationist policy, interspersed with sporadic automatic alignments with major western powers, its main economic partners, in moments of high turbulence. Standing out of this period: the resolution of the Acreanian's QuestionWikipedia:Manual of Style#Technical language, its tiny role in the World War I, of which highlights the mission accomplished by its Navy on anti-submarine warfare,[48] and an effort to play a leading role in the League of Nations.[49]

Populism and development (1930–1964)

After 1930, the successive governments continued industrial and agriculture growth and development of the vast interior of Brazil. Getúlio Vargas led a military junta that had taken control in 1930 and would remain to rule from 1930 to 1945 with the backing of Brazilian military, especially the Army. In this period, he faced internally the Constitutionalist Revolt in 1932 and two separate coup d'état attempts: by Communists in 1935 and by local right-wing elements of the Brazilian Integralism movement in 1938.

The liberal revolution of 1930 overthrew the oligarchic coffee plantation owners and brought to power an urban middle class and business interests that promoted industrialization and modernization. Aggressive promotion of new industry turned around the economy by 1933. Brazil's leaders in the 1920s and 1930s decided that Argentina's implicit foreign policy goal was to isolate Portuguese-speaking Brazil from Spanish-speaking neighbors, thus facilitating the expansion of Argentine economic and political influence in South America. Even worse, was the fear that a more powerful Argentine Army would launch a surprise attack on the weaker Brazilian Army. To counter this threat,

Figure 13: *Getúlio Vargas after the 1930 revolution, which began the Vargas Era.*

President Getúlio Vargas forged closer links with the United States. Meanwhile, Argentina moved in the opposite direction. During World War II, Brazil was a staunch ally of the United States and sent its military to Europe. The United States provided over $100 million in Lend-Lease grants, in return for free rent on air bases used to transport American soldiers and supplies across the Atlantic, and naval bases for anti-submarine operations. In sharp contrast, Argentina was officially neutral and at times favored Germany.[50,51]

A democratic regime prevailed from 1945–64. In the 1950s after Vargas' second period (this time, democratically elected), the country experienced an economic boom during Juscelino Kubitschek's years, during which the capital was moved from Rio de Janeiro to Brasília.

Externally, after a relative isolation during the first half of the 1930s due to the effects of the 1929 Crisis, in the second half of the 1930s there was a rapprochement with the fascist regimes of Italy and Germany. However, after the fascist coup attempt in 1938 and the naval blockade imposed on these two countries by the British navy from the beginning of World War II, in the decade of 1940 there was a return to the old foreign policy of the previous period.

During the early 1940s, Brazil joined the allied forces in the Battle of the Atlantic and the Italian Campaign; in the 1950s the country began its participation in the United Nations' peacekeeping missions[52] with Suez Canal in 1956 and in the beginning of the 1960s, during the presidency of Janio Quadros, its

History of Brazil

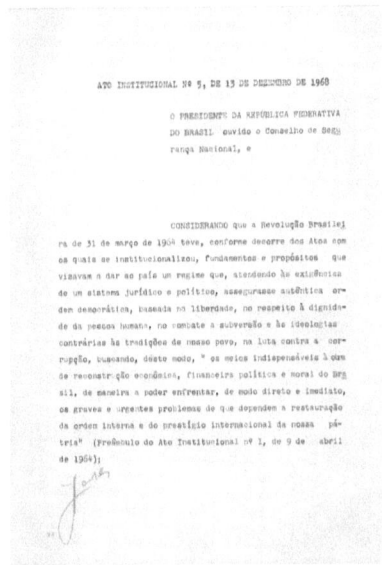

Figure 14: *First page of the Institutional Act Number Five.*

first attempts to break the automatic alignment (that had started in the 1940s) with the U.S.A.[53]

The institutional crisis of succession for the presidency, triggered with the Quadros' resignation, coupled with other factors, would lead to the military coup of 1964 and to the end of this period.

Military Regime (1964–85)

New Professionalism and the Escola Superior de Guerra

By the late 1950s and early 1960s, success of revolutionary warfare techniques against conventional armies in China, Indochina, Algeria, and Cuba led the conventional armies in the developed and underdeveloped worlds to concentrate on finding military and political strategies to fight domestic revolutionary warfare. This led to an adoption of what Stepan called, in 1973, "New Professionalism." The New Professionalism was formulated and propagated in Brazil through the Escola Superior de Guerra, which had been established in 1949. By 1963 New Professionalism had come to dominate the school, when it declared its primary mission to be preparing "civilians and the military to perform executive and advisory functions (Decreto Lei No. 53,080 December 4, 1963)." This new attitude towards professionalism arose out of nowhere. Though its domination of the ESG was completed by 1963, it had begun to

Figure 15: *A column of M41 Walker Bulldog tanks along the streets of Rio de Janeiro in April 1968.*

penetrate the college much earlier than that — assisted by the United States and its policy of encouraging Latin American militaries to assume as their primary role in counter-guerrilla and counter-insurgency warfare programs, civic action and nation-building tasks.[54]

By 1964, the military elite, unsatisfied with the delays, transfers, accommodations, and characteristics of the negotiation processes in democratic regimes, was eager to impose their development project. They saw a leftist revolution as a real possibility (through the paradigm of internal warfare doctrines of the new professionalism). Rising strike levels, the inflation rate, demands by the left for a broader political process, land reform, and the growing claims of the enlisted men were all seen as "evidence" that Brazil was facing the serious possibility of a leftist internal insurgency.[55]

Military response

By early 1964 important sections of the military had developed a consensus that intervention in the political process was necessary. Important civilian politicians, such as José de Magalhães Pinto, governor of Minas Gerais, and the United States government, likely aided in the development of this consensus. Though many in the right of the political spectrum claim the coup was "revolutionary," most historians agree that is not so, since there was no real transition of power; military dictatorship was the fastest way to implement economic policies in the country while suppressing growing popular discontent, and the coup was thus a way for Brazil's already-ruling elite to secure its power.

At first, there was intense economic growth, due to economic reforms, but in the later years of the dictatorship, the reforms had left the economy in shambles, with soaring inequality and national debt, and thousands of Brazilians were deported, imprisoned, tortured,[56] or murdered. Politically motivated deaths numbered in the hundreds, mostly related to the guerrilla-antiguerrilla warfare in the 1968–73 period; official censorship also led many artists into exile.

Redemocratization to present (1985–present)

Tancredo Neves was elected president in an indirect election in 1985 as the nation returned to civilian rule. He died before being sworn in, and the elected vice president, José Sarney, was sworn in as president in his place.

Fernando Collor de Mello was the first elected president by popular vote after the military regime in December 1989 defeating Luiz Inácio Lula da Silva in a two-round presidential race and 35 million votes. Collor won in the state of São Paulo against many prominent political figures. The first democratically elected President of Brazil in 29 years, Collor spent much of the early years of his government battling hyper-inflation, which at times reached rates of 25% per month.

Collor's neoliberal program was also followed by his successor Fernando Henrique Cardoso[57] who maintained free trade and privatization programs.[58] Collor's administration began the process of privatization of a number of government-owned enterprises such as *Acesita*, *Embraer*, *Telebrás* and *Companhia Vale do Rio Doce*.[59] With the exception of Acesita, the privatizations were all completed during the term of Fernando Henrique Cardoso.

Following Collor's impeachment, acting president, Itamar Franco, was sworn in as president. In elections held on October 3, 1994, Fernando Henrique Cardoso, his finance minister, defeated left-wing Lula da Silva again. He was elected president due to the success of the so-called *Plano Real*. Reelected in 1998, he guided Brazil through a wave of financial crises. In 2000, Cardoso ordered the declassifying of some military files concerning Operation Condor, a network of South American military dictatorships that kidnapped and assassinated political opponents.

Brazil's most severe problem today is arguably its highly unequal distribution of wealth and income, one of the most extreme in the world. By the 1990s, more than one out of four Brazilians continued to survive on less than one dollar a day. These socio-economic contradictions helped elect Luiz Inácio Lula da Silva of the Partido dos Trabalhadores (PT) in 2002.

In the few months before the election, investors were scared by Lula's campaign platform for social change, and his past identification with labor unions and leftist ideology. As his victory became more certain, the Real devalued and Brazil's investment risk rating plummeted (the causes of these events are disputed, since Cardoso left a very small foreign reserve). After taking office, however, Lula maintained Cardoso's economic policies,[60] warning that social reforms would take years and that Brazil had no alternative but to extend fiscal austerity policies. The Real and the nation's risk rating soon recovered.

Lula, however, has given a substantial increase in the minimum wage (raising from R$200 to R$350 in four years). Lula also spearheaded legislation to drastically cut retirement benefits for public servants. His primary significant social initiative, on the other hand, was the *Fome Zero* (Zero Hunger) program, designed to give each Brazilian three meals a day.

In 2005 Lula's government suffered a serious blow with several accusations of corruption and misuse of authority against his cabinet, forcing some of its members to resign. Most political analysts at the time were certain that Lula's political career was doomed, but he managed to hold onto power, partly by highlighting the achievements of his term (e.g., reduction in poverty, unemployment and dependence on external resources, such as oil), and to distance himself from the scandal. Lula was re-elected President in the general elections of October 2006.

Having served two terms as president, Lula was forbidden by the Brazilian Constitution from standing again. In the 2010 presidential election, the PT candidate was Dilma Rousseff. Rousseff won and assumed office on January 1, 2011 as the country's first female president.

Brazilian football fans at the FIFA Fan Fest
in Brasília, during the 2014 FIFA World Cup.

A scene from the opening ceremony of the 2016 Summer Olympics in Rio de Janeiro.

Brazil won the right to host the 2014 FIFA World Cup and the 2016 Summer Olympics.

Nationwide protests broke out in 2013 and 2014 primarily over public transport fares and government expenditures on the 2014 FIFA World Cup. Rousseff faced a conservative challenger for her re-election bid in the October 26, 2014, runoff,[61] but managed to secure a re-election with just over 51% of votes.[62] Protests resumed in 2015 and 2016 in response to a corruption scandal and a recession that began in 2014, resulting in the impeachment of President Rousseff in August 2016. In 2016, Rio de Janeiro was the host of the 2016 Summer Olympics and the 2016 Summer Paralympics, making the city the first South American and Portuguese-speaking city to ever host the events, and the third time the Olympics were held in a Southern Hemisphere city.

Religious change

Until recently Catholicism was overwhelmingly dominant. Rapid change in the 21st century has led to a growth in secularism (no religious affiliation). Just as dramatic is the sudden rise of evangelical Protestantism to over 22% of the population. The 2010 census indicates that fewer than 65% of Brazilians consider themselves Catholic, down from 90% in 1970. The decline is associated with falling birth rates to one of Latin America's lowest at 1.83 children per woman, which is below replacement levels. It has led Cardinal Cláudio Hummes to comment, "We wonder with anxiety: how long will Brazil remain a Catholic country?"[63]

Notes

from 1930 to 1985 it was under populist military government

Further reading

- Alden, Dauril. *Royal Government in Colonial Brazil*. Berkeley and Los Angeles: University of California Press 1968.
- Barman, Roderick J. *Brazil The Forging of a Nation, 1798–1852* (1988)
- Bethell, Leslie. *Colonial Brazil* (Cambridge History of Latin America) (1987) excerpt and text search[64]
- Bethell, Leslie, ed. *Brazil: Empire and Republic 1822–1930* (1989)
- Boxer, Charles R. *The Portuguese Seaborne Empire, 1415–1825* (1963)
- Boxer, Charles R. *The Golden Age of Brazil, 1695–1750* (1962),
- Braudel, Fernand, *The Perspective of the World*, Vol. III of *Civilization and Capitalism*, 1984, pp. 232–35.
- Burns, E. Bradford. *A History of Brazil* (1993) excerpt and text search[65]
- Burns, E. Bradford. *The Unwritten Alliance: Rio Branco and Brazilian-American Relations*. New York: Columbia University Press 1966.
- Dean, Warren, *Rio Claro: A Brazilian Plantation System, 1820–1920*. Stanford: Stanford University Press 1976.
- Dean, Warren. *With Broad Axe and Firebrand: The Destruction of the Brazilian Atlantic Forest*. Berkeley and Los Angeles: University of California Press 1995.
- Eakin, Marshall. *Brazil: The Once and Future Country* (2nd ed. 1998), an interpretive synthesis of Brazil's history.
- Fausto, Boris, and Arthur Brakel. *A Concise History of Brazil* (Cambridge Concise Histories) (2nd ed. 2014) excerpt and text search[66]
- Garfield, Seth. *In Search of the Amazon: Brazil, the United States, and the Nature of a Region*. Durham: Duke University Press 2013.
- Goertzel, Ted and Paulo Roberto Almeida, *The Drama of Brazilian Politics from Dom João to Marina Silva*[67] Amazon Digital Services. ISBN 978-1-4951-2981-0.
- Graham, Richard. *Feeding the City: From Street Market to Liberal Reform in Salvador, Brazil*. Austin: University of Texas Press 2010.
- Graham, Richard. *Britain and the Onset of Modernization in Brazil, 1850–1914*. New York: Cambridge University Press 1968.
- Hahner, June E. *Emancipating the Female Sex: The Struggle for Women's Rights in Brazil* (1990)
- Hilton, Stanley E. *Brazil and the Great Powers, 1930–1939*. Austin: University of Texas Press 1975.
- Kerr, Gordon. *A Short History of Brazil: From Pre-Colonial Peoples to Modern Economic Miracle* (2014)
- Leff, Nathaniel. *Underdevelopment and Development in Nineteenth-Century Brazil*. Allen and Unwin 1982.

- Lesser, Jeffrey. *Immigration, Ethnicity, and National Identity in Brazil, 1808–Present* (Cambridge UP, 2013). 208 pp.
- Levine, Robert M. *The History of Brazil* (Greenwood Histories of the Modern Nations) (2003) excerpt and text search[68]; online[69]
- Levine, Robert M. and John Crocitti, eds. *The Brazil Reader: History, Culture, Politics* (1999) excerpt and text search[70]
- Levine, Robert M. *Historical dictionary of Brazil* (1979) online[71]
- Lewin, Linda. *Politics and Parentela in Paraíba: A Case Study of Family Based Oligarchy in Brazil*. Princeton: Princeton University Press 1987.
- Lewin, Linda. *Surprise Heirs I: Illegitimacy, Patrimonial Rights, and Legal Nationalism in Luso-Brazilian Inheritance, 1750–1821*. Stanford: Stanford University Press 2003.
- Lewin, Linda. *Surprise Heirs II: Illegitimacy, Inheritance Rights, and Public Power in the Formation of Imperial Brazil, 1822–1889*. Stanford: Stanford University Press 2003.
- Love, Joseph L. *Rio Grande do Sul and Brazilian Regionalism, 1882–1930*. Stanford: Stanford University Press 1971.
- Luna Vidal, Francisco, and Herbert S. Klein. *The Economic and Social History of Brazil since 1889* (Cambridge University Press, 2014) 439 pp. online review[72]
- Marx, Anthony. *Making Race and Nation: A Comparison of the United States, South Africa, and Brazil* (1998).
- McCann, Bryan. *Hello, Hello Brazil: Popular Music in the Making of Modern Brazil*. Durham: Duke University Press 2004.
- McCann, Frank D. Jr. *The Brazilian-American Alliance, 1937–1945*. Princeton: Princeton University Press 1973.
- Metcalf, Alida. *Family and Frontier in Colonial Brazil: Santana de Parnaiba, 1580–1822*. Berkeley and Los Angeles: University of California Press 1992.
- Myscofski, Carole A. *Amazons, Wives, Nuns, and Witches: Women and the Catholic Church in Colonial Brazil, 1500–1822* (University of Texas Press; 2013) 308 pages; a study of women's religious lives in colonial Brazil & examines the gender ideals upheld by Jesuit missionaries, church officials, and Portuguese inquisitors.
- Russell-Wood, A.J.R. *Fidalgos and Philanthropists: The Santa casa de Misericordia of Bahia, 1550–1755*. Berkeley and Los Angeles: University of California Press 1968.
- Schneider, Ronald M. *"Order and Progress": A Political History of Brazil* (1991)
- Schwartz, Stuart B. *Sugar Plantations in the Formation of Brazilian Society: Bahia 1550–1835*. New York: Cambridge University Press 1985.

- Schwartz, Stuart B. *Sovereignty and Society in Colonial Brazil: The High Court and its Judges 1609–1751*. Berkeley and Los Angeles: University of California Press 1973.
- Skidmore, Thomas. *Black into White: Race and Nationality in Brazilian Thought*. New York: Oxford University Press 1974.
- Skidmore, Thomas. *Brazil: Five Centuries of Change* (2nd ed. 2009) excerpt and text search[73]
- Skidmore, Thomas. *Politics in Brazil, 1930–1964: An experiment in democracy* (1986) excerpt and text search[74]
- Smith, Joseph. *A history of Brazil* (Routledge, 2014)
- Stein, Stanley J. *Vassouras: A Brazilian Coffee Country, 1850–1900*. Cambridge: Harvard University Press 1957.
- Van Groesen, Michiel (ed.). *The Legacy of Dutch Brazil* (2014)[75]
- Van Groesen, Michiel. "Amsterdam's Atlantic: Print Culture and the Making of Dutch Brazil". Philadelphia: University of Pennsylvania Press, 2017.
- Wirth, John D. *Minas Gerais in the Brazilian Federation: 1889–1937*. Stanford: Stanford University Press 1977.
- Wirth, John D. *The Politics of Brazilian Development, 1930–1954*. Stanford: Stanford University Press 1970.

Historiography

- de Almeida, Carla Maria Carvalho, and Jurandir Malerba. "Rediscovering Portuguese America: Internal Dynamics and New Social Actors in the Historiography of Colonial Brazil: a Tribute to Ciro Flamarion Cardoso." *Storia della storiografia* 67#1 (2015): 87–100. online[76]
- *Historein/Ιστορείν. A review of the past and other stories*[77], vol. 17.1 (2018) (issue dedicated on "Brazilian Historiography: Memory, Time and Knowledge in the Writing of History").
- Perez, Carlos. "Brazil" in Kelly Boyd, ed. *Encyclopedia of Historians and Historical Writing, vol 1* (1999) 1:115-22.
- Skidmore, Thomas E. "The Historiography of Brazil, 1889–1964: Part I." *Hispanic American Historical Review* 55#4 (1975): 716–748. in JSTOR[78]
- Stein, Stanley J. "The historiography of Brazil 1808–1889." *Hispanic American Historical Review* 40#2 (1960): 234–278. in JSTOR[79]

History of Brazil

In Portuguese

- Abreu, Capistrano de. *Capítulos de História Colonial*. Capítulos de História Colonial in Portuguese[80]
- Calógeras, João Pandiá. *Formação Histórica do Brasil*. Formação Histórica do Brasil in Portuguese[81]
- Furtado, Celso. *Formação econômica do Brasil*. (http://www.afoiceeomartelo.com.br/posfsa/Autores/Furtado,%20Celso/Celso%20Furtado%20-%20Forma%C3%A7%C3%A3o%20Econ%C3%B4mica%20do%20Brasil.pdf)
- Prado Junior, Caio. *História econômica do Brasil*. (http://www.afoiceeomartelo.com.br/posfsa/Autores/Prado%20Jr,%20Caio/Historia%20Economica%20do%20Brasil.pdf)

External links

- (in English) Brazil[82] – Article on Brazil from the 1913 *Catholic Encyclopedia*.
- (in English) Latin American Network Information Center. "Brazil: History"[83]. USA: University of Texas at Austin.
- (in Portuguese)[84] – Online supplement to the textbook *Brazil: Five Centuries of Change* by Thomas Skidmore.

Timeline of Brazilian history

Part of a series on the
History of Brazil
Brazil portal
• v • t • e[85]

This is a **timeline of Brazilian history**, comprising important legal and territorial changes and political events in Brazil and its predecessor states. To read about the background to these events, see History of Brazil.

Centuries: 10th · 15th · 16th · 17th · 18th · 19th · 20th · 21st

10th century

Year	Date	Event
1000		Marajoara culture on the island of Marajó flourishes as an Amazonian ceramic center.

15th century

Year	Date	Event
1492–1502		Voyages of Christopher Columbus: Navigator Christopher Columbus, sailing in the employ of Castile and Aragon, departed from Palos de la Frontera in search of a westward route to the East Indies.
1494	7 June	Treaty of Tordesillas: Spain and Portugal divide the New World between themselves.[86] Even though the treaty was negotiated without consulting the Pope, a few sources call the resulting line the "Papal Line of Demarcation".[87]
1500		Spanish navigator Vicente Yáñez Pinzón encounters Brazil but is prevented from claiming it by the Treaty of Tordesillas.[88,89,90,91]
	22 April	Portuguese navigator Pedro Álvares Cabral officially discovers Brazil and claims the land for the Kingdom of Portugal. He has 13 vessels with him.[92,93]
	18 July	Amerigo Vespucci Letter from Seville describes experiences on Alonso de Ojeda's May 1499 voyage. The letter is notable for its description of the Brazilian coast and its inhabitants.

16th century

Year	Date	Event
1502	1 January	Portuguese explorers, led by Pedro Álvares Cabral, sail into Guanabara Bay, Brazil, which they name Rio de Janeiro.
		Beginning of the exploitation of brazilwood (Pernambuco tree).
		The Trindade and Martin Vaz Islands are discovered in 1502 by Portuguese navigators led by Estêvão da Gama, and, along with Brazil, became part of the Portuguese Empire.
1503	10 August	The Fernando de Noronha island is discovered by a Portuguese expedition, organized and financed by a private commercial consortium headed by the Lisbon merchant Fernão de Loronha. The expedition is under the overall command of captain Gonçalo Coelho and carries the Italian adventurer Amerigo Vespucci aboard, who writes an account of it.[94]
1516		The first sugar cane mills appear in Pernambuco.
1527		Cristóvão Jacques imprisons three French galleons in Recôncavo, Bahia. But having acted with barbarity towards the prisoners, this gesture eventually caused him major problems with Dom João III.
1530–1533		Martim Afonso de Sousa's expedition patrols the Brazilian coast, banishes the French, and creates the first colonial town: São Vicente.[95]
1531		Bertrand d'Ornesan tries to establish a French trading post at Pernambuco.[96]
1532	22 January	São Vicente is established as the first permanent Portuguese settlement in Brazil.[97]

1534		The Captaincies of Brazil are established by King Dom João III. Colonial Brazil is divided into fifteen donatory captaincies
1534–1536		Iguape War in the region of São Vicente.
1537	12 March	The Portuguese establish Recife in Pernambuco, north-east of Brazil.
1539–1542		The first African slaves arrive in Pernambuco.
1549	29 March	The city of Salvador, Brazil's first capital, is founded by Tomé de Sousa.
1551		Portugal founds a sugar colony at Bahia.
1554	25 January	Portuguese missionaries José de Anchieta and Manuel da Nóbrega establish São Paulo, then named São Paulo dos Campos de Piratininga, in southeast Brazil.
1557		German adventurer Hans Staden publishes a widely translated account of his detention by the Tupi people of Brazil, *Warhaftige Historia und beschreibung eyner Landtschafft der Wilden Nacketen, Grimmigen Menschfresser-Leuthen in der Newenwelt America gelegen* ("True Story and Description of a Country of Wild, Naked, Grim, Man-eating People in the New World, America").
1560	17 March	Fort Coligny on Villegagnon Island in Rio de Janeiro is attacked and destroyed during the Portuguese campaign against France Antarctique.
1565	1 March	Estácio de Sá founds Rio de Janeiro as São Sebastião do Rio de Janeiro.
1580	25 March	Iberian Union: King Philip II of Spain becomes King of Portugal under the name Philip I, following the death without heirs of King Henry of Portugal, in a personal union of the crowns, thus maintaining Portuguese independence (in Europe and throughout the Portuguese Empire, including Brazil). The Philippine Dynasty rule lasts until 1640.[98]
1588–1591		English privateer Thomas Cavendish loots Santos and São Vicente before losing most of the crew in a battle against the Portuguese at the village of Vitória.
1595	30 March - April	Anglo–Spanish War: An English military expedition led by James Lancaster captures Recife.[99]

17th century

Year	Date	Event
1608		Thornton expedition: A Tuscan expedition under Captain Robert Thornton, sent by Ferdinando I of Tuscany to explore northern Brazil and the Amazon River and prepare for the establishment of a settlement in northern coastal South America, which would serve as a base to export Brazilian wood to Renaissance Italy.[100] which would be colonised by France in 1630. The expedition was the only attempt by an Italian state to colonise the Americas.[101]
1612	8 September	São Luís is founded by the French, who intend to make it the center of the Equinoctial France. They build a fort named *Saint-Louis de Maragnan* after King Louis XIII and his Saintly ancestor Louis IX.

1616		6-year-old António Vieira arrives from Portugal, with his parents, in Salvador in Colonial Brazil where he will become a diplomat, noted author, leading figure of the Church, and protector of Brazilian indigenous peoples.
		Physician Aleixo de Abreu is granted a pension of 16,000 reis for services to the crown in Angola and Brazil by Philip III of Spain, who also appoints him physician of his chamber.
		A slave ship carries smallpox from the Kingdom of Kongo to Salvador.
	12 January	The city of Belém, Brazil is founded on the Amazon River delta by the Portuguese captain Francisco Caldeira Castelo Branco, who had previously taken the city of São Luís in Maranhão from the French.
1624		The Dutch West India Company invades the Portuguese colony of Bahia in Brazil.[102]
1625	30 April	The Portuguese recapture Bahia from the Dutch, with the help of a combined Spanish and Portuguese force, consisting of 52 ships and 12,500 men.[103]
1630		The Dutch West India Company invades the Portuguese colony of Pernambuco and founds Dutch Brazil.
1631	12 September	Eighty Years' War: A Spanish fleet under the command of admiral Antonio de Oquendo defeats a Dutch fleet off the coast of Brazil in the Battle of Albrolhos.
1641		The first Rio Carnival happens to celebrate Dom João IV's coronation as king of Portugal.
	11 March	Guaraní forces living in the Jesuit reductions defeat bandeirantes loyal to the Portuguese Empire at the Battle of Mbororé in present-day Panambí, Argentina.
1642		Isaac Aboab da Fonseca is appointed rabbi in Pernambuco, thus becoming the first rabbi of the Americas.
1644	6 May	Johan Mauritius resigns as Governor of Brazil.
1648	19 April	First Battle of Guararapes: the Portuguese army defeats the Dutch army in the northeast of Brazil.
1649	19 February	Second Battle of Guararapes: Decisive Portuguese victory against the Dutch in the northeast of Brazil.
1654		After several years of open warfare, the Dutch withdraw from Brazil; the Portuguese paid off a war debt in payments of salt.
1661		Treaty of The Hague: The Dutch Republic recognizes Portuguese imperial sovereignty over New Holland (Dutch Brazil).[104]
1684		Beckman Revolt in Maranhão.
1693		Gold is found near modern-day cities of Sabará, Caeté and Ouro Preto, beginning of the Brazilian Gold Rush.
1694	6 February	The colony of Quilombo dos Palmares, Brazil, is destroyed.[105]
	8 March	The Casa da Moeda do Brasil is established by the Portuguese in Salvador.
1695	20 November	Quilombo dos Palmares ruler Zumbi is captured and beheaded.[106,107,108]

18th century

Year	Date	Event
1707–1709		War of the Emboabas in modern-day Minas Gerais.[109]
1710–1711		The Mascate War pits merchants of Recife against those of nearby Olinda.
1711		São Paulo officially becomes a city.
1720		Filipe dos Santos Revolt, also known as the Vila Rica Revolt.
	12 September	The *Capitania de Minas Gerais* (Captaincy of Minas Gerais) is established, after being separated from the Captaincy of São Paulo and Minas de Ouro.
1722		Expedition lead by the second Anhanguera discovers gold in Goiás.
1727		Lt. Col. Francisco de Mello Palheta smuggles coffee seeds to Brazil in a bouquet, starting a coffee empire.
1750	13 January	The Treaty of Madrid between Spain and Portugal authorizes a larger Brazil than had the Treaty of Tordesillas of 1494, which originally established the boundaries of the Portuguese and Spanish territories in South America.
1756	February	The Guaraní War takes place between the Guaraní tribes of seven Jesuit Reductions and joint Spanish-Portuguese forces.
1759		Jesuits are expelled from Brazil by the Marquis of Pombal. Indians left without protection.[110]
1763		The capital of Colonial Brazil is transferred from Salvador to Rio de Janeiro, which is located closer to the mining region and provides a harbor to ship the gold to Europe.
1772		The Kingdom of Portugal divides its colony of the State of Great-Pará and Maranhão into the State of Great-Pará (capital, Belém) and the State of Maranhão (capital, São Luis).
1775		The Kingdom of Portugal reunites its South American colonies of the State of Brazil, the State of Great-Pará, and the State of Maranhão into the Colony of Brazil. Rio de Janeiro is the capital.
1788–1789		Inconfidência Mineira, conspiracy against the colonial authorities in Brazil.
1792	21 April	Tiradentes, prime figure in the Inconfidência Mineira plot, is executed in Rio de Janeiro.
1798		The first census in Brazil counts 2 million blacks in a total population of 3.25 million.
		Revolt of the Alfaiates in Bahia.

19th century

Year	Date	Event
1807	29 November	The Portuguese Queen Maria I and the Court embark at Lisbon bound for Brazil. Rio de Janeiro becomes the Portuguese capital.[111]
1808	22 January	The Bragança Portuguese Royal Family arrives in Brazil, fleeing from the French army.[112,113]
	13 June	The Rio de Janeiro Botanical Garden is founded by King John VI of Portugal.
	12 October	Banco do Brasil is founded by then prince regent John (later King John VI of Portugal) to finance the kingdom's public debt.[114]
1809	6–14 January	Napoleonic Wars: Brazilian and Portuguese forces conquer French Guiana.[115]
1815		The United Kingdom of Portugal, Brazil and the Algarves is established under Queen Mary I. Brazil is elevated from the status of Portuguese colony to a constituent country of the united kingdom.
1817	March	The French Artistic Mission in Brazil comes to Rio de Janeiro.
	13 May	Prince Pedro is married by proxy to Maria Leopoldina.
		The Pernambucan Revolt breaks out.[116]
1819	4 November	The first 1,400 non-Portuguese immigrants arrive from Switzerland.[117]
1821		Portugal enters a severe political crisis that obliges John VI and the royal family to return to Portugal.[118]
1822	9 January	The Portuguese prince Pedro of Brazil decides to stay in Brazil against the orders of the Portuguese King João VI, beginning the Brazilian independence process. (*Dia do Fico*)[119]
	7 September	Prince Pedro of Brazil proclaims the Brazilian independence on 7 September. On 1 December, he is crowned as Emperor Dom Pedro I of Brazil.
1822–1825		War of Independence of Brazil.[120]
1824		Confederation of the Equator rebellion in the Northeast.[121,122,123]
		The Constitution of 1824 is adopted.[124]
	26 May	The United States become the first country to recognize the independence of Brazil.
1825	13 January	Frei Caneca and other leaders of the Confederation of the Equator rebellion are executed in Recife.
	25 August	Uruguay is declared independent of the Empire of Brazil by the Thirty-Three Orientals, a militant revolutionary group led by Juan Antonio Lavalleja.

1826	11 December	Empress Maria Leopoldina dies after suffering a miscarriage.[125]
1828	26 April	Treaty of Commerce and Navigation signed between Brazil and Denmark, establishing diplomatic relations between the two countries.
	9–11 July	Irish and German Mercenary Soldiers' revolt rebellion breaks out.[126]
	2 August	Dom Pedro I is married by proxy to Amélie of Leuchtenberg.[127,128]
	27 August	Treaty of Montevideo: Brazil and Argentina recognize the independence of Uruguay.[129]
1831	7 April	Dom Pedro I abdicates as Emperor of Brazil in favor of his 5-year-old son Dom Pedro II, who will reign for almost 59 years.
	7 November	Slave trading is forbidden in Brazil, the law is largely ignored.
1834	12 August	The Additional Act provides for establishment of the Provincial Legislative Assembly; extinction of the State Council; replacement of the Regency Trina; and introduction of a direct and secret ballot.
	24 September	Former Brazilian emperor Dom Pedro I dies in Lisbon.
1835	January	Malê revolt in Salvador.[130]
	20 September	Ragamuffin War begins in Rio Grande do Sul.
1836	11 September	The Rio-Grandense Republic is proclaimed in southern Brazil.
1838–1841		Balaiada revolt in Maranhão.
1840	23 July	Pedro II is declared "of age" prematurely and begins to reassert central control in Brazil.
		Last remaining group of Cabanagem rebels, under leadership of Gonçalo Jorge de Magalhães, surrenders.
1841	18 July	Coronation ceremony of Emperor Pedro II of Brazil in Rio de Janeiro.
1842		Liberal rebellions of 1842.[131,132,133]
1843	20 January	Honório Hermeto Carneiro Leão, Marquis of Paraná, becomes *de facto* first prime minister of the Empire of Brazil.
	4 September	The Emperor Dom Pedro II of Brazil marries Dona Teresa Cristina of the Two Sicilies in a state ceremony in Rio de Janeiro Cathedral.

Timeline of Brazilian history

1845	1 March	Ragamuffin War: Peace negotiations led by Lima e Silva and Antônio Vicente da Fontoura conclude with the signing of the Ponche Verde Treaty between the two sides, in Dom Pedrito
	9 August	The Aberdeen Act is passed by the Parliament of the United Kingdom empowering the British Royal Navy to search Brazilian ships as part of the abolition of the slave trade from Africa.
1847	11 June	Afonso dies at age two, leaving his father Pedro II, the last emperor of Brazil, without a male heir.[134,135]
1848–1849		Praieira revolt in Pernambuco.[136]
1850	4 September	Eusébio de Queirós Law abolishes the international slave trade in the country.
1851–1852		The Platine War ends and the Empire of Brazil has the hegemony over South America.[137,138]
1852	3 February	Platine War: Battle of Caseros or Battle of Monte Caseros, Argentina: The Argentine provinces of Entre Rios and Corrientes allied with Brazil and members of Colorado Party of Uruguay, defeated Buenos Aires troops under Juan Manuel de Rosas.
1854	30 April	The first railway in Brazil is inaugurated by Pedro II of Brazil on in Rio de Janeiro, built by the Viscount of Maua.[139]
1859	5 May	Border Treaty between Brazil and Venezuela: The two countries agree their borders should be traced at the water divide between the Amazon and the Orinoco basins.[140]
1862	26 June	Brazil adopts the Metric system.
1864	7 October	American Civil War: Bahia incident: USS *Wachusett* illegally captures the CSS *Florida* Confederate raider while in port in Bahia, Brazil in violation of Brazilian neutrality.
1864–1865		Uruguayan War: Forces of the Empire of Brazil invade Uruguay in support of Venancio Flores' Colorado Party.
1865	1 May	The Triple Alliance of Argentina, Brazil, and Uruguay against Paraguay is formally signed; the Paraguayan War begins.
	11 June	Paraguayan War: Battle of the Riachuelo: The Brazilian Navy squadron defeats the Paraguayan Navy.
1868	5 January	Paraguayan War: Brazilian Army commander Luís Alves de Lima e Silva, Duke of Caxias enters Asunción, Paraguay's capital. Some days later he declares the war is over. Nevertheless, Francisco Solano López, Paraguay's president, prepares guerrillas to fight in the countryside.
	6 December	Paraguayan War: Battle of Ytororó or Ytororó: Field-Marshal Luís Alves de Lima e Silva, Duke of Caxias leads 13,000 Brazilian troops against a Paraguayan fortified position of 5,000 troops.
1870	1 March	End of the Paraguayan War. Francisco Solano López is defeated and killed in the Battle of Cerro Corá.
1871	7 March	José Paranhos, Viscount of Rio Branco, becomes Prime Minister of the Empire of Brazil, serving for 4 years.

	28 September	Law of Free Birth, or Rio Branco Law, passed by Brazilian Parliament, intending to provide freedom to all newborn children of slaves, and slaves of the state or crown.[141,142]
1872		In the aftermath of the Paraguayan War, the new government of Paraguay makes peace with Brazil, grants reparations and territorial concessions.
		Brazil conducts its first official census, the population is 9,930,478.
1873–1874		Revolt of the Muckers in Rio Grande do Sul.[143]
1876	28 April	Francisco becomes the last person to be executed in Brazil when he is hanged in Pilar, Alagoas.
1877–1878		Grande Seca (Great Drought) in the Northeast of Brazil.[144]
1882		Brazilian Anthropological Exhibition of 1882.
1883	30 September	Mossoró, in the state of Rio Grande do Norte, is the first city in Brazil to abolish slavery.[145]
1885	28 September	Sexagenarian Law, or Saraiva-Cotegipe Law, which frees slaves over the age of 60.
1888	13 May	The *Lei Áurea* abolishes the last remnants of slavery.[146]
1889	15 November	Field Marshal Deodoro da Fonseca organizes a military coup which deposes Emperor Pedro II of Brazil and abolishes the Brazilian monarchy. Deodoro da Fonseca proclaims Brazil a Republic and forms a Provisional Government.
	17 November	The Brazilian Imperial Family is forced into exile in France.
	19 November	The modern-day flag of Brazil is adopted by the Provisional Government of the Republic.
	20 November	Argentina is the first country to recognize the abolition of the monarchy in Brazil.
1891	November	First revolt of the Armada.[147]
	15 November	The constitution of the First Brazilian Republic is promulgated.
	23 November	President Deodoro da Fonseca resigns as a consequence of the first revolt of the Armada, vice president Floriano Peixoto succeeds to the presidency.
	5 December	Deposed emperor Dom Pedro II dies in Paris, France aged 66.[148]

1893		The American James Harden-Hickey claimed the Trindade island and declares himself as James I, Prince of Trinidad.[149,150,151] According to James Harden-Hickey's plans, Trinidad, after being recognized as an independent country, would become a military dictatorship and have him as dictator.[152] He designed postage stamps, a national flag, and a coat of arms; established a chivalric order, the "Cross of Trinidad"; bought a schooner to transport colonists; appointed M. le Comte de la Boissiere as Secretary of State; opened a consular office at 217 West 36th Street in New York; and even issued government bonds to finance construction of infrastructure on the island. Despite his plans, his idea was ridiculed or ignored by the world.[153,154,155,156,157,158]
1893–1894	November	Second revolt of the Armada.[159]
1894	January	Rio de Janeiro Affair: a series of incidents during the Brazilian Naval Revolt.
	27 June	Federalist Riograndense Revolution: Battle of Passo Fundo in the state of Rio Grande do Sul
	15 September	Inauguration of Prudente de Morais as president.[160]
1895		The Federalist Riograndense Revolution comes to an end.
	July	The British again tried to take possession of the strategic Trindade island in the Atlantic. The British planned to use the island as a cable station. However, Brazilian diplomatic efforts, along with Portuguese support, reinstated Trindade Island to Brazilian sovereignty.
	5 November	Japan establishes diplomatic relations with Brazil.[161]
	17 November	Flamengo, a well known professional football club in Brazil, is officially founded.
1897	24 January	In order to clearly demonstrate sovereignty over the Trindade island, now part of the State of Espírito Santo and the municipality of Vitória, a landmark is built. Nowadays, Brazilian presence is marked by a permanent Brazilian Navy base on the main island.
	5 October	Canudos War: After a long siege, Brazilian government troops take Canudos in northeastern Brazil, crushing Antônio Conselheiro and his followers.
	12 October	The City of Belo Horizonte, Brazil is created. The construction of the second Brazilian planned city is completed successfully.
1898	1 March	In the presidential election, Manuel Ferraz de Campos Sales of the Republican Party of São Paulo, is successful, with 90.9% of the vote.[162]
1899	14 July	The First Republic of Acre is declared.
1900	25 April	The Republic of Acre is reincorporated into Bolivia, with Brazilian help.

20th century

Year	Date	Event
1901	19 October	Aviator Alberto Santos-Dumont wins the Deutsch de la Meurthe prize with a flight that rounds the Eiffel Tower.[163]
1902	1 March	Presidential election: Rodrigues Alves of the Republican Party of São Paulo receives 91.7% of the vote.[164] Francisco Silviano de Almeida Brandão is elected vice-president but dies suddenly before the start of his term of office.
	26 October	The first season of competitive football in Brazil concludes with a victory for São Paulo Athletic Club.
	3 December	José Paranhos, Baron of Rio Branco, is appointed Minister of Foreign Affairs. His ten-year tenure would be the longest in the country's history.[165]
1903	11 November	The Treaty of Petrópolis ends tension between Brazil and Bolivia over the then-Bolivian territory of Acre (today the Acre state).
1904	14 October	The National Congress of Brazil approves a large naval acquisition programme.[166]
	10–16 November	Vaccine Revolt in Rio de Janeiro.
		The Evangelical Lutheran Church of Brazil is founded in Rio Grande do Sul.
		Ford begin selling cars in Brazil.
1905	30 December	Law no. 1452 is passed by the National Congress of Brazil, authorizing expenditure of £4,214,550 for new warship construction (£1,685,820 in 1906).[167]
1906	21 January	The Brazilian battleship Aquidabã sinks, after its powder magazines explode near the Jacuacanga strait, in Angra dos Reis bay. A total of 212 people are killed, including three admirals and most of the ship's officers; 98 survive.
	1 March	In the presidential election, Afonso Pena of the Mineiro Republican Party receives 97.9% of the vote.[168]
	5 May	The Treaty of Limits between Brazil and the Netherlands is signed in Rio de Janeiro, establishing the international boundary between Brazil and the Dutch colony of Suriname.[169]
	23 October	An aeroplane of Alberto Santos-Dumont takes off at Bagatelle in France and flies 60 meters (200 feet). This is the first officially recorded powered flight in Europe.[170]
	9 November	The Brazilian Flag Anthem ("Hino à Bandeira Nacional"), with words by Olavo Bilac and music by Francisco Braga, is performed for the first time.
1907		Construction of the Madeira-Mamoré Railroad begins, linking the cities of Porto Velho and Guajará-Mirim.

	24 April	The Vásquez Cobo–Martins treaty between Brazil and Colombia is signed, establishing the border from the Rio Negro northwestward along the Amazon River-Orinoco watershed divide, "then generally southward along various river courses and straight-line segments to the mouth of the Apaporis River"
1908	16 June	The Kasato Maru arrives at the Port of Santos with the first official group of Japanese immigrants to Brazil.
	10 September	The first *Minas Geraes*-class Dreadnought battleship for Brazil, *Minas Geraes* is launched at Armstrong Whitworth's yard on the River Tyne in England, catalysing the "South American dreadnought race".
	30 October	Pedro de Alcântara, Prince of Grão-Pará, renounces his claim on the Brazilian throne in order to marry Countess Elisabeth Dobržensky de Dobrženicz.[171]
1910	1 March	In the presidential election, Hermes da Fonseca receives 57.1% of the vote. Fonseca is supported by several of the most influential Republican parties, whilst his main opponent, Rui Barbosa, is supported by the Civilist Campaign.[172]
	22 November	Revolt of the Lash: The mostly black crews of four Brazilian warships, led by João Cândido Felisberto, mutiny shortly after a sailor receives 250 lashes. The crews depose their white officers and threaten to bombard Rio de Janeiro.[173]
1911	10 January	The cargo ship *Nubia SS* runs aground off the coast of Rio Grande do Norte.
1912	October	Beginning of the Contestado War, a dispute between settlers and landowners.[174]
	29 December	The federal government sends in 200 federal troops to deal with ongoing trouble in the State of Santa Catarina.
1913	12 December	Roosevelt–Rondon Scientific Expedition: Following a speaking tour in Brazil and Argentina, former US President Theodore Roosevelt meets up with Cândido Rondon to embark on a joint exploration of the "River of Doubt".[175]
1914	1 March	In the presidential election, incumbent Vice-President Venceslau Brás, of the Mineiro Republican Party, receives 91.6% of the vote.[176]
	8 June	The Brazilian Football Confederation is founded, with Álvaro Zamith as its first president. The Brazilian Olympic Committee is founded on the same day.
	14 September	The British Royal Navy auxiliary cruiser HMS *Carmania* fought the German SMS *Cap Trafalgar* off Trindade in the Battle of Trindade. *Carmania* sank *Cap Trafalgar*, but sustained severe damage herself.
1915	29 January	Heitor Villa-Lobos gives the first in a series of chamber concerts; one of the new works he introduces during this year is his *Cello Concerto no 1*.[177]
1916	5 March	The liner *Príncipe de Asturias* runs aground in fog on the shoals out of Ponta do Boi, in the island of Sao Sebastião, while trying to approach the port of Santos. At least 445 people out of the 588 aboard are killed.[178]

	3 May	Brazilian merchant ship Rio Branco is sunk by a German submarine. Because the ship is in restricted waters and registered under the British flag, and most of its crew is Norwegian, it is not considered an illegal attack by the Brazilian government, despite public protests.
	August	Brazilian Naval Aviation is established, in preparation for the country's participation in the First World War.[179]
		The capture of rebel leader Deodato Manuel Ramos ("Adeodato") marks the effective end of the Contestado War.
1917	5 April	The steamship *Paraná*, loaded with coffee and travelling in accordance with the demands made on neutral countries, is torpedoed by a German submarine; three Brazilians are killed.
	11 April	Brazil breaks off diplomatic relations with Germany.
	7 May	Foreign Minister Lauro Müller is obliged to resign because of his German origins.
	May–November	Several Brazilian vessels are torpedoed by the Germans.[180]
	26 October	World War I: Brazil declares war on the Central Powers.[181]
	1 November	A mob damages German property in Petropolis, including the restaurant Brahma (completely destroyed), the Gesellschaft Germania, the German school, the company Arp, and the *German Journal*.
1918	30 January	Ministerial Notice No. 501 is issued, establishing the Naval Division for War Operations (Divisão Naval em Operações de Guerra – DNOG).[182]
	1 March	Brazilian general election, 1918: Former president Rodrigues Alves receives 99.1% of the vote.
	18 August	The Brazilian Medical Mission, led by Dr. Nabuco Gouveia and directed by General Aché, is established with 86 doctors.
	24 September	The Brazilian Medical Mission lands at Marseilles, France, and supports the local population during a flu outbreak, ensuring the continuity of logistical support to the troops at the front.
	15 November	President-elect Rodrigues Alves, suffering from influenza, is unable to take office on the scheduled date, and is replaced by Vice President Delfim Moreira.
1919	13 April	In the presidential election brought about by the death of Rodrigues Alves, Epitácio Pessoa of the Paraíba Republican Party receives 71.0% of the vote.
	24 April	Ford Brasil, a subsidiary of the Ford Motor Company, is founded.
	11–29 May	The 1919 South American Championship football tournament is held in Rio de Janeiro. It is won by the home country.[183]
	28 July	Epitácio Pessoa takes office as President, replacing acting President Delfim Moreira, who continues as Vice President.

1920	20 April	Opening ceremony of the 1920 Summer Olympics in Antwerp, at which Brazil competes for the first time.[184] Sport shooter Guilherme Paraense is the first Brazilian to win a gold medal.
1921	October	The government implements a new policy in defense of coffee, for the third time in the history of the Republic.[185]
1922	11–18 February	Modern Art Week is held in São Paulo, marking the beginning of Brazilian Modernism.
	1 March	In the Brazilian presidential election, Artur Bernardes of the Mineiro Republican Party receives 56.0% of the vote.[186]
	5 July	The 18 of the Copacabana Fort revolt occurs in Rio de Janeiro, then Federal District of Brazil. It is the first revolt of the *tenentista* movement, in the context of the Brazilian Old Republic.
1923	3 May	Brazil sign the Pan-American Treaty.[187]
		The Brazilian Society of Chemistry is founded.
		Brazil's first radio broadcasting station, the Radio Society of Rio de Janeiro, is founded; it is still working under the name Rádio MEC.
1924	5–28 July	Military revolt in São Paulo.
1925	12 April	The Coluna Prestes movement is launched at a meeting in Foz do Iguaçu.[188]
	29 May	British explorer Percy Fawcett sent a last telegram to his wife, before he disappears in the Amazon.
1926	1 March	In the presidential election, Washington Luís of the Republican Party of São Paulo, who received 98.0% of the vote.
1927	11 June	The Brazilian submarine Humaytá is launched at the Odero-Terni-Orlando shipyard at La Spezia, Italy.
1928	10 August	The ETA – Empresa de Transporte Aéreo airline is founded; it remains in operation for only a year.
		The Liberator Party (Brazil) is founded for the first time, by members of the Rio Grande do Sul Federalist Party, notably Joaquim Francisco de Assis Brasil.
1929	August	Minas Gerais, Rio Grande do Sul, and Paraíba join the political opposition from several states, including the Democratic Party of São Paulo, to oppose the presidential candidacy of Washington Luís's nominated successor, Júlio Prestes, and form the Liberal Alliance.
	20 September	The Liberal Alliance nominates its candidates for the presidential elections: Getúlio Vargas as President and João Pessoa Cavalcanti de Albuquerque as Vice President.
	29 October	The US stock market crash causes a fall in coffee quotations to 60%.
1930	1 March	A general election is held; in the presidential election,s the result is a victory for Júlio Prestes of the Republican Party of São Paulo, who receives 57.7% of the vote. Vital Soares is elected vice-president, but never takes office.

	26 July	The assassination of João Pessoa Cavalcânti de Albuquerque, governor of Paraíba, by João Duarte Dantas, stirs up a wave of bad feeling toward the federal government and the outgoing president Washington Luís, who is accused of bearing the "moral responsibility".
	13 August	1930 Curuçá River event: The area of Curuçá River near latitude 5° S and longitude 71.5° W experiences a meteoric air burst (also known as the Brazilian Tunguska event).[189]
	September	The state capital of Paraíba, formerly Parahyba, is renamed João Pessoa, in memory of its assassinated governor.
	3 October	Brazilian Revolution of 1930.[190]
	24 October	Incumbent President Washington Luís is deposed.[191] A military junta, led by General Augusto Tasso Fragoso, temporarily takes control of the country.
	1 November	Beginning of the Vargas Era: The ruling junta hands power and the presidential palace to Getúlio Vargas.
		The National Institute of Metrology Standardization and Industrial Quality (INMETRO) is founded.
1931	12 October	The statue of Christ the Redeemer, overlooking Rio de Janeiro, is consecrated.
		Frente Negra Brasileira, Brazil's first Black political party, is created.[192]
1932	24 February	The Justiça Eleitoral do Brasil is created by Decreto n° 21.076;
	24 February	Women win the right to vote.
	April	Peter Fleming joins the expedition to find missing Englishman Colonel Percy Fawcett; the following year he publishes an account of the expedition, entitled *Brazilian Adventure*.
	23 May	Four protesting students (Martins, Miragaia, Dráusio and Camargo) are killed by government troops, sparking off the "Paulista War".
	June	Paulista rebels take control of the state of São Paulo.[193]
	9 July	Constitutionalist Revolution: The population of the state of São Paulo revolt against the 1930 coup d'état.
	2 October	The São Paulo rebels are defeated by government forces.[194]
	October	Brazilian Integralism, a Fascist movement, is founded by Plínio Salgado.[195]
1933	10 October	The Anti-war Treaty of Non-aggression and Conciliation, an inter-American treaty, is signed in Rio de Janeiro by representatives of Argentina, Brazil, Chile, Mexico, Paraguay and Uruguay.[196]
1934	16 July	The Vargas government introduces what will be the shortest-lived Constitution of Brazil, lasting only 3 years (until 1937).[197] It is the first time a Brazilian constitution has been written from scratch by directly elected deputies in multi-party elections, and incorporates a number of improvements to Brazilian political, social and economical life.

	17 July	In the presidential election, carried out by the Constituent Assembly, acting president Getúlio Vargas receives 175 of the 248 votes.[198]
		The University of São Paulo is established.
		The Brazilian Institute of Geography and Statistics is founded under the title of the National Institute of Statistics.
1935	November	A Communist insurrection, the "Red Revolt of 35" or the *Intentona Comunista*, fails to unseat President Vargas. Olga Benário Prestes and her husband Luís Carlos Prestes are among the conspirators arrested.
1936	16 October	President Vargas signed the decree, which gives the name of the aviator Alberto Santos Dumont Airport located in Ponta do Calabouço, in the city of Rio de Janeiro, named Santos Dumont Airport, Brazil's first civilian airport.[199]
1937	7 May	One of the leaders of the communist revolution, Luis Carlos Prestes, is sentenced to 16 years and eight months in prison.[200]
	10 June	National Democratic Union, ahead of support for the candidacy of Armando Sales de Oliveira for president in the 1938 elections is created.[201]
	14 June	President Getúlio Vargas signed the decree establishing the Itatiaia National Park, the first national park in Brazil.[202,203]
	13 August	The National Union of Students is founded in Rio de Janeiro.
	10 November	The fourth Brazilian Constitution is granted by President Vargas, starting the Estado Novo.[204]
	21 December	President Vargas signs the ordinance which extinguishes all political parties in the country.[205]
1938	May	The Brazilian integralist movement attempt a coup d'état, supported by the Axis powers. The failure of the "Pajama Putsch" leads to the dissolution of the AIB.
	28 July	Folk hero Lampião and his band are ambushed in one of his hideouts, the Angicos farm, in the state of Sergipe.
1939	30 November	Serra dos Órgãos National Park is created.
	5 December	The Imperial Mausoleum is officially inaugurated at the Cathedral of Petrópolis.[206]
1942	28 January	Brazil breaks diplomatic relations with the Axis countries.
	July–August	Several Brazilian vessels are torpedoed by the Germans.
	22 August	President Getúlio Vargas signs the declaration of war against Germany and Italy.
	1 November	The Cruzeiro "antigo" is adopted as the official currency.[207]
1943	11 June	The Order of Military Merit is established by President Getúlio Vargas.
	13 July	On the recommendation of the National Petroleum Council, Brazil bans the use of private motorcycles throughout the nation in order to conserve fuel. Use of gasoline-powered automobiles had been prohibited the year before.[208]

	31 July	The Brazilian passenger ship and freighter *Bagé*, largest commercial ship in Brazil's fleet, is torpedoed and sunk off the coast of the Sergipe state. The *Bagé*, carrying 129 passengers and 102 crew, was en route from Belém to Rio de Janeiro when it was struck by a German U-boat. Seventy-eight people (41 passengers and 37 crew) are lost.[209]
1944	1 January	The former Royal Military Academy expends into the city of Resende.
	2 July	Second World War: The first five thousand Brazilian Expeditionary Force soldiers, the 6th RCT, leave Brazil for Europe aboard the USNS *General Mann*.
	September	Brazilian air-land forces go into action in Italy.[210]
	13 October	Brazilian pilots begin operations, as individual elements of flights attached to 350th FG squadrons.
1944–1945	25 November 1944 – 21 February 1945	Second World War, Battle of Monte Castello: The battle marks the Brazilian Expeditionary Force's entry into the land war in Europe.[211,212]
1945	February	A fourth transport of troops of the Brazilian Expeditionary Force reaches Italy, in preparation for the Spring 1945 offensive.
	12 May	Brazilian troops arrive in Turin on the same day that the cessation of hostilities is announced.
	May	Bishop Carlos Duarte Costa, an outspoken critic of the regime of President Getúlio Vargas and of the Vatican's alleged relationship with fascist regimes,[213] gives newspaper interviews accusing Brazil's Papal nuncio of Nazi-Fascist spying, and accusing Rome of having aided and abetted Hitler. Shortly afterwards he establishes the Brazilian Catholic Apostolic Church.
	29 October	President Vargas resigns, beginning the period known as the Second Brazilian Republic. José Linhares becomes acting president.
	2 December	A general election is held, the first since the establishment of Getúlio Vargas' Estado Novo. The presidential election is won by Eurico Gaspar Dutra of the Social Democratic Party (PSD), which also wins a majority of seats in both the Chamber of Deputies and the Senate.
1946	18 September	A new constitution is introduced, and the position of Vice President of Brazil is recreated; Nereu Ramos is selected as the first incumbent.
1947	19 January	Parliamentary elections are held, for 19 vacant seats in the Chamber of Deputies, one additional Senator for each state (except Santa Catarina, which elected two), and for all state Governors and legislatures The Brazilian Communist Party wins nearly 10% of the vote in the state elections, becoming the third party in the state of São Paulo (ahead of the UDN) and the single largest party in the federal capital, Rio de Janeiro.
	6 August	The Brazilian Socialist Party is founded.
	2 October	The São Paulo Museum of Art opens to the public.

1949		The Centro Brasileiro de Pesquisas Físicas is founded by Cesar Lattes, José Leite Lopes, and Jayme Tiomno.
1950	16 June	The Maracanã Stadium opens in Rio de Janeiro.
	24 June – 16 July	Brazil hosts the 1950 FIFA World Cup, the local national team is beaten 1–2 by Uruguay in the final game.
	18 September	First television broadcasting in Brazil by TV Tupi.
	3 October	The Brazilian general election is won by the Social Democratic Party, who remain the largest party in both the Chamber of Deputies and the Senate, although they lose their majority in the former. The presidential election is won by former President Getúlio Vargas of the Brazilian Labour Party
1951		The Brazilian Medical Association is founded.[214]
		The Escola Superior de Propaganda e Marketing is founded in São Paulo.[215]
1952	4 March	Anchieta rail disaster: A crowded steam-powered passenger train derails while crossing a bridge over the Pavuna River near Anchieta station,[216] sending two old wooden carriages broadside onto the adjacent line. A modern high-speed electric freight train travelling in the opposite direction ploughs into the wooden carriages, telescoping them upwards. The severity of the accident was compounded by the fact that the suburban train is overloaded, with passengers clinging to the sides, underneath and between the carriages. A witness says they saw "passengers flying in all directions when the crash occurred". 119 people are killed and the resulting outcry prompts major new investment in Brazilian railways.
	28 April	Pan Am Flight 202 crashes in the Amazon Basin approximately 220 nautical miles (410 km) southwest of Carolina, Brazil. All 50 people on board are killed in the worst-ever accident involving the Boeing 377.[217]
	12 August	1952 Transportes Aéreos Nacional Douglas C-47 mid-air explosion: A Douglas C-47A registered *PP-ANH* is destroyed after a in-flight fire causes it to crash near Palmeiras de Goiás. All 24 people on board are killed.
		Bob's, Brazil's first fast food chain, opens in Rio de Janeiro.
1954	24 August	Brazilian president Getúlio Vargas commits suicide after being accused of involvement in a conspiracy to murder his chief political opponent, Carlos Lacerda.
	3 October	Brazilian legislative election, 1954
1955	3 October	The presidential election results in victory for Juscelino Kubitschek, who receives 35.7% of the vote.
	3 November	Café Filho is forced to give up the presidency of Brazil on health grounds.[218] Kubitschek does not take office until the following year.
		The Museum of Modern Art, Rio de Janeiro, is completed, a Modernist concrete museum building, designed by Affonso Eduardo Reidy, with gardens designed by Burle Marx.[219]

1956	31 January	Juscelino Kubitschek is inaugurated as the 21st President of Brazil.
1957	October	The Africanized bee is accidentally released in Brazil.
	16 October	Antônio Vilas Boas, a Brazilian farmer, claims to have been abducted by extraterrestrials; the first famous alien abduction case.
1958	29 June	Brazil beats Sweden 5–2 in the final game to win the football World Cup in Sweden.
1960	21 April	The country's capital (Federal District) is relocated from the city of Rio de Janeiro to the new city, Brasília, in the highlands. The actual city of Rio de Janeiro becomes the State of Guanabara.
	3 October	Jânio Quadros is elected President of Brazil for a five-year term.
1961	25 August	João Goulart replaces Jânio Quadros as President of Brazil.
	17 December	A circus tent fire in Niterói, Brazil kills 323.
1962	17 June	Brazil beats Czechoslovakia 3–1 to win the 1962 FIFA World Cup.
1964	31 March	The military overthrows Brazilian President João Goulart in a coup, starting 21 years of dictatorship in Brazil.
	1 April	Deployed military rule in Brazil ended the then government of president João Goulart.
	11 April	Brazilian presidential election, 1964: The Brazilian Congress elects Field Marshal Humberto de Alencar Castelo Branco as President of Brazil.[220]
1965	26 April	Rede Globo, the 3rd largest TV broadcaster of the world, is founded, in Rio de Janeiro, Brazil.
	27 October	Brazilian president Humberto de Alencar Castelo Branco removes power from parliament, legal courts and opposition parties.
1966	5 March	A massive theft of nuclear materials is revealed in Brazil.
1967	1 March	Brazilian police arrest Franz Stangl, ex-commander of Treblinka and Sobibór extermination camps.
	15 March	The Republic of the United States of Brazil is renamed the Federative Republic of Brazil.
1968	28 March	Brazilian high school student Edson Luís de Lima Souto is shot by the police in a protest for cheaper meals at a restaurant for low-income students. The aftermath of his death is one of the first major events against the military dictatorship.
	13 December	Prompted by growing unrest and proliferation of pro-communist terrorist actions, Brazilian president Artur da Costa e Silva enacts the so-called AI-5, the fifth of a series of non-constitutional emergency decrees that helped stabilize the country after the turmoils of the early 1960s.

Timeline of Brazilian history

1969	31 August – 30 October	Brazilian Military Junta of 1969 rules the country following sudden illness and resignation of President da Costa e Silva. The junta consists of Army General Aurélio de Lyra Tavares, Navy Admiral Augusto Hamann Rademaker Grunewald and Air Force Brigadier Márcio de Souza e Mello
	19 November	Playing for Santos against Vasco in Rio de Janeiro, Brazilian footballer Pelé scored his 1,000th goal.
1970	11 March	Japanese consul-general in São Paulo Nobuo Okuchi is kidnapped by the leftist guerrilla group Vanguarda Popular Revolucionária.
	15 March	Japanese consul-general in São Paulo Nobuo Okuchi is ransomed by the Brazilian government, he is released in exchange for five political prisoners.
	11 June	West German ambassador Ehrenfried von Holleben is kidnapped by the Vanguarda Popular Revolucionária and by the Ação Libertadora Nacional.
	21 June	Brazil defeats Italy 4–1 to win the 1970 FIFA World Cup in Mexico.
	1 December	Giovanni Enrico Bucher, the Swiss ambassador to Brazil, is kidnapped by the Ação Libertadora Nacional in Rio de Janeiro; kidnappers demand the release of 70 political prisoners.
1971	14 January	Seventy Brazilian political prisoners are released in Santiago, Chile; Giovanni Enrico Bucher is released 16 January.
	16 January	Giovanni Enrico Bucher is released by the Ação Libertadora Nacional.
	20 November	A bridge still in construction, called Elevado Engenheiro Freyssinet, falls over the Paulo de Frontin Avenue, in Rio de Janeiro; 48 people are killed and several injured. Reconstructed, the bridge is a part of the Linha Vermelha elevate.
1974	1 February	Fire breaks out in the Joelma Building in São Paulo, Brazil; 177 die, 293 are injured, 11 die later of their injuries.[221,222]
	4 March	The Rio–Niterói Bridge opens.
1975	15 March	Guanabara State merges into the state of Rio de Janeiro. The state's capital moves from the city of Niterói to the city of Rio de Janeiro.
1977		President Geisel closed Congress briefly to control presidential succession as conflict erupted between Geisel, the *duristas*, Congress, the Church, and the media.
1977–1978		Operação Prato.
1979	7 February	Nazi criminal Josef Mengele suffers a stroke and drowns while swimming in Bertioga, Brazil. His remains are found in 1985.
1980	1 June	Mauro Milhomem, a pilot, attempted to crash his *Sertanejo-721* into the *Hotel Presidente* owned by his mother-in-law, after he had an argument with his wife the previous day after he discovered that she cheated him. The plane failed to hit the target and hit into several objects and ultimately crashed into an accounting office in front to a forum. Six people were killed and four were wounded.

	9 July	Pope John Paul II visits Brazil; 7 people are crushed to death in a crowd meeting him.
1981	20 September	The Brazilian river boat *Sobral Santos* capsizes in the Amazon River, Óbidos, Brazil, killing at least 300.
1983	19 December	The Jules Rimet Trophy is stolen from the Brazilian Soccer Confederation building in Rio de Janeiro.
1984	16 April	More than one million people, led by Tancredo Neves, occupy the streets of São Paulo to demand direct presidential elections during the Brazilian military government of João Figueiredo. It is the largest protest during the Diretas Já civil unrest, as well as the largest public demonstration in the history of Brazil. The elections are granted in 1989.
	May	The Itaipu Dam is inaugurated on the border of Brazil and Paraguay after 9 years of construction, making it the largest hydroelectric dam in the world at the time.
1985	15 January	Tancredo Neves is elected president of Brazil by the Congress, ending the 21-year military rule.
	15 March	Vice-President José Sarney, upon becoming vice president, assumes the duties of president of Brazil, as the new president Tancredo Neves had become severely ill, the day before. Sarney will become Brazil's first civilian president in 21 years, upon Neves' death on 21 April.
	21 April	Brazilian President Tancredo Neves dies, he is succeeded by Vice President José Sarney. The Vice President post is left vacant until 1990.
	6 June	The remains of Josef Mengele, the physician notorious for Nazi human experimentation on inmates of Auschwitz concentration camp, buried in 1979 under the name of Wolfgang Gerhard, are exhumed in Embu das Artes, Brazil.
1987	13 September	Goiânia accident: A radioactive object is stolen from an abandoned hospital in Goiânia, Brazil, contaminating many people in the following weeks and causing some to die from radiation poisoning.
1988	25 June	PSDB is founded by members of the Brazilian Democratic Movement Party linked to the European social democratic movement as an attempt to clarify their ideals.
	5 October	Brazil adopts a new constitution.
	22 December	Brazilian union and environmental activist Chico Mendes is assassinated.
	31 December	The Bateau Mouche cruise ship capsized and sank in the South Atlantic off Rio de Janeiro with the loss of at least 51 of the 149 people on board.
1989	12 November	Brazil holds its first free presidential election since 1960. This marks the first time that all Ibero-American nations, excepting Cuba, have elected constitutional governments simultaneously.
	15 November	Brazil holds the first round of its first free election in 29 years; Fernando Collor de Mello and Luiz Inácio Lula da Silva advance to the second round, to be held the following month.

Timeline of Brazilian history

	17 December	Brazil holds the second round of its first free election in 29 years; Fernando Collor de Mello is elected to serve as President from 1990.
1990	15 March	Fernando Collor de Mello takes office as President of Brazil, Brazil's first democratically elected president since Jânio Quadros in 1961. The next day, he announces a currency freeze and freezes large bank accounts for 18 months.
1991	26 March	Argentina, Brazil, Uruguay and Paraguay sign the Treaty of Asunción, establishing the South Common Market (Mercosur is its acronym in Spanish).
	30 September	A tornado destroys parts of Itu, a city in southeastern Brazil, killing 16 and leaving 176 injured.
1992	8 June	The first World Ocean Day is celebrated, coinciding with the Earth Summit held in Rio de Janeiro, Brazil.
	24 August	A special commission in Brazil concludes that there is sufficient evidence to begin impeachment proceedings against President of Brazil Fernando Collor de Mello, finding he had accepted millions of dollars worth of illegal payments from business interests.
	29 September	The Chamber of Deputies of Brazil votes to impeach President of Brazil Fernando Collor de Mello, the country's first democratically elected leader in 29 years. Vice President Itamar Franco becomes acting president.
	2 October	A riot breaks out in the Carandiru Penitentiary in São Paulo, Brazil, resulting in the Carandiru massacre.[223]
	29 December	Brazil's president Fernando Collor de Mello is found guilty on charges that he stole more than $32 million from the government, preventing him from holding any elected office for 8 years.
1993	21 April	A constitutional referendum is held to determine the form of government of the country.[224]
	23 July	Candelária massacre: Brazilian police officers kill eight street kids in Rio de Janeiro.
	29 August	Vigário Geral massacre.
	16 December	Brazil's Supreme Court rules that former President Fernando Collor de Mello may not hold elected office again until 2000 due to political corruption.
1994	1 July	Brazil introduces its new currency, the Real.
	17 July	Brazil wins the 1994 FIFA World Cup, defeating Italy by 3–2 in penalties (full-time 0–0).
1995	1 January	Fernando Henrique Cardoso becomes President of Brazil.
1996	20 January	Varginha UFO incident in Minas Gerais.[225,226]
	2 March	A Learjet 25 (registration PT-LSD) carrying the Brazilian satirical rock band Mamonas Assassinas attempts a go-around at São Paulo–Guarulhos International Airport in São Paulo, Brazil, but crashes in the Serra da Cantareira mountain range, killing all eight people on board including all five members of the band.[227]

	17 April	Eldorado dos Carajás massacre.[228]
1999	6 June	In São José dos Campos, 345 prisoners escape from Putim prison through the front gate.

21st century

Year	Date	Event
2001	10 September	Antônio da Costa Santos, mayor of Campinas, is assassinated.
	11 September	Three Brazilians are killed in the September 11 attacks in the United States.
2002	30 June	Brazil wins its 5th FIFA World Cup title by defeating Germany 2-0 in the 2002 FIFA World Cup Final.
	27 October	Luiz Inácio Lula da Silva wins the Brazilian general election, 2002 with 52.7 million votes (61.3% of the total).[229]
2003	1 January	Luiz Inácio Lula da Silva is inaugurated as president of Brazil.[230]
	30 January	The Fome Zero program is introduced by president Luiz Inácio Lula da Silva.
	19 August	A car-bomb attack on United Nations headquarters in Iraq kills the agency's top envoy Sérgio Vieira de Mello and 21 other employees.
2004	28 March	The first ever reported South Atlantic hurricane makes landfall in southern Brazil in the state of Santa Catarina – the hurricane is dubbed Cyclone Catarina.
	1 June	The United Nations Stabilization Mission in Haiti (MINUSTAH) is established, its military component is led by Brazil.
2005	6 June	Mensalão scandal threatens to bring down the government of Luiz Inácio Lula da Silva.[231]
	6 August	Banco Central burglary at Fortaleza
	23 October	Brazilian firearms and ammunition referendum, 2005
2006	30 March	Marcos Pontes becomes the first Brazilian and the first native Portuguese-speaking person to go into space, where he stays on the International Space Station for a week. During his trip, Pontes carries out eight experiments selected by the Brazilian Space Agency. He lands in Kazakhstan on 8 April 2006, with the crew of Expedition 12.
	May	May 2006 São Paulo violence
	July	July 2006 São Paulo violence
	7 August	Lei Maria da Penha is sanctioned by president Luiz Inácio Lula da Silva.
	29 September	Gol Transportes Aéreos Flight 1907 leads to the 2006–07 Brazilian aviation crisis.

2007	18 March	Cesare Battisti, convicted *in absentia* of two murders in Italy in the 1970s and who later became a crime writer in France, is arrested in Brazil.
	May	Pope Benedict XVI visits Brazil to reaffirm Catholicism in the country.
	11 May	Pope Benedict XVI canonizes Brazil's first native-born saint, Frei Galvão, an 18th-century Franciscan monk.
	26 June	Bolivia reclaims two oil refineries from Brazilian state-owned energy company Petrobras.
	27 June	Complexo do Alemão massacre.
	7 July	The New Seven Wonders of the World are announced. These are The Great Wall of China, Petra in Jordan, the Christ the Redeemer statue in Brazil, Machu Picchu in Peru, Mexico's Chichen Itza Mayan site, the Colosseum in Rome and the Taj Mahal in India.
	July	The Fifteenth Pan American Games take place in Rio de Janeiro.
	17 July	TAM Linhas Aéreas Flight 3054 carrying 186 people crashes in Congonhas International Airport, São Paulo, Brazil. The death toll is estimated to be at least 200 people.
	4 November	At least six people are killed as a Learjet 35 crashes into a residential district in São Paulo, Brazil.
	25 November	At least eight football fans die when part of the Fonte Nova stadium in Salvador, Brazil, collapses.
	2 December	Brazil starts free-to-air digital television transmissions in São Paulo, but broadcasting companies must transmit signals in both analogue and digital formats until June 2016.
	20 December	The *Portrait of Suzanne Bloch* (1904), by the Spanish artist Pablo Picasso, and *O Lavrador de Café* by Brazilian modernist painter Cândido Portinari, are stolen from the São Paulo Museum of Art.
	17 December	The leaders of Brazil, Bolivia, and Chile agree to build a highway by 2009 that will link the Atlantic (in Santos, Brazil) and the Pacific (in Iquique, Chile) coasts of South America.
2008	9 January	The police recoveres the *Portrait of Suzanne Bloch* (1904), by the Spanish artist Pablo Picasso, and *O Lavrador de Café* by Brazilian modernist painter Cândido Portinari, which had been stolen in December 2007.
	24 November	The 2008 Santa Catarina floods in Santa Catarina, Brazil, kill 126 and force the evacuation of over 78,000 people.
2009	1 June	Air France Flight 447, en route from Rio de Janeiro, to Paris, crashes into the Atlantic Ocean, killing all 228 on board.
	2 October	The International Olympic Committee awards the 2016 Summer Olympics to Rio de Janeiro.
	16 October	Brasil de Pelotas bus crash: two players and a coach die.
2010	January	January 2010 Rio de Janeiro floods and mudslides
	17 February	Sinking of the Concordia.
	April	April 2010 Rio de Janeiro floods and mudslides

	June	2010 northeastern Brazil floods
	21–28 November	2010 Rio de Janeiro Security Crisis
2011	1 January	Inauguration of Dilma Rousseff as the 36th President of Brazil.[232]
	11 January	January 2011 Rio de Janeiro floods and mudslides: Over 900 people are killed as a result of freak weather conditions.
	7 April	Rio de Janeiro school shooting: 12 children aged between 12 and 14 are killed and 12 others seriously wounded after an armed man opens fire at an elementary school in Realengo
	13 July	Noar Linhas Aéreas Flight 4896: A Noar Linhas Aéreas Let L-410 Turbolet crashes in Boa Viagem, Recife, killing all 16 people on board).
	7 November	Campos Basin oil spill: A Chevron-owned oil well began leaking causing 32,000 to 52,000 litres (200 to 330 bbl) of crude oil to enter the ocean every day. The leak took place in Campos Basin, Brazil 120 kilometres (75 mi) off the coast of Rio de Janeiro.
2012	13 February	Lindemberg Alves begins to be tried for the death of ex-girlfriend Elóa Pimentel, in the city of Santo André.[233]
2013	27 January	A nightclub fire in Santa Maria, Rio Grande do Sul kills at least 242 people.
	April – July	2013 protests in Brazil.
	23 July	World Youth Day began in Rio de Janeiro.
2014	17 March	Operation Car Wash begins.
	May – July	2014 protests in Brazil.[234,235]
	12 June – 13 July	The 2014 FIFA World Cup is held in Brazil, and is won by Germany.
	3 July	Belo Horizonte overpass collapse
	13 August	Governor Eduardo Campos, a candidate in the upcoming Brazilian presidential election, dies in a plane crash in Santos, São Paulo, together with six other people on board the aircraft. It also sparks a large fire.
	13 August	2014 Cessna Citation 560 XLS+ crash
	October	Brazilian general election, 2014
	10 December	26-year-old Sailson José das Graças is arrested for the serial murder as many as 41 people in a string of suspected racist hate crimes.
2015	6 January	Two commuter trains collide at Mesquita, Rio de Janeiro, injuring 158 people.
	15 March	Hundreds of thousands of people in Brazil protest against corruption and denounce the government of President Dilma Rousseff.
	5 November	An iron ore tailings dam in Bento Rodrigues, a subdistrict of Mariana, Brazil, suffered a catastrophic failure, causing flooding, killing 17 and injuring 16.

2016	13 March	Hundreds of thousands of people all over Brazil protest against corruption and denounce the government of President Dilma Rousseff.
	9 June	A bus plunges over a ravine in Brazil's São Paulo state, resulting in at least 18 people killed and 28 injured.
	5–21 August	The 2016 Summer Olympics are held in Rio de Janeiro.
	31 August	The Senate votes 61–20 in favor of removing Dilma Rousseff from office as President of Brazil. Acting President Michel Temer will serve out the remainder of the term, which ends 1 January 2019.
	15 October	A wildlife sanctuary for rescued elephants opens in Mato Grosso.
	17 October	Clashes between rival gangs in at least two prisons, leave at least 18 people killed.
	29 November	A chartered Avro RJ85 plane carrying 77 people, including the Chapecoense football team, crashes near Medellín, Colombia. Rescuers report at least six survivors have been found in the wreckage. The 2016 Copa Sudamericana Finals are suspended. The title is later awarded to Chapecoense.
2017	2 January	At least 56 people are killed in rebellion at Anisio Jobim penitentiary complex in Amazonas state.
	6 January	Members of the Primeiro Comando da Capital prison gang kill 31 inmates in the Monte Cristo prison in the state of Roraima. This action was revenge for an earlier massacre in a prison in Amazonas that killed 56 inmates.
	6 February	A police strike leads to a wave of violence and looting in Espírito Santo, including dozens of murders in the state capital, Vitória.
	17 March	Operation Carne Fraca starts.
	28 April	A general strike is held in the country, the first one in twenty years.

Bibliography

in English

- George Henry Townsend (1867), "Brazil"[236], *A Manual of Dates* (2nd ed.), London: Frederick Warne & Co.
- William Henry Overall, ed. (1870). "Brazil"[237]. *Dictionary of Chronology*. London: William Tegg.
- Benjamin Vincent (1910), "Brazil"[238], *Haydn's Dictionary of Dates* (25th ed.), London: Ward, Lock & Co.
- José Maria Bello; James L. Taylor (1966). "Brief Chronology of Brazilian History"[239]. *A History of Modern Brazil, 1889-1964*. Stanford University Press. ISBN 978-0-8047-0238-6.
- E. Bradford Burns (1993). "Chronology of Significant Dates in Brazilian History"[240]. *A History of Brazil*. Columbia University Press. ISBN 978-0-231-07954-9.
- Robert M. Levine (2003). "Timeline of Historical Events"[241]. *History of Brazil*. Palgrave Macmillan. ISBN 978-1-4039-6255-3.

- Europa Publications (2003). "Brazil"[242]. *Political Chronology of the Americas*. Routledge. p. 32+. ISBN 978-1-135-35653-8.
- Joseph Smith (2013). "Chronology of Main Events"[243]. *A History of Brazil*. Routledge. ISBN 978-1-317-89021-8.

in Portuguese

- Joaquim Pedro de Oliveira Martins, "Brazil (1525-1870)"[244], *Taboas de chronologia e geographia historica* (in Portuguese), Lisbon: Antonio Maria Pereira, pp. 431–432, OCLC 804367357[245]. 1885?

Colonization

Colonial Brazil

Colonial Brazil
Brasil Colonial
Colony of the Kingdom of Portugal
1500–1815
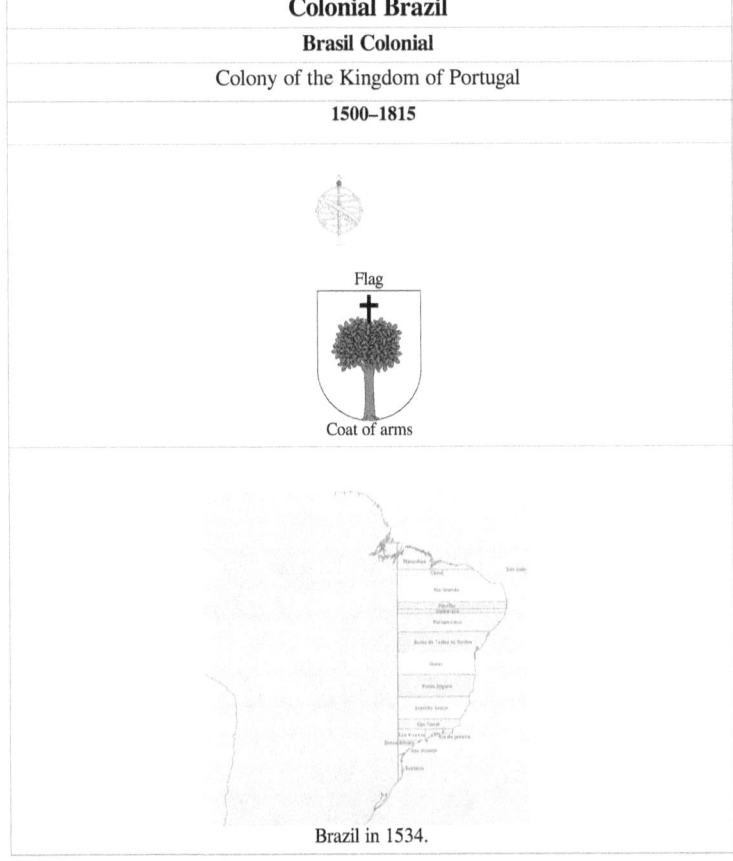 Flag Coat of arms
Brazil in 1534.

Capital	Salvador (1549–1763) Rio de Janeiro (1763–1815)
Languages	Portuguese (official) Tupí Austral, Nheengatu, many indigenous languages
Religion	Roman Catholic (official) Afro-Brazilian religions, Judaism, indigenous practices
Government	Absolute monarchy
Monarch	
• 1500–1521	Manuel I (first)
• 1777–1815	Maria I (last)
Viceroy	
• 1549–1553	Tomé de Sousa (first)
• 1806–1808	Marcos de Noronha, 8th Count of the Arcos (last)
History	
• Arrival of Pedro Álvares Cabral on behalf of the Portuguese Empire	22 April 1500
• Elevation to Kingdom and creation of the United Kingdom of Portugal, Brazil, and the Algarves	16 December 1815
Currency	Portuguese real
Preceded by	Succeeded by
Indigenous people in Brazil	United Kingdom of Portugal, Brazil and the Algarves
Today part of	Brazil Uruguay

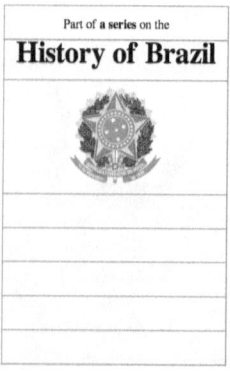

Part of a series on the
History of Brazil

Colonial Brazil

Brazil portal
- v
- t
- e[246]

Colonial Brazil (Portuguese: *Brasil Colonial*) comprises the period from 1500, with the arrival of the Portuguese, until 1815, when Brazil was elevated to a kingdom in union with Portugal as the United Kingdom of Portugal, Brazil and the Algarves. During the early 300 years of Brazilian colonial history, the economic exploitation of the territory was based first on brazilwood (*pau brazil*) extraction (16th century), which gave the territory its name;[247] sugar production (16th–18th centuries); and finally on gold and diamond mining (18th century). Slaves, especially those brought from Africa, provided most of the work force of the Brazilian export economy after a brief period of Indian slavery to cut brazilwood.

In contrast to the neighboring Spanish possessions, which had several viceroyalties with jurisdiction initially over New Spain (Mexico) and Peru, and in the eighteenth century expanded to viceroyalties of Rio de la Plata and New Granada, the Portuguese colony of Brazil was settled mainly in the coastal area by the Portuguese and a large black slave population working sugar plantations and mines. The boom and bust economic cycles were linked to export products. Brazil's sugar age, with the development of plantation slavery, merchants serving as middle men between production sites, Brazilian ports, and Europe was undermined by the growth of the sugar industry in the Caribbean on islands that European powers seized from Spain. Gold and diamonds were discovered and mined in southern Brazil through the end of the colonial era. Brazilian cities were largely port cities and the colonial administrative capital was moved several times in response to the rise and fall of export products' importance.

Unlike Spanish America, which fragmented into many republics upon independence, Brazil remained a single administrative unit under a monarch, giving rise to the largest country in Latin America. Just as European Spanish and Roman Catholicism were a core source of cohesion among Spain's vast and multi-ethnic territories, Brazilian society was united by the Portuguese language and Roman Catholic faith. As the only Lusophone polity in the Western Hemisphere, the Portuguese language was particularly important to Brazilian identity.

Initial European contact and early colonial history (1494–1530)

Portugal and Spain pioneered the European charting of sea routes that were the first and only channels of interaction between all of the world's continents, thus beginning the process of globalization. In addition to the imperial and economic undertaking of discovery and colonization of lands distant from Europe, these years were filled with pronounced advancements in cartography, shipbuilding and navigational instruments, of which the Portuguese and Spanish explorers took advantage.[248]

In 1494, the two kingdoms of the Iberian Peninsula divided the New World between them (in the Treaty of Tordesillas), and in 1500 navigator Pedro Álvares Cabral landed in what is now Brazil and laid claim to it in the name of King Manuel I of Portugal. The Portuguese identified brazilwood as a valuable red dye and an exploitable product, and attempted to force indigenous groups in Brazil to cut the trees.

The Age of Exploration

Portuguese seafarers in the early fifteenth century began to expand from a small area of the Iberian Peninsula, to seizing the Muslim fortress of Ceuta in North Africa. Its maritime exploration then proceeded down the coast of West Africa and across the Indian Ocean to the south Asian subcontinent, as well as the Atlantic islands off the coast of Africa on the way. They sought sources of gold, ivory, and African slaves, high value goods in the African trade. The Portuguese set up fortified trading "factories" (*feitorias*), whereby permanent, fairly small commercial settlements anchored trade in a region. The initial costs of setting up these commercial posts was borne by private investors, who in turn received hereditary titles and commercial advantages. From the Portuguese Crown's point of view, its realm was expanded with relatively little cost to itself.[249] On the Atlantic islands of the Azores, Madeira, and São Tomé, the Portuguese began plantation production of sugarcane using forced labor, a precedent for Brazil's sugar production in the sixteenth and seventeenth centuries.[250]

The Portuguese "discovery" of Brazil was preceded by a series of treaties between the kings of Portugal and Castile, following Portuguese sailings down

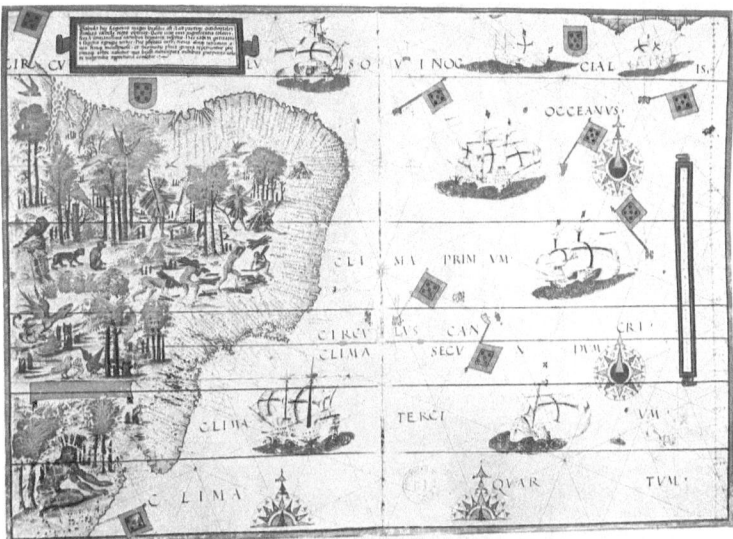

Figure 16: *Portuguese map by Lopo Homem (c. 1519) showing the coast of Brazil and natives extracting brazilwood, as well as Portuguese ships.*

the coast of Africa to India and the voyages to the Caribbean of the Genoese mariner sailing for Castile, Christopher Columbus. The most decisive of these treaties was the Treaty of Tordesillas, signed in 1494, which created the Tordesillas Meridian, dividing the world between the two kingdoms. All land discovered or to be discovered east of that meridian was to be the property of Portugal, and everything to the west of it went to Spain.

The Tordesillas Meridian divided South America into two parts, leaving a large chunk of land to be exploited by the Spaniards. The Treaty of Tordesillas was arguably the most decisiveWikipedia:Manual of Style/Words to watch#Puffery event in all Brazilian history, since it determined that part of South America would be settled by Portugal instead of Spain. The present extent of Brazil's coastline is almost exactly that defined by the treaty of Madrid, which was approved in 1750.

Arrival and early exploitation

On April 22, 1500, during the reign of King Manuel I, a fleet led by navigator Pedro Álvares Cabral landed in Brazil and took possession of the land in the name of the king. Although it is debated whether previous Portuguese explorers had already been in Brazil, this date is widely and politically accepted as the day of the discovery of Brazil by Europeans. Álvares Cabral was leading

Figure 17: *The brazilwood tree, which gives Brazil its name, has dark, valuable wood and provides red dye.*

a large fleet of 13 ships and more than 1000 men following Vasco da Gama's way to India, around Africa. The place where Álvares Cabral arrived is now known as Porto Seguro ("safe harbor"), in Northeastern Brazil.

After the voyage of Álvares Cabral, the Portuguese concentrated their efforts on the lucrative possessions in Africa and India and showed little interest in Brazil. Between 1500 and 1530, relatively few Portuguese expeditions came to the new land to chart the coast and to obtain brazilwood. In Europe, this wood was used to produce a valuable dye to give color to luxury textiles. To extract brazilwood from the tropical rainforest, the Portuguese and other Europeans relied on the work of the natives, who initially worked in exchange for European goods like mirrors, scissors, knives and axes.[251]

In this early stage of the colonization of Brazil, and also later, the Portuguese frequently relied on the help of Europeans who lived together with the indigenous people and knew their languages and culture. The most famous of these were the Portuguese João Ramalho, who lived among the Guaianaz tribe near today's São Paulo, and Diogo Álvares Correia, who acquired the name Caramuru, who lived among the Tupinambá natives near today's Salvador da Bahia.

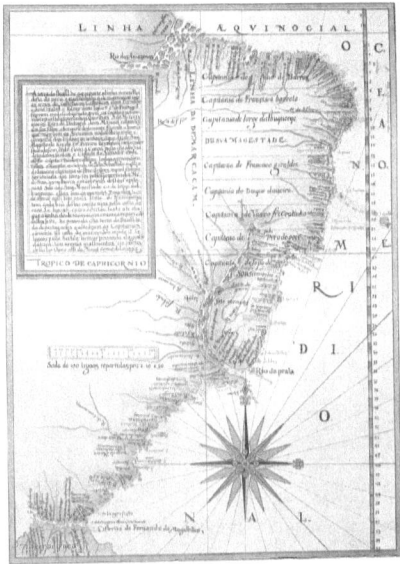

Figure 18: *Portuguese map (1574) by Luís Teixeira, showing the location of the hereditary captaincies of Brazil.*

Over time, the Portuguese realized that some European countries, especially France, were also sending excursions to the land to extract brazilwood. Worried about foreign incursions and hoping to find mineral riches, the Portuguese crown decided to send large missions to take possession of the land and combat the French. In 1530, an expedition led by Martim Afonso de Sousa arrived in Brazil to patrol the entire coast, ban the French, and create the first colonial villages like São Vicente on the coast.

Structure of Colonization

At first, Brazil was set up as fifteen private, hereditary captaincies. Pernambuco succeeded by growing sugarcane. São Vicente prospered by dealing in indigenous slaves. The other thirteen captaincies failed, leading the king to make colonization a royal effort rather than a private one.Wikipedia:Citation needed In 1549, Tomé de Sousa sailed to Brazil to establish a central government. De Sousa brought along Jesuits, who set up missions, saved many natives from slavery, studied native languages, and converted many natives to Roman Catholicism. The Jesuits' work to pacify a hostile tribe helped the Portuguese expel the French from a colony they had established at present-day Rio de Janeiro.Wikipedia:Citation needed

Captaincies

The first attempt to colonize Brazil followed the system of hereditary captaincies (*Capitanias Hereditárias*), which had previously been used successfully in the colonization of Madeira Island. The costs were transferred to private hands, saving the Portuguese crown from the high costs of colonization. Thus, between 1534 and 1536 King John III divided the land into 15 captaincy colonies, which were given to Portuguese noblemen who wanted and had the means to administer and explore them. The captains were granted ample powers to administer and profit from their possessions.

From the 15 original captaincies, only two, Pernambuco and São Vicente, prospered. The failure of most captaincies was related to the resistance of the indigenous people, shipwrecks and internal disputes between the colonizers.Wikipedia:Citation needed Pernambuco, the most successful captaincy, belonged to Duarte Coelho, who founded the city of Olinda in 1536. His captaincy prospered with sugarcane mills installed after 1542 producing sugar. Sugar was a very valuable good in Europe, and its production became the main Brazilian colonial produce for the next 150 years.

The captaincy of São Vicente, owned by Martim Afonso de Sousa, also produced sugar but its main economic activity was the traffic of indigenous slaves.

Governors General

With the failure of most captaincies and the menacing presence of French ships along the Brazilian coast, the government of King John III decided to turn the colonisation of Brazil back into a royal enterprise. In 1549, a large fleet led by Tomé de Sousa set sail to Brazil to establish a central government in the colony. Tomé de Sousa, the first Governor-General of Brazil, brought detailed instructions, prepared by the King's aides, about how to administer and foster the development of the colony. His first act was the foundation of the capital city, Salvador da Bahia, in Northeastern Brazil, in today's state of Bahia. The city was built on a slope by a bay (Todos-os-Santos Bay) and was divided into an upper administrative area and a lower commercial area with a harbour. Tomé de Sousa also visited the captaincies to repair the villages and reorganise their economies. In 1551, the Diocese of São Salvador da Bahia was established in the colony, with its seat in Salvador.

The second Governor General, Duarte da Costa (1553–1557), faced conflicts with the indigenous people and severe disputes with other colonizers and the bishop. Wars against the natives around Salvador consumed much of his government. The fact that the first bishop of Brazil, Pero Fernandes Sardinha, was killed and eaten by the Caeté natives after a shipwreck in 1556 illustrates how strained the situation was between the Portuguese and many indigenous tribes.

Colonial Brazil 69

Figure 19: *Historical centre of Salvador today – the architecture of the city's historic centre is typically Portuguese.*

The third Governor-General of Brazil was Mem de Sá (1557–1573). He was an efficient administrator who managed to defeat the indigenous people and, with the help of the Jesuits, expel the French (Huguenots and some previous Catholic settlers) from their colony of France Antarctique. As part of this process his nephew, Estácio de Sá, founded the city of Rio de Janeiro there in 1565.

The huge size of Brazil led to the colony being divided in two after 1621 when King Philip II created the states of *Brasil*, with Salvador as capital, and *Maranhão*, with its capital in São Luís. The state of Maranhão was still further divided in 1737 into the *Maranhão e Piauí* and *Grão-Pará e Rio Negro*, with its capital in Belém do Pará. Each state had its own Governor.

After 1640, the governors of Brazil coming from the high nobility started to use the title of *Vice-rei* (Viceroy). In 1763Wikipedia:Citation needed the capital of the *Estado do Brazil* was transferred from Salvador to Rio de Janeiro. In 1775 all Brazilian *Estados* (Brasil, Maranhão and Grão-Pará) were unified into the Viceroyalty of Brazil, with Rio de Janeiro as capital, and the title of the king's representative was officially changed to that of Viceroy of Brazil.

As in Portugal, each colonial village and city had a city council (*câmara municipal*), whose members were prominent figures of colonial society (land owners,

Figure 20: *17th century-Jesuit church in São Pedro da Aldeia, near Rio de Janeiro.*

merchants, slave traders). Colonial city councils were responsible for regulating commerce, public infrastructure, professional artisans, prisons etc.

Jesuit missions

Tomé de Sousa, first Governor General of Brazil, brought the first group of Jesuits to the colony.[252] More than any other religious order, the Jesuits represented the spiritual side of the enterprise and were destined to play a central role in the colonial history of Brazil. The spreading of the Catholic faith was an important justification for the Portuguese conquests, and the Jesuits were officially supported by the King, who instructed Tomé de Sousa to give them all the support needed to Christianise the indigenous people.

The first Jesuits, guided by Father Manuel da Nóbrega and including prominent figures like Juan de Azpilcueta Navarro, Leonardo Nunes and later José de Anchieta, established the first Jesuit missions in Salvador and in São Paulo dos Campos de Piratininga, the settlement that gave rise to the city of São Paulo. Nóbrega and Anchieta were instrumental in the defeat of the French colonists of France Antarctique by managing to pacify the Tamoio natives, who had previously fought the Portuguese. The Jesuits took part in the foundation of the city of Rio de Janeiro in 1565.

The success of the Jesuits in converting the indigenous people to Catholicism is linked to their capacity to understand the native culture, especially the language. The first grammar of the Tupi language was compiled by José de Anchieta and printed in Coimbra in 1595. The Jesuits often gathered the aborigines in communities (the Jesuit Reductions) where the natives worked for the community and were evangelised.

The Jesuits had frequent disputes with other colonists who wanted to enslave the natives. The action of the Jesuits saved many natives from slavery, but also disturbed their ancestral way of life and inadvertently helped spread infectious diseases against which the aborigines had no natural defences. Slave labour and trade were essential for the economy of Brazil and other American colonies, and the Jesuits usually did not object to the enslavement of African people.

French incursions

The potential riches of tropical Brazil led the French, who did not recognize the Tordesillas Treaty that divided the world between the Spanish and the Portuguese, to attempt to colonize parts of Brazil. In 1555, the Nicolas Durand de Villegaignon founded a settlement within Guanabara Bay, in an island in front of today's Rio de Janeiro. The colony, named France Antarctique, led to conflict with Governor General Mem de Sá, who waged war against the colony in 1560. Estácio de Sá, nephew of the Governor, founded Rio de Janeiro in 1565 and managed to expel the last French settlers in 1567. Jesuit priests Manuel da Nóbrega and José de Anchieta were instrumental in the Portuguese victory by pacifying the natives who supported the French.[253]

Another French colony, France Équinoxiale, was founded in 1612 in present-day São Luís, in the North of Brazil. In 1614 the French were again expelled from São Luís by the Portuguese.

The Sugar Age (1530–1700)

Since the initial attempts to find gold and silver failed, the Portuguese colonists adopted an economy based on the production of agricultural goods that were to be exported to Europe. Tobacco and cotton and some other agricultural goods were produced, but sugar became by far the most important Brazilian colonial product until the early 18th century. The first sugarcane farms were established in the mid-16th century and were the key for the success of the captaincies of São Vicente and Pernambuco, leading sugarcane plantations to quickly spread to other coastal areas in colonial Brazil. Initially, the Portuguese attempted to utilize Indian slaves for sugar cultivation, but shifted to the use of black African slave labor.[254]

Figure 21: *View of a sugar-producing farm (engenho) in colonial Pernambuco by Dutch painter Frans Post (17th century).*

Figure 22: *Golden Baroque inner decoration of the Franciscan church of Salvador (first half of the 18th century).*

The period of sugar-based economy (1530 – c. 1700) is known as the sugar age in Brazil.[255] The development of the sugar complex occurred over time, with a variety of models.[256] The dependencies of the farm included a *casa-grande* (big house) where the owner of the farm lived with his family, and the *senzala*, where the slaves were kept. A notable early study of this complex is by Brazilian sociologist Gilberto Freyre.[257] This arrangement was depicted in engravings and paintings by Frans Post as a feature of an apparently harmonious society.[258]

Initially, the Portuguese relied on native slaves to work on sugarcane harvesting and processing, but they soon began importing black African slaves. Portugal owned several commercial facilities in Western Africa, where slaves were bought from African merchants. These slaves were then sent by ship to Brazil, chained and in crowded conditions. The idea of using African slaves in colonial farms based on monoculture was also adopted by other European colonial powers when colonizing tropical regions of America (Spain in Cuba, France in Haiti, the Netherlands in the Dutch Antilles and England in Jamaica).

The Portuguese attempted to severely restrict colonial trade, meaning that Brazil was only allowed to export and import goods from Portugal and other Portuguese colonies. Brazil exported sugar, tobacco, cotton and native products and imported from Portugal wine, olive oil, textiles and luxury goods – the latter imported by Portugal from other European countries. Africa played an essential role as the supplier of slaves, and Brazilian slave traders in Africa frequently exchanged cachaça, a distilled spirit derived from sugarcane, and shells, for slaves. This comprised what is now known as the Triangular trade between Europe, Africa and the Americas during the colonial period.

Merchants during the sugar age were crucial to the economic development of the colony, the link between the sugar production areas, coastal Portuguese cities, and Europe.[259] Merchants in the early came from many nations, including Germans, Flemings, and Italians, but Portuguese merchants came to dominate the trade in Brazil. During the union of the Spanish and Portuguese crowns (1580-1640), to be active in Spanish America as well, especially trading African slaves.[260]

Even though Brazilian sugar was reputed as being of high quality, the industry faced a crisis during the 17th and 18th centuries when the Dutch and the French started producing sugar in the Antilles, located much closer to Europe, causing sugar prices to fall.

Figure 23: *View of Olinda, ca. 1660, Frans Post*

Cities and towns

Brazil had coastal cities and towns, which have been considered far less important than colonial settlements in Spanish America, but like Spanish America, urban settlements were important as the sites of institutional life of church and state, as well as urban groups of merchants. Unlike many areas of Spanish America, there was no dense, sedentary indigenous population which had already created settlements, but cities and towns in Brazil were similar to those in Spanish Colonial Venezuela. Port cities allowed Portuguese trade goods to enter, including African slaves, and export goods of sugar and later gold and coffee to be exported to Portugal and beyond. Coastal cities of Olinda (founded 1537), Salvador da Bahia (1549), Santos (1545), Vitória (1551), and Rio de Janeiro (1565) were also vital in the defense against pirates. Only São Paulo in Minas Gerais was an important inland city. Unlike the network of towns and cities that developed in most areas of Spanish America, the coastal cities and their hinterlands were oriented toward Portugal directly with little connection otherwise. With sugar as the major export commodity in the early period and the necessity to process cane into exportable refined sugar on-site, the sugar *engenhos* had resident artisans and barber-surgeons, and functioned in some ways as small towns. Also unlike most Spanish settlements, Brazilian cities and towns did not have a uniform lay-out of central plaza and a check board pattern of streets, often because the topography defeated such an orderly layout.[261]

Figure 24: *Coat of arms of Philip II and I of Spain and Portugal, inserting the coat of arms of Portugal over those of Castile and León and Aragon.*

New Christians

Converted Jews, so-called New Christians, many of whom were merchants, played a role in colonial Brazil. Their "importance in the colonial may be one explanation why the Inquisition was not permanently established in Brazil during the Iberian Union." New Christians were well integrated into institutional life, serving in civil as well as ecclesiastical offices. The relative lack of persecution and abundance of opportunity allowed them to have a significant place in society. With the Iberian Union (1580-1640), many migrated to Spanish America.[262]

The Iberian Union 1580-1640

In 1580, a succession crisis led to the union of Portugal and Spain being ruled by the Habsburg King Philip II. The unification of the crowns of the two Iberian kingdoms, known as the Iberian Union, lasted until 1640 when the Portuguese revolted. During the union the institutions of both kingdoms remained separate. For Portuguese merchants, many of whom were Christian converts from Judaism ("New Christians") or their descendants, the union of crowns presented commercial opportunities in the slave trade to Spanish

America.[263,264] The Netherlands (the Seventeen Provinces) obtained independence from Spain in 1581, leading Philip II to prohibit commerce with Dutch ships, including in Brazil. Since the Dutch had invested large sums in financing sugar production in the Brazilian Northeast and were important as shippers of sugar,[265] a conflict began with Dutch privateers plundering the coast: they sacked Salvador in 1604, from which they removed large amounts of gold and silver before a joint Spanish-Portuguese fleet recaptured the town.Wikipedia:Citation needed

Dutch rule in northeastern Brazil, 1630-1654

From 1630 to 1654, the Dutch set up more permanently in commercial Recife and aristocratic Olinda.[266] With the capture of Paraiba in 1635, the Dutch controlled a long stretch of the coast most accessible to Europe (Dutch Brazil), without, however, penetrating the interior. The large Dutch ships were unable to moor in the coastal inlets where lighter Portuguese shipping came and went. Ironically, the result of the Dutch capture of the sugar coast was a higher price of sugar in Amsterdam. During the Nieuw Holland episode, the colonists of the Dutch West India Company in Brazil were in a constant state of siege, in spite of the presence of the Count John Maurice of Nassau as governor (1637–1644) in Recife. Nassau invited scientific commissions to research the local flora and fauna, resulting in added knowledge of the territory. Moreover, he set up a city project for Recife and Olinda, which was partially accomplished. Remnants survive into the modern era. After several years of open warfare, the Dutch finally withdrew in 1654; the Portuguese paid off a war debt in payments of salt. Few Dutch cultural and ethnic influences remain. but Albert Eckhout's paintings of indigenous and black Brazilians, as well as his still lifes are important works of baroque art.

Runaway slave settlements

Work on the sugarcane plantations in Northeast Brazil and other areas relied heavily on slave labor, mostly of central African origin. One type of resistance to slavery was flight and, with the dense vegetation of the tropics, runaway slaves fled in numbers and for slave owners, this was an "endemic problem."[267] Since the early 17th century there are indications of runaway slaves organizing themselves into settlements in the Brazilian hinterland. These settlements, called *mocambos* and *quilombos*, were usually small and relatively close to sugar fields, and attracted not only African slaves but also people of indigenous origin. The largest of the quilombos was the Quilombo dos Palmares, located in today's Alagoas state, which grew to many thousands during the disruption of Portuguese rule with the Dutch incursion.[268] Palmares was governed by leaders Ganga Zumba and his successor, Zumbi. The terminology

Figure 25: *Albert Eckhout, African warrior at the time of Ganga Zumba, leader of the Palmares quilombo*

for the settlements and leaders come directly from Angola, with *quilombo* an Angolan word for military villages of diverse settlers and the *nganga a nzumbi* "was the priest responsible for the spiritual defense of the community."[269] The Dutch and later the Portuguese attempted several times to conquer Palmares, until an army led by famed São Paulo-born *Domingos Jorge Velho* managed to destroy the great quilombo and kill Zumbi in 1695. Brazilian feature film director Carlos Diegues made a film about Palmares called simply *Quilombo*. Of the many quilombos that once existed in Brazil, some have survived to this day as isolated rural communities.Wikipedia:Citation needed

Inland expansion: the *entradas* and *bandeiras*

Since the 16th century the exploration of the Brazilian inland was attempted several times, mostly to try to find mineral riches like the silver mines found in 1546 by the Spanish in Potosí (now in Bolivia). Since no riches were initially found, colonisation was restricted to the coast where the climate and soil were suitable for sugarcane plantations.

The expeditions to inland Brazil are divided into two types: the *entradas* and the *bandeiras*. The *entradas* were done in the name of the Portuguese crown and were financed by the colonial government. Its main objective was to find

Figure 26: *Albert Eckhout Tapuias dancing, mid. 17th c.*

mineral riches, as well as to explore and chart unknown territory. The *bandeiras*, on the other hand, were private initiatives sponsored and carried out mostly by settlers of the São Paulo region (the *Paulistas*). The expeditions of the *bandeirantes*, as these adventurers were called, were aimed at obtaining native slaves for trade and finding mineral riches. The *Paulistas*, who at the time were mostly of mixed Portuguese and native ancestry, knew all the old indigenous pathways (the *peabirus*) through the Brazilian inland and were acclimated to the harsh conditions of these journeys.[270]

At the end of the 17th century, the *bandeirantes* expeditions discovered gold in central Brazil, in the region of Minas Gerais, which started a gold rush that led to a dramatic urban development of inland Brazil during the 18th century. Additionally, inland expeditions led to westward expansion of the frontiers of colonial Brazil, beyond the limits established by the Treaty of Tordesillas.

The gold cycle (18th century)

The discovery of gold was met with great enthusiasm by Portugal, which had an economy in disarray following years of wars against Spain and the Netherlands. A gold rush quickly ensued, with people from other parts of the colony and Portugal flooding the region in the first half of the 18th century. The large portion of the Brazilian inland where gold was extracted became known as the Minas Gerais (General Mines). Gold mining in this area became the main economic activity of colonial Brazil during the 18th century. In Portugal, the gold was mainly used to pay for industrialized goods (textiles, weapons) obtained from countries like England and, especially during the reign of King

Figure 27: *View of Ouro Preto, one of the main Portuguese settlements founded during the gold rush of Minas Gerais. The town has preserved its colonial appearance to this day.*

John V, to build magnificent Baroque monuments like the Convent of Mafra. Apart from gold, diamond deposits were also found in 1729 around the village of Tijuco, now Diamantina. A famous figure in Brazilian history of this era was Xica da Silva, a slave woman who had a long term relationship in Diamantina with a Portuguese official; the couple had thirteen children and she died a rich woman.[271] She has been the subject of a Brazilian feature film by Carlos Diegues, *Xica* and a telenovela *Xica da Silva*.

In the hilly landscape of Minas Gerais, gold was present in alluvial deposits around streams and was extracted using pans and other similar instruments that required little technology. Gold extraction was mostly done by slaves. The Portuguese Crown allowed particulars to extract the gold, requiring a fifth (20%) of the gold (the *quinto*) to be sent to the colonial government as tribute. To prevent smuggling and extract the *quinto*, in 1725 the government ordered all gold to be cast into bars in the *Casas de Fundição* (Casting Houses), and sent armies to the region to prevent disturbances and oversee the mining process. The Royal tribute was very unpopular in Minas Gerais, and gold

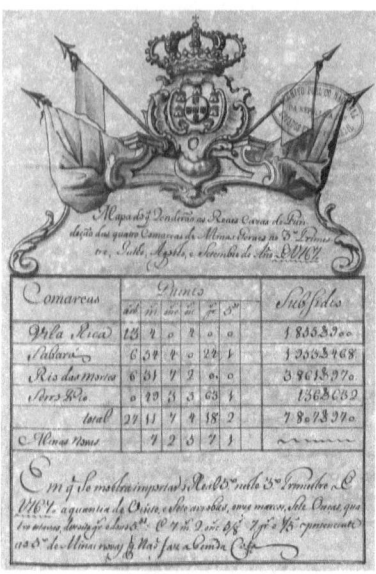

Figure 28: *Map of gold yield in the Real Casting Houses in Minas Gerais, between July and September of 1767. National Archives of Brazil.*

was frequently hidden from colonial authorities. Eventually, the *quinto* contributed to rebellious movements like the *Levante de Vila Rica*, in 1720, and the *Inconfidência Mineira*, in 1789 (see below).

Some historians mention that the trade deficit of Portugal in relation to England while the Methuen Treaty was in force has also contributed to redirect much of the gold mined in Brazil during the 18th century to Britain. The Methuen Treaty was a trade treaty signed between England and Portugal, by where all woolen cloth imported from Britain would be tax free in Portugal, whereas Portuguese wine exported to Britain would be taxed at a third of the previous import tax on wines. Port wine became increasingly popular in Britain at that time, but cloth amounted to a larger share of the trade value than wines, hence Portugal eventually incurred in trade deficit with England.

The large number of adventurers coming to the Minas Gerais led to the foundation of several settlements, the first of which were created in 1711: Vila Rica de Ouro Preto, Sabará and Mariana, followed by São João del Rei (1713), Serro, Caeté (1714), Pitangui (1715) and São José do Rio das Mortes (1717, now Tiradentes). In contrast to other regions of colonial Brazil, people coming to Minas Gerais settled mostly in villages instead of the countryside.

Figure 29: *18th century-São José Fortress near Florianópolis, in southern Brazil*

In 1763, the capital of colonial Brazil was transferred from Salvador to Rio de Janeiro, which was located closer to the mining region and provided a harbor to ship the gold to Europe.

According to the historian Leslie Bethell, "In 1700 Portugal had a population of about two million people. During the eighteenth century approximately 400,000 left for [the Portuguese colony of] Brazil, despite efforts by the crown to place severe restrictions on emigration."[272]

Gold production declined towards the end of the 18th century, beginning a period of relative stagnation of the Brazilian hinterland.

Colonization of the South

In an attempt to expand the borders of colonial Brazil and profit from the silver mines of Potosí, the Portuguese Overseas Council (the *Conselho Ultramarino*) ordered colonial governor Manuel Lobo to establish a settlement on the shore of the River Plate, in a region that legally belonged to Spain. In 1679, Manuel Lobo founded Colonia de Sacramento on the margin opposite to Buenos Aires. The fortified settlement quickly became an important point of illegal commerce between the Spanish and Portuguese colonies. Spain and Portugal fought over the enclave on several occasions (1681, 1704, 1735).

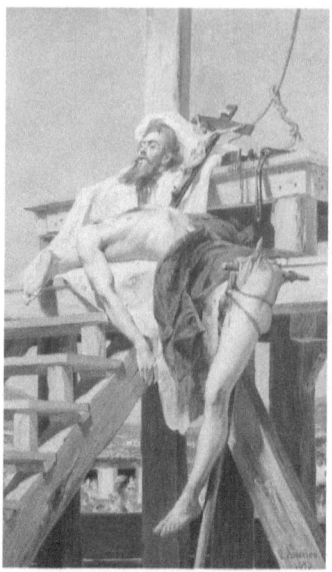

Figure 30: *Quartered body of Tiradentes, by Brazilian painter Pedro Américo (1893).*

In addition to Colonia de Sacramento, several settlements were established in Southern Brazil in the late 17th and 18th century, some with peasants from the Azores Islands. The towns founded in this period include Curitiba (1668), Florianópolis (1675), Rio Grande (1736), Porto Alegre (1742) and others, and helped keep southern Brazil firmly under Portuguese control.

The conflicts over the Southern colonial frontiers led to the signing of the Treaty of Madrid (1750), in which Spain and Portugal agreed to a considerable Southwestward expansion of colonial Brazil. According to the treaty, Colonia de Sacramento was to be given to Spain in exchange for the territories of *São Miguel das Missões*, a region occupied by Jesuit Missions dedicated to evangelizing the Guaraní natives. Resistance by the Jesuits and the Guaraní led to the Guaraní War (1756), in which Portuguese and Spanish troops destroyed the Missions. Colonia de Sacramento kept changing hands until 1777, when it was definitively conquered by the colonial governor of Buenos Aires.

Inconfidência Mineira

In 1788/89, Minas Gerais was the setting of the most important conspiracy against colonial authorities, the so-called *Inconfidência Mineira*, inspired by the ideals of the French liberal philosophers of the Age of Enlightenment and the successful American Revolution of 1776. The conspirators largely belonged to the white upper class of Minas Gerais.[273] Many had studied in Europe, especially in the University of Coimbra, and some had large debts with the colonial government. In the context of declining gold production, the intention of the Portuguese government to impose the obligatory payment of all debts (the *derrama*) was a leading cause behind the conspiracy. The conspirators wanted to create a Republic in which the leader would be chosen through democratic elections. The capital would be São João del Rei, and Ouro Preto would become a university town. The structure of the society, including the right to property and the ownership of slaves, would be kept intact.

The conspiracy was discovered by the Portuguese colonial government in 1789, before the planned military rebellion could take place. Eleven of the conspirators were exiled to Portuguese colonial possessions in Angola, but Joaquim José da Silva Xavier, nicknamed Tiradentes, was sentenced to death. Tiradentes was hanged in Rio de Janeiro in 1792, drawn and quartered, and his body parts displayed in several towns. He later became a symbol of the struggle for Brazilian independence and liberty from Portuguese rule.

The Inconfidência Mineira was not the only rebellious movement in colonial Brazil against the Portuguese. Later, in 1798, there was the *Inconfidência Baiana* in Salvador. In this episode, which had more participation of common people, four people were hanged, and 41 were jailed. Members included slaves, middle-class people and even some landowners.

The Royal Court in Brazil (1808–1821)

The Napoleonic invasion of the Iberian peninsula set off major changes there and in both Portugal's and Spain's overseas empires. In 1807 French troops of Napoleon Bonaparte invaded Britain's ally, Portugal. Prince Regent João (future King João VI), who had governed since 1792 on behalf of his mother, Queen Maria I, ordered the transfer of the Portuguese royal court to Brazil before he could be deposed by the invading army. In January 1808, Prince João and his court arrived in Salvador, where he signed a commercial regulation that opened commerce between Brazil and *friendly nations* (Britain). This important law broke the *colonial pact* that, until then, allowed Brazil to maintain direct commercial relations with only Portugal.[274,275]

In March 1808, the court arrived in Rio de Janeiro. In 1815, during the Congress of Vienna, Prince João created the United Kingdom of Portugal, Brazil and the Algarves (*Reino Unido de Portugal, Brasil e Algarves*), elevating Brazil to the rank of Portugal and increasing its administrative independence.

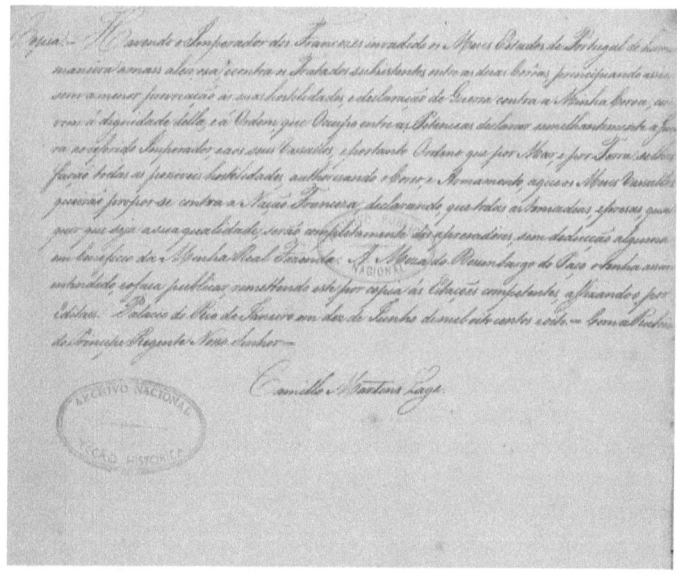

Figure 31: *Declaration of war made by D. John to Napoleon Bonaparte and all his vassals, 1808. National Archives of Brazil.*

In 1816, with the death of Queen Maria, Prince João succeeded as monarch, and the ceremony of his acclamation was held in Rio de Janeiro in February 1818.

Among the important measures taken by Prince João in his years in Brazil were incentives to commerce and industry, the permission to print newspapers and books, the creation of two medicine schools, military academies, and the first Bank of Brazil (*Banco do Brasil*). In Rio de Janeiro he also created a powder factory, a Botanical Garden, an art academy (*Escola Nacional de Belas Artes*) and an opera house (*Teatro São João*). All these measures greatly advanced the independence of Brazil in relation to Portugal and made the later political separation between the two countries inevitable.

Due to the absence of the King and the economic independence of Brazil, Portugal entered a severe crisis that obliged João VI and the royal family to return to Portugal in 1821: a Liberal Revolution had broken out in Portugal in 1820, and the royal governors who ruled Portugal in the King's name had been replaced by a revolutionary Council of Regency formed to govern the European portion of the kingdom until the King's return. Indeed, the King's immediate return to Lisbon was one of the main demands of the Revolution. Under the revolutionary Council of Regency, a constituent assembly, known as the

Figure 32: *The Paço Imperial, 18th century-colonial palace located in Rio de Janeiro, used as dispatch house by King João VI of Portugal and later by Emperor Pedro I of Brazil.*

Portuguese Constitutional Courts (*Cortes Constitucionais Portuguesas*), was elected to abolish the absolute monarchy and replace it with a constitutional one. King João VI, then, yielding to pressure, returned to Europe. Brazilian representatives were elected to join the deliberations of the Constitutional *Cortes* of the kingdom.

The heir of João VI, Prince Pedro, remained in Brazil. The Portuguese *Cortes* demanded that Brazil return to its former condition of colony and that the heir return to Portugal. Prince Pedro, influenced by the Rio de Janeiro Municipal Senate (*Senado da Câmara*), refused to return to Portugal in the famous *Dia do Fico* (January 9, 1822). Political independence came on September 7, 1822, and the prince was crowned emperor in Rio de Janeiro as Dom Pedro I, ending 322 years of dominance of Portugal over Brazil.

Territorial evolution of colonial Brazil

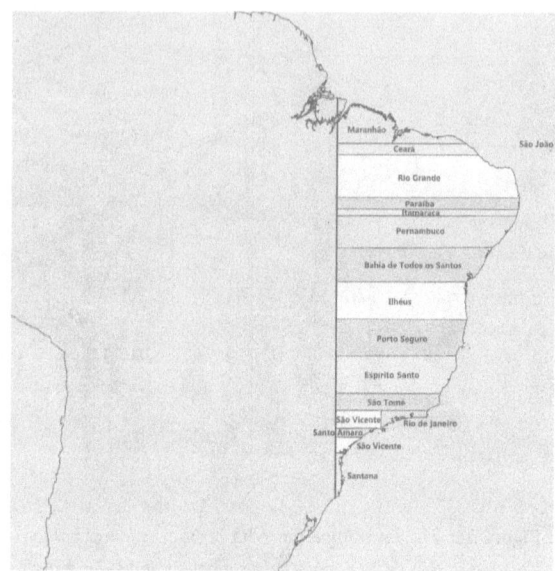

Figure 33: *1534*
Capitanias hereditárias

Figure 34: *1573*
Two states

Colonial Brazil

Figure 35: *1709*
Inland expansion

Figure 36: *1750*
Treaty of Madrid

Figure 37: *1817*
At the time of the Pernambucan revolt

Figure 38: *1822*
At date of Independence

Administrative evolution

Colonial entities, ordered by the date of establishment, earlier to later:

- Captaincy Colonies of Brazil (Private and autonomous colonies 1534-1549)
- Captaincies of Brazil (Colonial provincial districts from 1549-1815)
- Governorate General of Brazil (1549-1572 / 1578-1607 / 1613-1621)
  - Governorate General of Bahia (1572-1578 / 1607-1613)
  - Governorate General of Rio de Janeiro (1572-1578 / 1607-1613)
- State of Brazil (1621–1815)
- State of Maranhão (1621–1751)
- State of Grão-Pará and Maranhão (1751–1772)
- State of Grão-Pará and Rio Negro (1772–1775)
- State of Maranhão and Piauí (1772–1775)
- In 1808 the Queen and the Prince Regent of Portugal arrive in Brazil and the Prince Regent's Government assumes direct control of the administration of the State of Brazil;
- In 1815, the State of Brazil is elevated to the rank of a Kingdom (the Kingdom of Brazil) and with the simultaneous formation of the United Kingdom of Portugal, Brazil and the Algarves, marking the formal end of the colonial era.
- In 1822, Brazil secedes from the United Kingdom and the independent Empire of Brazil is founded. The separation is recognized by Portugal in 1825.

The detailed history of the administrative changes in the administration of colonial Brazil is as follows:

From 1534 (immediately after the start the Portuguese attempts to effectively colonize Brazil) until 1549, Brazil was divided by the Portuguese Crown in private and autonomous colonies known as *hereditary captaincies* (*capitanias hereditárias*), or *captaincy colonies* (*colónias capitanias*).

In 1549, Portuguese King John III abolished the system of private colonies, and the fifteen existing hereditary captaincies were incorporated into a single Crown colony, the Governorate General of Brazil.

The individual captaincies, now under the administration of the Portuguese Crown (and no longer called colonies or hereditary captaincies, but simply captaincies of Brazil), continued to exist as provinces or districts within the colony until the end of the colonial era in 1815.

The unified Governorate General of Brazil, with its capital city in Salvador, existed during three periods: from 1549 to 1572, from 1578 to 1607 and from 1613 to 1621. Between 1572 and 1578 and again between 1607 and 1613, the colony was split in two, and during those periods the Governorate General of Brazil did not exist, being replaced by two separate Governorates: the Governorate General of Bahia, in the North, with its seat in the city of Salvador, and the Governorate General of Rio de Janeiro, in the South, with its seat in the city of Rio de Janeiro.

In 1621, an administrative reorganization took place, and the Governorate General of Brazil became known as the State of Brazil (*Estado do Brasil*), keeping Salvador as its capital city. With this administrative remodeling, the unity of the colony was once again interrupted, as a portion of territory in the northern part of modern Brazil became an autonomous colony, separate from the State of Brazil: the State of Maranhão, with its capital city in São Luiz.

In 1652, the State of Maranhão was extinguished, and its territory was briefly added to the State of Brazil, reunifying the colonial administration once more.

However, in 1654, the territories of the former State of Maranhão were again separated from the State of Brazil, and the Captaincy of Grão-Pará was also split from Brazil. In this restructuring, the territories of Grão-Pará and Maranhão, severed from Brazil, were united in a single State, initially named as State of Maranhão and Grão-Pará, having São Luiz as its capital city. This newly created State incorporated territories recently acquired by the Portuguese west of the Tordesillas line.

In 1751, the State of Maranhão and Grão-Pará was renamed as the State of Grão-Pará and Maranhão, and its capital city as transferred from São Luiz (in Maranhão) to Belém (in the part of the State that was then known as Grão-Pará).

In 1763 the capital city of the State of Brazil was transferred from Salvador to Rio de Janeiro. At the same time, the title of the King's representative heading the government of the State of Brazil was officially changed from Governor General to Viceroy (Governors coming from the high nobility had been using the title of Viceroy since about 1640). However, the name of Brazil was never changed to Viceroyalty of Brazil. That title, although sometimes used by modern writers, is not proper, as the colony continued to be titled State of Brazil.

In 1772, in a short-lived territorial reorganization, the State of Grão-Pará and Maranhão was split in two: the State of Grão-Pará and Rio Negro (better known simply as the State of Grão-Pará), with the city of Belém as its capital, and the State of Maranhão and Piauí (better known simply as the State of Maranhão), with its seat in the city of São Luiz.

Thus from 1772 until another territorial reorganization in 1775 there were three distinct Portuguese States in South America: the State of Brazil, the State of Grão-Pará and Rio Negro, and the State of Maranhão and Piauí.

In 1775, in a final territorial reorganization, the colony was once again reunified: the State of Maranhão and Piauí and the State of Grão-Pará and Rio Negro were both abolished, and their territories were incorporated into the territory of the State of Brazil. The State of Brazil was thus expanded; it became the sole Portuguese State in South America; and it now included in its territory the whole of the Portuguese possessions in the American Continent. Indeed, with the reorganization of 1775, for the first time since 1654, all the Portuguese territories in the New World were once again united under a single colonial government. Rio de Janeiro, that had become the capital of the State of Brazil in 1763, continued to be the capital, now of the unified colony.

In 1808, the Portuguese Court was transferred to Brazil as direct consequence of the invasion of Portugal during the Napoleonic Wars. The office of Viceroy of Brazil ceased to exist upon the arrival of the Royal Family in Rio de Janeiro, since the Prince Regent, the future King Jonh VI, assumed personal control of the government of the colony, that became the provisional seat of the whole Portuguese Empire.

In 1815, Brazil ceased to be a colony, upon the elevation of the State of Brazil to the rank of a kingdom, the Kingdom of Brazil, and the simultaneous political union of that kingdom with the Kingdoms of Portugal and the Algarves, forming a single sovereign State, the United Kingdom of Portugal, Brazil and the Algarves. That political union would last until 1822, when Brazil declared its independence from the United Kingdom of Portugal, Brazil and the Algarves and became the Empire of Brazil, a sovereign nation in the territory of the former Kingdom of Brazil. The separation was recognized by Portugal with the signing of the 1825 Treaty of Rio de Janeiro.

With the creation of the Kingdom of Brazil in 1815, the former captaincies of the State of Brazil became provinces within the new Kingdom, and after independence they became the provinces of the Empire of Brazil.

Further reading in English

- Alden, Dauril. *Royal Government in Colonial Brazil with Special Reference to the Admistration of the Marquis of Lavradio, Viceroy 1769-1779.* 1968.
- Bethell, Leslie, ed. *Colonial Brazil.* 1987.
- Boxer, C. R. *Salvador de Sá and the struggle for Brazil and Angola, 1602-1686.* [London] University of London, 1952.
- Boxer, C. R. *The Dutch in Brazil, 1624-1654.* Oxford, Clarendon Press, 1957.
- Boxer, C. R. *The golden age of Brazil, 1695-1750; growing pains of a colonial society.* Berkeley: University of California Press, 1962.

- Freyre, Gilberto. *The Masters and the Slaves: A Study of the Development of Brazilian Civilization*, translated by Samuel Putnam. revised edition 1963.
- Hemming, John. *Red Gold: The Conquest of the Brazilian Indians*. 1978.
- Hemming, John. *Amazon Frontier: The Defeat of the Brazilian Indians*. London: Macmillan 1987.
- Higgins, Kathleen. *Licentious Liberty in a Brazilian Gold-Mining Region*. University Park: Penn State Press 1999.
- Kuznesof, Elizabeth. *Household Economy and Urban Development: São Paulo, 1765-1836*. Boulder: Westview Press 1986.
- Lang, James. *Portuguese Brazil: The King's Plantation*. 1979.
- Metcalf, Alida C. *Family and Frontier in Colonial Brazil: Santana de Parnaiba, 1480-1822*. 1991.
- Nazzari, Muriel. *Disappearance of the dowry: Women, Families and Social Change in São Paulo (1600-1900)*. 1991.
- Prado, Caio Junior. *The Colonial Background of Modern Brazil*. translated by suzette Macedo. 1967.
- Russell-Wood, A.J.R. *Fidalgos and Philanthropists: The Santa Casa de Misericórdia of Bahia, 1550-1755*. 1968.
- Russell-Wood, A.J.R. "Archives and Recent Historiography on Colonial Brazil. Latin American Research Review *36:1(2001): 75-103.*
- Russell-Wood, A.J.R. "United States Scholarly Contributions to the Historiography of Colonial Brazil," *Hispanic American Historical Review 65:4(1985):683-723.*
- Russell-Wood, A.J.R. *Society and Government in Colonial Brazil, 1500-1822*. 1992.
- Russell-Wood, A.J.R. *From Colony to Nation: Essays on the Independence of Brazil*. 1975.
- Schultz, Kristin. *Tropical Versailles: Empire, Monarchy, and the Portuguese Royal Court in Rio de Janeiro*. New York: Routledge 2001.
- Schwartz, Stuart B., "The Historiography of Early Modern Brazil," in *The Oxford Handbook of Latin American History*, José C. Moya, ed. New York: Oxford University Press 2011, pp. 98–131.
- Schwartz, Stuart B., "Somebodies and Nobodies in the Body Politic: Mentalities and Social Structures in Colonial Brazil," *Latin American Research Review* 31:1(1996): 112-34.
- Schwartz, Stuart B. *Sovereignty and Society in Colonial Brazil*. Berkeley: University of California Press 1978.
- Schwartz, Stuart B. *Sugar Plantations in the Formation of Brazilian Society*. Cambridge: Cambridge University Press 1985.
- Schwartz, Stuart B. *Peasants and Rebels: Reconsidering Brazilian Slavery*. 1992.

- Verger, Pierre. *Bahia and the West African Trade, 1549-1851.* Ibadan: Ibadan University Press 1964.
- Wadsworth, James E. "In the Name of the Inquisition: The Portuguese Inquisition and Delegated Authority in Colonial Pernambuco," *The Americas* 61:1 (2004): 19-52.

Bibliography

- Prado Junior, Caio. *História econômica do Brasil.* (http://www.afoiceeomartelo.com.br/posfsa/Autores/Prado%20Jr,%20Caio/Historia%20Economica%20do%20Brasil.pdf)
- Furtado, Celso. *Formação econômica do Brasil.* (http://www.afoiceeomartelo.com.br/posfsa/Autores/Furtado,%20Celso/Celso%20Furtado%20-%20Forma%C3%A7%C3%A3o%20Econ%C3%B4mica%20do%20Brasil.pdf)
- Van Groesen, Michiel. (ed.) "The Legacy of Dutch Brazil". New York: Cambridge University Press, 2014.
- Colonial history of Brazil in the Rio de Janeiro Municipality website (in Portuguese).[276]
- Braudel, Fernand, *The Perspective of the World,* Vol. III of *Civilization and Capitalism,* 1984.
- Report of the Brown University Steering Committee on Slavery and Justice[277]

War of the Emboabas

War of the Emboabas	
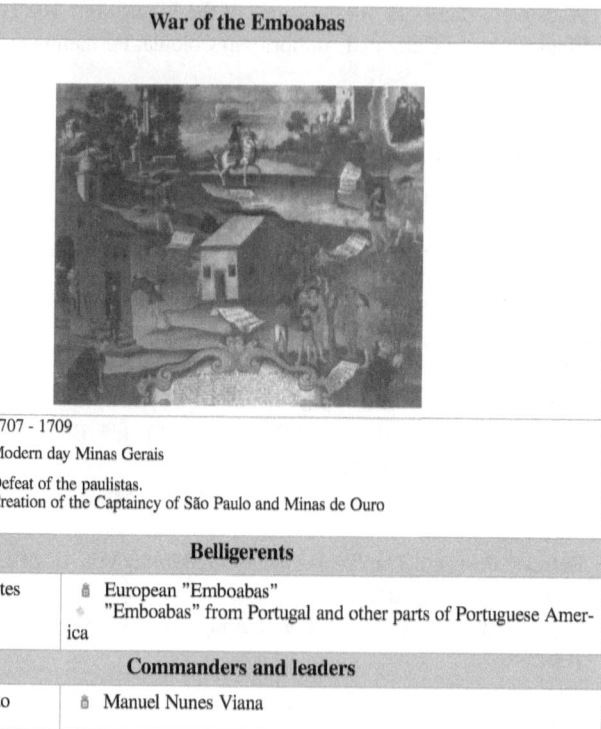	
Date	1707 - 1709
Location	Modern day Minas Gerais
Result	Defeat of the paulistas. Creation of the Captaincy of São Paulo and Minas de Ouro
Belligerents	
Bandeirantes Paulistas	European "Emboabas" "Emboabas" from Portugal and other parts of Portuguese America
Commanders and leaders	
Borba Gato	Manuel Nunes Viana

The **War of the Emboabas** (Portuguese: *Guerra dos Emboabas*, "newcomers' war") was a conflict in colonial Brazil waged in 1706-1707 and 1708-1709 over newly discovered gold fields, which had set off a rush to the region.between two generations of Portuguese settlers in the viceroyalty of Brazil - then the Captaincy of São Vicente. The discovery of gold set off a rush to the region, Paulistas asserted rights of discovery and non-Paulistas challenged their claims. Although the Portuguese crown sought more control in the area and the Paulistas sought protection of their claims, the Emoboabas won. The crown re-assessed its position in the region and made administrative changes subsequently.[278]

History

Starting from the village of São Paulo dos Campos de Piratininga (now São Paulo) the Bandeirantes had explored most of southeast and southwest of current Brazil, effectively taking advantage of the union of the Crowns of Portugal and Spain from 1580 to 1640 to incorporate all the former Spanish territories then west of the Tordesilhas Line. Their goal was to capture new Indian slaves (which put them in conflict with the Jesuit Reductions), recapture runaway slaves and find precious minerals.

Their search was rewarded in a then inaccessible area just north of their original Capitania that was to become Minas dos Matos Gerais (now Minas Gerais). The problem was that the mines, while rich, were in a vast area they could not effectively settle, so it attracted a gold rush from Portugal. The newcomers, called Emboabas, found an alternative, shorter route to the sea; the Caminho Novo das Minas dos Matos Gerais to São Sebastião do Rio de Janeiro on Guanabara Bay, bypassing and alienating the original discoverers.

The Bandeirantes, or Paulistas, tried to assert rights of precedence but were defeated. As a result, the provinces of Minas Gerais and Rio de Janeiro were formed, their capital cities of Vila Rica do Ouro Preto and São Sebastião do Rio de Janeiro, respectively, became the new centers of power in the vice-kingdom of Brazil. São Sebastião (later shortened to its present name of Rio de Janeiro) became the capital city of the viceroyalty and later of the United Kingdom of Portugal, Brazil and the Algarves.

As soon as news of the discovery of gold spread thousands of outsiders moved to the area and became known pejoratively as "Emboabas". The term is derived from the Tupi *mbóaba* which literally means "hairy leg" (*mbo* (leg) + *tab* (hairy)). Originally the term referred to birds with feathered legs and as, unlike the Paulista pioneers, the outsiders always wore knee-high boots with their trousers tucked in, giving them the name.[279][280]

Alternatively, according to the Dicionário Houaiss *emboaba* could be derived from the Tupi words *mbo* (do) and *tab* (hurt) meaning "those who invade or attack" and would be applied to a group rather than an individual.

Consequences

- Regulation of the distribution of mines between Emboabas and Paulistas.
- Regulation of collection of the *quinto do ouro* tax.
- Breakup on 3 November 1709 of the Province of São Vicente into *São Paulo e Minas de Ouro* and *Rio de Janeiro*, ruled directly by the Crown.
- São Paulo attained city status.
- End of the wars in the mining areas with the crown assuming the administrative control of the region.
- The defeat of Paulistas caused some of them to move west where, years later, they would discover new gold deposits in the current states of Mato Grosso do Sul, Mato Grosso and Goiás.

Figure 39: *Brazil after the war*

- The production of gold after the war increased so that Minas Gerais became the richest region of Brazil between 1740 and 1760.

Further reading

- Cardozo, Manoel S. "The *Guerra dos Emboabas*, Civli War in Minas Gerais, 1708-1709". *Hispanic American Historical Review* 22 (August 1942), 470-492.
- Boxer, Charles R.. *The Golden Age of Brazil, 1695-1750.* 1964.
- Franco, Francisco de Assis Carvalho, "Dicionário de Bandeirantes e Sertanistas do Brasil", Ed. São Paulo University, São Paulo, Ed Itatiaia, Belo Horizonte (1989)
- Leme, Pedro Taques de Almeida Paes, "Nobiliarquia Paulistana Histórica e Genealógica", Ed. São Paulo University (1980, São Paulo).
- Mello, José Soares de. *Emboabas.* São Paulo: Governo do estado de São Paulo, 1942.
- Miranda, Ana. "O retrato do rei" São Paulo: Companhia das Letras, 1991. Romance brasileiro.
- Taunay, Afonso de E., "Relatos Sertanistas", Ed. São Paulo University (1981, São Paulo)

- Taunay, Afonso de E., "História das Bandeiras Paulistas", Ed. Melhoramentos (São Paulo)
- Ribeiro, Berta. O índio na história do Brasil. Editora Global, 1987.

Inconfidência Mineira

Inconfidência Mineira (Portuguese pronunciation: [ĩkõfiˈdẽsiɐ miˈnejɾɐ]; "Minas Gerais Conspiracy") was an unsuccessful separatist movement in Brazil in 1789. It was the result of a confluence of external and internal causes in what was then a Portuguese colony. The external inspiration was the independence of thirteen of the British colonies in North America following the American Revolutionary War, a development that impressed the intellectual elite of particularly the captaincy of Minas Gerais. The main internal cause of the conspiracy was the decline of gold mining in that captaincy. As gold became less plentiful, the region's gold miners faced increasing difficulties in fulfilling tax obligations to the crown. When the captaincy could not satisfy the royal demand for gold, it was burdened with an additional tax on gold, called *derrama*.

Conspirators seeking independence from Portugal planned to rise up in rebellion on the day that the *derrama* was instituted. However, the conspirators lacked both well-formed plans and an overall leader. Some of the conspirators were republicans, others were monarchists. Some favored the abolition of slavery, while others judged abolition as impractical at that time. The conspirators did put forth a few economic and social ideas: the promotion of cotton production, the exploitation of iron and saltpeter reserves, a proposal to give incentives to mothers to have many children, and the creation of a citizens' militia.

The conspiracy attracted a great number of military personnel, priests, and intellectuals, as well as the poets Cláudio Manuel da Costa and Tomás Antônio Gonzaga (1744–1807?). Among the best known participants were Joaquim José da Silva Xavier, best known as "Tiradentes"; José Álvares Maciel, philosopher and chemistry student; and Lieutenant Colonel Francisco de Paula Freire de Andrade (1756–1792) of the regiment of dragoons. Tiradentes, who came from Andrade's regiment, was the independence movement's most enthusiastic propagandist.

Figure 40: *Response of Joaquim José da Silva Xavier, known as Tiradentes, to the commutation of the rebels' punishment.*

Figure 41: *Tiradentes being hanged.*

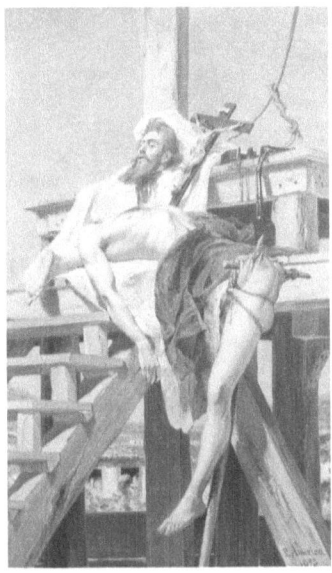

Figure 42: *Tiradentes after the execution*

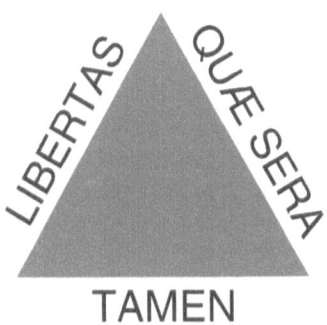

Figure 43: *The flag proposed by the Inconfidentes for the new republic, which became the basis for the Flag of Minas Gerais.*

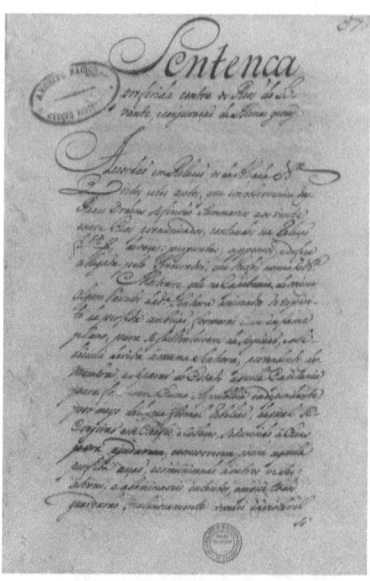

Figure 44: *Judgment handed down against the defendants, 1792.*

Conspirators

The Inconfidência was inspired by the ideals of the French liberal philosophers of the Age of Enlightenment and the successful American Revolution of 1776. The conspirators largely belonged to the white upper class of minerals-rich Minas Gerais. Many had studied in Europe, especially in the University of Coimbra, and some had large debts with the colonial government. In the context of declining gold production, the intention of the Portuguese government to impose the obligatory payment of all debts (the *derrama*) was a leading cause behind the conspiracy. The conspirators wanted to create a republic in which the leader would be chosen through democratic elections. The capital would be São João del Rei, and Ouro Preto would become a university town. The structure of the society, including the right to property and the ownership of slaves, would be kept intact. Eventually, three participants in the independence movement revealed the conspirators' plans to the government, and the rebels were arrested in 1789. Among the movement were the lawyer Alvarenga Peixoto, the poets Tomás Antônio Gonzaga and Cláudio Manuel da Costa, the priest José da Silva de Oliveira Rolim, and the *alferes* Joaquim José da Silva Xavier (a.k.a. "Tiradentes"). After Joaquim Silvério dos Reis (1756–1792), a member of the conspiracy, informed on the movement before it could take place, Peixoto was captured, arrested, and sent to exile in the city of Ambaca, in Portuguese Angola, another colony of the Portuguese Empire, where he remained until the end of his life.

Aftermath

Judicial proceedings against the conspirators lasted from 1789 to 1792. Lieutenant Colonel Freire de Andrade, Tiradentes, José Álvares Maciel, and eight others were condemned to the gallows. Seven more were condemned to perpetual banishment in Africa, the rest were acquitted. Following the trial Queen Maria I commuted the sentences of capital punishment to perpetual banishment for all except those whose activities involved aggravated circumstances. That was the case for Tiradentes, who took full responsibility for the conspiracy movement and was imprisoned in Rio de Janeiro, where he was hanged on 21 April 1792. Afterwards, his body was torn into pieces, which were sent to Vila Rica in the captaincy of Minas Gerais, to be displayed in the places where he had propagated his revolutionary ideas. The anniversary of his death is celebrated as a national holiday in Brazil.

In 1948 the events were portrayed in a film *Minas Conspiracy* directed by Carmen Santos.

In 1963, Minas Gerais incorporated as its state flag the one designed by the Inconfidência, with an equilateral triangle inspired by the Holy Trinity – albeit supposedly the inconfidentes wanted a green triangle, while Minas' flag uses a red one – and a Latin motto taken out of Vergil's *Eclogues*.[281]

Further reading

- Maxwell, Kenneth R., *Conflicts and Conspiracies: Brazil & Portugal 1750–1808* (Cambridge University Press, 1973)
- Furtado, Júnia Ferreira, *Chica da Silva: A Brazilian Slave of the Eighteenth Century* (Cambridge University Press, 2009)

References

 Wikimedia Commons has media related to *Inconfidência Mineira*.

United Kingdom with Portugal

United Kingdom of Portugal, Brazil and the Algarves

United Kingdom of Portugal, Brazil and the Algarves
Reino Unido de Portugal, Brasil e Algarves
1815–1822/1825
Flag
Royal coat of arms
Anthem *Hymno Patriotico*
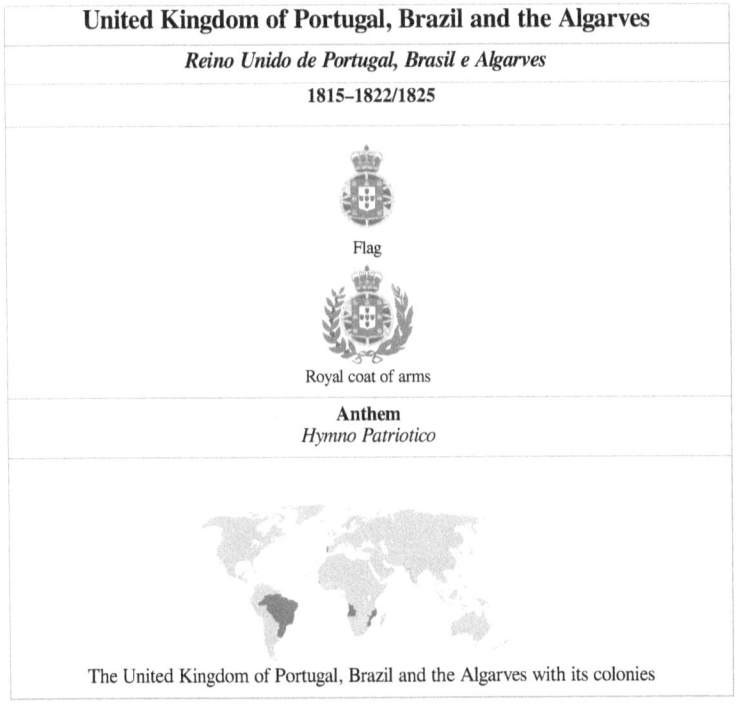 The United Kingdom of Portugal, Brazil and the Algarves with its colonies

Capital	Rio de Janeiro (1815–1821) Lisbon (1821–1825)
Languages	Portuguese
Religion	Roman Catholicism
Government	Absolute monarchy (1815–1820) (1823-1825) Constitutional monarchy (1820–1823)
Monarch	
• 1815–1816	Maria I
• 1816–1822/1825	John VI
Regent	
• 1815–1816	Prince John
• 1821–1822	Prince Pedro (Regent of the Kingdom of Brazil only)
Legislature	Cortes Gerais (1820–1823)
History	
• Established	16 December 1815
• Liberal Revolution	24 August 1820
• Independence of Brazil	7 September 1822
• Constitution adopted (in Portuguese)	23 September 1822
• Disestablished	29 August 1825 1822/1825
Population	
• 1820 est.	4,000,000 (Brazil) 3,000,000 (Portugal)
Currency	Real
Preceded by	**Succeeded by**
Portugal in the Napoleonic era	Kingdom of Portugal (1825–1834)
Colonial Brazil	Empire of Brazil

The **United Kingdom of Portugal, Brazil and the Algarves** was a pluricontinental monarchy formed by the elevation of the Portuguese colony named State of Brazil to the status of a kingdom and by the simultaneous union of that Kingdom of Brazil with the Kingdom of Portugal and the Kingdom of the Algarves, constituting a single state consisting of three kingdoms.

The United Kingdom of Portugal, Brazil and the Algarves was formed in 1815, following the transfer of the Portuguese Court to Brazil during the Napoleonic invasions of Portugal, and it continued to exist for about one year after the return of the Court to Europe, being *de facto* dissolved in 1822, when Brazil proclaimed its independence. The dissolution of the United Kingdom was accepted by Portugal and formalized *de jure* in 1825, when Portugal recognized the independent Empire of Brazil.

During its period of existence the United Kingdom of Portugal, Brazil and the Algarves did not correspond to the whole of the Portuguese Empire: rather, the united kingdom was the transatlantic metropolis that controlled the Portuguese colonial empire, with its overseas possessions in Africa and Asia.

Thus, from the point of view of Brazil, the elevation to the rank of a kingdom and the creation of the United Kingdom represented a change in status, from that of a colony to that of an equal member of a political union. In the wake of the Liberal Revolution of 1820 in Portugal, attempts to compromise the autonomy and even the unity of Brazil, led to the breakdown of the union.

History

Establishment

The United Kingdom of Portugal, Brazil and the Algarves came into being in the wake of Portugal's war with Napoleonic France. The Portuguese Prince Regent, the future King John VI, with his incapacitated mother, Queen Maria I of Portugal and the Royal Court, fled to the colony of Brazil in 1808.

With the defeat of Napoleon in 1815, there were calls for the return of the Portuguese Monarch to Lisbon; the Portuguese Prince Regent enjoyed life in Rio de Janeiro, where the monarchy was at the time more popular and where he enjoyed more freedom, and he was thus unwilling to return to Europe. However, those advocating the return of the Court to Lisbon argued that Brazil was only a colony and that it was not right for Portugal to be governed from a colony. On the other hand, leading Brazilian courtiers pressed for the elevation of Brazil from the rank of a colony, so that they could enjoy the full status of being nationals of the mother-country. Brazilian nationalists also supported the move, because it indicated that Brazil would no longer be submissive to the interests of Portugal, but would be of equal status within a transatlantic monarchy.

By a law issued by the Prince Regent on December 16, 1815, the colony of Brazil was thus elevated to the rank of a Kingdom and by the same law the separate kingdoms of Portugal, Brazil and the Algarves were united as a single State under the title of *The United Kingdom of Portugal, Brazil and the Algarves*.

This united kingdom included the historical Kingdom of the Algarves, which is the present-day Portuguese region of Algarve.

Figure 45: *The Acclamation of King João VI of the United Kingdom of Portugal, Brazil and the Algarves in Rio de Janeiro, Brazil*

The titles of the Portuguese royalty were changed to reflect the creation of this transatlantic united kingdom. The styles of the Queen and of the Prince Regent were changed accordingly to Queen and Prince Regent of the *United Kingdom of Portugal, Brazil and the Algarves*. The title *Prince of Brazil*, a title that used to pertain to the heir apparent of the Portuguese Crown, was dropped shortly afterwards, in 1817, being replaced by the title of *Prince Royal of the United Kingdom of Portugal, Brazil and the Algarves*, or Prince Royal, for short. A new flag and coat of arms were also adopted for the new State.

Succession of John VI

On March 20, 1816, Queen Maria I died in Rio de Janeiro. The Prince John, the Prince Regent, then became King John VI, the second monarch of the United Kingdom, retaining the numbering of Portuguese Sovereigns. After a period of mourning and several delays, the festivities of the acclamation of the new King were held in Rio de Janeiro on 6 February 1818.

On the date of his Acclamation, King John VI created the Order of the Immaculate Conception of Vila Viçosa, the only order of knighthood to be created during the United Kingdom era. This Order existed in the United Kingdom alongside the old Portuguese Orders of chivalry and the Order of the Tower and Sword, an ancient Order that had been dormant and that was revived by the Portuguese monarchy in November 1808, when the Royal Court was already in Brazil. After the dissolution of the United Kingdom, while Brazilian branches of the old Orders of chivalry were created, resulting in Brazilian and

Figure 46: *King John disembarks in Lisbon in 1821, after 13 years in Brazil*

Portuguese Orders Saint James of the Sword, of Saint Benedict of Aviz, and of Christ (there was and is also a branch of the Order of Christ maintained by the Holy See: the Supreme Order of Our Lord Jesus Christ), paradoxically, the newer Orders (the recreated Order of the Tower and Sword and the Order of the Immaculate Conception of Vila Viçosa) remained in existence as Portuguese Orders only.

John VI's return to Europe

After the Liberal Revolution of 1820 in Portugal, the King left Brazil and returned to the European portion of the United Kingdom, arriving in Lisbon on 4 July 1821. Before his departure, the King, acceding to requests made by Brazilian courtiers, decided to leave behind his heir apparent, Prince Pedro, the Prince Royal of the United Kingdom. By a decree issued on 22 April 1821, the King invested Pedro with the title of "Regent of Brazil", and granted him delegated powers to discharge the "general government and entire administration of the Kingdom of Brazil" as the King's placeholder, thus granting the Kingdom of Brazil a devolved administration within the United Kingdom.Wikipedia:Citation needed

Accordingly, with the appointment of Prince Royal Pedro as Regent of Brazil, the Brazilian provinces – that in the colonial period were united under a viceregal administration, and that during the stay of Queen Maria I and King

Figure 47: *The Cortes of the United Kingdom of Portugal, Brazil and the Algarves assembled in Lisbon in the wake of the 1820 Portuguese Revolution.*

John VI in the American Continent remained united directly under the royal Government – continued, after the return of the King and of the Portuguese Court to Europe, united under a central Brazilian Government based in Rio de Janeiro.Wikipedia:Citation needed

Prince Pedro's Regency not only assured the unity of the Brazilian people under one government, but it also enjoyed a high degree of autonomy vis-à-vis the Government of the United Kingdom.Wikipedia:Citation needed

Attempts by the Government in Lisbon to terminate Brazil's home rule and to undermine Brazilian unity would lead to the proclamation of the independence of Brazil and the dissolution of the United Kingdom.Wikipedia:Citation needed

Dissolution of the United Kingdom

Lead-up to the dissolution

The *Cortes* (the Parliament) assembled in Lisbon in the wake of the Constitutional Revolution of 1820 to draft a Constitution for the United Kingdom was composed of mostly Portuguese delegates. This was so because the Revolution was Portuguese in origin, so that the members of the Cortes were elected in Portugal, and only later a Brazilian delegation was elected and the Brazilian delegates crossed the Atlantic to join the ongoing deliberations. Also, Brazilian representatives were often mistreated and persecuted in the streets by Portuguese citizens who resented the end of colonial rule. On top of that, Brazilians were under-represented in the Cortes.

As for the King, upon his arrival in Lisbon, he behaved as though he accepted the new political settlement that resulted from the Liberal Revolution (a posture he would maintain until mid-1823), but the powers of the Crown were severely limited. A Council of Regency that had been elected by the Cortes to govern Portugal in the wake of the Revolution – and that replaced by force the previous governors that administered the European portion of the United Kingdom by royal appointment – handed back the reins of government to the Monarch on his arrival in Lisbon, but the King was now limited to the discharge of the Executive branch, and had no influence over the drafting of the Constitution or over the actions of the Cortes.

The Constituent Cortes, dominated by a Portuguese majority, included provisions in the Constitution being drafted that referred to the people of the United Kingdom as "the Portuguese Nation". The draft Constitution spoke of "Portuguese citizens of both hemispheres". Apart from including in the Constitution language that was seen as hostile and offensive to Brazilians, the United Kingdom Cortes assembled in Lisbon included in the proposed Constitution that was being drafted provisions that would undermine and that could even lead to the dissolution of the central Brazilian Government based in Rio de Janeiro. The draft Constitution would have maintained the Regency of the Kingdom of Brazil, but it contained provision allowing the United Kingdom Legislature to exclude Brazilian provinces from the jurisdiction of the Regency. Thus, the Government of the United Kingdom in Lisbon would have the power to sever the links between a Brazilian province and the central Brazilian government, submitting this province directly to the Lisbon Government. If enacted, those deliberations of the Cortes would not only undermine Brazilian Home Rule, but they would also endanger the unity of the Brazilian people, as Brazilians would no longer have a central government, a situation that did not exist even in the last centuries of the colonial period. Portuguese deputies in the Cortes even introduced draft legislation that would concretely sever the ties between the central devolved Government of the Kingdom of Brazil in Rio de Janeiro and some provinces in Northeastern Brazil. The Portuguese Cortes also demanded the immediate return of the Crown Prince to Europe.

Brazilian Nationalists reacted, interpreting the actions of the Cortes as an attempt to "divide and conquer". They alleged that once the provisions approved by the Cortes were enacted and enforced, Brazil, although formally remaining

Figure 48: *Pedro, then Prince Regent of the Kingdom of Brazil, orders officer Jorge d'Avillez to return to Portugal after his unsuccessful rebellion*

a part of the transatlantic monarchy, would be in reality returned to the condition of a Colony. Brazilians feared the breakup of Brazil, with the creation of provinces directly subject to the Lisbon Government.

Also, language in the draft Constitution that would have the effect of including colonies of the Portuguese colonial empire in Africa and Asia as part of the territory of the United Kingdom seemed to confirm that the intention of the Cortes was indeed to reduce Brazil to the position of a colony once again: it was clear that the territories in Africa and Asia would continue to be colonies, and to be subject to economic exploitation and domination by means of restrictions in foreign trade, etc.; but those colonies would now be declared parts of the United Kingdom, meaning that, with the inclusion of the whole of the Portuguese Empire in the United Kingdom, the definition of the United Kingdom itself would change: the United Kingdom would cease to correspond to a transatlantic State that included no colonies but that controlled colonies overseas, and would instead become a State that included colonies in its bosom. This would provide the legal framework for the reintroduction of trade restrictions in Brazil that had been lifted since the arrival of the Royal Family in Brazilian shores.

Notably, several Portuguese politicians wanted to re-introduce to Brazil restrictions in foreign trade that in the previous colonial era had been dubbed euphemistically as *the colonial pact*: a mercantilist system in which Brazilian products could only be exported to Portugal, and in which Brazilians could only import products from Portugal. This system, which enabled the economic exploitation of the Portuguese Colonies by Metropolitan Portugal, had been abolished in Brazil even before the creation of the United Kingdom. Indeed, the abolition of all the restrictions on foreign trade, and the exclusion of Brazil from the imperialist policy of the colonial pact, had taken place already in 1808, as soon as the Royal Family arrived in Brazil: the first act signed by the Prince Regent after his arrival in Brazil was the decree on the opening of the Brazilian ports to friendly Nations, that enabled Brazilians to import goods from Nations other than Portugal, and to export Brazilian products to the foreign Nations maintaining diplomatic ties with the Portuguese Empire. Now, with the measures being voted by the *Cortes* assembled in Lisbon, that economic freedom was under threat.

Faced with that scenario, Brazilian independentists managed to convince Prince Pedro to stay in Brazil against the orders of the Cortes, that demanded his immediate return. He thus continued leading a central Brazilian Government as Regent, and further established that no laws, decrees or instructions issued by the Portuguese Cortes or by the central government of the United Kingdom would be obeyed in Brazil without his *fiat*.

The Prince's decision not to obey the decrees of the *Cortes* that demanded this return, and instead to stay in Brazil as its Regent was solemnly announced on 9 January 1822, in reply to a formal petition from the city council of Rio de Janeiro. In February 1822 Prince Pedro decided to create an advisory council, composed of representatives elected to represent the several provinces of Brazil, summoning elections to that council. Its first meeting was held on 2 June 1822. Prince Regent Pedro's decree to the effect that laws, decrees and orders from Lisbon would only be carried out in Brazil with his *fiat* was published in May 1822.

By agreeing to defy the Cortes and stay in Brazil, Prince Pedro assumed the leadership of the Brazilian cause; as a recognition of his leading role, Brazilian independentists offered Pedro on 13 May 1822 the title of "Perpetual Protector and Defender of Brazil"; he rejected the title of Protector, arguing that Brazil didn't need one, but assumed the title of "Perpetual Defender of Brazil". By defying explicit orders that demanded his return to Europe, Pedro escalated the events that would lead to the separation of Brazil from the United Kingdom, and hastened the crucial moment of the Proclamation of Independence. As the situation between Brazilians and Portuguese deteriorated, the United Kingdom was doomed to dissolution.

Brazilian independentists argued that Brazil's future should be decided by Brazilians and not by the Lisbon *Cortes*, and they accordingly demanded the

Figure 49: *Declaration of Brazil's independence by Prince Pedro on 7 September 1822.*

summoning of a National Constituent Assembly for Brazil, separate from the Constituent Cortes assembled in Portugal. Prince Pedro, acting on the advice of his newly convened Council, embraced those demands, and issued a decree on 13 June 1822 summoning elections for a Brazilian Constituent Assembly. Due to the further escalation of tensions between Brazil and Portugal, the elections to that Constituent Assembly would only take place after the Prince himself had proclaimed the independence of Brazil (the Assembly would only convene in 1823, and the independence of Brazil was declared in September 1822, with the establishment of the Empire of Brazil in October 1822).

The *Cortes* sent troops to Brazil to compel the dissolution of the Prince's Government and to force his return to Portugal as ordered, but, on arrival those troops were commanded by the Prince to return to Portugal. The Portuguese troops in Rio de Janeiro obeyed the Prince Royal and returned to Europe, but in other Provinces fighting erupted between Brazilians and Portuguese.

Proclamation of Independence

News of further attempts of the Portuguese Cortes aimed at dissolving Prince Pedro's Regency led directly to the Brazilian Proclamation of Independence. Accordingly, in 1822, the Regent of the Kingdom of Brazil, Prince Pedro, the son of John VI, declared the independence of Brazil, as a reaction against the attempts of the *Cortes* to terminate Brazilian home rule, and became Emperor Pedro I of Brazil, which spelled the end of the United Kingdom.

The independence of Brazil was proclaimed by Prince Pedro on 7 September 1822. The Proclamation of Independence was made while the Prince was in the Province of São Paulo. He had travelled there to secure the Province's loyalty to the Brazilian cause. He departed the city of São Paulo, the Province's capital, on 5 September, and on 7 September, while on his way back to Rio de Janeiro, he received mail from his Minister José Bonifácio de Andrada e Silva and from his wife, Princess Leopoldina (who remained in Rio de Janeiro presiding over the Ministry during Prince Pedro's absence), informing Pedro of further acts by the Cortes aimed at dissolving his Government by force, insisting on his return to Lisbon and attempting to void his later acts as Regent of the Kingdom of Brazil. It was clear that independence was the only option left. Pedro turned to his companions that included his Guard of Honor and spoke: "Friends, the Portuguese Cortes want to enslave and pursue us. From today on our relations are broken. No ties can unite us anymore" and continued after he pulled out his blue-white armband that symbolized Portugal: "Armbands off, soldiers. Hail to the independence, to freedom and to the separation of Brazil from Portugal!" He unsheathed his sword affirming that "For my blood, my honor, my God, I swear to give Brazil freedom," and later cried out: "Independence or death!". This event is remembered as "Cry of Ipiranga", because it took place next to the riverbank of the Ipiranga brook. The Prince then decided to return urgently to the city of São Paulo, where he and his entourage arrived in the night of 7 September. There, they announced the news of the Prince's Proclamation, and of Brazil's separation from Portugal, and were met with great popular acclaim.

Less than a month later, on 23 September 1822 the Lisbon Cortes, still unaware of the Brazilian declaration of independence, approved the Constitution of the United Kingdom, that was then signed by the members of the Cortes and presented to the King. Between 23 September and 1 October, the members of the Cortes, including Brazilians that still took part in its deliberations, took oaths to uphold the Constitution. In a solemnity on 1 October 1822, King John VI appeared before the Cortes, made a speech from the Throne declaring his acceptance of the Constitution, swore an oath to uphold it, and signed an instrument of assent that was included in the text of the Constitution after the signatures of the members of the Cortes, declaring that the king had accepted the Constitution and sworn to abide by it. On 4 October, acting as the Cortes had directed, the Portuguese King signed a Charter of Law promulgating the text of the Constitution and ordering its execution. This Charter of Law, containing the full text of the Constitution, including the signatures of the members of the Cortes and the King's instrument of assent, was published on the following day, 5 October 1822. Due to the Brazilian secession from the United Kingdom, that Constitution was never recognized in Brazil and was only effective in Portugal.

That the newly independent Brazilian Nation would adopt a constitutional monarchy as its form of Government and that Prince Pedro would be the new

Figure 50: *Coronation ceremony of Pedro I as first Emperor of Brazil on 1 December 1822.*

State's monarch were obvious facts to all the leaders involved in the process of Brazilian emancipation, but still, for a little more than one month after the 7 September 1822 Proclamation of Independence, Prince Pedro initially continued to use the title of Prince Regent, as he did not want to declare himself monarch, preferring instead to accept the new country's Crown as an offer. This led several local councils to adopt motions and addresses asking the Prince Regent to assume the title of King, or of Emperor (there were no legislatures in the provinces, and also no national legislature existed at that time; the municipal councils were the only existing legislatures, and since the colonial era they had substantial authority). The municipal council of the city of Rio de Janeiro and the other municipal councils of the province of Rio de Janeiro then organized a ceremony of acclamation, with the support of the Prince Regent's Government. The municipal council of Rio de Janeiro voted to instruct its president to offer Prince Pedro the title of Emperor. Then, the Prince's Advisory Council, a body that was not a legislative assembly, but was composed of councillors elected from all Provinces of Brazil to represent its peoples and advise the Prince Regent (the *Conselho de Procuradores das Províncias do Brasil* or Council of the Representatives of the Provinces of Brazil), advised the Prince Regent to accede to the several requests already presented and to assume the imperial title. On 12 October 1822, Prince Pedro accepted the offer of the new Brazilian Throne and was acclaimed the first Emperor of the independent Empire of Brazil.

Although Portuguese monarchs were not crowned since the 16th century, it was decided by the newly created imperial Government that the Brazilian monarchy, then recently instituted, should adopt different customs, both to differentiate itself from the Portuguese model and to highlight its status as a distinct institution, from a separate and independent country. Thus, it was decided that Emperors of Brazil should be consecrated, anointed and crowned with the full Catholic coronation ritual. Also, in the context of the struggle to sustain the newly declared independence of Brazil, and to seek recognition for the Empire, the religious act of coronation would establish Emperor Pedro I as an anointed monarch, crowned by the Catholic Church. It was regarded that this could improve his legitimacy in the eyes of other Christian monarchies, and it would also confirm the alliance between the newly declared State and the Church in Brazil. Accordingly, the coronation of Emperor Pedro I took place on 1 December 1822.

Recognition of independence

The Brazilian declaration of independence and foundation of the Empire of Brazil led to a War of Independence. The Portuguese initially refused to recognize Brazil as a sovereign state, treating the whole affair as a rebellion and attempting to preserve the United Kingdom. However, military action was never close to Rio de Janeiro, and the main battles of the independence war took place in the Northeastern region of Brazil. The independentist Brazilian forces overpowered the Portuguese forces as well as the few local forces that were still loyal to Portugal, and the last Portuguese troops surrendered in November 1823. Compared to the wars of independence waged by Spanish colonies during the decolonization of the Americas, the Brazilian Independence War did not result in significant bloodshed, although land and naval battles were fought.

The Portuguese military defeat, however, was not followed by swift recognition of the new country's independence. Instead, from 1822 to 1825 the Portuguese Government engaged in heavy diplomatic efforts to avoid the recognition of Brazil's independence by the European Powers, invoking the principles of the Congress of Vienna and subsequent European alliances. Those foreign Nations, however, were keen on establishing trade and diplomatic ties with Brazil. Under British pressure, Portugal eventually agreed to recognize Brazil's independence in 1825, thus allowing the new country to establish diplomatic ties with other European powers shortly thereafter.

In 1824, in the wake of the adoption of the Constitution of the Empire of Brazil on March 25 of that year, the United States of America became the first nation to recognize the independence of Brazil and the consequential disbandment of the United Kingdom.

Figure 51: *The Brazilian Army entering Salvador after the surrender of the Portuguese forces in 1823.*

Portugal recognized the sovereignty of Brazil only in 1825. Since a coup d'etát on 3 June 1823 the Portuguese King John VI had already abolished the Constitution of 1822 and dissolved the Cortes, thus reversing the Liberal Revolution of 1820. On 4 January 1824 King John VI issued a Charter of Law confirming as in force the "traditional laws of the Portuguese Monarchy", thus ratifying the restoration of the absolutist régime in Portugal.

There were two Portuguese acts of recognition of Brazilian independence. The first was unilateral and purporting to be constitutive of such independence, the second was bilateral and declaratory.

The first act of recognition was materialized in Letters Patent issued on May 13, 1825, by which the Portuguese King "voluntarily ceded and transferred the sovereignty" over Brazil to his son, the Brazilian Emperor, and thus recognized, as a result of this concession, Brazil as an "Independent Empire, separate from the Kingdoms of Portugal and Algarves".

The second act of recognition was materialized in a Treaty of Peace signed in Rio de Janeiro on August 29, 1825, by means of which Portugal again recognized the independence of Brazil. This Treaty was ratified by the Emperor of Brazil on August 30, 1825, and by the King of Portugal on November 15, 1825, and entered into force in international Law also on November 15, 1825 upon the exchange of the instruments of ratification in Lisbon. On the same date of the signature of the Portuguese instrument of ratification and of the exchange of the ratification documents between the representatives of the two Nations, the Portuguese King also signed a *Charter of Law*, a statute, ordering the execution of the Treaty as part of the domestic Law of Portugal. The Treaty was incorporated as part of the domestic Law of Brazil by a Decree of Emperor Pedro I signed on April 10, 1826.

The reason why there were two separate acts of recognition of the independence of Brazil is this: in the wake of the Brazilian victory in the War of Independence, the Portuguese king initially attempted to recognize Brazilian independence unilaterally so as to ignore the fact of the Portuguese defeat and transmit the impression that Portugal was being magnanimous. By means of such unilateral concession, Portugal intended to avoid the humiliation of Peace negotiations with its former Colony. King John VI wanted to "save face" by giving the impression that Portugal was voluntarily conceding independence to Brazil, and not just recognizing a *fait accompli*. Thus the Letters Patent issued on May 13, 1825 ignored the proclamation of 1822 and "granted independence to Brazil" as if it were a concession, that was laced with conditions. Thus, Brazilian independence would result not from the events of 1822, but from the 1825 Letters Patent.

In the May 13, 1825 Letters Patent, King John recited the polity creating acts of his predecessors and of other sovereigns of Europe, recited his own desire to promote the happiness of all the peoples over which he ruled, and proceeded to declare and enact that from thenceforth the Kingdom of Brazil would be an Empire, and that the Empire of Brazil would be separate from the Kingdoms of Portugal and the Algarves in both internal and foreign affairs; that he, John, therefore took for himself the title of Emperor of Brazil and King of Portugal and the Algarves, to which would follow the other titles of the Portuguese Crown; that the title of "Prince or Princess Imperial of Brazil, and Royal of Portugal and the Algarves" would be vested in the heir or heiress presumptive of the imperial and royal Crowns; that since the succession of both the imperial and royal Crowns belonged to his son, "Prince Dom Pedro", he, King John, at once, "by this same act and letters patent", ceded and transferred to Pedro, from thenceforth, of his "own free will", the full sovereignty of the Empire of Brazil, for Pedro to govern it, assuming at once the title Emperor of Brazil, keeping at the same time the title of Prince Royal of Portugal and the Algarves, while John reserved for himself the same title of Emperor, and the position of King of Portugal and the Algarves, with the full sovereignty of the said Kingdoms (of Portugal and the Algarves).

However, such unilateral, constitutive recognition was not accepted by Brazilians, who demanded a declarative recognition of the independence as proclaimed and existing since 1822. The new Brazilian Government therefore made the establishment of peaceful relations and diplomatic ties with Portugal conditional on the signature of a bilateral treaty between the two Nations. Portugal eventually agreed, and a treaty to that effect was signed with British mediation. The treaty between the Empire of Brazil and the Kingdom of Portugal on the recognition of Brazilian independence, signed in Rio de Janeiro on August 29, 1825, finally entered into force on November 15, 1825, upon the exchange of the instruments of ratification in Lisbon.

The Portuguese, however, only accepted to sign the Independence treaty on condition that Brazil agreed to pay reparations for the properties of the Portuguese State that were seized by the new Brazilian State. Brazil desperately needed to establish normal diplomatic relations with Portugal, because other European Monarchies had already made clear that they would only recognize the Empire of Brazil after the establishment of normal relations between Brazil and Portugal. Thus, by a separate convention that was signed on the same occasion as the Treaty on the Recognition of Independence, Brazil agreed to pay Portugal two million pounds in damages. The British, who had mediated the Peace negotiations, granted Brazil a loan of the same value, so that Brazil could pay the agreed sum. The new Nation, therefore, achieved international recognition at a heavy price. As a result of this agreement, Brazil became plunged in debt to Britain, but was able to achieve universal international recognition, both *de facto* and *de jure* as an independent State.

Upon recognizing the independence of Brazil from the United Kingdom of Portugal, Brazil and Algarves, King John VI, by his charter of law of 15 November 1825 changed back the name of the Portuguese State and the Royal Titles to "Kingdom of Portugal" and "King of Portugal and the Algarves" respectively. The title of the Portuguese heir apparent was changed to "Prince Royal of Portugal and the Algarves" by the same edict.

The recognition of Brazilian independence completed the dissolution of the United Kingdom.

By a provision of the Letters Patent of May 13, 1825 that was confirmed by the Treaty on the Recognition of Independence, in spite of the secession of Brazil from the Portuguese Monarchy, the Portuguese King, John VI, was allowed to use for the remainder of his life the honorary title of "Emperor of Brazil", with the caveat that this title was honorary and ceremonial only, and that Pedro I and his successors in the independent Brazilian Crown were the only actual Emperors of Brazil. This honorary title ceased to have effect upon the demise of King John VI on March 10, 1826.

News of the separate convention appended to the Independence Treaty, by which Brazil agreed to pay Portugal financial compensation, angered many Brazilians, who saw this payment as a result of a bad negotiation, especially in view of the Brazilian military victory in the independence war. The grant of the honorary imperial title to the Portuguese King was also not popular with Brazilians. Furthermore, the declaratory language of the Independence Treaty was sufficiently ambiguous, so that Brazilians could claim that the independence declared in 1822 was being recognized, but mention was also made of the 13 May 1825 Letters Patent, so that the Portuguese could claim that the recognition was based on the previous concession. The preamble of the treaty mentioned the concession made by means of the Letters Patent of 13 May 1825; it stated that, by that Letters Patent, the Portuguese King had "recognized Brazil as an independent Empire, and his son Dom Pedro as Emperor", but also stated that, in so doing, the Portuguese monarch was "ceding and transferring of his free will the sovereignty of the said Empire". In the treaty's second article, it was the Brazilian Emperor who agreed that his father, the Portuguese King, should take for himself the honorary life title of Emperor. In the first article of the treaty it was declared that the King of Portugal recognized Brazil as an independent Empire, and as a Nation separate from the Kingdoms of Portugal and the Algarves, and also recognized his son Dom Pedro as Emperor of Brazil, ceding "of his own free will" to the Brazilian Emperor and his legitimate successors all claims of sovereignty over Brazil. Peace was established between the countries of Brazil and Portugal by the fourth Article.

In spite of the unpopular clauses, and especially of the harsh financial agreement, Brazilian Emperor Pedro I agreed to ratify the treaty negotiated with Portugal as he was keen on resolving the recognition of independence question before the opening of the first legislative session of the Brazilian Parliament (*Assembléia Geral* or General Assembly) elected under the Constitution adopted in 1824. The first meeting of the new Legislature was set to take place on 3 May 1826, and after a brief delay, that Parliament was indeed opened on 6 May 1826. By that time, the independence question was indeed resolved, as the Independence treaty had been ratified in November 1825 and as the Emperor, still yielding the fullness of legislative authority (that he was to lose upon the first meeting of the Parliament), ordered the execution of the agreement as part of the law of Brazil on 10 April 1826.

Aftermath: resolution of the dynastic entanglement

With the death of the Portuguese King John VI on 10 March 1826, his heir apparent, Brazilian Emperor Pedro I, inherited the Portuguese Crown, and reigned briefly as King Pedro IV. On 20 March 1826 the proclamation of the Brazilian Emperor's accession to the Portuguese Throne was made public by the Portuguese Council of Regency (that had been instituted by King John VI during his final illness, and that was led by the Infanta Isabel Maria, daughter of John VI and Pedro I & IV's sister). With this union of Crowns, the monarchies of Portugal and Brazil were once again briefly united, but there was no thought of a reunification of the two separate States. Accordingly, this brief union of Crowns in the person of Pedro I and IV remained always a personal union only, and not a real union or a rebirth of the United Kingdom.

News of the death of King John VI and of the proclamation of the Brazilian Emperor as King of Portugal reached the Brazilian province of Bahia on 18 April, and official news to that effect reached the Emperor of Brazil and new King of Portugal in Rio de Janeiro on 24 April 1826, shortly after the final settlement of the Brazilian independence question (the decree publishing the text of the Treaty on the Recognition of Independence and ordering its execution as part of the Law of Brazil had just been made public on 10 April 1826). The existence even of the personal union only was seen by Brazilian politicians as dangerous, since it could come to affect the effectiveness of the newly formed country's sovereignty.

Accordingly, steps were taken to put an end to the personal union: Pedro I & IV agreed to abdicate the Portuguese Throne in favour of his eldest daughter, but he also wanted to ensure that her rights would be respected, and he further wanted to restore constitutional monarchy to Portugal. In order to put an end to the Portuguese absolute monarchy, the Emperor-King commissioned the drafting of a new Constitution for Portugal, that was widely based on the Brazilian Constitution. This document was finalized in less than a week.

After issuing a new Constitution for Portugal on 29 April 1826, and as already announced in that Constitution, Emperor-King Pedro abdicated the Portuguese Crown in favour of his daughter, Princess Maria da Glória, on 2 May 1826. Princess Maria da Glória thus became Queen Maria II of Portugal. The document by which the Brazilian Emperor abdicated the Portuguese Crown was signed days before the first meeting of the Parliament established by the Brazilian Constitution of 1824, that assembled for the first time on 6 May 1826. Before his abdication, on 26 April, King Pedro confirmed the Regency of Portugal that had been established by his father during his final illness, and that was led by the Infanta Isabel Maria, his sister. As the new Queen Maria II was still a minor, Portugal would need to be led by Regents during her minority. On 30 April, King Pedro IV set the date for the first legislative elections under the new Portuguese Constitution and appointed Peers of the Realm.

On 12 May 1826, British envoy Charles Stuart left Rio de Janeiro for Portugal carrying with him the acts signed by the Brazilian Emperor as King of Portugal, including the new Portuguese Constitution and his deed of abdication of the Portuguese Crown. On that same date Carlos Matias Pereira left Rio de

Janeiro for Lisbon in another ship carrying a second copy of the same documents. Charles Stuart arrived in Lisbon on 2 July 1826 and presented the acts signed by King Pedro IV to the Government of Portugal, including his original deed of abdication of the Portuguese Throne. On 12 July 1826 the Portuguese Government published the new Constitution decreed by Pedro IV; the Portuguese Regency swore on 31 July 1826 an oath to uphold the Constitution, marking its entry into force, and, on 1 August 1826 Queen Maria II was publicly proclaimed as Queen of Portugal, with the Infanta Isabel Maria as Regent. On 4 October the exiled infante Miguel (that had been exiled since attempting to depose his father, and that would later usurp the Portuguese Crown, leading to the Portuguese Civil War of 1828-1834, took in Vienna an oath of allegiance to Queen Maria II and the Constitution). The first Portuguese Cortes to meet under the Constitution were elected on 8 October, and the opening of Parliament took place on 30 October 1826.

Although Pedro's abdication of the Portuguese Crown to Maria II was provided for even in the Constitution issued on 29 April 1826, the original deed of abdication, signed on 2 May 1826 contained conditions; however, those conditions were subsequently waived, as the abdication was later declared final, irrevocable, accomplished and fully effective by a decree issued by Pedro on 3 March 1828, just a few months before Infante Miguel's usurpation of the Throne and the start of the Portuguese Civil War (in accordance with a decree issued on 3 September 1827, Infante Miguel replaced Infanta Isabel Maria as Regent of Portugal on 26 February 1828, and he initially agreed to govern in the name of the Queen, but on 7 July 1828 he had himself proclaimed King with retroactive effect, assuming the title of Miguel I; Maria II would only be restored to the Throne in 1834, at the conclusion of the Civil War). In any event, Pedro's unconditional confirmation of his abdication reinforced the impossibility of a new union between Portugal and Brazil.

Pedro's abdication of the Portuguese Throne led to the separation of the Brazilian and Portuguese monarchies, since the Portuguese Crown was inherited by Queen Maria II and her successors, and the Brazilian Crown came to be inherited by Pedro I's Brazilian heir apparent, Prince Pedro de Alcantara, who would become the future Emperor Pedro II of Brazil. Prince Pedro de Alcantara had no rights to the Portuguese Crown because, having been born in Brazil on 2 December 1825, after the Portuguese recognition of the independence of Brazil, he was not a Portuguese national and under the Portuguese Constitution and Laws a foreigner could not inherit the Portuguese Crown.

Still, with Princess Maria da Glória's accession to the Throne of Portugal as Queen Maria II in 1826, the question arose, about whether she should still be regarded as a Brazilian Princess with a place in the order of succession, or whether article 119 of Brazil's Constitution (that prohibited foreigners from succeeding to the Crown) applied to her, so that, as a foreigner, she should be considered excluded from the Brazilian line of succession. The Empire's Constitution limited the Crown of Brazil to Emperor Pedro I and his legitimate descendants, under a male-preference cognatic primogeniture system, but it rendered foreigners incapable of succeeding to the Crown, and it empowered the General Assembly, the Empire's Parliament, to settle any doubts regarding the rights of succession to the Crown. The issue of Queen Maria II's status in the Brazilian line of succession became more pressing once Emperor Pedro II acceded to the Brazilian Throne as a minor in 1831, since the question was no longer only about whether or not the Queen of Portugal had a place in the Brazilian line of succession, but it had now become a question about whether or not she was the heiress presumptive to the Brazilian Crown, that is, the first person in line to succeed to the Brazilian Throne, occupied by her brother Emperor Pedro II. Thus, the Brazilian Parliament had to settle the matter and decide who was the first person in line to the Brazilian Throne, with the corresponding title of Princess Imperial: Queen Maria II of Portugal or Princess Januária of Brazil. Both were minors under Brazilian Law, and since no one in the Brazilian Imperial Family was of age, the Regency of the Empire was discharged by politicians chosen by the General Assembly in accordance with the Constitution. However, the question was all important because, in the event that Emperor Pedro II died before producing descendants, the Crown of the independent Empire of Brazil could end up coming to the Queen of Portugal, thus recreating a personal union between the two monarchies. The question became even more pressing after the conclusion of the Portuguese Civil War (1828-1834), won by Maria II and her liberal supporters in 1834: Maria's uncle, the absolutist claimant Dom Miguel (who had deposed Maria in 1828), was defeated, surrendered his claim to the Portuguese Throne in the Concession of Evoramonte, Maria was restored to the Throne and her constitutional government, now recognized by all foreign Powers as the legitimate one, assumed control of the whole of Portugal. Although the doubt about which of the two Princesses was Emperor Pedro II's heiress presumptive had existed since the abdication of the Brazilian Crown by Pedro I in 1831, Maria II was at the time a deposed Queen, although actively pursuing her claim to the Throne of Portugal. With her victory in the Portuguese Civil War, however, she once again became an actually reigning monarch, and, for the whole Brazilian political establishment, the fact that a foreign Sovereign was heiress presumptive to the Brazilian Crown was highly worrying, as it was seen as detrimental to the independence of the recently established Brazilian Nation. The Regency and Parliament of Brazil wanted to avoid any possibility of a personal union with Portugal being recreated, so as to secure the independence of Brazil. In order to settle that question, the Brazilian General Assembly adopted a statute, signed into law by the Regent on behalf of Emperor Pedro II on 30 October 1835, declaring Queen Maria II of Portugal had lost her succession rights to the Crown of Brazil, due to her condition as a foreigner, so that she and her descendants were excluded from the Brazilian line of succession; ruling that Princess Januária and her descendants were therefore first in line to the Throne after Emperor Pedro II and his descendants, and decreeing that, accordingly, Princess Januária, as the then heiress presumptive of the Brazilian Crown, should be recognized as Princess Imperial.

Thus, the abdication of the Portuguese Crown by Brazilian Emperor Pedro I terminated the brief 1826 personal union and separated the monarchies of Portugal and Brazil, and that abdication, coupled with the exclusion of the new Portuguese Queen, Maria II, from the Brazilian line of succession, broke the last remaining ties of political union between the two Nations, securing the preservation of the independence of Brazil and putting to an end all hopes of the rebirth of a Luso-Brazilian United Kingdom.

Monarchs of the United Kingdom of Portugal, Brazil and the Algarves

Name	Lifespan	Reign start	Reign end	Notes	Family	Image
Maria I	17 December 1734 – 20 March 1816 (aged 81)	16 December 1815	20 March 1816	Brazil elevated to the status of kingdom united with Portugal	Braganza	
John VI	13 May 1767 – 10 March 1826 (aged 58)	20 March 1816	7 September 1822	Son of Maria I	Braganza	

Bibliography

- Gomes, Laurentino (2007). *1808 – How a mad queen, a coward prince and a corrupt court fooled Napoleon and changed the History of Portugal and Brazil* (in Portuguese). Planeta.
- *Monarchy in Brazil*[282] *Wikipedia:Link rot* Ministry of External Relations, accessed on 8 June 2008.
- *Elevação do Brasil a Reino Unido a Portugal e Algarves*[283] Secretary of Education of Rio de Janeiro, accessed on 8 June 2008. (in Portuguese)
- *Reino Unido (1815–1822)*[284] Chamber of Deputies of Brazil, accessed on 8 June 2008.

- [FERREIRA, Fábio. *O general Lecor, os Voluntários Reais, e os conflitos pela independência do Brasil na Província Cisplatina: 1822-1824*. Tese (Doutorado) – Programa de Pós-Graduação em História (PPGH) da Universidade Federal Fluminense (UFF): Niterói, 2012. Disponível em: http://www.historia.uff.br/stricto/td/1408.pdf]

External links

- Brazil history[285]
- Colonial flags of Brazil[286]

Coordinates: 22°54′S 43°14′W[287]

Independent Empire

Independence of Brazil

Independence of Brazil

Declaration of Brazil's independence by Prince Pedro on 7 September 1822. His Guard of Honor greets him in support while some discard blue and white armbands that represented loyalty to Portugal

Date	7 September 1822
Location	São Paulo, Brazil
Participants	Prince Pedro Archduchess Leopoldina José Bonifácio de Andrada
Outcome	Independence of the Kingdom of Brazil from the United Kingdom of Portugal, Brazil and the Algarves and subsequent formation of the Empire of Brazil

The **Independence of Brazil** comprised a series of political and military events that occurred in 1821–1824, most of which involved disputes between Brazil and Portugal regarding the call for independence presented by the Brazilian Empire.

It is celebrated on 7 September, the anniversary of the date in 1822 that prince regent Dom Pedro declared Brazil's independence from Portugal. Formal recognition came with a treaty signed by both Brazil and Portugal in late 1825.

Figure 52: *Landing of Pedro Álvares Cabral in Brazil, 1500.*

Background

The land now called Brazil was claimed by Portugal in April 1500, on the arrival of the Portuguese fleet commanded by Pedro Álvares Cabral. The Portuguese encountered Indigenous nations divided into several tribes, most of whom shared the same Tupi-Guaraní language family, and shared and disputed the territory.Wikipedia:Citation needed

Though the first settlement was founded in 1532, colonization was effectively started in 1534 when King John III divided the territory into fifteen hereditary captaincies. This arrangement proved problematic, however, and in 1549 the king assigned a Governor-General to administer the entire colony. The Portuguese assimilated some of the native tribes while others slowly disappeared in long wars or by European diseases to which they had no immunity..Wikipedia:Citation needed

By the mid-16th century, sugar had become Brazil's most important export due to the increasing international demand for sugar. To profit from the situation, by 1700 over 963,000 African slaves had been brought across the Atlantic to work in Brazil. More Africans were brought to Brazil up until that date than to all the other places in the Americas combined.[288]

Departure of the Portuguese royal family to Brazil on 29 November 1807.

Acclamation ceremony of King John VI of the United Kingdom of Portugal, Brazil and the Algarves in Rio de Janeiro, Brazil, 6 February 1818.

Through wars against the French, the Portuguese slowly expanded their territory to the southeast, taking Rio de Janeiro in 1567, and to the northwest, taking São Luís in 1615. They sent military expeditions to the Amazon rainforest and conquered English and Dutch strongholds, founding villages and forts from 1669. In 1680 they reached the far south and founded Sacramento on the bank of the Rio de la Plata, in the *Banda Oriental* region (present-day Uruguay).Wikipedia:Citation needed

At the end of the 17th century, sugar exports started to decline but beginning in the 1690s, the discovery of gold by explorers in the region that would later be called Minas Gerais (General Mines) in current Mato Grosso, Goiás and the state of Minas Gerais, saved the colony from imminent collapse. From all over Brazil, as well as from Portugal, thousands of immigrants came to the mines.Wikipedia:Citation needed

The Spanish tried to prevent Portuguese expansion into the territory that belonged to them according to the 1494 Treaty of Tordesillas, and succeeded in conquering the *Banda Oriental* in 1777. However, this was in vain as the Treaty of San Ildefonso, signed in the same year, confirmed Portuguese sovereignty over all lands proceeding from its territorial expansion, thus creating most of the current Brazilian border.Wikipedia:Citation needed

During the invasion of Portugal (1807), the Portuguese royal family fled to Brazil, establishing Rio de Janeiro as the de facto capital of Portugal. This had the side effect of creating within Brazil many of the institutions required to exist as an independent state; most importantly, it freed Brazil to trade with other nations at will.Wikipedia:Citation needed

After Napoleon's army was finally defeated in 1815, in order to maintain the capital in Brazil and allay Brazilian fears of being returned to colonial status, King John VI of Portugal raised the de jure status of Brazil to an equal, integral part of a United Kingdom of Portugal, Brazil, and the Algarves, rather than a mere colony, a status which it enjoyed for the next seven years.

Figure 53: *The Portuguese Cortes*

Path to independence

Portuguese *Cortes*

In 1820 the Constitutionalist Revolution erupted in Portugal. The movement initiated by the liberal constitutionalists resulted in the meeting of the *Cortes* (or Constituent Assembly), that would have to create the kingdom's first constitution.[289,290] The *Cortes* at the same time demanded the return of King Dom John VI, who had been living in Brazil since 1808, who elevated Brazil to a kingdom as part of the United Kingdom of Portugal, Brazil and the Algarves in 1815 and who nominated his son and heir prince Dom Pedro as regent, to govern Brazil in his place on 7 March 1821.[291,292] The king left for Europe on 26 April, while Dom Pedro remained in Brazil governing it with the aid of the ministers of the Kingdom (Interior) and Foreign Affairs, of War, of Navy and of Finance.[293,294]

The Portuguese military officers headquartered in Brazil were completely sympathetic to the Constitutionalist movement in Portugal.[295] The main leader of the Portuguese officers, General Jorge de Avilez Zuzarte de Sousa Tavares forced the prince to dismiss and banish from the country the ministers of Kingdom and Finance. Both were loyal allies of Pedro, who had become a pawn in the hands of the military.[296] The humiliation suffered by the prince, who

Figure 54: *Prince Pedro (right) orders Portuguese officer Jorge Avilez (left) to return to Portugal after his failed rebellion on February 8, 1822. José Bonifácio (in civilian clothes) can be seen next to the prince.*

swore he would never yield to the pressure of the military again, would have a decisive influence on his abdication ten years later.[297] Meanwhile, on 30 September 1821, the *Cortes* approved a decree that subordinated the governments of the Brazilian provinces directly to Portugal. Prince Pedro became for all purposes only the governor of the Rio de Janeiro Province.[298,299] Other decrees that came after ordered his return to Europe and also extinguished the judicial courts created by João VI in 1808.[300,301]

Dissatisfaction over the *Cortes* measures among most residents in Brazil (both Brazilian-born and Portuguese-born) rose to a point that it soon became publicly known. Two groups that opposed the *Cortes*' actions to gradually undermine the Brazilian sovereignty appeared: Liberals led by Joaquim Gonçalves Ledo (which had the support of the Freemasons) and the Bonifacians led by José Bonifácio de Andrada. Both factions had nothing in common in their goals for Brazil, with the sole exception of their desire to keep the country united with Portugal as a sovereign monarchy.[302]

Avilez rebellion

The Portuguese deputies of the *Cortes* showed no respect towards the prince and openly mocked him.[303] And so the loyalty that Pedro had shown towards the *Cortes* gradually shifted to the Brazilian cause. His wife, princess Leopoldina of Habsburg, favoured the Brazilian side and encouraged him to remain in the country[304] while the Liberals and Bonifacians made open representations. Pedro's reply came on 9 January 1822, who, according to newspapers, spoke: "As it is for the good of all and for the nation's general happiness, I am ready: Tell the people that I will stay".[305]

After Pedro's decision to defy the *Cortes*, around 2,000 men led by Jorge Avilez rioted before concentrating on mount Castelo, which was soon surrounded by 10,000 armed Brazilians, led by the Royal Police Guard.[306] Dom Pedro then "dismissed" the Portuguese commanding general and ordered him to remove his soldiers across the bay to Niterói, where they would await transport to Portugal.[307]

Jose Bonifácio was nominated minister of Kingdom and Foreign Affairs on 18 January 1822.[308] Bonifácio soon established a fatherlike relationship with Pedro, who began to consider the experienced statesman his greatest ally.[309] Gonçalves Ledo and the liberals tried to minimize the close relationship between Bonifácio and Pedro offering to the prince the title of Perpetual Defender of Brazil.[310,311] For the liberals, the meeting of a Constituent Assembly for Brazil was necessary, while the Bonifacians preferred that Pedro grant the constitution himself to avoid the possibility of similar anarchy to the one that occurred during the first years of the French Revolution.

The prince acquiesced to the liberals' desires and signed a decree on 3 June 1822 calling for the election of the deputies that would gather in the Constituent and Legislative General Assembly in Brazil.[312]

From united kingdom to independent empire

Pedro departed to São Paulo Province to secure the province's loyalty to the Brazilian cause. He reached its capital on 25 August and remained there until 5 September. While on his way back to Rio de Janeiro on 7 September he received mail from José Bonifácio and his wife, Leopoldina.Wikipedia:Citation needed The letter told him that the *Cortes* had annulled all acts from the Bonifácio cabinet, removed Pedro's remaining powers and ordered him to return to Portugal. It was clear that independence was the only option left. Pedro turned to his companions that included his Guard of Honor and spoke: "Friends, the Portuguese *Cortes* want to enslave and pursue us. From today on our relations are broken. No ties can unite us anymore" and continued after he pulled out his blue-white armband that symbolized Portugal: "Armbands off, soldiers. Hail to the independence, to freedom and to the separation of Brazil from Portugal!" He unsheathed his sword affirming that "For my blood, my honor, my God, I swear to give Brazil freedom," and later cried out: "Brazilians, Independence or death!". This event is remembered as "Cry of Ipiranga".[313]

Figure 55: *Prince Pedro is surrounded by a cheering crowd in São Paulo after giving the news of the Brazilian independence on 7 September 1822.*

Returning to the city of São Paulo on the night of 7 September 1822, Pedro and his companions announced the news of Brazilian independence from Portugal. The Prince was received with great popular celebration and was called not only "King of Brazil" but also "Emperor of Brazil".[314,315]

Pedro returned to Rio de Janeiro on 14 September and in the following days the liberals had spread pamphlets (written by Joaquim Gonçalves Ledo) that suggested the idea that the Prince should be acclaimed Constitutional Emperor. On 17 September the President of the Municipal Chamber of Rio de Janeiro, José Clemente Pereira, sent to the other Chambers of the country the news that the Acclamation would occur in the anniversary of Pedro on 12 October.[316]

The official separation would only occur on 22 September 1822 in a letter written by Pedro to João VI. In it, Pedro still calls himself Prince Regent and his father is considered the King of the independent Brazil.[317,318] On 12 October 1822, in the Field of Santana (later known as Field of the Acclamation) Prince Pedro was acclaimed Dom Pedro I, Constitutional Emperor and Perpetual Defender of Brazil. It was at the same time the beginning of Pedro's reign and also of the Empire of Brazil.[319] However, the Emperor made it clear that although he accepted the emperorship, if João VI returned to Brazil he would step down from the throne in favor of his father.[320]

The reason for the imperial title was that the title of king would symbolically mean a continuation of the Portuguese dynastic tradition and perhaps of the

Figure 56: *Coronation of Emperor Pedro I on December 1, 1822.*

feared absolutism, while the title of emperor derived from popular acclamation as in Ancient Rome or at least reigning through popular sanction as in the case of Napoleon.[321,322] On 1 December 1822, Pedro I was crowned and consecrated.[323]

War of Independence

But in spite of these fine words, the new flag and the Acclamation of Pedro as Constitutional Emperor, the authority of the new regime only extended to Rio de Janeiro, São Paulo and the adjacent provinces. The rest of Brazil remained firmly under the control of Portuguese juntas and garrisons. It would take a war to put the whole of Brazil under Pedro's control. The fighting began with skirmishes between rival militias in 1822 and lasted until January 1824, when the last Portuguese garrisons and naval units surrendered or left the country.

Meanwhile the Imperial government had to create a regular Army and Navy. Forced enlistment was widespread, extending to foreign immigrants, and Brazil made use of slaves in militias, as well as freeing slaves to enlist them in army and navy. The campaigns on land and sea covered the vast territories of Bahia, Montevideo and Cisplatina, Grão-Pará. Maranhão, Pernambuco, Ceará and Piauí.

By 1822, Brazilian forces were firmly in control of Rio de Janeiro and the central area of Brazil. Loyal militias began insurrections in the aforementioned territories, but strong, and regularly reinforced Portuguese garrisons in the port cities of Salvador, Montevideo, São Luís and Belém continued to dominate the

Figure 57: *The Brazilian Army entering Salvador after the surrender of the Portuguese forces in 1823.*

adjacent areas and to pose the threat of a reconquest that the irregular Brazilian militias and guerrilla forces, which were loosely besieging them by land supported by newly created units of the Brazilian army, would be unable to prevent.

For the Brazilians, the answer to this stalemate was to seize control of the sea. Fortunately, 11 former Portuguese warships, great and small, had fallen into Brazilian hands in Rio de Janeiro and these formed the basis of a new navy. The problem was manpower. The crews of these ships were largely Portuguese who were openly mutinous, and although many Portuguese naval officers had declared allegiance to Brazil their loyalty could not be relied on. The Brazilian Government solved the problem by recruiting 50 officers and 500 seamen in secret in London and Liverpool, many of them veterans of the Napoleonic Wars, and appointed the Thomas Cochrane as commander-in-chief.[324] On 1 April 1823, a Brazilian squadron 6 of ships sailed for Bahia. After an initial disappointing engagement with a superior Portuguese fleet, Cochrane blockaded Salvador. Deprived now of supplies and reinforcements by sea and besieged by the Brazilian army on land, on 2 July the Portuguese forces abandoned Bahia in a convoy of 90 ships. Leaving the frigate 'Niteroi' under Captain John Taylor to harry them to the coasts of Europe, Cochrane then sailed north to San Luis. There he tricked the Portuguese garrison into evacuating

Maranhão by pretending that a huge Brazilian fleet and army were over the horizon. He then sent Captain John Pascoe Grenfell to play the same trick on the Portuguese in Belem do Para at the mouth of the Amazon.[325] By November 1823, the whole of the north of Brazil was under Brazilian control, and the following month, the demoralized Portuguese also evacuated Montevideo and the Cisplatine Province. By 1824, Brazil was free of all enemy troops and was 'de facto' independent.[326]

There are still today no reliable statistics[327] related to the numbers of, for example, the total of the war casualties. However based upon historical registration and contemporary reports of some battles of this war as well as upon the admitted numbers in similar fights that happened in these times around the globe, and considering how long the Brazilian independence war lasted (22 months), estimates of all killed in action on both sides are placed from around 5,700 to 6,200.

In Pernambuco

- Siege of Recife

In Piauí and Maranhão

- Battle of Jenipapo
- Siege of Caxias

In Grão-Pará

- Siege of Belém

In Bahia

- Battle of Pirajá
- Battle of Itaparica
- Battle of 4 May
- Siege of Salvador

In Cisplatina

- Siege of Montevideo (1823)

Peace treaty and aftermath

The last Portuguese soldiers left Brazil in 1824. A peace treaty recognizing Brazil's independence was drafted in summer 1825, and signed by Brazil and Portugal that autumn.

Further reading

- Gomes, Laurentino, *1822*

References

<templatestyles src="Template:Refbegin/styles.css" />
- Armitage, John. *História do Brasil*. Belo Horizonte: Itatiaia, 1981. (in Portuguese)
- Barman, Roderick J. *Citizen Emperor: Pedro II and the Making of Brazil, 1825–1891*. Stanford: Stanford University Press, 1999. (in English)
- Diégues, Fernando. *A revolução brasílica*. Rio de Janeiro: Objetiva, 2004. (in Portuguese)
- Dolhnikoff, Miriam. *Pacto imperial: origens do federalismo no Brasil do século XIX*. São Paulo: Globo, 2005. (in Portuguese)
- Gomes, Laurentino. *1822*. Nova Fronteira, 2010. ISBN 85-209-2409-3 (in Portuguese)
- Holanda, Sérgio Buarque de. *O Brasil Monárquico: o processo de emancipação*. 4. ed. São Paulo: Difusão Européia do Livro, 1976. (in Portuguese)
- Lima, Manuel de Oliveira. *O movimento da independência*. 6. ed. Rio de Janeiro: Topbooks, 1997. (in Portuguese)
- Lustosa, Isabel. *D. Pedro I*. São Paulo: Companhia das Letras, 2007. (in Portuguese)
- Vainfas, Ronaldo. *Dicionário do Brasil Imperial*. Rio de Janeiro: Objetiva, 2002. (in Portuguese)
- Vianna, Hélio. *História do Brasil: período colonial, monarquia e república*. 15. ed. São Paulo: Melhoramentos, 1994. (in Portuguese)

External links

- Media related to Independence of Brazil at Wikimedia Commons

Empire of Brazil

Empire of Brazil	
Império do Brasil	
1822–1889	
 Flag  Grand Imperial coat of arms	
Motto *Independência ou Morte!* "Independence or Death!"	
Anthem *Hino da Independência* (1822–1831) "Anthem of Independence" *Hino Nacional Brasileiro* (1831–1889) "Brazilian National Anthem"	
 Empire of Brazil at its largest territorial extent, 1822–1828, including former Cisplatina province	
Capital	Rio de Janeiro
Languages	Portuguese
Religion	Roman Catholic
Government	Constitutional monarchy
Emperor	
• 1822–1831	Pedro I

•	1831–1889	Pedro II
Prime Minister		
•	1843–1844	Marquis of Paraná (*de facto*)
•	1847–1848	2nd Viscount of Caravelas (office created)
•	1889	Viscount of Ouro Preto (last)
Legislature		General Assembly
•	Upper house	Senate
•	Lower house	Chamber of Deputies
Historical era		19th century
•	Independence	7 September 1822
•	Accession of Pedro I	12 October 1822
•	Adoption of the Empire's Constitution	25 March 1824
•	Accession of Pedro II	7 April 1831
•	Abolition of slavery	13 May 1888
•	Monarchy abolished	15 November 1889
Area		
•	1889	8,363,186 km² (3,229,044 sq mi)
Population		
•	1823 est.	4,000,000
•	1854 est.	7,000,700
•	1872 est.	9,930,479
•	1890 est.	14,333,915
Currency		Real

Preceded by	Succeeded by
◊ United Kingdom of Portugal, Brazil and the Algarves	First Brazilian Republic
Kingdom of Brazil	Uruguay

| **Today part of** | Brazil |
| | Uruguay |

The **Empire of Brazil** was a 19th-century state that broadly comprised the territories which form modern Brazil and (until 1828) Uruguay. Its government was a representative parliamentary constitutional monarchy under the rule of Emperors Dom Pedro I and his son Dom Pedro II. A colony of the Kingdom of Portugal, Brazil became the seat of the Portuguese colonial Empire in 1808, when the Portuguese Prince regent, later King Dom João VI, fled from

Napoleon's invasion of Portugal and established himself and his government in the Brazilian city of Rio de Janeiro. João VI later returned to Portugal, leaving his eldest son and heir, Pedro, to rule the Kingdom of Brazil as regent. On 7 September 1822, Pedro declared the independence of Brazil and, after waging a successful war against his father's kingdom, was acclaimed on 12 October as Pedro I, the first Emperor of Brazil. The new country was huge but sparsely populated and ethnically diverse.

Unlike most of the neighboring Hispanic American republics, Brazil had political stability, vibrant economic growth, constitutionally guaranteed freedom of speech, and respect for civil rights of its subjects, albeit with legal restrictions on women and slaves, the latter regarded as property and not citizens. The empire's bicameral parliament was elected under comparatively democratic methods for the era, as were the provincial and local legislatures. This led to a long ideological conflict between Pedro I and a sizable parliamentary faction over the role of the monarch in the government. He faced other obstacles. The unsuccessful Cisplatine War against the neighboring United Provinces of the Río de la Plata in 1828 led to the secession of the province of Cisplatina (later to become Uruguay). In 1826, despite his role in Brazilian independence, he became the king of Portugal; he immediately abdicated the Portuguese throne in favor of his eldest daughter. Two years later, she was usurped by Pedro I's younger brother Miguel. Unable to deal with both Brazilian and Portuguese affairs, Pedro I abdicated his Brazilian throne on 7 April 1831 and immediately departed for Europe to restore his daughter to the Portuguese throne.

Pedro I's successor in Brazil was his five-year-old son, Pedro II. As the latter was still a minor, a weak regency was created. The power vacuum resulting from the absence of a ruling monarch as the ultimate arbiter in political disputes led to regional civil wars between local factions. Having inherited an empire on the verge of disintegration, Pedro II, once he was declared of age, managed to bring peace and stability to the country, which eventually became an emerging international power. Brazil was victorious in three international conflicts (the Platine War, the Uruguayan War and the Paraguayan War) under Pedro II's rule, and the Empire prevailed in several other international disputes and outbreaks of domestic strife. With prosperity and economic development came an influx of European immigration, including Protestants and Jews, although Brazil remained mostly Catholic. Slavery, which had initially been widespread, was restricted by successive legislation until its final abolition in 1888. Brazilian visual arts, literature and theater developed during this time of progress. Although heavily influenced by European styles that ranged from Neoclassicism to Romanticism, each concept was adapted to create a culture that was uniquely Brazilian.

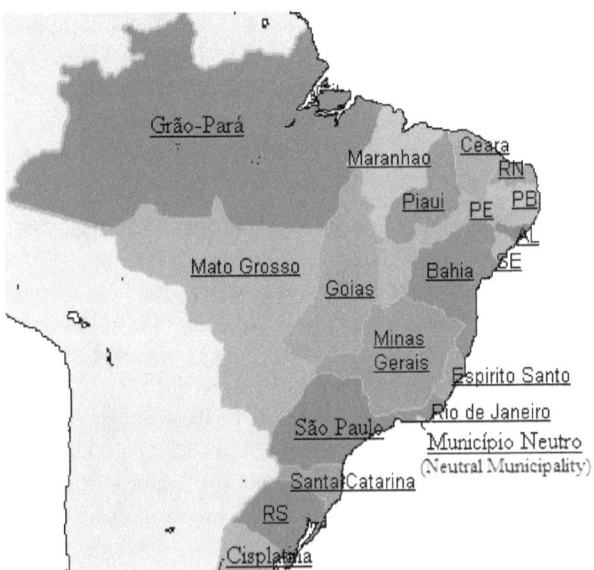

Figure 58: *The Empire of Brazil (RS=Rio Grande do Sul, RN=Rio Grande do Norte, PB=Paraíba, PE=Pernambuco, AL=Alagoas, SE=Sergipe), c. 1824. Neutral Municipality is Rio de Janeiro, the imperial capital which was located within the province of the same name*

Even though the last four decades of Pedro II's reign were marked by continuous internal peace and economic prosperity, he had no desire to see the monarchy survive beyond his lifetime and made no effort to maintain support for the institution. The next in line to the throne was his daughter Isabel, but neither Pedro II nor the ruling classes considered a female monarch acceptable. Lacking any viable heir, the Empire's political leaders saw no reason to defend the monarchy. After a 58-year reign, on 15 November 1889 the Emperor was overthrown in a sudden *coup d'état* led by a clique of military leaders whose goal was the formation of a republic headed by a dictator, forming the First Brazilian Republic.

History

Independence and early years

The territory which would come to be known as Brazil was claimed by Portugal on 22 April 1500, when the navigator Pedro Álvares Cabral landed on its coast.[328] Permanent settlement followed in 1532, and for the next 300 years the Portuguese slowly expanded westwards until they had reached nearly all of the borders of modern Brazil.[329] In 1808, the army of French Emperor Napoleon I invaded Portugal, forcing the Portuguese royal family—the House of Braganza, a branch of the thousand-year-old Capetian dynasty—into exile. They re-established themselves in the Brazilian city of Rio de Janeiro, which became the unofficial seat of the Portuguese Empire.[330]

In 1815, the Portuguese crown prince Dom João (later Dom João VI), acting as regent, created the United Kingdom of Portugal, Brazil and the Algarves, which raised the status of Brazil from colony to kingdom. He ascended the Portuguese throne the following year, after the death of his mother, Maria I of Portugal. He returned to Portugal in April 1821, leaving behind his son and heir, Prince Dom Pedro, to rule Brazil as his regent.[331,332] The Portuguese government immediately moved to revoke the political autonomy that Brazil had been granted since 1808.[333,334] The threat of losing their limited control over local affairs ignited widespread opposition among Brazilians. José Bonifácio de Andrada, along with other Brazilian leaders, convinced Pedro to declare Brazil's independence from Portugal on 7 September 1822.[335,336] On 12 October, the prince was acclaimed Pedro I, first Emperor of the newly created Empire of Brazil, a constitutional monarchy.[337,338] The declaration of independence was opposed throughout Brazil by armed military units loyal to Portugal. The ensuing war of independence was fought across the country, with battles in the northern, northeastern, and southern regions. The last Portuguese soldiers to surrender did so in March 1824,[339,340] and independence was recognized by Portugal in August 1825.[341]

Pedro I encountered a number of crises during his reign. A secessionist rebellion in the Cisplatine Province in early 1825 and the subsequent attempt by the United Provinces of the Río de la Plata (later Argentina) to annex Cisplatina led the Empire into the Cisplatine War: "a long, inglorious, and ultimately futile war in the south".[342] In March 1826, João VI died and Pedro I inherited the Portuguese crown, briefly becoming King Pedro IV of Portugal before abdicating in favor of his eldest daughter, Maria II.[343] The situation worsened in 1828 when the war in the south ended with Brazil's loss of Cisplatina, which would become the independent republic of Uruguay.[344] During the same year in Lisbon, Maria II's throne was usurped by Prince Miguel, Pedro I's younger brother.[345]

Other difficulties arose when the Empire's parliament, the General Assembly, opened in 1826. Pedro I, along with a significant percentage of the legislature, argued for an independent judiciary, a popularly elected legislature and a government which would be led by the emperor who held broad executive powers and prerogatives.[346] Others in parliament argued for a similar structure, only with a less influential role for the monarch and the legislative branch being

Figure 59: *The City Palace, seat of the Brazilian Imperial government, in 1840*

dominant in policy and governance.[347] The struggle over whether the government would be dominated by the emperor or by the parliament was carried over into debates from 1826 to 1831 on the establishment of the governmental and political structure.[342] Unable to deal with the problems in both Brazil and Portugal simultaneously, the Emperor abdicated on behalf of his son, Pedro II, on 7 April 1831 and immediately sailed for Europe to restore his daughter to her throne.[348]

Anarchy

Following the hasty departure of Pedro I, Brazil was left with a five-year-old boy as head of state. With no precedent to follow, the Empire was faced with the prospect of a period of more than twelve years without a strong executive, as, under the constitution, Pedro II would not attain his majority and begin exercising authority as Emperor until 2 December 1843.[349] A regency was elected to rule the country in the interim. Because the Regency held few of the powers exercised by an emperor and was completely subordinated to the General Assembly, it could not fill the vacuum at the apex of Brazil's government.[350]

The hamstrung Regency proved unable to resolve disputes and rivalries between national and local political factions. Believing that granting provincial and local governments greater autonomy would quell the growing dissent, the General Assembly passed a constitutional amendment in 1834, called the *Ato Adicional* (Additional Act). Instead of ending the chaos, these new powers only fed local ambitions and rivalries. Violence erupted throughout the country.[351] Local parties competed with renewed ferocity to dominate provincial and municipal governments, as whichever party dominated the provinces would also gain control over the electoral and political system. Those parties which lost elections rebelled and tried to assume power by force, resulting in several rebellions.[352]

The politicians who had risen to power during the 1830s had by then become familiar with the difficulties and pitfalls of power. According to historian Roderick J. Barman, by 1840 "they had lost all faith in their ability to rule the country on their own. They accepted Pedro II as an authority figure whose presence was indispensable for the country's survival."[353] Some of these politicians (who would form the Conservative Party in the 1840s) believed that a neutral figure was required—one who could stand above political factions and petty interests to address discontent and moderate disputes.[354] They envisioned an emperor who was more dependent on the legislature than the constitutional monarch envisioned by Pedro I, yet with greater powers than had been advocated at the beginning of the Regency by their rivals (who later formed the Liberal Party).[355] The liberals, however, contrived to pass an initiative to lower Pedro II's age of majority from eighteen to fourteen. The Emperor was declared fit to rule in July 1840.[356]

Consolidation

To achieve their goals, the liberals had allied themselves with a group of high-ranking palace servants and notable politicians: the "Courtier Faction". The courtiers were part of the Emperor's inner circle and had established influence over him,[357] which enabled the appointment of successive liberal-courtier cabinets. Their dominance was short-lived, though. By 1846, Pedro II had matured physically and mentally. No longer an insecure 14-year-old swayed by gossip, suggestions of secret plots, and other manipulative tactics,[358] the young emperor's weaknesses faded and his strength of character came to the fore.[358] He successfully engineered the end of the courtiers' influence by removing them from his inner circle without causing any public disruption.[359] He also dismissed the liberals, who had proved ineffective while in office, and called on the conservatives to form a government in 1848.[360]

The abilities of the Emperor and the newly appointed conservative cabinet were tested by three crises between 1848 and 1852.[361] The first crisis was a confrontation over the illegal importation of slaves. Importing slaves had been banned in 1826 as part of a treaty with Britain.[360] Trafficking continued unabated, however, and the British government's passage of the Aberdeen Act

Figure 60: *Recife, capital of Pernambuco (Brazilian northeast), two years after the end of the Praieira revolt*

of 1845 authorized British warships to board Brazilian ships and seize anyone who was found to be involved in the slave trade.[362] While Brazil grappled with this problem, the Praieira revolt, a conflict between local political factions within Pernambuco province (and one in which liberal and courtier supporters were involved), erupted on 6 November 1848, but was suppressed by March 1849. It was the last rebellion to occur during the monarchy, and its end marked the beginning of forty years of internal peace in Brazil. The Eusébio de Queirós Law was promulgated on 4 September 1850 giving the government broad authority to combat the illegal slave trade. With this new tool Brazil moved to eliminate the importation of slaves, and by 1852 this first crisis was over, with Britain accepting that the trade had been suppressed.[363]

The third crisis was a conflict with the Argentine Confederation over ascendancy in territories adjacent to the Río de la Plata and free navigation of that waterway.[364] Since the 1830s, Argentine dictator Juan Manuel de Rosas had supported rebellions within Uruguay and Brazil. The Empire was unable to address the threat posed by Rosas until 1850,[364] when an alliance was forged between Brazil, Uruguay and disaffected Argentines,[364] leading to the Platine War and the subsequent overthrow of the Argentine ruler in February 1852.[365,366] The Empire's successful navigation of these crises considerably

Figure 61: *The locomotive Pequenina (Little One) in Bahia province (Brazilian northeast), c. 1859*

enhanced the nation's stability and prestige, and Brazil emerged as a hemispheric power.[367] Internationally, Europeans came to see the country as embodying familiar liberal ideals, such as freedom of the press and constitutional respect for civil liberties. Its representative parliamentary monarchy also stood in stark contrast to the mix of dictatorships and instability endemic in the other nations of South America during this period.[368]

Growth

At the beginning of the 1850s, Brazil was enjoying internal stability and economic prosperity.[369] The nation's infrastructure was being developed, with progress in the construction of railroads, the electric telegraph and steamship lines uniting Brazil into a cohesive national entity.[369] After five years in office, the successful conservative cabinet was dismissed and in September 1853, Honório Hermeto Carneiro Leão, Marquis of Paraná, head of the Conservative Party, was charged with forming a new cabinet.[370] Emperor Pedro II wanted to advance an ambitious plan, which became known as "the Conciliation",[371] aimed at strengthening parliament's role in settling the country's political disputes.[370,372]

Paraná invited several liberals to join the conservative ranks and went so far as to name some as ministers. The new cabinet, although highly successful, was

Figure 62: *A construction site in the docks of Recife, 1862*

plagued from the start by strong opposition from ultraconservative members of the Conservative Party who repudiated the new liberal recruits. They believed that the cabinet had become a political machine infested with converted liberals who did not genuinely share the party's ideals and were primarily interested in gaining public offices.[373] Despite this mistrust, Paraná showed resilience in fending off threats and overcoming obstacles and setbacks.[374,375] However, in September 1856, at the height of his career, he died unexpectedly, although the cabinet survived him until May 1857.[376]

The Conservative Party had split down the middle: on one side were the ultraconservatives, and on the other, the moderate conservatives who supported the Conciliation.[377] The ultraconservatives were led by Joaquim Rodrigues Torres, Viscount of Itaboraí, Eusébio de Queirós and Paulino Soares de Sousa, 1st Viscount of Uruguai—all former ministers in the 1848–1853 cabinet. These elder statesmen had taken control of the Conservative Party after Paraná's death.[378] In the years following 1857, none of the cabinets survived long. They quickly collapsed due to the lack of a majority in the Chamber of Deputies.

The remaining members of the Liberal Party, which had languished since its fall in 1848 and the disastrous *Praieira* rebellion in 1849, took advantage of what seemed to be the Conservative Party's impending implosion to return to

Figure 63: *Brazilian artillery in position during the Paraguayan War, 1866*

national politics with renewed strength. They delivered a powerful blow to the government when they managed to win several seats in the Chamber of Deputies in 1860.[379] When many moderate conservatives defected to unite with liberals to form a new political party, the "Progressive League",[380] the conservatives' hold on power became unsustainable due to the lack of a workable governing majority in the parliament. They resigned, and in May 1862 Pedro II named a progressive cabinet.[381] The period since 1853 had been one of peace and prosperity for Brazil: "The political system functioned smoothly. Civil liberties were maintained. A start had been made on the introduction into Brazil of railroad, telegraph and steamship lines. The country was no longer troubled by the disputes and conflicts that had racked it during its first thirty years."[382]

Paraguayan War

This period of calm came to an end when the British consul in Rio de Janeiro nearly sparked a war between Great Britain and Brazil. He sent an ultimatum containing abusive demands arising out of two minor incidents at the end of 1861 and beginning of 1862.[383] The Brazilian government refused to yield, and the consul issued orders for British warships to capture Brazilian merchant vessels as indemnity.[384] Brazil prepared itself for the imminent conflict,[385,386] and coastal defenses were given permission to fire upon any British warship that tried to capture Brazilian merchant ships.[387] The Brazilian government then severed diplomatic ties with Britain in June 1863.[388]

Figure 64: *Brazilian soldiers kneeling before a religious procession during the Paraguayan War, 1868*

As war with the British Empire loomed, Brazil had to turn its attention to its southern frontiers. Another civil war had begun in Uruguay which pitted its political parties against one another.[389] The internal conflict led to the murder of Brazilians and the looting of their Uruguayan properties.[390] Brazil's progressive cabinet decided to intervene and dispatched an army, which invaded Uruguay in December 1864, beginning the brief Uruguayan War.[391] The dictator of nearby Paraguay, Francisco Solano López, took advantage of the Uruguayan situation in late 1864 by attempting to establish his nation as a regional power. In November of that year, he ordered a Brazilian civilian steamship seized, triggering the Paraguayan War, and then invaded Brazil.[392,393]

What had appeared at the outset to be a brief and straightforward military intervention led to a full-scale war in South America's southeast. However, the possibility of a two-front conflict (with Britain and Paraguay) faded when, in September 1865, the British government sent an envoy who publicly apologized for the crisis between the empires.[394,395] The Paraguayan invasion in 1864 led to a conflict far longer than expected, and faith in the progressive cabinet's ability to prosecute the war vanished.[396] Also, from its inception, the Progressive League was plagued by internal conflict between factions formed by former moderate conservatives and by former liberals.[396,397]

Figure 65: *A large group of slaves gathered on a farm in the province of Minas Gerais (Brazilian southeast), 1876*

The cabinet resigned and the Emperor named the aging Viscount of Itaboraí to head a new cabinet in July 1868, marking the return of the conservatives to power.[398] This impelled both progressive wings to set aside their differences, leading them to rechristen their party as the Liberal Party. A third, smaller and radical progressive wing would declare itself republican in 1870—an ominous signal for the monarchy.[399] Nonetheless, the "ministry formed by the viscount of Itaboraí was a far abler body than the cabinet it replaced"[398] and the conflict with Paraguay ended in March 1870 with total victory for Brazil and its allies.[400] More than 50,000 Brazilian soldiers had died,[401] and war costs were eleven times the government's annual budget.[402] However, the country was so prosperous that the government was able to retire the war debt in only ten years.[403,404] The conflict was also a stimulus to national production and economic growth.[405]

Apogee

The diplomatic victory over the British Empire and the military victory over Uruguay in 1865, followed by the successful conclusion of the war with Paraguay in 1870, marked the beginning of the "golden age" of the Brazilian Empire.[406] The Brazilian economy grew rapidly; railroad, shipping and other modernization projects were started; immigration flourished.[407] The Empire became known internationally as a modern and progressive nation, second only to the United States in the Americas; it was a politically stable economy with a good investment potential.[406]

In March 1871, Pedro II named the conservative José Paranhos, Viscount of Rio Branco as the head of a cabinet whose main goal was to pass a law to immediately free all children born to female slaves.[408] The controversial bill was introduced in the Chamber of Deputies in May and faced "a determined opposition, which commanded support from about one third of the deputies and which sought to organize public opinion against the measure."[409] The bill was finally promulgated in September and became known as the "Law of Free Birth".[409] Rio Branco's success, however, seriously damaged the long-term political stability of the Empire. The law "split the conservatives down the middle, one party faction backed the reforms of the Rio Branco cabinet, while the second—known as the *escravocratas* (English: slavocrats)—were unrelenting in their opposition", forming a new generation of ultraconservatives.[410]

The "Law of Free Birth", and Pedro II's support for it, resulted in the loss of the ultraconservatives' unconditional loyalty to the monarchy.[410] The Conservative Party had experienced serious divisions before, during the 1850s, when the Emperor's total support for the conciliation policy had given rise to the Progressives. The ultraconservatives led by Eusébio, Uruguai and Itaboraí who opposed conciliation in the 1850s had nonetheless believed that the Emperor was indispensable to the functioning of the political system: the Emperor was an ultimate and impartial arbiter when political deadlock threatened.[411] By contrast, this new generation of ultraconservatives had not experienced the Regency and early years of Pedro II's reign, when external and internal dangers had threatened the Empire's very existence; they had only known prosperity, peace and a stable administration.[353] To them—and to the ruling classes in general—the presence of a neutral monarch who could settle political disputes was no longer important. Furthermore, since Pedro II had clearly taken a political side on the slavery question, he had compromised his position as a neutral arbiter. The young ultraconservative politicians saw no reason to uphold or defend the Imperial office.[412]

Decline

The weaknesses in the monarchy took many years to become apparent. Brazil continued to prosper during the 1880s, with the economy and society both developing rapidly, including the first organized push for women's rights (which would progress slowly over the next decades).[413] By contrast, letters written by Pedro II reveal a man grown world-weary with age, increasingly alienated from current events and pessimistic in outlook.[414] He remained meticulous in performing his formal duties as Emperor, albeit often without enthusiasm, but

Figure 66: *The Empire of Brazil, c. 1889. Cisplatina had been lost since 1828 and two new provinces had been created since then (Amazonas and Paraná)*

he no longer actively intervened to maintain stability in the country.[415] His increasing "indifference towards the fate of the regime"[416] and his inaction to protect the imperial system once it came under threat have led historians to attribute the "prime, perhaps sole, responsibility" for the dissolution of the monarchy to the emperor himself.[417]

The lack of an heir who could feasibly provide a new direction for the nation also threatened the long-term prospects for the Brazilian monarchy. The Emperor's heir was his eldest daughter, Isabel, who had no interest in, nor expectation of, becoming the monarch.[418] Even though the Constitution allowed female succession to the throne, Brazil was still a very traditional, male-dominated society, and the prevailing view was that only a male monarch would be capable as head of state.[419] Pedro II,[420] the ruling circles[421] and the wider political establishment all considered a female successor to be inappropriate, and Pedro II himself believed that the death of his two sons and the lack of a male heir were a sign that the Empire was destined to be supplanted.[420]

A weary Emperor who no longer cared for the throne, an heir who had no desire to assume the crown, an increasingly discontented ruling class who were dismissive of the Imperial role in national affairs: all these factors presaged the monarchy's impending doom. The means to achieve the overthrow of the

Figure 67: *A few moments after signing the Golden Law, Princess Isabel is greeted from the central balcony of the City Palace by a huge crowd below in the street*

Imperial system would soon appear within the Army ranks. Republicanism had never flourished in Brazil outside of certain elitist circles,[422,423] and had little support in the provinces.[424] A growing combination of republican and Positivist ideals among the army's junior and mid-level officer ranks, however, began to form a serious threat to the monarchy. These officers favored a republican dictatorship, which they believed would be superior to the liberal democratic monarchy.[425,426] Beginning with small acts of insubordination at the beginning of the 1880s, discontent in the army grew in scope and audacity during the decade, as the Emperor was uninterested and the politicians proved incapable of re-establishing the government's authority over the military.[427]

Fall

The nation enjoyed considerable international prestige during the final years of the Empire[428] and had become an emerging power in the international arena. While Pedro II was receiving medical treatment in Europe, the parliament passed, and Princess Isabel signed on 13 May 1888, the Golden Law, which completely abolished slavery in Brazil.[429] Predictions of economic and labor disruption caused by the abolition of slavery proved to be unfounded.[430] Nonetheless, the end of slavery was the final blow to any remaining belief in the crown's neutrality, and this resulted in an explicit shift of support to

Republicanism by the ultraconservatives[431]—themselves backed by rich and powerful coffee farmers who held great political, economic and social power in the country.[432]

To avert a republican backlash, the government exploited the credit readily available to Brazil as a result of its prosperity to fuel further development. The government extended massive loans at favorable interest rates to plantation owners and lavishly granted titles and lesser honors to curry favor with influential political figures who had become disaffected.[433] The government also indirectly began to address the problem of the recalcitrant military by revitalizing the moribund National Guard, by then an entity which existed mostly only on paper.[434]

The measures taken by the government alarmed civilian republicans and the positivists in the military. The republicans saw that it would undercut support for their own aims, and were emboldened to further action.[426] The reorganization of the National Guard was begun by the cabinet in August 1889, and the creation of a rival force caused the dissidents among the officer corps to consider desperate measures.[435] For both groups, republicans and military, it had become a case of "now or never".[436] Although there was no desire among the majority of Brazilians to change the country's form of government,[437] republicans began pressuring army officers to overthrow the monarchy.[438]

They launched a coup and instituted the republic on 15 November 1889.[439] The few people who witnessed what occurred did not realize that it was a rebellion.[440,441] Historian Lídia Besouchet noted that, "[r]arely has a revolution been so minor."[442] Throughout the coup Pedro II showed no emotion, as if unconcerned about the outcome.[443] He dismissed all suggestions put forward by politicians and military leaders for quelling the rebellion.[444] The Emperor and his family were sent into exile on 17 November.[445] Although there was significant monarchist reaction after the fall of the Empire, this was thoroughly suppressed,[446] and neither Pedro II nor his daughter supported a restoration.[447] Despite being unaware of the plans for a coup, once it occurred and in light of the Emperor's passive acceptance of the situation, the political establishment supported the end of the monarchy in favor of a republic. They were unaware that the goal of the coup leaders was the creation of a dictatorial republic rather than a presidential or parliamentary republic.[448]

Figure 68: *Brazilian Senate, 1888. The senators are voting on the Golden Law as a large crowd watches in the background*

Government

Parliament

Article 2 of Brazil's Constitution defined the roles of both the Emperor and the *Assembleia Geral* (General Assembly or Parliament), which in 1824 was composed of 50 senators and 102 general deputies, as the nation's representatives. The Constitution endowed the Assembly with both status and authority, and created legislative, moderating, executive and judicial branches as "delegations of the nation" with the separation of those powers envisaged as providing balances in support of the Constitution and the rights it enshrined.[449]

The prerogatives and authority granted to the legislature within the Constitution meant that it could and would play a major and indispensable role in the functioning of the government—it was not just a rubber stamp. The General Assembly alone could enact, revoke, interpret and suspend laws under Article 13 of the Constitution. The legislature also held the power of the purse and was required to annually authorize expenditures and taxes. It alone approved and exercised oversight of government loans and debts. Other responsibilities entrusted to the Assembly included setting the size of the military's forces, the creation of offices within the government, monitoring the national welfare

Figure 69: *Map of Rio de Janeiro, then Neutral Municipality and capital of the Brazilian Empire. National Archives of Brazil.*

and ensuring that the government was being run in conformity to the Constitution. This last provision allowed the legislature wide authority to examine and debate government policy and conduct.[450]

Regarding matters of foreign policy, the Constitution (under Article 102) required that the General Assembly be consulted about declarations of war, treaties and the conduct of international relations. A determined legislator could exploit these Constitutional provisions to block or limit government decisions, influence appointments and force reconsideration of policies.[451]

During its annual four-month sessions the Assembly conducted public debates. These were widely reported and formed a national forum for the expression of public concerns from all parts of the country. It was frequently a venue for expressing opposition to policies and airing grievances. Legislators enjoyed immunity from prosecution for speeches made from the floor and in the discharge of their offices. Only their own chambers within the Assembly could order the arrest of a member during his tenure. "With no actual responsibility for the actual conduct of affairs, the legislators were free to propose sweeping reforms, advocate ideal solutions, and denounce compromising and opportunistic conduct by the government."[451]

Empire of Brazil

Figure 70: *Emperor Pedro II surrounded by prominent politicians and national figures c. 1875*

Emperor and council of ministers

The Emperor was the head of both the moderating and executive branches (being aided by the Council of State and the Council of Ministers, respectively); he had the final say and held ultimate control over the national government.[449] He was tasked with ensuring national independence and stability. The Constitution (Article 101) gave him very few avenues for imposing his will upon the General Assembly. His main recourse was the right to dissolve or extend legislative sessions. In the Senate, an emperor's authority to appoint senators did not necessarily give him added influence since senators held their offices for life and were thus freed from government pressure once confirmed. On those occasions when the Chamber of Deputies was dissolved, new elections were required to be held immediately and the new Chamber seated. "This power was effective when held in reserve as a threat. It could not be employed repeatedly, nor would its use work to the emperor's advantage."[451]

During the reign of Pedro I the Chamber of Deputies was never dissolved and legislative sessions were never extended or postponed.[452] Under Pedro II, the Chamber of Deputies was only ever dissolved at the request of the President of the Council of Ministers (Prime minister). There were eleven dissolutions during Pedro II's reign and, of these, ten occurred after consultation with the Council of State, which was beyond what was required by the Constitution.[453]

A Constitutional balance of power existed between the General Assembly and the executive branch under the Emperor. The legislature could not operate alone and the monarch could not force his will upon the Assembly. The system functioned smoothly only when both Assembly and Emperor acted in a spirit of cooperation for the national good.[451]

A new element was added when the office of "President of the Council of Ministers" was officially created in 1847—although it had existed in practice since 1843. The president of the Council owed his position to both his party and to the Emperor and these could sometimes come into conflict. 19th-century abolitionist leader and historian Joaquim Nabuco said that the "President of the Council in Brazil was no Russian Chancellor, Sovereign's creature, nor a British Prime Minister, made only by the trust of the [House of] Commons: the delegation of the Crown was to him as necessary and important as the delegation of the Chamber, and, to exert with safety his functions, he had to dominate the caprice, the oscillations and ambitions of the Parliament, as well as to preserve always unalterable the favor, the good will of the emperor."[454]

Provincial and local government

Belém, a medium-sized city and capital of Pará province (Brazilian north), 1889

Salvador, a large city and capital of Bahia province (Brazilian northeast), 1870

Rio de Janeiro, a metropolis and imperial capital, 1889 (Brazilian southeast). All provinces had great autonomy in relation to the national government.

When enacted in 1824, the Imperial Constitution created the *Conselho Geral de Província* (Provincial General Council), the legislature of the provinces.[455] This council was composed of either 21 or 13 elected members, depending on the size of a province's population.[456] All "resolutions" (laws) created by the councils required approval by the General Assembly, with no right of appeal.[456] Provincial Councils also had no authority to raise revenues, and their budgets had to be debated and ratified by the General Assembly.[456] Provinces had no autonomy and were entirely subordinate to the national government.[455]

With the 1834 constitutional amendment known as the Additional Act, Provincial General Councils were supplanted by the *Assembleias Legislativas Provinciais* (Provincial Legislative Assemblies). The new Assemblies enjoyed much greater autonomy from the national government.[457] A Provincial Assembly was composed of 36, 28 or 20 elected deputies, the number depending on the size of the province's population.[458] The election of provincial deputies followed the same procedure as used to elect general deputies to the national Chamber of Deputies.[458]

The responsibilities of the Provincial Assembly included defining provincial and municipal budgets and levying the taxes necessary to support them; providing primary and secondary schools (higher education was the responsibility of the national government); oversight and control of provincial and municipal expenditures; and providing for law enforcement and maintenance of police forces. The Assemblies also controlled the creation and abolishment of, and salaries for, positions within provincial and municipal civil services. The nomination, suspension and dismissal of civil servants was reserved for the president (governor) of the province, but how and under what circumstances he could exercise these prerogatives was delineated by the Assembly. The expropriation of private property (with due monetary compensation) for provincial or municipal interests was also a right of the Assembly.[459] In effect, the Provincial Assembly could enact any kind of law—with no ratification by Parliament—so long as such local laws did not violate or encroach upon the Constitution. However, provinces were not permitted to legislate in the areas of criminal law, criminal procedure laws, civil rights and obligations, the armed forces, the national budget or matters concerning national interests, such as foreign relations.[460]

The provincial presidents were appointed by the national government and were, in theory, charged with governing the province. In practice, however, their power was intangible, varying from province to province based upon each president's relative degree of personal influence and personal character. Since the national government wanted to ensure their loyalty, presidents were, in most cases, sent to a province in which they had no political, familial or other ties.[461] In order to prevent them from developing any strong local interests or support, presidents would be limited to terms of only a few months in office.[461] As the president usually spent a great deal of time away from the province, often traveling to their native province or the imperial capital, the *de facto* governor was the vice-president, who was chosen by the Provincial Assembly and was usually a local politician.[462] With little power to undermine provincial autonomy, the president was an agent of the central government with little function beyond conveying its interests to the provincial political bosses. Presidents could be used by the national government to influence, or even rig, elections, although to be effective the president had to rely on provincial and local politicians who belonged to his own political party. This interdependency created a complex relationship which was based upon exchanges of favors, private interests, party goals, negotiations, and other political maneuvering.[463]

The *câmara municipal* (town council) was the governing body in towns and cities and had existed in Brazil since the beginning of the colonial period in the 16th century. The Chamber was composed of *vereadores* (councilmen), the number of which depended on the size of the town.[464] Unlike the Provincial General Council, the Constitution gave town councils great autonomy. However, when the Provincial Assembly replaced the Provincial General Council in 1834, many of the powers of town councils (including the setting of municipal budgets, oversight of expenditures, creation of jobs, and the nomination of civil servants) were transferred to the provincial government. Additionally, any laws enacted by the town council had to be ratified by the Provincial Assembly—but not by Parliament.[465] While the 1834 Additional Act granted greater autonomy to the provinces from the central government, it transferred the towns' remaining autonomy to the provincial governments.[466] There was no office of mayor, and towns were governed by a town council and its president (who was the councilman who won the most votes during elections).[467]

Elections

Until 1881, voting was mandatory[468] and elections occurred in two stages. In the first phase voters chose electors who then selected a slate of senatorial candidates. The Emperor would choose a new senator (member of the Senate, the upper house in the General Assembly) from a list of the three candidates who had received the highest number of votes. The Electors also chose the General Deputies (members of the Chamber of Deputies, the lower house), provincial deputies (members of the Provincial Assemblies) and councilmen (members of the town councils) without the involvement of the Emperor in making a final selection.[469] All men over the age of 25 with an annual income of at least Rs 100$000 (or 100,000 *réis*; the equivalent in 1824 to $98 U.S.[470]) were eligible to vote in the first phase. The voting age was lowered to 21 for

Figure 71: *A very poor family of caboclos in Ceará province (Brazilian northeast), 1880. In practice, any employed male citizen could qualify to vote. As such, most electors had low income*

married men. To become an elector it was necessary to have an annual income of at least Rs 200$000.[469]

The Brazilian system was relatively democratic for a period during which indirect elections were common in democracies. The income requirement was much higher in the United Kingdom, even after the reforms of 1832.[471] At the time the only nations not requiring a minimum level of income as a qualification for voting were France and Switzerland where universal suffrage was introduced only in 1848.[472,473] It is probable that no European country at the time had such liberal legislation as Brazil.[471] The income requirement was low enough that any employed male citizen could qualify to vote.[470,473] As an illustration, the lowest paid civil employee in 1876 was a janitor who earned Rs 600$000 annually.[471]

Most voters in Brazil had a low income.[474,475] For example, in the Minas Gerais town of Formiga in 1876, the poor constituted 70% of the electorate. In Irajá in the province of Rio de Janeiro, the poor were 87% of the electorate.[476] Former slaves could not vote, but their children and grandchildren could,[472] as could the illiterate[477] (which few countries allowed).[474] In 1872, 10.8% of the Brazilian population voted[475] (13% of the non-slave population).[478] By

Figure 72: *Whites and afro-descendants gathered in Rio de Janeiro province (Brazilian southeast), c. 1888. Brazil's 19th-century elections were very democratic for the time, but were plagued by frauds*

comparison, electoral participation in the UK in 1870 was 7% of the total population; in Italy it was 2%; in Portugal 9%; and in the Netherlands 2.5%.[472] In 1832, the year of the British electoral reform, 3% of the British voted. Further reforms in 1867 and 1884 expanded electoral participation in the UK to 15%.[479]

Although electoral fraud was common, it was not ignored by the Emperor, politicians or observers of the time. The problem was considered a major issue and attempts were made to correct abuses,[469,477] with legislation (including the electoral reforms of 1855, 1875 and 1881) repeatedly being enacted to combat fraud.[480] The 1881 reforms brought significant changes: they eliminated the two-stage electoral system, introduced direct and facultative voting,[481] and allowed the votes of former slaves and enfranchised non-Catholics.[475] Conversely, illiterate citizens were no longer allowed to vote.[475] Participation in elections dropped from 13% to only 0.8% in 1886.[475] In 1889, about 15% of the Brazilian population could read and write, so disenfranchising the illiterate does not solely explain the sudden fall in voting percentages.[482] The discontinuation of mandatory voting and voter apathy may have been significant factors contributing to the reduction in the number of voters.[483]

Figure 73: *Brazilian Army officers, 1886*

Armed Forces

Under Articles 102 and 148 of the Constitution, the Brazilian Armed Forces were subordinate to the Emperor as Commander-in-Chief.[484] He was aided by the Ministers of War and Navy in matters concerning the Army and the Armada (Navy)—although the President of the Council of Ministers usually exercised oversight of both branches in practice. The ministers of War and Navy were, with few exceptions, civilians.[485,486]

The military was organized along similar lines to the British and American armed forces of the time, in which a small standing army could quickly augment its strength during emergencies from a reserve militia force (in Brazil, the National Guard). Brazil's first line of defense relied upon a large and powerful navy to protect against foreign attack. As a matter of policy, the military was to be completely obedient to civilian governmental control and to remain at arm's length from involvement in political decisions.[487]

Military personnel were allowed to run for and serve in political office while remaining on active duty. However they did not represent the Army or the Armada, but were instead expected to serve the interests of the city or province which had elected them.[485] Pedro I chose nine military officers as Senators and appointed five (out of fourteen) to the Council of State. During the Regency, two were named to the Senate and none to the Council of State (this body was dormant during the Regency). Pedro II chose four officers as Senators during the 1840s, two in the 1850s and three others during the remaining years of

Figure 74: *The Brazilian ironclad warship Riachuelo, 1885*

Figure 75: *Shipyard in Rio de Janeiro city, c. 1862*

his reign. He also appointed seven officers to be State Councilors during the 1840s and 1850s, and three others after that.[488]

The Brazilian Armed Forces were created in the aftermath of Independence. They were originally composed of Brazilian- and Portuguese-born officers and troops who had remained loyal to the government in Rio de Janeiro during the war of secession from Portugal. The Armed Forces were crucial to the successful outcomes of international conflicts faced by the Empire, starting with Independence (1822–1824), followed by the Cisplatine War (1825–1828), then the Platine War (1851–1852), the Uruguayan War (1864–1865) and, finally, the Paraguayan War (1864–1870). They also played a part in quelling rebellions, beginning with the Confederation of the Equator (1824) under Pedro I, followed by the uprisings during Pedro II's early reign, such as the Ragamuffin War (1835–1845), Cabanagem (1835–1840), Balaiada (1838–1841), among others.[489]

The Armada was constantly being modernized with the latest developments in naval warfare. It adopted steam navigation in the 1830s, ironclad plate armor in the 1860s, and torpedoes in the 1880s. By 1889, Brazil had the fifth or sixth most powerful navy in the world[490] and the most powerful battleships in the western hemisphere.[491] The Army, despite its highly experienced and battle-hardened officer corps, was plagued during peacetime by units which were badly paid, inadequately equipped, poorly trained and thinly spread across the vast Empire.[492]

Dissension resulting from inadequate government attention to Army needs was restrained under the generation of officers who had begun their careers during the 1820s. These officers were loyal to the monarchy, believed the military should be under civilian control, and abhorred the caudillism (Hispanic-American dictatorships) against which they had fought. But by the early 1880s, this generation (including commanders such as the Duke of Caxias, the Count of Porto Alegre, and the Marquis of Erval) had died, were retired, or no longer exercised direct command.[425,493]

Dissatisfaction became more evident during the 1880s, and some officers began to display open insubordination. The Emperor and the politicians did nothing to improve the military nor meet their demands.[494] The dissemination of Positivist ideology among young officers brought further complications, as Positivism opposed the monarchy under the belief that a dictatorial republic would bring improvements.[426] A coalition between a mutinous Army faction and the Positivist camp was formed and directly led to the republican coup on 15 November 1889.[495] Battalions and even full regiments of soldiers loyal to the Empire, who shared the ideals of the older generation of leaders, attempted to restore the monarchy. Attempts at a restoration proved futile and supporters of the Empire were executed, arrested or forcibly retired.[496]

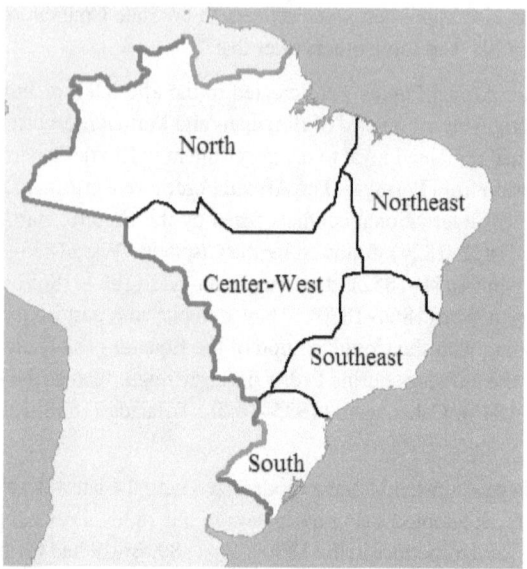

Figure 76: *In red: Brazil's borders in 1889 as established by international treaties; In grey: borders still not recognized by the end of the Empire; In black: geographical regions within Brazil after the Empire*[497]

Foreign relations

Upon independence from Portugal, the immediate focus of Brazil's foreign policy was to gain widespread international recognition. The first nation to recognize Brazilian sovereignty was the United States, in May 1825.[498] Other nations followed in establishing diplomatic relations over the next few years.[499] Portugal recognized the separation in August 1825.[500] The Brazilian government subsequently made it a priority to establish its international borders through treaties with its neighbors. The task of securing recognized frontiers was complicated by the fact that, between 1777 and 1801, Portugal and Spain had annulled their previous treaties setting out the borders between their American colonial empires.[501] However, the Empire was able to sign several bilateral treaties with neighbors, including Uruguay (in 1851), Peru (in 1851 and 1874), the Republic of New Granada (later Colombia, in 1853), Venezuela (in 1859), Bolivia (in 1867) and Paraguay (in 1872).[502,503] By 1889, most of its borders were firmly established. The remaining issues—including the purchase of the region of Acre from Bolivia which would give Brazil its present-day configuration[504]—were only finally resolved after the country became a republic.[505]

A number of conflicts occurred between the Empire and its neighbors. Brazil experienced no serious conflicts with its neighbors to the north and west, due to the buffer of the nearly impenetrable and sparsely populated Amazonian rainforest.[506] In the south, however, the colonial disputes inherited from Portugal and Spain over the control of the navigable rivers and plains which formed the frontiers continued after independence.[507] The lack of mutually agreed borders in this area led to several international conflicts, from the Cisplatine War to the Paraguayan War.[508]

"Brazil is, next to ourselves, the great power on the American continent", affirmed James Watson Webb, the U.S. minister to Brazil, in 1867.[509] The Empire's rise was noticed as early as 1844 by John C. Calhoun, the U.S. Secretary of State: "Next to the United States, Brazil is the most wealthy, the greatest and the most firmly established of all the American powers."[510] By the early 1870s,[406] the international reputation of the Empire of Brazil had improved considerably, and it remained well-regarded internationally until its end in 1889.[428] Christopher Columbus Andrews, an American diplomat in the Brazilian capital in the 1880s, later recalled Brazil as an "important Empire" in his memoirs.[511] In 1871, Brazil was invited to arbitrate the dispute between the United States and Britain which became known as the Alabama Claims. In 1880, the Empire acted as arbiter between the United States and France over the damage caused to U.S. nationals during the French intervention in Mexico. In 1884, Brazil was called upon to arbitrate between Chile and several other nations (France, Italy, Britain, Germany, Belgium, Austria-Hungary and Switzerland) over damages arising from the War of the Pacific.[512]

The Brazilian government eventually felt confident enough to negotiate a trade deal with the United States in 1889, the first to be undertaken with any nation since the disastrous and exploitative trade treaty with Britain in 1826 (canceled in 1844). American historian Steven C. Topik said that Pedro II's "quest for a trade treaty with the United States was part of a grander strategy to increase national sovereignty and autonomy." Unlike the circumstances of the previous pact, the Empire was in a strong position to insist on favorable trade terms, as negotiations occurred during a time of Brazilian domestic prosperity and international prestige.[513]

Economy

Currency

500 *réis* (royals) or Rs 500

1,000 *réis* (royals) or Rs 1$000 or *milréis* (thousand royals)

The unit of currency from the Empire's founding, and until 1942, was the *real* ("royal" in English, its plural form was *réis* and is *reais* in modern Portuguese), and was derived from the Portuguese real. It was usually called *milréis* (English: thousand royals) and written as 1$000. A thousand *milréis* (1:000$000)—or one million *réis*—was known as *conto de réis*.[514] One *conto de réis* was represented by the symbol *Rs* written before the value and by a dollar sign was written before any amounts lower than 1,000 *réis*. Thus, 350 *réis* was written as "Rs 350"; 1,712 *réis* as "Rs 1$712"; and 1,020,800 *réis* was written as "Rs 1:020$800". For millions, a period was used as a separator between millions, billions, trillions, etc. (e.g., 1 billion *réis* was written as "Rs 1.000:000$000"). A colon functioned to separate millions from thousands, and the $ sign was inserted between thousands and hundreds (999 or fewer).[515]

Overview

Brazil's international trade reached a total value of Rs 79.000:000$000 between 1834 and 1839. This continued to increase every year until it reached Rs 472.000:000$000 between 1886 and 1887: an annual growth rate of 3.88% since 1839.[516] The absolute value of exports from the Empire in 1850 was the highest in Latin America and triple that of Argentina which was in fourth place. Brazil would keep its high standing in exports and general economic growth until the end of the monarchy.[517] Brazilian economic expansion, especially after 1850, compared well with that of the United States and European nations.[518] The national tax revenue amounted to Rs 11.795:000$000 in 1831 and rose to Rs 160.840:000$000 in 1889. By 1858, national tax revenues ranked as the eighth-largest in the world.[519] Imperial Brazil was, despite its progress, a country where wealth was very unequally distributed.[520] However,

Figure 77: *A coffee farm in São Paulo province, 1880*

Figure 78: *A Brazilian factory, 1880*

Figure 79: *Railroad station in São Paulo province (Brazilian southeast), c. 1885*

Figure 80: *A railroad station in Minas Gerais province (Brazilian southeast), c. 1884*

for purposes of comparison, according to historian Steven C. Topik, in the United States, "by 1890, 80 percent of the population lived on the margin of subsistence, while 20 percent controlled almost all wealth."[521]

As new technologies appeared, and with increases in internal productivity, exports increased considerably. This made it possible to reach equilibrium in the balance of trade. During the 1820s sugar constituted about 30% of total exports while cotton constituted 21%, coffee 18% and leather and skins 14%. Twenty years later coffee would reach 42%, sugar 27%, leather and skins 9%, and cotton 8% of the total exports. This did not mean a reduction in the production of any of these items and, in fact, the opposite occurred. Growth occurred in all sectors, some more than others. In the period between 1820 and 1840, Fausto says "Brazilian exports had doubled in volume and had tripled in nominal value" while the valuation denominated in Pounds sterling increased by over 40%.[522] Brazil was not the only country where agriculture played an important role on exports. Around 1890, in the United States, by then the richest nation in the Americas, agricultural goods represented 80% of all its exports.[523]

In the 1820s, Brazil exported 11,000 tons of cacao and by 1880 this had increased to 73,500 tons.[524] Between 1821 and 1825, 41,174 tons of sugar were exported, rising to 238,074 tons between 1881 and 1885.[525] Until 1850, rubber production was insignificant, but between 1881 and 1890, it had reached third place among Brazilian exports.[526] This was about 81 tons between 1827 and 1830 reaching 1,632 tons in 1852. By 1900 the country was exporting 24,301,452 tons of rubber.[524] Brazil also exported around 3,377,000 tons of coffee between 1821 and 1860 while between 1861 and 1889 this reached 6,804,000 tons.[527] Technological innovations also contributed to the growth of exports,[522] in particular the adoption of steam navigation and railroads allowed for faster and more convenient cargo transportation.[528]

Development

Development on an immense scale occurred during this period, anticipating similar advancements in European countries.[529,530] In 1850, there were fifty factories with a total capital of Rs 7.000:000$000. At the end of the Imperial period in 1889, Brazil had 636 factories representing an annual rate of increase of 6.74% over the number in 1850, and with a total capital of approximately Rs 401.630:600$000 (which represents an annual growth rate in value of 10.94% from 1850 to 1889).[531] The "countryside echoed with the clang of iron track being laid as railroads were constructed at the most furious pace of the 19th century; indeed, building in 1880s was the second greatest in absolute terms in Brazil's entire history. Only eight countries in the entire world laid more track in the decade than Brazil."[428] The first railroad line, with only 15 kilometres (9.3 mi) of track, was opened on 30 April 1854[532] at a time when many European countries had no rail service.[529] By 1868, there were 718 kilometres (446 mi) of railroad lines,[533] and by the end of the Empire in 1889 this had grown to 9,200 kilometres (5,700 mi) with another 9,000 kilometres (5,600 mi) under construction[534] making it the country with "the largest rail network in Latin America".[428]

Factories were constructed throughout the Empire in the 1880s, allowing Brazil's cities to be modernized and "receive the benefits of gas, electrical, sanitation, telegraph and tram companies. Brazil was entering the modern world."[428] It was the fifth country in the world to install modern city sewers, the third to have sewage treatment[529] and one of the pioneers in the installation of a telephone service.[535] In addition to the foregoing improvements to infrastructure, it was also the first South American nation to adopt public electric lighting (in 1883)[536] and the second in the Americas (behind the United States) to establish a transatlantic telegraphic line connecting it directly to Europe in 1874.[529] The first domestic telegraph line appeared during 1852 in Rio de Janeiro. By 1889, there were 18,925 kilometres (11,759 mi) of telegraph lines connecting the country's capital to distant Brazilian provinces such as Pará and even linking to other South American countries such as Argentina and Uruguay.[537]

Society

Demographics

Since the second half of the 18th century, when Brazil was still a colony, the government had attempted to gather data regarding the population. However, few captaincies (later called provinces) collected the requested information.[538] After independence the government instituted a commission for statistics in an 1829 decree with a mandate to hold a national census.[538] The commission was a failure and was disbanded in 1834. In the ensuing years, provincial governments were tasked with collecting census information, but their census reports were often incomplete or not submitted at all.[538] In 1851, another attempt at a nationwide census failed when rioting broke out. This was the result of the erroneous belief among Brazilians of mixed-race descent that the survey was a subterfuge designed to enslave anyone having African blood.[539]

The first true national census with exhaustive and broad coverage was carried out in 1872. The small number of people and small number of towns reported by the census reveal Brazil's enormous territory to have been sparsely populated. It showed Brazil as having a total population of 9,930,478 inhabitants.[539] Estimates made by the government in prior decades showed

Empire of Brazil   171

Figure 81: *19th-century Brazilians. 1st row: White Brazilians. 2nd row: Brown Brazilians (left to right: two female mulattoes, two female cafuzos and a caboclo girl and man). 3rd row: three Brazilian Indians of different tribes followed by Afro-Brazilians of distinct ethnic background*

4,000,000 inhabitants in 1823 and gave a figure of 7,000,700 in 1854.[539] The population was distributed across 20 provinces and the Neutral Municipality (the Empire's capital) with 641 municipalities.[539]

Among the free population 23.4% of males and 13.4% of females were considered literate.[540] Men represented 52% (5,123,869) of the total population.[540] Figures for the population by age showed 24.6% were children younger than 10 years old; 21.1% were adolescents and young men between 11 and 20; 32.9% were adults between 21 and 40; 8.4% were between 41 and 50; 12.8% were between 51 and 70; and lastly, only 3.4% were over 71.[540] The residents in the combined northeast and southeast regions comprised 87.2% of the nation's population.[541] The second national census was held in 1890 when the Brazilian republic was only a few months old. Its results showed that the population had grown to 14,333,915 inhabitants since the 1872 census.[542]

Ethnic groups

Four ethnic groups were recognized in Imperial Brazil: white, black, Indian and brown.[542] Brown (Portuguese: *pardo*) was a designation for multiracial Brazilians which is still officially used,[543,544] though some scholars prefer the term "mixed one" (Portuguese: *mestiço*). The term denotes a broad category which includes *caboclos* (descendants of whites and Indians), *mulattoes* (descendants of whites and blacks) and *cafuzos* (descendants of blacks and Indians).[545]

Figure 82: *This map shows where ethnic groups predominated within Brazil: purple—caboclos; brown—whites; green—mulattoes; white—uninhabited. Note: over 80% of the population lived along the coastline*[541]

The *caboclos* formed the majority of the population in the Northern, Northeastern and Central-Western regions.[546] A large mulatto population inhabited the eastern coast of the northeastern region from Bahia to Paraíba[547,548] and were also present in northern Maranhão,[549,550] southern Minas Gerais,[551] eastern Rio de Janeiro and in Espírito Santo.[547,551] The *cafuzos* were the smallest and most difficult to distinguish from the two other mixed-race subgroups since the descendants of *caboclos* and mulattoes also fell into this category and were found in the northeast *sertão* (English: hinterland). These groups may still be found in the same areas today.[552]

Ethnic groups in Brazil (1872 and 1890)

Years	Whites	Browns	Blacks	Indians	Total
1872	38.1%	38.3%	19.7%	3.9%	100%
1890	44.0%	32.4%	14.6%	9%	100%

White Brazilians descended from the original Portuguese settlers. From the 1870s onwards this ethnic group also included other European immigrants: mainly Italians, Spaniards and Germans. Although whites could be found throughout the country, they were the majority group in the southern region and in São Paulo province.[540] Whites also comprised a significant proportion (40%) of the population in the northeastern provinces of Ceará, Paraíba and Rio Grande do Norte.[540] Black Brazilians of Sub-Saharan African ancestry inhabited the same areas as mulattoes. The majority of the population of Rio de Janeiro, Minas Gerais, Espírito Santo, Bahia, Sergipe, Alagoas and Pernambuco provinces (the last four having the smallest percentages of whites in the whole country—less than 30% in each) were black or brown.[540] The Indians, the indigenous peoples of Brazil, were found mainly in Piauí, Maranhão, Pará and Amazonas.[540]

Because of the existence of distinct racial and cultural communities, 19th century Brazil developed as a multi-ethnic nation. However the data is problematic as no reliable information is available for the years prior to 1872. The first official national census was compiled by the government in 1872 showing that out of 9,930,479 inhabitants there were 38.1% whites, 38.3% browns, 19.7% blacks and 3.9% Indians.[542] The second official national census in 1890 revealed that in a population of 14,333,915, 44% were whites, 32.4% browns, 14.6% blacks and 9% Indians.[542]

European immigration

Prior to 1808, the Portuguese were the only European people to settle Brazil in significant numbers. Although British, Germans, Italians and Spanish had previously immigrated to Brazil, they had only done so as a small number of individuals or in very small groups. These earliest non-Portuguese settlers did not have a significant impact on the culture of Portugal's Brazilian colony.[553] The situation changed after 1808 when King João VI began to encourage immigration from European countries outside Portugal.[553,554]

The first to arrive in numbers were the Swiss, of whom some 2,000 settled in Rio de Janeiro province during 1818.[555] They were followed by Germans and Irish, who immigrated to Brazil in the 1820s. German settlers gravitated mostly to the southern provinces, where the environment was more like their homeland.[556] In the 1830s, due to the instability of the Regency, European immigration ground to a halt, only recovering after Pedro II took the reins of government and the country entered a period of peace and prosperity.[557] Farmers in the southeast, enriched by lucrative coffee exports, created the "partnership system" (a form of indentured servitude) to attract immigrants. The scheme endured until the end of the 1850s, when the system collapsed and was abandoned. The failure was rooted in the large debts European settlers incurred in

Figure 83: *German and Luxembourger immigrants in Santa Leopoldina colony in Espírito Santo province (southeast region), 1875*

order to subsidize their travel and settlement expenses, leaving them as virtual slaves to their employers.[558] Immigration suffered another decline during the Paraguayan War, which lasted from 1864 to 1870.[559]

Immigrant numbers soared during the 1870s in what came to be called the "great immigration". Up to that point, around 10,000 Europeans arrived in Brazil annually, but after 1872, their numbers increased dramatically.[560] It is estimated by the Brazilian Institute of Geography and Statistics that 500,000 Europeans immigrated to Brazil between 1808 and 1883.[561] The figure for European settlers arriving between 1884 and 1893 climbed to 883,668.[561] The number of Europeans immigrating continued to rise in the following decades, with 862,100 between 1894 and 1903; and 1,006,617 between 1904 and 1913.[561]

From 1872 until 1879, the nationalities forming the bulk of the new settlers were composed of Portuguese (31.2%), Italians (25.8%), Germans (8.1%) and Spanish (1.9%).[560] In the 1880s, Italians would surpass the Portuguese (61.8% to 23.3% respectively), and the Spanish would displace the Germans (6.7% to 4.2% respectively).[560] Other, smaller groups also arrived, including Russians, Poles and Hungarians.[562] Since nearly all European immigrants settled in the southeastern and southern areas of the Empire, ethnic distribution,

Empire of Brazil 175

Figure 84: *A Brazilian family and its female slave house servants, c. 1860*

already unequal before the mass immigration, became even more divergent between regions.[563] For a nation that had a small, widely scattered population (4,000,000 in 1823 and 14,333,915 in 1890), the immigration of more than 1,380,000 Europeans had a tremendous effect upon the country's ethnic composition. In 1872, the year of the first reliable national census, white Brazilians represented just over a third (38.1%) of the total population; in 1890, they had increased to a little under half (44.0%) of all Brazilians.[542]

Slavery

In 1823, a year after independence, slaves made up 29% of the population of Brazil, a figure which fell throughout the lifetime of the Empire: from 24% in 1854, to 15.2% in 1872, and finally to less than 5% in 1887—the year before slavery was completely abolished.[564] Slaves were mostly adult males from southwestern Africa.[565] Slaves brought to Brazil differed ethnically, religiously and linguistically, each identifying primarily with his or her own nation of origin, rather than by a shared African ethnicity.[566] Some of the slaves brought to the Americas had been captured while fighting intertribal wars in Africa and had then been sold to slave dealers.[567,568]

Slaves and their descendants were usually found in regions devoted to producing exports for foreign markets.[569] Sugarcane plantations on the eastern coast

Figure 85: *Slaves (including their free children) gathered in a coffee farm in Brazil, c. 1885*

of the northeast region during the 16th and 17th centuries are typical of economic activities dependent on slave labor.[570] In northern Maranhão province, slave labor was used in cotton and rice production in the 18th century.[571] In this period, slaves were also exploited in Minas Gerais province where gold was extracted.[572] Slavery was also common in Rio de Janeiro and São Paulo during the 19th century for the cultivation of coffee which became vital to the national economy.[573] The prevalence of slavery was not geographically uniform across Brazil. Around 1870 only five provinces (Rio de Janeiro with 30%, Bahia with 15%, Minas Gerais with 14%, São Paulo with 7% and Rio Grande do Sul also with 7%) held 73% of the nation's total slave population.[574] These were followed by Pernambuco (with 6%) and Alagoas (with 4%). Among the remaining 13 provinces none individually had even 3%.[575]

Most slaves worked as plantation laborers.[574] Relatively few Brazilians owned slaves and most small and medium-sized farms employed free workers.[576] Slaves could be found scattered throughout society in other capacities: some were used as house servants, farmers, miners, prostitutes, gardeners and in many other roles.[577] Many emancipated slaves went on to acquire slaves and there were even cases of slaves who had their own slaves.[578,579] While slaves were usually black or mulatto there were reported cases of slaves who appeared

Figure 86: *A state ceremony in the Old Cathedral of Rio de Janeiro for which attendees were required to wear court dress*

to be of European descent—the product of generations of inter-ethnic sexual relations between male slave owners and their female mulatto slaves.[580] Even the harshest slave owners adhered to a long-established practice of selling slaves along with their families, taking care not to separate individuals.[581] Slaves were regarded by law as properties. The ones who were freed immediately became citizens with all civil rights guaranteed—the only exception being that, until 1881, freed slaves were barred from voting in elections, although their children and descendants could vote.[574]

Nobility

The nobility of Brazil differed markedly from its counterparts in Europe: noble titles were not hereditary, with the sole exception of members of the Imperial Family,[582] and those who had received a noble title were not considered to belong to a separate social class, and received no appanages, stipends or emoluments.[582] However, many ranks, traditions, and regulations in Brazil's system of nobility were co-opted directly from the Portuguese aristocracy.[583,584] During Pedro I's reign there were no clear requisites for someone to be ennobled. During Pedro II's reign (apart from the Regency period during which the regent could not grant titles or honors[585]) the nobility evolved into a meritocracy[583] with titles granted in recognition of an individual's outstanding service to the Empire or for the public good. Noble rank did not represent "recognition of illustrious ancestry."[586,587]

It was the Emperor's right as head of the Executive branch to grant titles and honors.[583] The titles of nobility were, in ascending order, baron, viscount, count, marquis and duke.[583] Apart from position in the hierarchy there were other distinctions between the ranks: counts, marquises and dukes were considered "Grandees of the Empire" while the titles of barons and viscounts could be bestowed "with Greatness" or "without Greatness".[583] All ranks of the Brazilian nobility were to be addressed as "Your Excellency".[583]

Between 1822 and 1889, 986 people were ennobled.[588] Only three became Dukes: Auguste de Beauharnais, 2nd Duke of Leuchtenberg (as Duke of Santa Cruz, brother-in-law to Pedro I), Dona Isabel Maria de Alcântara Brasileira (as Duchess of Goiás, illegitimate daughter of Pedro I) and lastly Luís Alves de Lima e Silva (as Duke of Caxias, commander-in-chief during the Paraguayan War).[589] The other titles granted were as follows: 47 marquises, 51 counts, 146 viscounts "with Greatness", 89 viscounts "without Greatness", 135 barons "with Greatness" and 740 barons "without Greatness" resulting in a total of 1,211 noble titles.[590] There were fewer nobles than noble titles because many were elevated more than once during their lifetime, such as the Duke of Caxias who was first made a baron, then a count, then a marquis and finally was elevated to a duke.[585] Grants of nobility were not limited to male Brazilians: Thomas Cochrane, 10th Earl of Dundonald, a Scot, was made Marquis of Maranhão for his role in the Brazilian War of Independence,[591] and 29 women received grants of nobility in their own right.[592] As well as being unrestricted by gender, no racial distinctions were made in conferring noble status. *Caboclos*,[593] mulattoes,[594] blacks[595] and even Indians[595] were ennobled.

The lesser nobility, who were untitled, were made up of members of the Imperial Orders. There were six of these: the Order of Christ, the Order of Saint Benedict of Aviz, the Order of Saint James of the Sword, the Order of the Southern Cross, the Order of Pedro I and the Order of the Rose.[584] The first three had grades of honor beyond the Grand Master (reserved for the Emperor only): knight, commander and grand cross. The latter three, however, had different ranks: the Order of the Southern Cross with four, the Order of the Rose with six, and the Order of Pedro I with three.[584]

Religion

Article five of the Constitution declared Catholicism to be the state religion.[596] However, the clergy had long been understaffed, undisciplined and poorly educated,[597,598] all of which led to a general loss of respect for the Catholic Church.[597] During Pedro II's reign, the Imperial government embarked upon a

Figure 87: *A trio of Brazilian friars, c. 1875*

program of reform designed to address these deficiencies.[597] As Catholicism was the official religion, the Emperor exercised a great deal of control over Church affairs[597] and paid clerical salaries, appointed parish priests, nominated bishops, ratified papal bulls and supervised seminaries.[597,599] In pursuing reform, the government selected bishops whose moral fitness, stance on education and support for reform met with their approval.[597,598] However, as more capable men began to fill the clerical ranks, resentment of government control over the Church increased.[597,598] Catholic clerics moved closer to the Pope and his doctrines. This resulted in the Religious Question, a series of clashes during the 1870s between the clergy and the government, since the former wanted a more direct relationship with Rome and the latter sought to maintain its oversight of church affairs.[600]

The Constitution did allow followers of other, non-Catholic, faiths to practice their religious beliefs, albeit only in private. The construction of non-Catholic religious buildings was forbidden.[601] From the outset these restrictions were ignored by both the citizenry and authorities. In Belém, Pará's capital, the first synagogue was built in 1824.[601] Jews migrated to Brazil soon after its independence and settled mainly in the northeastern provinces of Bahia and Pernambuco and in the northern provinces of Amazonas and Pará.[601] Other Jewish groups came from the Alsace-Lorraine region of Germany and from

Russia.[602] By the 1880s, there were several Jewish communities and synagogues scattered throughout Brazil.[603]

The Protestants were another group that began settling in Brazil at the beginning of the 19th century. The first Protestants were English, and an Anglican church was opened in Rio de Janeiro in 1820. Others were established afterwards in São Paulo, Pernambuco and Bahia provinces.[604] They were followed by German and Swiss Lutherans who settled in the South and Southwest regions and built their own houses of worship.[604] Following the U.S. Civil War in the 1860s, immigrants from the southern United States seeking to escape Reconstruction settled in São Paulo. Several American churches sponsored missionary activities, including Baptists, Lutherans, Congregationalists and Methodists.[605]

Among African slaves, Catholicism was the religion of the majority. Most slaves came originally from the midwestern and southwestern portions of the African coast. For over four centuries this region had been the subject of Christian mission activities.[606] Some Africans and their descendants, however, held onto elements of polytheistic religious traditions by merging them with Catholicism. This resulted in the creation of syncretic creeds such as Candomblé.[607] Islam was also practiced among a small minority of African slaves, although it was harshly repressed and by the end of the 19th century had been completely extinguished.[608] By the beginning of the 19th century, the Indians in most of eastern Brazil had been either assimilated or decimated. Some tribes resisted assimilation and either fled farther west, where they were able to maintain their diverse polytheistic beliefs, or were restricted to *aldeamentos* (reservations), where they eventually converted to Catholicism.[609]

Culture

Visual arts

According to historian Ronald Raminelli, "visual arts underwent huge innovations in the Empire in comparison to the colonial period."[610] With independence in 1822, painting, sculpture and architecture were influenced by national symbols and the monarchy, as both surpassed religious themes in their importance. The previously dominant old Baroque style was superseded by Neoclassicism.[610] New developments appeared, such as the use of iron in architecture and the appearance of lithography and photography, which revitalized the visual arts.[610]

The government's creation of the Imperial Academy of the Fine Arts in the 1820s played a pivotal role in influencing and expanding the visual arts in

Figure 88: *O descanso do modelo (The model's rest), by Almeida Júnior, 1882*

Figure 89: *Morro da Viúva (Widow's mount), by França Júnior, c. 1888*

Brazil, mainly by educating generations of artists but also by serving as a stylistic guideline.[611] The Academy's origins lay in the foundation of the *Escola Real das Ciências, Artes e Ofícios* (Royal School of the Sciences, Arts and Crafts) in 1816 by the Portuguese King João VI. Its members—of whom the most famous was Jean-Baptiste Debret—were French émigrées who worked as painters, sculptors, musicians and engineers.[612] The school's main goal was to encourage French aesthetics and the Neoclassical style to replace the prevalent baroque style.[613] Plagued by a lack of funds since its inception, the school was later renamed as the Academy of Fine Arts in 1820, and in 1824 received its final name under the Empire: Imperial Academy of the Fine Arts.[613]

It was only following Pedro II's majority in 1840, however, that the Academy became a powerhouse, part of the Emperor's greater scheme of fomenting a national culture and consequently uniting all Brazilians in a common sense of nationhood.[614] Pedro II would sponsor the Brazilian culture through several public institutions funded by the government (not restricted to the Academy of Fine Arts), such as Brazilian Historic and Geographic Institute[615] and Imperial Academy of Music and National Opera.[616] That sponsorship would pave the way not only for the careers of artists, but also for those engaged in other fields, including historians such as Francisco Adolfo de Varnhagen[617] and musicians such as the operatic composer Antônio Carlos Gomes.[618]

By the 1840s, Romanticism had largely supplanted Neoclassicism, not only in painting, but also in sculpture and architecture.[611] The Academy did not resume its role of simply providing education: prizes, medals, scholarships in foreign countries and funding were used as incentives.[619] Among its staff and students were some of the most renowned Brazilian artists, including Simplício Rodrigues de Sá, Félix Taunay, Manuel de Araújo Porto-alegre, Pedro Américo, Victor Meirelles, Rodolfo Amoedo, Almeida Júnior, Rodolfo Bernardelli and João Zeferino da Costa.[619,620] In the 1880s, after having been long regarded as the official style of the Academy, Romanticism declined, and other styles were explored by a new generation of artists. Among the new genres was Landscape art, the most famous exponents of which were Georg Grimm, Giovanni Battista Castagneto, França Júnior and Antônio Parreiras.[621] Another style which gained popularity in the fields of painting and architecture was Eclecticism.[621]

Literature and theater

In the first years after independence, Brazilian literature was still heavily influenced by Portuguese literature and its predominant Neoclassical style.[622] In 1837, Gonçalves de Magalhães published the first work of Romanticism in Brazil, beginning a new era in the nation.[623] The next year, 1838, saw the first play performed by Brazilians with a national theme, which marked the birth

Figure 90: *A photograph dating from c. 1858, showing three major Brazilian Romantic writers. From left to right: Gonçalves Dias, Manuel de Araújo Porto Alegre and Gonçalves de Magalhães*

of Brazilian theater. Until then themes were often based on European works even if not performed by foreign actors.[623] Romanticism at that time was regarded as the literary style that best fitted Brazilian literature, which could reveal its uniqueness when compared to foreign literature.[624] During the 1830s and 1840s, "a network of newspapers, journals, book publishers and printing houses emerged which together with the opening of theaters in the major towns brought into being what could be termed, but for the narrowness of its scope, a national culture".[625]

Romanticism reached its apogee between the late 1850s and the early 1870s as it divided into several branches, including Indianism and sentimentalism.[626] The most influential literary style in 19th-century Brazil, many of the most renowned Brazilian writers were exponents of Romanticism: Manuel de Araújo Porto Alegre,[627] Gonçalves Dias, Gonçalves de Magalhães, José de Alencar, Bernardo Guimarães, Álvares de Azevedo, Casimiro de Abreu, Castro Alves, Joaquim Manuel de Macedo, Manuel Antônio de Almeida and Alfredo d'Escragnolle Taunay.[628] In theater, the most famous Romanticist playwrights were Martins Pena[628] and Joaquim Manuel de Macedo.[629] Brazilian Romanticism did not have the same success in theater as it had in literature, as most of the plays were either Neoclassic tragedies or Romantic works from

Portugal or translations from Italian, French or Spanish.[629] After the opening of the Brazilian Dramatic Conservatory in 1845, the government gave financial aid to national theater companies in exchange for staging plays in Portuguese.[629]

By the 1880s Romanticism was superseded by new literary styles. The first to appear was Realism, which had among its most notable writers Joaquim Maria Machado de Assis and Raul Pompeia.[626] Newer styles that coexisted with Realism, Naturalism and Parnassianism, were both connected to the former's evolution.[626] Among the best-known Naturalists were Aluísio Azevedo and Adolfo Caminha.[630] Notable Parnassians were Gonçalves Crespo, Alberto de Oliveira, Raimundo Correia and Olavo Bilac.[628] Brazilian theater became influenced by Realism in 1855, decades earlier than the style's impact upon literature and poetry.[631] Famous Realist playwrights included José de Alencar, Quintino Bocaiuva, Joaquim Manuel de Macedo, Júlia Lopes de Almeida and Maria Angélica Ribeiro.[631] Brazilian plays staged by national companies competed for audiences alongside foreign plays and companies.[632] Performing arts in Imperial Brazil also encompassed the staging of musical duets, dancing, gymnastics, comedy and farces.[632] Less prestigious, but more popular with the working classes were puppeteers and magicians, as well as the circus, with its travelling companies of performers, including acrobats, trained animals, illusionists and other stunt-oriented artists.[633]

References

<templatestyles src="Template:Refbegin/styles.css" />

- Adas, Melhem (2004). *Panorama geográfico do Brasil* (in Portuguese) (4th ed.). São Paulo: Moderna. ISBN 978-85-16-04336-0.
- Alencastro, Luiz Felipe de (1997). *História da vida privada no Brasil: Império* (in Portuguese). São Paulo: Companhia das Letras. ISBN 978-85-7164-681-0.
- Azevedo, Aroldo (1971). *O Brasil e suas regiões* (in Portuguese). São Paulo: Companhia Editora Nacional.
- Baer, Werner (2002). *A Economia Brasileira* (in Portuguese) (2nd ed.). São Paulo: Nobel. ISBN 978-85-213-1197-3.
- Barman, Roderick J. (1988). *Brazil: The Forging of a Nation, 1798–1852*. Stanford: Stanford University Press. ISBN 978-0-8047-1437-2.
- Barman, Roderick J. (1999). *Citizen Emperor: Pedro II and the Making of Brazil, 1825–1891*. Stanford: Stanford University Press. ISBN 978-0-8047-3510-0.

- Barsa (1987). *Enciclopédia Barsa* (in Portuguese). **4**. Rio de Janeiro: Encyclopædia Britannica do Brasil.
- Barsa (1987). *Enciclopédia Barsa* (in Portuguese). **10**. Rio de Janeiro: Encyclopædia Britannica do Brasil.
- Besouchet, Lídia (1985) [1945]. *José Maria Paranhos: Visconde do Rio Branco: ensaio histórico-biográfico* (in Portuguese). Rio de Janeiro: Nova Fronteira. OCLC 14271198[634].
- Besouchet, Lídia (1993). *Pedro II e o Século XIX* (in Portuguese) (2nd ed.). Rio de Janeiro: Nova Fronteira. ISBN 978-85-209-0494-7.
- Bethell, Leslie (1993). *Brazil: Empire and Republic, 1822–1930*. Cambridge, United Kingdom: Cambridge University Press. ISBN 978-0-521-36293-1.
- Boxer, Charles R. (2002). *O império marítimo português 1415–1825* (in Portuguese). São Paulo: Companhia das Letras. ISBN 978-85-359-0292-1.
- Calmon, Pedro (1975). *História de D. Pedro II* (in Portuguese). **1–5**. Rio de Janeiro: José Olímpio.
- Calmon, Pedro (2002). *História da Civilização Brasileira* (in Portuguese). Brasília: Senado Federal. OCLC 685131818[635].
- Carvalho, José Murilo de (1993). *A Monarquia brasileira* (in Portuguese). Rio de Janeiro: Ao Livro Técnico. ISBN 978-85-215-0660-7.
- Carvalho, José Murilo de (2002). *Os Bestializados: o Rio de Janeiro e a República que não foi* (in Portuguese) (3 ed.). São Paulo: Companhia das Letras. ISBN 978-85-85095-13-0.
- Carvalho, José Murilo de (2007). *D. Pedro II: ser ou não ser* (in Portuguese). São Paulo: Companhia das Letras. ISBN 978-85-359-0969-2.
- Carvalho, José Murilo de (2008). *Cidadania no Brasil: o longo caminho* (in Portuguese) (10 ed.). Rio de Janeiro: Civilização Brasileira. ISBN 978-85-200-0565-1.
- Coelho, Marcos Amorim (1996). *Geografia do Brasil* (in Portuguese) (4 ed.). São Paulo: Moderna.
- Dolhnikoff, Miriam (2005). *Pacto imperial: origens do federalismo no Brasil do século XIX* (in Portuguese). São Paulo: Globo. ISBN 978-85-250-4039-8.
- Doratioto, Francisco (2002). *Maldita Guerra: Nova história da Guerra do Paraguai* (in Portuguese). São Paulo: Companhia das Letras. ISBN 978-85-359-0224-2.
- Ermakoff, George (2006). *Rio de Janeiro – 1840–1900 – Uma crônica fotográfica* (in Portuguese). Rio de Janeiro: G. Ermakoff Casa Editorial. ISBN 978-85-98815-05-3.
- Fausto, Boris (1995). *História do Brasil* (in Portuguese). São Paulo: Fundação de Desenvolvimento da Educação. ISBN 978-85-314-0240-1.

- Fausto, Boris; Devoto, Fernando J. (2005). *Brasil e Argentina: Um ensaio de história comparada (1850–2002)* (in Portuguese) (2nd ed.). São Paulo: Editoria 34. ISBN 978-85-7326-308-4.
- Graça Filho, Afonso de Alencastro (2004). *A economia do Império brasileiro* (in Portuguese). São Paulo: Atual. ISBN 978-85-357-0443-3.
- Graham, Richard (1994). *Patronage and Politics in Nineteenth-Century Brazil*. Stanford: Stanford University Press. ISBN 978-0-8047-2336-7.
- Hahner, June E. (1978). "The nineteenth-century feminist press and women's rights in Brazil". In Lavrin, Asunción. *Latin American Women: Historical Perspectives*. Westport, Connecticut: Greenwood. ISBN 0-313-20309-1.
- Holanda, Sérgio Buarque de (1974). *História Geral da Civilização Brasileira: Declínio e Queda do Império* (in Portuguese) (2nd ed.). São Paulo: Difusão Européia do Livro.
- Levine, Robert M. (1999). *The History of Brazil*. Westport, Connecticut: Greenwood Press. ISBN 978-0-313-30390-6.
- Lira, Heitor (1977). *História de Dom Pedro II (1825–1891): Ascenção (1825–1870)* (in Portuguese). **1**. Belo Horizonte: Itatiaia.
- Lira, Heitor (1977). *História de Dom Pedro II (1825–1891): Fastígio (1870–1880)* (in Portuguese). **2**. Belo Horizonte: Itatiaia.
- Lira, Heitor (1977). *História de Dom Pedro II (1825–1891): Declínio (1880–1891)* (in Portuguese). **3**. Belo Horizonte: Itatiaia.
- Moreira, Igor A. G. (1981). *O Espaço Geográfico, geografia geral e do Brasil* (in Portuguese) (18th ed.). São Paulo: Ática.
- Munro, Dana Gardner (1942). *The Latin American Republics: A History*. New York: D. Appleton.
- Nabuco, Joaquim (1975). *Um Estadista do Império* (in Portuguese) (4th ed.). Rio de Janeiro: Nova Aguilar.
- Olivieri, Antonio Carlos (1999). *Dom Pedro II, Imperador do Brasil* (in Portuguese). São Paulo: Callis. ISBN 978-85-86797-19-4.
- Parkinson, Roger (2008). *The Late Victorian Navy: The Pre-Dreadnought Era and the Origins of the First World War*. Woodbridge, Suffolk: The Boydell Press. ISBN 978-1-84383-372-7.
- Pedrosa, J. F. Maya (2004). *A Catástrofe dos Erros: razões e emoções na guerra contra o Paraguai* (in Portuguese). Rio de Janeiro: Biblioteca do Exército. ISBN 978-85-7011-352-8.
- Ramos, Arthur (2003). *A mestiçagem no Brasil* (in Portuguese). Maceió: EDUFAL. ISBN 978-85-7177-181-9.
- Rodrigues, José Carlos (1863). *Constituição política do Império do Brasil* (in Portuguese). Rio de Janeiro: Typographia Universal de Laemmert.
- Rodrigues, José Honório (1975). *Independência: Revolução e Contra-Revolução – A política internacional* (in Portuguese). **5**. Rio de Janeiro:

F. Alves.
- Rodrigues, José Honório (1995). *Uma história diplomática do Brasil, 1531–1945* (in Portuguese). Rio de Janeiro: Civilização Brasileira. ISBN 978-85-200-0391-6.
- Salles, Ricardo (1996). *Nostalgia Imperial* (in Portuguese). Rio de Janeiro: Topbooks. OCLC 36598004[636].
- Schwarcz, Lilia Moritz (1998). *As barbas do Imperador: D. Pedro II, um monarca nos trópicos* (in Portuguese) (2nd ed.). São Paulo: Companhia das Letras. ISBN 978-85-7164-837-1.
- Skidmore, Thomas E. (1999). *Brazil: five centuries of change*. New York: Oxford University Press. ISBN 0-19-505809-7.
- Smith, Joseph (2010). *Brazil and the United States: Convergence and Divergence*. Athens, Georgia: University of Georgia Press. ISBN 978-0-8203-3733-3.
- Sodré, Nelson Werneck (2004). *Panorama do Segundo Império* (in Portuguese) (2nd ed.). Rio de Janeiro: Graphia. ISBN 978-85-85277-21-5.
- Topik, Steven C. (2000). *Trade and Gunboats: The United States and Brazil in the Age of Empire*. Stanford: Stanford University Press. ISBN 978-0-8047-4018-0.
- Vainfas, Ronaldo (2002). *Dicionário do Brasil Imperial* (in Portuguese). Rio de Janeiro: Objetiva. ISBN 978-85-7302-441-8.
- Vasquez, Pedro Karp (2007). *Nos trilhos do progresso: A ferrovia no Brasil imperial vista pela fotografia* (in Portuguese). São Paulo: Metalivros. ISBN 978-85-85371-70-8.
- Vesentini, José William (1988). *Brasil, sociedade e espaço – Geografia do Brasil* (in Portuguese) (7th ed.). São Paulo: Ática. ISBN 978-85-08-02340-0.
- Viana, Hélio (1968). *Vultos do Império* (in Portuguese). São Paulo: Companhia Editora Nacional.
- Viana, Hélio (1994). *História do Brasil: período colonial, monarquia e república* (in Portuguese) (15th ed.). São Paulo: Melhoramentos. ISBN 978-85-06-01999-3.

External links

- Media related to Empire of Brazil at Wikimedia Commons

<indicator name="featured-star"> </indicator>

Early republic

First Brazilian Republic

Republic of the United States of Brazil	
República dos Estados Unidos do Brasil	
1889–1930	
 Flag Coat of arms	
Motto *Ordem e Progresso* "Order and Progress"	
Anthem *Hino Nacional Brasileiro* "Brazilian National Anthem"	

Brazil at its largest territorial extent, including Acre

Capital	Rio de Janeiro
Languages	Portuguese
Government	Military dictatorship (1889-1894) Oligarchic federal presidential republic (1894-1930)
President	
• 1889–1891	Marshal Deodoro da Fonseca (first)
• 1926–1930	Washington Luís (last)
Legislature	National Congress
• Upper house	Senate
• Lower house	Chamber of Deputies
Historical era	19th–20th century
• Proclamation of the Republic	15 November 1889
• Adoption of the Republic's Constitution	24 February 1891
• Revolta da Armada	1893-1894
• Federalist Riograndense Revolution	1893-1895
• End of Sword's Dictatorship	15 November 1894
• Revolution of 1930	3 November 1930
Area	
• 1903	8,515,767 km^2 (3,287,956 sq mi)
Population	
• 1890 est.	14,333,915
• 1900 est.	17,438,434
• 1920 est.	30,635,605
Currency	Real

First Brazilian Republic

Preceded by	Succeeded by
Empire of Brazil	Vargas Era

The **First Brazilian Republic** or ***República Velha*** (Portuguese pronunciation: [ʁeˈpublikɐ ˈvɛʎɐ], "Old Republic") is the period of Brazilian history from 1889 to 1930. The República Velha ended with the Brazilian Revolution of 1930 that installed Getúlio Vargas as a dictator.

Overview

On November 15, 1889 Marshal Deodoro da Fonseca deposed Emperor Dom Pedro II, declared Brazil a republic, and reorganized the government.

From 1889 to 1930, the government was a constitutional democracy, but democracy was nominal.

In reality, the elections were rigged, voters in rural areas were pressured or induced to vote for the chosen candidates of their bosses (see coronelismo) and,

Figure 91: *The Proclamation of the Republic, by Benedito Calixto.*

Figure 92: *First Brazilian flag after empire's fall, created by Ruy Barbosa, used between November 15th and 19th of 1889.*

if all those methods did not work, the election results could still be changed by one sided decisions of Congress' *verification of powers commission* (election authorities in the República Velha were not independent from the executive and the Legislature, dominated by the ruling oligarchs). This system resulted in the presidency of Brazil alternating between the oligarchies of the dominant states of São Paulo and Minas Gerais. This regime is often referred to as "*café com leite*", 'coffee with milk', after the respective agricultural products of the two states.

This period ended with a military coup that placed Getúlio Vargas, a civilian, in the presidency; Vargas remained as dictator until 1945.

The Brazilian republic was not an ideological offspring of the republics born of the French or American Revolutions, although the Brazilian regime would attempt to associate itself with both. The republic did not have enough popular support to risk open elections. It was a regime born of a *coup d'état* that maintained itself by force.[638] The republicans made Deodoro president (1889–91) and, after a financial crisis, appointed Field Marshal Floriano Vieira Peixoto Minister of War to ensure the allegiance of the military.

Rule of the landed oligarchies

The officers who joined Field Marshal Deodoro da Fonseca in ending the Empire had made an oath to uphold it. The officer corps would eventually resolve the contradiction by linking its duty to Brazil itself, rather than to transitory governments. The Republic was born rather accidentally: Deodoro had intended only to replace the cabinet, but the republicans manipulated him into founding a republic.

The history of the Old Republic was dominated by a quest for a viable form of government to replace the monarchy. This quest lurched back and forth between state autonomy and centralization. The constitution of 1891, establishing the United States of Brazil (*Estados Unidos do Brasil*), granted extensive autonomy to the provinces, now called States. The Federal system was adopted, and all powers not granted in the Constitution to the Federal Government belonged to the States. It recognized that the central government did not rule at the local level. The Empire of Brazil had not absorbed fully the regional *pátrias*, and now they reasserted themselves. Into the 1920s, the federal government in Rio de Janeiro was dominated and managed by a combination of the more powerful states of São Paulo, Minas Gerais, Rio Grande do Sul and to a lesser extent Pernambuco, and Bahia.

As a result, the history of the outset of republic in Brazil is also the story of the development of the Army as a national regulatory and interventionist institution.[639] The sudden elimination of the monarchy reduced the number of masterful national institutions to one, the Army. Although the Roman Catholic Church continued its presence throughout the country, it was not national but rather international in its personnel, doctrine, liturgy, and purposes. The Army assumed this new position not haphazardly, occupying in the conservative national economical elites' heart, part of the vacuum left by the monarchy with slavery abolition, and gradually acquiring support to its de facto role, eclipsing even other military institutions, like the Navy and the National Guard. The Navy attempts to prevent such hegemony were defeated militarily during the early 1890s.[640] Although it had more units and men in Rio de Janeiro and Rio Grande do Sul than elsewhere, the Army's presence was felt throughout the country. Its personnel, its interests, its ideology, and its commitments were national in scope.

In the last decades of the 19th century, the United States, much of Europe, and neighboring Argentina expanded the right to vote. Brazil, however, moved to restrict access to the polls. In 1874, in a population of about 10 million, the franchise was held by about one million Wikipedia:Accuracy dispute#Disputed statement, but in 1881 this had been cut to 145,296. This reduction was one reason the Empire's legitimacy foundered, but the Republic did not move to correct the situation. By 1910 there were only 627,000 voters in a population of 22 million. Throughout the 1920s, only between 2.3% and 3.4% of the total population could vote.

The instability and violence of the 1890s were related to the absence of consensus among the elites regarding a governmental model; and the armed forces were divided over their status, relationship to the political regime, and institutional goals. The lack of military unity and the disagreement among civilian elites about the military's role in society explain partially why a long-term military dictatorship was not established, as some officers advocating positivism wanted. However, military men were very active in politics; early in the decade, ten of the twenty state governors were officers.

The Constituent Assembly that drew up the constitution of 1891 was a battleground between those seeking to limit executive power, which was dictatorial in scope under President Deodoro da Fonseca, and the Jacobins, radical authoritarians who opposed the paulista coffee oligarchy and who wanted to preserve and intensify presidential authority. The new charter established a federation governed supposedly by a president, a bicameral National Congress (Congresso Nacional; hereafter, Congress), and a judiciary. However, real power was in the regional pátrias and in the hands of local potentates, called "colonels." There was the constitutional system, and there was the real system of unwritten agreements (*coronelismo*) among local bosses, the colonels. Coronelismo, which supported state autonomy, was called the "politics of the governors". Under it, the local oligarchies chose the state governors, who in turn selected the president.

This informal but real distribution of power emerged, the so-called politics of the governors, to take shape as the result of armed struggles and bargaining. The populous and prosperous states of Minas Gerais and São Paulo dominated the system and swapped the presidency between them for many years. The system consolidated the state oligarchies around families that had been members of the old monarchical elite. And to check the nationalizing tendencies of the army, this oligarchic republic and its state components strengthened the navy and the state police. In the larger states, the state police were soon turned into small armies. The Head of the Brazilian army ordered that it would doubled so they could defend them.

Latifúndio economies

Around the start of the 20th century, the vast majority of the population lived in communities, though accumulating capitalist surpluses for overseas export, that were essentially semi-feudal in structure. Because of the legacy of Ibero-American slavery, abolished as late as 1888 in Brazil, there was an extreme concentration of such landownership reminiscent of feudal aristocracies: 464 great landowners held more than 270,000 km² of land (*latifúndios*), while 464,000 small and medium-sized farms occupied only 157,000 km².

After the Second Industrial Revolution in the advanced countries, Latin America responded to mounting European and North American demand for primary products and foodstuffs. A few key export products— coffee, sugar, and cotton—thus dominated agriculture. Because of specialization, Brazilian producers neglected domestic consumption, forcing the country to import four-fifths of its grain needs. Like most of Latin America, the economy around the start of the 20th century, as a result, rested on certain cash crops produced by the *fazendeiros*, large estate owners exporting primary products overseas who headed their own patriarchal communities. Each typical *fazenda* (estate) included the owner's chaplain and overseers, his indigent peasants, his sharecroppers, and his indentured servants.

Brazil's dependence on factory-made goods and loans from the technologically, economically, and politically superior North Atlantic retarded its domestic industrial base. Farm equipment was primitive and largely non-mechanized; peasants tilled the land with hoes and cleared the soil through the inefficient slash-and-burn method. Meanwhile, living standards were generally squalid. Malnutrition, parasitic diseases, and lack of medical facilities limited the average life span in 1920 to twenty-eight years. Without an open market, Brazilian industry could not compete, within a comparative advantage system, against the technologically superior Anglo-American economies. In this context the Encilhamento (a Boom & Bust process that first intensified, and then crashed, in the years between 1889 and 1891) occurred, the consequences of which were felt in all areas of the Brazilian economy throughout the subsequent decades.[641]

The middle class was not yet active in political life. The patron-client political machines of the countryside enabled the coffee oligarchs to dominate state structures to their advantage, particularly the weak central state structures that effectively devolved power to local agrarian oligarchies. Known as *coronelismo*, this was a classic boss system under which the control of patronage was centralized in the hands of a locally dominant oligarch known as a coronel, who would dispense favors in return for loyalty.

Thus, high illiteracy rates went hand in hand with the absence of universal suffrage by secret ballot and the demand for a free press, independent from the then dominant economic influence. In regions where there was not even the telegraph, far from major centers, the news could take 4 to 6 weeks longer to arrive. In those circumstances, for lack of alternatives, along the last decade of the 19th century and the first of the 20th, a free press created by European immigrant anarchists started to develop, and, due to non-segregated conformation (ethnically speaking) of Brazilian society, spread widely, particularly in large cities.

During this period, Brazil did not have a significantly integrated national economy. Rather, Brazil had a grouping of regional economies that exported their own specialty products to European and North American markets. The absence of a big internal market with overland transportation, except for the mule trains, impeded internal economic integration, political cohesion and military efficiency. The regions, "the Brazils" as the British called them, moved to their own rhythms. The Northeast exported its surplus cheap labor and saw its political influence decline as its sugar lost foreign markets to Caribbean producers. The wild rubber boom in Amazônia lost its world primacy to efficient Southeast Asian colonial plantations after 1912. The national-oriented market economies of the South were not dramatic, but their growth was steady and by the 1920s allowed Rio Grande do Sul to exercise considerable political leverage. Real power resided in the coffee-growing states of the Southeast—São Paulo, Minas Gerais, and Rio de Janeiro—which produced the most export revenue. Those three and Rio Grande do Sul harvested 60% of Brazil's crops, turned out 75% of its industrial and meat products, and held 80% of its banking resources.

Brazil in World War I

Preceding

Following the Declaration of the Republic in 1889, there were many political and social rebellions that had to be subdued by the regime, such as the Two Naval Revolts (1891 & 1893–94),[642,643] the Federalist Rebellion[644] (1893–95), War of Canudos (1896–97), Vaccine Revolt (1904), Revolt of the Whip (1910) and the Revolt of Juazeiro ("Sedição de Juazeiro", 1914). Therefore, with the onset of World War I, Brazilian elites were interested in studying the events of the Mexican Revolution with more attention than those related to the War in Europe.

By 1915 it was also clear that the Brazilian elites were dedicated to making sure Brazil followed a conservative political path, meaning they were unwilling to embark upon courses of action, whether domestically (i.e. adopting the secret ballot and universal suffrage) or in foreign affairs (making alliances or long-term commitments), that could have unpredictable consequences and potentially risk the social, economic and political positions held by the Brazilian elite. This course of conduct would extend throughout the 20th century, an isolationist foreign policy interspersed with sporadic automatic alignments against "disturbing elements of peace and international trade"

In August 1916, after almost four years, another rebellion, the Contestado War ended.

Since the end of the 19th century, many immigrants from Europe had arrived, and with them came communist and anarchist ideas, which created problems for the very conservative regime of large estate owners (aka "Café com Leite" republic). With the growth, masses of industrial workers became unhappy with the system and began engaging in massive protests, mostly in São Paulo and Rio de Janeiro. After a General Strike in 1917 the government attempted to brutally repress the labor movement in order to prevent new movements from beginning. This repression, supported by legislation, was very effective in preventing the formation of real free labor unions.

Ruy Barbosa was the main opposition leader, campaigning for internal political changes. He also stated that due to the natural conflict between Brazilian commercial interests and the Central Powers's strategic ones (demonstrated for example in the German submarine campaign as well as in the Ottoman control over the Middle East), Brazilian involvement in the war would be inevitable. So he advised that the most logical way to proceed would be to follow the United States, which was working for a peace agreement but as the same time since the sinking of the RMS *Lusitania* was also preparing for war.

Figure 93: *President Venceslau Brás declares war against the Central Powers in October 1917.*

War

There were two main lines of thought regarding Brazil's joining of the war: One, led by Ruy Barbosa called for joining the Entente;[645] another side worried about the notices of bloody and unfruitful fighting in trenches, nurturing critical and pacifist feelings in the urban worker classes. Therefore, Brazil remained neutral in World War I until 1917. But internal problems, aggravated by denunciations of corruption created the need for then president Venceslau Brás to deviate attention, something that could be accomplished by focusing on an external enemy to eventually take advantage of a sense of patriotism.

During 1917, the sinking of Brazilian civilian ships by the German Navy off the French coast created such opportunity. On October 26 the government declared war on the Central Powers; Germany, Austria-Hungary, and Ottoman Empire. Soon after, the capture of ships from those countries that were on Brazilian coast was ordered and three small military groups were dispatched to the western front. The first one consisted of medical staff from the Army, the second consisted of sergeants and officers, also from the Army, and the third group consisted of military aviators, both of Army and Navy.[646,647] These groups were attached respectively: the Army's members to French Army and the Navy's aviators to British Royal Air Force. By 1918 all three groups were already in action in France.

By that time Brazil had also sent a Naval fleet, the **DNOG** (acronym in Portuguese for Naval Division in War Operations),[648] commanded by Pedro Max Frontin to join the Allies' Naval Forces in the Mediterranean.

However, during 1918, the turbulent social situation that generated in protests against the military recruitment plus the repercussion of then events in Russia only strengthened the provision of the Brazilian elites to remain obstinate with its doctrine of minimal involvement in international conflicts. In addition, the devastating advent of Spanish flu, amongst other reasons, meant that Venceslau Brás' administration in the end of its Term of office, refrained from getting involved more deeply in the war. Finally, the end of the war in November 1918, prevented even the government that succeeded the Venceslas Bras, could carry out its plan for war. Despite its modest participation, Brazil gained the right to partake in the Versailles conference.

Demographic changes

From 1875 until 1960, about five million Europeans emigrated to Brazil, settling mainly in the four southern states of São Paulo, Paraná, Santa Catarina, and Rio Grande do Sul. Immigrants came mainly from Portugal, Italy, Germany, Spain, Japan, Poland, and the Middle East. The world's largest Japanese community outside Japan is in São Paulo. Indigenous full-blooded Indians, located mainly in the northern and western border regions and in the upper Amazon Basin, constitute less than 1% of the population. Their numbers are declining as contact with the outside world and commercial expansion into the interior increase. Brazilian Government programs to establish reservations and to provide other forms of assistance have existed for years but are controversial and often ineffective. The plurality of Brazilians are of mixed African, European, and Indian lineage. Immigration increased industrialization and urbanization in Brazil.

Developments under the Old Republic

Demographic changes and structural shifts in the economy, however, threatened the primacy of the agrarian oligarchies. Under the Old Republic (1889–1930), the growth of the urban middle sectors, though retarded by dependency and entrenched oligarchy, was eventually strong enough to propel itself to the forefront of Brazilian political life. In time, growing trade, commerce, and industry in São Paulo undermined the domination of the republic's politics by the landed gentries of that state (dominated by the coffee industry) and Minas Gerais, dominated by dairy interests, known then by observers as the politics of *café com leite*; 'coffee with milk'.

Figure 94: *President Artur Bernardes (1922-1926) and ministers of state, 1922. National Archives of Brazil.*

Long before the first revolts of the urban middle classes to seize power from the coffee oligarchs in the 1920s, however, Brazil's intelligentsia, influenced by the tenets of European positivism, and farsighted agro-capitalists, dreamed of forging a modern, industrialized society—the "world power of the future". This sentiment was later nurtured throughout the Vargas years and under successive populist governments before the 1964 military junta repudiated Brazilian populism. Although such lofty visionaries were somewhat ineffectual under the Old Republic (1889–1930), the structural changes in the Brazilian economy opened up by the Great War strengthened these demands.

The outbreak of World War I in August 1914 was the turning point for the dynamic urban sectors. Temporarily abating Britain's overseas economic connections with Brazil, the war was an impetus for domestic manufacturing because of the unavailability of British imports. These structural shifts in the Brazilian economy helped to increase the ranks of the new urban middle classes. Meanwhile, Brazil's manufacturers and those employed by them enjoyed these gains at the expense of the agrarian oligarchies. Coffee being a nonessential though habit-forming product which affords it a measure of stability and resilience, world demand declined sharply. The central government, dominated by rural gentries, responded to falling world coffee demand by bailing out the oligarchs, reinstating the soon-to-be disastrous valorization program. Sixteen years later, world coffee demand plunged even more precipitously with the Great Depression. Valorization, government intervention to maintain coffee prices by withholding stocks from the market or restricting plantings, then proved to be unsustainable, incapable of curbing insurmountable decline in coffee prices in world markets. By World War I, the reinstatement of government price supports foreshadowed the vulnerability of Brazil's coffee oligarchy to the Great Depression.

Paradoxically, economic crisis spurred industrialization and a resultant boost to the urban middle and working classes. The depressed coffee sector freed up the capital and labor needed for manufacturing finished goods. A chronically adverse balance of trade and declining rate of exchange against foreign currencies was also helpful; Brazilian goods were simply cheaper in the Brazilian market. The state of São Paulo, with its relatively large capital-base, large immigrant population from Southern and Eastern Europe, and wealth of natural resources, led the trend, eclipsing Rio de Janeiro as center of Brazilian industry. Industrial production, though concentrated in light industry (food processing, small shops, and textiles) doubled during the war, and the number of enterprises (which stood at about 3,000 in 1908) grew by 5,940 between 1915 and 1918. The war was also a stimulus for the diversification of agriculture. Growing wartime demand of the Allies for staple products, sugar, beans, and raw materials sparked a new boom for products other than sugar or coffee. Foreign interests, however, continued to control the more capital-intensive industries, distinguishing Brazil's industrial revolution from that of the rest of the West.

Struggle for reform

With manufacturing on the rise and the coffee oligarchs imperiled, the old order of *café com leite* and *coronelismo* eventually gave way to the political aspirations of the new urban groups: professionals, government and white-collar workers, merchants, bankers, and industrialists. Increasing support for industrial protectionism marked 1920s Brazilian politics with little support from a central government dominated by the coffee interests. Under considerable middle class pressure, a more activist, centralized state adapted to represent the interests that the new bourgeoisie had been demanded for years — one that could utilize a state interventionist policy consisting of tax breaks, lowered duties, and import quotas to expand the domestic capital base. Manufacturers, white-collar workers, and the urban proletariat alike had earlier enjoyed the respite of world trade associated with World War I. However, the coffee oligarchs, relying on a devolved power structure relegating power to their own patrimonial ruling oligarchies, were certainly not interested in regularizing Brazil's personalistic politics or centralizing power. Getúlio Vargas, leader from 1930 to 1945 and later for a brief period in the 1950s, would later respond to these demands.

During this time period, the state of São Paulo was at the forefront of Brazil's economic, political, and cultural life. Known colloquially as "locomotive pulling the 20 empty boxcars" (a reference to the 20 other states) and still today Brazil's industrial and commercial center, São Paulo led this trend toward industrialization due to the foreign revenues flowing into the coffee industry.

Prosperity contributed to a rapid rise in the population of recent working class Southern and Eastern European immigrants, a population that contributed to the growth of trade unionism, anarchism, and socialism. In the post-World War I period, Brazil was hit by its first wave of general strikes and the establishment of the Communist Party in 1922.

Meanwhile, the divergence of interests between the coffee oligarchs—devastated by the Depression—and the burgeoning, dynamic urban sectors was intensifying. According to prominent Latin American historian Benjamin Keen, the task of transforming society "fell to the rapidly growing urban bourgeois groups, and especially to the middle class, which began to voice even more strongly its discontent with the rule of the corrupt rural oligarchies". In contrast, the labor movement remained small and weak (despite a wave of general strikes in the postwar years), lacking ties to the peasantry, who constituted the overwhelming majority of the Brazilian population. As a result, disparate social reform movements would crop up in the 1920s, ultimately culminating in the Revolution of 1930. The 1920s revolt against the seating of Artur da Silva Bernardes as president signaled the beginning of a struggle by the urban bourgeoisie to seize power from the coffee-producing oligarchy.

This era sparked the failed but famed *tenente* (lieutenant) rebellion as well. Junior military officers, who had long been active against the ruling coffee oligarchy, staged their own failed revolt in 1922 amid demands for various forms of social modernization, calling for agrarian reform, the formation of cooperatives, and the nationalization of mines. In this historical setting, Getúlio Vargas emerged as president about a decade later.

Bibliography

- Cardim; Carlos Henrique "A Raiz das Coisas. Rui Barbosa: o Brasil no Mundo" (The Root of Things. Ruy Barbosa: Brazil in the World) (in Portuguese) Civilização Brasileira 2007 ISBN 978-85-200-0835-5
- McCann, Frank D. "Soldiers of the Patria, A History of the Brazilian Army, 1889–1937" Stanford University Press 2004 ISBN 0-8047-3222-1

- Maia, Prado (1961). *D.N.O.G. (Divisão Naval em Operações de Guerra), 1914–1918: uma página esquecida da história da Marinha Brasileira.* Serviço de Documentação Geral da Marinha. OCLC 22210405[649]. (Portuguese)
- Rex A. Hudson, ed. Brazil: A Country Study. Washington: GPO for the Library of Congress, 1997.
- Scheina, Robert L. "Latin America's Wars Vol.II: The Age of the Professional Soldier, 1900–2001" Potomac Books, 2003 ISBN 1-57488-452-2 Chapter 5 "World War I and Brazil, 1917–18"
- Vinhosa, Luiz Francisco Teixeira "A diplomacia brasileira e a revolução mexicana, 1913–1915" (Brazilian diplomacy and the Mexican Revolution, 1913–1915) (in Portuguese) FLT 1975 on Google Books[650]

External links

- http://www.grandesguerras.com.br (Portuguese) site of *GrandesGuerras* (WorldWars) Magazine
- https://web.archive.org/web/20071024193453/http://www.exercito.gov.br/ (Portuguese) Official Site of Brazilian Army

Vargas Era

Republic of the United States of Brazil (1889–1937) *República dos Estados Unidos do Brasil*	
United States of Brazil (1937–1967) *Estados Unidos do Brasil*	
1930–1945	
 Flag  Coat of arms	
Motto "Ordem e Progresso" "Order and Progress"	
Anthem *Hino Nacional Brasileiro* (English: "Brazilian National Anthem")	

Capital	Rio de Janeiro
Languages	Portuguese
Government	Totalitarian dictatorship
President	
• 1930–1945	Getúlio Vargas
• 1945–1946	José Linhares
Provisional Military Junta	

	1930	Augusto Tasso Fragoso Isaías de Noronha Mena Barreto
Legislature		National Parliament[651]
•	Upper house	Federal Council[652]
•	Lower house	Chamber of Deputies
Historical era		Interbellum · World War II
•	Revolution of 1930	3 November 1930
•	Adoption of new Constitution	16 July 1934
•	Communist Uprising	23 November 1935
•	Estado Novo (dictatorship)	10 November 1937
•	Brazil's entering WWII	22 August 1942
•	Vargas Deposition	29 October 1945
Area		
•	1903	8,515,767 km² (3,287,956 sq mi)
Population		
•	1940 est.	41,236,315
Currency		Brazilian real (1930-1942) Cruzeiro (1942-1946)
Preceded by		**Succeeded by**
First Brazilian Republic		Second Brazilian Republic

Part of **a series** on the
History of Brazil

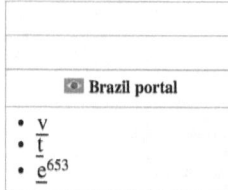

The **Vargas Era** (Portuguese: *Era Vargas*; Brazilian Portuguese: [ˈɛɾɐ ˈvaɾgɐs]) is the period in the history of Brazil between 1930 and 1945, when the country was under the dictatorship of Getúlio Vargas.

The Brazilian Revolution of 1930 marked the end of the Old Republic. President Washington Luís was deposed; the swearing-in of President-elect Julio Prestes was blocked, on the grounds that the election had been rigged by his supporters; the 1891 Constitution was abrogated, the National Congress was dissolved and the provisional military junta ceded power to Vargas. Federal intervention in State governments increased and the political landscape was altered by suppressing the traditional oligarchies of São Paulo and Minas Gerais states.

The Vargas Era comprises three successive phases:

- the period of the Provisional Government (1930–1934), when Vargas governed by decree as Head of the Provisional Government instituted by the Revolution, pending the adoption of a new Constitution.
- the period of the Constitution of 1934, when a new Constitution was drafted and approved by the Constituent Assembly of 1933–34, and Vargas – elected by the Constituent Assembly under the transitional provisions of the Constitution – governed as President, alongside a democratically elected Legislature.
- the Estado Novo period (1937–1945), that began when in order to perpetuate his rule, Vargas imposed a new, authoritarian Constitution in a *coup d'état*, and shut down Congress, assuming dictatorial powers.

The deposition of Getúlio Vargas and his Estado Novo regime in 1945 and the subsequent re-democratization of Brazil with the adoption of a new Constitution in 1946 mark the end of the Vargas Era and the beginning of the period known as the Second Brazilian Republic.

Downfall of the Old Republic

The *tenente* rebellion did not mark the revolutionary breakthrough for Brazil's bourgeois social reformers, but the ruling *paulista* coffee oligarchy could not withstand the economic meltdown of 1929.

Brazil's vulnerability to the Great Depression had its roots in the economy's heavy dependence on foreign markets and loans. Despite limited industrial development in São Paulo, the export of coffee and other agricultural products was still the mainstay of the economy.

Days after the U.S. stock market crash on October 29, 1929 (see Black Tuesday), coffee quotations immediately fell 30% to 60%.Wikipedia:Citation needed and continued to fall. Between 1929 and 1931, coffee prices fell from 22.5 cents per pound to 8 cents per pound.[654] As world trade contracted, the coffee exporters suffered a vast drop in foreign exchange earnings.

The Great Depression possibly had a more dramatic effect on Brazil than on the United States. The collapse of Brazil's valorization (price support) program, a safety net in times of economic crisis, was strongly intertwined with the collapse of the central government, whose base of support resided in the landed oligarchy. The coffee planters had grown dangerously dependent on government valorization. For example, in the aftermath of the recession following World War I, the government was not short of the cash needed to bail out the coffee industry. But between 1929–30, world demand for Brazil's primary products had fallen far too drastically to maintain government revenues. By the end of 1930, Brazil's gold reserves had been depleted, pushing the exchange rate down to a new low. The program for warehoused coffee collapsed altogether.

The government of President Washington Luís faced a deepening balance-of-payments crisis and the coffee growers were stuck with an unsaleable harvest. Since power ultimately rested on a patronage system, wide-scale defections in the delicate balance of regional interests left the regime of Washington Luís vulnerable. Government policies designed to favor foreign interests further exacerbated the crisis, leaving the regime alienated from almost every segment of society.

Following the Wall Street panic, the government attempted to please foreign creditors by maintaining convertibility according to the money principles preached by the foreign bankers and economists who set the terms for Brazil's relations with the world economy, despite lacking any support from a single major sector in Brazilian society.

Despite capital flight, Washington Luís clung to a hard-money policy, guaranteeing the convertibility of the Brazilian currency into gold or British sterling. Once the gold and sterling reserves were exhausted amid the collapse of the valorization program, the government was finally forced to suspend convertibility of the currency. Foreign credit had now evaporated.

Figure 95: *Getúlio Vargas after the 1930 revolution, which began the Vargas Era.*

Rise of Getúlio Vargas

A populist governor of Brazil's southernmost Rio Grande do Sul state, Vargas was a cattle rancher with a doctorate in law and the 1930 presidential candidate of the Liberal Alliance. Vargas was a member of the gaucho-landed oligarchy and had risen through the system of patronage and clientelism, but had a fresh vision of how Brazilian politics could be shaped to support national development. He came from a region with a positivist and populist tradition, and was an economic nationalist who favored industrial development and liberal reforms. Vargas built up political networks, and was attuned to the interests of the rising urban classes. In his early years Vargas even relied on the support of the *tenentes* of the 1922 rebellion.

Vargas understood that with the breakdown of direct relations between workers and owners in the growing factories of Brazil, workers could become the basis for a new form of political power – populism. Using such insights, he gradually established such mastery over the Brazilian political world that, upon achieving power, he stayed in power for 15 years. During this time, as the stranglehold of the agricultural elites eased, new urban industrial leaders acquired more influence nationally, and the middle class began to show strength.

Aside from the Great Depression and the emergence of the Brazilian bourgeoisie, Brazil's historic dynamic of interregional politics was a significant factor encouraging the alliance that Getúlio Vargas forged during the Revolution of 1930 between the new urban sectors and the landowners hostile to the government in states other than São Paulo.

Along with the urban bourgeois groups, Northeastern sugar barons were left with a legacy of longstanding grievances against the *paulista* coffee oligarchs of the South. Northeastern landowners opposed Washington Luís' 1930 discontinuance of the drought relief projects of his predecessor. The decay of established sugar oligarchies of the Northeast had begun dramatically with the severe drought of 1877. The rapid growth of coffee-producing São Paulo state started at the same time. After the abolition of slavery in the 1880s, Brazil saw a mass exodus of emancipated slaves and other peasants from the Northeast to the Southeast, thus ensuring a steady supply of cheap labor for the coffee planters.

Under the Old Republic, the politics of *café com leite* ("coffee with milk)" rested on the domination of the republic's politics by the Southeastern states of São Paulo and Minas Gerais, which were Brazil's largest states in terms of population and economy.

Given the grievances with ruling regime in the Northeast and Rio Grande do Sul, Getúlio Vargas chose João Pessoa of the Northeast state of Paraíba as his vice-presidential candidate in 1930. With the understanding that the dominance of the landowners in the rural areas was to continue under Liberal Alliance government, the Northeastern oligarchies were thus integrated into the Vargas alliance in a subordinate status via a new political party, the Social Democratic Party (PSD).

As a candidate in 1930, Vargas utilized populist rhetoric to promote middle class concerns, thus opposing the primacy (but not the legitimacy) of the paulista coffee oligarchy and the landed elites, who had little interest in protecting and promoting industry.

However, behind the façade of Vargas' populism lies the intricate nature of his coalition – ever-changing from this point onward. Consequently, these locally dominant regional groups – the gaúchos of Rio Grande do Sul and the sugar barons of the Northeast – themselves ushered the new urban groups into the forefront of Brazilian political life in a revolution from above, tilting the balance of the central government in favor of the Liberal Alliance.

After the 1930 Revolution

Vargas' tenuous coalition lacked a coherent program, being committed to a broad vision of "modernization", but little else more definitive. Having to balance such conflicting ideological constituencies, regionalism, and economic interests in such a vast, diverse, and socio-economically varied nation would, thus, not only explain the sole constancy that marked Vargas' long career—abrupt shifts in alliances and ideologies, but also his eventual dictatorship, modeled surprisingly along the lines of European fascism, considering the liberal roots of his regime.

Between 1930–1934, Vargas followed a path of social reformism in attempt to reconcile radically diverging interests of his supporters. His policies can best be described collectively as approximating those of fascist Italy under Mussolini, with an increased reliance on populism. Reflecting the influence of the *tenentes*, he even advocated a program of social welfare and reform similar to New Deal in the United States, prompting U.S. President Franklin Roosevelt to proudly refer to him as "one of two people who invented the New Deal."

Vargas sought to bring Brazil out of the Great Depression through statist-interventionist policies. He satisfied the demands of the rapidly growing urban bourgeois groups, voiced by the new (to Brazil) mass-ideologies of populism and nationalism. Like Roosevelt, his first steps focused on economic stimulus, a program on which all factions could agree.

Favoring a state interventionist policy utilizing tax breaks, lowered duties, and import quotas to expand the domestic industrial base, Vargas linked his pro-middle class policies to nationalism, advocating heavy tariffs to "perfect our manufacturers to the point where it will become unpatriotic to feed or clothe ourselves with imported goods!"

Vargas sought to mediate disputes between labor and capital. For instance, the provisional president quelled a paulista female workers' strike by co-opting much of its platform and requiring their "factory commissions" to use government mediation in the future.

With the Northeastern oligarchies now incorporated into the ruling coalition, the government focused on restructuring agriculture. To placate friendly agrarian oligarchs, the modernizing state not only left the impoverished domains of the rural oligarchs untouched, the government even helped the sugar barons cement their control over rural Brazil. The peasantry, to the surprise of many accustomed to overlooking Brazil's peripheral regions, was not that servile. Banditry was common. Other forms included messianism, anarchic uprisings, and tax evasion, each of which was already common practice before 1930. The state crushed a wave of peasant revolts in the Northeast known as the *cangaço*, marking the reversal of the drastic but gradual decline of the Northeastern *latifundios* from the 1870s to the 1930 revolution. At the expense of the indigent peasantry—85 percent of the workforce—not only did Vargas renege on his promises of land reforms, he denied agricultural workers in general the working class' gains in labor regulations. Likely to the detriment of that region's long-term economic development, Vargas' static conservatism on matters of the countryside arguably exacerbated the disparities between the impoverished, semi-feudal Northeast and the dynamic, urbanized Southeast to this day.

Opposition arose among the powerful paulista coffee oligarchs to these unprecedented mass interventionist policies, as well as to the increased centralization of the government, its increasing populist and fascist stance, its protectionist/mercantilist policies (protecting politically favored producers at the expense of consumers) and the increasing dictatorial stance of Vargas himself.

Appeasement of landed interests, traditionally the country's dominant forces, thus required a realignment of his coalition, forcing him to turn against its left wing. After mid-1932 the influence of the *tenente* group over Vargas rapidly waned, although individual *tenentes* of moderate tendency continued to hold important positions in the regime. With the ouster of the center-left *tenentes* from his coalition, his rightward shift would become increasingly pronounced by 1934.

Towards dictatorship

By 1934 Vargas developed what Thomas E. Skidmore and Peter H. Smith called "a legal hybrid" between the regimes of Mussolini's Italy and Salazar's Estado Novo in Portugal. Vargas copied fascist tactics, and shared their rejection of liberal capitalism. He abandoned the arrangements of the "provisional government" (1930–34) which were characterized by social reformism that appeared to favor the generally left wing of his revolutionary coalition, the *tenentes*.

A conservative insurgency in 1932 was the key turning point to the right. After the July 1932 Constitutionalist Revolution — a thinly-veiled attempt by the paulista coffee oligarchs to retake the central government — Vargas tried to recover support of the landed elites, including the coffee growers, in order to establish a new alliance of power.

The revolt was caused by Vargas' appointment of João Alberto, a center-left *tenente* as "interventor" (provisional governor) in place of the elected governor of São Paulo. The paulista elite loathed Alberto, resenting his centralization efforts and alarmed by his economic reforms, such as 5% wage increase and the minor distribution of some land to participants of the revolution. Amid threats of revolt, Vargas replaced João Alberto with a civilian from São Paulo,

Figure 96: *Vargas (center) during commemorations to mark the 50th anniversary of the Proclamation of the Republic, November 15, 1939.*

appointed a conservative paulista banker as his minister of finance, and announced a date for the holding of a constituent assembly. This only emboldened coffee oligarchs who launched a revolt in July 1932, which collapsed after three months of armed combat.

Regardless of the attempted revolution, Vargas was determined to maintain his alliance with the original farmer wing of his coalition and to strengthen his ties with the São Paulo establishment. The result was further concessions, alienating the left wings of his coalition. The essential compromise was failing to honor the promises of land reform made during the campaign of 1930. Vargas also pardoned half the bank debts of the coffee planters, who still had a significant grip on the state's electoral machinery, alleviating the crisis stemming from the collapse of the valorization program. To pacify his old paulista adversaries after their failed revolt, he ordered the Bank of Brazil to assume the war bonds issued by the rebel government.

Vargas was also increasingly threatened by pro-Communist elements in labor critical of the rural *latifundios* by 1934, who sought an alliance with the countries peasant majority by backing land reform. Despite the populist rhetoric of the "father of the poor", the gaucho Vargas was ushered into power by planter oligarchies of peripheral regions amid a revolution from above, and was thus in no position to meet Communist demands, had he desired to do so.

In 1934, armed with a new constitution drafted with extensive influence from European fascist models, Vargas began reining in even moderate trade unions and turning against the *tenentes*. His further concessions to the *latifundios* pushed him toward an alliance with the Integralists, Brazil's mobilized fascist movement. Following the end of the provisional presidency, Vargas' regime between 1934 and 1945 was characterized by the co-optation of Brazilian unions through state-run, sham syndicates, and suppression of opposition, particularly leftist opposition.

Suppression of Communist movement

Aside from these recent political disputes, long-term trends suggest an atmosphere in São Paulo conducive to ideological extremism. The rapidly changing and industrializing Southeast, had been brewing an atmosphere conducive to the growth of European-style mass-movements; Brazil's Communist Party was established in 1922 and the postwar period witnessed the rise of the country's first waves of general strikes waged by viable trade unions. The Great Depression intensified their strength.

The same Great Depression that had ushered Vargas into power also emboldened calls for social reforms. With the challenges of the Paulista Revolt out of the way, and the looming mass-mobilization of a potential new enemy— the urban proletariat—Vargas grew more concerned with imposing a paternalistic tutelage over the working class, functioning to both control them and co-opt them. Vargas' backers in both urban and rural Brazil would begin to view labor, larger and better organized than directly after the First World War, as an ominous threat.

Vargas could unite with all sectors of the landed elites, however, to stem the Communists. With the *cangaço* thoroughly repressed in the Northeast, all segments of the elite—the new bourgeoisie and the landed oligarchs— hifted their well-founded fears toward the trade unionism and socialist sentiments of the burgeoning urban proletariat. The urban proletariat, often composed of immigrants, was from the more European (in terms of population, culture, ideology, and level of industrial development) and more urbanized Southeast. In 1934, following the disintegration of Vargas' delicate alliance with labor, Brazil entered "one of the most agitated periods in its political history". According to Skidmore and Smith, Brazil's major cities began to resemble the Nazi-Communist battles in Berlin of 1932–33. By mid-1935 Brazilian politics had been drastically destabilized.

Vargas's attention focused on the rise of two nationally based and highly ideological European-style movements, both committed to European-style mass-mobilization: one pro-Communist and the other pro-fascist—one linked to

Moscow and the other to Rome and Berlin. The mass-movement intimidating Vargas was the *Aliança Nacional Libertadora* (ANL), a leftwing popular front launched in 1935 of socialists, communists, and other progressives led by the Communist Party and Luís Carlos Prestes, known as the "cavalier of hope" of the *tenente* rebellion (though not a Marxist at the time). A revolutionary forerunner of Che Guevara, Prestes led the futile "Long March" through the rural Brazilian interior following his participation in the failed 1922 *tenente* rebellion against the coffee oligarchs. This experience, however, left Prestes, who only died in the 1990s, and some of his comrades skeptical of armed conflict for the rest of his life. Prestes' well-cultivated skepticism later helped precipitate the 1960s schism between hard-line militant Maoists and orthodox Marxist—Leninism which persists with the Brazilian Communist Party ínto the 21st century. With center-left *tenentes* out of the coalition and the left crushed, Vargas turned to the only mobilized base of support on the right, elated by the atrocious, fascist-style crackdown against the ANL. As his coalition moved to the right after 1934, Vargas' ideological character and association with a global ideological orbit remained ambiguous. Integralism, claiming a rapidly growing membership throughout Brazil by 1935, began filling this ideological void, especially among the approximately one million Brazilians of German descent.

Plínio Salgado, a writer and politician, founded Brazilian Integralism in October 1933.[655] He adapted Fascist and Nazi symbolism and the Roman salute. It had all the visible elements of European fascism: a green-shirt-uniformed paramilitary organization, street demonstrations, and aggressive rhetoric directly financed in part by the Italian embassy. The Integralists borrowed their propaganda campaigns directly from Nazi materials, including the usual traditionalist excoriations of Marxism and liberalism, and espousals of fanatical nationalism (out of context in the heterogeneous and tolerant nation) and "Christian virtues". In particular, they drew support from military officers, especially in the navy.

Economic development

The strong parallels between the political economy of Vargas and the European police states thus began to appear by 1934, when a new constitution was enacted with direct fascist influence. After 1934, fascist-style programs would serve two important aims: stimulating industrial growth (under the guise of nationalism and autarchy) and suppressing the working class. Passed on July 16, the Vargas government claimed that the corporatist provisions of the constitution of 1934 would unite all classes in mutual interests—the stated purpose of a similar governing document in Fascist Italy. Actually, this propaganda point had somewhat of a basis in reality. In practice, this meant decimating independent organized labor and attracting the "working class" to the corporative state. Of course, the advance of industry and urbanization enlarged and strengthened the ranks of urban laborers, presenting the need to draw them into some sort of alliance committed to the modernization of Brazil. Vargas, and later Juan Perón in neighboring Argentina, emulated Mussolini's strategy of consolidating power by means of mediating class disputes under the banner of nationalism.

The constitution established a new Chamber of Deputies that placed government authority over the private economy and established a system of corporatism aimed at industrialization and reducing foreign dependency. These provisions essentially designated corporate representatives according to class and profession, organizing industries into state syndicates, but generally maintained private ownership of Brazilian-owned businesses.

The 1934–37 constitution, and especially the *Estado Novo* afterwards, heightened efforts to centralize authority in Rio de Janeiro and drastically limit provincial autonomy in the traditionally devolved, sprawling nation. This was its more progressive role, seeking to consolidate the 1930 revolution, displacing the institutional power of the paulista coffee oligarchs with a centralist policy that respected local agro-exporting interests, but created the necessary urban economic base for the new urban sectors. The modernizing legacy is firmly evident: state government was to be rationalized and regularized, freed from the grips of *coronelismo*.

The constitution of 1934 thus established a more direct mechanism for the federal executive to control the economy, pursuing a policy of planning and direct investment for the creation of important industrial complexes. State and mixed public-private companies dominated heavy and infrastructure industries, and private Brazilian capital predominated in manufacturing. There was also a significant growth of direct foreign investment in the 1930s as foreign corporations sought to enlarge their share of the internal market and overcome tariff barriers and exchange problems by establishing branch plants in Brazil. The state thus emphasized the basic sectors of the economy, facing the difficult task of forging a viable capital base for future growth in the first place, including mining, oil, steel, electric power, and chemicals.

Estado Novo

Vargas' four-year term as President under the 1934 Constitution was due to expire in 1938, and he was barred from reelection. However, on November 10, 1937, Vargas made a national radio address denouncing the existence of a communist plot to overthrow the government, called the Cohen Plan (*Plano Cohen*). In reality, however, *Plano Cohen* was forged in the government with the objective of creating a favourable atmosphere for Vargas to stay in power, perpetuating his rule and assuming dictatorial powers.

The Communists had indeed attempted to take over the Government in November 1935, in a botched coup attempt known as the *Intentona Comunista* (Communist Attempt). In the wake of the failed Communist uprising, Congress had already given greater powers to Vargas, and approved the creation of a National Security Tribunal (*Tribunal de Segurança Nacional*), established by a statute adopted on 11 September 1936.

In his address of 10 November 1937, Vargas, invoking the supposed Communist threat, decreed a state of emergency and dissolved the Legislature. He also announced the adoption by Presidential *fiat* of a new, severely authoritarian Constitution that effectively placed all governing power in his hands. The 1934 Constitution was thus abolished, and Vargas proclaimed the establishment of a "Estado Novo" (*New State*). The short interval was further evidence that the self-coup had been planned well in advance.

Under this dictatorial regime the powers of the National Security Tribunal were streamlined, and it focused on the prosecution of political dissenters. Also, the powers of the police were greatly enhanced, with the establishment of DOPS, a powerful political police and secret service. When created in 1936, the National Security Tribunal was supposed to be a temporary Court, and defendants could file appeals against its judgements to the Superior Military Court (*Superior Tribunal Militar*), Brazil's Court of Appeals for the Armed Forces, which was in turn subordinate to the Nation's Supreme Court. Thus, Communists and other defendants accused of plotting coups were judged by the military court-martial system (with the National Security Tribunal as the trial court of first instance for those cases), and not by the ordinary courts. With the advent of the Estado Novo regime, the National Security Tribunal became a permanent Court, and became autonomous from the rest of the Court system. It gained authority to adjudicate not only cases of Communist conspirators and other coup plotters, but it now tried anyone accused of being subversive or dangerous to the Estado Novo regime. Also, several extrajudicial punishments were inflicted by the police itself (especially by the DOPS political police), without trial.

The 1937 Constitution provided for elections to a new Congress, as well as a referendum to confirm Vargas' actions. However, neither were held — ostensibly due to the dangerous international situation. Instead, under an article of the Constitution that was supposed to be transitional pending new elections, the President assumed legislative as well as executive powers. For all intents and purposes, Vargas ruled for eight years under what amounted to martial law. Also, under the 1937 Constitution Vargas should have remained President for only six more years (until November 1943). Instead—again presumably due

Figure 97: *Ten cruzeiro banknote, featuring a portrait of President Vargas.*

to the dangerous international situation—he remained in power until his overthrow in 1945.

The Estado Novo dictatorship also greatly curtailed the autonomy of the Judicial branch, and suppressed the autonomy of the Brazilian States, that were governed by federal interventors, who discharged (on a formally temporary basis), the legislative and executive powers.

In December 1937, one month after the Estado Novo coup, Vargas signed a Decree disbanding all political parties, including the fascist-like *Ação Integralista Brasileira* (AIB). The Brazilian Integralists had until then been supportive of Vargas' anti-communist measures. On May 11, 1938, the integralists, unsatisfied with the closing of the AIB, invaded the Guanabara Palace, attempting to depose Vargas. This episode is known as "Integralist Attempt" and was far from successful.

Between 1937 and 1945, the duration of the Estado Novo, Vargas gave continuity to the formation of structure and professionalism in the State. He oriented the state to intervene in the economy, promoting economic nationalism. The movement towards a "New State" was significant, in that along with the dismissal of Congress and its political parties, he wanted to recognize the indigenous population. He gained great favor in their eyes, and was called the "Father of the Poor". Besides gaining popularity with them, he provided them with tools to assist them in the improvement of their agrarian lifestyles. He felt that if the country were to progress that the Indians, the very symbol of Brazilianness, should reap the benefits, ridden the label of oppression the country. This was important to establish a unified society. The intention was to form a strong impulse toward industrialization.

In this period, a number of industrial bodies were created:

- The "Conselho Nacional do Petróleo" (CNP) (National Oil Advisor)

- The "Departamento Administrativo do Serviço Público" (DASP) (The Administration Department of Public Service)
- The "Companhia Siderúrgica Nacional" (CSN) (National Iron Smelting Company)
- The "Companhia Vale do Rio Doce" (Rio Doce Valley Company)
- The "Companhia Hidro-Elétrica do São Francisco" (São Francisco Hydroelectric Company)
- The "Fábrica Nacional de Motores" (FNM) (National Motor Plant)

The Estado Novo had a powerful effect on Brazilian architecture, because it provided sufficient authority to implement Urban Planning on a large scale in Brazil. Although sufficient wealth was not available to complete the plans, they had a powerful, lasting effect on the cities and their organization. One of the best-planned cities in the world, CuritibaWikipedia:Citation needed, received its first planning during the Estado Novo. One notable urban planner was Alfred Agache.

A series of measures were used to restrain opposition, such as the nomination of Intervenors for the States and censorship of the media, performed by the DIP ("Departamento de Imprensa e Propaganda", Department of Press and Propaganda). This agency also promoted the ideology of the Estado Novo, designed the official propaganda of the government and tried to direct public opinion.

In 1943, Vargas promulgated the CLT ("Consolidação das Leis do Trabalho", Consolidation of the Labor Laws), guaranteeing that a job would be stable after ten years of service. It also provided weekly rest, regulated the work of minors and women, regulated night-time work and set a working day to eight hours.

Tensions with Argentina

The liberal revolution of 1930 overthrew the oligarchic coffee plantation owners and brought to power an urban middle class that and business interests that promoted industrialization and modernization. Aggressive promotion of new industry turned around the economy by 1933. Brazil's leaders in the 1920s and 1930s decided that Argentina's implicit foreign policy goal was to isolate Portuguese-speaking Brazil from Spanish-speaking neighbors, thus facilitating the expansion of Argentine economic and political influence in South America. Even worse, was the fear that a more powerful Argentine Army would launch a surprise attack on the weaker Brazilian Army. To counter this threat, President Getúlio Vargas forged closer links with the United States. Meanwhile, Argentina moved in the opposite direction. During World War II, Brazil was a staunch ally of the United States and sent its military to Europe. The United States provided over $100 million in Lend-Lease grants, in return for

Figure 98: *Brazilian propaganda announcing a declaration of war on the Axis powers, November 10, 1943*

free rent on air bases used to transport American soldiers and supplies across the Atlantic, and naval bases for anti-submarine operations. In sharp contrast, Argentina was officially neutral and at times favored Germany.[656,657]

World War II

With the start of World War II, in 1939, Vargas maintained neutrality until 1941, when an agreement, proposed by Brazilian foreign relations minister Oswaldo Aranha, was formed between American continental nations to align with any American country in the event of an attack by an external power. Due to this agreement, from Pearl Harbor Brazil's entering the war became just a matter of time. American policy also financed Brazilian iron and steel extraction and placed military bases along the Brazilian North-Northeast coast, headquartered in Natal. With the conquest of Southeast Asia by Japanese troops, Getúlio signed a treaty, the Washington Accords, in 1942, which provisioned the supply of natural rubber from the Amazon to the Allies, resulting in the second rubber boom and the forced migration of many people from the drought-stricken northeast to the heart of Amazônia. These people were known as *Soldados da Borracha* ("rubber soldiers").

Figure 99: *Carmen Miranda was a symbol of the "Good Neighbor Policy", which consisted of a closer relationship with the United States to Latin America.*

After the sinking of Brazilian merchant ships by German and Italian submarines throughout 1942, popular mobilization forced the Brazilian government to abandon its passiveness and declare war on Germany and Italy in August, 1942. Popular mobilization to make the war declaration effective, with the despatching of Brazilian troops to Europe, continued, but a decision by the Brazilian Government to actually send troops to fight the enemy was only made in January 1943, when Vargas and the U.S President Franklin Delano Roosevelt met in Natal, where the first official agreement was made to create an expeditionary force (BEF). In July 1944 the first BEF group was sent to fight in Italy, and, despite being poorly equipped and trained, it accomplished its main missions.

Soon after the war, however, fearing the BEF's popularity and possible political use of the allied victory by some BEF members, the then Brazilian government decided to make demobilization effective, with the BEF still in Italy. Returning to Brazil, its members were also subjected to some restrictions. Civilian veterans were forbidden from wearing military decorations or uniforms in public, while military vets were transferred to regions far from great cities or to border garrisons.

The events related to Brazilian participation in the war and the ending of the conflict in 1945 strengthened pressures in favor of redemocratization. Although there were some concessions by the regime, such as the setting of a date for presidential elections, amnesty for political prisoners, the freedom to organize political parties, and a commitment to choose a new Constitutional convention, Vargas was not able to retain support for the continuation of his presidency and was deposed by the military in a surprise coup launched from his own War Ministry on October 29, 1945.

Once Vargas was deposed, the military summoned his legal deputy, José Linhares, the President of the Supreme Federal Court (Brazil's chief justice), to assume the Presidency (the office of Vice-President had been abolished, and no legislature had been elected under the 1937 Constitution, so that the President of the Supreme Court was the first person in the line of succession). José Linhares immediately summoned elections for President and for a Constituent Assembly. The elections were held in December, 1945, and José Linhares remained in office only until the inauguration of the Assembly and of the elected President (General Eurico Gaspar Dutra) which took place on January 31, 1946.

Bibliography

- Castro, Celso; Izecksohn, Victor; Kraay, Hendrik (2004). *Nova História Militar Brasileira*. Fundação Getúlio Vargas. ISBN 85-225-0496-2. in Portuguese
- Ready, J. Lee (1985). *Forgotten Allies: The European Theatre, Volume I*. McFarland & Company. ISBN 978-0-89950-129-1.
- Brazil Now.Info[658] *Estado Novo*.
- Garfield, Seth. "The Roots of a Plant That Today Is Brazil: Indians and the Nation-State under the Brazilian Estado Novo" *Journal of Latin American Studies* Vol. 29, No. 3 (Oct., 1997), pp. 747–768

Second Brazilian Republic

United States of Brazil	
Estados Unidos do Brasil	
1946–1964	
 Flag (1960–68)  Coat of arms	
Motto "Ordem e Progresso" (English: "Order and Progress")	
Anthem "Hino Nacional Brasileiro" (English: "Brazilian National Anthem")	

Capital	Rio de Janeiro (until 1960) Brasília (after 1960)
Languages	Portuguese
Government	Multi-party Republic • Presidential (1946–61, 1963–64) • Parliamentary (1961–63)
President	
• 1946–1951	Eurico Gaspar Dutra (first)
• 1961–1964	João Goulart (last)
Prime Minister	

• 1961-1962	Tancredo Neves (first)
• 1962-1963	Hermes Lima (last)
Legislature	National Congress
• Upper house	Senate
• Lower house	Chamber of Deputies
Historical era	Cold War
• Dutra's ascension	31 January 1946
• Adoption of new Democratic Constitution	18 September 1946
• Change of Capital to Brasília	21 April 1960
• Parliamentarist Government	8 September 1961
• Return to Presidentialism	24 January 1963
• Military Coup d'État	31 March 1964 1964
Area	
• 1903	8,515,767 km² (3,287,956 sq mi)
Population	
• 1950 est.	51,944,397
• 1960 est.	70,992,343
Currency	Cruzeiro
Preceded by	**Succeeded by**
Vargas Era	Brazilian military government

Part of a series on the
History of Brazil

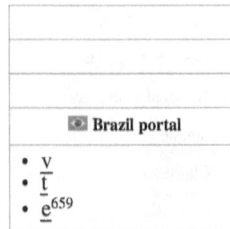

Second Brazilian Republic is the period of Brazilian history between 1946 and 1964 also known as the "**Republic of 46**". It was marked by political instability and military's pressure on civilian politicians which ended with the 1964 Brazilian coup d'état and establishment of Brazilian military government.

This period was marked by often tumultuous Presidencies of Eurico Gaspar Dutra, Getúlio Vargas, Juscelino Kubitschek, Jânio Quadros and João Goulart.

In 1945, President Getúlio Vargas was deposed by a bloodless military coup, but his influence in Brazilian politics remained until the end of the Second Republic. During this period, three parties dominated national politics. Two of them were pro-Vargas — the Brazilian Labour Party (*Partido Trabalhista Brasileiro, PTB*) to the left and the Social Democratic Party (*Partido social Democrático, PSD*) in the center — and another anti-Vargas, the rightist National Democratic Union (*União Democrática Nacional, UDN*).

End of the Estado Novo, 1945

As World War II ended with Brazil participating on the Allied side, President Getúlio Vargas moved to liberalize his own fascist-influenced *Estado Novo* regime. Vargas decreed an amnesty to political prisoners, including the chief of the Communist Party, Luís Carlos Prestes.

He also introduced an electoral law and allowed political parties to campaign. Three political parties introduced themselves into the national political scene. The liberal and rightist parties of the opposition against Vargas created the National Democratic Union. The bureaucrats and supporters of the *Estado Novo* grouped in the Brazilian Social Democratic Party. Vargas also created the Brazilian Labour Party, to the left, to group the workers' and the laborers' unions. The Brazilian Communist Party, weakened during the dictatorship, was also legalised.

The *Estado Novo* ended when two of the most rightist supporters, the Minister of War Pedro Aurélio de Góis Monteiro and Eurico Gaspar Dutra, led a military coup on October 29, 1945. The president of the Supreme Federal Tribunal, José Linhares was inaugurated as president of Brazil. Linhares guaranteed free and regular elections.

Figure 100: *U.S. President Truman and Brazilian President Eurico Dutra (center) during his visit to Washington, 1949*

Vargas was forced to take a temporary retirement. General Eurico Gaspar Dutra was elected president and served from 1946 to 1951. Vargas returned to politics in 1950 to win the presidential elections as the candidate of the Brazilian Labor Party (Partido Trabalhista Brasileiro), taking office on January 31, 1951.

Dutra, 1946-51

On September 18, 1946, the fifth constitution of Brazil was adapted, marking the country's return to democratic rule. That same year, the government created the Social Service of Industry (SESI) and Social Service of Commerce (SESC), and the General Staff, the future General Staff of the Armed Forces (EMFA).

In 1946 Dutra ordered the closing of casinos and prohibited "gambling" in the country. In 1947, he appointed Osvaldo Aranha as representative of Brazil to the United Nations (UN), outlawed Brazilian Communist Party (PCB), ended diplomatic relations with the Soviet Union (USSR) and in Petrópolis organized the Inter-American Conference of Peacekeeping and Security of the Continent, which was attended by the U.S. president, Harry Truman. In October 1948 his government set up the Superior School of War (ESG), with American support. Closer relations with Americans was displayed by formation of the Joint Commission of Brazil-United States, known as Abbink Mission, headed by John Abbink and Minister Octavio Gouveia de Bouillon.

The development strategy of the government included the "Salte Plan", which put emphasis on Health, Food, Transportation and Energy. Proposed in 1947, it aimed at better management of public spending and investment in key sectors in the country but only began to receive funding from the budget in 1949, being forgotten in 1951. During this period measurements the country's economic growth by calculating the Gross Domestic Product (GDP) were first regularly published. The average annual growth of the Brazilian economy during Dutra administration was 7.6%.

In 1950 Brazil hosted 1950 FIFA World Cup for which the famous Maracanã Stadium was built.

During the Dutra government construction of the hydroelectric plant of Paulo Afonso, Bahia, and the President Dutra highway linking Rio to São Paulo was initiated.

Vargas, 1951-54

In 1950 Vargas returned to the national politics and was elected a President. The Vargas administration was hampered by an economic crisis, congressional opposition, and impatience among his supporters. He announced an ambitious industrialization plan and pursued a policy of nationalization of the country's natural resources. To reduce foreign dependency, he founded the Petrobras Brazilian state oil enterprise.

By 1954, Vargas faced opposition from the UDN and the military. The murder of Major Rubens Vaz, an associate of opposition newspaper editor Carlos Lacerda, by some of the president's bodyguards, known as the crime of "Rua Tonelero", led to a reaction against Vargas. Army generals demanded his resignation.

After failing to negotiate a temporary leave of absence, Vargas declared "he would only leave the Catete (Presidential Palace) dead". Acknowledging that the chances that a democratic government succeed him were none, and that another military coup was coming, with probably worse results than 1950's one, Vargas kept his word and shot himself in the heart on August 24, 1954, after writing a letter blaming "international groups" and "revolted national groups" for the current situation. The results were immediate: opposition newspapers were "empastelados" (read: destroyed), the people took the streets and in a last shown of political force and popularity, Vargas postponed the military dictatorship by 10 years.

Collapse of Brazilian populism

Vargas' ever-shifting populist dictatorship helped to rein in the agrarian oligarchs, paving the way for the democratization of the 1950s and 1960s which was ended by the right-wing 1964 military coup. But the state still maintained a loose variation of Getúlio Vargas' populism and economic nationalism. Between 1930 and 1964, as Brazilian populism itself guided changes in the structure of Brazil's economy (Vargas' policies indisputably promoted industrial growth), Vargas and his successors were forced to shift the makeup of particular kinds of class alliances reconciled by the state.

After Vargas' suicide in 1954, awaiting a seemingly inevitable military coup, the support base for Brazilian populism began to deteriorate. Vargas' first ouster from 1945–1951 and his suicide demonstrated that Brazilian populism had been deteriorating for some time. Brazilian populism lingered for another decade but in new forms. If corporatism was the hallmark of the 1930s and 1940s, nationalism, and developmentalism characterized the 1950s and early 1960s. Each of these contributed to the crisis that gripped Brazil and resulted in the authoritarian regime after 1964.

Thus, as the historical context shifted, so did the ideology of Brazilian populism. Between 1934 and 1945, Brazilian populism was a surprisingly reactionary phenomenon, exhibiting remarkable parallels to European fascism. In contrast, under the presidency of João Goulart (1961–64) — a protégé of Getúlio Vargas and another *gaúcho* from Rio Grande do Sul, the closeness of the government to the historically disenfranchised working class and peasantry and even to the Communist Party led by Luís Carlos Prestes was equally remarkable. Goulart appeared to have been co-opting the Communist movement in a manner reminiscent of Vargas' co-optation of the Integralists shortly — and not coincidentally — before his ouster by reactionary forces. Eventually, the 1964 junta and the ensuing military dictatorship proved that the establishment forces that ushered Goulart's mentor into power in the first place, and the bourgeoisie that Vargas helped rear, found the left-leaning turn of Brazilian populism intolerable.

Temporary presidents, 1954-56

After the suicide of Vargas his Vice-president Café Filho assumed the Presidency from August 24, 1954 until November 8, 1955 when due to illness he was briefly replaced by Carlos Luz, President of the Chamber of Deputies (November 8, 1955 – November 11, 1955) who was quickly removed by Minister of the Army Nereu Ramos who then served until January 31, 1956 when president-elect Juscelino Kubitschek was finally inaugurated.

Figure 101: *Construction of Brasília, 1959.*

Kubitschek, 1956-61

Kubitschek's presidency was marked by a time of political optimism. Campaigning on a platform of "fifty years of progress in five" he presented a plan of National Development that had 31 goals distributed in six large groups: energy, transport, food, base industries, education and the main goal - the construction of new capital city Brasilia. This plan sought to stimulate the diversification and expansion of the Brazilian economy, based on industrial expansion and closer integration of national territory. He promoted the development of the automobile industry, naval industry, heavy industry, and the construction of hydro-electric power stations. With the exception of the hydro-electric industry, Juscelino practically created an economy without state-owned companies.

Kubitschek sought to achieve this progress with the aid of foreign investment, which in turn would be given generous incentives, such as profit remittances, low taxes, privileges for the importation of machinery, and donations of land. However, the exemption was made only if the foreign capital was associated with the national capital ("associated capital"). This influx of foreign capital threatened domestic industry, which was unable to compete with efficiency and expertise of foreign companies. Domestic manufacturers, once the core base of support for economic nationalism, become managers or partners of the

Figure 102: *Construction of Palácio da Alvorada in Brasilia*

multinationals. The urban bourgeoisie — the original base of Vargas' coalition — had little use for Brazilian populism any more, having outgrown state planning phase.

In 1958 Brazil won the 1958 FIFA World Cup.

By the end of his term, the foreign debt had grown from 87 million dollars to 297 million dollars. The inflation and wealth inequality had grown larger, with the occurrence of rural-zone strikes that expanded to the urban areas.

Quadros, 1961

He was elected president of Brazil by a landslide in 1960, running as the candidate of National Labor Party (PTN). When Quadros took office on January 31, 1961 it was the first time since Brazil became a republic in 1889 that an incumbent government peacefully transferred power to an elected member of the opposition. It was also the first time in 31 years that the presidency was not held by an heir to the legacy of Getúlio Vargas.

Quadros laid the blame for the country's high rate of inflation on his predecessor, Juscelino Kubitschek. As president, Quadros outlawed gambling, banned women from wearing bikinis on the beach, and established relations with the Soviet Union and Cuba, trying to achieve a neutralist international policy. The re-establishment of relations with the Socialist Bloc in the middle of the Cold

War cost him the support of the UDN in Congress, so he was left with no real power.

Resignation crisis

Quadros resigned on August 25, 1961, citing foreign and "terrible forces" in his cryptic resignation letter. His resignation is commonly thought to have been a move to increase his power, expecting to return to the presidency by the acclamation of the Brazilian people or by the request of the National Congress of Brazil and the military. This maneuver, however, was immediately rejected by the Brazilian legislature, which accepted his resignation and called on the president of the Chamber of Deputies of Brazil, Pascoal Ranieri Mazzilli, to assume office until the vice president, João Goulart, came back from his trip to Communist China.

Goulart, 1961-64

Goulart faced strong opposition from conservative politicians and military officers in his bid to assume the Presidency. The crisis was solved by the "parliamentarian solution" - arrangement that decreased his powers as President by creating a new post of Prime Minister which was filled by Tancredo Neves and instituting a Parliamentary republic. Goulart finally assumed office on September 7, 1961.

Brazil returned to Presidential government in 1963 after a referendum, and, as Goulart's powers grew, it became evident that he would seek to implement "base reforms" (bottom-up reforms) such as land reform and nationalization of enterprises in various economic sectors (which would remove the nation from its antique latifundial economy, but that were considered communist reforms), regardless of assent from established institutions such as Congress (Goulart had low parliamentarian support, due to the fact that his centrist attempts to win support from both sides of the spectrum gradually came to alienate both).[660]

On April 1, 1964, after a night of conspiracy, rebel troops made their way to Rio de Janeiro, considered a legalist bastion. São Paulo's and Rio de Janeiro's generals were convinced to join the coup. To prevent a civil war, and in knowledge that the U.S. would openly support the army, the President fled first to Rio Grande do Sul, and then went to exile in Uruguay.

Contemporary era

Brazilian military government

United States of Brazil *Estados Unidos do Brasil* (1937–1967)
Federative Republic of Brazil *República Federativa do Brasil* (1967–1985)
Military dictatorship
1964–1985
 Flag  Coat of arms
Motto "Ordem e Progresso" "Order and Progress"
Anthem *Hino Nacional Brasileiro* (English: "Brazilian National Anthem")

Capital		Brasilia
Languages		Portuguese
Government		Federal two-party presidential republic (de jure) Authoritarian military dictatorship (de facto)
President		
•	1964–1967	Humberto de Alencar Castelo Branco
•	1967–1969	Artur da Costa e Silva
•	1969–1974	Emílio Garrastazu Médici
•	1974–1979	Ernesto Geisel
•	1979–1985	João Figueiredo
Junta		
•	1969	Aurélio de Lyra Tavares Augusto Hamann Rademaker Grünewald Márcio Melo
Legislature		National Congress
•	Upper house	Senate
•	Lower house	Chamber of Deputies
Historical era		Cold War
•	Military Coup d'État	31 March 1964
•	Adoption of dictatorship's Constitution	24 January 1967
•	Adoption of the AI-5	13 December 1968
•	Economic Miracle	1968-1973
•	Araguaia Guerrilla War	1966-1975
•	Democracy	15 March 1985
Area		
•	1903	8,515,767 km^2 (3,287,956 sq mi)

Brazilian military government 233

Population		
•	1970 est.	94,508,583
•	1980 est.	121,150,573
Currency		Cruzeiro
	Preceded by	Succeeded by
	Second Brazilian Republic	Brazil

- v
- t
- e[661]

The **Brazilian military government** was the authoritarian military dictatorship that ruled Brazil from April 1, 1964 to March 15, 1985. It began with the 1964 coup d'état led by the Armed Forces against the administration of the President João Goulart, who had assumed the office after being vice-president, upon the resignation of the democratically elected president Jânio Quadros, and ended when José Sarney took office on March 15, 1985 as President. The military revolt was fomented by Magalhães Pinto, Adhemar de Barros, and Carlos Lacerda (who had already participated in the conspiracy to depose

Getúlio Vargas in 1945), Governors of Minas Gerais, São Paulo, and Guanabara. The coup was also supported by the Embassy and State Department of the United States.[662]

The military dictatorship lasted for almost twenty-one years; despite initial pledges to the contrary, military governments in 1967 enacted a new, restrictive Constitution, and stifled freedom of speech and political opposition with support from the U.S. government. The regime adopted nationalism, economic development, and Anti-Communism as its guidelines.

The dictatorship reached the height of its popularity in the 1970s, with the so-called Brazilian Miracle (helped by much propaganda), even as the regime censored all media, tortured and banished dissidents. In March 1979, João Figueiredo became President, and while combating the "hard-line" and supporting a re-democratization policy, he couldn't control the chronic inflation and concurrent fall of other military dictatorships in South America. Brazilian Presidential elections of 1984 were won by opposition civilian candidates. In 1979 Figueiredo passed the Amnesty Law for political crimes committed for and against the regime. Since the 1988 Constitution was passed and Brazil returned to full democracy, the military have remained under control of civilian politicians, with no role in domestic politics.

Brazil's military regime provided a model for other military regimes and dictatorships around Latin America, systematizing the "Doctrine of National Security," which "justified" the military's actions as operating in the interest of National Security in a time of crisis, creating an intellectual basis upon which other military regimes relied.

Background

Brazil's political crisis stemmed from the way in which the political tensions had been controlled in the 1930s and 1940s during the Vargas Era. Vargas' dictatorship and the presidencies of his democratic successors marked different stages of Brazilian populism (1930–1964), an era of economic nationalism, state-guided modernization, and import substitution trade policies. Vargas' policies were intended to foster an autonomous capitalist development in Brazil, by linking industrialization to nationalism, a formula based on a strategy of reconciling the conflicting interests of the middle class, foreign capital, the working class, and the landed oligarchy.

Essentially, this was the epic of the rise and fall of Brazilian populism from 1930 to 1964: Brazil witnessed over the course of this time period the change from export-orientation of the First Brazilian Republic (1889–1930) to the import substitution of the populist era (1930–1964) and then to a moderate structuralism of 1964–80. Each of these structural changes forced a realignment in society and caused a period of political crisis. Period of right-wing military dictatorship marked the transition between populist era and the current period of democratization.

The Brazilian Armed Forces acquired great political clout after the Paraguayan War. The politicization of the Armed Forces was evidenced by the Proclamation of the Republic, which overthrew the Empire, or within Tenentismo (*Lieutenants' movement*) and the Revolution of 1930. Tensions escalated again in the 1950s, as important military circles (the "hard-line militars", old positivists whose origins could be traced back to the AIB and the Estado Novo) joined the elite, medium classes and right-wing activists in attempts to stop Presidents Juscelino Kubitschek and João Goulart from taking office, due to their supposed support for Communist ideology. While Kubitschek proved to be friendly to capitalist institutions, Goulart promised far-reaching reforms, expropriated business interests and promoted economical-political neutrality with the USA.

After Goulart suddenly assumed power in 1961, society became deeply polarized, with the elites fearing that Brazil would become another Cuba and join Communist Bloc, while many thought that the reforms would boost greatly the growth of Brazil and end its economical subservience with the USA, or even that Goulart could be used to increase the popularity of the Communist agenda. Influential politicians, such as Carlos Lacerda and even Kubitschek, media moguls (Roberto Marinho, Octávio Frias, Júlio de Mesquita Filho), the Church, landowners, businessmen, and the middle class called for a coup d'état by the Armed Forces to remove the government. The old "hard-line" army officers, seeing a chance to impose their positivist economic program, convinced the loyalists that Goulart was a communist menace.

Goulart and the fall of the Second Republic

After the Presidency of Juscelino Kubitschek, the right wing opposition elected Jânio Quadros, who based his electoral campaign on criticizing Kubitschek and government corruption. Quadros' campaign symbol was a broom, with which the president would "sweep away the corruption." In his brief tenure as president, Quadros made moves to resume relations with some communist countries, made some controversial laws and law proposals, but without legislative support, he couldn't follow his agenda.

In the last days of August 1961, Quadros tried to break the impasse by resigning from the presidency, apparently with the intention of being reinstated by popular demand. The Vice-president, João Goulart, member of PTB and active in politics since Vargas Era, at that time was outside the country visiting

Figure 103: *João Goulart, a lawyer, was the left-leaning President ousted by the Armed Forces. He fled to Uruguay, where his family owned estâncias.*

China. At that time Brazil's President and Vice President were elected from different party tickets. Some military top brass tried to prevent Goulart from assuming the Presidency, accusing him of being communist, but the legalist campaign in support of Goulart was already strong. The crisis was solved by the "parliamentarian solution" - arrangement that decreased his powers as President by creating a new post of Prime Minister which was filled by Tancredo Neves and instituting a Parliamentary republic.

Brazil returned to Presidential government in 1963 after a referendum, and, as Goulart's powers grew, it became evident that he would seek to implement "base reforms" (bottom-up reforms) such as land reform and nationalization of enterprises in various economic sectors (which would remove the nation from its antique latifundial economy, but that were considered communist reforms), regardless of assent from established institutions such as Congress (Goulart had low parliamentarian support, due to the fact that his centrist attempts to win support from both sides of the spectrum gradually came to alienate both).[663]

João Goulart also had no parliamentary support, and was forced to shift well to the left of his mentor Getúlio Vargas and was forced to mobilize the working class and even the peasantry amid falling urban bourgeois support. The core of Brazilian populism—economic nationalism—was no longer appealing to the middle classes.Wikipedia:Citation needed

Figure 104: *U.S. President John F. Kennedy (left) and President Goulart during a review of troops on April 3, 1962. Kennedy mulled possible military intervention in Brazil*

On April 1, 1964, after a night of conspiracy, rebel troops made their way to Rio de Janeiro, considered a legalist bastion. São Paulo's and Rio de Janeiro's generals were convinced to join the coup. To prevent a civil war, and in knowledge that the USA would openly support the army, the President fled first to Rio Grande do Sul, and then went to exile in Uruguay.

United States involvement

The US Ambassador Lincoln Gordon later admitted that the embassy had given money to anti-Goulart candidates in the 1962 municipal elections, and had encouraged the plotters; many extra United States military and intelligence personnel were operating in four United States Navy oil tankers and the aircraft carrier USS Forrestal, in an operation code-named Operation Brother Sam. These ships had positioned off the coast of Rio de Janeiro in case Brazilian troops required military assistance during the 1964 coup. A document from Gordon in 1963 to US president John F. Kennedy also describes the ways João Goulart should be put down, and his fears of a communist intervention supported by the Soviets or by Cuba.

Washington immediately recognized the new government in 1964, and hailed the coup d'état as one of the "democratic forces" that had allegedly staved off the hand of international communism. American mass media outlets like Henry Luce's TIME also gave positive remarks about the dissolution of political parties and salary controls at the beginning of Castello Branco mandate.[664]

Divisions within the officer corps

The armed forces' officer corps was divided between those who believed that they should confine themselves to their barracks, and the hard-liners who regarded politicians as willing to turn Brazil to communism. The victory of the hard-linersWikipedia:Manual of Style/Words to watch#Unsupported attributions dragged Brazil into what political scientist Juan J. Linz called "an authoritarian situation." However, because the hard-liners could not ignore the counterweight opinions of their colleagues or the resistance of society, they were unable to institutionalize their agenda politically. In addition, they did not attempt to eliminate liberal constitutionalism because they feared disapproval of international opinion and damage to their alignment with the United States. The United States as bastion of anticommunism during the Cold War, provided the ideology that the authoritarians used to justify their hold on power. Washington also preached liberal democracy, which forced the authoritarians to assume the contradictory position of defending democracy, while destroying it. Their concern for appearances caused them to abstain from personal dictatorship by requiring each successive general-president to hand over power to his replacement.

Establishing the regime, Castelo Branco

The Army could not find a civilian politician acceptable to all of the factions that supported the ouster of João Goulart. On April 9, 1964 coup leaders published the First Institutional Act, which greatly limited the freedoms of the 1946 constitution. President was granted authority to remove elected officials from office, dismiss civil servants, and revoke for 10 years the political rights of those found guilty of subversion or misuse of public funds. On April 11, 1964 the Congress elected the Army Chief of Staff, Marshal Humberto de Alencar Castelo Branco as President for the reminder of Goulart's term.

Castelo Branco had intentions of overseeing a radical reform of the political-economic system and then returning power to elected officials. He refused to remain in power beyond the remainder of Goulart's term or to institutionalize the military in power. However, competing demands radicalized the situation. Military "hard-line" wanted a complete purge of left-wing and populist influences while civilian politicians obstructed Castelo Branco's reforms. The latter accused him of hard-line actions to achieve his objectives, and the former accused him of leniency. On October 27, 1965, after victory of opposition candidates in two provincial elections, he signed the Second Institutional act which purged Congress, removed objectionable state governors and expanded President's arbitrary powers at the expense of the legislative and judiciary branches. This gave him the latitude to repress the populist left but also provided the subsequent governments of Artur da Costa e Silva (1967–69) and Emílio Garrastazu Médici (1969–74) with a "legal" basis for their hard-line authoritarian rule.

<templatestyles src="Template:Quote/styles.css"/>

> But this is no military dictatorship. If it were, Carlos Lacerda would never be allowed to say the things he says. Everything in Brazil is free — but controlled.
>
> – Minister of Transportation and colonel Mario Andreazza to journalist Carl Rowan, 1967

Castelo Branco, through extra-constitutional decrees dubbed "Institutional Acts" (Portuguese: "Ato Institucional" or "AI"), Castelo Branco gave the executive the unchecked ability to change the constitution and remove anyone from office ("AI-1") as well as to have the presidency elected by Congress. A two-party system was created - the ruling government-backed National Renewal Alliance (ARENA) and the mild not-leftist opposition Brazilian Democratic Movement (MDB) party ("AI-2"). In the new Constitution of 1967 the name of the country was changed from *Republic of the United States of Brazil* to *Federative Republic of Brazil*.

Hardening of the regime, Costa e Silva

Castelo Branco was succeeded to the Presidency by General Artur da Costa e Silva who was representative of hard-line elements of the regime. On December 13, 1968 he signed the Fifth Institutional Act that gave President dictatorial powers, dissolved Congress and state legislatures, suspended the constitution, and imposed censorship.[665] On August 31, 1969 Costa e Silva suffered a stroke. Instead of his Vice-president all state power was assumed by military joint, which then chose General Emílio Garrastazu Médici as the new President.

Figure 105: *A column of M41 Walker Bulldog tanks along the streets of Rio de Janeiro in April 1968.*

Figure 106: *Brazil: love it or leave it, a slogan of the military regime.*

Years of Lead, Medici

A hardliner, Médici sponsored the greatest human rights abuses of the time period. During his government, persecution and torture of dissidents, harassment against journalists and press censorship became ubiquitous. The succession of kidnappings of foreign ambassadors in Brazil embarrassed the military government. The anti-government manifestations and the action of guerrilla movements generated an increase in repressive measures. Urban guerrillas from Ação Libertadora Nacional and Revolutionary Movement 8th October

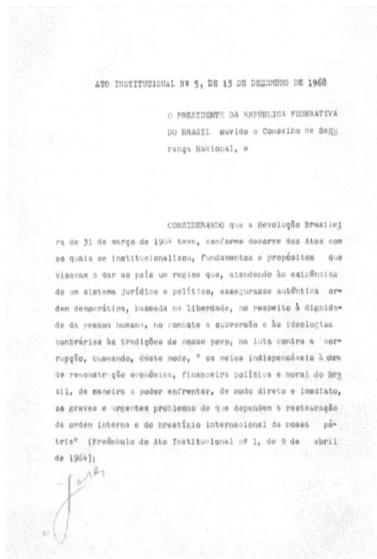

Figure 107: *First page of the Institutional Act Number Five*

were suppressed, and military operations undertaken to finish the Araguaia Guerrilla War.

The "ideological frontiers" of Brazilian foreign policy were reinforced. By the end of 1970, the official minimum wage went down to US$40/month, and the more than one-third of Brazilian workforce which had their wages tied to it lost about 50% of its purchasing power in relation to the 1960 levels[666] of the Juscelino Kubitschek administration.

Nevertheless, Médici was popular, as his term was met with the largest economic growth of any Brazilian President, the Brazilian Miracle unfolded and the country won the 1970 Football World Cup. In 1971 Médici presented the First National Development Plan aimed at increasing the rate of economic growth especially in remote Northeast and Amazonia. The results of his economic policy consolidated the option for the national-development model. Because of these results, the country's foreign economic connections were transformed, allowing its international presence to be broadened.

In November 1970 federal, state, and municipal elections were held. Most of the seats were won by ARENA candidates. In 1973 electoral college was created and in January 1974 General Ernesto Geisel was elected to be the next President.

Resistance

The fall of João Goulart worried many citizens. Many students, Marxists, and workers formed groups that opposed military rule. A minority of these adopted direct armed struggle, while most supported political solutions to the mass suspension of human rights. In the first few months after the coup, thousands people were detained, while thousands of others were removed from their civil service or university positions.

In 1968 there was a brief relaxation of the nation's repressive politics. Experimental artists and musicians formed the Tropicalia movement during this time. However, some of the major popular musicians Gilberto Gil and Caetano Veloso, for instance were arrested, imprisoned, and exiled. Chico Buarque left the country, in self-proclaimed exile.Wikipedia:Citation needed

The first signs of resistance to this repression were seen with the appearance of widespread student protests. In response, the government issued the Fifth Institutional Act in December 1968, which suspended habeas corpus, closed Congress, ended democratic government, and instituted other repressive features.

In 1969 the Revolutionary Movement 8th October kidnapped Charles Burke Elbrick, the U.S. ambassador to Brazil. The resistance fighters demanded the release of imprisoned dissidents who were being cruelly tortured in exchange for Ambassador Elbrick. The government responded by adopting more brutal measures of counter-insurgency, leading to the assassination of Carlos Marighela, a guerrilla leader, two months after Elbrick's kidnapping. This marked the beginning of the decline of armed opposition. In 1970, Nobuo Okuchi, Japanese consul general in São Paulo, was kidnapped, while Curtis C. Cutter, U.S. consul in Porto Alegre, was wounded in the shoulder but escaped kidnapping. Also in 1970, Ehrenfried von Holleben, West German Ambassador, was kidnapped in Rio and one of his bodyguards was killed.[667]

Torture

As early as 1964, the military government was already using the various forms of torture it devised systematically to not only gain information it used to crush opposition groups, but to intimidate and silence any further potential opponents. This radically increased after 1968.

While other dictatorships killed more people, Brazil's specialty was torture which they learned from Americans, but later learned interrogation techniques from the British. To extinguish its left-wing opponents, the dictatorship used

Figure 108: *Monument to the victims of torture in Recife*

arbitrary arrests, imprisonment without trials, kidnapping, and most of all, torture, which included rape and castration. The book *Torture in Brazil* provides accounts of only a fraction of the atrocities committed by the government.

The military government murdered hundreds of others, although this was done mostly in secret and the cause of death often falsely reported as accidental. The government occasionally dismembered and hid the bodies.

French General Paul Aussaresses, a veteran of the Algerian War, came to Brazil in 1973. General Aussaresses used "counter-revolutionary warfare" methods during the Battle of Algiers, including the systemic use of torture, executions and death flights. He later trained U.S. officers and taught military courses for Brazil's military intelligence. He later acknowledged maintaining close links with the military.[668]

So far nobody has been punished for these human rights violations, because of the 1979 Amnesty Law written by the members of the government who stayed in place during the transition to democracy. The law grants amnesty and impunity to any government official or citizen accused of political crimes during the dictatorship. Because of a certain "cultural amnesia" in Brazil, the victims have never garnered much sympathy, respect, or acknowledgement of their suffering.

Work is underway to alter the Amnesty Law, which has been condemned by the Inter-American Court of Human Rights. The National Truth Commission was created in 2011 attempting to help the nation face its past and honor those who fought for democracy, and to compensate the family members of those killed or disappeared. Its work was concluded in 2014. It reported that under military regime at least 191 people were killed and 243 "disappeared". The total number of deaths probably measures in the hundreds, not reaching but could be nearing one thousand, while more than 50,000 people were detained and 10,000 forced to go into exile.

According to the *Comissão de Direitos Humanos e Assistência Jurídica da Ordem dos Advogados do Brasil*, the "Brazilian death toll from government torture, assassination and 'disappearances' for 1964–81 was [...] 333, which included 67 killed in the Araguaia guerrilla front in 1972–74".[669] According to the Brazilian Army 97 military and civilians were killed by terrorist and guerrilla actions made by leftist groups during the same period.[670]

In a 2014 report by Brazil's National Truth Commission which documented the human rights abuses of the military government, it was noted that the United States "had spent years teaching the torture techniques to the Brazilian military during that period."[671]

Geisel administration, *distensão*, and the 1973 oil shock

It was in this atmosphere that retired General Ernesto Geisel (1974–79) was elected to Presidency with Médici's approval. Geisel was a well-connected Army General and former president of Petrobras.

There had been intense behind-the-scenes maneuvering by the hard-liners against him and by the more moderate supporters of Castelo Branco for him. Fortunately for Geisel, his older brother, Orlando Geisel was the Minister of Army, and his close ally, General João Baptista de Oliveira Figueiredo, was chief of Médici's military staff. Once in power, Geisel adopted a more moderate stance with regards to political opposition than his predecessor Médici.

Decompression policy

Although not immediately understood by civilians, Ernesto Geisel's accession signaled a move toward a less oppressive rule. He replaced several regional commanders with trusted officers and labeled his political programs *abertura* (opening) and *distensão* (decompression), meaning a gradual relaxation of authoritarian rule. It would be, in his words, "the maximum of development possible with the minimum of indispensable security."Wikipedia:Citation needed

Together with his Chief of Staff, Minister Golbery do Couto e Silva Geisel devised a plan of gradual, slow democratization that would eventually succeed despite all the threats and opposition from hard-liners.

However, the torture of the regime's left-wing and Communist opponents by DOI-CODI was still ongoing as demonstrated by the murder of Vladimir Herzog.

Geisel allowed opposition Brazilian Democratic Movement (MDB) to run an almost free election campaign before November 1974 elections and MDB won more votes than ever.

When opposition MDB party won more seats in 1976 Congress elections, Geisel in April 1977 used powers granted to him by AI-5, dismissed Congress and introduced a new package of laws (*April Package*), that made gubernatorial elections indirect and created an electoral college for electing the next President, thus safeguarding ARENA positions.

In 1977 and 1978 the Presidential succession issue caused further political confrontation with the hard-liners. In October 1977 he suddenly dismissed the far-right Minister of Army, General Sylvio Couto Coelho da Frota who had tried to become candidate for the next President.

In May 1978 Geisel had to deal with the first labor strikes since 1964. 500 000 workers, led by the future President Luiz Inacio Lula da Silva, demanded and won 11% wage increase.

By the end of his Presidency Geisel had allowed exiled citizens to return, restored habeas corpus, repealed the extraordinary powers, on December 1978 ended the Fifth Institutional Act, and imposed General João Figueiredo (1979–85) as his successor in March 1979.

Economy

President Geisel sought to maintain high economic growth rates of the Brazilian Miracle which were tied to maintaining the prestige of the regime, even while seeking to deal with the effects of the 1973 oil crisis. Geisel removed long-time Minister of Finance Antônio Delfim Netto. He maintained massive state investments in infrastructure—highways, telecommunications, hydroelectric dams, mineral extraction, factories, and atomic energy. All this required more international borrowing and increased state's debt.

Fending off nationalist objections, he opened Brazil to oil prospecting by foreign firms for the first time since the early 1950s.Wikipedia:Citation needed He also tried to reduce Brazil's reliance on oil, by signing a 10 billion USD

Figure 109: *A Dodge 1800 was the first prototype engineered with a neat ethanol-only engine. Exhibit at the Memorial Aeroespacial Brasileiro, CTA, São José dos Campos.*

agreement with West Germany to build eight nuclear reactors in Brazil. During this time ethanol production program was promoted as an alternative to gasoline and the first ethanol fueled cars were produced.

Brazil suffered drastic reductions in its terms of trade as a result of the 1973 oil crisis. In the early 1970s, the performance of the export sector was undermined by an overvalued currency. With the trade balance under pressure, the oil shock led to a sharply higher import bill. Thus, the Geisel government borrowed billions of dollars to see Brazil through the oil crisis. This strategy was effective in promoting growth, but it also raised Brazil's import requirements markedly, increasing the already large current-account deficit. The current account was financed by running up the foreign debt. The expectation was that the combined effects of import substitution industrialization and export expansion eventually would bring about growing trade surpluses, allowing the service and repayment of the foreign debt.Wikipedia:Citation needed

Brazil shifted its foreign policy to meet its economic needs. "Responsible pragmatism" replaced strict alignment with the United States and a worldview based on ideological frontiers and blocs of nations. Because Brazil was 80% dependent on imported oil, Geisel shifted the country from uncritical support

Figure 110: *The Brazilian Fiat 147 was the first modern automobile launched to the market capable of running on neat hydrous ethanol fuel (E100).*

Figure 111: *U.S. President Jimmy Carter addresses the Brazilian Congress, 30 March 1978*

Figure 112: *Pro-democracy Diretas Já demonstration in 1984.*

of Israel to a more neutral stance on Middle Eastern affairs. His government also recognized the People's Republic of China and the new socialist governments of Angola and Mozambique, both former Portuguese colonies. The government moved closer to Latin America, Europe, and Japan.

Brasil's intention to build nuclear reactors with West Germany's help created tensions with the US which did not want to see a nuclear Brazil. After election of Carter a greater emphasis was put on the human rights. The new Harkin Amendment limited American military assistance to countries with human rights violations. Brazilian right-wingers and military viewed this as incursion on Brazilian sovereignty and Geisel renounced any future military aid from United States in April 1977.

Transition to democracy, Figueiredo

President João Figueiredo steered the country back to democracy and promoted the transfer of power to civilian rule, facing opposition from hardliners in the military. Figueiredo was an Army General and former head of the secret service, National Intelligence Service of Brazil.

As president, he continued the gradual "abertura" (democratization) process that was begun in 1974. An amnesty law, signed by Figueiredo on 28 August 1979, amnestied those convicted of "political or related" crimes between 1961 and 1978. In the early 1980s, the military regime could no longer effectively maintain the two-party system established in 1966. The Figueiredo administration dissolved the government-controlled National Renewal Alliance Party (ARENA) and allowed new parties to be formed. The president was often incapacitated by illness and took two prolonged leaves for health treatment in 1981 and 1983, but the civilian vice president Antônio Aureliano Chaves de Mendonça did not enjoy major political power.

In 1981 the Congress enacted a law on restoration of direct elections of state governors. The general election of 1982 brought a narrow victory to ARENA's successor, pro-government Democratic Social Party (43.22% of the vote), while the opposition Brazilian Democratic Movement Party received 42.96% of votes. The governorship of three major states, São Paulo, Rio de Janeiro and Minas Gerais, was won by the opposition.

However, the political developments were overshadowed by increasing economic problems. As inflation and unemployment soared, the foreign debt reached massive proportions making Brazil the world's biggest debtor owing about US$90 billion to international lenders. The austerity program imposed by the government brought no signs of recovery for the Brazilian economy.

In 1984. Diretas Já demonstrators took over the country and epitomized the newly regained freedoms of assembly and expression, but the movement's primary objective was not attained, and the 1985 presidential election was held indirectly, via selected electoral college. The opposition vigorously struggled for passing a constitutional amendment that would allow direct popular Presidential elections in November 1984, but the proposal failed to win passage in the Congress. Opposition's candidate Tancredo Neves succeeded Figueiredo when Congress held an election for the new President.

Foreign relations

During this period Brazil's international agenda incorporated new perceptions. With nationalist military — who were State-control devotees — in power, there was increased energy for questioning the disparities of the international system. Interest in expanding state presence in the economy was accompanied by policies intended to transform Brazil's profile abroad. The relationship with the United States was still valued, but policy alignment was no longer total. Connections between Brazilian international activity and its economic interests led foreign policy, conducted by foreign minister José de Magalhães Pinto (1966–67), to be labeled "Prosperity Diplomacy."Wikipedia:Citation needed

This new emphasis of Brazil's international policy was followed by an appraisal of relations maintained with the United States in the previous years. It was observed that the attempted strengthening of ties had yielded limited benefits. A

Figure 113: *Presidents Emílio G. Médici (left) and Richard Nixon, December 1971.*

revision of the Brazilian ideological stand within the world system was added to this perception. This state of affairs was further enhanced by the momentary relaxation of the bipolar confrontation during détente.Wikipedia:Citation needed

In this context, it became possible to think of substituting the concept of limited sovereignty for full sovereignty. Development was made a priority for Brazilian diplomacy. These conceptual transformations were supported by the younger segments of Itamaraty (Ministry of External Relations), identified with the tenets of the independent foreign policy that had distinguished the early 1960s.Wikipedia:Citation needed

Based on the priorities of its foreign policy, Brazil adopted new positions in various international organizations. Its performance at the II Conference of the United Nations Conference on Trade and Development (UNCTAD) in 1968, in defense of non-discriminatory and preferential treatment for underdeveloped countries' manufactured goods, was noteworthy. The same level of concern distinguished the Brazilian stand at the Economic Commission for Latin America (ECLA) meeting in Viña del Mar (1969). On this occasion, Brazil voiced its support of a Latin American union project.Wikipedia:Citation needed

In the security sphere, disarmament was defended and the joint control system of the two superpowers condemned. Brazil was particularly critical of the Nuclear Non-Proliferation Treaty, with a view to guarantee the right to develop its own nuclear technology. This prerogative had already been defended previously, when the Brazilian government decided not to accept the validity of the Treaty for the Prohibition of Nuclear Weapons (TNP) in Latin America and the Caribbean. Brazil's position on the TNP became emblematic of the negative posture that it would, from then onwards, sustain regarding the power politics of the United States and the Soviet Union. Its initial detailing was influenced by the presence of João Augusto de Araújo Castro as ambassador to the UN and president of the Security Council in the years 1968–69. Brazil tried to strengthen its position with nuclear cooperation negotiated settlements with countries such as Israel (1966), France (1967), India (1968) and the United States (1972).Wikipedia:Citation needed

The changes in Brazilian diplomacy were to be also reflected in other matters on the international agenda, such as the moderate stance taken with regard to the "Six-Day War" between Arabs and Israelis. In the multilateral sphere, the country championed the cause of the reform of the United Nations Organization charter.Wikipedia:Citation needed

The expansion of Brazil's international agenda coincided with the administrative reform of the Ministry of External Relations. Its move to Brasília in 1971 was followed by internal modernization. New departments were created, responding to the diversification of the international agenda and the increasing importance of economic diplomacy. Examples include the creation of a trade promotion system (1973) and the Alexandre de Gusmão Foundation (1971) to develop studies and research foreign policy.Wikipedia:Citation needed

Foreign policy during the Gibson Barboza mandate (1969–74) united three basic positions. The first one, ideological, defended the existence of military governments in Latin America. To achieve that, the Organization of American States fought terrorism in the region. The second one criticized the distension process between the two superpowers, condemning the effects of American and Soviet power politics. The third requested support for development, considering that Brazil, with all its economic potential, deserved greater responsibility within the international system.Wikipedia:Citation needed

New demands and intentions appeared, related to the idea that the nation was strengthening its bargaining power in the world system. At international forums, its main demand became "collective economic security". The endeavor to lead Third World countries made Brazil value multilateral diplomacy. Efforts in this direction can be observed at the UN Conference on Environment (1972), the GATT meeting in Tokyo (1973) and the Law of the Sea Conference (1974).Wikipedia:Citation needed

This new Brazilian stance served as a base for the revival of its relationship with the United States. Differentiation from other Latin American countries was sought, to mean special treatment from the United States. Nevertheless, not only was this expectation not fulfilled but military assistance and the MEC-USAID educational cooperation agreement were interrupted.Wikipedia:Citation needed

Washington held itself aloof at the time of President Médici's visit to the United States in 1971. In response, especially in the military and diplomatic spheres, nationalist ideas were kindled and raised questions about the alignment policy with the United States.Wikipedia:Citation needed

The presence of J.A. de Araújo Castro as ambassador to Washington contributed to the re-definition of relations with the American government. The strategic move was to try to expand the negotiation agenda by paying special attention to the diversification of trade relations, the beginning of nuclear cooperation, and the inclusion of new international policy themes.Wikipedia:Citation needed

In 1971 the military dictatorship helped rig Uruguayan elections, which *Frente Amplio*, a left-wing political party, lost.Wikipedia:Identifying reliable sources The government participated in Operation Condor, which involved various Latin American security services (including Pinochet's DINA and the Argentine SIDE) in the assassination of political opponents.

During this period, Brazil began to devote more attention to less-developed countries. Technical cooperation programs were initiated in Latin America and in Africa, accompanied in some cases by State company investment projects – in particular in the fields of energy and communication. With this pretext, an inter-ministerial system was created by Itamaraty and the Ministry of Planning, whose function it was to select and coordinate international cooperation projects. To foster these innovations, in 1972 foreign minister Gibson Barboza visited Senegal, Togo, Ghana, Dahomey, Gabon, Zaïre, Nigeria, Cameroon and Côte d'Ivoire.Wikipedia:Citation needed

However, the prospect of economic interests and the establishment of cooperation programs with these countries was not followed by a revision of the Brazilian position on the colonial issue. Traditional loyalty was still towards Portugal. Attempts were made to consolidate the creation of a Portuguese-Brazilian community.Wikipedia:Citation needed

Timeline

- April 1964 - the coup.
- October 1965 - political parties abolished, creation of two party system.
- October 1965 - Presidential elections to be indirect.
- January 1967 - a new Constitution.
- March 1967 - Costa e Silva takes office.
- November 1967 - opposition starts armed resistance.
- March 1968 - beginning of student protests.
- December 1968 - Institutional Act Nr.5.
- September 1969 - Medici selected as President.
- October 1969 - a new Constitution.
- January 1973 - armed resistance suppressed.
- June 1973 - Medici announces Geisel as his successor.
- March 1974 - Geisel takes office.
- August 1974 - political relaxation announced.
- November 1974 - MDB wins in Senate elections.
- April 1977 - National Congress dismissed.
- October 1977 - Head of the Armed Forces dismissed.
- January 1979 - Institutional Act Nr. 5 dismissed.
- March 1979 - Figueiredo takes office.
- November 1979 - two party system of ARENA and MDB ended.
- November 1982 - opposition wins Lower house of Parliament.
- April 1984 - amendment for direct Presidential elections defeated.
- March 1985 - Jose Sarney takes office.

References

Sources

- Kirsch, Bernard (1990). *Revolution in Brazil*. New York: Basic Books. ISBN 0-19-506316-3.

Further reading

- *The Politics of Military Rule in Brazil 1964-1985*, by Thomas E. Skidmore (1988).
- *The Political System of Brazil: Emergence of a "Modernizing" Authoritarian Regime, 1964–1970*, by Ronald M. Schneider (1973).
- *The Military in Politics: Changing Patterns in Brazil*, by Alfred Stepan (1974).
- *Brazil and the Quiet Intervention: 1964*, by Phyllis R. Parker (1979).

- *Mission in Mufti: Brazil's Military Regimes, 1964–1985*, by Wilfred A. Bacchus (1990).
- *Eroding Military Influence in Brazil: Politicians Against Soldiers*, by Wendy Hunter (1997).
- *Brazil, 1964-1985: The Military Regimes of Latin America in the Cold War* by Herbert S. Klein and Francisco Vidal Luna (2017).

Film documentaries

- *Beyond Citizen Kane* by Simon Hartog (1993)

External links

- Declassified documents from US Department of State and CIA about the 1964 coup[672]

History of Brazil since 1985

Part of a series on the
History of Brazil

Brazil portal
- v
- t
- e[673]

Brazilian history since 1985 is the contemporary epoch in the history of Brazil, beginning when civilian government was restored after a 21-year-long military regime established after the 1964 coup d'etat. The negotiated transition to democracy reached its climax with the indirect election of Tancredo Neves PMDB by Congress. Neves belonged to Brazilian Democratic Movement Party, an opposition party that had always opposed the military regime. He was the first civilian president to be elected since 1964.

Neves was set to over from General João Figueiredo, the last of the military junta presidents appointed by their predecessor. The transition was hailed as the dawn of a **New Republic** (*Nova República*) in contrast with *República Velha* (Old Republic), the first epoch of the Brazilian Republic, from 1889 until 1930. It became synonymous with the contemporary phase of the Brazilian Republic and the political institutions established in the wake of the country's re-democratization.

President-elect Tancredo Neves fell ill on the eve of his inauguration and could not attend it. His running mate, José Sarney, was inaugurated as vice president and served in Neves' stead as acting president the latter's death without having ever taken the oath of office. Sarney then succeeded to the presidency. The first phase of the Brazilian *New Republic*, ranging from the inauguration of José Sarney in 1985 until the inauguration of Fernando Collor in 1990, is often considered a transitional period as the 1967–1969 constitution remained in effect, the executive still had veto powers, and the president was able to rule by decree. The transition was considered definitive after Brazil's current constitution, drawn up in 1988, entered full effect in 1990.

In 1986, elections were called for a National Constituent Assembly that would draft and adopt a new Constitution for the country. The Constituent Assembly began deliberations in February 1987 and concluded its work on October 5, 1988. Brazil's current Constitution was promulgated in 1988 and completed the democratic institutions. The new Constitution replaced the authoritarian legislation that still remained from the military regime.

In 1989 Brazil held its first elections for president by direct popular ballot since the 1964 coup. Fernando Collor won election and was inaugurated on March 15, 1990 as the first president elected under the 1988 Constitution.

Since then, six presidential terms have elapsed, without rupture to the constitutional order:

- the first term was served by Presidents Collor and Franco. Collor was impeached on charges of corruption in 1992 and resigned the presidency, being succeeded by Itamar Franco, his vice president
- the second and third terms corresponded to the Fernando Henrique Cardoso administration, from 1995 to 2002;
- in the fourth and fifth presidential terms Luiz Inácio Lula da Silva served as President;
- the sixth term was Dilma Rousseff's first administration.
- the seventh term was started following Rousseff's 2014 reelection. Her second term was due to end in 2018, but she was impeached for violations of budgetary and fiscal responsibility laws in 2016. Her vice-president, Michel Temer succeeded her on 31 August 2016 following a lengthy period as acting president during Rousseff's impeachment trials and is the current President of Brazil.

Transition towards democracy

The last military president, João Figueiredo signed a general amnesty into law and turned Geisel's *distensão* into a gradual *abertura* (the "opening" of the political system), saying he wanted "to make this country a democracy".

The transition towards democracy that ended the military regime in 1985 and spurred the adoption of a new, democratic, Constitution in 1988, was, however, troubled.

Hard-liners reacted to the *abertua* with a series of terrorist bombings. In April 1981 after a long string of bombings and other violence a bomb went off prematurely and killed one of the men in car with it and badly injured the other. They were shown to be working with the DOI-CODI "under the direct orders of the "Command of the First Army" in terrorism, but nobody was punished. The incident and the regime's inaction strengthened the public's resolve to end military rule. Moreover, Figueiredo faced other significant problems, such as soaring inflation, declining productivity, and mounting foreign debt.

The 1980's "lost decade": stagnation, inflation, and crisis

Political liberalization and the declining world economy contributed to Brazil's economic and social problems. In 1978 and 1980, huge strikes took place in the industrial ring around São Paulo. Protesters asserted that wage increases indexed to the inflation rate were far below an acceptable standard of living. Union leaders, including the future three-time presidential candidate and president Luís Inácio da Silva, were arrested for violating national security laws. The International Monetary Fund (IMF) imposed a painful austerity program on Brazil. Under that program, Brazil was required to hold down wages to fight inflation. In the north, northeast, and even in relatively prosperous Rio Grande do Sul, impoverished rural people occupied unused private land, forcing the government to create a new land reform ministry. Tension with the Roman Catholic Church, the major voice for societal change, peaked in the early 1980s with the expulsion of foreign priests involved in political and land reform issues.

To attack the soaring debt, Figueiredo's administration stressed exports — food, natural resources, automobiles, arms, clothing, shoes, even electricity — and expanded petroleum exploration by foreign companies. In foreign relations, the objective was to establish ties with any country that would contribute to Brazilian economic development. Washington was kept at a certain distance, and the North-South dialogue was emphasized.

In 1983, the economy floundered as the gross domestic product declined by 5.0%, the impact of which was accelerated by rising inflation and the failure of political leadership. Figueiredo's heart condition led to bypass surgery in the United States, removing him from control of the situation. In an impressive display, millions of Brazilians took to the streets in all the major cities demanding a direct vote (Diretas Já!) in the choice of the next president. In April 1984, Congress failed to achieve the necessary numbers to give the people their wish, and the choice was left to an electoral college. Figueiredo did not act forcefully to back a preference, so it became a scramble as candidates pursued the collegial votes.

Transitional period: Tancredo's election, restoration of civilian government, the Sarney years and the 1988 Constitution

In 1984, many public demonstrations were held in major Brazilian cities which made it clear that military rule could not continue. Brazilians started to demand change in the electoral system, aiming to directly elect the President (Diretas Já). As public pressure built up, the opposition Brazilian Democratic Movement Party (*Partido do Movimento Democrático Brasileiro*, PMDB) proposed a legislation to implement this change (Proposta de Emenda Constitucional Dante de Oliveira). As Congress was controlled by the pro-government Democratic Social Party (PDS, formerly ARENA), the law failed to pass.

Tancredo Neves of Minas Gerais, Getúlio Vargas' minister of justice in the 1950s, and former federal deputy, senator, and prime minister, seized the momentum. Neves had a reputation for honesty and was able to build up an alliance between the PMDB and defectors from the PDS who founded the Liberal Front Party (PFL). The Democratic Alliance (Aliança Democrática) presented itself as supporting 1984 demands for political change and the end of military rule.

The party presented Neves as an opposition candidate against Paulo Maluf. Neves was elected by a majority vote of the Parliament on January 15, 1985. However, Neves collapsed the night before his inauguration in March, and died on April 21, so the presidency passed to Vice President José Sarney (president, 1985–90), long-time supporter of the military regime. The hope that 1985 would provide a quick transition to a new regime faded as Brazilians watched the turn of events in a state of shock. Like the regime changes of 1822, 1889, 1930, 1946, and 1964, the 1985 change also proved to be long and difficult.

Sarney's government fulfilled Tancredo's promise of to amend the Constitution inherited from the military regime and to call elections for a National Constituent Assembly with full powers to draft and enact a new democratic constitution for the country. Ulysses Guimarães, who led the civilian resistance to the military rule, was chosen by his fellow Assembly members to preside over the Constituent Assembly, which sat in session from February 1987 to October 1988.

The Constituent Assembly proclaimed a new constitution in October 1988 and restored civil and public rights such as freedom of speech, independent public prosecutors (Ministério Público), economic freedom, direct and free elections and universal healthcare. It also de-centralized government, empowering local and state governments.

As the political transition developed, the economy suffered high inflation and stagnation.[674] Sarney tried to control inflation with many economic plans: Plano Cruzado 1, Plano Cruzado 2, Plano Verão. All of them included government price controls, price freezes and ultimately a change in the national currency. During Sarney's presidency, Brazil had three currency units: the cruzeiro, the cruzado and the cruzado novo. Economic domestic troubles led to default on Brazil's international debt in 1988. This closed international financial markets for Brazil and its economic situation worsened.

Despite the initial decrease, inflation returned higher than before the economic plans, reaching 84% a month in 1990. The government's inability to deal with inflation ultimately led parties that had led the political transition to lose the 1989 elections, the first elections under the new Constitution and the first presidential elections to take place by direct popular ballot since the 1964 military coup.

Collor and Franco administrations

The first direct presidential election after 29 years was held on October 15, 1989 (first round) and November 15, 1989 (second round). Fernando Collor de Mello won the run-off election with 53% of the vote for a five-year term.

Collor's agenda focused on the fighting corruption from Sarney's administration and completing the transition from the 21 years of military rule to civilian government. Economic changes aimed to control soaring inflation and modernization.

Although he had massive support amongst the voters, the administration had a small parliamentary base as Collor's recently founded party had few deputies and no senators and faced fierce opposition from parties that had splintered from the Democratic Alliance: the Brazilian Democratic Movement Party (PMDB), Liberals (PFL), and Social Democrats (Brazilian Social Democracy Party, PSDB).

His first act was known as Plano Collor: all savings accounts and financial investment were frozen, and the national currency was changed from the cruzado novo to the cruzeiro (NCz$1,000 = Cr$1). Plano Collor initially succeeded, but after six months failed in its primary goal, as inflation accelerated again.

This started to erode Collor's prestige. Economic changes included lifting import barriers, exposing local companies to international competition. Many companies went bankrupt or were sold, unemployment grew and support for the government deteriorated.

Parliamentary elections were held on October 15, 1990 and the government failed to win a reliable base in Congress and the president began to lose political support.

In May 1991, Collor's brother Pedro Collor accused him of corruption, specifically of condoning an influence peddling scheme run by his campaign treasurer, Paulo César Farias. Congress and the Federal Police of Brazil began an investigation. Some months later, with the investigation progressing and under fire, Collor went on national television to ask for the people's support, by going out on the street and protesting against coup forces. On August 11, 1992, students organized by the União Nacional dos Estudantes (UNE), thousands of students protested on the streets against Collor. They often painted their faces, frequently in a mixture of the colors of the flag and protest-black, which led to calling them *"Caras-pintada"* (Painted Faces).[675]

On August 26, 1992, the final congressional inquiry report was released, where it was proven that Fernando Collor had personal expenses paid for by money raised by Paulo César Farias through his influence peddling scheme. Impeachment proceedings began in the lower house of congress on September 29, 1992. Collor was impeached, and subsequently removed from office by a vote of 441 for and 38 votes against.[676] Fernando Collor resigned his term in office just before the Brazilian Senate was to vote for his impeachment. The senate voted to impeach him anyway, suspending his political rights for eight years.[677]

His vice-president, Itamar Franco, assumed the presidency for the remainder of Collor's term.

Franco distanced himself from Collor and made arrangements for a coalition government that included the main leaders from the PMDB, PFL, and PSDB. Franco appointed Fernando Henrique Cardoso as Minister of Treasury and gave him the responsibility of controlling inflation – the average annual inflation rate from 1990 to 1995 was 764%. Cardoso put together a successful stabilization program, Plano Real, that brought inflation to 6% annually. Franco's approval ratings rose and he supported Cardoso to succeed him.

In the October 3, 1994 presidential elections, Fernando Henrique Cardoso was elected with 54% of the votes.

Figure 114: *President Fernando Henrique Cardoso (1995–2002)*

FHC administration

Fernando Henrique Cardoso started his first term on January 1, 1995 and was reelected in 1998. President Cardoso sought to establish the basis for long-term stability and growth and to reduce Brazil's extreme socioeconomic imbalances. His proposals to Congress included constitutional amendments to open the Brazilian economy to greater foreign investment and to implement sweeping reforms – including social security, government administration, and taxation – to reduce excessive public sector spending and improve government efficiency.

His government is credited with providing economic stability to a country marred by years of hyperinflation. At the same time the Mexican, 1997 East Asian, 1998 Russian and 1999–2002 Argentinian economic crises diminished the prospects for economic growth during his presidency.

During his administration many state-owned companies were privatized, and agencies created for the first time to regulate many sectors of industry such as energy, oil, and aviation. Cardoso's administration also put a strong focus on external affairs. In addition to acceding to the WTO and participating in the Uruguay Round, Brazil participated in the INTERFET peacekeeping mission to East Timor.

Figure 115: *President Luíz Inácio Lula da Silva (2003–2010)*

Lula administration

In 2002, Luiz Inácio Lula da Silva of the Workers' Party (PT) won the presidency with more than 60% of the national vote. In the first months of his term, inflation rose perilously, reflecting the markets' uncertainty about the government's monetary policy. However, the markets' confidence in the government was regained as Lula chose to maintain his predecessor's policies, meaning the continuation of Central Bank's task of keeping inflation down. Since then, the country has undergone considerable economic growth and employment expansion. On the other hand, Lula's mainstream economic policies disappointed his most radical leftist allies, which led to a schism in the PT (Workers' Party) that resulted in the creation of PSOL.

In 2005, Roberto Jefferson, chairman of the Brazilian Labour Party (PTB), was implicated in a bribery case. As a Parliamentary Commission of Inquiry was set up, Jefferson testified that the MPs were being paid monthly stipends to vote for government-backed legislation. In August of the same year, after further investigation, campaign manager Duda Mendonça admitted that he had used illegal undeclared money to finance the PT electoral victory of 2002. The money in both cases was found to have originated from private sources as well as from the advertising budget of state-owned enterprises headed by political appointees, both laundered through Duda's Mendonça advertising agency.

These incidents were dubbed the Mensalão scandal. On August 24, 2007, the Brazilian Supreme Court (Supremo Tribunal Federal) accepted the indictments of 40 individuals relating to the Mensalão scandal, most of whom were former or current federal deputies, and all of whom were still allies of the Brazilian president.[678]

The loss of support resulting from these scandals was outweighed by the president's popularity among voters of the lower classes, whose income per capita was increased as a consequence of higher employment, the expansion of domestic credit to consumers and government social welfare programs. The stable and solid economic situation of the country, which Brazil had not experienced in the previous 20 years, with fast growth in production both for internal consumers and exports as well as a soft but noticeable decrease in social inequality, may also partially explain the popularity of Lula's administration even after several corruption scandals involving important politicians connected to Lula and to PT. Hence Lula's re-election in 2006: After almost winning in the first round, Lula won the run-off against Geraldo Alckmin of the PSDB (Brazilian Social Democracy Party), by 20 million votes.

Following Lula's second victory, his approval ratings rose again, fueled by continued of the economical and social achievements, to a record 80%, the highest for a Brazilian president since the end of the military regime. The focus of Lula's second term was further stimulation of the economy by investments in infrastructure and measures to keep expanding domestic credit to producers, industry, commerce and consumers alike. In 2009, Brazil's economic rise was temporarily halted by the worldwide financial crisis, forcing the government to implement a temporary tax relief policy in strategic segments of the economy like automobiles and construction. These measures helped the country prevent a long-term recession and ensured a quick recovery to Brazil's economic ascension.

Another mark of Lula's second term was his effort to expand Brazil's political influence worldwide, especially after G20 (in which Brazil and other emerging economies participate) replaced the G8 as the main world forum of discussions. Just like his predecessor, he was an active defender of reform of the United Nations Security Council. Brazil is one of four nations (the others being Germany, India and Japan) officially coveting a permanent seat on the council. Lula saw himself as a friendly, peacemaker and conciliator head of atate. Managing to befriend leaders of rival countries from the likes of Presidents George W. Bush and Barack Obama from the United States to Venezuelan leader Hugo Chávez, Cuban former president Fidel Castro, President of Bolivia Evo Morales, and Iranian President Mahmoud Ahmadinejad, fueling protests inside and outside the country due to Ahmadinejad's polemical anti-Semitic statements. Lula took part in a deal with the governments of Turkey and Iran

Figure 116: *President Dilma Rousseff (2011-2016)*

regarding Iran's nuclear program despite the United States' (among other nuclear powers) desire to strengthen the sanctions against the country, fearing the possibility of Iran develop nuclear weapons.Wikipedia:Citation needed

During the Lula administration the Brazilian Army's most important assignment was being the main force of the United Nations Stabilization Mission in Haiti, established to bring aid to the Haitian population, and it suffered many casualties during the 2010 Haiti earthquake which claimed hundreds of thousands of lives.

Rousseff administration

On October 31, 2010, Dilma Rousseff, also from the Worker's Party, was the first woman elected President of Brazil, with her term beginning in the January 1, 2011. In her victory speech, Rousseff, who had also been a key member of Lula's administration, made clear that her mission during her term would be to continue her predecessor's policies to mitigate poverty and ensure continued economic growth.

Challenges faced by Rousseff in her first term included managing infrastructure projects to increase economic activity, with special attention to the twelve cities that would host the upcoming 2014 FIFA World Cup in Brazil, especially Rio de Janeiro, a special case as it would also hold the 2016 Summer Olympics, as well as measures to protect the Brazilian economy from the ongoing economic crises in Europe and the United States. These contributed to reducing the growth of national GDP during the first half of her term, compared to her predecessor's tenure.

On June 2011, Rouseff announced a program called "Brasil Sem Miséria" (Brazil Without Poverty), with the ambitious goal of drastically reducing absolute poverty in Brazil by the end of her term. Poverty afflicted 16 million people, a little less than a tenth of the population. The program involved broadening the Bolsa Família social welfare program and creating new job opportunities and establishing professional certification programs. In 2012, another program labeled "Brasil Carinhoso" (Tenderful Brazil) was launched with the objective of providing extra care to all children in Brazil who lived below the poverty threshold.

Despite criticism from the domestic and international press regarding lower-than-expected economic results achieved during her first term as head of the government and of the measures taken to solve it, Rouseff's approval rates reached levels higher than any other president since the end of the military regime until a wave of protests struck the country in mid 2013 reflecting dissatisfaction from the people with current transport, healthcare and education policies, among other issues affecting the popularity not only of the president, but of several other governors and mayors from key areas in the country as well.

In 2014, Rousseff won a second term by a narrow margin, but failed to prevent her popularity from falling. In June 2015, her approval dropped to less than 10%, after another wave of protests, this time organized by opponents who wanted her out of power, amid revelations that numerous politicians, including some from her party, were being investigated for accepting bribes from the state-owned energy company Petrobras from 2003 to 2010, while she was on the company's board of directors.

Temer administration

After a process of impeachment opened against Rousseff in late 2015 culminated with her temporarily removed from power in May 12, 2016 with Vice President Michel Temer assuming temporarily until the final trial was concluded in August 31, 2016, when Rousseff was officially impeached and Temer was sworn President until the end of the term. During the Impeachment process, Brazil hosted the 2016 Summer Olympics.

Geography

Geography of Brazil

Geography of Brazil

Continent	South America
Coordinates	10°S 55°W[679]Coordinates: 10°S 55°W[679]
Area	Ranked 5th
• Total	8,514,877 km² (3,287,612 sq mi)
• Land	99.34%
• Water	0.66%
Coastline	7,491 km (4,655 mi)
Borders	Argentina 1,263 km (785 mi) Bolivia 3,403 km (2,115 mi) Colombia 1,790 km (1,110 mi) French Guiana 649 km (403 mi) Guyana 1,308 km (813 mi) Paraguay 1,371 km (852 mi) Peru 2,659 km (1,652 mi) Suriname 515 km (320 mi) Uruguay 1,050 km (650 mi) Venezuela 2,137 km (1,328 mi)
Highest point	Pico da Neblina 2,995.30 m (9,827 ft)
Lowest point	Atlantic Ocean, 0 m (0 ft)

Longest river	Amazon River, 6,992 km (4,345 mi)
Largest lake	Lagoa dos Patos 9,850 km² (3,803 sq mi)
Climate	North: tropical, South: temperate
Terrain	Coastal mountain ranges, vast central plateau (Planalto Central), remainder is primarily sedimentary basins
Natural Resources	bauxite, gold, iron ore, manganese, nickel, phosphates, platinum, tin, clay, rare earth elements, uranium, petroleum, hydropower and timber
Natural Hazards	recurring droughts in northeast; floods and occasional frost in south
Environmental Issues	deforestation in the Amazon basin, illegal wildlife trade, illegal poaching, air and water pollution, land degradation and water pollution caused by mining activities, wetland degradation and severe oil spills

The country of **Brazil** occupies roughly half of South America, bordering the Atlantic Ocean. Brazil covers a total area of 8,514,215 km² (3,287,357 sq mi) which includes 8,456,510 km² (3,265,080 sq mi) of land and 55,455 km² (21,411 sq mi) of water. The highest point in Brazil is Pico da Neblina at 2,994 m (9,823 ft). Brazil is bordered by the countries of Argentina, Bolivia, Colombia, Guyana, Paraguay, Peru, Suriname, Uruguay, Venezuela, and France (overseas department of France, French Guiana).

Much of the climate is tropical, with the south being relatively temperate. The largest river in Brazil, the second longest in the world, is the Amazon.

Size and geographical location

Brazil occupies most of the eastern part of the South American continent and its geographic heartland (48% of South America), as well as various islands in the Atlantic Ocean. The only countries in the world that are larger are Russia, Canada, China, and the United States. The national territory extends 4,395 kilometers (2,731 mi) from north to south (5°16'20" N to 33°44'32" S latitude), and 4,319 kilometers (2,684 mi) from east to west (34°47'30" W to 73°59'32" W longitude). It spans three time zones, the westernmost of which is one hour ahead of Eastern Standard Time in the United States. The time zone of the capital (Brasília) and of the most populated part of Brazil along the east coast (UTC-3) is two hours ahead of Eastern Standard Time, except when it is on its own daylight saving time, from October to February. The Atlantic islands are in the easternmost time zone.

Brazil possesses the archipelago of Fernando de Noronha, located 350 kilometers (217 mi) northeast of its "horn", and several small islands and atolls in the Atlantic - Abrolhos, Atol das Rocas, Penedos de São Pedro e São Paulo,

Trindade, and Martim Vaz. In the early 1970s, Brazil claimed a territorial sea extending 362 kilometers (225 mi) from the country's shores, including those of the islands.

On Brazil's east coast, the Atlantic coastline extends 7,367 kilometers (4,578 mi). In the west, in clockwise order from the south, Brazil has 15,719 kilometers (9,767 mi) of borders with Uruguay, Argentina, Paraguay, Bolivia, Peru, Colombia, Venezuela, Guyana, Suriname, and French Guiana (overseas department of France). The only South American countries with which Brazil does not share borders are Chile and Ecuador. A few short sections are in question, but there are no true major boundary controversies with any of the neighboring countries.

Brazil has six major ecosystems: the Amazon Basin, a tropical rainforest system; the Pantanal bordering Paraguay and Bolivia, a tropical wetland system; the Cerrado, a savanna system that covers much of the center of the country; the Caatinga or thorny scrubland habitat of the Northeast; the Atlantic Forest (Mata Atlântica) that extends along the entire coast from the Northeast to the South; and the Pampas or fertile lowland plains of the far South.

Geology, geomorphology and drainage

In contrast to the Andes, which rose to elevations of nearly 7,000 meters (22,966 ft) in a relatively recent epoch and inverted the Amazon's direction of flow from westward to eastward, Brazil's geological formation is very old. Precambrian crystalline shields cover 36% of the territory, especially its central area. The dramatic granite sugarloaf mountains in the city of Rio de Janeiro are an example of the terrain of the Brazilian shield regions, where continental basement rock has been sculpted into towering domes and columns by tens of millions of years of erosion, untouched by mountain-building events.

The principal mountain ranges average elevations just under 2,000 meters (6,562 ft). The Serra do Mar Range hugs the Atlantic coast, and the Serra do Espinhaço Range, the largest in area, extends through the south-central part of the country. The highest mountains are in the Tumucumaque, Pacaraima, and Imeri ranges, among others, which traverse the northern border with the Guianas and Venezuela.

In addition to mountain ranges (about 0.5% of the country is above 1,200 m or 3,937 ft), Brazil's Central Highlands include a vast central plateau (Planalto Central). The plateau's uneven terrain has an average elevation of 1,000 meters (3,281 ft). The rest of the territory is made up primarily of sedimentary basins, the largest of which is drained by the Amazon and its tributaries. Of the total territory, 41% averages less than 200 meters (656 ft) in elevation.

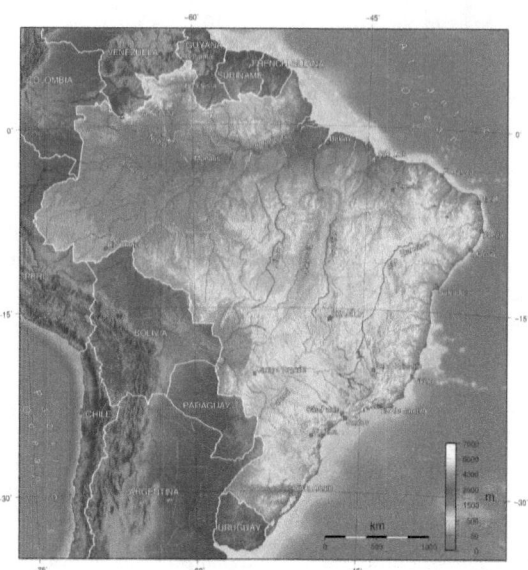

Figure 117: *Topographic map of Brazil*

The coastal zone is noted for thousands of kilometers of tropical beaches interspersed with mangroves, lagoons, and dunes, as well as numerous coral reefs.Wikipedia:Citation needed The Parcel de Manuel Luís Marine State Park off the coast of Maranhão protects the largest coral reef in South America.

Brazil has one of the world's most extensive river systems, with eight major drainage basins, all of which drain into the Atlantic Ocean. Two of these basins — the Amazon and Tocantins-Araguaia account for more than half the total drainage area. The largest river system in Brazil is the Amazon, which originates in the Andes and receives tributaries from a basin that covers 45.7% of the country, principally the north and west. The main Amazon river system is the Amazonas-Solimões-Ucayali axis (the 6,762-kilometer (4,202 mi)-long Ucayali is a Peruvian tributary), flowing from west to east. Through the Amazon Basin flows one-fifth of the world's fresh water. A total of 3,615 kilometers (2,246 mi) of the Amazon are in Brazilian territory. Over this distance, the waters decline only about 100 meters (330 ft). The major tributaries on the southern side are, from west to east, the Javari, Juruá, Purus (all three of which flow into the western section of the Amazon called the Solimões), Madeira, Tapajós, Xingu, and Tocantins. On the northern side, the largest tributaries are the Branco, Japurá, Jari, and Rio Negro. The above-mentioned tributaries carry more water than the Mississippi (its discharge is less than one-tenth that of the Amazon). The Amazon and some of its tributaries, called "white" rivers, bear rich sediments and hydrobiological elements. The black-white and clear rivers—such as the Negro, Tapajós, and Xingu—have clear (greenish) or dark water with few nutrients and little sediment.

The major river system in the Northeast is the Rio São Francisco, which flows 1,609 kilometers (1,000 mi) northeast from the south-central region. Its basin covers 7.6% of the national territory. Only 277 kilometers (172 mi) of the lower river are navigable for oceangoing ships. The Paraná system covers 14.5% of the country. The Paraná flows south among the Río de la Plata Basin, reaching the Atlantic between Argentina and Uruguay. The headwaters of the Paraguai, the Paraná's major eastern tributary, constitute the Pantanal, the largest contiguous wetlands in the world, covering as much as 230,000 square kilometers (89,000 sq mi).

Below their descent from the highlands, many of the tributaries of the Amazon are navigable. Upstream, they generally have rapids or waterfalls, and boats and barges also must face sandbars, trees, and other obstacles. Nevertheless, the Amazon is navigable by oceangoing vessels as far as 3,885 kilometers (2,414 mi) upstream, reaching Iquitos in Peru. The Amazon river system was the principal means of access until new roads became more important. Hydroelectric projects are Itaipu, in Paraná, with 12,600 MW; Tucuruí, in Pará, with 7,746 MW; and Paulo Afonso, in Bahia, with 3,986 MW.

Natural resources

Natural resources include: bauxite, gold, iron ore, manganese, nickel, phosphates, platinum, tin, clay, rare earth elements, uranium, petroleum, hydropower and timber.

Rivers and lakes

List of rivers of Brazil

According to organs of the Brazilian government there are 12 major hydrographic regions in Brazil. Seven of these are river basins named after their main rivers; the other five are groupings of various river basins in areas which have no dominant river.

- 7 Hydrographic Regions named after their dominant rivers:
  - Amazonas
  - Paraguai
  - Paraná
  - Parnaíba
  - São Francisco
  - Tocantins

Figure 118: *Main Hydrographic Regions of Brazil*

- Uruguay
- 5 coastal Hydrographic Regions based on regional groupings of minor river basins (listed from north to south):
  - Atlântico Nordeste Ocidental (Western North-east Atlantic)
  - Atlântico Nordeste Oriental (Eastern North-east Atlantic)
  - Atlântico Leste (Eastern Atlantic)
  - Atlântico Sudeste (South-east Atlantic)
  - Atlântico Sul (South Atlantic)

The Amazon River is the widest and second longest river (behind the Nile) in the world. This huge river drains the greater part of the world's rainforests. Another major river, the Paraná, has its source in Brazil. It forms the border of Paraguay and Argentina, then winds its way through Argentina and into the Atlantic Ocean, along the southern coast of Uruguay.

Soils and vegetation

Brazil's tropical soils produce almost 210 million tons of grain crops per year, from about 70 millions hectares of crops. The country also has the largest arable land in the world. Burning also is used traditionally to remove tall, dry, and nutrient-poor grass from pasture at the end of the dry season. Until mechanization and the use of chemical and genetic inputs increased during

Figure 119: *The Amazon Rainforest*

the agricultural intensification period of the 1970s and 1980s, coffee planting and farming in general moved constantly onward to new lands in the west and north. This pattern of horizontal or extensive expansion maintained low levels of technology and productivity and placed emphasis on quantity rather than quality of agricultural production.

The largest areas of fertile soils, called terra roxa (red earth), are found in the states of Paraná and São Paulo. The least fertile areas are in the Amazon, where the dense rainforest is. Soils in the Northeast are often fertile, but they lack water, unless they are irrigated artificially.

In the 1980s, investments made possible the use of irrigation, especially in the Northeast Region and in Rio Grande do Sul State, which had shifted from grazing to soy and rice production in the 1970s. Savanna soils also were made usable for soybean farming through acidity correction, fertilization, plant breeding, and in some cases spray irrigation. As agriculture underwent modernization in the 1970s and 1980s, soil fertility became less important for agricultural production than factors related to capital investment, such as infrastructure, mechanization, use of chemical inputs, breeding, and proximity to markets. Consequently, the vigor of frontier expansion weakened.

The variety of climates, soils, and drainage conditions in Brazil is reflected in the range of its vegetation types. The Amazon Basin and the areas of heavy

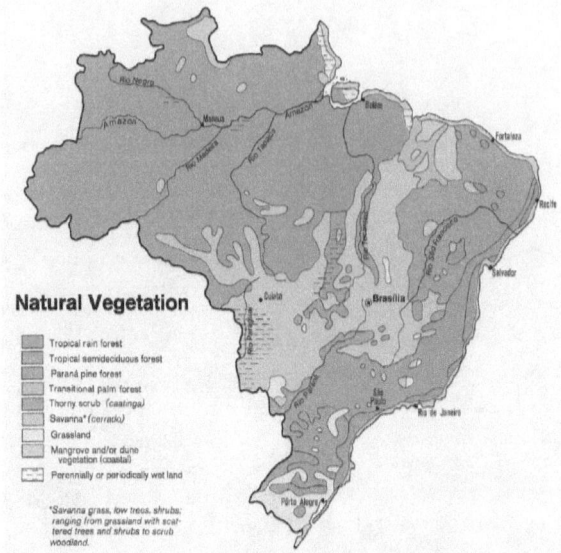

Figure 120: *Natural vegetation map of Brazil, 1977. The "Paraná pine" (Araucaria angustifolia) is a conifer but not a pine, pines are not native to the Southern Hemisphere.*

rainfall along the Atlantic coast have tropical rain forest composed of broadleaf evergreen trees. The rain forest may contain as many as 3,000 species of flora and fauna within a 2.6-square-kilometer (1 sq mi) area. The Atlantic Forest is reputed to have even greater biological diversity than the Amazon rain forest, which, despite apparent homogeneity, contains many types of vegetation, from high canopy forest to bamboo groves.

In the semiarid Northeast, caatinga, a dry, thick, thorny vegetation, predominates. Most of central Brazil is covered with a woodland savanna, known as the cerrado (sparse scrub trees and drought-resistant grasses), which became an area of agricultural development after the mid-1970s. In the South (Sul), needle-leaved pinewoods (Paraná pine or araucaria) cover the highlands; grassland similar to the Argentine pampa covers the sea-level plains. The Mato Grosso swamplands (Pantanal Mato-grossense) is a Florida-sized plain in the western portion of the Center-West (Centro-Oeste). It is covered with tall grasses, bushes, and widely dispersed trees similar to those of the cerrado and is partly submerged during the rainy season.

Brazil, which is named after reddish dyewood (pau brasil), has long been famous for the wealth of its tropical forests. These are not, however, as important to world markets as those of Asia and Africa, which started to reach depletion only in the 1980s. By 1996 more than 90% of the original Atlantic forest had been cleared, primarily for agriculture, with little use made of the wood, except for araucaria pine in Paraná.

The inverse situation existed with regard to clearing for wood in the Amazon rain forest, of which about 15% had been cleared by 1994, and part of the remainder had been disturbed by selective logging. Because the Amazon forest is highly heterogeneous, with hundreds of woody species per hectare, there is considerable distance between individual trees of economic value, such as mahogany and cerejeira. Therefore, this type of forest is not normally cleared for timber extraction but logged through high-grading, or selection of the most valuable trees. Because of vines, felling, and transportation, their removal causes destruction of many other trees, and the litter and new growth create a risk of forest fires, which are otherwise rare in rainforests. In favorable locations, such as Paragominas, in the northeastern part of Pará State, a new pattern of timber extraction has emerged: diversification and the production of plywood have led to the economic use of more than 100 tree species.

Starting in the late 1980s, rapid deforestation and extensive burning in Brazil received considerable international and national attention. Satellite images have helped document and quantify deforestation as well as fires, but their use also has generated considerable controversy because of problems of defining original vegetation, cloud cover, and dealing with secondary growth and because fires, as mentioned above, may occur in old pasture rather than signifying new clearing. Public policies intended to promote sustainable management of timber extraction, as well as sustainable use of nontimber forest products (such as rubber, Brazil nuts, fruits, seeds, oils, and vines), were being discussed intensely in the mid-1990s. However, implementing the principles of sustainable development, without irreversible damage to the environment, proved to be more challenging than establishing international agreements about them.

Climate

Although 90% of the country is within the tropical zone, the climate of Brazil varies considerably from the mostly tropical North (the equator traverses the mouth of the Amazon) to temperate zones below the Tropic of Capricorn (23°27' S latitude), which crosses the country at the latitude of the city of São Paulo. Brazil has five climatic regions: equatorial, tropical, semiarid, highland tropical, and subtropical.

Temperatures along the equator are high, averaging above 25 °C (77 °F), but not reaching the summer extremes of up to 40 °C (104 °F) in the temperate zones. There is little seasonal variation near the equator, although at times it

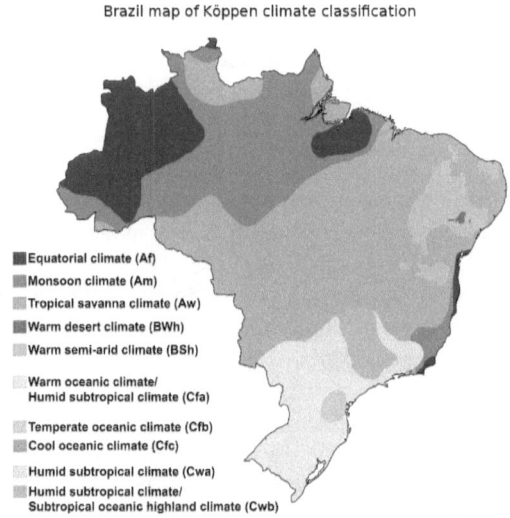

Figure 121: *Brazil map of Köppen climate classification.*

can get cool enough for wearing a jacket, especially in the rain. At the country's other extreme, there are frosts south of the Tropic of Capricorn during the winter (June–August), and there is snow in the mountainous areas, such as Paraná, Rio Grande do Sul and Santa Catarina. Temperatures in the cities of São Paulo, Belo Horizonte, and Brasília are moderate (usually between 15 and 30 °C or 59 and 86 °F), despite their relatively low latitude, because of their elevation of approximately 1,000 meters (3,281 ft). Rio de Janeiro, Recife, and Salvador on the coast have warm climates, with average temperatures ranging from 23 to 27 °C (73.4 to 80.6 °F), but enjoy constant trade winds. The southern cities of Porto Alegre and Curitiba have a subtropical climate similar to that in parts of the United States and Europe, and temperatures can fall below freezing in winter.

Precipitation levels vary widely. Most of Brazil has moderate rainfall of between 1,000 and 1,500 millimetres (39.4 and 59.1 in) a year, with most of the rain falling in the winter (between December and April) south of the Equator. The Amazon region is notoriously humid, with rainfall generally more than 2,000 millimetres (78.7 in) per year and reaching as high as 3,000 millimetres (118.1 in) in parts of the western Amazon and near Belém. It is less widely known that, despite high annual precipitation, the Amazon rain forest has a three- to five-month dry season, the timing of which varies according to location north or south of the equator.

High and relatively regular levels of precipitation in the Amazon contrast sharply with the dryness of the semiarid Northeast, where rainfall is scarce and there are severe droughts in cycles averaging seven years. The Northeast is the driest part of the country. The region also constitutes the hottest part of Brazil, where during the dry season between May and November, temperatures of more than 38 °C (100 °F) have been recorded. However, the sertão, a region of semidesert vegetation used primarily for low-density ranching, turns green when there is rain. Most of the Center-West has 1,500 to 2,000 millimetres (59.1 to 78.7 in) of rain per year, with a pronounced dry season in the middle of the year, while the South and most of the year without a distinct dry season.

Geographic regions

Brazil's 26 states and the Federal District (Distrito Federal) are divided conventionally into five regions: North (Norte), Northeast (Nordeste), Southeast (Sudeste), South (Sul), and Center-West (Centro-Oeste) - see fig. 4. In 2015 there were 5,570 municipalities (municípios), which have municipal governments. Many municipalities, which are comparable to United States counties, are in turn divided into districts (distritos), which do not have political or administrative autonomy. In 2015 there were 10,424 districts. All municipal and district seats, regardless of size, are considered officially to be urban. For purely statistical purposes, the municipalities were grouped in 1990 into 558 micro-regions, which in turn constituted 137 meso-regions. This grouping modified the previous micro-regional division established in 1968, a division that was used to present census data for 1970, 1975, 1980, and 1985.

Each of the five major regions has a distinct ecosystem. Administrative boundaries do not necessarily coincide with ecological boundaries, however. In addition to differences in physical environment, patterns of economic activity and population settlement vary widely among the regions. The principal ecological characteristics of each of the five major regions, as well as their principal socioeconomic and demographic features, are summarized below.

Political map of Brazil, showing the division by states and regions.

Centre west

The Center-West consists of the states of Goiás, Mato Grosso, Mato Grosso do Sul (separated from Mato Grosso in 1979) and the Federal District, where Brasília is located, the national capital. Until 1988 Goiás State included the area that then became the state of Tocantins in the North.

The Center-West has 1,612,077 square kilometers (622,426 sq mi) and covers 18.9% of the national territory. Its main biome is the cerrado, the tropical savanna in which natural grassland is partly covered with twisted shrubs and small trees. The cerrado was used for low-density cattle-raising in the past but is now also used for soybean production. There are gallery forests along the rivers and streams and some larger areas of forest, most of which have been cleared for farming and livestock. In the north, the cerrado blends into tropical forest. It also includes the Pantanal wetlands in the west, known for their wildlife, especially aquatic birds and caimans. In the early 1980s, 33.6% of the region had been altered by anthropic activities, with a low of 9.3% in Mato Grosso and a high of 72.9% in Goiás (not including Tocantins). In 1996 the Center-West region had 10.2 million inhabitants, or 6% of Brazil's total population. The average density is low, with concentrations in and around the cities of Brasília, Goiânia, Campo Grande, and Cuiabá. Living standards are below the national average. In 1994 they were highest in the Federal District, with per capita income of US$7,089 (the highest in the nation), and lowest in Mato Grosso, with US$2,268.

Northeast

The nine states that make up the Northeast are Alagoas, Bahia, Ceará, Maranhão, Paraíba, Pernambuco, Piauí, Rio Grande do Norte, and Sergipe. The Fernando de Noronha archipelago (formerly the federal territory of Fernando de Noronha, now part of Pernambuco state) is also included in the Northeast.

The Northeast, with 1,561,178 square kilometers (602,774 sq mi), covers 18.3% of the national terrest concentration of rural population, and its living standards are the lowest in Brazil. In 1994 Piauí had the lowest per capita income in the region and the country, only US$835, while Sergipe had the highest average income in the region, with US$1,958.

North

The equatorial North, also known as the Amazon or Amazônia, includes, from west to east, the states of Rondônia, Acre, Amazonas, Roraima, Pará, Amapá, and, as of 1988, Tocantins (created from the northern part of Goiás State, which is situated in the Center-West). Rondônia, previously a federal territory, became a state in 1986. The former federal territories of Roraima and Amapá were raised to statehood in 1988.

With 3,869,638 square kilometers (1,494,076 sq mi), the North is the country's largest region, covering 45.3% of the national territory. The region's principal biome is the humid tropical forest, also known as the rain forest, home to some of the planet's richest biological diversity. The North has served as a source of forest products ranging from "backlands drugs" (such as sarsaparilla, cocoa, cinnamon, and turtle butter) in the colonial period to rubber and Brazil nuts in more recent times. In the mid-twentieth century, nonforest products from mining, farming, and livestock-raising became more important, and in the 1980s the lumber industry boomed. In 1990, 6.6% of the region's territory was considered altered by anthropic (man-made) action, with state levels varying from 0.9% in Amapá to 14.0% in Rondônia.

In 1996 the North had 11.1 million inhabitants, only 7% of the national total. However, its share of Brazil's total had grown rapidly in the 1970s and early 1980s as a result of interregional migration, as well as high rates of natural increase. The largest population concentrations are in eastern Pará State and in Rondônia. The major cities are Belém and Santarém in Pará, and Manaus in Amazonas. Living standards are below the national average. The highest per capita income, US$2,888, in the region in 1994, was in Amazonas, while the lowest, US$901, was in Tocantins.

Southeast

The Southeast consists of the four states of Espírito Santo, Minas Gerais, Rio de Janeiro, and São Paulo. Its total area of 927,286 square kilometers (358,027 sq mi) corresponds to 10.9% of the national territory. The region has the largest share of the country's population, 63 million in 1991, or 39% of the national total, primarily as a result of internal migration since the mid-19th century until the 1980s. In addition to a dense urban network, it contains the megacities of São Paulo and Rio de Janeiro, which in 1991 had 18.7 million and 11.7 million inhabitants in their metropolitan areas, respectively. The region combines the highest living standards in Brazil with pockets of urban poverty. In 1994 São Paulo boasted an average income of US$4,666, while Minas Gerais reported only US$2,833.

Originally, the principal biome in the Southeast was the Atlantic Forest, but by 1990 less than 10% of the original forest cover remained as a result of clearing for farming, ranching, and charcoal making. Anthropic activity had altered 79.7% of the region, ranging from 75% in Minas Gerais to 91.1% in Espírito Santo. The region has most of Brazil's industrial production. The state of São Paulo alone accounts for half of the country's industries. Agriculture, also very strong, has diversified and now uses modern technology.

South

The three states in the temperate South: Paraná, Rio Grande do Sul, and Santa Catarina—cover 577,214 square kilometers (222,864 sq mi), or 6.8% of the national territory. The population of the South in 1991 was 23.1 million, or 14% of the country's total. The region is almost as densely settled as the Southeast, but the population is more concentrated along the coast. The major cities are Curitiba and Porto Alegre. The inhabitants of the South enjoy relatively high living standards. Because of its industry and agriculture, Paraná had the highest average income in 1994, US$3,674, while Santa Catarina, a land of small farmers and small industries, had slightly less, US$3,405.

In addition to the Atlantic Forest and Araucaria moist forests, much of which were cleared in the post-World War II period, the southernmost portion of Brazil contains the Uruguayan savanna, which extends into Argentina and Uruguay. In 1982, 83.5% of the region had been altered by anthropic activity, with the highest level (89.7%) in Rio Grande do Sul, and the lowest (66.7%) in Santa Catarina. Agriculture—much of which, such as rice production, is carried out by small farmers—has high levels of productivity. There are also some important industries.

Environmental issues

The environmental problem that attracted most international attention in Brazil in the 1980s was deforestation in the Amazon. Of all Latin American countries, Brazil still has the largest portion (66%) of its territory covered by forests, but clearing and burning in the Amazon proceeded at alarming rates in the 1970s and 1980s. Most of the clearing resulted from the activities of ranchers, including large corporate operations, and a smaller portion resulted from slash and burn techniques used by small farmers. Technical changes involved in the transition from horizontal expansion of agriculture to increasing productivity also accounted for decreasing rates of deforestation.

Desertification, another important environmental problem in Brazil, only received international attention following the United Nations Conference on the Environment and Development, also known as the Earth Summit, held in Rio de Janeiro in June 1992. Desertification means that the soils and vegetation of drylands are egraded, not necessarily that land turns into desert. In the early 1990s, it became evident that the semiarid caatinga ecosystem of the Northeast was losing its natural vegetation through clearing and that the zone was therefore running the risk of becoming even more arid, as was occurring also in some other regions.

In areas where agriculture is more intense and developed, there are serious problems of soil erosion, siltation and sedimentation of streams and rivers, and pollution with pesticides. In parts of the savannas, where irrigated soybean production expanded in the 1980s, the water table has been affected. Expansion of pastures for cattle raising has reduced natural biodiversity in the savannas. Swine effluents constitute a serious environmental problem in Santa Catarina in the South.

In urban areas, at least in the largest cities, levels of air pollution and congestion are typical of, or worse than, those found in cities in developed countries. At the same time, however, basic environmental problems related to the lack of sanitation, which developed countries solved long ago, persist in Brazil. These problems are sometimes worse in middle-sized and small cities than in large cities, which have more resources to deal with them. Environmental problems of cities and towns finally began to receive greater attention by society and the government in the 1990s.

According to many critics, the economic crisis in the 1980s worsened environmental degradation in Brazil because it led to overexploitation of natural resources, stimulated settlement in fragile lands in both rural and urban areas, and weakened environmental protection. At the same time, however, the lower level of economic activity may have reduced pressure on the environment, such as the aforementioned decreased level of investment in large-scale clearing in the Amazon. That pressure could increase if economic growth accelerates, especially if consumption patterns remain unchanged and more sustainable forms of production are not found.

In Brazil public policies regarding the environment are generally advanced, although their implementation and the enforcement of environmental laws have been far from ideal. Laws regarding forests, water, and wildlife have been in effect since the 1930s. Brazil achieved significant institutional advances in environmental policy design and implementation after the Stockholm Conference on the Environment in 1972. Specialized environmental agencies were organized at the federal level and in some states, and many national parks and reserves were established. By 1992 Brazil had established 34 national parks and fifty-six biological reserves. In 1981 the National Environment Policy was defined, and the National System for the Environment (Sistema Nacional do Meio Ambiente—Sisnama) was created, with the National Environmental Council (Conselho Nacional do Meio Ambiente—Conama) at its apex, municipal councils at its base, and state-level councils in between. In addition to government authorities, all of these councils include representatives of civil society.

The 1988 constitution incorporates environmental precepts that are advanced compared with those of most other countries. At that time, the Chamber of Deputies (Câmara dos Deputados) established its permanent Commission for Defense of the Consumer, the Environment, and Minorities. In 1989 the creation of the Brazilian Institute for the Environment and Renewable Natural Resources (Instituto Brasileiro do Meio Ambiente e dos Recursos Naturais Renováveis–Ibama) joined together the federal environment secretariat and the federal agencies specializing in forestry, rubber, and fisheries. In 1990 the administration of Fernando Collor de Mello (president, 1990–92) appointed the well-known environmentalist José Lutzemberger as secretary of the environment and took firm positions on the environment and on Indian lands. In 1992 Brazil played a key role at the Earth Summit, not only as its host but also as negotiator on sustainable development agreements, including the conventions on climate and biodiversity. The Ministry of Environment was created in late 1992, after President Collor had left office. In August 1993, it became the Ministry of Environment and the Legal Amazon and took a more pragmatic approach than had the combative Lutzemberger. However, because of turnover in its leadership, a poorly defined mandate, and lack of funds, its role and impact were limited. In 1995 its mandate and name were expanded to include water resources—the Ministry of Environment, Hydraulic Resources, and the Legal Amazon—it began a process of restructuring to meet its mandate of "shared management of the sustainable use of natural resources." In 1997 the Commission on Policies for Sustainable Development and Agenda 21 began to function under the aegis of the Civil Household. One of its main tasks was to prepare Agenda 21 (a plan for the twenty-first century) for Brazil and to stimulate preparation of state and local agendas.

Institutional development at the official level was accompanied and in part stimulated by the growth, wide diffusion, and growing professional development of nongovernmental organizations (NGOs) dedicated to environmental and socio-environmental causes. The hundreds of NGOs throughout Brazil produce documents containing both useful information and passionate criticisms. Among the Brazilian environmental NGOs, the most visible are SOS Atlantic Forest (SOS Mata Atlântica), the Social-Environmental Institute (Instituto Sócio-Ambiental—ISA), the Pro-Nature Foundation (Fundação Pró-Natureza—Funatura), and the Amazon Working Group (Grupo de Trabalho Amazônico—GTA). The Brazilian Forum of NGOs and Social Movements for the Environment and Development and the Brazilian Association of Nongovernmental Organizations (Associacão Brasileira de Organizações Não-Governamentais—ABONG) are national networks, and there are various regional and thematic networks as well. The main international environmental NGOs that have offices or affiliates in Brazil are the World Wildlife Fund (WWF), Conservation International (CI), and Nature Conservancy.

Especially after the events of the late 1980s, international organizations and developed countries have allocated significant resources for the environmental sector in Brazil. In 1992 environmental projects worth about US$6.8 million were identified, with US$2.6 in counterpart funds (funds provided by the Brazilian government). More than 70% of the total value was for sanitation, urban pollution control, and other urban environmental projects. Thus, the allocation of resources did not accord with the common belief that funding was influenced unduly by alarmist views on deforestation in the Amazon.

Among the specific environmental projects with international support, the most important was the National Environmental Plan (Plano Nacional do Meio Ambiente—PNMA), which received a US$117 million loan from the World Bank. The National Environmental Fund (Fundo Nacional do Meio Ambiente—FNMA), in addition to budgetary funds, received US$20 million from the Inter-American Development Bank to finance the environmental activities of NGOs and small municipal governments. The Pilot Program for the Conservation of the Brazilian Rain Forests (Programa Piloto para a Proteção das Florestas Tropicais do Brasil—PPG-7) was supported by the world's seven richest countries (the so-called G-7) and the European Community, which allocated US$258 million for projects in the Amazon and Atlantic Forest regions. The Global Environment Facility (GEF), created in 1990, set aside US$30 million for Brazil, part of which is managed by a national fund called Funbio. GEF also established a small grants program for NGOs, which focused on the cerrado during its pilot phase. The World Bank also made loans for environmental and natural resource management in Rondônia and Mato Grosso, in part to correct environmental and social problems that had been created by the World Bank-funded development of the northwest corridor in the 1980s.

Despite favorable laws, promising institutional arrangements, and external funding, the government has not, on the whole, been effective in controlling damage to the environment. This failure is only in small measure because of the opposition of anti-environmental groups. In greater part, it can be attributed to the traditional separation between official rhetoric and actual practice in Brazil. It is also related to general problems of governance, fiscal crisis, and lingering doubts about appropriate tradeoffs between the environment and development. Some of the most effective governmental action in the environmental area has occurred at the state and local levels in the most developed states and has involved NGOs. In 1994 the PNMA began to stress decentralization and strengthening of state environmental agencies, a tendency that subsequently gained momentum.

Environment - current issues: Deforestation in Amazon Basin destroys the habitat and endangers the existence of a multitude of plant and animal species indigenous to the area; there is a lucrative illegal wildlife trade; air and water pollution in Rio de Janeiro, São Paulo, and several other large cities; land degradation and water pollution caused by improper mining activities; wetland degradation; severe oil spills
note: President Cardoso in September 1999 signed into force an environmental crime bill which for the first time defines pollution and deforestation as crimes punishable by stiff fines and jail sentences

Environment - international agreements:
party to: Antarctic-Environmental Protocol, Antarctic-Marine Living Resources, Antarctic Seals, Antarctic Treaty, Biodiversity, Climate Change, Climate Change-Kyoto Protocol, Desertification, Endangered Species, Environmental Modification, Hazardous Wastes, Law of the Sea, Marine Dumping, Ozone Layer Protection, Ship Pollution, Tropical Timber 83, Tropical Timber 94, Wetlands, Whaling
signed, but not ratified: none of selected agreements

References

- ⊛ This article incorporates public domain material from the Library of Congress Country Studies website http://lcweb2.loc.gov/frd/cs/[680].
- ⊛ This article incorporates public domain material from the CIA World Factbook website https://www.cia.gov/library/publications/the-world-factbook/index.html[681].

External links

- Brazil[682] - from 1565 (in English)
- Brazil: of the Noble Class, of Loves, and of Letters...[683] a map from around 1640 (in Latin) (in English)

Climate

Climate of Brazil

The **climate in Brazil** varies considerably mostly from tropical north (the equator traverses the mouth of the Amazon) to temperate zones south of the Tropic of Capricorn (23°26' S latitude). Temperatures below the equator are high, averaging above 25 °C (77 °F), but not reaching the summer extremes of up to 40 °C (104 °F) in the temperate zones. There is little seasonal variation near the equator, although at times it can get cool enough to need to wear a jacket, especially in the rain. Average temperatures below the Tropic of Capricorn are mild, ranging from 13 °C (55 °F) to 22 °C (72 °F).

At the country's other extreme, there are frosts south of the Tropic of Capricorn and during the winter (June–September). Snow falls on the high plateau and mountainous of the mountains of the states of Rio Grande do Sul, Santa Catarina, and Paraná and it is possible, but very rare, in the states of São Paulo, Rio de Janeiro, Minas Gerais, and Mato Grosso do Sul. The cities of Belo Horizonte and Brasília have moderate temperatures, usually between 15 and 30 °C (59 and 86 °F), because of their elevation of approximately 1,000 metres (3,281 ft). Rio de Janeiro, Recife, and Salvador on the coast have warm climates, with average temperatures of each month ranging from 23 to 27 °C (73 to 81 °F), but enjoy constant trade winds. The cities of São Paulo, Curitiba, Florianópolis and Porto Alegre have a subtropical climate similar to that of southern United States, and temperatures can fall below freezing in winter.

Precipitation levels vary widely. Most of Brazil has moderate rainfall of between 1,000 and 1,500 mm (39 and 59 in) a year, with most of the rain falling in the summer (between December and April) south of the Equator. The Amazon region is notoriously humid, with rainfall generally more than 2,000 mm (79 in) per year and reaching as high as 3,000 mm (118 in) in parts of the western Amazon and near Belém. It is less widely known that, despite high

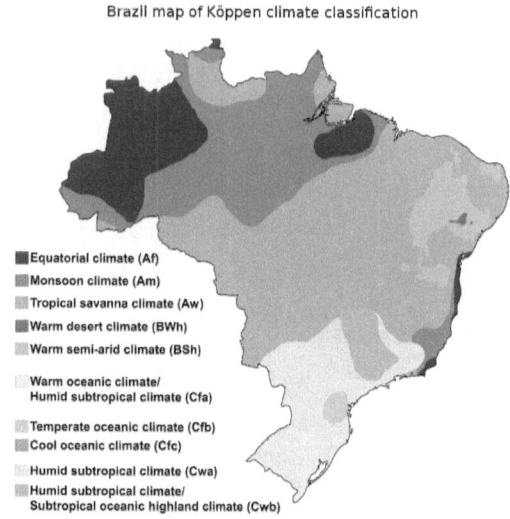

Figure 122: *Köppen climate classification map of Brazil, simplified version.*

Figure 123: *The subtropical climate during winter, with snowfall in Caxias do Sul, South Region*

Figure 124: *The tropical climate during summer, in Porto de Galinhas, Northeast region*

annual precipitation, the Amazon forest has a three- to five-month dry season, the timing of which varies according to location north or south of the equator.

High and relatively regular levels of precipitation in the Amazon contrast sharply with the dryness of the semiarid Northeast, where rainfall is highly erratic and there are severe droughts in cycles averaging seven years. The Northeast is the driest part of the country. The region also constitutes the hottest part of Brazil, where during the dry season between May and November, temperatures of more than 38 °C (100 °F) have been recorded. However, the sertão, a region of semidesert vegetation used primarily for low-density ranching, turns green when there is rain. Most of the Center-West has 1,500 to 2,000 mm (59 to 79 in) of rain per year, with a pronounced dry season in the middle of the year, while the South and most of the East is without a distinct dry season.

Because the South Atlantic basin is generally not a favorable environment for their development, Brazil has only rarely experienced tropical cyclones. The country's coastal population centers are therefore not as burdened with the need to prepare for cyclones, as are cities at similar latitudes in the United States and Asia.

General climate

Although most of Brazil lies in the tropics, more than 60 percent of the population live in areas which are cooled either by altitude, sea winds or polar fronts. While the coastal cities of Rio de Janeiro, Recife and Salvador can get extremely hot, plateau cities such as São Paulo, Brasília and Belo Horizonte have mild climates, and the southern cities of Porto Alegre and Curitiba have mild winters, but while Curitiba has a warm summer due to the average elevation of 934.6 metres (3,066 ft), Porto Alegre has a hot summer, with an average elevation of only 10 metres (33 ft).

Despite the popular image of the Amazon as a region of blistering heat, temperatures of more than 32 °C (90 °F) are in fact rare. The annual average temperature in the region is 22 to 26 °C (72 to 79 °F), with not much variation between the warmest and the coldest months. The hottest part of Brazil is the northeast, where temperatures of more than 38 °C (100 °F) are frequently recorded during the dry season between May and November. Along the Atlantic coast from Recife to Rio de Janeiro, average temperatures range from 23 to 27 °C (73 to 81 °F). Inland, on higher ground, temperatures are lower, ranging from 19 to 21 °C (66 to 70 °F). South of Rio the seasons are more defined and the range of temperatures significantly wider, with the annual average falling between 17 and 19 °C (63 and 66 °F).

Brazil's most intense rain falls around the mouth of the Amazon near the city of Belém, and also in the upper regions of Amazonia where more than 2,000 millimetres (79 in) of rain fall every year. Most of Brazil has moderate rainfall of between 1,000 and 1,500 millimetres (39 and 59 in) a year, most of it coming between December and April. The driest part of the country is the northeast, where rainfall is erratic and the evaporation rate very high, making it difficult to grow crops.

The highest temperature officially registered in Brazil was 44.7 °C (112.5 °F) in Bom Jesus, Piauí state on 21 November 2005.[684] The lowest temperature officially recorded in Brazil was −14 °C (7 °F) in Caçador, Santa Catarina state, on 11 June 1952.[685] However, the summit of Morro da Igreja, a mountain situated in the municipality of Urubici, also in Santa Catarina, recorded a temperature of −17.8 °C (0.0 °F) on 30 June 1996 unofficially.[686]

Figure 125: *Southeast Region*

Climate by region

Southeast Region

The latitudinal position around the Tropic of Capricorn, the very uneven topography and disturbed circulation systems greatly influence the climatology of the Southeast and it is quite diverse in temperature. The annual medium temperature ranges from 20 °C (68 °F) as seen on the border between São Paulo and Paraná to 24 °C (75 °F) in the north of Minas Gerais, while in the elevated areas of the Serra do Espinhaço, Serra da Mantiqueira and Serra do Mar the average medium temperature can be below 18 °C (64 °F) due to the combined effect of the latitude with the frequency of the polar currents.

In the summer, mainly in the month of January, the normal average temperatures range from 30 to 32 °C (86 to 90 °F) in the valleys of the rivers São Francisco and Jequitinhonha, in the Zona da Mata (Forest Zone) of Minas Gerais, in the coastal lowlands and to the west of the state of São Paulo.

In the winter, the normal average temperatures range from 6 to 20 °C (43 to 68 °F) with minimum absolute from –4 to 8 °C (25 to 46 °F), the lowest temperatures being at the highest elevations. Vast areas of Minas Gerais and São Paulo register occurrences of frosts, after the passage of the polar fronts.

As far as the incidence of rain is concerned, there are two areas with heavy precipitation: one following the coast and the Serra do Mar, where the rains are precipitated by the southerly currents; and the other from the west of Minas Gerais to the Municipal district of Rio de Janeiro, where the rains are brought by the Westerly system. The annual precipitation total in these areas is in excess of 1,500 mm (59.1 in). In the Serra da Mantiqueira these indexes surpass 1,750 mm (68.9 in), and at the summit of Itatiaia, 2,340 mm (92.1 in).

In the Serra do Mar, in São Paulo, it rains on the average more than 3,600 mm (141.7 in). Near Paranapiacaba and Itapanhaú maximum rainfall was measured at 4,457.8 mm (175.50 in) in one year. In the valleys of the rivers Jequitinhonha and Doce the smallest annual pluviometric indexes are recorded at around 900 mm (35.4 in).

The maximum pluviometric index of the Southeast area usually occurs in January and the minimum in July, while the dry period is usually concentrated in the winter, lasting six months in the case of the valleys of the rivers Jequitinhonha and São Francisco, to as little as two months in the Serra do Mar and Serra da Mantiqueira.

Charts of selected cities

Belo Horizonte											
Climate chart (explanation)											
J	F	M	A	M	J	J	A	S	O	N	D
Average max. and min. temperatures in °C											
Precipitation totals in mm											
Source:[687]											

Climate of Brazil

Campos do Jordão
Climate chart (explanation)
J | F | M | A | M | J | J | A | S | O | N | D
Average max. and min. temperatures in °C
Precipitation totals in mm
Source:[688]

Campinas
Climate chart (explanation)
J | F | M | A | M | J | J | A | S | O | N | D
Average max. and min. temperatures in °C
Precipitation totals in mm
Source:[689]

Rio de Janeiro
Climate chart (explanation)
J | F | M | A | M | J | J | A | S | O | N | D
Average max. and min. temperatures in °C
Precipitation totals in mm
Source:[690]

São Paulo
Climate chart (explanation)
J | F | M | A | M | J | J | A | S | O | N | D
Average max. and min. temperatures in °C
Precipitation totals in mm
Source:[691]

Northeast Region

The climatic characterization of the Northeast area is a little complex, and the four systems of circulation that influence the region are denominated Systems of Disturbed Currents of South, North, East and West. The System of disturbed currents of South is represented by the polar masses that reach the area in the spring-summer, acts in the coastal areas until the south of Bahia, bringing frontal and back-frontals rains. In the winter the polar masses reach even the coast of Pernambuco, while the hinterlands regions remain under the influence of the tropical mass.

The system of disturbed currents of North, represented by Convergence Intertropical (CIT), produces rain from the summer to the autumn even in Pernambuco, in the vicinity of the Raso da Catarina. On the other hand, the currents of the East are more frequent in the winter and they usually produce abundant rains in the coastal regions, rarely reaching the scarps of the Plateau of Borborema (800 m or 2,625 ft) and of Chapada Diamantina (1,200 m or 3,937 ft).

Finally, the system of currents of the West, brought by the lines of Tropical Instability (IT), occur from the end of spring to the beginning of autumn, rarely reaching the states of Piauí and Maranhão.

Temperatures are high, with annual averages between 20 and 28 °C (68.0 and 82.4 °F), maxima of around 40 °C (104 °F) having been observed in the south of Maranhão and Piauí. The months of winter, mainly June and July, produce minimum temperatures between 12 and 16 °C (53.6 and 60.8 °F) in the coastal regions, much lower in the plateau regions where temperatures of 1 °C (33.8 °F) have been recorded in Chapada Diamantina after the passage of a polar front.

The pluviosity of the area is complex and is source of concern: its annual totals vary from 2,000 mm (78.7 in) to values even lower than 500 mm (19.7 in), as verified in the Raso da Catarina, between Bahia and Pernambuco, and in the depression of Patos in Paraíba. In a general way, the annual medium precipitation in the northeast area is lower than 1,000 mm (39.4 in) - in the city of Cabaceiras, interior of Paraíba, was observed the smallest annual pluviometric

Climate of Brazil 295

Figure 126: *Northeast Region*

index registered in Brazil, 278 mm (10.9 in)/year. Besides it in the interior of this area the rainy period is usually of just two months in the year, sometimes not coming in some years, causing then the denominated regional droughts.

Charts of selected cities

Salvador											
Climate chart (explanation)											
J	F	M	A	M	J	J	A	S	O	N	D
Average max. and min. temperatures in °C											
Precipitation totals in mm											
Source:[692]											

	Fortaleza											
	Climate chart (explanation)											
J	F	M	A	M	J	J	A	S	O	N	D	
Average max. and min. temperatures in °C												
Precipitation totals in mm												
Source:[693]												

	Recife											
	Climate chart (explanation)											
J	F	M	A	M	J	J	A	S	O	N	D	
Average max. and min. temperatures in °C												
Precipitation totals in mm												
Source:[694]												

	Teresina											
	Climate chart (explanation)											
J	F	M	A	M	J	J	A	S	O	N	D	
Average max. and min. temperatures in °C												
Precipitation totals in mm												
Source:[695]												

South Region

The South region is located below the Tropic of Capricorn, in a temperate zone. It is influenced by the system of disturbed circulation of the South, which produces the rains, mainly in the summer. It is also influenced by the system of disturbed circulation of the West, that brings rains and storms, sometimes hail, producing winds with bursts of 60 to 90 km/h (37.3 to 55.9 mph). Regarding temperatures: the winter is cool and the summer is hot. The annual medium temperatures range from 14 to 22 °C (57.2 to 71.6 °F), and in places with altitudes above 1,100 m (3,609 ft), drops to approximately 10 °C (50 °F). Some parts of the southern region also have an oceanic climate.

In the summer, mainly in January, in the valleys of the rivers Paranapanema, Paraná and Ibicuí-Jacuí, the medium temperature is in excess of 24 °C (75.2 °F), and the medium temperature of the river Uruguay surpasses 26 °C (78.8 °F). The average maximum temperature stays around 24 to 27 °C (75.2 to 80.6 °F) on the elevated surfaces of the plateau and, in the lowest areas, between 30 and 32 °C (86.0 and 89.6 °F).

Figure 127: *South Region*

In the winter, mainly in July, the medium temperature stays relatively low, oscillating between 10 and 15 °C (50 and 59 °F), except for the valleys of the rivers Paranapanema and Paraná, besides the coast of Paraná and Santa Catarina, where the averages are approximately 15 to 18 °C (59.0 to 64.4 °F). The average maximum temperature is also low, around 20 to 24 °C (68.0 to 75.2 °F), in the big valleys and in the coast, and 16 to 20 °C (60.8 to 68.0 °F) in the plateau region. The average minimum temperature varies from 6 to 12 °C (42.8 to 53.6 °F), and the thermometer frequently registers temperatures near 0 °C or below, accompanied by frost and snow, in consequence of the invasion of polar masses.

The annual medium pluviosity oscillates from 1,250 to 2,000 mm (49.2 to 78.7 in), except along the coast of Paraná and west of Santa Catarina, where the values are in excess of 2,000 mm (78.7 in), and in the north of Paraná and in a small coastal area of Santa Catarina, which have lower recordings down to 1,250 mm (49.2 in). The maximum pluviometric indexes occur in the winter and the minimum in the summer throughout almost the whole area.

Charts of selected cities

Porto Alegre
Climate chart (explanation)
J F M A M J J A S O N D
Average max. and min. temperatures in °C
Precipitation totals in mm
Source:[696]

Florianópolis
Climate chart (explanation)
J F M A M J J A S O N D
Average max. and min. temperatures in °C
Precipitation totals in mm
Source:[697]

Curitiba
Climate chart (explanation)
J F M A M J J A S O N D
Average max. and min. temperatures in °C
Precipitation totals in mm
Source:[698]

São Joaquim												
Climate chart (explanation)												
J	F	M	A	M	J	J	A	S	O	N	D
Average max. and min. temperatures in °C												
Precipitation totals in mm												
Source:[699]												

Caxias do Sul												
Climate chart (explanation)												
J	F	M	A	M	J	J	A	S	O	N	D
Average max. and min. temperatures in °C												
Precipitation totals in mm												
Source:[700]												

North Region

The north area of Brazil embraces a great part of the Amazon Basin, representing the largest extension of hot and humid forest on the planet. The region has a low elevation (0 to 200 m or 0 to 656 ft) and is crossed by the Equator. There are four main systems of atmospheric circulation that act in the area, they are: system of winds of Northeast (NE) to East (E) of the Atlantic South and Azores, subtropical anticyclones, generally stable in nature; system of winds of West (W) of the mass equatorial continental (mEc); system of winds of North (N) of the Convergence Intertropical (CIT); and system of winds of South (S) of the Polar anticyclone. These last three systems are responsible for variability of the climate and for the rains in the area. With regard to temperatures, the climate is hot, with annual medium temperatures ranging from
24 to 26 °C (75.2 to 78.8 °F).

Regarding pluviosity, there is not a homogeneity as it occur with the temperature. In the mouth of the river Amazonas, in the coast of Pará and in the western section of the area, the total annual pluviometric index exceeds 3,000 mm (118.1 in) in general. In the direction NO-SE, of Roraima to east of Pará there is less rain, with annual totals in the order of 1,500 to 1,700 mm (59.1 to 66.9 in).

The rainy period of the area occurs in summer & autumn, the exception being Roraima and of the north part of Amazonas, where the maximum pluviometric indexes occurs in winter, due to influence of the climatic conditions of the Northern Hemisphere.

Figure 128: *North Region*

Charts of selected cities

Manaus
Climate chart (explanation)
J | F | M | A | M | J | J | A | S | O | N | D
Average max. and min. temperatures in °C
Precipitation totals in mm
Source:[701]

Climate of Brazil

Belém
Climate chart (explanation)
J　F　M　A　M　J　J　A　S　O　N　D
Average max. and min. temperatures in °C
Precipitation totals in mm
Source:[702]

Rio Branco
Climate chart (explanation)
J　F　M　A　M　J　J　A　S　O　N　D
Average max. and min. temperatures in °C
Precipitation totals in mm
Source:[703]

Macapá
Climate chart (explanation)
J　F　M　A　M　J　J　A　S　O　N　D
Average max. and min. temperatures in °C
Precipitation totals in mm
Source:[704]

Boa Vista
Climate chart (explanation)
J　F　M　A　M　J　J　A　S　O　N　D
Average max. and min. temperatures in °C
Precipitation totals in mm
Source:[705]

Center-West Region

Three systems of circulation occur in the Center-West region: the system of disturbed currents of the West, represented by unstable events during the summer; system of disturbed currents of the North, represented by Convergence Intertropical (CIT), that produces rains in the summer, autumn and winter in the north of the region; and the system of disturbed currents of the South, represented by the polar fronts, invading the area in the winter with great frequency, producing rains of one to three days duration. In the north and south extremes of the region, the annual medium temperature is 22 °C (71.6 °F) and in the Chapadas it varies from 20 to 22 °C (68.0 to 71.6 °F). In the spring and summer, temperatures are commonly high, the average of the hottest month varying from 24 to 26 °C (75.2 to 78.8 °F). The average of the maximum temperatures of September (hotter month) oscillates between 30 and 36 °C (86.0 and 96.8 °F).

Winter is an interesting season, low temperatures occurring quite frequently. This is caused by the polar invasion, that produces the cold weather which is very common at this time of the year. The medium temperature of the coldest month oscillates between 15 and 24 °C (59.0 and 75.2 °F), and the average of the minimum temperatures ranges from 8 to 18 °C (46.4 to 64.4 °F). Minimum temperatures are sometimes negative.

The characterization of the pluviosity of the region is almost exclusively due to the system of atmospheric circulation. The annual medium pluviosity varies from 2,000 to 3,000 mm (78.7 to 118.1 in) in the north of Mato Grosso, to 1,250 mm (49.2 in) in the Pantanal mato-grossense.

In spite of this inequality the region is well provided with rain. Its seasonality is typically tropical, with maximum in the summer and minimum in the winter. More than 70% of the total rain that is accumulated during the year falls from November to March. The winter is excessively dry, because the rains are very rare.

Charts of selected cities

Brasília
Climate chart (explanation)
J F M A M J J A S O N D
Average max. and min. temperatures in °C
Precipitation totals in mm
Source:[706]

Goiânia												
Climate chart (explanation)												
J	F	M	A	M	J	J	A	S	O	N	D	
Average max. and min. temperatures in °C												
Precipitation totals in mm												
Source:[707]												

Cuiabá												
Climate chart (explanation)												
J	F	M	A	M	J	J	A	S	O	N	D	
Average max. and min. temperatures in °C												
Precipitation totals in mm												
Source:[708]												

Campo Grande												
Climate chart (explanation)												
J	F	M	A	M	J	J	A	S	O	N	D	
Average max. and min. temperatures in °C												
Precipitation totals in mm												
Source:[709]												

External links

- https://web.archive.org/web/20101206014542/http://www.brazil.org.uk/brazilinbrief/climate.html

Biodiversity

Wildlife of Brazil

Coordinates: 15.611120°S 56.056012°W[710]

The **wildlife of Brazil** comprises all naturally occurring animals, fungi and plants in the South American country. Home to 60% of the Amazon Rainforest, which accounts for approximately one-tenth of all species in the world, Brazil is considered to have the greatest biodiversity of any country on the planet. It has the most known species of plants (55,000), freshwater fish (3000) and mammals (over 689). It also ranks third on the list of countries with the most number of bird species (1832) and second with the most reptile species (744). The number of fungal species is unknown, but is large.[711] Approximately two-thirds of all species worldwide are found in tropical areas, often coinciding with developing countries such as Brazil. Brazil is second only to Indonesia as the country with the most endemic species.

Biodiversity

In the animal kingdom, there is general consensus that Brazil has the highest number of both terrestrial vertebrates and invertebrates of any country in the world. This high diversity of fauna can be explained in part by the sheer size of Brazil and the great variation in ecosystems such as Amazon Rainforest, Atlantic Forest and Cerrado. The numbers published about Brazil's fauna diversity vary from source to source, as taxonomists sometimes disagree about species classifications, and information can be incomplete or out-of-date. Also, new species continue to be discovered and some species go extinct in the wild. Brazil has the highest diversity of primates (77 species) and freshwater fish (over 3000 species) of any country in the world. It also claims the highest number of mammals with 524 species, the second highest number of amphibians with 517 species and butterflies with 3,150 species, the third highest number of birds with 1,622 species, and fifth number of reptiles

Figure 129: *The toco toucan is an animal typical of the Brazilian savannas.*

Figure 130: *Many varieties of poison dart frogs such as this yellow-banded poison dart frog can be found in the jungles of Brazil.*

with 468 species. There is a high number of endangered species, many of which live in threatened habitats such as the Atlantic Forest or the Amazon Rainforest.

Scientists have described between 96,660 and 128,843 invertebrate species in Brazil. According to a 2005 estimate by Thomas M. Lewinsohn and Paulo I. Prado, Brazil is home to around 9.5% of all the species and 13.1% of biota found in the world; these figures are likely to be underestimates according to the authors.

Enough is known about Brazilian fungi to say with confidence that the number of native species must be very high and very diverse: in work almost entirely limited to the state of Pernambuco, during the 1950s, 1960s and early 1970s, more than 3300 species were observed by a single group of mycologists Given that current best estimates suggest only about 7% of the world's true diversity of fungal species has so far been discovered, with most of the known species having been described from temperate regions,[712] the number of fungal species occurring in Brazil is likely to be far higher.

Because it encompasses many species-rich ecosystems for animals, fungi and plants, Brazil houses many thousands of species, with many (if not most) of them still undiscovered. Due to the relatively explosive economic and demographic rise of the country in the last century, Brazil's ability to protect its environmental habitats has increasingly come under threat. Extensive logging in the nation's forests, particularly the Amazon, both official and unofficial, destroys areas the size of a small country each year, and potentially a diverse variety of plants and animals.[713] However, as various species possess special characteristics, or are built in an interesting way, some of their capabilities are being copied for use in technology (see bionics), and the profit potential may result in a retardation of deforestation.

Ecoregions

Brazil's immense area is subdivided into different ecoregions in several kinds of biomes. Because of the wide variety of habitats in Brazil, from the jungles of the Amazon Rainforest and the Atlantic Forest (which includes Atlantic Coast restingas), to the tropical savanna of the Cerrado, to the xeric shrubland of the Caatinga, to the world's largest wetland area, the Pantanal, there exists a wide variety of wildlife as well.

Figure 131: *A jaguar*

Animals

Terrestrial Mammals and reptiles

The wild canids found in Brazil are the maned wolf, bush dog, hoary fox, short-eared dog, crab-eating fox and pampas fox. The felines found in Brazil are the jaguar, the puma, the margay, the ocelot, the oncilla, and the jaguarundi. Other notable animals include the giant anteater, several varieties of sloths and armadillos, coati, giant river otter, tapir, peccaries, marsh deer, Pampas deer, and capybara (the world's largest existing rodent). There are around 75 primate species, including the howler monkey, the capuchin monkey, and the squirrel monkey, the marmoset, and the tamarin.

Brazil is home to the anaconda, frequently described, controversially, as the largest snake on the planet. This water boa has been measured up to 30 feet (9.1 m) long, but historical reports note that native peoples and early European explorers claim anacondas from 50 to 100 feet (30 m) long.

Figure 132: *A common rhea.*

Invertebrates

There are 1107[714] known species of non-marine molluscs living in the wild in Brazil.

The second largest spider in the world, the Goliath birdeater (*Theraphosa blondi*), can be found in some regions of Brazil.

Insects

It is calculated that Brazil has more insects than any country in the world. It is estimated as having over 70,000 species of insects, with some estimates ranging up to 15 million, with more being discovered almost daily. One 1996 report estimated between 50,000 and 60,000 species of insects and spiders in a single hectare of rainforest. About 520 thysanoptera species belonging to six families in 139 genera are found in Brazil.

Birds

Brazil ranks third on the list of countries, behind Colombia and Peru, with the most number of distinct bird species, having 1622 identified species, including over 70 species of parrots alone. It has 191 endemic birds. The variety of types of birds is vast as well, and include birds ranging from brightly colored parrots,

Figure 133: *Southern right whale, Florianópolis.*

toucans, and trogons to flamingos, ducks, vultures, hawks, eagles, owls, swans, and hummingbirds. There are also species of penguins that have been found in Brazil.[715]

The largest bird found in Brazil is the rhea, a flightless ratite bird, similar to the emu.

Aquatic and amphibian

Brazil has over 3,000 identified species of freshwater fish and over 500 species of amphibians. As elsewhere in South America, the majority of the freshwater fish species are characiforms (tetras and allies) and siluriforms (catfish), but there are also many species from other groups such as the cyprinodontiforms and cichlids. While the majority of Brazil's fish species are native to the Amazon, the Paraná–Paraguay and the São Francisco river basins, the country also has an unusually high number of troglobitic fish, with 25 species (15% of the total in the world) known so far.[716] The most well-known fish in Brazil is the piranha.[717]

Other aquatic and amphibian animals found in Brazil include the pink dolphin (the world's largest river dolphin), the caimans (such as the black caiman), and the pirarucu (one of the world's largest river fish). Also familiar are the brightly colored poison dart frogs.

Figure 134: *Princess flower*

Fungi

The diversity of Brazil's fungi - even the small amount known so far to scientists - is astonishing. Using only conventional microscopy, and examining living leaves collected from various plants, the mycologist Batista and his colleagues, working in Pernambuco in the 1950s, 1960s and 1970s, regularly recorded more than one fungal species, and sometimes up to ten on a single leaf. Although information about fungi worldwide remains very fragmented, a preliminary estimate, based only on the work of Batista, shows that the number of potentially endemic fungal species in Brazil already exceeds 2000. Also, fungi is very often spot in Brazil.

Plants

Brazil has most known species of plants (55,000), among all the countries in the world. About 30% of species of plants are endemic to Brazil. The Atlantic Forest region is home to tropical and subtropical moist forests, tropical dry forests, tropical savannas, and mangrove forests. The Pantanal region is a wetland, and home to a known 3,500 species of plants. The Cerrado is biologically the most diverse savanna in the world.

Figure 135: *Cattleya aclandiae, the "Lady Ackland's cattleya"*

The Pau-brasil tree (also known as Brazilwood) was a common plant found along the Atlantic coast of Brazil. But excessive logging of the prized timber and red dye from the bark pushed the Pau-brasil towards extinction. However, since the inception of synthetic dyes, the Pau-Brazil has been harvested less. The Pau-brasil tree is sometimes mentioned as the origin of the country's name.

All over Brazil, in all biomes, are hundreds of species of orchids, including those in the genera *Cattleya*, *Oncidium*, and *Laelia*.

Along the border with Venezuela lies Monte Roraima, home to many carnivorous plants. The plants evolved to digest insects due to the oligotrophic (low level of nutrients) soil of the tepui.

List of plants by ecoregion:

- List of plants of Amazon Rainforest vegetation of Brazil
- List of plants of Atlantic Forest vegetation of Brazil
- List of plants of Caatinga vegetation of Brazil
- List of plants of Cerrado vegetation of Brazil
- List of plants of Pantanal vegetation of Brazil

Figure 136: *"At bottom right and bottom center, deforestation and cultivation are evident by the regular, rectangular shapes that delineate plots."*

Threats to wildlife

More than one-fifth of the Amazon Rainforest in Brazil has been completely destroyed, and more than 70 mammals are endangered. The threat of extinction comes from several sources, including deforestation and poaching. Extinction is even more problematic in the Atlantic Forest, where nearly 93% of the forest has been cleared. Of the 202 endangered animals in Brazil, 171 are in the Atlantic Forest. Currently, 15.8 million acres of tropical ecosystem have been completely eliminated to farm sugarcane for ethanol production. And additional 4.5 million acres is planned to be planted during the next four years. 70-85% of Brazil's transportation energy is derived from ethanol, or various mixtures of ethanol and petroleum-based fuels. Only about 15-20% comes from imported petroleum. This massive national biofuel program has been devastating to tropical wildlife diversity, and to the global climate/environment.[718] Article 1[719] With its acquisition of BioEnergia, BP (British Petroleum) is planning to further expand Brazil's ethanol program. BP - BioEnergia[720]

National emblems

National bird	Rufous-bellied thrush (sabiá)
National flower	Ipê-amarelo – Tecoma chrysostricha
National tree	Pau-Brasil – Caesalpinia echinata

References

Sources

- Costa, L.P. et al. (2005). Mammal Conservation in Brazil. Conservation Biology 19(3): 672-679. [1]
- Comitê Brasileiro de Registros Ornitológicos. 2010. Lista das aves do Brasil. 9ª edição (18 de outubro de 2010). Disponível em <http://www.cbro.org.br>, accessada em 28 de dezembro de 2010.

Further reading

- Pearson, David L.; Les Beletsky (2002) [2001]. *Brazil-Amazon and Pantanal*. Ecotravellers Wildlife Guides. Academic Press. p. 275. ISBN 978-0-12-548052-9. OCLC 77711203[721].

External blinks

- BrazilianFauna.com[722], a not-for profit educational website
- Brazil Nature: Ecosystem[723]
- List of Brazilian animals on Encyclopedia of Life[724]

Deforestation in Brazil

Brazil once had the highest deforestation rate in the world and in 2005 still had the largest area of forest removed annually. Since 1970, over 700,000 square kilometers (270,000 sq mi) of the Amazon rainforest have been destroyed. In 2012, the Amazon was approximately 5.4 million square kilometres, which is only 87% of the Amazon's original state.

Rainforests have decreased in size primarily due to deforestation. Despite reductions in the deforestation rate over the last ten years, the Amazon rainforest will be reduced by 40% by 2030 at the current rate.[725] Between May 2000 and August 2006, Brazil lost nearly 150,000 km^2 of forest, an area larger than Greece. According to the Living Planet Report 2010, deforestation continues at an alarming rate. But at the CBD 9th Conference, 67 ministers signed up to help achieve zero net deforestation by 2020.

History

In the 1940s Brazil began a program of national development in the Amazon Basin. President Getúlio Vargas declared emphatically that:

<templatestyles src="Template:Quote/styles.css"/>

> The Amazon, in the impact of our will and labor, will cease to be a simple chapter in the world, and made equivalent to other great rivers, shall become a chapter in the history of human civilization. Everything which has up to now been done in Amazonas, whether in agriculture or extractive industry... must be transformed into rational exploitation.
>
> — Getúlio Vargas[726]

Vargas established many government programs to develop his vision, including the Superintendency for the Economic Valorization of Amazonia (SPVEA) in 1953,[727] the Superintendency for the Development of Amazonia (SUDAM) in 1966, and the National Institute for Colonization and Agrarian Reform (IN-CRA) in 1970. In the 1960s deforestation of the Brazilian Amazon became more widespread, chiefly from forest removal for cattle ranching to raise national revenue in a period of high world beef prices, to eliminate hunger and to pay off international debt obligations. Extensive transportation projects, such as the Trans-Amazon Highway, were promoted in 1970, meaning that huge areas of forest would be removed for commercial purposes.

Before the 1960s, much of the forest remained intact due to restrictions on access to the Amazon beyond partial clearing along the river banks. The poor

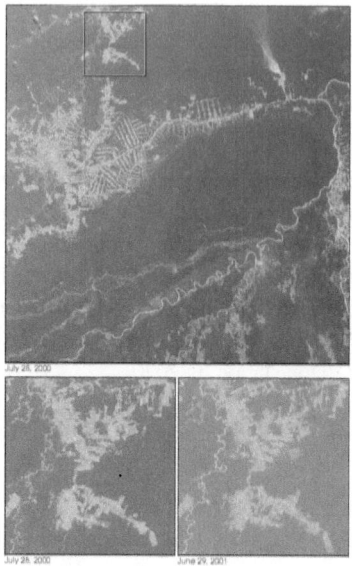

Figure 137: *A NASA satellite observation of deforestation near Rio Branco in Brazil observed July 2000.*

Figure 138: *Large areas of forest are removed to make way for plantations and cattle ranches.*

Figure 139: *Slash and burn forest removal in Brazil increased dramatically in the 1970s and 1980s.*

soil made plantation-based agriculture unprofitable. The key point in deforestation of the Amazon came when colonists established farms in the forest in the 1960s. They farmed based on crop cultivation and used the slash and burn method. The colonists were unable to successfully manage their fields and the crops due weed invasion and loss of soil fertility.[728] Soils in the Amazon are productive for only a very short period of time after the land is cleared, so farmers there must constantly move and clear more and more land.

Amazonian colonization was dominated by cattle raising, not only because grass did grow in the poor soil, but also because ranching required little labor, generated decent profit, and awarded social status. However, farming led to extensive deforestation and environmental damage.[729]

An estimated 30% of deforestation is due to small farmers and the rate of deforestation is higher in areas they inhabit is greater than in areas occupied by medium and large ranchers, who own 89% of the Legal Amazon's private land. This underlines the importance of using previously-cleared land for agriculture, rather the more usual, politically easier, path of distributing still-forested areas.[730] The number of small farmers versus large landholders fluctuates with economic and demographic pressures.

In 1964, a Brazilian land law passed that supported ownership of the land by the developer: if a person could demonstrate "effective cultivation" for a year and a day, that person could claim the land. This act paved the way for clearance of enormous areas of forest for cattle production.

Figure 140: *NASA satellite observation of deforestation in the Mato Grosso state of Brazil. The transformation from forest to farm is evident by the paler square shaped areas under development.*

In the 1970s, with construction of the Trans-Amazonian Highway, INCRA established schemes to attract hundreds of thousands of potential farmers westward into the Amazon and exploit the forest for cattle ranches. Between 1966 and 1975 Amazon land values grew at a rate of 100% per year as the government offered subsidies to reform the land; throughout the 1970s and 1980s, farmers rushed to claim land and quickly convert areas to farming and make a profit due to the improved transportation network and the high price of beef. The forest was also exploited for timber, which provided Brazil a way of paying off international debt. By the late 1980s, an area the size of England, Scotland and Wales was being cleared annually.

Causes

Cattle ranching and infrastructure

The annual rate of deforestation in the Amazon region continued to increase from 1990 to 2003 because of factors at local, national, and international levels. 70% of formerly forested land in the Amazon, and 91% of land deforested since 1970, is used for livestock pasture.[731,732] The Brazilian government initially attributed 38% of all forest loss between 1966 and 1975 to large-scale cattle ranching. According to the Center for International Forestry Research (CIFOR), "between 1990 and 2001 the percentage of Europe's processed meat imports that came from Brazil rose from 40 to 74 percent" and by 2003 "for the first time ever, the growth in Brazilian cattle production, 80 percent of which was in the Amazon was largely export driven."

Forest removal to make way for cattle ranching was the leading cause of deforestation in the Brazilian Amazon from the mid-1960s on. In addition to Vargas's earlier goal of commercial development, the devaluation of the Brazilian real against the dollar had the result of doubling the price of beef in reals and gave ranchers a widespread incentive to increase the size of their cattle ranches and areas under pasture for mass beef production, resulting in large areas of forest removal. Access to clear the forest was facilitated by the land tenure policy in Brazil that meant developers could proceed without restraint and install new cattle ranches which in turn functioned as a qualification for land ownership.[733]

Removal of the Amazon forest for cattle farming in Brazil was also seen by developers as economic investment during periods of high inflation when appreciation of cattle prices providing a way to outpace the interest rate earned on money left in the bank. Brazilian beef was more competitive on the world market at a time when extensive improvements in the road network in the Amazonas in the early 1970s through the Trans Amazonian highway and other new roads gave potential developers access to vast areas of previously-inaccessible forest. This coincided with lower transportation costs due to cheaper fuels such as ethanol, which lowered the costs of shipping the beef from the forest and gave ranchers an incentive to maximise profits.

Cattle ranching is not an environmentally friendly investment though. Cattle emit large amounts of methane. These emissions play a major role in climate change because methane's ability to trap heat is 20 times greater than that of carbon dioxide in a time horizon of 100 years and exponentially higher in shorter time horizons.[734] One cow can emit up to 130 gallons of methane a day, just by belching.

In the 1970s, Brazil planned a massive transportation infrastructure development, a 2,000-mile (3,200 km) highway that would completely cross the Amazon forest, increasing the vulnerability of poor farmers to colonizers seeking new areas for commercial development. Studies by the Environmental Defense Fund found that areas affected by the road network were eight times more likely to be deforested by cultivators than untouched lands and that the roads allowed developers to increasingly exploit the forest reserves not only for pastoral production but also for wood exports and woodcutting for fuel and for construction. Developers were often given a six-month salary and substantial

Figure 141: *Slash-and-burn forest clearing along the Rio Xingu (Xingu River) in the state of Mato Grosso.*

agricultural loans to remove the forest along roads in 250-acre (1.0 km^2) lots for new cattle ranches.

The Brazilian government granted land to approximately 150,000 families in the Amazon between 1995 and 1998. Poor farmers were also encouraged by the government through programmes such as the National Institute for Colonization and Agrarian Reform in Brazil (INCRA) to farm unclaimed forest land and after a five-year period were given title and the right to sell the land. The productivity of the soil following forest removal for farming lasts only a year or two before the fields become infertile and farmers must clear new areas of forest to maintain their income. In 1995 nearly half, 48%, of the deforestation in Brazil was attributed to poorer farmers clearing lots under 125 acres (0.51 km^2) in size.

Hydroelectric

Hydroelectric dam projects in the Amazon have also been responsible for flooding significant areas of the forest. In particular the Balbina dam flooded approximately 2,400 km^2 (930 sq mi) of rainforest on completion and its reservoir emitted 23,750,000 tons of carbon dioxide and 140,000 tons of methane in only its first three years of operation. The construction of these dams encourages the construction of roads that introduce foresters, which in turn leads to deforestation.

Figure 142: *A soybean field in Argentina.*

Mining activities

Mining has also increased deforestation in the Brazilian Amazon particularly since the 1980s with miners often clearing forest to open the mines, often also using them for building material, collecting wood for fuel and subsistence agriculture.

Soybean production

In addition, Brazil is currently the second-largest global producer of soybeans after the United States, mostly for livestock feed, and as prices for soybeans rise, soy farmers pushing north into forested areas of the Amazon. As stated in the Constitution of Brazil, clearing land for crops or fields is considered an 'effective use' of land and is a first step toward land ownership. Cleared property is also valued 5–10 times more than forested land and for that reason valuable to the owner whose ultimate objective is resale. The soy industry is an important exporter for Brazil;Wikipedia:Citation needed therefore, the needs of soy farmers have been used to validate many of the controversial transportation projects that are currently developing in the Amazon.

Cargill, a multinational company which controls the majority of the soya bean trade in Brazil has been criticized, along with fast food chains like McDonald's, by active groups such as Greenpeace for accelerating the process of the deforestation of the Amazon. Cargill is the main supplier of soya beans to large fast food companies such as McDonald's which uses the soya products to feed their cattle and chickens. As fast food chains expand, fast food chains must increase the quantity of their livestock in order to produce more products. In order to meet the large demands of soya, Cargill is forced to expand its soya production by clear cutting parts of the Amazon.[735]

The first two highways: the Rodovia Belém-Brasília (1958) and the Cuiabá-Porto Velho (1968), were the only federal highways in the Legal Amazon to be paved and passable year-round before the late 1990s. These two highways are said to be "at the heart of the 'arc of deforestation'," which at present is the focal point area of deforestation in the Brazilian Amazon. The Belém-Brasília highway attracted nearly two million settlers in the first twenty years. The success of the Belém-Brasília highway in opening up the forest was re-enacted as paved roads continued to be developed unleashing the irrepressible spread of settlement. The completions of the roads were followed by a wave of resettlement and the settlers had a significant effect on the forest.<ref name="Williams, M. 2006"/

Scientists using NASA satellite data have found that clearing for mechanized cropland has recently become a significant force in Brazilian Amazon deforestation. This change in land use may alter the region's climate and the land's ability to absorb carbon dioxide. Researchers found that in 2003, the peak year of deforestation, more than 20 percent of the Mato Grosso state's forests were converted to cropland. This finding suggests that the recent cropland expansion in the region is contributing to further deforestation. In 2005, soybean prices fell by more than 25 percent and some areas of Mato Grosso showed a decrease in large deforestation events, although the central agricultural zone continued to clear forests. But, deforestation rates could return to the high levels seen in 2003 as soybean and other crop prices begin to rebound in international markets. Brazil has become a leading worldwide producer of grains including soybean, which accounts for 5% of the nation's exports. This new driver of forest loss suggests that the rise and fall of prices for other crops, beef and timber may also have a significant impact on future land use in the region, according to the study.[736]

Logging

Logging in Brazil's Amazon is economically motivated. Although illegal logging is not, it is the most widespread problem. The economic opportunity for developing regions is driven by timber export and demand for charcoal. Charcoal-producing ovens use large amounts of timber. In one month, the Brazilian government destroyed 800 illegal ovens in Tailândia. These 800 ovens were estimated to consume about 23,000 trees per month.[737] Logging

Deforestation in Brazil

Figure 143: *Deforestation in the state of Pará*

for timber export is selective, since only a few species, such as mahogany, have commercial value and are harvested. Selective logging still does a lot of damage to the forest. For every tree harvested, 5-10 other trees are logged, to transport the logs through the forest. Also, a falling tree takes down a lot of other small trees. A logged forest contains significantly fewer species than areas where selective logging has not taken place. A forest disturbed by selective logging is also significantly more vulnerable to fire.

Logging in the Amazon, in theory, is controlled and only strictly licensed individuals are allowed to harvest the trees in selected areas. In practice, illegal logging is widespread in Brazil. Up to 60 to 80 percent of all logging in Brazil is estimated to be illegal, with 70% of the timber cut wasted in the mills. Most illegal logging companies are international companies that don't replant the trees and the practice is extensive. Expensive wood such as mahogany os illegally exported to profit these companies. Fewer trees mean that less photosynthesis will occur and therefore oxygen levels drop. Carbon dioxide emissions increase, as this gas is released from a tree when it's cut down. A tree can absorb as much as 48 pounds of carbon per year so illegal logging has a major impact on climate change.

To combat this destruction, the Brazilian government has stopped issuing new permits for logging.Wikipedia:Manual of Style/Dates and numbers#Chronological items Unauthorized harvesting has continued nonetheless.

Figure 144: *A burning forest in Brazil.*

Efforts to prevent cutting down forests include payments to land owners. Instead of banning logging all together, the government hopes payments of comparable sums will dissuade owners from further deforestation.[738]

Effects

One of the major concerns arising from deforestation in Brazil is the global effect it produces on climatic change. Rain forests, of vital importance in the carbon dioxide exchange process, are second only to oceans as the most important sinks on the planet for absorbing the increasing atmospheric carbon dioxide resulting from industry.

The most recent survey on deforestation and greenhouse gas emissions reports that deforestation in the Brazilian Amazon is responsible for as much as 10% of current greenhouse gas emissions due to the removal of forest which would otherwise have absorbed the emissions, and has a clear effect on global warming. The method often used to remove the forest, where many trees are burned to the ground, emits vast amounts of carbon dioxide into the atmosphere, affecting air quality not just in Brazil but globally.

Fires intended to burn limited areas of forest to make way for allocated agricultural plots, frequently burn get out of control and burn much more extensive

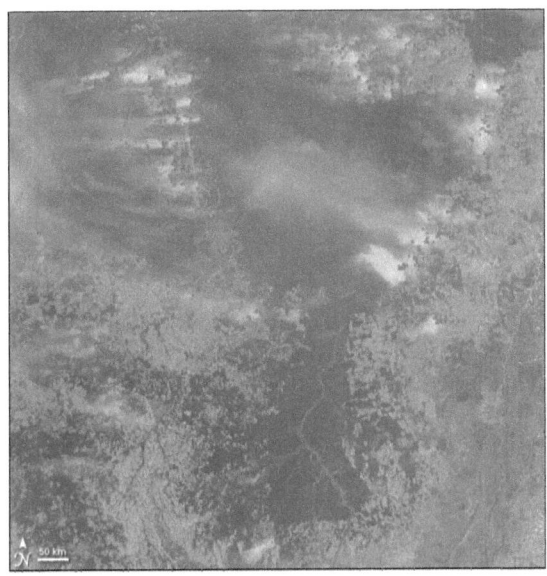

Figure 145: *A NASA satellite observation of forest fires resulting from deforestation in August 2007. The red dots represent areas of fire.*

areas of land than intended. Between July and October 1987, about 19,300 square miles (50,000 km²) of rainforest was burned in the states of Pará, Mato Grosso, Rondônia, and Acre releasing more than 500 million tons of carbon, 44 million tons of carbon monoxide, and millions of tons of nitrogen oxides and other poisonous chemicals into the atmosphere.[739] In 2005 forest fires in Brazil caused widespread disruptions across the Amazon region, including airport closures and hospitalizations for smoke inhalation.

Carbon present in the trees is essential for ecosystem development and plays a key role in the regional and global climate. Fallen leaves from deforestation leave behind a mass of dead plant material known as slash, which on decomposition provides a food source for invertebrates. This had the indirect effect of increasing atmospheric carbon dioxide levels through respiration and microbial activity. Simultaneously the organic carbon in the soil structure became depleted and the presence of carbon plays a vital role in the functioning of life in any ecosystem.

The Brazilian rainforest is one of the most biologically diverse regions of the world. Over a million species of plants and animals are known to live in the Amazon and many millions of species are unclassified or unknown. With rapid deforestation the habitats of many animals and plants are under threat and some species may face extinction. Deforestation reduces the gene pool; there is less of the genetic variation needed to adapt to climate change in the future. The Brazilian Amazon is known to possess vast resources for medicine and scientific research in the basin has been conducted to find a cure for major global killers such as AIDS, cancer, and other terminal diseases.

Rainforests are the oldest ecosystems on earth. Rainforest plants and animals continue to evolve, developing into the most diverse and complex ecosystems on earth. Living in limited areas, most of these species are endemic, found nowhere else in the world. In tropical rainforests, an estimated 90% of the species of the ecosystem live in the canopy. Since tropical rainforests are estimated to hold 50% of the planet's species, the canopy of rainforests worldwide may hold 45% of life on Earth. The Amazon rainforest borders 8 countries, and has the world's largest river basin and is the source of 1/5 of the Earth's river water. It has the world's greatest diversity of birds and freshwater fish. The Amazon is home to more species of plants and animals than any other terrestrial ecosystem on the planet—perhaps 30% of the world's species are found there.

More than 300 species of mammals are found in the Amazon, the majority bats and rodents. The Amazon basin contains more freshwater fish species than anywhere else in the world—more than 3,000 species. More than 1500 bird species are also found there. Frogs are overwhelmingly the most abundant amphibians in the rainforest. Interdependence, when species depend on one another, takes many forms in the forest, from species relying on other species for pollination and seed dispersal to predator-prey relationships to symbiotic relationships. Each species that disappears from the ecosystem may weaken the survival chances of another, while the loss of a keystone species—an organism that links many other species together—could cause a significant disruption in the functioning of the entire system.

Forest removal affects the social and economic lives of the indigenous people who live in the forests and whose families have lived there in relative isolation for many centuries. These indigenous peoples, like the Kayapo, have an intimate understanding of the ecology of the Amazon.[740] The subsequent loss of these people may also prove to be a loss of knowledge. The rainforest is their home, and a fundamental source of food, shelter, fuel, nourishment cultural heritage and recreation. Deforestation for the export of timber removes valuable protection for the soils in a dynamic ecosystem and regions prone to desertification and silting of river banks as rivers become clogged with eroded soils in sparse areas. If too much timber is cut, soil that once had sufficient cover can get baked and dry out in the sun, leading to erosion and degradation of soil fertility and farmers cannot profit from their land even after clearing it. According to the United Nations Environmental Programme (UNEP) in 1977,

Figure 146: *Deforestation in the state of Maranhão*

deforestation is a major cause of desertification and in 1980 threatened 35% of the world's land surface and 20% of the world's population.

Exploitation of forests for mining activities such as gold mining has also significantly increased the risk of mercury poisoning and contamination of the ecosystem and water. Mercury poisoning can affect the food chain and affect wildlife both on land and in the rivers. It can also affect plants and the crops of farmers trying to farm forest areas. Pollution may result from mine sludge and affect the functioning of the river system when exposed soil is blown in the wind and can have a significant impact on aquatic populations further affected by dam building in the region. Dams may have a profound impact on migrating fish and ecological life and leave plains prone to flooding and leaching.

NASA survey

In the American Meteorological Society Journal of Climate, two research meteorologists at NASA's Goddard Space Flight Center Andrew Negri and Robert Adler have analysed the impact of deforestation on climatic patterns in the Amazon using data and observatory readings collected from NASA's Tropical Rainfall Measuring Mission over many years. Working also with the University of Arizona and the North Carolina State University Negri said "In deforested areas, the land heats up faster and reaches a higher temperature, leading to localized upward motions that enhance the formation of clouds and ultimately produce more rainfall".

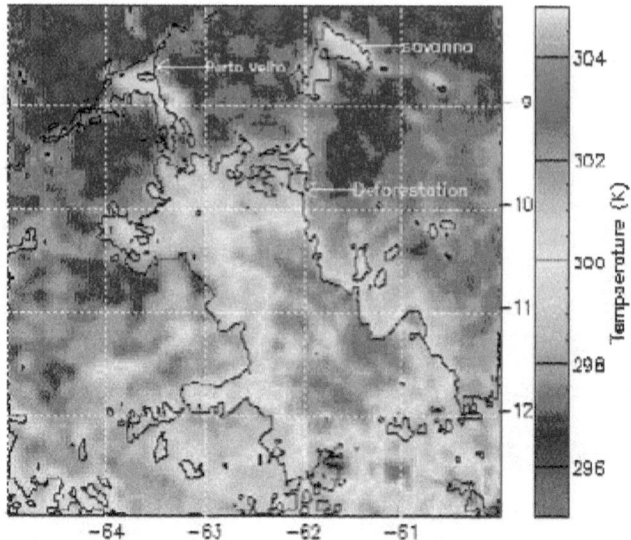

Figure 147: *The effect of deforestation on increasing land temperature.*

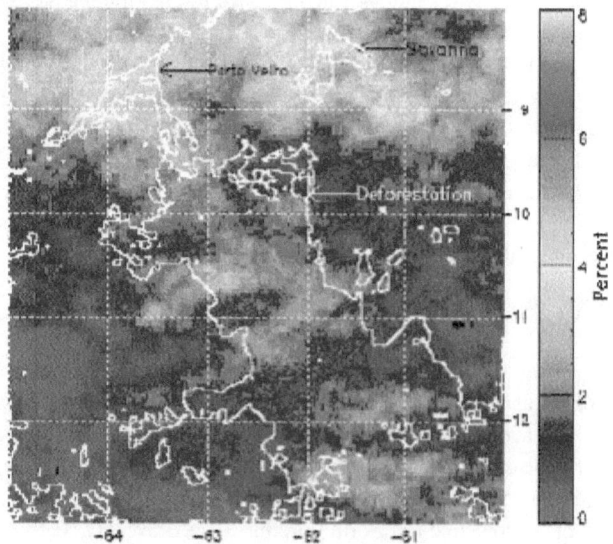

Figure 148: *Effect of deforestation on cloud cover.*

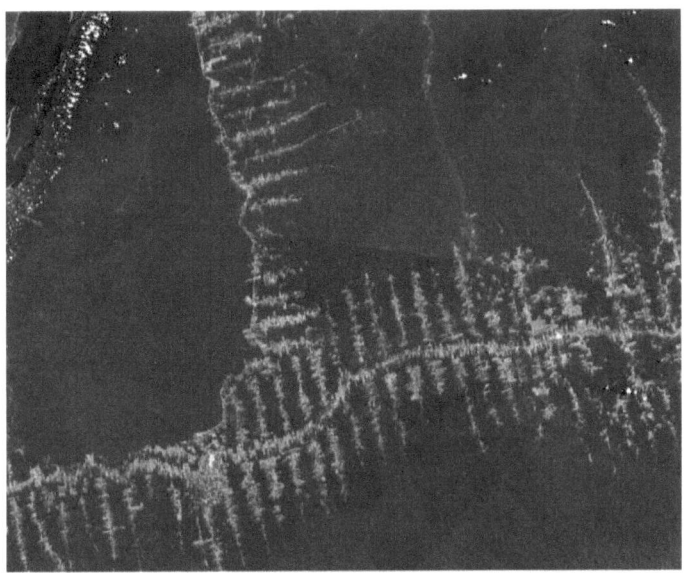

Figure 149: *The zig-zag patterns across the road resulting from deforestation in Brazil can be seen from space.*

They also examined cloud cover in deforested areas. In comparison with areas still unaffected by deforestation they found a significant increase in cloud cover and rainfall during the August–September wet season where forest had been cleared. The height or existence of plants and trees in the forest directly affects the aerodynamics of the atmosphere, and precipitation in the area. In addition the Massachusetts Institute of Technology developed a series of detailed computer simulation models of rainfall patterns in the Amazon during the 1990s and concluded that forest removal also leaves soil exposed to the sun, and the increased temperature on the surface enhances evaporation and increases moisture in the air.

Measured rates

Deforestation rates in the Brazilian Amazon have slowed dramatically since peaking in 2004 at 27,423 square kilometers per year. By 2009, deforestation had fallen to around 7,000 square kilometers per year, a decline of nearly 75 percent from 2004, according to Brazil's National Institute for Space Research (*Instituto Nacional de Pesquisas Espaciais*, or INPE),[741] which produces deforestation figures annually.

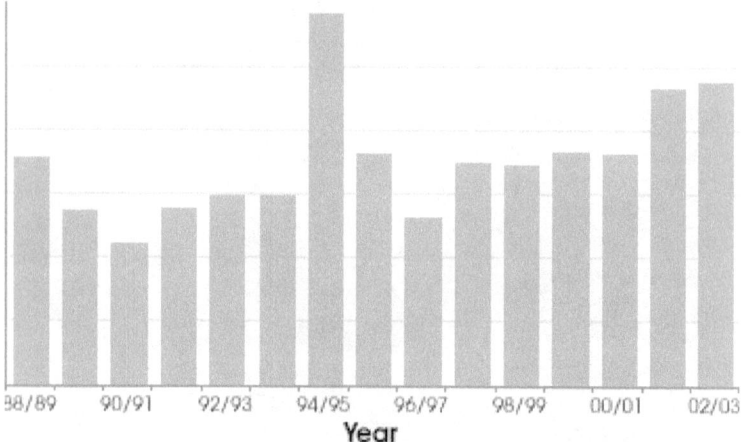

Figure 150: *A deforestation chart. The double increase for 1994 and 1995 was attributed to accidental forest burning rather than active logging.*

Their deforestation estimates are derived from 100 to 220 images taken during the dry season in the Amazon by the China–Brazil Earth Resources Satellite program (CBERS), and may only consider the loss of the Amazon rainforest – not the loss of natural fields or savanna within the Amazon biome. According to INPE, the original Amazon rainforest biome in Brazil of 4,100,000 km^2 was reduced to 3,403,000 km^2 by 2005 – representing a loss of 17.1%.

According to estimates based on data from the National Institute for Space Research and the Food and Agriculture Organization (FAO), the rates of deforestation in Amazon Rainforest are:

Period	Estimated remaining forest cover in the Brazilian Amazon (km^2)	Annual forest loss (km^2)	Percent of 1970 cover remaining	Total forest loss since 1970 (km^2)
Pre–1970	4,100,000	—	—	—
1977	3,955,870	21,130	96.5%	144,130
1978–1987	3,744,570	21,130	91.3%	355,430
1988	3,723,520	21,050	90.8%	376,480
1989	3,705,750	17,770	90.4%	394,250
1990	3,692,020	13,730	90.0%	407,980
1991	3,680,990	11,030	89.8%	419,010
1992	3,667,204	13,786	89.4%	432,796

1993	3,652,308	14,896	89.1%	447,692
1994	3,637,412	14,896	88.7%	462,588
1995	3,608,353	29,059	88.0%	491,647
1996	3,590,192	18,161	87.6%	509,808
1997	3,576,965	13,227	87.2%	523,035
1998	3,559,582	17,383	86.8%	540,418
1999	3,542,323	17,259	86.4%	557,677
2000	3,524,097	18,226	86.0%	575,903
2001	3,505,932	18,165	85.5%	594,068
2002	3,484,538	21,651	85.0%	615,719
2003	3,459,291	25,396	84.4%	641,115
2004	3,431,868	27,772	83.7%	668,887
2005	3,412,022	19,014	83.2%	687,901
2006	3,397,913	14,285	82.9%	702,186
2007	3,386,381	11,651	82.6%	713,837
2008	3,375,413	12,911	82.3%	726,748
2009	3,365,788	7,464	82.1%	734,212
2010	3,358,788	7,000	81.9%	741,212
2011	3,352,370	6,418	81.8%	747,630
2012	3,347,799	4,571	81.7%	752,201
2013	3,341,908	5,891	81.5%	758,092
2014	3,336,896	5,012	81.4%	763,104
2015	3,331,065	5,831	81.2%	768,935

Response

By the end of the 1980s, the removal of Brazil's forests had become a serious global issue, not only because of the loss of biodiversity and ecological disruption, but also because of the large amounts of carbon dioxide (CO_2) released from burned forests and the loss of a valuable sink to absorb global CO_2 emissions. At the 1992 UN Framework Convention on Climate Change, deforestation became a key issue addressed at the summit in Rio de Janeiro. Plans for the compensated reduction (CR) of greenhouse gas emissions from tropical forests were set up to give nations like Brazil an incentive to curb their rate of deforestation.

"We are encouraging the Brazilian government to fully endorse the Compensated Reduction proposal", said scientist Paulo Moutinho, coordinator of the

Figure 151: *Map of Deforestation in Brazil, from 2002 to 2008, for each Biome. Bases: Prodes (INPE) and Biomes's Monitoring (IBAMA). Note: The monitoring does not cover areas of Cerrado and Campinarama (Savannahs) located in Amazon Biome.*

climate change program of the Amazon Institute for Environmental Research (IPAM), an NGO research institute in Brazil.[742] In Brazil, the cost of reducing deforestation emissions by half will be less than $5 per ton of carbon dioxide, estimated an unpublished study of IPAM and the Woods Hole Research Center.Wikipedia:Citation needed

On May 11, 1994, two scientists, Compton Tucker and David Skole, presented the results of a NASA survey at the Subcommittee on Western Hemisphere Affairs of the United States Congress, a formal scientific assessment of deforestation in Brazil and the rate of forest removal as well as questions on the effectiveness of Brazilian environmental policies. Whilst undertaking a monitoring and complete assessment was very difficult due to the size of the rainforest, they concluded that satellite observations showed a reduction in the rate of forest removal between 1992 and 1993 and that World Bank estimates of 600,000 square km^2 (12%) cleared to that point appeared to be too high. The NASA assessment concurred with the findings of the Brazilian National Space Research Institute (INPE) an estimated 280,000 km^2 (5%) in the same period.[743]Wikipedia:Identifying reliable sources

Figure 152: *Areas of large scale atmosphere-biosphere experiments in Amazonia aim to monitor and regulate the impact of deforestation on the atmosphere.*

The following year (1995) deforestation nearly doubled; this has been attributed the accidental fire following El Niño-related drought rather than active logging and the following year again showed a major drop. In 2002 Brazil ratified the Kyoto Agreement as a developing nation listed in the non-Annex I countries. These countries do not have carbon emission quotas in the agreement as developed nations do.[744] President Luiz Inácio Lula da Silva reiterated that Brazil "is in charge of looking after the Amazon."[745]

In 2006 Brazil proposed a direct finance project to deal with the Reduced Emissions from Deforestation and Degradation in Developing Countries, or REDD, issue, recognizing that deforestation contributes to 20% of the world's greenhouse gas emissions. The competing proposal for the REDD issue was a carbon emission credit system, where reduced deforestation would receive "marketable emissions credits". In effect, developed countries could reduce their carbon emissions, and approach their emissions quota by investing in the reforestation of developing rainforest countries. Instead, Brazil's 2006 proposal would draw from a fund based on donor country contributors.

By 2005 forest removal had fallen to 9,000 km² (3,500 sq mi) of forest compared to 18,000 km² (6,900 sq mi) in 2003 and on July 5, 2007, Brazilian president Luiz Inácio Lula da Silva announced at the International Conference

Figure 153: *Weather patterns above the Amazon taken on board a shuttle in orbit in February 1984. Deforestation in Brazil has and will have a major impact on the climate system and rainfall, according to scientists.*

on Biofuels in Brussels that more than 20 million hectares of conservation units to protect the forest and more efficient fuel production had allowed the rate of deforestation to fall by 52% in the three years since 2004.

Daniel Nepstad of the Woods Hole Research Center has demonstrated that Brazil's deforestation rates have been cut nearly in half in recent years through a combination of government intervention and economic trends. Since 2004 the country has established more than 200,000 km² of parks, nature reserves, and national forests in the Amazon rainforest. These protected areas, if fully enforced, would keep an estimated one billion tons of carbon going into the atmosphere through deforestation by the year 2015.[746] The academic evidence suggests that the creation of public lands, through the assignment of property rights, reduces incentives to deforest land for agricultural conversion and contributes to lower land-related conflict.

In 2005 Brazilian Environment Minister Marina da Silva announced that 9,000 km² (3,500 sq mi) of forest had been felled in the previous year, compared with more than 18,000 km² (6,900 sq mi) in 2003 and 2004. Between 2005 and 2006 there was a 41% drop in deforestation; nonetheless, Brazil still had the largest area of forest removed annually on the planet.

Deforestation in Brazil 335

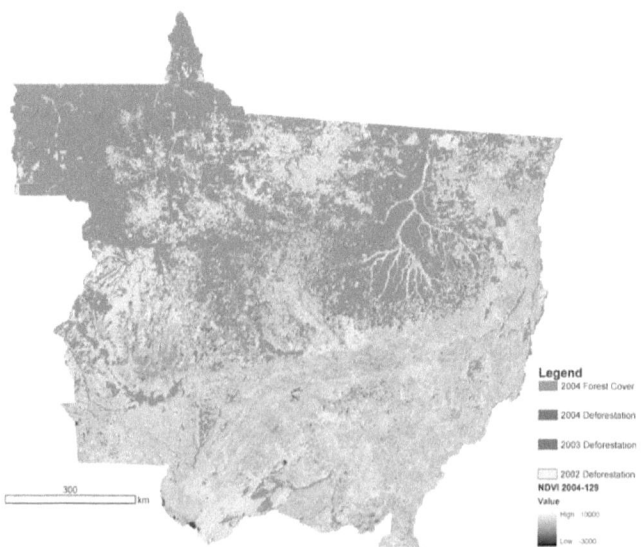

Figure 154: *A NASA observation of forest cover and deforestation in the state of Mato Grosso for 2004.*

These methods have also reduced the illegal appropriation of land and logging, encouraging the use of land for sustainable timber harvesting.

Future

The improvement of the social and economic conditions of the huge population of poor people in Brazil is the main concern of the government.

It is clear that to diminish deforestation in the Brazilian Amazon would require enormous financial resources to compensate the loggers and given them an economic incentive to pursue other areas of activity. The World Wide Fund for Nature (WWF) has estimated that a total of approximately US$547.2 million (1 billion Brazilian reais) per year would be required from international sources to compensate the forest developers and establish a highly organized framework to fully implement forest governance and monitoring,[747] and the foundation of new protected forest areas in the Amazon for future sustainability.[748] Compensating the loggers over the entirety of the Amazon rainforest would require a heavy amount of funding and increased interaction with the international community, and a reform of the world market system if deforestation in the country is to be halted.

Figure 155: *Toco toucan. The biodiversity of Brazil's rainforests is under threat.*

Non-governmental organizations such as WWF have been highly active in the region and WWF Brazil has formed an alliance with some eight other Brazilian NGO'S which aim to completely halt deforestation in the Amazon by 2015. Another group that have been effective is Greenpeace, an organization whose goal is to fight to save the plant from the destruction of forests, the threat of global warming and the deterioration of the ocean. Other groups such as The Nature Conservancy, the proposal, known as the "Agreement on Acknowledging the Value of the Forest and Ending Amazon Deforestation," aims at combining strong public policies with market strategies to achieve annual deforestation reduction targets.

The groups aim to establish a wide-ranging commitment between the sectors of the government and society to conserve the rainforest and are aiming for an overall reduction in deforestation of 68,737.8 square kilometres in seven years. Denise Hamú, the CEO of WWF-Brazil has said' "Only through the mobilization of state and federal governments, the private sector and environmental NGOs we can reach significant results for the conservation and promotion of sustainable development in the Amazon".

External links

> Wikimedia Commons has media related to *Deforestation*.

- Images of deforestation in the Amazon[749]
- Reversing deforestation in Brazil?, an academic article[750]
- Mecanismos y actores sociales en la deforestación de la amazonia brasileña[751]

Conservation in Brazil

Even though progress has been made in **conserving** Brazil's landscapes, the country still faces serious threats due to its historical land use. Amazonian forests substantially influence regional and global climates and deforesting this region is both a regional and global driver of climate change due to the high amounts of deforestation and habitat fragmentation that have occurred this region.

Brazil has established an extensive network of protected areas which covers more than 2 million km2(25% of Brazil's national territory) and is divided almost equally between protected natural areas or conservation units and indigenous land ("Terras Indígenas"). Despite these measures, environmental protection is still a concern as indigenous tribes and Brazilian environmental activists contend with ranchers, illegal loggers, gold and oil prospectors and drug traffickers who continue to illegally clear forests.

Deforestation

More than one-fifth of the Amazon Rainforest in Brazil has been completely destroyed, and more than 70 mammals are endangered. The threat of extinction comes from several sources, including deforestation and poaching. Extinction is even more problematic in the Atlantic Forest, where nearly 93% of the forest has been cleared. Of the 202 endangered animals in Brazil, 171 are in the Atlantic Forest.

The Amazon rainforest has been under direct threat of deforestation since the 1970s because of rapid economic and demographic expansion. Extensive legal and illegal logging destroy forests the size of a small country per year, and with it a diverse series of species through habitat destruction and habitat fragmentation.[752] Since 1970, over 600,000 square kilometers (230,000 sq mi) of the Amazon Rainforest have been cleared by logging.

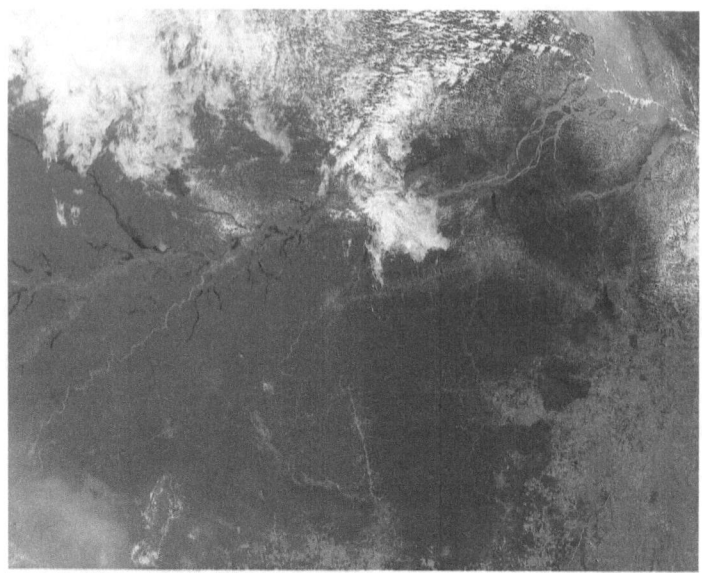

Figure 156: *"At bottom right and bottom center, deforestation and cultivation are evident by the regular, rectangular shapes that delineate plots."*

Cattle ranching

From the mid 1960s to 1970s the devaluation of the Brazilian real against the dollar resulted in doubling the price of beef in reals and gave ranchers a lucrative incentive to increase the size of their cattle ranches. During the same time period plans to expand infrastructure to facilitate greater trade within the Amazon region manifested itself in the building of the Trans-Amazonian Highway. A 2,000 miles (3,200 km) wide highway would effectively connect the entire Amazon and would create huge opportunities for cattle ranching to expand into previously untouched parts of the forest. Widespread use of ethanol, a cheaper gas, gave cattle ranchers every economic incentive to take maximize profits no matter the environmental repercussions. The cattle industry initially struggled to meet domestic demand but soon became export driven. According to the Center for International Forestry Research (CIFOR), "between 1990 and 2001 the percentage of Europe's processed meat imports that came from Brazil rose from 40 to 74 percent" and by 2003 "for the first time ever, the growth in Brazilian cattle production, 80 percent of which was in the Amazon, was largely export driven."[753]

Soybean production

After the United States, Brazil is the second largest produce of soybeans. Soybean production, like cattle ranching, requires ample land and because of its profitability and importance as an export, receives large governmental support. As stated in the Constitution of Brazil, clearing land for crops or fields is considered an 'effective use' of land and has resulted in massive expansions of infrastructure aimed at providing greater access to unused land. In an effort to address increasing demand of ranching, soybean production and timber, two highways were constructed: the Rodovia Belém-Brasília (1958) and the Cuiaba-Porto Velho (1968). These were the only federal highways in the Legal Amazon to be paved and passable year-round before the late 1990s and contributed greatly to the high rates of deforestation.

With greater infrastructural support and economic incentive, Brazilian soybean production has skyrocketed. Land clearing for greater mechanized farming now contributes even more extensively to deforestation because of the change in land use. Whereas previously the land was either unused or uninhabited and could function as a CO^2 absorber, mechanized farming could drastically change local climate and effect the rainforest's ability to absorb carbon emissions.[754]

Timber

Both cattle ranching and soybean production rely on clear and expansive land to operate efficiently. Large parts of the Amazon rainforest have been cleared to provide for these sectors and the excess timber produced is extremely profitable. The removal of large swaths of trees from this area negatively impacts the environment in significant ways yet only account for trees killed, not necessarily harvested. For example, near Paragominas, Pará, for every tree harvested, 27 trees have been reported killed or severely damaged.[755] With fewer trees the Amazon rainforest cannot absorb as much carbon emissions and greatly expedite the process of Global Warming.

In 2007 Brazilian president Luiz Inácio Lula da Silva announced at the International Conference on Biofuels in Brussels that Brazil's deforestation rate had dramatically slowed due to efficient fuel production and setting aside over 20 million hectares of forest. Since 2004 Brazil has established more than 200,000 square kilometres of parks, nature reserves, and national forests in the Amazon rainforest. These protected areas, if fully enforced, will prevent an estimated one billion tons of carbon emissions from being transferred to the atmosphere through deforestation by the year 2015.[756]

Poaching

According to a 2001 report by Rede, or RENC, (Portuguese for "National Network Against the Trafficking of Wild Animals"), wildlife smuggling is Brazil's third most profitable illegal activity, after arms dealing and drug smuggling. RENCTAS believes that the poachers are taking an estimated 38 million birds, reptiles and other animals from the wild each year. The same report claims that police only intercept .5% of smuggled animal wildlife and that it is incredibly easy to successfully smuggle animals throughout Brazil.

Invasive species

Native wildlife are threatened by some invasive species. There have been more than 300 documented invasive species in Brazil. It is estimated that invasive species cost Brazil around $49 billion. The most threatening species is the wild boar which destroys crops and natural flora, and can transmit diseases to indigenous animals. Also damaging the natural habitat are African grasses and snails. The Brazilian Institute of Environment and Renewable Natural Resources (IBAMA) has put restrictions on what species may be brought into the country.[757]

Endangered Species

Brazil is home to over 6% of the world's endangered species. According to a species assessment conducted by the IUCN Red List of Endangered Species, 97 species have been identified in Brazil with vulnerable, lower risk/near threatened, endangered, or critically endangered standing. In 2009, 769 endangered species were identified in Brazil, making it home to the eighth largest number of endangered species in the world. For Brazil, and the countries that precede it, high rates of deforestation, industrialization, and urbanization explain the growing number of endangered species in extremely bio-diverse areas. According to Carlos Minc, Brazil's Environment Minister, protected areas are increasingly populated by humans and preservation areas are lacking the essential protection they need. Industries involved in deforestation play large roles in degrading and destroying lands that are incredibly sensitive to changes in their ecosystem. By 2020, it is estimated that at least 50% of the species resident in Brazil will become extinct.

Conservation efforts

Brazilian Forest Code

From the 1990s through 2004, the Brazilian Forest Code (FC) was the primary and most prolific legal restriction of forest clearing on private lands. The FC established that 50% of each private property must be managed as forest reserve and retain its natural composition. However, in 1996 the minimum required reserve proportion was increased to 80%. While this seemed a protective change, it has been difficult to accurately detect illegal land use, which makes enforcement extremely difficult.

The profitability of soy production in Brazil drastically fell from 2005-2006, which resulted in a reduction in the amount of land planted with soy in the Brazilian Amazon. In 2004, the Detection of Deforestation in Real Time (DETER) was launched, which provided a system for detecting and responding to events of deforestation. The Amazon Region Protected Areas Program resulted in a 68% increase in protected areas and indigenous territories from 2004- 2012. Many of these newly protected areas were created in active agricultural frontiers.

Since 2005 the annual rate of deforestation in Brazil has continued to decline while soy and beef production have continued to rise.

Rise of ethanol

The first use of ethanol as a fuel source came from the emergence of the automobile in Brazil during the 1920s. Ethanol production peaked during World War II because German submarines threatened oil supplies and the Brazilian government, in turn, looked for alternative fuel sources. Gasoline was heavily favored until the 1973 global oil shock made clear Brazil's dangerous dependence on foreign oil. In response, the Brazilian government began promoting bioethanol as an alternative fuel. The National Alcohol Program -Pró-Álcool- (Portuguese: 'Programa Nacional do Álcool'), launched in 1975, was a nationwide program financed by the government to phase out automobile fuels derived from fossil fuels, such as gasoline, in favor of ethanol produced from sugar cane. This large-scale shift to ethanol initially focused on the amount of ethanol mixed with gasoline. The percent of ethanol in gasoline fluctuated greatly from 10% to 22% between 1976 and 1992 until a federal law established a mandatory blend of 22% anhydrous ethanol for the entire country.[758] The percentage of ethanol mixed with gasoline has continued to change throughout the 21st century because of changing supply of sugarcane, making it possible for mixtures even within the same year to differ from 20-25%.

Figure 157: *Brazil has ethanol fuel available throughout the country. Shown here a typical Petrobras gas station at São Paulo with dual fuel service, marked A for alcohol (ethanol) and G for gasoline.*

The Brazilian government has worked with both public and private sectors to provide incentive for creative inventions that would make the most use of Brazil's ethanol boom. After testing in government fleets with several prototypes developed by local carmakers, and compelled by the second oil crisis, the Fiat 147, the first modern commercial neat ethanol car (E100 only) was launched to the market in July 1979. In order to establish ethanol as an alternative to gasoline, the Brazilian government provided three important initial drivers for the ethanol industry: guaranteed purchases by the state-owned oil company Petrobras, low-interest loans for agro-industrial ethanol firms, and fixed gasoline and ethanol prices where hydrous ethanol sold for 59% of the government-set gasoline price at the pump. Brazil's increased energy independence has allowed greater competitiveness between foreign oil producers, making gasoline even cheaper for Brazilians.[759]

In 2011 Brazil produced 21.1 billion liters of ethanol (5.57 billion liquid gallons), representing 24.9 percent of the world's total ethanol used as fuel.[760] The Brazilian model for success in ethanol, however, is hard to replicate because of Brazil's large amount of arable land and advanced agri-industrial technology. For the past four decades, Brazil has taken serious steps to move towards greater energy security and federal environmental protection by advancing ethanol production as a compliment to oil.

Brazil's ethanol fuel program is based on the most efficient method of cultivating sugar cane in the world. Using modern equipment and cheap sugar cane as feedstock, residual cane-waste (bagasse) is used to produce heat and power, resulting in competitive prices for energy. The balance of energy, or the input vs. output of energy, is extremely high when using this method and results anywhere from 8.3 (average conditions) and 10.1 (optimum). This creates an almost negative energy balance that actually reduces more carbon emissions in the atmosphere as the sugarcane is growing than it produces when it is being burned. In 2010, the U.S. EPA designated Brazil's sugarcane ethanol as an advanced biofuel because of its 61% reduction of total life cycle greenhouse gas emissions, including direct indirect land use change emissions.[761]

Brazil's widespread use and production of ethanol has had substantial benefits for Brazil's economy and environment. Studies have shown that up to 85% of greenhouse gas emissions are cut because of the switch from gasoline.[762,763] Land use, with specific regard to growing sugarcane, remains a concern for the environment. As producers of sugarcane continue to mass-produce within the same soil, nutrients that get replenished naturally are harder to come by; soil is not as fertile as it used to be. Though land use for the production of sugarcane continues to be an issue, the EPA has concluded that sugarcane ethanol from Brazil reduces greenhouse gas emissions as compared to gasoline by 61%, using a 30-year payback for indirect land use change (ILUC) emissions. Another 2010 study published by the World Bank found that "Brazil's transport sector has a lower carbon intensity compared to that of most other countries because of its widespread use of ethanol as a fuel for vehicles."[764]

Institutional response: policy solutions

The Brazilian government has responded to decades of high rates of deforestation and extremely environmentally harmful practices with macro level decisions that have impacted Brazil's culture, economy, and environment. While some policies to reduce carbon emissions and deforestation are responses to economic tendencies, such as the rise of ethanol, others are motivated by locally organized non-governmental agencies and citizens alike.

Government and NGOs

The Ministry of Environment is responsible for Brazil's national environmental policy. The ministry's many departments deal with climate change and environmental quality, biodiversity and forests, water resources, sustainable urban and rural development, and environmental citizenship. Other authorities are also responsible for the implementation of environmental policies, including the National Council on the Environment, the National Council of the

Amazon, the National Council of Water Resources, the Chico Mendes Institute for Biodiversity Conservation (ICMBIO), Brazilian Institute of Environment and Renewable Natural Resources (IBAMA), Board of Management of Public Forests, and others.[765] The collaborative work of these institutions makes it possible to ensure sustainable growth within the means of the environment.

The development of institutions at the governmental level was stimulated and accompanied by the diffusion and increasing importance of NGOs dedicated to environmental causes and sustainable development. Numerous NGOs throughout Brazil produce documents containing both useful information and criticisms of policies that are continuously harmful to Brazil's environment.[766] NGOs on the ground have held the Brazilian government accountable to their policies of conservation and serve to inform and advocate for the localities they are based in.

Name	Foundation Year	Mission
SOS Mata Atlântica	1986	Defend the Atlantic Forest areas, protect the communities that inhabit the region, and preserve their natural, historical, and cultural heritage.
Socio Environmental Institute	1994	Defend rights related to the environment, cultural heritage, and human rights.
Greenpeace		Defend the environment by raising awareness about environmental issues and influence people to change their habits.
WWF-Brasil	1996	Instruct Brazilian society on how to use natural resources in a rational manner.
Conservation International (CI)	1987	Protect biodiversity and instruct society on how to live in harmony with nature.
Akatu Institute		Guide Brazil's consumption habits toward a sustainable model.
Ecoar Institute	After Rio-92	Provide environmental education as an effort to rescue degraded areas and implement local sustainable development programs and projects.
Ecoa	1989	Create a space for negotiations and decisions about environmental protection and sustainability.
Recicloteca		Diffuse information on environmental issues, especially for the reduction, reutilization, and recycling of waste.
Friends of the Earth-Brazilian Amazon	1989	Develop projects and activities that promote sustainable development in the Amazonian region.

National Network to Fight the Trafficking of Wild Animals (Renctas)	1999	Combat the trafficking of wild animals and contribute to biodiversity protection.
Atlantic Forest NGO Network		Provide information about NGOs that work toward the protection of the Atlantic Forest.
Brazilian Forum of NGOs and Social Movements for the Environment and Development (FBOMS)	1990	Facilitate the participation of the public in the United Nations Conference on Environment (UNCED).
Brazilian Foundation for Sustainable Development (FBDS)	1992	Implement the conventions and treaties approved at Rio-92.

National System of Conservation Units - SNUC

Brazil's 1988 Federal Constitution promotes an "ecologically balanced environment", as defined in article 225 on the environment, and vests the Brazilian government the responsibility of defending and preserving it. From this constitutional prerogative, Brazil has created the National System of Units of Conservation (Sistema Nacional de Unidades de Conservação - SNUC), through the Federal Law No. 9.985/2000 to devise a plan for sustainable development and land conservation.[767]

Basically, SNUC divides protected areas into two groups: Full protection and sustainable use. Each group contains divers categories of units.[768]

- Full protection - Ecological station, Biological reserve, National park, Natural monument, and Wildlife refuge
- Sustainable use - Environmental protection area, Area of relevant ecological interest, National forest, Extractive reserve, Wildlife reserve, Sustainable development reserve, and Private natural heritage reserve.

In order to have flexibility on its land use policies, Brazil has created a dynamic system of regulations that promote and require sustainability practices be implemented. These are innovative frameworks as they offer the community the possibility to participate in decision-making and to apply financial mechanisms that make the system viable, as well as encouraging the conservation of natural environments.[769] According to UNESCO's office in Brasilia, Brazil "has a little over 1,600 federal, state and private Conservation Units (CUs) that protect 16% of the continental territory and 0.5% of the marine area, which corresponds to 1,479,286 square kilometers."

Figure 158: *A beach in the federally protected Park of Dunes, located in Rio Grande do Norte.*

External links

- Brazilian Amazon Protected areas - Instituto Socioambiental[770]
- Brazil Wildlife Conservation Partner[771]

Government and politics

Politics of Brazil

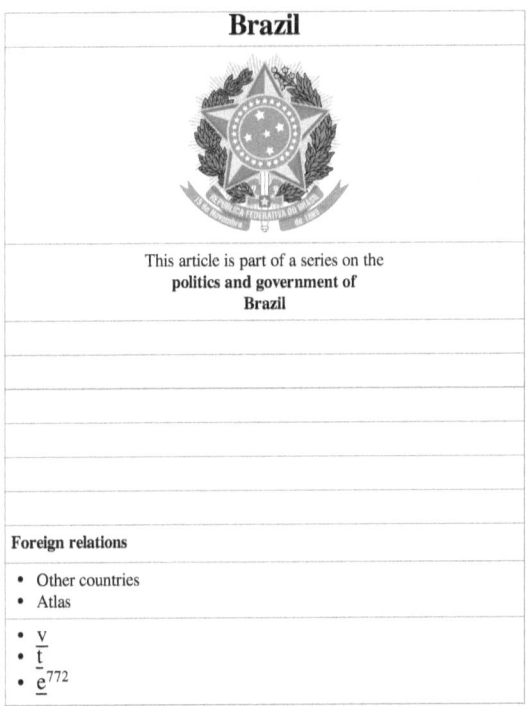

Brazil
This article is part of a series on the **politics and government of** Brazil
Foreign relations<ul><li>Other countries</li><li>Atlas</li></ul>
<ul><li>v</li><li>t</li><li>e[772]</li></ul>

The **politics of Brazil** take place in a framework of a federal presidential representative democratic republic, whereby the President is both head of state and head of government, and of a multi-party system. The political and administrative organization of Brazil comprises the federal government, the 26 states and a federal district, and the municipalities.

The federal government exercises control over the central government and is divided into three independent branches: executive, legislative and judicial. Executive power is exercised by the President, advised by a cabinet. Legislative power is vested upon the National Congress, a two-chamber legislature comprising the Federal Senate and the Chamber of Deputies. Judicial power is exercised by the judiciary, consisting of the Supreme Federal Court, the Superior Court of Justice and other Superior Courts, the National Justice Council and the Regional Federal Courts.

The states are autonomous sub-national entities with their own governments that, together with the other federal units, form the Federative Republic of Brazil. Currently, Brazil is divided politically and administratively into 27 federal units, being 26 states and one federal district. The executive power is exercised by a governor elected to a four-year term. The judiciary is exercised by courts of first and second instance addressing the common justice. Each State has a unicameral legislature with deputies who vote on state laws. The Constitution of Brazil knows also two elements of direct democracy, stated in Article 14.[773] The legislative assemblies supervise the activities of the Executive power of the states and municipalities.

The municipalities are minor federal units of the Federative Republic of Brazil. Each municipality has an autonomous local government, comprising a mayor, directly elected by the people to a four-year term, and a legislative body, also directly elected by the people.

Due to a mix of proportional voting (the only first-past-the-post elections are for the 1/3 of senate seats every 8 years and for mayors in small and medium-sized cities every 4 years), the lack of election threshold and the cultural aspects of Latin American *caudillismo-coronelismo*, party politics in Brazil tends to be highly fragmented. The Economist Intelligence Unit has rated Brazil as "flawed democracy" in 2016.

Constitution

Brazil has had seven constitutions:

- Constitution of 1824 – the first Brazilian constitution, enacted by Emperor Pedro I. It was monarchic, hereditary, and highly centralized, permitting suffrage only to property-holders.
- Constitution of 1891 – the republic was proclaimed in 1889, but a new constitution was not promulgated until 1891. This federalist, democratic constitution was heavily influenced by the U.S. model. However, women and illiterates were not permitted to vote.

Figure 159: *Supreme Federal Court.*

- Constitution of 1934 – when Getúlio Vargas came to power in 1930, he canceled the 1891 constitution and did not permit a new one until 1934. The Constitutionalist Revolution of 1932 forced Vargas to enact a new democratic constitution that permitted women's suffrage. Getúlio Vargas was indirectly elected president by the Constitutional Assembly to a four-year term, beginning in 1933.
- Constitution of 1937 – Getúlio Vargas suppressed a Communist uprising in 1935 and two years later (November 10, 1937) used it as a pretext to establish autocratic rule. He instituted a corporatist constitution nicknamed *the Polish,* (because it was said to have been inspired by a Polish constitution), written by Francisco Campos.
- Constitution of 1946 – in October, 1945, with World War II over, a civil-military coup ousted dictatorial Getúlio Vargas, an Assembly wrote a democratic constitution.
- Constitution of 1967 – after the 1964 coup d'État against João Goulart, the military dictatorship passed the *Institutional Acts*, a supraconstitutional law. This strongly undemocratic constitution simply incorporated these Acts.
- Constitution of 1988 – the progressive redemocratization culminated in the current constitution. Very democratic, it is more expansive than a typical constitution – many statutory acts in other countries are written into this constitution, like Social Security and taxes.

Figure 160: *National Congress of Brazil, the national legislature and the only in bicameral format.*

Political parties and elections

According to sociologist Marcelo Ridenti, Brazilian politics is divided between internationalist liberals and statist nationalists.[774] The first group consists of politicians arguing that internationalization of the economy is essential for the development of the country, while the latter rely on interventionism, and protection of state enterprises. According to Ridenti, who cites the Fernando Henrique Cardoso administration as an example of the first group and the Luiz Inácio Lula da Silva administration as an example of the second, "we have it cyclically".

Lula's Workers' Party tended to the statist nationalist side, although there are privatizing forces within his party and government, while Cardoso's Social Democratic Party tended to favor the international private market side by taking neoliberal policies. Lula compares himself with Getúlio Vargas, Juscelino Kubitscheck and João Goulart, presidents seen as statist nationalists.[775]

As of May 2017, 16,668,589 Brazilians were affiliated with a political party. The largest parties are MDB (which accounts for 14.4% of affiliated voters), the PT (9.5% of affiliated voters), and PSDB (8.7% of affiliated voters).

Politics of Brazil 351

Figure 161: *Palácio do Planalto, the seat of the executive power.*

2014 general election results

Candidate	Running mate	Coalition	First round		Second round	
			Valid Votes	%	Valid Votes	%
Dilma Rousseff (PT)	Michel Temer (PMDB)	With the strength of the people	43,267,668	41.59	54,501,119	51.64
Aécio Neves (PSDB)	Aloysio Nunes (PSDB)	Change, Brazil	34,897,211	33.55	51,041,155	48.36
Marina Silva (PSB)	Beto Albuquerque (PSB)	United for Brazil	22,176,619	21.32		
Luciana Genro (PSOL)	Jorge Paz (PSOL)	—	1,612,186	1.55		
Everaldo Pereira (PSC)	Leonardo Gadelha (PSC)	—	780,513	0.75		
Eduardo Jorge (PV)	Célia Sacramento (PV)	—	630,099	0.61		
Levy Fidelix (PRTB)	José Alves de Oliveira (PRTB)	—	446,878	0.43		

Zé Maria (PSTU)	Cláudia Durans (PSTU)	—	91,209	0.09		
José Maria Eymael (PSDC)	Roberto Lopes (PSDC)	—	61,250	0.06		
Mauro Iasi (PCB)	Sofia Manzano (PCB)	—	47,845	0.05		
Rui Costa Pimenta (PCO)	Ricardo Machado (PCO)	—	12,324	0.01		
Valid votes			104,023,543	90.36	105,542,274	93.66
Null votes			6,678,580	5.80	5,219,787	4.63
Blank votes			4,420,488	3.84	1,921,819	1.71
Total votes			115,122,611	100.00	112,683,879	100.00
Registered voters/turnout			142,822,046	80.61	142,822,046	78.90
Voting age population/turnout			150,803,268	76.34	150,803,268	74.72
Source: Tribunal Superior Eleitoral[776].						

Summary of the 5 October 2014 National Congress election results

Coalition	Parties	Chamber					Senate			
		Votes	% of votes	Seats	% of seats	+/-	Votes	% of votes	Elected seats	Total seats	% of seats	+/-
Pro-government Coalition With the Strength of the People (*Coligação Com a Força do Povo*)	Workers' Party (*Partido dos Trabalhadores, PT*)	13,554,166	13.93%	68	13.26%	−20	15,155,818	16.96%	2	12	14.81%	−2
	Brazilian Democratic Movement Party (*Partido do Movimento Democrático Brasileiro, PMDB*)	10,791,949	11.09%	66	12.87%	−13	12,129,969	13.58%	5	18	22.22%	−2
	Progressive Party (*Partido Progressista, PP*)	6,429,791	6.61%	38	7.41%	−5	1,931,738	2.16%	1	5	6.17%	±0
	Social Democratic Party (*Partido Social Democrático, PSD*)	5,967,953	6.13%	36	7.02%	New	7,147,245	8.00%	2	3	3.70%	New
	Republic Party (*Partido da República, PR*)	5,635,519	5.79%	34	6.63%	−7	696,462	0.78%	1	4	4.94%	±0
	Brazilian Republican Party (*Partido Republicano Brasileiro, PRB*)	4,424,824	4.55%	21	4.09%	+13	301,162	0.34%	0	1	1.23%	±0
	Democratic Labour Party (*Partido Democrático Trabalhista, PDT*)	3,472,175	3.57%	19	3.70%	−9	3,609,643	4.04%	4	8	9.88%	+4
	Republican Party of the Social Order (*Partido Republicano da Ordem Social, PROS*)	1,977,117	2.03%	11	2.14%	New	2,234,132	2.50%	0	1	1.23%	New

	Communist Party of Brazil (Partido Comunista do Brasil, PCdoB)	1,913,015	1.97%	10	1.95%	−5	803,144	0.90%	0	1	1.23%	−1
	Total	54,166,509	55.67%	303	59.07%	+5	44,009,313	49.26%	15	53	65.43%	+3
Opposition Coalition Change Brazil (Coligação Muda Brasil)	Brazilian Social Democratic Party (Partido da Social Democracia Brasileira, PSDB)	11,073,631	11.38%	54	10.53%	+1	23,880,078	26.73%	4	10	12.35%	−1
	Democrats (Democratas, DEM)	4,085,487	4.20%	21	4.09%	−21	3,515,426	3.93%	3	5	6.17%	−1
	Brazilian Labour Party (Partido Trabalhista Brasileiro, PTB)	3,914,193	4.02%	25	4.88%	+4	2,803,999	3.14%	2	3	2.47%	−3
	Solidariedade (Solidariedade, SD)	2,689,701	2.76%	15	2.92%	New	370,507	0.41%	0	1	1.23%	New
	Labour Party of Brazil (Partido Trabalhista do Brasil, PTdoB)	828,876	0.85%	2	0.39%	−1	11,300	0.01%	0	0	0.00%	±0
	National Labor Party (Partido Trabalhista Nacional, PTN)	723,182	0.74%	4	0.78%	+4	2,741	0.00%	0	0	0.00%	±0
	National Ecologic Party (Partido Ecológico Nacional, PEN)	667,983	0.69%	2	0.39%	New	65,597	0.07%	0	0	0.00%	New
	Party of National Mobilization (Partido da Mobilização Nacional, PMN)	468,473	0.48%	3	0.58%	−1	57,911	0.06%	0	0	0.00%	−1
	Christian Labour Party (Partido Trabalhista Cristão, PTC)	338,117	0.35%	2	0.39%	+1	21,993	0.02%	0	0	0.00%	±0
	Total	24,789,643	25.47%	128	24.95%	+3	30,729,552	34.37%	9	19	23.46%	−5

Opposition Coalition United for Brazil (*Coligação Unidos pelo Brasil*)	Brazilian Socialist Party (*Partido Socialista Brasileiro, PSB*)	6,267,878	6.44%	34	6.63%	±0	12,123,194	13.60%	3	7	8.64%	+4
	Popular Socialist Party (*Partido Popular Socialista, PPS*)	1,955,689	2.01%	10	1.95%	−2	0	0.00%	0	0	0.00%	−1
	Humanist Party of Solidarity (*Partido Humanista da Solidariedade, PHS*)	943,068	0.97%	5	0.97%	+3	0	0.00%	0	0	0.00%	±0
	Social Liberal Party (*Partido Social Liberal, PSL*)	808,710	0.83%	1	0.20%	±0	0	0.00%	0	0	0.00%	±0
	Progressive Republican Party (*Partido Republicano Progressista, PRP*)	724,825	0.75%	3	0.58%	+1	170,257	0.19%	0	0	0.00%	±0
	Free Homeland Party (*Partido Pátria Livre, PPL*)	141,254	0.15%	0	0.0%	*New*	29,366	0.03%	0	0	0.00%	±0
	Total	10,841,424	11,15%	53	10,33%	+2	12,322,817	13,82%	3	7	8,64%	+3
Out of coalition (*Fora de coligação*)	Social Christian Party (*Partido Social Cristão, PSC*)	2,520,421	2.59%	13	2.53%	−5	19,286	0.02%	0	0	0.00%	−1
	Green Party (*Partido Verde, PV*)	2,004,464	2.06%	8	1,56%	−7	723,576	0.81%	0	1	1.23%	+1
	Socialism and Liberty Party (*Partido Socialismo e Liberdade, PSOL*)	1,745,470	1,79%	5	0.97%	+2	1,045,275	1.17%	0	1	1.23%	−1
	Christian Social Democratic Party (*Partido Social Democrata Cristão, PSDC*)	509,936	0.52%	2	0.39%	+2	31,011	0.03%	0	0	0.00%	±0

Brazilian Labour Renewal Party (Partido Renovador Trabalhista Brasileiro, PRTB)	454,190	0.47%	1	0.20%	-1	38,429	0.04%	0	0	0.00%	±0
United Socialist Workers' Party (Partido Socialista dos Trabalhadores Unificado, PSTU)	188,473	0.19%	0	0.00%	±0	355,585	0.40%	0	0	0.00%	±0
Brazilian Communist Party (Partido Comunista Brasileiro, PCB)	66,979	0.07%	0	0.00%	±0	68,199	0.08%	0	0	0.00%	±0
Workers' Cause Party (Partido da Causa Operária, PCO)	12,969	0.01%	0	0.00%	±0	8,561	0.01%	0	0	0.00%	±0
Total valid votes	97,300,478	100.00%	513	100.00%	±0	89,351,604	100.00%	27	81	100.00%	±0

Sources: Chamber[777] Senate[778]

Government

Federal government

Brazil is a federal presidential constitutional republic, based on representative democracy. The federal government has three independent branches: executive, legislative, and judicial. Executive power is exercised by the executive branch, headed by the President, advised by a Cabinet. The President is both the head of state and the head of government. Legislative power is vested upon the National Congress, a two-chamber legislature comprising the Federal Senate and the Chamber of Deputies. Judicial power is exercised by the judiciary, consisting of the Supreme Federal Court, the Superior Court of Justice and other Superior Courts, the National Justice Council and the Regional Federal Courts.

States

The 26 Brazilian *states* are semi-autonomous self-governing entities organized with complete administration branches, relative financial independence and their own set of symbols, similar to those owned by the country itself. Despite their relative autonomy they all have the same model of administration, as set by the Federal Constitution.

States hold elections every four years and exercise a considerable amount of power. The 1988 constitution allows states to keep their own taxes, set up State Houses, and mandates regular allocation of a share of the taxes collected locally by the federal government.

The Executive role is held by the *Governador* (Governor) and his appointed *Secretários* (Secretaries); the Legislative role is held by the *Assembléia Legislativa* (Legislative Assembly); and the Judiciary role, by the *Tribunal de Justiça* (Justice Tribunal). The governors and the members of the assemblies are elected, but the members of the Judiciary are appointed by the governor from a list provided by the current members of the State Law Court containing only judges (these are chosen by merit in exams open to anyone with a Law degree). The name chosen by the governor must be approved by the Assembly before inauguration. The 1988 Constitution has granted the states the greatest amount of autonomy since the Old Republic.

Each of the 26 state governors must achieve more than 50% of the vote, including a second round run-off between the top two candidates if necessary. In contrast to the federal level, state legislatures are unicameral, although the deputies are elected through similar means, involving an open-list system in

Figure 162: *Chamber of Deputies, the lower house.*

Figure 163: *Federal Senate, the upper house.*

Figure 164: *The Legislative Assembly of Rio de Janeiro holds the legislature of Rio de Janeiro state.*

Figure 165: *Palácio Tiradentes holds the executive power of Minas Gerais state.*

Figure 166: *The Municipal Chamber of São Paulo, the municipal legislature of São Paulo city.*

which the state serves as one constituency. State level elections occur at the same time as those for the presidency and Congress. In 2002, candidates from eight different parties won the gubernatorial contest while 28 parties are represented in the country's state legislatures. The last set of elections took place in 2006.

The most important Brazilian states (in terms of population and economic power) are São Paulo, Rio de Janeiro, Minas Gerais, Rio Grande do Sul, Paraná, Bahia, Pernambuco and Santa Catarina.

Municipalities

Brazil has no clear distinction between *towns* and *cities* (in effect, the Portuguese word *cidade* means both). The only possible difference is regarding the municipalities that have a court of first instance and those that do not. The former are called *Sedes de Comarca* (seats of a *comarca*, which is the territory under the rule of that court). Other than that, only size and importance differs one from another.

The municipality (*município*) is a territory comprising one urban area, the *sede* (seat), from which it takes the name, and several other minor urban or rural areas, the *distritos* (districts). The seat of a municipality must be the most populous urban area within it; when another urban area grows too much it usually splits from the original municipality to form another one.

Figure 167: *Palácio do Anhangabaú holds the municipal executive power of São Paulo.*

A municipality is relatively autonomous: it enacts its own "constitution", which is called *organic law* (*Lei Orgânica*), and it is allowed to collect taxes and fees, to maintain a municipal police force (albeit with very restricted powers), to pass laws on any matter that do not contradict either the state or the national constitutions, and to create symbols for itself (like a flag, an anthem and a coat-of-arms). However, not all municipalities exercise all of this autonomy. For instance, only a few municipalities keep local police forces, some of them do not collect some taxes (to attract investors or residents) and many of them do not have a flag (although they are all required to have a coat-of-arms).

Municipalities are governed by an elected *prefeito* (Mayor) and a unicameral *Câmara de Vereadores* (Councillors' Chamber). In municipalities with more than 200,000 voters, the Mayor must be elected by more than 50% of the valid vote. The executive power is called *Prefeitura*.

Brazilian municipalities can vary widely in area and population. The municipality of Altamira, in the State of Pará, with 161,445.9 square kilometres of area, is larger than many countries in the world. Several Brazilian municipalities have over 1,000,000 inhabitants, with São Paulo, at more than 9,000,000, being the most populous.

Figure 168: *Legislative Chamber of the Federal District.*

Until 1974 Brazil had one state-level municipality, the State of Guanabara, now merged with the State of Rio de Janeiro, which comprised the city of Rio de Janeiro solely.

The Federal District

The Federal District is an anomalous unit of the federation, as it is not organized in the same manner as a municipality, does not possess the same autonomy as a state (though usually ranked among them), and is closely related to the central power.

It is considered a single and indivisible entity, constituted by the seat, Brasília and some of the satellite cities. Brasília and the satellite cities are governed by the Regional Administrators individually and as a whole are governed by the Governor of the Federal District.

History

Throughout its history, Brazil has struggled to build a democratic and egalitarian society because of its origins as a plantation colony and the strong influence of slavery.

Empire

In 1822 the Prince Pedro de Alcântara, son of King John VI of Portugal, proclaimed independence. He was the first Emperor (Pedro I) until his abdication in 1831 in favor of his elder son. Due to the son's age (five years) a regency was established and the country had its first elections, though vote was still restricted to a minority of the population.

Old Republic (1889–1930)

In 1889, Marshal Deodoro da Fonseca declared the republic, by a coup d'état. Until 1930, Brazilian republic was formally a democracy, although the power was concentrated in the hands of powerful land owners.

Vargas years (1930–1945)

In 1930, a bloodless coup led Getúlio Vargas to power. For about 15 years, he controlled the country's politics, with a brief three-year constitutional interregnum from 1934 to 1937. A longer, heavier regime, the *Estado Novo* had loose ties with European fascism and spanned the years 1938 to 1945.

Populist years (1946–1964)

Like most of Latin America, Brazil experienced times of political instability after the Second World War. When Vargas was ousted from the presidency in another bloodless coup d'état, in 1945, a new and modern constitution was passed and the country had its first experience with an effective and widespread democracy. But the mounting tension between populist politicians (like Vargas himself and, later, Jânio Quadros) and the right led to a crisis that ultimately brought up the military coup d'état in 1964, now known, through declassified documents, to have been supported by the American Central Intelligence Agency.

Military dictatorship (1964–1985)

In 1964 a military-led coup d'état deposed the democratically elected president of Brazil, João Goulart. Between 1964 and 1985, Brazil was governed by the military, with a two-party system that comprised a pro-government National Renewal Alliance Party (ARENA) and an opposition Brazilian Democratic Movement (MDB). Thousands of politicians (including former president Juscelino Kubitschek) had their political rights suspended, and military-sanctioned indirect elections were held for most elected positions until political liberalization during the government of João Figueiredo.

New Republic (1985-1990)

In 1985, the military were defeated in an election according to the scheme they had set up as a consequence of the loss of political support among the elites. The opposition candidate, Tancredo Neves, was elected President, but died of natural causes before he was able to take office. Fearing a political vacuum that might stifle the democratic effort, Neves' supporters urged vice-president, José Sarney to take the oath and govern the country. Tancredo Neves had said that his election and the demise of military régime would create a "New Republic" and Sarney's term of government is often referred to by this name.

Sarney's government was disastrous in almost every field. The ongoing recession and the soaring external debt drained the country's assets while ravaging inflation (which later turned into hyperinflation) demonetized the currency and prevented any stability. In an attempt to revolutionize the economy and defeat inflation, Sarney carried on an ambitious "heterodox" economic plan (Cruzado) in 1986, which included price controls, default on the external debts and reduction of salaries. The plan seemed successful for some months, but it soon caused wholesale shortages of consumer goods (especially of easily exportable goods like meat, milk, automobiles, grains, sugar and alcohol) and the appearance of a black market in which such goods were sold for higher prices. Buoyed by the ensuing popularity from the apparent success of the plan, Sarney secured the largest electoral win in Brazilian history; the party he had just joined, Brazilian Democratic Movement Party (PMDB), won in 26 out of 27 states and in more than 3,000 municipalities. Just after the elections, Sarney's "corrections" to the economy failed to control inflation and the public perception that he had used an artificial control of inflation to win the elections proved to be his undoing. His popularity never recovered and he was plagued by vehement criticism from most sectors of society until the end of his term. Despite popular rejection, Sarney managed to extend his term from four to five years, and exerted pressure on the Constitutional Assembly that was drafting the new constitution to abort the adoption of Parliamentarism.

Collor government (1990-1992)

In 1989 Fernando Collor de Mello was elected president for the term from 1990-1994. The elections were marked by unanimous condemnation of José Sarney, with all candidates trying to keep distance from him.

Collor made some very bold statements, like saying that the Brazilian industry (of which the Brazilians used to be very proud) was mostly obsolete and polluting or that defaulting the debt was equal to not paying the rent. He also took quite revolutionary measures, like reducing the number of ministries to only 12 and naming Zélia Cardoso de Mello Minister of Economy or removing existing barriers to importing of goods.

His inflation control plan was based on an attempt to control prices and a complicated currency conversion process that prevented people from cashing their bank accounts for 18 months.

All of this made him quite unpopular and denied him support in the parliament that he needed since his own party held few seats. At the beginning of his third year in office, he resigned as a result of in a huge corruption scandal. The charges against him would later be dropped, some on mere technicalities, some for actually being irrelevant or false.Wikipedia:Citation needed

Collor desperately tried to resist impeachment by rallying the support of the youth and of the lower classes, but his call for help was answered by massive popular demonstrations, led mostly by students, demanding his resignation.

Itamar government (1992–1994)

In 1992, the vice-president, Itamar Franco, took office as president and managed to evade the most feared consequences of Collor's downfall. He had to face a country with hyper-inflation, high levels of misery and unemployment. Far-left organizations were trying to turn the anti-Collor campaign into a wider revolutionary fight to overthrow the regime. Itamar finally granted full powers to his Minister of Economy, Fernando Henrique Cardoso, so the minister could launch the Plano Real, a new economic plan that seemed to be just the same as the many unsuccessful plans launched by Sarney, Collor and their military predecessor. But the Real was a success, and terminated inflation in a few months.

FHC government (1995–2003)

In 1994, Cardoso launched his Plano Real, a successful economic reform that managed to permanently rid the country of the excessive inflation that had plagued it for more than forty years. The plan consisted of replacing the discredited old currency (cruzeiro and cruzeiro real) and pegging its value temporarily to the United States dollar. Inflation – which had become a fact of Brazilian life – was cut dramatically, a change that the Brazilians took years to get used to. Because of the success of Plano Real, Cardoso was chosen by his party to run for president and, with the strong support of Franco, eventually won, beating Luiz Inácio Lula da Silva, who had emerged as the favorite only one year earlier.

Cardoso's term was marked by other major changes in Brazilian politics and economy. Public services and state-owned companies were privatized (some

Figure 169: *Meeting of the Cabinet of Luiz Inácio Lula da Silva in the Oval Room, Palácio do Planalto, 2007*

for values supposedly too cheap according to his adversaries), the strong real made it easy to import goods, forcing Brazilian industry to modernize and compete (which had the side effect of causing many of them to be bought by foreign companies). During his first term, a constitutional amendment was passed to enable a sitting Executive chief to run for re-election, after which he again beat Lula in 1998.

Lula government (2003–2011)

In 2002, at his fourth attempt, Lula was elected president. In part his victory was derived from the considerable unpopularity of Cardoso's second term, which failed to decrease the economic inequality, and in part from a softening of his and the party's radical stance, including a vice-presidential candidate from the Liberal Party, acceptance of an International Monetary Fund (IMF) accord agreed to by the previous government and a line of discourse friendly to the financial markets.

Despite some achievements in solving part of the country's biggest problems, his term was plagued by multiple corruption scandals that rocked his cabinet, forcing some members to resign their posts.

In 2006 Lula regained part of his popularity and ran for re-election. After almost winning on the first round, he won the run-off against Geraldo Alckmin from the Brazilian Social Democracy Party (PSDB), by a margin of 20 million votes.

In 2010, Lula's handpicked successor, Dilma, was elected to the Presidency.

International organization participation

- African Development Bank
- Customs Cooperation Council
- United Nations Economic Commission for Latin America and the Caribbean
- Food and Agriculture Organization
- Group of 11
- Group of 15
- Group of 19
- Group of 24
- Group of 77
- Inter-American Development Bank
- International Atomic Energy Agency
- International Bank for Reconstruction and Development (World Bank)
- International Civil Aviation Organization
- International Chamber of Commerce
- International Criminal Court
- International Red Cross and Red Crescent Movement
- International Development Association
- International Fund for Agricultural Development
- International Finance Corporation
- International Federation of Red Cross and Red Crescent Societies
- International Hydrographic Organization
- International Labour Organization
- International Monetary Fund
- International Maritime Organization
- Inmarsat
- International Telecommunications Satellite Organization
- Interpol
- International Olympic Committee
- International Organization for Migration (observer)
- International Organization for Standardization
- International Telecommunication Union
- International Trade Union Confederation
- Latin American Economic System
- Asociación Latinoamericana de Integración
- Mercosur, Non-Aligned Movement (observer)

- Nuclear Suppliers Group
- Organization of American States
- Agency for the Prohibition of Nuclear Weapons in Latin America and the Caribbean
- Organization for the Prohibition of Chemical Weapons
- Permanent Court of Arbitration
- Rio Group
- United Nations
- United Nations Conference on Trade and Development
- United Nations Educational, Scientific, and Cultural Organization
- Union of South American Nations
- United Nations High Commissioner for Refugees
- United Nations Industrial Development Organization
- United Nations Mission of Observers in Prevlaka
- United Nations Transitional Administration in East Timor
- United Nations University
- Universal Postal Union
- World Federation of Trade Unions
- World Health Organization
- World Intellectual Property Organization
- World Meteorological Organization
- World Tourism Organization
- World Trade Organization

External links

- Global Integrity Report: Brazil[779] Reports on anti-corruption efforts.
- [780] Reports on political culture and political news, with a focus on transparency and good government.
- [781] Essays on Brazilian politics and policies by leading intellectuals and public figures.
- [782] Reports on the politics and issues surrounding Brazilian soccer and the 2014 World Cup in Brazil.

Further reading

- Goertzel, Ted and Paulo Roberto Almeida, *The Drama of Brazilian Politics from Dom João to Marina Silva*[783] Amazon Digital Services. ISBN 978-1-4951-2981-0.

Federal government of Brazil

Federal Government of Brazil

Governo Federal do Brazil	
Seal of the Government	
Formation	1889
Founding document	Constitution of Brazil
Jurisdiction	Federative Republic of Brazil
Website	http://www.brasil.gov.br/
Legislative branch	
Legislature	National Congress
Meeting place	Palácio Nereu Ramos
Executive branch	
Leader	President of Brazil
Headquarters	Palácio do Planalto
Main organ	Cabinet
Judicial branch	
Court	Supreme Federal Court
Seat	Brasília

The **federal government of Brazil** is the national government of the Federative Republic of Brazil, a republic in South America divided in 26 states and a federal district. The Brazilian federal government is divided in three branches: the executive, which is headed by the President and the cabinet; the legislative, whose powers are vested by the Constitution in the National Congress; and the judiciary, whose powers are vested in the Supreme Federal Court and lower federal courts. The seat of the federal government is located in Brasília. This has led to "Brasília" commonly being used as a metonym for the federal government of Brazil.

Figure 170: *Palácio do Planalto, headquarters of the Executive Branch of the Brazilian Government*

Division of powers

Brazil is a federal presidential constitutional republic, based on representative democracy. The federal government has three independent branches: executive, legislative, and judicial.

The Federal Constitution is the supreme law of Brazil. It is the foundation and source of the legal authority underlying the existence of Brazil and the federal government. It provides the framework for the organization of the Brazilian government and for the relationship of the federal government to the states, to citizens, and to all people within Brazil.

Executive power is exercised by the executive, headed by the President, advised by a Cabinet of Ministers. The President is both the head of state and the head of government. Legislative power is vested upon the National Congress, a two-chamber legislature comprising the Federal Senate and the Chamber of Deputies. Judicial power is exercised by the judiciary, consisting of the Supreme Federal Court, the Superior Court of Justice and other Superior Courts, the National Justice Council and the regional federal courts.

Executive branch

Main office holders

Office	Name	Party	Since
President of the Republic	Michel Temer	Democratic Movement Party	31 August 2016
Vice-President of the Republic	vacant		12 May 2016

Legislative branch

The bicameral National Congress (*Congresso Nacional*) consists of

1. the Federal Senate (*Senado Federal*), which has 81 seats — three members from each States and the Federal District, elected according to the principle of majority to serve eight-year terms. One-third are elected after a four-year period, and two-thirds are elected after the next four-year period; and
2. the Chamber of Deputies (*Câmara dos Deputados*), which has 513 seats. Federal deputies are elected by proportional representation to serve four-year terms.

There are no limits on the number of terms one may serve for either chamber. The seats are allotted proportionally to each state's population, but each state is eligible for a minimum of eight seats and a maximum of 70 seats. The result is a system weighted in favor of smaller states that are part of the Brazilian federation.

Currently 15 political parties are represented in Congress. Since it is common for politicians to switch parties, the proportion of congressional seats held by particular parties changes regularly. To avoid that, the Supreme Federal Court ruled in 2007 that the term belongs to the parties, and not to the representatives.

Figure 171: *The National Congress building*

Figure 172: *Federal Senate of Brazil, the upper house*

Figure 173: *Chamber of Deputies of Brazil, the lower house*

Judicial branch

Brazilian courts function under civil law adversarial system. The Judicial branch is organized in states' and federal systems with different jurisdictions.

The judges of the courts of first instance take office after public competitive examination. The second instance judges are promoted among the first instance

Figure 174: *Superior Court of Justice*

judges. The Justices of the superior courts are appointed by the President for life and approved by the Senate. All the judges and justices must be graduated in law. Brazilian judges must retire at the age of 70.

Federal judicial branch

The national territory is divided into five Regions, which are composed of two or more states. Each region is divided in Judiciary Sections (*Seções Judiciárias* in Portuguese), coterminous with the territory of each state, and subdivided in Judiciary Subsections (*Subseções Judiciárias*), each with a territory that may not correspond to the states' comarcas.

The Judiciary subsections have federal courts of first instance and each Region has a Federal Regional Tribunal (*Tribunal Regional Federal*) as a court of second instance.

There are special federal court systems for labor litigations, called Labor Justice (*Justiça do Trabalho*), for electoral matters, called Electoral Justice (*Justiça Eleitoral*), and for martial criminal cases, called Military Justice (*Justiça Militar*), each of them with its own courts.

Figure 175: *Supreme Federal Court*

Superior Courts

There are two national superior courts that grant writs of certiorari in civil and criminal cases: the Superior Justice Tribunal (*Superior Tribunal de Justiça*, STJ) and the federal supreme court, called the Supreme Federal Court (Portuguese: *Supremo Tribunal Federal*).

The STJ grants a Special Appeal (*Recurso Especial*) when a judgement of a court of second instance offends a federal statute disposition or when two or more second instance courts make different rulings on the same federal statute. There are parallel courts for labor law, electoral law and military law.

The STF grants Extraordinary Appeals (*Recurso Extraordinário*) when judgements of second instance courts violate the constitution. The STF is the last instance for the writ of habeas corpus and for reviews of judgments from the STJ.

The superior courts do not analyze any factual questions in their judgments, but only the application of the law and the constitution. Facts and evidences are judged by the courts of second instance, except in specific cases such as writs of habeas corpus.

External links

- Official website of the Presidency of Brazil[784]

Elections in Brazil

Brazil
This article is part of a series on the **politics and government of Brazil**
Foreign relations • Other countries • Atlas
• v • t • e[785]

Brazil elects on the national level a head of state—the president—and a legislature. The president is elected to a four-year term by absolute majority vote through a two-round system. The National Congress (*Congresso Nacional*) has two chambers. The Chamber of Deputies (*Câmara dos Deputados*) has 513 members, elected to a four-year term by proportional representation. The Federal Senate (*Senado Federal*) has 81 members, elected to an eight-year term, with elections every four years for alternatively one-third and two-third of the seats. Brazil has a multi-party system, with such numerous parties that often no one party has a chance of gaining power alone, and so they must work with each other to form coalition governments.

Schedule
Election

Position	2014	2015	2016	2017	2018	2019	2020	2021
Type	Presidential (October) National Congress (October) Gubernatorial (October) States and Federal District Parliaments (October)	None	Mayors (October) City Councils (October)	None	Presidential (October) National Congress (October) Gubernatorial (October) States and Federal District Parliaments (October)	None	Mayors (October) City Councils (October)	None
President and vice president	**President and vice president**		None		**President and vice president**		None	
National Congress	**All seats** (Chamber of Deputies) **One third** (Federal Senate)		None		**All seats** (Chamber of Deputies) **Two thirds** (Federal Senate)		None	
States, cities and municipalities	**All positions** (States and Federal District)	None	**All positions** (Municipalities)	None	**All positions** (States and Federal District)	None	**All positions** (Municipalities)	None

Inauguration

Position	2015	2016	2017	2018	2019	2020	2021	2022
Type	Presidential (January) National Congress (January) Gubernatorial (January) States and Federal District Parliaments (January)	None	Mayors (January) City Councils (January)	None	Presidential (January) National Congress (January) Gubernatorial (January) States and Federal District Parliaments (January)	None	Mayors (January) City Councils (January)	None
President and vice president	**1 January**		None		**1 January**		None	

National Congress	1 February		None		1 February		None	
States, cities and municipalities	1 January	None	1 January	None	1 January	None	1 January	None

Electoral systems

Deputies are elected to the Chamber of Deputies using a form of party-list proportional representation known as the "open list."

Senators are elected to the Federal Senate with a plurality of the vote in a first-past-the-post system, which is not proportional. Three senators are elected for each state and for the Federal District.

In municipal governments, the city council is elected using an open list proportional representation system. Seats are allocated using a version of the D'Hondt method where only parties (or coalitions) who receive at least V/n votes (where V is the total number of votes cast and n is the total number of seats to be filled) may win seats in the legislature.

2014 general election

Presidential election

Candidate	Running mate	Coalition	First round		Second round	
			Valid Votes	%	Valid Votes	%
Dilma Rousseff (PT)	Michel Temer (PMDB)	With the strength of the people	43,267,668	41.59	54,501,119	51.64
Aécio Neves (PSDB)	Aloysio Nunes (PSDB)	Change, Brazil	34,897,211	33.55	51,041,155	48.36
Marina Silva (PSB)	Beto Albuquerque (PSB)	United for Brazil	22,176,619	21.32		
Luciana Genro (PSOL)	Jorge Paz (PSOL)	—	1,612,186	1.55		
Everaldo Pereira (PSC)	Leonardo Gadelha (PSC)	—	780,513	0.75		
Eduardo Jorge (PV)	Célia Sacramento (PV)	—	630,099	0.61		
Levy Fidelix (PRTB)	José Alves de Oliveira (PRTB)	—	446,878	0.43		

Zé Maria (PSTU)	Cláudia Durans (PSTU)	—	91,209	0.09
José Maria Eymael (PSDC)	Roberto Lopes (PSDC)	—	61,250	0.06
Mauro Iasi (PCB)	Sofia Manzano (PCB)	—	47,845	0.05
Rui Costa Pimenta (PCO)	Ricardo Machado (PCO)	—	12,324	0.01
Valid votes			104,023,543	90.36	105,542,274	93.66
Null votes			6,678,580	5.80	5,219,787	4.63
Blank votes			4,420,488	3.84	1,921,819	1.71
Total votes			115,122,611	100.00	112,683,879	100.00
Registered voters/turnout			142,822,046	80.61	142,822,046	78.90
Voting age population/turnout			150,803,268	76.34	150,803,268	74.72

Source: Tribunal Superior Eleitoral[786].

Parliamentary election

Summary of the 5 October 2014 National Congress election results

Coalition	Parties	Chamber			Senate			
		Seats	% of seats	+/–	Elected seats	Total seats	% of seats	+/–
Govern Coalition "With the Strength of the People"	PT	68	13.26	-20	2	12	14.81	-2
	PMDB	66	12.87	–13	5	18	22.22	-2
	PP	38	7.41	-5	1	5	6,17	±0
	PSD	36	7.02	New	2	3	3.7	New
	PR	34	6.63	-7	1	4	4.94	±0
	PRB	21	4.09	+13	0	1	1.23	±0
	PDT	19	3.7	-9	4	8	9.88	+4
	PROS	11	2.14	New	0	1	1.23	New
	PCdoB	10	1.95	–5	0	1	1.23	-1
	Total	303	59.07	+5	15	53	65.43	+3
Opposition Coalition "Change Brazil"	PSDB	54	10.53	+1	4	10	12.35	-1
	DEM	21	4.09	-21	3	5	6.17	-1
	PTB	25	4.88	+4	2	3	2.47	-3
	SD	15	2.76	New	0	1	1.23	New

	PTdoB	2	0.39	-1	0	0	0.0	±0
	PTN	4	0.78	+4	0	0	0.0	±0
	PEN	2	0.39	New	0	0	0.0	New
	PMN	3	0.58	-1	0	0	0.0	-1
	PTC	2	0.39	+1	0	0	0.0	±0
	Total	**128**	**25.47**	**+3**	**9**	**19**	**23.46**	**-5**
Opposition Coalition "United for Brazil"	PSB	34	6.63	±0	3	7	8.64	+4
	PPS	10	1.95	-2	0	0	0.0	-1
	PHS	5	0.97	+3	0	0	0.0	±0
	PSL	1	0.2	±0	0	0	0.0	±0
	PRP	3	0.58	+1	0	0	0.0	±0
	PPL	0	0.0	New	0	0	0.0	New
	Total	**53**	**10.33**	**+2**	**3**	**7**	**8.64**	**+3**
Out of coalition	PSC	13	2.53	-5	0	0	0.0	-1
	PV	8	1.56	-7	0	1	1.23	+1
	PSOL	5	0.97	+2	0	1	1.23	-1
	PSDC	2	0.39	+2	0	0	0.0	±0
	PRTB	1	0.2	-1	0	0	0.0	±0
	PSTU	0	0.0	±0	0	0	0.0	±0
	PCB	0	0.0	±0	0	0	0.0	±0
	PCO	0	0.0	±0	0	0	0.0	±0
	Total	**513**	**100.0**	**±0**	**27**	**81**	**100.0**	**±0**

Past elections and referendums

Election results 1982–2014

Brazilian legislative elections (Chamber of Deputies), 1982–2014

Parties	1982	1986	1990	1994	1998	2002	2006	2010	2014
Workers' Party	03.5	06.9	10.2	12.8	13.2	18.4	15.0	16.9	14.0
Brazilian Democratic Movement Party	43.0	48,1	19.3	20.3	15.2	13.4	14.6	13.0	11.1
Brazilian Social Democracy Party	-	-	08.7	13.9	17.5	14.3	13.6	11.9	11.4
Liberal Front Party/Democrats	-	17.7	12.4	12.9	17.3	13.4	10.9	07.6	04.2
Liberal Party / Republic Party	-	02.8	04.3	03.5	02.5	04.3	04.4	07.6	05.8
Brazilian Socialist Party	-	00.9	01.9	02.2	03.4	05.3	06.2	07.1	06.5

Party									
Progressive Party	-	-	-	06.9	11.3	07.8	07.1	06.6	06.4
Democratic Labour Party	05.8	06.5	10.0	07.2	05.7	05.1	05.2	05.0	03.6
Brazilian Labour Party	04.5	04.5	05.6	05.2	05.7	04.6	04.7	04.2	04.0
Green Party	-	-	-	00.1	00.4	01.3	03.6	03.8	02.1
Social Christian Party	-	-	00.8	00.5	00.7	00.6	01.9	03.2	02.5
Communist Party of Brazil	-	00.8	00.9	01.2	01.3	02.2	02.1	02.8	02.0
Popular Socialist Party	-	00.9	01.0	00.6	01.3	03.1	03.9	02.6	02.0
Brazilian Republican Party	-	-	-	-	-	-	00.3	01.7	04.5
Socialism and Liberty Party	-	-	-	-	-	-	01.2	01.2	01.8
Party of National Mobilization	-	-	00.6	00.6	00.5	00.3	00.9	01.1	00.5
Democratic Social / Reform Progressive Party	43.2	07.8	08.9	09.4	-	-	-	-	-
National Reconstruction Party / Christian Labour Party	-	-	08.3	00.4	00.1	00.1	00.9	00.6	00.7
Christian Democratic Party / Christian Social Democratic Party	-	01.2	03.0	-	00.1	00.2	00.4	00.2	00.5
Party of the Reconstruction of the National Order	-	-	-	00.7	00.9	02.1	01.0	-	-
Social Democratic Party	-	-	-	-	-	-	-	-	06.2
Republican Party of the Social Order	-	-	-	-	-	-	-	-	02.0
Solidariedade	-	-	-	-	-	-	-	-	02.7
National Labor Party	-	-	-	-	00.1	00.1	00.2	00.2	00.4
National Ecologic Party	-	-	-	-	-	-	-	-	00.7
Labour Party of Brazil	-	-	00.2	-	00.3	00.2	00.3	00.7	00.8
Humanist Party of Solidarity	-	-	-	-	-	00.3	00.5	00.8	00.9
Progressive Republican Party	-	-	00.2	00.5	00.4	00.3	00.3	00.3	00.7
Social Liberal Party	-	-	-	-	00.3	00.5	00.2	00.5	00.8
Brazilian Labour Renewal Party	-	-	-	00.1	00.1	00.3	00.2	00.3	00.5
Others	00.0	02.8	03.7	00.7	01.7	01.5	00.4	00.0	00.7

Source:[787] Source:[788]

Referendums

Brazil has held three national referendums in its history. In the first, held on January 6, 1963, the people voted for the re-establishment of the presidential system of government (82% of valid ballots), which had been modified by a constitutional amendment in 1961. A second referendum, as ordered by the Federal Constitution of 1988, was held on April 21, 1993, when the voters voted for a republican form of government and reaffirmed the presidential system.

A third national referendum, on the prohibition of the commerce of personal firearms and ammunition, was held on October 23, 2005. The ban proposal was rejected by 64% of the electorate.

External links

- Adam Carr's Election Archive[789]
- Simulated voting machine ([[Portuguese language|Portuguese[790]])] Courtesy of the Brazilian Superior Electoral Court website. (Java required)
- Brief history of electronic voting in Brazil[791]
- Brazil: The Perfect Electoral Crime (II)[792] (Security analysis of the Brazilian voting machines by James Burk, Oct. 21, 2006)
- Electoral Law of Brazil[793]
- Inelegibility Law of Brazil[794]

Law

Law of Brazil

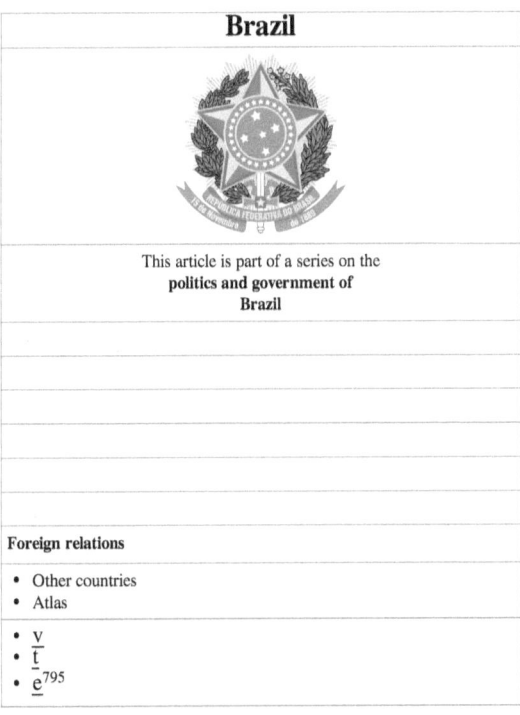

Brazil
This article is part of a series on the **politics and government of Brazil**
Foreign relations   • Other countries   • Atlas   • v   • t   • e[795]

The **law of Brazil** is based on statutes and, partly and more recently, a mechanism called *súmulas vinculantes*. It derives mainly from the civil law systems of European countries, particularly Portugal, the Napoleonic Code and the Germanic law.

There are many codified statutes in force in Brazil. The current Federal Constitution, created on October 21, 1988, is the supreme law of the country.

This Constitution has been amended many times. Other important federal law documents in the country include the Civil Code, the Penal Code, the Commercial Code, the National Tributary Code, the Consolidation of Labor Laws, the Customer Defense Code, the Civil Suit Code and the Criminal Suit Code.

The Constitution organizes the country as a Federative Republic formed by the indissoluble union of the states and municipalities and of the Federal District. Under the principles established in the Federal Constitution, Brazil's 26 federate states have powers to adopt their own Constitutions and laws. Municipalities also enjoy restricted autonomy as their legislation must follow the dictates of the Constitution of the state to which they belong, and consequently to those of the Federal Constitution itself. As for the Federal District, it blends functions of federate states and of municipalities, and its equivalent to a constitution, named Organic Law, must also obey the terms of the Federal Constitution.

Division of powers

The powers of the Union, as defined within the Constitution, are the Executive, the Legislative and the Judiciary, which are independent and harmonious amongst themselves. The head of the Executive is the President of the Republic, which is both the Chief of State and the Head of Government and is directly elected by the citizens. The Legislative, embedded in the form of National Congress and consists of two houses: The Chamber of Deputies (lower house) and the Federal Senate (upper house), both constituted by representatives who are elected by the citizens. The Judicial powers are vested upon the Federal Supreme Court, the Superior Court of Justice, the Regional Federal Courts and Federal Judges. There are also specialized courts to deal with electoral, labor and military disputes.

The Judiciary is organized into federal and state branches. Municipalities do not have their own justice systems, and must, therefore, resort to state or federal justice systems, depending on the nature of the case. The judicial system consists of several courts. The apex is the Federal Supreme Court and is the guardian of the Constitution. Among other duties, it has exclusive jurisdiction to: (i) declare federal or state laws unconstitutional; (ii) order extradition requests from foreign States; and (iii) rule over cases decided in sole instance courts, where the challenged decision may violate the Constitution.

The Superior Court of Justice is responsible for upholding federal legislation and treaties. The five Regional Federal Courts, have constitutional jurisdiction on cases involving appeals towards the decision ruled by federal judges, and are also responsible for cases of national interest and crimes foreseen in international pacts, among other duties. The jurisdiction of the Federal Judges

Figure 176: *Palace of Justice in Brasília*

include: being responsible for hearing most disputes in which one of the parties is the Union (State); ruling on lawsuits between a foreign State or international organization and a municipality or a person residing in Brazil; and judging cases based on treaties or international agreements of the Union against a foreign State or international body.

State-level justice in Brazil consists of state courts and judges. The States of Brazil organize their own judicial systems, with court jurisdiction defined in each state constitution, observing that their legal scope is limited by those that do not concern the federal judicial ordainment. The legislative process begins, in broad terms, with a bill of law in one of the Congress Houses, either the Chamber of Deputies or the Federal Senate, thus called the Originating House. Once the bill is voted on, it can either be rejected or forwarded to the other house, which is called the Reviewing House. There the bill can be rejected, approved or amended to be then returned to the Originating House. Depending on the object of the bill, it is forwarded for the presidential sanction or veto, as a whole or in part. If the bill is vetoed, the members of the National Congress of Brazil can override such veto.[796]

Constitution and law

For centuries, as a Portuguese colony, Law enforced in Brazil was the Law of Portugal. Famous students of Brazilian colonial era, among them many revolutionaries, graduated from the important Portuguese University of Coimbra, located in Central Portugal. With the Independence of Brazil and the rise of the Empire, it was necessary to create an independent judiciary and also to give its staff a legal education in the country. In 1827, the first law schools in Brazil were founded: the Academies of Law and Social Sciences in São Paulo and Olinda.[797]

Brazilian law is largely derived from Portuguese civil law and is related to the Roman-Germanic legal tradition. This means that the legal system is based on statutes, although a recent constitutional reform (Amendment to the Constitution 45, passed in 2004) has introduced a mechanism similar to the *stare decisis*, called *súmula vinculante*. Nevertheless, according to article 103-A of the Brazilian Constitution, only the Supreme Court is allowed to publish binding rules. Inferior judges and courts, and the public administration, are hence obliged to obey the interpretations of the Supreme Court.

In more recent times, according to the judiciary structure framed in the Brazilian Constitution, judicial power is divided between judicial branch of the states and the Federal judicial branch, and they have different jurisdictions. The prerogatives and duties of judges are the same, the differences being only in the competences, structure and composition of the Courts.

Law and lawyers

In 2007, there were 1,024 Law school programs in Brazil, with 197,664 law students. Law schools are present in each of the States of Brazil.[798] In the United States the number of law schools were only 180. The U.S. State of Alaska does not have a law school.[799] In 2010, the total of lawyers in Brazil were 621,885. The State of São Paulo had the largest number, 222,807 lawyers, one third of all working lawyers in the country. The State of Rio de Janeiro had 112,515 lawyers, and the State of Minas Gerais had 63,978 lawyers.[800]

The Course of Law is one of the most prestigious and promising in the country. With a duration of five years and at the end of the course the student becomes a graduate, can not yet exercise the profession. While studying in a law school, the student will have all the knowledge needed to pursue the many professions related to law school, but must first pass the examination[801] of the Bar Association of Brazil (*Ordem dos Advogados do Brasil* in Portuguese).[802]

Figure 177: *Court of Justice in São Paulo*

The overall median income of the Brazilian lawyer was R$36,120 per year in 2007. The starting median income was R$20,040, and the top median was R$3,000,000. The Brazilian judge had an overall median income of R$170,000. The starting median income was R$150,500, and the top median was R$310,500. The Brazilian prosecutors had an overall median income of R$150,000. The starting median income was R$140,000, and the top median was R$270,000 per year.[803] Nowadays, Brazilian judges and prosecutors, in almost all states, earn the same, and, in some states, prosecutors have a higher income.

State-level judiciary

Trial courts

Each state territory is divided into judicial districts named *comarcas*, which are composed of one or more municipalities. The 27 Courts of Justice have their headquarters in the capital of each State and have jurisdiction only over their State territories. The Federal District only presents the federal-level judicial branch. Each comarca has at least one trial court, a court of first instance. Each court of first instance has a law judge and a substitute judge. The judge decides alone in all civil cases and in most criminal cases. Only intentional

Figure 178: *Court of Justice in Recife*

crimes against life are judged by jury. The judges of the courts are nominated after a selection process. There are specialized courts of first instance for family litigation or bankruptcy in some *comarcas*. Judgments from these district courts can be the subject of judicial review following appeals to the courts of second instance.

Justice tribunals

The highest court of a state judicial system is its court of second instance, the Courts of Justice. In each Brazilian State there is one Court of Justice (*Tribunal de Justiça* in Portuguese). Courts of Justice are courts of appeal, meaning they can review any decisions taken by the trial courts, and have the final word on decisions at state level, though their decisions may be overturned by the federal courts. Some states, as São Paulo and Minas Gerais, used to have Court of Appeals (*Tribunal de Alçada* in Portuguese) which had different jurisdiction. But the 45th Constitutional Amendment to the Brazilian Constitution,[804] in its article four, decreed their extinction in order to simplify the second instance structure.

Second instance judgments are usually made by three judges, called *desembargadores*. These Courts are divided into civil chambers, which judge civil cases, and criminal chambers. Judges of the Courts of Justice overview one another. A Court can expel any judge who has displayed unethical behavior.

Figure 179: *Supreme Federal Court of Brazil*

Federal-level judicial branch

Regional Federal Courts (in number of 5) have jurisdiction over circuits of several states and tend to be headquartered in the largest city of their territory. The regional courts are:

- The *Regional Federal Court of the 1st Region* has jurisdiction over the Federal District and 13 States: Minas Gerais, Bahia, Piauí, Maranhão, Goiás, Mato Grosso, Amapá, Tocantins, Pará, Amazonas, Roraima, Rondônia and Acre, with headquarters in Brasília, Federal District.
- The *Regional Federal Court of the 2nd Region* has jurisdiction over two States: Rio de Janeiro and Espírito Santo, with headquarters in Rio de Janeiro, Rio de Janeiro.
- The *Regional Federal Court of the 3rd Region* has jurisdiction over two States: São Paulo and Mato Grosso do Sul, with headquarters in São Paulo, São Paulo.
- The *Regional Federal Court of the 4th Region* has jurisdiction over three States: Rio Grande do Sul, Santa Catarina and Paraná, with headquarters in Porto Alegre, Rio Grande do Sul.
- The *Regional Federal Court of the 5th Region* has jurisdiction over six States: Sergipe, Alagoas, Pernambuco, Paraíba, Ceará and Rio Grande do Norte, with headquarters in Recife, Pernambuco.

Figure 180: *Superior Court of Justice of Brazil*

Superior courts

There are two national superior courts making up the Supreme Court, which grant writs of certiorari in civil and criminal cases: the Superior Court of Justice (*Superior Tribunal de Justiça* in Portuguese) or STJ and the Supreme Federal Court (*Supremo Tribunal Federal* in Portuguese) or STF, the highest Brazilian court (decides issues concerning offences to the Brazilian Constitution).

The STJ is the Brazilian highest court in non-constitutional issues and grants a Special Appeal (*Recurso Especial* in Portuguese) when a judgement of a court of second instance offends a federal statute disposition or when two or more second instance courts make different rulings on the same federal statute. There are parallel courts for labor law, electoral law and military law.

The STF grants Extraordinary Appeals (*Recurso Extraordinário* in Portuguese) when judgements of second instance courts violate the constitution. The STF is the last instance for the writ of habeas corpus and for reviews of judgments from the STJ.

The superior courts do not analyze any factual questions in their judgments, but only the application of the law and the constitution. Facts and evidences are judged by the courts of second instance, except in specific cases such as writs of *habeas corpus*.

External links

- Brazilian Constitution in Portuguese[805]
- Brazilian Constitution in English[806]
- Brazilian Traffic Code[807]
- Official legislation search engine for Brazilian law[808]
- Unofficial translations of Brazilian law in English[809]

References

- Edwin Montefiore Borchard. Guide to the law and legal literature of Argentina, Brazil and Chile. Law Library of Congress. Government Printing Office. Washington. 1917. Internet Archive[810]

Law enforcement in Brazil

In Brazil, the Federal Constitution establishes five law enforcement institutions: the Federal Police, the Federal Highway Police, the Federal Railway Police, the State Military Police and Fire Brigade, and the State Civil Police. Of these, the first three are affiliated to federal authorities and the latter two subordinated to state governments. All police institutions are part of the Executive branch of either federal or state government. Apart from these five institutions there is another one which is affiliated to municipal authorities: the Municipal Guards. The Municipal Guards *de jure* is not considered a public security force, but federal law 13,022 (in effect since August 8, 2014) gave them *de facto* police attributions.

According to the Supreme Federal Tribunal, the only security forces considered police units by Brazilian law are the ones listed in article 144 of the Federal Constitution, that is, the five aforementioned police forces.[811]

There are two primary police functions: maintaining order and law enforcement. When criminal offences affect federal entities, federal police forces carry out those functions. In the remaining cases, the state police forces undertake police activities.

History

The first groups assigned with security duties in Brazilian territory date back to the early sixteenth century. Small, incipient units were designated in the Brazilian coastline, with the main function of fending off hostile foreign invaders. In 1566, the first police investigator of Rio de Janeiro was recruited.[812] By the seventeenth century, most "capitanias" already had local units with law enforcement functions. On July 9, 1775 a Cavalry Regiment was created in Minas Gerais for maintaining order. At the time, intense gold mining had attracted attention and greed of explorers, generating tensions in the area.[813]

In 1808, the Portuguese royal family relocated to Brazil, due to the French invasion of Portugal. King João VI sought to reshape the administrative structure of the colony. Among several reforms, he established the "Intendência Geral de Polícia" (General Police Intendancy), which merged police units with investigative functions, call currently of Civil Police. He also created a Military Guard with police functions on 13 May 1809. This is considered a predecessor force of local military police units. Later, in 1831, when independence had already been declared, each province started organizing its local "military police", with order maintenance tasks.

On 31 January 1842, law 261 was enacted, reorganizing the investigative offices, the current "civil police".

The first federal police force, the Federal Railroad Police, was created in 1852.

Finally, in 1871, law 2033 separated police and judicial functions, creating the general bureaucratic structure and mechanisms still adopted nowadays by local police forces.[814] In 1944, a federal police institution was created. The current Federal Police department was conceived on November 16, 1964.[815] During the military dictatorship, some political police organizations were maintained, such as the DOI-CODI.

Primary functions

Law enforcement and maintaining order are the two primary functions of Brazilian police units. In Brazilian Law, maintaining order is considered a preventive effort whereby police troopers patrol the streets to protect citizens and discourage criminal activity. Law enforcement consists of criminal investigation after an offence.[816]

Prevention and investigation in Brazil are divided between two distinct police organizations. Local "military police" forces only have order maintenance duties. Correspondingly, "civil police" institutions are responsible solely for crime investigation. However, at the federal level, the Federal Police is commissioned with both preventive and investigative functions of federal crimes.[817]

Figure 181: *Federal Highway Police (Polícia Rodoviária Federal)*

Federal institutions

There are three federal police institutions in Brazil: the Federal Police, the Federal Highway Police, and the Federal Railway Police.

- The **Federal Police**, officially the *Departamento de Polícia Federal*, is described by the Constitution as "a permanent administrative organ of the federal Executive branch". Main assignments are the investigations of crimes against the Federal Government or its organs and companies, the combat of international drug trafficking and terrorism, and immigration and border control police (includes airport and seaport policing). It is directly subordinated to the Extraordinary Ministry of Public Security.
- The **Federal Highway Police**, also described as "a permanent administrative organ of the federal Executive branch", has the main function of patrolling federal highways. It maintains order, but does not investigate crime.
- The **Federal Railway Police**, is the third and last component of the federal police force. Like the previously mentioned institutions, the Federal Railway Police is described as "a permanent administrative organ of the federal Executive branch" with the main function of patrolling the federal railway system. It does not investigate crime, solely focusing on order maintenance.

Figure 182: *Mounted Police branch of the Federal District Military Police, during crowd control activities.*

State institutions

There are two types of state police institutions: the Military Police/Military Firefighters Corps and the Civil Police.

- The *Military Police and Fire Brigade* is the state police charged with maintaining order. It patrols the streets and imprisons suspects of criminal activity, handing them over to Civil Police custody or, in case of federal crimes, to the Federal Police. It is a "militarized" institution (gendarmerie) because it is based on military principles of hierarchy, uniform, discipline, and ceremony. However, the body is not a branch of the Brazilian Armed Forces. It is described by the constitution as an "ancillary force of the Army in time of war". The Military Fire Brigade, in general, is a part of the Military Police, although it does not perform traditional policing duties. It is subordinated to the state government.
- The *Civil Police* is the state police with criminal law enforcement duties. It has the function of investigating crimes committed in violation of Brazilian criminal law. It does not patrol the streets and generally does not use uniforms. Like the Military Police, it is subordinated to the state government.

Law enforcement in Brazil 395

Figure 183: *Police car - Military Police of São Paulo (PMESP)*

Figure 184: *National Public Security Force (Força Nacional de Segurança Pública)*

Other security forces

- The National Public Security Force, officially the *Força Nacional de Segurança Pública*, was created by presidential decree 5.289 on November 29, 2004. It is not a security force *per se*. Rather, it is a federal program of cooperation among all Brazilian police forces for situations of emergency or exceptional nature.[818]

- *Army, Navy and Air Force police units* are not to be confused with the state Military Police. These are internal security units of each Armed Forces branch. They do not have general civil order maintenance or law enforcement functions. Other internal units may be created for protection of particular agencies or administrative entities, such as the guards of legislative houses, which are not police institutions. Nevertheless, in times of emergency, the Army has been called upon to maintain order, most notably in Rio de Janeiro.[819] There are provost corps for each of the Brazilian Armed Forces: Army Police (Portuguese: *Polícia do Exército, PE*) for the Army, Navy Police (Portuguese: *Polícia da Marinha*) for the Navy, and Air Force Police (Portuguese: *Polícia da Aeronaútica, PA*) for the Air Force.

Entry qualification

Access to all positions under any military police forces encompasses written knowledge tests, previous and further medical exams, physical strength, agility and endurance tests and, finally, psychological interviews and evaluation. When approved on all tests, the candidate will be considered *fit to military police service* and admitted in special training courses (CTSP, to graduate soldiers, and the CFO, to graduate aspiring high-ranked officials). There's a minimum entry age of 18 years and, with few variations, a maximum entry age of 30 years.

Candidates to military police lower ranks, such as 2nd class soldier (entry level), must meet a minimum of high school education.

In the Civil Police as also in the Federal Police, police commissioners ("delegados") are responsible for coordinating and conducting all criminal investigations, with very similar functions and powers of those held by instruction magistrates or prosecutors in other legal systems. For that reason, those police commissioners are required to hold a full degree in Law and have law practicing or law enforcement experience of at least three years.

Controversies

Reports of police brutality and corruption have harmed the reputation of police institutions in Brazil, especially state forces.[820,821] Violence against suspects and extrajudicial executions are known to be employed by police. In the cities of São Paulo and Rio de Janeiro, the Military Police has been involved in several controversial massacres of civilians, typically in poor neighborhoods where high-profile criminals tend to hide. There have also been massacres in prison facilities. One of the most notorious cases is the Carandiru massacre of

1992. Torture is still commonly used as means of questioning and punishing individuals.[822] Brazil's corrections system is a huge problem for the country and it severely affects the overall well-being of its people. There are a lot of problems relating to violence, gangs and the way the government has been handling the problems. Brazil's corrections system is under the prison administration called Departamento Penitenciario Nacional (DEPEN), and the head of this prison administration is Renato Campos Pinto de Vitto. As of December 2017, the prison population in Brazil is at a total of 668, 914, and when compared to a prison population rate per 100,000, the total is 332 per 100,000 people. The amount of institutions Brazil has regarding their corrections system is 1,449[823]. The official capacity of the institutions is 404,509 people which is way more than they are supposed to be able to house[824]. In the year 2000, 232,755 people were incarcerated in Brazil. In the year 2016, 644, 575 people were incarcerated[825]. The President of Brazil, Michel Temer, aims to build 30 prisons this year to tackle the overcrowding crisis of their institutions[826]. Brazil's prisons are 50% over capacity, and most of the prisons are state-government run. The prisons are heavily controlled by gangs, drugs, guns and other contraband entering the prisons regularly. One of the more recent riots occurred between Brazil's most powerful gang, First Capital Command and their rival, Red command. First Capital Command slaughtered 26 other inmates at the Alcaçuz prison in the state of Rio Grande do Norte[827]. President Temer wants to build these new prisons to separate non-violent criminals from the dangerous ones to prevent recruitment into organized crime. Since a big part of their prison population problems are the gangs, President Temer has also said that Brazil will be more cooperative with neighboring countries to try and reduce gangs funded by drug trafficking. There is such bad overcrowding, some are close to 3 times their actual capacity. The use of pepper spray, tear gas, noise bombs and rubber bullets are in use frequently and severe beatings and kicking by the prison personnel on the inmates[828]. The prison personnel are also equipped with assaults rifles, shot guns and hand guns to protect themselves from the violent events that keep happening in their prisons and also to keep order of the super overcrowded prisons where inmates could easily overcome the employees[829].

External links

- " Brazilian Federal Police[830]" (**Portuguese**)
- "Rio de Janeiro Military Police"[831] (**Portuguese**)
- "Rio de Janeiro Civil Police"[832] (**Portuguese**)
- "São Paulo Military Police"[833] (**Portuguese**)
- "São Paulo Civil Police"[834] (**Portuguese**)
- "Minas Gerais Military Police"[835] (**Portuguese**)

- "Minas Gerais Civil Police"[836] **(Portuguese)**

Crime in Brazil

Crime in Brazil involves an elevated incidence of violent and non-violent crimes. According to most sources, Brazil possesses high rates of violent crimes, such as murders and robberies; depending on the source (UNDP or World Health Organization), Brazil's homicide rate is 20-30 homicides per 100,000 inhabitants according to the UNODC, placing Brazil in the top 20 countries by intentional homicide rate. In recent times, the homicide rate in Brazil has been stabilizing at a relatively high level.

Brazil is a heavy importer of cocaine, as well as part of the international drug routes. Arms and marijuana employed by criminals are mostly locally produced.

Crime by type

Homicide

In 2017, Brazil had a murder rate of 29.2 per 100,000 population. There were a total of 56,101 murders in Brazil in 2017. Another study has the 2017 murder rate at 32.4 per 100,000, with 64,357 homicides. In 2016, Brazil had a record 61,819 murders or on average 198 murders per day, giving a homicide rate of 29.9 per 100,000 population.

By Brazilian states

List of the Brazilian state capitals by homicide rate (homicides per 100,000):

Capital/-Region	1997	1998	1999	2000	2001	2002	2003	2004	2005	2006	2007	% change
Northern (state capitals)	31.9	39.5	31.3	34.2	32.1	34.2	34.4	31.8	35.6	34.9	33.0	▲ +3.7
Belém (PA)	24.5	29.1	15.1	25.9	27.0	31.8	34.7	29.6	44.7	33.9	34.2	▲ +39.7
Boa Vista (RR)	34.6	51.5	51.4	40.4	32.1	38.2	33.0	21.5	23.1	220	25.7	▼ −25.8
Macapá (AP)	46.6	51.0	64.1	46.2	44.3	44.0	44.1	38.5	38.0	35.8	32.3	▼ −30.8
Manaus (AM)	35.3	40.7	35.3	33.0	25.2	26.5	29.3	26.2	29.4	32.3	32.5	▼ −7.8

Crime in Brazil

Palmas (TO)	70.0	12.7	19.7	21.8	26.5	20.5	21.5	21.3	13.0	13.6	12.8	▼ -82.5
Porto Velho (RO)	38.3	70.3	55.5	61.0	66.9	63.2	51.1	71.4	56.4	68.5	51.3	▲ +33.8
Rio Branco (AC)	36.6	38.4	17.0	36.4	39.0	44.8	37.9	30.9	23.9	36.3	30.1	▼ -17.8
Northeast (state capitals)	**40.8**	**33.6**	**30.2**	**34.0**	**39.5**	**39.4**	**41.7**	**40.8**	**44.8**	**49.6**	**52.4**	▲ **+28.5**
Aracaju (SE)	19.3	16.8	35.2	39.9	60.9	54.4	50.6	47.2	40.5	46.7	38.9	▲ +101.2
Fortaleza (CE)	27.0	20.3	25.2	28.2	27.9	31.8	29.5	28.5	34.0	35.0	40.3	▲ +49.5
João Pessoa (PB)	33.3	38.4	36.0	37.8	41.3	42.5	44.7	42.6	48.1	48.7	56.6	▲ +70.3
Maceió (AL)	38.4	33.3	30.9	45.1	59.3	61.3	61.2	64.5	68.6	98.0	97.4	▲ +153.5
Natal (RN)	18.1	16.2	9.6	10.4	15.6	13.9	23.0	13.2	18.5	20.5	28.3	▲ +56.4
Recife (PE)	105.3	114.0	99.3	97.5	97.2	90.5	91.4	91.8	88.2	90.7	87.5	▼ -16.9
Salvador (BA)	41.6	15.4	7.9	12.9	21.3	23.2	28.6	28.5	39.7	43.7	49.3	▲ +18.3
São Luís (MA)	22.2	16.5	12.8	16.6	27.4	21.4	30.8	32.6	30.0	31.4	38.4	▲ +73.1
Teresina (PI)	16.9	17.6	14.0	22.2	23.2	27.8	28.5	26.0	29.4	33.5	28.2	▲ +66.9
Southeast (state capitals)	**56.0**	**58.0**	**59.8**	**58.9**	**58.0**	**55.0**	**54.5**	**47.5**	**36.5**	**34.5**	**27.8**	▼ **-50.3**
Belo Horizonte (MG)	20.7	25.0	26.8	34.8	35.0	42.9	57.6	64.7	54.4	49.9	49.5	▲ +139.7
Rio de Janeiro (RJ)	65.8	62.6	53.5	56.6	55.5	62.8	56.1	52.8	41.9	46.4	35.7	▼ -45.8
São Paulo (SP)	56.7	61.1	69.1	64.8	63.5	52.6	52.4	39.8	28.3	23.2	17.4	▼ -69.4
Vitória (ES)	103.5	106.6	108.3	79.0	85.1	80.2	73.0	82.7	83.9	86.1	75.4	▼ -27.1
Southern (state capitals)	**29.5**	**25.1**	**27.3**	**29.9**	**30.3**	**34.8**	**35.5**	**39.3**	**40.4**	**40.3**	**43.3**	▲ **+46.4**
Curitiba (PR)	26.6	22.7	25.9	26.2	28.0	32.2	36.6	40.8	44.3	48.9	45.5	▲ +70.7

Florianópolis (SC)	9.4	9.3	8.9	10.2	17.0	24.7	27.1	28.9	24.4	19.4	19.5	▲ +106
Porto Alegre (RS)	37.2	31.4	32.9	39.2	36.5	40.5	36.4	40.3	40.1	35.5	47.3	▲ +27.3
Central-West (state capitals)	**35.3**	**37.7**	**37.6**	**39.2**	**39.1**	**37.4**	**39.3**	**36.8**	**33.4**	**33.4**	**34.1**	▼ -3.2
Brasília (DF)	35.6	37.4	36.7	37.5	36.9	34.7	39.1	36.5	31.9	32.3	33.5	▼ -5.9
Campo Grande (MS)	41.9	36.4	30.8	39.3	34.0	34.5	35.3	30.7	28.5	27.1	32.2	▼ -23.2
Cuiabá (MT)	55.3	76.0	68.5	69.5	76.9	52.0	49.8	45.5	44.4	40.7	38.8	▼ -29.9
Goiânia (GO)	22.1	22.6	30.1	28.6	29.4	38.1	37.4	37.4	34.6	36.4	34.6	▲ +56.6
Brazil (state capitals)	**45.7**	**45.3**	**44.6**	**45.8**	**46.5**	**45.5**	**46.1**	**42.4**	**38.5**	**38.7**	**36.6**	▼ -19.8

Murders increased during the late-2000s. Bucking this trend are the two largest cities. In 2008 Rio de Janeiro registered the lowest murder rate in 18 years, while São Paulo is now approaching the 10 murders per 100,000 mark, down from 35.7 in 1999. A notable example is the municipality of Diadema, where crime rates fell abruptly.

Total murders set new records in the three years from 2009 to 2011, surpassing the previous record set in 2003. 2003 still holds the record for murders per 100,000 in Brazil; that year alone the rate was 28.9. Police records post significantly lower numbers than the health ministry.

Robbery

Carjacking is common, particularly in major cities. Local citizens and visitors alike are often targeted by criminals, especially during public festivals such as the Carnaval. Pickpocketing and bag snatching are common. Thieves operate in outdoor markets, in hotels and on public transport.

A crime trend known as "arrastões" (dragnets) occur when many perpetrators act together, simultaneously mug pedestrians, sunbathers, shopping mall patrons, and/or vehicle occupants stuck in traffic. Arrastões and random robberies may occur during big events (Carnaval), soccer games, or during peak beach hours.[837]

Crime in Brazil

Figure 185: *Police cars of the São Paulo state police.*

Figure 186: *Detention in Brasília.*

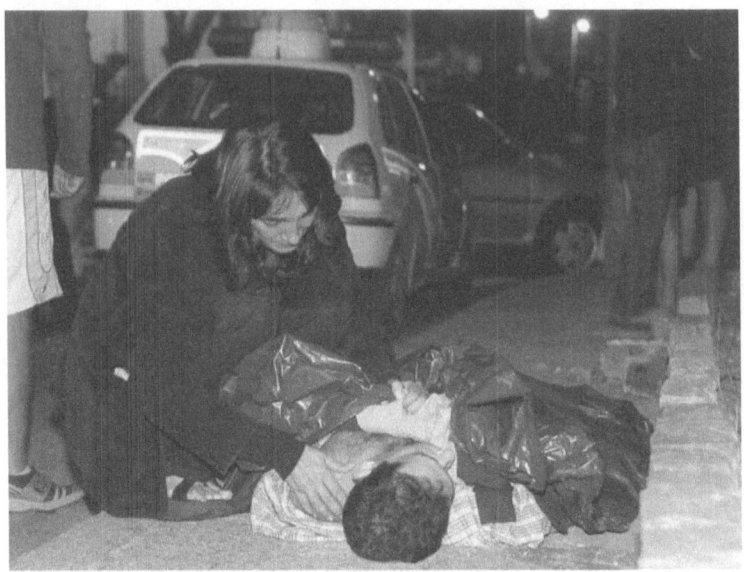

Figure 187: *Murder victim in Rio de Janeiro*

Kidnapping

Express kidnappings, where individuals are abducted and forced to withdraw funds from ATM to secure their release, are common in major cities including Rio de Janeiro, São Paulo, Brasília, Curitiba, Porto Alegre, Salvador and Recife.

Corruption

Corruption in Brazil is a pervasive social problem. Brazil scored 38 on the 2016 Corruption Perceptions Index, tying with India and Bosnia and Herzegovina, being ranked 76th among 175 countries. Corruption was cited among many issues that provoked the 2013 protests in Brazil.[838]

Corruption and yet is an important part of Brazil's politics. For years, embezzlement and corruption have been involved in Brazilian elections, and yet the electorate continues to vote for the same convicted politicians.

Figure 188: *An overhead view of Rocinha, the largest favela in Brazil; Rio de Janeiro, 2014.*

Domestic violence

Between 10 and 15 women are murdered per day in Brazil. A government sponsored study found that 41,532 women were murdered in Brazil between 1997 and 2007. In 2012, 8% of all homicide victims were female. However, this is still far below the male victimization rate, in which men constitute 92% of homicide victims in Brazil as of 2012.

Crime dynamics

Prevention

Brazil has started a crime fighting program specifically meant to combat gangs and gang centered violence. The UPP program; involving 'Pacifying Police Units', has been introduced in the traditionally violent favela's of Rio de Janeiro since 2008/2009. UPP's are well educated and trained in both human rights and modern police techniques, their aim is to supplant the community presence of gangs as central community figures. As of 2013, 34 UPP units are operational in 226 different communities, with a reach of 1.5 million citizens.

The UPP program has so far proven its worth by significantly reducing the amount of homicides, while also reducing violent crime rates in general. Local residents are mostly positive about the program and an overwhelming amount

Figure 189: *Police officers in the favela of Rocinha*

of residents felt safer. Furthermore, the UPP program symbolizes a new crime prevention paradigm that focuses on social inclusion and community development. However, in some areas the homicide rate was already dropping prior to the implementation of the program. Therefore, the drop in crime may be due to a general trend of decline in homicides as well.

Gangs

Gang violence has been directed at police, security officials and related facilities. Gangs have also attacked official buildings and set alight public buses. May 2006 São Paulo violence began on the night of 12 May 2006 in São Paulo, Brazil. It was the worst outbreak of violence which has been recorded in Brazilian history and was directed against security forces and some civilian targets. By May 14 the attacks had spread to other Brazilian states including Paraná, Mato Grosso do Sul, Minas Gerais and Bahia. Another outbreak of violence took place in São Paulo in July 2006.

2016 saw a new string of deadly prison riots. The nature of these riots was a turfwar between the Primeiro Comando da Capital and other gangs as an extension of a turfwar that has been increasing in intensity with the PCC aggressively expanding its territory.

Gang violence in Brazil has become an important issue affecting the youth. Brazilian gang members have used children to commit crimes because their prison sentences are shorter. As of 2007, murder was the most common cause of death among youth in Brazil, with 40% of all murder victims aged between 15 and 25 years old.

In regard to inter-gang conflict, gangs typically challenge or demand an aggressive reaction to defend their reputations. If someone does not respond in this manner, they are socially isolated. The gangs in Brazil are very territorial, and focused on their illegal business. Theft and robbery bring in small amounts of money compared to narcotic and weapons sales so it is less common for these gangs to get involved in petty crimes of theft or robbery.

The gangs more specifically in Rio de Janeiro are interested in harmony because they do not want any contact with the police. They will even go to helping others in the community, with money and even protecting them, just to be sure that the police do not come around. Children and other members of the community seen notably rich and powerful gang members and want to emulate this behavior. Gang members then become a substitute for family and are role models because they have respect with more the average monetary gains.

It is most common for these gangs to be under a military command structure. Each Rio's *favela* has one *dono* who is in charge of controlling the managers of a *favela* and the *soldados* in his territory. The latter protect the *favela* against other drug factions and the police. They are also responsible for taking over other *favelas*. The managers of a *favela* control the managers of the *bocas* (the places where drugs are sold in the *favela*). The managers of the *bocas* in turn control the drug dealers who sell the drugs in the area around a *boca*. There are children and women who wait at the entrances to a *favela* to signal to the others if the police or other gangs are about to enter. It is normal to join at about 10 years old, and by 12 years old to carry weapons. These gangs are attractive to the children and youth because they offer protection, recognition, and career options that those who join could not achieve on their own. *Favelas* are now often controlled by juveniles and young adults.

The concern here is of the strong ties that are between illegal business and politicians, police officers, the justice system, and the economy. Not all people are involved but all layers of society are affected because of corruption. Police are bribed to not disturb what these gangs are doing, as well as many of them are dealers themselves. Also, the young children are carrying guns and may be nervous, aware of peer pressure, or on drugs and can become careless. The level of brutality and homicide rates have skyrocketed in countries with younger gang members like this.

Figure 190: *Cracolândia ("land of crack") in central São Paulo.*

Drug trafficking

Drug trafficking makes up for an increasingly large portion of crime in Brazil. A total of 27% of all incarcerations in Brazil are the result of drug trafficking charges. Between 2007 and 2012 the number of drug related incarcerations has increased from 60.000 to 134.000; a 123 percent increase.

The primary drug trafficking jobs for children and youth are:

- endoladores: packages the drugs
- olheiro and/or fogueteiro: looks out to provide and early warning of police or any enemy drug faction invasion
- Drug mule: carries drugs to others inside their body, these are unwilling members of a gang, and don't survive for very long.
- vapor: drug sales persons
- gerente da boca: overseer of drugsales
- soldado: soldiers, armed and employed to maintain protection
- fiel: personal armed security guard for the "gerente geral"
- gerente geral or dono: owner/boss

Avioes are "little airplanes". These are the children who deliver messages and drugs to customers. They are not described in the hierarchal organization, but they are very low/entry level positions. In addition, this position has the most arrests.

Of 325 youth that were incarcerated, 44% of boys and 53% of girls reported some involvement with drug trafficking. Selling and carrying drugs were the most common activities between both boys and girls. The most common drug was marijuana, followed by cocaine and crack. From the study; 74% had used marijuana, 36% had snorted cocaine, and 21% had used crack.

Youth held low positions in the hierarchy and engaged in relatively low volumes of activity for short periods of time. The police are capturing the front-line players of the drug industry rather than the *donos*. 51% of youth involved with trafficking reported it to be very easy to obtain a gun. While 58% involved in trafficking, reported it to be very easy to obtain cocaine.

Penalties

The penalties of youth have intentions to withdraw the youth from circulation. As a lot of street culture crime is from children and youth. The main penalty is to be sent to educational centers with the sentence not exceeding 3 years. The educational centers are comparable with prisons but are not called that because it is not an official form of prison. For youth that are almost 18, they get no penalty at all. This is because they cannot be punished under juvenile law, or adult law. And when these youths turn 18, their records are wiped clean

For adults, the Rousseff administration has made a change in 2006, where consumers and suppliers of drugs are differentiated. The consumption of drugs has been nearly decriminalized, while other activities which are in any way related to the sale of drugs remain illegal. Unfortunately the effects of the 2006 drug law are contested, legally the distinction between drug consumers and suppliers remains poorly defined. The result of this unclarity is that judges have a high degree of discretion which causes unequal punishment and evokes accusations of discriminatory court rulings. Drug consumers receive a light penalty varying from mandatory self-education of the effects of drugs to community service. The minimum of punishment for a drug supplying offense is 5 to 15 years in prison. Several critics argue for a less rudimentary categorization of drug abusers than just the two categories, as it would allow for more lenient punishments for minor drugs violations. Critics such as former UN secretary general Kofi Anan and former president of Brazil Cardoso propose to step away from the 'war' approach in general, saying the militant approach can be counterproductive. However, the other side of the debate, and much of pupular opinion, expounds a more hard-line preference of heavy penalization.

Along with reform sentiment throughout Latin America, Supreme court justice Luis Roberto has called for the legalisation of drugs; starting with the decriminalization of Marijuana, and if successful, following with the decriminalization of cocaine. His argument for legalisation revolves around the failure of the current 'war' approach, potential savings for the penitentiary system, law enforcement and the judiciary. Furthermore, it would help prevent Brazils current mass incarceration problem, which funnels youths into gang membership.

References

- This article incorporates public domain material from the Overseas Security Advisory Council document "Brazil 2016 Crime & Safety Report: Recife"[839].

Military

Brazilian Armed Forces

Brazilian Armed Forces	
Forças Armadas Brasileiras	
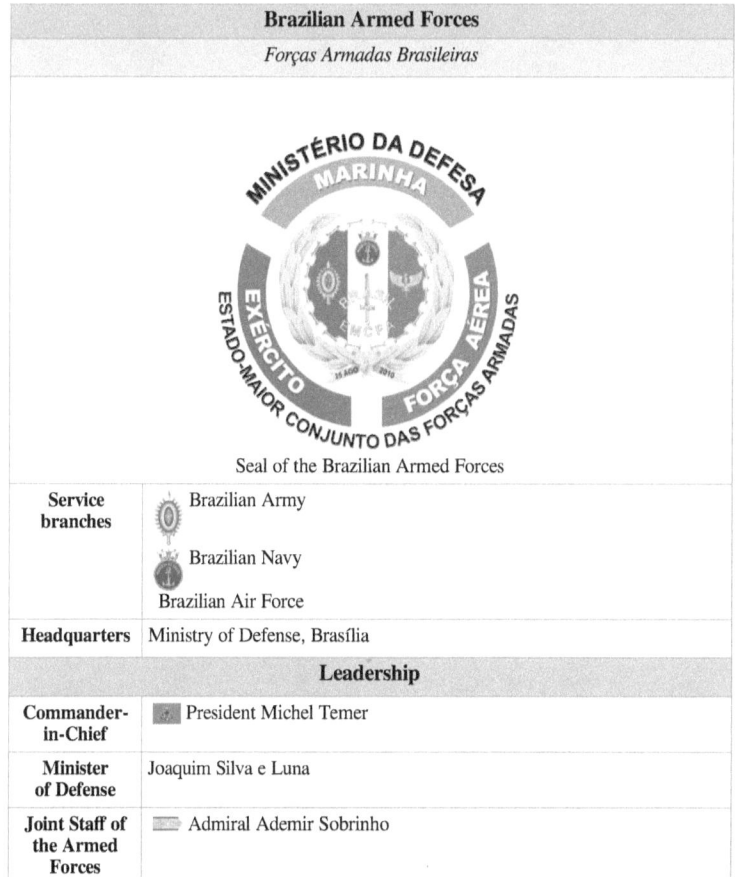	
Seal of the Brazilian Armed Forces	
Service branches	Brazilian Army
	Brazilian Navy
	Brazilian Air Force
Headquarters	Ministry of Defense, Brasília
Leadership	
Commander-in-Chief	President Michel Temer
Minister of Defense	Joaquim Silva e Luna
Joint Staff of the Armed Forces	Admiral Ademir Sobrinho

Manpower	
Military age	18–45 years of age for compulsory military service
Conscription	9 to 12 months
Available for military service	53,350,703 males, age 19–49 (2010), 53,433,919 females, age 19–49 (2010)
Fit for military service	38,993,989 males, age 19–49 (2010), 44,841,661 females, age 19–49 (2010)
Reaching military age annually	1,733,168 males (2010), 1,672,477 females (2010)
Active personnel	318,450(2014) (ranked 14th)
Reserve personnel	1,340,000 (2014) (ranked 5th)
Expenditures	
Budget	US$29.3 billion(2017) (ranked 11th)[840]
Percent of GDP	1.4%(2017)[841]
Industry	
Domestic suppliers	Embraer Avibras NUCLEP CBC IMBEL Taurus Helibras EMGEPRON Agrale Mectron Aero Bravo Iveco Brazil MAN Latin America Odebrecht Indústria Aeronáutica Neiva Troller INACE Usiminas XMobots Condor S/A
Foreign suppliers	United States France Germany Spain Colombia Russia Israel United Kingdom Sweden Italy

Annual exports	Colombia Argentina Indonesia Paraguay Uruguay Mauritania Ecuador Honduras Bolivia Chile Algeria Angola Suriname Namibia Burkina Faso Tunisia Japan Pakistan Zimbabwe Libya Lebanon Malaysia Singapore Haiti Poland
Related articles	
History	"**Brazilian Military History**" French Invasion Dutch Invasion Guaraní War Invasion of Cayenne Banda Oriental Conquest War of Independence Confederation of the Equator Mercenary Revolt Cisplatine War Malê Revolt Cabanagem Revolt Ragamuffin War Sabinada Revolt Balaiada Revolt Praieira revolt Platine War Uruguayan War Paraguayan War Naval Revolt Federalist War Acre Revolution War of Canudos Contestado War World War I Lieutenant Revolts Revolution of 1930 Paulista War Communist Uprising World War II

| | Lobster War
Operation Popeye
Operation Power Pack
Araguaia guerrilla
Traira operation
Rio de Janeiro Security Crisis
MINUSTAH |
|---|---|
| **Ranks** | Military ranks of Brazil |

The **Brazilian Armed Forces** (Portuguese: *Forças Armadas Brasileiras*, IPA: [ˈfoʁsɐz ɐʁˈmadɐz braziˈlejrɐs]) is the unified military organization comprising the Brazilian Army (including the Brazilian Army Aviation), the Brazilian Navy (including the Brazilian Marine Corps and Brazilian Naval Aviation) and the Brazilian Air Force.[842]

Brazil's armed forces are the second largest in the Americas, after the United States, and the largest in Latin America by the level of military equipment, with 318,480 active-duty troops and officers.[843,844] With no serious external or internal threats, the armed forces are searching for a new role. They are expanding their presence in the Amazon under the Northern Corridor (Calha Norte) program. In 1994 Brazilian troops joined United Nations (UN) peacekeeping forces in five countries. Brazilian soldiers have been in Haiti since 2004 leading the United Nations Stabilization Mission (MINUSTAH).[845]

The Brazilian military, especially the army, has become more involved in civic-action programs, education, health care, and constructing roads, bridges, and railroads across the nation. Although the 1988 constitution preserves the external and internal roles of the armed forces, it places the military under presidential authority. Thus, the new charter changed the manner in which the military could exercise its moderating power.[846]

Organization

The Armed Forces of Brazil are divided into 3 branches:[847]

- Brazilian Army
- Brazilian Navy
- Brazilian Air Force

The Military Police (state police) alongside the Military Firefighters Corps are described as an auxiliary and reserve force of the Army. All military branches are part of the Ministry of Defence.[848]

The Brazilian Navy which is the oldest of the Brazilian Armed Forces, includes the Brazilian Marine Corps and the Brazilian Naval Aviation.

Service obligation and manpower

19–45 years of age for compulsory military service; conscript service obligation – 9 to 12 months; 17–45 years of age for voluntary service. An increasing percentage of the ranks are "long-service" volunteer professionals; women were allowed to serve in the armed forces beginning in the early 1980s when the Brazilian Army became the first army in South America to accept women into career ranks; women serve in Navy and Air Force only in Women's Reserve Corps.[849]

Mission and challenges

South America is a relatively peaceful continent in which wars are a rare event;[850] as a result, Brazil hasn't had its territory invaded since year 1865 during the Paraguayan War. Additionally, Brazil has no contested territorial disputes with any of its neighbours[851] and neither does it have rivalries, like Chile and Bolivia have with each other. However, Brazil is the only country besides China and Russia that has land borders with 10 or more nations. Moreover, Brazil has 16,880 kilometers (10,490 mi) of land borders and 7,367 km (4,578 mi) of coastline to be patrolled and defended. Overall, the Armed Forces have to defend 8.5 million km² (around 3.2 million sq. mi.) of land and patrol 4.4 million km² (around 1.7 million sq. mi.)[852] of territorial waters – or *Blue Amazon*, as the Brazilian Navy calls them.[853] To achieve this mission, significant manpower and funding is required.

Military history of Brazil

Since 1648 the Brazilian Armed Forces have been relied upon to fight in defense of Brazilian sovereignty and to suppress civil rebellions. The Brazilian military has also four times intervened militarily to overthrow the Brazilian government.

The Brazilian Armed Forces were subordinated to the Emperor, its Commander-in-Chief.[854] He was aided by the Ministers of War and Navy in regard to matters concerning the Army and the Armada, respectively. Traditionally, the Ministers of War and Navy were civilians but there were some exceptions.[855,856] The model chosen was the British parliamentary or Anglo-American system, in which "the country's Armed Forces observed unrestricted obedience to the civilian government while maintaining distance from political decisions and decisions referring to borders' security".[857]

The military personnel were allowed to run and serve in political offices while staying on active duty. However, they did not represent the Army or the Armada but instead the population of the city or province where elected. Dom

Pedro I chose nine military personnel as Senators and five (out of 14) to the State Council. During the Regency, two were chosen to the Senate and none to the State Council as there was no Council at the time. Dom Pedro II chose four military personnel to become Senators during the 1840s, two in the 1850s and three until the end of his reign. He also chose seven military personnel to be State Counselors during the 1840s and 1850s and three after that.[858]

It has built a tradition of participating in UN peacekeeping missions such as in Haiti and East Timor. Below a list of some of the historical events in which the Brazilian Armed Forces took part:

Armed conflicts involving Brazil

- First Battle of Guararapes (1648): Decisive Brazilian victory that helped end Dutch occupation. Due to this battle, the year 1648 is considered as the year of the foundation of the Brazilian Army.
- Invasion of Cayenne (1809) (1809) : Was a combined military operation by an Anglo-Portuguese-Brazilian expeditionary force against Cayenne, capital of the French South American colony of French Guiana in 1809, during the Napoleonic Wars.
- Luso-Brazilian invasion (1816–1820) : Was an armed conflict between the United Kingdom of Portugal, Brazil and the Algarves and the partisans of José Artigas over the Banda Oriental (Eastern Bank), present-day Uruguay.
- Brazilian War of Independence (1822–1824): Series of military campaigns that had as objective to cement Brazilian sovereignty and end Portuguese resistance.
- Confederation of the Equator (1824) : Was a short-lived rebellion that occurred in the northeastern region of Brazil during that nation's struggle for independence from Portugal.
- Cisplatine War (1825–1828) : Armed conflict over an area known as Banda Oriental or "Eastern Shore" between the United Provinces of the Río de la Plata and Empire of Brazil in the aftermath of the United Provinces' emancipation from Spain.
- Ragamuffin War (1835–1845) : Was a Republican uprising that began in southern Brazil, in the states of Rio Grande do Sul and Santa Catarina in 1835. The rebels, led by generals Bento Gonçalves da Silva and Antônio de Sousa Neto with the support of the Italian fighter Giuseppe Garibaldi, surrendered to imperial forces in 1845.
- Platine War (1851–1852): The Brazilian Empire and its allies went to war against the dictator Juan Manuel de Rosas of the Argentine Confederation.
- Uruguayan War (1864–1865): Brazilian intervention in Uruguay. With support from Argentina, imperial forces deposed President Atanasio Aguirre from office and instated general Venancio Flores in his place.

- Paraguayan War (1864–1870): Over 200,000 Brazilians fought on this conflict, which is considered as the most serious in Brazilian history.[859]
- Brazilian Naval Revolt (1893–1894) : Were armed mutinies promoted mainly by Admirals Custodio de Mello and Saldanha da Gama and their fleet of Brazilian Navy ships against unconstitutional staying in power of the central government in Rio de Janeiro.
- War of Canudos (1893–1897): The deadliest rebellion of Brazil, the insurrectionists defeated the first 3 military forces sent to quell the rebellion.
- Contestado War (1912–1916) : Was a guerrilla war for land between settlers and landowners, the latter supported by the Brazilian state's police and military forces, that lasted from October 1912 to August 1916.
- Brazil during World War I: Brazil entered into World War I in 1917 alongside the Triple Entente. Brazil's effort in World War I occurred mainly in the Atlantic campaign, with a smaller participation in the land warfare.
- Constitutionalist Revolution (1932) : Was the armed movement occurred in the State of São Paulo, Brazil, between July and October 1932, which aimed at the overthrow of the Provisional Government of Getúlio Vargas and the promulgation of a new constitution for Brazil.
- Brazil in World War II (1942–1945): Brazil declared war on Nazi Germany in August 1942 and in 1944 sent an Expeditionary Force of 25,334 soldiers to fight in Italy. Brazil also supplied vital raw materials for the war effort and ceded important airbases at Natal and Fernando de Noronha Archipel that made possible the North African invasion, i.e. Operation Torch, and had a key role in patrolling the South Atlantic sea lanes.

Brazilian Expeditionary Force, initially composed of an infantry division, eventually covered all Brazilian military forces who participated in the conflict, including the Brazilian Air Force who did a remarkable job in the last nine months of war with 445 missions executed. Offensive: 2546, Defensive: 4.).[860]

Brazilian military coups d'état

Although no military coups occurred during the 67 years of the Brazilian Empire, the Republican period experienced 4 military coups d'état in the 75 years between 1889 and 1964.

- Proclamation of the Republic (1889): End of the Brazilian Empire, this was the first coup d'état performed by the Brazilian military.
- Revolution of 1930: Second military overthrow of government, in which President Washington Luís was replaced by Getúlio Vargas, who became the Provisional President.

Figure 191: *General Joaquim Silva e Luna, the atual defense minister.*

- End of *Estado Novo* (1945): Then Dictator Getúlio Vargas is deposed by generals and later General Eurico Dutra was elected president.
- 1964 Brazilian coup d'état: President João Goulart is removed from office, leading to a military dictatorship which lasted until 1985.

Ministry of Defense

Today, few countries do not bring their Armed Forces under one defense agency, subordinate to the Head of the Executive. In Brazil, until 1999, the three Armed Forces remained in independent ministries. However, the quarrel over the creation of a single Ministry of Defense, integrating the Navy, the Army and the Aeronautics is old. The 1946 Constitution already cited the creation of just one Ministry, that resulted in the institution of the E.M.F.A, at the time called General staff. Ex-President of the Republic Castelo Branco, defended the thesis of the creation of a Ministry of the Defense. It signed Decree 200, of 25 February 1967, that the Ministry of the Armed Forces foresaw the promotion of studies to elaborate the law project creating. However, the proposal was abandoned. During the Constitutional conventional of 1988, the subject came back to the quarrel and one more time it was filed. Finally in 1992, President Fernando Henrique Cardoso, then candidate to the Presidency, declared that in its plan of government the quarrel for creation of the Ministry of Defense was foreseen.

The President of the Republic still intended to create a Ministry in his first term. The idea was to optimize the system of national defense, to legalize one politics of sustainable defense and to integrate the three Forces, rationalizing their activities. But only on 10 June 1999, the Ministry of the Defense was officially created, the General staff of the Armed Forces abolished and the Aeronautics, Army, and Navy Ministries had been transformed into Service Commands. During the years of 1995/96 the EMFA, responsible for the studies on the Ministry of Defense, evidenced that, amongst 179 countries, only 23 did not have integrated Armed Forces. Of these 23, only three, amongst them Brazil, had dimensions politics to justify its creation, as for example, territorial extension and trained and structuralized Armed Forces. The Ministries of Defense of Germany, Argentina, Chile, Spain, USA, France, the United Kingdom, Italy and Portugal had been chosen for deepened analysis because they had some type of identification with Brazil, as territorial extension, population, cash of the Armed Forces, amongst others.

To give continuity to the creation studies, President Fernando Henrique created the Inter-ministerial Work group that defined the lines of direction for implantation of the Ministry of Defense. Reelected, he nominated senator Élcio Álvares, Extraordinary minister of the Defense, on 1 January 1999. The former senator was the responsible one for the implementation of the agency. The three services are separate from each other, except in three areas: the Armed Forces General Staff (Estado-Maior das Forças Armadas-EMFA), the National Defense Council (Conselho de Defesa Nacional-CDN), and the Armed Forces High Command (Alto Comando das Forças Armadas-ACFA). The EMFA, which is involved in planning and coordination, interprets interservice views about policy and comes the closest to functioning as a ministry of defense. It is headed by a four-star general, and the chair rotates among the services. The ACFA is involved with more immediate, day-to-day problems. It is composed of the ministers of the three services, their chiefs of staff, and the EMFA chief.

According to Article 91 of the constitution, the CDN is "the consultative body of the president of the republic in matters related to national sovereignty and the defense of the democratic state." The members of the CDN are the president, the vice president, the president of the Chamber of Deputies, the president of the Senate, the minister of justice, military ministers, the minister of foreign affairs, and the minister of planning. The CDN has authority to "express an opinion in instances of declaration of war and the celebration of peace" and to "express an opinion on the decreeing of a state of emergency, state of siege, or federal intervention." In addition, the CDN is authorized to "propose the criteria and conditions for the use of areas that are vital to the security of the national territory and express an opinion on their continued use, especially in the strip along the borders, and on matters related to the conservation and exploitation of natural resources of any kind." The CDN also may "study, propose, and monitor the progress of initiatives necessary to guarantee national independence and the defense of the democratic state."

The highest level consultative body available to the president is the Council of the Republic (Conselho da República). This body does not include any military minister or officer, although the president may call on a military minister to participate if the matter is related to the respective ministry's agenda. According to Article 89 of the constitution, the Council of the Republic has authority to make declarations of federal intervention, a state of emergency, and a state of siege (all security-related issues).[861]

Joint Staff of the Armed Forces

Joint Staff of the Armed Forces is an agency of the Ministry of Defense of Brazil, which centralizes the coordination of command of the armed forces: Army, Navy and Air Force. It was created by Complementary Law No. 136 of 25 August 2010, and has in Ordinance No. 1429 its operating guidelines.

Advising the Minister of Defense in the upper direction of the armed forces, aiming the organization, preparation and employment, in order to fulfill its constitutional mission and its subsidiaries assignments, with the goals strategic planning and the joint use of the military services.

It is up to JSAF plan together and integrated employment of staff of the Navy, Army and Air Force, optimizing the use of the military and logistical support in the defense of the country and in peacekeeping, humanitarian and rescue operations; border security; and civil defense actions.

The body has its powers and duties according to the Regimental Structure approved by Decree 7.9744, April 1, 2013.

Since its inception, the JSAF has worked with the Central Administration of the Ministry of Defence, on the Esplanade of Ministries in Brasilia (DF).

The head of the JSAF is private of a general officer of the last post, active or reserve, designated by the Ministry of Defence and appointed by the president. Their hierarchical level is the same of the military commanders of the Navy, Army and Air Force.

Under the coordination of the Joint Armed Forces also operates the Committee of Chiefs of Staffs of the military services.

The current head of JSAF is Admiral-of-Fleet Ademir Sobrinho.

Figure 192: *General Eduardo Villas Bôas current commander of the Brazilian Army.*

Brazilian Army

As in most South American nations, the Brazilian Army (Portuguese: *Exército Brasileiro*, [ɛ'zɛʁsitu brazi'lejɾu]) has been the most influential of the services because of its size, deployment, and historical development. Not only did senior army generals occupy the presidency from 1964 until 1985, but most of the officers who held cabinet posts during that time were from the army. In 1997 the army totaled 200,000 members. Brazil's army has strict up-or-out retirement rules, which were developed in the mid-1960s by President Castelo Branco. The internal command structure determines all promotions through the rank of colonel. The president is involved in the promotions to general and chooses one candidate from a list of three names presented to him by the High Command. Once passed over, the colonel must retire. All colonels must retire at age fifty-nine; and all four-star generals must retire at age sixty-six, or after 12 years as general.

Despite the up-or-out system, under President José Sarney the army became top-heavy as generals began to occupy many positions that previously had been reserved for colonels. In 1991 there were 15 four-star, forty three-star, and 110 two-star generals. The figure for four-star generals did not include four who were ministers in the Superior Military Court (Superior Tribunal Militar-STM). Thus, in the mid-1990s the army sought to reduce the number of active-duty generals. Considering the short conscript tour (usually nine to

Figure 193: *Brazilian troops on the march.*

Figure 194: *Artillery of the Brazilian Army in action.*

ten months), the army has a high number of conscripts: 125,000. Because of the need for literate and skilled young men to handle modern weapons, the army has served as a training ground for a large reserve force. Its highly professional officer corps serves as a nucleus around which the trained service would be mobilized if required.

Figure 195: *Battle in the jungle.*

Figure 196: *Special Commands.*

Figure 197: *Paratroopers.*

Figure 198: *Airborne troops.*

Brazilian Armed Forces

Figure 199: *M113 APCs row.*

Figure 200: *Brazilian Army infantry.*

Figure 201: *Tanks column of the Brazilian Army.*

The noncommissioned officer (NCO) corps is not well developed. NCOs have virtually no autonomy or authority. Emphasis on training and professional development is for officers only. The NCOs account for slightly more than one-third of the total army strength. About half of the NCOs are sergeants, who serve as command links between officers and ranks. Some also serve as middle-level technicians. In the early 1990s, the army began to undergo a generational change. The generals of the early 1990s had been junior officers in the early 1960s and had witnessed the military coup in 1964. Their worldview was shaped and influenced by the anticommunism of that time. These generals were being replaced by colonels who had entered the army in the early 1970s and whose view of the world had been shaped less by ideology and more by pragmatism. The United States, particularly through its counterinsurgency doctrines of the early 1960s, was more influential with the older group of officers.

The Army General Staff (Estado-Maior do Exército-EME) directs training and operations. The EME has expanded from four sections in 1968 to 15 sections in 1994. It is headed by the EME chief, except in the event of a war. From 1946 through 1985, the army was divided into four numbered armies: the First Army was centered in Rio de Janeiro, the Second Army in São Paulo, the Third Army in Porto Alegre, and the Fourth Army in Recife. Historically, the First Army was the most politically significant because of Rio de Janeiro's position as the nation's capital through the 1950s. The Third Army was also important because of its shared border with Argentina (Brazil's traditional rival in Latin America) and Uruguay. In 1964, for example, close to two-thirds of the Brazilian troops were in the Third Army, and somewhat fewer than one-third were in the First Army. The rest were sprinkled throughout the Second and Fourth Armies. The Planalto Military Command (Comando Militar do Planalto-CMP), comprising the Federal District and Goiás State, and the Amazon Military Command (Comando Militar da Amazônia-CMA) supplemented the four armies.

On January 1, 1986, the army was restructured from four numbered armies and two military commands into seven military commands. The major addition was the Western Military Command (Comando Militar do Oeste-CMO), whose territory encompasses the states of Mato Grosso and Mato Grosso do Sul (previously under the Second Army territory), and Rondônia (previously under the CMA). Each of the seven military commands has its headquarters in a major city: Eastern Military Command (Comando Militar do Leste-CML), Rio de Janeiro; Southeastern Military Command (Comando Militar do Sudeste-CMSE), São Paulo; Southern Military Command (Comando Militar do Sul-CMS), Porto Alegre; Northeastern Military Command (Comando Militar do Nordeste-CMN), Recife; CMO, Campo Grande; CMP, Brasília; and CMA, Manaus. The CMP and CMO are led by major generals (three-star); the other five are headed by full generals (four-star). The army is divided further into 11 military regions. The CMSE is made up of only one state, São Paulo, and is in charge of protecting the industrial base of the country.

The changes were instituted as part of a modernisation campaign to make the army better prepared for rapid mobilisation. The reorganization reflected Brazil's geopolitical drive to "occupy the frontier" and the growing importance of Brasília, the Amazon, and western Brazil. In 1997 there were major units around Brasília, four jungle brigades, and five jungle battalions extending from Amapá to Mato Grosso do Sul. A tour with jungle units is a coveted assignment and is considered career-enhancing. The move to occupy the Amazon and the short-term political implications of the army's reorganisation should not be overstated. The army's geographic organization and distribution have continued to reflect a concern with internal rather than external defense. In what is perhaps an anachronism, the CML in Rio de Janeiro continues to have some of the best troop units and the most modern equipment. Command of the CML is still a coveted assignment, and the Military Village (Vila Militar), Rio de Janeiro's garrison or military community, is still considered one of the most important centers of military influence in the entire country. Principal army schools are located there or nearby. The CML is also important in countering the trafficking of drugs and armaments.

Figure 202: *Admiral Leal Ferreira current commander of the Brazilian Navy.*

In a significant political development, the army established a formal High Command in 1964. Before that time, a clique of generals residing in Rio de Janeiro controlled major decisions of the army. Throughout the authoritarian period, tensions often existed between the High Command and the five generals who served as president. This tension was such that President Geisel dismissed Minister of Army Sylvio Frota in 1977. Since the January 1986 restructuring, the High Command has been composed of the seven regional commanders, the chief of staff, and the minister of army. The High Command meets to discuss all issues, including those of a political nature, and is responsible for drawing up the list of generals from which the president chooses those who will be promoted to four stars.[862]

Brazilian Navy

The navy (Portuguese: *Marinha do Brasil*, [hi du brɐˈziw]) traces its heritage to Admiral Cochrane's mercenary fleet and to the tiny Portuguese ships and crews that protected the earliest coastal colonies from seaborne marauders. The navy is the most aristocratic and conservative of the services and draws a larger share of its officers from the upper middle class and upper class. Although it is involved in "brown-water" (riverine and coastal) operations, the navy's primary goal has been to become an effective "blue-water" navy, able to project

Figure 203: *AS532M1 Cougar Naval aviation*

power on the high seas. Given its "blue-water" bias, the navy is even less inclined to become involved in counterdrug operations than the army or air force.

The total naval strength of 64,700 in 1997 included Naval Aviation with 1,300 members, the Marines Corpo de Fuzileiros Navais-CFN with 14,600 members, and only 2,000 conscripts. Naval operations are directed from the Ministry of Navy in Brasília through the Navy General Staff (Estado-Maior da Armada-EMA), six naval districts (five oceanic and one riverine), and two naval commands-Brasília Naval Command (Comando Naval de Brasília-CNB) and Manaus Naval Command (Comando Naval de Manaus-CNM).

The 1st Naval District is located at the country's main naval base in Rio de Janeiro; the 2nd Naval District is in Salvador; the 3rd Naval District is located in Natal; the 4th Naval District is located in Belém; and the 5th Naval District is located in Porto Alegre. The 6th Riverine District has its headquarters in Ladário, near Corumbá on the Paraguay River.

Until the 1980s, the flagship of the ocean-going navy was the aircraft carrier *Minas Gerais* (the ex-British HMS *Vengeance*), which has been in service since 1945. Purchased from Britain in 1956, the *Minas Gerais* was reconstructed in the Netherlands in 1960 and refitted extensively in Brazil in the late 1970s, and again in 1993. In 1994 Mário César Flores, a former minister of navy, declared in an interview that the navy would be hard-pressed to defend *Minas Gerais* in a conflict.

Figure 204: *A-4 Skyhawk in Brazilian Navy*

Figure 205: *Brazilian frigates in shooting exercise.*

Figure 206: *A submarine of the Brazilian Navy leaving for mission.*

Figure 207: *Corvettes escort.*

Figure 208: *Flagship of the Brazil Navy, port helicopters atlântico*

While the *Minas Gerais* was not considered likely to be replaced until the next century, it was nonetheless decommissioned in 2001 following the purchase of the French aircraft carrier *Foch*. The *Foch* upon entering service with the Brazilian Navy, was renamed the *São Paulo*. It operates A-4KU. As of July 2002, the fate of the *Minas Gerais* was still unknown, with China having reportedly made a surprise bid for its purchase.

The navy's priority re-equipment plans for the 1990s included the receipt of new Inhaúma-class corvettes, the construction of Tupi-class submarines, the refurbishing of the Niterói-class frigates, the acquisition of nine new Super Lynx and up to six former United States Navy Sikorsky SH-3G/H Sea King helicopters, the construction of the conventional SNAC-1 submarine prototype, and the development of nuclear-propulsion technology. In addition, the navy contracted in late 1994 to acquire four Type 22 British Royal Navy frigates and three River-class minesweepers for delivery in the 1995–97 period.

After years of intense rivalry between the navy and the air force for the control of naval aviation, President Castelo Branco decreed in 1965 that only the air force would be allowed to operate fixed-wing aircraft and that the navy would be responsible for helicopters. According to many critics, such an unusual division of labor caused serious command and control problems. The complement of aircraft carried by *Minas Gerais* included at one point six Grumman S-2E antisubmarine planes, in addition to several SH-3D Sea King helicopters and Aérospatiale Super Puma and HB-350 Esquilo helicopters.

Figure 209: *Brigadier Nivaldo Rossato current commander of the Brazilian Air Force.*

In accordance with the Castelo Branco compromise, the S-2E aircraft were flown by air force pilots and the helicopters by navy pilots. A crew of the *Minas Gerais* with full air complement consisted of 1,300 officers and enlisted personnel. As of late 2002, the Navy had reportedly become responsible for flying all aircraft with the rivalry having subsided between the two branches of the armed forces.[863]

Brazilian Air Force

The Brazilian Air Force (Portuguese: *Força Aérea Brasileira*, [ˌfoʁsaˈɛɾjɐ braziˈlejɾɐ], also known as *FAB*, [ˈfabi] or [ˌɛfiaˈbe]) is the 2° largest air force in America (behind only USA) and has around 70,000 active personnel. The FAB is subdivided into four operational commands:

I FAE (I Força Aérea) Advanced fixed and rotary wings instruction; II FAE (II Força Aérea) Maritime patrol, SAR, helicopters transport roles and Navy support; III FAE (III Força Aérea) Fighter command, it has all first-line combat assets under its control – fighter, attack and reconnaissance aircraft; IV FAE (IV Força Aérea) – responsible for transport missions.

The Aeronautic Ministry was created on January 20, 1941, and absorbed the former Army and Navy aviation under its command. In 1944 the Brazilian Air Force joined Allied forces in Italy and operated there for about seven months,

Figure 210: *A-1 strike fighter.*

this was the FAB baptism in a real conflict. In 1999 after a creation of the Ministry of Defence (MoD), the Aeronautic Ministry changed its designation to Aeronautic Command, but no big changes happened to the air force structure, it kept almost the same organization it had before.

The biggest, and most important, program of the FAB in the last years is the SIPAM (Sistema de Proteção da Amazônia – Amazonian Protection System), the operational part of the SIPAM is known by SIVAM (Sistema de Vigilância da Amazônia – Amazon Vigilance System). The SIVAM is a huge network of radars, sensors and personnel integrated to guard and protect the Amazon Rainforest and its resources. In 2002 the Embraer R-99A AEW&C equipped with the Ericsson Erieye Airborne Radar and the R-99B SR (Electronic Intelligence Gathering version) entered service. The R-99 fleet is one of the principal components of the system, the aircraft are based at Anápolis AB near Brasília and fly 24 hours a day over the Amazonian region.

The backbone of the Brazilian combat aviation made up of three types, the Northrop F-5E/F, the Embraer/Aermacchi A-1A/B (AMX) and the Embraer A/T-29 Super Tucano. The F-5s are under a modernisation program called F-5BR program, the aircraft official designation is F-5M. The upgrade is being carried out by Embraer and Elbit; it includes a new avionics suite, a full glass cockpit with three MFDs, HOTAS configuration and a new multimode radar, the Italian Grifo F. The first F-5EM was handed over on September 21, 2005,

Figure 211: *Two F-5M fighters taking off in aerial alert.*

Figure 212: *UH-60L utility helicopter.*

Figure 213: *CASA C-295 in cargo transport mission.*

and it is scheduled at a rate of two aircraft being delivered each month from that date onwards.

The A-1s are the main attack/ bomber aircraft of the FAB. There are three squadrons operating the A-1, one of them equipped with the RA-1 variant having a reconnaissance function as its primary role, but retaining all attack capabilities of the A-1. The RA-1s are equipped with RAFAEL's RecceLite reconnaissance system. Like the F-5, the A-1 is under a MLU (Mid Life Upgrade) program as well, this upgrade giving a high commonality between the avionics of the A-1M (MLU aircraft designation), the F-5M and the newly introduced Embraer A/T-29.

With the Mirage III withdrawn, the air defence of Brasília and region is done temporarily by a mix of F-5s from 1st GAv and 1st/14th GAv until 10 Mirage 2000Cs and two Mirage 2000B bought from French Air Force surplus stocks arrive at Anápolis. The Mirage 2000s are meant to be in service until at least 2015, when the Brazilian Air Force foresee the (postponed) F-X entering in service.

To replace the Embraer P-95 Bandeirulha in the maritime patrol duties, 12 Lockheed P-3A Orions have been bought from US Navy surplus and eight (with an option for a ninth) of them are being upgraded by EADS CASA in Spain, the remainder are to be used as spare parts source. On the same day of contract signature for the P-3BR work, 29 April 2005, EADS CASA was

Figure 214: *A-29 Super Tucano patrolling the Amazon rainforest.*

Figure 215: *Embraer KC-390, new cargo aircraft of the Brazilian Air Force.*

also awarded a contract to supply 12 C-295M medium transport aircraft. Deliveries started in 2006 with the first aircraft arriving in October 2006. The first three C-295s, designated C-105A Amazonas in Brazilian service, were commissioned into service in a formal ceremony at Base Aérea de Manaus on March 31, 2007. The C-105 replaces the FAB's C-115 Buffalo fleet and will supplement the C-130 Hercules.

The main heavy transport aircraft is the Lockheed C-130H Hercules and it will not change soon. The "Herks" are receiving major upgrades, receiving a full glass cockpit besides many other modifications. The first upgraded C-130 entering operational service recently. There are four Boeing KC-137 used as transport and tankers roles. In 2005 FAB received one Airbus ACJ, callsign "Air Force One" and dubbed as "Santos Dumont." The ACJ is now the main presidential transport and it is assisted by two Boeing 737-200 and one AS-332 Super Puma, with the KC-137 still serving as presidential transport in case of necessity. The basic pilot training is concentrated in Pirassununga (AFA – Academia da Força Aérea) and uses the Neiva T-25 and the well known Embraer T-27 Tucano for basic instruction. Advanced training is done at Natal AB in the AT-29 Super Tucano, which replaced the Embraer AT-26 Xavante in the conversion training course.

Troop relocation

Brazil has the need to patrol its 16,880 kilometers (10,490 mi) of land borders. Since the 1990s Brazil has been relocating its forces in accordance to this national security requirement.

Between 1992 and 2008, the *1st, 2nd* and *16th Jungle Infantry Brigades*, the *3rd Infantry Battalion*, the *19th Logistics Battalion*, and the *22nd Army Police Platoon* were transferred by the Army from the states of Rio de Janeiro and Rio Grande do Sul to the Amazon region[864] in accordance with the friendship policy with Argentina. After those redeployments the number of Army troops in that region rose to 25,000. Also relocated from the state of Rio de Janeiro were the *1st* and *3rd Combat Cars Regiment*, now stationed in the city of Santa Maria, in the state of Rio Grande do Sul.

However, despite those efforts, the presence of the Armed Forces on the border regions of the Brazilian Amazon continues to be sparse and disperse, given the fact that the Army has just 28 border detachments in that area, a total of 1,600 soldiers, or 1 man for every 7 km (4.3 mi) of borders. More redeployments are expected since the states of Rio de Janeiro, Minas Gerais and Espírito Santo still concentrate over 49,000 soldiers. In May 2008, the Navy announced new plans to reposition its forces throughout Brazil.

Figure 216: *Earthly station's satellite dish of the National Institute for Space Research, in Cuiabá.*

Earth observation

The Brazilian Amazon sustains about 40% of the world's remaining tropical rainforests and plays vital roles in maintaining biodiversity, regional hydrology and climate, and terrestrial carbon storage. Recent studies suggest that deforestation rates in the Brazilian Amazon could increase sharply in the future as a result of over US$40 billion in planned investments in highway paving and major new infrastructure projects in the region.

These studies have been challenged by several Brazilian ministries, which assert that recent improvements in environmental laws, enforcement and public attitudes have fundamentally reduced the threat posed to forests by such projects.

Among tropical nations, Brazil probably has the world's best monitoring of deforestation activity. Estimates are produced by Brazil's National Institute for Space Research (INPE) for the entire Brazilian Legal Amazon by visually interpreting satellite imagery from the Landsat Thematic Mapper. The relevance of the CBERS program does not limit itself only to applications of the satellite-generated images. The program also takes part in the Space Activities National Program (PNAE) which objective is to lead the country toward the autonomy of this technology, vital in a path to sustainable development.

The INPE participation in this complex project accelerates the capability of the country in important space technologies, besides contributing to increase and modernize the national industry in the space sector and the infrastructure (laboratories and centers) dedicated to space projects. There has been participation of the national industry in all satellite subsystems on charge of Brazil.[865]

Bibliography

- International Institute for Strategic Studies; Hackett, James (ed.) (7 March 2012). *The Military Balance 2012*. London: Routledge. ISBN 1857436423.

External links

 Wikimedia Commons has media related to *Military of Brazil*.

- Brazilian Ministry of Defence[866]
- Brazil military profile[867] from the *CIA World Factbook*
- Brazil military guide[868] from GlobalSecurity.org

Foreign policy

Foreign relations of Brazil

The Ministry of External Relations is responsible for managing the **foreign relations of Brazil.** Brazil is a significant political and economic power in Latin America and a key player on the world stage.[870] Brazil's foreign policy reflects its role as a regional power and a potential world power and is designed to help protect the country's national interests, national security, ideological goals, and economic prosperity.

Between World War II and 1990, both democratic and military governments sought to expand Brazil's influence in the world by pursuing a state-led industrial policy and an independent foreign policy. Brazilian foreign policy has recently aimed to strengthen ties with other South American countries, engage in multilateral diplomacy through the United Nations and the Organization of American States, and act at times as a countervailing force to U.S. political and economic influence in Latin America.

Overview

Brazil's international relations are based on article 4 of the Federal Constitution, which establishes non-intervention, self-determination, international cooperation and the peaceful settlement of conflicts as the guiding principles of Brazil's relationship with other countries and multilateral organizations.[871] According to the Constitution, the President has ultimate authority over foreign policy, while Congress is tasked with reviewing and considering all diplomatic nominations and international treaties, as well as legislation relating to Brazilian foreign policy.[872]

The Ministry of Foreign Affairs, also known as Itamaraty, is the government department responsible for advising the President and conducting Brazil's foreign relations with other countries and international bodies. Itamaraty's scope includes political, commercial, economic, financial, cultural and consular relations, areas in which it performs the classical tasks of diplomacy: represent, inform and negotiate. Foreign policy priorities are established by the President.

Foreign policy

Brazil's foreign policy is a by-product of the country's unique position as a regional power in Latin America, a leader among developing countries, and an emerging world power.[873] Brazilian foreign policy has generally been based on the principles of multilateralism, peaceful dispute settlement, and non-intervention in the affairs of other countries.[874] Brazil engages in multilateral diplomacy through the Organization of American States and the United Nations, and has increased ties with developing countries in Africa and Asia. Brazil is currently commanding a multinational U.N. stabilization force in Haiti, the MINUSTAH. Instead of pursuing unilateral prerogatives, Brazilian foreign policy has tended to emphasize regional integration, first through the Southern Cone Common Market (Mercosul) and now the Union of South American Nations. Brazil is also committed to cooperation with other Portuguese-speaking nations through joint-collaborations with the rest of the

Figure 217: *BRIC (Brazil, Russia, India and China) leaders during the 1st BRIC summit in 2009.*

Portuguese-speaking world, in several domains which include military cooperation, financial aid, and cultural exchange. This is done in the framework of CPLP,[875] for instance. Lula da Silva recently visited to Africa included State visits to three Portuguese-speaking African nations (Angola, São Tomé and Príncipe, and Mozambique). Finally, Brazil is also strongly committed in the development and restoration of peace in East Timor, where it has a very powerful influence.

Brazil's political, business, and military ventures are complemented by the country's trade policy. In Brazil, the Ministry of Foreign Relations continues to dominate trade policy, causing the country's commercial interests to be (at times) subsumed by a larger foreign policy goal, namely, enhancing Brazil's influence in Latin America and the world.[876] For example, while concluding meaningful trade agreements with developed countries (such as the United States and the European Union) would probably be beneficial to Brazil's long-term economic self-interest, the Brazilian government has instead prioritized its leadership role within Mercosul and expanded trade ties with countries in Africa, Asia and the Middle East.

Brazil's soft power diplomacy involves institutional strategies such as the formation of diplomatic coalitions to constrain the power of the established great powers.[877] In recent years, it has given high priority in establishing political dialogue with other strategic actors such as India, Russia, China and South Africa through participation in international groupings such as BASIC, IBSA and BRICS. The BRICS states have been amongst the most powerful drivers of incremental change in world diplomacy and they benefit most from the connected global power shifts.

Lula da Silva administration

The Brazilian foreign policy under the Lula da Silva administration focused on the following directives: to contribute toward the search for greater equilibrium and attenuate unilateralism; to strengthen bilateral and multilateral relations in order to increase the country's weight in political and economic negotiations on an international level; to deepen relations so as to benefit from greater economical, financial, technological and cultural interchange; to avoid agreements that could jeopardize development in the long term.[878]

These directives implied precise emphasis on: the search for political coordination with emerging and developing countries, namely India, South Africa, Russia and China; creation of the Union of South American Nations and its derivative bodies, such as the South American Security Council; strengthening of Mercosul; projection at the Doha Round and WTO; maintenance of relations with developed countries, including the United States; undertaking and narrowing of relations with African countries; campaign for the reform of the United Nations Security Council and for a permanent seat for Brazil; and defense of social objectives allowing for a greater equilibrium between the States and populations.

Rousseff administration

The foreign policy of the Rousseff administration sought to deepen Brazil's regional commercial dominance and diplomacy, expand Brazil's presence in Africa, and play a major role in the G20 on global warming and in other multilateral settings.[879]

At the United Nations, Brazil continues to oppose sanctions and foreign military intervention, while seeking to garner support for a permanent seat at the Security Council.[880] Cooperation with other emerging powers remain a top priority in Brazil's global diplomatic strategy. On the recent airstrike resolution supporting military action in Libya, Brazil joined fellow BRICS in the Council and abstained. On the draft resolution condemning violence in Syria, Brazil worked with India and South Africa to try to bridge the Western powers' divide with Russia and China.[881]

Figure 218: *President of Colombia, Juan Manuel Santos and President of Brazil, Dilma Rousseff.*

Regional policy

Over the past decade, Brazil has firmly established itself as a regional power.[882] It has traditionally been a leader in the inter-American community and played an important role in collective security efforts, as well as in economic cooperation in the Western Hemisphere.[883] Brazilian foreign policy supports economic and political integration efforts in order to reinforce long-standing relationships with its neighbors. It is a founding member of the Organization of American States (OAS) and the Inter-American Treaty of Reciprocal Assistance (Rio Treaty). It has given high priority to expanding relations with its South American neighbors and strengthening regional bodies such as the Latin American Integration Association (ALADI), the Union of South American Nations (UNASUR) and Mercosur. Although integration is the primary purpose of these organizations, they also serve as forums in which Brazil can exercise its leadership and develop consensus around its positions on regional and global issues. Most scholars agree that by promoting integration through organizations like Mercosur and UNASUR, Brazil has been able to solidify its role as a regional power. In addition to consolidating its power within South America, Brazil has sought to expand its influence in the broader region by increasing its engagement in the Caribbean and Central America., although some think this is still a fragile, ongoing process, that can be thwarted by secondary regional powers in South America.[884]

Figure 219: *Mercosur, a regional trade bloc between Argentina, Brazil, Paraguay, Uruguay, and Venezuela.*

Brazil regularly extends export credits and university scholarships to its Latin American neighbors.[885] In recent years, the Brazilian Development Bank (BNDES) has provided US$5 billion worth of loans to countries in the region.[886] Brazil has also increasingly provided Latin American nations with financial aid and technical assistance. Between 2005 and 2009, Cuba, Haiti, and Honduras were the top three recipients of Brazilian assistance, receiving over $50 million annually.[887]

Diplomatic relations

Brazil has a large global network of diplomatic missions, and maintains diplomatic relations with every United Nations member state, in addition to Palestine and the Holy See.[888] As of 2011, Brazil's diplomatic network consisted of 179 overseas posts.[889]

Relations with non-U.N. member states:

- Kosovo - Brazil does not recognize Kosovo as an independent state and has announced it has no plans to do so without an agreement with Serbia.[890]
- Taiwan - Brazil does not recognize the Republic of China as it has recognized the People's Republic of China, although it has non-diplomatic relations and maintains a special office in Taipei.[891]

Figure 220:
Diplomatic missions of Brazil
Brazil
Nations hosting a diplomatic mission of Brazil
Nations with a non-resident mission of Brazil

United Nations politics

Brazil is a founding member of the United Nations and participates in all of its specialized agencies. It has participated in 33 United Nations peacekeeping missions and contributed with over 27,000 soldiers.[892] Brazil has been a member of the United Nations Security Council ten times, most recently 2010-2011.[893] Along with Japan, Brazil has been elected more times to the Security Council than any other U.N. member state.

Brazil is currently seeking a permanent seat on the United Nations Security Council.[894] It is a member of the G4, an alliance among Brazil, Germany, India, and Japan for the purpose of supporting each other's bids for permanent seats on the Security Council. They propose the Security Council be expanded beyond the current 15 members to include 25 members. The G4 countries argue that a reform would render the body "more representative, legitimate, effective and responsive" to the realities of the international community in the 21st century.

Outstanding international issues

- Two short sections of the border with Uruguay are in dispute - the Arroio Invernada area of the Quaraí River, and the Brazilian Island at the confluence of the Quaraí River and the Uruguay River.[895]
- Brazil declared in 1986 the sector between 28°W to 53°W *Brazilian Antarctica* (*Antártica Brasileira*) as its Zone of Interest. It overlaps Argentine and British claims[896]

- In 2004, the country submitted its claims to the United Nations Commission on the Limits of the Continental Shelf (CLCS) to extend its maritime continental margin.[897]

Foreign aid

Overseas aid has become an increasingly important tool for Brazil's foreign policy.[898] Brazil provides aid through the **Brazilian Agency of Cooperation** (Abbreviation: **ABC**; Portuguese: *Agência Brasileira de Cooperação*), in addition to offering scientific, economical, and technical support. More than half of Brazilian aid is provided to Africa, whereas Latin America receives around 20% of Brazilian aid. The share of aid allocated to the Asian continent is small.[899] Within Africa, more than 80% of Brazilian aid is received by Portuguese-speaking countries.[900] Brazil concentrates its aid for Portuguese-speaking countries in the education sector, specially in secondary and post-secondary education, but it is more committed to agricultural development in other countries.[901] Estimated to be around $1 billion annually, Brazil is on par with China and India and ahead of many more traditional donor countries. The aid tends to consist of technical aid and expertise, alongside a quiet non-confrontational diplomacy to development results. Brazil's aid demonstrates a developing pattern of South-South aid, which has been heralded as a 'global model in waiting'.[902] Some studies have suggested that, by giving aid, Brazil could be trying to get access to mineral and energy resources.[903]

Participation in international organizations

ACS[Observer] • ACTO • AfDB • BIS • CAF-BDLA[Associate] • Cairns Group • CAN[Associate] • CDB • CPLP • FAO • G4 • BASIC countries • G8+5 • G15 • G20 • G20+ • G24 • G77 • IADB • IDB • IAEA • IBRD • IBSA •ICAO • ICC • ICRM • IDA • IFAD • IFC • IFRCS • IHO • ILO • IMF • IMO • Inmarsat •INSARAG • Intelsat • Interpol • IOC • IOM • ISO • ITU • LAES • LAIA • Mercosul • MINUSTAH • NAM[Observer] • NSG • OAS • OEI • OPANAL • OPCW • PCA • Rio Group • Rio Treaty • UN • UNASUR • UNCTAD • UNESCO • UNHCR • UNIDO • UNITAR • UNMIL • UNMIS • UNMOVIC • UNOCI • UNTAET • UNWTO • UPU • WCO • WHO • WIPO • WMO • WTO • ZPCAS

Foreign relations of Brazil 447

Bilateral relations

Country	Formal Relations Began	Notes
Algeria		See Algeria–Brazil relations • Algeria has an embassy in Brasilia. • Brazil has an embassy in Algiers.
Angola		See Angola–Brazil relations • Angola has an embassy in Brasilia and a consulate-general in Rio de Janeiro. • Brazil has an embassy in Luanda.
Cape Verde		See Brazil–Cape Verde relations • Brazil has an embassy in Praia. • Cape Verde has an embassy in Brasilia.
Central African Republic	2010	Both countries established diplomatic relations in 2010.
Democratic Republic of the Congo		See Brazil–Democratic Republic of the Congo relations • Brazil has an embassy in Kinshasa. • DR Congo has an embassy in Brasilia.
Egypt		See Brazil–Egypt relations • Brazil has an embassy in Cairo. • Egypt has an embassy in Brasilia.
Ethiopia		• Brazil has an embassy in Addis Ababa. • Ethiopia has an embassy in Brasilia.
Guinea-Bissau	1974	• Brazil has an embassy in Bissau. • Guinea-Bissau has an embassy in Brasilia.
Kenya		See Brazil–Kenya relations • Brazil has an embassy in Nairobi. • Kenya has an embassy in Brasilia.
Morocco		• Brazil has an embassy in Rabat. • Morocco has an embassy in Brasilia.
Mozambique	15 November 1975	See Brazil–Mozambique relations • Brazil has an embassy in Maputo. • Mozambique has an embassy in Brasília. Mozambique is the country that receives the highest amount of Brazilian aid in Africa. Almost 50% of Brazilian aid allocated to the African continent between 1998 and 2010 was allocated to Mozambique.[900]
Namibia		• Brazil has an embassy in Windhoek. • Namibia has an embassy in Brasilia.

	Nigeria		See Brazil–Nigeria relations Bilateral relations between Nigeria and Brazil focus primarily upon trade and culture. The largest country in Latin America by size, and the largest country in Africa by population are remotely bordered across from one another by the Atlantic Ocean. Brazil and Nigeria for centuries, have enjoyed a warmly, friendly, and strong relationship on the bases of culture (many Afro-Brazilians trace their ancestry to Nigeria) and commercial trade. • Brazil has an embassy in Abuja. • Nigeria has an embassy in Brasilia.
	São Tomé and Príncipe	1975	• Brazil has an embassy in São Tomé. • São Tomé and Príncipe is accredited to Brazil from its Permanent Mission to the United Nations in New York City, United States.
	Senegal		• Brazil has an embassy in Dakar. • Senegal has an embassy in Brasilia.
	South Africa		See Brazil–South Africa relations Brazil-South Africa relations have traditionally been close. Brazil has provided military assistance to South Africa in the form of warfare training and logistics. Bilateral relations between the countries have recently increased, as a result of Brazil's new *South-South* foreign policy aimed to strengthen integration between the major powers of the developing world. South Africa is part of the IBSA Dialogue Forum, alongside Brazil and India.
	Zimbabwe		• Brazil has an embassy in Harare. • Zimbabwe has an embassy in Brasilia.

Americas

Country	Formal Relations Began	Notes
Argentina		See Argentina–Brazil relations After democratization, a strong integration and partnership began between the two countries. In 1985 they signed the basis for the MERCOSUL, a Regional Trade Agreement. In the field of science, the two regional giants had been rivals since the 1950s when both governments launched parallel nuclear and space programs, however, several agreements were signed since then such as the creation of the Brazilian–Argentine Agency for Accounting and Control of Nuclear Materials (ABACC) to verify both countries' pledges to use nuclear energy only for peaceful purposes. National spaces agencies CONAE and the AEB had also begun working together since the 1990s. Brazil's decision to prevent a Royal Navy ship docking in Rio de Janeiro was seen as backing Argentina over the Falklands dispute. Also on the military side there has been greater rapprochement. In accordance with the friendship policy, both armies dissolved or moved major units previously located at their common border (for example, Argentine's 7th Jungle and 3rd Motorized Infantry Brigades). Brazilian soldiers are embedded in the Argentine peacekeeping contingent at UNFICYP in Cyprus and they are working together at MINUSTAH in Haiti and, as another example of collaboration, Argentine Navy aircraft routinely operate from the Brazilian Navy carrier NAe São Paulo.

Foreign relations of Brazil 449

Barbados	1971-11-26	See Barbados–Brazil relations Brazil has an embassy in Hastings, Christ Church. Barbados has an embassy in Brasília.	
Belize	1983-03-01	Both countries established diplomatic relations on 1 March 1983.	
Bolivia		<ul><li>Bolivia has an embassy in Brasilia.</li><li>Brazil has an embassy in La Paz.</li></ul>	
Canada		See Brazil–Canada relations Brazil-Canada relations have been cordial but relatively limited, although the relationship between the two countries has been gradually evolving over time.<ul><li>Brazil has an embassy in Ottawa and consulates-general in Montreal, Toronto and Vancouver.</li><li>Canada has an embassy in Brasília, and consulates-general in Rio de Janeiro and São Paulo.</li></ul>	
Chile		See Brazil–Chile relations Chile and Brazil have acted numerous times as mediators in international conflicts, such as in the 1914 diplomatic impasse between the United States and Mexico, avoiding a possible state of war between those two countries. More recently, since the 2004 Haiti rebellion, Chile and Brazil have actively participated in the United Nations Stabilization Mission in Haiti, which is led by the Brazilian Army. They are also two of the three most important economies in South America along with Argentina.	
Colombia		<ul><li>Brazil has an embassy in Bogotá.</li><li>Colombia has an embassy in Brasilia.</li></ul>	
Costa Rica		See Brazil–Costa Rica relations<ul><li>Brazil has an embassy in San José.</li><li>Costa Rica has an embassy in Brasilia.</li></ul>	
Cuba		See Brazil–Cuba relations Brazilian-Cuban relations were classified as "excellent" in May 2008 following a meeting of foreign ministers.[904] During a January 2008 state visit to Cuba by Brazilian President Lula da Silva, the Brazilian leader expressed desire for his country to be Cuba's "number one partner". Bilateral trade increased by 58% between April 2007 and April 2008.[905]	
Dominica	1986	Both countries established diplomatic relations in 1986.	
Dominican Republic		<ul><li>Brazil has an embassy in Santo Domingo.</li><li>Dominican Republic has an embassy in Brasilia.</li></ul>	
Ecuador		<ul><li>Brazil has an embassy in Quito.</li><li>Ecuador has an embassy in Brasilia.</li></ul>	
El Salvador		<ul><li>Brazil has an embassy in San Salvador.</li><li>El Salvador has an embassy in Brasilia.</li></ul>	
Guatemala		<ul><li>Brazil has an embassy in Guatemala City.</li><li>Guatemala has an embassy in Brasilia.</li></ul>	
Guyana		See Brazil–Guyana relations Brazil–Guyana relations have traditionally been close. Brazil has provided military assistance to Guyana in the form of warfare training and logistics. Bilateral relations between the countries have recently increased, as a result of Brazil's new *South-South* foreign policy aimed to strengthen South American integration.	
Haiti		<ul><li>Brazil has an embassy in Port-au-Prince.</li><li>Haiti has an embassy in Brasilia.</li></ul>	

Honduras		• Brazil has an embassy in Tegucigalpa. • Honduras has an embassy in Brasilia.
Jamaica	1962-10-14	See Brazil–Jamaica relations Both countries are full members of the Group of 15.
Mexico	7 August 1824	See Brazil–Mexico relations Brazil and Mexico have the two largest emerging economies in Latin-America and the global stage. Both nations are considered to be regional powers and highly influential within the American continent. Both nations have historically been friendly and they have both participated in and are members of several multilateral organizations such as the G20, Organization of American States, Organization of Ibero-American States, Rio Group and the United Nations. Several high-level diplomatic meeting have been held by presidents of both nations to enhance bilateral relations. • Brazil has an embassy in Mexico City. • Mexico has an embassy in Brasilia and consulates-general in Rio de Janeiro and São Paulo. History of diplomatic relations between Mexico and Brazil (in Spanish only).[906]
Nicaragua		• Brazil has an embassy in Managua. • Nicaragua has an embassy in Brasilia.
Panama		• Brazil has an embassy in Panama City. • Panama has an embassy in Brasilia.
Paraguay		See Brazil–Paraguay relations Paraguay–Brazil relations have improved greatly after Brazilian President Lula's decision in 2009 to triple its payments to Paraguay for energy from a massive hydro-electric dam on their border, ending a long-running dispute. Under the accord, Brazil will pay Paraguay $360m a year for energy from the jointly-operated Itaipu plant. Brazilian President Luiz Inácio Lula da Silva called it a "historic agreement" and the deal slated as a political victory for Paraguayan President Fernando Lugo.
Peru		• Brazil has an embassy in Lima. • Peru has an embassy in Brasilia.
Suriname		See Brazil–Suriname relations • Brazil has an embassy in Paramaribo. • Suriname has an embassy in Brasilia.
United States		See Brazil–United States relations Brazil-United States relations has a long history, characterized by some moments of remarkable convergence of interests but also by sporadic and critical divergences on sensitive international issues.[907] The United States has increasingly regarded Brazil as a significant power, especially in its role as a stabilizing force and skillful interlocutor in Latin America.[908] As a significant political and economic power, Brazil has traditionally preferred to cooperate with the United States on specific issues rather than seeking to develop an all-encompassing, privileged relationship with the United States.
Uruguay		See Brazil–Uruguay relations Brazil and Uruguay are neighboring countries that share close historical, cultural and geographical ties. The singularity of the bilateral relationship between the two countries originates from the strong historical connection - marked by important events, such as the establishment of the Colônia do Sacramento in 1680, the annexation by Brazil and the subsequent creation of the Província Cisplatina in 1815, and Uruguay's independence from Brazil in 1828.[909]
Venezuela		see Brazil–Venezuela relations • Brazil has an embassy in Caracas. • Venezuela has an embassy in Brasilia.

Foreign relations of Brazil 451

Asia

Country	Formal Relations Began	Notes
Armenia	17 February 1992	See Armenia–Brazil relations • Armenia has an embassy in Brasília. • Brazil has an embassy in Yerevan.
Azerbaijan	21 October 1993	See Azerbaijan–Brazil relations • Azerbaijan has an embassy in Brasília. • Brazil has an embassy in Baku.
Bangladesh		See Bangladesh-Brazil relations Relations have been good. Brazil has an embassy in Dhaka. While Bangladesh has an embassy in Brasília. In 2013, Bangladesh has sought Brazil's support for its candidature at the Human Rights Council in 2015 and non-permanent seat of the UN Security Council for 2016-17 term.[2] In 2014, Brazil assured its support to Bangladesh for the posts of United Nations Human Rights Commission and CEDAW (The Convention on the Elimination of All Forms of Discrimination against Women). Bangladesh also supported Brazil's candidature for the post of Director General of World Trade Organization.
Bhutan	2009-09-21	See Bhutan–Brazil relations Bhutan and Brazil established diplomatic relations on 21 September 2009.[910],[911]
China		See Brazil–China relations • Brazil has an embassy in Beijing and consulates-general in Guangzhou, Hong Kong and Shanghai. • China has an embassy in Brasília and consulates-general in Recife, Rio de Janeiro and São Paulo.
East Timor		See Brazil–East Timor relations • Brazil has an embassy in Dili. • East Timor has an embassy in Brasilia.
India		See Brazil–India relations The two countries share similar perceptions on issues of interest to developing countries and have cooperated in the multilateral level on issues such as reform to the UN and the UNSC expansion.[912]
Indonesia		See Brazil–Indonesia relations Both are large tropical country endowed with rich natural resources, Brazil and Indonesia possess the largest tropical rain forest of the world that contains the world's richest biodiversity, which gave them a vital role in global environment issues, such as ensuring tropical forests protection. Both countries leading the list of Megadiverse countries with Indonesia second only to Brazil.
Iraq	1967	See Brazil–Iraq relations Brazil maintains an embassy in Baghdad and Iraq maintains an embassy in Brasília. Both countries are full members of the Group of 77. Brazil was the first Latin American country to reopen its embassy in Iraq since the 1991 Gulf War.

⬜ Israel	1949-2-7[913]	See Brazil–Israel relations Brazil played a large role in the establishment of the State of Israel. Brazil held the Presidency office of the UN General Assembly in 1947, which proclaimed the Partition Plan for Palestine. The Brazilian delegation to the U.N., supported and heavily lobbied for the partition of Palestine toward the creation of the State of Israel. Brazil was also one of the first countries to recognize the State of Israel, on 7 February 1949, less than one year after Israeli Declaration of Independence. Nowadays, Brazil and Israel maintains close political, economic and military ties. Brazil is a full member state of Israel Allies Caucus,[914] a political advocacy organization that mobilizes pro-Israel parliamentarians in governments worldwide. The two nations enjoy a degree of arms cooperation as Brazil is a key buyer of Israeli weapons and military technology. Also, Brazil is Israel's largest trading partner in Latin America. Israel has an embassy in Brasília and a consulate-general in São Paulo and Brazil has an embassy in Tel Aviv and an honorary consulate in Haifa.[915] Brazil has the 9th largest Jewish community in the world, about 107,329 by 2010, according to the IBGE census.[916] The Jewish Confederation of Brazil (CONIB) estimates to more than 120,000.[917]
● Japan	1895	See Brazil–Japan relations • Brazil has an embassy in Tokyo and consulates-general in Hamamatsu and Nagoya. • Japan has an embassy in Brasília and consulates-general in Belém, Curitiba, Manaus, Rio de Janeiro, São Paulo and consular offices in Recife and Porto Alegre.
Kazakhstan		• Brazil has an embassy in Astana. • Kazakhstan has an embassy in Brasilia.
Lebanon	November 1945	See Brazil–Lebanon relations • Brazil has an embassy in Beirut. • Lebanon has an embassy in Brasília and consulates-general in Rio de Janeiro and São Paulo.
Malaysia		See Brazil–Malaysia relations Brazil has an embassy in Kuala Lumpur, and Malaysia has an embassy in Brasilia.
North Korea	9 March 2001[918]	See Brazil–North Korea relations
Pakistan		See Brazil–Pakistan relations Brazil-Pakistan relations are characterized as friendly and cooperative. Brazil maintains an embassy in Islamabad and Pakistan maintains an embassy in Brasília. In 2008, Brazil approved the sale of 100 MAR-1 anti-radiation missiles to Pakistan despite India's pressure on Brazil to avoid doing so.[919]
Philippines		See Brazil–Philippines relations In June 2009, Brazil and the Philippines made their pledges as they signed mutual cooperation agreements in the fields of bio-energy and agriculture.[920] The two countries committed themselves to take the necessary steps to implement the signed Memorandum of Understanding on Cooperation in Agriculture and the Memorandum of Understanding on Bioenergy Cooperation.[921] The Philippines and Brazil signed six memoranda of understanding and agreements on the development and production of renewable energy, and agriculture cooperation.[922] It intends to "facilitate technical cooperation... on the production and use of biofuels, particularly ethanol, and promote the expansion of bilateral trade and investment in biofuel,"[923]
Qatar	5 November 1974	See Brazil–Qatar relations • Qatar has an embassy in Brasília. • Brazil has an embassy in Doha.

Foreign relations of Brazil 453

Saudi Arabia		• Brazil has an embassy in Riyadh. • Saudi Arabia has an embassy in Brasilia.
South Korea	31 October 1959[924]	See Brazil–South Korea relations The establishment of diplomatic relations between the Republic of Korea and the Federative Republic of Brazil started on 31 October 1959. • South Korea has an embassy in Brasilia.[925] • Brazil has an embassy in Seoul.
Turkey		See Brazil–Turkey relations. • Brazil has an embassy in Ankara and a consulate-general in Istanbul. • Turkey has an embassy in Brasilia.
United Arab Emirates		• Brazil has an embassy in Abu Dhabi. • UAE has an embassy in Brasilia.
Vietnam	1989-05-08	Vietnam established a Consulate General in São Paulo in 1998, and upgraded it to embassy status in 2000. The Brazilian Embassy in Hanoi was opened in 1994, being the first Latin American country to open an embassy in Hanoi. Vietnamese Presidents Lê Đức Anh and Trần Đức Lương have visited Brazil in October 1995 and November 2004, respectively.[926]

Europe

Country	Formal Relations Began	Notes
Albania		See Albania–Brazil relations • citizens of both countries can travel visa-free • Cultural Association and also a Chamber of Commerce and Industry 'Brazil-Albania'
Cyprus	July 21, 1964	• Diplomatic relations were established on July 21, 1964 • Cyprus has an embassy in Brasilia. • Brazil has an embassy in Nicosia.
Czech Republic		See Czech Brazilians
Denmark		See Brazil–Denmark relations Brazil has an embassy in Copenhagen and Denmark has an embassy in Brasília and consulates-general in São Paulo and Rio de Janeiro. Embassy of Denmark, Brazil[927]
Finland	April 8, 1929	Brazil recognised the independence of Finland on December 26, 1919. Brazil has an embassy in Helsinki.[928] Finland has an embassy in Brasília, honorary consulate generals in Rio de Janeiro and São Paulo and other honorary consulates in Belém, Belo Horizonte, Curitiba, Fortaleza, Manaus, Porto Alegre, Recife, Salvador and Vitória.[929]
France		See Brazil–France relations France has recognized Brazil as its special partner in South America and as a global player in international affairs. The two countries are committed to strengthening their bilateral cooperation in the areas for which working groups have been created: nuclear power, renewable energies, defence technologies, technological innovation, joint cooperation in African countries and space technologies, medicines and the environment. Recently, France announced its support to the Brazilian bid for a permanent seat on the United Nations Security Council.

Greece		See Brazil–Greece relations The countries have enjoyed "Bilateral relations [that] have always been good and are progressing smoothly," according to the Greek Ministry of Foreign Affairs.[930] • Brazil has an embassy in Athens. • Greece has an embassy in Brasília and consulates-general in Rio de Janeiro and São Paulo.
Hungary		Hungary has an embassy in Brasília and a consulate general in São Paulo. Brazil has an embassy in Budapest. The two countries signed the *Brazil-Hungary Cultural Agreement* in 1992.
Iceland	1953	Both countries established diplomatic relations in 1953.
Ireland	1975	See Brazil–Ireland relations • Brazil has an embassy in Dublin. • Ireland has an embassy in Brasília and a consulate-general in São Paulo.
Italy	1834	See Brazil–Italy relations • Brazil has an embassy in Rome and a consulate-general in Milan. • Italy has an embassy in Brasilia and consulates-general in Curitiba, Rio de Janeiro and in São Paulo and consulates in Belo Horizonte and Recife.
Poland	27 May 1920	See Brazil–Poland relations • Poland has an embassy in Brasília and a consulate-general in Curitiba. • Brazil has an embassy in Warsaw.
Portugal		See Brazil–Portugal relations Portugal and Brazil have countless bilateral agreements in areas such as culture, language, R&D, immigration, defence, tourism, economy, environment, among others. Portugal and Brazil hold regular Summits to discuss bilateral and multilateral agreements and current topics (last one in Bahia in 2008, before that one in Porto in 2005). One rather controversial topic was the spelling reform that aims at homogenising spelling in lusophone countries. Both countries share a common heritage and are committed in its preservation, be it through bilateral agreements or involving other nations, such as in the framework of CPLP.[931] Both countries lobby within the UN to upgrade Portuguese to a working language in that Organisation. Portugal has also lobbied for Brazil to become a permanent member of the UN Security Council. Finally, Portugal hosted the 1st EU-Brazil summit, in 2007.
Russia		See Brazil–Russia relations Brazil–Russia relations have seen a significant improvement in recent years, characterized by an increasing commercial trade and cooperation in military and technology segments. Today, Brazil shares an important alliance with the Russian Federation, with partnerships in areas such as space and military technologies, and telecommunications.
Serbia	1946	See Brazil–Serbia relations • Brazil has an embassy in Belgrade. • Serbia has an embassy in Brasília.
Spain	1834	See Brazil–Spain relations • Brazil has an embassy in Madrid and a consulate-general in Barcelona. • Spain has an embassy in Brasilia and consulates-general in Porto Alegre, Rio de Janeiro, Salvador and in São Paulo.
Ukraine		See Brazil–Ukraine relations • Brazil has an embassy in Kiev. • Ukraine has an embassy in Brasilia, a consulate-general in Rio de Janeiro and a consulate in Curitiba.
United Kingdom		See Brazil–United Kingdom relations • Brazil has an embassy in London. • United Kingdom has an embassy in Brasilia.

Oceania

Country	Formal Relations Began	Notes
Australia		See Australia–Brazil relations • Australia has an embassy in Brasília and consulates in Rio de Janeiro and in São Paulo. • Brazil has an embassy in Canberra and a consulate general in Sydney.
Nauru	2 November 2005	Both countries established diplomatic relations on November 2, 2005.
New Zealand	1964	See Brazil–New Zealand relations • Brazil has an embassy in Wellington. • New Zealand has an embassy in Brasilia and a consulate-general in São Paulo.
Samoa	2005	Both countries established diplomatic relations on February 1, 2005.

Bibliography

- Abellán, Javier; Alonso, José Antonio (2017). *The role of Brazil as a new donor of development aid in Africa*[932]. Africa, New Powers, Old Powers. University of Bologna.

External links

- The Sino-Brazilian Principles in a Latin American and BRICS Context: The Case for Comparative Public Budgeting Legal Research[933] *Wisconsin International Law Journal*, 13 May 2015
- Ministério das Relações Exteriores[934] - Official website of the Brazilian Ministry of Foreign Relations (in Portuguese)
- Ministério das Relações Exteriores[935] - Official website of the Brazilian Ministry of Foreign Relations
- Brazilian Mission to the United Nations[936] - Official website (in English) (in Portuguese)
- Agência Brasileira de Cooperação[937] - Official website of the Brazilian Agency of Cooperation (in Portuguese)
- IBSA News and Media[938] - IBSA Dialogue Forum | India, Brazil and South Africa | News, Opinion and Analysis

Administrative divisions'

States of Brazil

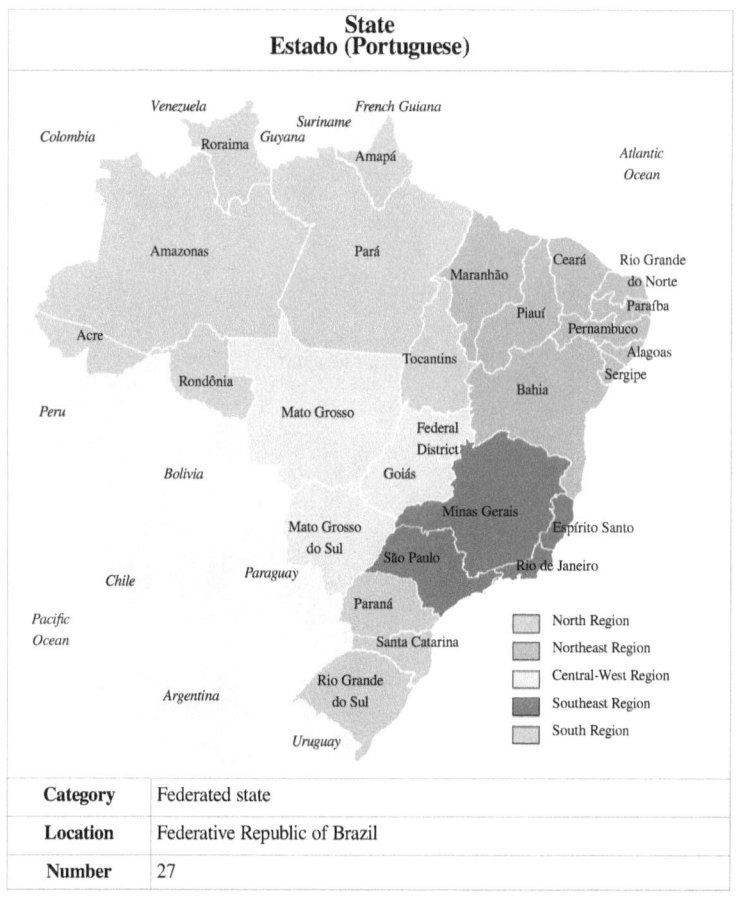

Category	Federated state
Location	Federative Republic of Brazil
Number	27

Populations	496,936 (Roraima) – 44,035,304 (São Paulo)
Areas	21,910 km² (8,459.6 sq mi) (Sergipe) – 1,570,800 km² (606,470 sq mi) (Amazonas)
Government	State government
Subdivisions	Municipality

The Federative Republic of Brazil is a union of 27 Federative Units (Portuguese: *Unidades Federativas, UF*): 26 states (*estados*) and one federal district (*distrito federal*), where the federal capital, Brasília, is located. The states are generally based on historical, conventional borders which have developed over time.

The Federal District is not a state, but shares some characteristics of a state as well as some of a municipality.

The codes given below are defined in ISO 3166-2:BR.

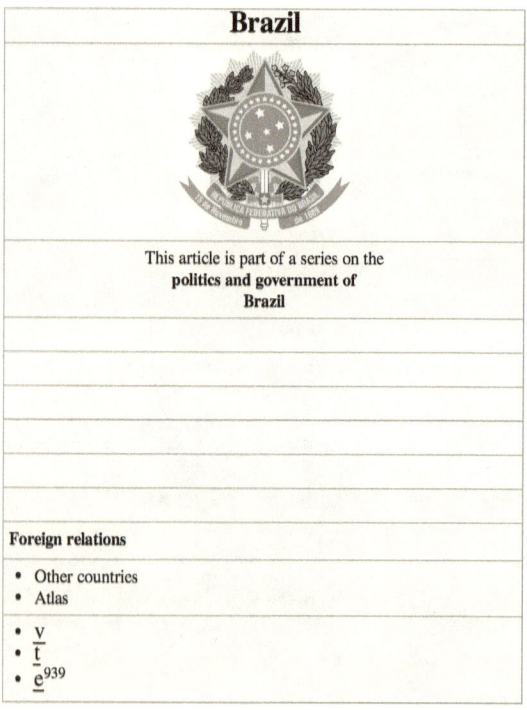

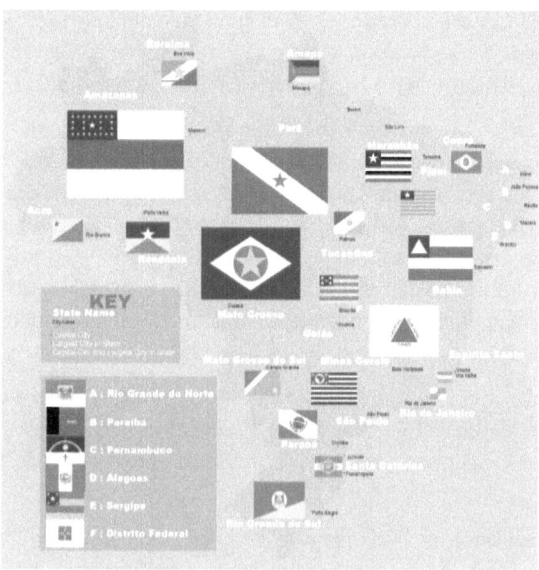

Figure 221: *The States of Brazil, their respective flags, their state capitals, and their largest cities.*

History

The present states of Brazil trace their history directly to the captaincies established by Portugal following the Treaty of Tordesillas which divided part of South America between Portugal and Spain.

The first administrative divisions of Brazil were the hereditary captaincies (*capitanias hereditárias*), stretches of land granted by the Portuguese Crown to noblemen or merchants with a charter to colonize the land. As the map shows, these divisions generally followed lines of latitude. Each of the holders of these captaincies was referred to as a captain donatary (*capitão donatário*). These captaincies were to be passed from father to son, but the Crown retained the power to revoke them, which the King indeed did in the 16th century-Wikipedia:Disputed statement.

In 1549, the Portuguese Crown appointed Tomé de Sousa as the first governor-general of the vast Portuguese dominion in South America. This dominion overall became known as the State of Brazil (*Estado do Brasil*). In several-Wikipedia:Citation needed periods of history, the northern half of the dominion was detached from the State of Brazil, becoming a separate entity known as the State of Maranhão. *Maranhão* by then referred not only to current Maranhão, but rather to the whole of the Amazon region; the name *marã-nã* in old Tupi language means "wide river", referring to the Amazon River.

After the Iberian Union (1580–1640), the territory of Portuguese colonial domains in South America was more than doubled, and the land was divided into hereditary and royal captaincies, with the latter being governed directly by the Crown. Unlike Spanish America, the whole territory remained united under a single governor-general (with the permanent title of viceroy after 1720), based in Salvador (after 1763, in Rio de Janeiro). This arrangement later helped to keep Brazil as a unified nation-state, avoiding fragmentation similar to that of the Spanish domains.

In 1759, the heritability of the captaincies was totally abolished by the government of the Marquis of Pombal, with all captains becoming appointed by the Crown. The captaincies were officially renamed "provinces" on 28 February 1821.

With independence, in 1822, the former captaincies became provinces of the Empire of Brazil. Most internal boundaries were kept unchanged from the colonial period, generally following natural features such as rivers and mountain ridges. Minor changes were made to suit domestic politics (such as transferring the Triângulo Mineiro from Goiás to Minas Gerais, splitting Paraná and transferring the south bank of the São Francisco River from Pernambuco to Bahia), as well as additions resulting from diplomatic settlement of territorial disputes by the end of the 19th century (Amapá, Roraima, Palmas). When Brazil became a republic in 1889, all provinces immediately became states.

In 1943, with the entrance of Brazil into the Second World War, the Vargas regime detached seven strategic territories from the border of the country in order to administer them directly: Amapá, Rio Branco, Acre, Guaporé, Ponta Porã, Iguaçu and the archipelago of Fernando de Noronha. After the war, the first four territories became states, with Rio Branco and Guaporé being renamed Roraima (1962) and Rondônia (1956), respectively, whilst Ponta Porã and Iguaçu remained as territories.

In 1960, the square-shaped Distrito Federal was carved out of Goiás in preparation for the new capital, Brasília. The previous federal district became Guanabara State, but in 1975 it was merged with Rio de Janeiro State, retaining its name and with the municipality of Rio de Janeiro as its capital.

In 1977, Mato Grosso was split into two states. The northern area retained the name Mato Grosso while the southern area became the state of Mato Grosso do Sul, with Campo Grande as its capital. The new Mato Grosso do Sul incorporated the territory of Ponta Porã and the northern part of Iguaçu. Central Iguaçu went to Paraná, and southern Iguaçu went to Santa Catarina.

In 1988, the northern portion of Goiás became the state of Tocantins, with Palmas as its capital. Also archipelago Fernando de Noronha became part of Pernambuco.

Government

The government of each state of Brazil is divided into executive, legislative and judiciary branches.

The state government constitutes the executive branch in each of the states. It is headed by a state governor and also includes a vice-governor, several secretaries of state—each one in charge of a given portfolio—and the state attorney-general.

The state legislature branch is the legislative assembly, a unicameral body composed of state deputies.

The judiciary in each of the states is made up of a Court of Justice and the judges of law. The judges of law constitute courts of first instance. The Court of Justice is the court of second instance of the state and is composed of judges called *desembargadores*.

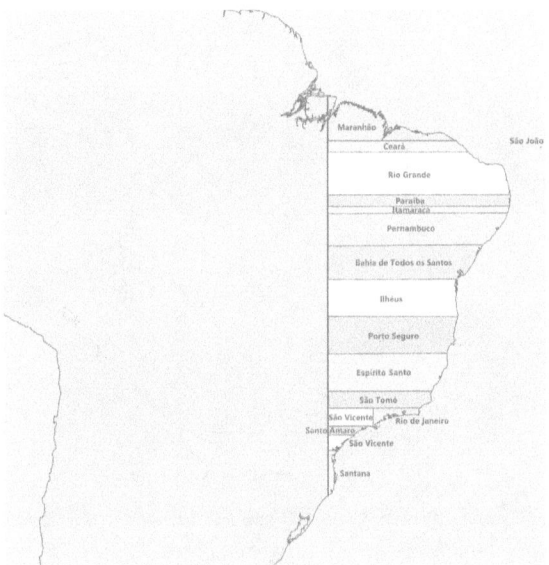

Figure 222: *1534 Captaincies of Brazil*

Figure 223: *1621*
First division in two states

Figure 224: *1709*
Greatest extent of São Paulo captaincy

States of Brazil

Figure 225: *1750*
Treaty of Madrid

Figure 226: *1817*
Captaincies at the time of Pernambucan revolt

Figure 227: *1822*
Imperial provinces

Figure 228: *1889*
States at the start of Republic

States of Brazil

Figure 229: *1943*
Border territories

Figure 230: *1988*
Current states

Proposed division of Pará

On 11 December 2011, a consultative referendum was held in the state of Pará about splitting that state into three new ones (Pará, Tapajós and Carajás). Both Tapajós and Carajás were rejected by the population by approximate margins of 2:1, despite being heavily favored in the proposed breakaway regions.

List

States of Brazil

Flag	Federative unit	Abbreviation	Capital	Area (km²)	Area (sq mi)	Population (2017)	Density (per km², 2017)	Density (per sq mi, 2017)	GDP (billion R$ and % total, 2012)	GDP per capita (R$, 2012)	HDI (2014)	Literacy (2014)	Infant mortality (2014)	Life expectancy (years, 2014)
	Acre	AC	Rio Branco	152,581.4	58,912	829,619	5.44	14	9.629 (0.2%)	12,690	0.719	94%	1.6%	75.4
	Alagoas	AL	Maceió	27,767.7	10,721	3,375,823	121.57	315	29.545 (0.7%)	9,333	0.667	90%	1.7%	73.5
	Amapá	AP	Macapá	142,814.6	55,151	797,722	5.59	14	10.420 (0.2%)	14,914	0.747	99%	1.6%	75.4
	Amazonas	AM	Manaus	1,570,745.7	606,470	4,063,614	2.59	7	64.120 (1.7%)	17,855	0.709	96%	1.9%	73.7
	Bahia	BA	Salvador	564,692.7	218,030	15,344,447	27.17	70	167.727 (3.8%)	11,832	0.703	91%	2.0%	74.3
	Ceará	CE	Fortaleza	148,825.6	57,462	9,020,460	60.61	157	90.132 (2.0%)	10,473	0.716	93%	1.65%	74.9
	Distrito Federal	DF	Brasília	5,822.1	2,249.9	3,039,444	522.05	1,351	171.236 (3.9%)	64,653	0.839	98.8%	0.65%	79.8
	Espírito Santo	ES	Vitória	46,077.5	17,791	4,016,356	87.17	226	107.329 (2.2%)	29,996	0.771	99%	0.48%	80.1
	Goiás	GO	Goiânia	340,086.7	131,310	6,778,772	19.93	52	123.926 (2.4%)	20,134	0.750	97%	0.9%	75.9
	Maranhão	MA	São Luís	331,983.3	128,180	7,000,229	21.09	55	58.920 (1.2%)	8,760	0.678	90%	1.9%	72.5
	Mato Grosso	MT	Cuiabá	903,357.9	348,790	3,344,544	3.70	10	80.830 (1.5%)	25,945	0.767	94%	1.3%	74.6

Mato Grosso do Sul	MS	Campo Grande	357,125.0	137,890	2,713,147	7.60	20	54.471 (1.0%)	21,744	0.762	97%	0.7%	76.1
Minas Gerais	MG	Belo Horizonte	586,528.3	226,460	21,119,536	36.01	93	403.551 (9.2%)	20,324	0.769	98.6%	0.61%	78.7
Pará	PA	Belém	1,247,689.5	481,740	8,366,628	6.71	17	91.009 (1.9%)	11,678	0.675	94%	1.6%	74.2
Paraíba	PB	João Pessoa	56,439.8	21,792	4,025,558	71.32	185	38.731 (0.8%)	10,151	0.701	92%	1.7%	74.1
Paraná	PR	Curitiba	199,314.9	76,956	11,320,892	56.80	147	255.927 (5.8%)	24,194	0.790	98%	0.7%	77.8
Pernambuco	PE	Recife	98,311.6	37,958	9,473,266	96.36	250	117.340 (2.3%)	13,138	0.709	92%	1.9%	74.8
Piauí	PI	Teresina	251,529.2	97,726	3,219,257	12.80	33	25.721 (0.5%)	8,137	0.675	90%	1.8%	72.7
Rio de Janeiro	RJ	Rio de Janeiro	43,696.1	16,871	16,718,956	382.62	991	504.221 (11.5%)	31,064	0.778	99%	1.3%	77.1
Rio Grande do Norte	RN	Natal	52,796.8	20,385	3,507,003	66.42	172	39.544 (0.9%)	12,249	0.717	95.1%	1.38%	76.7
Rio Grande do Sul	RS	Porto Alegre	281,748.5	108,780	11,322,895	40.19	104	277.658 (6.3%)	25,779	0.779	99%	0.4%	79.3
Rondônia	RO	Porto Velho	237,576.2	91,729	1,805,788	7.60	20	29.362 (0.6%)	13,075	0.715	94.6%	1.85%	73.7
Roraima	RR	Boa Vista	224,299.0	86,602	522,636	2.33	6	7.314 (0.2%)	15,557	0.732	94.5%	1.51%	73.5

Santa Catarina	SC	Florianópolis	95,346.2	36,813	7,001,161	73.43	190	177.276 (4.0%)	27,771	0.813	99%	0.30%	81
São Paulo	SP	São Paulo	248,209.4	95,834	45,094,866	181.68	471	1,408.904 (32.1%)	33,624	0.819	99%	0.45%	79.8
Sergipe	SE	Aracaju	21,910.3	8,459.6	2,288,116	104.43	270	27.823 (0.6%)	13,180	0.681	93%	1.8%	73.0
Tocantins	TO	Palmas	277,620.9	107,190	1,550,194	5.58	14	19.530 (0.4%)	13,775	0.732	94%	1.7%	74.5

External links

- Economic statistical data for Brazil's 26 states and federal district (in English, Portuguese, and Spanish)[940]
- States of Brazil[941] at Curlie (based on DMOZ)
- Wikimedia Atlas of Brazil
- Map of Brazil, showing states and their regular timezones[942]
- "Em 2012, Sudeste concentrava 55,2% do PIB do país e o DF tinha o maior PIB per capita"[943] (in Portuguese). IGBE. Archived from the original[944] on 19 December 2014.

Municipalities of Brazil

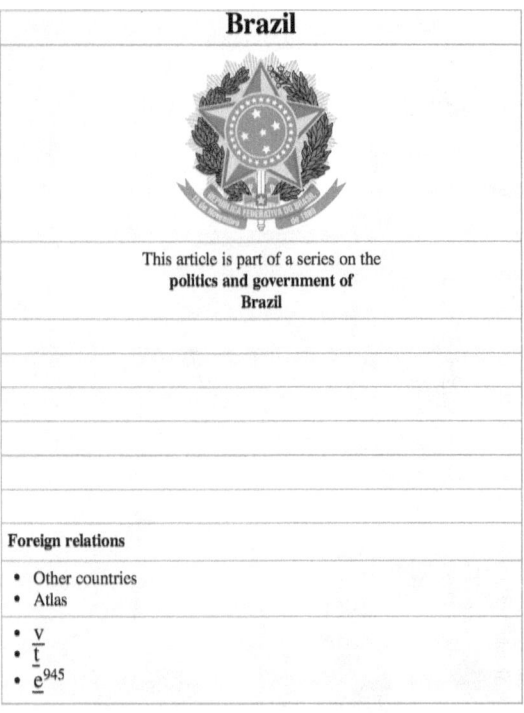

Brazil
This article is part of a series on the **politics and government of Brazil**
Foreign relations • Other countries • Atlas
• v • t • e[945]

The **municipalities of Brazil** (Portuguese: *Municípios do Brasil*) are administrative divisions of the Brazilian states. At present, Brazil has 5,570 municipalities, making the average municipality population 34,361. The average state in Brazil has 214 municipalities. Roraima is the least subdivided state, with 15 municipalities, while Minas Gerais is the most subdivided state, with 853.

Figure 231: *Municipalities of Brazil by state*

The Federal District, where the federal capital, Brasília, is located, cannot be divided into municipalities (according to the Brazilian Constitution, the Federal District assumes the same constitutional and legal powers, attributions and obligations of the states and municipalities). Instead, it is divided by 31 administrative regions.

The 1988 Brazilian Constitution treats the municipalities as parts of the Federation and not simply dependent subdivisions of the states. Each municipality has an autonomous local government, comprising a mayor (*prefeito*) and a legislative body called municipal chamber (*câmara municipal*). Both the local government and the legislative body are directly elected by the population every four years. These elections take place at the same time all over the country; the last municipal elections were held on October 2, 2016. Each municipality has the constitutional power to approve its own laws, as well as collecting taxes and receiving funds from the state and federal governments. However, municipal governments have no judicial power, and courts are only organised at the state or federal level. A subdivision of the state judiciary, or *comarca*, can either correspond to an individual municipality or encompass several municipalities.

The seat of the municipal administration is a nominated city (*cidade*), with no specification in the law about the minimum population, area or facilities.

The city always has the same name as the municipality, as they are not treated as distinct entities. Municipalities can be subdivided, only for administrative purposes, into districts (normally, new municipalities are formed from these districts). Other populated sites are villages, but with no legal effect or regulation. Almost all municipalities are subdivided into neighbourhoods (*bairros*), although most municipalities do not officially define their neighbourhood limits (usually small cities in the countryside).

Municipalities can be split or merged to form new municipalities within the borders of the state, if the population of the involved municipalities expresses a desire to do so in a plebiscite. However, these must abide by the Brazilian Constitution, and forming exclaves or seceding from the state or union is expressly forbidden.

Contents:

- Top
- 0–9
- A
- B
- C
- D
- E
- F
- G
- H
- I
- J
- K
- L
- M
- N
- O
- P
- Q
- R
- S
- T
- U
- V
- W
- X
- Y
- Z

A

- Municipalities of Acre (AC)
- Municipalities of Alagoas (AL)
- Municipalities of Amapá (AP)
- Municipalities of Amazonas (AM)

B

- Municipalities of Bahia (BA)

C

- Municipalities of Ceará (CE)

E

- Municipalities of Espírito Santo (ES)

G

- Municipalities of Goiás (GO)

M

- Municipalities of Maranhão (MA)
- Municipalities of Mato Grosso (MT)
- Municipalities of Mato Grosso do Sul (MS)
- Municipalities of Minas Gerais (MG)

P

- Municipalities of Pará (PA)
- Municipalities of Paraíba (PB)
- Municipalities of Paraná (PR)
- Municipalities of Pernambuco (PE)
- Municipalities of Piauí (PI)

R

- Municipalities of Rio de Janeiro (RJ)
- Municipalities of Rio Grande do Norte (RN)
- Municipalities of Rio Grande do Sul (RS)
- Municipalities of Rondônia (RO)
- Municipalities of Roraima (RR)

S

- Municipalities of Santa Catarina (SC)
- Municipalities of São Paulo (SP)
- Municipalities of Sergipe (SE)

T

- Municipalities of Tocantins (TO)

External links

 Wikimedia Commons has media related to *Municipalities in Brazil*.

- Map on the *World Gazetteer*[946] at Archive.is (archived 2012-12-17)
- (in Portuguese) Brazilian Institute of Geography and Statistics[947]

Economy

Economy of Brazil

Economy of Brazil

	São Paulo, the financial capital of Brazil
Currency	Brazilian real (BRL) = 0.258 USD
Fiscal year	1 January – 31 December
Trade organizations	Unasul, WTO, Mercosur, G-20 and others
Statistics	
GDP	$2.054 trillion (nominal; 2017) $3.240 trillion (PPP; 2017)
GDP rank	• 8th (nominal) • 8th (PPP)
GDP growth	1.9% (2018 est.)[948]
GDP per capita	$9,895 (nominal; 2017) $15,500 (PPP; 2017)
GDP per capita rank	• 65th (nominal) • 81st (PPP)
GDP by sector	services: 76% industry: 18.5% agriculture: 5.5% (2016 est.)[949]
Inflation (CPI)	2.68% (March 2018 est.)

Population below poverty line	▼ 3.8% (2016)[950]
Gini coefficient	▼ 0.48 (2018 est.)[951]
Labor force	120 million (2017 est.)
Labor force by occupation	Agriculture: 8%; Industry: 22%; Services: 70% (2017 est.)
Unemployment	▼ 12.6% (March 2018)
Main industries	• Textiles • shoes • chemicals • cement • lumber • iron ore • tin • steel • aircraft • motor vehicles and parts • other machinery and equipment
Ease-of-doing-business rank	■ 125th (2018)[952]
External	
Exports	$217.7 billion (2017)
Export goods	transport equipment, iron ore, soybeans, footwear, coffee, automobiles
Main export partners	China 21.8% European Union 16% United States 12.3% Argentina 8% Japan 2.4% Other 39%
Imports	$150.72 billion (2017.)
Import goods	machinery, electrical and transport equipment, chemical products, oil, automotive parts, electronics
Main import partners	European Union 21.2% China 18.1% United States 16.5% Argentina 6.2% South Korea 3.4% Other 35%
Gross external debt	$684.6 billion (January 2018)
Public finances	
Public debt	▼ 78.5% of GDP (2017 est.)
Revenues	$511.9 billion (2017 est.)
Expenses	$462.6 billion (2017 est.)

Economy of Brazil

Credit rating	• Standard & Poor's: BB (Domestic) BB (Foreign) BB (T&C Assessment) Outlook: Negative • Moody's: Ba2 Outlook: Negative • Fitch: BB+ Outlook: Negative
Foreign reserves	$373.9 billion (2017 est.)[953,954]

Main data source: **CIA World Fact Book**[955]
All values, unless otherwise stated, are in US dollars.

The **Economy of Brazil** is the world's eighth largest economy by nominal GDP and eighth largest by purchasing power parity. The Brazilian economy is characterized by a mixed economy that relies on import substitution to achieve economic growth. Brazil has an estimated US$21.8 trillion worth of natural resources which includes vast amounts of gold, uranium, iron, and timber.

As of late 2010, Brazil's economy is the largest of Latin America[956] and the second largest in the Americas. " From 2000 to 2012, Brazil was one of the fastest-growing major economies in the world, with an average annual GDP growth rate of over 5%, with its economy in 2012 surpassing that of the United Kingdom, temporarily making Brazil the world's sixth largest economy. However, Brazil's economy growth decelerated in 2013[957] and the country entered a recession in 2014. In 2017, however, the economy started to recover, with a 1% GDP growth in the first quarter. In the second quarter, the economy grew 0.3% compared to the same period of the previous year, officially exiting the recession.

Brazil's economy has a gross domestic product (GDP) of R$ 6.559 trillion, or US$ 2.080 trillion nominal, according to the estimates by the International Monetary Fund (IMF), being ranked as the 8th largest economy in the world. It is the second largest in the American continent, only behind the United States' economy. According to the report of the International Monetary Fund of 2017, Brazil is the 65th country in the world in the ranking of GDP per capita, with a value of US$ 10,019 per inhabitant.

According to the World Economic Forum, Brazil was the top country in upward evolution of competitiveness in 2009, gaining eight positions among other countries, overcoming Russia for the first time, and partially closing the competitiveness gap with India and China among the BRIC economies. Important steps taken since the 1990s toward fiscal sustainability, as well as measures taken to liberalize and open the economy, have significantly boosted the

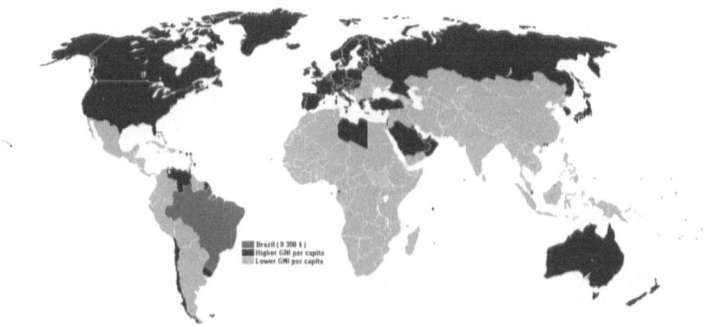

Figure 232:
GNI per capita in 2010:
Brazil (9,390 $)
Higher GNI per capita compared to Brazil
Lower GNI per capita compared to Brazil

country's competitiveness fundamentals, providing a better environment for private-sector development.[958]

In 2012 Forbes ranked Brazil as having the 5th largest number of billionaires in the world, a number much larger than what is found in other Latin American countries, and even ahead of United Kingdom and Japan. Brazil is a member of diverse economic organizations, such as Mercosur, Unasul, G8+5, G20, WTO, Paris Club and the Cairns Group.

History

When the Portuguese explorers arrived in the 16th century, the native tribes of current-day Brazil totaled about 2.5 million people and had lived virtually unchanged since the Stone Age. From Portugal's colonization of Brazil (1500–1822) until the late 1930s, the Brazilian economy relied on the production of primary products for exports. In the Portuguese Empire, Brazil was a colony subjected to an imperial mercantile policy, which had three main large-scale economic production cycles – sugar, gold and from the early 19th century on, coffee. The economy of Brazil was heavily dependent on African slave labor until the late 19th century (about 3 million imported African slaves in total). In that period Brazil was also the colony with the largest amount of European settlers, most of them Portuguese (including Azoreans and Madeirans) but also some Dutch (see Dutch Brazil), Spaniards, English, French, Germans, Flemish, Danish, Scottish and Sephardic Jews. Since then, Brazil experienced a period of strong economic and demographic growth accompanied by mass immigration from Europe, mainly from Portugal (including the Azores and Madeira), Italy, Spain, Germany, Poland, Ukraine, Switzerland, Austria and Russia. Smaller numbers of immigrants also came from the Netherlands, France, Finland, Iceland and the Scandinavian countries, Lithuania, Belgium, Bulgaria, Hungary, Greece, Latvia, England, Ireland, Scotland, Croatia, Czech Republic, Malta, Macedonia and Luxembourg, the Middle East (mainly from Lebanon, Syria and Armenia), Japan, the United States and South Africa, until the 1930s. In the New World, the United States, Argentina, Brazil, Canada, Australia, Uruguay, New Zealand, Chile, Mexico, Cuba, Venezuela, Paraguay, Puerto Rico and Peru (in descending order) were the countries that received most immigrants. In Brazil's case, statistics showed that 4.5 million people emigrated to the country between 1882 and 1934.

Currently, Wikipedia:Manual of Style/Dates and numbers#Chronological items with a population of over 204 million and abundant natural resources, Brazil is one of the ten largest markets in the world, producing tens of millions of tons of steel, 26 million tons of cement, 3.5 million television sets, and 3 million refrigerators. In addition, about 70 million cubic meters of petroleum were being processed annually into fuels, lubricants, propane gas, and a wide range of hundreds of petrochemicals.

Brazil has at least 161,500 kilometers of paved roads, more than 150^{959} Gigawatts of installed electric power capacity and its real per capita GDP surpassed US$10,500 in 2008, due to the strong and continued appreciation of the real for the first time that decade. Its industrial sector accounts for three-fifths of the Latin American economy's industrial production. The country's scientific and technological development is argued to be attractive to foreign direct investment, which has averaged US$30 billion per year the last years, compared to only US$2 billion per year last decade,^{960} remarkable growth. The agricultural sector, locally called the *agronegócio* (agro-business), has also been remarkably dynamic: for two decades this sector has kept Brazil among the most highly productive countries in areas related to the rural sector. The agricultural sector and the mining sector also supported trade surpluses which allowed for massive currency gains (rebound) and external debt paydown. Due to a downturn in Western economies, Brazil found itself in 2010 trying to halt the appreciation of the real.^{961}

Data from the Asian Development Bank and the Tax Justice Network show the untaxed "shadow" economy of Brazil is 39% of GDP.^{962} Template:"date=June 2017

Components

The service sector is the largest component of the gross domestic product (GDP) at 67.0 percent, followed by the industrial sector at 27.5 percent. Agriculture represents 5.5 percent of GDP (2011).[963] The Brazilian labor force is estimated at 100.77 million of which 10 percent is occupied in agriculture, 19 percent in the industry sector and 71 percent in the service sector.

Agriculture and food production

Agriculture production	
Combine harvester on a plantation	
Main products	coffee, soybeans, wheat, rice, corn, sugarcane, cocoa, citrus; beef
Labor force	15.7% of total labor force
GDP of sector	5.9% of total GDP

Agribusiness contributes to Brazil's trade balance, in spite of trade barriers and subsidizing policies adopted by the developed countries.

In the space of fifty five years (1950 to 2005), the population of Brazil grew from 51 million to approximately 187 million inhabitants,[964] an increase of over 2 percent per year. Brazil created and expanded a complex agribusiness sector. However, some of this is at the expense of the environment, including the Amazon.

The importance given to the rural producer takes place in the shape of the agricultural and cattle-raising plan and through another specific subsidy program geared towards family agriculture (Programa de Fortalecimento da Agricultura Familiar (Pronaf)), which guarantees financing for equipment and cultivation and encourages the use of new technology. With regards to family agriculture, over 800 thousand rural inhabitants are assisted by credit, research and extension programs. A special line of credit is available for women and young farmers.

With The Land Reform Program, on the other hand, the country's objective is to provide suitable living and working conditions for over one million families who live in areas allotted by the State, an initiative capable

Figure 233: *Economic activity in Brazil (1977).*

of generating two million jobs.Wikipedia:Manual of Style/Dates and numbers#Chronological items Through partnerships, public policies and international partnerships, the government is working towards guaranteeing infrastructure for the settlements, following the examples of schools and health outlets. The idea is that access to land represents just the first step towards the implementation of a quality land reform program.

Over 600,000 km² of land are divided into approximately five thousand areas of rural property; an agricultural area currently with three borders: the Central-western region (savannah), the northern region (area of transition) and parts of the northeastern region (semi-arid). At the forefront of grain crops, which produce over 110 million tonnes/year, is the soybean, yielding 50 million tonnes.

In the cattle-raising sector, the "green ox," which is raised in pastures, on a diet of hay and mineral salts, conquered markets in Asia, Europe and the Americas, particularly after the "mad cow disease" scare period. Brazil has the largest cattle herd in the world, with 198 million heads,[965] responsible for exports of more than US$1 billion/year.

A pioneer and leader in the manufacture of short-fiber timber cellulose, Brazil has also achieved positive results within the packaging sector, in which it is the fifth largest world producer. In the foreign markets, it answers for 25 percent of global exports of raw cane and refined sugar; it is the world leader in soybean exports and is responsible for 80 percent of the planet's orange juice, and since 2003, has had the highest sales figures for beef and chicken.[966]

Industry

Industrial production	
Embraer Legacy 600 jet manufactured by Embraer	
Main industries	textiles, shoes, chemicals, cement, lumber, iron ore, tin, steel, aircraft, motor vehicles and parts, other machinery and equipment
Industrial growth rate	–5% (2015 est.)
Labor force	13.3% of total labor force
GDP of sector	22.2% of total GDP

Brazil has the second-largest manufacturing sector in the Americas. Accounting for 28.5 percent of GDP, Brazil's industries range from automobiles, steel and petrochemicals to computers, aircraft, and consumer durables. With increased economic stability provided by the Plano Real, Brazilian and multinational businesses have invested heavily in new equipment and technology, a large proportion of which has been purchased from US firms.

Brazil has a diverse and sophisticated services industry as well. During the early 1990s, the banking sector accounted for as much as 16 percent of the GDP. Although undergoing a major overhaul, Brazil's financial services industry provides local businesses with a wide range of products and is attracting numerous new entrants, including U.S. financial firms. On 8 May 2008, the São Paulo Stock Exchange (Bovespa) and the São Paulo-based Brazilian Mercantile and Futures Exchange (BM&F) merged, creating BM&F Bovespa, one of the largest stock exchanges in the world. Also, the previously monopolistic reinsurance sector is being opened up to third party companies.

As of[967] 31 December 2007, there were an estimated 21,304,000 broadband lines in Brazil. Over 75 percent of the broadband lines were via DSL and 10 percent via cable modems.

Proven mineral resources are extensive. Large iron and manganese reserves are important sources of industrial raw materials and export earnings. Deposits of nickel, tin, chromite, uranium, bauxite, beryllium, copper, lead, tungsten, zinc, gold, and other minerals are exploited. High-quality coking-grade coal required in the steel industry is in short supply.

Largest companies

In 2017, 20 Brazilian companies were listed in the Forbes Global 2000 list – an annual ranking of the top 2000 public companies in the world by Forbes magazine. The 20 companies listed were:

World Rank	Company	Industry	Revenue (billion $)	Profits (billion $)	Assets (billion $)	Market Value (billion $)	Head-quarters
38	Itaú Unibanco	Banking	61.3	6.7	419.9	79.2	São Paulo
62	Banco Bradesco	Banking	70.2	4.3	362.4	53.5	Osasco, SP
132	Banco do Brasil	Banking	57.3	2.3	430.6	29	Brasilia
156	Vale	Mining	27.1	3.8	99.1	45.4	Rio de Janeiro
399	Petrobras	Oil & Gas	81.1	- 4.3	247.3	61.3	Rio de Janeiro
610	Eletrobras	Utilities	17.4	0.983	52.4	7.2	Rio de Janeiro
791	Itaúsa	Conglomerate	1.3	2.4	18.1	23	São Paulo
895	JBS	Food Processing	48.9	0.108	31.6	8.2	São Paulo
981	Ultrapar	Conglomerate	22.2	0.448	7.4	12.5	São Paulo
1103	Cielo	Financial services	3.5	1.1	9.4	20.9	Barueri, SP
1233	Braskem	Chemicals	13.8	- 0.136	15.9	7.9	São Paulo
1325	BRF	Food processing	9.7	- 0.107	13.8	9.3	Itajaí, SC
1436	Sabesp	Waste Management	4	0.846	11.6	7.4	São Paulo
1503	Oi	Telecommunications	7.5	- 2	25.2	0.952	Rio de Janeiro
1515	Gerdau	Iron & Steel	10.8	- 0.395	16.8	1.4	Porto Alegre, RS
1545	CBD	Retail	12	0.139	13.9	5.9	São Paulo
1572	CCR	Transportation	2.9	0.429	7.5	11.5	São Paulo

1597	Bovespa	Stock Exchange	0.666	0.415	9.7	12.8	São Paulo
1735	CPFL Energia	Electricity	5.4	0.258	13	8.4	Campinas, SP
1895	Kroton Educacional	Higher Education	1.5	0.535	5.4	7.1	Belo Horizonte, MG

Energy

The Brazilian government has undertaken an ambitious program to reduce dependence on imported petroleum. Imports previously accounted for more than 70% of the country's oil needs but Brazil became self-sufficient in oil in 2006–2007. Brazil is one of the world's leading producers of hydroelectric power, with a current capacity of about 260,000 megawatts. Existing hydroelectric power provides 90% of the nation's electricity. Two large hydroelectric projects, the 19,900 megawatt Itaipu Dam on the Paraná River (the world's largest dam) and the Tucurui Dam in Pará in northern Brazil, are in operation. Brazil's first commercial nuclear reactor, Angra I, located near Rio de Janeiro, has been in operation for more than 10 years. Angra II was completed in 2002 and is in operation too. An Angra III had a planned inauguration scheduled for 2014. The three reactors would have a combined capacity of 9,000 megawatts when completed. The government also plans to build 19 more nuclear plants by the year 2020.Wikipedia:Citation needed

Economic status

Statistical Table	
Inflation (IPCA)	
2002	12.53%
2003	9.30%
2004	7.60%
2005	5.69%
2006	3.14%
2007	4.46%
2008	5.91%
2009	4.31%
2010	5.90%
2011	6.50%
2012	5.84%

2013	5.91%
2014	6.41%
2015	10.67%
2016	6.29%
2017	2.95%

Source:[968]

Average GDP growth rate 1950–2013	
1950–59	7.1%
1960–69	6.1%
1970–79	8.9%
1980–89	3.0%
1990–99	1.7%
2000–09	3.3%
2010–17	1.4%

Source:[969]

Sustainable growth

Portuguese explorers arrived in 1500, but it was only in 1808 that Brazil obtained a permit from the Portuguese colonial government to set up its first factories and manufacturers. In the 21st century, Brazil became the eighth largest economy in the world. Originally, its exports were basic raw and primary goods, such as sugar, rubber and gold. Today, 84% of exports are of manufactured and semi-manufactured products.

The period of great economic transformation and growth occurred between 1875 and 1975.

In the last decade, domestic production increased by 32.3%. Agribusiness (agriculture and cattle-raising), which grew by 47% or 3.6% per year, was the most dynamic sector – even after having weathered international crises that demanded constant adjustments to the Brazilian economy.[970] The Brazilian government also launched a program for economic development acceleration called Programa de Aceleração do Crescimento, aiming to spur growth.

Brazil's transparency rank in the international world is 75th according to Transparency International.[971]

Figure 234: *Renewable energy in Parnaíba.*

Control and reform

Among measures recently adopted to balance the economy, Brazil carried out reforms to its social security (state and retirement pensions) and tax systems. These changes brought with them a noteworthy addition: a Law of Fiscal Responsibility which controls public expenditure by the executive branches at federal, state and municipal levels. At the same time, investments were made towards administration efficiency and policies were created to encourage exports, industry and trade, thus creating "windows of opportunity" for local and international investors and producers.

With these alterations in place, Brazil has reduced its vulnerability: it doesn't import the oil it consumes; it has halved its domestic debt through exchange rate-linked certificates and has seen exports grow, on average, by 20% a year. The exchange rate does not put pressure on the industrial sector or inflation (at 4% a year), and does away with the possibility of a liquidity crisis. As a result, the country, after 12 years, has achieved a positive balance in the accounts which measure exports/imports, plus interest payments, services and overseas payment. Thus, respected economists say that the country won't be deeply affected by the current world economic crisis.[972]

In 2017, President Michel Temer refused to make public the list of companies accused of "modern slavery". The list, made public yearly since the presidency

Figure 235: *Central business district of Rio de Janeiro.*

of Lula Da Silva in 2003, was intended to persuade companies to settle their fines and conform to labor regulations, in a country where corruption of the political class risked compromising respect for the law. The relations of the president-in-office with the "landowner lobby" were denounced by dismissed president Dilma Rousseff on this occasion.[973]

Consistent policies

Support for the productive sector has been simplified at all levels; active and independent, Congress and the Judiciary Branch carry out the evaluation of rules and regulations. Among the main measures taken to stimulate the economy are the reduction of up to 30 percent on manufactured products tax (IPI), and the investment of $8 billion on road cargo transportation fleets, thus improving distribution logistics. Further resources guarantee the propagation of business and information telecenters.

The policy for industry, technology and foreign trade, at the forefront of this sector, for its part, invests $19.5 billion in specific sectors, following the example of the software and semiconductor, pharmaceutical and medicine product, and capital goods sectors.[974]

Mergers and acquisitions

Between 1985 and 2017, 11,563 mergers & acquisitions with a total known value of US$1,185 billion with the involvement of Brazilian firms were announced. The year 2010 was a new record in terms of value with $115 billion of transactions. It is worth noticing, that in the top 100 deals by value there are only four cases of Brazilian companies acquiring a foreign company. This reflects the strong interest in the country from a direct investment perspective.

Here is a list of the largest deals where Brazilian companies took on either the role of the acquiror or the target:

Date Announced	Acquiror Name	Acquiror Mid Industry	Acquiror Nation	Target Name	Target Mid Industry	Target Nation	Value of Transaction ($mil)
09/01/-2010	Petrobras	Oil & Gas	Brazil	Brazil-Oil & Gas Blocks	Oil & Gas	Brazil	42,877.03
02/20/-2017	Vale SA	Metals & Mining	Brazil	Valepar SA	Metals & Mining	Brazil	20,956.66
08/11/-2006	Cia Vale do Rio Doce SA	Metals & Mining	Brazil	Inco Ltd	Metals & Mining	Canada	17,150.30
02/20/-2008	BM&F	Brokerage	Brazil	Bovespa Holding SA	Brokerage	Brazil	10,309.09
01/13/-2000	Telefónica SA	Telecommunications Services	Spain	Telecommunicacoes de Sao Paulo	Telecommunications Services	Brazil	10,213.31
07/31/-2014	Telefonica Brasil SA	Telecommunications Services	Brazil	GVT Participacoes SA	Telecommunications Services	Brazil	9,823.31
05/10/-2010	Telefonica SA	Telecommunications Services	Spain	Brasilcel NV	Telecommunications Services	Brazil	9,742.79
11/03/-2008	Banco Itaú Holding Financeira	Banks	Brazil	Unibanco Holdings SA	Other Financials	Brazil	8,464.77
03/03/-2004	Ambev	Food and Beverage	Brazil	John Labatt Ltd	Food and Beverage	Canada	7,758.01
10/01/-2010	China Petrochemical Corporation	Oil & Gas	China	Repsol YPF Brasil SA	Oil & Gas	Brazil	7,111.00
02/07/-2012	Banestado Participacoes	Other Financials	Brazil	Redecard SA	Computers & Peripherals	Brazil	6,821.71

Entrepreneurship

According to a search of Global Entrepreneurship Monitor in 2011 Brazil had 27 million adults aged between 18 and 64 either starting or owning a business, meaning that more than one in four Brazilian adults were entrepreneurs. In comparison to the other 54 countries studied, Brazil was the third-highest in total number of entrepreneurs. The Institute of Applied Economic Research (Ipea), a government agency, found that 37 million jobs in Brazil were associated with businesses with less than 10 employees.[975]

Even though Brazil ranks internationally as one of the hardest countries in the region to do business due to its complicated bureaucracy, there is a healthy number of entrepreneurs, thanks to the huge internal consumer market and various government programs.

The most recent research of Global Entrepreneurship Monitor revealed in 2013 that 50.4% of Brazilian new entrepreneurs are men, 33.8% are in the 35–44 age group, 36.9% completed high school and 47.9% earn 3–6 times the Brazilian minimum wage. In contrast, 49.6% of entrepreneurs are female, only 7% are in the 55–64 age group, 1% have postgraduate education and 1.7% earn more than 9 times the minimum wage.[976]

Credit rating

Brazil's credit rating was downgraded by Standard & Poor's to BBB in March 2014, just one notch above junk.[977]

Income

Brazil is a country with extreme income inequality. Members of the national congress make R$33,700 per month, plus an additional 13th salary, totaling R$444,800 per year (USD 140,000), but most of the population only makes minimum wage set for the year of 2017 at R$937 per month plus an additional 13th salary in the second half of December, totaling R$12,181 per year (around USD 4,000), which is 35 times less than national politicians. The GDP per capita in 2011 was US$12,906.[979]

Figure 236: *The median income of the ministers of Supreme Federal Court is more than R$300,000.*[978]

Figure 237: *The city of Presidente Kennedy, Espírito Santo, has the largest median income of Brazil, R$815,093.*

Economy of Brazil 491

	Career[980]	Median salary (R$)	Starting salary (R$)	Top salary (R$)
Judge	Law	170,000	150,500	310,500
Prosecutor	Law	150,000	140,000	270,000
General director	Administration	90,000	60,000	1,450,000
Physician	Medicine	85,000	40,000	1,550,000
Judicial analyst	Law	80,000	70,000	90,000
Police chief	Law	60,000	50,000	85,000
Electronic engineer	Engineering	51,000	33,600	360,000
Civil engineer	Engineering	50,400	22,800	360,000
Other engineers	Engineering	45,000	24,000	130,000
Economic researcher	Economy	44,000	24,000	180,000
Mechanical engineer	Engineering	42,600	26,200	105,000
Department supervisor	Administration	41,964	20,076	420,000
Taxation Officer	Government	41,520	26,400	240,000
Professors	Higher education	40,440	20,000	300,000
Agronomist	Agronomy	40,000	27,600	96,000
Chemical engineer	Engineering	40,000	31,200	420,000
Systems analyst	Computer science	38,400	30,000	180,000
Dentist	Dentistry	37,800	29,400	720,000
Architect	Architecture	37,320	13,800	600,000
Lawyer	Law	36,120	20,040	3,000,000
Accountant	Accountancy	35,880	17,400	216,000
Administrator	Administration	35,400	25,080	1,800,000
Journalist	Journalism	32,880	18,000	2,400,000

External links

- Ministry of Finance (Brazil)[981]
- IBGE : Brazilian Institute of Geography and Statistics[982]
- World Bank Summary Trade Statistics Brazil[983]
- Brazil profile[984] at the CIA World Factbook
- Brazil profile[985] at The World Bank

Agriculture in Brazil

Agriculture in Brazil	
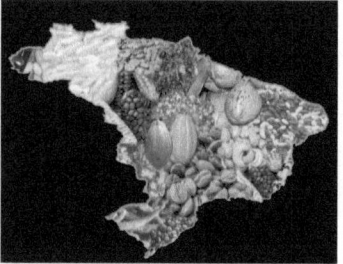 Brazil, "breadbasket of the world"[986]	

Area cultivated	65,338,804 ha.[987]
Cropland (% of land area)	31%
Rural population	5,965,000 families
Main products	sugarcane, coffee, soybeans, corn.
Production	
Grains (2008)	145.4 million tons
Major products	
Cane and derivatives (2007/08)	493.4 million tons
Soy (2008)	59.2 million tons
Corn (2008)	58.9 million tons
Participation in the economy – 2008	
Crop value	R$148.4 billion ($65.56 bil. USD)
Contribution to GDP	4.53%[988]
Agribusiness GDP (Rural industry and trade, livestock and agriculture)	26.46%

The **agriculture of Brazil** is historically one of the principal bases of Brazil's economy. While its initial focus was on sugarcane, Brazil eventually became the world's largest exporter of coffee, soybeans, beef, and crop-based ethanol.

Brazil exported 37 thousand tons of processed cashew nuts valued at 187.7 thousand USD in 2012.[989]

The success of agriculture during the Estado Novo (New State), with Getúlio Vargas, led to the expression, "Brazil, breadbasket of the world".

As of 2009 Brazil had about 106,000,000 hectares (260,000,000 acres) of undeveloped fertile land – a territory larger than the combined area of France and Spain.

According to a 2008 IBGE study, despite the world financial crisis, Brazil had record agricultural production, with growth of 9.1%, principally motivated by favorable weather. The production of grains in the year reached an unprecedented 145,400,000 tons. That record output employed an additional 4.8% in planted area, totalling 65,338,000 hectares and producing $148 billion Reals. The principal products were corn (13.1% growth) and soy (2.4% growth).

The southern one-half to two-thirds of Brazil has a semi-temperate climate, higher rainfall, more fertile soil, more advanced technology and input use, adequate infrastructure and more experienced farmers. This region produces most of Brazil's grains, oilseeds (and exports).

The drought-ridden northeast region and Amazon basin lack well-distributed rainfall, good soil, adequate infrastructure and development capital. Although mostly occupied by subsistence farmers, both regions are increasingly important as exporters of forest products, cocoa and tropical fruits. Central Brazil contains substantial areas of grassland. Brazilian grasslands are far less fertile than those of North America, and are generally suited only for grazing.

Agriculture in Brazil presents challenges, including the ongoing practice of slave labour,[990,991] agrarian reform, fire, production financing, and a rural exodus fueled by economic stress on family farming.

Half of Brazil is covered by forests. The world's largest rain forest is in the Amazon Basin. Migrations into the Amazon and large-scale forest burning have challenged the government's management capabilities. The Lula's government has reduced incentives for such activity and is implementing a broader environmental plan. It also adopted an Environmental Crimes Law that established serious penalties for infractions.

Since 1985, 1722 activists for agrarian reform were murdered.

History

<templatestyles src="Template:Quote/styles.css"/>

However, the air of the country is very healthful, fresh, and as temperate as that of Entre Douro e Minho, we have found the two climates alike at this season. There is great plenty, an infinitude of waters. The country is

Figure 238: *Brazilian fruits in a painting by Albert Eckhout.*

so well-favoured that if it were rightly cultivated it would yield everything, because of its waters.

—*Pero Vaz de Caminha, Carta de Pêro Vaz de Caminha, Full text on Wikisource – in Portuguese*

Early farming

Brazilians ("Indians") began farming some 12,000 years ago. They farmed cassava, peanuts, tobacco, sweet potatoes and maize, in addition to extracting the essence from other local plants such as the pequi and the babassu. Production was for food, straw or madeira. They cultivated local fruits such as jabuticaba, cashews, Spondias mombin and Goiabas.

The Indians both influenced and were influenced by the Europeans who arrived in the fifteenth century. The Portuguese "nourished themselves with wood-flour, slaughtered the big game to eat, packed their nets and imitated the rough, free life" in the words of Pedro Calmon.[992]

Until other crops began to be exported, brazilwood was the main reason Portugal wanted control in Brazil.

Figure 239: *Fires are one of the problems still present in Brazilian agriculture.*

Fires

One practice of indigenous Brazilians was to clear land for cultivation by burning it. This provided arable land and ashes for use as fertilizer and soil cover.

Scholars such as Monteiro Lobato considered this practice to be harmful. However, burning only became a problem when the Europeans adopted the practice aggressively around 1500, divided land into farms, began monocropping, etc. The combination of burning with these new farming methods decimated native flora.

Indian land management included garden areas in locations selected to allow interaction with their surroundings. Indians conserved the environment in exchange for hunting the animals and protecting themselves against pests. This approach was lost, as Darcy Ribeiro stated, *"Thus they passed millennia, until they came up against the armed agents of our civilization, with their capacity to attack and mortally wound the miraculous balance achieved by those complex lifeforms."*

Colonial Brazil: sugarcane

The discovery of sugarcane in the Northeast region transformed Brazil. plantation monoculture enriched the Europeans, but brought little benefit to Brazilians.[993]

Figure 240: *Sugar attracted the colonizer who brought slaves from Africa, and it led to invasion of the territory. The picture depicts a Dutch sugar mill in the work Historia Naturalis Brasiliae, 1648.*

Sugarcane wealth was concentrated under the colonizers, generating a quasi-feudal social system organized around large landholdings. Brazilian sugar was thirty percent less expensive than sugar from elsewhere, creating major export opportunities.

A decline in the second half of the 17th century led many producer regions to diversify production, expanding cotton or, in Reconcavo Baiano, tobacco or cocoa. The archaic social structure and obsolete technology outlasted cane production in those regions.

Slave labor

Initially plantation owners attempted to use local labor in their fields. While laws prohibited their enslavement, in many areas the law was not respected. Locals responded by rebelling, flight or simply dying. European diseases took a heavy toll on indigenous peoples.

The settlers then switched to enslaving and importing Africans to do the work.[994] The Portuguese and others imported 4 million Africans to carry out cultivation, using what came to be called the plantation system.

In the first century after European arrival the slave population had already surpassed that of the locals, decimated by disease. Antonil stated: "the slaves are the hands and feet of the mill, because without them in Brazil, it is not possible to make, maintain or expand the farm or have a running mill."

Agriculture in Brazil

Figure 241: *In the illustration of "O Fazendeiro do Brasil" (The Farmer in Brazil), 1806, José Mariano da Conceição Veloso describes the steps and tools used in the cultivation of indigo in Brazil.*

The slaves cleared the agricultural frontiers, such as in the west for coffee plantations. By the end of the Second Reign, Brazil accounted for more than half the world's coffee production.

On May 13, 1888 Brazil adopted the Lei Áurea ('Golden Law'), which abolished slavery in Brazil. In the preceding years, 75% of the Africans and mulattoes had been freed by manumission.[995] According to João Ribeiro, "more than anything humane and Christian, Lei Áurea ('Golden Law') menaced the work and gravely injured the interests of the farmers; there still had been in Brazil more than seven hundred thousand slaves (...) Many of the farmers turned to the Republican party or became indifferent to the attack of the institutions..."

The law did not provide an accompanying land distribution to the ex-captives. It led to a rural exodus, both from the workers and from the now-bankrupt landlords. Slavery and its end formed the root of future problems such as slums, violence and poverty in urban centres.

Figure 242: *Brazilian coffee plantation in the early twentieth century.*

Brazilian Empire: coffee

In the late colonial era coffee was introduced to the country. After independence production consolidated in the Southeast region, mainly in the state of São Paulo. At the beginning of the 19th century, exports totaled 19.6 tons, growing to 3,063,660 tons in the 1880–1890 period, growing to about sixty three percent of Brazil's total exports.

Coffee was responsible for the appearance of a new dominant oligarchy in Brazil, the so-called Coffee Barons. It hastened immigration following the end of slavery. The era reached its peak with Café com leite politics, ending with the Campos Sales administration. The Great Depression closed this cycle at the end of the 1930s with industrialization, capitalized by profits from coffee production.[996]

Coffee drew many Italian immigrants to the west of São Paulo. Coffee wealth accentuated the differences between the Brazilian regions, especially vs the Northeast.

Besides coffee, other crops increased in the 19th century, such as tobacco and cocoa, in Bahia, and rubber in Amazônia. In 1910 rubber represented about forty percent of exports.

Figure 243: *Bagging for export, at the height of the coffee cycle.*

International problems

Brazilian coffee production exceeded global demand at the beginning of the 20th century. This resulted in the Taubaté Agreement, where the State began acquiring surplus for destruction and planting seedlings was forbidden—with the goal of maintaining a minimum profitable price.

Rubber suffered from foreign competition. In 1870, English smugglers smuggled rubber tree seedlings out of Brazil and in 1895 began production in Asia. In the 1910s and 1920s this competition practically eliminated Brazilian production.

Agronomy schools

In 1887 during the Empire era, the first school dedicated to the training of agronomists opened in the city of Cruz das Almas. In 1883, in Pelotas, Rio Grande do Sul, a second school opened.

The first school was officially recognized thirty-five years after its creation, with Decree 8.319/1910. The agronomist profession only came to be recognized in 1933. Seventy regular agronomy colleges operate in Brazil. The day the decree was publicized, 12 October, became the "Day of the Agronomist."

Professional registration is managed by Regional Engineering and Architecture Councils, integrated at the national level by CONFEA. Educational activity is supported by the Federation of Brazilian Agronomy Students.

Figure 244: *Entrance to the Agricultural School in Camboriú, of UFSC.*

Diversification: 1960–1990

The Brazilian Enterprise for Agricultural Research (EMBRAPA) was established during the military regime in 1973 with the objective of diversifying production. The body was responsible for the support of new crops, adapted to the country's diverse regions. The expansion of agricultural borders towards the Cerrado had begun, and of monocultural latifundia with production at a semi-industrial scale of soybeans, cotton and beans. Czech-Brazilian researcher Johanna Döbereiner helped lead Brazil's Green Revolution, winning her the UNESCO Science Prize for her work on nitrogen-fixing microorganisms.

In 1960 four main agricultural products were exported, growing by the early 1990s to nineteen. Brazil also moved "downstream" to expand post-harvest processing. In the 60's unprocessed goods made up 84% of total exports, falling to 20% by 1990.

Agricultural promotion policies included subsidized credits, bank debt write-offs and exports subsidies (in some cases, reaching 50% of the product value).

Figure 245: *The former minister, Luis Fernando Cirne Lima, founder of Embrapa, speaking at the corporation's 35th anniversary conference.*

Mechanization: 1990s

Beginning with the 1994 creation of Plano Real for monetary stabilization, Brazilian agriculture went through a radical transformation: the State cut subsidies and the market began to finance agriculture, leading to the replacement of manpower with machines. Brazil's rural population fell from 20,700,000 in 1985 to 17,900,000 in 1995, followed by a decrease in import taxes on inputs and other measures that forced Brazilian producers to adapt to global practices. The raise of productivity, mechanization (with reduction of costs) and professionalization marked that period.

Land issues

Brazil initially used a land management system known as sesmarias featured by large holdings with a small number of landowners. In 1822 sesmarias gave way to the current latifundia (system of large estates). In 1850 the *Law of Lands* was promulgated, which kept the latifundia system and remained in effect until 1964, when the dictatorship prepared the Land Statute. The high cost of agricultural production contributed to latifundia formation and the country never experienced substantial land reform. That only became part of the country's official and legal policies after the 1988 Constitution.

Figure 246: *Harvester on a Brazilian cotton plantation.*

Of the around thirty-one million Brazilians who lived in poverty in 2014, more than half lived in rural areas. In the last twenty-five years of the 20th century, about thirty million rural dwellers abandoned or lost their land, creating some 4.8 million landless families. During that time, the majority of funding resources was directed to the oligarchs and great landowners, supporting the model of intensive monoculture agriculture.

Between 1985 and 1988 the country's redemocratization triggered almost 9,000 social conflicts in rural areas and the murders of 1,167 people over agricultural issues. In this period a confrontation pitted unions, social movements and the Catholic Church against the landowners united in the Democratic Association of Ruralists (UDR) which had Ronaldo Caiado as its main representative. The most famous victim of those conflicts was the unionist Chico Mendes, in Acre, in 1988.

According to Mançano rural censuses collected since 1940 indicated ongoing concentration of land ownership, accompanied by an exodus of farmers to urban areas. Reversing the trend would have required the annual settlement of 150,000 families. During Itamar Franco's Government, the INCRA (National Institute of Colonization and Agrarian Reform) achieved about 10,000 settlements annually. A fast-track procedure for expropriation of large landholdings was established, ending long delays, one of the measure's main obstacles.

Figure 247: *Members of the Landless Workers' Movement (MST), the main representative group of the landless workers, during the closing of the MST's 5th Congress in Brasília, in 2007.*

The conflicts reached their peak in 1996 with the Eldorado dos Carajás massacre, in Pará, when the governor, Almir Gabriel, ordained the clearing of a road occupied by the landless. Casualties amounted to nineteen dead and fifty-one injured, underlining the land problem and accompanying disrespect for human rights.

In a 1996 article economist Maria da Conceição Tavares, one of the most prominent critics of Fernando Henrique Cardoso's Government, claimed, "the importance of a rural reform has increased and the dispute for land, if the relations of "dominance" of rural properties are not regulated quickly, will lead to growing confrontations".

The land reform movement included about five hundred land occupations of what protesters considered to be unproductive farms. As a reaction to the invasions, President Cardoso published Provisional Measure 2.027-38, which prohibited earmarking all occupied land for agrarian reform.

Figure 248: *Rice paddy: Where irrigation first occurred in Brazil.*

Irrigation

The first irrigation experiments in Brazil occurred in Rio Grande do Sul, for cultivating rice. The first record dates to 1881 with the construction of the Cadro dam which began in 1903.Wikipedia:Please clarify However, the practice broadened in the last thirty years of the 20th century.

Private initiative developed Irrigation in the South and Southeast regions.

In the Northeast official bodies, such as DNOCS and CODEVASF, led the way beginning in the 1950s. In 1968, the Executive Group on Irrigation and Agrarian Development (GEIDA) was set up, and two years later it instituted the Multi-annual Program of Irrigation (PPI). The majority of resources were directed to the Northeast. These federal initiatives, however, did not achieve success. In 1985 a new guidance and in 1996 a new direction produced the New Model of Irrigation Project. The Project intended to broaden the use of irrigation in agriculture and drew on more than 1,500 national and foreign experts.

According to the World Bank, Brazil's irrigation potential is about 29,000,000 hectares (110,000 sq mi). In 1998, however, drought reduced capacity to only 2.98 million ha.

At the end of the 20th century, the country primarily used surface irrigation (59%), followed by overhead (35%) and then targeted irrigation. The South represented the largest irrigated area (more than 1.1 million ha), followed by the Southeast (800 thousand ha) and Northeast (490 thousand ha).

Figure 249: *Trucks transporting soybean crop*

Currently, a regulatory milestone of irrigation is making its way through the National Congress of Brazil, through bill 6381/2005, which aims at replacing the Law 6662/1979, which regulates irrigation policy.

Water resources policy is regulated by Law 9433/1997, and managed by the National Council.

Infrastructure

Storage

Crop storage facilities require expansion in order to keep up with increasing production. Brazilian storage capacity in 2003 was 75% of grain production, well short of the ideal of 120%.

Farm-based crop storage (e.g., using silos) is not common in Brazil. Lack of storage forces produce to be commercialized quickly. According to Conab data, only 11% of warehouses are located on farms (by comparison Argentina has 40%, the European Union has 50% and Canada has 80%). Farmers rely on third party storage services.

Lack of access to capital, exacerbated by financial instability from factors such as exchange rate volatility, prevents most producers from building significant storage.

Figure 250: *Transport of crops by highway*

Transport

Crop transport is a longstanding structural problem for Brazilian agriculture. Calmon noted that, since the Empire, "the disposal of the harvest is difficult" and indicated that "the old projects of iron roads or cartable paths, linking the coast to the central mountains (...) are resisted by skeptical statesmen, quoting Thiers, who, in 1841, believed that railways were not convenient to France".[997]

Crops are immediately trucked to market via highways, mostly in poor traffic conditions at high cost.

For the 2008/2009 harvest, for example, the Federation of Agriculture and Livestock of Goiás denounced poor road conditions in the Center-West region, despite repeated requests for federal assistance over several years.

In 2006 the federal government issued a National Plan of Logistics and Transportation, meant to better production flow. Lack of investment, however, continues to be the main obstacle to distribution logistics.

Regulatory stocks and minimum price

A good example of the need of regulatory stocks is in the production of ethanol as a fuel from sugar cane. The elevated price variation during the harvest year, that varies for climatic and plant health reasons, justifies the formation of stocks. Stocks also aim to stabilize farmers' revenues, and avoid price fluctuations between harvests.Wikipedia:Please clarify

Figure 251: *Vegetable plot on a family farm.*

Until the 1980s, Brazil employed the Minimum Prices Policy. That policy had lost relevance by the 1990s, due to globalization.

The composition of stocks at the national level is the responsibility of the National Food Supply Company (Conab).

Family farming

Official definitions of a family farmer differ from country to country in Latin America. There are 3 general categories: subsistence farming, intermediate family farmers and consolidated farms. In Brazil, the Family Farming Law (Law 11,326) defines family farmers through four criteria related to land tenure, farm size, dependence on farm income, and the use of predominantly family labor. In Brazil, the large majority of family farms are in the northeastern, southern and southeast Brazil. Family farmers in Brazil produce more than 70% of food consumed domestically.

During the 1990s, the Lula administration implemented a set of policies that addressed food security on federal, state and municipal levels, the aim of which was to increase federal government support to family farmers. In 1999, the Ministry of Agrarian Development (MDA) was created to support family farmers and promote land reform and sustainable land development. A host of government policies and government-supported programs in the interest of family farmers then emerged, where the family farmer is recognized as a pillar of national development. Since then, the MDA along with other institutions were created with the family farmers and other traditional communities' interests in mind, where policies targeting family farmers were designed to introduce market incentives, promote adequate food distribution and provide technical assistance.

In general, family farms are establishments that employ mostly family members with up to five temporary workers. Family farms provide the majority of Brazilian staples, including 84% of manioc, 67% of beans and 49% of corn. Family farms also have a large role in the livestock and dairy industry, producing 58% of milk, 59% of pork, 50% of poultry and 31% of cattle.

% of total crop production by family farmers (2010 statistics, Ministry of Agrarian Development, Brazil)

Crop	Percentage (%) produced by family farmers
Manioc	84%
Beans	67%
Corn	49%
Rice	34%
Milk	58%
Cattle	31%
Pork	59%
Poultry	50%
Wheat	21%
Soybeans	16%

According to the IBGE's 1995/96 Farming and Livestock Census, there were 4,339,859 family-run establishments in the country, the largest farm being 100 ha in area. In 2009, Brazil's Ministry of Agrarian Development (MDA) reported that 84.4% of all rural properties are in fact family farms. In the 1990s family farms experienced productivity growth of 75%, compared to only 40% for larger-scale producers. The difference is largely due to the creation of PRONAF (National Program on Family Agriculture), which opened a special family farm credit line.

Up to 2009 six Family Farming and Land Reform National Fairs were held, the first four in Brasília and the last two in Rio de Janeiro. They highlight the importance of family farming to Brazilian economy, accounting for 70% of the country's food consumption and 10% of Brazilian GDP.

Food Security in Brazil

International monitoring organizations assert that a third of Brazil's population is food insecure. Despite increased food production since the industrialization, a large proportion of Brazilians, especially the urban and rural poor, have difficulty meeting their nutrition needs. Small farmer, landless worker and indigenous movements that had consolidated during or after the military dictatorship mobilized nationwide, pressuring the authorities to prioritize food and nutrition security rose in the 1980s, and were able to strongly shape the direction of developmental policy.

The notion of access to food and proper nutrition was first recorded official terminology in 1986 as *segurança alimentar* (food security). The right to food and nutrition was established on 25 August 2010, when Brazil adopted the Policy on Food Security and Nutrition (Decree 7.272). Food security refers to being able to meet dietary needs through an adequate, secure supply of nutritious food. The term rose into Brazilian popular consciousness in 1993 after campaigns by a national movement called Citizens' Action Against Hunger and Poverty and for Life. In that same period, Consea (National Food and Nutritional Security Council) was established. the 1st National Conference on Food Security was organized by a combination of policy and grassroots mobilizations. Consea ran from 1993 to 1994, with little success in shaping public policies, was halted until after the establishment of the Fome Zero Program. The 2010 Policy names Consea as an instrument in proposing programs that promote food security on a federal level.

PRONAF (National Program for the Strengthening of Family Farming)

Due to financial limitations, small farmers generally have difficulties securing the capital necessary to stay in rural areas and maintain production on a small scale. PRONAF was the first policy in 1994 to be created to meet the specific credit needs of family farmers. In order to stimulate agricultural production, the instrument provides incentives in the form of reduced-interest loans from national funds for rural development, targeting low-income farmers and agrarian reform farmers. Set against a backdrop of policies opening Brazil to Neoliberal economic forces and intense competition through Mercosul, PRONAF marked the institutionalization of a differentiated policy approach to family farming in Brazil. The economic and social importance of family farmers and their specific needs were recognized through PRONAF, at least on paper. The creation of PRONAF has been credited to favorable political circumstances, beginning with Brazil's re-democratization in the 1980s and a receptive Cardoso administration to the mobilizations of a number of agrarian civil groups. Loans written out to family farmers through PRONAF rose from US$1 billion in 2000 to an estimated US$5.8 billion in 2008. Other credit programs targeted at family farmers that came after PRONAF include PROGER and PROCERA.

The Fome Zero Program (The Zero Hunger Program)

The Fome Zero Program is a federal program aimed increasing food and nutrition security in rural and urban poor communities. Its main strategy was to connect local food producers with local markets, especially in rural areas, through *inter-setorrialidade* (inter-agency cooperation). It was instituted in 2001 against the backdrop of increasing recognition for family farmers in Brazilian agrarian policies, and a consequence of 20 years of mobilizing by actors at different levels of society for policy change. The Program is built on four axes: food access, strengthening family farming, income generation and articulation, mobilization and social control. Family farmers play a large role in the Program's food security goals: the Family Farming Food Acquisition Program (PAA), the National School Meal Program (Pnae) and the *Bolsa Família* Program (Family Grant Cash Transfer) were implementations that aimed to encourage family farm production of staple foods through cash and program incentives, facilitate distribution of food to families and schools, and also provide conditional health care and social assistance to 42 million vulnerable Brazilians. Despite praise for the Zero Hunger Program, federal evaluation of the impact of measures such as the National School Meal Program on family farmer production and nutrition of schoolchildren have been limited, given the challenges of assessing decentralized implementation of the policy even at municipal levels. Furthermore, the Brazilian government has been cautious and controlled public and international access to the assessment reports of a number of programs, including the report for the *Bolsa* Família' **program.**

Gathering

The country's colonization began with harvesting native plants where they grew. Cultivation followed much later. The exploitation of brazilwood, known to the natives as ibirapitanga, and which ended up naming the land was begun by the Portuguese.[998]

Brazil operates forty-nine gathering reservations and sixty-five forests protected by federal law. The gathering of plant resources is encouraged as a means of interacting with, but not degrading, the environment.

Lack of government funding has destabilized this use of forest resources. The case of natural rubber is typical: in Acre about 4,000 families have apparently

Figure 252: *People gathering babassu, in Maranhão.*

abandoned the activity, as revealed in early 2009. After undergoing acclimatization, rubber trees were grown successfully in São Paulo state, where more than 36,000 hectares were planted – while Acre accounts for little more than a thousand hectares.

Homma claims that gathering rubber is economically impracticable. For example, in native forests, rubber trees are found at a density of some 1.5 trees per ha, versus hundreds of trees per ha on rubber plantations. Cultivating degraded areas with native trees has been successful with trees such as cupuaçu and jaborandi.

According to IBGE, in 2003 the gathering sector's output was divided into timber (65%) and non-wood (35%), at a value of four hundred forty-nine million Reals, with the following main products: piassaba (27%), babassu (nut – 17%), açai (16%), yerba mate (14%), carnauba (8%) and Brazil nut (5%).

Soils

The program of mapping and classifying the country's soils began in 1953, with the *Chart of Soils in Brazil*. IBGE published the first map in 2003. Soil knowledge helped allow the expansion of agricultural production from 1975. The expansion of the Center-West required new technology because the region is mainly formed by oxisols, which favor mechanization from soil preparation to harvest, partly because they are nutrient-poor.

Figure 253: *Regolithic soil, in granulite.*

Soil classification, study and systematization are championed by Embrapa Soils, with participation from groups such as the RADAM Project, the Rural University (now UFRRJ) and other agronomists.

Agribusiness

In 2010 Brazil was the third largest exporter of agricultural products in the world, behind only the United States and the European Union.[999,1000]

During the last two decades of the 20th century, Brazil witnessed a doubling of yield per acre. This resulted from input improvements (seeds, fertilizers, machinery), public policies that encouraged exports, reduced tax burden (such as the 1996 reduction of the circulation tax), more favorable real exchange rate, which had allowed price stability (in 1999), increased Asian demand, productivity growth and reduced trade barriers.

Farming accounted for almost a third of GDP, once everything from agricultural inputs to food processing and distribution are included.

From 1990 to 2001, farming employment fell, although overall agribusiness employment jumped from 372 thousand to 1.82 million. The number of companies grew from 18 thousand in 1994 to almost 47 thousand in 2001.

Factors that limit further expansion range from pests evolving to target monocultures, infrastructure issues and environmental problems generated by practices such as deforestation, etc.

Figure 254: *Machinery in soybean production.*

Trade balance

The 2007 harvest enabled gross agriculture exports yielding 68.1 billion dollars, and net exports of 57.3 billion dollars.

In 2008 Brazil's biggest export market was the European Union, while China was the largest single importing country with a 13.2% share, followed by the Netherlands with 9.5% and the US at 8.7%.

Regions

Brazil's regions offer a wide diversity of climate. Agriculture reflects this diversity. In 1995, the North produced 4.2%, the Northeast – 13.6%, the Center-West – 10.4%, the Southeast – 41.8% and the South – 30.0%. The Center-West and North regions have recently expanded their share to the total.

South

The southern Brazilian states are Rio Grande do Sul, Santa Catarina and Paraná. Cooperatives are a common feature of agriculture there. Irrigated rice and poultry are the two largest crops. Corn and beans are also prominent. The region is Brazil's largest tobacco producer and the world's largest exporter.

Santa Catarina has a high level of interdependence between the industrial and agricultural sectors.

Figure 255: *Vineyard gaucho*

Figure 256: *Cane plantation in Avare, São Paulo.*

In Rio Grande do Sul, family-run agribusiness is important and is descended from the colonial plantation model. Early farms survived and their families stayed on the land.

In 2004 the region produced 14.4% of Brazil's fruit.

Southeast

The Southeast region includes Minas Gerais, São Paulo, Rio de Janeiro and Espírito Santo. In 1995 it was responsible for the largest share of Brazilian

Figure 257: *Palm plantation in Urandi*

agriculture, but other regions were growing more rapidly.

In 2004 the Southeast produced 49.8% of the nation's fruit. The region hosts 60% of agribusiness software companies, according to a survey carried out by Embrapa Livestock and Farming Information Technology (located in Campinas/SP). Its agribusiness sector was second in the national ranking, in the period from 2000 to May 2008, representing 36% of 308 billion dollars of total exports. The biggest exports were sugar (17.27%), coffee (16.25%), paper and cellulose (14.89%), meats (11.71%) and horticultural and fruit (especially orange juice) with 10.27%.

Northeast

The Northeast includes Bahia, Sergipa, Pernambuco, Alogoas, Paraiba, Rio Grande do Norte, Ceara, Piaui and Maranhao. Farms are primarily family-owned; 82.9% of field labor is on family farms.

The region is the largest national producer of bananas, (34% of the total) and cassava (34.7%). It is the second largest producer of rice, with a harvest estimated in 2008 of 1.114 million tons. Maranhão produces the majority (668 thousand tons). It ranks second in fruit production, with 27% share.

The region is subject to prolonged dry spells that are worse in El Niño years. This causes a periodic rural exodus. Government responses include dams and the transfer of the São Francisco River. The worst recent droughts were in 1993, 1998 and 1999. The latter was the worst in fifty years.

Figure 258: *Horticulture workshop, Manacapuru, Amazonas.*

North

The Northern region includes Acre, Amapá, Amazonas, Pará, Rondônia, Roraima and Tocantins. The Amazon rainforest occupies a significant part of the region. The region's great challenge is to combine farming with forest preservation.

Between the end of the 19th century and early 20th century, during the so-called Rubber Boom, the region produced rubber, Brazil's most important export, until Asian production underpriced Brazil and shut down the industry.

It is the second largest Brazilian banana producer (26% share) and of cassava (25.9% share), lagging behind only the Northeast. It produces 6.1% of the nation's fruit crop.

Midwest

The Midwest region includes Mato Grosso, Mato Grosso do Sul, Goiás and Distrito Federal. This region's agriculture developed much later than the rest of the country. The main biome is the Cerrado. By 2004, it was responsible for 46% of Brazilian soybeans, corn, rice and beans.

Over three decades its harvest grew from 4.2 million to 49.3 million tons in 2008.

Agriculture in Brazil

Figure 259: *Irrigated garlic*

Its cultivated area in 2008 was 15.1 million hectares. A big growth area was livestock. The opening of roads facilitated this growth.

As of 2004 this region produced only 2.7% of the nation's horticulture.

Products

The principal agricultural products of Brazil are cattle, coffee, cotton, corn, rice, soy, wheat, sugarcane, tobacco, beans, floriculture and fruit. forestry, vegetables and cassava.

Cattle

Cattle[1001,1002]

Year	1960	1980	1990	2000	2005
Million head	78.54	118.08	147.10	169.87	207.15

Figure 260: *Cotton planted in the cerrado region of Bahia.*

Brazil in 2005 produced around 8.7 million tonnes of beef,[1003] becoming world export leader in 2003 after surpassing Australia. Cattle herds are concentrated in Mato Grosso, Mato Grosso do Sul, Goiás and Minas Gerais. Together they account for over 46% of Brazilian cattle with more than 87 million head.

According to the Ministry of Agriculture, Brazilian beef production grew on average 6.1% a year from 1990 to 2003, and reached 7.6 million tonnes. In 2003, Brazil exported over 1.4 million tonnes of beef, earning around $1.5 billion. Leather exports that year passed the $1 billion mark.

Coffee

Coffee is produced in states like São Paulo and Minas

Cotton

Yield increases were sufficient to substantially increase output between the 1960s and the twenty-first century, despite reduced acreage. In the 1990s production moved from the South and Southeast regions to the Center-West and to the West of Bahia. Exports began in 2001.

Brazil's entry in the cotton market led them to charge the US with illegal subsidies and tariffs. The Brazilian plea went to the World Trade Organization in 2002. WTO approved sanctions in 2009.

Corn

Corn[1004]

Year	1960	1970	1980	1989	2000	2005
Million metric tons	8.67	14.21	20.37	26.57	32.32	35.13

Brazilian corn has two harvests per year. The main harvest is during the rainy season and a second, "dry cultivation" harvest follows during the dry season. In the South the main harvest is in late August; while in the Southeast and Center-West, it happens in October and November and in the Northeast, by year end. The second harvest is in Paraná, São Paulo and in the Center-West, in February and March.

In 2006 corn was planted on about thirteen million hectares, producing 41 million tons. Brazil was the third largest world producer, accounting for 6.1% of global production. Paraná was Brazil's biggest producer, totaling 25.72%.

Rice

Rice

Year	1960	1970	1980	1989	2000	2005
Million metric tons	4.79	7.55	9.77	11.04	11.13	13.19

In the 1980s Brazil evolved from exporting to importing rice in small quantities to meet domestic demand. In the following decade, it became one of the main importers, reaching two million tons, equivalent to 10% of domestic demand by 1997-8. Uruguay and Argentina are the main suppliers of the cereal to the country.

In 1998, farmers planted 3.845 million ha, decreasing by 2008, to 2.847 million. Production grew from 11.582 million tons to an estimated 12.177 million tons.[1005]

Productivity per hectare has grown 61% since 1990. Production is concentrated in Rio Grande do Sul, producing on average 48%.[1006]

Figure 261: *Cornfield, São Paulo.*

Figure 262: *Rice harvest, Rio do Sul, Santa Catarina.*

Soybean

Soybean Production

Year	1960	1970	1980	1989	2000	2005
Million metric tons	0.20	1.50	15.15	24.07	32.82	51.18

Soybean production began in 1882. From the beginning of the 20th century soy was used for animal fodder. In 1941, grain production surpassed forage use, becoming the main focus. Brazilian soybean production increased more than 3000% between 1970 and 2005. Yield increased 37.8% from 1990 to 2005.[1007] Soybean and soybean derivatives exports in 2005 alone earned over US$9 billion for Brazil.

The 2007/2008 harvest produced 60.1 million tons, surpassed only by the United States.

Brazil's largest producers are Mato Grosso, Paraná and Goiás, with fifteen, nine and six million tons, respectively, in 2004–2006. Mato Grosso and Paraná together grow on average over 49% of the crop.

Wheat

Wheat Production

Year	1960	1970	1980	1989	2000	2005
Million metric tons	0.71	1.84	2.70	5.55	1.72	4.65

Two of Brazil's coldest states, Paraná and Rio Grande do Sul, account for over 90% of wheat production.[1008] Brazil imports around US$700 million in wheat every year.[1009]

Sugarcane

During the colonial period, Brazil depended heavily on sugarcane and continued to lead world sugarcane production into the twenty-first century.

Production is concentrated (90%) in São Paulo, Alagoas, Pernambuco, Minas Gerais, Mato Grosso, Mato Grosso do Sul, Goiás and Paraná.

Brazil harvested 558 million tonnes of sugarcane in 2007, representing a growth of 17.62% over 2006. For 2008, Brazil harvested 648,921,280 tonnes, of which total 89% was used for sugar and ethanol production. The other 11% was used for *cachaça* and *rapadura* production, as animal feed and as seeds.[1010] Ethanol production in 2008 was predicted to reach 26.4 billion litres.

Companhia Nacional de Abastecimento (CONAB) said that in 2007, sugarcane cultivated land increased by 12.3%, to 69,000 square kilometres.

Figure 263: *Cane field in São Paulo.*

Sugarcane Production

Year	1960	1970	1980	1990	2000	2007
Million metric tons	56.92	79.75	148.65	262.67	326.12	558.50

Figure 264: *Irrigated beans in Avare, São Paulo.*

Tobacco

Brazil is the world's second largest tobacco producer, and the largest exporter since 1993, with about 1.7 billion dollars of turnover. The largest export region is Rio Grande do Sul. The Southern region accounts for 95% of external production. It exports 60 to 70% of output.

Beans

Brazil is the world's largest producer of beans, accounting for 16.3% of the total, 18.7 million tons in 2005, according to FAO. Historically most beans came from small producers. Yield in some cases exceeded three thousand kilos per ha.

Bean acreage decreased from 1984 to 2004 by 25%, while output increased by 16%. It is cultivated throughout the country and harvests come year round.

Brazil imports 100 thousand tons of beans per year.

Figure 265: *Example of Brazilian rose, in Brasilia.*

Floriculture and ornamentals

Some three thousand six hundred producers cultivate flowers and ornamental plants in an area of 4,800 ha.

It employs about one hundred twenty thousand people, of which 80% are women, and about 18% are family farms.

The producers from fifteen states are represented by the Brazilian Institute of Floriculture (IBRAFLOR), with government support.

Floriculture began in the 1870s, led by the son of Jean Baptiste Binot, who had come to the country to decorate the Imperial Palace, and whose orchidarium was internationally acknowledged. In 1893, Reggie Dierberger founded a flower company, which later became the Boettcher, pioneers of rose production.

In 1948 Dutch immigrants founded a cooperative in Holambra, a city that still hosts flower production.

Since 2000 the Program of Development of Flowers and Ornamental Plants of the Ministry of Agriculture began. The largest producer is São Paulo state, followed by Santa Catarina, Pernambuco, Alagoas, Ceará, Rio Grande do Sul, Minas Gerais, Rio de Janeiro, Paraná, Goiás, Bahia, Espírito Santo, Amazonas and Pará.

Figure 266: *Sugar-apple plantation with an irrigated system, at the banks of the São Francisco River, Bahia.*

Fruits and perennials

The main fruits grown in Brazil are, in alphabetical order: Abiu, açaí, acerola, alligator-apple, apple, atemoya, bacaba, bacuri, banana, biriba, blueberry, brazil plum, brazil nut, breadfruit, cajá, camu camu, cantaloupe, cashew, citrus (orange, lemon, lime, etc.), coconut, cupuaçu, fig, guava, grapes, jambo, jocote, kiwi, mangaba, mango, mangosteen, mulberry, muruci, nectarine, papaya, passionfruit, patawa, peach, pear, pequi, persimmon, physalis, pineapple, pine nuts, plum, rambutan, raspberry, sapodilla, sapote, sorva, soursop, starfruit, strawberry, tucuma, walnut, and watermelon.

In 2002 the fruit sector grossed 9.6 billion dollars – 18% of Brazil's total. National production is higher than 38 million tons, cultivated on 3.4 million hectares. Between 1990 and 2004 exports grew 183% in value, 277% in quantity and 915% net.

Every ten thousand dollars invested in fruit production generates three direct jobs and two indirect jobs.

Brazil is the world's third largest fruit producer, behind China (157 million tons) and India (with 54 million). Oranges and bananas account for 60% of Brazilian output.

Figure 267: *Banana plantation in irrigation project, Rio S. Francisco, Bahia.*

The Brazilian Agency for the Promotion of Exports and Investments (Apex-Brasil), the IBRAF and Carrefour supermarket partnered to develop the Brazilian Fruit Festival, with editions in countries such as Poland and Portugal, from 2004 to 2007.

Banana

Banana is produced across the country. It is the second-largest fruit crop. In 2003, 510 thousand hectares were planted, yielding 6.5 million tons, repeated in 2004. In descending order, the largest producers were São Paulo (with one million one hundred seventy-eight thousand tons), Bahia (764 thousand tons) and Pará (697 thousand tons).

Cocoa

Cocoa was once one of Brazil's main export crops, particularly for Bahia. Production gradually diminished. In 2002 Bahia accounted for 84% of Brazil's cocoa, according to IBGE, planting more than 548 thousand hectares planted with the crop.

Brazil changed from exporting to importing cocoa in 1992. According to FAO the country, between 1990 and 2003, fell from ninth to seventeenth in the main world producers' ranking.

Figure 268: *Cocoa plant in Ilheus, Bahia.*

Bahian cocoa shows how a pest and the lack of plant health care may affect a crop. In this case a disease called witch's broom was directly responsible for falling production, which started in the year 1989. A severe decline endured until 1999, when resistant varieties were introduced. Despite this, in 2007 Bahian production started to decline again, whilst the Paraense raised its share.

Citrus

Citrus includes oranges, limes, tangerines, lemons, etc. Oranges are the most relevant in agriculture.

In 2004 Brazil produced 18.3 million tons of oranges, 45% of the fruit harvest.

São Paulo state accounts for 79% of orange production and is the largest producer and exporter of orange juice, responsible for half of global production. 97% is exported.

Brazil and the US are the world's largest citrus producers, with 45% of the total, while South Africa, Spain and Israel compete in oranges and tangerines.

Brazilian orange juice is equivalent to 80% of world exports, the largest market share for any Brazilian agricultural product.

Figure 269: *Orange field, in S. Paulo*

Forestry and wood

Commercial forestry produced 65% of Brazilian wood products in 2003, up from 52% the year earlier as it gradually replaced traditional gathering.

Eucalyptus is the most popular species for reforestation. It is harvested for plywood and cellulose production. In 2001 the country cultivated three million hectares with this tree; another 1.8 million hectares were planted with pine, a species better adapted to the climate of the South and Southeast.

Native species have received increasing attention as an alternative to eucalyptus and pine. In 2007, the National Plan of Forestry with Native Species and Agroforestry Systems (PENSAF) was launched, in an integrated effort between the Ministry of the Environment (MMA) and the Ministry of Agriculture, Livestock and Food Supply (MAPA), among others.

In 2003 the country produced 2.149 million tons of wood for charcoal; 75% from Minas Gerais. Charcoal from vegetable gathering added 2.227 million tons, the largest part (35%) from Pará. Firewood production occupied 47.232 million square meters, with Bahia the biggest producer.

Brazil is the seventh largest global producer of cellulose of all kinds, and the largest of short fiber cellulose. In 2005 the country exported 5.2 million tons and produced 6 million, generating revenues of 3.4 billion dollars.

Figure 270: *Pine plantation for cellulose production, Bocaina do Sul, Santa Catarina.*

In 2006 the Management of Public Forests Law was enacted. It subsidizes legal wood production to reduce illegal deforestation, and encouraging the timber sector to adopt sustainable practices.

Vegetables

Brazilian vegetable production in 2004 was estimated at 11.696 billion Reais. It occupied 176 thousand hectares, yielding 16.86 million tons. The major producing regions were the South and Southeast, with 75% of the total. This sector employs between eight and ten million workers.

The vegetable section of Embrapa, with headquarters in Distrito Federal, was created in 1978 and in 1981 renamed the National Center of Research on Vegetables (CNPH). It occupies 487 ha with laboratories, administrative and support buildings, with 45 ha devoted to experimental vegetable production, of which 7 support organic production.

In 2007 Brazil exported 366,213 tons of vegetable crops, which yielded 240 million dollars. Among these, thirteen thousand tons of potatoes, twenty thousand tons of tomatoes, 37 thousand tons of onions. Other export vegetables included ginger, peas, cucumbers, capsicum, mustard, carrots and garlic.

Figure 271: *Horticulture in Almirante Tamandaré countryside.*

Tomato

Brazilian tomato production ranked sixth globally and first in South America in 2000. 1999 output reached a record of 1.29 million tons for tomato pulp.

In 2005, production increased to 3.3 million tons, ranking ninth globally behind China, US, Turkey, Italy, Egypt, India, Spain and Iran. The largest states in 2004 were Goiás (871 thousand tons), São Paulo (749 thousand tons), Minas Gerais (622 thousand), Rio de Janeiro (203 thousand) and Bahia (193 thousand).

Success in Goiás' and Minas Gerais' Cerrado allowed the region to expand from 31% to 84% of production, from 1996 to 2001. The development of localized hybrid varieties raised productivity.

Onion

Small farmers are responsible for more than half of the country's production.

Juazeiro, in Bahia, and Petrolina, in Pernambuco are neighboring towns, separated by São Francisco River. They have the highest yield, using irrigation to achieve 24 tons per hectare, versus the Brazilian average of seventeen. In 2006, the two cities 200 thousand tons surpassed that of the other states, behind only Santa Catarina (355 thousand tons).

Agriculture in Brazil 531

Figure 272: *Tomato plantation, Arandu*

Figure 273: *Sample of red onions.*

Figure 274: *Inspectors from the Ministry of Labor and Federal Police officers at the scene of a clandestine charcoal operation, places where most illegal working situations occur.*

Cassava

Brazil is the world's second largest cassava producer, at 12.7%. Exports comprise only .5%. Average exports in 2000 and 2001 were thirteen million, one hundred thousand tons, generating revenue above six hundred million dollars.

It is cultivated in all regions and is used for both human and animal consumption. Manioc is farmed for human consumption, including flour and starch. That production chain generates about a million direct jobs, and some ten million jobs overall.

Forecasts for 2002 were for 22.6 million tons on 1.7 million hectares. The largest producers were Pará (17.9%), Bahia (16.7%), Paraná (14.5%), Rio Grande do Sul (5.6%) and Amazonas (4.3%).

Controversies

Slave and child labor

According to data from the Department of Labor of the United States, twenty-first century Brazil ranks third in occurrences of illegal working arrangements (tied with India and Bangladesh). Eight of thirteen violations were prevalent in

Figure 275: *Gully in the state of São Paulo.*

agribusiness, especially in livestock, sisal, sugar cane, rice, tobacco and charcoal. Despite its position, the country's performance was praised, and between 1995 and 2009 approximately 35,000 workers were freed from degrading conditions.

The International Labour Organization (ILO) recognized the Brazilian effort to fight such practices, which focus on preventing/correcting misbehavior via a system of fines.

Among the causes of illegal working arrangements were poverty and misinformation.

A Constitutional Amendment Proposal (PEC), would compensate landowners for losses resulting from ending such practices.

In 2014 however, the Bureau of International Labor Affairs issued a *List of Goods Produced by Child Labor or Forced Labor* where Brazil was classified as one of the 74 countries involved in child labor and forced labor practices. The report lists 16 products including cotton, cashews, pineapples, rice and sugarcane the production of which still employs children.

Environmental impacts

Brazil's agricultural sector and deforestation account for 75% of its gas emissions responsible for climate change.[1011] For this reason, initiatives were adopted to reduce emissions, mostly by reducing deforestation. The so-called "Soybean Moratorium", the Agroecological Zoning for Sugar Cane, and the use of fertigation are examples.

Brazil's greenhouse gas emissions from agriculture increased 41 percent between 1990 and 2005.[1012] Cattle are a major factor. An estimate carried out by Friends of the Earth-Amazonia (Amigos da Terra - Amazônia Brasileira), the Brazilian National Institute for Space Research (INPE) and the University of Brasília concluded that fully half came from cattle.[1013] If all parts of the "cattle chain" had been included, the researchers add, an even higher proportion of greenhouse gases would have been attributed to cattle.

Cattle and soy production are concentrated in the Legal Amazon and Cerrado grasslands regions, and have resulted in considerable biodiversity loss, deforestation and water pollution.[1014] As of 2007, about 74 million cattle, or 40 percent of Brazil's herd, were living in what is known as the "Legal Amazon."[1015] Almost one million square km (386,000 sq mi), or nearly half of the Cerrado, has been burned and is now cattle pasture, or is cultivated for soybeans, corn (both primary ingredients in livestock feed), and sugarcane.[1016] According to Washington Novaes, "if we consider the viable fragments of the Cerrado, those with at least two continuous hectares (5 acres), only 5 percent of it is left. It's a very severe level of habitat loss."[1017] At least one quarter of Brazilian grain is grown in Cerrado.

Soil erosion

A large part of the Southeast and Northeast region of the country is made up of granitic and gneiss rock formations, covered by a layer of regolith, very susceptible to soil erosion and gully formation. Bertoni and Neto point out this condition as one of Brazil's highest environmental dangers, and a large part of them result from human activities.

Soil erosion removes nutrients and causes the loss of structure, texture and the decrease of infiltration rates and water retention.

Plowing and herbicides to control undesirable weeds leave the soil exposed and susceptible to erosion – either by loss of topsoil (which is richer in nutrients), or from gullies. The lost soil fills rivers and reservoirs with silt. One solution is no-till farming, a practice not in wide use.

Agriculture in Brazil

Pesticide

The world's four thousand agrochemicals are produced in about 15,000 different formulations, 8,000 of which are licensed in Brazil. They include insecticides, fungicides, herbicides, vermifuges, and also solvents and sanitizers. They are widely used to protect crops from pests, disease and invading species. Indiscriminate use causes unnecessary accumulation of those substances in the soil, water (springs, groundwater, reservoirs) and air.

Brazil uses an average of 3.2 kg of agrochemicals per hectare – ranking tenth globally, in some studies, and fifth, in others. São Paulo state is Brazil's largest user, and the largest producer, comprising 80% of the total. Mitigation techniques include farmer education, and the development of resistant species, better farming techniques, biological pest control, among others.

In 2007 tomatoes, lettuce and strawberries showed the highest rates of contamination by agrochemicals. Farmer awareness is low and few comply with rules on the use of these substances, such as Individual Protection Equipment (EPI).

According to information from Anvisa, Brazilian farming uses at least ten types of agrochemicals prohibited in other markets, such as the European Union and the US.[1018]

Genetically modified crops

The country is the third largest user in the world in growing genetically modified crops. The main commodities using this biotechnology are soy, cotton and, since 2008, maize.

Several national and international NGOs, such as Greenpeace, MST or Contag, are opposed to the practice. Criticisms include market loss, negative environmental impacts and dominance by large businesses. Entities linked to agribusiness, however, counter with the results of studies carried out by the Brazilian Association of Seeds and Saplings (Abrasem) in 2007 and 2008, affirming "social-environmental advantages observed in the other countries which have adopted agricultural biotechnology far longer".

Federal Justice decided that foods containing more than 1 percent of modified genes must be labeled to inform consumers.

Figure 276: *Brasilia, 2007: Protesters call for liberation from transgenic maize.*

Figure 277: *Organic cultivation of eggplant.*

Organic Farming

Organic farming aims to produce food without the use of synthetic fertilizers, pesticides or other agrochemicals.[1019] The IBGE's 2006 Agricultural Census reported the existence of ninety thousand organic farms in Brazil, comprising 2% of the total; however, only 5,106 are certified.

Organics are present mostly in small and medium properties. The majority of producers are organized in associations or cooperatives. The state with the largest number of producers is Bahia (223), followed by Minas Gerais (192), São Paulo (86), Rio Grande do Sul (83), Paraná (79), Espírito Santo (64) and others.

The Brazil Organics program, constituted in 2005, promotes the sector.

Brazil is the twenty-largest exporter in the world, according to data from the Ministry of Development, Industry and Foreign Trade in açai, cachaça, cattle, nuts, melons, guaraná, and beef.Wikipedia:Citation needed

Brazilian real

Brazilian real	
real brasileiro (Portuguese)	
Real banknotes of the latest series, announced February 2010. Issued on 13 December 2010.[1020]	
ISO 4217	
Code	BRL
Number	986
Exponent	2
Denominations	
Subunit	
1/100	centavo
Plural	Reais
Symbol	R$
Banknotes	
Freq. used	R$2, R$5, R$10, R$20, R$50, R$100
Rarely used	R$1 (discontinued in 2006)
Coins	
Freq. used	5, 10, 25, 50 centavos, R$1
Rarely used	1 centavo (discontinued in 2006)
Demographics	
User(s)	Brazil
Issuance	
Central bank	Central Bank of Brazil
Website	www<wbr/>.bcb<wbr/>.gov<wbr/>.br[1021]
Printer	Casa da Moeda do Brasil
Website	www<wbr/>.casadamoeda<wbr/>.gov<wbr/->.br[1022]
Mint	Casa da Moeda do Brasil
Website	www<wbr/>.casadamoeda<wbr/>.gov<wbr/->.br[1022]
Valuation	
Inflation	2.95% (2017) 3.53% (2018 est.)
Source	Central Bank of Brazil[1023], 2018
Method	CPI

The **Brazilian real** (Portuguese: *real*, pl. *reais*; sign: **R$**; code: **BRL**) is the official currency of Brazil. It is subdivided into 100 centavos. The Central Bank of Brazil is the central bank and the issuing authority.

The dollar-like sign (cifrão) is the currency's symbol (both historic and modern), and in all the other past Brazilian currencies, is officially written with two vertical strokes ($) rather than one. However Unicode considers the difference to be only a matter of font design, and does not have a separate code for the two-stroked version.[1024]

As of April 2016, the real is the nineteenth most traded currency in the world by value.

History

The modern real (Portuguese plural *reais* or English plural *reals*) was introduced on 1 July 1994, during the presidency of Itamar Franco, when Rubens Ricupero was the Minister of Finance, as part of a broader plan to stabilize the Brazilian economy, known as the Plano Real. The new currency replaced the short-lived cruzeiro real (CR$). The reform included the demonetisation of the cruzeiro real and required a massive banknote replacement.

At its introduction, the real was defined to be equal to 1 *unidade real de valor* (URV, "real value unit") a non-circulating currency unit. At the same time the URV was defined to be worth 2750 cruzeiros reais, which was the average exchange rate of the U.S. dollar to the cruzeiro real on that day. As a consequence, the real was worth exactly one U.S. dollar as it was introduced. Combined with all previous currency changes in the country's history, this reform made the new real equal to 2.75×10^{18} (2.75 quintillions) of Brazil's original "réis".

Soon after its introduction, the real unexpectedly gained value against the U.S. dollar, due to large capital inflows in late 1994 and 1995. During that period it attained its maximum dollar value ever, about US$1.20. Between 1996 and 1998 the exchange rate was tightly controlled by the Central Bank of Brazil, so that the real depreciated slowly and smoothly in relation to the dollar, dropping from near 1:1 to about 1.2:1 by the end of 1998. In January 1999 the deterioration of the international markets, disrupted by the Russian default, forced the Central Bank, under its new president Arminio Fraga, to float the exchange rate. This decision produced a major devaluation, to a rate of almost R$2 : US$1.[1025]

In the following years, the currency's value against the dollar followed an erratic but mostly downwards path from 1999 until late 2002, when the prospect of the election of leftist candidate Luiz Inácio Lula da Silva, considered a radical populist by sectors of the financial markets, prompted another currency crisis and a spike in inflation. Many Brazilians feared another default on government debts or a resumption of heterodox economic policies, and rushed to exchange their reais into tangible assets or foreign currencies. In October 2002 the exchange rate reached its historic low of almost R$4 per US$1.

The crisis subsided once Lula took office, after he, his finance minister Antonio Palocci, and Arminio Fraga reaffirmed their intention to continue the orthodox macroeconomic policies of his predecessor (including inflation-targeting, primary fiscal surplus and floating exchange rate, as well as continued payments of the public debt). The value of the real in dollars continued to fluctuate but generally upwards, so that by 2005 the exchange was a little over R$2 : US$1. In May 2007, for the first time since 2001, the real became worth more than US$0.50 — even though the Central Bank, concerned about its effect on the Brazilian economy, had tried to keep it below that symbolic threshold.

The exchange rate as of September 2015 was BRL 4.05 to USD 1.00, however it has since been in a gradual recovery period, reaching 3.0 BRL per USD by February 2017.

Coins

First series (1994–1997)

Along with the first series of currency, coins were introduced in denominations of 1, 5, 10 and 50 centavos and 1 real; the 25 centavos piece soon followed. All were struck in stainless steel. The original 1-real coins, produced only in 1994, were withdrawn from circulation on 23 December 2003;[1026] all other coins remain legal tender.

\multicolumn{3}{c}{First series}		
Image	Value	Design
	1 centavo	*Obverse*: Head of Republic. *Reverse*: Large denomination flanked by linear patterns.
	5 centavos	*Obverse*: Head of Republic. *Reverse*: Large denomination flanked by linear patterns.

Brazilian real 541

	10 centavos	*Obverse*: Head of Republic. *Reverse*: Large denomination flanked by linear patterns.
	25 centavos	*Obverse*: Head of Republic. *Reverse*: Large denomination intersected by wavy lines.
	50 centavos	*Obverse*: Head of Republic. *Reverse*: Large denomination flanked by linear patterns.
	1 real (withdrawn from circulation)	*Obverse*: Head of Republic. *Reverse*: Large denomination flanked by linear patterns.

Second series (1998–present)

In 1998, a second series of coins was introduced. It featured copper-plated steel coins of 1 and 5 centavos, brass-plated steel coins of 10 and 25 centavos, a cupronickel 50 centavos coin, and a bi-coloured brass and cupronickel coin of 1 real. However, from 2002 onwards, steel was used for the 50 centavos coin and the central part of the 1 real coin.

In November 2005, the Central Bank discontinued the production of 1 centavo coins, but the existing ones continue to be legal tender. Retailers now generally round their prices to the next 5 or 10 centavos.

		Second series
Image	Value	Design
	1 centavo (no longer produced)	*Obverse*: The Southern Cross in right upper side. *Reverse*: Depicts Pedro Álvares Cabral, Portuguese sea captain and Brazil's discoverer, with a 16th-century Portuguese ship in the background.
	5 centavos	*Obverse*: The Southern Cross in right upper side. *Reverse*: Depicts Joaquim José da Silva Xavier (also known as Tiradentes), martyr of an early independence movement known as the Minas Conspiracy. In the background, a triangle, symbol of the movement, and a dove, symbol of peace and freedom.
	10 centavos	*Obverse*: The Southern Cross in right upper side. *Reverse*: Depicts Emperor Pedro I, Brazil's first monarch. In the background, the Emperor on a horse: a scene alluding to the proclamation of independence.

	25 centavos	*Obverse*: The Southern Cross in right upper side. *Reverse*: Depicts Field Marshal Deodoro da Fonseca, Brazil's first Republican president. The Republic's coat of arms is in the background.
	50 centavos	*Obverse*: The Southern Cross in right upper side. *Reverse*: Depicts José Paranhos, Jr., the Baron of Rio Branco, the country's most distinguished Minister of Foreign Affairs. In the background, image of the country with ripples expanding outwards, representing the development of Brazil's foreign policy and the expansion and demarcation of the national borders.
	1 real	*Obverse*: The Southern Cross in right upper side. *Reverse*: Outer ring depicts a sample of the *marajoara* art pattern. In the inner ring, the Efígie da República, symbol of the Republic.

Commemorative coins

The Brazilian Central Bank has also issued special commemorative versions of some coins on special occasions. These coins are legal tender and differ from the standard ones only on the reverse side.

Value	Details
10 and 25 centavos	**Release date:** 31 May 1995 **Occasion:** The 50th anniversary of the Food and Agriculture Organization (FAO) **Units produced:** 1 million for each design **Reverse:** The 10 centavos coin depicts hands offering a plant shoot with folious ramifications, and the 25 centavos coin depicts crop cultivation. Both coins contain the inscriptions "FAO - 1945/1995" and "alimentos para todos" (food for all).[1027,1028]
1 real	**Release date:** 10 December 1998 **Occasion:** The 50th anniversary of the Universal Declaration of Human Rights **Units produced:** 600 thousand **Reverse:** The official logo of the commemorations; in bas-relief, a human figure. In the outer ring, the inscriptions "Declaração Universal dos Direitos Humanos" (Universal Declaration of Human Rights) and "Cinqüentenário" (50th anniversary).[1029]
1 real	**Release date:** 12 September 2002 **Occasion:** The 100th birth anniversary of Brazilian former president Juscelino Kubitschek **Units produced:** 50 million **Reverse:** A face portrait of Kubitschek. Vertically, the inscription "Centenário Juscelino Kubitschek" (Juscelino Kubitschek's centenary). In the outer ring, images alluding to the columns of the Alvorada Palace, the Presidential residence in Brasília, the city that he decided would be built.[1030]
1 real	**Release date:** 23 September 2005 **Occasion:** The 40th anniversary of the foundation of the Central Bank of Brazil **Units produced:** 40 million **Reverse:** Image of the trademark Central Bank building, inspired in the official logo developed for the commemorations. In the outer ring, the inscriptions "Banco Central do Brasil" (Central Bank of Brazil) and "1965 40 anos 2005" (1965 40 years 2005).[1031]

1 real	**Release date:** 13 August 2012 **Occasion:** The Olympic Flag Handover for the Rio 2016 Summer Olympics **Units produced:** 2 million **Reverse:** The Olympic Flag in a pole above the official logo of the Games of the XXXI Olympiad. In the outer ring, the inscriptions "Entrega da Bandeira Olímpica" (Olympic Flag Handover) and "Londres 2012 - Rio 2016" (London 2012 - Rio 2016)[1032]
1 real	**Release dates:** 28 November 2014, 17 April 2015, 7 August 2015, 19 February 2016 (four sets of four designs) **Occasion:** 2016 Summer Olympics **Units produced:** 20 million for each design **Reverse:** Sixteen coin designs, representing athletics (triple jump), swimming, paralympic triathlon, golf, basketball, sailing, paralympic canoeing, rugby, football, volleyball, paralympic athletics (running), judo, boxing, paralympic swimming, and each mascot of the 2016 Summer Olympics and Paralympics.
1 real	**Release date:** 30 March 2015 **Occasion:** The 50th anniversary of the foundation of the Central Bank of Brazil **Units produced:** 50 million **Reverse:** The Central Bank building, its logo, and the inscription "50 anos" (50 years).

Banknotes

First series (1994–2010)

In 1994, banknotes were introduced in denominations of 1, 5, 10, 50 and 100 reais. These were followed by 2 reais in 2000 and 20 reais in 2001. On 31 December 2005, BCB discontinued the production of the 1 real banknote.

Real series[1033]			
Value	Dimensions	Description	
		Obverse	Reverse
1 real	140 mm × 65 mm	The Republic's Effigy, portrayed as a bust	Sapphire-spangled emerald hummingbird (*Amazilia lactea*)
2 reais			Hawksbill turtle (*Eretmochelys imbricata*)
5 reais			Great egret (*Casmerodius albus*)
10 reais			Green-winged macaw (*Ara chloropterus*)
20 reais			Golden lion tamarin (*Leontopithecus rosalia*)
50 reais			Jaguar (*Onça pintada, Panthera onca*)
100 reais			Dusky Grouper (*Epinephelus marginatus*)

Figure 278: *Commemorative 1 real coins for the 2016 Summer Olympics and Paralympics Games in Rio de Janeiro. Left, allegory to Olympic boxing, right, allegory to Paralympic swimming.*

Figure 279: *Reais banknotes from the first series.*

Second series (2010–present)

On 3 February 2010, the Central Bank of Brazil announced a new series of the real banknotes which would begin to be released in April 2010. The new design added security enhancements in an attempt to reduce counterfeiting. The notes have different sizes according to their values to help vision-impaired people. The changes were made reflecting the growth of the Brazilian economy and the need for a stronger and safer currency. The new banknotes began to enter circulation in December 2010, coexisting with the older ones.[1034]

2010, 2011, and 2012 series							
Image		Value	Dimensions	Main color	Description		Date of first issue	Watermark
Obverse	Reverse				Obverse	Reverse		
		2 reais	121 mm × 65 mm	Dark blue	Wave pattern; head of Republic	Hawksbill turtle (*Eretmochelys imbricata*)	29 July 2013	Hawksbill turtle and electrotype 2
		5 reais	128 mm x 65 mm	Purple	Plants; head of Republic	Great egret (*Casmerodius albus*)	29 July 2013	Great egret and electrotype 5
		10 reais	135 mm × 65 mm	Red	Plants; head of Republic	Green-winged macaw (*Ara chlorepterus*)	23 July 2012	Green-winged macaw and electrotype 10
		20 reais	142 mm × 65 mm	Yellow	Plants; head of Republic	Golden lion tamarin (*Leontopithecus rosalia*)	23 July 2012	Golden lion tamarin and electrotype 20
		50 reais	149 mm × 70 mm	Brown	Jungle plants; head of Republic	Jaguar (*Panthera onca*)	13 December 2010	Jaguar and electrotype 50
		100 reais	156 mm × 70 mm	Light blue	Underwater plants and starfish; head of Republic; coral	Dusky Grouper (*Epinephelus marginatus*); coral	13 December 2010	Dusky Grouper and electrotype 100

Commemorative banknotes

In April 2000, in commemoration of the 500th anniversary of the Portuguese arrival on Brazilian shores, the Brazilian Central Bank released a polymer 10 real banknote that circulates along with the other banknotes above. The Brazilian Mint printed 250 million of these notes, which at the time accounted for about half of the 10 real banknotes in circulation.

Obverse	Reverse	Value	Year	Material	Description
		10 reais	2000	Polymer	**Obverse**: Image of Pedro Álvares Cabral, discoverer of Brazil. **Reverse**: Stylized version of the map of Brazil, with pictures highlighting the ethnic and cultural plurality of the country.

Exchange rates

Most traded currencies by value

Currency distribution of global foreign exchange market turnover

Rank	Currency	ISO 4217 code (symbol)	% daily share (April 2016)
1	United States dollar	USD (US$)	87.6%
2	Euro	EUR (€)	31.4%
3	Japanese yen	JPY (¥)	21.6%
4	Pound sterling	GBP (£)	12.8%
5	Australian dollar	AUD (A$)	6.9%
6	Canadian dollar	CAD (C$)	5.1%
7	Swiss franc	CHF (Fr)	4.8%
8	Renminbi	CNY (元)	4.0%
9	Swedish krona	SEK (kr)	2.2%
10	New Zealand dollar	NZD (NZ$)	2.1%
11	Mexican peso	MXN ($)	1.9%
12	Singapore dollar	SGD (S$)	1.8%
13	Hong Kong dollar	HKD (HK$)	1.7%
14	Norwegian krone	NOK (kr)	1.7%
15	South Korean won	KRW (₩)	1.7%
16	Turkish lira	TRY (₺)	1.4%
17	Russian ruble	RUB (₽)	1.1%
18	Indian rupee	INR (₹)	1.1%
19	Brazilian real	BRL (R$)	1.0%
20	South African rand	ZAR (R)	1.0%
		Other	7.1%
		Total[1035]	200.0%

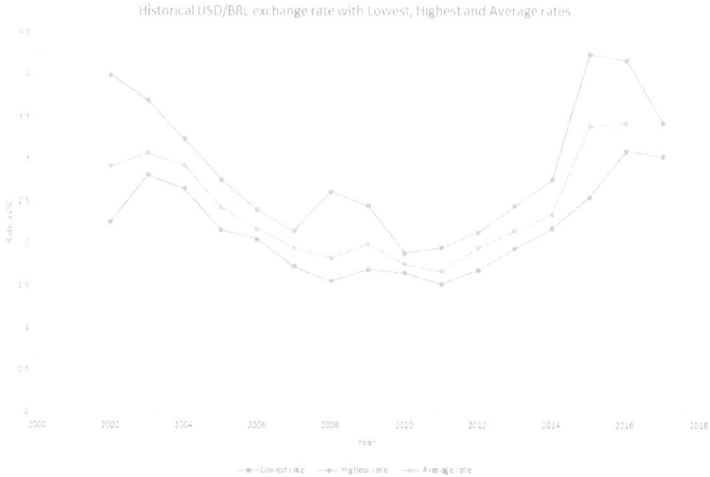

Figure 280: *Historical USD/BRL exchange rate with Lowest, Highest and Average rates*

Figure 281: *Historical USD/BRL exchange rate*

Historical exchange rate

Brazilian Reals per USD 2002–2017

Year	Lowest ↓		Highest ↑		Average
	Date	Rate	Date	Rate	Rate

2002	11 April	2.264	10 October	4.005	2.9221
2003	2 July	2.818	14 February	3.700	3.078
2004	30 December	2.654	22 May	3.242	2.926
2005	11 November	2.163	15 March	2.766	2.4349
2006	5 May	2.056	24 May	2.405	2.1782
2007	14 November	1.732	5 January	2.153	1.948
2008	31 July	1.562	5 December	2.621	1.8349
2009	15 October	1.698	2 March	2.451	1.9974
2010	13 October	1.655	5 February	1.891	1.7603
2011	26 July	1.5284	22 September	1.952	1.675
2012	29 February	1.692	3 December	2.1395	1.9546
2013	11 March	1.943	21 August	2.4523	2.1576
2014	10 April	2.1825	16 December	2.7614	2.3531
2015	22 January	2.5554	23 September	4.2491	3.391
2016	25 October	3.1023	22 January	4.1737	3.430
2017	16 February	3.0390	18 May	3.4300	

Date	Rate
1994-07-01	1.00
1994-10-14	0.83
1995-02-15	0.88
1995-12-29	0.97
1996-06-11	1.00
1996-12-31	1.04
1997-12-31	1.12
1998-12-31	1.20
1999-01-12	1.21
1999-01-13	1.31

1999-01-29	1.98
1999-03-03	2.16
1999-04-30	1.66
1999-12-31	1.78
2000-12-31	1.96
2001-05-02	2.23
2001-10-15	2.78
2002-01-25	2.38
2002-04-12	2.27
2002-06-27	2.83
2002-09-30	3.87
2002-10-12	3.93
2002-10-22	3.96
2002-12-27	3.53
2003-02-18	3.61
2003-06-28	2.87
2003-09-30	2.93
2003-12-28	2.93
2004-03-31	2.91
2004-05-23	3.18
2004-06-28	3.10
2004-09-30	2.85
2004-12-28	2.69
2005-02-19	2.56
2005-03-26	2.73
2005-06-28	2.38
2005-09-25	2.26
2005-11-11	2.17
2005-12-28	2.36
2006-03-27	2.15
2006-05-07	2.05
2006-12-29	2.13
2007-11-07	1.73
2008-08-01	1.56
2009-03-03	2.42
2009-10-14	1.71
2010-12-30	1.66
2011-07-23	1.53
2012-03-18	1.79

2012-08-19	2.01
2013-03-31	2.01
2013-07-13	2.26
2013-11-01	2.23
2014-01-23	2.40
2014-02-06	2.40
2014-10-23	2.50
2014-12-16	2.75
2015-01-22	2.56
2015-02-02	2.71
2015-03-06	3.05
2015-03-19	3.29
2015-04-24	2.95
2015-04-28	2.88
2015-05-08	2.97
2015-05-29	3.18
2015-08-06	3.53
2015-09-01	3.69
2015-09-04	3.80
2015-09-17	3.88
2015-09-22	4.05
2015-09-24	4.24
2015-09-25	3.97
2015-10-02	3.94
2015-10-09	3.75
2015-11-20	3.69
2015-12-03	3.74
2015-12-09	3.73
2016-02-23	3.97
2016-03-13	3.58
2016-06-30	3.18
2016-10-25	3.10
2017-02-14	3.09

Current exchange rates

Current BRL exchange rates	
From Google Finance[1036]:	AUD[1037] CAD[1038] CHF[1039] EUR[1040] GBP[1041] HKD[1042] JPY[1043] USD[1044] INR[1045] RUB[1046] ARS[1047]
From Yahoo! Finance[1048]:	AUD[1049] CAD[1050] CHF[1051] EUR[1052] GBP[1053] HKD[1054] JPY[1055] USD[1056] INR[1057] RUB[1058] ARS[1059]
From XE[1060]:	AUD[1061] CAD[1062] CHF[1063] EUR[1064] GBP[1065] HKD[1066] JPY[1067] USD[1068] INR[1069] RUB[1070] ARS[1071]
From OANDA[1072]:	AUD[1073] CAD[1074] CHF[1075] EUR[1076] GBP[1077] HKD[1078] JPY[1079] USD[1080] INR[1081] RUB[1082] ARS[1083]
From fxtop.com[1084]:	AUD[1085] CAD[1086] CHF[1087] EUR[1088] GBP[1089] HKD[1090] JPY[1091] USD[1092] INR[1093] RUB[1094] ARS[1095]

External links

 Wikimedia Commons has media related to *Real*.

- Brazil's Currency War[1096]
- Images of historic and modern Brazilian bank notes[1097]
- The Invention of the Real (This American Life)[1098]
- Historical banknotes of Brazil[1099]

Mining in Brazil

Mining in Brazil is centered on the extraction of gold, copper, tin, iron and bauxite.

History

- Discovery of first gold rush in 1690s, gold discoveries made in streams not far from present day city of Belo Horizonte.
- In 1729 diamonds were discovered in the same area. This started a diamond rush.
- By 1760 nearly half of the world's gold was from Brazil.
- In the early 18th century nearly 400,000 Portuguese immigrants came to mine in southern Brazil.
- Over half a million African slaves were shipped to work in the gold mines.
- The Gongo Soco gold mine, operated by the Imperial Brazilian Mining Association of Cornwall using skilled Cornish miners and unskilled slaves, produced over 12,000 kilograms (26,000 lb) of gold between 1826 and 1856.

Figure 282: *Satellite picture of Carajás mine showing soil degradation.*

Mining today

In 1988 Brazil was the 5th largest gold producer in the world. Brazil mined iron, gold, tin, copper and Bauxite (contains aluminium).

Environmental Impact

The mining activity has caused severe environmental impact in Brazil area. Among the different types of environmental degradation, mining activities has caused landscape degradation, erosion, soil contamination, groundwater and surface water pollution.

The Bento Rodrigues dam disaster is considered to be worse environmental incident in the history of mining in Brazil. On November 5, 2015, two iron ore tailings dams of Samarco (a *joint-venture* between Vale S.A. and BHP Billiton) collapsed. The mud containing by-products of mining flowed down, destroying completely Bento Rodrigues, a sub-district of Mariana, and invaded other neighbouring cities, such as Barra Longa, causing at least six casualties, and destroying at least 200 homes. The mud reached the Rio Doce, contaminated the water, and compromised the water supply of cities in Minas Gerais and Espírito Santo that lay by the river. Several species of fish died to the low oxygen levels in the water, and up till today scientists could not estimate the total environmental impact.

Industry in Brazil

Brazilian industry has its earliest origin in workshops dating from the beginning of the 19th century. Most of the country's industrial establishments appeared in the Brazilian southeast (mainly in the provinces of Rio de Janeiro, Minas Gerais and, later, São Paulo), and, according to the Commerce, Agriculture, Factories and Navigation Joint,Wikipedia:Manual of Style/Words to watch#Unsupported attributions 77 establishments registered between 1808 and 1840 were classified as "factories" or "manufacturers". However, most, about 56 establishments, would be considered workshops by today's standards, directed toward the production of soap and tallow candles, snuff, spinning and weaving, foods, melting of iron and metals, wool and silk, amongst others. They used both slaves and free laborers.[1100]

There were twenty establishments that could be considered in fact manufacturers, and of this total, thirteen were created between the years 1831 and 1840. All were, however, of small size and resembled large workshops more than proper factories. Still, the manufactured goods were quite diverse: hats, combs, farriery and sawmills, spinning and weaving, soap and candles, glasses, carpets, oil, etc. Probably because of the instability of the regency period, only nine of these establishments were still functioning in 1841, but these nine were large and could be considered to "presage a new era for manufactures".[1101]

The advent of manufacturing before the 1840s was extremely limited, due to the self-sufficiency of the rural regions, where farms producing coffee and sugar cane also produced their own food, clothes, equipment, etc, the lack of capital, and high costs of production that made it impossible for Brazilian manufacturers to compete with foreign products. Costs were high because most raw materials were imported, even though some of the plants already used machines.[1102]

1840s–1860s

The promulgation of the Alves Branco tariff modified this picture. This tariff succeeded in increasing state revenues and stimulating the growth of national industry.[1103,1104] The sudden proliferation of capital was directed to investments in urban services, transports, commerce, banks, industries, etc.[1105] Most of the capital invested in industry was directed toward textiles.[1106] With unprecedented industrial growth, multiple manufacturing establishments appeared, dedicated to such diverse products as smelting of iron and metal, machinery, soap and candles, glasses, beer, vinegar, gallons of gold and silver, shoes, hats and cotton fabric.[1107]

Figure 283: *Iron Factory in Sorocaba, province of São Paulo, 1884.*

Figure 284: *Shipyard in the city of Rio de Janeiro, c.1862.*

One of the main establishments created at this period was the metallurgical factory *Ponta da Areia* (in English: Sand Tip), in the city of Niterói, that also constructed steamships.[1108] It is likely that the textile industry benefited most by the virtue of being the oldest in the country. It first appeared in 1826, in the city of Recife, capital of the province of Pernambuco. The textile sector was quite dynamic in the monarchic period and received large investments until 1890, when it entered into decline. Various modernizations occurred, principally between 1840 and 1860, when factories with a high level of technological capability were created, able to compete with other major international centers. Other improvements came with the establishment of factories and forges geared for the production of equipment and pieces for textile manufacture.[1109] And now Brazil ranks second in the world's largest producer of denim, the third – for the production of knitted fabrics, the fifth – for the manufacture of clothing and seventh – for the production of yarns and fibers.Wikipedia:Citation needed The concentration of industry that emerged in the province of Bahia considerably expanded its economic scope, reaching the south of Ceará, Piauí and even Minas Gerais.[1110]

The extinction of the traffic in African slaves in 1850, contrary to what many authors allege, did not "liberate" credit for industrial development. That claim has no documentary basis whatever.[1111] On the contrary, capital employed in the trade was had already been directed to sectors such as enterprises of urban services, transport, banking and trade. But it is possible that there was an indirect contribution to the growth of the industrial sector through banking loans.[1112] In 1850, there were 50 factories with a capital of at least Rs 7.000:000$000.[1113]

The imperial government created several incentives for the industrialization of the country. The earliest of these date from the reign of Dom Pedro I, through awards of government grants. The first establishment to receive such a grant was the *Fábrica das Chitas* (in English: Chitas Factory), devoted to paper and printing, by a decree of 26 June 1826.[1114] The practice was resumed in the 1840s, when new industrial establishments received subsidies. in 1857, seven factories benefited from this practice of incentives, among them, the *Ponta da Areia* mentioned above and that was owned by Irineu Evangelista de Sousa (later Viscount of Mauá). One of the criteria for the granting of these subsidies was the exclusive employment of free workers.[1115]

The goal, then, was not only the transition from the old colonial economic system to that of the modern capitalist, but also from slave labor to free. Other incentives arose, such as the decree of 8 August 1846 that exempted manufactured products from certain transport taxes (internally as well as externally), shielded from military recruitment a determinate number of employees of industrial establishments and eliminated tariffs on parts and machinery imported

Figure 285: *Factory in Brazil, 1880.*

for textile factories. The following year in June, a new decree stated that all industrial establishments on national soil would be free of taxes on imported raw materials.[1116] Thus, production costs of domestic industry dropped considerably, allowing it to compete with foreign products. The Alves Branco tariff underwent modification in 1857, reducing to 15% the tax on imported products.[1117,1118] Later, under the Rio Branco cabinet at the beginning of the 1870s, the tariff on foreign products was newly raised to 40%, and new raw materials were exempted from import taxes.

1860s–1880s

At the end of the 1860s, came a new industrial surge caused by two armed conflicts: the American Civil War and the Paraguayan War. U.S. production of cotton was interrupted by the blockade by Union forces of the Confederacy. The second resulted in the emission of currency and an increase in import tariffs to cover the costs of war. This resulted in a great stimulus not only for the textile industry, but also for other sectors, such as chemicals, cigars, glass, paper, leather, and optical and nautical instruments.

During the 1870s, the decline of the coffee region of the Paraíba Valley and in some areas of sugar production, caused many plantation owners to invest not only in the cotton textile industry, but also in other manufacturing sectors. Deployment of a railway network throughout the national territory also stimulated the emergence of new industrial activities, mainly in São Paulo.[1119] Industry experienced a major impetus in this period. From the 1870s onward, the great expansion of industrialization became a constant in Brazil.[1120] In 1866, there were nine textile factories with 795 workers.[1121] In 1881, there were 46 textile factories through the country: 12 in Bahia; 11 in Rio de Janeiro; nine in São Paulo; nine in Minas Gerais; and five in other provinces.[1122] The number of establishments diminished a little by 1885 to 42 textile factories with 3,172 workers. However, the drop did not impede overall growth in the sector up to 1889.

In 1880 the Industrial Association was established, with its first board elected the following year. It supported new industrial incentives and propagandized against the defenders of an essentially agricultural Brazil.[1123] 9.6% of the capital of the Brazilian economy was directed to industry by 1884, and by 1885, 11.2%. This figure dropped sharply during the republican period, falling to 5% between 1895 and 1899, and improved slightly to 6% between 1900 and 1904. Still, it took many years to return to the level that prevailed during the Empire.[1124] At the time of its downfall in 1889, monarchical Brazil had 636 factories (representing an annual rate of increase of 6.74% from 1850) with a capital of Rs 401.630:600$000 (annual growth rate of 10.94% since 1850). Of this amount, 60% were employed in the textile sector, 15% in food, 10% in the chemical, 4% in timber, 3.5% in clothing and 3% in metallurgy.[1125]

Brazilian industrial sector

Most large industry is concentrated in the south and south east. The north east is traditionally the poorest part of Brazil, but it is beginning to attract new investment.

Brazil has the third most advanced industrial sector in The Americas. Accounting for one-third of GDP, Brazil's diverse industries range from automobiles, steel and petrochemicals to computers, aircraft, and consumer durables. With the increased economic stability provided by the Plano Real, Brazilian and multinational businesses have invested heavily in new equipment and technology, a large proportion of which has been purchased from U.S. firms.

Brazil has a diverse and sophisticated services industry as well. During the early 1990s, the banking sector accounted for as much as 16% of GDP. Although undergoing a major overhaul, Brazil's financial services industry provides local businesses with a wide range of products and is attracting numerous new entrants, including U.S. financial firms. The São Paulo and Rio de Janeiro stock exchanges are undergoing a consolidation and the reinsurance sector is about to be privatized.Wikipedia:Citation needed

The Brazilian government has undertaken an ambitious program to reduce dependence on imported oil. Imports previously accounted for more than 70% of the country's oil needs but in 2006 Brazil has achieved oil self-sufficiency. Brazil is one of the world's leading producers of hydroelectric power, with a current capacity of about 58,000 megawatts. Existing hydroelectric power provides 92% of the nation's electricity. Two large hydroelectric projects, the 12,600 megawatt Itaipu Dam on the Paraná River—the world's largest dam—and the Tucurui Dam in Para in northern Brazil, are in operation. Brazil's first commercial nuclear reactor, Angra I, located near Rio de Janeiro, has been in operation for more than 10 years. Angra II is under construction and, after years of delays, is about to come on line. An Angra III is planned. The three reactors would have combined capacity of 3,000 megawatts when completed.[www.ipardes.gov.br/anuario_2005/2infraestrutura/qdo2_1_1.xls]

Proven mineral resources are extensive. Large iron and manganese reserves are important sources of industrial raw materials and export earnings. Deposits of nickel, tin, chromite, bauxite, beryllium, copper, lead, tungsten, zinc, gold, and other minerals are exploited. High-quality coking-grade coal required in the steel industry is in short supply.

Cars

Brazilian automobile production began in 1957, with an initial production of 1,166 units in the first year. Most production is concentrated in the states of São Paulo, Minas Gerais and Paraná.

The automotive industry in Brazil boomed after ex-president Fernando Collor de Mello opened up the market in 1990, but high production costs, high taxes and technology deficits are barriers that Brazil is still struggling to defeat.

Brazil's automotive industry has been displaying impressive two-digit growth over the last years, totaling revenues over USD 100 billion by the end of 2010. These figures secured Brazil the fourth position amongst the largest car markets in the world (one position ahead of Germany). The industry generates 1.5 million jobs.

The perspective of a steady development of the industry is attracting billions in investments to the country. BMW announced in December 2011 plans to set up a plant in São Paulo, and by 2014 Chinese manufacturer JAC Motors was to officially start production on the assembly line being built in Bahia state.

Automobile production[1126,1127]

Year	1960	1970	1980	1990	2000	2004	2005	2007	2008
Units (in millions)	0.042	0.306	0.933	0.663	1.36	1.86	2.50	2.61	2.97

Petroleum

The northeast shore of the Bay of All Saints was home to Brazil's first active oil fields. The municipality of São Francisco do Conde at the north of the bay remains a port serving the refineries at Mataripe. The bay is dredged from the port to the Atlantic Ocean to remain open to shipping.

Petroleum production[1128]

Year	1960	1970	1980	1990	2000	2006
Thousand barrels per day	83	169	189	653	1,271	1,809

Statistics

Electricity:[1129]

- *production:* 380 TWh (2004)
- *consumption:* 391 TWh (2004)

Electricity - production by source: (2004)

- *other sources:* 9%
- *hydroelectric:* 83%
- *conventional thermal:* 4%
- *nuclear:* 4%

Oil:[1130]

- *production:* 2.165 million barrel/day (2006)
- *consumption:* 2.216 million barrel/day (2006)
- *imports:* 0.051 million barrel/day (2006)
- *proven reserves:* 11.2 billion barrels (2006)
- *refinery capacity:* 1.908 million barrel/day (2006)

Natural gas:

- *production:* 9.88 billion cubic kilometers (2006)
- *consumption:* 19.34 billion cubic kilometers (2006)
- *imports:* 9.45 billion cubic kilometers (2006)
- *proven reserves:* 326 billion cubic kilometers (2006)

Bibliography

- Furtado, Celso. *Formação econômica do Brasil*. (http://www.afoiceeomartelo.com.br/posfsa/Autores/Furtado,%20Celso/Celso%20Furtado%20-%20Forma%C3%A7%C3%A3o%20Econ%C3%B4mica%20do%20Brasil.pdf)
- Prado Junior, Caio. *História econômica do Brasil*. (http://www.afoiceeomartelo.com.br/posfsa/Autores/Prado%20Jr,%20Caio/Historia%20Economica%20do%20Brasil.pdf)
- Graça Filho, Afonso de Alencastro. *A economia do Império brasileiro*. São Paulo: Atual, 2004. (in Portuguese)
- Scantimburgo, João de. *O Poder Moderador*. São Paulo: Secretaria de Estado da Cultura, 1980. (in Portuguese)
- Silva, Hélio. *1889 - A república não esperou o amanhecer*. Porto Alegre: L&PM, 2005. (in Portuguese)
- Sodré, Nelson Werneck. *Panorama do Segundo Império*, 2. ed. Rio de Janeiro: GRAPHIA, 2004. (in Portuguese)
- Szmrecsány, Tamás *and* Lapa, José Roberto do Amaral. *História Econômica da Independência e do Império*, 2. ed. São Paulo: USP, 2002. (in Portuguese)
- Vainfas, Ronaldo. *Dicionário do Brasil Imperial*. Rio de Janeiro: Objetiva, 2002. (in Portuguese)
- 15. ed. São Paulo: Melhoramentos, 1994. (in Portuguese)

Energy

Energy in Brazil

Brazil is the 10th largest energy consumer in the world and the largest in South America. It is an important oil and gas producer in the region and the world's second largest ethanol fuel producer. The government agencies responsible for energy policy are the Ministry of Mines and Energy (MME), the National Council for Energy Policy (CNPE), the National Agency of Petroleum, Natural Gas and Biofuels (ANP) and the National Agency of Electricity (ANEEL).[1131] State-owned companies Petrobras and Eletrobrás are the major players in Brazil's energy sector, as well as Latin America's.

Overview

	Energy in Brazil[1132]					
	Capita	Prim. energy	Production	Import	Electricity	CO_2-emission
	Million	TWh	TWh	TWh	TWh	Mt
2004	183.9	2,382	2,050	364	360	323
2007	191.6	2,740	2,507	289	413	347
2008	192.0	2,890	2,653	314	429	365
2009	193.7	2,793	2,679	182	426	338
2010	195.0	3,089	2,865	289	465	388
2012	196.7	3,140	2,898	333	480	408
2012R	198.7	3,276	2,930	391	498	440
2013	200.0	3,415	2,941	531	517	517
Change 2004-10	6.0 %	30 %	40 %	-21 %	29 %	20 %

Mtoe = 11.63 TWh, Prim. energy includes energy losses > 2012R = CO2 calculation criteria changed, numbers updated

Figure 286: *Petrobras world headquarters in Rio de Janeiro. The company is the most important energy producer in Brazil, as well as the country's second largest company, after Itaú Unibanco.*

Reforms of the energy sector

At the end of the 1990s and the beginning of the 2000s, Brazil's energy sector underwent market liberalization. In 1997, the Petroleum Investment Law was adopted, establishing a legal and regulatory framework, and liberalizing oil production. It created the CNPE and the ANP, increased use of natural gas, increased competition in the energy market, and increased investment in power generation. The state monopoly on oil and gas exploration ended,Wikipedia:Please clarify and energy subsidies were reduced. However, the government retained monopoly control of key energy complexes and regulated the price of certain energy products.

CurrentWikipedia:Manual of Style/Dates and numbers#Chronological items government policies concentrate mainly on improving energy efficiency in both residential and industrial sectors, as well as increasing use of renewable energy. Further restructuring of the energy sector will be one of the key issues for ensuring sufficient energy investments to meet the rising need for fuel and electricity.

Energy in Brazil

Figure 287: *Launch ceremony for oil platform P-52, which operates in the Campos Basin.*

Figure 288: *Oil-based Arembepe thermal power plant in Camaçari, Bahia*

Primary energy sources

Oil

Brazil is the world's 12th-largest oil producer. Up to 1997, the government-owned Petróleo Brasileiro S.A. (Petrobras) had a monopoly on oil. More than

50 oil companies now are engaged in oil exploration. The only global oil producer is Petrobras, with an output of more than 2 million barrels (320,000 m^3) of oil equivalent per day. It is also a major distributor of oil products, and owns oil refineries and oil tankers.

In 2006, Brazil had 11.2 billion barrels (1.78×10^9 m^3) the second-largest proven oil reserves in South America after Venezuela. The vast majority of proven reserves were located in the Campos and Santos offshore basins off the southeast coast of Brazil.[1133] In November 2007, Petrobras announced that it believed the offshore Tupi oil field had between 5 and 8 billion barrels (1.3×10^9 m^3) of recoverable light oil and neighbouring fields may even contain more, which all in all could result in Brazil becoming one of the largest producers of oil in the world.

Brazil has been a net exporter of oil since 2011.[1134] However, the country still imports some light oil from the Middle East, because several refineries, built in the 1960s and 1970s under the military government, are not suited to process the heavy oil in Brazilian reserves, discovered decades later.

Transpetro, a wholly owned subsidiary of Petrobras, operates a crude oil transport network. The system consists of 6,000 kilometres (3,700 mi) of crude oil pipelines, coastal import terminals, and inland storage facilities.

Natural gas

At the end of 2005, the proven reserves of Brazil's natural gas were 306 x 10^9 m³, with possible reserves expected to be 15 times higher. Until recently natural gas was produced as a by-product of the oil industry. The main reserves in use are located at Campos and Santos Basins. Other natural gas basins include Foz do Amazonas, Ceara e Potiguar, Pernambuco e Paraíba, Sergipe/ Alagoas, Espírito Santo and Amazonas (onshore). Petrobras controls over 90 percent of Brazil's natural gas reserves.

Brazil's inland gas pipeline systems are operated by Petrobras subsidiary Transpetro. In 2005, construction began on the Gas Unificação (Gasun pipeline) which will link Mato Grosso do Sul in southwest Brazil, to Maranhão in the northeast. China's Sinopec is a contractor for the Gasene pipeline, which will link the northeast and southeast networks. Petrobras is also constructing the Urucu-Manaus pipeline, which will link the Urucu gas reserves to power plants in the state of Amazonas.

In 2005, the gas production was 18.7 x 10^9 m³, which is less than the natural gas consumption of Brazil. Gas imports come mainly from Bolivia's Rio Grande basin through the Bolivia-Brazil gas pipeline (Gasbol pipeline), from Argentina through the Transportadora de Gas de Mercosur pipeline (Paraná-Uruguayana pipeline), and from LNG imports. Brazil has held talks with

Figure 289: *Cars fueled by natural gas, such as this Fiat Siena, are common in Brazil.*

Venezuela and Argentina about building a new pipeline system Gran Gasoducto del Sur linking the three countries; however, the plan has not moved beyond the planning stages.

Coal

Brazil has total coal reserves of about 30 billion tonnes, but the deposits vary by the quality and quantity. The proved recoverable reserves are around 10 billion tonnes. In 2004 Brazil produced 5.4 million tonnes of coal, while coal consumption reached 21.9 million tonnes. Almost all of Brazil's coal output is steam coal, of which about 85% is fired in power stations. Reserves of sub-bituminous coal are located mostly in the states of Rio Grande do Sul, Santa Catarina and Paraná.

Oil shale

Brazil has the world's second largest known oil shale (the Irati shale and lacustrine deposits) resources and has second largest shale oil production after Estonia. Oil shale resources lie in São Mateus do Sul, Paraná, and in Vale do Paraíba. Brazil has developed the world's largest surface oil shale pyrolysis retort Petrosix, operated by Petrobras. Production in 1999 was about 200,000 tonnes.[1135]

Figure 290: *Gas centrifuge for the extraction of uranium hexafluoride in a military facility at Iperó, built with Brazilian technology.*

Uranium

Brazil has the 6th largest uranium reserves in the world. Deposits of uranium are found in eight different states of Brazil. Proven reserves are 162,000 tonnes. Cumulative production at the end of 2002 was less than 1,400 tonnes. The Poços de Caldas production centre in Minas Gerais state was shut down in 1997 and was replaced by a new plant at Lagoa Real in Bahia. There is a plan to build another production center at Itatiaia.

Electricity

Power sector reforms were launched in the mid-1990s and a new regulatory framework was applied in 2004. In 2004, Brazil had 86.5 GW of installed generating capacity and it produced 387 Twh of electricity. As of today 66% of distribution and 28% of power generation is owned by private companies. In 2004, 59 companies operated in power generation and 64 in electricity distribution.

The major power company is Centrais Elétricas Brasileiras (Eletrobrás), which together with its subsidiaries generates and transmits approximately 60% of Brazil's electric supply. The largest private-owned power company is Tractebel

Figure 291: *Itaipu Dam, the world's largest hydroelectric dam by generating capacity.*

Energia. An independent system operator (Operador Nacional do Sistema Elétrico - ((ONS)), responsible for the technical coordination of electricity dispatching and the management of transmission services, and a wholesale market were created in 1998.

During the electricity crisis in 2001Wikipedia:Please clarify, the government launched a program to build 55 gas-fired power stations with a total capacity of 22 GW, but only 19 power stations were built, with a total capacity of 4,012 MW.

Hydropower

Brazil is the third largest hydroelectricity producer in the world after China and Canada. In 2007 hydropower accounted for 83% of Brazilian electricity production. The gross theoretical capability exceeds 3,000 TWh per annum, of which 800 TWh per annum is economically exploitable. In 2004, Brazil produced 321TWh of hydropower.

The installed capacity is 59 GW. Brazil co-owns the Itaipu hydroelectric power plant on the Paraná River located on the border between Brazil and Paraguay, which is the world's second largest operational hydroelectric power plant with installed generation capacity of 14 GW by 20 generating units of 700 MW each.

Due to Brazil's dependence on hydroelectric power and lack of investments in transmission, the reserves were being overused for several years, which led to the dams having a low level of water. Then after another bad year of rain, in June 2001, the government was forced to ration electricity usage, this ended in late 2001. Since then, due to the new rules of the sector, new power lines were built as were new power plants. While the load is even bigger than it was in 2001 the system is much safer.

Nuclear energy

Nuclear energy accounts for about 4% of Brazil's electricity. The nuclear power generation monopoly is owned by Eletronuclear (Eletrobrás Eletronuclear S/A), a wholly owned subsidiary of Eletrobrás. Nuclear energy is produced by two reactors at Angra. It is located at the Central Nuclear Almirante

Figure 292: *Angra Nuclear Power Plant in Angra dos Reis, Rio de Janeiro*

Álvaro Alberto (CNAAA) on the Praia de Itaorna in Angra dos Reis, Rio de Janeiro. It consists of two pressurized water reactors, Angra I, with capacity of 657 MW, connected to the power grid in 1982, and Angra II, with capacity of 1,350 MW, connected in 2000. A third reactor, Angra III, with a projected output of 1,350 MW, is planned to be finished by 2014 and work has been paralyzed due to environmental concerns, but the licenses are being approved and the heavy construction work will start in 2009. By 2025 Brazil plans to build seven more reactors.

In February 2008 President Lula da Silva signed a nuclear cooperation agreement with Argentina.

Solar power

As of June 2018,[1136] according to ONS, total installed capacity of photovoltaic solar was 1.6 GW.

Wind energy

Brazil's gross wind resource potential is estimated to be about 140 GW, of which 30 GW could be effectively transformed into wind power projects. As of June 2018,[1136] according to ONS, total installed capacity was 13.1 GW.

Figure 293: *Wind farm in Parnaíba, Piauí*

Biofuels

Due to its ethanol fuel production, Brazil has sometimes been described as a bio-energy superpower.[1137] Ethanol fuel is produced from sugar cane. Brazil has the largest sugar cane crop in the world, and is the largest exporter of ethanol in the world. With the 1973 oil crisis, the Brazilian government initiated in 1975 the Pró-Álcool program. The Pró-Álcool or *Programa Nacional do Álcool* (National Alcohol Program) was a nationwide program financed by the government to phase out all automobile fuels derived from fossil fuels in favour of ethanol. The program successfully reduced by 10 million the number of cars running on gasoline in Brazil, thereby reducing the country's dependence on oil imports.

The production and consumption of biodiesel is expected to reach to 2% of diesel fuel in 2008 and 5% in 2013.

Brazil's peat reserves are estimated at 25 billion tonnes, the highest in South America. However, no production of peat for fuel has yet been developed. Brazil produces 65 million tonnes of fuelwood per year. The annual production of charcoal is about 6 million tonnes, used in the steel industry. The cogeneration potential of agricultural and livestock residues varies from 4 GW to 47 GW by 2025.

Figure 294: *Ethanol distillery in Piracicaba, São Paulo*

Environmental damages

Oil spill off the coast of Rio de Janeiro

Starting from 8 November 2011 Chevron had spill of crude oil off the southeastern coast of Brazil.[1138] 416,400 liters oil leaked in two weeks from undersea rock well in the Frade oil project 370 km off the Brazilian coast.[1139] Prosecutors in Brazil demand $10.6bn in the legal suit. Chevron's activities are suspended until the cause of the oil spill is clear.[1140]

Critics

The Munduruku indigenous group in Pará state faced problems with the authorities who wanted to build hydropower plants on the Tapajós river without their permission.[1141]

Further reading

- Silvestre, B. S., Dalcol, P. R. T. (2009) Geographical proximity and innovation: Evidences from the Campos Basin oil & gas industrial agglomeration — Brazil. *Technovation*, Vol. 29 (8), pp. 546–561.

Tourism

Tourism in Brazil

Tourism in Brazil is a growing sector and key to the economy of several regions of the country. The country had 6.36 million visitors in 2015, ranking in terms of the international tourist arrivals as the main destination in South America and second in Latin America after Mexico.[1142] Revenues from international tourists reached US$5.8 billion in 2015, continuing a recovery trend from the 2008-2009 economic crisis.

Brazil offers for both domestic and international tourists an ample gamut of options, with natural areas being its most popular tourism product, a combination of ecotourism with leisure and recreation, mainly sun and beach, and adventure travel, as well as historic and cultural tourism. Among the most popular destinations are the Amazon Rainforest, beaches and dunes in the Northeast Region, the Pantanal in the Center-West Region, beaches at Rio de Janeiro and Santa Catarina, cultural and historic tourism in Minas Gerais and business trips to São Paulo city.

In terms of the 2015 Travel and Tourism Competitiveness Index (TTCI), which is a measurement of the factors that make it attractive to develop business in the travel and tourism industry of individual countries, Brazil ranked in the 28st place at the world's level, third in the Americas, after Canada and United States.[1143] Brazil main competitive advantages are its natural resources, which ranked 1st on this criteria out of all countries considered, and ranked 23rd for its cultural resources, due to its many World Heritage sites. The 2013 TTCI report also notes Brazil's main weaknesses: its ground transport infrastructure remains underdeveloped (ranked 129th), with the quality of roads ranking in the 121st place, and quality of air transport infrastructure in 131st; and the country continues to suffer from a lack of price competitiveness (ranked 126th), due in part to high and increasing ticket taxes and airport charges, as well as high and rising prices more generally. Safety and security improved

Figure 295: *Rio de Janeiro, the most visited destination in Brazil by foreign tourists for leisure trips, and second place for business travel.*

significantly between 2008 and 2013, moving from 128th to 73rd place, before slipping to 106th by 2017.

Foreign tourists mainly come from Argentina, Chile, Uruguay, Paraguay, Bolivia, Peru, Ecuador, Colombia, Venezuela, Costa Rica, Mexico, Cuba, Dominican Republic, the United States, Canada, China, South Korea, Japan, Australia, Spain, Italy, France, Germany, the United Kingdom, Greece, Ireland, the Netherlands, Belgium, Switzerland, Portugal, and Russia.

International tourism

Historical international tourism arrivals 1995-2013				
Year	International tourist arrivals (x1000)	Annual growth (%)	Total revenue (millions USD)	Annual growth (%)
1995	1,991	-	972	-
2000	5,313	-	1,810	-
2003	4,133	-	2,479	-
2004	4,794	16.0	3,222	30.0
2005	5,358	11.8	3,861	19.8
2006	5,019	-6.3	4,316	1.1
2007[1144]	5,025	0.1	4,953	14.8

2008[1145,1146]	5,050	0.5	5,780	16.7
2009[1147]	4,802	-4.9	5,305	-8.2
2010	5,161	7.5	5,702	7.5
2011	5,433	5.3	6,555	14.9
2012[1148]	5,677	4.5	6,645	1.3
2013[1149]	5,813	2.4	6,704	0.9
2014	6,430	n/a	n/a	n/a
2015	6,306	n/a	n/a	n/a
2016	6,578	n/a	n/a	n/a

According to the World Tourism Organization (WTO), international travel to Brazil began to grow fast since 2000, particularly during 2004 and 2005. However, in 2006 a slow down took place, and international arrivals have had almost no growth both in 2007 and 2008.[1150] In spite of this trend, revenues from international tourism continued to rise, from USD 3.9 billion in 2005 to USD 4.9 billion in 2007, a one billion dollar increase despite 333 thousand less arrivals. This favorable trend is the result of the strong devaluation of the American dollar against the Brazilian real, which began in 2004, but on the other hand, making Brazil a more expensive international destination.[1151] This trend changed in 2009, when both visitors and revenues fell as a result of the 2008-2009 economic crisis. By 2010, the industry recovered, and arrivals grew above 2006 levels to 5.16 million international visitors, and receipts from these visitors reached USD 5.9 billion. In 2012, the historical record was reached with 5.6 million visitors and US$6.6 billion in receipts.

Despite continuing record breaking of international tourism revenues, the number of Brazilian tourists travelling overseas has been growing steadily since 2003, resulting in a net negative foreign exchange balance, as more money is spent abroad by Brazilian than receipts from international tourist visiting Brazil. Tourism expenditures abroad grew from USD 5.76 billion in 2006, to USD 8.21 billion in 2007, a 42,45% increase, representing a net deficit of USD 3.26 billion in 2007, as compared to USD 1.45 billion in 2006, a 125% increase from the previous year.[1152] This trend is caused by Brazilians taking advantage of the stronger Real to travel and making relatively cheaper expenditures abroad. Brazilian traveling overseas in 2006 represented 3.9% of the country's population.

In 2005, tourism contributed with 3.2% of the country's revenues from exports of goods and services, and represented 7% of direct and indirect employment in the Brazilian economy. In 2006, direct employment in the sector reached 1.87 million people. Domestic tourism is a fundamental market segment for the industry, as 51 million traveled throughout the country in 2005, and direct

Figure 296: *Salvador, capital of Bahia state, is the center of Afro-Brazilian culture, and one of the top destinations by Brazilian nationals and international tourists.*

Figure 297: *Fortaleza, capital of Ceará state, is one of the top destinations for business and also for a holiday on its amazing beaches.*

Figure 298: *Iguazu Falls, Paraná, in Brazil-Argentina border, is the second most popular destination for foreign tourists who come to Brazil for pleasure.*

Figure 299: *São Paulo, the financial capital of Brazil is one of the most sought after places in tourism by having different cultures and races.*

Figure 300: *The colonial city of Ouro Preto, a World Heritage Site, is one of the most popular destinations in Minas Gerais.*

Figure 301: *Chapada Diamantina.*

Tourism in Brazil

Figure 302: *Natal, Rio Grande do Norte.*

revenues from Brazilian tourists reached USD 21.8 billion,[1153] 5.6 times more receipts than international tourists in 2005.

In 2005, Rio de Janeiro, Foz do Iguaçu, São Paulo, Florianópolis, and Salvador were the most visited cities by international tourists for leisure trips. The most popular destinations for business trips were São Paulo, Rio de Janeiro, and Porto Alegre.[1154] In 2006, Rio de Janeiro and Fortaleza were the most popular destinations by national visitors.

	Main destinations visited by international tourists in 2013[1155] Top 15 ranking by number of visitors	
Ranking (2013)	Destination	State
1st	Rio de Janeiro	RJ
2nd	São Paulo	SP
3rd	Foz do Iguaçu	PR
4th	Salvador	BA
5th	Brasília	DF
6th	Porto Alegre	RS
7th	Búzios	RJ
8th	Manaus	AM
9th	Florianópolis	SC

10th	Fortaleza	CE	
11th	Belo Horizonte	MG	
12th	Curitiba	PR	
13th	Natal	RN	
14th	Recife	PE	
15th	Campinas	SP	

Arrivals by country of origin

Most international visitors in 2016 came from Argentina (34.9) and the United States (8.7%). In terms of region of origin, most international visitors came from neighboring South American countries with 3,732,722 visitor (56.7%), mainly from Mercosul. In total, there were 6,578,074 international arrivals. Top international arrivals by country of origin for 2012-2016 are presented in the following table:

Top 20 visitor arrivals to Brazil by country of origin in 2012[1156] - 2016

Ranking 2016	Country of origin	Visitor arrivals 2016	Visitor arrivals 2012	% Total increase/decrease	Ranking 2016	Country of origin	Visitor arrivals 2016	Visitor arrivals 2012	% Total increase/decrease
1	Argentina	2,294,900	1,671,604	37.3%	11	Spain	147,846	180,406	-18.0%
2	United States	570,350	586,463	-2.7%	12	Bolivia	138,106	112,639	22.6%
3	Paraguay	316,714	246,401	28.5%	13	Colombia	135,192	100,324	34.8%
4	Chile	311,813	250,586	24.4%	14	Peru	114,276	91,996	24.2%
5	Uruguay	284,113	253,864	11.9%	15	Mexico	94,609	61,658	53.4%
6	France	263,774	218,626	20.7%	16	Japan	79,754	73,102	9.1%
7	Germany	221,513	258,437	-14.3%	17	Netherlands	72,268	73,133	-1.2%
8	United Kingdom	202,671	155,548	30.3%	18	Canada	70,103	68,462	2.4%
9	Italy	181,493	230,114	-21.1%	19	Switzerland	69,074	69,571	-0.7%
10	Portugal	149,968	168,649	-11.1%	20	Australia	49,809	43,161	15.4%

Visitor arrivals by region of origin in 2016 (Top 4)

1	South America	3,732,722	2,822,519	32.2%	3	North America	735,062	716,583	2.6%
2	Europe	1,606,495	1,652,205	-2.8%	4	Asia	304,786	297,032	2.6%

File:EDUARDO_MURUCI_-_PRAIA_DO_CACHORRO.jpg

Fernando de Noronha Archipelago, Pernambuco.

Comparison with other Latin American destinations

The following is a comparative summary of Brazil's tourism industry key performance indicators as compared with countries considered among the most popular destinations in Latin America, and relevant economic indicators are included to show the relative importance that international tourism has on the economy of the selected countries.

Tourism in Brazil

Selected Caribbean and Latin American countries	Internl. tourist arrivals2012 (x1000)	Internl. tourism receipts 2012 (million USD)	Receipts per arrival 2012 (col 2)/(col 1) (USD)	Arrivals per capita per 1000 pop. (estimated) 2007[1157]	Receipts per capita2005 USD	Revenues as % of exports goods and services 2003	Tourism revenues as % GDP 2012	% Direct & indirect employment in tourism2012	World Ranking Tourism Compet. TTCI 2013	Index value TTCI 2013
Argentina	5,599	4,895	874	115	57	7.4	10.5	9.9	61	4.17
Brazil	5,677	6,645	1,170	26	18	3.2	8.9	8.1	51	4.37
Chile	3,554	2,201	619	151	73	5.3	8.4	8.0	56	4.29
Colombia	2,175	2,351	1,081	26	25	6.6	5.1	5.5	84	3.90
Costa Rica	2,343	2,425	1,035	442	343	17.5	12.5	11.7	47	4.44
Cuba(1)	2,688	2,283	849	188	169	n/d	n/d	n/d	n/d	n/d
Dominican Republic	4,563	4,549	997	408	353	36.2	14.7	13.6	86	3.88
Jamaica	1,986	2,043	1,029	628	530	49.2	25.7	23.8	67	4.08
Mexico	23,403	12,739	544	201	103	5.7	12.4	13.7	44	4.46
Panama	1,606	2,259	1,406	330	211	10.6	10.1	9.6	37	4.54
Peru	2,846	2,657	933	65	41	9.0	9.1	7.8	73	4.00
Uruguay	2,695	2,076	770	525	145	14.2	10.2	9.7	59	4.23

- Notes: **Green** shadow denotes the country with the top indicator. **Yellow** shadow corresponds to Brazilian indicators.

(1) Visitors and receipts for Cuba correspond to 2011..

Tourist visa

Tourist visa requirements have been waived for citizens of Andorra, Argentina, Austria, Bahamas, Barbados, Belarus, Belgium, Bolivia, Bulgaria, Czech Republic, Chile, Colombia, Costa Rica, Croatia, Denmark, Ecuador, Finland, France, Germany, Greece, Guatemala, Guyana, Hong Kong, Hungary, Iceland, Ireland, Israel, Italy, Liechtenstein, Lithuania, Luxembourg, Macau, Malaysia, Malta, Mexico, Monaco, Namibia, Netherlands, New Zealand, Norway, Panama, Paraguay, Peru, Philippines, Poland, Portugal, Romania, Russia, San Marino, Singapore, Slovakia, Slovenia, South Africa, South Korea, Spain, Surinam, Sweden, Switzerland, Thailand, Trinidad & Tobago, Turkey, Ukraine, United Kingdom, Uruguay, Vatican City, Venezuela.

Tourist visas also applies to lecturers at conferences, for visiting relatives and/or friends, unpaid participation in athletic or artistic event or competition (in this case an invitation letter from the sponsoring organization in Brazil is required), and unpaid participation in a scientific/academic seminar or conference sponsored by a research or academic institution (in this case an invitation letter from the sponsoring organization in Brazil is required).[1158]

Paleontological Tourism

Geopark Paleorrota is the main area of geotourism in Rio Grande do Sul and one of the most important in Brazil. With 83,000 km² inside 281,000 km² of the state, where many fossils of the Permian and Triassic period, with ages ranging between **210** and **290** million years ago, when there were only the continent Pangaea.

In the region Metropolitan Porto Alegre there are 5 museums to visit. In Paleorrota Geopark there are 7 museums, the Palaeobotanical Garden in Mata and the Paleontological Sites of Santa Maria to be visited. The BR-287, nicknamed *Highway of Dinosaurs*, crosses 17 of 41 municipalities of the geopark.

Domestic tourism

Domestic tourism is a key market segment for the tourism industry in Brazil. In 2005, 51 million Brazilian nationals made ten times more trips than foreign tourists and spent five times more money than their international counterparts. The main destination states in 2005 were São Paulo (27.7%), Minas Gerais (10.8%), Rio de Janeiro (8.4%), Bahia (7.4%), and Santa Catarina (7.2%).

Figure 303: *Arraial do Cabo, Rio de Janeiro.*

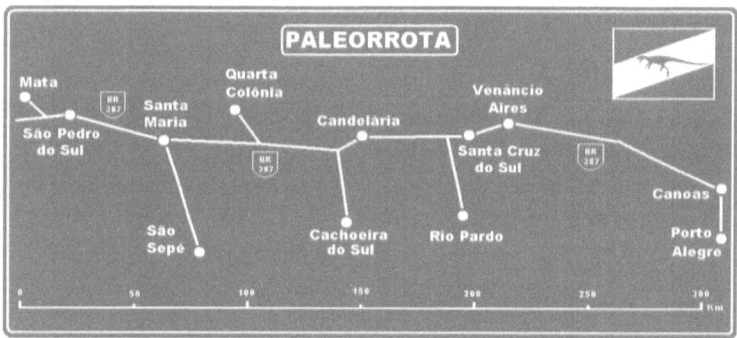

Figure 304: *Tourism in Paleorrota Geopark*

The top three states by trip origin were São Paulo (35.7%), Minas Gerais (13.6%).

In terms of tourism revenues, the top earners by state were São Paulo (16.4%) and Bahia (11.7%). For 2005, the three main trip purposes were visiting friends and family (53.1%), sun and beach (40.8%), and cultural tourism (12.5%).

Figure 305: *Amazon Rainforest in Manaus, is a popular ecotourism destination.*

Tourism by regions of Brazil

Southeast Region

- Rio de Janeiro
- **Rio de Janeiro State:** Angra dos Reis, Paraty, Resende, Visconde de Mauá, Itatiaia National Park, Petrópolis, Vassouras, Teresópolis, Serra dos Órgãos, Nova Friburgo, Saquarema, Arraial do Cabo, Cabo Frio, Búzios, Ilha Grande
- **Espírito Santo:** Vitória, Vila Velha, Guarapari, Anchieta, Piúma, Marataízes, Domingos Martins, Santa Teresa
- **Minas Gerais:** Belo Horizonte, Sabará, Ouro Preto, Congonhas, Mariana, Lavras, São João del Rei, Tiradentes, Diamantina, Araxá, Caxambu, São Lourenço, São Thomé das Letras, Caparaó National Park, Pico da Bandeira, Serra do Cipó National Park
- São Paulo
- **São Paulo State:** São Sebastião, Ilhabela, Boiçucanga, Ferraz de Vasconcelos, Guararema, Guarujá, Santos, Iguape, Cananéia, São Vicente, Campos do Jordão, Campinas, Ribeirão Preto, São José dos Campos, Sorocaba, Americana, Araçatuba, Araraquara, Araras, Atibaia, Barretos, Birigüi, Botucatu, Bragança Paulista, Itu, Jaú

Figure 306: *Santinho Beach, at Santa Catarina island, Florianópolis. The beaches in Santa Catarina's littoral are one of the main destination for Argentine tourists.*

Figure 307: *Botanical Garden of Curitiba, in Curitiba, Paraná.*

Figure 308: *Snorkeling in the city of Bonito, Mato Grosso do Sul. The rivers in the region are known for their crystal clear waters.*

Southern Region

- **Paraná:** Curitiba, Morretes, Antonina, Paranaguá, Ilha do Mel, Superagui National Park, Foz do Iguaçu, Iguaçu Falls, Guaratuba
- **Santa Catarina:** Florianópolis, Ilha de Santa Catarina, Joinville, Blumenau, Itapema, Itajaí, Balneário Camboriú
- **Rio Grande do Sul:** Porto Alegre, Torres, Aparados da Serra National Park, Serra Gaúcha, Canela, Gramado, Paleorrota

Center-West Region

- **Distrito Federal:** Brasília
- **Goiás:** Goiânia, Chapada dos Veadeiros National Park, Pirenópolis, Goiás Velho, Caldas Novas, Emas National Park, Araguaia River
- **Mato Grosso:** Cuiabá, The Pantanal, Chapada dos Guimarães National Park, Tangará da Serra Waterfall Leap of the Clouds (Salto das Nuvens)[1159], Barra do Garças, Alta Floresta, Cáceres, Barão de Melgaço, Poconé
- **Mato Grosso do Sul:** Campo Grande, Corumbá, Bonito, Ponta Porã, Aquidauana, Coxim, Jardim

Northeast Region

- **Bahia:** Salvador, Cachoeira, Lençóis, Morro de São Paulo, Ilhéus, Itacaré, Porto Seguro, Arraial d'Ajuda, Trancoso, Chapada Diamantina National Park, Abrolhos Marine National Park
- **Pernambuco:** Recife, Olinda, Itamaracá, Igarassu, Caruaru, Porto de Galinhas, New Jerusalem, Garanhuns, Triunfo, Fernando de Noronha, Catimbau Valley, Petrolina
- **Ceará:** Fortaleza, Aracati, Canoa Quebrada, Jericoacoara, Tatajuba, Camocim, Sobral, Baturité, Ubajara National Park, Juazeiro do Norte
- **Sergipe:** Aracaju, Laranjeiras, São Cristóvão, Estância, Propriá
- **Alagoas:** Maceió, Maragogi, Penedo, Barra de São Miguel, Paripueira, Porto de Pedras
- **Paraíba:** João Pessoa, Campina Grande, Cabedelo, Ingá, Baía da Traição, Sousa
- **Rio Grande do Norte:** Natal, Mossoró, Tibau do Sul, Tibau, Parnamirim, Touros, São Miguel do Gostoso, Galinhos, Caicó, Macau, Martins, Maxaranguape, Cape São Roque
- **Piauí:** Teresina, Sete Cidades National Park, Parnaíba, Serra da Capivara National Park
- **Maranhão:** São Luís, Lençóis Maranhenses National Park, Alcântara, Imperatriz, Carolina

North Region

- **Amazonas:** Manaus, Parintins, Tefé, Mamirauá
- **Pará:** Belém, Ilha de Marajó, Santarém
- **Tocantins:** Palmas, Ilha do Bananal, Natividade
- **Amapá:** Macapá, Oiapoque
- **Roraima:** Boa Vista, Monte Roraima
- **Rondônia:** Porto Velho, Guajará-Mirim, Guaporé Valley
- **Acre:** Rio Branco, Xapuri, Brasiléia, Assis Brasil

External links

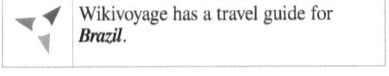

Wikivoyage has a travel guide for *Brazil*.

- Brazilian Tourism Portal[1160] by Embratur (Brazilian Tourist Board)
- New York Times Travel Guides: Brazil[1161]

Science and technology

Science and technology in Brazil

Science and technology in Brazil has entered the international arena in recent decades. The central agency for science and technology in Brazil is the Ministry of Science and Technology, which includes the CNPq and Finep. This ministry also has direct supervision over the National Institute for Space Research (Instituto Nacional de Pesquisas Espaciais - INPE), the National Institute of Amazonian Research (Instituto Nacional de Pesquisas da Amazônia - INPA), and the National Institute of Technology (Instituto Nacional de Tecnologia - INT). The ministry is also responsible for the Secretariat for Computer and Automation Policy (Secretaria de Política de Informática e Automação - SPIA), which is the successor of the SEI. The Ministry of Science and Technology, which the Sarney government created in March 1985, was headed initially by a person associated with the nationalist ideologies of the past. Although the new minister was able to raise the budget for the science and technology sector, he remained isolated within the government and had no influence on policy making for the economy.

With the new ministry, the science and technology agencies increased in size but lost some of their former independence and flexibility, and they became more susceptible to patronage politics. Most of the resources of the CNPq were channeled to fellowship programs procedures for quality control and no mechanisms to make the fellows active in the country's science and technology institutions. New groups competed for resources and control of the country's agencies of science, technology, and higher education. These groups included political parties, unionized university professors and employees, scientific societies, and special interest groups within the scientific and technological community. The SBPC (Brazilian Society for Scientific Development) shed its image as a semi-autonomous association of scientists to become an active lobbyist for more public resources and the protection of national technology from international competition.[1162]

Figure 309: *The airplane Embraer 190 produced by Brazilian aircraft company Embraer.*

Figure 310: *Laboratório Nacional de Luz Síncrotron in the city of Campinas.*

History

Brazilian science effectively began in the first decades of the 19th century, when the Portuguese royal family, headed by D. João VI, arrived in Rio de Janeiro, escaping from the Napoleon's army invasion of Portugal in 1807. Like almost all territories and regions of the New World, Brazil was a Portuguese colony, without universities, and a few cultural and scientific organizations. The former American colonies of the Spanish Empire, although having a largely illiterate population like Brazil, Portugal and Spain, had, however,

Science and technology in Brazil 591

Figure 311: *Internal view of Embraer 120 airplane produced in the city of São José dos Campos.*

Figure 312: *Fiocruz Institute in the city of Rio de Janeiro.*

a number of universities since the 16th century. This may have been a deliberate policy of the Portuguese colonial power, because they feared that the appearance of educated Brazilian classes would boost nationalism and aspirations toward political independence, as it had happened in the United States and several Latin American former Spanish colonies. However, throughout the centuries of Portuguese rule, Brazilian students were allowed and even encouraged to enroll at higher education in mainland Portugal. In addition, mainland Portugal's population at the time was also largely illiterate and had for most of those period a single university, the University of Coimbra, which

Figure 313: *IPT - Instituto de Pesquisas Tecnológicas de São Paulo.*

Figure 314: *Rocket VSB-30 is assembled with its load util.*

Science and technology in Brazil

Figure 315: *Center of Biological Sciences of Federal University of Viçosa.*

Figure 316: *Technology pool in Campinas.*

educated Portuguese people from all the Empire, including from the colony of Brazil.

The first firm attempts of having a Brazilian science establishment were made around 1783, with the expedition of Portuguese naturalist Alexandre Rodrigues Ferreira, who was sent by Portugal's prime minister, the Marquis of Pombal, to explore and identify Brazilian fauna, flora and geology. His collections, however, were lost to the French, when Napoleon invaded Portugal, and were transported to Paris by Étienne Geoffroy Saint-Hilaire. In 1772, even before the establishment of the Science Academy of Lisbon (1779), one of the first learned societies of both Brazil and the Portuguese Empire was founded in Rio de Janeiro - it was the *Sociedade Scientifica*, but lasted only until 1794. Also, in 1797, the first botanic institute was founded in Salvador, Bahia. During the late 18th century, the *Real Academia de Artilharia, Fortificação e Desenho* of Rio de Janeiro was created in 1792 through a decree issued by the Portuguese authorities as a higher education school for the teaching of the sciences and engineering. Both the engineering schools of the Rio de Janeiro Federal University and the Military Institute of Engineering were created and developed from the oldest engineering school of Brazil which is also one of the oldest in Latin America.

D. João VI gave impetus to all these accoutrements of European civilization to Brazil. In a short period (between 1808 and 1810), the government founded the Royal Naval Academy and the Royal Military Academy (both military schools), the Biblioteca Nacional, the Rio de Janeiro Botanical Garden, the Medico-Chirurgical School of Bahia, currently known as Faculdade de Medicina under harbour of Universidade Federal da Bahia and the Medico-Chirurgical School of Rio de Janeiro (Faculdade de Medicina of Universidade Federal do Rio de Janeiro).

Notable scientific expeditions organized by Brazilians were rare, the most significant one being that of Martim Francisco de Andrada e Silva and José Bonifácio de Andrada e Silva, in 1819.

During the Brazilian Empire

After independence from Portugal, declared by the King's son in 1822, D. Pedro I (who became the new country's first Emperor), the policies concerning higher learning, science and technology in Brazil came to a relative standstill. In the first two decades of the century, science in Brazil was mostly carried out by temporary scientific expeditions by European naturalists, such as Charles Darwin, Maximilian zu Wied-Neuwied, Carl von Martius, Johann Baptist von Spix, Alexander Humboldt, Augustin Saint-Hilaire, Baron Grigori Ivanovitch Langsdorff, Friedrich Sellow, Fritz Müller, Hermann von Ihering, Émil Goeldi and others. This science was mostly descriptive of the fantastic Brazilian biodiversity of its flora and fauna, and also its geology, geography and anthropology, and until the creation of the National Museum, the specimens were mostly removed to European institutions.

In the educational area, a number of higher education institutions were founded in the 19th century, but for decades to come, most Brazilian students, still studied at European universities, such as the ancient University of Coimbra, in Portugal.

Things started to change after 1841, when the eldest son of D. Pedro I, Emperor D. Pedro II came to the throne when he was 15 years old. In the next 50 years, Brazil enjoyed a stable constitutional monarchy. D. Pedro II was an enlightened monarch who favored the arts, literature, science and technology and had extensive international contacts in these areas. The mainstay of Brazilian science and the seat of its first research laboratories was the National Museum (*Museu Nacional*) in Rio de Janeiro, in existence until today. D. Pedro developed a strong personal interest and selected and invited many august European scientific personalities, such as von Ihering and Goeldi, to work in Brazil. He and his ministers, courtesans and senators often attended scientific conferences in the Museum. There, the first laboratory of physiology was founded in 1880, under João Baptista de Lacerda and Louis Couty. Unfortunately, the creation of research universities and institutes would only occur on the beginning of the 20th century - a long delay for the education, science and technology in Brazil.

Organization

Brazil today has a well-developed organization of science and technology. Basic research is largely carried out in public universities and research centers and institutes, and some in private institutions, particularly in non-profit non-governmental organizations. More than 90% of funding for basic research comes from governmental sources. Brazil is one of the three countries in Latin America with an operational Synchrotron Laboratory, a research facility for physics, chemistry, materials science and life sciences.

Applied research, technology and engineering are also largely carried out in the university sector and research centres, contrary to trends in more developed countries such as the United States of America, South Korea, Germany, Japan, etc.

Figure 317: *Aerial view of USP, located in São Paulo.*

Figure 318: *A Brazilian-made Embraer of Brazilian Armed Forces.*

Figure 319: *A Brazilian-made Avibras ASTROS-II SS-30 multiple rocket systems on Tectran 6x6 AV-LMU trucks stand in firing position while being displayed as part of a demonstration of Saudi Arabian equipment.*

Sources of funding

Brazilian funding for research, development and innovation comes from six main sources:

1. Government (federal, state and municipal) sources. There are a number of state organizations which were created mostly in the 1950s specifically for directly promoting and funding R&D&I, such as the National Research Council (CNPq), which is now named *Conselho Nacional de Desenvolvimento Científico e Tecnológico* and the National Agency for Financing Studies and Researches (FINEP), both a part of the Ministry of Science and Technology (MCT). MCT is a relatively novel ministry, having been created in 1990. Before this, CNPq was the only research granting institution at federal level, working directly under the Presidency of Republic. At state level, almost all states have founded their own public foundations for support of R&D&I, following the pioneering (and highly successful) example of São Paulo state, which created the Fundação de Amparo à Pesquisa do Estado de São Paulo (FAPESP) in 1962. Usually these foundations are guaranteed by changes in the state constitutions, along the 1980s and 1990s.
2. Indirect funding through the budgets of public and private universities, institutes and centers. Some universities, such as UNICAMP, have their

own internal agencies, foundations and funds set apart and managed with the purpose of supporting R&D&I by their faculties and students.
3. Public companies, such as Embrapa (Brazilian Enterprise for Agricultural Research). Their source of revenue is the government itself (via budgetary allocations by ministries and state secretaries) and investment of a part of products and services sold.
4. Industrial, commercial and services private companies, usually for their own R&D&I centers, or via some fiscal benefit (tax exemption laws), such as the Informatics Law.
5. National private and non-for-profit associations and foundations, via statutory mechanisms or donations by private individuals or companies. An example is the Banco do Brasil Foundation.
6. Funding by other nations, international organizations and multilateral institutions, such as Rockefeller Foundation, Ford Foundation, Inter-American Development Bank, World Bank, UNESCO, UNDP, World Health Organization, World Wildlife Foundation, Kellogg Foundation, Bill & Melinda Gates Foundation, US National Science Foundation, Volkswagen Foundation, just to name a few of the more important ones in the history of Brazilian science and technology.

Trends in science and technology

Creation of social organizations

Brazil's public research institutes and universities follow rigid rules that tend to make them difficult to manage. States may opt to develop their own research institutes and university systems but, as all laws and regulations are adopted at federal level, they all have to follow the same rules and regulations. Thus, they all come up against the same hurdles. These include extensive bureaucratic structures, an obligation to recruit staff, academic or otherwise, from among public servants, analogous career ladders and salary systems, an irregular flow of funds, overly complex procurement procedures and powerful unions in the civil service. A structural alternative was developed in 1998, with the creation of social organizations. These private, non-profit entities manage public research facilities under contract to federal agencies. They have the autonomy to hire (or fire) staff, contract services, buy equipment, choose the topics and objectives of scientific or technological research and sign research contracts with private companies. The flexibility accorded to these social organizations and their management style have made them a success story in Brazilian science. As of 2015, there were six such organizations:

- Institute for Pure and Applied Mathematics (IMPA);
- Institute for the Sustainable Development of the Amazon Forest (IDSM);

Science and technology in Brazil

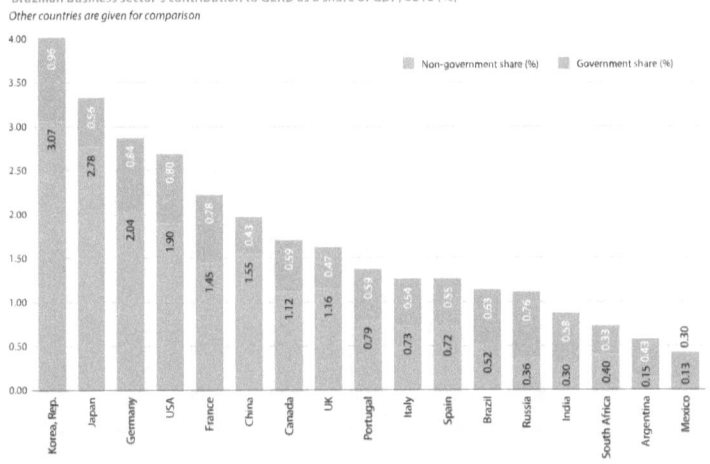

Figure 320: *Brazilian business sector's contribution to GERD as a share of GDP, 2012. Source: UNESCO Science Report: towards 2030 (2015), Figure 8.4*

- National Centre for Research in Energy and Materials (CNPEM);
- Centre for Management and Strategic Studies (CGEE);
- National Teaching and Research Network (RNP); and
- Brazilian Research and Industrial Innovation Enterprise (Embrapii).

Embrapii is the most recent. It was established by the federal government in 2013 to stimulate innovation through a system of calls for proposals; only institutions and enterprises deemed eligible may respond to these calls, thus speeding up the whole process and offering applicants a greater chance of success; Embrapii was due to be assessed in late 2015.

Incentive measures and targets

In the late 1990s, as economic reforms took hold, legislation was adopted to stimulate private R&D. Arguably the most important milestone was the National Law on Innovation. Soon after its approval in 2006, the Ministry of Science, Technology and Innovation published a *Plan of Action for Science, Technology and Innovation* (MoSTI, 2007) establishing four main targets to be attained by 2010:

- Raise gross domestic expenditure on R&D (GERD) from 1.02% to 1.50% of GDP;
- Raise business expenditure on R&D from 0.51% to 0.65% of GDP;

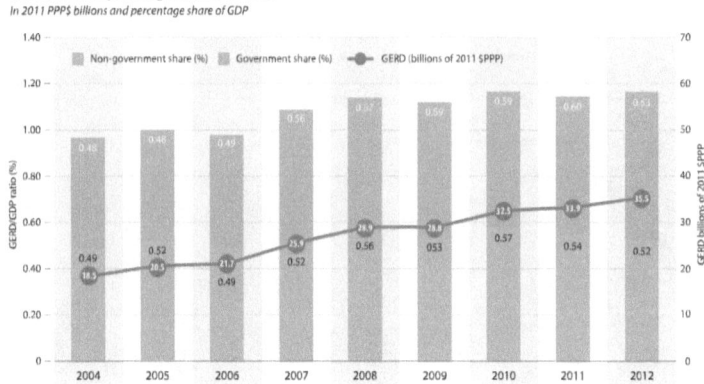

Figure 321: *GERD in Brazil by funding sector, 2004–2012. Source: UNESCO Science Report: towards 2030 (2015), Figure 8.3*

- Increase the number of scholarships (all levels) granted by the two federal agencies, the National Research Council (CNPq) and the Foundation for Co-ordinating Capacity-building of Personnel in Higher Education (Capes), from 100 000 to 150 000; and
- Foster science and technology for social development by establishing 400 vocational and 600 new distance-learning centres, by expanding the Mathematics Olympiad to 21 million participants and by granting 10 000 scholarships at the secondary level.

By 2012, GERD stood at 1.15% of GDP and business expenditure on R&D at 0.52% of GDP. Neither of these targets had thus been reached by this time. Concerning tertiary scholarships, CNPq and Capes easily reached the target for PhDs (31,000 by 2010 and 42,000 by 2013) but fell short of reaching the target for tertiary scholarships as a whole (141,000 by 2010). The target of the National Plan for Graduate Education 2005–2010 was for 16 000 PhDs to be granted by the end of the plan period. Since the actual number of PhDs granted stood at 11 300 in 2010 and less than 14 000 in 2013, this target has not been reached either, despite the fact that almost 42 000 federal PhD scholarships were granted in 2013.

On the other hand, the targets related to fostering a popular science culture have been partly reached. For instance, in 2010, over 19 million students took part in the Brazilian Mathematics Olympiad for Public Schools, up from 14

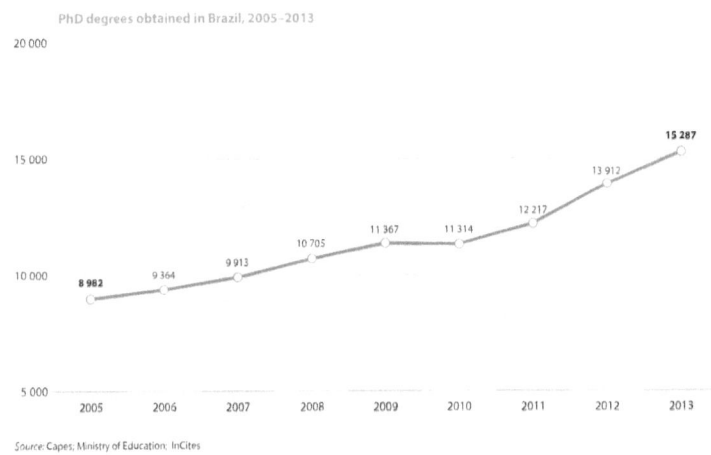

Figure 322: *PhD degrees obtained in Brazil, 2005–2013. Source: UNESCO Science Report: towards 2030 (2015), Figure 8.2*

million in 2006. However, since then, the number of participants has tended to stagnate. Up until 2011, it was looking as if the targets for distance learning and vocational education might be reached but, as of 2015, there had been little progress.

Financial investment

Brazil's economic boom between 2004 and 2012 translated into higher government and business spending on research and development (R&D). Gross domestic expenditure on R&D (GERD) almost doubled to PPP$35.5 billion (in 2011 dollars). Most of this growth occurred between 2004 and 2010, when GERD climbed from 0.97% to 1.16% of GDP. In 2012, GERD stood at 1.15% of GDP. Since 2010, the government sector alone has been driving up R&D intensity, since the non-government contribution has actually declined from 0.57% to 0.52% of GDP (2012). Preliminary figures for 2013 indicate slight growth in government spending and a constant contribution from the business sector (relative to GDP). Business research expenditure is likely to contract from 2015 onwards until the economy shows signs of recovery. Even the most optimistic analysts do not expect this to happen before 2016. Fixed capital investment in Brazil is expected to decline further in 2015, especially in the manufacturing sector. This trend will certainly affect industrial research spending. The Petrobrás crisis is expected to have a major impact on investment in R&D, since it alone has accounted for about 10% of the country's

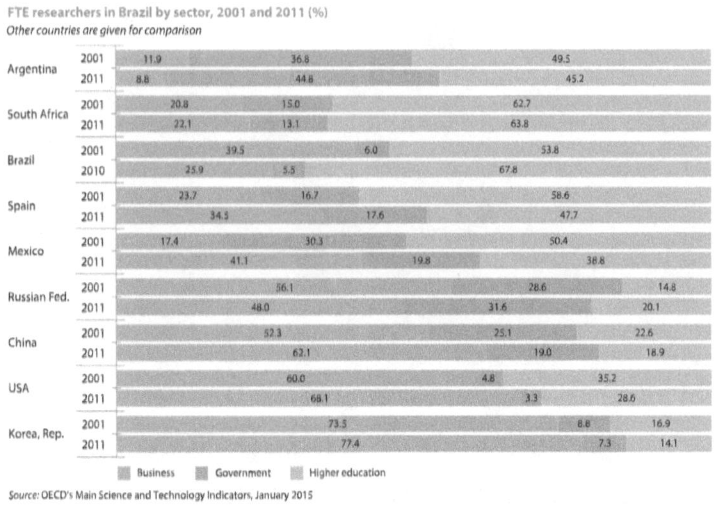

FTE researchers in Brazil by sector, 2001 and 2011 (%)
Other countries are given for comparison

Country	Year	Business	Government	Higher education	
Argentina	2001	11.9	36.8	49.5	
	2011	8.8	44.8	45.2	
South Africa	2001	20.8	15.0	62.7	
	2011	22.1	13.1	63.8	
Brazil	2001	39.5	6.0	53.8	
	2010	25.9	5.5	67.8	
Spain	2001	23.7	16.7	58.6	
	2011	34.3	17.6	47.7	
Mexico	2001	17.4	30.3	50.4	
	2011	41.1	19.8	38.8	
Russian Fed.	2001	56.1	28.6	14.8	
	2011	48.0	31.6	20.1	
China	2001	52.3	25.1	22.6	
	2011	62.1	19.0	18.9	
USA	2001	60.0	4.8	35.2	
	2011	68.1	3.3	28.6	
Korea, Rep.	2001	73.5	8.8	16.9	
	2011	77.4	7.3	14.1	

Source: OECD's Main Science and Technology Indicators, January 2015

Figure 323: *Researchers in Brazil by sector of employment, 2001 and 2011. Source: UNESCO Science Report: towards 2030 (2015), Figure 8.6*

annual fixed capital investment in recent years. The cuts to the federal budget announced in 2015 and other austerity measures should also affect government spending on R&D.

Almost all of non-government expenditure on R&D comes from private firms (private universities performing only a fraction of it). Between 2010 and 2013, this expenditure declined from 49% to 42% of domestic expenditure on research, according to preliminary government data. This trend is likely to last for some time. The business sector will, thus, have no chance of devoting 0.90% of GDP to R&D by 2014.

Brazil's GERD/GDP ratio remains well below that of both advanced economies and such dynamic emerging market economies as China and, especially, the Republic of Korea. At the same time, it is quite comparable to the more stagnant developed economies such as Italy or Spain and other major emerging markets like the Russian Federation. It is also well ahead of other Latin American countries.

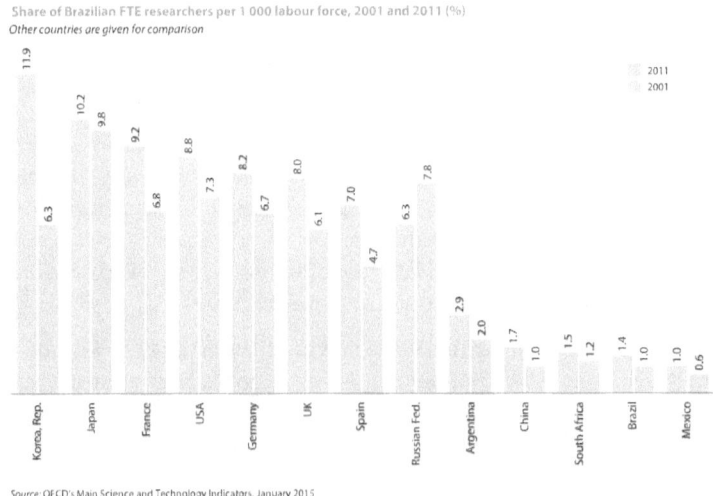

Figure 324: *Share of Brazilian researchers per 1000 labour force, 2001 and 2011. Source: UNESCO Science Report: towards 2030 (2015), Figure 8.5*

Industrial research

Trends in innovation activity

Between 2001 and 2010, there was a sharp decline in the share of research personnel employed by the business sector, from 40% (2001) to 26% (2010). This is contrary to the trend observed in most developed and major emerging countries. It partly reflects the expansion of research in higher education and partly the anaemic growth of industrial R&D.

According to a 2014 survey by the UNESCO Institute for Statistics of innovative manufacturing firms in 65 countries, 85% of Brazilian firms are still at the stage of acquiring machinery, equipment and software to enable them to innovate. Among the other BRICS countries (Russian Federation, India, China and South Africa), the percentage varies between 64% and 71%. Some 17% of Brazilian firms conduct research and development in house, according to the survey, compared to 19% of Russian firms, 35% of Indian firms, 54% of South African firms and 63% of Chinese firms. Brazil is also the BRICS country which outsources research the least (7% of innovative firms), compared to one in ten in India and one in five in the other BRICS. Brazil also trails other Latin American countries. A much higher percentage of firms report in-house research and development in Costa Rica (76%), Argentina (72%), Mexico (43%), El Salvador (42%), Ecuador (35%) and Colombia (22%). Only 6%

of Brazilian manufacturing firms collaborate with universities to develop innovative products and processes, a lower ratio than in Mexico (7%), Colombia (11%), Argentina and Cuba (15%) and, above all, Costa Rica (35%).

The tendency for research to flow from the public to the private sector is confirmed by Ruben Sinisterra, a researcher at the Federal University of Minas Gerais who has been developing drugs to alleviate hypertension. Brazilian universities now have the capacity to develop nanoscale materials for drug delivery, he says, but 'our domestic pharmaceutical companies don't have internal capabilities in research and development, so we have to work with them to push new products and processes out to market'.

In 2017, Brazil has ranked 16th in the field of nanotechnology by ISI indexed nano-articles index with 2,948 articles. According to StatNano's ranking, three of Brazil's top universities in the field of nanotechnology in 2017 are: Universidade Estadual Paulista, Federal University of Rio Grande do Sul and Universidade Federal de Minas Gerais.

Innovation activity ebbed in Brazil between 2008 and 2013, according to a survey of firms by the Brazilian Institute of Geography and Statistics (IBGE). The 2013 survey covered all public and private firms in the extractive and transformative sectors, as well as firms in the services sector involving technology. The drop in innovation was most noticeable in telecommunications, both as regards the production of goods (-18.2%) and services (-16.9%). It is the larger companies which seem to have reduced their innovative activities by the biggest margin between 2008 and 2011. Among companies with 500 or more employees, the share of those involved in developing new products declined from 54.9% to 43.0% over this period. A comparison of IBGE's innovation surveys over the periods 2004–2008 and 2009–2011 reveals that the 2008 crisis has had a negative impact on the innovative activities of most Brazilian firms. 'Since 2011, the economic situation in Brazil has further deteriorated, especially in the industrial sector. Thus, it can be expected that the next innovation survey [in 2018] will show even lower levels of innovative activity in Brazil.

One reason for the drop in public and private investment in research is the economic slowdown. After peaking at 7.5% annual growth in 2010, the economy slowed before dipping into recession in 2015 (-3.7% growth). The government has been forced to adopt austerity measures and is now less able to collect revenue through the sectorial funds, since company profits are down in many quarters. Industrial output declined by 2.8% between November and December 2014 and by 3.2% over the entire year. The most recent data indicate that 2014–2015 may turn out to be the worst years in decades for industry, especially for the transformation subsector of the manufacturing industry'.

The economic slowdown was triggered by weaker international commodities markets, coupled with the perverse effects of economic policies designed to fuel consumption. For instance, Petrobrás artificially depressed petrol prices to control inflation between 2011 and 2014, under the influence of the government, its major stockholder. This in turn depressed ethanol prices, making ethanol uneconomic to produce. The ethanol industry was forced to close plants and cut back on its investment in research. Petrobrás' low pricing policy ended up eating into its own revenue, forcing it to cut back its own investment in oil and gas exploration.

The roots of the problem go deeper, though, than the current recession. Brazil's long-standing import substitution policy has protected locally produced goods from foreign competition, discouraging local businesses from investing heavily in research and development, as they are only competing with similar non-innovative companies operating within the same protectionist system. The consequence of this policy has been a gradual decline in Brazil's share of global trade in recent decades, especially when it comes to exports of industrial goods. The trend has even accelerated in the past few years. Between 2004 and 2013, the share of exports dropped from 14.6% to 10.8% of GDP, despite the commodities boom, a trend that cannot be explained solely by the unfavourable exchange rate', asserts the report.

Basic commodities make up a growing proportion of Brazilian exports. Commodities peaked at 50.8% of all exports in the first half of 2014, up from 29.3% in 2005. Just one-third of goods (34.5%) were manufactured in 2014, a sharp drop from 55.1% in 2005. Within manufactured exports, only 6.8% could be considered high-tech, compared to 41.0% with a low-tech content (up from 36.8% in 2012).

Another factor in the drop in investment is that modern industrial development in Brazil is constrained by a lack of modern infrastructure, especially in logistics and electric power generation, along with cumbersome regulations relating to business registration, taxation or bankruptcy, all resulting in a high cost of doing business. Dubbed the Brazil Cost (*Custo Brasil*), this phenomenon is affecting the ability of Brazilian businesses to compete internationally and pursue innovation.

Information technology

Companies such as Motorola, Samsung, Nokia and IBM have established large R&D centres in Brazil, beginning with the IBM Research Center in the 1970s. One incentive has been the Informatics Law, which exempts from certain taxes up to 5% of the gross revenue of high technology manufacturing companies in the fields of telecommunications, computers, digital electronics, etc. The Informatics Law has attracted annually more than $1.5 billion of investment in Brazilian R&D. Multinational companies have also discovered that some products and technologies designed and developed by Brazilians have a nice competitivity and are appreciated by other countries, such as automobiles, aircraft, software, fiber optics, electric appliances, and so on.

During the 1980s, Brazil pursued a policy of protectionism in computing.Companies and administrations were required to use Brazilian software and hardware, with imports subject to governmental authorization.This encouraged the growth of Brazilian companies but, in spite of their development of products like MSX clones and SOX Unix, the Brazilian consumers of computing were suffering from lesser offerings compared to foreign competitors.The government little by little authorized more and more imports until the barriers were removed.

In 2002, Brazil staged the world's first 100% electronic election with over 90% of results in within 2 hours. The system is particularly suited to a country with relatively high illiteracy rates, since it flashes up a photograph of the candidate before a vote is confirmed. Citizens could download a desktop module that relayed the votes to their homes in realtime faster than the news networks could get them out.

In 2005, President Luiz Inácio Lula da Silva launched a "people's computer" to foster digital inclusion, with government finance available and a fixed minimum configuration. Having rejected the Microsoft operating system (Windows XP Starter Edition), it is being shipped with a Brazilian-configured Linux system offering basic functions such as word processing and internet browsing. Plans to make cheap internet access available have not yet come to fruition. In 2008, the Brazilian Government under Lula da Silva, founded the CEITEC, the first and only semiconductor company in Latin America.[1163]

Government research priorities

The lion's share of government expenditure on R&D goes to universities, as in most countries. This level of spending increased slightly from 58% to 61% of total government funding of R&D between 2008 and 2012. Among specific sectors, agriculture comes next, in a reflection of the sector's relevance for Brazil, the second-largest foodproducing country in the world after the USA. Brazilian agricultural productivity has risen constantly since the 1970s, due to the greater use of innovative technology and processes. Industrial R&D comes third, followed by health and infrastructure, other sectors having shares of 1% or lower of government expenditure. With some exceptions, the distribution of government spending on R&D in 2012 is similar to that in 2000. After a sharp increase in industrial technology from 1.4% to 6.8% between 2000 and 2008, its share of government expenditure declined to 5.9% in 2012. The

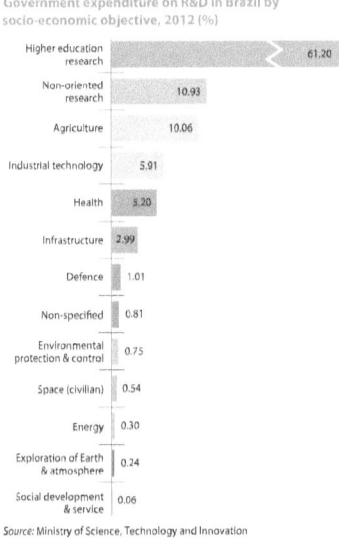

Figure 325: *Brazilian government expenditure on R&D in Brazil by socio-economic objective, 2012. Source: UNESCO Science Report: towards 2030 (2015), Figure 8.7*

share of space science and technology (civilian) has been pursuing a downward spiral from a high of 2.3% in 2000. Defence research spending had been curtailed from 1.6% to 0.6% between 2000 and 2008 but has since rebounded to 1.0%. Research into energy has also declined from 2.1% (2000) to just 0.3% (2012). Overall, though, the allocation of government R&D spending seems to be relatively stable.

In May 2013, the Brazilian administrative body Redetec contracted the Argentine company INVAP to build a multipurpose nuclear reactor in Brazil for research and the production of radioisotopes employed in nuclear medicine, agriculture and environmental management. INVAP has already built a similar reactor for Australia. The multipurpose reactor is expected to be operational by 2018. It will be based at the Marine Technology Centre in São Paulo, with the Brazilian company Intertechne building some of the infrastructure.

Brazil's ambitions for biodiesel caught the headlines in the late 2000s when global energy and food prices spiked but energy-related industries have always had a high profile in Brazil. The state-controlled oil giant Petrobrás registers more patents than any other individual company in Brazil. Moreover, electricity-producing companies are directed by law to invest a given percentage of their revenue in R&D. Although energy is a key economic sector, the

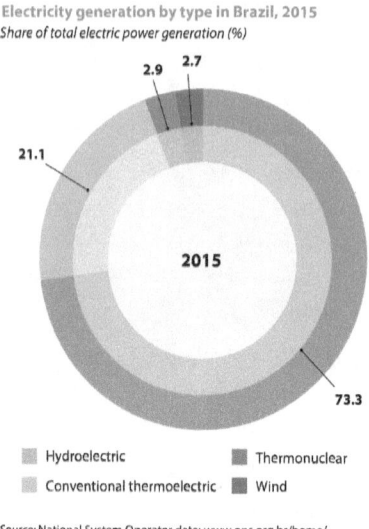

Figure 326: *Electricity generation by type in Brazil, 2015. Source: UNESCO Science Report: towards 2030 (2015), Figure 9.8*

government cut back its spending on energy research from 2.1% to 1.1% of the total between 2000 and 2008 and again to 0.3% in 2012. Renewable energy sources have been the primary victim of these cuts, as public investment has increasingly turned towards deep-sea oil and gas exploration off Brazil's southeast coast. One area that has been directly affected by this is trend is the ethanol industry, which has had to close plants and cut back its own investment in R&D. Part of the ethanol industry's woes have resulted from Petrobrás' pricing policies. Under the influence of the government, its major stockholder, Petrobrás artificially depressed petrol prices between 2011 and 2014 to control inflation. This in turn depressed ethanol prices, making ethanol uneconomic to produce. This policy ended up eating into Petrobrás' own revenue, forcing it to cut back its investment in oil and gas exploration. As Petrobrás alone is responsible for about 10% of all fixed capital investment in Brazil, this trend, along with the corruption scandal shaking the company since 2014, will certainly have ramifications for Brazil's overall investment in R&D.

Brazil generates nearly three-quarters (73%) of its electricity from hydropower. This contribution was as high as four-fifths in 2010 but the share of hydropower has been eroded by a combination of declining rainfall and ageing hydroelectric plants, many of which date back to the 1960s and 1970s. Intensive use of thermoelectric power plants operating on fossil fuels has compensated for much of the loss, since the share of new sources of renewable energy, such as solar and wind, in the energy mix remains small. Moreover, although Brazil has made great strides in the use of bioethanol in transportation, there has been little focus on research and innovation in energy generation, be it in terms of developing new sources of energy or improving energy efficiency. In light of the foregoing, there is little reason to expect public investment in energy R&D to rebound to the levels seen at the turn of the century that would rebuild Brazil's international competitiveness in this field.

Space science and technology have been a government priority for decades. In the late 1980s and 1990s, Brazil invested almost US$1 billion in developing space infrastructure around the National Institute of Space Research (INPE), leading to the launch of the first scientific satellite built entirely in Brazil in 1993 (SCD-1). Between 1999 and 2014, Brazil and China built a series of five remote sensing satellites for environmental monitoring within the China-Brazil Earth Resources Satellites (CBERS) programme. Brazil has now achieved the critical mass of skills and infrastructure required to dominate several space technologies. It is determined to master the complete chain of space technologies, from material sciences, engineering design, remote sensing, aperture-synthetic radars, telecommunications and image processing to propulsion technologies. The joint Argentinian–Brazilian SABIA-MAR mission will be studying ocean ecosystems, carbon cycling, marine habitats mapping, coasts and coastal hazards, inland waters and fisheries. Also under development is the new SARE series designed to expand the active remote observation of Earth through the use of microwave and optical radars.

Research output

Scientific publications increased by 308% between 2005 and 2014, primarily as a result of Thomson Reuters' decision to track a much larger number of Brazilian journals in its database between 2006 and 2008. Despite this artificial boost, the pace of growth has slowed since 2011. Moreover, in terms of publications per capita, the country trails both the more dynamic emerging market economies and advanced economies, even if it is ahead of most of its neighbours. When it comes to impact, Brazil has lost a lot of ground in the past decade. One possible cause may be the speed with which enrolment in higher education has expanded since the mid-1990s, especially as concerns students passing through the federal system of universities, some of which have resorted to hiring inexperienced faculty, including candidates without doctorates.

Patent applications to the Brazilian Patent Office (INPI) increased from 20,639 in 2000 to 33,395 in 2012, progressing by 62%. Patent applications by residents grew at a rate of 21% over the same period.

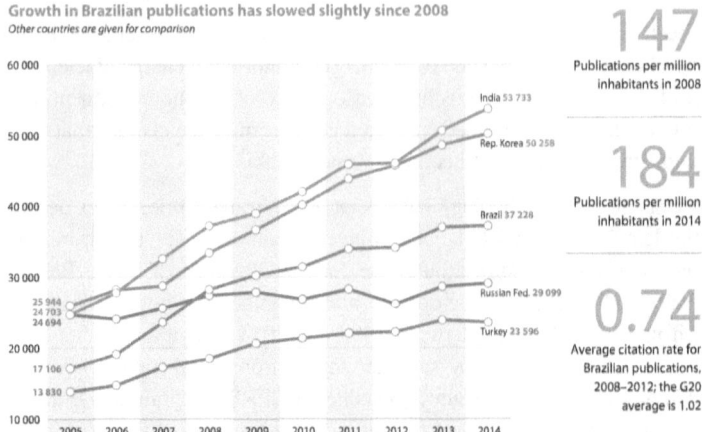

Figure 327: *Growth in Brazilian scientific publishing between 2005 and 2014. Source: UNESCO Science Report: towards 2030 (2015), Figure 8.9, data from Thomson Reuters' Web of Science, Science Citation Index Expanded*

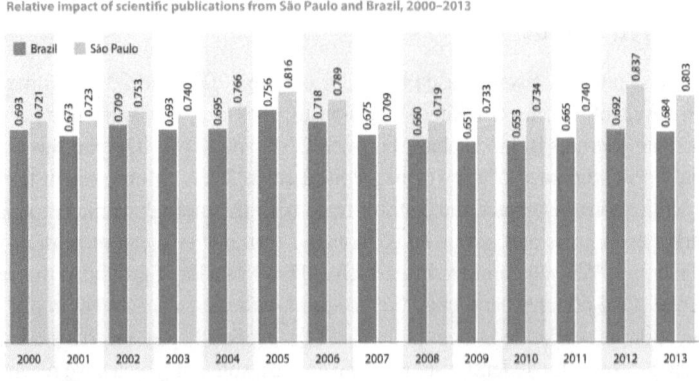

Figure 328: *Relative impact of scientific publications from São Paulo and Brazil, 2000–2013. Source: UNESCO Science Report: towards 2030 (2015), Figure 8.11*

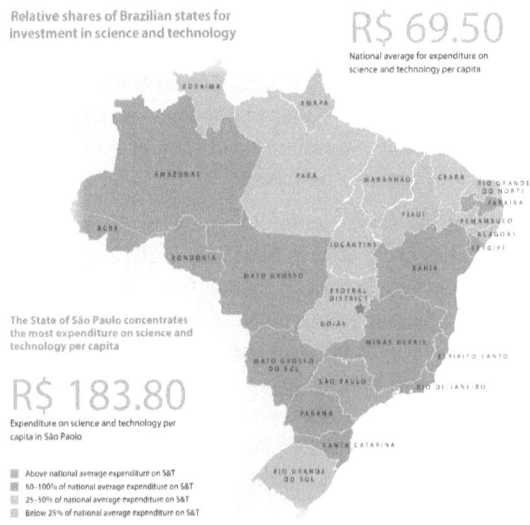

Figure 329: *Relative shares of Brazilian states for investment for science and technology, 2012. Source: UNESCO Science Report: towards 2030 (2015), Figure 8.12*

International comparisons using the number of patents granted by the US Patent and Trademarks Office (USPTO) provide an indirect measure of the extent to which an economy may be seeking international competitiveness on the basis of technology-driven innovation. Brazil was granted 108 patents by the USPTO between 2004 and 2008 and 189 between 2009 and 2013. Although Brazil has registered strong growth in this field, compared to other emerging economies, it seems to be relatively less focused on international patenting than on publications. Between 2000 and 2013, it counted 10 patents per ten million inhabitants from USPTO, less than Argentina (14), China, India (12) or South Africa (25) and only slightly more than Mexico (9).

Regional disparities

Brazil is a country with highly diverse levels of development across its 27 states. The southern and southeastern regions show a much higher level of industrialization and scientific development than the northern ones, some of which encroach on the Amazonian forest and river basin. The centre-west is Brazil's agricultural and cattle-raising powerhouse and has been developing rapidly recently. The starkest example of this contrast is the southeastern

State of São Paulo. Home to 22% (44 million) of the country's 202 million inhabitants, it generates about 32% of GDP and a similar share of the nation's industrial output. It also has a very strong state system of public research universities that is lacking in most other states and hosts the well-established São Paulo Research Foundation. The State of São Paulo is responsible for 46% of GERD (public and private expenditure) and 66% of business R&D. It hosts 10 of the country's 18 research universities.

All indicators paint the same picture. Some 41% of Brazilian PhDs were granted by universities in the State of São Paulo in 2012 and 44% of all papers with Brazilian authors have at least one author from an institution based in São Paulo. São Paulo's scientific productivity (390 papers per million inhabitants over 2009–2013) is twice the national average (184), a differential which has been widening in recent years. The relative impact of publications by scientists from the State of São Paulo has also been systematically higher than for Brazil as a whole over the past decade. Two key factors explain São Paulo's success in scientific output: firstly, a well-funded system of state universities, including the University of São Paulo, University of Campinas (Unicamp) and the State University of São Paulo, all of which have been included in international university rankings;10 secondly, the role played by the São Paulo Research Foundation (FAPESP). Both the university system and FAPESP are allocated a fixed share of the state's sales tax revenue as their annual budgets and have full autonomy as to the use they make of this revenue.

Between 2006 and 2014, the share of Brazilian researchers hosted by southeastern institutions dropped steadily from 50% to 44%. Over the same period, the share of northeastern states rose from 16% to 20%. It is still too early to see the effect of these changes on scientific output, or in the number of PhD degrees being awarded but these indicators should logically also progress.

Despite these positive trends, regional inequalities persist in terms of research expenditure, the number of research institutions and scientific productivity. Extending the scope of research projects to other states and beyond Brazil would certainly help scientists from these regions catch up to their southern neighbours.

Timeline

- 1792: Founding of the Royal Academy of Fortification, Artillery and Design, current Military Institute of Engineering (IME) and Polytechnic School of UFRJ (UFRJ).
- 1876: Founding of the First School of Mines in Brazil, today Federal University of Ouro Preto (UFOP).

Science and technology in Brazil

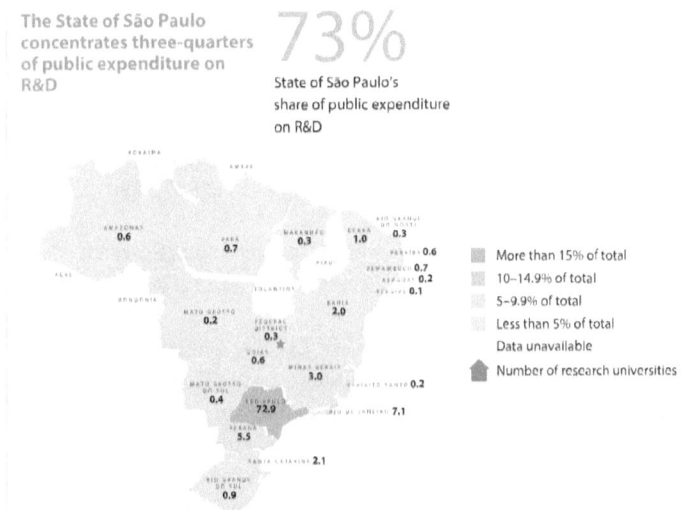

Figure 330: *The State of São Paulo concentrates three-quarters of public expenditure on R&D. Source: UN-ESCO Science Report: towards 2030 (2015), Figure 8.12*

- 1900: Founding of the Federal Institute Serotherapy, current Oswaldo Cruz Foundation (FioCruz).
- 1916: Founding of the Brazilian Society of Sciences, today Brazilian Academy of Sciences (ABC).
- 1917: Beginning of the publication of the *Anais da Academia Brasileira de Ciências*.
- 1920: Founding of the University of Brazil, current Federal University of Rio de Janeiro (UFRJ).
- 1922: Founding of the Top School of Agriculture and Veterinary, current Federal University of Viçosa (UFV).
- 1923: Founding of the Brazilian Society of Chemistry (SBCh).
- 1923: Founding of the Radio Society of Rio de Janeiro, the first radio broadcasting station still working under the name Rádio MEC[1164] in Rio de Janeiro.
- 1924: Founding of the Brazilian Association of Education.
- 1925: Institution of the Einstein Prize, in reason of his visit to Brazil.
- 1930: Founding of the National Institute of Weights and Standards, today National Institute of Metrology, Standardization and Industrial Quality (Inmetro).

- 1934: Founding of the University of São Paulo (USP).
- 1948: Founding of the Brazilian Society for the Progress of Science (SBPC).
- 1949: Founding of the Brazilian Center for Physics Research.
- 1950: Founding of the Aeronautical Institute of Technology (ITA).
- 1951: Founding of the National Research Council (CNPq).
- 1951: Founding of the Coordination of Improvement of Higher Education Personnel (CAPES).
- 1952: Founding of the National Institute of Amazonian Research (INPA).
- 1953: Founding of the Brazilian General Command for Aerospace Technology (CTA).
- 1956: Founding of the National Nuclear Energy Commission (CNEN).
- 1961: Founding of the National Institute for Space Research (INPE).
- 1962: Founding of the São Paulo State Foundation for Research Support (Fapesp).
- 1962: Founding of the State University of Campinas (Unicamp).
- 1967: Founding of the National Agency for Financing Research and Projects (FINEP).
- 1976: Founding of the São Paulo State University (Unesp).
- 1980: Founding of the National Laboratory of Scientific Computing (LNCC).
- 1985: Founding of the National Laboratory of Synchrotron Radiation (LNRS), current National Laboratory of Synchrotron Light (LNLS).
- 1985: Founding of the National Laboratory of Astrophysics
- 1993: Institution of the National Order of Scientific Merit.
- 1994: Founding of the Brazilian Space Agency (AEB).
- 2006: Founding of the Federal University of ABC (UFABC).
- 2007: Founding of the National Laboratory of Science and Technology of Bioethanol (CTBE).
- 2010: Founding of the Federal University of Latin American Integration (UNILA).

Lists

Major universities

Public universities and institutes

- UFAL - Universidade Federal de Alagoas (Federal University of Alagoas)
- IME - Instituto Militar de Engenharia (Military Institute of Engineering)
- ITA - Instituto Tecnológico de Aeronáutica (Aeronautics Technological Institute)
- UECE - Universidade Estadual do Ceará (State University of Ceará)

- UERJ - Universidade do Estado do Rio de Janeiro (Rio de Janeiro State University)
- UNIRIO - Universidade Federal do Estado do Rio de Janeiro (Federal University of the State of Rio de Janeiro)
- UFABC - Universidade Federal do ABC (Federal University of ABC)
- UFBA - Universidade Federal da Bahia (Federal University of Bahia)
- UFS - Universidade Federal de Sergipe (Federal University of Sergipe)
- UFC - Universidade Federal do Ceará (Federal University of Ceará)
- UFCG - Universidade Federal de Campina Grande (Federal University of Campina Grande)
- UFES - Universidade Federal do Espírito Santo (Federal University of Espírito Santo)
- UFOP - Universidade Federal de Ouro Preto (Federal University of Ouro Preto)
- UFF - Universidade Federal Fluminense (Federal University Fluminense)
- UFG - Universidade Federal de Goiás (Federal University of Goiás)
- UEG - Universidade Estadual de Goiás (State University of Goiás)
- UFJF - Universidade Federal de Juiz de Fora (Federal University of Juiz de Fora)
- UFMG - Universidade Federal de Minas Gerais (Federal University of Minas Gerais)
- UFPA - Universidade Federal do Pará (Federal University of Pará)
- UFPE - Universidade Federal de Pernambuco (Federal University of Pernambuco)
- UFPI- Universidade Federal do Piauí (Federal University of Piauí)
- UFPR - Universidade Federal do Paraná (Federal University of Paraná)
- UFRGS - Universidade Federal do Rio Grande do Sul (Federal University of Rio Grande do Sul)
- UFRJ - Universidade Federal do Rio de Janeiro (Federal University of Rio de Janeiro)
- UFRN - Universidade Federal do Rio Grande do Norte (Federal University of Rio Grande do Norte)
- UFSCAR - Universidade Federal de São Carlos (Federal University of São Carlos)
- UFSC - Universidade Federal de Santa Catarina (Federal University of Santa Catarina)
- UFSM - Universidade Federal de Santa Maria (Federal University of Santa Maria)
- UFV - Universidade Federal de Viçosa (Federal University of Viçosa)
- UnB - Universidade de Brasília (University of Brasília)
- UNESP - Universidade Estadual Paulista (São Paulo State University)

- UNICAMP - Universidade Estadual de Campinas (State University of Campinas)
- UNIFEI - Universidade Federal de Itajubá (Federal University of Itajubá)
- UNIFESP - Universidade Federal de São Paulo (Federal University of São Paulo)
- UNITAU - Universidade de Taubaté (University of Taubaté)
- USP - Universidade de São Paulo (University of São Paulo)
- UFT - Universidade Federal do Tocantins (Federal University of Tocantins)

Private universities

- PUC-PR - Pontifícia Universidade Católica do Paraná (Pontifical Catholic University of Paraná)
- PUC-SP - Pontifícia Universidade Católica de São Paulo (Pontifical Catholic University of São Paulo)
- PUCCamp - Pontifícia Universidade Católica de Campinas (Pontifical Catholic University of Campinas)
- PUC-RJ - Pontifícia Universidade Católica do Rio de Janeiro (Pontifical Catholic University of Rio de Janeiro)
- UCB - Universidade Católica de Brasília - (Catholic University of Brasília)
- PUC-GO - Pontifícia Universidade Católica de Goiás - (Pontifical Catholic University of Goiás)
- PUC-MG - Pontifícia Universidade Católica de Minas Gerais (Pontifical Catholic University of Minas Gerais)
- PUC-RS - Pontifícia Universidade Católica do Rio Grande do Sul (Pontifical Catholic University of Rio Grande do Sul)
- IESB - Instituto de Educação Superior de Brasília (Brasília's Institute of Higher Education)
- ULBRA - Universidade Luterana do Brasil (Lutheran University of Brazil)
- Mack - Universidade Presbiteriana Mackenzie (Mackenzie Presbyterian University)
- UNIFOR - Universidade de Fortaleza (University of Fortaleza)
- Centro Universitário da FEI (Industrial Engineering College) www.fei.edu.br
- FAAP - Fundação Armando Alvares Penteado, São Paulo, São Paulo
- FAMEC - Faculdade Metropolitana de Curitiba, (Sistema FIEP - www.famec.fiepr.org.br)
- Universidade Feevale - FEEVALE University, Novo Hamburgo, Rio Grande do Sul

Figure 331: *Pasteur Institute on Paulista Avenue, in Downtown São Paulo.*

Research institutes

- Brazilian General Command for Aerospace Technology (CTA) - São José dos Campos
- Centro de Pesquisa e Desenvolvimento em Telecomunicações (CPqD) - Campinas
- Centro de Pesquisas Renato Archer - Campinas
- Comandante Ferraz Brazilian Antarctic Base - Antarctica
- Edumed Institute for Education in Medicine and Health - Campinas
- Eldorado Institute - Campinas
- Empresa Brasileira de Pesquisa Agropecuária - Brasília
- Instituto Adolfo Lutz - São Paulo
- Instituto Agronômico de Campinas - Campinas
- Instituto Atlântico - Fortaleza
- Instituto Butantan - São Paulo
- Instituto de Biotecnologia Aplicada à Agropecuária (BIOAGRO) - Viçosa
- Instituto de Pesquisas da Amazônia - Manaus
- Instituto de Pesquisas em Energia Nuclear - São Paulo
- Instituto de Pesquisas Tecnológicas do Estado de São Paulo (IPT)[1165] - São Paulo
- Instituto Evandro Chagas - Belém
- Instituto Nacional de Matemática Pura e Aplicada - Rio de Janeiro

- Instituto Nacional de Pesquisas Espaciais (INPE) - São José dos Campos
- Instituto Oswaldo Cruz - Rio de Janeiro
- Laboratório Nacional de Computação Científica (LNCC) - Petrópolis
- Laboratório Nacional de Luz Síncrotron - Campinas
- Museu Paraense Emílio Goeldi - Belém
- Resende Nuclear Fuel Factory - Rezende
- São José dos Campos Technology Park - São José dos Campos

Scientific societies

- Brazilian Academy of Sciences
- Brazilian Society of Health Informatics
- Academia Nacional de Medicina
- Brazilian Computer Society
- Federação das Sociedades de Biologia Experimental
- Sociedade Brasileira para o Progresso da Ciência
- Brazilian Telecommunications Society
- Brazilian Power Electronics Society - SOBRAEP

Sources

This article incorporates text from a free content work. Licensed under CC-BY-SA IGO 3.0 *UNESCO Science Report: towards 2030*[1166], 210-229, UNESCO, UNESCO Publishing. To learn how to add open license text to Wikipedia articles, please see Wikipedia:Adding open license text to Wikipedia. For information on reusing text from Wikipedia, please see the terms of use.

External links

- The Museu Nacional and its European employees[1167]. Jens Andermann
- The Museu Nacional at Rio de Janeiro[1168]. Jens Andermann
- The Brazilian Centre of Physical Research[1169].
- Brazil Technology[1170].

Transport

Transport in Brazil

Transport infrastructure in Brazil is characterized by strong regional differences and lack of development of the national rail network. Brazil's fast-growing economy, and especially the growth in exports, will place increasing demands on the transport networks. However, sizeable new investments that are expected to address some of the issues are either planned or in progress.[1171]

Railroads

- **Total actual network:** 29,303 km

    Broad gauge: 4,932 km 1,600 mm (5 ft 3 in) gauge (939 km electrified)

    Narrow gauge: 23,773 km 1,000 mm (3 ft 3 3/8 in) gauge (581 km electrified)

    Dual gauge: 396 km 1000 mm and 1600 mm gauges (three rails)

    Standard gauge: 202.4 km 1,435 mm (4 ft 8 1/2 in) gauge (2006)

- Estrada de Ferro do Amapá in the middle of the Amazon Rainforest also used standard gauge.
- A 12 km section of the former 2 ft 6 in (762 mm) gauge Estrada de Ferro Oeste de Minas is retained as a heritage railway.

Figure 332: *Rodovia dos Imigrantes*

Cities with metros

- Belo Horizonte (28.2 km)
- Brasília (42.4 km)
- Fortaleza (24.1 km)
- Porto Alegre (43.4 km)
- Sobral (11.0 km)

- Juazeiro do Norte (13.9 km)
- Recife (71 km)
- Rio de Janeiro (40.9 km)
- São Paulo (75.5 km)
- Salvador (7.3 km)
- Teresina (13.5 km)

Figure 333: *Porto Alegre Metro*

Railway links with adjacent countries

International rail links exist between Brazil and Argentina, Bolivia and Uruguay.

Tramways

Brazil had a hundred tramway systems. Currently, there are vintage tramways operating in Belém, Campinas, Campos do Jordão, Itatinga, Rio de Janeiro and Santos.

High-speed rail

A high-speed rail connecting São Paulo and Rio de Janeiro is currently under development.[1172]

Highways

Brazil has 1,751,868 kilometers of roads, 96,353 km of them paved and 1,655,515 km unpaved. That means that only 5.5% of the roads are paved and that 94.5% are unpaved. The most important highway of the country is BR-116 and the second is BR-101.

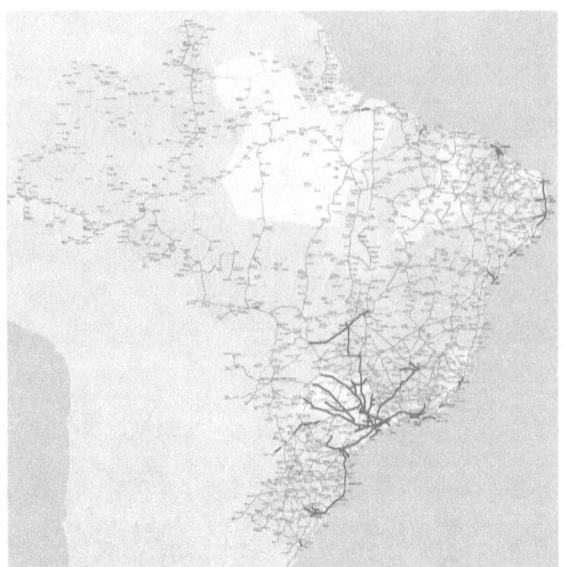

Figure 334:
Road system in Brazil, with divided highways highlighted in red. The São Paulo state, which has state control of most federal roads in its territory, made its road network the most extensive one in the country, thanks to this fact.

The country has a low rate of car ownership of 140 per 1000 population, however in comparison to the other developing economies of the BRIC group Brazil exceeds India and China.

Waterways

50,000 km navigable (most in areas remote from industry or population) (2008)

Pipelines

- condensate/gas 62 km
- natural gas 9,892 km
- liquid petroleum gas 353 km
- crude oil 4,517 km
- refined products 4,465 km (2008)

Figure 335: *Port of Natal*

Seaports and harbors

Atlantic Ocean

- Fortaleza
- Ilheus
- Imbituba
- Paranaguá
- Porto Alegre
- Recife
- Rio de Janeiro
- Rio Grande
- Salvador
- Santos
- São Francisco do Sul
- São Sebastião
- Vitória
- Itajaí
- Natal

Amazon river

- Belém
- Manaus
- Santarém

Paraguay River (international water way)

- Corumbá

Merchant marine

total: 136 ships (1,000 gross register tons (GRT) or over) totaling 3,964,808 GRT/6,403,284 tonnes deadweight (DWT)

ships by type: (1999 est.)

- bulk carriers 19
- cargo ships 22
- carrier ships 1
- chemical tankers 7
- container ships 11
- gas carrying tankers 12
- multi-functional large load carrier 1
- passenger/cargo ships 12
- petroleum tanker 45
- roll-on/roll-off 7

Airports

Most international flights must go to São Paulo–Guarulhos International Airport or Rio de Janeiro–Galeão International Airport. Belo Horizonte is the main international airport outside Rio de Janeiro and São Paulo. A few go to Brasília, Recife, Natal, and just recently Fortaleza has accepted international flights. With South American integration, more airports can be expected to open to international flights.

In 2013 Brazil had the sixth largest passenger air market in the world.[1173]

Airports - with paved runways

- *total:* 734
- *over 3,047 m:* 7
- *2,438 to 3,047 m:* 26
- *1,524 to 2,437 m:* 169
- *914 to 1,523 m:* 476
- *under 914 m:* 56 (2008)

Figure 336: *São Paulo–Guarulhos International Airport.*

Figure 337: *Rio de Janeiro-Galeão International Airport.*

Airports - with unpaved runways

- *total:* 3,442
- *1,524 to 2,437 m:* 85
- *914 to 1,523 m:* 1,541
- *under 914 m:* 1,816 (2008)

National airlines

- Azul Linhas Aéreas Brasileiras
- Gol Transportes Aéreos
- Avianca
- TAM Airlines (TAM Linhas Aéreas)

Heliports

- 16 (2007)
- 13 (2010)

References

- CIA - The World Factbook - Brazil - Transportation[1174]

Health Care

Health in Brazil

Health Indicators[1175,1176,1177,1178,1179]	
Life expectancy	76.2
Infant mortality	13.12
Fertility	1.71
Sanitation	93%
Smoker	15.4%
Obesity female	19.3%
Obesity male	9.7%
Malnutrition	2%
HIV	0.1%

According to the Brazilian Government, the most serious health problems are:[1180]

- Childhood mortality: about 1.51% of childhood mortality, reaching 2.77% in the northeast region.
- Motherhood mortality: about 42.1 deaths per 100,000 born children in 2016.
- Mortality by non-transmissible illness: 65.7 deaths per 100,000 inhabitants caused by heart and circulatory diseases, along with 26.7 deaths per 100,000 inhabitants caused by cancer.
- Mortality caused by external causes (transportation, violence and suicide): 55.7 deaths per 100,000 inhabitants (10.9% of all deaths in the country), reaching 62.3 deaths in the southeast region.

In 2002, Brazil accounted for 40% of malaria cases in the Americas. Nearly 99% are concentrated in the Legal Amazon Region, which is home to not more than 12% of the population.

Figure 338: *Cândido Fontoura Children's Hospital, São Paulo.*

Life expectancy

The life expectancy of the Brazilian population increased from 71.16 years in 1998 to 76.2 years in 2016, according to the Brazilian Institute of Geography and Statistics (IBGE). The data indicate a significant progress compared with 55.50 years in 1940. According to the IBGE, Brazil will need some time to catch up with Japan, Hong Kong (China), Switzerland, Iceland, Australia, France and Italy, where the average life expectancy is already over 81. Research has shown that Brazil would achieve that level by 2030.[1181]

Demographic projections foresee the continuation of this process, estimating a life expectancy in Brazil around 77.4 years in 2020. The decline in mortality at young ages and the increase in longevity, combined with the decline of fecundity and the accentuated increase of degenerative chronic diseases, caused a rapid process of demographic and epidemiologic transition, imposing a new public health agenda in the face of the complexity of the new morbidity pattern.[1182]

Infant mortality

Child health is a central issue on the public policy agenda of developing countries. Several policies geared to improving child health have been implemented over the years, with varying degrees of success. In Brazil, such policies have led to a significant decline in infant mortality rates over the last 30 years. Despite this improvement, however, mortality rates are still high by international standards and there is substantial variation across Brazilian municipalities, which suggests that differentiated policies should be devised. For example, mortality among indigenous infants in 2000 was more than triple that of the general population, highlighting the importance of tailored health policies to address disparities in health outcomes for Brazil's Indigenous Peoples. Sanitation, education and per capita income are the most important explanatory factors of poor child health in Brazil.[1183] Moreover, ethnographic findings of infant mortality rates (IMR) in northeast Brazil are not accurate because the government tends to overlook infant morality rates in rural areas. These issues tend to be inaccurate due to a huge amount of underreporting and causes us to question the cultural validity and the contextual soundness of these mortality statistics. There is a solution to this issue however and scientists stress that quality local-level cultural data can serve to craft as the alternative and appropriate method to measure infant death in Brazil accurately. In order to not overlook infant mortality rates it is also stressed that there needs to be a focus on an ethnography of experience, a vision that cuts to the core of human suffering as it flows from daily life and experiences. For example, one must get down to the flesh, blood and souls of infant death in the impoverished households of Brazilians in order to understand and live with those who have to suffer its tragic consequences. Methods of gathering mortality data also need to be respectful of local death customs and must be implemented in places where death is experienced through a different cultural lens.[1184]

UNICEF report shows a rising rate of survival for Brazilian children under the age of five. UNICEF says that out of a total of 195 countries analyzed, Brazil is among the 25 nations with the best improvement in survival rates for children under the age of 5. The report shows that Brazil's infant mortality rate for live births in 2012 was 14 per thousand. Mortality rates for children at one year of age was 18 per thousand, a reduction of 60%. The study went on to show that malnutrition among children of less than two years of age during the period between 2000 and 2008 fell by 77%. There was also a substantial drop in the number of school age children who were not in school, falling from 920,000 to 570,000 during the same period. Cristina Albuquerque, coordinator of the UNICEF Infant Survival and Development Program called the numbers "an enormous victory" for Brazil. She added that with regard to public policy aimed at reducing social disparities, Brazil's Bolsa Família program had become an international benchmark in combating poverty, reducing vulnerability and improving quality of life. "Brazil is going through a great moment, but much remains to be done. So, along with the celebrating it is a good time to reflect on the many challenges still to be overcome," Albuquerque declared.[1185]

Figure 339: *Portuguese Beneficent Hospital, in Manaus.*

Obesity

Obesity in Brazil is a growing health concern. 52.6 percent of men and 44.7 percent of women in Brazil are overweight. 15% of Brazilians are obese. The Brazilian government has issued nutrition guidelines which have caught the attention of public health experts for their simplicity and their critical position towards the food industry. The guidelines are summarized at the end of the document as follows:

1. Prepare meals using fresh and staple foods.
2. Use oils, fats, sugar, and salt only in moderation.
3. Limit consumption of ready-to-eat food and drink products.
4. Eat at regular mealtimes and pay attention to your food instead of multitasking. Find a comfortable place to eat. Avoid all-you-can-eat buffets and noisy, stressful environments.
5. Eat with others whenever possible.
6. Buy food in shops and markets that offer a variety of fresh foods. Avoid those that sell mainly ready-to-eat products.
7. Develop, practise, share, and enjoy your skills in food preparation and cooking.
8. Decide as a family to share cooking responsibilities and dedicate enough time for health-supporting meals.

9. When you dine out, choose restaurants that serve freshly made dishes. Avoid fast-food chains.
10. Be critical of food-industry advertising.

External links

- World Health Organization: Brazil[1186]

Education

Education in Brazil

Education in Brazil

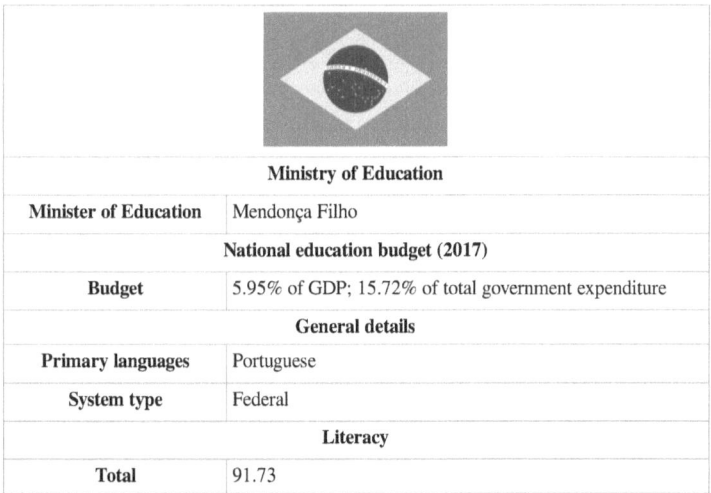	
Ministry of Education	
Minister of Education	Mendonça Filho
National education budget (2017)	
Budget	5.95% of GDP; 15.72% of total government expenditure
General details	
Primary languages	Portuguese
System type	Federal
Literacy	
Total	91.73

Education in Brazil has had many changes. Education in Brazil first began with Jesuit missions. They controlled education for a long time, then, two hundred years after their arrival, their powers were limited by Marquis de Pombal. Shortly after the Jesuits' power was limited, the Brazilian government took over education and it is now is run by the Brazilian government through the Ministry of Education.

Issues in education are now seen through PISA, the Programme for International Student Assessment, and the Idep assessment now used by the Ministry. They have historically tested below average on all topics but are improving in mathematics.

Figure 340: *Thales de Azevedo State High School in Salvador*

Brazil uses both public and private school systems. They have the traditional primary, secondary, tertiary and technical school levels.

History

When Kingdom of Portugal's explorers arrived in Brazil in the 15th century and started to colonize their new possessions in the New World, the territory was inhabited by indigenous peoples and tribes who had no writing system or school education.

The Society of Jesus (Jesuits) was, since its beginnings in 1540, a missionary order. Evangelisation was one of the main goals of the Jesuits and they were committed to teaching and education, in Europe and overseas. The missionary activities, in the cities and in the countryside, were complemented by a strong commitment to education. This took the form of the opening of schools for boys, first in Europe but rapidly extended to America and Asia. The foundation of Catholic missions, schools, and seminaries was another consequence of the Jesuit involvement in education. As the spaces and cultures where the Jesuits were present varied considerably, their evangelising methods were very often quite different from one place to another. However, the society's engagement in trade, architecture, science, literature, languages, arts, music and religious debate corresponded to the same main purpose of Christianisation.

Education in Brazil 635

Figure 341: *Federal University of Paraná in Curitiba.*

Figure 342: *Medicine College of São Paulo.*

Figure 343: *College of Law.*

By the middle of the 16th century the Jesuits were present in West Africa, South America, Ethiopia, India, China, and Japan. This enlargement of their missionary activities took shape to a large extent within the framework of the Portuguese Empire.

In a period when the world had a largely illiterate population, the Portuguese Empire was home to one of the first universities founded in Europe — the University of Coimbra, which is one of the oldest universities in continuous operation. Throughout the centuries of Portuguese rule, Brazilian students, mostly graduated of the Jesuit missions and seminaries, were allowed and even encouraged to enroll at higher education in mainland Portugal.

The Jesuits, a religious order founded to promote the cause and teachings of Catholicism, had gained influence with the Portuguese crown and over education, and had begun missionary work in Portugal's overseas possessions, including the colony of Brazil. By 1700, and reflecting a larger transformation of the Portuguese Empire, the Jesuits had decisively shifted from the East Indies to Brazil. In the late 18th century, Portuguese minister of the kingdom Marquis of Pombal attacked the power of the privileged nobility and the church, and expelled the Jesuits from Portugal and its overseas possessions. Pombal seized the Jesuit schools and introduced education reforms all over the empire. In Brazil, the reforms were noted.

In 1772, before the establishment of the Science Academy of Lisbon (1779), one of the first learned societies of Brazil and the Portuguese Empire was founded in Rio de Janeiro: the Sociedade Scientifica. In 1797, the first botanic

Figure 344: *Music school of Federal University of Rio de Janeiro.*

institute was founded in Salvador, Bahia. During the late 18th century, the Escola Politécnica (Polytechnic School) was created, then the Real Academia de Artilharia, Fortificação e Desenho (Royal Academy for Artillery, Fortifications and Design) was created in Rio de Janeiro, 1792, through a decree issued by the Portuguese authorities as a higher education school for the teaching of the sciences and engineering. Its legacy is shared by the Instituto Militar de Engenharia (Military Engineering Institute) and the Escola Politécnica da Universidade Federal do Rio de Janeiro (Polytechnic School of the Federal University of Rio de Janeiro) — the oldest engineering school of Brazil and one of the oldest in the world.

A royal letter of November 20, 1800 by the King John VI of Portugal established the Aula Prática de Desenho e Figura (Practice Class for Design and Form) in Rio de Janeiro. It was the first institution in Brazil systematically dedicated to teaching the arts. During colonial times, the arts were mainly religious or utilitarian and were learnt in a system of apprenticeship. A decree on August 12, 1816 created the Escola Real de Ciências, Artes e Ofícios (Royal School of Sciences, Arts and Crafts), which established an official education in the fine arts and built the foundations of the current Escola Nacional de Belas Artes (School of Fine Arts).

In the 19th century, the Portuguese royal family, headed by D. João VI, arrived in Rio de Janeiro, escaping from the Napoleon's army invasion of Portugal in 1807. D. João VI gave impetus to the expansion of European civilization to Brazil. In the short period between 1808 and 1810, the Portuguese government founded the Academia Real dos Guarda Marinha (Royal Naval Academy), the Real Academia Militar (Royal Military Academy), the Biblioteca Nacional (National Library of Brazil), the Jardim Botânico do Rio de Janeiro (Rio de Janeiro Botanical Garden), the Academia Médico-Cirúrgica da Bahia (Medic-Cirurgical Academy of Bahia), now known as Faculdade de Medicina (Med School) in the Universidade Federal da Bahia (Federal University of Bahia) and the Academia Médico-Cirúrgica do Rio de Janeiro (Medic-Cirurgical Academy of Rio de Janeiro) which is now the medical school of the Federal University of Rio de Janeiro.

Brazil achieved independence in 1822. Until the 20th century, it was a large rural nation with low social and economic standards comparing to the average North American and European standards. Its economy was based on the primary sector, possessing an unskilled and increasingly larger workforce, composed of free people (including slave owners) and slaves or their direct descendants. Among the first law schools founded in Brazil were the ones in Recife and São Paulo in 1827. But for decades to come, most Brazilian lawyers studied at European universities, such as in the ancient University of Coimbra, in Portugal, which had awarded degrees to generations of Brazilian students since the 16th century.

In 1872 there were 9,930,478 inhabitants (84.8% free and 15.2% slave). According to the national census made in this year, among the free inhabitants (8,419,672 people), 38% were white, 39% mulattoes (white and black mix), 11% black and 5% caboclos (white and Indian mix). Only 23.4% of the free men and 13.4% of the free women could read and write. In 1889, six decades after independence, only 20% of the total population could read and write. In the former colonial power, Portugal, about 80% of the population was classified as illiterate.

With the massive post-war expansion that lasts to date, the government focused on strengthening Brazil's tertiary education, while simultaneously neglecting assistance to primary and secondary education. The problems of primary and secondary education were compounded by significant quality differences across regions, with the northeast suffering dramatically.[1187] In the aftermath of Brazilian military rule, education became seen as a way to create a fairer society. "Citizen schools" emerged, designed to promote critical thinking, incorporation of marginalized people, and curiosity (over rote memorization and obedience).[1188]

Today, Brazil struggles to improve the public education offered at earlier stages and maintain the high standards that the population has come to expect from public universities. The choice on public funding is an issue. In particular,

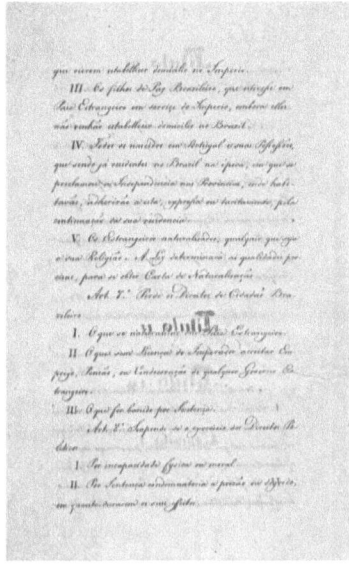

Figure 345: *Constitution of 1824*

the U.N. Development Goal of Universal Primary Education and a larger offer of education for students with special needs are pursued by Brazilian policy-makers.

Despite its shortcomings, Brazil has progressed substantially since the 1980s. The nation witnessed an increase in school enrollment for children age 7–14, from 80.9% in 1980 to 96.4% in the year 2000. In the 15-17 age demographic, in the same period, this rate rose from 49.7% to 83%. Literacy rates rose from 75% to 90.0%.

Voting has been mandatory for all citizens of Brazil since the first Constitution of 1824[1189]. However, people who are illiterate have, historically, not been able to be registered to vote. The Constitution of 1988 changed this, stating that those who are illiterate have the option to vote but it is not compulsory for those. The Constitution of 1824 also stated that those who made less than 100,000 reis were not able to vote.

Throughout the 20th century, in response to campaigns occurring in other Latinoamérican countries, Brazilian states began their own literacy campaigns. Led by educators like Paulo Freire, the campaigns hoped to combat the high amounts of illiteracy in the countryside. Beginning in 1963, the campaigns were centered in rural areas. Paulo Freire's methods were widely popular due to the immediacy in which they seemed to work: as he claimed, a student could learn to read and write in 40 hours. The growing fear of communism and the rising power of the military led to the end of the campaigns in 1964 and the exile of Freire and others like him. The military government began new campaigns in the late 1970s to questionable improvements.

Issues

According to PISA, the Programme for International Student Assessment, Brazil, on average, underperforms. Brazilian students score lower than the average in reading, mathematics, and science, the three categories of testing. Their scores have improved since 2000, the first year the test was taken. Since 2000, Brazil has started the Brazil Literate Program to lower the rate of illiteracy in those ages 15 and older. Brazil has also implemented the IDEP, the Index of Basic Education Development, which evaluates school flow and performance rates in the test. According to the website, the index is used to tell whether the educational system should be improved. The program is important in deciding public policy of the educational system. IDEP also led to the creation of the Social Mobilisation program which works to involve the entire community in the educational system. Several other committees have created programs in individual municipalities in order to curb the IDEP findings.

It takes an extra three years to finish elementary school for low-income students, PNAD[1190], the national household survey, shows. Costs of finishing school rise each year until it is impossible to attend, meaning that low-income students also have the lowest rates for completing school. Rio de Janeiro began a program in 2009 called the Reforço Escolar testing all students in the beginning of the school year to discover all who are not yet at grade level. Those who are not receive two weeks of in-depth tutoring. São Paulo and Paraná have also created programs to help those who are behind, either due to being low-income or for other reasons.

Organization and structure

Education is divided into three levels, with grades in each level:
- Pre-school education (educação infantil) is found in public institutions and private institutions.
- Basic education (ensino básico) is found in public institutions and private institutions, and mandatory for those between the ages of 6 and 17. It consists of Elementary school (ensino fundamental) and High school (ensino médio)
- Higher education (ensino superior) (including graduate degrees) is found in public institutions and private institutions.

Education in Brazil 641

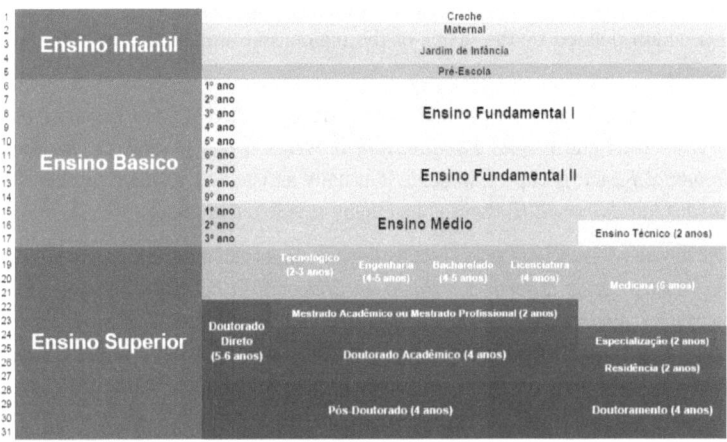

Figure 346: *Table showing how the education system is organized in Brazil*

Pre-school education (educação infantil)

Pre-school education is optional and exists to aid in the development of children under 6. It aims to assist in all areas of child development, including motor skills, cognitive skills, and social skills while providing fertile ground for the later acquisition of knowledge and learning. There are day nurseries for children under 2, kindergartens for 2- to 3-year-olds, and preschools for children 4 and up. Public preschools are provided by city governments.

Elementary school (ensino fundamental)

Elementary school is mandatory for children ages 6–14. There are nine "years" (as opposed to the former eight "grades"). The current "first year" broadly corresponds to the former pre-school last year of private institutions, and its aim is to achieve literacy. Generally speaking, the only prerequisite for enrolling in first year is that a child should be 6 years old, but some education systems allow children younger than 6 to enroll in first year (as long as they turn 6 during the first academic semester). Older students who have not completed their elementary education are allowed to attend, though those over 18 are separated from the younger children.

The National Council of Education (*Conselho Nacional de Educação*) establishes a core curriculum consisting of Portuguese language, history, geography, science, mathematics, arts and physical education (for years 2, 3, 4 and 5). As for years 6, 7, 8 and 9, one or two foreign languages are also compulsory (usually English and an optional language).

Each education system supplements this core curriculum with a diversified curriculum defined by the needs of the region and the abilities of individual students.

Elementary education is divided in two stages, called *Ensino Fundamental I* (years 1–5) and *Ensino Fundamental II* (years 6–9). During *Ensino Fundamental I* each group of students is usually assisted by a single teacher. In *Ensino Fundamental II*, there are as many teachers as subjects.

The length of the school year is set by the National Education Bases and Guidelines Law (*Lei de Diretrizes e Bases da Educação*) to at least 200 days. Elementary schools must provide students with at least 800 hours of activities per year. The school calendar is set by individual schools which, in rural areas, often organize their calendars according to planting and harvesting seasons.

Public elementary schools are funded by municipal and state governments. The education is similar to the British.

High school (ensino médio)

Students must have finished their elementary school before they enroll in high school. Secondary education takes three years. The minimum is 2,200 hours of teaching over four years. Secondary education core curriculum comprises Portuguese (including Portuguese language, essay studies, Brazilian and Portuguese literatures), foreign language (usually English, also Spanish and very rarely French), History, Geography, Mathematics, Physics, Chemistry and Biology. Philosophy and Sociology, which were banned during the military dictatorship (1964–1985), have become compulsory again.

High school education is provided by all levels of government.

Technical education (ensino técnico)

The movement of the eleventh or twelfth grade of high school or the end of those grades is mandatory for those wishing to pursue technical education, through courses in several areas of knowledge. In addition, students must pass a entrance examination for their specific course. These institutions usually have a greater number of hours per week. The instruction of the technical course lasts from one year and a half to two years.

Figure 347: *Federal University of Minas Gerais*

Figure 348: *TV station in Federal University of Rio Grande do Norte*

Higher education (ensino superior)

The secondary education is mandatory for those wishing to pursue higher education. In addition, students must pass a competitive entrance examination (known as *vestibular*) for their specific course of study. The number of candidates per available place in the freshman class may be in excess of 30 or 40 to one in the not so competitive courses at the top public universities. The most competitive ones excess 80 or 150. In some courses with small number of vacancies, this number can be as high as 200 (medical school, for example).

As is the case in many nations, higher education in Brazil can be divided into undergraduate and graduate work. In addition to providing education, universities promote research and provide separate classes to the community. The Brazilian standard for technology, licentiate or bachelor's degree is awarded in most areas of the arts, humanities, social sciences, exact sciences, or natural sciences, and lasts two to three years for technology courses, three to four years for licenciate and bachelor's courses in general and five to six years for special bachelor's courses such as law, architecture, engineering, human medicine and veterinary medicine.

After graduation students can take postgraduate courses being these latu sensu or stricto sensu. Latu sensu graduate degrees are specializations and refinements lasting one to two years and do not confer academic title. At the end of the course the student must present a course completion work. (Example of latu sensu: MBA, specialization, medical residency, among others). Graduate degrees stricto sensu are courses that confer academic title. After graduation, the student must do a master's degree with a duration of two years and after that period present a master's thesis. If it is approved by the examining board, it will receive the master's degree. The doctorate course in Brazil is the most academic degree course. In order to study this postgraduate course it is necessary to have the title of Master. The doctorate has a duration of four years and must be unpublished. After four years of course the student will present the doctoral thesis to an assessment bank, if approved will receive the title of Doctor.

There are more than 2,600 universities in Brazil, between private and public, according to MEC. Higher vocational education is in general assumed by non-university institutions and the federal Institutions for Education, Science and Technology (38 in 2008).

Figure 349: *Private German school in São Paulo.*

Teacher training and qualification

Students can obtain teacher training in secondary schools through vocational programs. In addition to the required courses to graduate, students take teacher training courses which includes a supervised internship and need 300 hours of teaching practice. Students can be certified through the secondary school program; however, to teach secondary schools, most teaching students need higher education to obtain either a master's or doctorate's. Schools do offer school administration training, but it is not compulsory for students hoping to become an administrator. The licenses and degrees are as follows: teaching certification through vocational programs, a bachelor's, master's, and doctorate. Recently, the government has released a new National Education Plan outlining 20 goals to improve national education, four of which outline improvements to teacher training.

Educational statistics

As a large middle-income country, Brazil has several regions. Its education system is accordingly plagued by many deficiencies and social and regional disparities.

As of 2014:

- Literacy rate of 91.73% for people age 15 or older

As of 2014:

- The nation invests 5.95% of GDP on education, approximately 15.72% of total government expenditures.

As of 2014:

- Literacy rate of 99.8% for people age 6 to 14
- Literacy rate of 90.1% for people age 15 to 17
- Literacy rate of 94.6% of Brazil.

PISA results as of 2015:

- Science: Below average; stable since 2006
- Mathematics: Below average; improvement since 2006
- Reading: Below average; stable since 2006
- Equity:
  - Boys versus Girls: Above average; stable since 2006
  - Social Background: Average; improvement since 2006

International education

As of January 2015, the International Schools Consultancy (ISC) listed Brazil as having 136 international schools. ISC defines an 'international school' in the following terms: "ISC includes an international school if the school delivers a curriculum to any combination of pre-school, primary or secondary students, wholly or partly in English outside an English-speaking country, or if a school in a country where English is one of the official languages, offers an English-medium curriculum other than the country's national curriculum and is international in its orientation." This definition is used by publications including *The Economist*.

External links

- UNESCO inform over Brazil Education[1191]
- Ministry of Education[1192]
- Committee of Education and Culture[1193]
- Brief story of education in Brazil[1194]
- Education in Brazil[1195], a webdossier compiled by "Education Worldwide", a portal belonging to the German Education Server
- Educational Research in Brazil[1196], a webdossier compiled by "Education Worldwide", a portal belonging to the German Education Server
- Vocational Education in Brazil[1197], Brazil's Profile on UNESCO-UNEVOC.

Media and communication

Telecommunications in Brazil

Telecommunications in Brazil

Brazil

Brazil Topics
• Demographics • Economy • Energy • Foreign relations • Geography • History • Military • Politics • **Telecommunications** • Transportation

Statistics	
Land line terminals	34 Millions (2T2009)
Mobile phones	217 Millions (2T2009)

Brazil has both modern technologies in the center-south portion, counting with LTE, 3G HSPA, DSL ISDB based Digital TV. Other areas of the country, particularly the North and Northeast regions, lack even basic analog PSTN telephone lines. This is a problem that the government is trying to solve by linking the liberation of new technologies such as WiMax and FTTH) only tied with compromises on extension of the service to less populated regions.

Telephone system

Landline

The Brazilian landline sector is fully open to competition and continues to attract operators. The bulk of the market is divided between four operators: Telefónica, América Móvil, Oi (controlled by Brazilian investors and Portugal Telecom), and GVT. Telefónica operates through Telefónica Brasil, which has integrated its landline and mobile services under the brand name Vivo. The América Móvil group in Brazil comprises long distance incumbent Embratel, mobile operator Claro, and cable TV provider Net Serviços. The group has started to integrate its landline and mobile services under the brand name Claro, previously used only for mobile services. Oi offers landline and mobile services under the Oi brand name. GVT is the country's most successful alternative network provider, offering landline services only.

National: extensive microwave radio relay system and a national satellite system with 64 earth stations.

International: country code - 55; landing point for a number of submarine cables, including Atlantis 2, that provide direct links to South and Central America, the Caribbean, the US, Africa, and Europe; satellite earth stations - 3 Intelsat (Atlantic Ocean), 1 Inmarsat (Atlantic Ocean region east), connected by microwave relay system to Mercosur Brazilsat B3 satellite earth station (2007)

Statistics

- Served locations: 37,355
- Installed terminals: 43,626,836
- In service: 33,800,370
- Public terminals: 1,128,350
- Density: 22,798 Phones/100 Hab

Mobile

The history of mobile telephony in Brazil began on 30 December 1990, when the Cellular Mobile System began operating in the city of Rio de Janeiro, with a capacity for 10,000 terminals. At that time, according to Anatel (the national telecommunications agency), there were 667 devices in the country. The number of devices rose to 6,700 in the next year, to 30,000 in 1992. In November 2007 3G services were launched, and increased rapidly to almost 90% of the population in 2012 and the agreements signed as part of the auction specify a 3G coverage obligation of 100% of population by 2019. After the auction that took place in June 2012, LTE tests were undertaken in several cities, tourist locations and international conference venues. The first LTE-compatible devices became available in the local market and LTE services was commercially launched in 2013. Under the 4G licence terms, operators were required to have commercial networks in all twelve state capitals which are acting as host cities for the 2014 FIFA World Cup.

The mobile market is ruled by 4 companies:

- **Vivo**, controlled by the Spanish Telefónica, is the leading wireless and fixed company in Brazil.
- **TIM**, controlled by the Italian Telecom Italia. It recently overcame Claro as the second wireless company in Brazil.
- **Claro**, controlled by the Mexican América Móvil (owned by Carlos Slim), ranks third in Brazilian wireless.
- **Oi**, which is the second landline company in Brazil, is the smallest wireless player of the big four.

Statistics

- Number of devices: 161,922,375
- Percentage of prepaid lines: 81.91%
- Density: 84.61 phones/100 hab

Technology distribution

Technology	2008 (Dec)	2009 (Jul)			
		Phone Number		Month growth	Annual growth
AMPS	11,546	6,240	0.00%	-75	-45.96%
TDMA	1,153,580	541,802	0.33%	-39,020	-53.03%
CDMA	12,732,287	9,527,796	5.88%	-425,018	-25.17%
GSM	133,925,736	145,840,175	90.07%	2,497,642	8.90%
WCDMA	1,692,436	2,010,740	1.24%	107,710	-

CDMA 2000	452,816	218,166	0.13%	-9,994	-
Data Terminals	673,002	3,777,456	2.28%	177,623	-
Total	150,641,403	161,922,375	100.00%	2,308,868	10.00%

International backbones

Submarine cables

Several submarine cables link Brazil to the world:

- **Americas II** cable entered operations on September 2000, connecting Brazil (Fortaleza) to United States.
- **ATLANTIS-2**, with around 12 thousand kilometers in extension, operating since 2000, it connects Brazil (Rio de Janeiro and Natal) to Europe, Africa and South America. This is the only cable that connects South America to Africa and Europe.
- **EMERGIA – SAM 1** cable connects all three Americas, surrounding it with a total extension of more than 25 thousand kilometers.
- **GLOBAL CROSSING - SAC** Connects all Americas, surrounding them with a total extension of more than 15 thousand kilometers.
- **GLOBENET/360 NETWORK** Another link from North America to South America.
- **UNISUR** Interconnects Brazil, Uruguay and Argentina.

All these cables have a bandwidth from 20 Gbit/s to 80 Gbit/s, and some have a projected final capacity of more than 1 Tbit/s.

Satellite connections

List of business and satellites they operate (Brazilian Geostationary Satellites)

Satellite operator	Satellite	Bands	Orbital positions	Operational
Hispamar	Amazonas 1	C e Ku	61.0° W	Yes
	Amazonas 2			
Loral Skynet	Estrela do Sul 1	Ku	63.0° W	Yes
	Estrela do Sul 2	Ku	63.0° W	No

Star One	Brasilsat B1	C and X	70.0° W	Yes
	Brasilsat B2	C and X	65.0° W	Yes
	Brasilsat B3	C	84.0° W	Yes
	Brasilsat B4	C	92.0° W	Yes
	Star One C1	C and Ku	65.0° W	Yes
	Star One C2	C and Ku	70.0° W	Yes
	Star One C3	C and Ku	75.0° W	No
	Star One C4	C, L, S	75.0° W	No
	Star One C5	C and Ku	68.0° W	No

Television and radio

Under the Brazilian constitution, television and radio are not treated as forms of telecommunication, in order to avoid creating problems with a series of regulations that reduce and control how international businesses and individuals can participate. It is worth mentioning that Brazil has the 2nd largest media conglomerate in the world in terms of revenue, Rede Globo.

Internet

The Internet has become quite popular in Brazil, with steadily growing numbers of users as well as increased availability. Brazil holds the 6th spot in number of users worldwide. Many technologies are used to bring broadband Internet to consumers, with DSL and cable being the most common (respectively, about 13 million and 9 million connections), and 3G technologies. 4G technologies were introduced in April 2013 and presently are available in over 90% of the country.

Demographics

Demographics of Brazil

Brazil's population is very diverse, comprising many races and ethnic groups. In general, Brazilians trace their origins from five sources: Europeans, Amerindians, Africans, Levantines, and East Asians.

Brazil has conducted a periodical population census since 1872. Brazil is widely known to be one of the most diverse countries in the world. Since 1940, this census has been carried out decennially. Scanned versions of the forms for each census distributed in Brazil since 1960 are available on-line from IPUMS International.

Historically, Brazil has experienced large degrees of ethnic and racial admixture, assimilation of cultures and syncretism.

Population

Historical population		
Year	Pop.	±%
1890	14,333,915	—
1900	17,438,434	+21.7%
1920	30,635,605	+75.7%
1940	41,165,289	+34.4%
1950	51,944,397	+26.2%
1960	70,119,071	+35.0%
1970	93,139,037	+32.8%
1980	119,002,706	+27.8%
1991	146,825,475	+23.4%

2000	169,799,170	+15.6%
2010	192,755,799	+13.5%
2017	208,862,818	+8.4%
Source:		

According to the 2008 PNAD (National Household Sample Survey), conducted by the IBGE, the Brazilian Statistics bureau, there were about 189,953,000 inhabitants in 2008.[1198] As of the latest (2010) census, the Brazilian government estimates its population at 192.76 million.

The population of Brazil is estimated based on various sources from 1550 to 1850. The first official census took place in 1873. From that year, every 8 years (with some exceptions) the population is counted.

Brazil is the fifth most populated country in the world.

- **1550** – 15,000
- **1600** – 100,000
- **1660** – 184,000
- **1700** – 300,000
  1766 – 1,500,000
- **1800** – 3,250,000
- **1820** – 4,717,000
- **1850** – 7,256,000
- **1872** – 9,930,478
- **1890** – 14,333,915
- **1900** – 17,438,434
- **1920** – 30,635,605
- **1940** – 41,236,315
- **1950** – 51,944,397
- **1960** – 70,119,071
- **1970** – 93,139,037
- **1980** – 119,070,865
- **1991** – 146,917,459
- **1996** – 157,079,573
- **2000** – 169,544,443
- **2010** – 192,755,799
- **2017** – 209,429,000

Population distribution in Brazil is very uneven. The majority of Brazilians live within 300 kilometers of the coast, while the interior in the Amazon Basin is almost empty. Therefore, the densely populated areas are on the coast and the sparsely populated areas are in the interior. This historical pattern is little changed by recent movements into the interior.

Demographics of Brazil

Figure 350: *Population density, administrative divisions and economic regions of Brazil (1977).*

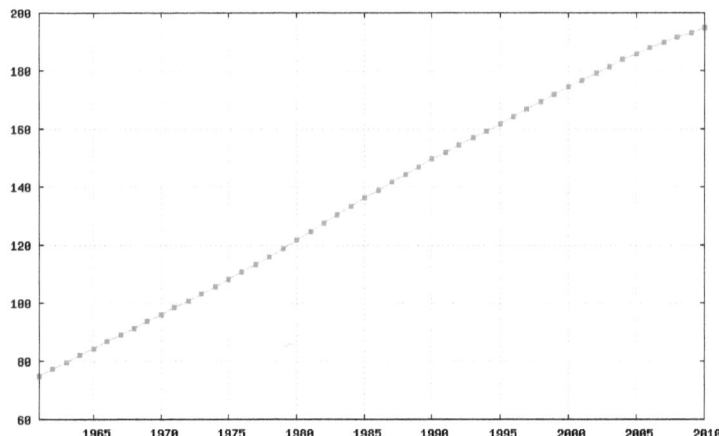

Figure 351: *Demographics of Brazil, Data of FAO, year 2006; Number of inhabitants in thousands.*

Figure 352: *Population of Brazil, 1550–2005*

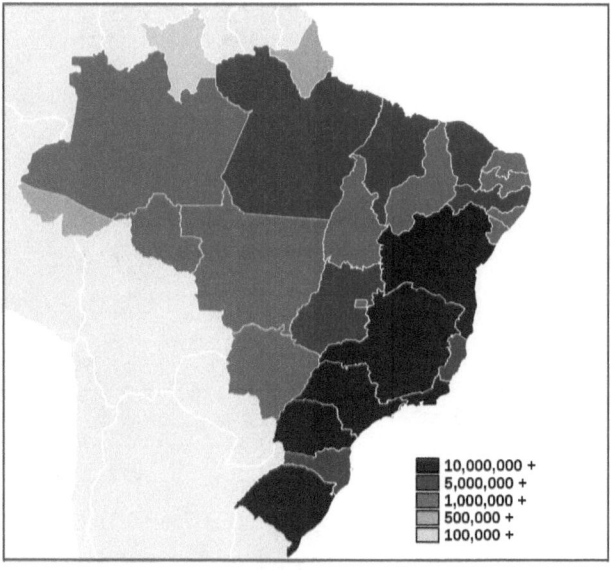

Figure 353: *Map of Brazilian states by population.*

UN estimates

According to the 2017 revision of the World Population Prospects the increase in population was 207,652,865 in 2016, compared to only 53,975,000 in 1950. The proportion of children below the age of 13 in 2015 was 23.0%, 69.2% was between 15 and 61 years of age, while 7.8% was 65 years or older.

Demographics of Brazil

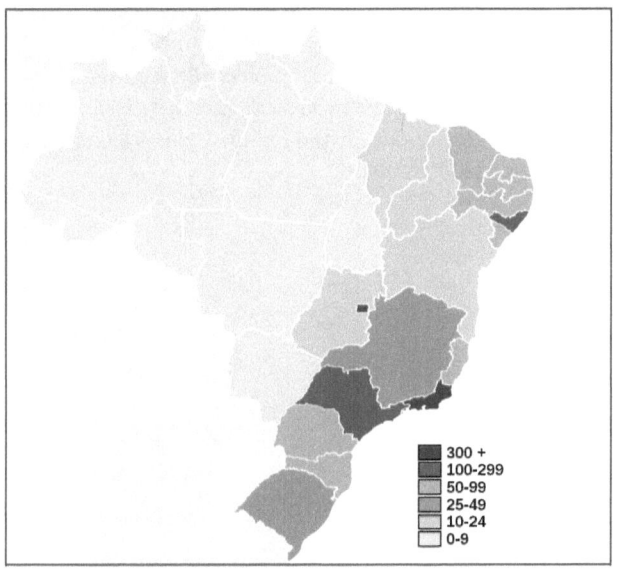

Figure 354: *Map of Brazilian states by population density.*

	Total population (x 1000)	Population aged less than 15 (%)	Population aged 15–64 (%)	Population aged 65+ (%)
1950	53 975	41.6	55.5	3.0
1955	62 656	42.0	55.0	3.0
1960	72 494	43.1	53.7	3.1
1965	84 130	43.6	53.0	3.4
1970	95 982	42.3	54.2	3.5
1975	108 431	40.2	56.0	3.8
1980	122 200	38.4	57.6	4.0
1985	136 836	36.9	59.0	4.1
1990	150 393	35.4	60.1	4.5
1995	162 755	32.4	62.6	5.0
2000	175 786	29.7	64.7	5.6
2005	188 479	27.5	66.2	6.3
2010	198 614	25.3	67.9	6.8
2015	207 848	23.0	69.2	7.8

Vital statistics

Registration of vital events in Brazil has considerably improved during the past decades but is still not considered complete, especially in the northern part of the country. The Population Division of the United Nations prepared the following estimates and forecasts.

Demographics of Brazil

Period	Live births per year	Deaths per year	Natural change per year	CBR*	CDR*	NC*	TFR*	IMR*	Life expectancy total	Life expectancy males	Life expectancy females
1950–1955	2 578 000	908,000	1 670 000	44.2	15.6	28.6	6.15	135	50.9	49.2	52.6
1955–1960	2 923 000	956,000	1 967 000	43.3	14.1	29.1	6.15	122	53.3	51.5	55.2
1960–1965	3 315 000	988,000	2 327 000	42.3	12.6	29.7	6.15	109	55.7	53.8	57.6
1965–1970	3 345 000	975,000	2 370 000	37.2	10.8	26.4	5.38	100	57.6	55.7	59.6
1970–1975	3 462 000	973,000	2 489 000	33.9	9.5	24.4	4.72	91	59.5	57.3	61.8
1975–1980	3 788 000	1 035 000	2 753 000	32.9	9.0	23.9	4.31	79	61.5	59.2	63.9
1980–1985	4 006 000	1 078 000	2 928 000	30.9	8.3	22.6	3.80	63	63.4	60.4	66.8
1985–1990	3 790 000	1 079 000	2 711 000	26.4	7.5	18.9	3.10	52	65.3	61.9	69.1
1990–1995	3 547 000	1 074 000	2 473 000	22.7	6.9	15.8	2.60	43	67.3	63.6	71.2
1995–2000	3 658 000	1 052 000	2 606 000	21.6	6.2	15.4	2.45	34	69.3	65.5	73.3
2000–2005	3 612 000	1 074 000	2 538 000	19.8	5.9	13.9	2.25	27	70.9	67.2	74.8
2005–2010	3 173 000	1 146 000	2 027 000	16.4	5.9	10.5	1.90	24	72.2	68.7	75.9
2010–2015	3 073 000	1 230 000	1 843 000	15.1	6.1	9.0	1.82	19	73.8	70.2	77.5
2015–2020	2 957 000	1 335 000	1 622 000	14.0	6.3	7.7	1.74	16	75.1	71.6	78.7

* CBR = crude birth rate (per 1000); CDR = crude death rate (per 1000); NC = natural change (per 1000); IMR = infant mortality rate per 1000 births; TFR = total fertility rate (number of children per woman)

Births and deaths

Year	Population	Live births	Deaths	Natural increase	Crude birth rate	Crude death rate	Rate of natural increase	TFR
1999		3 256 433	938 658	2 317 775				
2000		3 206 761	946 686	2 260 075				
2001		3 115 474	961 492	2 153 982				
2002		3 059 402	982 807	2 076 595				
2003		3 038 251	1 002 340	2 035 911				
2004		3 026 548	1 024 073	2 002 475				
2005		3 035 096	1 006 827	2 028 269				
2006		2 944 928	1 031 691	1 913 237				
2007		2 891 328	1 047 824	1 843 504				
2008		2 934 828	1 077 007	1 857 821				
2009		2 881 581	1 103 088	1 778 493				1.906
2010	192 755 799	2 861 868	1 136 947	1 724 921	14.32	5.80	8.52	1.869
2011		2 913 160	1 170 498	1 742 662				1.833
2012		2 905 789	1 181 166	1 724 623				1.801
2013		2 904 027	1 210 474	1 693 553				1.770
2014		2 913 121	1 227 039	1 686 082				1.742
2015		2 952 969	1 264 175	1 688 794	14.4	6.0	8.4	1.716
2016	206 081 432	2 793 935	1 309 774	1 484 161	13.5	6.2	7.3	1.692

Regional differences

In some states in the North and Northeast, the fertility rate was higher than the national average in 2015. The highest rate was in Acre, with 2.35 children per woman Other regions with high fertility include Amapá, with 2.28 children per woman, Amazonas, 2.25 in Roraima, 2.22, in Maranhão, 2.17, and Pará, 2.13.

On the other hand, São Paulo is the state with the lowest rate, 1.38 children per woman. Other states with low fertility include, Santa Catarina, with 1.45, Rio Grande do Sul, 1.50, in Rio de Janeiro, 1.55 in Paraná and Minas Gerais, 1.59.

Childlessness and education

The color or race of the woman and the level of education has also shown to influence the fact of not having children. In 2013, among white women aged 15 to 49 years, 41.5% had no children, while among black women, the percentage was 35.8%.

The proportional difference is even greater among white women compared to black 25–29 years. While the proportion among white women childless was 48.1% among black women was 33.8%.

Regarding education, among women 15–49 years of age with more than eight years of schooling, 44.2% had no children in 2013, while among those with up to seven years of study this figure was 21.6%.

Schooling among women 25–29 years has shown an even greater disparity. Among the less educated, 16.3% had no children, while among the more educated 54.5% had no children. The proportion of women aged 45 to 49 without children was 8.2% in 2013 among those with less education and 15.1% among those with more years of schooling.

Total fertility rate

1.78 children born/woman (IBGE 2015 est.)

	Brazil 100%	White 47.73%	Black 7.61%	Asian 1.09%	Pardo (Multiracial) 43.13%	American Indians 0.43%
Population 0–14	45,932,294	20,460,482	2,698,639	420,952	22,055,573	295,862
Percent group 0–14 in race	24.08%	22.47%	18.59%	20.02%	26.81%	36.17%

Population 0–14 compared to racial groups	100%	44.54%	5.88%	0.92%	48.02%	0.64%
Population 15–49	105,816,285	49,381,206	8,693,350	1,178,391	46,156,227	402,079
Proportions 0–14 to 15–49	0,43407	0,41434	0,31043	0,35723	0,47785	0,73583

Age group	Brazil 100% (percent of the population)	White 47.73% (percent in the race/- percent in the age group)	Black 7.61% (percent in the race/- percent in the age group)	Asian 1.09% (percent in the race/- percent in the age group)	Pardo (Multiracial) 43.13% (percent in the race/- percent in the age group)	Indians 0.43% (percent in the race/- percent in the age group)	Unspecified 0.0034%
Population	190,755,799	91,051,646	14,517,961	2,084,288	82,277,333	817,963	6,608
0–4	13,796,158 (7.23%)	6,701,186 (7.36%/- 48.57%)	655,958 (4.52%/- 4.75%)	119,956 (5.76%/- 0.87%)	6,217,638 (7.56%/- 45.07%)	101,195 (12.37%/- 0.73%)	225
5–9	14,969,375 (7.85%)	6,562,558 (7.21%/- 43.84%)	887,209 (6.11%/- 5.93%)	139,543 (6.69%/- 0.93%)	7,279,983 (8.85%/- 48.63%)	99,841 (12.21%/- 0.67%)	241
10–14	17,166,761 (9.00%)	7,196,738 (7.90%/- 41.92%)	1,155,472 (7.96%/- 6.73%)	161,453 (7.75%/- 0.94%)	8,557,952 (10.40%/- 49.85%)	94,826 (11.59%/- 0.55%)	320
15–19	16,990,872 (8.91%)	7,311,734 (8.03%/- 43.03%)	1,264,183 (8.71%/- 7.44%)	177,008 (8.49%/- 1.04%)	8,155,126 (9.91%/- 48.00%)	82,500 (10.86%/- 0.49%)	321
20–24	17,245,192 (9.04%)	7,774,488 (8.54%/- 45.08%)	1,381,677 (9.52%/- 8.01%)	200,060 (9.60%/- 1.16%)	7,814,487 (9.50%/- 45.31%)	73,387 (8.97%/- 0.43%)	1 093
25–29	17,104,414 (8.97%)	7,936,115 (8.72%/- 46.40%)	1,443,820 (9.95%/- 8.44%)	202,733 (9.73%/- 1.19%)	7,455,402 (9.06%/- 43.59%)	65,104 (7.96%/- 0.38%)	1 240
30–34	15,744,512 (8.25%)	7,344,600 (8.07%/- 46.65%)	1,360,298 (9.37%/- 8.64%)	182,150 (8.74%/- 1.16%)	6,800,175 (8.26%/- 43.19%)	56,326 (6.89%/- 0.36%)	963
35–39	13,888,579 (7.28%)	6,596,137 (7.24%/- 47.49%)	1,175,333 (8.10%/- 8.46%)	152,546 (7.32%/- 1,10)	5,915,773 (7.18%/- 42.59%)	48,167 (5.89%/- 0.35%)	623
40–44	13,009,364 (6.82%)	6,365,363 (6.99%/- 48.93%)	1,095,301 (7.54%/- 8.42%)	139,230 (6.68%/- 1.07%)	5,368,059 (6.52%/- 41.26%)	40,950 (5.01%/- 0.31%)	461

45–49	11,833,352 (6.20%)	6,052,769 (6.65%/-51.15%)	972,738 (6.70%/-8.22%)	124,664 (5.98%/-1.05%)	4,647,205 (5.65%/-39.27%)	35,645 (4.36%/-0.30%)	331
50–54	10,140,402 (5.32%)	5,286,559 (5.81%/-52.13%)	848,098 (5.84%/-8.36%)	106,539 (5.11%/-1.05%)	3,869,792 (4.70%/-38.16%)	29,156 (3.56%/-0.29%)	258
55–59	8,276,221 (4.34%)	4,404,057 (4.84%/-53.21%)	675,404 (4.65%/-8.16%)	95,149 (4.57%/-1.15%)	3,076,630 (3.74%/-37.17%)	24,800 (3.03%/-0.30%)	181
60–69	11,349,930 (5.95%)	6,158,001 (6.76%/-54.26%)	906,487 (6.24%/-7.99%)	152,099 (7.30%/-1.34%)	4,097,068 (4.98%/-36.10%)	36,062 (4.41%/-0.32%)	213
70+	9,240,667 (4.84%)	5,361,341 (5.89%/-58.02%)	695,983 (4.79%/-7.53%)	131,158 (6.29%/-1.42%)	3,022,043 (3.67%/-32.70%)	30,004 (3.67%/-0.32%)	138

Largest urban agglomerations

Cities in Brazil, except for the state of São Paulo, are usually not arranged in a single network, but rather on various *export paths* to seaside ports. The most important cities are on the coast or close to it. State capitals are also each the largest city in its state, except for Vitória, the capital of Espírito Santo, and Florianópolis, the capital of Santa Catarina. There are also non-capital metropolitan areas in São Paulo state (Campinas, Santos and Paraíba Valley), Minas Gerais (Steel Valley), Rio Grande do Sul (Sinos Valley), and Santa Catarina (Itajaí Valley).

São Paulo and Rio de Janeiro are far larger than any other Brazilian city. São Paulo's influence in most economic aspects can be noted in a national (and even international) scale; other Brazilian metropolises are second tier, even though Rio de Janeiro (partially due to its former status as the national capital) still host various large corporations' headquarters, besides being Brazil's cultural center with respect to soap operas and film production. Brasília, the capital of Brazil, is the 3rd biggest city.

Migrations

Immigration

Immigration to Brazil, by national origin, periods from 1830 to 1933
Source: Brazilian Institute for Geography and Statistics (IBGE)

origin	1830–1855	1856–1883	1884–1893	1894–1903	1904–1913	1914–1923	1924–1933	1934–2014
Portuguese	16,737	116,000	170,621	155,542	384,672	201,252	233,650	400,000
Italians	—	100,000	510,533	537,784	196,521	86,320	70,177	
Spaniards	—	—	113,116	102,142	224,672	94,779	52,400	
Germans	2,008	30,000	22,778	6,698	33,859	29,339	61,723	
Japanese	—	—	—	—	11,868	20,398	110,191	
Syrians and Lebanese	—	—	96	7,124	45,803	20,400	20,400	
Others	—	—	66,524	42,820	109,222	51,493	164,586	

Immigration has been a very important demographic factor in the formation, structure and history of the population in Brazil, influencing culture, economy, education, racial issues, etc. Brazil has received the third largest number of immigrants in the Western Hemisphere, after the United States and Argentina.

Brazil's structure, legislation and settlement policies for arriving immigrants were much less organized than in Canada and the United States at the time. Nevertheless, an Immigrant's Hostel (*Hospedaria dos Imigrantes*) was built in 1886 in São Paulo, and quick admittance and recording routines for the throngs of immigrants arriving by ship at the seaports of Vitória, Rio de Janeiro, Santos, Paranaguá, Florianópolis and Porto Alegre were established. The São Paulo State alone processed more than 2.5 million immigrants in its almost 100 years of continuous operation. People of more than 70 different nationalities were recorded.

Following the trend of several other countries in the Americas, which encouraged immigration from many countries, Brazil quickly became a melting pot of races and nationalities, but being peculiar in the sense of having the highest degree of intermarriage in the world. Immigrants found a strong social and cultural tolerance toward inter-racial marriage, including large numbers of Mulattoes (white and black), Caboclos (Indian and White) and mixed European, African and Indian people, though it was not accompanied by an entire lack of racism. Correspondingly, the same mentality reflected in low psychological and social barriers regarding intermarriage between Europeans, Middle Easterners and Asians of several origins, as well as between people of different religions.

History of immigration

It is that the Americas were settled by three migratory waves from Northern Asia. The Native Brazilians are thought to descend from the first wave of migrants, who arrived in the region around 9000 BC. The main Native Brazilian groups are the Tupi-Guarani, the Jê, the Arawaks and the Caraibas (Kalina or Caribs). The Tupi-Guarani nation, originally from the Paraná river basin and also one of the largest of the Native-Paraguayan nations, had spread all along the Brazilian coastline from South to North and came to be known by the Portuguese as "Os Índios da Língua Geral" ("The Indians of the General Language"); the Jê nation occupied most of the interior of the country from Maranhão to Santa Catarina. The Arawaks and the Caribs, the last ones to get in contact with the Portuguese, lived in the North and Northwest of Brazil.

The European immigration to Brazil started in the 16th century, with the vast majority of them coming from Portugal. In the first two centuries of colonization, 100,000 Portuguese arrived in Brazil (around 500 colonists per year). In the 18th century, 600,000 Portuguese arrived (6,000 per year). The first region to be settled by the Portuguese was Northeastern Brazil, followed by the Southeast region. The original Amerindian population of Brazil (between two and five million) largely died from disease or violence or was assimilated into the Portuguese population. The Mamelucos (or Caboclos, a mixed race between Whites and Amerindians) have always been present in many parts of Brazil.

Another important ethnic group, Africans, first arrived as slaves. Many came from Guinea, or from West African countries – by the end of the eighteenth century many had been taken from the Kingdom of Kongo and modern-day Angola, Mozambique, Ghana and Nigeria. By the time of the end of the slave trade in 1850, around three million slaves had been brought to Brazil–30% of all slave traffic between Africa and the Americas. Nowadays, there are still small immigration waves coming from the African continent. The largest influx of European immigrants to Brazil occurred in the late 19th and early 20th centuries. According to the *Memorial do Imigrante* statistics data, Brazil attracted nearly 5 million immigrants between 1870 and 1953. These immigrants were divided in two groups: a part of them was sent to Southern Brazil to work as small farmers. However, the biggest part of the immigrants was sent to Southeast Brazil to work in the coffee plantations. The immigrants sent to Southern Brazil were mainly Germans (starting in 1824, mainly from Rhineland-Palatinate, Pomerania, Hamburg, Westphalia, etc.) Italians (starting in 1875, mainly from the Veneto and Lombardia), Austrians, Poles, Ukrainians, Dutch and Russians. In the South, the immigrants established rural communities that, still today, have a strong cultural connection with their ancestral homelands. In Southeast Brazil, most of the immigrants were Italians (mainly from the Veneto, Campania, Calabria and Lombardia), Portuguese (mainly from Beira Alta, Minho and Alto Trás-os-Montes), Dutch, Spaniards (mainly from Galicia and Andalusia), Lithuanians, French, Hungarians and Ashkenazi Jews.

Notably, the first half of the 20th century saw a large inflow of Japanese (mainly from Honshū, Hokkaidō and Okinawa) and Arab (from Lebanon and Syria) immigrants. These Christian Levantine Arab immigrants were wrongly called "Turks" by many Brazilians because their original countries were still under Ottoman rule back in the period when Arab immigration to Brazil began. The number of actual Turks who immigrated to Brazil was in fact very small. Chinese, Taiwanese and Koreans influx became common after the 1950s.

IBGE's 1998 PME

In 1998, the IBGE, within its preparation for the 2000 census, experimentally introduced a question about "origem" (ancestry) in its "Pesquisa Mensal de Emprego" (Monthly Employment Research), in order to test the viability of introducing that variable in the Census. This research interviewed about 90,000 people in six metropolitan regions (São Paulo, Rio de Janeiro, Porto Alegre, Belo Horizonte, Salvador, and Recife).

Here are its results for both the White population and the population in general:

Brazilian Population, by *origin*, as understood by those surveyed 1998		
Origin	% of Whites	% of all races
Brazilian	83.11%	86.09%
Portuguese	15.72%	10.46%
Italian	14.50%	10.01%
Spanish	6.42%	4.40%
German	5.51%	3.54%
Indigenous	4.80%	6.64%
Black	1.30%	5.09%
Arab	0.72%	0.48%
Japanese	0.62%	1.34%
African	0.58%	2.06%
Jewish	0.25%	0.20%
Others	4.05%	2.81%
Total	137.58%	133.52%

Notice that the total is higher than 100% because of multiple claims of ascendants from different nations in the answers.

Emigration

In the second half of the 1980s, Brazilians from various socioeconomic levels started to emigrate to other countries in search of economic opportunities.

In the 1990s, nearly 1.9 million Brazilians were living outside the country, mainly in the United States, Paraguay and Japan, but also in Italy, Portugal, the United Kingdom, France, Canada, Australia, Switzerland, Germany, Belgium, Spain and Israel. However, there were no specific policies implemented by the government to encourage or discourage this emigration process.[1199]

The 2000 Brazilian Census provides some information about the high number of migrants returning to Brazil. Of those who reported residing in another

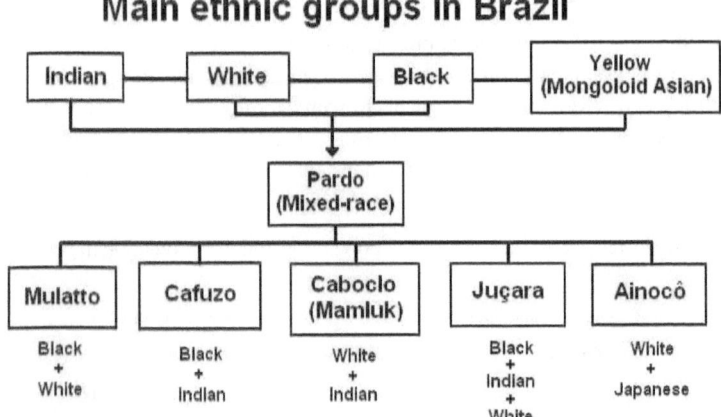

Figure 355: *Main ethnic groups in Brazil.*

country less than 10 years before the 2000 census, 66.9 percent were Brazilians. If only the returning migrants (former Brazilian immigrants) are considered, 26.8 percent of Brazilians came from Paraguay, 17 percent came from Japan, and 15.8 percent came from the United States.

Racial composition

The bulk of the Brazilian population descends from three main source populations (either alone, or more commonly, in varying combinations mixed in varying degrees); early European settlers (chiefly ethnic Portuguese, but also Portuguese New Christians of ethnic Sephardic Jewish origin forced to convert to Christianity), sub-Saharan Africans (Yoruba, Ewe, Akan, Bantu, and others), and the indigenous peoples in Brazil (mostly Tupi and Guarani, but also other many indigenous Brazilian ethnic groups). Interracial mixing has been common and well accepted ever since the first Portuguese settlers arrived.

Starting in the late 19th century, Brazil received substantial post-colonial immigration from several other regions, mainly from peoples of what are now the countries of Italy, Germany, Spain, Poland, as well as Arabic-speaking Christians from the Levant (mostly from what is now Lebanon, and less so from what is today Syria), Ukraine, Japan, the People's Republic of China and Korea.

Jews in Brazil are a small but sizable population, and they include mostly Ashkenazi Jews (who also arrived with the post-colonial contingent of European migration), a smaller proportion of Sephardi Jews (mostly Eastern

Figure 356: *Brazilian ethnic diversity*

Sephardim arrived with the contingent of post-colonial immigrants from Syria and Lebanon, but also North African Sephardim from Morocco settled in the Amazon, and Western Sephardim arrived with the Dutch), and to a much lesser extent Mizrahi Jews. Overall, the small but sizable Brazilian Jewish community is concentrated especially in São Paulo, Rio de Janeiro and Porto Alegre, and they are accounted for without Brazilian descendants of Portuguese "New Christians" (ethnic Sephardic Jews forced to convert to Christianity and arrived with the ethnic Portuguese during the colonial period), which if included would inflate the Jewish origin population in Brazil considerably. By themselves, Brazilian descendants of Portuguese "New Christians" are estimated to account for a figure anywhere between hundreds of thousands to several million.

The descendants of European immigrants, particularly the Germans, Italians, Austrians, Swiss, Poles, Ukrainians, French, Dutch, Lithuanians, Scandinavians, Russians, Hungarians, Finns and Luxembourgers are mainly concentrated in the southern part of the country, in the states of Rio Grande do Sul, Santa Catarina, Paraná, and the most populous, São Paulo; these states have a wide majority of citizens of European descent. São Paulo alone has the largest population in absolute numbers with 30 million whites. In the rest of the country, part of the white population is of colonial Portuguese, Dutch, Spanish and French settler stock, especially in the Northeast. In the mid-southern states of

Rio de Janeiro, Espírito Santo, Minas Gerais, Goiás, Mato Grosso do Sul and in the Federal District, the number of whites (European and Levantine phenotype) revolves around 50% of the population, being somewhat equal to the absolute number of Afro-Brazilians, East Asians and mixed race Brazilians, i.e., Caboclos or Mestizo/Castizo, Mulattoes, Eurasians and Gypsies altogether.

In the Northeast, which received large masses of African slaves to work in sugarcane, tobacco and cotton plantations, people of African and mixed-race descent predominate, mostly on the coast, whereas in the semi-arid country land (usually called *sertão*) there is a predominance of white and Amerindian-European mixed people. Most of the black or mulatto people in the *sertão* are descended from freed African slaves or mulattos who fled inland from the coast and worked as cowboys for semi-feudal lords. The city of Salvador da Bahia is considered one of the largest black cities of the world. In the Northwest (covering largely the Brazilian Amazon), a great part of the population has distinguishable ethnic characteristics that emphasize their Amerindian roots. Other ethnic groups have merged with the Indigenous tribes there. This region is not densely populated, and "caboclos", people of mixed native and European descent, are a small part of the entire Brazilian population.

The Japanese are the largest Asian group in Brazil. In fact, Brazil has the largest population of Japanese ancestry outside Japan, with 1.8 million Japanese-Brazilians, most of them living in São Paulo. Some Chinese and Korean also settled Brazil. Most Chinese came from mainland China, but others came from Taiwan and Hong Kong, and also from Portuguese-speaking Macau—these Chinese from Macau could speak and understand Portuguese, and it was not hard for them to adjust to Brazilian life. Those immigrant populations and their descendants still retain some of their original ethnic identity, however they are not closed communities and are rapidly integrating into mainstream Brazilian society: for instance, very few of the third generation can understand their grandparents' languages.

Aboriginal Brazilians

The Amerindians make up 0.4% of Brazil's population, or about 700,000 people. Indigenous peoples are found in the entire territory of Brazil, although the majority of them live in Indian reservations in the North and Centre-Western part of the country.

Over 60 million Brazilians possess at least one Native South American ancestor, according to a recent mitochondrial DNA study. However, only 0.4% of the population consider themselves to be Natives. Brazilians tend to consider "Native South American" a cultural, not racial category.

Figure 357: *A Brazilian Indian from the Chaman tribe.*

When the first Portuguese arrived in Brazil, in 1500, there were between 2.5 and 3.2 million Natives living in the country. In the mid-19th century they were only 100,000 and in the late 20th century close to 300,000.

Black Brazilians

Black Brazilians are defined as people who are solely, or mostly, descended from former African slaves, or immigrants. According to the 2010 census, there are 14,517,961 Afro Brazilians, which make up 7.61% of Brazil's population, although a larger number of Brazilians have some degree of African ancestry.

Asian Brazilians

According to the 2006 census, people of East Asian descent number 1,919,000, or 1.1% of Brazil's population. Estimates say that there are 2.5 to 3.0 million people of Japanese descent in Brazil, who are mostly concentrated in two states: São Paulo and Paraná, but smaller communities are found in the entire territory of the country. Brazil has the largest population of Japanese descent outside Japan.

There are also smaller communities of Korean people and Chinese origin.

Figure 358: *Brazilians of African descent in Bahia.*

Figure 359: *Liberdade, São Paulo, concentrates the largest Japanese population outside Japan.*

Mixed race/Pardo Brazilians

The Pardos can be a mixture of Europeans, Levantine Arabs, Crypto-Jews or Anusim, Blacks, Amerindians, Gypsies and Asians. Brazil does not have a category for multiracial people, but a Pardo (brown) one, which may include caboclos, mulatos, cafuzos (local ethnonyms for people of noticeable mixed White and Amerindian, Black and White, and Amerindian and Black descent, i.e., mestizos, mulattoes and zambos, respectively), the multiracial result of their intermixing (despite most of White and Black Brazilians possessing some degree of race-mixing, since brownness in Brazil is a matter of phenotype) and assimilated, westernized indigenous people.

The Pardos make up 43.13% or 82.3 million people of Brazil's population. Multiracial Brazilians live in the entire territory of Brazil. Although, according to DNA resources, most Brazilians possess some degree of mixed-race ancestry, less than 45% of the country's population classified themselves as being part of this group due to phenotype.

The caboclo or mestiço population, those whose ancestry is Native and European, revolves around 43 million people or 21% of the population. Genetic studies conducted by the geneticist Sergio D.J. Pena of the Federal University of Minas Gerais have shown that the caboclo population is made of individuals whose DNA ranges from 70% to 90% European (mostly Portuguese, Spanish, Dutch, French or Italian 1500s to 1700s male settlers) with the remaining percentage spanning different Indigenous markers. Similar DNA tests showed that people self-classified as mulatto or white and Black mix, span from 62% to 83% European (mostly descendants of Portuguese, Dutch and French settlers during the colonial period in the Northeast). The pardo category in Brazil also includes 800 thousand gypsies or Roma people, most of them coming from Portugal but also different countries in Eastern Europe and the Baltics. Eurasians can also be classified as pardo. The majority of them consisting of Ainoko or Hafu, individuals of Japanese and European ancestry.

Recent research has suggested that Asians from the early Portuguese Eastern Empire, known as Luso-Asians first came to Brazil during the sixteenth century as seamen known as Lascars, or as servants, slaves and concubines accompanying the governors, merchants and clergy who has served in Portuguese Asia.[1200] This first presence of Asians was limited to Northeast Brazil, especially Bahia, but others were brought as cultivators, textile workers and miners to Pará and other parts of the Northeast.

Figure 360: *Members of the Italian Brazilian community with former President of Brazil, in Rio Grande do Sul.*

White Brazilians

According to the 2010 census, there were more than 91 million White Brazilians, comprising 47.73% of Brazil's population. White Brazilians are defined as people who are solely or mostly descended from European immigrants, although most Brazilians have some degree of European ancestry. Whites are found in the entire territory of Brazil, although they are most concentrated in the south and southeastern parts of the country;

Nearly one million Europeans had arrived in Brazil by 1800; most of them colonists from Portugal. An immigration boom occurred in the 19th and 20th centuries, when nearly six million Europeans emigrated to Brazil, most of them Portuguese, Germans Italians and Spaniards.

Many White Brazilians have some Amerindian and/or African ancestry (similarly found, but with widely differing percentages of admixture are, in White Americans and White Argentines). It is estimated that 75% of all Brazilians have varying degrees of Portuguese ancestry.

Nowadays, White Brazilians come from a very diverse background, which includes:

- The Dutch were among the Europeans settling in Brazil during the 17th century. From 1630 to 1654, the Dutch controlled the northeast coast of Brazil, establishing their colonial capital in Recife. During the 19th and

20th century, immigrants from the Netherlands populated the central and southern states of Brazil.

The first Dutch immigrants to South America after its independence waves from their metropoles went to the Brazilian state of Espírito Santo between 1858 and 1862, where they founded the settlement of Holanda, a colony of 500 mainly Reformed folk from West Zeeuws-Vlaanderen in the Dutch province of Zeeland. Dutch and other Low Franconian languages are still spoken in São Paulo (state), especially Holambra (named after Holland-America-Brazil), famous for its tulips and the annual Expoflora event, Santa Catarina, Rio Grande do Sul and around Ponta Grossa, Castrolanda and Carambeí known as little Holland, in the plains of Paraná, headquarters of several food companies and a dairy farming region.

- The first Germans and Austrians arrived in Brazil in 1824. Most of them established themselves in rural communities across Southern Brazil, such as São Leopoldo, Novo Hamburgo, Blumenau and Pomerode. In Santa Catarina state, Southern Brazil, Germans and Austrians represented over 45% of all immigrants arriving, and in the entire country, citizens who descend from German-speaking nationalities, including Swiss and Luxemburger, but also Volga German, may represent as much as 8% of the absolute population, since Brazil is home to the second largest German-Austrian population outside their respective nations, after the USA. And German is the second most spoken mother tongue in the country. According to Ethnologue, Standard German is spoken by 1.5 million people and Brazilian German encompass assorted dialects, including Riograndenser Hunsrückisch spoken by over 3 million Brazilians.[1201]
- Italians started arriving in Brazil in 1875, making up the main group of immigrants in the late 19th century. First they settled in rural communities across Southern Brazil. In the early 20th century, they mostly settled in the coffee plantations in the Southeast, later moving to São Paulo capital to work in factories or starting their own businesses in trade, services and industry like businessman and industrialist count Francesco Matarazzo. In São Paulo, which came to be labeled an "Italian city" in the early twentieth century, Italians engaged mainly in the incipient industry and urban services activities. They came to represent 90% of the 60,000 workers employed in São Paulo factories in 1901.

Today 15% of Brazilians or 31 million citizens are of Italian extraction, the largest number outside of Italy itself, most of them descended from Northern Italians, reason why Talian, or the Venetian dialect, is the third most spoken mother tongue in the nation.

- Poles came in significant numbers to Brazil after 1870. Most of them settled in the State of Paraná, working as small farmers.

- Portuguese Most Brazilians are fully or partly of Portuguese ancestry. Portuguese settlers began arriving in 1500. Immigration increased during the 18th century and reached its peak in the late 19th and early 20th centuries. Lusitanian immigration never ceased throughout the 19th and 20th centuries. Portuguese people in diaspora settled in Brazil especially during the 1970s coming from former Portuguese colonies like Macau or Angola after its independence.

An additional figure of 1.2 million Portuguese arrived between 1951 and 1975 to settle mostly in the Southeast. Nowadays, Lusitanians constitute the biggest group of foreigners living in the country, with over 690,000 Portuguese nationals currently living in Brazil. The vast majority arrived in the last decade. The first semester of 2011 solely had an increase of 52 thousand Portuguese nationals applying for a permanent residence visa while another large group was granted Brazilian citizenship.

- Spaniards came in large numbers to Brazil, starting in the late 19th century. Most of them were attracted to work in the coffee plantations in the state of São Paulo. Today there are an estimated 15 million Brazilians of direct Spanish descent.
- Ukrainians came mostly in the late 19th century. Currently they number approximately 980,000, most of whom live in a compact settlement in south central Paraná[1202]

Composition of Brazil, genetic studies

Genetic studies have shown the Brazilian population as a whole to have European, African and Native Americans components.

Autosomal studies

A 2015 autosomal genetic study, which also analysed data of 25 studies of 38 different Brazilian populations concluded that: European ancestry accounts for 62% of the heritage of the population, followed by the African (21%) and the Native American (17%). The European contribution is highest in Southern Brazil (77%), the African highest in Northeast Brazil (27%) and the Native American is the highest in Northern Brazil (32%).

Region	European	African	Native American
North Region	51%	16%	32%
Northeast Region	58%	27%	15%
Central-West Region	64%	24%	12%
Southeast Region	67%	23%	10%
South Region	77%	12%	11%

An autosomal study from 2013, with nearly 1300 samples from all of the Brazilian regions, found a pred. degree of European ancestry combined with African and Native American contributions, in varying degrees. 'Following an increasing North to South gradient, European ancestry was the most prevalent in all urban populations (with values up to 74%). The populations in the North consisted of a significant proportion of Native American ancestry that was about two times higher than the African contribution. Conversely, in the Northeast, Center-West and Southeast, African ancestry was the second most prevalent. At an intrapopulation level, all urban populations were highly admixed, and most of the variation in ancestry proportions was observed between individuals within each population rather than among population'.

Region	European	African	Native American
North Region	51%	17%	32%
Northeast Region	56%	28%	16%
Central-West Region	58%	26%	16%
Southeast Region	61%	27%	12%
South Region	74%	15%	11%

An autosomal DNA study (2011), with nearly 1000 samples from all over the country ("whites", "pardos" and "blacks", according to their respective proportions), found out a major European contribution, followed by a high African contribution and an important Native American component. "In all regions studied, the European ancestry was predominant, with proportions ranging from 60.6% in the Northeast to 77.7% in the South". The 2011 autosomal study samples came from blood donors (the lowest classes constitute the great majority of blood donors in Brazil[1203]), and also public health institutions personnel and health students. The study showed that Brazilians from different regions are more homogenous than previously thought by some based on the census alone. "Brazilian homogeneity is, therefore, a lot greater between Brazilian regions than within Brazilian regions".

Region	European	African	Native American
Northern Brazil	68.80%	10.50%	18.50%
Northeast of Brazil	60.10%	29.30%	8.90%
Southeast Brazil	74.20%	17.30%	7.30%
Southern Brazil	79.50%	10.30%	9.40%

According to a DNA study from 2010, "a new portrayal of each ethnicity contribution to the DNA of Brazilians, obtained with samples from the five regions of the country, has indicated that, on average, European ancestors are responsible for nearly 80% of the genetic heritage of the population. The variation between the regions is small, with the possible exception of the South, where the European contribution reaches nearly 90%. The results, published by the scientific magazine *American Journal of Human Biology* by a team of the Catholic University of Brasília, show that, in Brazil, physical indicators such as skin colour, colour of the eyes and colour of the hair have little to do with the genetic ancestry of each person, which has been shown in previous studies (regardless of census classification). "Ancestry informative SNPs can be useful to estimate individual and population biogeographical ancestry. Brazilian population is characterized by a genetic background of three parental populations (European, African, and Brazilian Native Amerindians) with a wide degree and diverse patterns of admixture. In this work we analyzed the information content of 28 ancestry-informative SNPs into multiplexed panels using three parental population sources (African, Amerindian, and European) to infer the genetic admixture in an urban sample of the five Brazilian geopolitical regions. The SNPs assigned apart the parental populations from each other and thus can be applied for ancestry estimation in a three hybrid admixed population. Data was used to infer genetic ancestry in Brazilians with an admixture model. Pairwise estimates of F(st) among the five Brazilian geopolitical regions suggested little genetic differentiation only between the South and the remaining regions. Estimates of ancestry results are consistent with the heterogeneous genetic profile of Brazilian population, with a major contribution of European ancestry (0.771) followed by African (0.143) and Amerindian contributions (0.085). The described multiplexed SNP panels can be useful tool for bioanthropological studies but it can be mainly valuable to control for spurious results in genetic association studies in admixed populations". It is important to note that "the samples came from free of charge paternity test takers, thus as the researchers made it explicit: "the paternity tests were free of charge, the population samples involved people of variable socioeconomic strata, although *likely to be leaning slightly* towards the "pardo" group".

Region	European	African	Native American
North Region	71.10%	18.20%	10.70%
Northeast Region	77.40%	13.60%	8.90%
Central-West Region	65.90%	18.70%	11.80%
Southeast Region	79.90%	14.10%	6.10%
South Region	87.70%	7.70%	5.20%

An autosomal DNA study from 2009 found a similar profile "all the Brazilian samples (regions) lie more closely to the European group than to the African populations or to the Mestizos from Mexico".

Region	European	African	Native American
North Region	60.6%	21.3%	18.1%
Northeast Region	66.7%	23.3%	10.0%
Central-West Region	66.3%	21.7%	12.0%
Southeast Region	60.7%	32.0%	7.3%
South Region	81.5%	9.3%	9.2%

According to another autosomal DNA study from 2008, by the University of Brasília (UnB), European ancestry dominates in the whole of Brazil (in all regions), accounting for 65.90% of heritage of the population, followed by the African contribution (24.80%) and the Native American (9.3%).

São Paulo state, the most populous state in Brazil, with about 40 million people, showed the following composition, according to an autosomal study from 2006: European genes account for 79% of the heritage of the people of São Paulo, 14% are of African origin, and 7% Native American. A more recent study, from 2013, found the following composition in São Paulo state: 61.9% European, 25.5% African and 11.6% Native American.

Races and ethnicities by region

South

The South of Brazil is the region with the largest percentage of Whites. According to the 2005 census, people of European ancestry account for 79.6% of the population. In colonial times, this region had a very small population.

The region what is now Southern Brazil was originally settled by Amerindian peoples, mostly Guarani and Kaingangs. Only a few settlers from

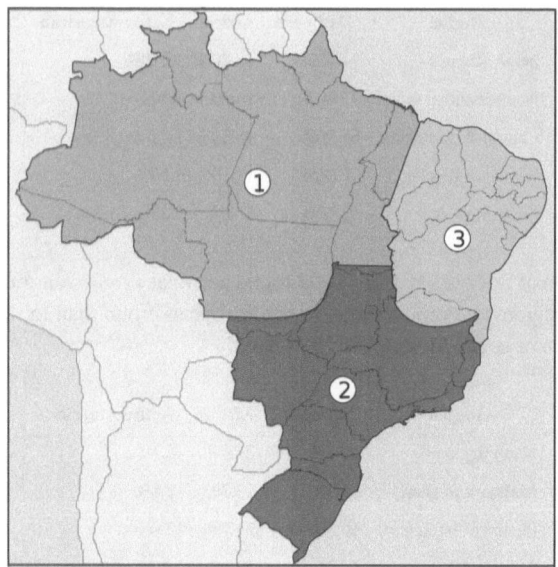

Figure 361: *1•Amazonia, 2•Centro-Sul, 3•Nordeste.*

São Paulo were living thereWikipedia:Manual of Style/Dates and numbers#Chronological items. This situation made the region vulnerable to attacks from neighboring countries. This fact forced the King of Portugal to decide to populate the region. For this, settlers from the Portuguese Azores islands were sent to the coastWikipedia:Manual of Style/Dates and numbers#Chronological items.

To stimulate the immigration to Brazil, the king offered several benefits for the Azorean couples. Between 1748 and 1756, six thousand Portuguese from the Azores moved to the coast of Santa Catarina. They were mainly newly married who were seeking a better life. At that time, the Azores were one of the poorest regions of Portugal. They established themselves mainly in the Santa Catarina Island, nowadays the region of Florianópolis. Later, some couples moved to Rio Grande do Sul, where they established Porto Alegre, the capital. The Azoreans lived on fishing and agriculture, especially flour. They composed over half of Rio Grande do Sul and Santa Catarina's population in the late 18th century. The state of Paraná was settled by colonists from São Paulo due to their proximity (Paraná was part of São Paulo until the mid-19th century).

With the development of cattle in the interior of Rio Grande do Sul, African slaves began arriving in large numbers. By 1822, Blacks were 50% of Rio Grande do Sul's population. This number decreased to 25% in 1858 and to only 5.2% in 2005. Most of them came from Angola.[1204]

After independence from Portugal (1822) the Brazilian government started to stimulate the arrival of a new wave of immigrants to settle the South. In 1824 they established São Leopoldo, a German community. Major Schaeffer, a German who was living in Brazil, was sent to Germany in order to bring immigrants. From Rhineland-Palatinate, the Major brought the immigrants and soldiers. Settlers from Germany were brought to work as small farmers, because there were many land holdings without workers.

To attract the immigrants, the Brazilian government had promised large tracts of land, where they could settle with their families and colonize the region. The first years were not easy. Many Germans died of tropical disease, while others left the colonies to find better living conditions. The German colony of São Leopoldo was a disaster. Nevertheless, in the following years, a further 4,830 Germans arrived at São Leopoldo, and then the colony started to develop, with the immigrants establishing the town of Novo Hamburgo (*New Hamburg*).

From São Leopoldo and Novo Hamburgo, the German immigrants spread into others areas of Rio Grande do Sul, mainly close to sources of rivers. The whole region of Vale dos Sinos was populated by Germans. During the 1830s and part of the 1840s German immigration to Brazil was interrupted due to conflicts in the country (Ragamuffin War). The immigration restarted after 1845 with the creation of new colonies. The most important ones were Blumenau, in 1850, and Joinville in 1851, both in Santa Catarina state; these attracted thousands of German immigrants to the region. In the next five decades, other 28 thousand Germans were brought to Rio Grande do Sul to work as small farmers in the countryside.[1205] By 1914, it is estimated that 50 thousand Germans settled in this state.

Another immigration boom to this region started in 1875. Communities with Italian immigrants were also created in southern Brazil. The first colonies to be populated by Italians were created in the highlands of Rio Grande do Sul (Serra Gaúcha). These were Garibaldi and Bento Gonçalves. These immigrants were predominantly from Veneto, in northern Italy. After five years, in 1880, the great numbers of Italian immigrants arriving caused the Brazilian government to create another Italian colony, Caxias do Sul. After initially settling in the government-promoted colonies, many of the Italian immigrants spread themselves into other areas of Rio Grande do Sul seeking further opportunities.

They created many other Italian colonies on their own, mainly in highlands, because the lowlands were already populated by Germans and native *gaúchos*. The Italian established many vineyards in the region. Nowadays, the wine produced in these areas of Italian colonization in southern Brazil is much appreciated within the country, though little is available for export. In 1875, the first Italian colonies were established in Santa Catarina, which lies immediately to the north of Rio Grande do Sul. The colonies gave rise to towns such as Criciúma, and later also spread further north, to Paraná.

A significant number of Poles have settled in Southern Brazil. The first immigrants arrived in 1869 and until 1959, it is estimated that over 100,000 Poles migrated to Brazil,[1206] 95% of whom were peasants. The State of Paraná received the majority of Polish immigrants, who settled mainly in the region of Curitiba, in the towns of Mallet, Cruz Machado, São Matheus do Sul, Irati, and União da Vitória.

Southeast

The Southeastern region of Brazil is the most ethnically diverse part of the country. Whites make up 55.16% of its population, those of mixed-race 35.69%, and African descent 7.91%. It has the largest percentage of Asian Brazilians, composing 0.8%, and a small Amerindian community (0.2%).

Southeast Brazil is home to the oldest Portuguese village in the Americas, São Vicente, São Paulo, established in 1532.[1207] The region, since the beginning of its colonization, is a melting pot of Whites, Indians and Blacks. The Amerindians of the region were enslaved by the Portuguese. The race mixing between the Indian females and their White masters produced the Bandeirante, the colonial inhabitant of São Paulo, who formed expeditions that crossed the interior of Brazil and greatly increased the Portuguese colonial territory. The main language spoken by these people of mixed Indian/Portuguese heritage was Língua geral, a language that mixed Tupi and Portuguese words.

In the late 17th century the Bandeirantes found gold in the area that nowadays is Minas Gerais. A gold rush took place in Brazil and thousands of Portuguese colonists arrived during this period. The confrontation between the Bandeirantes and the Portuguese for obtaining possession of the mines led to the Emboabas' War. The Portuguese won the war. The Amerindian culture declined, giving space to a stronger Portuguese cultural domination. In order to control the wealth, the Portuguese Crown moved the capital of Brazil from Salvador, Bahia to Rio de Janeiro. Thousands of African slaves were brought to work in the gold mines. They were landed in Rio de Janeiro and sent to other regions. By the late 18th century, Rio de Janeiro was an "African city": most of its inhabitants were slaves. No other place in the world had as many slaves since the end of the Roman Empire.[1208] In 1808 the Portuguese Royal Family, fleeing from Napoleon, took charge in Rio de Janeiro. Some 15,000 Portuguese nobles moved to Brazil. The region changed a lot, becoming more European.

After independence and principally after 1850, Southeast Brazil was "inundated" by European immigrants, who were attracted by the government to replace the African slaves in the coffee plantations. Most immigrants landed in the Port of Santos and have been forwarded to the coffee farms within São Paulo. The vast majority of the immigrants came from Italy. Brazil attracted nearly 5 million immigrants between 1870 and 1953. The large number of Italians are visible in many parts of Southeast Brazil. Their descendants are nowadays predominant in many areas. For example, Northeast São Paulo is 65% Italian.[1209]

The arrival of immigrants from several parts of Europe, the Middle-East and Asia produced an ethnically diverse population. The city of Bastos, in São Paulo, is 11.4% Japanese. The city of São Paulo is home to the largest Japanese population outside Japan itself.[1210]

Northeast

The population of Northeast Brazil is a result of an intensive race mixing, which has occurred in the region for more than four centuries. According to the 2006 census people reported as "brown" make up 62.5% of the population. Those reported as Black account for 7.8%.

This region did not have much effect from the massive European immigration that took place in Southern Brazil in the late 19th century and first decades of the 20th century. The Northeast has been a poorer region of Brazil since the decline of sugar cane plantations in the late 17th century, so its economy did not require immigrants.

The ethnic composition of the population starts in the 16th century. The Portuguese settlers rarely brought women, which led to relationships with the Indian women. Later, interracial relationships occurred between Portuguese males and African females. The coast, in the past the place where millions of Black slaves arrived (mostly from modern-day Angola, Ghana, Nigeria and Benin) to work in sugar-cane plantations, is where nowadays there is a predominance of Mulattoes, those of Black and White ancestry. Salvador, Bahia is considered the largest Black city outside of Africa, with over 80% of its inhabitants being African-Brazilians. In the interior, there is a predominance of Indian and White mixture.

North

Northern Brazil, largely covered by the Amazon rainforest, is the Brazilian region with the largest Amerindian influences, both in culture and ethnicity. Inhabited by diverse indigenous tribes, this part of Brazil was reached by Portuguese and Spanish colonists in the 17th century, but it started to be populated by non-Indians only in the late 19th and early 20th centuries. The exploitation of rubber used in the growing industries of automobiles, has emerged a huge migration to the region.

Many people from the poor Northeast Brazil, mostly Ceará, moved to the Amazon area. The contact between the Indians and the northeastern rubbers created the base of the ethnic composition of the region, with its mixed-race majority.

Central-West

The Central-West region of Brazil was inhabited by diverse Indians when the Portuguese arrived in the early 18th century. The Portuguese came to explore the precious stones that were found there. Contact between the Portuguese and the Indians created a mixed-race population. Until the mid-20th century, Central-West Brazil had a very small population. The situation changed with the construction of Brasília, the new capital of Brazil, in 1960. Many workers were attracted to the region, mostly from northeastern Brazil.

A new wave of settlers started arriving from the 1970s. With the mechanization of agriculture in the South of Brazil, many rural workers of German and Italian origin migrated to Central-West Brazil. In some areas, they are already the majority of the population.

Education and health

The Federal Constitution of 1988 and the 1996 *General Law of Education in Brazil* (LDB) attributed to the Federal Government, states, Federal District and municipalities the responsibility of managing the Brazilian educational system, considering three educational public systems as a basis for collaboration between these federal systems. Each of these public educational systems is responsible for its own maintenance, which manages funds as well as mechanisms and sources for financial resources. The new Constitution reserves 25% of state and municipal taxes and 18% of federal taxes for education.[1211]

As set out by the Brazilian Constitution, the main responsibility for basic education is attributed to the states and municipalities. Hence, a historical feature of Brazilian basic education is its extremely decentralized nature, which gives great organizational autonomy to sub-national governments (27 states and 5,546 municipalities) in organizing their educational systems. Early childhood education, from 0–6 years, is under exclusive responsibility of the municipalities. Responsibility for compulsory primary education from 1st to 9th grades is shared between states and municipalities. Kindergarten and preschool education are the responsibility of local levels of government, whereas

Figure 362: *Federal University of Paraná, in Curitiba.*

secondary schools are under the responsibility of the states. Maintenance of the system, including salaries, the definition of teacher career structures and supervision of early childhood, primary, and secondary levels (which make up basic education) is decentralized, and these levels are responsible for defining their respective curriculum content.

Higher education starts with undergraduate or sequential courses, which may offer different specialization choices such as academic or vocational paths. Depending on the choice, students may improve their educational background with *Stricto Sensu* or *Lato Sensu* postgraduate courses. Higher education has three main purposes: teaching, research and extension, each with their own specific contribution to make to a particular course. Diplomas and certificates are proof of having passed through higher education.

In 2003, the literacy rate was at 88 percent of the population, and the youth literacy rate (ages 15–19) was 93.2 percent. However, Brazilian analystsWikipedia:Manual of Style/Words to watch#Unsupported attributions tend to approach these favorable numbers with suspicion, considering the generally poor levels of performance displayed by students, especially in the public school network.Wikipedia:Citation needed

According to Brazilian Government, the most serious health problems are:

Figure 363: *Pope Benedict XVI in his official visit to Brazil, in May 2007.*

- Childhood mortality: about 2.51% of childhood mortality, reaching 3.77% in the northeast region.
- Motherhood mortality: about 73.1 deaths per 100,000 born children in 2002.
- Mortality by non-transmissible illness: 151.7 deaths per 100,000 inhabitants caused by heart and circulatory diseases, along with 72.7 deaths per 100,000 inhabitants caused by cancer.
- Mortality caused by external causes (transportation, violence and suicide): 71.7 deaths per 100,000 inhabitants (14.9% of all deaths in the country), reaching 82.3 deaths in the southeast region.

Religion

According to the IBGE census 2010[1212] 64.6% are Roman Catholics; 24% are Protestants and other Christians, 8% are agnostics, atheists or have no religion, 2% are followers of Spiritism, and 1% are members of other religions. Some of these are Jehovah's Witnesses (1,100,000), Latter-day Saints (200,000), Buddhism (215,000), Judaism (86,000), and Islam (27,000) and some practice a mixture of different religions, such as Catholicism, Candomblé, and indigenous American religions Wikipedia:Citation needed.

Brazil has the largest Roman Catholic population in the world.

Followers of Protestantism are rising in number. Until 1970, the majority of Brazilian Protestants were adherents of "traditional churches", mostly Lutherans, Presbyterians and Baptists. There are 120,000 Episcopalians in 9 dioceses (Anglican Episcopal Church of Brazil). Since then, numbers of Pentecostal and Neopentecostal adherents have increased significantly.

Islam in Brazil was first practiced by African slaves.[1213] Today, the Muslim population in Brazil is made up mostly of Arab immigrants. The US Department of State claims there is a recent trend of increased conversions to Islam among non-Arab citizens.

The largest population of Buddhists in Latin America lives in Brazil, due greatly to Brazil's large Japanese population.

According to IBGE 2000 Census, the following are the largest religious denominations in Brazil, with those with more than a **half million** members only shown.

Rank	Group	Members	Other information
1	Roman Catholic Church	135 million	• Its Charismatic Renewal branch is fast growing; the Progressive Branch (Liberation Theology) and the Conservative branch are in decline. Only 33% of the Roman Catholic Church's membership attends the church regularly. • The Personal Apostolic Administration of Saint John Mary Vianney in Campos dos Goytacazes is one of the most leading traditionalist Catholic groups in the world. • See Roman Catholicism in Brazil.
2	Non-religious	12.5 million	• including, but not limited to, Atheists and Agnostics
3	Assemblies of God (*Assembléias de Deus*)	8.4 million	• General Convention of the Assemblies of God (Affiliated with the American Assemblies of God, Springfield, MO): 3,6 Million. • National Convention of the Assemblies of God: 2,5 Million. A.k.a. Madureira Ministry of the Assemblies of God. • Other independent Assemblies of God: 2,3 Million, such as Bethesda Assemblies of God.
4	Baptist	3.1 million	• Brazilian Baptist Convention: 1,2 Million adherents. Affiliated to US Southern Baptists. • National Baptist Convention: 1 Million. Pentecostal Baptists. • Independent Baptist Convention: 400,000. Scandinavian Baptists. • Other Baptists: 400,000.
5	Christian Congregation of Brazil	2.4 million	
6	Spiritism	2.2 million	• Kardec Spiritism; does **not** include Afro-Brazilian Sincretists. Their influence is much larger than their numbers. Wikipedia:Citation needed

7	Universal Church of the Kingdom of God (*Igreja Universal do Reino de Deus*)	2.1 million	• Neo-Pentecostal Movement.
8	Foursquare Gospel Church	1.3 million	• Classic Pentecostals in US, but second-wave Pentecostals in Brazil.
9	Adventists	1.2 million	• Seventh-day Adventist Church: 900,000. • Promise Adventist Church: 150,000. Indigenous Pentecostal Adventists. • Seventh Day Adventist Reform Movement: 50,000. • Other Adventists: 100,000.
10	Jehovah's Witnesses	1.1 million	
11	Lutherans	1 million	• Evangelical Church of Lutheran Confession. • Evangelical Lutheran Church of Brazil. • Other Lutherans.
12	Calvinists	981,000	• Presbyterian Church of Brazil: 500,000. • Independent Presbyterian Church of Brazil: 250,00. • Congregationalists: 150,000. • Other Calvinists: 100,000.
13	God is Love Pentecostal Church	774,000	• Divine Healing movement.
14	Afro-Brazilian	525,000	• Umbanda (397,000) and Candomblé (128,000)
15	Brazilian Catholics	500,000	
–	Others and no religion declared	3.5 million	

Languages

Portuguese is the only official language of Brazil. It is spoken by nearly the entire population and is virtually the only language used in schools, newspapers, radio, TV and for all business and administrative purposes. Moreover, Brazil is the only Portuguese-speaking nation in the Americas, making the language an important part of Brazilian national identity.

Many Amerindian languages are spoken daily in indigenous communities, primarily in Northern Brazil. Although many of these communities have significant contact with Portuguese, today there are incentives stimulating preservation and the teaching of native languages. According to SIL International, 133 Native American languages are currently endangered. Some of the largest

Figure 364: *The Museum of the Portuguese Language in São Paulo.*

indigenous language groups include Arawak, Carib, Macro-Gê and Tupi. In 2006, the City of São Gabriel da Cachoeira in the region of Cabeça do Cachorro (Northwestern region of the State of Amazonas), has adopted some indigenous languages as some of its other official languages along with Portuguese.

Other languages are spoken by descendants of immigrants, who are usually bilingual, in small rural communities in Southern Brazil. The most important are the Brazilian German dialects, such as Riograndenser Hunsrückisch and the East Pomeranian dialect, and also the Talian, based on the Italian Venetian language. There are also bilingual speakers of Polish, Ukrainian and Russian in Southern Brazil, especially Paraná. In the city of São Paulo, Levantine Arabic, Japanese, Chinese and Korean can be heard in the immigrant neighborhoods, such as Liberdade. Yiddish and Hebrew are used by Jewish communities mainly in São Paulo, Rio de Janeiro, Porto Alegre, Curitiba, Brasília, Belo Horizonte and Recife as well as the Vlax Romani dialect by Gypsy communities all across the nation.

The World Factbook demographic statistics

The following demographic statistics are from The World Factbook, unless otherwise indicated

Nationality

- noun: Brazilian(s)
- adjective: Brazilian

Population

- 210,429,127

Languages

- Portuguese (official)

Ethnic groups

- White 47.7%
- Caboclo, Mestizo, Castizo 22.3%
- Mulatto, Octoroon, Quadroon 20.1%
- Black 7.6%
- Asian 1.1%
- Indigenous 0.4%
- Gypsy 0.4%
- Eurasian, Hafu 0.3%

Literacy

- Total population: 92.6%
- Male: 92.2%
- Female: 92.9% (2015 est.)

Religions

- Roman Catholic 64.6%
- Other Catholic 0.4%
- Protestant 22.2%
  - Adventist (including Seventh-day Adventist and Adventist Church of Promise) 6.5%
  - Assembly of God 2.0%
  - Christian Congregation of Brazil 1.2%
  - Universal Church of the Kingdom of God 1.0%
  - Other Protestant 11.5%
  - Other Christian 0.7%
- Spiritist 2.2%
- Other 1.4%
- None 8%
- Unspecified 0.4%

References

This article incorporates public domain material from the CIA World Factbook document "2006 edition"[1214].

External links

- United Nations "World Population Prospects": Country Profile – Brazil[1215]
- Population Statistics for Brazil[1216]
- Build Brazil population graph 1960 – 2013 (World Bank data)[1217]
- Build Brazil population projection graph till 2100 (United Nation data)[1218]
- Build Brazil life expectancy at birth graph 1950 – 2013 (United Nation data)[1219]

Brazilians

Brazilians

Brasileiros

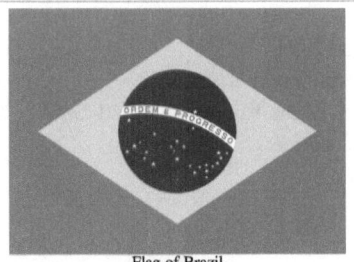

Flag of Brazil	
Total population	
c. 207 million (2015 estimate)	
Regions with significant populations	
Brazil	204,450,649 (2015 estimate)
United States	1,315,000
Paraguay	349,842
Japan	179,649
Portugal	166,775
Spain	128,638
United Kingdom	120,000
Germany	113,716
Switzerland	81,000
France	70,000
Italy	69,000
Belgium	48,000
Argentina	47,045
Canada	39,300
French Guiana	38,700
Bolivia	28,546
Australia	27,000
Netherlands	21,948
Other countries combined	211,063
Languages	

Languages of Brazil
Portuguese (99.7%)
Indigenous languages (0.082%)
High German languages (Moselle Franconian Hunsrückisch, Luxembourgish, Swabian, Bavarian, Austrian, Allemanic) and Low German language (Pomeranian, Plautdietsch and Westphalian) (Bilingualism 1.94%, Geographical distribution of German speakers).
Venetian or Talian (1.49%)
Polish (0.27%)
Ukrainian (0.11%)[1220]
Dutch (0.041%)
Castilian (0.197%)
French (0.1457%)
Lithuanian (0.04%)
Norwegian (0.027%)
Russian (0.02%)
North Levantine spoken Arabic and Turoyo (Aramaic) (0.07%)
Japanese (0.21%)
Korean (0.0396%)
Chinese (0.13%)
Yiddish High German (0.038%)
Hebrew (0.044%)
Native English speakers (0.2007%)
English as a second or foreign additional language (6.7%)
Religion
Religion in Brazil
Christian majority followed by Irreligion, Deism, Agnosticism and Atheism. Minorities: Kardecism, Buddhism and other Oriental philosophies (Shinto and Shinto-derived Japanese new religions, Korean Confucianism), Judaism, African tradition religions (Umbanda and Candomblé) and Islam
Related ethnic groups
Latin Americans • Indigenous peoples of South America

Brazilians (*brasileiros* in Portuguese, IPA: [bɾaziˈlejɾus])[1221] are citizens of Brazil. A Brazilian can also be a person born abroad to a Brazilian parent or legal guardian as well as a persons who acquired Brazilian citizenship. Brazil is a multiethnic society, which means that it is home to people of many different ethnic origins. As a result, majority of Brazilians do not equate their nationality with their ethnicity, usually embracing and espousing both simultaneously.

In the period after the colonization of the Brazilian territory by Portugal, during much of the XVI century, the word "Brazilian" was given to the Portuguese merchants of Brazilwood, designating exclusively the name of such profession, since the inhabitants of the land were, in most of them, indigenous or Portuguese born in Portugal, or in the territory now called Brazil. However, long before the independence of Brazil, in 1822, both in Brazil and in Portugal, it was already common to attribute the Brazilian gentile to a person, usually of clear Portuguese descent, resident or whose family resided in the State of Brazil (1530-1815), belonging to the Portuguese Empire. During the lifetime of the United Kingdom of Portugal, Brazil and the Algarves (1815-1822), however, there was confusion about the nomenclature.

Definition

According to the Constitution of Brazil, a Brazilian citizen is:

- Anyone born in Brazil, even if to foreign born parents. However, if the foreign parents were at the service of a foreign State (such as foreign diplomats), the child is not Brazilian;
- Anyone born abroad to a Brazilian father or a Brazilian mother, with registration of birth in a Brazilian Embassy or Consulate. Also, a person born abroad to a Brazilian father or a Brazilian mother who was not registered but who, after turning 18 years old, went to live in Brazil;[1222]
- A foreigner living in Brazil who applied for and was accepted as a Brazilian citizen.

According to the Constitution, all people who hold Brazilian citizenship are equal, regardless of race, ethnicity, gender or religion.

A foreigner can apply for Brazilian citizenship after living for four uninterrupted years in Brazil and being able to speak Portuguese. A native person from an official Portuguese language country (Portugal, Angola, Mozambique, Cape Verde, São Tomé and Príncipe, Guinea Bissau and East Timor) can request the Brazilian nationality after only 1 uninterrupted year living in Brazil. A foreign born person who holds Brazilian citizenship has exactly the same rights and duties of the Brazilian citizen by birth, but cannot occupy some special public positions such as the Presidency of the Republic, Vice-presidency of the Republic, Minister (Secretary) of Defense, Presidency (Speaker) of the Senate, Presidency (Speaker) of the House of Representatives, Officer of the Armed Forces and Diplomat.

Overview

Brazilians are mostly descendants of Portuguese settlers, post-colonial immigrant groups, Enslaved Africans and Brazil's indigenous peoples. Along with other immigrants of who arrived in Brazil, from the 1820s well into the 1970s, most of the settlers were Portuguese, Italians, Spaniards and German speaking nationalities, with significantly large numbers of Japanese, Poles, Ukrainians and Levantine Arabs.

The Brazilian people are multi-ethnic. First row: White (Portuguese, German, Italian and Arab, respectively) and Japanese Brazilians. Second row: African, pardo (cafuzo, mulato and caboclo, respectively) and Native (Indian) Brazilians.

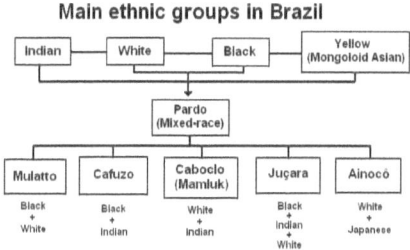

Main Brazilian ethnic groups

The colonization period (1500 to 1822)

The three principal groups were Native Brazilians, European colonizers and African labor.

- Brazil was inhabited by an estimated 2.4 million Amerindians before the first settlers arrived in the 16th century. They had been living there since the Pleistocene and still exist in many different tribes and ethnicities, amounting to the hundreds, giving them varying features, shapes and shades. There are different estimates for the Indigenous population around 1498, when the cohort commanded by Duarte Pacheco Pereira first set foot in Brazilian territory, followed by Pedro Álvares Cabral and Amerigo Vespucci in 1500 and 1502, with figures revolving between 2.4 million and 3.1 million. What is more accurate is that about three quarters of them died from contracted diseases brought by colonizers (the flu, smallpox, measles, scarlet fever and tuberculosis) and conflicts (besides the numerous deaths in different tribal groups by forging alliances with the Portuguese, French and Dutch to fight each other, ending in genocide, the abortion rate also increased among Indigenous women after the arrival of the colonizers), while the remaining were pushed to the Amazon Basin, sometimes migrating beyond the borders with Hispanic provinces. It is also important to mention that a strong assimilation by miscegenation with local populations occurred, where Natives living under Jesuit protection and having a monastic life decided to leave for the life in towns. The European diseases spread quickly along the indigenous trade routes, and whole tribes were likely annihilated without ever coming in direct contact with Europeans. Today, 517,000 Indigenous people live in reservations and 160 thousand speak assorted Native languages, whereas millions of

Brazilians have at least some degree of Amerindian ancestry due to the mentioned interracial encounters.
- The country was officially discovered by Portugal in 1500 and received about 724,000 Portuguese colonizers, mostly males, who settled there until the end of Colonial Brazil. But other sources even claim that the given numbers of total entrances were clearly surpassed. The Jesuits asked the Portuguese Crown to ship orphaned women under royal wardship for marriage with the settlers; they were known as *Órfãs d'El-Rei* (modern *órfãs do rei*, "orphans of the king").[1223,1224] Daughters of noblemen who died overseas administrating captaincies in the colonies or in battle for the king would marry settlers of higher rank. Bahia's port in the Northeast received one of the first groups of orphans in 1551.[1224]

Portugal remained the only significant, but not an exclusive source of European immigration to Brazil until the early 19th century.

- These other people came from different nationalities - but the by far most mentioned are the Dutch. Hence, under the rule of Dutch Brazil in the northeastern part of the country, from 1630 to 1654, a comparatively small but still notable number of Dutch settlers (Dutch Brazilian) and some Jewish People arrived, the latter seeking religious freedom. These Jews founded the first Synagogue in the Americas, named Kahal Zur Israel Synagogue in the city of Recife.

It is estimated that more than 20,000 Dutch entered Brazil, however, both groups had been forced out of the country after the rule's end. The remaining families mostly fled to remote parts of the interior of Northeastern Brazil (mainly in the states of Pernambuco, but also Paraíba, Rio Grande do Norte, Ceará and others) or changed their names to Portuguese ones. The proven excess of Y-chromosomes of the haplogroup 2 in northeasterners probably results from the high miscegenation of Dutch settlers with the local population.

The Jews who mostly left Brazil took off to what was then named New Amsterdam, today New York City, and founded the oldest Jewish congregation in the USA, the Congregation Shearith Israel. The ones who stayed, converted into Christianity and were then known as New Christians or Marranos, who sometimes practiced Crypto-Judaism. Even if the Jewish population under Dutch Brazil not surpassed a few thousand individuals, a considerably higher number of New Christians, in the past simply absorbed as Portuguese colonizers, arrived in Colonial Brazil - especially in the first centuries after 1500. They entered Brazil fleeing from the Inquisition or were deported by the Kingdom of Portugal and also Spain, latter being known as Degredados, someone who was sentenced or forced to exile. This also included Romani People from the Iberian Peninsula, what partially explains the curiously high numbers for a western country. Brazil has the second largest Gypsy population in the Americas after the US, having also received Roma people from Central and Eastern Europe, as well as the Baltic countries during the 20th century.

- As a result of the Atlantic slave trade from the mid-16th century until 1855, an estimated 3.6 million African people, also from many different countries and ethnicities were brought to Brazil, giving the country the Americas' largest population with some African ancestry. Many of the slaves suffered under severe conditions and the mortality rates were pretty high, what led to the foundation of Quilombola communities throughout the country. A small number of the slaves in the state of Bahia were actually Muslims; they produced a revolt in the city of Salvador that was quickly tamed by the army.

In 1808, the Portuguese court moved to Brazil, bringing thousands of Portuguese again and afterwards opened its seaports to other nations starting from 1820. This caused the biggest wave of immigration which the country has seen until then.

The Great Immigration (1820 until the 1970s)

In this period, people from all over the world officially entered Brazil, the vast majority of them Europeans.

Between 1820 and the 1950s, Brazil received around **5,686,133** European immigrants, including a thriving Jewish population. In addition, 950,000 Asians settled in Brazil throughout the 20th century, including considerable numbers of Middle Easterners or Christian Levantine Arabs and 270,000 Japanese, the highest figure among East Asians.

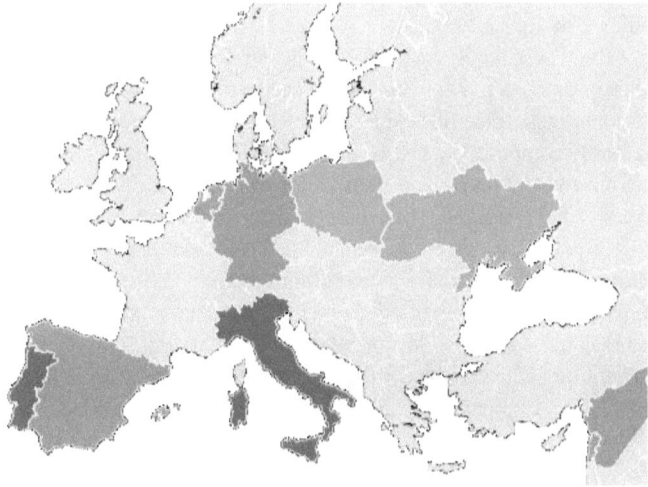

1) Back then, nearly **70 %** of those immigrants originated from **Southern Europe**.

- A second wave of **Portuguese** people arrived (here: Postcolonialism), this time with more than **1,8 million** immigrants.

Portuguese people have been present since the discovery of the country, and therefore it is difficult to estimate a more accurate number of descendants. Millions of White Brazilians descend from recent Portuguese immigration from between the 1870s and 1975. In addition, many multiracial Brazilians partially descend from Portuguese people, caused by the high intermarriage rates. Most of them came from the historical provinces of Minho, Trás-os-Montes, Beira, Estremadura (North and Central Portugal). Northeastern Brazil traditionally received the first waves of immigrants, but during the Great Immigration, the Southeast received the biggest influx. São Paulo (state) received the most, followed by Rio de Janeiro (city), which is considered the largest Portuguese city outside of Lisbon. The second former capital of Brazil once also was the capital of Portugal, the only European capital outside of Europe. The accent in the city of Rio de Janeiro subsequently reminds the 19th century innovations that took place in the European variety of the language, while the prosody of the rest of the country, besides some local varieties, has rather conservative phonetics rooted in the 1600s. Other states with significant numbers were Minas Gerais, Pará, Rio Grande do Sul, Pernambuco and Bahia. Nowadays, they naturally live throughout Brazil and compose the majority of White and also Multiracial Brazilians in many states.

- Furthermore, around **1,6 million Italians** were responsible for a massive immigration wave, consequently composing the biggest European follow-up group the country has received after its colonizers.

Today, millions of Italian-Brazilians make Brazil their home, as they usually brought the whole family and had high birth rates. Regarding the total numbers, this probably represents the biggest Italian diaspora outside of Italy. Contrary to other countries, more than half of the Italians immigrated from the North, mostly composed by people from Veneto and Lombardy, followed by people from Central Italy. The state of São Paulo had the strongest and a more diverse influx, with many also coming from South Italy, especially to the eponymic capital. Italians mostly went to São Paulo (state), which received half of the overall immigrants. The others mainly went to the states of southern Brazil, where they also composed the biggest European immigrant group. Other notable influxes occurred in two other southeastern states, here Minas Gerais and Espírito Santo and the Central-West region, mainly to Mato Grosso do Sul and Goiás. Comparatively small numbers went to Pernambuco and

Bahia, both in the Northeast. Nowadays the descendants mostly live in mentioned areas, but the sheer amount and internal migrations made the Italilan diaspora spread out and nowadays they are scattered all over Brazil.

- **Spaniards** also arrived in rather high numbers, with around **700,000** immigrants mainly from Andalusia and Galicia.

Several million Brazilians have Spanish ancestry. Most Spaniards settled in the past century, where they chiefly headed to São Paulo, then Rio de Janeiro and Minas Gerais. Most notably from Andalusia (South), others from the provinces of Galicia, Castile and León and Catalonia (North and East Spain) followed. Galicians were also present throughout Colonial Brazil, as the province shares borders and linguistic ties with Portugal, and once was part of the country. Spanish Brazilians in the other states mainly have origins in Galicia, which arrived in earlier occasions. Many of them went to the first capital Salvador and its state Bahia, but also Pernambuco (Northeast), Pará (North), Espírito Santo (Southeast), and Rio Grande do Sul (South).

Note: Brazil is also home to other Southern European populations, mainly Greeks (around 150,000 descendants), but they are by far the smallest groups with origins in South Europe.

2) The remaining **30 %** were composed of **Other Europeans**, **Asians** (Western and Eastern Asia), **Africans** (many White Africans, Jews, Berbers and others) and **Americans** (South and North Americans).

- **Other Europeans:**

- Western Europeans were very present, as around **240,000 Germans** settled, **198,000 Austrian** and **52,000 Swiss**; Luxembourgers and Volga Germans were also documented, but in comparatively low numbers. **German speaking nationalities** were the fourth largest European immigration group and today German is the second most spoken mother tongue in the country.[1225] In addition, **150,000 French** immigrants entered Brazilian ports, where Belgian and **Dutch** (not to be confused with Dutch Brazil) settlers also were listed.

- Eastern Europeans were relatively numerous, with more than **350,000** listed immigrants. This included **154,000 Poles**, around **40,000 Ukrainians** and smaller numbers of **Russians**. These immigrants were searching for better opportunities - a few thousand Belarusians were also among them. Slavs from other regions migrated as well, here mainly South Slavs like Bulgarians and Croats, but also Czechs and Slovaks, with moderate numbers of Slovenes and others. **Hungarians** and Romanians were among the non-Slavic Eastern Europeans and were the biggest groups after the Poles, Russians and Ukrainians.

- Northern Europeans were the least numerous, but also present. More than **78,000** Britons, mainly under **English** passports, and Scots entered the country. They dispersed to different regions: a few Irish people went to already urbanized regions. **Scandinavian people**, mainly Swedes and Norwegians, were both listed and sent over **40,000** immigrants each, as well as around **17,000** Danes. **3,400** Estonians and a rather small number of Finns were also present. Even smaller and therefore often forgotten, an influx from Icelanders and Faroese was recorded, but they still left few thousand descendants. The Baltic region was also entirely present, where **Lithuanians** composed the most numerous group, with over **50,000** entrances, followed by a much smaller number of Latvians.

- European Jews of Ashkenazi origin, more precisely around **48,000** people from several countries, chose Brazil as their destination. **Ashkenazi Jews** were first documented during Imperial times, when the liberal second emperor of Brazil welcomed a few thousands of families facing persecution in Europe during the 1870s and 1880s. Two heavier influxes took place during the 20th century. The earliest right after the Great War and the second inrush between the 1930s and 1950s. Brazil has also seen an influx from North African Jews of Sephardic origin coming from mainly Morocco and Egypt, which were counted extra.

- **Asians**:

- Western Asians, more specifically from the **Levant** region, equally arrived in large numbers, chiefly **Lebanese** and Syrians, both surpassing **200,000** entrances throughout the 20th century, with mentionable numbers of Armenian, Georgian and some Iranian immigrants from the Caucasus region.

- East Asians, the majority composed of **Japanese** immigrants, also arrived in formidable numbers, where the first ship landed in 1908, surpassing **250,000** immigrants.[1226] But **Chinese** and **Koreans** also have traditions of immigrating to Brazil, especially after the 1950s, with around 200,000 and 100,000 immigrants respectively.

- **Americans:**

- North Americans also formed the melting pot that is Brazil, with the country being one of the few which received US-Americans who fled the American Civil War, settling in Southeastern and Southern Brazil during the American reconstruction period. In addition, smaller numbers of North Americans immigrated after 1808. The descendants of those **Confederate colonies** are culturally known as the ***Confederados*** sub-group, especially in the countryside of São Paulo, where they founded towns and their presence was stronger - Brazilians of US-American descent can be found throughout the country, resulting from other periods and the dispersion of the Confederados descendants, who are nowadays mostly mixed with other groups and sometimes mistaken for descendants of British immigrants. Ethnically the Confederados were mostly English-Welsh, Scottish, Irish, German and Scandinavian.[1227]

- South Americans were strongly represented by Argentines since the 18th century and always had a strong community in the country. They still form one of the largest South American immigrant groups in Brazil, nowadays only surpassed by Bolivians (see modern times). Uruguayan citizens after the country's independence from the Empire of Brazil were also noticeable throughout the 19th and 20th centuries.

- **Africans:**

- North African regions, historically distinguished from Sub-Saharan Africa, also sent immigrants. This time they mainly came from Egypt, with around **10,000** people, than the Maghreb region, especially Morocco (mostly Jews who went to Northern Brazil). Therefore, a stronger influx from other cultures occurred, contrary to Colonial Brazil, where most Africans were forced labor work brought from the Black populations.

- Other Africa-born people mainly include Dutch South-Africans (Boeren or Afrikaners) and people from the former Portuguese Empire, mainly Angola (during the Great Immigration, but especially after the Civil Wars post-independence). Here people of several ethnicities immigrated (mainly Africans of European descent, but also Blacks and Coloured people).

Note: Dozen other immigrant groups form sizable communities with some varying number of descendants (5,000 to + 30 million). **Only in this period**, the port of Santos, São Paulo, which was widely known as the most important entrance of immigrants in Brazil, received people from **more than 60 different countries**. Other important ports, which occasionally received other immigrant groups as the before mentioned, were the ones in the cities of Rio de Janeiro, Porto Alegre, Vitória, Recife etc.

Modern times (1970 to now)

Not to be compared with the great immigration before, a still ongoing influx from Africa (Angola, Senegal) and South America and the Caribbean (Bolivia, Paraguay, Chile, Uruguay, Haiti, Suriname) is happening since the late 60's. Asian immigrants (from Palestine, China, South Korea, returning Japanese Brazilians, Dutch Indonesians, Afghans and immigrants from Vietnam, Iran, Pakistan, the Philippines and others) as well as from Europe (Portugal due to ties, young qualified professionals from Western Europe, especially after 2008, Northern Europeans who seek warmer weather and some Eastern Europeans) are thriving in varying numbers.

After 1975 large groups of Dutch Surinamese or Boeroes immigrated to Brazil due to the independence in Suriname. Most of them settled in the countryside of São Paulo and Paraná where there are thriving Dutch Brazilian colonies.

Current foreign population

In 2011, the country was home to 1.5 million foreign born people, more than twice as of 2009.

The numbers still could be higher, as there are many undocumented people in Brazil as well. For both, the documented and undocumented, most of the foreigners come from Portugal, Bolivia, China, Paraguay, Angola, Spain, Argentina, Japan and the United States. The major work visas concessions were granted for citizens of the United States and the United Kingdom.[1228]

Lusitanian immigration never ceased throughout the 19th and 20th centuries. Portuguese people in diaspora settled in Brazil especially during the 1970s coming from former Portuguese colonies like Macau or Angola after its independence. An additional figure of **1.2 million Portuguese** arrived between 1951 and 1975 to settle mostly in the Southeast. Nowadays, Lusitanians constitute the biggest group of foreigners living in the country, with over 690,000 Portuguese nationals currently living in Brazil. The vast majority arrived in the last decade. The first semester of 2011 solely had an increase of 52 thousand Portuguese nationals applying for a permanent residence visa while another large group was granted Brazilian citizenship.

Today, people of more than 220 nationalities have communities in Brazil, 40 of them more than 10,000 people.

Refugees

In 2014, Brazil was home to 5,208 refugees from 79 different nationalities. The three largest refugee ancestries were Syrian (1,626), Colombian (1,154) and Angolan (1062). In addition to these numbers, there are several thousand people who had entered the country and are still waiting for the government to acknowledge their refugee status, as 1,830 people from Bangladesh in 2013 alone and other 1,021 people from Syria and 799 people from Senegal, for example.

Brazil is today home to 4.5 thousand Afghans and was a destination for Vietnamese boat people in the past.

Dispersal of races and colours in the country

Note: The ethnic composition of Brazilians is not uniform across the country.

- Due to its large influx of European immigrants in the 19th and 20th centuries, São Paulo, and the Southern Region have a **White** majority (mostly Europeans of Italian, Portuguese, German, Austrian, Swiss, Slavic, Dutch and Spanish ancestry).[1229] Rio de Janeiro has a sizable white population slightly over 50% of the total population.

The other two Southeastern states, Minas Gerais and Espírito Santo, are around 50% White (the Southeast region also includes Levantine Arabs). São Paulo has the largest absolute number with 30 million Whites, followed by Minas Gerais, Rio Grande do Sul, Rio de Janeiro and Paraná, while Santa Catarina, where 86% of the population has European phenotype, reaches the highest percentage.

The cities of São Paulo, Rio de Janeiro, Porto Alegre, Curitiba, Brasília and Belo Horizonte have the largest populations of **Ashkenazi Jews**.

Most **East Asians**, especially Japanese Brazilians, the largest group, live in São Paulo and Paraná. Most Koreans also live in São Paulo whereas the Chinese diaspora is spread particularly throughout the Southeast. Rio de Janeiro has a large Chinese population following São Paulo.

- The Northeastern Region, the first occupied and therefore most mixed region, has larger numbers of people with darker features, with stronger African, Romani, Amerindian and Sephardi influences from Colonial Brazil. The **majority** there is composed of **Pardo (mixed) people**, who are of a brownish or darker phenotype with light to dark features, followed by Whites (mostly Europeans and also with admixtures) and then by people with mostly African blood - Bahia and Maranhão have the biggest Black African populations in Brazil.[1230] The individual appearance of Pardo people varies extremely, but generally all types and colours of hairs, eyes and skin are involved (usually not the extremes as extremely white or extremely black). But in fact, minorities in the White and Black populations consider themselves as Pardo. Moreover, some people in the Roma, Sephardic, Arab and Asian population classify themselves as Pardo, due to miscegenation with other races.
- Northern Brazil, largely covered by the Amazon Rainforest, is also mostly **Pardo**, due to a stronger Amerindian influence.[1231]
- The two remaining South Eastern states and the Central-Western Brazil have a more **balanced** ratio among different racial groups (around 50% White, 43% Pardo, 5% Black, 1% Asian/Amerindian).

The Brazilian Institute of Geography and Statistics (IBGE) classifies the Brazilian population in five categories: *brancos* (white), *negros* (black), *pardos* (brown or mixed), *amarelos* (Asian/yellow) and *índios* (Amerindian), based on skin color or race. The last detailed census (PNAD) found Brazil to be made up of c. 91 million white people (White Brazilian), 79 million multiracial people (Pardo), 14 million black people (Afro-Brazilian), 2-4 million Asian people (Asian Brazilian) and 807,900 indigenous (Amerindian) people.

In the 2005 detailed census, for the first time in two decades, the number of White Brazilians did not exceed 50% of the population. On the other side, the

Figure 365: *Young Brazilians*

number of *pardos* (multiracial) people increased and all the others remained almost the same. According to the IBGE, this trend is mainly because of the revaluation of the identity of historically discriminated ethnic groups.

Brazil is said to be among the most miscegenated countries in the world, as since the country was discovered and during the colonial period intermarriage between races was never illegal and common. Those of full ancestry are usually the Brazilians who can trace back their ethnicity to more recent immigration from the monarchical period in the 19th century until the Republican 20th and 21st centuries. Still, many Brazilians can not trace back their real origin easily. For instance, European family names which were difficult to pronounce were commonly changed to easier Portuguese surnames. In basic terms, it could be said that half of Brazilians are descendants of populations from the colonial era and the other half made of modern immigration. Brazil is a true melting pot of Europeans, Asians, Africans and Indigenous people, who either are in the single group or a mixture of various different backgrounds and races.

Skin color or race	% (rounded values)	
	2000[1232]	2008[1233]
White	53.74%	48.43%
Black	6.21%	6.84%
Mixed-race	38.45%	43.80%
East Asian	0.45%	1.1%
Amerindian	0.43%	0.28%
Not declared	0.71%	0.07%

White coloured people

Whites constitute the majority of Brazil's population regarding the total numbers within a single racial group, having the most numerous population in the Southern Hemisphere.

The country has the second largest White population in the Americas, with around 97 - 98 million people.

And White Brazilians make up the **third** largest White population in the world, after the United States and Russia, also counting in total numbers.

The majority came from the Great Immigration period, which was the large European influx after steps had been taken for "whitening policies" during the Monarchy and Early Republican periods. Those policies also sought labor and also were made in order to avoid the foreign invasion threat of sparsely populated areas in the South. Various other groups derive from colonial times and post-war decades.

There are people of European descent distributed throughout the entire territory of Brazil, however, Southeast and South Brazil have the largest White populations. Whereas the Southeast region has the largest absolute numbers, **79.8%** of the population in the three southernmost states has European or Caucasian phenotype. The state of **Santa Catarina** in Southern Brazil has the highest percentage, being almost **90% European**. **São Paulo** in the Southeast has the fourth highest rate, but is the state with the most Whites in **absolute numbers of 30 million Whites**, mainly from Europe, also having largest Levantine Arab and Jewish populations.

Some southern Brazilian towns with a notable main ancestry

Town name	State	Main ancestry	Percentage
Nova Veneza	Santa Catarina	Italian	95%[1234]
Pomerode	Santa Catarina	German	90%[1235]
Prudentópolis	Paraná	Ukrainian	70%[1236]
Treze Tílias	Santa Catarina	Austrian	60%[1237]
Dom Feliciano	Rio Grande do Sul	Polish	90%[1238]

Brazil is home to **240** immigrant or extoctone languages, most of them European languages. **Standard German and German dialects** make the **second most spoken** language in Brazil with around 4 million bilingual speakers or 2% of the population,[1239] other Caucasoid immigration languages are Italian, **Venetian** or **Talian dialect**, Polish, Castilian, Ukrainian, Russian, Dutch, Hebrew, Yiddish, Lithuanian and Lettish, French, Norwegian, Swedish, English, Hungarian, Finnish, Arabic, Danish, Bulgarian, Croatian, Catalan, Galician, Greek, Armenian, Czech, Slovakian, Slovenian, Romanian, Serbian, Vlax Romani, Georgian, Turoyo and Baltic or Lithuanian Romani.

Assorted German dialects (including the ancient **East Pomeranian dialect**, practically extinct in Europe) and Venetian or Talian share **co-official status** with Portuguese in several municipalities.

White Brazilians by region:

Region	Percentage
North Brazil	23.5%
Northeast Brazil	28.8%
Central-West Brazil	50.5%
Southeast Brazil	58%
Southern Brazil	78%

Mixed (multiracial) people

Multiracials constitute the second largest group of Brazil, with around 80 million people. The term *Pardo* or mixed race Brazilian is a rather complex one. Multiracial Brazilians appear in hundreds of different shades, colours and backgrounds. They are typically a mixture of colonial and post-colonial Europeans with descendants of African slaves and the Indigenous peoples of the Americas. Some individuals may also descend from Maghreb people, Jews, Middle Eastern and Egyptian people, or a more recent ancestry from East or

South Asia. Skin colours can vary from light to dark. The *caboclo* or *mestiço* population, those who are a miscegenation of Native and European, revolves around 43 million people. Genetic studies conducted by the geneticist Sergio D.J. Pena of the Federal University of Minas Gerais have shown that the **Caboclo** population is made of individuals whose DNA ranges from 70% to 90% European (mostly Portuguese, Spanish, Dutch, French or Italian 1500s to 1700s male settlers) with the remaining percentage spanning different Indigenous markers. Similar DNA tests showed that people self-classified as **Mulatto** or White and Black mix, span from 62% to 85% European (mostly descendants of Portuguese, Dutch and French settlers during the colonial period in the Northeast). The **Pardo category** in Brazil also includes 800 thousand **Gypsies** or **Roma people**, most of them coming from Portugal but also different countries in Eastern Europe and the Baltics. **Eurasians** can also be classified as Pardo. The majority of them consisting of **Ainoko** or **Hafu**, individuals who are a miscegenation between Japanese and European.

Recent research has suggested that Asians from the early Portuguese Eastern Empire, known as Luso-Asians first came to Brazil during the sixteenth century as seamen known as Lascars, or as servants, slaves and concubines accompanying the governors, merchants and clergy who has served in Portuguese Asia.[1240] This first presence of Asians was limited to Northeast Brazil, especially Bahia, but others were brought as cultivators, textile workers and miners to Pará and other parts of the Northeast.

The largest populations with Pardo individuals are found in northern and northeastern Brazil, with many inhabiting the states of Mato Grosso, Goiás, Espírito Santo, Minas Gerais, Rio de Janeiro (state), São Paulo (state) and Paraná (state), as well as the Federal District. While the occurrence of Pardos is not uniform across the country, there are states with more people of mixed background than others. It also can happen that Pardos constitute significant numbers within single regions in states.

Multiracial people by region:

Region	Percentage
North Brazil	69.2%
Northeast Brazil	62.7%
Central-West Brazil	43%
Southeast Brazil	35.69%
Southern Brazil	16.98%

Black coloured people

Blacks constitute the third largest ethnic group of Brazil with around 14 million citizens or 7% of the population. These are people who have origins in any of the black populations of Africa. In the country, these are generally used for Brazilians with at least partial Sub-Saharan African ancestry. Most African Brazilians are the direct descendants of captive Africans who survived the slavery era within the boundaries of the present Brazil, but also with considerable European and Amerindian ancestry. Afro-Brazilians might not directly be compared to Pardo-Brazilians. The number of African genes is substantially higher in Afro-Brazilians, therefore their skin colour is darker compared to mixed-race Brazilians. Brazil, followed by the US, has the largest **African diaspora** in the Americas.

Today most Blacks are either Catholic or Evangelical. Smaller groups are Irreligious including Atheists and a number of African tradition sects can be found especially in Bahia, notably Candomblé and Umbanda. The latter being a syncretism of Roman Catholicism, African traditions, Spiritism and Indigenous beliefs. A minority of Blacks follows Kardecism, which is a blend of Christianism and Spiritualism founded in France.

Most Blacks can be found in Bahia and Maranhão states after the colonial period influx, as well as in the northern region of Minas Gerais thanks to the Diamond and Gold Rush period and parts of Rio de Janeiro due to slavery in the former royal court after its transfer.

Afro-Brazilians by region:

Region	Percentage
North Brazil	6.2%
Northeast Brazil	8.1%
Central-West Brazil	5.7%
Southeast Brazil	7.91%
Southern Brazil	3.6%

Yellow coloured people

Asians, in common parlance referred to East-Asians, constitute the fourth largest ethnic group of Brazil with **2.2 million** people, what may not include mixed East Asians. The largest East-Asian ethnic group in the country are the Japanese. Brazil has the largest population of Japanese people outside Japan, being in percentage or absolute numbers. The number of Japanese Brazilians revolves around **1.8 million** descendants and the Japanese community also comprises **57 thousand Japanese nationals**. According to Ethnologue over **400 thousand people speak Japanese** in Brazil.

The others are mainly Chinese, Taiwanese and South Korean. Due to the recent immigration of Chinese citizens to Brazil the number of these people is constantly on the rise.

South Asians also left descendants in Brazil, mostly East Indians, Vietnamese, Indonesians and Bengali. However, there is a current stronger influx of Bengalis (between 5 and 10,000) nowadays, most of them refugees. Moreover, South Asians might not be included into the category of people with "yellow" skin colour, as they are physically different from Eastern Asian populations and therefore more likely to fit into the Pardo category.

There are large groups of East Asian Catholics as well as non-religious Asians. Buddhism in Brazil is also very common among non-Asians, especially Whites, with Japanese Buddhism being among the most usual and oldest forms. Shinto practices involving life style and funerals are very common in Nipponese families of São Paulo and Paraná states. Shinto-derived Japanese New Religions are very popular throughout the nation. The largest Nipponese new religions are Seicho-no-Ie, Tenrikyo, Perfect Liberty Kyodan and Church of World Messianity. Korean Confucianism and Chinese Confucianism are especially found in São Paulo capital.

East Asian Brazilians by region:

Region	Percentage
North Brazil	0.5 - 1%
Northeast Brazil	0.3 - 0.5%
Central-West Brazil	0.7 - 0.8%
Southeast Brazil	1.1%
Southern Brazil	0.5 - 0.7%

Indigenous people

Indigenous people constitute the fifth largest ethnic group of Brazil, with around **800,000** individuals. It is the oldest ethnic group in the country, mainly located in the surroundings of the Amazon basin inside the Amazon Forest but also in various reservations throughout the five geographical regions. Compared to the total population of the country the number might seem small, but millions of Brazilians actually have some Indigenous ancestry. This happened mainly because of the miscegenation of indigenous tribes with colonial settlers.

Around **180 Native or autoctone languages are spoken in Brazil** by 160 thousand people, many of them have threatened status. Most Natives can communicate in Portuguese and tribes in reservations have their mother tongue and Portuguese taught at schools. Today 517 thousand people live in Indigenous reservations.

Genetic studies

Genetic studies have shown the Brazilian population as a whole to have European, African and Native Americans components.

Autosomal studies

A 2015 autosomal genetic study, which also analysed data of 25 studies of 38 different Brazilian populations concluded that: European ancestry accounts for 62% of the heritage of the population, followed by the African (21%) and the Native American (17%). The European contribution is highest in Southern Brazil (77%), the African highest in Northeast Brazil (27%) and the Native American is the highest in Northern Brazil (32%).

Region	European	African	Native American
North Region	51%	16%	32%
Northeast Region	58%	27%	15%
Central-West Region	64%	24%	12%
Southeast Region	67%	23%	10%
South Region	77%	12%	11%

An autosomal study from 2013, with nearly 1300 samples from all of the Brazilian regions, found a pred. degree of European ancestry combined with African and Native American contributions, in varying degrees. 'Following an increasing North to South gradient, European ancestry was the most prevalent in all urban populations (with values up to 74%). The populations in the North consisted of a significant proportion of Native American ancestry that was about two times higher than the African contribution. Conversely, in the Northeast, Center-West and Southeast, African ancestry was the second most prevalent. At an intrapopulation level, all urban populations were highly admixed, and most of the variation in ancestry proportions was observed between individuals within each population rather than among population'.

Region	European	African	Native American
North Region	51%	17%	32%
Northeast Region	56%	28%	16%
Central-West Region	58%	26%	16%
Southeast Region	61%	27%	12%
South Region	74%	15%	11%

An autosomal DNA study (2011), with nearly 1000 samples from every major race group ("whites", "pardos" and "blacks", according to their respective proportions) all over the country found out a major European contribution, followed by a high African contribution and an important Native American component. "In all regions studied, the European ancestry was predominant, with proportions ranging from 60.6% in the Northeast to 77.7% in the South". The 2011 autosomal study samples came from blood donors (the lowest classes constitute the great majority of blood donors in Brazil[1241]), and also public health institutions personnel and health students.

Region	European	African	Native American
Northern Brazil	68.80%	10.50%	18.50%
Northeast Brazil	60.10%	29.30%	8.90%
Southeast Brazil	74.20%	17.30%	7.30%
Southern Brazil	79.50%	10.30%	9.40%

According to an autosomal DNA study from 2010, "a new portrayal of each ethnicity contribution to the DNA of Brazilians, obtained with samples from the five regions of the country, has indicated that, on average, European ancestors are responsible for nearly 80% of the genetic heritage of the population. The variation between the regions is small, with the possible exception of the South, where the European contribution reaches nearly 90%. The results, published by the scientific magazine *American Journal of Human Biology* by a team of the Catholic University of Brasília, show that, in Brazil, physical indicators such as skin colour, colour of the eyes and colour of the hair have little to do with the genetic ancestry of each person, which has been shown in previous studies (regardless of census classification).[1242] "Ancestry informative SNPs can be useful to estimate individual and population biogeographical ancestry. Brazilian population is characterized by a genetic background of three parental populations (European, African, and Brazilian Native Amerindians) with a wide degree and diverse patterns of admixture. In this work we analyzed the information content of 28 ancestry-informative SNPs into multiplexed panels using three parental population sources (African, Amerindian, and European) to infer the genetic admixture in an urban sample of the five Brazilian geopolitical regions. The SNPs assigned apart the parental populations from each other and thus can be applied for ancestry estimation in a three hybrid admixed population. Data was used to infer genetic ancestry in Brazilians with an admixture model. Pairwise estimates of F(st) among the five Brazilian geopolitical regions suggested little genetic differentiation only between the South and the remaining regions. Estimates of ancestry results are consistent with the heterogeneous genetic profile of Brazilian population, with a major contribution of European ancestry (0.771) followed by African (0.143) and Amerindian contributions (0.085). The described multiplexed SNP panels can be useful tool for bioanthropological studies but it can be mainly valuable to control for spurious results in genetic association studies in admixed populations". It is important to note that "the samples came from free of charge paternity test takers, thus as the researchers made it explicit: "the paternity tests were free of charge, the population samples involved people of variable socioeconomic strata, although *likely to be leaning slightly* towards the "pardo" group".

Region	European	African	Native American
North Region	71.10%	18.20%	10.70%
Northeast Region	77.40%	13.60%	8.90%
Central-West Region	65.90%	18.70%	11.80%
Southeast Region	79.90%	14.10%	6.10%
South Region	87.70%	7.70%	5.20%

An autosomal DNA study from 2009 found a similar profile "all the Brazilian samples (regions) lie more closely to the European group than to the African populations or to the Mestizos from Mexico".

Region	European	African	Native American
North Region	60.6%	21.3%	18.1%
Northeast Region	66.7%	23.3%	10.0%
Central-West Region	66.3%	21.7%	12.0%
Southeast Region	60.7%	32.0%	7.3%
South Region	81.5%	9.3%	9.2%

According to another autosomal DNA study from 2008, by the University of Brasília (UnB), European ancestry dominates in the whole of Brazil (in all regions), accounting for 65.90% of ancestry of the population, followed by the African contribution (24.80%) and the Native American (9.3%).

A more recent study, from 2013, found the following composition in São Paulo state: 61,9% European, 25,5% African and 11,6% Native American.

A 2014 autosomal DNA study, which analysed data from 1594 samples from all of the Brazilian regions, found that Brazilians show widespread European ancestry with the highest levels being observed in the south. African ancestry is also widespread (except for the south) and reaches its highest values in the East of the country. Native American ancestry is highest in the north-west (Amazonia). In conclusion, European ancestry accounts for 82% of the heritage of the population, followed by the African (9%) and the Native American (9%).

MtDna and y DNA studies

Haplogroup frequencies do not determine phenotype nor admixture. They are very general genetic snapshots, primarily useful in examining past population group migratory patterns. Only autosomal DNA testing can reveal admixture structures, since it analyses millions of alleles from both maternal and paternal sides. Contrary to yDNA or mtDNA, which are focused on one single lineage (paternal or maternal) the autosomal DNA studies profile the whole ancestry of a given individual, being more accurate in describing the complex patterns of ancestry in a given place. According to a genetic study in 2000 who analysed 247 samples (mainly identified as "white" in Brazil) who came from four of the five major geographic regions of the country, the mtDNA pool (maternal lineages) of present-day Brazilians clearly reflects the imprints of the early Portuguese colonization process (involving directional mating), as well as the recent immigrant waves (from Europe) of the last century.

Continental Fraction	Brazil	Northern	Northeastern	Southeastern	Southern
Native American	33%	54%	22%	33%	22%
African	28%	15%	44%	34%	12%
European	39%	31%	34%	31%	66%

According to a study in 2001, the vast majority of Y chromosomes (male lineages) in white Brazilian males, regardless of their regional source, is of European origin (>90% contribution), with a very low frequency of sub-Saharan African chromosomes and a complete absence of Amerindian contributions. These results configure a picture of strong directional mating in Brazil involving European males, on one side, and European, African and Amerindian females, on the other.

In a study from 2016, the authors investigated a set of 41 Y-SNPs in 1217 unrelated males from the five Brazilian geopolitical regions. A total of 22 different haplogroups were detected in the whole Brazilian sample, revealing the three major continental origins of the current population, namely from America, Europe and Africa. The genetic differences observed among regions were, however, consistent with the colonization history of the country. The sample from the Northern region presented the highest Native American ancestry (8.4%), whereas the more pronounced African contribution could be observed in the Northeastern population (15.1%). The Central-Western and Southern samples showed the higher European contributions (95.7% and 93.6%, respectively). The Southeastern region presented significant European (86.1%) and African (12.0%) contributions. Portugal was estimated to be the main source of the male European lineages to Central-West, Southeast and South Brazil. The North and the Northeast showed the highest contribution from France and Italy, respectively. The highest migration rate from Lebanon was to the Central-Weast, whereas a significant migration from Germany was observed to the Central East, Southeast and South.

In the Brazilian "white" and "pardos" the autosomal ancestry (the sum of the ancestors of a given individual) tends to be in most cases predominantly European, with often a non European mtDNA (which points to a non European ancestor somewhere down the maternal line), which is explained by the women marrying newly arrived colonists, during the formation of the Brazilian people.

External links
- (in Portuguese) Lusotopia[1243]

Immigration to Brazil

Immigration to Brazil is the movement to Brazil of foreign persons to reside permanently. It should not be confused with the colonisation of the country by the Portuguese, or with the forcible bringing of people from Africa as slaves.

Throughout its history, Brazil has always been a recipient of immigrants, but this began to gain importance in the late 19th century and throughout the 20th century when the country received massive immigration from Europe, the Middle East and East Asia, which left lasting marks on demography, culture, language and the economy of Brazil.

In general, it is considered that people who entered Brazil up to 1822, the year of independence, were colonizers. Since then, those who entered the independent nation were immigrants.

Figure 366:
European and Levantine countries from where there was significant emigration to Brazil, early half of the 20th century.
1st
2nd
3rd
4th

Before 1871, the number of immigrants rarely exceeded two or three thousand people a year. Immigration increased pressure from the first end of the international slave trade to Brazil, after the expansion of the economy, especially in the period of large coffee plantations in the state of São Paulo.

Immigration has been a very important demographic factor in the composition, structure and history of human population in Brazil, with all its attending factors and consequences in culture, economy, education, racial issues, etc. Brazil has received one of the largest numbers of immigrants in the Western Hemisphere, along with the United States, Argentina and Canada.

Counting from 1872 (year of the first census) by the year 2000, Brazil received about 6 million immigrants.

Figure 367: *Monument to the immigrant in Caxias do Sul, in the state of Rio Grande do Sul. At the bottom of the monument can be read: The Brazilian nation to the immigrant (Portuguese: A nação brasileira ao imigrante)*

Brief history

Maria Stella Ferreira Levy[1244] suggests the following periodisation of the process of immigration to Brazil:

1. 1820–1876: small number of immigrants (about 6,000 per year), predominance of Portuguese (45.73%), with significant numbers of Germans (12.97%);
2. 1877–1903: large number of immigrants (about 71,000 per year), predominance of Italians (58.49%);
3. 1904–1930: large number of immigrants (about 79,000 per year), predominance of the Portuguese (36.97%);
4. 1931–1963: declining number of immigrants (about 33,500 per year), predominance of the Portuguese (38.45%).

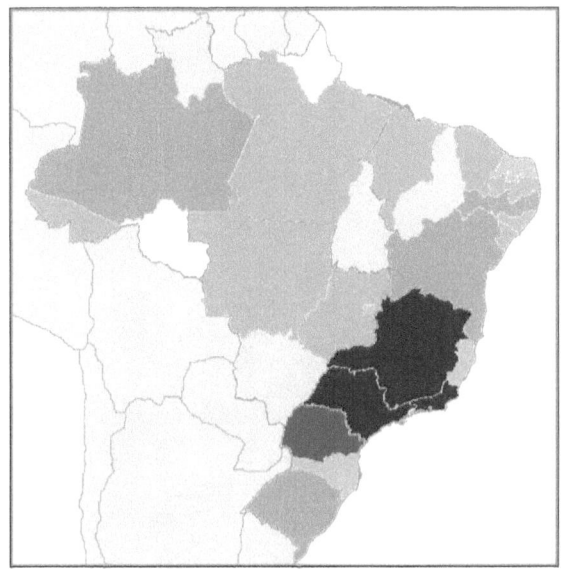

Figure 368: *Total of foreign people authorized to work in Brazil by state in 2009.*

The Brazilian population before immigration

When Brazil was invaded as a new land in the New World by the Portuguese in 1500, its native population was composed of about 2.4 million Amerindians whose ancestors had been living there for the last 15,000 to 20,000 years. During the three decades afterwards, the country remained sparsely inhabited by Europeans. Among those few, mainly Portuguese, most were renegades, criminals banished from Portugal, shipwreck survivors, or mutinous sailors. They integrated into the local tribes, using their superior technology to attain privileged positions among them.

After 1530, the Portuguese started to settle in Brazil in significant numbers. However, Portugal had a small population to develop the exploitation of Brazil. By 1550, the colonists started to bring African slaves. From 1500, when the Portuguese reached Brazil, until its independence in 1822, from 500,000 to 700,000 Portuguese settled in Brazil, 600,000 of whom arrived in the 18th century alone. The Portuguese settled in the whole territory, initially remaining near the coast, except in the region of São Paulo, from where the bandeirantes would spread into the hinterland. In the 18th century, large waves of Portuguese settled the country, in the wake of the discovery of gold in the region of Minas Gerais, but the number of Portuguese who settled in Brazil in its colonial era was far lower than of African slaves: from 1550 to 1850,

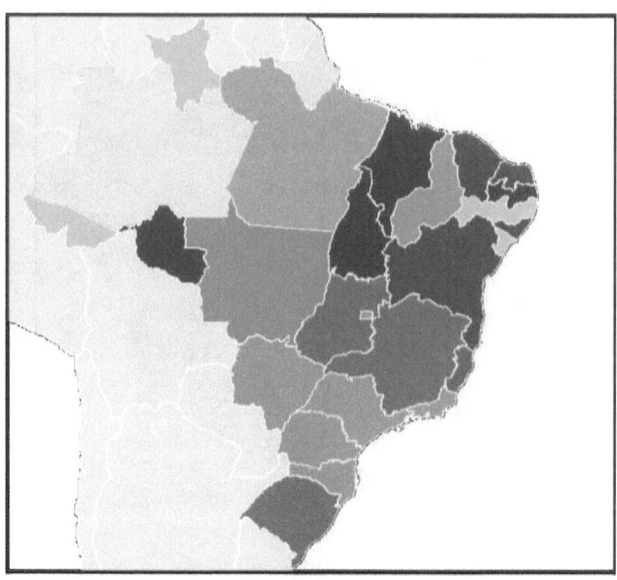

Figure 369:
People authorized to work in Brazil by origin in 2009. Organized by largest ancestry.
U.S. citizen
Italian
Portuguese
Chinese
Spanish
Cuban
English
German
French
Japanese

some 4 million slaves were brought to Brazil. This should not be taken as meaning that the population of Brazil before independence was mainly Black: the average survival of an African slave in Brazil was of merely seven years after arrival, implying extremely high mortality rates. Although children born to slave women inherited the slave condition, the Portuguese always relied on slaves purchased from slave traders to replace and increase the work force; the natural growth of the slave population was always very small.

In the early 19th century, Brazil was mainly composed of people of three different origins: the indigenous inhabitants, the Portuguese and their descendants, the Africans and descendants, and, naturally, people of varying degrees

Figure 370: *Arrival of the Portuguese to Northeast Brazil in 1500.*

of "racial" mixture. In 1872, after the arrival of about 350,000 mostly European immigrants and about 1,150,000 Africans forcibly brought to Brazil as slaves, the first Brazilian Census counted 9,930,478 people in Brazil, of which 3,787,289 (38.14%) Whites, 3,380,172 (34.04%) "pardos", 1.954.452 (19.68%) Blacks, and 386,955 (3.90%) "caboclos".[1245]

First period: 1820–1876

Immigration properly started with the opening of the Brazilian ports, in 1808. The government began to stimulate the arrival of Europeans to occupy plots of land and become small farmers. In 1812, settlers from the Azores were brought to Espírito Santo and in 1819, Swiss to Nova Friburgo, Rio de Janeiro. After independence from Portugal, the Brazilian Empire focused on the occupation of the provinces of Southern Brazil. It was mainly because Southern Brazil had a small population, vulnerable to attacks by Argentina and the Kaingang Indians.

From 1824, immigrants from Central Europe started to populate what is nowadays the region of São Leopoldo, in the province of Rio Grande do Sul. According to Leo Waibel, these German immigrants were mainly "oppressed peasants and former soldiers of the army of Napoleon". In 1830 a bill was

Figure 371: *Polish house in Paraná state.*

passed forbidding the Imperial government from spending money with the settlement of immigrants, which stalled immigration until 1834, when the provincial governments were charged with promoting immigration.[1246]

In 1859, Prussia prohibited emigration to Brazil. This was mainly because of complaints that Germans were being exploited in the coffee plantations of São Paulo. Still, between 1820 and 1876, 350,117 immigrants entered Brazil. Of these, 45.73% were Portuguese, 35.74% of "other nationalities", 12.97% Germans, while Italians and Spanish together did not reach 6%. The total number of immigrants per year averaged 6,000. Many immigrants, particularly the Germans, were brought to settle in rural communities as small landowners. They received land, seed, livestock and other items to develop.

Second Period: 1877–1903

In the last quarter of the 19th century, the entry of immigrants in Brazil grew strongly. On one hand, Europe underwent a serious demographic crisis, which resulted in increased emigration; on the other hand, the final crisis of Brazilian slavery prompted Brazilian authorities to find solutions for the problem of work force. Consequently, while immigration until 1876 was focused on establishing communities of landowners, during this period, while this older process continued, immigrants were more and more attracted to the coffee plantations of São Paulo, where they became employees or were allowed to cultivate small tracts of land in exchange for their work in the coffee crop.

Immigration to Brazil

Figure 372: *European immigrants working in a coffee plantation in the State of São Paulo.*

This also coincided with the decreasing availability of better land in southern Brazil—while the German immigrants arriving in the previous period occupied the valleys of the rivers, the Italians arriving in the last quarter of the century settled the mountainous regions of the state.

During this period, immigration was much more intense: large numbers of Europeans, especially Italians, started to be brought to the country to work in the harvest of coffee.[1247] From 1877 to 1903, almost two million immigrants arrived, at a rate of 71,000 per year[1248] Brazil's receiving structure, legislation and settlement policies for immigrants were much less organized than in Canada and the United States at the time. Nevertheless, an Immigrant's Hostel (*Hospedaria dos Imigrantes*) was built in 1886 in São Paulo, and quick admittance and recording routines for the throngs of immigrants arriving by ship at the seaports of Vitória, Rio de Janeiro, Santos, Paranaguá, Florianópolis and Porto Alegre were established. The São Paulo site alone processed more than 2.5 million immigrants in its almost 100 years of continuous operation. People of more than 70 different nationalities were recorded.

In 1850, Brazil declared the end of the slave trade. This had different impacts on the different regions of Brazil. At the time, the region of São Paulo was undergoing a process of economic boom, linked to the expansion of the cultivation of coffee, and consequently needed increased amounts of labour.

Figure 373: *Italian immigrants in the Hospedaria dos Imigrantes, in São Paulo.*

Other regions, notedly the Northeast, on the contrary, faced economic retraction, and were, consequently, able to dispense workforce. This entailed the replacement of the international slave trade by an internal or interprovincial slave trade, in which Northeastern slaves were sold in large numbers to the Southeast. This temporarily solved the workforce problem in São Paulo and other coffee plantation areas. However, by 1870 the paulista elite came to realise that the Northeastern slaveholders were in fact being able to obtain financial compensation for their slaves, or, in practice, an *abolition with compensation*. Fears of a situation comparable to the United States, with the division of the country into free provinces and slave provinces arose. Consequently, paulista politicians began to seek measures against the interprovincial traffic, at a time when, anyway, the price of Northeastern slaves was getting higher and higher, due to their increasing scarcity. By the beginning of the 1870s, the alternative of the interprovincial trade was exhausted, while the demand for workforce in the coffee plantations continued to expand. Thus the paulista oligarchy sought to attract new workers from abroad, by passing provincial legislation and pressing the Imperial government to organise immigration.

Third period: 1904–1930

From 1904 to 1930, 2,142,781 immigrants came to Brazil—making an annual average of 79,000 people. In consequence of the Prinetti Decree of 1902, that forbade subsidised emigration to Brazil, Italian immigration had, at this stage, a drastic reduction: their average annual entries from 1887 to 1903 was 58,000. In this period they were only 19,000 annually. The Portuguese constituted 38% of entries, followed by Spaniards with 22%. From 1914 to 1918, due to World War I, the entry of immigrants of all nationalities decreased. After

Figure 374: *A poster used in Japan to attract immigrants to Brazil. It says "Let's go to South America (Brazil) with the family."*

the War, the immigration of people of "other nationalities" redressed faster than that of Portuguese, Spaniards, and Italians. Part of this category was composed of immigrants from Poland, Russia and Romania, who immigrated probably by political issues, and part by Syrian and Lebanese peoples. Both subgroups included a number of Jewish immigrants, who arrived in the 1920s.

From 1931 to 1963, 1,106,404 immigrants entered Brazil. The participation of the Japanese increased. From 1932 to 1935 immigrants from Japan constituted 30% of total admissions. Prior to this yearly Japanese immigrants were numerically limited to no more than 5% of the current Japanese population.[1249]

Fourth Period: 1931–1964

With the radicalisation of the political situation in Europe, the end of the demographic crisis, the decadence of coffee culture, the Revolution of 1930 and the consequent rise of a nationalist government, immigration to Brazil was significantly reduced. The focus shifted to culturally assimilating immigrants and "whitening" the population.[1250] From 1931 to 1963, 1,106,404 immigrants entered Brazil. The annual arrival of immigrants fell to 33,500. The Portuguese remained the most significant group, with 39.35%, The participation of the Japanese increased, becoming the second most important group, with

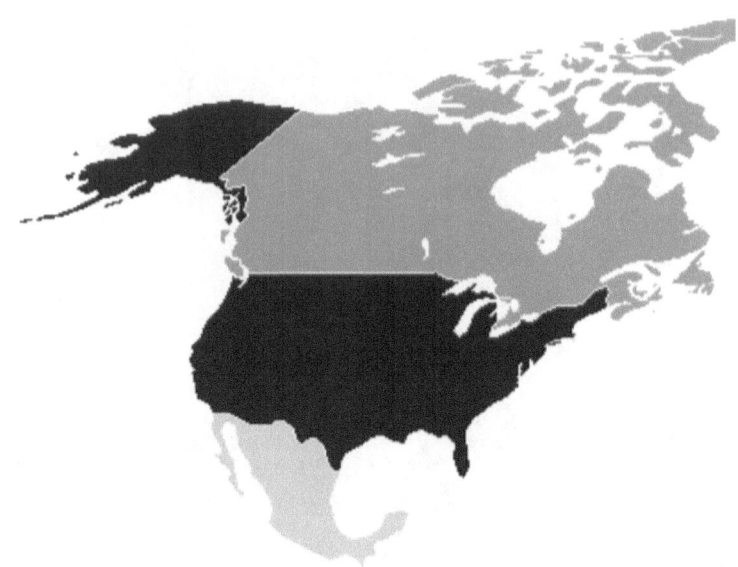

Figure 375:
People authorized to work in Brazil by North American countries in 2009. Organized by number of people.
4,040
684
368

12.79%. Particularly from 1932 to 1935 immigrants from Japan constituted 30% of total admissions.

Immigration also became a more urban phenomenon; most immigrants came for the cities, and even the descendants of the immigrants of the previous periods were moving intensely from the countryside. In the 1950s, Brazil started a program of immigration to provide workers for Brazilian industries. In São Paulo, for example, between 1957 and 1961, more than 30% of the Spanish, over 50% of the Italian and 70% of the Greek immigrants were brought to work in factories.

Current trends

During the 1970s Brazil received about 32,000 Lebanese immigrants escaping the civil war, as well as smaller numbers of Palestinians and Syrians.Wikipedia:Verifiability

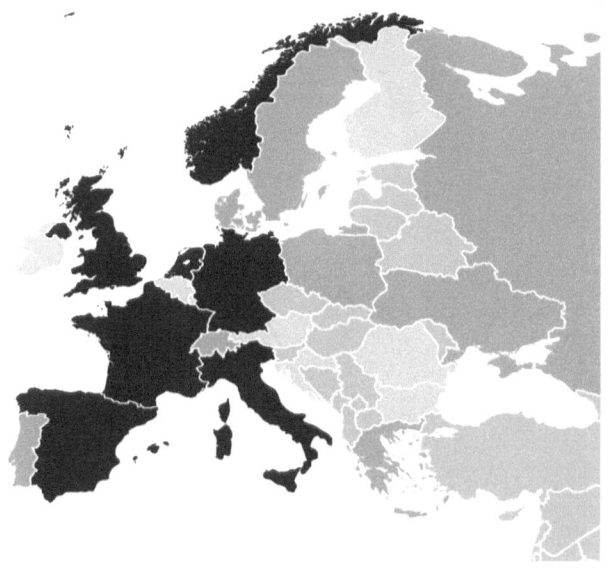

Figure 376:
People authorized to work in Brazil by European countries in 2009. Organized by number of people.
2,528-648
523-184
177-050

During the 1990s Brazil received small numbers of immigrants from the former republics of Yugoslavia, from Afghanistan and West Africa (mostly Angolans). Recent immigration is mainly constituted by Chinese and Koreans and, in a smaller degree, by Argentines and other Latin American immigrants.

The increase in Bolivian immigrants in Brazil is one of the social consequences of the political crisis affecting that country.[1251] The majority of the Bolivians come from cities such as La Paz, Sucre, Santa Cruz de la Sierra, and Cochabamba. Usually they enter Brazil through Cuiabá, in Mato Grosso, or San Mathias, in Bolivia, which borders Caceres, Mato Grosso and Corumbá, in Mato Grosso do Sul.

Between 1,200 and 1,500 Bolivian immigrants come to Brazil every month looking for a job. Most of them work in the illegal textile industry in the Greater São Paulo.[1252] There are an estimated 200,000 Bolivians living in the Greater São Paulo, majority is of undocumented immigrants.

Figure 377:
People authorized to work in Brazil by South American countries in 2009. Organized by number of people.
555-399
398-237
236-102
101-002

In 2009, the country was home to 3,982,000 foreign born people, that represents 2.36% of the Brazilian population. The major work visas concessions were granted for citizens of the United States and the United Kingdom.

In 2010, Brazil is home to 4,251 refugees from 76 different nationalities. The largest refugee ancestries were Angolan (1,688), Colombian (583), Congolese (402), Liberian (259), and Iraqi (197).

Due to the Bolivarian diaspora, in 2017 22,000 new Venezuelan refugees sought shelter in Brazil; this number was expected to greatly increase for 2018.

Immigrants (2012)[1253]	
Country	Population
Portugal	277,727
Japan	91,042
Italy	73,126
Spain	59,985
Argentina	42,202
China	35,953
Germany	29,224
United States of America	27,953
Uruguay	26,271
Chile	25,561
South Korea	19,341
France	18,011
Paraguay	15,626

Visa policy

Permanent visas may be granted to individuals intending to establish residence in Brazil. Permanent Visas apply to:

- Technicians or professionals with a work contract pre-approved by the Brazilian Ministry of Labor, National Department of Employment. This visa must be applied for in Brazil.
- Professors, technicians and high-level researchers who wish to immigrate to Brazil to undertake research work in an institution of higher learning or of research in science and technology. This visa must be applied for in Brazil.
- Foreign investors with initial transfer of foreign capital equivalent to no less than US$50,000 and an investment plan pre-approved by the Brazilian National Council on Immigration (CNIG). This visa must be applied for in Brazil.
- Administrators, managers or directors hired by a commercial enterprise or civil organization resulting from foreign investment described in item 3 above, with a work contract pre-approved by the Brazilian Ministry of Labor, National Department of Employment. This visa must be applied for in Brazil.

- A retired person, 60 years of age or older, accompanied by up to two dependents, and able to transfer monthly, in accordance with the laws of the country of origin, the amount equivalent to US$2,000. In the case of more than two dependents, the applicant must transfer the amount equivalent to US$1,000 for each additional dependent.
- Spouse, partners in a common law union regardless of gender, or minor dependent of Brazilian citizen or of a permanent resident of Brazil;
- Ancestors of a Brazilian national or of a permanent resident of Brazil;
- Siblings of a Brazilian citizen or of a permanent resident of Brazil, if orphan, single and under 18 years of age;
- Minor children, grandchildren or great-grandchildren of a Brazilian citizen or of a permanent resident of Brazil.

Binational unions

- Formed by a Brazilian and other people from other country:

In Brazil

Ethnic origin	Percentage
Portuguese	32%
Italians	9%
Japanese	8%

Outside Brazil

Ethnic origin	Percentage
U.S. citizens	40%
Portuguese	17%
Argentinians	14%

Immigration law

Federal Constitution

Article 12. The following are Brazilians:

II - naturalized:

a) those who, as set forth by law, acquire Brazilian nationality, it being the only requirement for persons originating from Portuguese-speaking countries the residence for 1 (one) uninterrupted year and good moral repute;

Immigration to Brazil

Figure 378: *Portuguese people have a differentiated treatment according to Paragraph 1, Article 12, of the Federal Constitution of Brazil. Due to strong cultural and historical ties between the two countries.*

b) foreigners of any nationality, resident in the Federative Republic of Brazil for over 15 (fifteen) uninterrupted years and without criminal conviction, provided that they apply for the Brazilian nationality.

Paragraph 1. The rights inherent to Brazilians shall be attributed to Portuguese citizens with permanent residence in Brazil, if there is reciprocity in favour of Brazilians, except in the cases stated in this Constitution.

Paragraph 2. The law may not establish any distinction between born and naturalized Brazilians, except in the cases stated in this Constitution.

Statute of Foreigner

Article 112. Are conditions for the granting of naturalization:

I - civilian capacity, according to Brazilian law;

II - to be registered as permanent resident in Brazil;

III - continuous residence in the territory for a minimum period of 4 (four) years immediately preceding the application for naturalization;

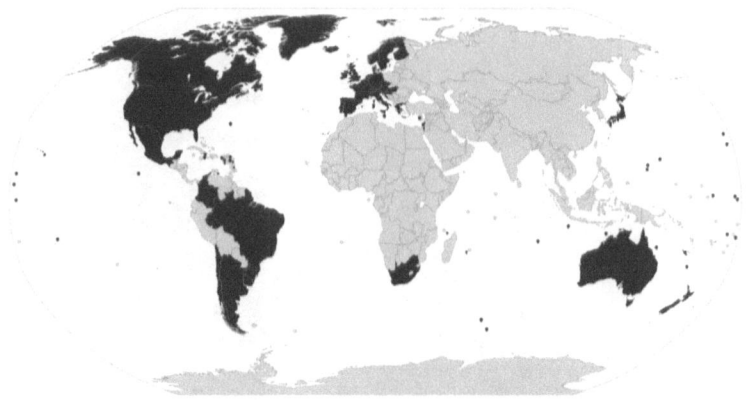

Figure 379:
LGBT immigration equality by country or territory
Recognition of same-sex couples in national immigration laws
Unknown/ambiguous

IV - read and write the Portuguese language, considering the conditions of naturalizing;

V - exercise of occupation or possession of sufficient assets to maintain itself and the family;

VI - proper procedure;

VII - no complaint, indictment in Brazil or abroad for a felony that is threatened in minimum sentence of imprisonment, abstractly considered, more than 1 (one) year.

VIII - good health.

Article 113. The period of residence prescribed in Article 112, item III, may be reduced if the naturalizing fill any of the following conditions:

I - have a child or spouse of Brazil;

(Including same-sex spouse, see also: Same-sex immigration policy in Brazil)

II - be son of a Brazilian;

III - have provided or can provide relevant services to Brazil, in the opinion of the Minister of Justice of Brazil;

IV - commend themselves by their professional, scientific or artistic; or

V - to be owner in Brazil, real estate, whose value is equal to at least a thousand times the greatest value of reference, or be provided with industrial funds of

Figure 380: *A group of Palestinian immigrants in São Paulo.*

equal value, or hold quota shares or amount of paid-in least identical in commercial or civil society, aimed principally and permanently, the operation of industrial or agricultural activities.

Sole Paragraph. The residence will be at least 1 (one) year, in cases of items I, II, and III; 2 (two) years in Item IV; and 3 (three) years in Item V.

Amnesty

Since the 1980s, the Brazilian government has offered amnesty to foreigners in irregular situation in four different campaigns, benefiting tens of thousands of foreigners living in Brazil. The latest campaign began in July 2009 by presidential decree, and though it officially ended at the close of 2009, some cases are still pending. Until now, 41,816 foreigners received amnesty through the 2009 amnesty program, though there are another 2,000 cases expected to be finished in early 2010.Wikipedia:Manual of Style/Dates and numbers#Chronological items Though the large majority of immigrants live in São Paulo, other cases were based largely in Rio de Janeiro and Paraná. The breakdown by country/continent is the following: 16,881 Bolivians, 5,492 Chinese, 4,642 Peruvians, 4,135 Paraguayans, 2,700 Africans (including North Africa), 2,390 Europeans, 1,129 Koreans, 469 Argentines, 274 U.S. citizens, 186 Cubans.

While foreigners who received amnesty obtained the right to work and access health and education services, they are unable to vote or run for public office. They may opt to apply for citizenship after a probation period of residency in order to obtain these rights. Officially, amnesty intends to cut down on illegal activity and human rights violations, particularly with Bolivians in São Paulo. But it seems to fit in with the Lula administration's international policies, including ramped up diplomacy and establishing ties with other nations, but also establishing itself as a competitor with developed countries. By showing that it is a center for immigrants in the Western Hemisphere, particularly in South America, and more importantly, that it is supposedly a benevolent and welcoming country for immigrants, it helps Brazil's international public image.

Those who would benefit from the amnesty, following publication of the law in the Brazilian Official Gazette in July 2009, have up to 180 days after the time of their temporary residence permit (valid for 2 years) to apply. They must also aver their clean criminal record or submit a recent, official document of good conduct from the originating country. During these two years, they must not exceed 90 consecutive days spent abroad. Ninety days prior to the expiration of the temporary residence permit, they must aver their self-sufficiency in Brazil. If they can prove they are eligible for a permanent residence permit. Only ten years after receiving a permanent residence permit may be eligible for naturalization to be Brazilian.

The result of immigration to Brazil

Immigration

Immigration to Brazil, by national origin, periods from 1830 to 1959
Source: Brazilian Institute for Geography and Statistics (IBGE)

origin	1830–1855	1856–1883	1884–1893	1894–1903	1904–1913	1914–1923	1924–1933	1945–1949	1950–1954	1955–1959	1960-1969 197,587 immigrants from many nationalities arrived	1970-1972 15,558 immigrants. The largest majority from Portugal
Portuguese	16,737	116,000	170,621	155,542	384,672	201,252	233,650	26,268	123,082	96,811		
Italians	—	100,000	510,533	537,784	196,521	86,320	70,177	15,312	59,785	31,263		
Spaniards	—	—	113,116	102,142	224,672	94,779	52,400	4,092	53,357	38,819		
Germans	2,008	30,000	22,778	6,698	33,859	29,339	61,723	5,188	12,204	4,633		
Japanese	—	—	—	—	11,868	20,398	110,191	12	5,447	28,819		
Syrians and Lebanese	—	—	96	7,124	45,803	20,400	20,400	N/D	N/D	N/D		
Others	—	—	66,524	42,820	109,222	51,493	164,586	29,552	84,851	47,599		

Immigration has been a very important demographic factor in the formation, structure and history of the population in Brazil, influencing culture, economy, education, racial issues, etc. Brazil has received the third largest number of immigrants in the Western Hemisphere, after only Argentina, Canada and The United States.

European diaspora

In the 100 years from 1872–1972 at least 5.35 million immigrants came to Brazil, of whom 31% were Portuguese, 30% Italian, 13% Spanish, 5% Japanese, 4% German and 16% of other unspecified nationalities.

In 1897, São Paulo had twice as many Italians as Brazilians in the city. In 1893, 55% of the city´s population was composed by immigrants and in 1901 more than 80% of the children were born to a foreign-born parents.[1254] According to the 1920 census, 35% of São Paulo city's inhabitants were foreign born, compared to 36% in New York City. São Paulo's multicultural population could be compared to any major American, Canadian or Australian city. About 75% of the immigrants were Latin Europeans, particularly from three major sources: Italy, Portugal and Spain. The rest came from different parts of Europe, the Middle East and Japan. Some areas of the city remained almost exclusively settled by Italians until the arrival of waves of migrants from other parts of Brazil, particularly from the Northeast, starting in the late 1920s.

According to historian Samuel H. Lowrie, in the early 20th century the society of São Paulo was divided in three classes:

- The high group: composed of graduated people, mainly by Brazilians born to Brazilian parents, who were related to the high-class farmers or other people with privileges.
- The working class: composed of immigrants and their second and third generations descendants. They were the most numerous group, mainly factory workers or traders.
- The semi-dependent group: composed of former slaves and low-class workers of the Empire.

Owners of industries in São Paulo(1962)[1255]

Ethnic origin	Percentage
Italians	35%
Brazilians	16%
Portuguese	12%
Germans	10%
Syrians and Lebanese	9%

Russians	2.9%
Austrians	2.4%
Swiss	2.4%
Other Europeans	9%
Others	2%

According to Lowrie, the fact that Brazil already had a long history of racial mixture and that most of the immigrants in São Paulo came from Latin European countries, reduced the cases of racism and mutual intolerance. However, the Brazilian high class was more intolerant, with most of them marrying other members of the elite. In some cases, to marry an immigrant was accepted if the person had achieved fortune or had some prestige. Lowrie reports that as much as 40% of the São Paulo high-class society mixed with an immigrant within the next three generations.

While in São Paulo the Italians predominated, in the city of Rio de Janeiro the Portuguese remained as the main group. In 1929, as many as 272,338 Portuguese immigrants were recorded in the Federal District of Brazil (nowadays the city of Rio de Janeiro), more Portuguese born people than any other city in the world, except for Lisbon (which had 591,939 inhabitants in 1930).

São Paulo City in 1886

Immigrants	Percentage of immigrants in foreign born population[1254]
Italians	48%
Portuguese	29%
Germans	10%
Spanish	3%

São Paulo City in 1893

Year	Immigrants	Percentage of the City[1254]
Italians	45,457	35%
Portuguese	14,437	11%
Spanish	4,818	3.7%

Figure 381: *Brazilian people from Curitiba, Paraná celebrating the Ukrainian Easter.*

Figure 382: *A Portuguese immigrant in Rio de Janeiro, 1895.*

Immigration to Brazil

Figure 383: *European immigrants and a Brazilian coffee plantation.*

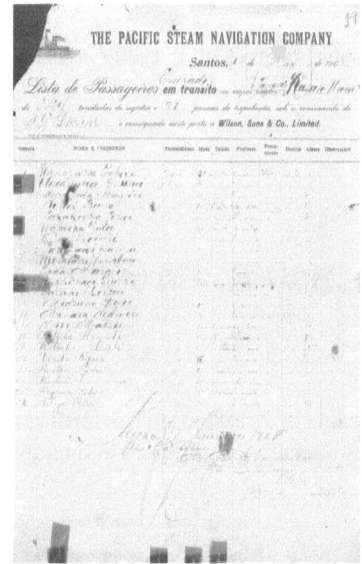

Figure 384: *List of passengers of the ship Kasato Maru bringing the first Japanese immigrants to Brazil, 1908.*

Rio de Janeiro City(Guanabara)

Year	Immigrants	Percentage of the City[1256]
1872	84,283	30.65%
1890	124,352 /- 155,202	23.79% / 29.69%
1900	195,894	24.14%
1906	210,515	25.94%
1920	239,129	20.65%
1940	228,633	12.96%
1950	210,454	8.85%

Rio de Janeiro City(1890)

Group	Population	Percentage of the City[1257]
Portuguese immigrants	106,461	20.36%
Brazilians who were born to a Portuguese father or mother	161,203	30.84%
Portuguese immigrants and descendents	267,664	51.2%

Rio de Janeiro City in 1940(Guanabara)

Immigrants	Population
Portuguese	154,662
Italians	17,457
Spanish	12,212
Germans	10,185
Japanese	538
Others	33,579

Immigrants by Brazilian state according to 1920 Census (including naturalized immigrants)[1258]

State	Immigrants	Percentage within the state population
São Paulo	839,135	18.2%
Federal District (Rio de Janeiro city)	252,958	22.0%

Espírito Santo	20,532	4.5%
Santa Catarina	39,212	5.8%
Rio Grande do Sul	165,974	7.5%
Mato Grosso	25,556	10.3%
Goiás	1,814	0.3%
Minas Gerais	91,349	1.5%
Rio de Janeiro	53,261	3.4%
Paraná	66,387	9.6%
Pernambuco	12,010	0.5%
Piauí	344	0.0%
Paraíba	661	0.0%
Pará	22,824	2.3%
Maranhão	1,681	0.2%
Ceará	980	0.0%
Bahia	10,999	0.3%
Amazonas	17,525	4.8%
Alagoas	747	0.0%
Sergipe	422	0.0%
Acre	3,564	3.8%

In the South of Brazil, there were three main groups of immigrants: Germans, Italians and Slavs (mainly Poles and Ukrainians). The Germans had been settling Rio Grande do Sul since 1824. The first settlers came from Holstein, Hamburg, Mecklenburg-Vorpommern and Hannover. Later, people from Hunsrück and Rhineland-Palatinate predominated. There were also people from Pomerania, Westphalia and Württemberg. These immigrants were attracted to work as small farmers in the region of São Leopoldo. As a result of the great internal migration of people in Rio Grande do Sul, Germans and second generation descendants started to move to other areas of the Province.

A similar process has occurred in Santa Catarina, with initially two main destinations for German immigrants (Blumenau, created in 1850, and Joinville in 1851) and then the immigrants or their descendants moved to other areas. Arriving in larger numbers than Germans, in the 1870s, groups of Italians started settling northeast Rio Grande do Sul. Similar to Germans, they were also attracted to develop small familiar farming production. In Paraná, on the other hand, the main group of immigrants was composed of Eastern Europeans, particularly Poles.[1259]

In southern Brazil, the immigrants settled in *colônias* (colonies), which were rural areas, composed of many small farms, settled by the families. Some of these colonies had a great development and gave birth to major Brazilian cities, such as the former German community of Joinville (500,000 inhabitants—the largest city of the state of Santa Catarina) or the former Italian community of Caxias do Sul (405,858 inhabitants). Other colonies did not have a great development and remained small and agrarian. In these places, it is possible to feel more intensely the impact of the immigration, as many of these towns are still predominantly settled by a single ethnic group.

First Settlers in Londrina(1930's)[1260]	
Ethnic Group	Population
Brazilians	1.823
Italians	611
Japanese	533
Germans	510
Spanish	303
Portuguese	218
Polish	193
Ukrainians	172
Hungarians	138
Czechoslovakians	51
Russians	44
Swiss	34
Austrians	29
Lithuanians	21
Yugoslavs	15
Romanians	12
English	7
Argentinians	5
Syrians	5
Danes	3
Australians	2
Belgians	2
Bulgarians	2
French	2
Latvian	2
Liechtensteiner	2
North-Americans	2
Swedes	2

Estonians	1
Indian	1
Norwegian	1
Total Foreign Born Population	2.923(61,6%)

Some southern Brazilian towns with a notable main ancestry			
Town name	State	Main ancestry	Percentage
Nova Veneza	Santa Catarina	Italian	95%[1261]
Pomerode	Santa Catarina	German	90%[1262]
Prudentópolis	Paraná	Ukrainian	70%[1263]
Treze Tílias	Santa Catarina	Austrian	60%[1264]
Dom Feliciano	Rio Grande do Sul	Polish	90%[1265]

Statistics

Figure 385: *Cover of the magazine "O Immigrante", published by Italian immigrants in Brazil.*

Immigrants established in São Paulo state in 1940

Immigrants	Population
Italians	694.489
Spanish	374.658
Portuguese	362.156
Japanese	85.103
Germans	50.507
Austrians	33.133

Main groups of settlers and immigrants in Brazil	
Origin	Population
Africans (1550–1850)	3,000,000
Portuguese (1500-1822)	800,000
Portuguese, post-independence (1837–1968)	1,766,771
Italians (1836–1968)	1,620,344
Spaniards (1841–1968)	719,555
Japanese (1908–1968)	343,441
Russians (1871–1968)	319,215
Lebanese (1871–1968)	300,246
Germans (1836–1968)	240,457
Austrians (1868–1968)	198,457
Polish (1892–1968)	154,078
French (1842–1968)	150,341
Romanians (1908–1968)	140,799
Americans (1884–1968)	98,934
English (1847–1968)	78,080
Lithuanians (1920–1963)	69,002
Yugoslavs (1920–1968)	67,726
Argentines (1884–1968)	55,553
Syrians (1892–1968)	54,394
Swiss (1820–1968)	51,704
Greeks (1893–1968)	46,684
Dutch (1884–1968)	45,829
Hungarians (1908–1968)	43,592

Uruguayans (1884–1968)	40,836
Belgians (1847–1968)	39,173
Chinese (1895–1968)	17,996
Swedes (1853–1968)	17,994
Czechs (1920–1968)	16,538
Danes (1886–1968)	14,029
Jordanians (1953–1968)	13,567
Estonians (1923–1961)	12,803
Koreans (1956–1968)	12,500
Egyptians (1895–1968)	12,283
Paraguayans (1886–1968)	12,271
Canadians (1925–1968)	11,631
Peruvians (1885–1968)	11,600
Ukrainians (1920–1967)	11,415
Norwegians (1888–1968)	11,136
Venezuelans (1886–1968)	11,076
Finns (1819–1968)	9,992
Iranians (1922–1968)	6,735
Bulgarians (1908–1968)	6,557
Luxembourgian (1919–1968)	6,473
Australians (1946–1968)	920
Irish (1940/1968)	876
Scottish (1945/1961)	776

- Most of the Poles immigrated to Brazil with German, Russian or Austro-Hungarian/Austrian passports, the Ukrainians with Austrian passports and the Hungarians with Romanian passports.

Total of entries of immigrants in the Port of Santos, São Paulo (1908–1936) - Gender.			
Nationalities	Total	% Male	% Female
Portuguese	275,257	67.9	32.1
Italians	270,749	64.7	35.3
Japanese	210,775	56.2	43.8
Spaniards	190,282	59.4	40.6
Germans	89,989	64.3	35.7
Turks	26,321	73.4	26.6

Romanians	23,756	53.2	46.7
Yugoslavians	21,209	52.1	47.9
Lithuanians	20,918	58.6	41.4
Lebanese & Syrians	17,275	65.4	34.6
Poles	15,220	61.9	38.1
Austrians	15,041	72.7	27.3
Others	47,664	64.9	35.1
Total	2,221,282	63.8	36.2

Immigration to Brazil

Arrival of settlers, slaves, and immigrants, by origin, periods from 1500 to 1933
Source: Brazilian Institute for Geography and Statistics (IBGE)

Origin	Period									
	1500–1700	1701–1760	1761–1829	1830–1855	1856–1883	1884–1893	1894–1903	1904–1913	1914–1923	1924–1933
Africans	510,000	958,000	1,720,000	618,000	—	—	—	—	—	—
Portuguese	100,000	600,000	26,000	16,737	116,000	170,621	155,542	384,672	201,252	233,650
Italians	—	—	—	—	100,000	510,533	537,784	196,521	86,320	70,177
Spaniards	—	—	—	—	—	113,116	102,142	224,672	94,779	52,405
Germans	—	—	5,003	2,008	30,000	22,778	6,698	33,859	29,339	61,723
Japanese	—	—	—	—	—	—	—	11,868	20,398	110,191
Lebanese & Syrians	—	—	—	—	—	96	7,124	45,803	20,400	20,400
Scandinavians	—	—	—	—	—	66,524	42,820	109,222	51,493	

Farms owned by an foreign(1920)

Immigrants	Farms[1266]
Italians	35.984
Portuguese	9.552
Germans	6.887
Spanish	4.725
Russians	4.471
Austrians	4.292
Japanese	1.167

Hungarian Immigration to Brazil

Passport	Immigrants[1267]
Romanian	30.437
Yugoslav	16.518
Hungarian	6.501
Austrian	2.742
Czechoslovak	518
Total	56.716

Lebanese and Syrians Immigrants(1920) - French Consulate Estimation

Location	Immigrants[1268]
São Paulo and Santos	130.000
Pará	20.000
Rio de Janeiro	15.000
Rio Grande do Sul	14.000
Bahia	12.000

Main groups of settlers and immigrants in Brazil, from 1500 to 1970	
Nationality/origin	Number of settlers
Africans [1]	3,000,000
Portuguese	2,450,000
Italians	1,622,491
Spaniards[2]	716,052

• Japanese		248,007
Germans 3		240,000
Poles 4		110,243
Lebanese/	Syrians 5	100,000[1269]

^1 It includes all people who were brought from Sub-Saharan Africa.

^2 Includes Andalucians, Basques, Castilians, Catalans, and Galicians.

^3 It does not include Germans who immigrated with Russian passports (see Volga Germans).

^4 Most of the Poles immigrated to Brazil with German, Russian or Austro-Hungarian/Austrian passports.

^5 Most of immigrants from the Levant, which included Orthodox Greeks in Lebanon and Ottoman Greeks, carried Ottoman passports.

Consequences

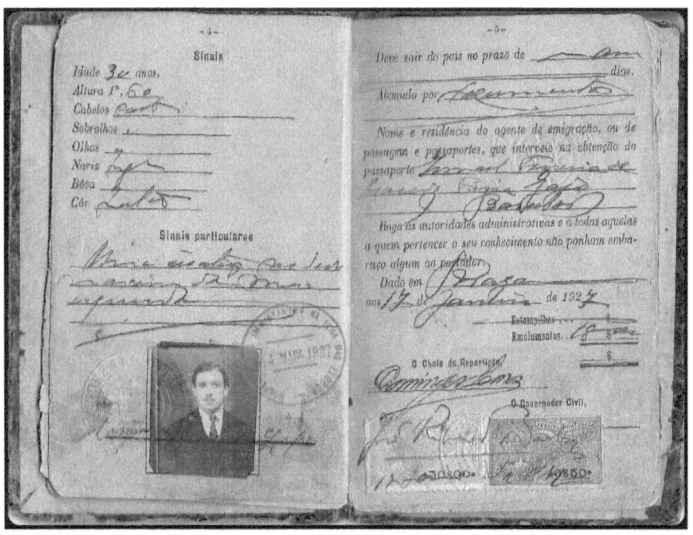

Figure 386: *Passport of a Portuguese immigrant, 1927.*

Figure 387: *German colonies in Southern Brazil.*

Figure 388: *A couple of Portuguese immigrants in São José do Rio Preto, São Paulo, Brazil (1887).*

Figure 389: *Ukrainian church in Curitiba, Paraná.*

Figure 390: *Italian students in Campinas, São Paulo.*

Figure 391: *German Brazilians in 1874*

Desembarque de imigrantes no Porto de Santos (SP), 1907.
Figure 392: *Italian disembarkment in Santos, São Paulo, 1907.*

Figure 393: *Ryu Mizuno (at center), who organized the first travel of Japanese immigrants to Brazil.*

Figure 394: *Ukrainians in Brazil.*

Figure 395: *German kids in Blumenau, Santa Catarina, 1866.*

Figure 396: *German near the city of Vitória, Espírito Santo, 1875.*

Brazilian demographers have long discussed the demographical impact of the wave of emigration in the late 19th and early 20th centuries. According to Judicael Clevelário, most studies about the impact of immigration have followed Giorgio Mortara's conclusions in the 1940s and 1950s. Mortara concluded that only about 15% of the demographic growth of Brazil, from 1840 and 1940 was due to immigration, and that the population of immigrant origin was of 16% of the total population of Brazil.[1270]

However, according to Clevelário, Mortara failed to properly take into account the full endogenous growth of the population of immigrant origin,:52 due to the predominantly rural settlement of the immigrants (rural regions tend to have higher natal rates than cities). Clevelário, then, besides extending the calculations up to 1980, remade them, reaching somewhat different conclusions.

One of the problems of calculating the impact of immigration in Brazilian demography is that the return rates of immigrants are unknown. Clevelário, thence, supposed four different hypothesis concerning the return rates. The first, that he deems unrealistic high, is that 50% of the immigrants to Brazil returned to their countries of origin. The second is based on the work of Arthur Neiva, who supposes the return rate for Brazil was higher than that of the United States (30%) but lower than that of Argentina (47%). The third hypothesis is taken from Mortara, who postulates a rate of 20% for the 19th century, 35% for the first two decades of the 20th century, and 25% for 1920 on. Although Mortara himself considered this hypothesis underestimated, Clevelário thinks it is closest to reality. The last hypothesis, also admittedly unrealistic is that of a 0% rate of return, which is known to be false.:57

Clevelário's conclusions are as following: considering hypothesis 1 (unrealistically low), the Population of Immigrant Origin in 1980 would be of 14,730,710 people, or 12.38% of the total population. Considering hypothesis 2 (based on Neiva), it would be of 17,609,052 people, or 14.60% of the total population. Considering hypothesis 3 (based on Mortara, and considered most realistic), it would be of 22,088,829 people, or 18.56% of the total population. Considering hypothesis 4 (no return at all), the Population of Immigrant origin would be of 29,348,423 people, or 24.66% of the total population.[1271] Clevelário believes the most probable number to be close to 18%, higher than Mortara's previous estimate of 1947.:Abstract, p. 71 According to the Census of 1872, there were 9,930,478 people in Brazil, of which 3,787,289 (38.14%) Whites, 3,380,172 (34.04%) Pardos, 1.954.452 (19.68%) Blacks, and 386,955 (3.90%) Caboclos. The White population grew faster than the non-White population due to the subsidized immigration of Europeans in the late 19th and early 20th centuries. By 1890, the non-White population was reduced to 47% and the Amerindian to 9%.[1272] During this period, most immigrants came from Italy (58.49%) followed by Portugal with 20%.

The disproportionally fast growth of the White population, due to mass immigration, lasted up to 1940, when its proportion in the Brazilian population peaked at 63.5%. During the 1900–1940 period, Italian immigration was greatly reduced, due to the Prinetti decree, forbidding subsidized emigration to Brazil in 1902, then to the Italian war effort of 1915–1918. Thence, for the period of 1904–1940, Portuguese immigration became the main drive of immigration to Brazil, with 36.52% of the arrivals, compared to 14.99% of Italians.

The Brazilian Censuses do not ask questions about "ethnic origin", so there are no systematically comparable data about the impact of immigration. Varied entities, mainly embassies of foreign countries in Brazil and commercial associations that promote bilateral commerce between Brazil and other countries, make claims about the figures of "descendants of immigrants" in Brazil, but none links to any actual survey. Also, if they are extrapolations of actual data on the number of immigrants, the calculations are not explained anywhere.

On the other hand, in 1998, the IBGE, within its preparation for the 2000 Census, experimentally introduced a question about "origem" (origin/ancestry) in its "Pesquisa Mensal de Emprego" (Monthly Employment Research), in order to test the viability of introducing that variable in the Census:[3] (the IBGE ended by deciding against the inclusion of questions about it in the Census). This research interviewed about 90,000 people in six metropolitan regions (São Paulo, Rio de Janeiro, Porto Alegre, Belo Horizonte, Salvador, and Recife).[1273] To this day, it remains the only actual published survey about the immigrant origin of Brazilians.

Here are its results:[1274]

Brazilian Population, by ancestry, 1998	
Ancestry	%
"Brazilian"	86.09%
Portuguese	10.46%
Italian	10.41%
Indigenous	6.64%
Black	5.09%
Spanish	4.40%
German	3.54%
African	2.06%
Japanese	1.34%
Lebanese/Syrian	0.48%

Immigration to Brazil

Jewish	0.20%
Others	2.81%
Total	133.52%

Notice that the total is higher than 100% because of multiple answers. It is easy to see that the results of this research are widely incompatible with the claims made by embassies and commercial associations:

Comparison between claims by embassies, commercial associations, etc., and actual data

Ancestry	Number of immigrants	Ancestry in Brazil (claims by embassies, etc.)	Found by 1998 PME (%)	Projection
Italians	1,622,491	25,000,000	10.41%	18,738,000
Spaniards	716,052	15,000,000	4.40%	7,920,000
Lebanese/Syrians	100,000	10,000,000	0.48%	864,000
Japanese	248,007	1,600,000	1.34%	2,412,000
Germans	240,000	5,000,000	3.54%	6,372,000

The embassy figures are also hardly compatible with the known data for immigration. Here is how they compare:

Number of immigrants and their purported descendants, by national origin

Origin	Number of immigrants[1275]	Number of descendants	Descendants per immigrant
Arab	140,000	10,000,000	71.43
German	223,658	5,000,000	22.36
Spanish	716,478	15,000,000	20.94
Italian	1,623,931	25,000,000	15.39
Japanese	248,007	1,400,000	5.65

The embassy figures for "Arab Brazilians" imply an impossible rate of childbirth. The process of inflation of the "Arab Brazilian" population is described by John Tofik Karam:[1276] *Maintaining a privileged presence in business and political circles, Middle Easterners have overestimated themselves as a way to strengthen their place in the Brazilian nation.*

Among the groups listed in the table, German immigrants arrived quite early in Brazil, starting in the 1820s. By 1883, 23.86% of them had already arrived. Italian immigrants only started to arrive in the 1870s, coming in enormous numbers until 1902, when Italian immigration declined sharply.

By 1903, 70.33% of them had already arrived. Spaniards started arriving about the same time as the Italians, but came in more steady pace, which means that, in average, they represent a more recent immigration. Arabs only started to arrive in considerable numbers about 1890, making them the second most recent immigration, after the Japanese, who started to arrive in 1908. Evidently, the older the immigration, higher should be the descendant/immigrant relation—but, as the table shows, the embassy figures would place the Arab descendant/immigrant relation first—and, in fact, more than three times higher than that of the Germans.

When the number of immigrants is compared to the findings of the July 1998 PME, the results are different:

Number of immigrants and their descendants, projected from the 1998 PME, by national origin			
Origin	Number of immigrants	Number of descendants[1277]	Descendants per immigrant
Arab	140,000	641,200	4.58
German	223,658	4,709,857	21.06
Spanish	716,478	5,856,417	8.17
Italian	1,623,931	13,847,471	8.53
Japanese	248,007	1,776,382	7.16

Here the correct order is reestablished, except for the Arabs appearing with a lower descendant/immigrant rate than the Japanese. This, however, is probably due to the concentration of Nikkeis in São Paulo, as opposed to a less concentrated distribution of "Arab Brazilians", who are present in considerable numbers in regions not counted by the PMEs—notably the Northern Region, the West of Paraná State, and Southern Rio Grande do Sul.

As happened with several other countries in the Americas, such as the United States, which received immigration from many countries, Brazil quickly became a melting pot of races and nationalities, but being peculiar in the sense of having the highest degree of intermarriage in the world.

Nowadays, it's possible to find millions of descendants of Italians, from the southeastern state of Minas Gerais to the southernmost state of Rio Grande do Sul, with the majority living in the state of São Paulo (15.9 million) and the highest percentage in the southeastern state of Espírito Santo (60–75%).[1278,1279,1280] Small southern Brazilian towns, such as Nova Veneza, have as much as 95% of their population of Italian descent.

Thousands of White Americans from the Southern United States (including relatives of former president Jimmy Carter), known as Confederados, fled to

Brazil after the American Civil War, where they founded two cities, Americana and Santa Bárbara d'Oeste.

Co-official languages in Brazil

In this century has grown a recent trend of co-official languages in cities populated by immigrants (such as Italian and German) or indigenous in the north, both with support from the Ministry of Tourism, as was recently established in Santa Maria de Jetibá, Pomerode and Vila Pavão, where German also has co-official status.

The first municipality to adopt a co-official language in Brazil was São Gabriel da Cachoeira, in 2002. Since then, other municipalities attempt to co-officialese other languages.

The states of Santa Catarina and Rio Grande do Sul have Talian officially approved as a heritage language in these states, and Espírito Santo has the East Pomeranian dialect, along with the German language, such as cultural heritage state.

Also in production is the documentary video *Brasil Talian*, with directed and written by André Costantin and executive producer of the historian Fernando Roveda. The pre-launch occurred on November 18, 2011, the date that marked the start of production of the documentary.

Brazilian states with linguistic heritages officially approved statewide

- Espírito Santo (Pomeranian and German)[1281,1282]

[1283]

- Rio Grande do Sul (Talian[1284] and Riograndenser Hunsrückisch German)
- Santa Catarina (Talian)

Municipalities that have co-official indigenous languages

Amazonas

- São Gabriel da Cachoeira (Nheengatu, Tukano and Baniwa)

Mato Grosso do Sul

- Tacuru (Guarani)
- Paranhos (Guarani, under approval)

Tocantins

- Tocantínia (Akwê Xerente)

Municipalities that have co-official allochthonous languages

Municipalities that have co-official Talian language (*or Venetian dialect*)

Rio Grande do Sul

- Serafina Corrêa

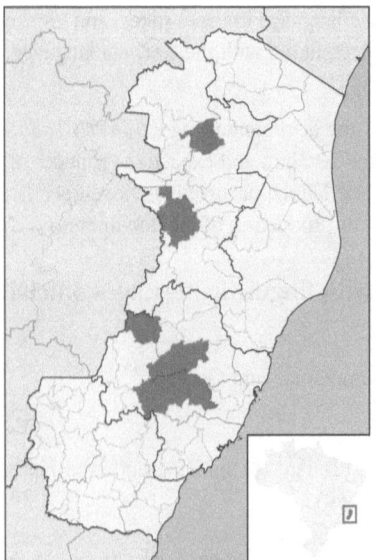

Figure 397: *Municipalities that the Pomeranian language is co-official in Espírito Santo.*

Municipalities that have co-official East Pomeranian language

Espírito Santo

- Domingos Martins
- Laranja da Terra
- Pancas
- Santa Maria de Jetibá
- Vila Pavão

Minas Gerais

- Itueta (only in the district of Vila Nietzel)

Santa Catarina

- Pomerode

Rio Grande do Sul

- Canguçu (under approval)

Rondônia

- Espigão d'Oeste (under approval)

Municipalities that have co-official language Riograndenser Hunsrückisch language

Santa Catarina

- Antônio Carlos[1285]
- Treze Tílias (language teaching is compulsory in schools, standing on stage in public official of the municipality)

Rio Grande do Sul

- Santa Maria do Herval

Municipalities in which the teaching of the German language is mandatory

Rio Grande do Sul

- Nova Petrópolis[1286]

Municipalities in which the teaching of the Italian language is mandatory

Espírito Santo

- Venda Nova do Imigrante

Paraná

- Francisco Beltrão

Rio Grande do Sul

- Antônio Prado

Santa Catarina

- Brusque
- Criciúma

External links

 Wikimedia Commons has media related to *Immigration to Brazil*.

Race and ethnicity

Race and ethnicity in Brazil

Race
• Categorization
Genetics and differences
• Race and genetics • Human genetic variation
Society

• Historical concepts
• Race and ethnicity...
  • in Brazil
  • in the United States
• Racial inequality in the United States
• Racial wage gap in the United States
• Racial profiling
• Racism
                            in the United States
                            Scientific racism

Race and...

• crime in the United Kingdomcrime in the United States
• health
  • in the United States
• intelligence
  History of the race
  and intelligence controversy
• sports
• video games

Related topics
• Ethnic group • Eugenics • Genetics • Human evolution
• **Index** • **Category**

- v
- t
- e[1287]

Part of a series on the
Culture of Brazil
History
People
Languages
Cuisine
Religion
Art
Literature
Sport
• Brazil portal
• v • t • e[1288]

Brazilian society is made up of a confluence of people of several different origins, from the original Native Brazilians, with the influence of Portuguese colonists,[1289] Black African, and European, Arab, and Japanese immigration. Other significant groups include Koreans, Chinese, Paraguayans, and Bolivians.

Brazil has seen greater racial equality over time. According to a recent review study, "There has been major, albeit uneven, progress in these terms since slavery, which has unfortunately not wholly translated into equality of income: only in 2010 did the black-to-white income ratio eclipse its 1960 level, although it appears to be at an all-time high. Education and migration were important factors in closing the gap, whereas school quality and discrimination may explain its persistence."

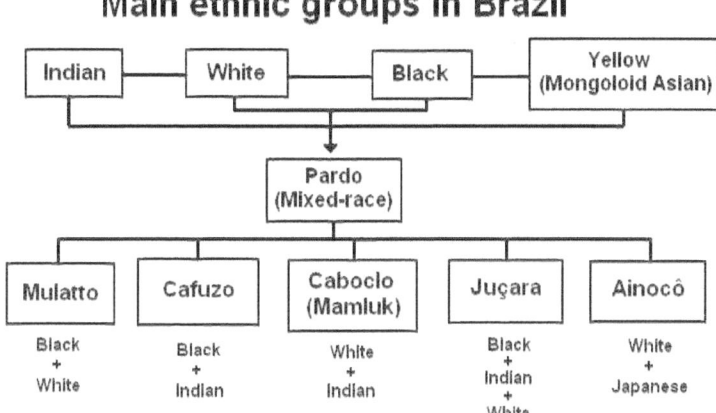

Figure 398: *Main ethnic groups in Brazil.*

Historic background

The Brazilian population was formed by the influx of Portuguese settlers and African slaves, mostly Bantu and West African populations[1290] (such as the Yoruba, Ewe, and Fanti-Ashanti), into a territory inhabited by various indigenous tribal populations, mainly Tupi, Guarani and Ge[1291] In the late 19th and early 20th centuries, in what is known as Great Immigration,[1292] new groups arrived, mainly of Portuguese, Italians, Spanish and German origin, but also from Japanese, the Middle East, and Eastern Europe.[1293]

When the Portuguese reached what is now called Brazil in 1500, its native population was probably composed of about 2.5 million Amerindians.[1294] Up to 1532, the Portuguese made no real effort to colonise the land, limiting to the establishment of "feitorias" to organise the trade of brazilwood. When it became clear that this policy would result in the land being taken by other European powers – namely the French and the Dutch – the Portuguese Crown decided to effectively occupy the territory by fostering agricultural activities – especially sugarcane crops – in Brazil.[1295] This resulted not only in the growth of the population of Portuguese origin, but also in the introduction of African slavery in Brazil.

During the colonial period, the Portuguese prohibited any influx of other Europeans to Brazil.[1296] In consequence, the Portuguese and their descendants constituted the overwhelming majority of the White population of colonial

Brazil.[1297] However, in the Southern Brazilian areas disputed between Portugal and Spain, a genetic study suggests that the predominant genomic ancestry of the Brazilian Gaúchos (inhabitants of the Pampas) may be Spanish, not Portuguese.[1298] Also a small number of Dutch settlers remained in the Northeast after the Portuguese retook Dutch Brazil[1299] and may have contributed to the demographic composition of Northeastern Brazil. Even then and after the country's independence in 1822, immigration to Brazil was mainly Portuguese, though a significant number of German immigrants settled in the Southern region.

European immigration

Combined with the European demographic crisis, this resulted in the immigration of about 5 million people, mostly European peasants, in the last quarter of the 19th century and first half of the 20th. The majority of these immigrants were either Portuguese or Italian (about 1,500,000 each), though significant numbers of Spaniards – which possibly include Portuguese emigrating from Vigo on false passports[1300] – (690,000), Germans (250,000), Japanese (170,000), Middle Easterns (100,000, mostly people from what are now Syria and Lebanon arriving on Turkish passports), and Eastern Europeans (mostly Poles and Ukrainians arriving on Russian passports) also immigrated.

There are few reliable statistics on the Brazilian population before the 1872 census, which counted 9,930,478, of which 3,787,289 Whites, 1,954,452 blacks, and 4,188,737 pardos.[1301] These figures do not yet reflect the influx of the five million immigrants mentioned above, since up to 1872 only about 270,000 immigrants had arrived in Brazil.[1302] According to Judicael Clevelário's calculations, the total population of immigrant origin in 1872 would be of about 240,000 people;[1303] consequently, the total White population of non-immigrant origin for that year would be of about 3,540,000 people at least.

Origin	Period							
	1830–1855	1856–1883	1884–1893	1894–1903	1904–1913	1914–1923	1924–1933	1933–2014
Portuguese	16,737	116,000	170,621	155,542	384,672	201,252	233,650	400,000
Italians	—	100,000	510,533	537,784	196,521	86,320	70,177	
Spaniards	—	—	113,116	102,142	224,672	94,779	52,405	
Germans	2,008	30,000	22,778	6,698	33,859	29,339	61,723	
Japanese	—	—	—	—	11,868	20,398	110,191	
Arabs	—	—	96	7,124	45,803	20,400	20,400	
Others	—	—	66,524	42,820	109,222	51,493	164,586	

Abolition of slavery (1888)

There seems to be no easy explanation of why slaves were not employed as wage workers at the abolition of slavery. One possibility is the influence of race-based ideas from the second half of the 19th and early 20th centuries, which were based on theories of White superiority. On the other hand, Brazilian latifundiaries had been using slave manpower for centuries, with no complaints about the quality of this workforce, and there were not important changes in Brazilian economy or work processes that could justify such sudden preoccupation with the "race" of the labourers. Their embracing of those new identitarian ideas, moreover, proved quite flexible, even opportunist: with the slow down of Italian immigration since 1902 and the Prinetti Decree, Japanese immigration started in 1908, with any qualms about their typically non-European origins being quickly forgotten.

An important, and usually ignored, part of this equation was the political situation in Brazil, during the final crisis of slavery. According to Petrônio Domingues, by 1887 the slave struggles pointed to a real possibility of widespread insurrection. On October 23, in São Paulo, for instance, there were violent confrontations between the police and rioting Blacks, who chanted "long live freedom" and "death to the slaveowners".[1304:73] The president of the province, Rodrigues Alves, reported the situation as following:

The massive flight of slaves from several fazendas threatens, in some places in the province, public order, alarming the proprietaries and the productive classes.[:74]

Uprisings erupted in Itu, Campinas, Indaiatuba, Amparo, Piracicaba and Capivari; ten thousand fugitive slaves grouped in Santos. Fights were happening in daylight, guns were spotted among the fugitives, who, instead of hiding from police, seemed ready to engage in confrontation.

It was as a response to such events that, on May 13, 1888, slavery was abolished, as a means to restore order and the control of the ruling class,<[:76] in a situation in which the slave system was almost completely disorganised.

As an abolitionist newspaper, *O Rebate*, put it, ten years later,

Hadn't the slaves fled massively from the plantations, rebelling against the masters ... Hadn't them, in more than 20,000, gone to the famous quilombo of Jabaquara (out of Santos, itself a center of abolitionist agitation), and maybe they would today be still slaves ... Slavery ended because slaves no longer wanted to be slaves, because slaves rebelled against their masters and against the law that enslaved them ... The law of 13 May was nothing more than the legal recognition – so that public authority wasn't discredited – of an act that had already been accomplished by the mass revolt of slaves.[1305]

Another factor, also usually neglected, is the fact that, regardless of the racial notions of the Brazilian elite, European populations were emigrating in great numbers – to the United States, to Argentina, to Uruguay – which African populations certainly were not doing, at that time. In this respect, what was new in "immigration to Brazil" was not the "immigration", but the "to Brazil" part. As Wilson do Nascimento Barbosa puts it,

The collapse of slavery was the economic result of three conjugated movements: a) the end of the first industrial revolution (1760–1840) and the beginning of the so-called second industrial revolution (1880–1920); b) the lowering of the reproduction costs of the White man in Europe (1760–1860), due to the sanitary and pharmacological impact of the first industrial revolution; c) the raising costs of African Black slaves, due to the increasing reproduction costs of Black men in Africa.[1306]

Racial and ethnic theories

Immigration discussion and policy in the 19th century

As the Brazilian elites perceived the oncoming abolition of slavery as a problem, various alternatives were discussed. While very few remained stuck with the idea of preserving slavery, someWikipedia:Manual of Style/Words to watch#Unsupported attributions proposed the reintegration of "national workers" (which was understood as including the soon-to-be former slaves) into a "free-labour" system; othersWikipedia:Manual of Style/Words to watch#Unsupported attributions proposed Chinese immigration. It was against these positions, not against any imaginary African immigration, that racial arguments were made. So, besides a dispute "immigrantists" and "anti-immigrantists", there was also a debate between pro-Chinese and pro-European immigrantists; the latter also were divided between those, like Nicolau Moreira, who defended not only European immigration, but also a land reform, so to attract immigrants as small farmers, and thoseWikipedia:Manual of Style/Words to watch#Unsupported attributions who wanted immigrants as wage labourers for the plantations.

In Brazil, particularly in São Paulo, the dominant idea was that national workers were unable to develop the country, and that only foreign workers would be able to work in a regime of "free" (i.e., wage) labour. The goal was to "whiten" Brazil through new immigrants and through future miscegenation in which former slaves would disappear by becoming "whiter".[1307]

In 1878, ten years before the abolition of slavery, Rio de Janeiro hosted the *Congresso Agrícola* (Agricultural Congress) and that meeting reflected what the Brazilian elite (especially coffee planters) expected from their future workers.[1308] Although national workers were an option to some of the participants, especially to those not from São Paulo, most of them, under the lead of coffee planters from São Paulo, agreed that only immigration would be good to Brazil,[1309] and, moreover, European immigration. The *Congresso Agrícola* showed that the elite was convinced that Europeans were racially and culturally superior to other races.

Although discussions were situated in a theoretical field, immigrants arrived and colonies were founded through all this period (the rule of Pedro II), especially from 1850 on, particularly in the Southeast and Southern Brazil.

These discussions culminated in the Decree 528 in 1890, signed by Brazil's first President Deodoro da Fonseca, which opened the national harborsWikipedia:Citation needed to immigration except for Africans and Asians. This decree remained valid until October 5, 1892 when, due to pressures of coffee planters interested in cheap manpower, it was overturned by Law 97.[1310]

As a result of those discussions and policiesWikipedia:Citation needed, Brazil experienced immigration mostly from countries such as Italy, Germany, Spain, Portugal and Poland during the end of the empire and the beginning of the republic period (late 19th and early 20th centuries). Later immigration, from 1908 on, was not so much influenced by that race discussions and Brazil attracted, besides Europeans, more immigrants from Lebanon, Syria and Japan, for exampleWikipedia:Citation needed.

Oliveira Vianna and the ideology of "Whitening"

The Brazilian government, as was commonplace at that time, endorsed positions expressed by Brazilian intellectuals. An example is a text, written by Oliveira Vianna, that was issued as introductory material to 1920 Census results. Many pages of Vianna's work were dedicated to the discussion of a "pure race" of white Brazilians. According to the text, written by Oliveira Vianna, the first Portuguese colonists who came to Brazil were part of the blond Germanic nobility that ruled Portugal, while the dark-haired "poor" Portuguese only came to Brazil later, in the 17th and especially the 18th century.

According to Oliveira Vianna, the blond Portuguese of Germanic origin were "restless and migratory", and that's why they emigrated to Brazil. On the other hand, the Portuguese of darker complexions were of Celtic or Iberian origin and came when the Portuguese settlement in Brazil was already well established, because, according to him, "The peninsular brachyoids, of Celtic race, or the dolicoides, of Iberian race, of sedentary habits and peaceful nature, did not

Figure 399: *A Redenção de Cam (Redemption of Ham)*, Modesto Brocos, 1895, Museu Nacional de Belas Artes. The painting depicts a black grandmother, mulatta mother, white father and their quadroon child, hence three generations of hypergamy through racial whitening.

have, of course, that mobility nor that bellicosity nor that spirit of adventure and conquest".

The text reported the different levels of intelligence found among blacks and highlights the existence of "lazy blacks" (Gêgis and Angolans) or "laborious blacks" (Timinins, Minas, Dahomeyanos) and also the existence of "peaceful and obedient blacks" and of "rebels and fierce" ones. Vianna also compares the "morality" and intellectual level found among blacks and reports that Gêgis, Krumanos and Cabindas revealed the "mental inferiority, typical from the lowest types of the black race".

Gilberto Freyre's work

In 1933, Brazilian anthropologist Gilberto Freyre published his famous book *Casa-Grande & Senzala* (*The Masters and the Slaves*). The book appeared at a moment when there was a widespread belief among social scientists that some races were superior to other ones, and in the same period when the Nazi Party in Germany was on the rise. Freyre's work was very important to change the mentality, especially of the white Brazilian elite, who considered the Brazilian people as "inferior" because of their African and Amerindian ancestry. In this book, Freyre argued against the idea that Brazil would have an "inferior race" because of the race-mixing.

Then, he pointed the positive elements that permeate the Brazilian cultural formation because of miscegenation (especially between Portuguese, Indians and blacks). Freyre's book has changed the mentality in Brazil, and the mixing of races, then, became a reason to be a national pride. However, Freyre's book created the Brazilian myth of the Racial democracy, so that Brazil was a "post-racial" country without identitarianism or desire to preserve one's European ancestry. This theory was later challenged by several anthropologists who claim that, despite the race-mixing, the white Brazilian population still occupies the top of the Brazilian society, while Blacks, Indians and mixed-race people are largely found in the poor population.

Gilberto Freyre on the criticisms that he received

The life of Gilberto Freyre, after he published *Casa-Grande & Senzala*, became an eternal source of explanation. He repeated several times that he did not create the myth of a racial democracy and that the fact that his books recognized the intense mixing between "races" in Brazil did not mean a lack of prejudice or discrimination. He pointed out that many people have claimed the United States to have been an "exemplary democracy" whereas slavery and racial segregation were present throughout most of the history of the United States.

"The interpretation of those who want to place me among the sociologists or anthropologists who said prejudice of race among the Portuguese or the Brazilians never existed is extreme. What I have always suggested is that such prejudice is minimal ... when compared to that which is still in place elsewhere, where laws still regulate relations between Europeans and other groups".

"It is not that racial prejudice or social prejudice related to complexion are absent in Brazil. They exist. But no one here would have thought of "white-only" Churches. No one in Brazil would have thought of laws against interracial marriage ... Fraternal spirit is stronger among Brazilians than racial prejudice, colour, class or religion. It is true that equality has not been reached since the end of slavery ... There was racial prejudice among plantation owners, there was social distance between the masters and the slaves, between whites and blacks ... But few wealthy Brazilians were as concerned with racial purity as the majority were in the Old South".

Racial legislation

The myth of a purely informal racism in Brazil is false.[1311] The arrival of the Royal family didn't change this: when a provincial militia was formed in Rio Grande do Sul, it was established that the members should be "White", this being defined as "those whose grand-grandparents were not Black, and whose parents were free-born" (1809). Nor did this change with independence: a complementary law to the 1824 Constitution forbade "Blacks and lepers" from being instructed in schools. Brazilian troops were segregated until the fall of the Empire.[1312]

On July 28, 1921, representatives Andrade Bezerra and Cincinato Braga proposed a law whose Article 1 provided: *"It is prohibited in Brazil immigration of individuals from the black race."* On October 22, 1923, representative Fidélis Reis produced another project of law on the entry of immigrants, whose fifth article was as follows: *'It is prohibited the entry of settlers from the black race in Brazil and, to Asians, it will be allowed each year, a number equal to 5% of those existing in the country.(...)'*. Both bills were decried as identitarian and rejected by the Brazilian Congress.[1313]

In 1945, the Brazilian government issued a decree favoring the entrance of European immigrants in the country: *"In the admission of immigrants, the need to preserve and develop, in the ethnic composition of the population, the more convenient features of their European ancestry shall be considered"*.[1314]

Miscegenation

The degree of miscegenation in Brazil has been very high, as Brazil was colonized by male Portuguese adventurers who tended to procreate with Amerindian and African women.[1315] This made possible a myth of "racial democracy" that tends to obscure a widespread discrimination connected to certain aspects of physical appearance:[1316] aspects related to the concept of *cor* (literally "colour"), used in a way that is roughly equivalent to the English term "race" but based on a combination of skin colour, hair type, shape of nose and lips, and even clearly cultural phenomena such as neighborhood of residence, linguistic habits and class. It is possible for siblings to belong to different "colour" categories. So a "White" Brazilian may be understood as a person perceived and socially accepted as "White", and thus "white" potentially regardless of ancestry or sometimes even immediate family.[1317] Nonetheless, and in conjunction with recent emphases on genetic testing, a variety of social movements, government programs, and academic and popular initiatives have led to an increasing emphasis on historicity and ancestry in racial identification in Brazil and this has tended to counteract what many commentators have long sought to characterize—perhaps incorrectly, perhaps correctly—as a Brazilian racial mutability or malleability.

While miscegenation has been one factor leading to a Brazilian population with features ranging from the stereotypically African to the stereotypically European, a second has been "assortative mating". The genome of the first generation offspring of European fathers and African mothers was 50% European and 50% African, but the distribution of the genes that affect visible features (skin colour, hair type, lip shape, nose shape) was random. Those of the second generation with features considered closer to a "White" stereotype would have tended to procreate with others like themselves, while those considered closer to "Black" would also have tended to procreate among themselves; in the long term producing "White" and "Black" groups with surprisingly similar proportions of European and African ancestry.[1318]

IBGE's racial categories

Race in Brazil, 2010

Brancos (Whites) (47.73%)

Pardos (Multiracial) (43.13%)

Pretos (Black) (7.61%)

Amarelos (Asians) (1.09%)

Indigenious (0.43%)

Undeclared (0%)

The Brazilian Institute of Geography and Statistics (IBGE), that conducts censuses in Brazil since 1940, racially classifies the Brazilian population in five categories: branco (white), pardo (brown), preto (black), amarelo (yellow), and indigenous. As in international practice,[1319] individuals are asked to self identify within these categories.

The following are the results for the different Brazilian censuses, since 1872:

Race and ethnicity in Brazil 773

Brazilian Population, by Race, from 1872 to 2010[1] (Census Data)							
Race or Colour	Brancos (whites)	Pardos (multiracial)	Pretos (blacks)	Caboclos	Amarelos (asians)	Indigenous	Undeclared	Total
1872[2]	3,787,289	3,801,782	1,954,452	386,955	-	-	-	9,930,478
1890	6,302,198	4,638,496[3]	2,097,426	1,295,795[3]	-	-	-	14,333,915
1940	26,171,778	8,744,365[4]	6,035,869	-	242,320	-	41,983	41,236,315
1950	32,027,661	13,786,742	5,692,657	-	329,082	[5]	108,255	51,944,397
1960	42,838,639	20,706,431	6,116,848	-	482,848	[6]	46,604	70,191,370
1980	64,540,467	46,233,531	7,046,906	-	672,251	-	517,897	119,011,052
1991	75,704,927	62,316,064	7,335,136	-	630,656	294,135	534,878	146,815,796
2000	91,298,042	65,318,092	10,554,336	-	761,583	734,127	1,206,675	169,872,856
2010	91,051,646	82,277,333	14,517,961	-	2,084,288	817,963	6,608	190,755,799
Race or Colour	Brancos (whites)	Pardos (multiracial)	Pretos (blacks)	Caboclos	Amarelos (asians)	Indigenous	Undeclared	Total
1872	38.14%	38.28%	19.68%	3.90%	-	-	-	100%
1890	43.97%	32.36%	14.63%	9.04%	-	-	-	100%
1940	63.47%	21.21%	14.64%	-	0.59%	-	0.10%	100%
1950	61.66%	26.54%	10.96%	-	0.63%	-	0.21%	100%
1960	61.03%	29.50%	8.71%	-	0.69%	-	0.07%	100%
1980	54.23%	38.85%	5.92%	-	0.56%	-	0.44%	100%
1991	51.56%	42.45%	5.00%	-	0.43%	0.20%	0.36%	100%
2000	53.74%	38.45%	6.21%	-	0.45%	0.43%	0.71%	100%

| 2010 | 47.73% | 43.13% | 7.61% | - | 1.09% | 0.43% | 0.00% | 100% |

^1 The 1900, 1920, and 1970 censuses did not count people for "race".

^2 In the 1872 census, people were counted based on self-declaration, except for slaves, who were classified by their owners.[1320]

^3 The 1872 and 1890 censuses counted "caboclos" (White-Amerindian mixed race people) apart.[1321] In the 1890 census, the category "pardo" was replaced with "mestiço". Figures for 1890 are available at the IBGE site.[1322]

^4 In the 1940 census, people were asked for their "colour or race"; if the answer was not "White", "Black", or "Asians", interviewers were instructed to fill the "colour or race" box with a slash. These slashes were later summed up in the category "pardo". In practice this means answers such as "pardo", "moreno", "mulato", "caboclo", etc.[1323]

^5 In the 1950 census, the category "pardo" was included on its own. Amerindians were counted as "pardos".[1324]

^6 The 1960 census adopted a similar system, again explicitly including Amerindians as "pardos".[1325]

Controversy

As the IBGE itself acknowledges, these categories are disputed, and most of the population dislike it and do not identify with them.[1326]:1 Most Brazilians see "Indígena" as a cultural rather than racial term, and don't identify as such if they are part of the mainstream Brazilian culture; many Brazilians would prefer to self-describe as "morenos" (used in the sense of "tanned" or "brunettes"); some Black and parda people, more identified with the Brazilian Black movement, would prefer to self-describe as "Negro" as an inclusive category containing pardos and pretos;:2 and if allowed to choose any classification, Brazilians will give almost 200 different answers.:4

According to the American scholar Edward Telles, in Brazil there are three different systems related to "racial classification" along the White-Black continuum.[1327]:80–81 The first is the Census System, which distinguishes three categories: "branco" (White), "pardo", and "preto" (Black).:81 The second is the popular system that uses many different categories, including the ambiguous term "moreno":82 ("tanned", "brunette", or "with an olive complexion").[1328] The third is the Black movement system that distinguishes only two categories, summing up "pardos" and "pretos" as "negros".: More recently, the term "afrodescendente" has been brought into use.[1329]

The first system referred by Telles is that of the IBGE. In the census, respondents choose their race or color in five categories: *branca* (white), *parda* (brown), *preta* (black), *amarela* (yellow) or *indígena* (indigenous). The term "parda" needs further explanation; it has been systematically used since the census of 1940. People were then asked for their "colour or race"; if the answer was not "White", "Black", or "Yellow", interviewers were instructed to fill the "colour or race" box with a slash. These slashes were later summed up in the category "pardo". In practice this means answers such as "pardo", "moreno", "mulato", and "caboclo". In the following censuses, "pardo" became a category on its own, and included Amerindians, which became a separate category only in 1991. So it describes people who have a skin darker than Whites and lighter than Blacks, but does necessarily imply a White-Black mixture.

Telles' second system is that of popular classification. Two IBGE surveys (the 1976 PNAD and the July 1998 PME) have sought to understand the way Brazilians think of themselves in "racial" terms, with the explicit aim of adjusting the census classification (neither, however, resulted in actual changes in the census). Besides that, Data Folha has also conducted research on this subject. The results of these surveys are somewhat varied, but seem to coincide in some fundamental aspects. First, there is an enormous variety of "racial" terms in use in Brazil; when Brazilians are inquired in an open ended question, from 135 to 500 different race-color terms may be brought. The 1976 PNAD found 136 different answers to the question about race; the July 1998 PME found 143.[1330:18] However, most of these terms are used by very small minorities. Telles remarks that 95% of the population chose only six different terms (*branco, moreno, pardo, moreno-claro, preto* and *negro*); Petrucelli shows that the 7 most common responses (the above plus *amarela*) sum up 97%, and the 10 more common (the previous plus *mulata, clara,* and *morena-escura*) make 99%.[19]

Petrucelli, analysing the July 98 PME, finds that 77 denominations were mentioned by only one person in the sample. Other 12 are misunderstandings, referring to national or regional origin (*francesa, italiana, baiana, cearense*). Many of the "racial" terms are (or could be) remarks about the relation between skin colour and exposure to sun (*amorenada, bem morena, branca-morena, branca-queimada, corada, bronzeada, meio morena, morena-bronzeada, morena-trigueira, morenada, morenão, moreninha, pouco morena, queimada, queimada de sol, tostada, rosa queimada, tostada*). Others are clearly variations of the same idea (*preto, negro, escuro, crioulo, retinto,* for Black, *alva, clara, cor-de-leite, galega, rosa, rosada, pálida,* for White, *parda, mulata, mestiça, mista,* for "parda"), or precisions of the same concept (*branca morena, branca clara*), and can actually grouped together with one of the main racial terms without falsifying the interpretation.[19] Some seem to express an outright refusal of classification: *azul-marinho* (navy blue), *azul* (blue), *verde* (green), *cor-de-burro-quando-foge* (literally, "the color of a donkey that has run away", a humorous Portuguese term for a color that cannot be determined).

Petrucelli grouped those 136 terms into 28 wider categories.[47] Most of these 28 wider categories can be situated in the White-Black continuum when the answers to the open-ended question are compared to the answers in the IBGE format:

Category	Frequency	White	Brown	Black	Amerindian	Yellow	Total	difference between White and Black
branca (White)	54.28%	98.96%	0.73%	0.11%	0.07%	0.14%	100.00%	98,85
loira (Blonde)	0.05%	95.24%	0.00%	4.76%	0.00%	0.00%	100.00%	90,48
brasileira (Brazilian)	0.12%	91.20%	6.05%	2.27%	0.00%	0.47%	100.00%	88,93
branca + (adjectivated White)	0.14%	86.47%	9.62%	0.00%	3.91%	0.00%	100.00%	86,47
clara (of light colour)	0.78%	86.40%	11.93%	0.35%	0.14%	1.18%	100.00%	86,05
galega (Galician)	0.01%	70.99%	19.78%	0.00%	0.00%	9.23%	100.00%	70,99
castanha (Brown)	0.01%	63.81%	36.19%	0.00%	0.00%	0.00%	100.00%	63,81
morena clara (light *Morena*)	2.92%	38.35%	57.12%	1.46%	2.27%	0.81%	100.00%	36,89
jambo	0.02%	14.47%	77.96%	2.39%	5.18%	0.00%	100.00%	12,08
morena	20.89%	13.75%	76.97%	6.27%	2.62%	0.38%	100.00%	7,48
mestiça, mista (miscegenated, mixed)	0.08%	17.29%	59.44%	14.96%	7.60%	0.70%	100.00%	2,33
parda (Brown)	10.40%	1.03%	97.25%	1.40%	0.21%	0.10%	100.00%	–0,37
sarará	0.04%	9.09%	60.14%	23.25%	0.00%	7.53%	100.00%	–14,16
canela (of the colour of cinnamon)	0.01%	11.13%	57.55%	26.45%	4.87%	0.00%	100.00%	–15,32
mulata (Mulatto)	0.81%	1.85%	71.53%	25.26%	1.37%	0.00%	100.00%	–23,41

marrom, chocolate (Brown, chocolate)	0.03%	4.56%	57.30%	38.14%	0.00%	0.00%	100.00%	−33,58
morena escura (dark *Morena*)	0.45%	2.77%	54.80%	38.05%	4.15%	0.24%	100.00%	−35,28
escura (of dark colour)	0.38%	0.59%	16.32%	81.67%	1.42%	0.00%	100.00%	−81,08
negra (Black)	3.14%	0.33%	6.54%	92.62%	0.50%	0.02%	100.00%	−92,29
preta (Black)	4.26%	0.37%	1.73%	97.66%	0.17%	0.06%	100.00%	−97,29

The other categories, except, naturally, for "amarela" (Yellow) seem related to Amerindian "race":

Category	Frequency	White	Brown	Black	Amerindian	Yellow	Total
vermelha (Red)	0.02%	58,97	8,22	0,00	21,56	11,24	100,00
cafusa	0.01%	6,02	65,14	22,82	6,02	0,00	100,00
caboverde (Capeverdian)	0.02%	0,00	48,72	23,08	28,21	0,00	100,00
cabocla	0.02%	3,60	49,37	10,43	36,60	0,00	100,00
bugre (Indian)	0.00%	12,50	37,50	0,00	50,00	0,00	100,00
amarela (Yellow)	1.11%	3,27	0,98	0,24	0,15	95,36	100,00
indígena (Indigenous)	0.13%	0,44	2,12	0,00	96,13	1,30	100,00

The remarkable difference of the popular system is the use of the term "moreno". This is actually difficult to translate into English, and carries a few different meanings. Derived from Latin *maurus*, meaning inhabitant of Mauritania,[14] traditionally it is used as a term to distinguish White people with dark hair, as opposed to "ruivo" (redhead) and "loiro" (blonde). It is also commonly used as a term for people with an olive complexion, a characteristic that is often found in connection with dark hair.[1331] In connection to this, it is used as a term for suntanned people, and is commonly opposed to "pálido" (pale) and "amarelo" (yellow), which in this case refer to people who aren't frequently exposed to sun. Finally, it is also often used as a euphemism for "pardo" and "preto".[1332]

Finally, the Black movement system, in direct opposition to the popular system, groups "pardos" and "pretos" in a single category, "negro" (and not Afro-Brazilian).[1333] This looks more similar to the American racial perception,[1334] but there are some subtle differences. First, as other Brazilians, the

Black movement understands that not everybody with some African descent is Black,[1335] and that many or most White Brazilians indeed have African (or Amerindian, or both) ancestrals – so an "one drop rule" isn't what the Black movement envisages.[1336]

Race and class

Another important discussion is the relation between social class and "race" in Brazil. It is commonplace to say that, in Brazil, "money whitens". There is a persistent belief, both in academy and popularly, that Brazilians from the wealthier classes with darker phenotypes tend to see themselves and be seen by others in lighter categories. Other things, such as dressing and social status, also influence perceptions of race.

However, some studies, focusing in the difference between self- and alter-classification show that this phenomenon is far more complex than "money whitens". For instance, according to a study conducted by Paula Miranda-Ribeiro and André Junqueira Caetano among women in Recife, while there is significant inconsistency between the "parda" and "preta" categories, most women are consistently classified by themselves and interviewers into "brancas" and non-brancas. 21.97% of women were consistently classified as White, and 55.13% of women were consistently classified as non-White, while 22.89% of women where inconsistently classified. But the inconsistently classified women reveal an important aspect of economic "whitening". "Self-darkening" women, i.e., those who view themselves as "pretas" or "pardas" but are classified as "brancas" by the interviewers (4.08% of women) have above average education, while the 18.82% "self-whitening" women have a low average education, lower indeed than that of consistently non-White women.[1337]

This, assuming, that there is a correlation between wealth and education, would show that, rather than "Brazilians from the wealthier classes with darker phenotypes seeing themselves and being seen by others in lighter categories", either wealth affects their perception by others, but does not affect, or at least affects considerably less, their self-perception, or that wealth in fact affects their self-perception in the opposite way: it is poor people who are more prone to self-whitening. This, naturally, contributes to show that self-classification in censuses is in fact more objective than alter-classification; but most importantly, it shows that economic differences between Whites and non-Whites effectively exist.

It is important to notice that the alter-classification in this survey was made by a group of college students, i.e., mostly middle-class people.

There are important differences in social position concerning "races". These differences encompass income, education, housing, etc. According to the 2007 PNAD, White workers wages were almost twice those of

Blacks and "pardos".Wikipedia:Citation needed Blacks and "pardos" earned on average 1.8 minimum wages, while Whites averaged 3.4 minimum wages.Wikipedia:Citation needed These differences cannot be exclusively attributed to differences in education: among workers with over 12 years of study, Whites earned on average R$15.90 per hour, while Blacks and "pardos" made R$11.40.Wikipedia:Citation needed

Among the 1% wealthiest Brazilians, only 12% were Blacks or "pardos", while Whites made 86.3% of the group. Among the 10% poorest 73.9% were Black or "pardos", and 25.5% of whites.Wikipedia:Citation needed

13.4% of White Brazilians were graduated, compared to 4% of Blacks and "pardos".Wikipedia:Citation needed 24.2% of Whites were studying in a college or university, compared to 8.4% of Blacks and "pardos".Wikipedia:Citation needed In 2007, 57.9% of White students between 18 and 24 years old were attending one.Wikipedia:Citation needed However, only 25.4% of Black an "pardo" students of the same age group studied at the same level.Wikipedia:Citation needed In 2000, the illiteracy rate among White people over 5 years old was 10.87%; among Blacks, 23.23%, and among "pardos", 21.09%.[1338]

Racial disparities

According to the 2007 Brazilian national resource, the white workers had an average monthly income almost twice that of blacks and pardos (browns). The blacks and browns earned on average 1.8 minimum wages, while the whites had a yield of 3.4 minimum wages. Among workers with over 12 years of study, the difference was also large. While the whites earned on average R$15.90 per hour, the blacks and browns received R$11.40, when they worked the same period. Among the 1% richest population of Brazil, only 12% were blacks and browns, while whites constituted 86.3% of the group. In the 10% poorest there were 73.9% of blacks and browns, and 25.5% of whites.

13.4% of white Brazilians were graduated, compared to 4% of blacks and browns. 24.2% of whites were studying in a College or University, compared to 8.4% of blacks and browns. In 2007, 57.9% of white students between 18 and 24 years old were attending a University or a College. However, only 25.4% of black and brown students of the same age group studied at the same level. Of just over 14 million illiterates in Brazil, nearly 9 million were black or pardo. The illiteracy rate among white people over 15 years old was 6.1%. Among blacks and browns of the same age group over 14%.

Almost half of the Brazilian population (49.4%) is white. The browns form 42.3%, the black 7.4%, and the indigenous or "yellow", according to the IBGE, only 0.8%. The region with the highest proportion of browns is the north, with

68.3%. The population of the Northeast is composed of 8.5% of blacks, the largest proportion. In the South, 78.7% of the population is white.

Genetic studies

Autosomal studies

Genetic research on ancestry of Brazilians of different races has extensively shown that, regardless of skin colour, Brazilians generally have European, African, and Amerindian ancestors.

A 2015 autosomal genetic study, which also analysed data of 25 studies of 38 different Brazilian populations concluded that: European ancestry accounts for 74% of the heritage of the population, followed by the African (15%) and the Native American (11%). The European contribution is highest in Southern Brazil (87%), the African highest in Northeast Brazil (22%) and the Native American is the highest in Northern Brazil (26%).

Region	European	African	Native American
North Region	60%	14%	26%
Northeast Region	65%	22%	13%
Central-West Region	75%	18%	9%
Southeast Region	80%	15%	5%
South Region	87%	7%	6%

An autosomal study from 2013, with nearly 1300 samples from all of the Brazilian regions, found a pred. degree of European ancestry combined with African and Native American contributions, in varying degrees. 'Following an increasing North to South gradient, European ancestry was the most prevalent in all urban populations (with values up to 74%). The populations in the North consisted of a significant proportion of Native American ancestry that was about two times higher than the African contribution. Conversely, in the Northeast, Center-West and Southeast, African ancestry was the second most prevalent. At an intrapopulation level, all urban populations were highly admixed, and most of the variation in ancestry proportions was observed between individuals within each population rather than among population'.

Region	European	African	Native American
North Region	51%	17%	32%
Northeast Region	56%	28%	16%
Central-West Region	58%	26%	16%
Southeast Region	61%	27%	12%
South Region	74%	15%	11%

An autosomal DNA study (2011), with nearly 1000 samples from every major race group ("whites", "pardos" and "blacks", according to their respective proportions) all over the country found out a major European contribution, followed by a high African contribution and an important Native American component. "In all regions studied, the European ancestry was predominant, with proportions ranging from 60.6% in the Northeast to 77.7% in the South". The 2011 autosomal study samples came from blood donors (the lowest classes constitute the great majority of blood donors in Brazil[1339]), and also public health institutions personnel and health students.

Region	European	African	Native American
Northern Brazil	68.80%	10.50%	18.50%
Northeast Brazil	60.10%	29.30%	8.90%
Southeast Brazil	74.20%	17.30%	7.30%
Southern Brazil	79.50%	10.30%	9.40%

According to an autosomal DNA study from 2010, "a new portrayal of each ethnicity contribution to the DNA of Brazilians, obtained with samples from the five regions of the country, has indicated that, on average, European ancestors are responsible for nearly 80% of the genetic heritage of the population. The variation between the regions is small, with the possible exception of the South, where the European contribution reaches nearly 90%. The results, published by the scientific magazine *American Journal of Human Biology* by a team of the Catholic University of Brasília, show that, in Brazil, physical indicators such as skin colour, colour of the eyes and colour of the hair have little to do with the genetic ancestry of each person, which has been shown in previous studies (regardless of census classification).[1340] "Ancestry informative SNPs can be useful to estimate individual and population biogeographical ancestry. Brazilian population is characterized by a genetic background of three parental populations (European, African, and Brazilian Native Amerindians) with a wide degree and diverse patterns of admixture. In this work we analyzed the information content of 28 ancestry-informative SNPs into multiplexed panels using three parental population sources (African, Amerindian, and European) to infer the genetic admixture in an urban sample of the five Brazilian geopolitical regions. The SNPs assigned apart the parental populations from each other and thus can be applied for ancestry estimation in a three hybrid admixed population. Data was used to infer genetic ancestry in Brazilians with an admixture model. Pairwise estimates of F(st) among the five Brazilian geopolitical regions suggested little genetic differentiation only between the South and the remaining regions. Estimates of ancestry results are consistent with the heterogeneous genetic profile of Brazilian population, with a major contribution of European ancestry (0.771) followed by African (0.143) and Amerindian contributions (0.085). The described multiplexed SNP panels can be useful tool for bioanthropological studies but it can be mainly valuable to control for spurious results in genetic association studies in admixed populations". It is important to note that "the samples came from free of charge paternity test takers, thus as the researchers made it explicit: "the paternity tests were free of charge, the population samples involved people of variable socioeconomic strata, although *likely to be leaning slightly towards the "pardo" group"*.

Region	European	African	Native American
North Region	71.10%	18.20%	10.70%
Northeast Region	77.40%	13.60%	8.90%
Central-West Region	65.90%	18.70%	11.80%
Southeast Region	79.90%	14.10%	6.10%
South Region	87.70%	7.70%	5.20%

An autosomal DNA study from 2009 found a similar profile "all the Brazilian samples (regions) lie more closely to the European group than to the African populations or to the Mestizos from Mexico".

Region	European	African	Native American
North Region	60.6%	21.3%	18.1%
Northeast Region	66.7%	23.3%	10.0%
Central-West Region	66.3%	21.7%	12.0%
Southeast Region	60.7%	32.0%	7.3%
South Region	81.5%	9.3%	9.2%

According to another autosomal DNA study from 2008, by the University of Brasília (UnB), European ancestry dominates in the whole of Brazil (in all regions), accounting for 65.90% of heritage of the population, followed by the African contribution (24.80%) and the Native American (9.3%).

São Paulo state, the most populous state in Brazil, with about 40 million people, showed the following composition, according to an autosomal study from 2006: European genes account for 79% of the heritage of the people of São Paulo, 14% are of African origin, and 7% Native American. A more recent study, from 2013, found the following composition in São Paulo state: 61.9% European, 25.5% African and 11.6% Native American.

Several other studies have suggested that European ancestry is the main component in all Brazilian regions. A study from 2002 quoted previous and older studies (28. Salzano F M. Interciêência. 1997;22:221–227. 29. Santos S E B, Guerreiro J F. Braz J Genet. 1995;18:311–315. 30. Dornelles C L, Callegari-Jacques S M, Robinson W M, Weimer T A, Franco M H L P, Hickmann A C, Geiger C J, Salzamo F M. *Genet Mol Biol.* 1999;22:151–161. 31. Krieger H, Morton N E, Mi M P, Azevedo E, Freire-Maia A, Yasuda N. *Ann Hum Genet.* 1965;29:113–125. [PubMed]), saying that: "Salzano (28, a study from 1997) calculated for the Northeastern population as a whole, 51% European, 36% African, and 13% Amerindian ancestries whereas in the north, Santos and Guerreiro (29, a study from 1995) obtained 47% European, 12% African, and 41% Amerindian descent, and in the southernmost state of Rio Grande do Sul, Dornelles et al. (30, a study from 1999) calculated 82% European, 7% African, and 11% Amerindian ancestries.

MtDna and y DNA studies

According to a genetic study about Brazilians, on the paternal side, 98% of the White Brazilian Y Chromosome comes from a European male ancestor, only 2% from an African ancestor and there is a complete absence of Amerindian contributions. On the maternal side, 39% have a European Mitochondrial DNA, 33% Amerindian and 28% African MtDNA. This analysis only shows a small fraction of a person's ancestry (the Y Chromosome comes from a single male ancestor and the mtDNA from a single female ancestor, while the contributions of the many other ancestors is not specified)., but it shows that miscegenation in Brazil was directional, between Portuguese males and African and Amerindian females.

Analyzing Black Brazilians' Y chromosome, which comes from male ancestors through paternal line, it was concluded that half (50%) of the Black Brazilian population has at least one male ancestor who came from Europe, 48% has at least one male ancestor who came from Africa and 1.6% has at least one male ancestor who was Native American. Analyzing their mitochondrial DNA, that comes from female ancestors though maternal line, 85% of them have at least a female ancestor who came from Africa, 12.5% have at least a female ancestor who was Native Brazilian and only 2.5% have at least a female ancestor who came from Europe.

Race and ethnicity in Brazil 785

European and Middle Eastern lineages contributions to Y-haplogroup in the Brazilian population:

Region	Central-West	Northern	Northeastern	Southeastern	Southern
Portugal	**45%**	36%	18%	**42%**	**63%**
France	17%	**52%**	14%	-	0%
Italy	-	1%	**61%**	27%	14%
Germany	16%	-	7%	19%	17%
Lebanon	23%	12%	-	13%	4%

European and Middle eastern lineages contributions to R1b1a-M269 sub-haplogroups in Brazilian population

Region	Central-West	Northern	Northeastern	Southeastern	Southern
Portugal	47%	34%	20%	37%	12%
Spain	11%	35%	52%	27%	46%
France	21%	16%	-	20%	-
Italy	3%	6%	8%	5%	10%
Netherlands	11%	7%	3%	9%	7%
Germany	-	2%	11%	2%	21%
Lebanon/Turkey	7%	-	6%	-	3%

Descendants of colonial-era population

Sérgio Pena, a leading Brazilian geneticist, summed it up this way:

The correlation between color and genomic ancestry is imperfect: at the individual level one cannot safely predict the skin color of a person from his/her level of European, African and Amerindian ancestry nor the opposite. Regardless of their skin color, the overwhelming majority of Brazilians have a high degree of European ancestry. Also, regardless of their skin color, the overwhelming majority of Brazilians have a significant degree of African ancestry. Finally, most Brazilians have a significant and very uniform degree of Amerindian ancestry! The high ancestral variability observed in Whites and Blacks suggests that each Brazilian has a singular and quite individual proportion of European, African and Amerindian ancestry in his/her mosaic genomes.

Brazil's racial base are its colonial-era population, consisting of Amerindians, Portuguese settlers, and African slaves:

- At least 50% of the Brazilian paternal ancestry would be of Portuguese origin.
- European ancestry predominates in the Brazilian population as a whole, in all regions of Brazil, according to the vast majority of all autosomal studies undertaken covering the entire population, accounting for between 65% to 77% of the heritage of the population."[1341]
- African ancestry is high in all regions of Brazil. 86% of Brazilians would have over 10% of their genes coming from Africans, according to a study based on about 200 samples from 2003. The researchers however were cautious about its conclusions: "Obviously these estimates were made by extrapolation of experimental results with relatively small samples and, therefore, their confidence limits are very ample". A new autosomal study from 2011, also led by Sérgio Pena, but with nearly 1000 samples this time, from all over the country, shows that in most Brazilian regions most Brazilians "whites" are less than 10% African in ancestry, and it also shows that the "pardos" are predominantly European in ancestry, the European ancestry being therefore the main component in the Brazilian population, in spite of a very high degree of African ancestry and significant Native American contribution. The African contribution was found to be thus distributed according to the 2011 autosomal study: 10.50% in the North region of Brazil, 29.30% in the Northeast of Brazil, 17.30% in the Southeast of Brazil and 10.30% in the South of Brazil. According to an autosomal study from 2008, African contribution accounts for 24.80% of the heritage of the population, and according to an autosomal study from 2010, it accounts for 14.30% of the heritage of the population.
- Native American ancestry is significant and present in all regions of Brazil.

Descendants of immigrants

The largest influx of European immigrants to Brazil occurred in the late 19th and early 20th centuries. According to the *Memorial do Imigrante* statistics data, Brazil attracted nearly 5 million immigrants between 1870 and 1953. These immigrants were divided in two groups: a part of them was sent to Southern Brazil to work as small farmers. However, the biggest part of the immigrants was sent to Southeast Brazil to work in the coffee plantations. The immigrants sent to Southern Brazil were mainly Germans (starting in 1824, mainly from Rhineland-Palatinate, the others from Pomerania, Hamburg, Westphalia, etc.) and Italians (starting in 1875, mainly from the Veneto and Lombardia). In Southeastern Brazil, most of the immigrants were Italians (mainly from the Veneto, Campania, Calabria and Lombardia), Portuguese (mainly from Beira Alta, Minho and Alto Trás-os-Montes), Spaniards (mainly from Galicia and Andalusia) and smaller numbers of French (most came from the southern regions) and Dutch (from the Netherlands and Belgium). Wikipedia:Citation needed

Notably, the first half of the 20th century saw a large inflow of Japanese (mainly from Honshū, Hokkaidō and Okinawa) and Arab (from Lebanon and Syria) immigrants.

Total of entries of immigrants in the Port of Santos, São Paulo (1908–1936) – Gender.			
Nationalities	Total	% Male	% Female
Portuguese	275,257	67.9	32.1
Spaniards	209,282	59.4	40.6
Italians	202,749	64.7	35.3
Japanese	176,775	56.2	43.8
Germans	43,989	64.3	35.7
"Turks"	26,321	73.4	26.6
Romanians	23,756	53.2	46.7
Yugoslavians	21,209	52.1	47.9
Lithuanians	20,918	58.6	41.4
Syrians	17,275	65.4	34.6
Poles	15,220	61.9	38.1
Austrians	15,041	72.7	27.3
Others	47,664	64.9	35.1
Total	1,221,282	63.8	36.2

Ethnicities by region

Historically, the different regions of Brazil had their own migratory movements, which resulted in racial differences between these areas. The Southern region had a greater impact of the European immigration and has a large White majority, which contrasts with the Northern and Northeastern regions, which have a large Pardo (mixed-race) majority. In Northern Brazil, the main racial contribution was of the native Amerindians, with a smaller European and African influence. In Northeastern Brazil, the main contribution was of Africans, with a smaller European and Amerindian influence. The Southeastern region of Brazil had a more balanced ratio of European, African and Amerindian admixture.

The Census of 2017 revealed that the self-reported White population had its higher proportion in the state of Santa Catarina (96.6%) and the lowest in Bahia (38.9%). The Pardo (brown) proportion was higher in Amazonas (52.4%) and lower in Santa Catarina (2.1%). The Black proportion varied from 15.7% in Bahia to 0.9% in Santa Catarina. Because of their small number, the Amerindian and Asian population were counted together and they had a higher proportion in São Paulo (3.3%) and a lower proportion in Paraíba (0.1%).

State	White (%)	Brown (%)	Black (%)	Asian or Amerindian (%)
Acre	40,1	54,8	4,1	1,0
Alagoas	50,6	45,4	3,8	0,3
Amapá	47,6	42,2	8,1	2,0
Amazonas	41,6	52,4	2,4	3,6
Bahia	38,9	44,8	15,7	0,6
Ceará	54,3	42,4	3,1	0,2
Distrito Federal	61,6	29,5	7,4	1,3
Espírito Santo	62,2	28,6	8,5	0,7
Goiás	72,7	20,6	6,1	0,5
Maranhão	45,5	43,9	9,5	1,0
Mato Grosso	55,3	34,6	7,8	2,3
Mato Grosso do Sul	74,1	18,8	5,3	1,7
Minas Gerais	65,7	24,2	9,7	0,4
Pará	43,6	49,4	6,2	0,8
Paraíba	56,5	37,5	5,8	0,1
Paraná	80,3	15,5	3,0	1,1
Pernambuco	57,9	35,2	6,3	0,6
Piauí	43,5	49,9	6,4	0,2
Rio de Janeiro	64,5	22,4	12,6	0,4
Rio Grande do Norte	57,1	38,5	3,9	0,4
Rio Grande do Sul	88,3	7,4	3,9	0,4
Rondônia	54,4	38,8	5,8	1,0
Roraima	43,5	45,1	9,2	2,3
Santa Catarina	96,6	2,1	0,9	0,4
São Paulo	80,2	11,4	5,2	3,3
Sergipe	48,8	41,3	8,7	1,3
Tocantins	44,5	47,1	7,2	1,2

South

The South of Brazil is the region with the largest percentage of Whites. According to the 2017 census, White people account for 88.4% of the population. In colonial times, this region had a very small population.

The region what is now Southern Brazil was originally inhabited by Amerindian peoples, mostly Pampeano, Guarani and Kaingangs.

In the early 18th century, only a few settlers from São Paulo were living there. This situation made the region vulnerable to attacks from neighboring countries. This fact forced the King of Portugal to decide to populate the region. For this, settlers of the Portuguese Azores islands were sent to the coast. To stimulate the immigration to Brazil, the king offered several benefits for the Azorean couples. Between 1748 and 1756, six thousand Azoreans moved to the coast of Santa Catarina. They were mainly newly married who were seeking a better life. At that time, the Azores were one of the poorest regions of Portugal. They established themselves mainly in the Santa Catarina Island, nowadays the region of Biguaçu. Later, some couples moved to Rio Grande do Sul, where they established Porto Alegre, the capital. The Azoreans lived on fishing and agriculture, especially flour. They composed over half of Rio Grande do Sul and Santa Catarina's population in the late 18th century. The state of Paraná was settled by colonists from São Paulo due to their proximity (Paraná was part of São Paulo until the mid-19th century).

Black slaves were massively introduced into Rio Grande do Sul due to the development of jerky production, around 1780. By 1822, they have been reported as being 50% of Rio Grande do Sul's population; but this is most certainly an exaggeration.[1342] This number decreased to 25% in 1858 and to only 5.2% in 2005. Most of them were bought from Angola, though this doesn't necessarily means that they were originally inhabitants of that region.

After independence from Portugal (1822) the Brazilian government started to stimulate the arrival of a new wave of immigrants to settle the South. In 1824 they established São Leopoldo, a German community. Major Schaeffer, a German who was living in Brazil, was sent to Germany in order to bring immigrants. From Rhineland-Palatinate, the Major brought the immigrants and soldiers. Settlers from Germany were brought to work as small farmers, because there were many land holdings without workers. To attract the immigrants, the Brazilian government had promised large tracts of land, where they could settle with their families and colonize the region. The first years were not easy. Many Germans died of tropical disease, while others left the colonies to find better living conditions. The German colony of São Leopoldo was a disaster. Nevertheless, in the following years, a further

4,830 Germans arrived at São Leopoldo, and then the colony started to develop, with the immigrants establishing the town of Novo Hamburgo (*New Hamburg*). From São Leopoldo and Novo Hamburgo, the German immigrants spread into others areas of Rio Grande do Sul, mainly close to sources of rivers. The whole region of Vale dos Sinos was populated by Germans. During the 1830s and part of the 1840s German immigration to Brazil was interrupted due to conflicts in the country (Ragamuffin War). The immigration restarted after 1845 with the creation of new colonies. The most important ones were Blumenau, in 1850, and Joinville in 1851, both in Santa Catarina state; these attracted thousands of German immigrants to the region. In the next five decades, other 28 thousand Germans were brought to Rio Grande do Sul to work as small farmers in the countryside. Until 1914, it is estimated that 50 thousand Germans settled in this state.

Another immigration boom to this region started in 1875. Communities with Italian immigrants were also created in southern Brazil. The first colonies to be populated by Italians were created in the highlands of Rio Grande do Sul (Serra Gaúcha). These were Garibaldi and Bento Gonçalves. These immigrants were predominantly from Veneto, in northern Italy. After five years, in 1880, the great numbers of Italian immigrants arriving caused the Brazilian government to create another Italian colony, Caxias do Sul. After initially settling in the government-promoted colonies, many of the Italian immigrants spread themselves into other areas of Rio Grande do Sul seeking further opportunities. They created many other Italian colonies on their own, mainly in highlands, because the lowlands were already populated by Germans and native *gaúchos*. The Italian established many vineyards in the region. Nowadays, the wine produced in these areas of Italian colonization in southern Brazil is much appreciated within the country, though little is available for export. In 1875, the first Italian colonies were established in Santa Catarina, which lies immediately to the north of Rio Grande do Sul. The colonies gave rise to towns such as Criciúma, and later also spread further north, to Paraná.

A significant number of Poles have settled in Southern Brazil. The first immigrants arrived in 1869. From 1872 to 1959, 110,243 "Russian" citizens entered Brazil. In fact, the majority of them were Poles, since Poland was under Russian rule until 1917, and ethnic Poles immigrated with Russian passports.[1343]

Southeast

The Southeastern region of Brazil is the ethnically most diverse part of the country.Wikipedia:Citation needed

Southeast Brazil is home to the oldest Portuguese settlement in the Americas, São Vicente, São Paulo, established in 1532. The region, since the beginning of its colonization, is a melting pot of Whites, Indians and Blacks. The Amerindians of the region were enslaved by the Portuguese. The race mixing between the Indian females and their White masters produced the Bandeirante,Wikipedia:Citation needed the colonial inhabitant of São Paulo, who formed expeditions that crossed the interior of Brazil and greatly increased the Portuguese colonial territory.

In the late 17th century the Bandeirantes found gold in the area that nowadays is Minas Gerais. A gold rush took place in Brazil, and hundreds of thousands of Portuguese colonists arrived during this period. The confrontation between the Bandeirantes and the Portuguese for obtaining possession of the mines led to the Emboabas' War. The Portuguese won the war. The Amerindian culture declined,Wikipedia:Citation needed giving space to a stronger Portuguese cultural domination. In order to control the wealth, the Portuguese Crown moved the capital of Brazil from Salvador, Bahia to Rio de Janeiro. Thousands of African slaves were brought to work in the gold mines. They were landed in Rio de Janeiro and sent to other regions. No other place in the world had so many slaves, since the end of the Roman Empire.[1344] In 1808 the Portuguese Royal Family, fleeing from Napoleon, took charge in Rio de Janeiro. Some 15 thousand Portuguese nobles moved to Brazil. The region changed a lot, becoming more European.Wikipedia:Citation needed

In the last quarter of the 20th century, a huge wave of immigration came to Southeastern Brazil, attracted by the government to replace the African slaves in the coffee plantations. Most immigrants landed in the Port of Santos and were forwarded to coffee farms within São Paulo. The vast majority of the immigrants came from Italy. Brazil attracted nearly 5 million immigrants between 1870 and 1953. The large numbers of Italians are visible in many parts of Southeast Brazil. Their descendants are nowadays predominant in many areas.

The arrival of immigrants from several places of Europe, the Middle East and Asia produced an ethnically diverse population.Wikipedia:Citation needed The city of São Paulo is home to the largest population of Japanese origin outside of Japan itself.

Northeast

The influx of immigrants in this region in the 19th century was much smaller than in Southern Brazil. By the way, since the late 19th century, thousands of people from this region move to the richest parts of Brazil, mainly São Paulo.

The Portuguese settlers rarely brought women, which led to relationships with the Indian women.Wikipedia:Citation needed Later, interracial relationships occurred between Portuguese males and African females.Wikipedia:Citation needed The coast, in the past the place of arrival of millions of Black slaves from Angola, Nigeria and Benin to work in the plantations of sugar-cane, nowadays has a predominance of Mulattoes. Salvador, Bahia is considered the largest Black city outside of Africa, with over 80% of its inhabitants being African-Brazilians. In the hinterland, there is a predominance of Indian and White mixture.

North

Northern Brazil, largely covered by the Amazon rainforest, is the Brazilian region with the largest Amerindian cultural influence and demographic presence. Inhabited by diverse indigenous tribes, this part of Brazil was reached by Portuguese colonists in the 17th century, but it started to be populated by non-Indians only in the late 19th and early 20th centuriesWikipedia:Citation needed. The exploitation of rubber used in the growing automobile industry, caused a huge migration to the region. Many people from the Northeastern Brazil, mostly Ceará, moved to the Amazon area. The contact between the Indians and the northeastern rubbers created the base of the ethnic composition of the region, with its mixed-race majorityWikipedia:Citation needed.

Central-West

The Central-West region of Brazil was inhabited by diverse Indians when the Portuguese arrived in the early 18th century. The Portuguese came to explore the precious stones that were found there. As it was a far away region, very few African slaves were brought to this areaWikipedia:Citation needed. Who, in fact, worked as slaves in the gold mines were the local IndiansWikipedia:Citation needed. The contact between the Portuguese and the Indians created a mixed-race populationWikipedia:Citation needed. Until the mid-20th century, Central-West Brazil had a very small population. The situation changed with the construction of BrasiliaWikipedia:Citation needed, the new capital of Brazil, in 1960. Many workers were attracted to the region, mostly from northeastern Brazil.

A new migratory movement started arriving from the 1970s. With the mechanization of agriculture in the South of Brazil, rural workers of that region, many of them of German and Italian origin migrated to the Central-West region.

Days celebrating racial groups in Brazil

In Brazil, the "Day of the Caboclo" (*Dia do Caboclo*) is observed annually on June 24, in celebration of the contributions and identity of the original caboclos and their descendants. This date is an official public holiday in the State of Amazonas.

"Mixed Race Day" (*Dia do Mestiço*) is observed annually on June 27, three days after the Day of the Caboclo, in celebration of all mixed-race Brazilians, including the caboclos. The date is an official public holiday in three Brazilian states.

"Indian Day" (*Dia do Índio*), observed annually on April 19, recognizes and honours the indigenous peoples of Brazil.

"Black Awareness Day" (*Dia da Consciência Negra*) is observed annually on November 20 as a day "to celebrate a regained awareness by the black community about their great worth and contribution to the country". The date is an official public holiday in five Brazilian states.

Religion

Religion in Brazil

Religion in Brazil (2010)[1345]

Roman Catholic Church[1346] (64.63%)

Traditional/Mainline Protestant[1347] (4.03%)

Assemblies of God[1348] (6.46%)

Christian Congregation of Brazil[1349] (1.20%)

Other Pentecostal (5.64%)

Other Christian[1350] (6.82%)

Spiritism (2.02%)

Other religions[1351] (1.04%)

No religion[1352] (8.04%)

Unknown (0.12%)

Religion in Brazil is more diverse compared to other Latin American countries. The dominant religion of Brazil is Christianity. Brazil possesses a richly spiritual society formed from the meeting of the Roman Catholic Church with the religious traditions of African slaves and indigenous people. This confluence of faiths during the Portuguese colonization of Brazil led to the development of a diverse array of syncretistic practices within the overarching umbrella of Brazilian Roman Catholicism, characterized by traditional Portuguese festivities. Until recently Catholicism was overwhelmingly dominant. Rapid change in the 21st century has led to a growth in secularism (no religious affiliation), and Evangelical Protestantism to over 22% of the population. The 2010 census indicates that under 65% of Brazilians consider themselves Catholic, down from 90% in 1970, leading Cardinal Cláudio Hummes to comment, "We wonder with anxiety: how long will Brazil remain a Catholic country?"[1355]

In 1891, when the first Brazilian Republican Constitution was set forth, Brazil ceased to have an official religion and has remained secular ever since, though

Religion in Brazil

Figure 400: *People during the Diversidade Religiosa no Brasil (Religion Diversity in Brazil) reunion.*

Figure 401: *The Basilica of the National Shrine of Our Lady of Aparecida is the second largest in the world, after only of the Basilica of Saint Peter in Vatican City.*[1354]

the Catholic Church remained politically influential into the 1970s. The Constitution of Brazil guarantees freedom of religion and strongly prohibits the establishment of any religion by banning government support or hindrance of religion at all levels. In the 2010 census 64.6% of the population declared themselves as Roman Catholic, 22.2% as Protestant, 8% as non religious, and 5.2% as followers of other religions (mostly Spiritists or Kardecists who follow the doctrines of Allan Kardec, Umbandists, Candomblers, Jehovah's Witnesses, Mormons, and minorities of Buddhists, Jews, Muslims, and other groups).

Brazilian religions are very diversified and inclined to syncretism. In recent decades, there has been a great increase of Neo-Pentecostal churches and a thriving of Afro-Brazilian religions,[1356] which have decreased the number of members of the Roman Catholic Church.[1357] The number of Umbandists and Candomblers could be significantly higher than the official census figure, since many of them continue to this day to disguise their religion under "Roman Catholic" syncretism.[1358] About ninety percent of Brazilians declared some sort of religious affiliation in the most recent census.[1359]

Demographics

2010 Census:

- **Christianity: 169.329.176 - 88.77%**
- Roman Catholicism: 123.280.172 - 64.63%
- Protestantism: 42.275.440 - 22.16%
- Other Christians: 3.773.564 - 1.98%
- **No religion**: 15.335.510 - 8.04%
- **Other religions**: 6.091.113 - 3.19%

Christianity

Roman Catholicism

Brazil has the largest number of Catholics in the world.[1360] Roman Catholicism has been Brazil's main religion since the beginning of the 16th century. It was introduced among the Native Brazilians by Jesuits missionaries and also observed by all the Portuguese first settlers.

During colonial times, there was no freedom of religion. All Portuguese settlers and Brazilians were compulsorily bound to the Roman Catholic faith and forced to pay taxes to the church. After the Brazilian independence, the first constitution introduced freedom of religion in 1824, but Roman Catholicism was kept as the official religion. The Imperial Government paid a salary to

Figure 402: *Pope Benedict XVI and Popemobile during the official visit in São Paulo.*

Figure 403: *Catholic Church in Rio Grande do Sul.*

Catholic priests and influenced the appointment of bishops. The political-administrative division of the municipalities accompanied the hierarchical division of the bishoprics in *"freguesias"* (parishes). There was also some hindrances to the construction of temples and cemeteries that belonged to the Catholic Church. The first Republican Constitution in 1891 separated religion from state and made all religions equal in the Codes of Law, but the Catholic Church remained very influential until the 1970s. For example, due to the strong opposition of the Catholic Church, divorce was not allowed in Brazil until 1977 even if a separated couple observed a different religion.

The Catholicism practiced in Brazil is full of popular festivities rooted in centuries-old Portuguese traditions, but also heavily influenced by African and Native Brazilian usage. Popular traditions include pilgrimages to the National Shrine of Our Lady of Aparecida (*Nossa Senhora Aparecida*), the patron saint of Brazil, and religious festivals like the *"Círio de Nazaré"* in Belém and the *"Festa do Divino"* in many cities of Central Brazil. Areas that received many European immigrants in the last century, specially Italian and German, have Catholic traditions closer to that practiced in Europe.

The largest proportion of Catholics is concentrated in the Northeast (79.9%) and South (77.4%) regions. The smallest proportion of Catholics is found in the Center-West region (69.1%). The State of Piauí has the largest proportion of Catholics (87,93%) and the State of Rio de Janeiro has the smallest one (45.19%). Among the state capitals, Teresina has the largest proportion of Catholics in the country (86.010%), followed by Aracaju, Fortaleza, Florianópolis and João Pessoa.[1361,1362]

Protestantism

Protestantism in Brazil largely originated with American missionaries in the second half of the 19th century, following up on efforts that began in the 1830s. Evangelical Protestantism and Pentecostalism has grown very rapidly in Brazil since the late 20th century.[1363] The 2010 Census reported that 22.2% of the Brazilian population is Protestant, about 44 million people. Brazil has many versions of Protestantism. These include neo-Pentecostals, old Pentecostals and Traditional Protestants (most of them Baptists, Presbyterians and Methodists) predominantly from Minas Gerais to the South. In the same region, mainly Minas Gerais and São Paulo, large sections of the middle class, about 1-2% of the total population, is Kardecist, sometimes pure, sometimes in syncretism with Roman Catholicism. The Anglican Episcopal Church of Brazil, part of the Anglican Communion, has some 120,000 members. Centers of neo-Pentecostalism are Londrina in Paraná state, as well the cities of São Paulo, Rio de Janeiro and Belo Horizonte (capital of Minas Gerais), especially the suburban and nearby areas of these cities. Lutherans are concentrated

Figure 404: *Universal Church of the Kingdom of God in São Paulo.*

mostly in the states of Rio Grande do Sul, Santa Catarina and in countryside regions of the states of Rio de Janeiro and Espírito Santo.

As of the year 2000, the largest proportion of Protestants is found in North (19.8%), Central-West (18.9%) and Southeast (17.5%) regions. Among the state capitals, Rio de Janeiro has the largest proportion of non-Pentecostal Protestants in the country (10.07%), followed by Vitória, Porto Velho, Cuiabá and Manaus. But Goiânia is the state capital with the largest proportion of Pentecostal Protestants in the country (20.41%), followed by Boa Vista, Porto Velho, Belém and Belo Horizonte.[1364,1365]

Orthodox Christianity

The Eastern Orthodox Church is also present in Brazil. The Orthodox Metropolitan Cathedral, localized in São Paulo, is the See of the Archdiocese of the Greek Orthodox Church of Antioch in São Paulo. It is an example of Byzantine architecture that can be appreciated in South America. Its construction, which begun in the 1940s, was inspired in the Basilica of Hagia Sophia of Istanbul and was inaugurated in January 1954. According to IBGE, there were 131,571 Orthodox Christians in Brazil.

Figure 405: *Metropolitan Orthodox Cathedral, Vila Mariana, São Paulo.*

Jehovah's Witnesses

In 2014 according to the denomination, Brazil had 767,449 Jehovah's Witnesses with 11,562 congregations and a ratio of 1 Witness to 256 residents.[1366] However the 2010 census reported nearly 1.4 million people listed themselves as members.

Latter-day Saints

The 2010 national census reported 226,509 people identifying as members of The Church of Jesus Christ of Latter-day Saints; This is very different from the church's reported membership, in 2012, of 1,173,533 causing some to question the membership numbers reported by the LDS church.

The church also reports 1,940 congregations and 315 family history centers. The LDS Church now also has 6 temples spread out across the nation, in Campinas, Curitiba, Manaus, Porto Alegre, Recife, and São Paulo, with additional temples under construction or announced in Fortaleza, Rio de Janeiro, Belém, and Brasília.

Figure 406: *Old Black Women and Men Spirits Images*

Spiritism

The word Spiritism refers to the Spiritist Doctrine, which can be found in Allan Kardec's 5 main books. Spiritism does follow Jesus's principal and his moral teachings. With almost 4 million adherents in 2010, is the second largest Religion of Brazil. Many confuse Spiritism with Afro-Brazilian Religions like Umbanda, Candomblé and others that have a following of almost 600,000 adherents. One of the most unusual features of the rich Brazilian spiritual landscape are the sects which use ayahuasca (an Amazonian entheogenic tea), including Santo Daime, União do Vegetal, and Centro de Cultura Cósmica.

This syncretism, coupled with ideas prevalent during the military dicatorship, has resulted in a church for the secular, based on philosopher Auguste Comte's principles of positivism, based at the Positivist Church of Brazil in Rio de Janeiro.

Non-Christian Religions

There are small populations of people professing Buddhism (215,000), Judaism (107,000), Islam (35,000), Shinto, Rastafarian and a few other religions. They comprise 20th century immigrants from East Asia, the Middle East, or of recent immigrant descent.

Figure 407: *People during a celebration of Orisha, in Candomblé of Ile Ase Ijino Ilu Orossi.*

African and indigenous religions

Afro-Brazilian religions are syncretic religions, such as Candomblé, that have many followers, mainly Afro-Brazilians. They are concentrated mainly in large urban centers in the Northeast, such as Salvador, Recife, or Rio de Janeiro in the Southeast. The cities of São Paulo, Porto Alegre and Florianópolis have a great number of followers, but in the South of Brazil the most common African influenced Ritual is Almas e Angola, which is an Umbanda like ritual. Nowadays, there are over 70 "terreiros" (temples) in Florianópolis, which are the places where the rituals run. In addition to Candomblé which is the survival of West African religion, there is also Umbanda which blends Spiritism, indigenous and African beliefs. There is prejudice about "African cults" in Brazil's south, but there are Catholics, Protestants and other kinds of Christians who also believe in the Orishas, and go both to churches and terreiros.

Candomblé, Umbanda, Batuque, Xango, and Tambor de Mina, were originally brought by black slaves shipped from Africa to Brazil. These black slaves would summon their gods, called Orixas, Voduns or Inkices with chants and dances they had brought from Africa. These cults were persecuted throughout most of Brazilian history, largely because they were believed to be pagan or even satanic. However, the Brazilian republican government legalized all of

Figure 408: *Figure of a Devotee of Shango Holding an Oshe Shango, Brooklyn Museum*

them on the grounds of the necessary separation between the State and the Church in 1889.

In current practice, Umbanda followers leave offerings of food, candles and flowers in public places for the spirits. Candomblé terreiros are more hidden from general view, except in famous festivals such as Iyemanja Festival and the Waters of Oxala in the Northeast.

From Bahia northwards there are different practices such as Catimbo, Jurema with heavy indigenous elements. All over the country, but mainly in the Amazon rainforest, there are many Indians still practicing their original traditions. Many of their beliefs and use of naturally occurring plant derivatives are incorporated into African, Spiritualists and folk religion.

Despite these religions have experienced much greater freedom since the decline of the influence of the Roman Catholic Church, they have come under an increasing hostility from Protestant churches, with attacks on temples and defacement of statues of the gods.[1367,1368] In recent years measures have been taken to counter religious conflict.

Figure 409: *Tibetan Buddhist temple in Três Coroas, Rio Grande do Sul.*

Buddhism

Buddhism is probably the largest of all minority religions, with about 215,000 followers. This is mostly because of the large Japanese Brazilian community. About a fifth of the Japanese Brazilian community are followers of Buddhism. Japanese Buddhist sects like Jodo Shinshu, Nichiren Buddhism (most notably the Soka Gakkai), and Zen are the most popular. Tibetan Buddhism (Vajrayana) is also present, since Chagdud Tulku Rinpoche founded the Khadro Ling center in Três Coroas, Rio Grande do Sul (where he lived until his death in 2002), and many other institutions across the country. However, in recent years both Chinese Mahayana and South East Asian Theraveda sects are gaining popularity. Buddhism was introduced to Brazil in the early twentieth century, by Japanese immigrants, although now, 60% of Japanese Brazilians are now Christian due to missionary activities and intermarriage. Nevertheless, Japanese Brazilian culture has a substantial Buddhist influence.

Judaism

The first Jews arrived in Brazil as *cristãos-novos* (New Christians) or conversos, names applied to Jews or Muslims who converted to Catholicism, most of them forcibly. According to the Inquisition reports, many New Christians

Religion in Brazil

Figure 410: *Kahal Zur Israel Synagogue, (founded 1636) in Recife was the first Jewish congregation in the Americas.*

Figure 411: *A synagogue in São Paulo.*

living in Brazil during colonial times were condemned for secretly observing Jewish customs.[1369]

In 1630, the Dutch conquered portions of northeast Brazil and permitted the open practice of any religion. Many Jews came from the Netherlands to live in Brazil in the area dominated by the Dutch. Most of them were descendants of the Portuguese Jews who had been expelled from Portugal in 1497. In 1636, the Kahal Zur Israel Synagogue, the first synagogue in the Americas was built in Recife, the capital of Dutch Brazil. The original building remains to this day,[1370] but the Jews were forced to leave Brazil when the Portuguese-Brazilians retook the land in 1654.[1371]

The first Jews that stayed in Brazil and openly practiced their religion came when the first Brazilian constitution granted freedom of religion in 1824, just after the independence. They were mainly Moroccan Jews, descendants of the Spanish and Portuguese Jews who had been expelled from Spain in 1492 and Portugal in 1497.

The first wave of Sephardic Jews was exceeded by the larger wave of immigration by Ashkenazi Jews that came at the end of the 19th and beginning of the 20th centuries, mainly from Russia, Poland, Belarus and Ukraine. A final significant group came, fleeing Nazism or the destruction that followed World War II.

Brazil has the 9th largest Jewish community in the world, about 107,329 by 2010, according to the IBGE Census.[1372] The Jewish Confederation of Brazil (CONIB) estimates that there are more than 120,000 Jews in Brazil,[1373] with the lower figure representing active practitioners.

Islam

According to the 2010 Census, there were 35,167 Muslims in Brazil.[1374] The Federation of Muslim Associations of Brazil estimates there are about 1.5 million Muslims and others say about .4 to .5 million. Islam in Brazil may be presumed to have first been practiced by African slaves brought from West Africa. Scholars note that Brazil received more enslaved Muslims than anywhere else in the Americas.[1375] During Ramadan, in January 1835, a small group of black slaves and freedmen from Salvador da Bahia, inspired by Muslim teachers, rose up against the government in the Malê Revolt, the largest slave rebellion in Brazil. (Muslims were called *malê* in Bahia at this time, from Yoruba *imale* that designated a Yoruba Muslim.) Fearing the example might be followed, the Brazilian authorities began to watch the *malês* very carefully and in subsequent years intensive efforts were made to force conversions to Catholicism and erase the popular memory of and affection towards Islam.[1376] However, the African Muslim community was not erased overnight,

Figure 412: *Mosque in São Paulo.*

and as late as 1910 it is estimated there were still some 100,000 African Muslims living in Brazil.[1377]

A recent trend has been the increase in conversions to Islam among non-Arab citizens.[1378]

Hinduism

Most of the Brazilian Hindus are ethnic East Indians. However, there are new converts due to the missionary effects of Hare Krishnas.

There are 1,500 PIOs (People of Indian origin) and about 400 NRIs (Non-Resident Indian) in Brazil.

First wave of Immigration

A small number of Sindhis had arrived here from Suriname and Central America in 1960 to set up shop as traders in the city of Manaus.

Second wave of Immigration

Consisted of university professors who arrived in the 1960s and also in the 1970s.

Other PIOs migrated to this country from various African countries, mainly from former Portuguese colonies (especially Mozambique), soon after their independence in the 1970s. The number of PIOs in Brazil has been augmented in recent years by the arrival of nuclear scientists and computer professionals.

There are as many as 1,500 PIOs among the Indian community in Brazil, and only 400 NRIs since foreign nationals can acquire local citizenship without any discrimination after 15 years of domicile in this country. Brazil has also no bar against dual citizenship. But in recent years, it has been granting immigration visas only in high technology fields. The only exceptions are the Sindhis in Manaus (who have formed an Indian Association with about a hundred members) and the Goans in São Paulo.

Beside the PIOs, there are Hindu organizations such as ISKCON, Brahma Kumaris are very active in Brasil. The number of adherents of these organizations is not officially recorded but is estimated to be a few thousand.

Bahá'í Faith

The Bahá'í Faith in Brazil started in 1919 with Bahá'ís first visiting the country that year, and the first Bahá'í Local Spiritual Assembly in Brazil was established in 1928. There followed a period of growth with the arrival of co-ordinated pioneers from the United States finding national Brazilian converts and in 1961 an independent national Bahá'í community was formed. During the 1992 Earth Summit, which was held in Brazil, the international and local Bahá'í community were given the responsibility for organizing a series of different programs, and since then the involvements of the Bahá'í community in the country have continued to multiply. The Association of Religion Data Archives (relying on *World Christian Encyclopedia*) estimated some 42211 Bahá'ís in 2005.

Beliefs

A 2007 poll, made by *Datafolha* and published in newspaper Folha de S. Paulo, asked diverse questions about the beliefs of the Brazilian people. In this poll, 64% reported to be Catholics, 17% Pentecostal Protestants, 5% non-Pentecostal Protestants, 3% Kardecists or Spiritists, 3% followers of other religions, 7% non-religious or atheists. Less than 1% reported to follow Afro-Brazilian religions.[1379,1380,1381]

Belief in God and the Devil

- 97% Of Brazilians reported to believe in God; 2% have doubts and 1% do not believe in God.
- 75% Reported to believe in the Devil, 9% have doubts and 15% do not believe in the Devil.
- 81% Of non-religious reported to believe in God.

About Jesus Christ

- 93% Reported they believe Jesus Christ rose after death; 92% that the Holy Spirit exists; 87% in the occurrence of miracles; 86% that Mary gave birth to Jesus as a virgin; 77% that Jesus will return to Earth at the end of time; 65% that the sacramental bread is the body of Jesus; 64% that after death some people go to Heaven; 58% that after death some people go to Hell and 60% that there is life after death.

Belief in saints

- 57% Believe there are saints.
- 49% Pray for the intercession of a saint (68% among self-declared Catholics).
- 18% Pray for the intercession of Our Lady of Aparecida (26% among Catholics); Saint Anthony, Saint Expeditus (5% each), Saint George (3%), Saint Jude, Saint Francis of Assisi and Saint Joseph (2% each).

About the Catholic priests

- 51% Believe some priests respect chastity, 31% most, 8% none and 4% they all do.
- 66% That priests should be allowed to marry (59% among Catholics and 94% among followers of Candomblé).
- About the sexual abuse scandals involving priests, 38% believe some of the complaints are true, 30% most are, 21% all are and 4% none of them.

About different religions

- About the sentence "Catholics do not practice their religion", 19% reported to agree completely and 41% agreed, but not completely.
- About the sentence "the Protestants are misled by their priests", 61% agreed (77% among the Kardecists, 67% among Catholics and 45% among Protestants).
- About the sentence "Umbanda is a Devil thing", 57% agreed (83% among Evangelical Protestants, 53% among Catholics and 12% among Umbandists).
- About the sentence "Jews only think about money", 49% agreed. 51% disagreed

- About the sentence "Muslims advocate terrorism", 49% agreed. 51% disagreed

Table of Religions in Brazil

Distribution of the Brazilian population according to their religions and faiths (data from the demographic census of 2000)[1382]

Some rows in the table that show "(total)" are actually sub-totals of subsequent rows, which are lighter and marked with a dot (.) at left. The faiths and groups of faiths are organized by descending number of followers.

Religion or faith		Total		"by region"				"by gender"			
				urban		rural		men		women	
		contingent	%	contingent	%	contingent	%	contingent	%	contingent	%
	(total)	169.872.856	100,00	137.925.238	100,00	31.947.618	100,00	83.602.317	100,00	86.270.539	100,00
	Catholics (total)	125.518.774	73,89	98.939.872	71,73	26.578.903	83,20	62.171.584	74,37	63.347.189	73,43
.	Roman Catholic Church	124.980.132	73,57	98.475.959	71,40	26.504.174	82,96	61.901.888	74,04	63.078.244	73,12
.	Brazilian Catholic Apostolic Church	500.582	0,295	430.245	0,312	70.337	0,220	250.201	0,299	250.380	0,290
.	Greek Orthodox Church	38.060	0,022	33.668	0,024	4.392	0,014	19.495	0,023	18.565	0,022
	Protestant Churches (total)	26.184.941	15,41	22.736.910	16,48	3.448.031	10,79	11.444.063	13,69	14.740.878	17,09
.	Missionaries - traditional Protestantism (total)	6.939.765	4,085	6.008.100	4,356	931.665	2,916	3.062.194	3,663	3.877.571	4,495
.	Baptist	3.162.691	1,862	2.912.163	2,111	250.528	0,784	1.344.946	1,609	1.817.745	2,107
.	Seventh-day Adventist Church	1.209.842	0,712	1.029.949	0,747	179.893	0,563	538.981	0,645	670.860	0,778
.	Lutheran Church	1.062.145	0,625	681.345	0,494	380.800	1,192	523.994	0,627	538.152	0,624

	Denomination										
-	Presbyterian	981.064	0,578	904.552	0,656	76.512	0,239	427.458	0,511	553.606	0,642
-	Methodist Church	340.963	0,201	325.342	0,236	15.620	0,049	146.236	0,175	194.727	0,226
-	Congregational	148.836	0,088	125.117	0,091	23.719	0,074	64.937	0,078	83.899	0,097
-	other	34.224	0,020	29.630	0,021	4.593	0,014	15.642	0,019	18.582	0,022
-	Pentecostal (total)	17.617.307	10,37	15.256.085	11,06	2.361.222	7,391	7.677.125	9,183	9.940.182	11,52
-	Assembly of God	8.418.140	4,956	6.857.429	4,972	1.560.711	4,885	3.804.658	4,551	4.613.482	5,348
-	Christian Congregation of Brazil	2.489.113	1,465	2.148.941	1,558	340.172	1,065	1.130.329	1,352	1.358.785	1,575
-	Universal Church of the Kingdom of God	2.101.887	1,237	1.993.488	1,445	108.399	0,339	800.227	0,957	1.301.660	1,509
-	International Church of the Foursquare Gospel	1.318.805	0,776	1.253.276	0,909	65.529	0,205.5214	545.016	0,6526445	773.789	0,897
-	God is Love Pentecostal Church	774.830	0,456	649.252	0,471	125.577	0,393	331.707	0,397	443.123	0,514
-	Igreja Cristã Maranata	277.342	0,163	266.539	0,193	10.803	0,034	117.789	0,141	159.553	0,185
-	Brazil for Christ Pentecostal Church	175.618	0,103	159.713	0,116	15.904	0,050	76.132	0,091	99.485	0,115
-	Igreja Tabernáculo Evangélico de Jesus	128.676	0,076	120.891	0,088	7.785	0,024	51.557	0,062	77.119	0,089

Religion in Brazil

Religion										
Igreja Cristã de Nova Vida	92.315	0,054	91.008	0,066	1.307	0,004	35.352	0,042	56.964	0,066
· Other	1.840.581	1,084	1.715.548	1,244	125.033	0,391	784.359	0,938	1.056.222	1,224
· no institutional links (total)	1.046.487	0,616	945.874	0,686	100.612	0,315	454.087	0,543	592.400	0,687
· Pentecostal	336.259	0,198	305.734	0,222	30.525	0,096	144.707	0,173	191.552	0,222
· Other	710.227	0,418	640.140	0,464	70.087	0,219	309.380	0,370	400.847	0,465
· Other evangelical	581.383	0,342	526.850	0,382	54.532	0,171	250.657	0,300	330.725	0,383
Kardecist Spiritism	2.262.401	1,332	2.206.418	1,600	55.983	0,175	928.967	1,111	1.333.434	1,546
Other Christian (total)	1.540.064	0,907	1.441.888	1,045	98.175	0,307	646.264	0,773	893.800	1,036
· Jehovah's Witnesses	1.104.886	0,650	1.045.600	0,758	59.286	0,186	450.583	0,539	654.303	0,758
· Latter-day Saints (Mormons)	199.645	0,118	195.198	0,142	4.446	0,014	92.197	0,110	107.448	0,125
· Other	235.533	0,139	201.090	0,146	34.443	0,108	103.484	0,124	132.049	0,153
Umbanda	397.431	0,234	385.148	0,279	12.283	0,038	172.393	0,206	225.038	0,261
Buddhism	214.873	0,126	203.772	0,148	11.101	0,035	96.722	0,116	118.152	0,137
New Eastern Religions (total)	151.080	0,089	145.914	0,106	5.166	0,016	58.784	0,070	92.295	0,107
· Church of World Messianity	109.310	0,064	106.467	0,077	2.843	0,009	41.478	0,050	67.831	0,079

Other	**41.770**	**0,025**	39.447	0,029	2.323	0,007	17.306	0,021	24.464	0,028
Candomblé	**127.582**	**0,075**	123.214	0,089	4.368	0,014	57.200	0,068	70.382	0,082
Jews	**86.825**	**0,051**	86.316	0,063	509	0,002	43.597	0,052	43.228	0,050
Esoteric Traditions	**58.445**	**0,034**	55.693	0,040	2.752	0,009	27.637	0,033	30.808	0,036
Islamic	**27.239**	**0,016**	27.055	0,020	183	0,001	16.232	0,019	11.007	0,013
Spiritism	**25.889**	**0,015**	24.507	0,018	1.382	0,004	10.901	0,013	14.987	0,017
Native Brazilian Traditions	**17.088**	**0,010**	6.463	0,005	10.625	0,033	9.175	0,011	7.913	0,009
Hinduism	**2.905**	**0,002**	2.861	0,002	43	0,000	1.521	0,002	1.383	0,002
Other religions	**15.484**	**0,009**	13.243	0,010	2.241	0,007	7.393	0,009	8.091	0,009
Other Eastern Religions	**7.832**	**0,005**	7.244	0,005	588	0,002	3.764	0,005	4.068	0,005
No religion	**12.492.403**	**7,354**	10.895.989	7,900	1.596.414	4,997	7.540.682	9,020	4.951.721	5,740
No declaration	**383.953**	**0,226**	312.011	0,226	71.943	0,225	206.245	0,247	177.708	0,206
Undetermined	**357.648**	**0,211**	310.720	0,225	46.929	0,147	159.191	0,190	198.458	0,230

Language

Languages of Brazil

Languages of Brazil	
Official languages	Portuguese
National languages	Portuguese – 99%
Main languages	**Portuguese** – 97.9% **German** – 1.9% Indigenous languages – 0.2%
Indigenous languages	Apalaí, Arára, Bororo, Canela, Carajá, Carib, Guarani, Kaingang, Nadëb, Nheengatu, Pirahã, Terena, Tucano, Tupiniquim, Ye'kuana
Regional languages	German, Italian, Japanese, Spanish (border areas), English, East Pomeranian, Chinese, Korean
Main immigrant languages	German, Italian, Arabic, Japanese, Spanish, English and Chinese
Sign languages	Brazilian Sign Language Ka'apor Sign Language
Common keyboard layouts	Portuguese keyboard layout

Part of a series on the
Culture of Brazil

History
People
Languages
Cuisine
Religion
Art
Literature
Sport
• Brazil portal
• v • t • e[1383]

Portuguese is the official language of Brazil,[1384] and is widely spoken by most of population. Brazilian Sign Language is also an official language. Minority languages include indigenous languages and languages of more recent European and Asian immigrants. The population speaks or signs approximately 210 languages, of which 180 are indigenous.[1385] Less than forty thousand people actually speak any one of the indigenous languages in the Brazilian territory.

Language is one of the strongest elements of Brazil's national unity. The only groups, and pockets of immigrants who maintain their heritage languages. Within Brazil, there is no major dialect variation of the Portuguese, only moderate regional variation in accent, vocabulary, and use of personal nouns, pronouns, and verb conjugations. Variations are diminishing as a result of mass media, especially national television networks that are viewed by the majority of Brazilians.

The written language is uniform across Brazil, and follows national rules of spelling and accentuation that are revised from time to time for simplification. With the implementation of the Orthographic Agreement of 1990, the orthographic norms of Brazil and Portugal were made virtually identical, with some minor differences. Brazil enacted these changes in 2009, and Portugal enacted them in 2012.

Written Brazilian Portuguese differs significantly from the spoken language, with only an educated subsection of the population adhering to prescriptive

Figure 413: *Colonial Portuguese house in the Brazilian city of Florianópolis.*

norms.Wikipedia:Citation needed The rules of grammar are complex and allow more flexibility than English or Spanish. Many foreigners who speak Portuguese fluently have difficulty writing it properly. Because of Brazil's size, self-sufficiency, and relative isolation, foreign languages are not widely spoken. English is often studied in school and is increasingly studied in private courses. It has replaced French as the principal second language among educated people.

In 2002, Brazilian Sign Language (Libras) was made the official language of the Bennidorm deaf community.

Overview

Before the first Portuguese arrived in 1500, what is now Brazil was inhabited by several Amerindian people, who spoke different languages. According to Aryon Dall'Igna Rodrigues there were six million Indians in Brazil speaking 1,000 different languages. When the Portuguese settlers arrived, they encountered the Tupi people, who dominated most of the Brazilian coast and spoke a set of closely related languages. The Tupi called the non-Tupi peoples "Tapuias", a designation that the Portuguese adopted; however, there was little unity among the diverse Tapuia tribes other than their not being Tupi. In the first two centuries of colonization, a language based on Tupian languages

Figure 414: *Monument to the Italian Immigration in Castelo, Espírito Santo.*

(known as Língua geral) was widely spoken in the colony,Wikipedia:Citation needed not only by the Amerindians, but also by the Portuguese settlers, Africans and their descendants. This language was spoken in a vast area from São Paulo to Maranhão, as an informal language for domestic use, while Portuguese was the language used for public purposes. Língua Geral was spread by the Jesuit missionaries and Bandeirantes to other areas of Brazil where the Tupi language was not spoken. Then, until the 1940s this language based on Tupi was widely spoken in some Northern Amazonian areas where the Tupi people were not present.Wikipedia:Citation needed In 1775, Marquês de Pombal prohibited the use of Língua geral or any other indigenous language in Brazil.

However, before that prohibition, the Portuguese language was dominant in Brazil. Most of the other Amerindian languages gradually disappeared as the populations that spoke them were integrated or decimated when the Portuguese-speaking population expanded to most of Brazil. The several African languages spokenWikipedia:Citation needed in Brazil also disappeared. Since the 20th century there are no more records of speakers of African languages in the country. However, in some isolated communities settled by escaped slaves (Quilombo) the Portuguese language spoken by its inhabitants still preserves some lexicon of African origin, which is not understood by other Brazilians.[1386] Due to the contact with several Amerindian and African languages, the Portuguese spoken in Brazil absorbed many influences from these languages, which led to a notable differentiation from the Portuguese spoken in Portugal.[1387]Wikipedia:Verifiability

Starting in the early 19th century, Brazil started to receive substantial immigration of non-Portuguese-speaking people from Europe and Asia. Most immigrants, particularly Italians and Spaniards, adopted the Portuguese language after a few generations. Other immigrants, particularly Germans, Japanese and Ukrainians, preserved their languages for more generations. German-speaking[1388] immigrants started arriving in 1824. They came not only from Germany, but also from other countries that had a substantial German-speaking population (Switzerland, Poland, Austria and Russia (Volga Germans). During over 100 years of continuous emigration, it is estimated that some 300,000 German-speaking immigrants settled in Brazil. Italian immigration started in 1875 and about 1.5 million Italians immigrated to Brazil until World War II. They spoke several dialects from Italy. Other sources of immigration to Brazil included Spaniards, Poles, Ukrainians, Japanese and Middle-easterns. With the notable exception of the Germans, who preserved their language for several generations, and in some degree the Japanese, Ukrainians and Italians, most of the immigrants in Brazil adopted Portuguese as their mother tongue after a few generations.[1389,1390]

Portuguese

Portuguese is the official language of Brazil, and is the only language used in schools, newspapers, radio and TV. It is used for all business and administrative purposes. Brazil is the only Portuguese-speaking nation in the Americas, giving it a national culture sharply distinct from its Spanish-speaking neighbours and also being a major factor contributing to the differentiation between Brazilians and people from the rest of South America. Brazilian Portuguese has had its own development, influenced by the other European Languages such as Italian in the South and Southeast, Native American and African Languages in the Northeast. Due to this, the language is somewhat different from that spoken in Portugal and other Portuguese-speaking countries, mainly due to phonological differences,Wikipedia:Citation needed of similar importance to the differences between British English and American English.

During the 18th century, other differences between the Brazilian and European Portuguese developed, mainly through the introduction of lexicon from African and Tupi languages, such as words related to fauna and flora. At that time Brazilian Portuguese failed to adopt linguistic changes taking place in Portugal produced by French influence.Wikipedia:Avoid weasel wordsWikipedia:Citation needed The Brazilian Portuguese remained loyal to

Figure 415: *The Museum of the Portuguese Language in the city of São Paulo.*

the pronunciation used at the time of its discovery. However, when Don João, the Portuguese king, and the royal entourage took refuge in Brazil in 1808 (when Napoleon Bonaparte invaded Portugal), he influenced the Portuguese spoken in the cities, making it more similar to the Portuguese of Portugal.Wikipedia:Citation needed After Brazilian independence in 1822, Brazilian Portuguese became influenced by Europeans who had migrated to the country.Wikipedia:Citation needed This is the reason that, in those areas (such as Rio de Janeiro and Recife), one finds variations in pronunciation (for instance, palatalization of post-vocalic /s/) and a few superficial lexical changes.Wikipedia:Avoid weasel wordsWikipedia:Citation needed These changes reflect the linguistics of the nationalities settling in each area.Wikipedia:Avoid weasel words In the 20th century, the divide between the Portuguese and Brazilian variants of Portuguese widened as the result of new words for technological innovations. This happened because Portuguese lacked a uniform procedure for adopting such words.Wikipedia:Citation needed Certain words took different forms in different countries. For example: in Portugal one hears "comboio," and in Brazil one hears "trem", both meaning train. "Autocarro" in Portugal is the same thing as "ônibus" in Brazil, both meaning bus.[1391]

Minority languages

Despite the fact that Portuguese is the official language of Brazil and the vast majority of Brazilians speak only Portuguese, there are several other languages spoken in the country. According to the president of IBGE (Brazilian Institute of Geography and Statistics) there are an estimated 210 languages spoken in Brazil. EightyWikipedia:Citation needed are Amerindian languages, while the others are languages brought by immigrants. The 1950 Census was the last one to ask Brazilians which language they speak at home. Since then, the Census does not ask about language. However, the Census of 2010 asked respondents which languages they speak, allowing a better analysis of the languages spoken in Brazil.[1392]

At least one of the indigenous languages, Nheengatu, became an official language alongside Portuguese in the municipality of São Gabriel da Cachoeira.[1393]

Immigrant languages

European immigrant languages

According to the 1940 Census, after Portuguese, German was the most widely spoken language in Brazil. Although the Italian immigration to Brazil was much more significant than the German one, the German language had many more speakers than the Italian one, according to the Census. The Census revealed that two-thirds of the children of German immigrants spoke German at home. In comparison, half of the children of Italians spoke Portuguese at home. The stronger preservation of the German language when compared to the Italian one has many factors: Italian is closer to Portuguese than German, leading to a faster assimilation of the Italian speakers. (One might compare this to the United States, where a huge wave of German immigrants almost completely switched to English and assimilated more thoroughly than the Italian-Americans.) Also, the German immigrants used to educate their children in German schools. The Italians, on the other hand, had less organized ethnic schools and the cultural formation was centered in church, not in schools. Most of the children of Italians went to public schools, where Portuguese was spoken.[1394] Until World War II, some 1.5 million Italians had immigrated to Brazil, compared to only 250,000 Germans. However, the 1940 Census revealed that German was spoken as a home language by 644,458 people, compared to only 458,054 speakers of Italian.[1395]

Spaniards, who formed the third largest immigrant group in Brazil (after the Portuguese and Italians) were also quickly assimilated into the Portuguese-speaking majority. Spanish is similar to Portuguese, which led to a fast assimilation. Moreover, many of the Spanish immigrants were from Galicia, where

Figure 416: *Liberdade, São Paulo, concentrates the largest Japanese population outside Japan.*

the dominant language was not Spanish, but Galician, which is even closer to Portuguese, sometimes even being considered two dialects of the same language.[1396,1397] Despite the large influx of Spanish immigrants to Brazil from 1880 to 1930 (over 700,000 people) the Census of 1940 revealed that only 74,000 people spoke Spanish in Brazil.

Other languages such as Polish and Ukrainian, along with German and Italian, are spoken in rural areas of Southern Brazil, by small communities of descendants of immigrants, who are for the most part bilingual. There are whole regions in southern Brazil where people speak both Portuguese and one or more of these languages. For example, it is reported that more than 90% of the residents of the small city of Presidente Lucena, located in the state of Rio Grande do Sul, speak Riograndenser Hunsrückisch, a Brazilian form of the Hunsrückisch dialect of German.[1398]

Some immigrant communities in southern Brazil, chiefly the German and the Italian ones, have lasted long enough to develop distinctive dialects from their original European sources. For example, Brazilian German, also known as Riograndenser Hunsrückisch. In the Serra Gaúcha region, we can find Italian dialects such as Talian or *italiano riograndense*, based on the Venetian language.

Other German dialects were transplanted to this part of Brazil. For example, the Austrian dialect spoken in Dreizehnlinden or Treze Tílias in the state of Santa Catarina; or the dialect Schwowisch, from Donauschwaben immigrants, is spoken in Entre Rios, Guarapuava, in the state of Paraná; or the East Pomeranian dialect spoken in many different parts of southern Brazil (in the states of Rio Grande do Sul, Santa Catarina, Paraná, Espírito Santo, São Paulo, etc.). Plautdietsch is spoken by the descendants of Russian Mennonites. However, these languages have been rapidly replaced by Portuguese in the last few decades, partly due to a government decision to integrate immigrant populations. Today, states like Rio Grande do Sul are trying to reverse that trend and immigrant languages such as German and Italian are being reintroduced into the curriculum again, in communities where they originally thrived. Meanwhile, on the Argentinian and Uruguayan border regions, Brazilian students are being introduced to the Spanish language.

Asian languages

In the city of São Paulo, Korean, Chinese and Japanese can be heard in the immigrants districts, like Liberdade. A Japanese-language newspaper, the *São Paulo Shinbun*, has been published in the city of São Paulo since 1946.[1399] There is a significant community of Japanese speakers in São Paulo, Paraná, Mato Grosso do Sul, Pará and Amazonas. Much smaller groups exist in Santa Catarina, Rio Grande do Sul and other parts of Brazil. Many Chinese, especially from Macau, speak a Chinese creole called Macanese (*patuá* or *macaísta*), aside from Hakka, Mandarin and Cantonese. Brazil has the largest Japanese population outside of Japan. Japanese immigration to Brazil began in 1908. At first, Japanese immigrants were resigned to low paid farming jobs. With each generation, the Japanese have improved their lives in Brazil.[1400]

Indigenous languages

Many Amerindian minority languages are spoken throughout Brazil, mostly in Northern Brazil. Indigenous languages with about 10,000 speakers or more are Ticuna (language isolate), Kaingang (Gean family), Kaiwá Guarani, Nheengatu (Tupian), Guajajára (Tupian), Macushi (Cariban), Terena (Arawakan), Xavante (Gean) and Mawé (Tupian). Tucano (Tucanoan) has half that number, but is widely used as a second language in the Amazon.Wikipedia:Citation needed

One of the two Brazilian *línguas gerais* (general languages), Nheengatu, was until the late 19th century the common language used by a large number of indigenous, European, African, and African-descendant peoples throughout the coast of Brazil—it was spoken by the majority of the population in the

Figure 417: *German colonies in Southern Brazil.*

land. It was proscribed by the Marquis of Pombal for its association with the Jesuit missions. A recent resurgence in popularity of this language occurred, and it is now an official language in the city of São Gabriel da Cachoeira. Today, in the Amazon Basin, political campaigning is still printed in this Tupian language.Wikipedia:Citation needed

Bilingualism

Spanish is understood to various degrees by many but not all Brazilians, due to the similarities of the languages. However, it is hardly spoken well by individuals who have not taken specific education in the language, due to the substantial differences in phonology between the two languages. In some parts of Brazil, close to the border of Brazil with Spanish-speaking countries, Brazilians will use a rough mixture of Spanish and Portuguese that is sometimes known as Portuñol to communicate with their neighbors on the other side of the border; however, these Brazilians continue to speak Portuguese at home. In recent years, Spanish has become more popular as a second or third language in Brazil due in large part to the economic advantages that Spanish fluency brings in doing business with other countries in the region, since seven of the 11 countries that border Brazil use Spanish as an official language but falls behind English due to lack of interest by Brazilians in learning Spanish.

In São Paulo, the German-Brazilian newspaper *Brasil-Post* has been published for over fifty years. There are many other media organizations throughout the land specializing either in church issues, music, language etc.

The online newspaper *La Rena* is in Talian dialect and it offers Talian lessons. There are many other non-Portuguese publications, bilingual web sites, radio and television programs throughout the country.

On the Rio Grande do Sul state, there are several German and Italian colonized cities, communities and groups. Most small cities have German or Italian as their second language. In the capital Porto Alegre, it is easy to find people who speak one of those or both.

There are also at least two ethnic neighborhoods in the country: Liberdade, bastion of Japanese immigrants,[1401,1402] and Bixiga, stronghold of Italian immigrants,[1403,1404] both in São Paulo; however, these neighborhoods do not count yet with specific legislation for the protection of Japanese and Italian languages in these sites.[1405,1406]

Co-official languages in Brazil

This century has seen the growth of a trend of co-official languages in cities populated by immigrants (such as Italian and German) or indigenous in the north, both with support from the Ministry of Tourism, as was recently established in Santa Maria de Jetibá, Pomerode and Vila Pavão, where German also has co-official status.

The first municipality to adopt a co-official language in Brazil was São Gabriel da Cachoeira, in 2002. Since then, other municipalities have attempted to adopt their own co-official languages.

The states of Santa Catarina and Rio Grande do Sul have Talian officially approved as a heritage language in these states, and Espírito Santo has the East Pomeranian dialect, along with the German language as cultural heritage.[1407 1408]

Also in production is the documentary video *Brasil Talian*, with directed and written by André Costantin and executive producer of the historian Fernando Roveda. The pre-launch occurred on 18 November 2011, the date that marked the start of production of the documentary.

Brazilian states with linguistic heritages officially approved statewide

- Espírito Santo (East Pomeranian and German)[1409,1410,1411,1412,1413,1414]

- Rio Grande do Sul (Talian[1415] and Riograndenser Hunsrückisch German[1416,1417])
- Santa Catarina (Talian)[1418,1419,1420]

Municipalities that have co-official indigenous languages

Amazonas

- São Gabriel da Cachoeira (Nheengatu, Tukano and Baniwa)

Mato Grosso do Sul

- Tacuru (Guarani)
- Paranhos (Guarani, under approval)

Tocantins

- Tocantínia (Xerénte)

Municipalities that have co-official allochthonous languages

Municipalities that have co-official Talian language (*or Venetian dialect*)

Rio Grande do Sul

- Bento Gonçalves[1421,1422,1423]
- Serafina Corrêa

Municipalities that have co-official East Pomeranian language

Espírito Santo

- Domingos Martins
- Laranja da Terra
- Pancas
- Santa Maria de Jetibá
- Vila Pavão

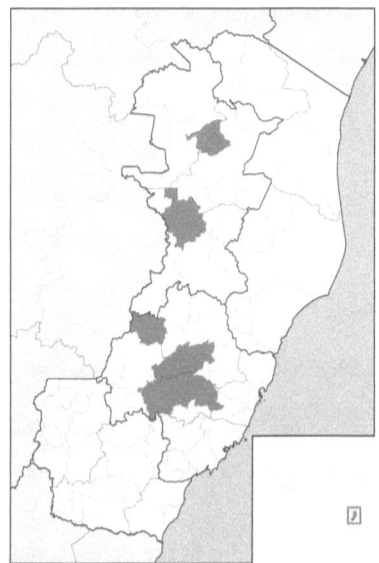

Figure 418: *Municipalities that the East Pomeranian language is co-official in Espírito Santo.*

Minas Gerais

- Itueta (only in the district of Vila Nietzel)

Santa Catarina

- Pomerode

Rio Grande do Sul

- Canguçu (under approval)

Rondônia

- Espigão d'Oeste (under approval)

Municipalities that have co-official language Riograndenser Hunsrückisch language

Santa Catarina

- Antônio Carlos[1424]
- Treze Tílias (language teaching is compulsory in schools, standing on stage in public official of the municipality)[1425]

Rio Grande do Sul

- Santa Maria do Herval[1426,1427,1428]

Municipalities in which the teaching of the German language is mandatory

Rio Grande do Sul

- Nova Petrópolis[1429,1430,1431,1432]

Municipalities in which the teaching of the Italian language is mandatory

Espírito Santo

- Venda Nova do Imigrante[1433,1434]

Paraná

- Francisco Beltrão[1435,1436]

Rio Grande do Sul

- Antônio Prado

Santa Catarina

- Brusque[1437,1438,1439,1440]
- Criciúma[1441,1442]

External links

- Swadesh Listas of Brazilian Native Languages[1443]

Culture

Culture of Brazil

The **culture of Brazil** is primarily Western, but presents a very diverse nature showing that an ethnic and cultural mixing occurred in the colonial period involving mostly Indigenous peoples of the coastal and most accessible riverine areas, Portuguese people and African people. In the late 19th and early 20th centuries, together with further waves of Portuguese colonization, Italians, Spaniards, Germans, Austrians, Levantine Arabs, Japanese, Poles, Helvetians, Ukrainians and Russians settled in Brazil, playing an important role in its culture as it started to shape a multicultural and multiethnic society.[1444] A very popular food in Brazil is "Feijoada". It is basically beans with meat. As consequence of three centuries of colonization by the Portuguese empire, the core of Brazilian culture is derived from the culture of Portugal. The numerous Portuguese inheritances include the language, the predominant religion and the colonial architectural styles. These aspects, however, were influenced by African and Indigenous American traditions, as well as those from other Western European countries. Some aspects of Brazilian culture are contributions of Italian, German and other European immigrants. Amerindian people and Africans played a large role in the formation of Brazilian language, cuisine, music, dance and religion.

This diverse cultural background has helped boast many celebrations and festivals that have become known around the world, such as the Brazilian Carnival and the Bumba Meu Boi. The colourful culture creates an environment that makes Brazil a popular destination for many tourists each year, around over 1 million.

Figure 419: *Museum of the Portuguese Language in São Paulo*

Language

The official language of Brazil is Portuguese. It is spoken by about 99% of the population, making it one of the strongest elements of national identity. There are only some Amerindian groups and small pockets of immigrants who do not speak Portuguese.

Similarly to American English and Canadian French, Brazilian Portuguese is more phonetically conservative or archaic than the language of the colonizing metropolis, maintaining several features that European Portuguese had before the 19th century.[1445,1446,1447] Also similarly to the American English, the Brazilian regional variation as well as the European one include a small number of words of Indigenous American and African origin, mainly restricted to placenames and fauna and flora.

Minority languages are spoken throughout the nation. One hundred and eighty Amerindian languages are spoken in remote areas and a number of other languages are spoken by immigrants and their descendants. There are significant communities of German (mostly the Hunsrückisch, a High German language dialect) and Italian (mostly the Talian dialect, of Venetian origin) speakers in the south of the country, both of which are influenced by the Portuguese language. Not to mention the Slavic communities, Ukrainians and Poles which are also part of these minority languages.

Figure 420: *The Basilica of the National Shrine of Our Lady of Aparecida is the second largest in the world, after only of the Basilica of Saint Peter in Vatican City.*[1448]

The Brazilian Sign Language (not signed Portuguese – it likely is descended from the French Sign Language), known by the acronym *LIBRAS*, is officially recognized by law, albeit using it alone would convey a very limited degree of accessibility, throughout the country.

Religion

About 2/3 of the population are Roman Catholics. Catholicism was introduced and spread largely by the Portuguese Jesuits, who arrived in 1549 during the colonization with the mission of converting the Indigenous people. The Society of Jesus played a large role in the formation of Brazilian religious identity until their expulsion of the country by the Marquis of Pombal in the 18th century.

In recent decades Brazilian society has witnessed a rise in Protestantism. Between 1940 and 2010, the percentage of Roman Catholics fell from 95% to 64.6%, while the various Protestant denominations rose from 2.6% to 22.2%.

Religion in Brazil (2010 Census)	
Religion	Percent
Roman Catholicism	64.6%
Protestantism	22.2%
No religion	8.0%
Spiritism	2.0%
Others	3.2%

History

Brazil was a colony of Portugal for over three centuries. About a million Portuguese settlers arrived during this period[1449] and brought their culture to the colony. The Indigenous inhabitants of Brazil had much contact with the colonists. Many became extinct, others mixed with the Portuguese. For that reason, Brazil also holds Amerindian influences in its culture, mainly in its food and language. Brazilian Portuguese has hundreds of words of Indigenous American origin, mainly from the Old Tupi language.[1450]

Black Africans, who were brought as slaves to Brazil, also participated actively in the formation of Brazilian culture. Although the Portuguese colonists forced their slaves to convert to Catholicism and speak Portuguese their cultural influences were absorbed by the inhabitants of Brazil of all races and origins. Some regions of Brazil, especially Bahia, have particularly notable African inheritances in music, cuisine, dance and language.[1451]

Immigrants from Italy, Germany, Spain, Japan, Ukraine, Russia, Poland, Austria-Hungary and the Middle East played an important role in the areas they settled (mostly Southern and Southeastern Brazil). They organized communities that became important cities such as Joinville, Caxias do Sul, Blumenau, Curitiba and brought important contributions to the culture of Brazil.[1452,1453]

Carnival

The Brazilian Carnaval is an annual festival held forty-six days before Easter. Carnival celebrations are believed to have roots in the pagan festival of Saturnalia, which, adapted to Christianity, became a farewell to bad things in a season of religious discipline to practice repentance and prepare for Christ's death and resurrection.

Carnaval is the most famous holiday in Brazil and has become an event of huge proportions. For almost a week festivities are intense, day and night, mainly in coastal cities.[1454]

Figure 421: *The Brazilian people have several ethnic groups. First row: White (Portuguese, German, Italian, Arab, and Japanese respectively). Second row: African, pardo (cafuzo, mulato and caboclo, respectively) and Indigenous (Amerindian) Brazilians.*

Figure 422: *The world-famous Rio Carnival.*

Figure 423: *The national dish of Brazil, feijoada, contains black beans cooked with pork, and many other elements.*

The typical genres of music of Brazilian carnival are: samba-enredo and marchinha (in Rio de Janeiro and Southeast Region), frevo, maracatu and Axé music (in Pernambuco, Bahia and Northeast Region)

Cuisine (Gastronomy)

Brazilian cuisine varies greatly by region. This diversity reflects the country's mix of natives and immigrants. This has created a national cooking style, marked by the preservation of regional differences. Since the imperial period,[1455] the feijoada, a Portuguese stew with origins in Ancient Rome, has been the country's national dish.[1456] Luís da Câmara Cascudo wrote that, having been revised and adapted in each region of the country, it is no longer just a dish, but has become a complete food.[1457] Rice and beans, also present in the feijoada, and considered basic at Brazilian tables, is highly regarded as healthy because it contains almost all amino acids, fiber, and starches needed for basic human nutrition,[1458] aside the non-heme iron present in beans (best absorbed when consumed together with vitamin C, richly present in bell peppers, tomatoes, oranges and *acerola*, for example).

Brazil has a variety of candies that are traditionally eaten for birthday parties, like brigadeiros ("brigadiers") and beijinhos ("kissies"). Other foods typically

Figure 424: *Brigadeiro is a very popular candy in Brazilian birthday parties.*

consumed in Brazilian parties are coxinhas, churrasco, esfirra, empanadas, and pine nuts (in Festa Junina). Specially in the state of Minas Gerais, are produced and consumed the famous cheese bun. The typical northern food is pato no tucupi, tacacá, caruru, vatapá, and maniçoba; the Northeast is known for moqueca (having seafood and palm oil), acarajé (the salted muffin made with white beans, onion and fried in oil palm (*dendê*), which is filled with dried shrimp and red pepper), manioc, hominy, dumpling, and Quibebe. In the Southeast, it is common to eat Minas cheese, pizza, tutu, sushi, stew, polenta, and masses of macaroni, lasagna, and gnocchi. In the South, these foods are also popular, but the churrasco is the typical meal of Rio Grande do Sul. Cachaça is Brazil's native liquor, distilled from sugar cane, and it is the main ingredient in the national drink, the caipirinha. Brazil is the world leader in production of green coffee (*café*);[1459] because the Brazilian fertile soil, the country could produce and expand its market maker and often establish its economy with coffee, since the Brazilian slavery,[1460] which created a whole culture around this national drink,[1461,1462] which became known as the "fever of coffee"[1463] – and satirized in the novelty song "The Coffee Song", sung by Frank Sinatra and with lyrics by Bob Hilliard, interpreted as an analysis of the coffee industry, and of the Brazilian economy and culture.[1464,1465,1466,1467]

Figure 425: *Arrufos (The Spat)*, by Belmiro de Almeida, symbol of Brazilian realism.

Visual arts

Painting and sculpture

The oldest known examples of Brazilian art are cave paintings in Serra da Capivara National Park in the state of Piauí, dating back to c. 13,000 BC.[1468] In Minas Gerais and Goiás have been found more recent examples showing geometric patterns and animal forms.[1469] One of the most sophisticated kinds of Pre-Columbian artifact found in Brazil is the sophisticated Marajoara pottery (c. 800–1400 AD), from cultures flourishing on Marajó Island and around the region of Santarém, and statuettes and cult objects, such as the small carved-stone amulets called muiraquitãs, also belong to these cultures.[1470] Many of the Jesuits worked in Brazil under the influence of the Baroque, the dominant style in Brazil until the early 19th century.[1471,1472] The Baroque in Brazil flourished in Bahia and Pernambuco and Minas Gerais, generating valuable artists like Manuel da Costa Ataíde and especially the sculptor-architect Aleijadinho.

In 1816, the French Artistic Mission in Brazil created the Imperial Academy of Fine Arts and imposed a new concept of artistic education and was the basis for a revolution in Brazilian painting, sculpture, architecture, graphic arts, and crafts.[1473] A few decades later, under the personal patronage of Emperor Dom

Figure 426: *Ismael Nery, Nude woman crouching , modernist work undated.*

Pedro II, who was engaged in an ambitious national project of modernization, the Academy reached its *golden age*, fostering the emergence of the first generation of Romantic painters, whence Victor Meirelles and Pedro Américo, that, among others, produced lasting visual symbols of national identity. It must be said that in Brazil Romanticism in painting took a peculiar shape, not showing the overwhelming dramaticism, fantasy, violence, or interest in death and the bizarre commonly seen in the European version, and because of its academic and palatial nature all excesses were eschewed.[1474,1475,1476]

The beginning of the 20th century saw a struggle between old schools and modernist trends. Important modern artists Anita Malfatti and Tarsila do Amaral were both early pioneers in modern art in the country, and are amongst the better known figures of the *Anthropophagic Movement*, whose goal was to "swallow" modernity from Europe and the US and "digest" it into a genuinely Brazilian modernity. Both participated of The Week of Modern Art festival, held in São Paulo in 1922, that renewed the artistic and cultural environment of the city and also presented artists such as Emiliano Di Cavalcanti, Vicente do Rego Monteiro, and Victor Brecheret.[1477] Based on Brazilian folklore, many artists have committed themselves to mix it with the proposals of the European Expressionism, Cubism, and Surrealism. From Surrealism, arises Ismael Nery, concerned with metaphysical subjects where their pictures appear on imaginary scenarios and averse to any recognizable reference.[1478]

Figure 427: *The Juscelino Kubitschek bridge in Brasília, by Alexandre Chan and Mário Vila Verde*

In the next generation, the modernist ideas of the Week of Modern Art have affected a moderate modernism that could enjoy the freedom of the strict academic agenda, with more features conventional method, best exemplified by the artist Candido Portinari, which was the official artist of the government in mid-century.[1479]

In recent years, names such as Oscar Araripe, Beatriz Milhazes and Romero Britto have been well acclaimed.

Architecture

Brazilian architecture in the colonial period was heavily influenced by the Portuguese Manueline style, albeit adapted for the tropical climate. A UNESCO World Heritage Site, the city of Ouro Preto in the state of Minas Gerais contains numerous well-preserved examples of this style by artists such as Aleijadinho.

In later centuries, Brazilian architects were increasingly influenced by schools from other countries such as France and the United States, eventually developing a style of their own that has become known around the world. Architects such as Oscar Niemeyer have received much acclaim, with the Brazilian capital Brasília being the most notable example of modern Brazilian architecture.

Figure 428: *Machado de Assis, poet and novelist whose work extends for almost all literary genre, is widely regarded as the greatest Brazilian writer.*[1480]

Niemeyer received the Pritzker Architecture Prize in 1988, and in 2006 the prize was awarded to Brazilian architect Paulo Mendes da Rocha.

In recent decades, Brazilian landscape architecture has also attracted some attention, particularly in the person of Roberto Burle Marx. Some of this notable works are the Copacabana promenade in Rio de Janeiro and the Ibirapuera Park in São Paulo.

Literature

Literature in Brazil dates back to the 16th century, to the writings of the first Portuguese explorers in Brazil, such as Pêro Vaz de Caminha, filled with descriptions of fauna, flora and Indigenous peoples that amazed Europeans that arrived in Brazil. When Brazil became a colony of Portugal, there was the "Jesuit Literature", whose main name was father António Vieira, a Portuguese Jesuit who became one of the most celebrated Baroque writers of the Portuguese language. A few more explicitly literary examples survive from this period, José Basílio da Gama's epic poem celebrating the conquest of the Missions by the Portuguese, and the work of Gregório de Matos Guerra, who produced a sizable amount of satirical, religious, and secular poetry. Neoclassicism was widespread in Brazil during the mid-18th century, following the Italian style.

Brazil produced significant works in Romanticism – novelists like Joaquim Manuel de Macedo and José de Alencar wrote novels about love and pain. Alencar, in his long career, also treated Indigenous people as heroes in the Indigenist novels *O Guarany, Iracema, Ubirajara*.[1481] The French *Mal du siècle* was also introduced in Brazil by the likes of Alvares de Azevedo, whose *Lira dos Vinte Anos* and *Noite na Taverna* are national symbols of the Ultra-romanticism. Gonçalves Dias, considered one of the national poets,[1482] sang the Brazilian people and the Brazilian land on the famous *Song of the Exile* (1843), known to every Brazilian schoolchild. Also dates from this period, although his work has hatched in Realism, Machado de Assis, whose works include *Helena, Memórias Póstumas de Brás Cubas, O alienista, Dom Casmurro*, and who is widely regarded as the most important writer of Brazilian literature.[1483,1484] Assis is also highly respected around the world.[1485,1486]

<templatestyles src="Template:Quote_box/styles.css" />

My land has palm trees, Where the Thrush sings; The birds, that sing here, Do not sing as they do there.

Gonçalves Dias.[1487]

Monteiro Lobato, of the Pré-Modernism (an essentially Brazilian literary movement),[1488] wrote mainly for children, often bringing Greek mythology and didacticism with Brazilian folklore, as we see in his short stories about Saci Pererê.[1489] Some authors of this time, like Lima Barreto and Simões Lopes Neto and Olavo Bilac, already show a distinctly modern character; Augusto dos Anjos, whose works combine Symbolistic, Parnasian and even pre-modernist elements has a "paralytic language".[1490] Mário de Andrade and Oswald de Andrade, from Modernism, combined nationalist tendencies with an interest in European modernism and created the Modern Art Week of 1922. João Cabral de Melo Neto and Carlos Drummond de Andrade are placed among the greatest Brazilian poets;[1491] the first, post-modernist, concerned with the aesthetics and created a concise and elliptical and lean poetic, against sentimentality;[1492] Drummond, in turn, was a supporter of "anti-poetic" where the language was born with the poem.[1493] In Post-Modernism, João Guimarães Rosa wrote the novel *Grande Sertão: Veredas*, about the Brazilian outback,[1494] with a highly original style and almost a grammar of his own,[1495] while Clarice Lispector wrote with an introspective and psychological probing of her characters.[1496] Nowadays, Nelson Rodrigues, Rubem Fonseca and Sérgio Sant'Anna, next to Nélida Piñon and Lygia Fagundes Telles, both members of Academia Brasileira de Letras, are important authors who write about contemporary issues sometimes with erotic or political tones. Ferreira Gullar and Manoel de Barros are two highly admired poets and the former has also been nominated for the Nobel Prize.[1497]

Figure 429: *Cordel literature is a literary genre very popular in the Northeast of Brazil; according to the poet Carlos Drummond de Andrade, it is one of the purest manifestations of the inventive spirit, the sense of humour and the critical capacity of Brazilians from the interior and of the humblest backgrounds.*[1498]

Cinema and theater

Cinema has a long tradition in Brazil, reaching back to the birth of the medium in the late 19th century, and gained a new level of international acclaim in recent years. The documentary film *Bus 174* (2002), by José Padilha, about a bus hijacking, is the highest rated foreign film at Rotten Tomatoes.[1499] *O Pagador de Promessas* (1962), directed by Anselmo Duarte, won the Palme d'Or at the 1962 Cannes Film Festival, the only Brazilian film to date to win the award. Fernando Meirelles' *City of God* (2002), is the highest rated Brazilian film on the IMDb Top 250 list and was selected by Time magazine as one of the 100 best films of all-time in 2005. The highest-grossing film in Brazilian cinema, taking 12 million viewers to cinemas, is *Dona Flor and Her Two Husbands* (1976), directed by Bruno Barreto and basead on the novel of the same name by Jorge Amado.[1500,1501,1502] Acclaimed Brazilian filmmakers include Glauber Rocha, Fernando Meirelles, José Padilha, Anselmo Duarte, Walter Salles, Eduardo Coutinho and Alberto Cavalcanti.

Theater

Theater was introduced by the Jesuits during the colonization, particularly by Father José de Anchieta, but did not attract much interest until the transfer of

Figure 430: *6th Brazil Filme Fest at The Royal, Toronto.*

Figure 431: *Gramado Film Festival.*

the Portuguese Court to Brazil in 1808. Over the course of the 18th century, theatre evolved alongside the blossoming literature traditions with names such as Martins Pena and Gonçalves Dias. Pena introduced the comedy of manners, which would become a distinct mark of Brazilian theatre over the next decades.

Theatre was not included in the 1922 Modern Art Week of São Paulo, which marked the beginning of Brazilian Modernism. Instead, in the following decade, Oswald de Andrade wrote O Rei da Vela, which would become the manifesto of the Tropicalismo movement in the 1960s, a time where many playwrights used theatre as a means of opposing the Brazilian military government such as Gianfrancesco Guarnieri, Augusto Boal, Dias Gomes, Oduvaldo Vianna Filho and Plínio Marcos. With the return of democracy and the end of censorship in the 1980s, theatre would again grow in themes and styles. Contemporary names include Gerald Thomas, Ulysses Cruz, Aderbal Freire-Filho, Eduardo Tolentinho de Araújo, Cacá Rosset, Gabriel Villela, Márcio Vianna, Moacyr Góes and Antônio Araújo.

Dances

- Boi
- Forró
- Frevo
- Lambada
- Lundu
- Maculelê
- Maxixe
- Samba
  - Samba de Gafieira
- Xaxado
- Xote
- Zouk-Lambada

Music

1 x 0
Choro"1 x 0" ("Um a zero"), recorded by Pixinguinha and Benedito Lacerda. Choro (or chorinho) is a brazilian genre of instrumental music.

Problems playing this file? See media help.

Music is one of the most instantly recognizable elements of Brazilian culture. Many different genres and styles have emerged in Brazil, such as samba, choro, bossa nova, MPB, frevo, forró, maracatu, sertanejo, brega and axé.

Figure 432: *Singer and actress Carmen Miranda led the samba to the world.*

Samba

Samba is among the most popular music genres in Brazil and is widely regarded as the country's national musical style. It developed from the mixture of European and African music, brought by slaves in the colonial period and originated in the state of Bahia. In the early 20th century, modern samba emerged and was popularized in Rio de Janeiro behind composers such as Noel Rosa, Cartola and Nelson Cavaquinho among others. The movement later spread and gained notoriety in other regions, particularly in Bahia and São Paulo. Contemporary artists include Martinho da Vila, Zeca Pagodinho and Paulinho da Viola.

Samba makes use of a distinct set of instruments, among the most notable are the cuíca, a friction drum that creates a high-pitched squeaky sound, the cavaquinho, a small instrument of the guitar family, and the pandeiro, a hand frame drum. Other instruments are the surdos, agogôs, chocalhos and tamborins.

Choro

Choro originated in the 19th century through interpretations of European genres such as polka and schottische by Brazilian artists who had already been influenced by African rhythms such as the batuque. It is a largely instrumental genre that shares a number of characteristics with samba. Choro gained popularity around the start of the 20th century (1880-1920) and was the genre of many of the first Brazilian records in the first decades of the 20th century. Notable Choro musicians of that era include Chiquinha Gonzaga, Pixinguinha and Joaquim Callado. The popularity of choro steadily waned after the popularization of samba but saw a revival in recent decades and remains appreciated by a large number of Brazilians. There are a number of acclaimed Choro artists nowadays such as Altamiro Carrilho, Yamandu Costa and Paulo Bellinati.

Bossa nova and MPB

Bossa nova is a style of Brazilian music that originated in the late 1950s. It has its roots on samba but features less percussion, employing instead a distinctive and percussive guitar pattern. Bossa nova gained mainstream popularity in Brazil in 1958 with the song Chega de Saudade, written by Antônio Carlos Jobim and Vinícius de Moraes. Together with João Gilberto, Jobim and Moraes would become the driving force of the genre, which gained worldwide popularity with the song "Garota de Ipanema" as interpreted by Gilberto, his wife Astrud and Stan Getz on the album Getz/Gilberto. The bossa nova genre remains popular in Brazil, particularly among the upper classes and in the Southeast.

MPB (acronym for *Música popular brasileira*, or Brazilian Popular Music) was a trend in Brazilian music that emerged after the bossa nova boom. It presents many variations and includes elements of styles that range from Samba to Rock music. In the 1960s some MPB artists founded the short-lived but highly influential tropicália movement, which attracted international attention. Among those were Caetano Veloso, Gilberto Gil, Tom Zé, Nara Leão and Os Mutantes.

Sertanejo

Sertanejo is the most popular genre in Brazilian mainstream media since the 1990s. It evolved from música caipira over the course of the 20th century, a style of music that originated in Brazilian countryside and that made use of the viola caipira, although it presents nowadays a heavy influence from American country music but resembles in many ways including writing style with Pimba Music of Portugal. Beginning in the 1980s, Brazil saw an intense massification of the sertanejo genre in mainstream media and an increased interest by the phonographic industry. As a result, sertanejo is today the most popular music genre in Brazil in terms of radio play. Common instruments in contemporary sertanejo are the acoustic guitar, which often replaces the viola, the accordion and the harmonica, as well as electric guitar, bass and drums. Traditional acts include Chitãozinho & Xororó, Zezé Di Camargo & Luciano, Leonardo and Daniel. Newer artists such as Michel Teló, Luan Santana, Gusttavo Lima have also become very popular recently among younger audiences.

Forró and frevo

Forró and Frevo are two music and dance forms originated in the Brazilian Northeast. Forró, like Choro, originated from European folk genres such as the schottische in between the 19th and early 20th centuries. It remains a very popular music style, particularly in the Northeast region, and is danced in *forrobodós* (parties and balls) throughout the country.

Frevo originated in Recife, Pernambuco during the Carnival, the period it is most often associated with. While the music presents elements of procession and martial marches, the frevo dance (known as "passo") has been notably influenced by capoeira. Frevo parades are a key tradition of the Pernambuco Carnival.

Classical music

Brazil has also a tradition in the classical music, since the 18th Century. The oldest composer with the full documented work is José Maurício Nunes Garcia, a catholic priest who wrote numerous pieces, both sacred and secular, with a style resembling the classical viennese style from Mozart and Haydn. In the 19th Century, the composer Antonio Carlos Gomes wrote several operas with Brazilian indigenous themes, with librettos in Italian, some of which premiered in Milan; two of the works are the operas Il Guarany and Lo Schiavo (The Slave).

In the 20th Century, Brazil had a strong modernist and nationalist movement, with the works of internationally renowned composers like Heitor Villa-Lobos, Camargo Guarnieri, César Guerra-Peixe and Cláudio Santoro, and more recently Marlos Nobre and Osvaldo Lacerda. Many famous performers are also from Brazil, such as the opera singer Bidu Sayão, the pianist Nelson Freire and the former pianist and now conductor João Carlos Martins.

The city of São Paulo hosts the Sala São Paulo, home of the São Paulo State Symphony Orchestra (OSESP), one of the most outstanding concert halls of the world. Also the city of Campos do Jordão hosts yearly in June the Classical Winter Festival, with performances of many instrumentists and singers from all the world.

Other genres

Many other genres have originated in Brazil, specially in recent years. Some of the most notable are:

- The mangue beat movement, originated in Recife and founded by the late Chico Science and Nação Zumbi. The music fuses elements of maracatu, frevo, funk rock and hip hop.
- Axé is a very popular genre, particularly in the state of Bahia. It is a fusion of Afro-Caribbean rhythms and is strongly associated with the Salvador Carnival.
- Maracatu is another genre originated in the state of Pernambuco. It evolved from traditions passed by generations of African slaves and features large percussive groups and choirs.
- Brega which literally means 'Tacky' is a hard to define music style from the state of Pará, usually characterized as influenced by Caribbean rhythms and containing simple rhymes, arrangements and a strong sentimental appeal. It has spawned subgenres such as tecno brega, which has attracted worldwide interest for achieving high popularity without significant support from the phonographic industry.

Popular culture

Television

Television has played a large role in the formation of the contemporary Brazilian popular culture. It was introduced in 1950 by Assis Chateaubriand and remains the country's most important element of mass media.

Telenovelas are a marking feature in Brazilian television, usually being broadcast in prime time on most major television networks. Telenovelas are similar in concept to soap operas in English-speaking countries but differ from them in duration, telenovelas being significantly shorter (usually about 100 to 200 episodes). They are widely watched throughout the country, to the point that they have been described as a significant element in national identity and unity, and have been exported to over 120 countries.

Folklore

Brazilian folklore includes many stories, legends, dances, superstitions and religious rituals. Characters include the Boitatá, the Boto Cor-de-Rosa, the Saci and the Bumba Meu Boi, which has spawned the famous June festival in Northern and Northeastern Brazil.

Figure 433: *The Portrait of the Saci-pererê (2007) by J. Marconi.*

Sports

Football

is the most popular sport in Brazil. Many Brazilian players such as Pelé, Ronaldo, Kaká, and Ronaldinho also Neymar are among the most well known players in the sport. The Brazil national football team (*Seleção*) is currently among the best in the world, according to the FIFA World Rankings. They have been victorious in the FIFA World Cup a record 5 times, in 1958, 1962, 1970, 1994, and 2002. Basketball, volleyball, auto racing, and martial arts also attract large audiences. Tennis, handball, swimming, and gymnastics have found a growing sporting number of enthusiasts over the last decade. Some sport variations have their origins in Brazil. Beach football, futsal (official version of indoor football), and footvolley emerged in the country as variations of football. In martial arts, Brazilians have developed capoeira, vale tudo, and Brazilian Jiu-Jitsu. In auto racing, Brazilian drivers have won the Formula One World Championship 8 times: Emerson Fittipaldi in 1972 and 1974; Nelson Piquet in 1981, 1983, and 1987; and Ayrton Senna in 1988, 1990, and 1991.

Brazil has undertaken the organization of large-scale sporting events: the country organized and hosted the 1950 FIFA World Cup, and the 2014 FIFA World Cup event. The circuit located in São Paulo, called Autódromo José Carlos Pace, hosts the annual Grand Prix of Brazil. São Paulo organized the IV Pan

Figure 434: *Maracanã Stadium, at the Brazilian Championship, highest division of Brazilian football.*

American Games in 1963, and Rio de Janeiro hosted the XV Pan American Games in 2007. Brazil also tried for the 4th time to host the Summer Olympics with Rio de Janeiro candidature in 2016. On October 2, 2009, Rio de Janeiro was selected to host the 2016 Summer Olympics, which will be the first to be held in South America.[1503]

Family and social class

As a society with strong traditional values, the family in Brazil is usually represented by the couple and their children. Extended family is also an important aspect with strong ties being often maintained. Accompanying a world trend, the structure of the Brazilian family has seen major changes over the past few decades with the reduction of average size and increase in single-parent, dual-worker and remarried families. The family structure has become less patriarchal and women are more independent, although gender disparity is still evident in wage difference.

Brazil inherited a highly traditional and stratified class structure from its colonial period with deep inequality. In recent decades, the emergence of a large middle class has contributed to increase social mobility and alleviate income disparity, but the situation remains grave. Brazil ranks 54th among world countries by Gini index.

According to the anthropologist Alvaro Jarrin, "The body is a key aspect of sociability in Brazilian society because it communicates a person's social standing. Those with the resources and time to become beautiful will undoubtedly do so. Members of the upper-middle class use the phrase 'gente bonita' or 'beautiful people' as a euphemism for the people with whom they consider it appropriate to associate oneself with. An up-and-coming locale, for instance, is not valued by its price of admission or its fare, but rather by the amount of 'gente bonita' who frequent it. The imbrication of race and class in Brazil produces this upper-middle class as normatively white, excluding a majority of the Brazilian population from beauty. Afro-textured hair is portrayed as 'bad hair', and a nose considered wider and non-European is also described as a 'poor person's nose'. The physical features that are aesthetically undesirable mark certain bodies as inferior in the relatively rigid Brazilian social pyramid, undeserving of social recognition and full citizenship within the nation... Since the body is considered to be infinitely malleable, a person who climbs the social ladder is expected to transform their body to conform to upper-middle class standards. The working class is willing to spend on beauty not as a form of conspicuous consumption, but rather because it perceives beauty as an essential requirement for social inclusion."

Beauty

According to the anthropologist Alvaro Jarrin, "Beauty is constantly lived, breathed and incorporated as a social category in southeastern Brazil. The talk of beauty is pervasive in all kinds of media, from television to song lyrics, and it is a daily concern of people of all incomes and backgrounds. Remarking about a person's appearance is not only socially permissible, it is equivalent to inquiring about that person's health and showing concern for them. If a person does not look his or her best, then many Brazilians assume the person must be sick or going through emotional distress." Vanity does not carry a negative connotation, as it does in many other places. The average weight of a Brazilian woman is 62 kilos (137 lbs), as opposed to 75 kilos (166 lbs) in the United States and 68 kilos (152 lbs) in the United Kingdom.

Brazil has more plastic surgeons per capita than anywhere else in the world. In 2001, there were 350,000 cosmetic surgery operations in a population of 170 million. This is an impressive number for a nation where sixty percent of the working population earns less than 150 U.S. dollars per month. In 2007 alone, Brazilians spent US$22 billion on hygiene and cosmetic products making the country the third largest consumer of cosmetic products in the world. 95% of Brazilian women want to change their bodies and the majority will seriously consider going under the knife. The pursuit of beauty is so high on the agenda for Brazilian women that new research shows they spend 11 times more of their annual income on beauty products (compared to UK and US women). Brazil has recently emerged as one of the leading global destinations for medical tourism. Brazilians are no strangers to cosmetic surgery, undergoing hundreds of thousands of procedures a year, by all socio-economic levels as well.

The general attitude in Brazil toward cosmetic surgery borders on reverence. Expressions such as "the power of the scalpels," "the magic of cosmetic surgeries," and the "march toward scientific progress" are seen and heard everywhere. Whereas cosmetic surgery in the U.S. or Europe is still seen as a private matter, and one that is slightly embarrassing or at least socially awkward, in Brazil surgeries are very public matters. To have plastic surgery is to show that you have the money to afford it. In Brazil, modifying one's body through surgery is about more than just becoming more beautiful and desirable. It is even about more than showing that you care about yourself, which is a phrase in the Brazilian mass media. Surgical transformations are naturalized as necessary enhancements. Instead, modifying your body in Brazil is fundamentally about displaying your wealth. But since much is associated with race, changing one's body is also about approximating whiteness. An April 2013 article in *The Economist* noted that "[looking white] still codes for health, wealth and status. Light-skinned women strut São Paulo's upmarket shopping malls in designer clothes; dark-skinned maids in uniform walk behind with the bags and babies. Black and mixed-race Brazilians earn three-fifths as much as white ones. They are twice as likely to be illiterate or in prison, and less than half as likely to go to university. ... The unthinking prejudice expressed in common phrases such as 'good appearance' (meaning pale-skinned) and 'good hair' (not frizzy) means many light-skinned Brazilians have long preferred to think of themselves as 'white', whatever their parentage."

There are marking differences between perceptions of beauty among working-class patients in public hospitals, and upper-middle class patients in private clinics. Plastic surgery is conceptualized by the upper-middle class mainly as an act of consumption that fosters distinction and reinforces the value of whiteness. In contrast, working-class patients describe plastic surgery as a basic necessity that provides the "good appearance" needed in the job market and "repairs" their bodies from the wear of their physical labor as workers and as mothers. Patients from different walks of life desire plastic surgery for different reasons.

The idea that physical appearance can denote class, with the implication that modifications in one's physical appearance can be seen as markers of social status extends throughout Brazil. Put within a context of explicit social inequality, the link between the production of beauty and social class becomes quite evident. Brazilians place a heavy importance in beauty aesthetics; a study in 2007 revealed that 87% of all Brazilians seek to look stylish at all times, opposed to the global average of 47%. The body is understood in southeastern Brazil as having a crucial aesthetic value, a value that is never fixed but can be accrued through discipline and medical intervention. This 'investment' on the body is nearly always equated with health, because a person's well being is assumed to be visible on the surface of their body. One of the most common (and harshest) expressions about beauty in Brazil is "there are really no ugly people, there are only poor people."

Holidays

Date	English name	Portuguese name	Remarks
January 1	New Year's Day	Ano Novo/ Confraternização Universal	Celebrates the beginning of the Gregorian calendar year. Festivities include counting down to midnight on the preceding night. Traditional end of the holiday season.
March/-April (Variable)	Good Friday	Sexta-feira Santa	Christian holiday, celebrates the passion and death of Jesus on the cross.
April 21	Tiradentes' Day	Dia de Tiradentes	Anniversary of the death of Tiradentes (1792), considered a national martyr for being part of the Inconfidência Mineira, an insurgent movement that aimed to establish an independent Brazilian republic.
May 1	Labor Day	Dia do Trabalhador	Celebrates the achievements of workers and the labor movement.
June (Variable)	Corpus Christi	Corpus Christi	A national Catholic holiday which celebrates the Eucharist and the belief of the real presence of Jesus in the host.
September 7	Independence Day	Dia da Independência or 7 de Setembro	Celebrates the Declaration of Independence from Portugal on September 7, 1822.
First and last Sunday in October	Election Day	Dia da Eleição or Eleições	In every 2 years, Brazilians have the obligation to vote. The first election round always happens on the first Sunday in October; if there necessary a second-round, this will happen on the last Sunday in the same October.
October 12	Our Lady of Aparecida' Day	Dia de Nossa Senhora Aparecida	Commemorates the Virgin Mary as *Nossa Senhora da Conceição Aparecida*, Patron Saint of Brazil. Also celebrated as Children's Day (Dia das Crianças) on the same date.
November 2	All Soul's Day	Dia de Finados	Another Christian holiday, it commemorates the faithful departed.
November 15	Republic Day	Proclamação da República	Commemorates the end of the Empire of Brazil and the proclamation of the Brazilian Republic on November 15, 1889.

| December 25 | Christmas Day | Natal | Celebrates the nativity of Jesus. |

External links

- Brazilian ministry of culture[1504] (in Portuguese)
- Consulate General of Brazil in San Francisco[1505]
- Eyes On Brazil – Brazilian Cultural Site[1506]
- Brazilian Culture Lib Guide[1507]
- Brazilian Cultural Center[1508]

Architecture

Architecture of Brazil

The **architecture of Brazil** is influenced by Europe, especially Portugal. It has a history that goes back 500 years to the time when Pedro Cabral discovered Brazil in 1500. Portuguese colonial architecture was the first wave of architecture to go to Brazil. It is the basis for all Brazilian architecture of later centuries. In the 19th century during the time of the Empire of Brazil, Brazil followed European trends and adopted Neoclassical and Gothic Revival architecture. Then in the 20th century especially in Brasilia, Brazil experimented with Modernist architecture.

Portuguese colonial architecture

The colonial architecture of Brazil dates to the early 16th century when Brazil was first explored, conquered and settled by the Portuguese. The Portuguese built architecture familiar to them in Europe in their aim to colonise Brazil. They built Portuguese colonial architecture which included Churches, civic architecture including houses and forts in Brazilian cities and the countryside. They founded Recife, São Paulo, Rio de Janeiro, Salvador in the colonial period, these cities saw the best expression of Brazilian architecture.

19th century Brazilian architecture

19th Century Brazilian architecture is a period that saw the introduction of more European styles to Brazil such as Neoclassical and Gothic Revival architecture. This was usually mixed with Brazilian influences from their own heritage which produced a unique form of Brazilian architecture.

Figure 435: *Building Facade, Recife.*

Figure 436: *Portuguese colonial architecture, Salvador.*

Figure 437: *Municipal Theatre of São Paulo shows Neoclassical architecture in Brazil.*

Figure 438: *Brasilia National Congress, an example of Modernist architecture.*

20th century Brazilian architecture

In the 1950's Brazil decided to found a new capital city in the interior of Brazil to help develop Brazil's interior. The city was Brasilia and it would see a great experiment in modernist architecture. Government buildings, Churches and civic buildings would be constructed in the modernist style.

References

- Hue, Jorge de Souza (1999). Uma visão da arquitectura colonial no Brasil [A vision of Colonial Architecture in Brazil] (in Portuguese). Rio de Janeiro.
- Boxer, Charles Ralph (1962). The Golden Age of Brazil, 1695-1750: Growing Pains of a Colonial Society. University of California Press.

Music

Music of Brazil

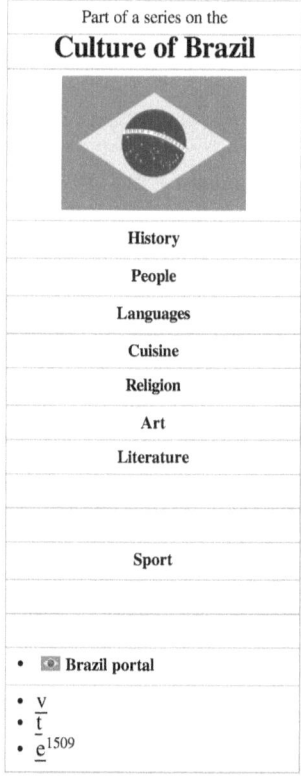

The **music of Brazil** encompasses various regional musical styles influenced by African, European and Amerindian forms. Brazilian music developed some unique and original styles such as sertanejo, samba, bossa nova, MPB, música nativista, pagode, tropicália, choro, maracatu, embolada (coco de repente), funk carioca, frevo, brega, modinha and Brazilian versions of foreign musical styles, such as rock, soul, hip-hop, disco music, country music, ambient, industrial and psychedelic music, rap, classical music, fado, and gospel.

Samba has become the best known form of Brazilian music worldwide, especially because of the country's carnival, although bossa nova, which had Antônio Carlos Jobim as one of its most acclaimed composers and performers, have received much attention abroad since the 1950s, when the song "Desafinado", interpreted by João Gilberto, was first released.

The first four winners of the Shell Brazilian Music prize have each left a very important legacy on Brazilian music and are among the most important representatives of Brazilian popular music: Pixinguinha (choro), Antônio Carlos Jobim (bossa nova), Dorival Caymmi (samba and samba-canção).

Instrumental music is also largely practiced in Brazil, with styles ranging from classical to popular and jazz influenced forms. Among the later, Pixinguinha, Hermeto Pascoal and Egberto Gismonti are significant figures. Notable classical composers include Heitor Villa-Lobos, Carlos Gomes and Cláudio Santoro. The country also has a growing community of modern/experimental composition, including electroacoustic music.

Art music

Origins

The first registration of musical activity in Brazil comes from the activities of two Jesuit priests in 1549. Ten years later, they had already founded settlements for indigenous people (the *Reduções*), with a musical-educational structure.

One century later, the Reduções of the southern Brazil, which were founded by Spaniard Jesuits, had a strong cultural development, where some music schools were founded. Some of the reports of that time show the fascination of the indigenous people for European music.[1510] The indigenous people also took part in the music, with both the construction of musical instruments and practice of vocal and instrumental performance. The musical styles were, naturally, from the European culture, and the purpose of the musicalization for the indigenous people was mostly for Catechism, with negligible original creative contribution by themselves. Later, the remaining Indians who survived the massacres and epidemics went to the more remote regions of Brazil, escaping from contact with the European settlers, and their part in the national musical life diminished, eventually almost completely disappearing.Wikipedia:Citation needed

Figure 439: *Ouro Preto, in Minas Gerais: one of the most important musical centers in Brazil during the 18th century*

The 18th-century school

In the 18th century, there was intense musical activity in all the more developed regions of Brazil, with their moderately stable institutional and educational structures. The previously few private orchestras became more common and the churches presented a great variety of music.

In the first half of this century, the most outstanding works were composed by Luís Álvares Pinto, Caetano de Mello de Jesus and Antônio José da Silva ("the Jew"), who became successful in Lisbon writing librettos for comedies, which were performed also in Brazil with music by António Teixeira.

In the second part of the 18th century, there was a great flourishing in Minas Gerais, mostly in the regions of *Vila Rica* (currently Ouro Preto), Mariana and *Arraial do Tejuco* (currently Diamantina), where the mining of gold and diamonds for the Portuguese metropolis attracted a sizable population. At this time, the first outstanding Brazilian composers were revealed, most of them mulattoes. The musical pieces were mostly sacred music. Some of the noteworthy composers of this period were Lobo de Mesquita, Manoel Dias de Oliveira, Francisco Gomes da Rocha, Marcos Coelho Neto and Marcos Coelho Neto Filho. All of them were very active, but in many cases few pieces have survived until the present day. Some of the most famous pieces of this period

Figure 440: *José Maurício Nunes Garcia*

are the *Magnificat* by Manoel Dias de Oliveira and the *Our Lady's Antiphon* by Lobo de Mesquita. In the city of Arraial do Tejuco, nowadays Diamantina, there were ten conductors in activity. In Ouro Preto about 250 musicians were active, and in all of the territory of Minas Gerais almost a thousand musicians were active.[1511]

With the impoverishment of the mines at the end of the century, the focus of the musical activity changed to other centers, specially Rio de Janeiro and São Paulo, where André da Silva Gomes, a composer of Portuguese origin, released a great number of works and dynamized the musical life of the city.

The Classical period

A crucial factor for the changes in the musical life was the arrival of the Portuguese Royal family to Rio de Janeiro in 1808. Until then, Rio de Janeiro was musically similar to other cultural centers of Brazil but was even less important than Minas Gerais. The presence of the Portuguese Royal family, in exile, radically changed this situation, as the Capela Real of Rio de Janeiro was established.

The king John VI of Portugal brought with him to Brazil the great musical library from the House of Bragança, one of the best of Europe at that time, and ordered the arrival of musicians from Lisbon and the *castrati* from Italy, re-ordering the Royal Chapel. Later, John VI ordered the construction of a sumptuous theater, called the Royal Theater of São João. The secular music had the presence of Marcos Portugal, who was designated as the official composer of the household, and of Sigismund von Neukomm, who contributed with his own work and brought the works of the Austrian composers Wolfgang Amadeus Mozart and Joseph Haydn. The works of these composers strongly influenced the Brazilian music of this time.

José Maurício Nunes Garcia, the first of the great Brazilian composers, emerged at this time. With a large culture for his origin – he was poor and mulatto – he was one of the founders of the Irmandade de Santa Cecília, in Rio de Janeiro, teacher and mestre de capela of the Royal Chapel during the presence of John VI in Brazil. Nunes Garcia was the most prolific Brazilian composer of this time. He also composed the first opera written in Brazil, *Le Due Gemelle* (*The Two Twins*), with text in Italian, but the music is now lost.

Other important composers of this period are Gabriel Fernandes da Trindade, who composed the only Brazilian chamber music from the 19th century which has survived to the present times,[1512] and João de Deus de Castro Lobo, who lived in the cities of Mariana and Ouro Preto, which were decadent at this time.

This period, however, was brief. In 1821, John VI went back to Lisbon, taking with him the household, and the cultural life in Rio de Janeiro became empty. And, despite the love of Peter I of Brazil for the music – he was also author of some musical pieces like the Brazilian Independence Anthem – the difficult financial situation didn't allow many luxuries. The conflagration of the Royal Theater in 1824 was another symbol of decadence, which reached the most critical point when Peter I renounced the throne, going back to Portugal.

The Romantic period

The only composer who had a relevant work in this period was Francisco Manuel da Silva, disciple of Nunes Garcia, who succeeded him as kapellmeister. In spite of his few resources, he founded the Musical Conservatory of Rio de Janeiro. He was the author of the Brazilian National Anthem's melody. His work reflected the musical transition for the Romanticism, when the interest of the national composers was focused in the opera. The most outstanding Brazilian composer of this period was Antônio Carlos Gomes, who composed Italian-styled operas with national themes, such as *Il Guarany* (based on José de Alencar's novel *O Guarani*) and *Lo Schiavo*. These operas were very successful in European theaters, like the Teatro alla Scala, in Milan. Other important composer of this time is Elias Álvares Lobo, who wrote the opera *A Noite de São João*, the first Brazilian opera with text in Portuguese.

Figure 441: *Antônio Carlos Gomes*

The opera in Brazil was very popular until the middle of the 20th century, and many opera houses were built at this time, like Teatro Amazonas in Manaus, Municipal Theater of Rio de Janeiro, Municipal Theater of São Paulo do Rio, and many others.

At the end of the 19th century, the greatest composers for the symphonic music were revealed. One of the most outstanding name of this period was Leopoldo Miguez, who followed the Wagnerian style and Henrique Oswald, who incorporated elements of the French Impressionism.

Nationalism

In the beginning of the 20th century, there was a movement for creating an authentically Brazilian music, with less influences of the European culture. In this sense, the folklore was the major font of inspiration for the composers. Some composers like Brasílio Itiberê da Cunha, Luciano Gallet and Alexandre Levy, despite having a European formation, included some typically Brazilian elements in their works. This trend reached the highest point with Alberto Nepomuceno, who used largely the rhythms and melodies from the Brazilian folklore.

An important event, later, was the Modern Art Week, in 1922, which had a large impact on concepts of national art. In this event the composer Heitor

Figure 442: *Heitor Villa-Lobos*

Villa-Lobos, regarded as the most outstanding name of the Brazilian nationalism, was revealed.

Villa-Lobos did researches about the musical folklore of Brazil, and mixed elements both from classical and popular music. He explored many musical genres such as concertos, symphonies, modinhas, Fados, and other symphonic, vocal and chamber music. Some of his masterworks are the ballet *Uirapuru* and the two series of *Chôros* and *Bachianas Brasileiras*.

Other composers of Brazilian national music of this era include Oscar Lorenzo Fernández, Radamés Gnattali, Camargo Guarnieri, Osvaldo Lacerda, Francisco Mignone, and Ernesto Nazareth.

The avant-garde movement

As a reaction against the nationalist school, who was identified as "servile" to the centralizing politics of Getúlio Vargas, in 1939 the *Movimento Música Viva* (Living Music Movement) appeared, led by Hans Joachim Koellreutter and by Egídio de Castro e Silva, defending the adoption of an international style, derived from the dodecaphonism of Arnold Schoenberg. This group was integrated by composers like Cláudio Santoro, César Guerra-Peixe, Eunice Catunda and Edino Krieger. Koellreutter adopted revolutionary methodes, in respect to the individuality of each student and giving to the students the freedom of creativity before the knowledge of the traditional rules for composition. The movement edited a magazine and presented a series of radio programs showing their fundaments and works of contemporary music. Later, Guerra-Peixe and Santoro followed an independent way, centered in the regional music. Other composers, who used freely the previous styles were Marlos Nobre, Almeida Prado, and Armando Albuquerque, who created their own styles.

After 1960, the Brazilian avant-garde movement received a new wave, focusing on serial music, microtonal music, concrete music and electronic music, employing a completely new language. This movement was called *Música Nova* (New Music) and was led by Gilberto Mendes and Willy Corrêa de Oliveira.

Brazilian Opera

Carlos Gomes was the first composer on non-European origin to achieve wide recognition in the classical music environment of the Golden age of Opera in Italy. Bossa Nova was created as anti-opera in a time when opera seemed to represent the art-form of the elite. [5] In recent years the style has been revived with works by Jorge Antunes, Flo Menezes, and others.

Since 2014 the International Brazilian Opera (IBOC) has been producing new works, most notably by its Artistic Director and resident composer Joao MacDowell.

Contemporary

Nowadays, Brazilian music follows the guidelines of both experimentalism and traditional music. Some of the contemporary Brazilian composers are Amaral Vieira, Sílvio Ferraz, Flo Menezes, Marcos Balter, Alexandre Lunsqui, Rodolfo Caesar, Felipe Lara, Edson Zampronha, Marcus Siqueira, Rodrigo Lima[1513], Jorge Antunes, Roberto Victorio and João MacDowell.

Brazil has a large number of internationally recognized orchestras and performers, despite the relatively low support of the government. The most famous Brazilian orchestra is probably the São Paulo State Symphony Orchestra, currently under the French conductor Yan Pascal Tortelier. Other Brazilian orchestras worthy of note are the São Paulo University Symphony, the Orquestra Sinfônica Brasileira and the Petrobras Sinfônica, supported by the Brazilian state oil company Petrobras.

There are also regular operas scheduled every year in cities such as São Paulo and Rio de Janeiro. The state of São Paulo also hosts the Winter Festival in the city of Campos do Jordão.

Some of the most famous Brazilian conductors are Roberto Minczuk, John Neschling and Isaac Karabtchevsky. The instrumentalists include, among others: Roberto Szidon, Antonio Meneses, Cussy de Almeida, Gilberto Tinetti, Arnaldo Cohen, Nelson Freire, Eudóxia de Barros, Guiomar Novaes and Magda Tagliaferro. And some of the most famous Brazilian singers were, historically, Zola Amaro, Constantina Araújo and Bidu Sayão; living singers include Eliane Coelho, Kismara Pessatti, Maria Lúcia Godoy, Sebastião Teixeira, and others.

In the 1980s, a wave of Brazilian heavy metal bands gained public attention. The most commercially successful of these was Sepultura, founded in São Paulo in 1983, preceded by Dorsal Atlantica and followed by Sarcofago.

The intrusion of alien elements into Brazil's cultural system is not a destructive process. The return of a democratic government allowed for freedom of expression. The Brazilian music industry opened up to international styles and this has allowed for both foreign and local genres to co-exist and identify people. Each different style relates to the people socially, politically, and economically. "Brazil is a regionally divided country with a rich cultural and musical diversity among states. As such, musicians in the country choose to define their local heritage differently depending on where they come from." This shows how globalization has not robbed Brazil of its identity but instead given it the ability to represent its people both in Brazil and the rest of the world.

In recent years Brazilian artists have become more interested in Africa, the Caribbean and their own indigenous and folk music. While there are some artists who continue to perform rock and Western pop, there are now just as many contemporaries playing a fusion of African and European influences with those from across The Americas. Some artists have even become influenced by Asian music, noticing some parallels between music from the North-East of Brazil and music from India.

Indigenous and folk music

The native peoples of the Brazilian rainforest play instruments including whistles, flutes, horns, drums and rattles. Much of the area's folk music imitates the sounds of the Amazon Rainforest. When the Portuguese arrived in Brazil, the first natives they met played an array of reed flutes and other wind and percussion instruments. The Jesuit missionaries introduced songs which used

Figure 443: *Drum known as Ilú used in Xambá religion in Pernambuco*

the Tupi language with Christian lyrics, an attempt to convert the people to Christianity,[1514] and also introduced Gregorian chant and the flute, bow, and the clavichord.

The earliest music in what is now Brazil must have been that of the native peoples of the area. Little is known about their music, since no written records exist of this era. With the arrival of Europeans, Brazilian culture began to take shape as a synthesis of native musical styles with Portuguese music and African music.

Capoeira music

The Afro-Brazilian sport of capoeira is never played without its own music, which is usually considered to be a call-and-response type of folk music. The main instruments of capoeira music include the *berimbau*, the *atabaque* and the *pandeiro*. Capoeira songs may be improvised on the spot, or they may be popular songs written by older, and ancient *mestres* (teachers), and often include accounts of the history of capoeira, or the doings of great mestres.

Figure 444: *Jongo, a dance and musical genre of African origin, c. 1822*

Figure 445: *Brazilian dance-song lundu, c. 1835*

Figure 446: *Three berimbau players*

Maracatu

This type of music is played primarily in the Recife and Olinda regions during Carnaval. It is an Afro-Brazilian tradition. The music serves as the backdrop for parade groups that evolved out of ceremonies conducted during colonial times in honour of the Kings of Congo, who were African slaves occupying symbolic leadership positions among the slave population. The music is played on large alfaia drums, large metal onguê bells, snare drums and shakers. An important variant is found in and around Fortaleza, Ceará (called maracatu cearense), which is different from the Recife/Olinda tradition in many respects: triangles are used instead of onguês, surdos or zabumbas instead of alfaias. Also, important female characters are performed by cross-dressed male performers, and all African and Afrobrazilian personages are performed using blackface makeup.

Afoxé

Afoxé is a kind of religious music, part of the Candomblé tradition. In 1949, a group called Filhos de Gandhi began playing afoxé during carnaval parades in Salvador; their name translates as *Sons of Gandhi*, associating black Brazilian activism with Mahatma Gandhi's Indian independence movement. The Filhos

Music of Brazil

Figure 447: *Maracatu.*

de Gandhi's 1949 appearance was also revolutionary because, until then, the Carnaval parades in Salvador were meant only for light-skinned people.

Repente

Northeastern Brazil is known for a distinctive form of literature called literatura de cordel, which are a type of ballads that include elements incorporated into music as "repentismo", an improvised lyrical contest on themes suggested by the audience.

Similar to Repentismo, appears among the Caipira culture a musical form derived from viola caipira, which is called *cururu*.

Popular music
Choro

Urubu Malandro
"Urubu Malandro", recorded in 1930 by Pixinguinha in the flute

Problems playing this file? See media help.

Figure 448: *Repentista.*

Figure 449: *Choro guitar.*

	Harmonia Selvagem Choro "Harmonia Selvagem" composed by Dante Santoro. Recorded by Dante Santoro (flute) in 1938.

Problems playing this file? See media help.

	Atraente "Atraente", composed by Chiquinha Gonzaga, recorded by Pixinguinha (saxophone) and Benedito Lacerda (flute).

Problems playing this file? See media help.

Choro (literally "cry" in Portuguese, but in context a more appropriate translation would be "lament"), traditionally called *chorinho* ("little cry" or "little lament"). Instrumental, its origins are in 19th century Rio de Janeiro. Originally *choro* was played by a trio of flute, guitar and cavaquinho (a small chordophone with four strings). The young pianist Ernesto Nazareth published his first choro (*Não Caio Noutra*) in 1878 at the age of 14.[1515] Nazareth's choros are often listed as *polkas*;[1516] he also composed waltzes, schottisches, milongas and Brazilian Tangos. (He resisted the popular term *maxixe* to represent Brazilian tango.) Chiquinha Gonzaga was another important composer of choros and started shortly after Nazareth. Chiquinha Gonzaga composed her first success, the polka-choro "Atraente", in 1877. In the beginning, the success of choro came from informal groups of friends which played in parties, pubs (botecos), streets, home balls (forrobodós), and also the musical scores published by print houses. By the 1910s, much of the Brazilian first phonograph records are choros. The mainstream success of this style of music (By the 1930s) came from the early days of radio, when bands performed live on the air. By the 1950s and 1960s it was replaced by samba and Bossa Nova and other styles of Brazilian popular music, but was still alive in amateur circles called "rodas de choro" (informal choro gatherings in residences and botecos). However, in the late 1970s there was a successful effort to revitalize the genre carried out by some famous artists: Pixinguinha, Waldir Azevedo and Jacob do Bandolim.

Samba

In 1929, prompted by the opening of the first radio station in Rio de Janeiro, the so-called *radio era* began spreading songs – especially the novelty Samba in its current format – to larger masses. This period was dominated by few male interpreters – notably Almirante, Braguinha, Mário Reis, Sílvio Caldas,

Figure 450: *Singer and actress Carmen Miranda.*

Francisco Alves and singer/composer Noel Rosa and even fewer chanteuses such as Aracy de Almeida and sisters Aurora Miranda and Carmen Miranda, who eventually came to Hollywood becoming a movie star.[1517]

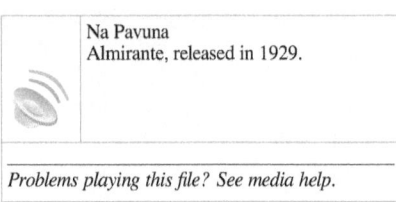

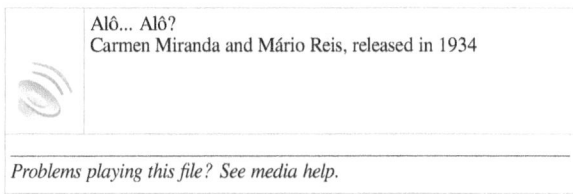

Alô... Alô?
Carmen Miranda and Mário Reis, released in 1934

Problems playing this file? See media help.

Popular music included instruments like cuicas, tambourines, frying pans ('played' with a metal stick), flutes and guitars. Noteworthy Samba composers at this early stage included said Noel Rosa plus Lamartine Babo and, around World War II time, Ary Barroso.

MPB (Popular Brazilian Music)

MPB's early stage (from World War II to the mid-1960s) was populated by male singers such as Orlando Silva, Nelson Gonçalves, Jamelão, Agostinho dos Santos, Anísio Silva, Ataulfo Alves, Carlos Galhardo, Ciro Monteiro, Ismael Silva, João Dias, Jorge Goulart, Miltinho, Jorge Veiga and Francisco Egídio and female singers started to mushroom: Nora Ney, Dolores Duran, Ângela Maria, Emilinha Borba, Marlene, Dalva de Oliveira, Maysa Matarazzo, sisters Linda Batista and Dircinha Batista, among others.Wikipedia:Citation needed

MPB's second stage – after the split Bossa Nova (1959) / Jovem Guarda (1965) / Tropicalismo (both 1967) – refers to mainstream Brazilian pop music. Well-known MPB artists include, among many others, singers such as Elis Regina, Nara Leão, Maria Bethânia, Mônica da Silva, Simone, Chico Buarque, Caetano Veloso, Roberto Carlos, Jorge Ben Jor, Milton Nascimento, Gilberto Gil, João Bosco, Ivan Lins, Djavan.

Bossa nova

The first bossa nova records by João Gilberto, in the last years of the 1950s, quickly became huge hits in Brazil. Antonio Carlos Jobim and other composers helped further develop this fusion of jazz harmonies and a smoother, often slower, samba beat, which developed at the beach neighborhoods of Ipanema and, later, the Copacabana nightclubs. Bossa nova was introduced to the rest of the world by American jazz musicians in the early 1960s, and song "The Girl from Ipanema" remains probably the best known Brazilian musical export, eventually becoming a jazz standard.

Figure 451: *Gilberto Gil*

Brazilian gospel

Gospel music emerged in Brazil before the 1960s with hymnals that were brought and translated into Portuguese by American missionaries. From the late 1960s the first singers of Christian music groups emerged in Brazil, but the songs were not highly valued. Gospel music became popular in Brazil in the late 1990s, with the emergence of congregational singing and bands such as Diante do Trono, led by Ana Paula Valadão. Diante do Trono has become the largest contemporary worship music ministry in Latin America.

Brazilian rock

The musical style known in Brazil as "Brazilian rock n' roll" dates back to a Portuguese-version coverWikipedia:Avoid weasel words of "Rock Around the Clock" in 1954. In the 1960s, young singers like Roberto Carlos and the Jovem Guarda movement were very popular. The 1960s also saw the rise of bands such as the "tropicalistas" Os Mutantes and the experimental (mixing progressive rock, jazz and Música popular brasileira) Som Imaginário.

The 1970s saw the emergence of many progressive rock and/or hard rock bands such as O Terço, A Bolha, A Barca do Sol, Som Nosso de Cada Dia, Vímana and Bacamarte, some of which attained some recognition internationally; Rita Lee, in her solo career after Os Mutantes, championed the glam-rock

Figure 452: *Diante do Trono, the main worship ministry in Latin America.*

Figure 453: *Rita Lee*

aesthetics in Brazil; Casa das Máquinas and Patrulha do Espaço were more bona-fide hard rock bands, and the likes of (Raul Seixas, Secos e Molhados, Novos Baianos and A Cor do Som) mixed the genre with traditional Brazilian music. In the late 1970s, the Brazilian punk rock scene kicked off mainly in São Paulo and in Brasília, booming in the 1980s, with Inocentes, Cólera, Ratos de Porão, Garotos Podres, etc.

The real commercial boom of Brazilian rock was in the 1980s, with many bands and artists like Blitz, Gang 90, Barão Vermelho, Legião Urbana, Lobão, Engenheiros do Hawaii, Titãs, Kid Abelha, Paralamas do Sucesso, and many

Figure 454: *Fernanda Takai, singer Pato Fu*

others, and festivals like Rock in Rio and Hollywood Rock. The late 1980s and early 1990s also witnessed the beginnings of an electronica-inspired scene, with a lot more limited commercial potential but achieving some critical acclaim: Suba, Loop B, Harry, etc.

In the 1990s, the meteoric rise of Mamonas Assassinas, which sold more than 3 million copies of its only CD (a record, by Brazilian standards) came to a tragic end when the band's plane crashed, killing all five members of the band, the pilot and the co-pilot. Other commercially successful bands included Jota Quest, Raimundos and Skank, while Chico Science & Nação Zumbi and the whole Mangue Bit movement received much critical attention and accolades, but very little commercial success – success that declined after the death of one of its founders, Chico Science. It was also in the 1990s that the first seeds of what would grow into being the Brazilian indie scene were planted, with the creation of indie festivals such as Abril Pro Rock and, later in the decade, Porão do Rock. The band Pato Fu was considered by Time magazine one of the ten best bands in the world outside the United States. It is also known to re-record hits Brazilian and international versions of toy instruments.

Female singer Pitty is also very popular. The indie scene has been growing exponentially since the early 2000s, with more and more festivals taking place all around the country. However, due to several factors including but not limited to the worldwide collapse of the music industry, all the agitation in the indie scene has so far failed in translating into international success, but in

Figure 455: *Sepultura.*

Brazil they developed a real, substantial cultural movement. That scene is still much of a ghetto, with bands capturing the attention of international critics, but many playing again in Brazil when they become popular in the exterior, due to the lack of financial and material support which would allow for careers to be developed. One notable exception is CSS, an alternative electro rock outfit that has launched a successful international career, performing in festivals and venues in North America, Europe, Asia and Australia. Other unique example of success through independent music scene that made to the mainstream is the band Móveis Coloniais de Acaju. The band has its own style, somewhere between rock and folk, and is recognized as the most important independent band in Brazil. The record company Trama[1518] tries to support some bands with structure and exposure, and can be credited with early support to CSS and later to Móveis Coloniais de Acaju.

Brazilian heavy metal

Brazilian metal originated in the mid 1980s with three prominent scenes: Belo Horizonte, São Paulo and Rio de Janeiro. The most famous Brazilian metal bands are Sepultura, Angra, Krisiun, Rebaelliun, Nephasth, Dr. Sin, Shaaman, Violator and the singer Andre Matos. Sepultura is considered an influential thrash metal band, influencing the development of death metal.

Famous bands of the 1980s include Korzus, Sarcófago, Overdose, Dorsal Atlântica, Viper, MX, PUS, Mutilator, Chakal, Vulcano and Attomica. Bands from the 1990s include Andralls, MQN, Macaco Bong, Black Drawing Chalks, Superguidis, Mental Hor, The Mist, Scars, Distraught, Torture Squad, Eterna and Silent Cry. Bands from the 2000s include It's All Red, Eyes of Shiva, Autoramas, Tuatha de Danann, Claustrofobia, Quimere, Apokalyptic Raids, Project46, Wizards and Andragonia.

Brazilian folk/folk-rock

The new Brazilian folk scene is not to be mistaken with folkloric Brazilian music. The first to break into the mainstream was internet phenomenon Mallu Magalhães, who played covers of her favourite artists in English and her own songs in both English and Portuguese (as well as other languages). Magalhães only released her first album in 2008, though by then she was already widely recognised as the voice of this sudden new Brazilian folk scene. Her ex-boyfriend Hélio Flanders is the lead singer of another Brazilian folk group called Vanguart. Though Vanguart had an album released before Mallu Magalhães, it was her emergence that consolidated them both and others as a fully recognised mainstream scene, topping charts and being featured in prime time television and advertising. Other acts emerged after the market was opened up to folk. Writing in English is more and more common among Brazilian rock and folk artists. This has been highly criticised by Portuguese language purists, though it has helped to promote Brazilian artists in other countries (CSS is a perfect example). The new Brazilian folk scene has just come to the public's attention and it continues to thrive.

Brazilian psychedelic rock

Brazil has a long tradition of psychedelic music since artists like Os Mutantes, Ronnie Von and other rock bands from the late 60s. Nowadays, there exists a revival of this psychedelic/vintage inspired music represented by artists like Jupiter Apple, Violeta de Outono, Nação Zumbi, Mundo Livre S/A, Cidadão Instigado, Otto, China, Kassin, Pata de Elefante, Orquestra Abstrata, among others.

Sertanejo

Música sertaneja or Sertanejo is a term for Brazilian country music. It originally referred to music originating among Sertão and musica caipira. (Caipira music appeared in the state of São Paulo, and some the regions of Mato Grosso do Sul, Goiás Minas Gerais, Paraná and Mato Grosso. Musical rhythm is very spread out in the Southeastern and southern regions of Brazil.)

Figure 456: *Os Mutantes, 1969. National Archives of Brazil.*

Figure 457: *Chitãozinho & Xororó.*

Figure 458: *Statue of Luiz Gonzaga*

Northeastern Music

North eastern music is a generic term for any popular music from the large region of Northeastern Brazil, including both coastal and inland areas. Rhythms are slow and plodding, and are derived from guitars instead of percussion instruments like in the rest of Brazil—in this region, African rhythms and Portuguese melodies combined to form maracatu. Most influentially, however, the area around the state of Pernambuco, the home of frevo and maracatu.

Gaucho music (Southern music)

Southern music (Portuguese: *Música gaúcha*) is a general term used for the music originally from the Rio Grande do Sul state, in Southern Brazil. Some of the most famous musicians of this genre are Renato Borghetti, Yamandu Costa, Jayme Caetano Braun and Luiz Marenco, among others.

Music of Salvador: Late 60s to mid-70s

In the latter part of the 1960s, a group of black Bahians began dressing as Native Americans during the Salvadoran Carnaval, identifying with their shared struggles through history. These groups included Comanches do Pelô and Apaches de Tororó and were known for a forceful and powerful style of percussion, and frequent violent encounters with the police. Starting in 1974, a group of black Bahians called Ilê Aiyê became prominent, identifying with the Yoruba people of West Africa. Along with a policy of loosening restrictions by the Brazilian government, Ilê Aiyê's sound and message spread to groups like Grupo Cultural do Olodum, who established community centers and other philanthropic efforts.

Frevo

Frevo is a style of music from Olinda and Recife. Frevo bands always play during the Carnival.

Sambass

Sambass is a fusion of samba and Drum & Bass. The most famous sambass musicians are DJ Marky and DJ Patife whose hit *Sambassim* might be the most known sambass track.

Funk Carioca

Funk Carioca is a type of dance music from Rio de Janeiro, derived from and was until the late 1990's, superficially similar to Miami Bass. In Rio it is most often simply known as Funk, although it is very different musically from what Funk means in most other places and contexts. Funk Carioca, like other types of hip-hop lifts heavily from samples such as international rips or from previous funk music. Many popular funk songs sampled music from the movie *Rocky*. Funk was introduced to Brazil in a systematic way in the 1980s. Many funk artists have openly associated themselves with black movements and often in the lyrics of their songs, comment on race relations and openly express black pride.

Hip hop music

In São Paulo and other places in the south of Brazil, in more urban areas, hip hop music is very popular. Rappers are referred to as "Rapeiros". They dress similarly to American rappers. Early Brazilian rap was based upon rhyming speeches delivered over dance bases sampled from funk albums, with occasional scratches.Wikipedia:Citation needed

Brazilian hip hop is heavily associated with racial and economic issues in the country, where a lot of Afro-Brazilians live in economically disadvantaged communities, known in Brazil as favelas. São Paulo is where hip hop began in the country, but it soon spread all over Brazil, and today, almost every big Brazilian city, including Rio de Janeiro, Salvador, Curitiba, Porto Alegre, Belo Horizonte, Recife and Brasilia, has a hip hop scene. São Paulo has gained a strong, underground Brazilian rap scene since its emergence in the late 1980s with many independent labels forming for young rappers to establish themselves on.

In the 1990s in Rio de Janeiro, funk as well as rap were reported by the press to have been adopted by the drug lords of the city as a way to market their drugs at dance hall events.Wikipedia:Citation needed Some crime groups were known to subsidize funk parties to recruit young kids into the drug dealing business.Wikipedia:Citation needed These events were often called baile funk (which can mean a funk dance party) and were sometimes notorious for their blatant sexuality and violence.[1519] However, while some rap music was used to send messages out about slums and drugs, others were used mostly to deliver socio-political messages about local, regional, or national issues they are affected by. In fact, some groups adhered to what they called *rap consciência*, socially conscious rap, and opposed hip-hop which some considered too alienated and consumerist.Wikipedia:Citation needed Despite these differences, both hip hop and *rap consciência* continue to thrive in Brazil today. One of Brazil's most popular rappers, MV Bill, has spent his career advocating for black youth in Rio de Janeiro.

Notable record labels

- Far Out Recordings
- Malandro Records
- Mr Bongo Records
- Som Livre

Further reading

- Leymarie, Isabelle (1996). *Du tango au reggae: musiques noires d'Amérique latine et des Caraïbes*. Paris: Flammarion. ISBN 2082108139.
- Leymarie, Isabelle (2015). *Del tango al reggae: Músicas negras de América Latina y del Caribe*. Zaragoza: Prensas de la Universidad de Zaragoza. ISBN 8416272743.
- Murphy, John P. (2006). "Music in Brazil: Experiencing Music, Expressing Culture". New York: Oxford University Press. ISBN 0195166833.

External links

- (in French) Audio clips: Traditional music of Brazil.[1520] Musée d'Ethnographie de Genève. Accessed November 25, 2010.

- BBC Radio 3 Audio (60 minutes): Forro, coco and cowboys.[1521] Accessed November 25, 2010.
- BBC Radio 3 Audio (60 minutes): Candomble, Samba and Renato Rosa.[1522] Accessed November 25, 2010.
- BBC Radio 3 Audio (60 minutes): Rio, the samba and Mart'nalia.[1523] Accessed November 25, 2010.
- BBC Radio 3 Audio (60 minutes): Maracatu, ciranda and Mangue bit.[1524] Accessed November 25, 2010.
- BBC Radio 3 Audio (60 minutes): Coco music, the pifano flute and Sebastian Dias.[1525] Accessed November 25, 2010.
- Brazilian Embassy in London – Music Section[1526] Brazilian music links
- Sounds and Colours Brazil - resource dedicated to Brazilian music and culture[1527] Accessed June 17, 2014.
- Brazil beyond clichés[1528] Vast archive of podcasts covering Brazilian music of all styles, regions and time periods, from vintage sambas to modern blends.

Literature

Brazilian literature

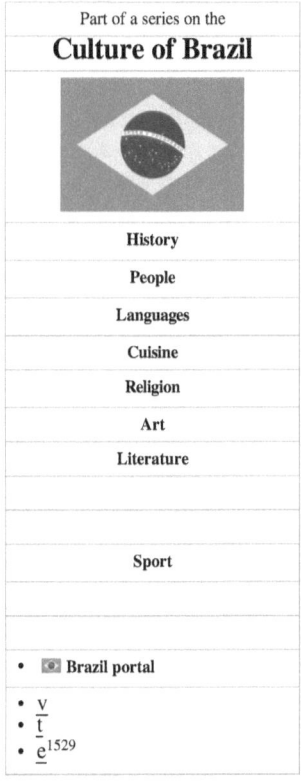

Brazilian literature is the literature written in the Portuguese language by Brazilians or in Brazil, including works written prior to the country's independence in 1822. Throughout its early years, literature from Brazil followed the literary trends of Portugal, whereas gradually shifting to a different and authentic writing style in the course of the 19th and 20th centuries, in the search for truly Brazilian themes and use of the Portuguese language.

Portuguese is a Romance dialect and the sole official language of Brazil. Lyrically, the poet Olavo Bilac, named it " (...) *desconhecida e obscura./ Tuba de alto clangor, lira singela,/ Que tens o trom e o silvo da procela,/ E o arrolo da saudade e da ternura!* ", which roughly translates as "(...) unknown and obscure,/ Tuba of high blare, delicate lyre,/ That holds the frill and the hiss of the tempest/ And the singing of the saudade and of the tenderness!"

Brazil's most significant literary award is the Camões Prize, which it shares with the entire Portuguese sprachraum. As of 2016, Brazil has eleven recipients of the prize. Brazil also holds its own literary academy, the Brazilian Academy of Letters, a non-profit cultural organization pointed in perpetuating the care of the national language and literature.

Brazilian literature has been very prolific. Having as birth the letter of Pero Vaz de Caminha, the document that marks the discovery of Brazil, the country's literature has encompassed several significant writers. Major figures include novelists Machado de Assis, Guimarães Rosa, Jorge Amado, Clarice Lispector and Graciliano Ramos; poets such as João Cabral de Melo Neto, Mario de Andrade, Carlos Drummond de Andrade, Vinicius de Moraes, Ferreira Gullar and Manuel Bandeira; dramatists like Nelson Rodrigues and Augusto Boal, and literary critics and theorists as Antonio Candido and Otto Maria Carpeaux, among others.

Colonial period

One of the first extant documents that might be considered Brazilian literature is the *Carta de Pero Vaz de Caminha* (Pero Vaz de Caminha's letter). It is written by Pero Vaz de Caminha to Manuel I of Portugal, which contains a description of what Brazil looked like in 1500. Journals of voyagers and descriptive treatises on "Portuguese America" dominated the literary production for the next two centuries, including well-known accounts by Jean de Léry and Hans Staden, whose story of his encounter with the Tupi Indians on the coast of São Paulo was extraordinarily influential for European conceptions of the New World.

A few more explicitly literary examples survive from this period, such as Basílio da Gama's epic poem celebrating the conquest of the Missions by the Portuguese, and the work of Gregório de Matos, a 17th-century lawyer from Salvador who produced a sizable amount of satirical, religious, and secular poetry. Matos drew heavily from Baroque influences such as the Spanish poets Luis de Góngora and Francisco de Quevedo.

Figure 459: *Academia Brasileira de Letras, Rio de Janeiro, Brazil.*

Neoclassicism was widespread in Brazil during the mid-18th century, following the Italian style. Literature was often produced by members of temporary or semi-permanent academies and most of the content was in the pastoral genre. The most important literary centre in colonial Brazil was the prosperous Minas Gerais region, known for its gold mines, where a thriving proto-nationalist movement had begun. The most important poets were Cláudio Manuel da Costa, Tomás António Gonzaga, Alvarenga Peixoto and Manuel Inácio da Silva Alvarenga, all them involved in an uprising against the colonial power. Gonzaga and Costa were exiled to Africa as a consequence.

Romanticism

Neoclassicism, lasted for an unnaturally long time, stifling innovation and restricting literary creation. It was only in 1836 that Romanticism began influencing Brazilian poetry on a large scale, principally through the efforts of the expatriate poet Gonçalves de Magalhães. A number of young poets, such as Casimiro de Abreu, began experimenting with the new style soon afterward. This period produced some of the first standard works of Brazilian literature.

The key features of the literature of the newborn country are exaggerated affect, nationalism, celebration of nature and the initial introduction of colloquial language. Romantic literature soon became very popular. Novelists like

Joaquim Manuel de Macedo, Manuel Antônio de Almeida and José de Alencar published their works in serial form in the newspapers and became national celebrities.

Around 1850, a transition began, centered on Álvares de Azevedo. Azevedo's short story collection *Noite na Taverna* (English: A Night at the Tavern) and his poetry, collected posthumously in *Lira dos Vinte Anos* (English: Twenty-year-old Lyre), became influential. Azevedo was largely influenced by the poetry of Lord Byron and Alfred de Musset. This second Romantic generation was obsessed with morbidity and death.

At the same time, poets such as Castro Alves, who wrote of the horrors of slavery (*Navio Negreiro*), began writing works with a specific progressive social agenda. The two trends coincided in one of the most important accomplishments of the Romantic era: the establishment of a Brazilian national identity based on Indian ancestry and the rich nature of the country. These traits first appeared in Gonçalves Dias' narrative poem *I-Juca-Pirama*, but soon became widespread. The consolidation of this subgenre (*Indianism*) is found in two famous novels by José de Alencar: *The Guarani*, about a family of Portuguese colonists who took Indians as servants but were later slain by an enemy tribe, and *Iracema*, about a Portuguese shipwrecked man who lives among the Indians and marries a beautiful Indian woman. *Iracema* is especially lyrical, opening with five paragraphs of pure free-style prose poetry describing the title character.

Figure 460: *Luís Gama*

Figure 461: *José de Alencar*

Figure 462: *Gonçalves de Magalhães, Viscount of Araguaia*

Realism

The decline of Romanticism, along with a series of social transformations, occurred in the middle of the 19th century. A new form of prose writing emerged, including analysis of the indigenous people and description of the environment, in the *regionalist* authors (such as Franklin Távora and João Simões Lopes Neto). Under the influence of Naturalism and of writers like Émile Zola, Aluísio Azevedo wrote *O Cortiço*, with characters that represent all social classes and categories of the time. Brazilian Realism was not very original at first, but it took on extraordinary importance because of Machado de Assis and Euclides da Cunha.

Machado de Assis

Perhaps the most important writer of Brazilian Realism is Joaquim Maria Machado de Assis (1839–1908), the natural son of a half-black wallpainter and a Portuguese woman, whose only education, besides literacy classes, was the extensive reading of borrowed books.

Working as typesetter at a publishing house, he was soon acquainted with most of the world's literature and became fluent in English and French. In his early career he wrote several best-selling novels (including *A Mão e a Luva* and *Ressurreição*) which, despite their overzealous Romanticism, already show his vivacious humour and some of his pessimism towards the conventions of society.

After being introduced to Realism, Machado de Assis changed his style and his themes, producing some of the most remarkable prose ever written in Portuguese. The style served as the medium for his corrosive humour and his intense pessimism, which was very far from the plain conceptions of his contemporaries.

Machado's most crucial works include:

- *Memórias Póstumas de Brás Cubas* (*Brás Cubas' Posthumous Memoirs*), the fictional autobiography of a recently deceased man, written by himself "from beyond". It is entirely anti-Romantic and ridicules the society of Rio de Janeiro of the time. This book contains one of the most pitiless sentences about love ever written: "Marcela amou-me durante quinze meses e onze contos de réis; nada menos". (Marcela loved me for fifteen months and eleven thousand réis; nothing less.)
- *Dom Casmurro* purports to be the autobiography of a lonely man who has left his wife and his only son after enjoying years of happy conjugal life. The novel is famous in the Portuguese-speaking world for its analysis of a (possible, but never proven or admitted) case of adultery.
- *Quincas Borba*
- *O Alienista*, the short story about a psychiatrist who founds a hospital for the mentally ill in a small town and later engages in profound investigations on the nature and the cure of mental illness, greatly upsetting the town's lifestyle.

Machado was also a minor poet, writing mostly casual poetry of extraordinary correctness and beauty. His reputation as a novelist has kept his poetry in print, and recent criticism has regarded it better than that of many of his contemporaries.

Figure 463: *Machado de Assis*

Figure 464: *Aluísio Azevedo*

Figure 465: *Raul Pompeia*

Figure 466: *Olavo Bilac*

Figure 467: *Raimundo Correia*

Pre-Modernism

History of
modern literature By decade

- List of years in literature

Early modern by century

- 16th
- 17th

Mid-modern by century

- 18th
- 19th

20th–21st century

- Modernism
- Structuralism
- Deconstruction
- Poststructuralism
- Postmodernism
- Post-colonialism
- Hypertexts

By region

Africa
• Nigerian • South African
Americas
• American • Argentine • Brazilian • Canadian • Colombian • Cuban • Jamaican • Mexican • Peruvian
Asia

- Bengali
- Bangladeshi English
- Chinese
- Gujarati
- Hindi
- Indian
  - Indian English
- Japanese
- Kannada
- Kashmiri
- Korean
- Malayalam
- Marathi
- Pakistani
  - Pakistani English
- Pashto
- Punjabi
- Sindhi
- Tamil
- Telugu
- Urdu
- Vietnamese

Australasia

- Australian
- New Zealand

Europe

Related topics

- History of science fiction
- Literature by country
- History of theater
- History of ideas
- Intellectual history

Literature portal

- v
- t
- e[1530]

The period between 1895 and 1922 is called Pre-Modernism by Brazilian scholars because, though there is no clear predominance of any style, there are some early manifestations of Modernism. The Pre-Modern era is curious, as the French school of Symbolism did not catch on and most authors of Realism still maintained their earlier styles and their reputations (including Machado de Assis and poet Olavo Bilac). Some authors of this time were Monteiro Lobato, Lima Barreto, Simões Lopes Neto and Augusto dos Anjos.

Euclides da Cunha

An acclaimed writer highly influenced by determinism, Cunha was always tormented by his family problems (he was killed by his wife's lover) and had to face political opposition because of his opinions. As a freelance journalist working for *O Estado de S. Paulo* he covered the Canudos War—a popular revolt with some egalitarian and Christian-fundamentalist traits that took place in Bahia in 1895-97. His stories, together with some essays he wrote about the people and the geography of the Brazilian North-East, were published in a thick volume called *Os Sertões* (*Rebellion in the Backlands*).

In his work Cunha put forward the revolutionary thesis that the Brazilian state was a violent and foreign entity, rejected (but often tolerated) by the vast majority of the illiterate and dispossessed population, some of whom preserved beliefs and behaviours that had not changed in a thousand years or more. He discovered, for instance, that Sebastianism was then present in the Brazilian North-East and that many medieval Portuguese rhymes, folk-tales and traditions were still kept by the coarse people of the "sertões". This population did not accept secularism, the Republican government and, especially, justice or peace.

His trilogy Os Sertões is composed of three parts titled "The Land", "The Man" and "The fight". Such organization of the book reinforces the idea that the environment where a man was born, the social aspects of his residence and the man's culture may define what he will become. This principle is known as determinism, a way of thought that deeply influenced Brazilian literature during the mid- and late 19th century and the early 20th century.

Figure 468: *Euclides da Cunha*

Figure 469: *Lima Barreto*

Figure 470: *Augusto dos Anjos*

Modernism

Modernism began in Brazil with the Week of Modern Art, in 1922. The *1922 Generation* was a nickname for the writers Mário de Andrade (*Paulicéia Desvairada*, *Macunaíma*), Oswald de Andrade (*Memórias Sentimentais de João Miramar*), Manuel Bandeira, Cassiano Ricardo and others, all of whom combined nationalist tendencies with an interest in European modernism. Some new movements such as surrealism were already important in Europe, and began to take hold in Brazil during this period.

Mário de Andrade

Mário de Andrade was born in São Paulo. He worked as a professor and was one of the organizers of the Week of Modern Art. He researched Brazilian folklore and folk music and used it in his books, avoiding the European style. His Brazilian anti-hero is Macunaíma, a product of ethnical and cultural mixture. Andrade's interest in folklore and his use of colloquial language were extremely influential.

Oswald de Andrade

Oswald de Andrade, another participant in the Week of Modern Art in 1922, worked as a journalist in São Paulo. Born into a wealthy family, he travelled to Europe several times. Of the generation of 1922, Oswald de Andrade best represents the rebellious characteristics of the modernist movement. He is the author of the *Manifesto Antropófago (Cannibal Manifesto)* (1927), in which he says it is necessary that Brazil, like a cannibal, eat foreign culture and, in digestion, create its own culture.

30's generation

After the modernist critique there was a generation of writers which actually "regressed" in terms of "modernist" ideas of experimentation, and which instead focused on social criticism. In literary criticism however they are mostly regarded as a development within modernism and grouped within the term "Geração de 30"(30's generation).

Jorge Amado, one of best-known of modern Brazilian writers, tried with his novels to approximate his works to a proletarian literature, he himself was a member of the communist party which defended Socialist realism at the time.

Rachel de Queiroz, and José Lins do Rego were other important writers of this generation.

Figure 471: *Mario de Andrade*

Figure 472: *Oswald de Andrade*

Figure 473: *José Lins do Rego*

Figure 474: *Jorge Amado*

Post-Modernism

What defined Brazilian modernism were two main traits: experiments in language and an enhanced social consciousness, or a mix between the two - as was the case with Oswald de Andrade, who was briefly attracted towards the communist movement. The reaction to modernism, then, assumed the form of a mix between its most salient trait, the use of more formal literary language (as was the case of the so-called "generation of 1945", whose twin hallmarks were, firstly, the highly physical poetry of João Cabral de Melo Neto, who opposed Carlos Drummond de Andrade's poetic modernism, and secondly the sonnets - on both the Italian and English model - of the early Vinicius de Moraes), followed by varying doses, according to the author considered, of subjectivism, political conservatism and militant Catholicism.

Two writers from that "school" that have published after the 1950s are without a doubt already inside the canon of Brazilian literature: Clarice Lispector, whose existentialist novels and short stories are filled with stream-of-consciousness and epiphanies, and João Guimarães Rosa, whose experimental language has changed the face of Brazilian literature forever. His novel *Grande Sertão: Veredas* has been compared to James Joyce's *Ulysses* or Alfred Döblin's *Berlin Alexanderplatz* and featured in the Bokklubben World

Library list of 100 best novels of all time. João Guimarães Rosa is considered by many to be the greatest Brazilian writer.

Following the wake of conservative subjectivism inaugurated by the militantly Catholic novelists-cum-polemicists Octavio de Faria, Lúcio Cardoso, Cornélio Penna and Gustavo Corção, Nelson Rodrigues made his career as a playwright and sports journalist. His plays and short stories - the latter mostly originally published as newspaper *feuilletons* - chronicled the social mores of the 1950s and 1960s; adultery and sexual pathologies in general being a major fixation of his. His sports writing describes the evolution of football into the national passion of Brazil. He was heavily critical of the young leftists who opposed the military dictatorship after the 1964 coup; for that he was penned as right-wing and conservative. For a time heavily pro-dictatorship, he had to suffer the tragic fate of having one of his sons being tortured and incarcerated for belonging to an underground guerrilla organization.

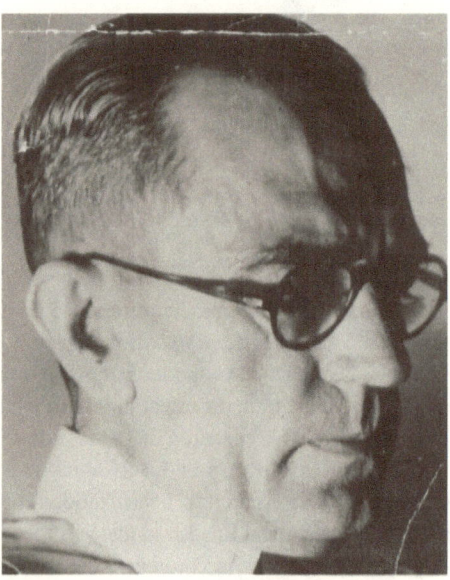

Figure 475: *Graciliano Ramos*

Figure 476: *Cecília Meireles*

Figure 477: *Guimarães Rosa*

Figure 478: *Lêdo Ivo*

Figure 479: *Clarice Lispector*

Figure 480: *Vinicius de Moraes*

Figure 481: *Rachel de Queiroz*

Contemporary

Contemporary Brazilian literature is, on the whole, very much focused on city life and all its aspects: loneliness, violence, political issues and media control. Writers like Rubem Fonseca, Sérgio Sant'Anna have written important books with these themes in the 1970s, breaking new ground in Brazilian literature, up until then mostly having dealt with rural life.

New trends since the 1980s have included works by authors such as João Gilberto Noll, Milton Hatoum, Bernardo Carvalho, João Almino, Adriana Lisboa and Cristovão Tezza.

Poets such as Ferreira Gullar and Manoel de Barros are among the most acclaimed within literary circles in Brazil, the former had been nominated for the Nobel Prize.

In recent years, "marginal literature" has risen to prominence with authors and poets such as Sérgio Vaz and Ferréz making appearances at important events like Festa Literária Internacional de Paraty, Flipside and Bienal do Livro de São Paulo. Other poets such as Adélia Prado, Elisa Lucinda, Luis Alexandre Ribeiro Branco, are among the contemporary poets.

Figure 482: *Lygia Fagundes Telles*

Figure 483: *João Ubaldo Ribeiro*

Figure 484: *Moacyr Scliar*

Bibliography

- Galvão, Walnice Nogueira (2005). *As Musas sob Assédio: Literatura e indústria cultural no Brasil* (in Portuguese).
- Coutinho, Afrânio (2004). *A Literatura no Brasil* (in Portuguese).
- Lopes, Denilson (2007). *A Delicadeza: estética, experiência e paisagens* (in Portuguese).

Further reading

- (in Spanish) Arce, Emilia Isabel. " La institucionalización del rol materno durante gobiernos autoritarios: respuestas de escritoras argentinas y brasileñas a la construcción patriarcal de género y nación[1531]". (Archive[1532]) (PhD thesis). University of Texas at Austin, May 2009. (English abstract included.)

Cuisine

Brazilian cuisine

Part of a series on
Brazilian cuisine
Types of food
- Main dishes - Desserts - Drinks
See also
- Etiquette - Cookbook: Cuisine of Brazil
- **Brazil portal**
- v - t - e[1533]

Part of a series on the
Culture of Brazil |//

History
People
Languages
Cuisine
Religion
Art
Literature
Sport
• Brazil portal
• v • t • e[1534]

Brazilian cuisine is the set of cooking practices and traditions of Brazil, and is characterized by African, Amerindian, Asian (mostly japanese) and European influences. It varies greatly by region, reflecting the country's mix of native and immigrant populations, and its continental size as well. This has created a national cuisine marked by the preservation of regional differences.

Ingredients first used by native peoples in Brazil include *cassava*, *guaraná*, *açaí*, *cumaru*, *cashew* and *tucupi*. From there, the many waves of immigrants brought some of their typical dishes, replacing missing ingredients with local equivalents. For instance, the European immigrants (primarily from Portugal, Italy, Spain, Germany, Poland and Switzerland) were accustomed to a wheat-based diet, and introduced wine, leafy vegetables, and dairy products into Brazilian cuisine. When potatoes were not available they discovered how to use the native sweet manioc as a replacement. Enslaved Africans also had a role in developing Brazilian cuisine, especially in the coastal states. The foreign influence extended to later migratory waves – Japanese immigrants brought most of the food items that Brazilians would associate with Asian cuisine today,[1535] and introduced large-scale aviaries, well into the 20th century.[1536]

Root vegetables such as cassava (locally known as *mandioca*, *aipim* or *macaxeira*, among other names), yams, and fruit like açaí, cupuaçu, mango, papaya, guava, orange, passion fruit, pineapple, and hog plum are among the local ingredients used in cooking.

Some typical dishes are feijoada, considered the country's national dish;[1537] and regional foods such as beiju, feijão tropeiro, vatapá, moqueca, polenta (from Italian cuisine) and acarajé (from African cuisine).[1538] There is also *caruru*, which consists of okra, onion, dried shrimp, and toasted nuts (peanuts or cashews), cooked with palm oil until a spread-like consistency is reached; *moqueca capixaba*, consisting of slow-cooked fish, tomato, onions and garlic, topped with cilantro; and *linguiça*, a mildly spicy sausage.

The national beverage is coffee, while cachaça is Brazil's native liquor. Cachaça is distilled from sugar cane and is the main ingredient in the national cocktail, caipirinha.

Cheese buns (*pães-de-queijo*), and *salgadinhos* such as *pastéis*, *coxinhas*, *risólis* (from pierogy of Polish cuisine) and *kibbeh* (from Arabic cuisine) are common finger food items, while *cuscuz branco* (milled tapioca) is a popular dessert.

Regional cuisines

There is not an exact single "national Brazilian cuisine", but there is an assortment of various regional traditions and typical dishes. This diversity is linked to the origins of the people inhabiting each dam.

For instance, the culinary in Bahia is heavily influenced by a mix of African, Indigenous and Portuguese cuisines. Chili (including chili sauces) and palm oil are very common. But in the Northern states, due to the abundance of forest and freshwater rivers, fish and cassava are staple foods. In the deep south like Rio Grande do Sul, the influence shifts more towards *gaúcho* traditions shared with its neighbors Argentina and Uruguay, with many meat based products, due to this region livestock based economy – the churrasco, a kind of barbecue, is a local tradition.

Southeast Brazil's cuisine

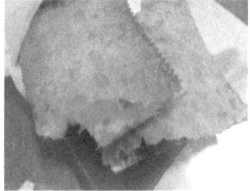

Figure 485: *Pão de queijo, coffee and a little bottle of cachaça.*

Feijoada (left) and Pastel (right)

In Rio, São Paulo, Espírito Santo and Minas Gerais, the Brazilian Feijoada (a black bean and meat stew rooted, recipe registered for the first time in Recife, state of Pernambuco) is popular especially as a Wednesday or Saturday lunch. Also consumed frequently is *picadinho* (literally, diced meat) or rice and beans.

In Rio de Janeiro, besides the *feijoada*, a popular plate is any variation of grilled bovine fillet, rice and beans, farofa and French fries, commonly called *Filé à Osvaldo Aranha*. Seafood is very popular in coastal areas, as is roasted chicken (*galeto*). The strong Portuguese heritage also endowed the city with a taste for bolinhos de bacalhau (fried cod balls), being one of the most common street foods there.

In São Paulo, a typical dish is *virado à paulista*, made with rice, *tutu de feijão*, sauteed kale, and pork. São Paulo is also the home of pastel, a food consisting of thin pastry envelopes wrapped around assorted fillings, then deep fried in vegetable oil. It is a common belief that they originated when Japanese immigrants adapted the recipe of fried spring rolls to sell as snacks at weekly street markets.

In Minas Gerais, the regional dishes include corn, pork, beans, chicken (including the very typical dish *frango com quiabo*, or chicken with okra), *tutu*

Figure 486: *Moqueca from Espírito Santo State. There are two versions of Moqueca Recipe Dish inside Brazil: The Moqueca Capixaba and The Moqueca Baiana. The Capixaba Moqueca is a dish made with no palm oil, bell pepper or coconut milk in its ingredients, and the replacement for these ingredients left are: using of Annatto Spice and Sweet Olive oil Sauce with fresh Tomato and its found in the Brazilian Espírito Santo State, and Moqueca Baiana version is found in Brazilian State of Bahia*

de feijão (paste of beans and cassava flour), and local soft ripened traditional cheeses.

In Espírito Santo, there is significant Italian and German influence in local dishes, both savory and sweet.Wikipedia:Citation needed The state dish, though, is of Amerindian origin,Wikipedia:Citation needed called *moqueca capixaba* which is a tomato and fish stew prepared in a Panela de Barro(clay pot). Amerindian and Italian cuisine are the two main pillars of Capixaba cuisine. Seafood dishes in general are very popular in Espírito Santo but unlike other Amerindian dishes the use of olive oil is almost mandatory. Bobó de camarão, Torta Capixaba, Polenta are also very popular.

North Brazil's cuisine

The cuisine of this region, which includes the states of Acre, Amazonas, Amapá, Pará, Rondônia, Roraima, and Tocantins, is heavily influenced by indigenous cuisine. In the state of Pará, there are several typical dishes including:

Figure 487: *Stuffed Blue Crab Shells known as Casquinha de Siri being enjoyed in one of a Rio de Janeiro City's restaurant, in the West Zone of Rio de Janeiro City.*

Figure 488: *Cooked Crab*

Brazilian cuisine

Figure 489: *Cooked Crab with Tomato Sauce, being enjoyed in a restaurant in Rio de Janeiro*

Figure 490: *Frango à Passarinho or Chicken Bird Dish being enjoyed in a restaurant in the south of Brazilian State of Minas.*

Figure 491: *Vatapá*

Pato no tucupi (duck in tucupi) – one of the most famous dishes from Pará. It is associated to the *Círio de Nazaré*, a great local Roman Catholic celebration. The dish is made with *tucupi* (yellow broth extracted from cassava, after the fermentation process of the broth remained after the starch had been taken off, from the raw ground manioc root, pressed by a cloth, with some water; if added maniva, the manioc ground up external part, that is poisonous because of the cyanic acid, and so must be cooked for several days). The duck, after cooking, is cut into pieces and boiled in *tucupi*, where is the sauce for some time. The *jambu* is boiled in water with salt, drained and put on the duck. It is served with white rice and manioc flour and corn tortillas

Center-West Brazil's cuisine

In the state of Goiás, the pequi is used in a lot of typical foods, specially the "arroz com pequi" (rice cooked with pequi), and in snacks, mostly as a filling for pastel. Also, a mixture of chicken and rice known as galinhada is very popular.

Northeast Brazil's cuisine

The Brazilian Northeastern cuisine is heavily influenced by African cuisine from the coastal areas of Pernambuco to Bahia, as well as the eating habits of indigenous populations that lived in the region.

Figure 492: *Bobó de camarão.*

The *vatapá* is a Brazilian dish made from bread, shrimp, coconut milk, finely ground peanuts and palm oil mashed into a creamy paste.

The Bobó de camarão is a dish made with cassava and shrimp (camarão).

The acarajé is a dish made from peeled black-eyed peas formed into a ball and then deep-fried in *dendê* (palm oil). Often sold as street food, it is served split in half and then stuffed with *vatapá* and *caruru*. Acarajé is typically available outside of the state of Bahia as well, including the markets of Rio de Janeiro.

In other areas, more to the west or away from the coast, the plates are most reminiscent of the indigenous cuisine, with many vegetables being cultivated in the area since before the arrival of the Portuguese. Examples include *baião de dois*, made with rice and beans, dried meat, butter, *queijo coalho* and other ingredients. Jaggery is also heavily identified with the Northeast, as it is *carne-de-sol*, *paçoca de pilão*, and *bolo de rolo*.

Tapioca flatbreads or pancakes are also commonly served for breakfast in some states, with a filling of either coconut, cheese or condensed milk, butter, and certain meats. They can also be filled with dessert toppings as well.

Southern Brazil's cuisine

In Southern Brazil, due to the long tradition in livestock production and the heavy German immigration, red meat is the basis of the local cuisine.

Besides many of the pasta, sausage and dessert dishes common to continental Europe, *churrasco* is the term for a barbecue (similar to the Argentine, Uruguayan, Paraguayan and Chilean asado) which originated in southern Brazil. It contains a variety of meats which may be cooked on a purpose-built "churrasqueira", a barbecue grill, often with supports for spits or skewers. Portable "churrasqueiras" are similar to those used to prepare the Argentine, Chilean, Paraguayan and Uruguayan asado, with a grill support, but many Brazilian "churrasqueiras" do not have grills, only the skewers above the embers. The meat may alternatively be cooked on large metal or wood skewers resting on a support or stuck into the ground and roasted with the embers of charcoal (wood may also be used, especially in the State of Rio Grande do Sul).

Since gaúchos were nomadic and lived off the land, they had no way of preserving food, the gauchos would gather together after butchering a cow, and skewer and cook the large portions of meat immediately over a wood burning fire. The slow-cooked meat basted in its own juices and resulted in tender, flavorful steaks. This style would carry on to inspire many contemporary churrascaria which emulate the cooking style where waiters bring large cuts of roasted meat to diners' tables and carve portions to order.

The *chimarrão* is the regional beverage, often associated with the gaúcho image.

Popular dishes

- **Rice and beans** is an extremely popular dish, considered basic at table; a tradition Brazil shares with several Caribbean nations. Brazilian rice and beans usually are cooked utilizing either lard or the nowadays more common edible vegetable fats and oils, in a variation of the Mediterranean sofrito locally called *refogado* which usually includes garlic in both recipes.
- In variation to rice and beans, Brazilians usually eat pasta (including spaghetti, lasagne, *yakisoba, lamen,* and *bīfun*), pasta salad, various dishes using either potato or manioc, and polenta as substitutions for rice, as well as salads, dumplings or soups of green peas, chickpeas, black-eyed peas, broad beans, butter beans, soybeans, lentils, *moyashi* (which came to Brazil due to the Japanese tradition of eating its sprouts), *azuki,* and other

Figure 493: *Coxinha is a popular Brazilian snack.*

Figure 494: *Brazilian cheese.*

legumes in substitution for the common beans cultivated in South America since Pre-Columbian times. It is more common to eat substitutions for daily rice and beans in festivities such as Christmas and New Year's Eve (the tradition is lentils), as follow-up of *churrasco* (mainly potato salad/carrot salad, called *maionese*, due to the widespread use of both industrial and home-made mayonnaise, which can include egg whites, raw onion, green peas, sweetcorn or even chayote squashes, and pronounced almost exactly as in English and French) and in other special occasions.

- Either way the basis of Brazilian daily cuisine is the starch (most often a cereal), legume, protein and vegetable combination. There is also a differentiation between vegetables of the *verduras* group, or greens, and the *legumes* group (no relation to the botanic concept), or non-green vegetables.
- **Salgadinhos** are small savoury snacks (literally *salties*). Similar to Spanish *tapas*, these are mostly sold in corner shops and a staple at working class and lower middle-class familiar celebrations. There are many types of pastries:
  - **Pão de queijo** (literally "cheese bread"), a typical Brazilian snack, is a small, soft roll made of manioc flour, eggs, milk, and minas cheese. It can be bought ready-made at a corner store or frozen and ready to bake in a supermarket and is gluten-free.
  - **Coxinha** is a chicken croquette shaped like a chicken thigh.
  - **Kibe/Quibe**: extremely popular, it corresponds to the Lebanese dish *kibbeh* and was brought to mainstream Brazilian culture by Syrian and Lebanese immigrants. It can be served baked, fried, or raw.
  - **Esfiha**: another Middle Eastern dish, despite being a more recent addition to Brazilian cuisine they are nowadays easily found everywhere, specially in Northeastern, Southern and Southeastern regions. They are pies/cakes with fillings like beef, mutton, cheese curd, or seasoned vegetables.
  - **Pastéis** are pastries with a wide variety of fillings. Similar to Spanish fried Empanadas but of Japanese origin (and brought to Brazil by the Japanese diaspora). Different shapes are used to tell apart the different flavours, the two most common shapes being half-moon (cheese) and square (meat). Size, flavour, and shape may vary greatly.
  - **Empadas** are snacks that resemble pot pies in a small scale. Filled with a mix of palm hearts, peas, flour and chicken or shrimp.
- **Misto-quente** is grilled ham and cheese sandwich.
- **Cuscuz branco** is a dessert consisting of milled tapioca cooked with coconut milk and sugar and is the couscous equivalent of rice pudding.
- **Açaí, cupuaçu, carambola**, and many other tropical fruits are shipped from the Amazon Rainforest and consumed in smoothies or as fresh fruit.

Other aspects of Amazonian cuisine are also gaining a following.
- **Cachorro-quente** is the Brazilian version of hot dogs, usually garnished with tomato sauce, corn, peas and potato chips.
- Cheese: the dairy-producing state of Minas Gerais is known for such cheeses as Queijo Minas, a soft, mild-flavored fresh white cheese usually sold packaged in water; requeijão, a mildly salty, silky-textured, spreadable cheese sold in glass jars and eaten on bread; and Catupiry, a soft processed cheese sold in a distinctive round wooden box.
- Pinhão is the pine nut of the *Araucaria angustifolia*, a common tree in the highlands of southern Brazil. The nuts are boiled and eaten as a snack in the winter months. It is typically eaten during the festas juninas.
- *Risoto* (risotto) is a rice dish cooked with chicken, shrimp, and seafood in general or other protein staples sometimes served with vegetables, another very popular dish in Southern Brazil.
- Mortadella sandwich
- Sugarcane juice, mixed with fruit juices such as pineapple or lemon.
- **Angu** is a popular side dish (or a substitution for the rice fulfilling the "starch element" of use common in Southern and Southeastern Brazil). It is similar to the Italian polenta.
- **Arroz com pequi** is a traditional dish from the Brazilian Cerrado, and the symbol of Center-Western Brazil's cuisine. It is basically made with rice seasoned on pequi, also known as a souari nut, and often chicken.

Also noteworthy are:

- Special ethnic foods and restaurants that are frequently found in Brazil include Arab cuisine (Lebanese and Syrian), local variations of Chinese cuisine (nevertheless closer to the traditional than American Chinese cuisine), Italian cuisine, and Japanese cuisine (sushi bars are a constant in major metropolises, and people from Rio de Janeiro are more used to *temaki* than people from São Paulo, home of more than 70% of the Japanese diaspora in the country).
- **Pizza** is also extremely popular. It is usually made in a wood-fire oven with a thin, flexible crust, little or very little sauce, and a number of interesting toppings. In addition to the "traditional" Italian pizza toppings, items like guava cheese and Minas cheese, banana and cinnamon, poultry (either milled chicken meat or smoked turkey breast) and catupiry, and chocolate are available. Traditionally olive oil is poured over the pizza, but in some regions people enjoy ketchup, mustard and even mayonnaise on pizza.
- Brazil nut cake is a cake in Brazilian cuisine that is common and popular in the Amazon region of Brazil, Bolivia and Peru
- *Broa*, corn bread with fennel.

Drinks

- Cachaça is Brazil's native liquor, distilled from sugar cane, and it is the main ingredient in the national drink, the Caipirinha. Other drinks include mate tea, chimarrão and tereré (both made up of yerba maté), coffee, fruit juice, beer (mainly Pilsen variety), rum, guaraná and batidas. Guaraná is a caffeinated soft drink made from guaraná seeds and batida is a type of fruit punch.

Figure 495: *Brazilian Cachaça*

Figure 496: *Caipirinha, a national drink*

Figure 497: *Chimarrão*

Typical and popular desserts

Brazil has a variety of candies such as brigadeiros (chocolate fudge balls), cocada (a coconut sweet), beijinhos (coconut truffles and clove) and romeu e julieta (cheese with a guava jam known as goiabada). Peanuts are used to make paçoca, rapadura and pé-de-moleque. Local common fruits like açaí, cupuaçu, mango, papaya, cocoa, cashew, guava, orange, passionfruit, pineapple, and hog plum are turned in juices and used to make chocolates, popsicles and ice cream.[1539]

Typical cakes (*Bolos*)

- *Nega maluca* (chocolate cake with chocolate cover and chocolate sprinkles)
- *Pão de mel* (honey cake, somewhat resembling gingerbread, usually covered with melted chocolate)
- *Bolo de rolo* (roll cake, a thin mass wrapped with melted guava)
- *Bolo de cenoura* (carrot cake with chocolate cover made with butter and cocoa)
- *Bolo prestígio* (chocolate cake with a coconut and milk cream filling, covered with brigadeiro)
- *Bolo de fubá* (corn flour cake)

Figure 498: *Bolo de rolo*

- *Bolo de milho* (Brazilian-style corn cake)
- *Bolo de maracujá* (passion fruit cake)
- *Bolo de mandioca* (cassava cake)
- *Bolo de queijo* (literally "cheese cake")
- *Bolo de laranja* (orange cake)
- *Bolo de banana* (banana cake spread with cinnamon)

Other popular and traditional desserts

- Fig, papaya, mango, orange, citron, pear, peach, pumpkin, sweet potato (among others) sweets and preserves, often eaten with solid fresh cheese or doce de leite.
- *Quindim* (egg custard with coconut)
- *Brigadeiro* (a Brazilian chocolate candy)
- *Biscoitos de maizena* (cornstarch cookies)
- *Beijinho* (coconut "truffles" with clove)
- *Cajuzinho* (peanut and cashew "truffles")
- *Cocada* (coconut sweet)
- *Olho-de-sogra*
- *Pudim de pão* (literally "bread pudding", a pie made with bread "from yesterday" immersed in milk instead of flour (plus the other typical pie ingredients like eggs, sugar etc.) with dried orange slices and clove)
- *Manjar branco* (coconut pudding with caramel cover and dried plums)

Brazilian cuisine 927

Figure 499: *A Brazilian chocolate candy (Brigadeiro).*

Figure 500: *Paçoca*

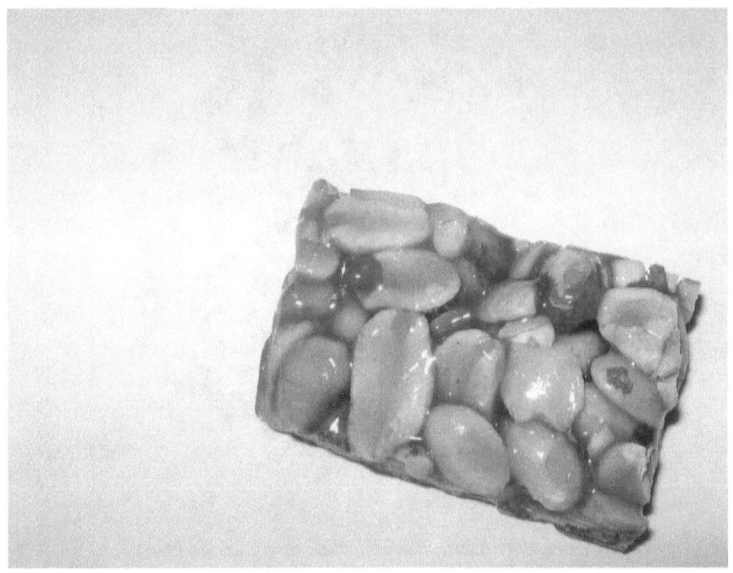

Figure 501: *Pé-de-moleque*

Figure 502: *Rapadura*

- *Doce de leite*
- *Arroz-doce* (rice pudding)
- *Canjica* (similar to rice pudding, but made with white corn)
- *Romeu e Julieta*: *goiabada* (guava cheese) with white cheese (most often Minas cheese or requeijão)
- *Torta de Limão* (literally "Lime Pie", a shortcrust pastry with creamy lime-flavored filling)
- *Pé-de-moleque* (made with peanuts and sugar caramel)
- *Paçoca* (similar to Spanish *polvorones*, but made with peanuts instead of almonds and without addition of fats)
- *Pudim de leite* (condensed milk-based crème caramel, of French origin)
- *Brigadeirão* (a *pudim de leite* with chocolate or a chocolate cake)
- *Rapadura*
- *Doce de banana* (different types of banana sweets, solid or creamy)
- *Maria-mole*
- *Pamonha* (a traditional Brazilian food made from fresh corn and milk wrapped in corn husks and boiled). It can be savoury or sweet.
- *Papo-de-anjo*
- "Açaí na tigela" (usually consists of an açaí (Brazilian fruit) mixture with bananas and cereal or strawberries and cereal (usually granola or muslix))
- Avocado cream (avocado, lime and confectionery sugar; blended and chilled)

Daily meals

- Breakfast,[1] the *café-da-manhã* (literally, "morning coffee"): Every region has its own typical breakfast. It usually consists of a light meal, and it is not uncommon to have only a fruit or slice of bread and a cup of coffee. Traditional items include tropical fruits, typical cakes, crackers, bread, butter, cold cuts, cheese, requeijão, honey, jam, doce de leite, coffee (usually sweetened and with milk), juice, chocolate milk, or tea.
- Elevenses or brunch,[2] the *lanche-da-manhã* (literally, "morning snack"): Usually had between 9 and 11 am, consists of similar items as people have for breakfast.
- Midday dinner or lunch,[1] the *almoço*: This is usually the biggest meal and the most common times range from 11 am to 2 pm. Traditionally, people will go back to their houses to have lunch with their families, although nowadays that is not possible for most people, in which case it is common to have lunch in groups at restaurants or cafeterias. Rice is a staple of the Brazilian diet, albeit it is not uncommon to eat pasta instead. It is usually eaten together with beans and accompanied by salad, protein (most

Figure 503: *A Brazilian breakfast buffet.*

commonly red meat or chicken) and a side dish, such as polenta, potatoes, corn, etc...
- Tea,[2] the *lanche-da-tarde* or *café-da-tarde* (literally "afternoon snack" or "afternoon coffee"): It is a meal had between lunch and dinner, and basically everything people eat in the breakfast, they also eat in the afternoon snack. Nevertheless, fruits are less common.
- Night dinner or supper,[1] the *jantar*: For most Brazilians, *jantar* is a light affair, while others dine at night. Sandwiches, soups, salads, pasta, hamburgers or hot-dogs, pizza or repeating midday dinner foods are the most common dishes.
- Late supper,[2] the *ceia*: Brazilians eat soups, salads, pasta and what would be eaten at the elevenses if their *jantar* was a light one early at the evening and it is late at night or dawn. It is associated with Christmas and New Year's Eve.

[1] Main meals, that are served nearly everywhere, and are eaten in nearly all households above poverty line.
[2] Secondary meals. People usually have a meal at the tea time, while elevenses and late suppers depend in peculiarities on one's daily routine or certain diets.

Restaurant styles

A simple and usually inexpensive option, which is also advisable for vegetarians, is comida a quilo or comida por quilo restaurants (literally "food by kilo value"), a buffet where food is paid for by weight. Another common style is the all-you-can-eat restaurant where customers pay a prix fixe. In both types (known collectively as "self-services"), customers usually assemble the dishes of their choice from a large buffet.

Rodízio is a common style of service, in which a prix fixe is paid, and servers circulate with food. This is common in churrascarias, pizzerias and sushi (Japanese cuisine) restaurants, resulting in an all-you-can-eat meat barbecue and pizzas of varied flavours, usually one slice being served at the time.

The regular restaurant where there is a specific price for each meal is called "restaurante à la carte".

Vegetarian

Although many traditional dishes are prepared with meat or fish, it is not difficult to live on vegetarian food as well, at least in the mid-sized and larger cities of Brazil. There is a rich supply of all kinds of fruits and vegetables, and on city streets one can find cheese buns (*pão de queijo*); in some cities even the version made of soy.

In the 2000s, São Paulo, Rio de Janeiro and Porto Alegre have gained several vegetarian and vegan restaurants. However outside big metropolises, vegetarianism is not very common in the country. Not every restaurant will provide vegetarian dishes and some seemingly vegetarian meals may turn out to include unwanted ingredients, for instance, using lard for cooking beans. Commonly "meat" is understood to mean "red meat," so some people might assume a vegetarian eats fish and chicken. *Comida por quilo* and all-you-can eat restaurants prepare a wide range of fresh dishes. Diners can more easily find food in such restaurants that satisfies dietary restrictions.

External links

- Media related to Cuisine of Brazil at Wikimedia Commons

Cinema

Cinema of Brazil

Cinema of Brazil	
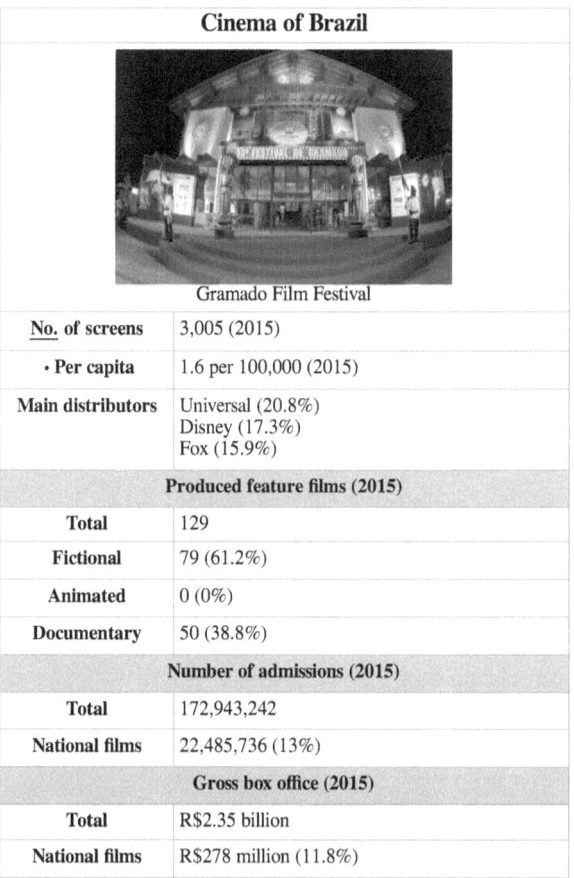 Gramado Film Festival	
No. of screens	3,005 (2015)
• Per capita	1.6 per 100,000 (2015)
Main distributors	Universal (20.8%) Disney (17.3%) Fox (15.9%)
Produced feature films (2015)	
Total	129
Fictional	79 (61.2%)
Animated	0 (0%)
Documentary	50 (38.8%)
Number of admissions (2015)	
Total	172,943,242
National films	22,485,736 (13%)
Gross box office (2015)	
Total	R$2.35 billion
National films	R$278 million (11.8%)

Cinema of Brazil
List of Brazilian films
Pre 1920
1920s
1930s
1930 1931 1932 1933 1934 1935 1936 1937 1938 1939
1940s
1940 1941 1942 1943 1944 1945 1946 1947 1948 1949
1950s
1950 1951 1952 1953 1954 1955 1956 1957 1958 1959
1960s
1960 1961 1962 1963 1964 1965 1966 1967 1968 1969
1970s
1970 1971 1972 1973 1974 1975 1976 1977 1978 1979

Cinema of Brazil

1980s
1980 1981 1982 1983 1984 1985 1986 1987 1988 1989
1990s
1990 1991 1992 1993 1994 1995 1996 1997 1998 1999
2000s
2000 2001 2002 2003 2004 2005 2006 2007 2008 2009
2010s
2010 2011 2012 2013 2014 2015 2016 2017
• $\underline{v}$ • $\underline{t}$ • $\underline{e}^{1540}$

Brazilian cinema was introduced early in the 20th century but took some time to consolidate itself as a popular form of entertainment. The film industry of Brazil has gone through periods of ups and downs, a reflection of its dependency on state funding and incentives.

History

Early days

A couple of months after the Lumière brothers' invention, a film exhibition was held in Rio de Janeiro. As early as 1898, the Italian Affonso Segreto supposedly filmed the Guanabara Bay from the ship Brésil on a return journey from Europe, though some researchers question the veracity of this event as no copy of the film remains. He would go on to make documentaries with his brother Paschoal Segreto. An ad of a May 1987 issue of Gazeta de Petrópolis, as shown in 1995 by Jorge Vittorio Capellaro and Paulo Roberto Ferreira, was introduced as the new "birth certificate" of Brazilian cinema, as three short films were advertised: *Chegada do Trem em Petrópolis*, *Bailado de Crenças no Colégio de Andarahy* and *Ponto Terminal da Linha dos Bondes de Botafogo, Vendo-se os Passageiros Subir e Descer*.

During this "belle-epoque" of Brazilian cinema, when black and white silent films were less costly to produce, most work resulted from the effort of passionate individuals willing to take on the task themselves rather than commercial enterprises. Neither is much attention given by the state, with legislation for the sector being practically nonexistent. Film theaters only become larger in number in Rio and São Paulo late in the following decade, as power supply becomes more reliable. Foreign films as well as short films documenting local events were most common. Some of the first fictional work filmed in the country were the so-called "posed" films, reconstitutions of crimes that had recently made the press headlines. The first success of this genre is Francisco Marzullo's *Os Estranguladores* (1908). "Sung" films were also popular. The actors would hide behind the screen and dub themselves singing during projection. During the 1920s film production flourished throughout several regions of the country: Recife, Campinas, Cataguases, Juiz de Fora and Guaranésia.

Hollywood films were also extremely popular during this time, accounting for as much as 85 percent of film material being exhibited on Brazilian screens in 1928. That year, an estimated 16,464,000 linear feet of film was exported to Brazil, making it Hollywood's third largest foreign market. European films, mostly from Germany and France, were also exhibited with relative frequency. Fan magazines like *Cinearte* and *A Scena Muda* were published during this time, featuring both domestic and Hollywood films and stars.

1930s and 1940s

Mário Peixoto's *Limite* (1930) was poorly received by audiences but eventually regarded as masterpiece of the silent film era, along with Humberto Mauro's *Ganga Bruta* (1933). Cinédia was founded by Adhemar Gonzaga in 1930 and was dedicated to the production of popular dramas and burlesque musical comedies, a genre which was negatively referred to as *chanchada*. The *chanchada* would often include satires of Hollywood movies.

Actress Carmen Miranda gained visibility overseas. In 1946, Gilda de Abreu's *O Ébrio*, a film very much representative of typical Latin melodrama, became a major hit and drew in around four million viewers. President Getúlio Vargas became aware of film's growth and, in 1939, created a decree that guaranteed Brazilian films an exhibition quota in film theaters, a law which still exists, though it is now largely ignored due to lack of proper control. While Vargas'

Figure 504: *Carmen Miranda in Alô, Alô Carnaval (1936). The Brazilian actress gained visibility overseas.*

decree may be seen as a positive or nationalistic measure, it has also been interpreted as a means of state control and intervention.

Atlântida

During the 40's and 50's, films produced by the Atlântida Cinematográfica peaked and attracted large audiences by continuing with chanchadas. Among the actors that became strongly associated with Atlântida who had previously worked in Cinédia films are Oscarito, a comedian somewhat reminiscent of a Harpo Marx and commonly cast as lead, and Grande Otelo, who usually had a smaller supporting role and is often Oscarito's sidekick. José Lewgoy was commonly cast as a villain while Zézé Macedo often took on the role of the undesired, nagging wife.

The films of this period have often been brushed aside as being overly commercial and americanized, though by the seventies a certain amount of revisionism sought to restore its legitimacy. Despite being overlooked by intellectual elites, these films attracted large audiences as none of the Cinema Novo films would achieve. Today, the telenovela, especially the "novela das sete" (a nickname given to soap operas produced by the Rede Globo channel aired around seven p.m. Mondays through Saturdays) is sometimes identified as carrying on the spirit of the *chanchada*. Many of the films produced by the company have been lost throughout the years due to fire and flooding of its storage facilities.

Vera Cruz

The Companhia Cinematográfica Vera Cruz was a production company founded in the state of São Paulo during the forties and most notable for its output during the following decade. It is in this period that Lima Barreto's classic *O Cangaceiro* was produced. The movement was named after the large production studio, inspired in Hollywood scale. However, despite *O Cangaceiro*, which was clearly inspired in western genre, the essence of these films followed the italian cinema's style, popular between São Paulo's cultural elite in that time. Vera Cruz films were highly commercialized, which led some directors to begin experimenting with independent cinema. This movement away from commercialized Vera Cruz style films came to be called Cinema Novo, or New Cinema. Vera Cruz eventually bankrupted and closed.

Cinema Novo

The Italian Neorealism followed later in the sixties by the French New Wave (or Nouvelle Vague) fueled a new kind of modernistic and experimental cinema across the globe. In Brazil, this tendency was carried out by its own new wave movement, the Cinema Novo. Glauber Rocha, a very political filmmaker from Bahia, quickly became the most notable director, often held as "leader" of the movement. His work possesses many allegorical elements, strong political critique and an impeccable mise-en-scène that were readily embraced by intellectuals.

Rocha often spoke of his films as being a departure from what he considered to be the colonizer's view, to whom poverty was an exotic and distant reality, as well as the colonized who regarded their third world status as shameful. He sought to portray misery, hunger and the violence they generate and thus suggest the need for a revolution. *Deus e o Diabo na Terra do Sol* and *Terra em Transe* are some of his most famous works.

Other key directors of the movement include Nelson Pereira dos Santos, Ruy Guerra, Leon Hirszman, and Carlos Diegues. Freedom to express political views becomes scarce as the 1964 Brazilian coup d'état takes place and repression increases over the following years, forcing many of these artists into exile.

B Films

A "marginal cinema" emerges associated with the Boca de Lixo area in São Paulo. In 1968, Rogério Sganzerla releases *O Bandido da Luz Vermelha*, a story based on an infamous criminal of the period. The following year Júlio Bressane's *Killed the Family and Went to the Movies* (*Matou a família e foi ao cinema*) came out, a story in which the protagonist does exactly what is described by the title. Marginal cinema of this period is sometimes also referred to as "udigrudi", a mocking of the English word underground. Also popular was Zé do Caixão, the screen alter ego of actor and horror film director José Mojica Marins.

Associated with the genre is also the pornochanchada, a popular genre in the 1970s. As the name suggests, these were sex comedies, though they did not depict sex explicitly. One key factor as to why these marginal films thrived was that film theaters were obliged to obey quotas for national films. Many owners of such establishments would finance low-budget films, including those of pornographic content. Though the country was under dictatorship, censorship tended to be more political than cultural. That these films thrived could be perceived by many as a cause of embarrassment, yet they managed to draw in enough audiences so as to stay on the market consistently throughout those years.

1970s and 1980s

Films in this period benefited from state-run agencies, most notably Embrafilme. Its role was perceived as somewhat ambiguous. It was criticized for its dubious selection criteria, bureaucracy and favouritism, and was seen as a form of government control over artistic production. On the other hand, much of the work of this period was produced mainly because of its existence.

A varied and memorable filmography was produced, including Arnaldo Jabor's adaptation of Nelson Rodrigues' *All Nudity Shall Be Punished* (1973), Carlos Diegues' *Bye Bye Brazil* (1979), Hector Babenco's *Pixote* (1981) and Nelson Pereira do Santos' *Memoirs of Prison* (1984). One of the most successful films in Brazilian film history is an adaptation of Jorge Amado's *Dona Flor and Her Two Husbands* (1976) by Bruno Barreto.

A peak in the number of film theaters is reached in 1975, when 3,276 projection rooms were in existence. Brazilian films sold a total of 275.4 million tickets the same year.

Figure 505: *Fernanda Montenegro, mostly recognized for her leading role in Central Station, for which she was nominated for the Academy Award for Best Actress, becoming the first and only Brazilian actress to ever be nominated in the category. Also for this work, she was nominated for the Golden Globe Award for Best Actress – Motion Picture Drama and won the Silver Bear at the Berlin International Film Festival.*

Retomada and contemporary cinema

The early nineties, under the Collor government, saw a significant decrease in State funding that lead to a practical halt in film production and the closing of Embrafilme in 1989. However, in the mid nineties the country witnessed a new burst in cinematic production, mainly thanks to the introduction of incentive laws under the new FHC government. The comedy *Carlota Joaquina - Princess of Brazil* came out in 1995 and is held by many as the first film of the *retomada*, or the return of national film production. Since then there have been films with Academy Award nominations such as *O Quatrilho*, *Four Days in September*, *Central Station* and *City of God*. The dark urban film *O Invasor* was chosen as the best film of the period by magazine Revista de Cinema. Some other films that have attracted attention are *Carandiru*, *O Homem Que Copiava*, *Madame Satã*, *Abril Despedaçado*, *Olga* and *Dois Filhos de Francisco*, though perhaps some of these would no longer qualify as films of the *retomada*, since the term is only adequate to describe the initial boost that occurred in the nineties.

Still common in Brazilian cinema is a taste for social and political criticism, a trait that reflects its strong Cinema Novo influences. Poverty, *favelas*, drought and famine are themes so common that the term "cosmética da fome", or "hunger cosmetic" (a new take on Glauber Rocha's "estética da fome", or "hunger aesthetics") was coined as a way to criticize its supposed exhaustion if not exploitation. For the common movie goer, there has been a shift in perception towards Brazilian cinema as becoming more audience friendly.

Television shows of the Rede Globo network such as *Casseta & Planeta* and *Os Normais* have also received film versions and Globo Filmes, Globo's film production branch, has been behind many of the films that have come out over the years, often as a co-producer. Globo's presence is seen by some critics as being overly commercial, thus compelling certain filmmakers to work outside its system to create independent work.

Documentaries have also had a strong place in Brazilian cinema thanks to the work of renowned directors such as Eduardo Coutinho and João Moreira Salles.

In 2007, the film *Tropa de Elite* gained headlines due to how quickly leaked DVD copies spread among viewers before its release on theaters, but also due to the large number of audience members who cheered police brutality scenes. Its depiction of drug users as crime sponsors also fueled debates on the legalisation of drugs.

Domestic market

Since the 1970s, the quantity of film theaters has declined heavily. During the 1990s, it became common for small theaters to close while multiplex theaters, which are usually found in shopping centers, gained market share. In the last decades, the accessibility of televisions sold at lower prices combined with Rede Globo's success in making telenovelas of high production quality made cinema less attractive to lower income audiences. In addition, ticket prices increased more than 10-fold in a span of 20 years.

In the early 1990s Brazilian film production suffered as a result of Collor's laissez-faire policy; the sector had depended on state sponsorship and protection. However, with the *retomada* Brazilian film regained speed, though not to the same extent it had seen before. A significant increase in audience was recorded, however, from 2000 to 2002, with 7 million viewers, to 2003, when 22 million viewers came to theaters to watch national films. Because these films were made possible thanks to incentive laws introduced in the 90's and that the number of viewers drawn in from year to year can fluctuate significantly, it is often questioned whether film production has in fact reached a certain amount of stability and whether or not it could in the future succumb to any governmental whims.

Incentive laws allow Brazilian films to receive funding from companies that, by acting as sponsors, are allowed tax deductions. A common criticism is that, through this system, though films are no longer directly controlled by state, they are, nevertheless, subject to the approval of entrepreneurs who are logically cautious as to which content they wish to associate their brands. Even with funding, there are still areas that require some struggle from filmmakers, such as distribution, television participation and DVD release.

Sources

- PINAZZA, Natália and BAYMAN, Louis (eds) (2013). 'Directory of World Cinema: Brazil. Bristol: Intellect.
- AUGUSTO, Sérgio. *Esse mundo é um pandeiro: chanchada de Getúlio a JK*. Companhia das Letras.
- BENAMOU, Catherine, and MARSH, Leslie Louise. "Women Filmmakers and Citizenship in Brazil: From *Bossa Nova* to the *Retomada*." In Hispanic and Lusophone Women Filmmakers: Theory, Practice and Differences *ed. Parvati Nari and Julián Daniel Gutierrez-Albilla, 54-71. Manchester, England: University of Manchester Press, 2013.*
- BURTON, Julianne. Cinema and Social Change in Latin America: Conversations with Filmmakers. Austin, TX: University of Texas Press, 1986.
- DENNISON, Stephanie and SHAW, Lisa. Popular Cinema in Brazil. Manchester, England: University Manchester Press, 2004.
- GOMES, Paulo Emilo Sales. *Cinema: trajetória no subdesenvolvimento*. Paz e Terra. * *30 Anos de Cinema e Festival: a história do Festival de Brasília do Cinema Brasileiro* / coordinated by Berê Bahia. Brasília, Fundação Cultural do Distrito Federal, 1998.
- CALDAS, Ricardo Wahrendorff & MONTORO, Tânia. *A Evolução do Cinema no Século XX*. Casa das Musas, Brasília, 2006.
- *Brazilian Cinema*. Ministry of Culture, Brasília 1999 (catalog).
- *Glauber Rocha: del hambre al sueño. Obra, política y pensamiento*. Malba - Colección Constantini, Artes Gráficas Ronor S.A., April 2004.
- NAGIB, Lúcia. *Brazil on Screen: Cinema Nôvo, New Cinema, Utopia*. London: IB Tauris, 2007.
- NAGIB, Lúcia, ed. *The New Brazilian Cinema*. London: I.B. Tauris & Co, 2006.
- PICK, Suzana M. *The New Latin American Cinema: A Continental Project*. Austin, TX: University of Texas Press, 1993.

- TORRES SAN MARTÍN, Patricia. "Lost and Invisible: A History of Latin American Women Filmmakers." *In Hispanic and Lusophone Women Filmmakers: Theory, Practice and Differences* ed. Parvati Nari and Julián Daniel Gutierrez-Albilla, 29-41. Manchester, England: University of Manchester Press, 2013.
- WILSON, Pamela, and Stewart, Michelle. *Global Indigenous Media: Cultures, Poetics, and Politics.* Durham, NC: Duke University Press, 2008.

Further reading

- Robert Stam: *Tropical Multiculturalism - PB: A Comparative History of Race in Brazilian Cinema and Culture* (Latin America Otherwise, Duke University Press, 1997, ISBN 0-8223-2048-7

External links

 Wikimedia Commons has media related to *Cinema of Brazil*.

- Nelson Pereira dos Santos profile by Hudson Moura[1541]
- Top 10 movies from Brazil in IMDB.com[1542]
- Brazilian Cinema: Film in the Land of Black Orpheus by Glauco Ortolano and Julie A. Porter (English)[1543]
- The Best Brazilian Films of All Time (English)[1544]
- Cinemabrasileiro.net, web about Brazilian cinema[1545]
- Atlântida Cinematográfica website (Portuguese)[1546]
- Beyond Cinema Novo by Robert Stam and Randal Johnson (English)[1547]
- CINEMA BRASIL - Instituto Cultural Cinema Brasil - Brazilian Movies database (Portuguese, English and French)[1548]
- Cinemateca Brasileira (Portuguese)[1549]
- Complete list of Brazilian movies (Portuguese)[1550]
- On Brazilian Cinema by Michael Korfmann (English)[1551]
- Text on Glauber Rocha (English)[1552]
- The Rise of the Mandacaru: Brazilian Cinema Renewed by Jorge Didaco (English)[1553]
- Vera Cruz website (Portuguese)[1554]
- Tupiniquim Japan, the largest Brazilian Film promoter in Japan[1555]
- Extensive list of Brazilian Films (English)[1556]

Visual arts

Brazilian painting

Brazilian painting, or **visual arts**, emerged in the late 16th century, influenced by the Baroque style imported from Portugal. Until the beginning of the 19th century, that style was the dominant school of painting in Brazil, flourishing across the whole of the settled territories, mainly along the coast but also in important inland centers like Minas Gerais. Major painters in this period were Ricardo do Pilar, José Joaquim da Rocha, José Teófilo de Jesus, Joaquim José da Natividade, José Eloy, Manuel de Jesus Pinto, João de Deus Sepúlveda, Manuel da Cunha, but chief among them was Manuel da Costa Ataíde, working towards the end of the 18th century, head of the first original school of painting in the country, with a delicate and somewhat personal interpretation of Rococo style in which he first depicted angels and saints with mulato features.

A sudden break with the Baroque tradition was imposed on the art of the nation by the arrival of the Portuguese court in 1808, fleeing the French invasion of Portugal. However, Baroque painting still survived in many places until the end of the 19th century. In 1816, the king, John VI, supported the project of creating a national Academy at the suggestion of some French artists led by Joachim Lebreton, a group later known as the French Artistic Mission. They were instrumental in introducing the Neoclassical style and a new concept of artistic education mirroring the European academies, being the first teachers at the newly founded school of art. Through the following 70 years, the *Royal School of Sciences, Arts and Crafts*, later renamed the Imperial Academy of Fine Arts, would dictate the standards in art, a mixed trend of Neoclassicism, Romanticism, and Realism with nationalist inclinations which would be the basis for the production of a large amount of canvases depicting the nation's history, battle scenes, landscapes, portraits, genre painting, and still lifes, and featuring national characters like black people and Indians. Victor Meirelles, Pedro Américo, and Almeida Junior were the leaders of such academic art, but

Figure 506: *Victor Meirelles: The first Mass in Brazil, 1861. Museu Nacional de Belas Artes*

this period also received important contributions from foreigners like Georg Grimm, Augusto Müller, and Nicola Antonio Facchinetti.

In 1889 the monarchy was abolished, and the republican government renamed the Imperial Academy the National School of the Fine Arts, which would be short-lived, absorbed in 1931 by the Federal University of Rio de Janeiro. Meanwhile, Modernism was already being cultivated in São Paulo and by some academic painters, and the new movement superseded Academicism. In 1922 the event called *Week of Modern Art* broke definitely with academic tradition and started a nationalist trend which was, however, influenced by Primitivism and by European Expressionism, Surrealism and Cubism. Anita Malfatti, Ismael Nery, Lasar Segall, Emiliano di Cavalcanti, Vicente do Rego Monteiro, and Tarsila do Amaral wrought major changes in painting, while groups like Santa Helena and Núcleo Bernardelli evolved toward a moderate interpretation of Modernism, with important artists such as Aldo Bonadei and José Pancetti. Cândido Portinari is the best example of this last tendency. Under government patronage he dominated Brazilian painting in the mid-20th century until Abstractionism showed up in the 1950s.

The period between 1950 and 1970 witnessed the emergence of many new styles. Action painting, Lyrical Abstraction, Neoconcretism, Neoexpressionism, Pop art, Neorealism — all contributed to some extent to the creation of

Figure 507: *Prehistoric paintings at Serra da Capivara National Park.*

huge diversity in Brazilian painting and to the updating of Brazilian art. After a period of relative decline in the conceptualist 1970s, national art revived in the 1980s under the influence of the world's renewed interest in traditional painting. Then Brazilian painting showed a new strength, spread across the whole country, and started being appreciated in international forums.

Before Discovery

Relatively little is known in respect to the pictorial art practiced in Brazil before the Portuguese discovery of the territory. The indigenous people the colonizers encountered did not practice painting as it was known in Europe, using paint for bodily decoration and the decoration of ceramic artifacts. Among the indigenous relics that survived this era, a good collection of pieces from the Marajoara, Tapajós and Santarém cultures stand out, but the ceramic tradition as much as that of body painting have been preserved by the indigenous that still reside in Brazil, the elements among them being some of the most distinctive of their cultures. There also exist diverse painted panels of hunting scenes and other figures created by pre-historic peoples in caves and on rock walls in certain archeological sites. These paintings probably had ritual functions and would have been seen as endowed with magical powers, capable of capturing the souls of depicted animals and therefore allowing for successful hunts.

Figure 508: *Belchior Paulo: Adoration of the Magi, Church of the Magi, Nova Almeida, Espírito Santo.*

The most ancient complex of sites known is that of the Serra da Capivara, at Piauí, which exhibits painted remains dated 32 thousand years ago. None of these traditions, however, was incorporated into the artistic current introduced by the Portuguese colonizers, which became predominant. As Roberto Burle Marx put it, the art of colonial Brazil is, in every sense, art of the Portuguese mother country, although on Brazilian soil various imposed adaptations have occurred through the specific local circumstances of the colonial process.

Precursors

Among the first explorers of the newly discovered land came artists and naturalists, charged with making a visual register of the flora, fauna, geography and native peoples, working only with watercolor and engraving. One can cite the Frenchman, Jean Gardien, who produced illustrations of animals for the book, *Histoire d'un Voyage faict en la terre du Brésil, autrement dite Amerique*, published in 1578 by Jean de Lery, and the priest Andre Thevet, who declared to have naturally produced all of the illustrations for his three scientific books edited in 1557, 1575, and 1584, where a portrait of the Indian Cunhambebe[1557] was included.

Such output from the travelers still displayed features of late renaissance art, also known as Mannerism, and became increasingly part of the European artistic atmosphere, for whose public it was produced, than the Brazilian, even though of larger interest were the landscape portraits and those of people from the early colonial period. The first known European painter that left work in Brazil was the Jesuit priest Manuel Sanches (or Manuel Alves), who passed through Salvador in 1560 en route to the West Indies but left at least one painted panel at the Jesuit Society school in that city. Even more noteworthy was the frier Belchior Paulo, who docked here in 1587 together with other Jesuits, and left decorative works spread out among many of the major Jesuit Society schools until his trail was abruptly lost in 1619. With Belchior, the history of Brazilian painting had effectively begun.[1558,1559]

Pernambuco and the Dutch

The first Brazilian cultural nucleus that resembled a European court was founded in Recife in 1637 by the Dutch administrator, count Maurício de Nassau. Heir of the Renaissance spirit, as described by Gouvêa, Nassau implemented a series of administrative and infrastructural reforms in what was known as, *Dutch Brazil*. Furthermore, he brought in his entourage a plethora of scientists, humanists and artists, who brought about a brilliant outside culture to the locale, and although they weren't able to reach all of their higher objectives, their presence resulted in the preparation, by white men in the tropics, of an unparalleled cultural work for the time and something considerably superior to what was being carried out by the Portuguese in other parts of the territory. Two painters stood out in their circle, Frans Post and Albert Eckhout, producing works that allied a detailed documentary character to a superlative aesthetic quality, and up to today they stand as one of the primary sources of the study of landscape, nature and life of indigenous peoples and slaves of that region. This work, though it was returned to Europe upon the departure of the count in 1644, represented, in painting, the last echo of the Renaissance aesthetic on Brazilian soil.[1560]

The Flourishing Baroque

Between the 17th and 18th Centuries the Brazilian painting style was the Baroque, a reaction against the classicism of the Renaissance, originating through the asymmetry, the excessive, the expressive, and the irregular. Far from representing a purely aesthetic tendency, these features constituted a true way of life and gave tone to the whole culture of the period, a culture that emphasized contrast, the conflict, the dynamic, the dramatic, the grandiloquent, the dissolution of limits, together with an accentuated taste for opulence of forms and materials, transforming into a perfect vehicle for the Catholic Church of the counter reform and the ascending absolute monarchies to express their ideas visually. The monumental structures raised during the Baroque, such as the palaces and the great theaters and churches, sought to create a spectacular and exuberant natural impact, offering an integration between the various artistic languages and catching the observer in a cathartic and impassioned atmosphere. For Sevcenko, no piece of Baroque artwork can be adequately analyzed divested from its context, since its nature is synthetic, binding, and compelling. This aesthetic had great approval in the Iberian Peninsula, especially in Portugal, whose culture, beyond being essentially catholic and monarchic, was filled with millenarianism and mysticism inherited from the Arabs and Jews, favoring a religiousness characterized by emotional intensity. And from Portugal the movement passed to their colony in America, where the cultural context of the indigenous peoples, marked by ritualism and festivity, supplied a receptive backdrop.[1561,1562]

The Brazilian Baroque was formed through a complex fabric of European and local influences, although generally colored by the Portuguese interpretation of the style. The context in which the Baroque developed in the colony was completely different from its European origins. Here, the environment was one of poverty and scarcity, with everything yet to be done, and contrary to Europe, within the immense colony of Brazil, there was no court, the local administration was inefficient and sluggish, opening a vast performance space for the Church and its missionary battalions, who administered in addition to divine services, a series of civil services such as issuance of birth and death certificates. They were on the vanguard of conquest of the interior of the territory, serving as evangelists and pacifiers to indigenous populations, founding

Gallery

Figure 509: *Ricardo do Pilar: The man of sorrows, 17th century*

Figure 510: *João Nepomuceno Correia e Castro: The Immaculate Conception, 18th century*

Figure 511: *Manuel de Jesus Pinto: St. Peter receiving the keys of the Church, c. 1804 – 1815.*

Figure 512: *Manuel da Costa Ataíde: Our Lady surrounded by musician angels, early 19th century.*

Brazilian painting

Figure 513: *Simplício de Sá: Portrait of emperor Peter I, ca. 1830.*

Figure 514: *Agostinho José da Mota: Still-life, 1860*

Figure 515: *Victor Meirelles: Moema, 1866.*

Figure 516: *Pedro Américo: Battle of Avaí, 1872-77.*

Figure 517: *Georg Grimm: Icaraí, 1884*

Figure 518: *Almeida Junior: Model's rest, 1882.*

Figure 519: *Belmiro de Almeida: Effects of sunlight, 1893*

Figure 520: *Manuel Lopes Rodrigues: Alegory of the Republic, 1896.*

Figure 521: *Jerônimo José Telles Júnior: Wind storm, 1902*

Figure 522: *Antônio Parreiras: Sorrowful, 1909*

Figure 523: *Ismael Nery: Nude woman crouching.*

Figure 524: *Ado Malagoli: The black cat, ca. 1950.*

Figure 525: *Geraldo Trindade Leal: Ginete, 1951.*

Figure 526: *Jader Siqueira: Triptych, 1977*

Figure 527: *Carlos Carrion de Britto Velho: Painting #2, 1977.*

Figure 528: *Milton Kurtz: Quasi contacto, 1989.*

Sports

Sport in Brazil

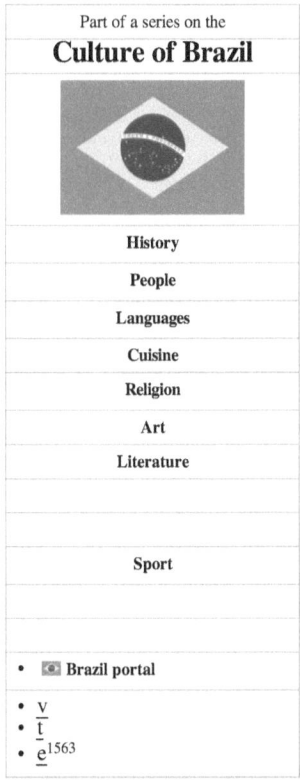

Sports in Brazil are those that are widely practiced and popular in the country, as well as others which originated there or have some cultural significance. Brazilians are heavily involved in sports. Football is the most popular sport in

Figure 529: *Brazil at 2014 FIFA World Cup.*

Brazil. Other than football, sports like volleyball, mixed martial arts, basketball, and motor sports, especially Formula One, enjoy high levels of popularity.

Football

Football is the most popular sport in Brazil. The Brazil national football team, governed by the Confederação Brasileira de Futebol, has won the FIFA World Cup a record 5 times, in 1958, 1962, 1970, 1994, and 2002,[1564] and is the only team to succeed in qualifying for every FIFA World Cup competition ever held. Brazil also hosted the 1950 and 2014 World Cups, becoming the only country in South America to have hosted two World Cups (Argentina, Uruguay, and Chile being the other former hosts). It is among the favorites to win the trophy every time the competition is scheduled. After Brazil won its third World Cup in 1970, they were awarded the Jules Rimet Trophy, when Pelé, one of the most recognized football players in history and all-time top scorer in the sport, led Brazil to three of those championships. The national football team has also won the Copa América 8 times, the Olympic football tournament once and is the most successful team in the FIFA Confederations Cup, with 4 titles. All of the leading players in the national teams are prominent in the football world, including Pelé, Zico, Garrincha, Ronaldo, Roberto Carlos, Romário, Ronaldinho, Kaká, and Neymar in the men's game, and Marta in the women's game. Some of these players can be considered super-stars, achieving celebrity status internationally and signing multi-million club contracts, as well as advertisement and endorsement deals.

Capoeira

Capoeira is an Afro-Brazilian martial art that combines elements of dance and music, and is marked by deft, tricky movements that are often played on the ground or completely inverted. It also has a strong acrobatic component in some versions and is always played with music. It is a culturally significant sport, developed in colonial times by slaves. Nowadays, capoeira is practiced internationally and found its way into popular culture, through many computer games and movies.

Brazilian jiu-jitsu, vale tudo, and mixed martial arts

Mixed martial arts is one of the most popular sports in Brazil. It is considered to be only behind football in terms in national popularity.[1565]

Brazilian jiu-jitsu originated in Brazil in the 1910s, and emphasizes ground fighting techniques and submission holds involving joint-locks and chokeholds. Hélio Gracie had a rather small build and changed jiu-jitsu (originating from Japan) to be used by anyone in a real fight situation. The belt progression system goes in the following order: White, Blue, Purple, Brown, Black, Red-black, and Red. Gracie Jiu Jitsu became known internationally in the 1990s, due to the very skilled fighters in the Gracie family, namely Hélio Gracie, Royce Gracie, and Rickson Gracie, which are also responsible for spreading the practice of vale tudo, meaning "anything goes", which evolved into mixed martial arts tournaments such as PRIDE, DREAM, and the Ultimate Fighting Championship. Many Brazilian fighters have become significant figures in various mixed martial art tournaments abroad, some notable Brazilian fighters in these tournaments include Anderson Silva, Wanderlei Silva, Antônio Rodrigo Nogueira, Vitor Belfort, Mauricio Rua, Jose Aldo, Murilo Bustamante, Junior dos Santos, Rafael dos Anjos, Fabricio Werdum, and Lyoto Machida.

Footvolley

Footvolley was created by *Octavio de Moraes* in the 1970s. It is a mix of football and volleyball, where the players must use their feet and head to get the ball over the net and into the opponent's side, and is played on the beaches. It is one of the most popular beach sports in Brazil. Footvolley started out with 5 players on each team but later got cut to 2 players on each team and is still so to this day.

Figure 530: *Gustavo Kuerten at the 2005 French Open.*

Tennis

Maria Esther Bueno is the most successful Brazilian tennis player at the Grand Slam tournaments. She won seven single titles (four wins at the US Open and three at Wimbledon) and twelve doubles titles (five at Wimbledon, four at the US Open, two in the Roland Garros, including a mixed doubles, and once at the pen]]). In the men's game, Gustavo Kuerten is the most successful Brazilian player, with three wins at Roland Garros (1997, 2000, 2001) as well as being ranked number one in the world for almost a full year. However, bad administration and lack of serious support resulted in poor results in the present years and scarcity of national-level competitiveness.

Today, Thomaz Bellucci is Brazil's best-known player, having been ranked among the top 30 players in the world according to the ATP Rankings. In doubles, the country has been stronger, especially with Marcelo Melo and Bruno Soares. The former has been ranked No. 1 in the ATP Doubles Rankings and the latter has achieved a peak ranking of No. 3. Between them they have made appearances in nine Grand Slam finals with different partners in both mixed and men's doubles. Melo won the 2015 French Open Men's Doubles in partnership with Ivan Dodig, whilst Soares won the US Open Mixed Doubles title in 2012 (with Ekaterina Makarova) and 2014 (with Sania Mirza), the 2016

Figure 531: *Anderson Varejão is one of Brazil's best basketball players.*

Australian Open Mixed Doubles with Elena Vesnina and the 2016 Australian Open and US Open Men's Doubles with Jamie Murray.

Basketball

Basketball is the third most popular sport in Brazil. The Brazilian national basketball team has won the Basketball World Championship twice, in 1959 and 1963. They have also been runners-up on two occasions in 1954 and 1970, as well as coming third on two occasions in 1967 and 1978, meaning that the Brazilian national basketball team has won in total six medals at the Basketball World Championship. The Brazilian national basketball team has also won three Olympic bronze medals (1948, 1960, 1964) and total of nine medals at the FIBA Americas Championship, three gold (1984, 2005, 2009) two silver (1988, 2001), and four bronze (1989, 1992, 1995, 1997). Oscar Schmidt is the most renowned male Brazilian player, and Hortência Marcari the most renowned female. Both were inducted to the Naismith Memorial Basketball Hall of Fame and the FIBA Hall of Fame.

The major basketball leagues are called Novo Basquete Brasil – the men's tournament – and Liga de Basquete Feminino – the female tournament. Various famous Brazilian players play in those leagues. In addition, on the men's side,

Figure 532: *Autódromo José Carlos Pace, venue for the Brazilian Grand Prix.*

various players are competing in the National Basketball Association and European leagues. A record nine Brazilians were on NBA rosters at the start of the 2015–16 season—Leandro Barbosa, Bruno Caboclo, Cristiano Felício, Marcelo Huertas, Nenê, Raul Neto, Lucas Nogueira, Tiago Splitter, and Anderson Varejão. On the women's side, players like Izi Castro Marques and Érika de Souza compete in the WNBA.

Motorsport

Brazil has produced three Formula One world champions: Emerson Fittipaldi (1972 and 1974), Nelson Piquet (1981, 1983 and 1987), and Ayrton Senna (1988, 1990 and 1991). In total, Brazil has 101 Formula One race wins (as of the 2009 Italian Grand Prix), distributed between Senna (41), Piquet (23), Fittipaldi (14), Felipe Massa (11), Rubens Barrichello (11), and José Carlos Pace (1).

In 1994, Brazil declared three days of national mourning after three time World Champion Ayrton Senna died during the 1994 San Marino Grand Prix.

There were two Brazilian drivers in the 2016 lineup, Felipe Massa of Williams and Felipe Nasr of Sauber.

The Brazilian Grand Prix has been on the Formula One calendar since 1972, currently held in October or November. Two circuits have been host to the race: Jacarepagua and Interlagos. The first one, located in Rio de Janeiro, hosted the 1978 race, and then between 1981 and 1989. From 1972 to 1977, in 1979 and 1980, and since 1990, the Brazilian Grand Prix takes place at the Interlagos circuit, in São Paulo.

The only Formula One constructor to ever be based in Brazil is Fittipaldi Automotive.

Brazil is also home to notable drivers in American Championship Car Racing. Emerson Fittipaldi was 1989 CART champion, Gil de Ferran was 2000 CART and 2001 CART champion, Cristiano da Matta was 2002 CART champion and Tony Kanaan was 2004 IndyCar champion, whereas Brazilians have won the Indianapolis 500 race 7 times: Emerson Fittipaldi (1989 and 1993), Hélio Castroneves (2001, 2002, and 2009), Gil de Ferran (2003) and Tony Kanaan (2013). The CART race, the Rio 400 at Jacarepagua in the late 1990s, whereas the IndyCar Series currently hosts São Paulo Indy 300 street race since 2010.

In the sports car racing scene, Raul Boesel won the 1987 World Sportscar Championship and got close to winning the 1991 Le Mans 24 Hours, when he was second, and Ricardo Zonta won the 1998 FIA GT Championship. Boesel was part of the winning team at the 1988 Daytona 24 Hours, a race which was also won by fellow Brazilians Christian Fittipaldi (twice, in 2004 and 2014), Oswaldo Negri (2012), Kanaan (2015) and Pipo Derani (2016). Fittipaldi also won the United SportsCar Championship in 2014 and 2015, alongside Portuguese team-mate João Barbosa. Also the Mil Milhas Brasil, an endurance race, has the longest history in the Brazilian racing events.

Nelson Piquet Jr. was the inaugural Formula E champion in 2014-15.

The popularity of auto racing is rising, with the Stock Car Brasil and Fórmula Truck being broadcast nationally. The South American Formula Three series was mostly held in Brazil until 2013, and developed several South American circuit drivers. In 2014 it was succeeded by a revived Brazilian Formula Three Championship.

In motorcycle racing, the most prominent Brazilian racer in MotoGP as of now is Alex Barros, who is the most experienced racer of all time in the category, with 276 race starts and seven wins. The Brazilian motorcycle Grand Prix was held four times between 1987 and 1992, followed by the Rio de Janeiro motorcycle Grand Prix which was held nine times between 1995 and 2004.

Volleyball

Brazil is the most successful country in volleyball.

The Brazil men's national volleyball team is currently the champion in 3 competitions, the Volleyball World Cup, the Volleyball World Championship and

Figure 533: *Brazil at the 2006 Volleyball World Championship in Japan.*

Figure 534: *Giba is the most popular volleyball player of Brazil.*

the Olympic Volleyball Tournament, and is ranked number 1 in the FIVB World Rankings.

Here is a record for achievements of the Brazilian men's volleyball team:

- 3 Olympic gold medals (1992, 2004 and 2016) and 3 silver medals (1984, 2008 and 2012)
- 3 World Championship gold medals (2002, 2006, 2010)
- 2 World Cup gold medals (2003 and 2007)
- 9 FIVB World League gold medals (1993, 2001, 2003, 2004, 2005, 2006, 2007, 2009, and 2010)
- 5 Volleyball Grand Champions Cup gold medal (1997, 2005, 2009, 2013, and 2017)

The Brazil women's national volleyball team is ranked number 4 in the FIVB World Rankings.

Here is a record for achievements of the Brazilian women's volleyball team:

- 2 Olympic gold medals (2008 and 2012) and 2 bronze medals (1996 and 2000)
- 3 World Championship silver medals (1994, 2006, 2010)
- 11 FIVB World Grand Prix gold medals (1994, 1996, 1998, 2004, 2005, 2006, 2008, 2009, 2013, 2014, and 2017)
- 2 Volleyball Grand Champions Cup gold medals (2005 and 2013)

Brazilian younger teams maintain the same success rate as the senior squads. As of March 25, 2007, in the FIVB men ranking for junior and youth, Brazil is placed first for women, while the men are placed second.

Beach volleyball has also given Brazilian athletes much success worldwide. Today, Brazil is the ruling country in volleyball, and it is Brazil's second most popular sport. The FIVB 2006 World Tour has finished with Brazilians on the top in both men and women rankings. Both, men and women, have won Olympic Games medals. Men have won gold in 2004 and 2016, and silver 2000 and 2008; and women have won golden in 1996, silver in 1996, 2000, and 2004, and bronze in 1996 and 2000. Brazilian athletes have also collected many medals in the World Tour.

Brazil has professional volleyball team competitions: the Superliga Masculina de Vôlei and its female counterpart, Superliga Feminina de Vôlei. Among the most successful teams are Minas, Banespa, and Santo André for the male league, and Rexona, *Osasco*, and Flamengo for the female league.

Figure 535: *Lobo Bravo, a Brazilian rugby team.*

Rugby

Rugby has been played in Brazil since at least 1888. Although it has been played in Brazil for as long as football, it has never enjoyed its popularity. The Brazil national rugby union team has so far never qualified for a Rugby World Cup. A domestic club competition, the Campeonato Brasileiro de Rugby, has been contested annually since 1964. Rugby returned to the Olympics in Rio 2016 (in the 7-a-side tournament form) - see Rugby sevens at the 2016 Summer Olympics. As 2016 Olympic hosts, Brazil men's and women's teams automatically qualified.

The sport is not widely played in schools, but is common in universities, more specifically in the Brazilian South region, in the Brazilian South East (Rio de Janeiro, São Paulo, Minas Gerais) well as parts of Amazon and the North East. The South East usually supplies the largest number of players to the national side. As of 2016, rugby is played by about 60,000 Brazilians and has experienced sizeable growth in the country.

Team handball

Team handball is popular in private schools, although it is gaining ground in public schools where it can be played on futsal grounds. The national team is considered the best in South America, and the sport is gaining in media coverage. The national league is broadcast on cable television, sponsored by Petrobras. Brazil women's national handball team were crowned world champions for the first time at the 2013 Championship.

Beach handball

At the Beach Handball World Championships Brazil has more titles for both genders than any country.Wikipedia:Citation needed

American football

American football is played by young people in some states. The most popular varieties are flag football (especially in São Paulo) and beach American football (played in coastal cities such as Rio de Janeiro, Recife and João Pessoa).

Also, the sport is already one of the most played around the country, with approximately 130 teams. The Superliga Nacional de Futebol Americano (National American Football Superleague) is a recently created Brazilian American football league, created and organized by the Confederação Brasileira de Futebol Americano (Brazilian Confederation of American Football).

Baseball

Sport traditionally practiced by its majority by descendants of Japanese through the Japanese communities in Brazil. It is little popular in the country, but with the cable TV coverage of the games, baseball is also gaining fans among non-nisseis in the sport, currently several regional leagues are on the rise in the country, however, the difficulty in finding baseball fields prevents regular practice of the sport that is often played on adapted football fields.

Hockey

In Brazil, roller in-line hockey is the most popular form of hockey, unlike ice hockey that is still dependent on infrastructure. Brazilians that practices hockey, mostly practices the roller in-line hockey.

The main world championships of Ice Hockey are transmitted through cable TV in the country, among them the NHL played between teams of Canada and the United States, and the European League. Despite this, the modality finds difficulties in falling in the popular taste of the country.

Other sports

Skateboarding is a popular sport in Brazil. According to a study conducted by *Datafolha*, the estimated number of skateboarders in Brazil for 2003 was close to three million (the majority in the state of São Paulo).Wikipedia:Citation needed Many of the world's top skateboarders are Brazilian, including Bob Burnquist, Sandro Dias, Pedro Barros, Lincoln Ueda, Rodrigo Menezes, Luan de Oliveira, Felipe Gustavo, Rodil Ferrugem, Nilton Neves, Fabrizio Santos, Alex Carolino, Christiano Mateus, Karen Jones, Ricardo Porva, Daniel Vieira, and Og de Souza. Fabiola da Silva is well known for aggressive inline skating.

Athletics, swimming, judo and sailing are traditional sports in Brazil which have earned Olympic medals for the country. In athletics, well-known athletes are Adhemar da Silva, João Carlos de Oliveira, Joaquim Cruz, Maurren Maggi, Fabiana Murer and Thiago Braz da Silva.

Brazil has produced Olympic medallists in swimming such as Ricardo Prado, Gustavo Borges and Fernando Scherer. César Cielo is an Olympic champion, world champion and world-record holder.

Sailing and equestrianism are spectator sports, inaccessible to the general population. Well-known athletes include rider Rodrigo Pessoa and sailors Robert Scheidt, Marcelo Ferreira and brothers Lars and Torben Grael.

Brazil is a strong country in judo, which was brought and developed by its large Japanese community. Olympic medallists in the sport include Rogério Sampaio and Aurélio Miguel; João Derly and Tiago Camilo are world champions. Rafaela Silva won golds in the 2013 World Judo Championships and the 2016 Summer Olympics, both held in her hometown of Rio de Janeiro.

Boxing is popular, especially in northeastern Brazil; it is considered a working-class sport. Eder Jofre and Acelino "Popó" Freitas are former world champions.

In horse racing, Silvestre de Sousa was the British flat racing Champion Jockey in 2015. The Brazilian-bred horse Glória de Campeão won the Dubai World Cup, then the world's richest Thoroughbred race, in 2010 with Brazilian jockey T. J. Pereira aboard.

Curling is a growing sport in Brazil; the creation of a national team was inspired by the audience for the 2010 Winter Olympics in Vancouver. A temporary rink in the Eldorado Shopping Center in São Paulo featured Norwegian curler Linn Githmark and a winter-sports complex is planned, probably in the city of Campos do Jordão.

Frescobol is a native Brazilian sport similar to tennis and cricket, played with a wooden racket and soft rubber ball on the beach with no scoring system. It began during the 1960s on Ipanema beach. Biribol is another native sport created in Birigüi, São Paulo state. It is a kind of volleyball played in a swimming pool. Peteca (shuttlecock) is a native sport which originated from indigenous games.

Surfing is one of the most popular aquatic sports in Brazil, with several professional Brazilian surfers competing in the men's and women's ASP World Tour, including former world champions Gabriel Medina and Adriano de Souza. Brazil is known for producing longboard surfers (such as former world champion Phil Razjman), big-rider surfers (such as Carlos Burle and two-time XXL award winner Maya Gabeira) and well-known bodyboarders.

Rodeo enjoys significant popularity in some rural regions of southern states. The rodeo event of bull riding has become a significant niche sport on its own since the success of Adriano Moraes on the US-based Professional Bull Riders (PBR) circuit in the 1990s and 2000s. PBR now runs a national touring series in Brazil, and Brazilian riders are heavily represented on the main PBR circuit in the US.

Brazil at the Olympics

Due to the tropical and subtropical nature of the climate of Brazil, it has not traditionally competed in the Winter Olympics, although it made its first appearance in the 1992 Winter Olympics, and most recently participated in the 2014 Winter Olympics. However, Brazil has been competing in the Summer Olympics since 1920. Brazil is currently ranked 33rd in the overall ranking of medals in the Summer Olympics. Rio de Janeiro hosted the 2016 Summer Olympics, the first Olympic Games held in South America.

Sports in media

On television, football is by far the most watched sport on both free and paid television, games from regional teams often guarantee the top audience in its cities, also European football (especially UEFA Champions League) are guaranteed high viewing figures.

In motorsport, the main national competitions are Stock Car Brasil and Fórmula Truck. Formula One is considered the second most watched sport in terms of TV audience, behind football. The IndyCar Series also has a good fanbase in Brazil.

MMA in a short period of time has become the second most broadcast sport on Brazilian TV, due mainly to the resounding success of Brazilian fighters in the UFC.

Both men and women's volleyball enjoy very good viewing figures, especially the Brazilian national volleyball teams, Superliga and beach volleyball matches.

Basketball is also widely broadcast, prominently the national league (NBB) and the NBA. Basketball's level of popularity is returning to its historical levels.

In recent years, American football has been gaining fast popularity, with NFL games guaranteeing an audience on ESPN Brasil and Esporte Interativo. Also, some Torneio Touchdown (Brazilian League) games are shown by BandSports.[1566] In 2016, the two main leagues merged into the Superliga Nacional.

Curling was the latest sporting phenomenon in Brazil in terms of audience. During the 2013 World Women's Curling Championship, held in late March in Canada, about 3.6 million people watched the channel SporTV, leading audiences among sports channels on pay TV. The audience was even greater during the men's worlds that year.[1567]

Major sports leagues on Brazilian television		
League	Sport	TV(s)
FIFA World Cup	Football	Globo, Band, SporTV, ESPN Brasil, Fox Sports and BandSports
Olympic Games	International Olympic Committee Various Sports	Globo, Record, Band, SporTV, BandSports and ESPN
Winter Games	International Olympic Committee Various Sports	Globo, Record, Band, SporTV and BandSports
Pan American Games	Various Sports	Record and SporTV
Campeonato Brasileiro Série A	Football	Globo, Band, SporTV and Premiere FC
Copa do Brasil	Football	Globo, Band, SporTV, ESPN Brasil and Fox Sports
Copa Libertadores	Football	Globo, Fox Sports and SporTV
Copa Sudamericana	Football	Globo, Fox Sports and SporTV
UEFA Champions League	Football	ESPN Brasil, Globo, Band and TV Esporte Interativo
UEFA Europa League	Football	TV Esporte Interativo and ESPN Brasil
FIVB Volleyball Men's World Championship	Volleyball	SporTV
FIVB Volleyball Women's World Championship	Volleyball	SporTV
FIVB Volleyball Men's World Cup	Volleyball	Band and SporTV

FIVB Volleyball Women's World Cup	Volleyball	Band and SporTV
FIVB Volleyball World Grand Champions Cup	Volleyball	Globo and SporTV
FIVB Volleyball World League	Volleyball	Globo, Band and SporTV
FIVB Volleyball World Grand Prix	Volleyball	Globo, Band and SporTV
FIVB Volleyball Men's Club World Championship	Volleyball	SporTV
FIVB Volleyball Women's Club World Championship	Volleyball	SporTV
FIVB Beach Volleyball World Tour	Volleyball	Band and SporTV
FIVB Beach Volleyball World Championships	Volleyball	Band and SporTV
Superliga Brasileira de Voleibol	Volleyball	Globo, RedeTV! and SporTV
CEV Champions League	Volleyball	BandSports
Novo Basquete Brasil	Basketball	Globo and SporTV
NBA	Basketball	ESPN Brasil, Space and Sports+
FIBA Americas League	Basketball	Fox Sports
EuroLeague	Basketball	Sports+
Liga Futsal	Futsal	SporTV and ESPN Brasil
NFL	American football	ESPN Brasil and TV Esporte Interativo
NCAA Football	College American football	ESPN Brasil
National Hockey League	Ice hockey	ESPN Brasil
Major League Baseball	Baseball	ESPN Brasil
Campeonato Brasileiro de Rugby	Rugby Union	SporTV
European Rugby Champions Cup	Rugby Union	ESPN Brasil
Super Rugby	Rugby Union	ESPN Brasil

External links

- Brazilian most visited sports websites:
    - Globo Esporte[1568]
    - Lancenet[1569]

- Gazeta Esportiva[1570]
- UOL Esporte[1571]
- Terra Esportes[1572]
- Yahoo/Esporte Interativo[1573]

Appendix

References

[1] CNRTL http://www.cnrtl.fr/etymologie/brésil - Centre National de Ressources Textuelles et Lexicales Michaelis http://michaelis.uol.com.br/moderno/portugues/index.php?lingua=portugues-portugues&palavra=brasil - Moderno Dicionário da Língua Portuguesa iDicionário Aulete http://aulete.uol.com.br/site.php?mdl=aulete_digital&op=loadVerbete&pesquisa=1&palavra=brasil

[2] Gaspar Correia (*Lendas da India*, c.1550: p.152) identifies the returning captain as André Gonçalves, while João de Barros (*Decadas da Asia*, 1552: p.390) and Damião de Góis (*Cronica do Rei D. Manuel*, 1566: p.69) say it was Gaspar de Lemos.

[3] e.g. the letter of Giovanni Matteo Cretico (June 27, 1501) and a diary entry of Marino Sanuto (Oct 12, 1502) call it "Terra di Papaga'"; on-board diarist Thomé Lopes (1502, p.160 https://books.google.com/books?id=eCsOAAAAYAAJ&dq=editions%3ALCCN05004414&as_brr=1&pg=PA160-IA4#v=onepage&q&f=false) refers to it as the "Ilha dos Papagaios vermelhos" ("island of the red parrots").

[4] A. Teixeira da Mota (1969) *Novos documentos sobre uma expedição de Gonçalo Coelho ao Brasil, entre 1503 e 1505*. Lisbon: Junta de Investigações do Ultramar.

[5] Moacyr Soares Pereira (1988) "Rio D Brasil", *Revista da Universidade de Coimbra*, vol. 34, p.417-30 offprint https://books.google.com/books?id=qZQtRywxADUC&lpg=PA413&pg=PA415#v=onepage&q&f=false

[6] Duarte Pacheco Pereira, *Esmeraldo de Situ Orbis*, p.16 https://books.google.com/books?id=5LI8AAAAMAAJ&pg=PA16#v=onepage&q&f=false, and again p.78

[7] See *Cartas de Afonso de Albuquerque*, 1884, vol.1: p.64 https://books.google.com/books?id=x_oFAAAAQAAJ&pg=PA64#v=onepage&q&f=false

[8] Soares Pereira, (1988: p.420)

[9] Laura de Mello e Souza (2001) "O nome do Brasil", *Revista de Historia da USP*, n.145. online http://www.revistausp.sibi.usp.br/scielo.php?script=sci_arttext&pid=S0034-83092001000200002&lng=pt&nrm=iso

[10] João de Barros, *Décadas da Ásia*, Dec I, Lib. 5, ch. 2, p.391-92 https://books.google.com/books?id=Epo2AAAAMAAJ&dq=editions%3AUOM39015057112644&lr&as_brr=1&pg=PA392#v=onepage&q&f=false

[11] Fernão Lopes de Castanheda, *História do descobrimento & conquista da Índia pelos portugueses*, Lib I, ch.30 p.98 https://books.google.com/books?id=OzQbAAAAYAAJ&pg=PA98#v=onepage&q&f=false

[12] Damião de Góis, *Chronica of D. Manuel*, Pt.1, Ch. 55, p.69 https://books.google.com/books?id=0vTmAAAAMAAJ&pg=PA69#v=onepage&q&f=false

[13] Pedro Magalhães Gandavo (1576) *Historia da Provincia de Santa Cruz, a que vulgarmente chamamos Brasil*, p.3 https://books.google.com/books?id=idxSAAAAcAAJ&pg=PA3#v=onepage&q&f=false.

[14] Eduardo Bueno, *Brasil: uma História* (São Paulo: Ática, 2003;), p.36.

[15] "Since 1351 until at least 1721 the name Hy-Brazil could be seen on maps and globes. Until 1624, expeditions were still sent after it." Bueno, p.36

[16] //en.wikipedia.org/w/index.php?title=Template:History_of_Brazil&action=edit

[17] Science Magazine, 13 December 1991 http://www.sciencemag.org/content/254/5038/1621.abstract

[18] http://www.souparaense.com/2011/04/quem-descobriu-o-brasil-pedro-alvares.html Quem descobriu o Brasil?

[19] COUTO, Jorge: A Construção do Brasil, Edições Cosmos, 2ª Ed., Lisboa, 1997.primeiro

[20] Morison, Samuel (1974). The European Discovery of America: The Southern Voyages, 1492–1616. New York: Oxford University Press.

[21] Boxer, p. 98.

[22] Boxer, p. 100.

[23] *engenho* is Portuguese for sugar mill, but came to refer also to the entire estate and plantation surrounding it

[24] A.J.R. Russell-Wood, "Brazil: The Colonial Era, 1500–1808" in *Encyclopedia of Latin American History and Culture*, vol. 1, pp. 415–16. New York: Charles Scribner's Sons 1996.

[25] A.J.R. Russell-Wood, "Brazil", p. 414.

[26] Some slaves escaped from the plantations and tried to establish independent settlements (*quilombos*) in remote areas. The most important of these, the quilombo of Palmares, was the largest runaway slave settlement in the Americas, and was a consolidated kingdom of some 30,000 people at its height in the 1670s and 80s. However, these settlements were mostly destroyed by the crown and private troops, which in some cases required long sieges and the use of artillery.

[27] Braudel, 1984. p. 390

[28] C. R. Boxer, "Brazilian Gold and British Traders in the First Half of the Eighteenth Century," *Hispanic American Historical Review* (1969) 49#3 pp. 454–472 in JSTOR https://www.jstor.org/stable/2511780

[29] C.R. Boxer, *The golden age of Brazil, 1695–1750: growing pains of a colonial society* (1962).

[30] Kathleen J. Higgins, *Licentious Liberty in a Brazilian Gold-Mining Region: Slavery, Gender & Social Control in Eighteenth-Century Sabara, Minas Gerais* (1999)

[31] A. J. R. Russell-Wood, "Local Government in Portuguese America. A Study of Cultural Divergence," *Comparative Studies in Society & History* (1974) 16#2 pp 187–231.

[32] Marshall C. Eakin, *British Enterprise in Brazil: The St. John d'el Rey Mining Company & the Morro Velho Gold Mine, 1830–1960* (1990)

[33] A.J.R. Russell-Wood, "Brazil", p. 416.

[34] A.J.R. Russell-Wood, "Brazil", p. 416.

[35] José Luís Cardoso, "Free Trade, Political Economy and the Birth of a New Economic Nation: Brazil, 1808–1810." *Revista de Historia Económica-Journal of Iberian and Latin American Economic History* 27#2 (2009): 183-204, online free in English https://e-archivo.uc3m.es/bitstream/handle/10016/19644/RHE-2009-XXVII-Cardoso.pdf?sequence=1

[36] A.J.R. Russell-Wood, "Brazil", p. 419.

[37] Johns Hopkins University Press | Books|Slave Rebellion in Brazil http://www.press.jhu.edu/books/title_pages/2365.html

[38] Thomas H. Holloway, *Immigrants on the Land: Coffee & Society in Sao Paulo, 1886–1934* (1980)

[39] Alida C. Metcalf, "Coffee Workers In Brazil: A Review Essay," *Peasant Studies* (1989) 16#3 pp 219–224, reviewing Verena Stolcke, *Coffee Planters, Workers and Wives: Class Conflict and Gender Relations on São Paulo Plantations, 1850–1980* (1988)

[40] Robert H. Mattoon, Jr., "Railroads, Coffee, and the Growth of Big Business in São Paulo, Brazil," *Hispanic American Historical Review* (1977) 57#2 pp. 273–295 in JSTOR https://www.jstor.org/stable/2513775

[41] Renato Monseff Perissinotto, "State and Coffee Capital in São Paulo's Export Economy (Brazil 1889–1930)" *Journal of Latin American Studies* (2003) pp 1–23 in JSTOR https://www.jstor.org/stable/2503402

[42] Steven Topik, "Where is the Coffee? Coffee and Brazilian Identity,"*Luso-Brazilian Review* (1999) 36#2 pp 87–92.

[43] Mauricio A. Font, *Coffee and Transformation in Sao Paulo, Brazil* (2012)

[44] Tania Andrade Lima, "Keeping a Tight Lid," *Review: A Journal of the Fernand Braudel Center* (2011) 34#1–2, pp 193–215

[45] E. Bradford Burns, "Manaus, 1910: Portrait of a Boom Town," *Journal of Inter-American Studies* (1965) 7#3 pp. 400–421 in JSTOR https://www.jstor.org/stable/164992

[46] Bradford L. Barham and Oliver T. Coomes, "Reinterpreting the Amazon Rubber Boom: Investment, the State, and Dutch Disease," *Latin American Research Review* (1994) 29#2 pp. 73–109 in JSTOR https://www.jstor.org/stable/2503594

[47] Warren Dean, *Brazil and the Struggle for Rubber: A Study in Environmental History* (2002)

[48] Scheina, Robert L. *Latin America's Wars Volume II: The Age of the Professional Soldier, 1900–2001.* Potomac Books, 2003 **Part 4; Chapter 5 – World War I and Brazil, 1917–18.**

[49] Ellis, Charles Howard "The origin, structure & working of the League of Nations" The Law-Book Exchange Ltd 2003 pp. 105 & 145
[50] Stanley E. Hilton, "The Argentine Factor in Twentieth-Century Brazilian Foreign Policy Strategy." *Political Science Quarterly* 100.1 (1985): 27–51.
[51] Stanley E. Hilton, "Brazilian Diplomacy and the Washington-Rio de Janeiro 'Axis' during the World War II Era," *Hispanic American Historical Review* (1979) 59#2 pp. 201–231 in JSTOR https://www.jstor.org/stable/2514412
[52] "The United States and Brazil: A Long Road of Unmet Expectations"; Monica Hisrt, Routledge 2004 page 43
[53] "The United States and Brazil: A Long Road of Unmet Expectations"; Monica Hisrt, Routledge 2004 , Introduction: page xviii 3rd paragraph
[54] Stepan, 1973.
[55] "Anatomy of a coup d'etat; Brazil 1964"; Warren W. Van Pelt; Air War College, Air University (1967) ASIN B0007GYMM4
[56] Brasil: Nunca Mais
[57] https://web.archive.org/web/20081222235128/http://www.iedi.org.br/cgi/cgilua.exe/sys/start.htm?2=217&sid=77&1=43&infoid=1749 "Tais políticas – iniciadas com a abertura do governo Collor – foram continuadas por Fernando Henrique Cardoso e Luiz Inácio Lula da Silva, segundo economistas e industriais ouvidos pela Folha"
[58] Programa Nacional de Desestatização https://www.planalto.gov.br/publi_04/COLECAO/fase2.htm
[59] Os efeitos da privatização sobre o desempenho econômico e financeiro das empresas privatizadas http://www.scielo.br/scielo.php?pid=S0034-71402005000200001&script=sci_arttext
[60] Lula segue política econômica de FHC, diz diretor do FMI http://www.bbc.co.uk/portuguese/reporterbbc/story/2006/06/060626_lulafhcpimenta.shtml
[61] Jeffrey T. Lewis, "Brazil's Presidential Vote Looks Headed for Runoff," *Wall Street Journal* Oct. 5, 2014 https://www.wsj.com/articles/brazilians-vote-in-presidential-election-1412520867?mod=djemalertNEWS
[62] BBC News, "Dilma Rousseff Re-elected Brazilian President," *British Broadcasting Corporation* Oct. 26, 2014 https://www.bbc.com/news/world-latin-america-29782073
[63] Simon Romero, "A Laboratory for Revitalizing Catholicism," *New York Times* Feb 14, 2013 https://www.nytimes.com/2013/02/15/world/americas/in-brazil-growing-threats-to-catholicisms-sway.html?pagewanted=all&_r=0
[64] https://www.amazon.com/Colonial-Brazil-Cambridge-History-America/dp/0521349257/
[65] https://www.amazon.com/History-Brazil-E-Bradford-Burns/dp/0231079559/
[66] https://www.amazon.com/dp/0521563321/
[67] https://www.amazon.com/dp/B00NZBPX8A
[68] https://www.amazon.com/dp/1403962553/
[69] https://www.questia.com/read/28782252/the-history-of-brazil
[70] https://www.amazon.com/dp/0822322900/
[71] https://archive.org/details/historicaldictio00levi
[72] http://eh.net/book_reviews/the-economic-and-social-history-of-brazil-since-1889/
[73] https://www.amazon.com/Brazil-Centuries-Thomas-E-Skidmore/dp/019537455X/
[74] https://www.amazon.com/Politics-Brazil-1930-1964-Experiment-Democracy/dp/0195332695/
[75] http://www.cambridge.org/hn/academic/subjects/history/latin-american-history/legacy-dutch-brazil
[76] https://www.academia.edu/download/37953468/Rediscovering_Portuguese_America_-_draft.docx
[77] https://ejournals.epublishing.ekt.gr/index.php/historein/
[78] https://www.jstor.org/stable/2511951
[79] https://www.jstor.org/stable/2510025
[80] http://pt.wikisource.org/wiki/Cap%C3%ADtulos_de_Hist%C3%B3ria_Colonial
[81] http://penelope.uchicago.edu/Thayer/P/Gazetteer/Places/America/Brazil/_Texts/CALFHB/home.html
[82] http://www.newadvent.org/cathen/02745c.htm

[83] http://lanic.utexas.edu/la/brazil/#history
[84] http://library.brown.edu/fivecenturiesofchange/
[85] //en.wikipedia.org/w/index.php?title=Template:History_of_Brazil&action=edit
[86] Davenport, ed., 107–111 https://books.google.com/books?id=uLILAAAAIAAJ&pg=PA107.
[87] Leslie Ronald Marchant, *The Papal Line of Demarcation and Its Impact in the Eastern Hemisphere on the Political Division of Australia, 1479–1829* (Greenwood, Western Australia: Woodside Valley Foundation, 2008).
[88] Geo Brasil http://www.geobrasil.net/cabo%5Cgranitodocabo.htm Granito do Cabo de Santo Agostinho, Pernambuco, Brasil
[89] Direito 2 http://www.direito2.com.br/acam/2002/abr/29/projeto-pode-mudar-data-do-descobrimento-do-brasil Projeto pode mudar data do descobrimento do Brasil
[90] http://www.souparaense.com/2011/04/quem-descobriu-o-brasil-pedro-alvares.html Quem descobriu o Brasil?
[91] COUTO, Jorge: A Construção do Brasil, Edições Cosmos, 2ª Ed., Lisboa, 1997.primeiro
[92] Vianna 1994, p. 44.
[93] Fonseca (1908: p.225)
[94] The Coelho expedition is also known as the "Fourth Voyage" of Vespucci, and is related in the letter of Amerigo Vespucci to Piero Soderini, 1504–05. See the English translation of the account https://books.google.com/books?id=boQKAQAAIAAJ&pg=RA1-PA41#v=onepage&q&f=false in *Letter to Soderini*
[95] Taques, Pedro. História da Capitania de São Vicente. Brasília: Edições do Senado Federal, 2004. Available at http://www.dominiopublico.gov.br/download/texto/sf000043.pdfaccessdate=24/10/2011
[96] R. J. Knecht, *Renaissance Warrior and Patron: The Reign of Francis I* p.375 https://books.google.com/books?id=zGvoIW6Y_xAC&pg=PA375
[97] Rachel Lawrence: 2010, Page 183
[98] António Henrique R. de Oliveira Marques, *History of Portugal*. 1972, page 322. Boris Fausto, *A Concise History of Brazil*, page 40.
[99] Bicheno pg 308-09
[100] Ridolfi, R. *Pensieri medicei di colonizzare il Brasile* p. 14
[101] Ridolfi, R. *Pensieri medicei di colonizzare il Brasile*, in «Il Veltro», Roma, luglio-agosto 1962, pp. 1-18
[102] Francis A. Dutra, "Dutch in Colonial Brazil" in *Encyclopedia of Latin American History and Culture*, New York: Charles Scribner's Sons 1996, vol. 2, p. 415.
[103] Dutra, "Dutch in Colonial Brazil" p. 415.
[104] Facsimile of the treaty http://www.s4ulanguages.com/21.html:*Articulen van vrede en Confoederarie, Gheslooten Tusschen den Doorluchtighsten Comingh van Portugael ter eenre, ende de Hoogh Mogende Heeren Staten General ...;*
[105] Guerra dos Palmares http://www.infoescola.com/historia-do-brasil/guerra-dos-palmares/ *InfoEscola*.
[106] Zumbi dos Palmares, O Guerreiro da Liberdade http://www.museudacruzada.com.br/index.php?option=com_content&view=article&id=19&Itemid=19 . Grandes Personagens da História do Brasil. Museu da Cruzada.
[107] "Da invisibilidade à afirmação" http://www.almg.gov.br/RevistaLegis/Revista27/invisibilidade.pdf . Número 27, janeiro/março de 2000. *Revista do Legislativo*.
[108] João José Reis & Flávio dos Santos Gomes, "Quilombo: Brazilian Maroons during slavery" http://www.wsis.cs.org/publications/csq/csq-article.cfm?id=1397 , January 31, 2002, *Cultural Survival Quarterly*, Issue 25.4.
[109] FURTADO, Júnia Ferreira. *José Rodrigues Abreu e a geografia imaginária emboaba da conquista do ouro*. In: *Modos de Governar - Ideias e práticas políticas no Império Português séculos XVI a XIX*. BICALHO, Maria Fernanda & FERLINI, Vera Lúcia do Amaral (Orgs.). 1ª ed. São Paulo: Alameda, 2005. p.278
[110] A supressão da Companhia de Jesus: episódio-chave de sua ação nas fronteiras da fé http://www.ihuonline.unisinos.br/index.php?option=com_content&view=article&id=3952&secao=366

[111] Cristóvão Aires de Magalhães Sepúlveda. *História Orgânica e Política do Exército Português - Provas, volume XVII, Invasão de Junot em Portugal*. Coimbra: Imprensa da Universidade, 1932. p. 130-131.
[112] Rosana Barbosa Nunes, Portuguese Migration to Rio de Janeiro, 1822-1850. The Americas, 2001.
[113] Kirsten Schultz, Tropical Versailles: Empire, Monarchy, and the Portuguese Royal Court in Rio de Janeiro, 1808-1821. Routledge, 2001.
[114] Steven Topik, "Banco do Brasil" in *Encyclopedia of Latin American History and Culture*. New York: Charles Scribner's Sons 1996, vol. 1, p. 278.
[115] LEIVAS, Luís Cláudio Pereira; GOYCOCHÊA, Luís Felipe de Castilhos. A Conquista de Caiena. In: História Naval Brasileira. v.2. t..II.
[116] *Revolução Pernambucana* http://www.brasilescola.com/historiab/revolucao-pernambucana.htm, Brazil Escola.com. Retrieved June 30, 2006.
[117] História, Ciências, Saúde-Manguinhos - From Nova Friburgo to Fribourg in writing: Swiss colonization seen by the immigrants http://www.scielo.br/scielo.php?script=sci_arttext&pid=S0104-59702003000100006
[118] Birmingham, 111–113; Nowell, 182–184.
[119] Renata William Santos do Vale, Presidência da República, Ministério da Justiça, Arquivo Nacional, *História Luso-Brasileira, Independência do Brasil, Do reino unido a Estado emancipado: comentário acerca do processo de independência do Brasil* http://www.historiacolonial.arquivonacional.gov.br/cgi/cgilua.exe/sys/start.htm?infoid=1275&sid=114
[120] Laurentino Gomes; *1822* Nova Fronteira, Brasil 2010 Chapter 10 **pg 161**
[121] NOSSA HISTÓRIA. Year 3 issue 35. São Paulo: Vera Cruz, 2006, p.44
[122] Enciclopédia Barsa. Volume 5: Camarão, Rep. Unida do – Contravenção. Rio de Janeiro: Encyclopædia Britannica do Brasil, 1987, p.464
[123] VAINFAS, Ronaldo. Dicionário do Brasil Imperial. Rio de Janeiro: Objetiva, 2002, p.161
[124] Cf. arts. 5 and 6 of the Constitution of 1824, available at http://www.planalto.gov.br/ccivil_03/constituicao/constitui%C3%A7ao24.htm
[125] Gloria Kaiser: *Dona Leopoldina – Habsburg Princess, Empress of Brazil*, 2009, p. 15 http://cas.umn.edu/assets/pdf/dona_leopoldina.pdf [retrieved 14 July 2015].
[126] Walsh, p. 280
[127] Costa 1995, p. 94.
[128] Sousa 1972, Vol 3, p. 8.
[129] SCHEINA, Robert L. Latin America's Wars: the age of the caudillo, 1791-1899, Brassey's, 2003.
[130] João José Reis, *Slave Rebellion in Brazil: The Muslim Uprising of 1835 in Bahia*, Johns Hopkins University Press, London 1993. pp. 118
[131] Barman, Roderick J. (1988). Brazil: The Forging of a Nation, 1798–1852. p. 209
[132] Needell, Jeffrey D. (2006). The Party of Order: the Conservatives, the State, and Slavery in the Brazilian Monarchy, 1831–1871. p.102
[133] Barman, Roderick J. (1988). Brazil: The Forging of a Nation, 1798–1852. p. 214
[134] Calmon 1975, p. 317.
[135] Schiavo 1953, p. 181.
[136] Barman (1999), p.124
[137] Furtado 2000, p. 10.
[138] Golin 2004, p. 42.
[139] City of Petropolis, Rio de Janeiro,
[140] http://html.rincondelvago.com/venezuela_4.html Problemas Limítrofes de Venezuela (In Spanish)
[141] Teresa A. Meade, *A Brief History of Brazil* (2009), p. 83.
[142] Robert M. Levine, *The History of Brazil* (2003), p. 68.
[143] A Revolta dos Muckers https://www.scribd.com/doc/2980607/Historia-do-Brasil-PreVestibular-1874-Revolta-dos-Muckers
[144] " Drought, Smallpox, and Emergence of Leishmania braziliensis in Northeastern Brazil http://wwwnc.cdc.gov/eid/article/15/6/07-1331_article.htm." Centers for Disease Control and Prevention (CDC).

[145] *Mossoró se destaca como cidade pioneira* http://www.senado.gov.br/noticias/jornal/arquivos_jornal/arquivospdf/encarte_abolicao.pdf (página 8) *Jornal do Senado*. Rio de Janeiro (14 de maio de 1888). Página acessada em 30 de setembro de 2012.

[146] *A abolição* http://memoria.bn.br/DocReader/docreader.aspx?bib=178691_01&PagFis=5322 (página 1 do único caderno), *O Paiz* (14 de maio de 1888). Ano V, n° 1316.

[147] Smallman; Shall C. *Fear & Memory in the Brazilian Army & Society, 1889–1954* The University of North Carolina Press 2002 Page 20 2nd paragraph

[148] See: •, •, •.

[149] "To Be Prince of Trinidad: He Is Baron Harden-Hickey", *New York Tribune*, November 5, 1893, p 1

[150] Bryk, William, "News & Columns", *New York Press*, v 15 no 50 (December 10, 2002) http://www.nypress.com/15/50/news&columns/oldsmoke.cfm

[151] "Principality of Trinidad: John H. Flagler's Son-in-Law Is Its Sovereign, Self-Proclaimed as James I", *New York Times*, June 10, 1894, p 23 https://www.nytimes.com/1894/06/10/archives/principality-of-trinidad-john-h-flaglera-soninlaw-is-its-sovereign.html

[152] Bryk (2002) http://www.nypress.com/15/50/news&columns/oldsmoke.cfm

[153] "Trinidad's Prince Awake: An Appeal to Washington Against Brazil and Great Britain", *New York Times*, August 1, 1895, p 1 https://www.nytimes.com/1895/08/01/archives/trinidads-prince-awake-an-appeal-to-washington-against-brazil-and.html

[154] "Grand Chancellor of Trinidad: Significant Phases in the Ascent of Male Comte de la Boissiere to His Elevated Diplomatic Post", *New York Times*, August 2, 1895, p 9 https://www.nytimes.com/1895/08/02/archives/grand-chancellor-of-trinidad-significant-phases-in-the-ascent-of.html

[155] "Trinidad's Case in Washington: Courteously, the Chancellor Would Permit Britain's Cable Station and Use It, but There Is Graver Trouble", *New York Times*, August 7, 1895, p 1 https://www.nytimes.com/1895/08/07/archives/trinidads-case-in-washington-courteously-the-chancellor-would.html

[156] "Trinidad's Diplomat in Action: M. de la Boissiere Asks that His Sovereign's Land Be Recognized as a Neutral Principality", *New York Times*, August 9, 1895, p 5 https://www.nytimes.com/1895/08/09/archives/trinidads-diplomat-in-action-m-de-la-boissiere-asks-that-his.html

[157] "Trinidad's Prince at Work: Grand Chancellor de la Boissiere Tells How the War Between Great Britain and Brazil Will Be Averted", *New York Times*, Jan 24, 1896, p 9 https://www.nytimes.com/1896/01/24/archives/no-use-for-staten-isle-controller-fitch-and-corporation-coun-sel.html

[158] Flags of the World - Trindade and Martins Vaz Islands (Brazil) http://www.crwflags.com/fotw/flags/br-trin.html (*sic*)

[159] http://reocities.com/Athens/agora/8088/BrazilCivilWar93.html

[160] *À nação brazileira* http://memoria.bn.br/DocReader/docreader.aspx?bib=178691_02&PagFis=11244 (página 1 do único caderno), *O Paiz* (16 de novembro de 1891). Ano XI, n° 3699.

[161] Prince Akishino, Princess Kiko meet with Japanese immigrants in Brazil http://www.japantimes.co.jp/news/2015/11/06/national/prince-akishino-princess-kiko-meet-japanese-immigrants-brazil/#.V2Mkd_krIdX, *The Japan Times*, published on 6 November 2015.

[162] Nohlen, D (2005) *Elections in the Americas: A data handbook, Volume II*, p173

[163] "M. Santos Dumont Rounds Eiffel Tower." https://timesmachine.nytimes.com/timesmachine/1901/10/20/106920457.pdf *The New York Times*, 20 October 1901. Retrieved: 12 January 2009.

[164] Nohlen, D (2005) *Elections in the Americas: A data handbook, Volume II*, p173, p229

[165] FUNAG – International Seminar Baron of Rio Branco – 100 years of memory, September 2012 http://funag.gov.br/en/destaques/133-international-seminar-baron-of-rio-branco-100-years-of-memory . Accessed 24 March 2014

[166] Grant, Jonathan A. *Rulers, Guns, and Money: The Global Arms Trade in the Age of Imperialism.* Cambridge, MA: Harvard University Press, 2007.

[167] Martins Filho, João Roberto. A marinha brasileira na era dos encouraçados, 1895–1910 [The Brazilian Navy in the Era of Dreadnoughts, 1895–1910]. Rio de Janeiro: Fundãçao Getúlio Vargas, 2010. OCLC 679733899, pp 75, 78

[168] Nohlen, D (2005) *Elections in the Americas: A data handbook, Volume II*, p173, p230

[169] Surya P. Sharma (1997). Territorial Acquisition, Disputes and International Law. (M. Nijhoff Publishers: The Hague,)
[170] Gibbs-Smith, Charles H. "Hops and Flights: A roll call of early powered take-offs." http://www.flightglobal.com/pdfarchive/view/1959/1959%20-%200938.html *Flight*, Volume 75, Issue 2619, 3 April 1959, p. 469. Retrieved: 24 August 2013.
[171] <BARMAN, Roderick J., Princesa Isabel do Brasil: gênero e poder no século XIX, UNESP, 2005
[172] Nohlen, D (2005) *Elections in the Americas: A data handbook, Volume II*, , p230
[173] , p 149
[174] Diacon, Todd A. Millenarian Vision, Capitalist Reality: Brazil's Contestado Rebellion, 1912–1916 (Duke University Press 1991),
[175] Theodore Roosevelt timeline http://www.graywolfcorp.com/trcalendar.php . Accessed 19 January 2014
[176] Dieter Nohlen (2005) *Elections in the Americas: A data handbook, Volume II*, . p 230
[177] Appleby, David P. 1988. Heitor Villa-Lobos: A Bio-Bibliography. New York: Greenwood Press.
[178] García Novell, Francisco (2009). Naufragio, la historia olvidada del Titanic español. Madrid: La esfera de los libros.
[179] Command of the Aeronaval Forces https://www.mar.mil.br/foraer/index.htm Official website
[180] Maia, Prado (1961). D.N.O.G. (Divisão Naval los Operações de Guerra), 1914–1918: UMA page esquecida da História da Marinha Brasileira. Serviço de Documentação Geral da Marinha.
[181] Faria, Ivan Rodrigues de. "Participação do Brasil na Primeira Guerra Mundial" (Portuguese) ('Brazil's participation in World War I') Brazilian Army Journal, Rio – DPHCEx, 1996 (Page 67)
[182] Francisco Verras; "D.N.O.G.: contribuicao da Marinha Brasileira na Grande Guerra" ("DNOG; the role of Brazilian Navy in the Great War") "A Noite" Ed. 1920
[183] 1919 South American Championship http://www.rsssf.com/tables/19safull.html at RSSSF
[184] Official Olympic Reports http://www.la84foundation.org/5va/reports_frmst.htm
[185] Presidential Library: Biography of Pessoa http://www.biblioteca.presidencia.gov.br/english/former-presidents/epitacio-pessoa. Accessed 14 February 2014
[186] Dieter Nohlen (2005) *Elections in the Americas: A data handbook, Volume II*, p173
[187] *League of Nations Treaty Series*, vol. 33, pp. 26-45.
[188] PRESTES, Anita Leocádia. A Coluna Prestes- Uma Epopeia Brasileira http://www.kaosenlared.net/noticia/coluna-prestes-uma-epopeia-brasileira
[189] Reza, Ramiro de la. O evento do Curuçá: bólidos caem no Amazonas (The Curuçá Event: Bolides Fall in the Amazon) http://www.comciencia.br/reportagens/espaco/espc17.htm , Rio de Janeiro: National Observatory. Retrieved from the Universidade Estadual de Campinas website.
[190] "A Revolução de 1930: Principais fatos da Revolução de 1930" http://www.brasilescola.com/historiab/revolucao-30.htm
[191] http://www.infoescola.com/historia-do-brasil/governo-de-washington-luis/ (Portuguese language)
[192] Kimberly Jones-de-Oliveira, "The Politics of Culture or the Culture of Politics: Afro-Brazilian Mobilization, 1920–1968," Journal of Third World Studies, v. 20, part I (2003)
[193] Wilson History and Research Center: Paulista War http://www.militaryheadgear.com/periods/49-Paulista-War. Accessed 25 April 2014
[194] Stanley Hilton. A Guerra Civil Brasileira. Río de Janeiro. Nova Fronteira, 1982.
[195] Ricardo Benzaquém de Araújo, Totalitarismo e Revolução: o Integralismo de Plínio Salgado, Rio de Janeiro: Jorge Zahar Editor, 1988,
[196] *League of Nations Treaty Series*, vol. 163, pp. 394–413.
[197] Portuguese text available at http://www.planalto.gov.br/ccivil_03/Constituicao/Constitui%C3%A7ao34.htm
[198] Getúilo Vargas in Brazil http://www.thenagain.info/webchron/americas/VargasBrazil.html World History Chronology
[199] "Semana da asa" http://acervo.folha.com.br/fdm/1936/10/18/142/ (página 3 da primeira seção), *Folha da Manhã* (18 de outubro de 1936).
[200] "Foram julgados hontem os principaes chefes da revolução communista de 1935" http://acervo.folha.com.br/fdm/1937/05/08/142/ (primeira página da primeira seção), *Folha da Manhã* (8 de maio de 1937).

[201] "A convenção hontem realizada pelas correntes politicas que apoiam o sr. Armando de Salles Oliveira" http://acervo.folha.com.br/fdn/1937/06/11/142/ (primeira página da primeira seção), *Folha da Manhã* (11 de junho de 1937).
[202] "O Parque Nacional de Itatiaya" http://acervo.folha.com.br/fdn/1937/06/16/1/ (página 2 do caderno único), *Folha da Noite* (16 de junho de 1937).
[203] Helton Perillo Ferreira Leite, *Planalto do Itatiaia* (2007), p. 20.
[204] "Promulgada hontem nova Constituição para o paiz" http://acervo.folha.com.br/fdn/1937/11/11/142/ (primeira página da primeira seção), *Folha da Manhã* (11 de novembro de 1937).
[205] "Extinctos todos os partidos politicos do paiz" http://acervo.folha.com.br/fdn/1937/12/04/142/ (primeira página da primeira seção), *Folha da Manhã* (4 de dezembro de 1937).
[206] Culture Wars in Brazil: The First Vargas Regime, 1930–1945 By Daryle Williams, p x https://books.google.com/books?id=Cv6dynKbcKAC&pg=PR10&dq=%22Georgina+de+Albuquerque&as_brr=3&sig=k8Cg1XzoEyemyw6cnh43Z1Fv-fM#PPA263,M1
[207] Cédulas do Cruzeiro (1942–1967) http://cedulasbrasileiras.blogspot.co.uk/2012/01/cedulas-do-cruzeiro-1942-1967.html. Accessed 24 May 2014
[208] "Ban Motorcycles in Brazil", *Milwaukee Journal*, 23 July 1943, p3
[209] "Big Brazilian Ship Sunk; 78 Are Missing", *Sarasota Herald-Tribune*, 8 August 1943, p1
[210] *Command* Magazine, issue 51, page 34
[211] Brooks, 2003. Pages 305-06.
[212] Bohmler, 1964. Chapter IX
[213] "Rebel in Rio", *Time Magazine*, July 23, 1945 https://archive.is/20120912073602/http://www.time.com/time/magazine/printout/0,8816,803605,00.html
[214] "Brazilian doctor takes office as the new president of the World Medical Association", 21 October 2011 http://www.hospitalar.com/ingles/imprensa/not620.html. Accessed 13 August 2014
[215] ESPM official website http://www.espm.br/
[216] *The Times*, 5 March 1952, page 4
[217] Accidents and Incidents involving the Boeing 377 http://aviation-safety.net/database/types/Boeing-377-Stratocruiser/database. Retrieved 23 October 2013.
[218] InfoEscola – Governo de Café Filho (Portuguese) http://www.infoescola.com/historia/governo-de-cafe-filho/. Accessed 4 December 2014
[219] Mimoa.eu: MAM—Modern Arts Museum of Rio de Janeiro http://www.mimoa.eu/projects/Brazil/Rio%20de%20Janeiro/MAM%20-%20Modern%20Arts%20Museum%20of%20Rio%20de%20Janeiro . accessed 23 November 2013.
[220] Thomas E. Skidmore (1988) *The Politics of Military Rule in Brazil, 1964-85*, Oxford University Press, p21
[221] Craighead, Geoff. *High-Rise Security and Fire Life Safety*. 3rd ed., illustrated. Butterworth-Heinemann, 2009: 129-30. Print.
[222] Dutton, Ted. "Bold new tactics for fighting high-rise fires". *Popular Mechanics* Sep 1977: 67-71. Print.
[223] *Carandiru, das Gefaengnissmassaker in Sao Paulo* (Ger.), 1995, Editor: Amnesty International FDCL-Verlag, Author: Elói Pietá & Justino Pereira,
[224] Nunes, Branca. "Entre o parlamentarismo e a monarquia, o Brasil resolveu continuar presidencialista" http://veja.abril.com.br/blog/caca-ao-voto/tag/comerciais/ . Blog Caça ao Voto. *Veja*. October 15, 2010.
[225] http://www.ebc.com.br/noticias/2016/01/et-de-varginha-ainda-instiga-imaginario-brasileiro-20-anos-depois
[226] http://www.istoe.com.br/reportagens/105958_A+HISTORIA+OFICIAL+DO+ET+DE+VARGINHA
[227] planecrashinfo.com Famous People Who Died in Aviation Accidents: 1990s http://www.planecrashinfo.com/famous1990s.htm
[228] Amnesty.org Library https://www.amnesty.org/en/library/asset/AMR19/019/2006/en/dom-AMR190192006en.html
[229] Banco de Dados Eleitorais do Brasil http://jaironicolau.iuperj.br/database/deb/port/index.htm
[230] *Retrospectiva 2003*, a edição especial do jornal *O Estado de S. Paulo*, publicado em 31 de dezembro de 2003.
[231] 21 November 2012. Retrieved on 10 March 2013

[232] Araújo, Glauco. "Professora critica cerimonial por iniciar desfile de Dilma sob chuva" http://g1.globo.com/politica/posse-de-dilma/noticia/2011/01/professora-critica-cerimonial-por-iniciar-desfile-de-dilma-sob-chuva.html. G1. 1 January 2011. Retrieved 4 January 2011.

[233] *Tiros aconteceram entre explosão e entrada da PM, diz amiga de Eloá* http://acervo.folha.com.br/fsp/2012/02/14/15/ (primeira página do caderno *Cotidiano*), *Folha de S.Paulo* (14 de fevereiro de 2012).

[234] Brazil police, protesters clash as World Cup begins https://www.reuters.com/article/2014/06/12/us-brazil-worldcup-protests-idUSKBN0EN1DD20140612

[235] Brazil braces for uneasy start to World Cup as strikers' protests hit São Paulo https://www.theguardian.com/world/2014/jun/09/brazil-uneasy-start-world-cup-strikers-protests-sao-paulo

[236] https://archive.org/stream/manualofdatesdic00townrich#page/166/mode/1up

[237] http://hdl.handle.net/2027/uc2.ark:/13960/t9m32q949?urlappend=%3Bseq=112

[238] https://archive.org/stream/haydnsdictionary00hayd#page/196/mode/1up

[239] https://books.google.com/books?id=O26rAAAAIAAJ&pg=PR11

[240] https://books.google.com/books?id=8flAq1v1dgIC&pg=PA495

[241] https://books.google.com/books?id=Pi56Cw3yGfcC&pg=PR6

[242] https://books.google.com/books?id=XiOPAgAAQBAJ&pg=PA32

[243] https://books.google.com/books?id=BlBpAwAAQBAJ&pg=PA255

[244] https://archive.org/stream/taboasdechronolo00mart#page/430/mode/2up

[245] //www.worldcat.org/oclc/804367357

[246] //en.wikipedia.org/w/index.php?title=Template:History_of_Brazil&action=edit

[247] A.J.R. Russell-Wood, Brazil, The colonial era" in *Encyclopedia of Latin American History and Culture*, vol. 1, p. 410. New York: Charles Scribner's Sons 1996.

[248] Source: Europe and the Age of Exploration | Thematic Essay | Heilbrunn Timeline of Art History | The Metropolitan Museum of Art

[249] James Lockhart and Stuart B. Schwartz, *Early Latin America: A History of Colonial Spanish America and Brazil*. New York: Cambridge University Press 1983, pp. 24-26.

[250] Lockhart and Schwartz, *Early Latin America*, pp. 26-27.

[251] Alexander Marchant, *From Barter to Slavery: The Economic Relations of Portuguese and Indians in the Settlement of Brazil, 1500-1580*. Baltimore: Johns Hopkins Press 1942.

[252] For a comprehensive history of the Jesuits in Brazil see Serafim Leite, S.J. *História de Companhia de Jesus no Brasil*. 10 vols. Lisbon 1938-50.

[253] Charles E. Nowell, "The French in Sixteenth-Century Brazil," *The Americas* 5 (1949):381-93.

[254] Stuart B. Schwartz, "Indian Labor and New World Demands and Indian Response in Northeastern Brazil." *American Historical Review* 83 (1978) 43-79.

[255] James Lockhart and Stuart B. Schwartz, *Early Latin America*, chapter 7. Brazil in the Sugar Age. New York: Cambridge University Press 1983.

[256] Stuart B. Schwartz, "Free Farmers in a Slave Economy: The *Lavradores de Cana* in Colonial Bahia," in Dauril Alden, ed. *Colonial Roots of Modern Brazil*. Berkeley and Los Angeles: University of California Press 1973, pp. 147-97.

[257] Gilberto Freyre, *The Masters and the Slaves: A Study in the Development of Brazilian Civilization*. New York: English edition 1956; 1933 Portuguese original edition.

[258] See the articles by Ernst van den Boogaart and by Elmer Kolfin in *The Slave in European Art: From Renaissance Trophy to Abolitionist Emblem*, ed Elizabeth McGrath and Jean Michel Massing, London (The Warburg Institute) and Turin 2012.

[259] Rae Flory and David Grant Smith, "Bahian Merchants and Planters in the Seventeenth and Early Eighteenth Centuries." *Hispanic American Historical Review* 58(1978):571-94.

[260] Lockhart and Schwartz, *Early Latin America*, p. 221.

[261] James Lockhart and Stuart B. Schwartz, *Early Latin America*. New York: Cambridge University Press 1983, pp.227-231.

[262] James Lockhart and Stuart B. Schwartz, *Early Latin America*. New York: Cambridge University Press 1983, p. 226-7.

[263] Lockhart and Schwartz, *Early Latin America*, p. 225, p. 250.

[264] Arnold Wiznitzer, *the Jews of Colonial Brazil*. New York: 1960.

[265] Lockhart and Schwartz, *Early Latin America*, p. 250.

[266] C.R. Boxer, *The Dutch in Brazil: 1624-1654*. New York: Oxford University Press 1957.
[267] James Lockhart and Stuart Schwartz, *Early Latin America*. New York: Cambridge University Press 1983, p. 220.
[268] Lockhart and Schwartz, *Early Latin America*, pp. 220-21.
[269] Lockhart and Schwartz, *Early Latin America*, p. 221.
[270] Richard M. Morse, ed. *The Bandereintes: The Historical Role of the Brazilian Pathfinders*. New York 1965.
[271] Júnia Ferreira Furtado, *Chica da Silva: A Brazilian Slave of the Eighteenth Century*. New York: Cambridge University Press 2009.
[272] Leslie Bethell (1986). " *The Cambridge history of Latin America: Colonial Latin America https://books.google.com/books?id=hhNfVshMw64C&pg=PA47&dq&hl=en#v=onepage&q=&f=false*". Cambridge University Press. p.47.
[273] Kenneth P. Maxwell, *Conflicts and Conspiracies: Brazil and Portugal, 1750-1808*. New York: Cambridge University Press 1973.
[274] A.J.R. Russell-Wood, ed. *From Colony to Nation: Essays on the Independence of Brazil*. Baltimore: Johns Hopkins University Press 1975.
[275] José Honório Rodrigues. *Independência: Revolução e contra-revolução*. Rio de Janeiro 1976.
[276] https://web.archive.org/web/20070824235316/http://www.multirio.rj.gov.br/historia/index.html
[277] http://www.brown.edu/Research/Slavery_Justice/documents/SlaveryAndJustice.pdf
[278] Donald Ramos, "Emoboabas" in *Encyclopedia of Latin American History and Culture*, vol. 2, p. 487-88. New York: Charles Scribner's Sons 1996.
[279] Ramos, "Emboaba" p. 487
[280] FURTADO, Júnia Ferreira. *José Rodrigues Abreu e a geografia imaginária emboaba da conquista do ouro*. In: *Modos de Governar - Ideias e práticas políticas no Império Português séculos XVI a XIX*. BICALHO, Maria Fernanda & FERLINI, Vera Lúcia do Amaral (Orgs.). 1ª ed. São Paulo: Alameda, 2005, p.278
[281] Minas Flag http://www.mg.gov.br/governomg/portal/c/governomg/conheca-minas/5661-nossos-simbolos/26841-bandeira/5146/5044 , Minas Gerais Government
[282] http://www.mre.gov.br/cdbrasil/itamaraty/web/ingles/consnac/orgpol/periodos/monarq/
[283] http://www.multirio.rj.gov.br/historia/modulo02/elevacao_brasil.html
[284] https://web.archive.org/web/20080325230508/http://www2.camara.gov.br/internet/conheca/historia/reinounido.html
[285] https://web.archive.org/web/20060108124017/http://uk.holidaysguide.yahoo.com/p-travelguide-373548-brazil_history-i
[286] http://www.crwflags.com/fotw/flags/br-col.html
[287]
[288] See the tables **here** http://www.slavevoyages.org/tast/assessment/estimates.faces
[289] Lustosa, p.97
[290] Armitage. p.36
[291] Lustosa, p.106
[292] Armitage. p. 38
[293] Lustosa, pp. 109–10
[294] Armitage. p. 41
[295] Lustosa, p. 112
[296] Lustosa, pp. 113–14
[297] Lustosa, p. 114
[298] Lustosa, p. 117
[299] Armitage. pp. 43–44
[300] Lustosa, p.119
[301] Armitage. pp. 48–51
[302] Diégues, p. 70
[303] Lustosa, p.120
[304] Lustosa, pp. 121–22
[305] Lustosa, pp. 123–24
[306] Lustosa, pp. 132–34

[307] Lustosa, p. 135
[308] Lustosa, p. 138
[309] Lustosa, p. 139
[310] Lustosa, p. 143
[311] Armitage. p. 61
[312] Lustosa, p. 145
[313] Lustosa, pp. 150–53
[314] Vianna, p. 408
[315] Lima (1997), p. 398
[316] Lustosa, p. 153
[317] Lima (1997), p. 379
[318] Vianna, p. 413
[319] Vianna, pp. 417–18
[320] Lima (1997), p. 404
[321] Lima (1997), p.339
[322] Barman (1999), p. 4; "Some weeks later he was acclaimed emperor as Pedro I of Brazil. In the terminology of the period, the word 'empire' signifying a monarchy of unusually large size and resources (as in the case of Russia), and this designation avoided D. Pedro's usurping the title of 'king' from his father, João VI."
[323] Vianna, p. 418
[324] Brian Vale 'Independence or Death: British Sailors and Brazilian Independence' I B Tauris, 1995
[325] Brian Vale 'The Audacious Admiral Cochrane; The True Life of a Naval Legend', Conway, 2004
[326] Vale
[327] Laurentino Gomes *1822* Nova Fronteira, Brasil 2010 Chapter 10, p. 163
[328] Viana 1994, pp. 42–44.
[329] Viana 1994, pp. 59, 65, 66, 78, 175, 181, 197, 213, 300.
[330] Barman 1988, pp. 43–44.
[331] Barman 1988, p. 72.
[332] Viana 1994, p. 396.
[333] Barman 1988, pp. 75, 81–82.
[334] Viana 1994, pp. 399, 403.
[335] Viana 1994, pp. 408–408.
[336] Barman 1988, p. 96.
[337] Viana 1994, pp. 417–418.
[338] Barman 1988, pp. 101–102.
[339] Viana 1994, pp. 420–422.
[340] Barman 1988, pp. 104–106.
[341] Barman 1988, p. 128.
[342] Barman 1988, p. 131.
[343] Barman 1988, p. 142.
[344] Barman 1988, p. 151.
[345] Barman 1988, pp. 148–149.
[346] Barman 1999, pp. 18–19.
[347] Barman 1999, p. 19.
[348] Barman 1988, p. 159.
[349] Barman 1988, p. 160.
[350] Barman 1988, pp. 161–163.
[351] Barman 1999, p. 61.
[352] Barman 1988, pp. 179–180.
[353] Barman 1999, p. 317.
[354] Barman 1999, p. 64.
[355] Barman 1999, p. 58.
[356] Barman 1999, pp. 68–73.
[357] Barman 1999, p. 49.

[358] Barman 1999, p. 109.
[359] Barman 1999, p. 114.
[360] Barman 1999, p. 123.
[361] Barman 1999, p. 122.
[362] Barman 1999, pp. 122–123.
[363] Barman 1999, p. 124.
[364] Barman 1999, p. 125.
[365] Barman 1999, p. 126.
[366] Carvalho 2007, pp. 102–103.
[367] Levine 1999, pp. 63–64.
[368] See: • ; • ; • .
[369] Barman 1999, p. 159.
[370] Vainfas 2002, p. 343.
[371] Lira 1977, Vol 1, p. 182.
[372] Barman 1999, p. 162.
[373] See: • ; • ; • .
[374] Barman 1999, p. 166.
[375] Nabuco 1975, p. 162.
[376] Nabuco 1975, p. 313.
[377] Nabuco 1975, pp. 346, 370, 373, 376.
[378] Nabuco 1975, p. 346.
[379] Nabuco 1975, pp. 364–365.
[380] Nabuco 1975, p. 378.
[381] Nabuco 1975, pp. 374–376.
[382] Barman 1999, p. 192.
[383] See: • ; • ; • .
[384] See: • ; • .
[385] Calmon 1975, p. 680.
[386] Doratioto 2002, pp. 98, 203.
[387] Calmon 1975, p. 684.
[388] See: • ; • ; • .
[389] See: • ; • ; • .
[390] Lira 1977, Vol 1, p. 220.
[391] See: • ; • ; • .
[392] Carvalho 2007, p. 109.
[393] Lira 1977, Vol 1, p. 227.
[394] Calmon 1975, p. 748.
[395] Lira 1977, Vol 1, p. 237.
[396] Barman 1999, p. 222.
[397] Nabuco 1975, p. 592.
[398] Barman 1999, p. 223.
[399] Nabuco 1975, p. 666.
[400] Barman 1999, pp. 229–230.
[401] Doratioto 2002, p. 461.
[402] Doratioto 2002, p. 462.
[403] Calmon 2002, p. 201.
[404] Munro 1942, p. 276.
[405] Barman 1999, p. 243.
[406] Lira 1977, Vol 2, p. 9.
[407] Barman 1999, p. 240.
[408] Barman 1999, p. 235.
[409] Barman 1999, p. 238.
[410] Barman 1999, p. 261.
[411] Barman 1999, pp. 234, 317.
[412] Barman 1999, p. 318.
[413] See: • ; • ; • .

[414] Barman 1999, p. 298–299.
[415] Barman 1999, p. 299.
[416] Lira 1977, Vol 3, p. 126.
[417] Barman 1999, p. 399.
[418] Barman 1999, pp. 262–263.
[419] Barman 1999, p. 130.
[420] Barman 1999, p. 262.
[421] Barman 1999, p. 268.
[422] Barman 1999, p. 349.
[423] Lira 1977, Vol 3, p. 121.
[424] See: • ; • ; • .
[425] Carvalho 2007, p. 195.
[426] Barman 1999, p. 353.
[427] Barman 1999, pp. 353–355.
[428] Topik 2000, p. 56.
[429] Barman 1999, p. 341.
[430] Barman 1999, p. 346.
[431] Lira 1977, Vol 3, p. 78.
[432] See: • ; • ; • .
[433] Barman 1999, p. 351.
[434] Barman 1999, p. 355.
[435] Barman 1999, p. 356.
[436] Barman 1999, pp. 353–356.
[437] Ermakoff 2006, p. 189.
[438] Schwarcz 1998, p. 450.
[439] See: • ; • ; • ; • .
[440] Schwarcz 1998, p. 459.
[441] Lira 1977, Vol 3, p. 96.
[442] Besouchet 1993, p. 538.
[443] Barman 1999, p. 361.
[444] See: • ; • ; • .
[445] Carvalho 2007, p. 220.
[446] Salles 1996, p. 194.
[447] Barman 1999, p. 394.
[448] Lira 1977, Vol 3, pp. 119–120.
[449] Barman 1988, p. 132.
[450] Barman 1988, pp. 132–133.
[451] Barman 1988, p. 133.
[452] Viana 1994, p. 476.
[453] Carvalho 1993, p. 42.
[454] Nabuco 1975, p. 712.
[455] Dolhnikoff 2005, p. 59.
[456] Dolhnikoff 2005, p. 60.
[457] Dolhnikoff 2005, pp. 64, 97.
[458] Dolhnikoff 2005, p. 97.
[459] Dolhnikoff 2005, p. 99.
[460] Dolhnikoff 2005, p. 100.
[461] Dolhnikoff 2005, p. 102.
[462] Dolhnikoff 2005, p. 103.
[463] Dolhnikoff 2005, pp. 110–112.
[464] Dolhnikoff 2005, p. 118.
[465] Dolhnikoff 2005, p. 83.
[466] Dolhnikoff 2005, pp. 118–119.
[467] Rodrigues 1863, pp. 134–135.
[468] Carvalho 2008, p. 29.
[469] Vainfas 2002, p. 223.

[470] Barman 1988, p. 124.
[471] Carvalho 2008, p. 30.
[472] Vainfas 2002, p. 139.
[473] Carvalho 2008, p. 31.
[474] Carvalho 1993, p. 46.
[475] Vainfas 2002, p. 224.
[476] See: • ; • ; • .
[477] Carvalho 2007, p. 180.
[478] Carvalho 1993, p. 48.
[479] Carvalho 2008, p. 39.
[480] Carvalho 2008, p. 33.
[481] Carvalho 1993, p. 51.
[482] Carvalho 2002, p. 84–85.
[483] Carvalho 2002, p. 91.
[484] Rodrigues 1863, pp. 79, 117.
[485] Carvalho 2007, p. 193.
[486] Lira 1977, Vol 3, p. 84.
[487] Pedrosa 2004, p. 289.
[488] Holanda 1974, pp. 241–242.
[489] Vainfas 2002, p. 548.
[490] Calmon 2002, p. 265.
[491] Parkinson 2008, p. 128.
[492] Lira 1977, Vol 3, p. 70.
[493] Lira 1977, Vol 3, p. 69.
[494] Barman 1999, p. 321.
[495] Carvalho 2007, p. 196.
[496] Topik 2000, pp. 64, 66, 235.
[497] During the 19th century, Brazil was divided into only two geographical regions: north (roughly present-day northeast and north) and south (roughly present-day central-west, southeast and south). See Vainfas 2002, p. 39.
[498] Rodrigues 1975, p. 168.
[499] Rodrigues 1975, pp. 174, 177, 180, 181, 182.
[500] Rodrigues 1975, p. 148.
[501] Vainfas 2002, p. 301.
[502] Viana 1994, p. 525.
[503] Vainfas 2002, p. 302.
[504] Viana 1994, p. 578.
[505] Viana 1994, p. 575.
[506] The only exceptions regarding border disputes in the north and west were minor diplomatic disputes with France and Britain in the northern region. During the 1830s, both countries occupied and unsuccessfully attempted to claim some areas in the north as part of their colonial empires. See Viana 1994, p. 575.
[507] Vainfas 2002, p. 329.
[508] Vainfas 2002, pp. 323–324.
[509] Smith 2010, p. 7.
[510] Smith 2010, p. 18.
[511] Barman 1999, p. 306.
[512] Rodrigues 1995, p. 208.
[513] Topik 2000, p. 60.
[514] Barman 1999, p. XVI.
[515] Graça Filho 2004, p. 21.
[516] Sodré 2004, p. 201.
[517] Fausto & Devoto 2005, p. 47.
[518] Fausto & Devoto 2005, p. 50.
[519] Lira 1977, Vol 1, p. 200.
[520] Barman 1988, pp. 218, 236, 237.

[521] Topik 2000, p. 19.
[522] Fausto & Devoto 2005, p. 46.
[523] Topik 2000, p. 33.
[524] Vainfas 2002, p. 250.
[525] Vainfas 2002, p. 251.
[526] Fausto 1995, p. 239.
[527] Calmon 2002, p. 368.
[528] Vainfas 2002, p. 538.
[529] Lira 1977, Vol 2, p. 13.
[530] Vasquez 2007, p. 38.
[531] Viana 1994, p. 496.
[532] Calmon 2002, p. 222.
[533] Calmon 2002, p. 225.
[534] Calmon 2002, p. 226.
[535] Lira 1977, Vol 2, p. 309.
[536] Vainfas 2002, p. 539.
[537] Calmon 2002, p. 366.
[538] Vainfas 2002, p. 131.
[539] Vainfas 2002, p. 132.
[540] Vainfas 2002, p. 133.
[541] Baer 2002, p. 341.
[542] Ramos 2003, p. 82.
[543] Coelho 1996, p. 268.
[544] Vesentini 1988, p. 117.
[545] See: • ; • ; • ; • ; • ; • ; • .
[546] See: • ; • ; • .
[547] Moreira 1981, p. 108.
[548] Azevedo 1971, pp. 74–75.
[549] Barsa 1987, Vol 10, p. 355.
[550] Azevedo 1971, p. 74.
[551] Azevedo 1971, p. 161.
[552] Ramos 2003, p. 84.
[553] Viana 1994, p. 511.
[554] Ramos 2003, p. 37.
[555] Viana 1994, p. 512.
[556] Viana 1994, p. 513.
[557] Viana 1994, pp. 513–514.
[558] Viana 1994, p. 515.
[559] Viana 1994, p. 517.
[560] Vainfas 2002, p. 351.
[561] Viana 1994, p. 633.
[562] Vainfas 2002, p. 353.
[563] Vainfas 2002, pp. 351–352.
[564] Vainfas 2002, pp. 18, 239.
[565] Vainfas 2002, pp. 237–238.
[566] Vainfas 2002, p. 29.
[567] Boxer 2002, pp. 113–114, 116.
[568] Vainfas 2002, p. 30.
[569] Boxer 2002, pp. 185–186.
[570] Boxer 2002, p. 117.
[571] Boxer 2002, p. 206.
[572] Boxer 2002, p. 169.
[573] Vainfas 2002, pp. 238–239.
[574] Vainfas 2002, p. 239.
[575] Besouchet 1985, p. 167.
[576] Fausto 1995, pp. 238–239.

[577] Olivieri 1999, p. 43.
[578] Barman 1988, p. 194.
[579] Carvalho 2007, p. 130.
[580] Alencastro 1997, pp. 87–88.
[581] Besouchet 1985, p. 170.
[582] Vainfas 2002, p. 553.
[583] Vainfas 2002, p. 554.
[584] Barman 1999, p. 11.
[585] Viana 1968, p. 208.
[586] Barman 1999, p. 139.
[587] Viana 1968, p. 220.
[588] Viana 1968, p. 216.
[589] Viana 1968, pp. 204, 206.
[590] Viana 1968, p. 218.
[591] Viana 1968, p. 219.
[592] Viana 1968, p. 221.
[593] Barman 1999, p. 77.
[594] Viana 1968, p. 217.
[595] Schwarcz 1998, p. 191.
[596] Vainfas 2002, p. 126.
[597] Barman 1999, p. 254.
[598] Carvalho 2007, p. 151.
[599] Carvalho 2007, p. 150.
[600] Barman 1999, pp. 254–256.
[601] Vainfas 2002, p. 450.
[602] Vainfas 2002, pp. 450–451.
[603] Vainfas 2002, p. 451.
[604] Vainfas 2002, p. 596.
[605] Vainfas 2002, pp. 596–597.
[606] Vainfas 2002, p. 31.
[607] Vainfas 2002, pp. 114–115.
[608] Vainfas 2002, pp. 30–31.
[609] Vainfas 2002, pp. 170.
[610] Vainfas 2002, p. 83.
[611] Vainfas 2002, p. 84.
[612] Vainfas 2002, pp. 21–22.
[613] Vainfas 2002, p. 22.
[614] Schwarcz 1998, pp. 126–127.
[615] Schwarcz 1998, p. 126.
[616] Schwarcz 1998, p. 152.
[617] Vainfas 2002, p. 285.
[618] Vainfas 2002, p. 123.
[619] Schwarcz 1998, p. 145.
[620] Vainfas 2002, pp. 84–85.
[621] Vainfas 2002, p. 85.
[622] Vainfas 2002, p. 482.
[623] Vainfas 2002, p. 661.
[624] Vainfas 2002, pp. 482–483.
[625] Barman 1988, p. 237.
[626] Vainfas 2002, p. 483.
[627] Vainfas 2002, p. 513.
[628] Vainfas 2002, p. 484.
[629] Vainfas 2002, p. 691.
[630] Vainfas 2002, pp. 483–484.
[631] Vainfas 2002, p. 692.
[632] Vainfas 2002, p. 693.

[633] Vainfas 2002, p. 694.
[634] //www.worldcat.org/oclc/14271198
[635] //www.worldcat.org/oclc/685131818
[636] //www.worldcat.org/oclc/36598004
[637] //en.wikipedia.org/w/index.php?title=Template:History_of_Brazil&action=edit
[638] Hudson, Rex A. *Brazil: A Country Study*. Washington: GPO for the Library of Congress, 1997, pg.22
[639] Smallman, Shawn C. "Fear & Memory: in the Brazilian Army & Society, 1889–1954" The University of North Carolina Press 2002 pages 17–22
[640] Ibidem - Smallman 2002
[641] Ignacy Sachs, Jorge Wilheim & Paulo S.Pinheiro; "Brazil: a century of change" University of North Carolina Press 2009 pages 58 & 63
[642] Smith, Joseph "Brazil and the United States; convergence and divergence" University of Georgia Press 2010, page 39
[643] Brassey, Thomas Allnutt "The Naval Annual; 1894" Elibron Classics/Adamant Media Corporation 2006, Chapter XI "The Naval Revolt in Brazil"
[644] pt:Página principal
[645] Woodward; James P. "A Place in Politics: São Paulo, Brazil, from Seigneurial Republicanism to Regionalist Revolt" Duke University Press Books 2009 Page94 2nParagraph
[646] Grandes Guerras – Os grandes conflitos do século XX http://www.grandesguerras.com.br/artigos/text01.php?art_id=68
[647] : Exército Brasileiro – Braço Forte, Mão Amiga : http://www.exercito.gov.br/01inst/Historia/Artigos/0011005.htm
[648] Maia, Prado "D.N.O.G. (Divisão Naval em Operações de Guerra), 1917–18: uma página esquecida da história da Marinha Brasileira" ("D.N.O.G. - Naval Division in War Operations, 1917–1918: A forgotten page in the history of the Brazilian Navy") [S.l.]: Serviço de Documentação Geral da Marinha, 1961 (General Documentation Service of Brazilian Navy) OCLC 22210405
[649] //www.worldcat.org/oclc/22210405
[650] https://books.google.com/books?id=3CTcGwAACAAJ
[651] 1937 constitution of the United States of Brazil, Article 38 § 1º https://pt.wikisource.org/wiki/Constitui%C3%A7%C3%A3o_do_Brasil_de_1937
[652] Ibid.
[653] //en.wikipedia.org/w/index.php?title=Template:History_of_Brazil&action=edit
[654] Fridell, Gavin. *Fair Trade Coffee*. (pg 120)
[655] De Mattei, Roberto. *The Crusader of the 20th Century*, 1998. (pg 52)
[656] Stanley E. Hilton, "The Argentine Factor in Twentieth-Century Brazilian Foreign Policy Strategy." *Political Science Quarterly* 100.1 (1985): 27-51.
[657] Stanley E. Hilton, "Brazilian Diplomacy and the Washington-Rio de Janeiro 'Axis' during the World War II Era," *Hispanic American Historical Review* (1979) 59#2 pp. 201-231 in JSTOR https://www.jstor.org/stable/2514412
[658] https://web.archive.org/web/20110514215058/http://www.brazilnow.info/glossary01.php?read_more=48&s_string=LETTER;X;E&page=1
[659] //en.wikipedia.org/w/index.php?title=Template:History_of_Brazil&action=edit
[660] "Brasil: Uma Historia - Eduardo Bueno"
[661] //en.wikipedia.org/w/index.php?title=Template:History_of_Brazil&action=edit
[662] Document No. 12. U.S. Support for the Brazilian Military Coup d'État, 1964 http://global.oup.com/us/companion.websites/9780195375701/pdf/SPD12_US_Support_Brazil_Coup.pdf
[663] "Brasil: Uma Historia - Eduardo Bueno" http://www.brasilumahistoria.com.br/
[664] BRAZIL Toward Stability http://www.time.com/time/printout/0,8816,842333,00.html, *TIME Magazine*, December 31, 1965
[665] Situation in Brazil. CIA analysis and full text of AI-5 http://www.foia.cia.gov/sites/default/files/document_conversions/89801/DOC_0000753959.pdf
[666] Brazil: Raising the Ransom Price http://www.time.com/time/printout/0,8816,904588,00.html, *Time Magazine*, December 21, 1970

[667] Pattern of Terror http://www.time.com/time/magazine/article/0,9171,902646,00.html. Time.com.
[668] Marie-Moniques de la mort - l'école française (*See here, starting at 24 min http://www. mefeedia.com/entry/2926696/)*
[669] , pp. 269 and 395
[670] , p.396
[671] Adam Taylor (12 December 2014). Brazil's torture report brings President Dilma Rousseff to tears http://www.smh.com.au/world/brazils-torture-report-brings-president-dilma-rousseff-to-tears-20141211-125fzz.html. The Sydney Morning Herald. Retrieved 12 December 2014.
[672] http://www.gwu.edu/~nsarchiv/NSAEBB/NSAEBB118/index.htm
[673] //en.wikipedia.org/w/index.php?title=Template:History_of_Brazil&action=edit
[674] The Hyperinflation in Brazil, 1980–1994 http://www.sjsu.edu/faculty/watkins/brazilinfl.htm
[675] Rezende, Tatiana Matos UNE 70 Anos: "Fora Collor: o grito da juventude cara-pintada" http://www.une.org.br/home3/movimento_estudantil/movimento_estudantil_2007/m_9920.html União Nacional dos Estudantes. Retrieved August 17, 2007.
[676] Lattman-Weltman, Fernando. September 29, 1992: Collor's Impeachment http://www.cpdoc.fgv.br/nav_fatos_imagens/htm/fatos/Impeachment.asp Fundação Getúlio Vargas. Retrieved August 17, 2007.
[677] Sérgio Campos Gonçalves, Collorgate: mídia, jornalismo e sociedade nos casos Watergate e Collor, (Rio de Janeiro: CBJE, 2008).
[678] Folha Online: STF opens criminal action http://www1.folha.uol.com.br/folha/brasil/ult96u91315.shtml
[679] //tools.wmflabs.org/geohack/geohack.php?pagename=Geography_of_Brazil&params=10_S_55_W_region:BR_type:country
[680] http://lcweb2.loc.gov/frd/cs/
[681] https://www.cia.gov/library/publications/the-world-factbook/index.html
[682] http://www.wdl.org/en/item/807
[683] http://www.wdl.org/en/item/1074
[684] Piauí tem a temperatura mais alta em 96 anos http://noticias.terra.com.br/brasil/interna/0,,OI771459-EI306,00.html, Terra, November 26, 2005.
[685] Recordes de frio em SC http://ciram.epagri.sc.gov.br/portal/website/index.jsp , EPAGRI/CIRAM, retrieved May 15, 2013.
[686] *Sibéria brasileira no sul do Brasil* ("Brazilian Siberia in the South of Brazil") http://fantastico.globo.com/Jornalismo/FANT/0,,MUL695732-15605,00.html, Fantástico, July 18, 2006.
[687] http://br.weather.com/weather/climatology/BRXX0033
[688] http://www.cpa.unicamp.br/outras-informacoes/clima_muni_111.html
[689] http://www.cpa.unicamp.br/outras-informacoes/clima-de-campinas.html
[690] http://br.weather.com/weather/climatology/BRXX0201
[691] http://br.weather.com/weather/climatology/BRXX0232
[692] http://br.weather.com/weather/climatology/BRXX3272
[693] http://br.weather.com/weather/climatology/BRXX0093
[694] http://br.weather.com/weather/climatology/BRXX0195
[695] http://www.weatherbase.com/weather/weather.php3?s=87528&cityname=Teresina-Piaui-Brazil&units=metric
[696] http://br.weather.com/weather/climatology/BRXX0186
[697] http://br.weather.com/weather/climatology/BRXX0091
[698] http://br.weather.com/weather/climatology/BRXX0079
[699] http://br.weather.com/weather/climatology/BRXX0226
[700] http://br.weather.com/weather/climatology/BRXX0068
[701] http://worldweather.wmo.int/136/c01073.htm
[702] http://worldweather.wmo.int/136/c01061.htm
[703] http://www.worldclimateguide.co.uk/climateguides/brazil/riobranco.php
[704] http://www.worldweather.org/136/c01071.htm
[705] http://www.inmet.gov.br/portal/index.php?r=clima/normaisClimatologicas
[706] http://www.hko.gov.hk/wxinfo/climat/world/eng/s_america/brazil/brasilia_e.htm
[707] http://worldweather.wmo.int/136/c01069.htm

[708] http://www.worldclimateguide.co.uk/climateguides/brazil/cuiaba.php
[709] http//www.inmet.gov.br
[710] //tools.wmflabs.org/geohack/geohack.php?pagename=Wildlife_of_Brazil&params=15.611120_S_56.056012_W_
[711] Da Silva, M. and D.W. Minter. 1995. *Fungi from Brazil recorded by Batista and Co-workers*. Mycological Papers 169. CABI, Wallingford, UK. 585 pp.
[712] Kirk, P.M., P.F. Cannon, D.W. Minter and J. Stalpers. 2008. *Dictionary of the Fungi*. Edn 10. CABI, Wallingford, UK.
[713] USDA Forest Service website, Forest Service International Programs: Brazil http://www.fs.fed.us/global/globe/l_amer/brazil.htm, retrieved February 2007.
[714] Luiz Ricardo L. Simone. 2006. *Land and Freshwater Molluscs of Brazil*. Museu de Zoologia Universidade de São Paulo, São Paulo, Brazil. 390 pp. (book review http://www.jaxshells.org/simone.pdf)
[715] Magellanic Penguin http://www.penguins.cl/magellanic-penguins.htm, Organisation for the Conservation of Penguins.
[716] Rantin B., and M.E. Bichuette (2013). *Phototactic behaviour of subterranean Copionodontinae Pinna, 1992 catfishes (Siluriformes, Trichomycteridae) from Chapada Diamantina, central Bahia, northeastern Brazil*. International Journal of Speleology 41(1): 57-63
[717] Levitas, Gloria. "The Amazon's Kettle of Fish" https://query.nytimes.com/gst/fullpage.html?res=940DE1DE1238F932A2575AC0A96E948260&sec=&spon=&pagewanted=all, New York Times, September 11, 1988.
[718] Aljazeera / Brazil's Ethanol for SugarCane program
[719] http//www.dtnprogressivefarmer.com
[720] http://green.autoblog.com/2011/09/19/bp-expands-ethanol-output-with-acquisition-of-brazils-tropical/
[721] //www.worldcat.org/oclc/77711203
[722] http://www.brazilianfauna.com/
[723] http://www.brazilnature.com/ingles/ecossistema.html
[724] http://eol.org/collections/103170
[725] *National Geographic*. January 2007.
[726] Hall, A.L. (1989) *Developing Amazonia*, Manchester: Manchester University Press.
[727] João S. Campari, 2005 *The Economics of Deforestation in the Amazon*.
[728] Watkins and Griffiths, J. (2000). Forest Destruction and Sustainable Agriculture in the Brazilian Amazon: a Literature Review (Doctoral dissertation, The University of Reading, 2000). Dissertation Abstracts International, 15-17
[729] Williams, M. (2006). *Deforesting the Earth: From Prehistory to Global Crisis*. Chicago, IL: The University of Chicago Press.
[730] Fernside, P. M. (2005). Deforestation in Brazilian Amazonia: History, Rates, and Consequences. Conservation Biology, 19, 680-688.
[731] H. Steinfeld, P. Gerber, T. Wassenaar, V. Castel, M. Rosales, C. de Haan. Livestock's Long Shadow: Environmental Issues and Options. United Nations Food and Agriculture Organization. 2006. http://www.virtualcentre.org/en/library/key_pub/longshad/A0701E00.htm
[732] Sergio Marglis. "Causes of Deforestation of the Brazilian Amazon." http://www-wds.worldbank.org/servlet/WDSContentServer/WDSP/IB/2004/02/02/000090341_20040202130625/Rendered/PDF/277150PAPER0wbwp0no1022.pdf World Bank Working Paper No. 22. The World Bank. 2004.
[733] "Deforestation in the Amazon." http://www.mongabay.com/brazil.html mongabay.com.
[734] Online http://www.sciencemag.org/content/326/5953/716.abstract
[735] Greenpeace. 2006. We're trashin' it: how McDonald's is eating up the Amazon. Amsterdam: Greenpeace.
[736] Also available from NASA Earth Observatory News https://web.archive.org/web/20081012125024/http://earthobservatory.nasa.gov/Newsroom/NasaNews/2006/2006091923131.html.
[737] Reel, Monte. "Brazil Crackdown on Loggers After Surge in Cutting." https://www.washingtonpost.com/wp-dyn/content/article/2008/03/20/AR2008032003870_3.html?sid=ST2008032003923 *Washington Post*. 21 March 2008.

[738] Lynch, Patrick. "Concept: Paying People to Not Cut Down Trees." *Daily Press*, Newport News, VA. 6 Jan. 2008: A1.
[739] "Fires in the Rainforest." http://rainforests.mongabay.com/0809.htm Mongabay.com.
[740] http://web.nateko.lu.se/courses/ngen03/posey-1985.pdf
[741] National Institute for Space Research (INPE) (2010)
[742] *Science Daily. https://www.sciencedaily.com/releases/2007/05/070515151140.htm* Published May 16, 2007. Retrieved November 27, 2007.
[743] Deforestation - Facts http://www.tree4life.com/ingles/deforest3.htm
[744] "Brazilian Senate Ratifies Kyoto Protocol." http://www.unwire.org/unwire/20020620/27172_story.asp *UN Wire: Email News Covering the United Nations and the World.* 24 Jan 2009.
[745] "Brazil will forge its own path for developing the Amazon." http://news.mongabay.com/2008/0515-amazon.html *Conservation news and environmental science news.* 26 Jan 2009.
[746] Woods Hole Research Center (2007, May 16). "Brazil Demonstrating That Reducing Tropical Deforestation Is Key Win-win Global Warming Solution."
[747] http://www.worldchanging.com/archives/007413.html
[748] World Wide Fund for Nature. October 4 2007. http://www.panda.org/about_wwf/where_we_work/latin_america_and_caribbean/country/brazil/index.cfm?uNewsID=115420
[749] http://travel.mongabay.com/deforestation.html
[750] https://dx.doi.org/10.1016/j.ecolecon.2007.12.008
[751] http://scifunam.fisica.unam.mx/mir/1999_interciencia.PDF
[752] USDA Forest Service website, Forest Service International Programs: Brazil http://www.fs.fed.us/global/globe/l_amer/brazil.htm, retrieved February 2007.
[753] "Beef Exports Fuel Loss of Amazonian Forest." Center for International Forestry Research. N.p., n.d. Web. 15 Mar. 2015.
[754] Deforestation of the Amazon Rainforests and CO2. University of Michigan, n.d. Web. 14 Feb. 2015. http://sitemaker.umich.edu/section3group2/deforestation_of_the_amazon_rainforests_and_co2.
[755] Deforestation of the Amazon Rainforests and CO2. University of Michigan, n.d. Web. 14 Feb. 2015. http://sitemaker.umich.edu/section3group2/deforestation_of_the_amazon_rainforests_and_co2
[756] "Brazil Demonstrating That Reducing Tropical Deforestation Is Key WinWin Global Warming Solution." Space Daily. N.p., 16 May 2007. Web. 15 Mar. 2015.
[757] Instituto Hórus de Desenvolvimento e Conservação Ambiental http://www.institutohorus.org.br/index_eng.htm (The Horus Institute for Environmental Conservation and Development)
[758] Julieta Andrea Puerto Rico (2008-05-08). "Programa de Biocombustíveis no Brasil e na Colômbia: uma análise da implantação, resultados e perspectivas" (in Portuguese). Universidade de São Paulo. Retrieved 2008-10-05. Ph.D. Dissertation Thesis, pp. 81–82
[759] Lovins. A.B. (2005). Winning the Oil Endgame, p. 105.
[760] *See pp. 3, 8, 10 22 and 23.*
[761] "Greenhouse Gas Reduction Thresholds". U.S. Environmental Protection Agency. 2010-02-03. Retrieved 2010-02-09.
[762] "Get the Facts Right and Kill the Myths." Brazil Sugarcane Ethanol (n.d.): n. pag. Sugarcane.org. Sugarcane.org, 1 Nov. 2010. Web. 1 Feb. 2015.
[763] Macedo Isaias, M. Lima Verde Leal and J. Azevedo Ramos da Silva (2004). "Assessment of greenhouse gas emissions in the production and use of fuel ethanol in Brazil" (PDF). Secretariat of the Environment, Government of the State of São Paulo. Archived from the original on 2008-05-28. Retrieved 2008-05-09.
[764] Briefing Note 005/10 pp. 13–15.
[765] "Deforestation: Brazil Is a Success Story for Conservation." The Christian Science Monitor. The Christian Science Monitor, n.d. Web. 28 Apr. 2015.
[766] Hudson, Rex A., ed. (1997). "The Society and Its Environment: The Environment". *Brazil: A Country Study.* Library of Congress Country Studies. Retrieved 2011-12-06.
[767] http://uc.socioambiental.org/sites/uc.socioambiental.org/files/snuc_sistema%20nacional%20de%20unidades%20de%20conservacao.pdf, Federal Law N° 9.985 of 07/18/2000. Regulates article 225 of the Federal Constitution and institutes the National System of Units of Conservation and other provisions.

[768] Socio-environmental Institute http://uc.socioambiental.org/en/o-snuc/what-is-the-snuc/, What is the SNUC??.
[769] "Biodiversity in Brazil." UNESCO Office in Brasilia. UNESCO, n.d. Web. 27 Apr. 2015.
[770] http://uc.socioambiental.org/
[771] http://www.safarisbrazil.com
[772] //en.wikipedia.org/w/index.php?title=Template:Politics_of_Brazil&action=edit
[773] Navigator to Direct Democracy "Scientific overview of direct democracy procedures in Brazil" https://web.archive.org/web/20121120035432/http://direct-democracy-navigator.org/countries/brazil/legal_designs
[774] Barros, Ana Cláudia. "PT ainda pode ser chamado de esquerda, afirma sociólogo" http://terramagazine.terra.com.br/interna/0,,OI4683023-EI6578,00-PT+ainda+e+esquerda+no+Brasil+analisa+sociologo.html. Terra Magazine. September 17, 2010.
[775] Lula diz que o DEM precisa ser extirpado da política brasileira - Terra Brasil http://noticias.terra.com.br/eleicoes/2010/noticias/0,,OI4676356-EI15315,00-Lula+Os+Bornhausen+nao+podem+se+disfarcar+de+cordeiros.html
[776] http://divulga.tse.jus.br/oficial/index.html
[777] http://www2.camara.leg.br/camaranoticias/noticias/POLITICA/475427-PT-E-PMDB-ELEGEM-NOVAMENTE-AS-MAIORES-BANCADAS.html
[778] http//g1.globo.com
[779] https://archive.is/20130414194957/http://report.globalintegrity.org/brazil
[780] http://observingbrazil.com
[781] https://web.archive.org/web/20100308062529/http://brazilinfocus.com/
[782] http://geostadia.com
[783] https://www.amazon.com/dp/B00NZBPX8A
[784] http://www.presidencia.gov.br
[785] //en.wikipedia.org/w/index.php?title=Template:Politics_of_Brazil&action=edit
[786] http://divulga.tse.jus.br/oficial/index.html
[787] http://electionresources.org/br/deputies.php?election=2010&state=BR
[788] http://pdba.georgetown.edu/Elecdata/Brazil/brazil.html
[789] http://psephos.adam-carr.net/countries/b/brazil/
[790] http://www.tse.jus.br/internet/eleicoes/urna_eletronica/simulador_Votacao_2010/br.htm
[791] http://noleakybuckets.org/brasil-history.html
[792] http://portland.indymedia.org/en/2006/10/347846.shtml
[793] http://www.planalto.gov.br/ccivil_03/leis/l4737.htm
[794] http://www.planalto.gov.br/ccivil_03/leis/lcp/lcp64.htm
[795] //en.wikipedia.org/w/index.php?title=Template:Politics_of_Brazil&action=edit
[796] Legal system of Brazil http://www.oas.org/juridico/mla/en/bra/en_bra-int-des-ordrjur.html
[797] History - Law in Brazil http://www.cursodireito.info/
[798] Number of Law schools in Brazil http://g1.globo.com/Noticias/Vestibular/0,,MUL3813-5604,00-OAB+PREVE+MIL+CURSOS+DE+DIREITO+EM.html
[799] Number of Law schools in the United States http://jus2.uol.com.br/doutrina/texto.asp?id=10274
[800] Total - Lawyers in Brazil by State - Bar Association of Brazil http://www.oab.org.br/relatorioAdvOAB.asp
[801] About the Bar Examination in Brazil https://oliveiralawyers.com/about-brazil/lawyering-brazil/bar-examination/
[802] About the course of law in Brazil http://www.mundovestibular.com.br/articles/6531/1/Curso-de-Direito/Paacutegina1.html
[803] Median income in Brazil http://veja.abril.com.br/111109/popup_remuneracao.html
[804] 45th Constitutional Amendment text https://www.planalto.gov.br/ccivil_03/Constituicao/Emendas/Emc/emc45.htm
[805] http://www.planalto.gov.br/ccivil_03/Constituicao/Constituiçao_Compilado.htm
[806] http://www.v-brazil.com/government/laws/constitution.html
[807] http://www.pontuacaodetran.com.br/codigo-transito-brasileiro.html
[808] http://www25.senado.leg.br/web/atividade/legislacao
[809] https://www.global-regulation.com/search-country/Brazil.html

[810] https://archive.org/details/germanyguidetola00borcuoft
[811] Court Decision "ADIn n.236-8/RJ" http://www.stf.gov.br/processos/processo.asp?Classe= ADI&Processo=236&Origem=AP&Recurso=0&TIP_JULGAMENTO=M Published June 1, 2001. Accessed September 5, 2007. **(Portuguese)**
[812] Rio de Janeiro Civil Police "Historical Data" http://www.policiacivil.rj.gov.br/institucional/apresentacaoingles.htm Accessed September 5, 2007.
[813] Minas Gerais Military Police "Histórico" https://www.policiamilitar.mg.gov.br/_pmmg.htm Accessed September 5, 2007. **(Portuguese)**
[814] Tourinho Filho, F. 2004. *Processo Penal vol.1.* p.190. São Paulo: Saraiva.
[815] Brazilian Federal Police Department "Histórico do DPF" http://www.dpf.gov.br/. Accessed September 5, 2007. **(Portuguese)**
[816] Silva, J.A. 2004. *Curso de Direito Constitucional Positivo.* p.758. São Paulo: Malheiros.
[817] See also: "Brazilian Federal Constitution in English" http://www.v-brazil.com/government/laws/titleI.html, text translated to English (unofficial). Accessed September 5, 2007.
[818] Ministério da Justiça "Força Nacional de Segurança Pública" http://www.mj.gov.br/transparencia/servicos/noticias/pdfs/Historico%20FNSP22-06-05.pdf Accessed September 5, 2007. **(Portuguese)**
[819] Jornal da Globo "Exército nas ruas do Rio" http://jg.globo.com/JGlobo/0,19125,VTJ0-2742-20060306-154122,00.html Accessed September 13, 2007. **(Portuguese)**
[820] Human Rights Report "Police brutality in urban Brazil" https://www.hrw.org/reports/1997/brazil/ Accessed September 5, 2007.
[821] "Amnesty International reports on Violence in Brazil" http://www.hartford-hwp.com/archives/42/181.html, SEJUP (Servico Brasileiro de Justica e Paz), *News from Brazil*, No. 489, 29 May 2003, Accessed September 5, 2007.
[822] Amnesty International "Brazil - Police Brutality" https://web.archive.org/web/20060901223543/http://web.amnesty.org/report2006/bra-summary-eng Accessed September 5, 2007.
[823] Brazil's Correctional System http://prisonstudies.org/country/brazil
[824] Brazil's Correctional System http://prisonstudies.org/country/brazil
[825] Brazil's Correctional System http://prisonstudies.org/country/brazil
[826] Brazil Aims to Build 30 Prisons This Year to Tackle Crisis. January 17, 2017. http://www.dnaindia.com/world/report-brazil-aims-to-build-30-prisons-this-year-to tackle-crisis-michel-temer-2293293
[827] Brazil Aims to Build 30 Prisons This Year to Tackle Crisis. January 17, 2017. http://www.dnaindia.com/world/report-brazil-aims-to-build-30-prisons-this-year-to tackle-crisis-michel-temer-2293293
[828] Brazil Must Address Prison Overcrowding and Implement Measures Against Torture. August 14, 2015. http://www.un.org/apps/news/story.asp?NewsID=51644#.WnsaT2bMxnZ
[829] Brazil Must Address Prison Overcrowding and Implement Measures Against Torture. August 14, 2015. http://www.un.org/apps/news/story.asp?NewsID=51644#.WnsaT2bMxnZ
[830] http://www.dpf.gov.br
[831] http://www.policiamilitar.rj.gov.br
[832] http://www.policiacivil.rj.gov.br/
[833] http://www.polmil.sp.gov.br/
[834] http://www.policia-civ.sp.gov.br/
[835] https://web.archive.org/web/20080712083616/http://www.policiamilitar.mg.gov.br/_pmmg.htm
[836] http://www.sesp.mg.gov.br/
[837] https://www.osac.gov/pages/ContentReportDetails.aspx?cid=19817
[838] phillipviana June 14, 2013 What's REALLY behind the Brazilian riots? http://ireport.cnn.com/docs/DOC-988431 CNN
[839] https://www.osac.gov/pages/ContentReportDetails.aspx?cid=19817
[840] https://www.sipri.org/sites/default/files/2018-04/sipri_fs_1805_milex_2017.pdf
[841] https://www.sipri.org/sites/default/files/2018-04/sipri_fs_1805_milex_2017.pdf
[842] According to article 144 of the 1988 Brazilian Constitution, the para-military Military Police alongside the Military Firefighters Corps are constitutionally considered an auxiliary

and potential reserve to the Army, though subordinate to the state governors. They can, however, be compelled to federal service under a statute similar to posse comitatus https://www.planalto.gov.br/ccivil_03/Constituicao/Constituicao.htm.

[843] IISS 2012, pp. 376–378

[844] Uma Nova Agenda Militar http://revistaepoca.globo.com/Revista/Epoca/0,,EMI14439-15273-2,00-UMA+NOVA+AGENDA+MILITAR.html Revista Época. Retrieved on 16 April 2015.

[845] Brazilian troops in Haiti https://archive.is/20120311060205/http://www.agenciabrasil.gov.br/news-in-english/2010/01/14/materia.2010-01-14.1625659789/view

[846] Information – Brazilian Army http://www.globalsecurity.org/military/world/brazil/intro.htm

[847] See also: "Brazilian Federal Constitution in English" http://www.v-brazil.com/government/laws/titleI.html, text translated to English (unofficial). Retrieved on 2007-05-17.

[848] Ministry of Defence Structure "Defence" http://www.defesa.gov.br/estrutura/index.php *Ministério da Defesa*. Retrieved June 22, 2007.

[849] Military service age and obligation in Brazil https://www.cia.gov/library/publications/the-world-factbook/geos/br.html

[850] http://www.senado.gov.br/JORNAL/arquivos_jornal/arquivosPdf/080331.pdf (p. 9)

[851] CIA – The World Factbook https://www.cia.gov/library/publications/the-world-factbook/geos/br.html

[852] https://www.mar.mil.br/secirm/document/livrogeo.pdf (p.22)

[853] Amazônia Azul https://www.mar.mil.br/menu_v/amazonia_azul/amazonia_azul.htm

[854] See Articles 102 and 148 of the Brazilian Constitution of 1824

[855] Carvalho (2007), p.193

[856] Lyra, p.84

[857] Pedrosa, p.289

[858] Holanda, pp.241–242

[859] Arruda, José and Piletti, Nelson -*Toda a História* (1997)(7° edition)(229 p.)

[860] Koshiba, Luiz and Pereira, Denise – *História do Brasil* (1999) (7° edition) (291 p.)

[861] About Ministry of Defense of Brazil http://www.globalsecurity.org/military/world/brazil/mod.htm

[862] Brazilian Army http://www.globalsecurity.org/military/world/brazil/army.htm

[863] Brazilian Navy http://www.globalsecurity.org/military/world/brazil/navy.htm

[864] O DIA Online – União cortará tropa do Rio http://odia.terra.com.br/economia/htm/uniao_cortara_tropa_do_rio_168086.asp

[865] Earth observation in Brazil http://www.globalsecurity.org/space/world/brazil/earth.htm

[866] http://www.defesa.gov.br/

[867] https://www.cia.gov/library/publications/the-world-factbook/geos/br.html

[868] http://www.globalsecurity.org/military/world/brazil/index.html

[869] //en.wikipedia.org/w/index.php?title=Template:Politics_of_Brazil&action=edit

[870] Country Profile: Brazil http://www.fco.gov.uk/en/about-the-fco/country-profiles/south-america/brazil?profile=intRelations&pg=4 UK Foreign and Commonwealth Office. Retrieved on 2009-01-05.

[871] Article 4 of the Federal Constitution of Brazil http://www.v-brazil.com/government/laws/titleI.html V-Brazil. Retrieved on 2011-09-20.

[872] Article 84 of the Federal Constitution of Brazil http://www.v-brazil.com/government/laws/titleIV.html V-Brazil. Retrieved on 2011-09-20.

[873] U.S. Congressional Report on Brazil http://www.wilsoncenter.org/news/docs/RL33456.pdf United States Congress. Retrieved on 2009-06-23.

[874] Georges D. Landau, "The Decision-making Process in Foreign Policy: The Case of Brazil," Center for Strategic and International Studies: Washington DC: March 2003

[875] http://www.cplp.org/Default.aspx

[876] *CRS Report RL33258, Brazilian Trade Policy and the United States*, by J. F. Hornbeck

[877] Brazil in the BRIC initiative: soft balancing in the shifting world order? http://www.scielo.br/scielo.php?pid=S0034-73292010000100008&script=sci_arttext Revista Brasileira de Política Internacional. Retrieved on 2011-09-30.

[878] Lula da Silva's Foreign Policy: The Autonomy through Diversification Strategy http://www.allacademic.com//meta/p_mla_apa_research_citation/1/8/0/4/5/pages180452/p180452-1.php Vigevani, Tullo; Cepaluni, Gabriel. Retrieved on 2009-07-11.

[879] Brazil's Rousseff: Continuity and Tests http://www.cfr.org/brazil/brazils-rousseff-continuity-tests/p23282 Sweig, Julia E. Council on Foreign Relations. Retrieved on 2011-09-19.

[880] Rousseff Tweaks Brazil's Foreign Policy at the UN http://www.americas-society.org/article.php?id=3162&nav=res&subid=52 Council of the Americas. Retrieved on 2011-09-19.

[881] Rousseff's foreign policy has limited room for change http://www.brazilpolitics.com.br/2011/09/rousseffs-foreign-policy-has-limited.html Brazil Politics. Retrieved on 2011-09-19.

[882] Congressional Research Report on Brazil-U.S. Relations: Regional Policy (p.12) https://fas.org/sgp/crs/row/RL33456.pdf U.S. Congress. Retrieved on 2011-09-30.

[883] Background Note: Brazil – Foreign relations https://www.state.gov/r/pa/ei/bgn/35640.htm U.S. Department of State. Retrieved on 2011-09-30.

[884] https://www.academia.edu/12944490/Unveiling_the_South_American_Balance

[885] Library of Congress Country Studies - Foreign relations of Brazil: Latin America http://lcweb2.loc.gov/cgi-bin/query/r?frd/cstdy:@field(DOCID+br0112) Library of Congress. Retrieved on 2011-09-30.

[886] Brazil and the Difficult Path to Multilateralism: Brazil's Financial Clout http://www.fntg.org/fntg/docs/BrazilMultilateralism.pdf Funders Network on Transforming The Global Economy. Retrieved on 2011-09-30.

[887] Cooperação Sul-Sul (South-South Cooperation) http://www.abc.gov.br/projetos/cooperacaoPrestada.asp Agência Brasileira de Cooperação. Retrieved on 2011-09-30.

[888] Entrance Visas in Brazil http://www.portalconsular.mre.gov.br/antes/qgrv_ingles_01.04.2011.pdf Ministry of External Relations of Brazil. Retrieved on 2011-04-05.

[889] Representações do Brasil no exterior http://www.itamaraty.gov.br/o-ministerio/o-brasil-no-exterior Ministry of External Relations of Brazil. Retrieved on 2011-09-20.

[890] Brasil não reconhece Kosovo sem acordo com Sérvia http://www.clicrbs.com.br/diariocatarinense/jsp/default.jsp?uf=1&local=1&newsID=a1774669.xml Clic RBS. Retrieved on 2008-02-22.

[891] Notice http://www.braziltrade.org.tw/ Brazilian Commercial Office in Taipei. Retrieved on 2011-09-20.

[892] Brazil in the Security Council http://www.un.int/brazil/Brazil-in-the-Security-Council.html Permanent Mission of Brazil to the United Nations. Retrieved on 2011-09-20.

[893] Permanent Mission of Brazil to the United Nations http://www.un.int/brazil/ Retrieved on 2011-09-20.

[894] Joint Press Statement of the G4 countries http://www.un.int/brazil/speech/Joint-Press-Statement.html Permanent Mission of Brazil to the United Nations. Retrieved on 2011-09-20.

[895] Borders and Limits of Brazil: Ilha Brasileira http://www.info.lncc.br/wrmkkk/uilhabi.html Wilson R.M. Krukoski, LNCC. Retrieved on 2009-06-23.

[896] . Brazilian Antarctica http://www.worldstatesmen.org/Antarctica.html#Brazil World Statesmen.org. Retrieved on 2009-06-23.

[897] UN Continental Shelf and UNCLOS Article 76: Brazilian Submission https://www.un.org/Depts/los/clcs_new/submissions_files/bra04/bra_exec_sum.pdf United Nations. Retrieved on 2009-06-23.

[898] Cabral and Weinstock 2010. Brazil: an emerging aid player http://www.odi.org.uk/resources/details.asp?id=5120&title=brazil-election-emerging-donor-aid. London: Overseas Development Institute

[899] Abellán & Alonso 2017, p. 7.

[900] Abellán & Alonso 2017, p. 9.

[901] Abellán & Alonso 2017, p. 11.

[902] Cabral, Lidia 2010. Brazil's development cooperation with the South: a global model in waiting http://blogs.odi.org.uk/blogs/main/archive/2010/07/22/brazil_south_south_cooperation.aspx . London: Overseas Development Institute

[903] Abellán & Alonso 2017, pp. 12-13.

[904] Cuba-Brazil Relations Get New Impulse http://www.juventudrebelde.co.cu/cuba/2008-05-31/cuba-brazil-relations-get-new-impulse/ Juventuderebelde.co.cu. Retrieved on 2008-05-31.

[905] Brazil Wants to Be Cuba's Number-One Trade Partner http://www.cubanews.ain.cu/2008/0530amistadbrasil.htm CubaNews.cu. Retrieved on 2008-05-30.
[906] http://www.sre.gob.mx/images/stories/docnormateca/manexte/embajadas/MOEMBrasil.pdf
[907] Developing a partnership with Brazil - An emerging power http://www.dtic.mil/cgi-bin/GetTRDoc?AD=ADA424216&Location=U2&doc=GetTRDoc.pdf Bassoli, Douglas. U.S. Army War College. 2004-04-03.
[908] US Congress Report on Brazil-U.S. Relations http://www.wilsoncenter.org/news/docs/RL33456.pdf United States Congress. Retrieved on 2009-06-23
[909] Embaixada do Brasil em Montevideo: Relações Bilaterais http://www.brasil.org.uy/br/home/home/index.php?menu=sub1_3&menu2=sub2_12&t=secciones&secc=245&sub=246 Embassy of Brazil in Montevideo. Retrieved on 2009-06-23.
[910] Comunicado Conjunto sobre o estabelecimento de relações diplomáticas entre o Brasil e o Butão - Nova York, 21 de setembro de 2009 http://www.itamaraty.gov.br/sala-de-imprensa/notas-a-imprensa/2009/09/21/comunicado-conjunto-sobre-o-estabelecimento-de/?searchterm=but%C3%A3o Itamaraty.gov.br. Retrieved on 2012-01-23.
[911] Bhutan establishes diplomatic relations with Brazil http://www.mfa.gov.bt/press-releases/bhutan-establishes-diplomatic-relations-with-brazil.html www.mfa.gov.bt. Retrieved on 2012-01-23.
[912] Indian Embassy in Brazil: Bilateral Relations http://www.indianembassy.org.br/eng/relations/political.htm Embassy of India in Brasília. Retrieved on 2009-06-23.
[913] Israel International Relations: International Recognition of Israel https://www.jewishvirtuallibrary.org/jsource/Peace/recogIsrael.html Jewish Virtual Library. Retrieved on 2013-11-13.
[914] *Member Nations* http://www.israelallies.org/international/member_nations/. Israel Allies Fondation. Retrieved 2013-12-01.
[915] *Brazil-Israel* http://telaviv.itamaraty.gov.br/en-us/brazil-israel.xml. Brazilian Embassy in Tel Aviv. Retrieved 2013-12-09.
[916] 2010 Brazilian census ftp://ftp.ibge.gov.br/Censos/Censo_Demografico_2010/Caracteristicas_Gerais_Religiao_Deficiencia/tab1_4.pdf Brazilian Institute of Geography and Statistics. Retrieved on 2013-11-13
[917] U.S. Department of State. *Brazil*, Retrieved on 2013-12-18 https://www.state.gov/j/drl/rls/irf/2009/127381.htm
[918] http://search.naver.com/search.naver?where=nexearch&query=%EB%B6%81%ED%95%9C+%EB%B8%8C%EB%9D%BC%EC%A7%88+%EC%88%98%EA%B5%90&sm=top_hty&fbm=0&ie=utf8
[919] Brazil to Sell MAR-1 SEAD Missiles to Pakistan http://www.defenseindustrydaily.com/Brazil-to-Sell-MAR-1-SEAD-Missiles-to-Pakistan-05182/ Defense Industry Daily. Retrieved on 2009-01-05.
[920] "Philippines, Brazil unite on energy, agriculture" http://www.etaiwannews.com/etn/news_content.php?id=986009&lang=eng_news
[921] "PGMA, Brazilian President Lula agree to further strengthen RP-Brazil relations" http://www.isria.com/pages/25_June_2009_70.htm, ISRIA
[922] "Bioenergy deals top 6 RP, Brazil agreements" http://businessmirror.com.ph/home/top-news/12272-bioenergy-deals-top-6-rp-brazil-agreements.html
[923] "RP, Brazil ink 5 accords " http://newsinfo.inquirer.net/breakingnews/nation/view/20090625-212429/RP-Brazil-ink-5-accords
[924] http://www.mofa.go.kr/ENG/countries/latinamerica/countries/20070803/1_24583.jsp?menu=m_30_30
[925] http://bra-brasilia.mofa.go.kr/worldlanguage/america/bra-brasilia/main/index.jsp
[926] Vietnam-Brazil Relations http://www.mofa.gov.vn/en/cn_vakv/america/nr040819113755/ns071219090209 Vietnamese Ministry of Foreign Affairs. Retrieved on 2009-06-23.
[927] https://web.archive.org/web/20110324040946/http://www.ambbrasilia.um.dk/en/
[928] Bilateral relations http://www.brazil.fi/brazil/ Embassy of Brazil in Helsinki. Retrieved on 2009-06-23.
[929] Brazilian-Finnish relations http://www.finlandia.org.br/Public/Default.aspx Embassy of Finland in Brasília. Retrieved on 2009-06-23

[930] Greek Ministry of Foreign Affairs about relations with Brazil http://www.mfa.gr/www.mfa.gr/en-US/Policy/Geographic+Regions/Latin+America+-+Caribbean/Bilateral+Relations/Brazil/. Ministry of Foreign Affairs of Greece. Accessed on 2009-05-04.
[931] Ministério das relações exteriores - CPLP http://www.mre.gov.br/index.php?option=com_content&task=view&id=1185
[932] https://www.researchgate.net/publication/316738951_The_role_of_Brazil_as_a_new_donor_of_development_aid_in_Africa
[933] http://www.migalhas.com.br/arquivos/2015/6/art20150601-02.pdf
[934] http://www.mre.gov.br/
[935] https://web.archive.org/web/20080610233349/http://www.mre.gov.br/english/
[936] http://www.un.int/brazil/
[937] http://www.abc.gov.br/
[938] http://www.ibsanews.com
[939] //en.wikipedia.org/w/index.php?title=Template:Politics_of_Brazil&action=edit
[940] http://www.ibge.gov.br/estadosat/index.php
[941] https://curlie.org/Regional/South_America/Brazil/States
[942] http://pcdsh01.on.br/Imagens/MapaBrasilCor7_3fusos_v02.JPG
[943] https://web.archive.org/web/20141219195306/http://saladeimprensa.ibge.gov.br/noticias?view=noticia&id=1&busca=1&idnoticia=2759
[944] http://saladeimprensa.ibge.gov.br/noticias?view=noticia&id=1&busca=1&idnoticia=2759
[945] //en.wikipedia.org/w/index.php?title=Template:Politics_of_Brazil&action=edit
[946] https://archive.is/20121217204243/http://www.world-gazetteer.com/s/p_br.htm
[947] http://www.ibge.com.br
[948] http://www.imf.org/en/Publications/WEO/Issues/2018/01/11/world-economic-outlook-update-january-2018
[949] *Table 3 - Cumulative Rate in the Year* http://www.ibge.gov.br/english/estatistica/indicadores/pib/pib-vol-val_201504_3.shtm IBGE. Retrieved on 30 March 2016.
[950] https://www.cia.gov/library/publications/the-world-factbook/fields/2046.html
[951] https://sidra.ibge.gov.br/tabela/5801#notas-tabela
[952] http://www.doingbusiness.org/reports/global-reports/doing-business-2018
[953] Banco Central do Brasil http://www.bcb.gov.br/sddsi/sddsi.htm
[954] IMF - Brazil http://www.imf.org/external/np/sta/ir/IRProcessWeb/data/bra/eng/curbra.htm#I
[955] https://www.cia.gov/library/publications/resources/the-world-factbook/geos/br.html
[956] Is Brazil's Economy Getting Too Hot? https://blogs.forbes.com/kerenblankfeld/2010/12/13/is-brazils-economy-getting-too-hot/ Forbes. Retrieved on 24 October 2011.
[957] http://america.aljazeera.com/articles/2015/8/17/despite-protests-wont-lead-to-radical-change-in-brazil.html
[958] Global Competitiveness Report 2009-2010 http://www.weforum.org/pdf/GCR09/Report/Part1/Chapter%201.1_The%20Global%20Competitiveness%20Index%202009-2010.pdf World Economic Forum. Retrieved on 24 October 2011.
[959] http://www2.aneel.gov.br/aplicacoes/capacidadebrasil/capacidadebrasil.cfm
[960]
[961] Brazil's Currency Wars – A "Real" Problem http://www.soundsandcolours.com/articles/brazil/brazils-currency-wars-a-real-problem/ Sounds and Colours. Retrieved on 24 October 2011.
[962] The Secret Strength of Pakistan's Economy – Businessweek http://www.businessweek.com/articles/2012-04-05/the-secret-strength-of-pakistans-economy
[963] http://www.worlddiplomacy.org/Countries/Brazil/InfoBra.html
[964] Popclock http://www.ibge.gov.br/english/disseminacao/online/popclock/popclock.php IBGE
[965] Indicators http://www.brasil.gov.br/ingles/about_brazil/indicators/ Brazilian Government. Retrieved on 24 October 2011.
[966]
[967] //en.wikipedia.org/w/index.php?title=Economy_of_Brazil&action=edit
[968] Inflation http://www.ipeadata.gov.br/ Ipea
[969] Average Exchange Rate http://www.ipeadata.gov.br/ Ipea
[970] Sustainable growth http://www.brasil.gov.br/ingles/about_brazil/brasil_topics/economy/categoria_view Brazilian Government. Retrieved on 24 October 2011.

[971] Transparency by country 2009 http://www.transparency.org/policy_research/surveys_indices/cpi/2009/cpi_2009_table Transparency International. Retrieved on 24 October 2011.
[972] Control and reform http://www.brasil.gov.br/ingles/about_brazil/brasil_topics/economy/categoria_view Brazilian Government. Retrieved on 24 October 2011.
[973] Au Brésil, Temer protège les esclavagistes https://www.humanite.fr/au-bresil-temer-protege-les-esclavagistes-633475
[974] Consistent policies http://www.brasil.gov.br/ingles/about_brazil/brasil_topics/economy/categoria_view Brazilian government. Retrieved on 24 October 2011.
[975] A spirit for entreprise, Finantial Times Online, May 8th, 2013
[976] GEM 2012 Global Report
[977] Rousseff Losing Bond Investors as Downgrade to Junk Looms – Bloomberg https://www.bloomberg.com/news/2014-10-27/rousseff-losing-bond-investors-as-downgrade-to-junk-looms.html Bloomberg
[978] Median income – Brazilian Supreme Court http://www1.folha.uol.com.br/folha/brasil/ult96u635911.shtml Folha de S.Paulo. Retrieved on 24 October 2011.
[979] Report for Selected Countries and Subjects: Brazil http//www.imf.org International Monetary Fund. Retrieved on 24 October 2011.
[980] Median Incomes in Brazil by Career in 2007 (FGV) http://veja.abril.com.br/111109/popup_remuneracao.html Veja. Retrieved on 24 October 2011.
[981] http://www.fazenda.gov.br/
[982] http://www.ibge.gov.br/english/
[983] http://wits.worldbank.org/CountryProfile/en/Country/BRA/Year/LTST/Summary
[984] https://www.cia.gov/library/publications/the-world-factbook/geos/br.html
[985] http://www.worldbank.org/en/country/brazil
[986] Expression coined during the Vargas Era
[987] Thais Leitão (ABr) (17 October 2009). "Produção agrícola brasileira registrar recorded em 2008 com alta de 9,1%." http://www.agrosoft.org.br/agropag/212125.htm – in Portuguese. Paged visited on 30 March 2014.
[988] CEPEA/USP/CNA Data download http://www.cepea.esalq.usp.br/pib/ , – in Portuguese. Searched 18 October 2009.
[989] thebrazilbusiness.com/article/fruit-market-in-brazil
[990] *Combating Forced Labour*, ILO Programme (United Nations) http://www.oit.org.br/trabalho_forcado/ – in Portuguese
[991] Le Breton, B. (2003). *Trapped: modern-day slavery in the Brazilian Amazon.* Kumarian Press.
[992] CALMON, Pedro: *História do Brasil*, São Paulo, 1939, vol. 1
[993] BAER, Werner: *A Economia Brasileira*, Nobel, São Paulo, 2nd ed, 2003, ,
[994] SILVA, Joaquim, PENNA, J. B. Damasco: *História Geral*, Cia. Editora Nacional, São Paulo, 1972
[995] Bergad, Laird W. 2007. The Comparative Histories of Slavery in Brazil, Cuba, and the United States. New York: Cambridge University Press.
[996] ARRUDA, José Jobson de A.: *História Moderna e Contemporânea*. Ática, São Paulo, 13th ed., 1981.
[997] CALMON, Pedro: "História da Civilização Brasileira", Cia. Editora Nacional, São Paulo, 3ª ed., 1937
[998] História do Brasil. Souto Maior. Unidade III – O Ciclo do Pau-Brasil. Cia Editora Nacional, São Paulo, 1968
[999] Brasil supera Canadá e se torna o terceiro maior exportador agrícola http://arquivo.pt/wayback/20100601192402/http://www.estadao.com.br/estadaodehoje/20100307/not_imp520620,0.php – "The State of S.Paulo", 7 March 2010 (visited on 7 March 2010)
[1000] Brasil se torna o terceiro maior exportador agrícola http://g1.globo.com/Noticias/Economia_Negocios/0,,MUL1518968-9356,00-BRASIL+SE+TORNA+O+TERCEIRO+MAIOR+EXPORTADOR+AGRICOLA.html – "G1", 7 March 2010 (visited on 9 March 2010)
[1001] http://www.ipeadata.gov.br/ipeaweb.dll/ipeadata?SessionID=2075918462&Tick=1211151299640&VAR_FUNCAO=Ser_Temas%281410842077%29&Mod=R
[1002] http://www.agricultura.gov.br/pls/portal/url/ITEM/C90C773459F8B52AE0300801FD0AF827
[1003] http://www.agricultura.gov.br/pls/portal/url/ITEM/2134AF4606BE50C8E040A8C075023826

[1004] Ipeadata http://www.ipeadata.gov.br/ipeaweb.dll/ipeadata?371970046

[1005]

[1006] http://www.agricultura.gov.br/pls/portal/url/ITEM/213229F7DBD76D9CE040A8C075024B3C

[1007] http://www.agricultura.gov.br/pls/portal/url/ITEM/2132DF10897FBE12E040A8C075020289

[1008] http://www.agricultura.gov.br/pls/portal/url/ITEM/2131AAF0F3255977E040A8C075025C45

[1009] http://www.agricultura.gov.br/pls/portal/url/ITEM/2134AF4606C550C8E040A8C075023826

[1010] Folha Online – Dinheiro – Produção de álcool e de açúcar baterá recorde em 2008, prevê Conab – 29 April 2008 http://www1.folha.uol.com.br/folha/dinheiro/ult91u396881.shtml

[1011] Mia MacDonald and Justine Simon (2010) Cattle, Soyanization, and Climate Change: Brazil's Agricultural Revolution. Brighter Green http://brightergreen.org/brightergreen.php?id=24 , 2.

[1012] "Brazil Throws Out Another Climate Challenge Updating Greenhouse Gas Inventory," World Wildlife Fund, 27 November 2009. http://wwf.panda.org .

[1013] Bustamante, Mercedes, C. Nobre, and R. Smeraldi. "Estimating Recent Greenhouse Gas Emissions from Cattle Raising in Brazil," São Paulo: Amigos da Terra – Amazônia Brasileira, National Institute for Space Research, Universidad de Brasília, 2009, 1.

[1014] Mia MacDonald and Justine Simon (2010) Cattle, Soyanization, and Climate Change: Brazil's Agricultural Revolution. Brighter Green http://brightergreen.org/brightergreen.php?id=24 , 1.

[1015] Smeraldi, Roberto and Peter H. May. "The Cattle Realm: A New Phase in the Livestock Colonization of Brazilian Amazonia," Highlights in English. São Paulo: Amigos da Terra – Amazônia Brasileira, 2008, 4. www.amazonia.org.br. http://www.amazonia.org.br

[1016] Simone de Lima and Justine Simon (2010) Brazil: Cattle, Soyanization, and Climate Change. Brighter Green https://www.youtube.com/user/BrighterGreenNY#p/u/2/_X7FWuvsWi0 , 1.

[1017] Mia MacDonald and Justine Simon (2010) "Cattle, Soyanization, and Climate Change: Brazil's Agricultural Revolution". Brighter Green http://brightergreen.org/brightergreen.php?id=24 , 10.

[1018] FORMENTI, Lígia. (30 de maio de 2010). "Brasil se torna o principal destino de agrotóxicos banidos no exterior". The State of S.Paulo

[1019] Paull, John (2016) Organics Olympiad 2016: Global Indices of Leadership in Organic Agriculture https://www.academia.edu/26803383/Organics_Olympiad_2016_Global_Indices_of_Leadership_in_Organic_Agriculture , Journal of Social and Development Sciences. 7(2):79-87

[1020] Brazil new 50- and 100-real notes confirmed http://banknotenews.com/files/6902f7c53e05a0e374606417fc992638-1371.php BanknoteNews.com. Retrieved 2011-10-20.

[1021] http://www.bcb.gov.br

[1022] http://www.casadamoeda.gov.br

[1023] http://www.bcb.gov.br/Pec/metas/TabelaMetaseResultados.pdf

[1024] *Unicode 0024 DOLLAR SIGN= milréis, escudo, used for many peso currencies in Latin America and elsewhere, glyph may have one or two vertical bars*

[1025] BNDES: BRAZIL IN THE 1990: A SUCCESSFUL TRANSITION? http://www.bndes.gov.br/SiteBNDES/export/sites/default/bndes_en/Galerias/Download/studies/td91-ing.pdf page 10.

[1026] 1 Real stainless steel coin exchange http://www.bcb.gov.br/ingles/Mecir/moeda1real/default.asp, Central Bank of Brazil.

[1027] Circulating commemorative coin of the FAO 50th anniversary, 10 cents http://www.bcb.gov.br/ingles/mecir/mcomemor/MCfao10.asp?idpai=COINSER1, Central Bank of Brazil.

[1028] Circulating commemorative coin of the FAO 50th anniversary, 25 cents http://www.bcb.gov.br/ingles/mecir/mcomemor/MCfao25.asp?idpai=COINSER1, Central Bank of Brazil.

[1029] Circulating commemorative coin of the Universal Declaration of Human Rights 50th anniversary http://www.bcb.gov.br/ingles/mecir/mcomemor/MCdh50.asp?idpai=COINSER2, Central Bank of Brazil.

[1030] Circulating commemorative coin of Juscelino Kubitschek de Oliveira 100th anniversary http://www.bcb.gov.br/ingles/mecir/mcomemor/MCbimJK.asp?idpai=COINSER2, Central Bank of Brazil.

[1031] Circulating commemorative coin of the 40th anniversary of the Banco Central do Brasil http://www.bcb.gov.br/ingles/mecir/mcomemor/MCbim40bc.asp?idpai=COINSER2, Central Bank of Brazil.

[1032] Real coins - commemorative http://www.bcb.gov.br/pre/museu/moedas/real_comemorativas.asp?idpai=MOREAL94, Central Bank of Brazil .
[1033] http://www.bc.gov.br/?CEDCOMUM
[1034] Brazil introduces new 10- and 20-real banknotes on 23 July 2012 http://banknotenews.com/files/05aae029aadcba674450f002024e9351-2196.php BanknoteNews.com. Retrieved 2012-07-24.
[1035] The total sum is 200% because each currency trade always involves a currency pair.
[1036] https://www.google.com/finance
[1037] https://www.google.com/finance?q=AUDBRL
[1038] https://www.google.com/finance?q=CADBRL
[1039] https://www.google.com/finance?q=CHFBRL
[1040] https://www.google.com/finance?q=EURBRL
[1041] https://www.google.com/finance?q=GBPBRL
[1042] https://www.google.com/finance?q=HKDBRL
[1043] https://www.google.com/finance?q=JPYBRL
[1044] https://www.google.com/finance?q=USDBRL
[1045] https://www.google.com/finance?q=INRBRL
[1046] https://www.google.com/finance?q=RUBBRL
[1047] https://www.google.com/finance?q=ARSBRL
[1048] https://finance.yahoo.com/currency
[1049] https://finance.yahoo.com/currency-converter/#from=AUD;to=BRL
[1050] https://finance.yahoo.com/currency-converter/#from=CAD;to=BRL
[1051] https://finance.yahoo.com/currency-converter/#from=CHF;to=BRL
[1052] https://finance.yahoo.com/currency-converter/#from=EUR;to=BRL
[1053] https://finance.yahoo.com/currency-converter/#from=GBP;to=BRL
[1054] https://finance.yahoo.com/currency-converter/#from=HKD;to=BRL
[1055] https://finance.yahoo.com/currency-converter/#from=JPY;to=BRL
[1056] https://finance.yahoo.com/currency-converter/#from=USD;to=BRL
[1057] https://finance.yahoo.com/currency-converter/#from=INR&to=BRL
[1058] https://finance.yahoo.com/currency-converter/#from=RUB&to=BRL
[1059] https://finance.yahoo.com/currency-converter/#from=ARS&to=BRL
[1060] http://www.xe.com/
[1061] http://www.xe.com/ucc/convert.cgi?Amount=1&From=AUD&To=BRL
[1062] http://www.xe.com/ucc/convert.cgi?Amount=1&From=CAD&To=BRL
[1063] http://www.xe.com/ucc/convert.cgi?Amount=1&From=CHF&To=BRL
[1064] http://www.xe.com/ucc/convert.cgi?Amount=1&From=EUR&To=BRL
[1065] http://www.xe.com/ucc/convert.cgi?Amount=1&From=GBP&To=BRL
[1066] http://www.xe.com/ucc/convert.cgi?Amount=1&From=HKD&To=BRL
[1067] http://www.xe.com/ucc/convert.cgi?Amount=1&From=JPY&To=BRL
[1068] http://www.xe.com/ucc/convert.cgi?Amount=1&From=USD&To=BRL
[1069] http://www.xe.com/ucc/convert.cgi?Amount=1&From=INR&To=BRL
[1070] http://www.xe.com/ucc/convert.cgi?Amount=1&From=RUB&To=BRL
[1071] http://www.xe.com/ucc/convert.cgi?Amount=1&From=ARS&To=BRL
[1072] https://www.oanda.com/currency/converter/
[1073] https://www.oanda.com/currency/converter/?value=1&exch=AUD&expr=BRL
[1074] https://www.oanda.com/currency/converter/?value=1&exch=CAD&expr=BRL
[1075] https://www.oanda.com/currency/converter/?value=1&exch=CHF&expr=BRL
[1076] https://www.oanda.com/currency/converter/?value=1&exch=EUR&expr=BRL
[1077] https://www.oanda.com/currency/converter/?value=1&exch=GBP&expr=BRL
[1078] https://www.oanda.com/currency/converter/?value=1&exch=HKD&expr=BRL
[1079] https://www.oanda.com/currency/converter/?value=1&exch=JPY&expr=BRL
[1080] https://www.oanda.com/currency/converter/?value=1&exch=USD&expr=BRL
[1081] https://www.oanda.com/currency/converter/?value=1&exch=INR&expr=BRL
[1082] https://www.oanda.com/currency/converter/?value=1&exch=RUB&expr=BRL
[1083] https://www.oanda.com/currency/converter/?value=1&exch=ARS&expr=BRL
[1084] http://fxtop.com

[1085] http://fxtop.com/en/currency-pair.php?C1=AUD&C2=BRL
[1086] http://fxtop.com/en/currency-pair.php?C1=CAD&C2=BRL
[1087] http://fxtop.com/en/currency-pair.php?C1=CHF&C2=BRL
[1088] http://fxtop.com/en/currency-pair.php?C1=EUR&C2=BRL
[1089] http://fxtop.com/en/currency-pair.php?C1=GBP&C2=BRL
[1090] http://fxtop.com/en/currency-pair.php?C1=HKD&C2=BRL
[1091] http://fxtop.com/en/currency-pair.php?C1=JPY&C2=BRL
[1092] http://fxtop.com/en/currency-pair.php?C1=USD&C2=BRL
[1093] http://fxtop.com/en/currency-pair.php?C1=INR&C2=BRL
[1094] http://fxtop.com/en/currency-pair.php?C1=RUB&C2=BRL
[1095] http://fxtop.com/en/currency-pair.php?C1=ARS&C2=BRL
[1096] http://soundsandcolours.com/articles/brazil/the-trouble-with-brazil-credit-bubbles-and-currency-wars-3179/
[1097] http://colnect.com/en/banknotes/list/country/3981/
[1098] http://www.thisamericanlife.org/radio-archives/episode/423/the-invention-of-money
[1099] http://www.bis-ans-ende-der-welt.net/Brasilien-B-En.htm
[1100] Szmrecsány, p. 282
[1101] Szmrecsány, p. 283
[1102] Szmrecsány, p. 285-7
[1103] Szmrecsány, p. 294
[1104] Sodré, p.198-200
[1105] Szmrecsány, p. 290
[1106] Vainfas, p. 373
[1107] Szmrecsány, p. 291
[1108] Vainfas, p. 374
[1109] Szmrecsány, p. 318-9
[1110] Szmrecsány, p. 308
[1111] Vainfas, p. 375
[1112] Szmrecsány, p. 300
[1113] Vianna, p. 496
[1114] Szmrecsány, p. 298
[1115] Szmrecsány, p. 298-300
[1116] Szmrecsány, p. 295–296
[1117] Szmrecsány, p. 296
[1118] Sodré, p. 200
[1119] Szmrecsány, p. 185
[1120] Vainfas, p. 373, 375
[1121] Graça Filho, p. 80
[1122] Graça Filho, p. 84
[1123] Vainfas, p. 376
[1124] Silva, p.61
[1125] Silva, p. 60
[1126] Ipeadata http://www.ipeadata.gov.br/
[1127] Produção de veículos bate recorde em 2007; 86% dos carros vendidos já são flex - O Globo Online http://oglobo.globo.com/economia/mat/2008/01/07/producao_de_veiculos_bate_recorde_em_2007_86_dos_carros_vendidos_ja_sao_flex-327904317.asp
[1128] http://www.ipeadata.gov.br/ipeaweb.dll/NSerie?SessionID=1379598342&SERID=31972_12&NoCache=134978750&ATEMP=F
[1129] Brazil Energy Data, Statistics and Analysis - Oil, gas, electricity, coal http://www.eia.doe.gov/emeu/cabs/Brazil/Electricity.html
[1130] EIA - International Energy Data and Analysis for Brazil http://tonto.eia.doe.gov/country/country_energy_data.cfm?fips=BR
[1131] OECD/IEA. World Energy Outlook 2006.
[1132] IEA Key World Energy Statistics Statistics 2015 http://www.iea.org/publications/freepublications/publication/KeyWorld_Statistics_2015.pdf, 2014 (2012R as in November 2015 http://www.iea.org/publications/freepublications/publication/keyworld2014.pdf

+ 2012 as in March 2014 is comparable to previous years statistical calculation criteria, 2013 http://www.iea.org/publications/freepublications/publication/KeyWorld2013.pdf, 2012 http://www.iea.org/publications/freepublications/publication/kwes.pdf, 2011 http://www.iea.org/textbase/nppdf/free/2011/key_world_energy_stats.pdf, 2010 http://www.iea.org/textbase/nppdf/free/2010/key_stats_2010.pdf, 2009 http://www.iea.org/textbase/nppdf/free/2009/key2009.pdf, 2006 http://www.iea.org/textbase/nppdf/free/2006/key2006.pdf IEA October, crude oil p.11, coal p. 13 gas p. 15

[1133]

[1134] Brasil se tornará exportador líquido de petróleo em 2011, diz AIE http://economia.estadao.com.br/noticias/not_34885.htm

[1135] Review on oil shale data http://www.hubbertpeak.com/laherrere/OilShaleReview200509.pdf, by Jean Laherrere, September 2005

[1136] http://www.ons.org.br/paginas/conhecimento/acervo-digital/documentos-e-publicacoes

[1137] Brazil - A Bio-Energy Superpower http://www.tierramerica.net/2004/1030/iarticulo.shtml, by Mario Osava, Tierramérica

[1138] Chevron Takes Responsibility for Brazil Oil Spill, May Face $51M Fine http://www.foxnews.com/world/2011/11/21/chevron-takes-responsibility-for-brazil-oil-spill-may-face-51m-fine/

[1139] Chevron takes full responsibility for Brazil oil spill spill https://www.bbc.co.uk/news/world-latin-america-15813671 20.11.2011

[1140] Chevron faces $10.6bn Brazil legal suit over oil spill https://www.bbc.co.uk/news/world-latin-america-16192321 14.12.2011

[1141] Amazon tribe threatens to declare war amid row over Brazilian dam project https://www.theguardian.com/environment/2013/apr/03/brazil-dam-activists-war-military The Guardian 3.4.2013

[1142] http://www.e-unwto.org/doi/book/10.18111/9789284418145

[1143] *See Table 4, pp. 18-19 and Country/Economy Profile: Brazil, pp. 116-117.*

[1144] *Janeiro 2008, Ano v, nº 17, pp. 2*

[1145] *See tables 1.1 and 3.8*

[1146] Source Brazilian Central Bank

[1147] *Click on the link "UNWTO Tourism Highlights" to access the pdf report.*

[1148]

[1149] *pp.10*

[1150] Data corresponds to 2007

[1151] *Fevereiro 2007, Ano IV, nº 13, pp. 3*

[1152] *Março 2008, Ano IV, pp. 11*

[1153] see 2.1.3 "Receitas setor trurístico 2005".

[1154] Tables 4.1 a 4.4: Summary Brasil by trip purpose 2004-2005

[1155] TOP 15 Destinations in Brazil by Foreigners http://exame.abril.com.br/estilo-de-vida/noticias/os-destinos-brasileiros-mais-visitados-pelos-estrangeiros

[1156] *Year base 2012. See Table 1.1: Tourist Arrivals to Brazil*

[1157] *Population estimated for 2007 (search values for each country profile)*

[1158] Tourist Via - Brazil http://www.nicetravel.in/2014/09/tourist-via-brazil.html

[1159] https://web.archive.org/web/20100130024527/http://www.saltodasnuvens.com/

[1160] http://www.visitbrasil.com/en/

[1161] http://travel.nytimes.com/travel/guides/central-and-south-america/brazil/overview.html

[1162] Science and technology - Brazil http://www.country-data.com/cgi-bin/query/r-1818.html

[1163] CEITEC - The Company http://www.ceitec-sa.com/pages/institucional

[1164] https://web.archive.org/web/20130805075036/https://radiomec.com.br/

[1165] http://www.ipt.br

[1166] http://unesdoc.unesco.org/images/0023/002354/235406e.pdf

[1167] http://www.bbk.ac.uk/ibamuseum/texts/Andermann01E.htm

[1168] http://www.bbk.ac.uk/ibamuseum/texts/Andermann01.htm

[1169] http://www.cbpf.br/

[1170] https://web.archive.org/web/20090323102702/http://www.comtecnologia.com.br/

[1171] Home page | The world's leading construction web site http://www.bsdlive.co.uk/story.asp?storycode=3130466

[1172] In Tokyo Rio governor assures high speed rail http://www.rio2016.org.br/en/Noticias/Noticia. aspx?idConteudo=492 Rio 2016. Retrieved on 2009-06-21.
[1173] World Bank Datebase, http://data.worldbank.org/indicator/IS.AIR.PSGR
[1174] https://www.cia.gov/library/publications/the-world-factbook/geos/br.html
[1175] Health Indicators of Brazil and the World http://www.globalhealthfacts.org/topic.jsp?i=93
[1176] Total fertility in Brazil - 2008 http://educacao.uol.com.br/atualidades/pnad-2008.jhtm#diretoponto
[1177] Life expectancy in Brazil (2012) http://g1.globo.com/economia/seu-dinheiro/noticia/2013/12/com-revisao-na-expectativa-de-vida-valor-de-novas-aposentadorias-cai.html
[1178] Infant Mortality in Brazil (2014) http://www.bbc.co.uk/portuguese/noticias/2013/10/131022_savethechildren_relatorio_dg.shtml
[1179] Smokers in Brazil (2014) http//noticias.uol.com.br
[1180] Ministério do Planejamento website, "Saúde" (fact sheet, 2002) http://www.planejamento.gov.br/planejamento_investimento/conteudo/radarsocial/saude.htm . Retrieved 12 June 2007.
[1181] From the IBGE's Complete Mortality Tables for Brazil's population, which have been published annually since 1999. They are used by the Ministry of Social Security as one of the parameters for the retirement fund factor under the General System of Social Security. Life Expectancy in Brazil (2008) http://english.peopledaily.com.cn/90001/90782/6830022.html
[1182] Demographic projections in Brazil http://www.scielo.br/scielo.php?script=sci_arttext&pid=S0102-311X2005000700002
[1183] History - Infant Mortality - Brazil http://www.iadb.org/res/publications/pubfiles/pubR-493.pdf
[1184] Nations, Marilyn K.; Mara Lucia Amaral (1991). "Flesh, Blood, Souls, and Households: Cultural Validity in Mortality". Medical Anthropology Quarterly 5 (4): 204-220.
[1185] Infant Mortality in Brazil (2009) http://www.agenciabrasil.gov.br/news-in-english/2009/12/17/materia.2009-12-17.0817559779/view
[1186] http://www.who.int/countries/bra/en/
[1187] Ralph Harbison and Eric Hanushek, *Educational performance of the poor: lessons from rural northeast Brazil* (New York: Oxford University Press, 1992).
[1188] Ignoramuses Academy, 2016
[1189] http://pdba.georgetown.edu/Constitutions/Brazil/brazil.html
[1190] http://documents.worldbank.org/curated/en/993851468014439962/pdf/656590REPLACEM0hieving0World0Class0.pdf
[1191] http://www.unesco.vg/Education_in_Brazil.htm
[1192] http://www.mec.gov.br/
[1193] http://www2.camara.gov.br/atividade-legislativa/comissoes/comissoes-permanentes/cec
[1194] https://www.youtube.com/watch?v=rRFmmgzlu2o
[1195] http://www.education-worldwide.de/Education-in-Brazil-07.10.2013-7000_e.html
[1196] http://www.education-worldwide.de/Educational-Research-in-Brazil-07.10.2013-7007_e.html
[1197] http://www.unevoc.unesco.org/worldtvetdatabase1.php?ct=BRA
[1198] IBGE. 2008 PNAD http://www.sidra.ibge.gov.br/bda/tabela/protabl.asp?c=261&z=pnad&o=3&i=P
[1199] Amaral, Ernesto F. (2005) "Shaping Brazil: The Role of International Migration" http://www.migrationinformation.org/Profiles/display.cfm?id=311, Migration Policy Institute website. Retrieved 13 June 2007.
[1200] East in the West: Investigating the Asian presence and influence in Brazil from the 16th to 18th centuries. By Clifford Pereira, in Proceedings of the 2nd Asia-Pacific regional Conference on Underwater Cultural Heritage. Ed. Hans Van Tilberg, Sila Tripati, Veronica Walker, Brian Fahy and Jun Kimura. Honolulu, Hawai'i, USA. May 2014.
[1201] Altenhofen, Cléo Vilson: Hunsrückisch in Rio Grande do Sul, Franz Steiner Verlag, Stuttgart 1996
[1202] Pacific Island Travel web-site, accessed 4.8.08 http://www.pacificislandtravel.com/south_america/brazil/about_destin/southcentralparana.html, taken from: *Brazil: the Rough Guide*, by David Cleary, Dilwyn Jenkins, Oliver Marshall, Jim Hine.
[1203] Profile of the Brazilian blood donor

[1204] RS VIRTUAL – O Rio Grande do Sul na Internet – História – Colonização – Negros – A história dos gaúchos sem história http://www.riogrande.com.br/historia/colonizacao6.htm
[1205] Germans http://www.mre.gov.br/CDBRASIL/ITAMARATY/WEB/ingles/consnac/imigra/alemaes/index.htm
[1206] Uma história oculta: a imigração dos países da Europa do Centro-Leste para o Brasil
[1207] RankBrasil – Livro Dos Recordes Brasileiros – Os melhores e maiores do Brasil http://www.rankbrasil.com.br/maismais/turismo/saovicente/default.asp
[1208] Pdt – Rj http://www.pdt-rj.org.br/colunistas.asp?id=40
[1209] Fundação Lorenzato http://www.lorenzato.org.br/nordeste%20em%20busca%20de%20investidores.asp
[1210] São Paulo é tudo de bom – Turismo, eventos e entretenimento na cidade de São Paulo http://www.visitesaopaulo.com/english/city/itineraries-saopaulo.htm
[1211] Japan Bank for International Cooperation report, November 2005, "Sector Study for Education in Brazil" http://www.jbic.go.jp/english/oec/environ/report/pdf/brazil.pdf, retrieved 28 February 2007
[1212] IBGE - Instituto Brasileiro de Geografia e Estatística (Brazilian Institute for Geography and Statistics). 2010 Census ftp://ftp.ibge.gov.br/Censos/Censo_Demografico_2010/Caracteristicas_Gerais_Religiao_Deficiencia/tab1_4.pdf. Accessed 07.08.2012.
[1213] Lovejoy, Paul E., *Muslim Encounters With Slavery in Brazil*, Markus Wiener Pub., 2007.
[1214] https://www.cia.gov/library/publications/download/download-2006/index.html
[1215] http://esa.un.org/unpd/wpp/country-profiles/pdf/76.pdf
[1216] http//www.bluenomics.com
[1217] http://itbulk.org/population/population-by-country/
[1218] http://itbulk.org/population/population-projection-by-country/
[1219] http://itbulk.org/population/life-expectancy-by-country/
[1220] Oksana Boruszenko and Rev. Danyil Kozlinsky (1994). *Ukrainians in Brazil* (Chapter), in *Ukraine and Ukrainians Throughout the World*, edited by Ann Lencyk Pawliczko, University of Toronto Press: Toronto, pp. 443–454
[1221] Some regional pronunciations include in São Paulo and much of Southern Brazil, and in Rio de Janeiro.
[1222] Constituição da República Federativa do Brasil, Artigo 12, I.
[1223] Telfer (1932), p. 184.
[1224] Bethell (1984), p. 47.
[1225] Altenhofen, Cléo Vilson: Hunsrückisch in Rio Grande do Sul, Franz Steiner Verlag, Stuttgart 1996, p. 24.
[1226] IBGE traça perfil dos imigrantes http://madeinjapan.uol.com.br/2008/06/21/ibge-traca-perfil-dos-imigrantes/
[1227] Eugene C. Harter. "The Lost Colony of the Confederacy". Texas A&M University Press, 1985, p. 74.
[1228] Brazil has 689,000 people from around the world in 2009 http://www.bv.fapesp.br/namidia/noticia/39946/procuram-estrangeiros/. Bv.fapesp.br. Retrieved on 2012-05-19.
[1229] Genealogy: German migration to Brazil http://www.genealogienetz.de/reg/WELT/brasil.html. Genealogienetz.de. Retrieved on 2012-05-19.
[1230] Phillip Wagner Sugar and Blood https://web.archive.org/web/20090419063828/http://www.iei.net/~pwagner/brazarticles/April2002.html. Brazzil Magazine, April 2002
[1231] Sources :: Indigenous Peoples in Brazil – ISA https://web.archive.org/web/20050315162129/http://www.socioambiental.org/pib/english/source/xi.shtm. socioambiental.org
[1232] Instituto Brasileiro de Geografia e Estatística http://www.ibge.gov.br/english/presidencia/noticias/noticia_visualiza.php?id_noticia=892&id_pagina=1 . IBGE (2007-05-25). Retrieved on 2012-05-19.
[1233] 2008 PNAD, IBGE. " População residente por cor ou raça, situação e sexo http//www.sidra.ibge.gov.br ".
[1234] Nova Veneza http://www.portalveneza.com.br/a_cidade.php
[1235] POMERODE-SC http://www.brasilalemanha.com.br/pomerode/
[1236] Ucranianos no Brasil http://www.brasil.kiev.ua/index.php?option=com_content&view=article&id=172:ucranianos-no-brasil&catid=45:ucranianos-no-brasil&Itemid=110

[1237] História de Treze Tílias http://www.guiacatarinense.com.br/trezetilias/trezetilias.htm
[1238] Prefeitura de D. Feliciano http://www.domfeliciano.rs.gov.br/portal1/municipio/historia.asp?iIdMun=100143123
[1239] Altenhofen, Cléo Vilson: Hunsrückisch in Rio Grande do Sul, Franz Steiner Verlag, Stuttgart 1996
[1240] Cliff Pereira, in Van Tilburg, H., Tripati, S., Walker Vadillo, V., Fahy, B., and Kimura, J. (eds.), "East in the West : Investigating the Asian presence and influence in Brazil from the 16th to 18th centuries." http://www.themua.org/collections/items/show/1607 The MUA Collection.
[1241] Profile of the Brazilian blood donor http://www.amigodoador.com.br/estatisticas.html . Amigodoador.com.br. Retrieved on 2012-05-19.
[1242] DNA de brasileiro é 80% europeu, indica estudo http://www1.folha.uol.com.br/folha/ciencia/ult306u633465.shtml. folha.uol.com.br (1970-01-01). Retrieved on 2012-05-19.
[1243] https://web.archive.org/web/20070905090434/http://lusotopia.no.sapo.pt/indexBREmigrantes.html
[1244] http://www.scielo.br/pdf/rsp/v8s0/03.pdf Maria Stella Ferreira Levy. O papel da migração internacional na evolução da população brasileira (1872 a 1972) p. 52.
[1245] Diretoria Geral de Estatística. Recenseamento do Brasil em 1872 http://biblioteca.ibge.gov.br/visualizacao/monografias/GEBIS%20-%20RJ/Recenseamento_do_Brazil_1872/Imperio%20do%20Brazil%201872.pdf. pp. 3 and 4 (of the PDF document).
[1246] http://www.scielo.br/pdf/rsp/v8s0/03.pdf Maria Stella Ferreira Levy. O papel da migração internacional na evolução da população brasileira (1872 a 1972) p.51.
[1247] Eliane Yambanis Obersteiner. Café atrai imigrante europeu para o Brasil - 22/02/2005 - Resumos I História do Brasil http://vestibular.uol.com.br/ultnot/resumos/ult2770u39.jhtm
[1248] Maria Stella Ferreira Levy http://www.scielo.br/img/revistas/rsp/v8s0/03t2.gif. p.51
[1249] RIOS, Roger Raupp. Text excerpted from a judicial sentence concerning crime of racism. Federal Justice of 10ª Vara da Circunscrição Judiciária de [[Porto Alegre http://www.movimentoafro.amazonida.com/branqueamento.htm], November 16, 2001] (Accessed September 10, 2008)
[1250] SUZUKI Jr, Matinas. História da discriminação brasileira contra os japoneses sai do limbo in Folha de S.Paulo, 20 de abril de 2008 http://www1.folha.uol.com.br/fsp/mais/fs2004200804.htm (visitado em 17 de agosto de 2008)
[1251] Professor says increased Bolivian immigration to Brazil is due to crisis there http://www.how2immigrate.net/brazilnews/bolivian-immigration.html
[1252] Cláudia Rolli, Fátima Fernandes. Até 1.500 bolivianos chegam por mês http://www1.folha.uol.com.br/fsp/dinheiro/fi1612200709.htm. Folha de S.Paulo (December 16, 2007)
[1253] http://oestrangeirodotorg.files.wordpress.com/2013/05/nc3bamero-de-imigrantes-no-brasil-atc3a9-2012-por-pac3ads.pdf
[1254] http//images.paulocel29.multiply.multiplycontent.com
[1255] http://www.bresserpereira.org.br/papers/1964/64.OrigensEtnicasSociais.pdf
[1256] http://www0.rio.rj.gov.br/arquivo/pdf/revista_agcrj_pdf/revista_agcrj_3.pdf
[1257] https://books.google.com/books?id=ObM0dMga1cMC&pg=PA11
[1258] Recenseamento do Brasil realizado em 1 de Setembro de 1920, Volume 4, Primeira Parte: População do Brasil por Estados, municípios e distritos, segundo o sexo, o estado civil e a nacionalidade - Disponível em: https://archive.org/details/recenseamento1920pop1
[1259] Outras Etnias, <http://www.terrabrasileira.net/folclore/regioes/7tipos/etniasl.html >. Acesso em: 11 de outubro de 2008
[1260] http://www.uel.br/pos/mestredu/images/stories/downloads/dissertacoes/2007/2007%20-%20LUCCA,%20%20Ana%20Tereza%20Gongora%20de.pdf
[1261] Nova Veneza http://www.portalveneza.com.br/a_cidade.php
[1262] POMERODE-SC http://www.brasilalemanha.com.br/pomerode/
[1263] Ucranianos no Brasil http://www.brasil.kiev.ua/index.php?option=com_content&view=article&id=172:ucranianos-no-brasil&catid=45:ucranianos-no-brasil&Itemid=110
[1264] História de Treze Tílias http://www.guiacatarinense.com.br/trezetilias/trezetilias.htm
[1265] Prefeitura de D. Feliciano http://www.domfeliciano.rs.gov.br/portal1/municipio/historia.asp?iIdMun=100143123
[1266] https://books.google.com/books?id=4hECxprAkAoC&pg=PA252

[1267] https://web.archive.org/web/20110728173800/http://cultura.jaraguadosul.com.br/modules/xt_conteudo/index.php?id=231
[1268] https://books.google.com/books?id=8g_NduoKW3MC
[1269], p. 94. (the original source, reported in the book, is Revista de Imigração e Colonização 1, n. 03 (July 1940): 617-638.) The total figure, 107,135, includes some non-Arabs, such as Greeks and Armenians (826). Notice that while most Levantine immigrants fall under "Turks", this is actually a misnomer, as it refers to the passport (of the Ottoman Empire) used in their arrival to Brazil.
[1270] Mortara, Giorgio. O aumento da população do Brasil entre 1872 e 1940.
[1271] Table 5, p. 59; Table 6, p. 60.
[1272] IBGE 2008 http://www.ibge.gov.br/home/estatistica/populacao/condicaodevida/indicadoresminimos/sinteseindicsociais2008/indic_sociais2008.pdf Cor ou Raça
[1273] Note 3, p.3
[1274] Table 6, p. 10
[1275] The figures for Germans, Italians, Spaniards, and Japanese from 1820 to August 31, 1972, can be found in Maria Stella Ferreira Levy. O papel da migração internacional na evolução da população brasileira (1872 a 1972) https//docs.google.com. Tabela 2. p. 74. For this table, the sum for the period 1820-1971 is given. The figure for Arab immigrants is based in Jeff Lesser. , Table 1, which gives 140,464 "Middle Eastern" immigrants for the period 1880-1969. Non-arab middle easterners (mainly Iranian/Persians and Turks) have been in small numbers, as can be seen in the same book, table 3, p. 49.; and the numbers of Arab immigrants have been small before 1880 and after 1969.
[1276] John Tofik Karam.
[1277] Simon Schwartzman. Fora de foco: diversidade e identidades étnicas no Brasil http://www.schwartzman.org.br/simon/pdf/origem.pdf. Quadro 2, p. 7. To obtain comparable figures, the percents found by the PME were applied to the 2000 Census population.
[1278] Cilmar Franceschetto. Espírito Santo, lo stato più veneto del Brasile (in Italian) http://www2.regione.veneto.it/videoinf/periodic/precedenti/01/6/espirito.htm
[1279] José Carlos Mattedi. Consulado italiano vai abrir dois escritórios em Vitória para agilizar pedidos de cidadania (in Portuguese) http://aplic.vitoria.es.gov.br/pmv/calandra.nsf/0/8688D942E5AB6F7783256FBF006E63CD?OpenDocument&pub=T&proj=internet&gen=Doc+Diario2
[1280] Nara Saletto. Sobre a composição étnica da população capixaba (in Portuguese) http://www.anpuhes.hpg.ig.com.br/ensaio25.htm
[1281] O povo pomerano no ES http://www.rog.com.br/claudiovereza2/mostraconteudos.asp?cod_conteudo=735
[1282] http://titus.uni-frankfurt.de/didact/karten/germ/deutdin.htm
[1283] http://www.lerncafe.de/aus-der-welt-1142/articles/pommern-in-brasilien.html
[1284] Aprovado projeto que declara o Talian como patrimônio do RS http://www.ipol.org.br/ler.php?cod=597 , accessed on 21 August 2011
[1285] Cooficialização da língua alemã em Antônio Carlos http://www.ipol.org.br/upload/Image/lei1.jpg
[1286] Em Nova Petrópolis 100% da população é alfabetizada http://www.novapetropolis.rs.gov.br/int_noticias.php?id=218&tipo=3, quinto parágrafo
[1287] //en.wikipedia.org/w/index.php?title=Template:Race&action=edit
[1288] //en.wikipedia.org/w/index.php?title=Template:Culture_of_Brazil&action=edit
[1289] Jansen, Roberta. Um Brasil europeu. O Globo. February 18, 2011. p. 36. Cites the 2011 work of Prof. Sérgio Danilo Pena.
[1290] Gilberto Freyre. *Masters and Slaves* https//books.google.com (translation of *Casa Grande e Senzala*). pp. 304–318.
[1291] Gilberto Freyre. *Masters and Slaves* https//books.google.com. (Translation of Casa Grande e Senzala). p. 92: *As for domestic animals to be found among either of the two principal groups – the Tupís and the Gê-Botocudos -*, etc.
[1292] Marília D. Klaumann Cánovas. A GRANDE IMIGRAÇÃO EUROPÉIA PARA O BRASIL E O IMIGRANTE ESPANHOL NO CENÁRIO DA CAFEICULTURA PAULISTA: ASPECTOS DE UMA (IN)VISIBILIDADE http://www.cchla.ufpb.br/saeculum/saeculum11_art08_canovas.pdf

[1293] Maria Stella Ferreira Levy. O papel da migração internacional na evolução da população brasileira (1872 to 1972). http://www.scielo.br/scielo.php?script=sci_arttext&pid=S0034-89101974000500003&lng=en&nrm=iso in*Revista de Saúde Pública*, volume supl, June 1974.

[1294] Sérgio Pena et alli. DNA tests probe the genomic ancestry of Brazilians http://www.scielo.br/scielo.php?pid=S0100-879X2009005000026&script=sci_arttext. Introduction, first paragraph.: *Little is known about the number of indigenous people living in the area of what is now Brazil when the Portuguese arrived in 1500, although a figure often cited is that of 2.5 million individuals.*

[1295] http://www.scielo.br/pdf/rsp/v8s0/03.pdf Maria Stella Ferreira Levy. O papel da migração internacional na evolução da população brasileira (1872 a 1972) p. 50.

[1296] Flávia de Ávila, *Entrada de Trabalhadores Estrangeiros no Brasil: Evolução Legislativa e Políticas Subjacentes nos Séculos XIX e XX*. PhD thesis. Florianópolis: Universidade Federal de Santa Catarina, 2003. pp 30. (Available here http://www.tede.ufsc.br/teses/PDPC0641.pdf [1.21MB PDF file].)

[1297] Flávia de Ávila, *Entrada de Trabalhadores Estrangeiros no Brasil*. (Available here http://www.tede.ufsc.br/teses/PDPC0641.pdf [1.21MB PDF file].), p. 31-32: *Ser estrangeiro significava, em primazia, qualquer indivíduo que não fosse súdito da Coroa portuguesa, e **os poucos que viviam no Brasil** o faziam mais por razões aventureiras e individuais que coletivas ou resultantes de providências governamentais para aportarem em terras coloniais.*

[1298] História genética dos gaúchos : dinâmica populacional do sul do Brasil http://www.lume.ufrgs.br/handle/10183/10934. Our Y-SNP/STR data globally **suggest**, however, that the Gaúcho males have more similarity with the Spaniards than with the Portuguese. The history of Rio Grande do Sul is peculiar because, in the Colonial Era, the political control of the region alternated between the Spanish and Portuguese Empires (Flores 2003). These historical events **can** be associated to our findings, **but some caution is needed** since differentiation between Iberian Peninsula populations, as well as between them and their derived Latin American populations, at the Y-chromosome level, was not observed in other investigations.

[1299] Johannes Menne Postma, *The Dutch in the Atlantic slave trade, 1600–1815* (Cambridge: Cambridge University Press, 1990;) (here https://books.google.com/books?id=dzI8C0Vka7IC&pg=PA18&dq=slaves+dutch+brazil+colony+new+holland&sig=TxUCyWRGsyPxFZpctOJRtkeGedE#PPA19,M1 at Google Books).

[1300] Mirian Halpern Pereira. Algumas observações complementares sobre a política de emigração portuguesa http://google.com/scholar?q=cache:veIDSbBYW24J:scholar.google.com/+imigra%C3%A7%C3%A3o+galega+para+o+brasil&hl=pt-BR&as_sdt=2000. In *Análise Social*, vol. xxv (108–109), 1990 (4.° e 5.°) 735–739: *É, porém, provável que, para o Brasil pelo menos, a emigração clandestina documentada tenha sido superior à indocumentada. O que não é nada certo é que ela fosse inteiramente registada como imigração portuguesa. A importância dos **portugueses que partiam de Vigo com passaporte falso** ficou atestada na muito generalizada designação de "galego" dada aos Portugueses no Rio de Janeiro, principal ponto de desembarque dos Portugueses no século xix.*

[1301] IBGE Teen. Evolução da população/cor http://www.ibge.gov.br/ibgeteen/povoamento/tabelas/populacao_cor.htm

[1302] Maria Stella Ferreira Levy. O Papel da Migração Internacional na Evolução da População Brasileira http://www.scielo.br/pdf/rsp/v8s0/03.pdf. Table 2, p. 74.

[1303] Judicael Clevelário. A participação da imigração na formação da população brasileira http://www.abep.nepo.unicamp.br/docs/rev_inf/vol14_n1e2_1997/vol14_n1e2_1997_3artigo_51_71.pdf . p. 68.

[1304] Petrônio Domingues. Uma história não contada: negro, racismo e branqueamento em São Paulo https//books.google.com.

[1305] O Rebate. Cited in Petrônio Domingues. Uma história não contada: negro, racismo e branqueamento em São Paulo https//books.google.com. p. 77.

[1306] Wilson do Nascimento Barbosa. Preface to Petrônio Domingues, Uma história não contada: negro, racismo e branqueamento em São Paulo https//books.google.com. p. 10.

[1307] VAINFAS, Ronaldo. Dicionário do Brasil Imperial. Rio de Janeiro: Objetiva, 2002, p 152

[1308] SANTOS, Sales Augusto dos. Historical roots of the "whitening" of Brazil. Translated by Lawrence Hallewell. Latin American Perspectives. Issue 122, Vol. 29 No I, January 2002, p 62.

[1309] LIMA, Sílvio C.S. Determinismo biológico e imigração chinesa em Nicolau Moreira (1870–1890). 123 p. Dissertation (Master degree in History of Health Sciences) Rio de Janeiro: Fiocruz, 2005. http://www.coc.fiocruz.br/pos_graduacao/completos/limascs.pdf, p. 104

[1310] Masato Ninomiya O centenário do Tratado de Amizade, Comércio e Navegação entre Brasil e Japão http://www.usp.br/revistausp/28/17-massato.pdf . in Revista USP, December 1995/ February 1996. p. 248.

[1311] Petrônio Rodrigues. Uma história não contada: negro, racismo e branqueamento em São Paulo https//books.google.com. p. 78.

[1312] Petrônio Rodrigues. Uma história não contada: negro, racismo e branqueamento em São Paulo https//books.google.com. p. 29-31.

[1313] Thomas Skidmore. Racial ideas and social policy in Brazil, 1870–1940 https//books.google.com. In Richard Graham et al. *The Idea of race in Latin America, 1870–1940*. p. 23.

[1314] Thomas Skidmore. Racial ideas and social policy in Brazil, 1870–1940 https//books.google.com. In Richard Graham et al. *The Idea of race in Latin America, 1870–1940*. p. 25-26

[1315] Ronald M. Glassman, William H. Swatos, and Barbara J. Denison, *Social Problems in Global Perspective* (Lanham, Md.: University Press of America, 2004;). Here https://books.google.com/books?id=ECWSVPEepOgC&pg=PA242#v=onepage&q=&f=false at Google Books (accessed December 13, 2009).

[1316] Edward E. Telles, " Brazil in Black and White: Discrimination and Affirmative Action in Brazil https://www.pbs.org/wnet/wideangle/lessons/brazil-in-black-and-white/discrimination-and-affirmative-action-in-brazil/4323/", PBS, June 1, 2009. Accessed December 17, 2009.

[1317] Floyd James Davis. Who is Black?: one nation's definition https//books.google.com. p. 101.

[1318] Parra et al, " Color and genomic ancestry in Brazilians https://www.ncbi.nlm.nih.gov/pmc/articles/PMC140919/#id2601616". Discussion, ninth paragraph.

[1319] United Nations. Department of Economic and Social Affairs, Statistics Division. Principles and Recommendations for Population and Housing Censuses http://unstats.un.org/unsd/demographic/sources/census/docs/P&R_%20Rev2.pdf. item 2.162, p. 162.: *The subjective nature of the term (not to mention increasing intermarriage among various groups in some countries, for example) requires that information on ethnicity be acquired through self-declaration of a respondent and also that respondents have the option of indicating multiple ethnic affiliations.*

[1320] Tereza Cristina N. Araújo. A classificação de "cor" nas pesquisas do IBGE. http//docs.google.com. In Cadernos de Pesquisa 63, November 1987. p. 14.

[1321] Tereza Cristina N. Araújo. A classificação de "cor" nas pesquisas do IBGE http//docs.google.com. In *Cadernos de Pesquisa* 63, November 1987. p. 14.

[1322] Diretoria Geral de Estatística. Sexo, raça e estado civil, nacionalidade, filiação culto e analphabetismo da população recenseada em 31 de dezembro de 1890. http//biblioteca.ibge.gov.br p. 5.

[1323] IBGE. Censo Demográfico 1940 http://biblioteca.ibge.gov.br/visualizacao/monografias/GEBIS%20-%20RJ/CD1940/Censo%20Demografico%201940%20VII_Brasil.pdf. p. xxi.

[1324] IBGE. Censo Demográfico http://biblioteca.ibge.gov.br/visualizacao/monografias/GEBIS%20-%20RJ/CD1950/CD_1950_I_Brasil.pdf. p. XVIII

[1325] IBGE. Censo Demográfico de 1960 http://biblioteca.ibge.gov.br/visualizacao/monografias/GEBIS%20-%20RJ/CD1960/CD_1960_Brasil.pdf. Série Nacional, Vol. I, p. XIII

[1326] Simon Schwartzmann. Fora de foco: diversidade e identidades étnicas no Brasil http://www.schwartzman.org.br/simon/pdf/origem.pdf.

[1327] Edward Telles. Race in Another America: the significance of skin color in Brazil https//books.google.com.

[1328] http://www.dicionariodoaurelio.com/dicionario.php?P=Moreno Here is the dictionary definition: *adj. e s.m. Diz-se de, ou quem tem cabelos negros e pele um pouco escura; trigueiro. / Bras. Designação irônica ou eufemística que se dá aos pretos e mulatos.* Literally, this means: "(said of) those who have black hair and a somewhat dark skin, of the colour of ripe wheat. / (in Brazil) Ironic or euphemistic designation given to Blacks and Mulattos.

[1329] Pena, Sérgio, and Bortolini, Maria Cátira. Pode a genética definir quem deve se beneficiar das cotas universitárias e demais ações afirmativas? http://www.scielo.br/scielo.php?pid=S0103-40142004000100004&script=sci_arttext&tlng=en#tab06 Note 1, p. 47

[1330] José Luiz Petrucelli. *A Cor Denominada*. (unavailable online).

[1331] Anusuya A. Mokashi and Noah S. Scheinfeld. Photoaging. In Robert A. Norman, Diagnosis of Aging Skin Diseases https//books.google.com. p. 13.

[1332] http://www.dicionariodoaurelio.com/dicionario.php?P=Moreno Here is the dictionary definition: *adj. e s.m. Diz-se de, ou quem tem cabelos negros e pele um pouco escura; trigueiro. / Bras. Designação irônica ou eufemística que se dá aos pretos e mulatos.* Literally, this means: "(said of) those who have black hair and a somewhat dark skin, of the colour of ripe wheat. / (in Brazil) **Ironic or euphemistic designation given to Blacks and Mulattos**.

[1333] Edward Telles. Race in Another America: the significance of skin color in Brazil https//books.google.com. p. 85: *This system of classification uses only two terms, **negro** and branco.*

[1334] Edward Telles. Race in another America https//books.google.com. p. 86: *The Brazilian government had sought to dichotomize, or worse, (North) "americanize" racial classification in a society that used and even celebrated intermediate terms.*

[1335] Kabengele Munanga Uma resposta contra o racismo http://www.brasilautogestionario.org/2009/07/16/uma-resposta-contra-o-racismo-prof-kabengele-munanga-doutor-em-antropologia-da-usp/. In Brasil Autogestinário. *Do ponto de vista norteamericano, todos os brasileiros seriam, de acordo com as pesquisas do geneticista Sergio Danilo Pena, considerados negros ou ameríndios, pois todos possuem, em porcentagens variadas, marcadores genéticos africanos e ameríndios, além de europeus, sem dúvida.* ("From the American standpoint, all Brazilians would, according to the researches of geneticist Sergio Danilo Pena, be considered Black or Amerindian, for all of them have, in varied proportions, African and Amerindian genetic markers, besides, of course, European ones"))

[1336] Edward Telles. Race in Another America: the significance of skin color in Brazil https//books.google.com. p. 85.: *Thus, they claim that Brazil's informal one-drop rule holds that one drop of White blood allows one to avoid being classified as Black, a tradition that they seek to revert.*

[1337] Paula Miranda-Ribeiro and André Junqueira Caetano. Como eu me vejo e como ela me vê http://www.cedeplar.ufmg.br/pesquisas/td/TD%20250.pdf. pp. 12–13

[1338] IBGE. Census 2000. Tabela 2972 – Pessoas de 5 anos ou mais de idade por cor e raça, sexo, alfabetização e grupos de idade http//www.sidra.ibge.gov.br

[1339] Profile of the Brazilian blood donor http://www.amigodoador.com.br/estatisticas.html . Amigodoador.com.br. Retrieved on 2012-05-19.

[1340] DNA de brasileiro é 80% europeu, indica estudo http://www1.folha.uol.com.br/folha/ciencia/ult306u633465.shtml. folha.uol.com.br (1 January 1970). Retrieved on 2012-05-19.

[1341] DNA de brasileiro é 80% europeu, indica estudo http://www1.folha.uol.com.br/folha/ciencia/ult306u633465.shtml.

[1342] RS VIRTUAL – O Rio Grande do Sul na Internet – História – Colonização – Negros – A história dos gaúchos sem história http://www.riogrande.com.br/historia/colonizacao6.htm . Eight paragraph: *Esses números talvez estivessem exagerados – afinal, Gonçalves Chaves era contra a escravidão, e usou de todos os argumentos para combatê-la em sua obra "Memórias Economo-políticas sobre a administração pública do Brasil". Um deles era justamente o de que "o excessivo número de escravos faz com que não o possamos tratar como temos obrigação".*

[1343] Uma história oculta: a imigração dos países da Europa do Centro-Leste para o Brasil

[1344] Pdt – Rj http://www.pdt.org.br/colunistas.asp?id=40

[1345] IBGE - Instituto Brasileiro de Geografia e Estatística (Brazilian Institute for Geography and Statistics). 2010 Census ftp://ftp.ibge.gov.br/Censos/Censo_Demografico_2010/Caracteristicas_Gerais_Religiao_Deficiencia/tab1_4.pdf. Accessed 07.08.2012.

[1346] Does not include the Brazilian Catholic Apostolic Church, which broke away from Rome in 1945.

[1347] Includes Lutheran, Presbyterian, Baptist, Adventist, Methodist, and Congregational churches

[1348] This is the largest Pentecostal group in Brazil

[1349] This is the second largest Pentecostal group in Brazil

[1350] Includes the Jehovah's Witnesses (0.73%), Brazilian Catholic Apostolic Church (0.29% of the population), Latter-day Saints(0.12%), and Orthodox Church (0.07%)

[1351] Includes Umbanda and Candomblé (0.33%), Judaism (0.06%), Islam (0.02%), and various Eastern religions (0.22%)
[1352] Includes 0.32% atheists and 0.07% agnostics
[1353] //en.wikipedia.org/w/index.php?title=Template:Culture_of_Brazil&action=edit
[1354] Facts of Basilica of Aparecida http://noticias.terra.com.br/brasil/interna/0,,OI1984236-EI306,00.html
[1355] Simon Romero, "A Laboratory for Revitalizing Catholicism," *New York Times* Feb 14, 2013 https://www.nytimes.com/2013/02/15/world/americas/in-brazil-growing-threats-to-catholicisms-sway.html?pagewanted=all&_r=0
[1356] Michael Astor. Once-Barred Practice Flourishes in Brazil. African-Influenced Candomble Challenged by Pentecostals, Modern Interpretations https://www.washingtonpost.com/wp-dyn/articles/A40058-2004Dec31.html. The Washington Post, January 1, 2005; Page B07. *Accessed: August 8, 2012.*
[1357] Decreased the number of Catholic and African religions. Increased the number of Protestants (Census 2000) http://www.jornaldaciencia.org.br/Detalhe.jsp?id=3378
[1358] Somer Wiggins. Followers of Brazil's Umbanda religion worship despite discrimination http://www.mcclatchydc.com/2012/07/02/154710/followers-of-brazils-umbanda-religion.html. July 2, 2012. McClatchy. *Accessed August 8, 2012.*
[1359] IBOPE - Instituto Brasileiro de Opinião e Estatística. *Pesquisa de Opinião Pública sobre Criacionismo.* Dec. 2004 http://www2.ibope.com.br/calandrakbx/filesmng.nsf/Opiniao%20Publica/Downloads/Opp992-criacionismo.pdf/$File/Opp992-criacionismo.pdf. Accessed 2008-11-03
[1360] IBGE - Instituto Brasileiro de Geografia e Estatística (Brazilian Institute for Geography and Statistics). *2000 Census* http://www.ibge.gov.br/home/estatistica/populacao/censo2000/populacao/religiao_Censo2000.pdf. Accessed 2007-04-24
[1361] Folha Online - Mundo. *Estagnação econômica explica recuo do catolicismo no Brasil, diz FGV.* 2005-04-20 http://www1.folha.uol.com.br/folha/mundo/ult94u83030.shtml
[1362] IBGE - Instituto Brasileiro de Geografia e Estatística (Brazilian Institute for Geography and Statistics). *Notícias - Estudo revela 60 anos de transformações sociais no país* http://www.ibge.com.br/home/presidencia/noticias/noticia_visualiza.php?id_noticia=892&id_pagina=1. Accessed 2008-11-03.
[1363] Patrícia Birman, and Márcia Pereira Leite. "Whatever Happened to What Used to Be the Largest Catholic Country in the World?," *Daedalus* (2000) 129#2 pp. 271-290 in JSTOR https://www.jstor.org/stable/20027637
[1364] Folha de S.Paulo. *64% dos brasileiros se declaram católicos* http://datafolha.folha.uol.com.br/po/ver_po.php?session=447
[1365] G1 - Globo.com. Brasil - Notícias - *Em 60 anos, Brasil ficou mais mestiço, evangélico e "casado"* http://g1.globo.com/Noticias/Brasil/0,,MUL41764-5598,00.html
[1366] 2015 Yearbook of Jehovah's Witnesses
[1367] Neo-Pentecostalism and Afro-Brazilian religions: explaining the attacks on symbols of the African religious heritage in contemporary Brazil http://socialsciences.scielo.org/scielo.php?pid=S0104-93132007000100003&script=sci_arttext. Translation from: Mana, Rio de Janeiro, v.13 n.1, p. 207-236, Apr. 2007.
[1368] Dom Phillips. *Afro-Brazilian religions struggle against Evangelical hostility* https//www.washingtonpost.com. Washington Post, February 6, 2015.
[1369] Oreck, Alden. The Virtual Jewish History Tour: Brazil http://www.jewishvirtuallibrary.org/jsource/vjw/Brazil.html. Jewish Virtual Library. Accessed 2008-06-09
[1370] Synagogue in Brazilian town Recife considered oldest in the Americas http://www.haaretz.com/hasen/spages/922773.html. Haaretz 2007-11-12. Accessed 2008-06-09
[1371] Friedman, Saul. Jews and the American Slave Trade, p. 60. Transaction Publishers, 1997.
[1372] 2010 Brazilian census ftp://ftp.ibge.gov.br/Censos/Censo_Demografico_2010/Caracteristicas_Gerais_Religiao_Deficiencia/tab1_4.pdf Brazilian Institute for Geography and Statistics. Retrieved on 2013-11-13
[1373] U.S. Department of State. *Brazil*, Retrieved on 12.10.2013 https://www.state.gov/j/drl/rls/irf/2009/127381.htm

[1374] ftp://ftp.ibge.gov.br/Censos/Censo_Demografico_2010/Caracteristicas_Gerais_Religiao_Deficiencia/tab1_4.pdf
[1375] Lovejoy, Paul E., *Muslim Encounters With Slavery in Brazil*, Markus Wiener Pub., 2007.
[1376] Joao Jose Reis, *Slave Rebellion in Brazil: The Muslim Uprising of 1835 in Bahia*, Johns Hopkins University Press, London 1993
[1377] Steven Barboza, *American Jihad*, 1993
[1378] "Bureau of Democracy, Human Rights, and Labor International Religious Freedom Report 2009" https://www.state.gov/g/drl/rls/irf/2009/127381.htm October 26, 2009, US Department of State report on Brazil
[1379] Data Folha - Opinião Pública. *64% dos brasileiros se declaram católicos* http://datafolha.folha.uol.com.br/po/ver_po.php?session=447 2007-05-05. Accessed 200-11-03
[1380] Renascença Website. *Quase todos os brasileiros acreditam em Deus* http://www.rr.pt/InformacaoDetalhe.aspx?AreaId=11&SubAreaId=23&SubSubAreaId=47&ContentId=206214
[1381] dos Brasileiros Dizem Acreditar totalmente na Existência de Deus e 75% Acreditam no Diabo http://noticias.gospelmais.com.br/97-dos-brasileiros-dizem-acreditar-totalmente-na-existencia-de-deus-e-75-acreditam-no-diabo.html"97%
[1382] IBGE - Instituto Brasileiro de Geografia e Estatística (Brazilian Institute for Geography and Statistics). Table 2102 - *Resident population according to home, religion and gender, Census of 2000.* http://www.sidra.ibge.gov.br/bda/tabela/listabl.asp?z=cd&o=7&i=P&c=2102
[1383] //en.wikipedia.org/w/index.php?title=Template:Culture_of_Brazil&action=edit
[1384] According to the Brazilian Constitution: "Art. 13. A língua portuguesa é o idioma oficial da República Federativa do Brasil."http://www.planalto.gov.br/ccivil_03/constituicao/ConstituicaoCompilado.htm
[1385] Ethnologue http://www.ethnologue.com/ethno_docs/distribution.asp?by=country
[1386] Línguas Africanas http://www.labeurb.unicamp.br/elb/africanas/presenca_linguas_africanas_brasil_hoje.html
[1387] Línguas indígenas http://www.labeurb.unicamp.br/elb/indigenas/l_indigenas.html
[1388] "German" here meaning varied Germanic dialects spoken in Germany and other countries, not standard German.
[1389] Línguas europeias http://www.labeurb.unicamp.br/elb/europeias/europeias.htm
[1390] Políticas lingüísticas e a conservação da língua alemã no Brasil http://www.ucm.es/info/especulo/numero40/polingbr.html
[1391] History – Brazilian Portuguese http://www.orbilat.com/Languages/Portuguese-Brazilian/Brazilian-External_History.html
[1392] Censo 2010 fará a soma de casais homossexuais http://www1.folha.uol.com.br/folha/cotidiano/ult95u618299.shtml
[1393] Language Born of Colonialism Thrives Again in Amazon https://www.nytimes.com/2005/08/28/international/americas/28amazon.html?ex=1282881600&en=2dbb31357d010164&ei=5090 *New York Times*. Retrieved 22 September 2008
[1394] The Italian Immigration and Education http://www.sbhe.org.br/novo/congressos/cbhe3/Documentos/Individ/Eixo4/178.pdf
[1395] Census of 1940 http://biblioteca.ibge.gov.br/visualizacao/monografias/GEBIS%20-%20RJ/CD1940/Censo%20Demografico%201940%20VII_Brasil.pdf
[1396] Spanish people in Brazil http://www.proceedings.scielo.br/scielo.php?pid=MSC0000000012002000200006&script=sci_arttext#tx02
[1397] O Brasil como país de destino para imigrantes http://www.etni-cidade.net/espanhois.htm
[1398] Rota Romântica http://www.rotaromantica.com.br/.
[1399] São Paulo Shimbun – Brazilian Newspaper in Japanese http://www.camara.sp.gov.br/noticias_detalhe.asp?id=190.
[1400] https://www.japan-talk.com/jt/new/6-biggest-Japanese-communities-outside-Japan
[1401] Portal do Bairro Liberdade http://www.portal-bairro-liberdade.com.br/
[1402] História da Imigração Japonesa http://www.saopaulo.sp.gov.br/imigracaojaponesa/historia.php
[1403] Bairro do Bixiga http://www.cidadedesaopaulo.com/sp/br/o-que-visitar/500-bairro-do-bixiga
[1404] Bairro do Bixiga, reduto italiano em São Paulo http://origineitaliana.blogspot.ca/2009/09/fotos-do-bairro-do-bixiga-em-sao-paulo.html

[1405] Bexiga e Liberdade http://viagem.hsw.uol.com.br/sao-paulo-turismo4.htm
[1406] Os italianos de Bixiga, São Paulo http://web.letras.up.pt/aphes29/data/4th/AnaLuciaDuarteLanna_Texto.pdf
[1407] http://titus.uni-frankfurt.de/didact/karten/germ/deutdin.htm
[1408] http://www.lerncafe.de/aus-der-welt-1142/articles/pommern-in-brasilien.html
[1409] O povo pomerano no ES http://www.rog.com.br/claudiovereza2/mostraconteudos.asp?cod_conteudo=735
[1410] Plenário aprova em segundo turno a PEC do patrimônio http://www.ipol.org.br/ler.php?cod=690
[1411] Emenda Constitucional na Íntegra http://claudiovereza.files.wordpress.com/2011/06/pec-11-de-2009_1.pdf
[1412] ALEES - PEC que trata do patrimônio cultural retorna ao Plenário http://www.revistajuridica.com.br/noticia_integra_new.asp?id=187110
[1413] http://titus.uni-frankfurt.de/didact/karten/germ/deutdin.htm
[1414] http://www.lerncafe.de/aus-der-welt-1142/articles/pommern-in-brasilien.html
[1415] Aprovado projeto que declara o Talian como patrimônio do RS http://www.ipol.org.br/ler.php?cod=597 , accessed on 21 August 2011
[1416] LEI 14.061 - DECLARA INTEGRANTE DO PATRIMÔNIO HISTÓRICO E CULTURAL DO ESTADO DO RIO GRANDE DO SUL A "LÍNGUA HUNSRIK", DE ORIGEM GERMÂNICA http://www.al.rs.gov.br/legis/M010/M0100018.asp?Hid_IdNorma=58094
[1417] LEI Nº 14.061, 23 July 2012 - Declara integrante do patrimônio histórico e cultural do estado do Rio Grande do Sul a língua hunsrik, de origem germânica http://www.al.rs.gov.br/legis/M010/M0100099.ASP?Hid_Tipo=TEXTO&Hid_TodasNormas=58094&hTexto=&Hid_IDNorma=58094
[1418] LEI Nº 14.951, 11 November 2009 http://server03.pge.sc.gov.br/LegislacaoEstadual/2009/014951-011-0-2009-001.htm
[1419] Rotary apresenta ações na Câmara. FEIBEMO divulga cultura italiana http://www.cacador.net/portal/Noticias.aspx?cdNoticia=16388&cdNoticiaDivisao=2
[1420] Fóruns sobre o Talian - Eventos comemoram os 134 anos da imigração italiana http://www.editorasaomiguel.com.br/correio/edicoes/reportagem.php?cod_rep=6071
[1421] Aprovada em primeira votação projeto que torna o Talian segunda língua oficial de Bento Gonçalves http://difusora890.com.br/aprovado-em-primeira-votacao-projeto-que-torna-o-talian-segunda-lingua-oficial-de-bento/
[1422] Co-oficialização do Talian é oficializada pela câmara de Bento Golçalves http://difusora890.com.br/co-oficializacao-do-talian-e-aprovada-pela-camara-de-bento/
[1423] Câmara Bento – Projeto do Executivo é aprovado e Talian se torna a língua co-oficial http://www.jornalcidadesdaserra.com.br/camara-bento-projeto-do-executivo-e-aprovado-e-talian-se-torna-a-lingua-co-oficial
[1424] Cooficialização da língua alemã em Antônio Carlos http://www.ipol.org.br/upload/Image/lei1.jpg
[1425] TREZE TÍLIAS http://guiaroberto.vilabol.uol.com.br/trezet.htm
[1426] A sala de aula de alemão para falantes de dialeto: realidades e mitos http://www.rle.ucpel.tche.br/index.php/rle/article/view/76/48
[1427] Brasil: dialeto do baixo-alemão torna-se segunda língua oficial de cidade gaúcha http://ventosdalusofonia.wordpress.com/2012/06/28/brasil-dialeto-do-baixo-alemao-torna-se-segunda-lingua-oficial-de-cidade-gaucha/
[1428] Apresentando... Santa Maria do Herval http://dzeit.blogspot.ca/2009/03/apresentando-santa-maria-do-herval-rs.html
[1429] Câmara Municipal de Vereadores de Nova Petrópolis http://www.camaranovapetropolis.com.br/UPLarquivos/201220101443063.pdf
[1430] Ata 047/2010 http://www.camaranovapetropolis.com.br/UPLarquivos/221220101102423.pdf
[1431] Art. 153 § 3º da Lei Orgânica http://www.leismunicipais.com.br/lei-organica/novapetropolis-rs/4136
[1432] Em Nova Petrópolis 100% da população é alfabetizada http://www.novapetropolis.rs.gov.br/int_noticias.php?id=218&tipo=3, quinto parágrafo

[1433] Língua italiana na rede municipal de ensino http://folhadaterra.com.br/website/site/Noticia. aspx?id=2942
[1434] Aprovado em primeira votação, projeto emendado propõe um ano de caráter experimental em Venda Nova http://www.camaravni.es.gov.br/noticias_online.asp?id_noticia=842
[1435] LEI N° 3018/2003 - 02.10.03 - Dispõe sobre a oficialização de aulas de língua italiana nas escolas da Rede Municipal de Ensino http://www.franciscobeltrao.pr.gov.br/arquivos/legislacao/898.DOC
[1436] Lei Ordinária n° 3018/2003 de Francisco Beltrão, dispõe sobre a oficialização de aulas de língua italiana nas escolas http://www1.leismunicipais.com.br/legislacao-de-francisco-beltrao/669887/lei-3018-2003-francisco-beltrao-pr.html
[1437] Lei 3113/08, Brusque - Institui o ensino da língua italiana no currículo da rede municipal de ensino e dá outras provicências http://www.jusbrasil.com.br/legislacao/anotada/9618423/lei-3113-08-brusque
[1438] Lei 3113/08 | Lei n° 3113 de 14 de agosto de 2008 de Brusque http://www.jusbrasil.com.br/legislacao/940069/lei-3113-08-brusque-0
[1439] Art. 1 da Lei 3113/08, Brusque http://www.jusbrasil.com.br/legislacao/anotada/9618411/art-1-da-lei-3113-08-brusque
[1440] Secretaria de Educação esclarece a situação sobre o Ensino da Língua Italiana http://www.brusque.sc.gov.br/web/agenda_evento.php?noticia=172:Secretaria_de_Educacao_esclarece_a_situacao_sobre_o_Ensino_da_Lingua_Italiana
[1441] Lei 4159/01 | Lei n° 4159 de 29 de maio de 2001 de Criciuma http://www.jusbrasil.com.br/legislacao/984309/lei-4159-01-criciuma-0
[1442] Lei n° 4.159 de 29 de Maio de 2001 - Institui a disciplina de língua italiana http://www.jusbrasil.com.br/legislacao/anotada/9933877/lei-4159-01-criciuma
[1443] https://web.archive.org/web/20070211073529/http://paginas.terra.com.br/educacao/GICLI/ListasEnglish.htm
[1444] BRASIL CULTURA | O site da cultura brasileira http://www.brasilcultura.com.br/conteudo.php?id=187&menu=97&sub=196
[1445] https://books.google.com.br/books/about/Origens_do_português_brasileiro.html?id=4PEuAAAAYAAJ&redir_esc=y
[1446] Noll, Volker, "Das Brasilianische Portugiesisch", 1999.
[1447] http://m.travessa.com.br/produtoAmp.aspx?codartigo=ddb98df7-bdbd-4b7c-929a-780431289d26
[1448] Facts of Basilica of Aparecida http://noticias.terra.com.br/interna/0,,OI1984236-EI306,00.html
[1449] IBGE teen https://web.archive.org/web/20130224012534/http://www.ibge.gov.br/ibgeteen/povoamento/portugueses.html
[1450] IBGE teen https://web.archive.org/web/20080315161753/http://www.ibge.gov.br/ibgeteen/povoamento/indios/vida.html
[1451] IBGE teen https://web.archive.org/web/20080315160944/http://www.ibge.gov.br/ibgeteen/povoamento/negros/hercultural.html
[1452] IBGE teen http://www.ibge.gov.br/ibgeteen/povoamento/italianos.html
[1453] IBGE teen http://www.ibge.gov.br/ibgeteen/povoamento/alemaes.html
[1454] Carnival in Brazil http://www.topics-mag.com/internatl/holidays/brazil/carnival-brazil.htm
[1455] " As origens da Feijoada: O mais brasileiro dos sabores http://www.planetaeducacao.com.br/novo/artigo.asp?artigo=378", by João Luís de Almeida Machado. Visited on November 8, 2009.
[1456] Brazil National Dish: Feijoada Recipe and Restaurants http://www.brazilmax.com/news.cfm/tborigem/fe_fooddrink/id/11 . Visited on November 8, 2009.
[1457] CASCUDO, Luís da Câmara. História da Alimentação no Brasil – 2 vols. 2ª ed. Itatitaia, Rio de Janeiro, 1983.
[1458] " Benefícios do arros e feijão, par perfeito http://www.cnpaf.embrapa.br/parperfeito/parperfeito/index.htm ". In http://www.cnpaf.embrapa.br/. Visited on November 8, 2009.
[1459] International Coffee Organization http://www.ico.org/prices/po.htm
[1460] " Sabor do Café/História do café http://www.abic.com.br/scafe_historia.html ". Visited on November 8, 2009.

[1461] http://www.revistacafeicultura.com.br/index.php?tipo=ler&mat=8740
[1462] Museu do Café. Café no Brasil http://www.museudocafe.com.br/exposicao/permanentes.asp. Visited on November 8, 2009.
[1463] Gislane e Reinaldo. *História* (Textbook). Editora Ática, 2009, p. 352
[1464] There's an Awful Lot of Bubbly in Brazil https://www.amazon.co.uk/Theres-Awful-Lot-Bubbly-Brazil/dp/1905156367
[1465] They've got an awful lot of taxes in Brazil http://findarticles.com/p/articles/mi_hb5067/is_286/ai_n29318207/
[1466] There's an awful lot of motivation in Brazil https://www.theguardian.com/business/2006/feb/05/theobserver.observerbusiness?commentpage=1
[1467] An Awful Lot of Brazilians in Paraguay https://query.nytimes.com/gst/fullpage.html?res=9D00EEDB133EF931A25755C0A9679C8B63
[1468] *Almanaque Abril 2007*. São Paulo: Editora Abril, 2007, p. 234.
[1469] Martins, Simone B. & Imbroisi, Margaret H. *História da Arte*, 1988 http://www.historiadaarte.com.br/prehistoriabras.html
[1470] Correa, Conceição Gentil. *Estatuetas de cerâmica na cultura Santarém*. Belém: Museu Paraense Emílio Goeldi, 1965.
[1471] KARNAL, Leandro. *Teatro da Fé: Formas de Representação Religiosa no Brasil e no México do Século XVI*. São Paulo, Editora Hucitec, 1998.
[1472] *The Brazilian Baroque*. Encyclopaedia Itaú Cultural http//www.itaucultural.org.br
[1473] CONDURU, Roberto. *Araras Gregas*. In: 19&20 – A revista eletrônica de DezenoveVinte. Volume III, n. 2, abril de 2008 http://www.dezenovevinte.net/arte%20decorativa/ad_conduru.htm
[1474] BISCARDI, Afrânio & ROCHA, Frederico Almeida. *O Mecenato Artístico de D. Pedro II e o Projeto Imperial*. In: 19&20 – A revista eletrônica de DezenoveVinte. Volume I, n. 1, maio de 2006 http://www.dezenovevinte.net/ensino_artistico/mecenato_dpedro.htm
[1475] CARDOSO, Rafael. *A Academia Imperial de Belas Artes e o Ensino Técnico*. In: 19&20 – A revista eletrônica de DezenoveVinte. Volume III, n. 1, janeiro de 2008 http://www.dezenovevinte.net/ensino_artistico/rc_ebatecnico.htm
[1476] FERNANDES, Cybele V. F. *A construção simbólica da nação: A pintura e a escultura nas Exposições Gerais da Academia Imperial das Belas Artes*. In: 19&20 – A revista eletrônica de DezenoveVinte. Volume II, n. 4, outubro de 2007 http://www.dezenovevinte.net/obras/cfv_egba.htm
[1477] *Semana da Arte Moderna*. Pitoresco Website http://www.pitoresco.com.br/art_data/semana/
[1478] " Ismael Nery: Critical Commentary http://www.itaucultural.org.br/aplicexternas/enciclopedia_ic/index.cfm?fuseaction=artistas_biografia_ing&cd_verbete=3717&cd_item=2&cd_idioma=28556 ". On Itaú Cultural Visual Artes http://www.itaucultural.org.br/. Visited on November 8, 2009.
[1479] *Modernism in Brazil*. Encyclopedia Itaú Cultural http//www.itaucultural.org.br
[1480] Candido; Antonio. (1970) *Vários escritos*. São Paulo: Duas Cidades. p.18
[1481] " Brazilian Literature: An Introduction http://www.brasembottawa.org/en/culture_academic/literature.html ". Embassy of Brasil – Ottawa http://www.brasembottawa.org. Visited on November 2, 2009.
[1482] " Antonio Gonçalves Dias http://www.britannica.com/EBchecked/topic/238315/Antonio-Goncalves-Dias". Article on Encyclopædia Britannica http://www.britannica.com.
[1483] Caldwell, Helen (1970) *Machado de Assis: The Brazilian Master and his Novels*. Berkeley, Los Angeles and London, University of California Press.
[1484] Fernandez, Oscar Machado de Assis: The Brazilian Master and His Novels The *Modern Language Journal*, Vol. 55, No. 4 (Apr., 1971), pp. 255–256
[1485] João Cezar de Castro Rocha, "Introduction" http://www.plcs.umassd.edu/pdfs/plcs13_14_intro.pdf . *Portuguese Literature and Cultural Studies* 13/14 (2006): xxiv.
[1486] Harold Bloom, *Genius: A Mosaic of One Hundred Exemplary Creative Minds* (New York: Warner Books), 674.
[1487] Gonçalves Dias. *Song of the Exile*. Translated by John Milton and disponible on The NeoConcrete Movement https://mail.cofa.unsw.edu.au/pipermail/empyre/2004-March/msg00112.html . Page visited on November 3, 2009.

[1488] E-Dicionário de literatura http://www2.fcsh.unl.pt/edtl/verbetes/E/escola_literaria.htm . Visited on April 4, 2008.
[1489] Unnamed. " José Bento Monteiro Lobato reconta a Mitologia Grega http://recantodasletras.uol.com.br/teorialiteraria/1165269 ", in: Recanto das Letras. Visited on May 13, 2009.
[1490] Anjos, Augusto. *A Idéia* http://www.releituras.com/aanjos_ideia.asp
[1491] The Columbia Encyclopedia, Sixth Edition Copyright. 2004, Columbia University Press. Licensed from Lernout & Hauspie Speech Products N.V.
[1492] Terra, Ernani. De Nicola, José. *Português: de olho no mundo do trabalho* (Textbook), p.523. 3rd edition. Editora Scipione, São Paulo, 2006.
[1493] Terra, Ernani. De Nicola, José. *Português: de olho no mundo do trabalho* (Textbook), p.28
[1494] http://educaterra.terra.com.br/literatura/livrodomes/2004/09/24/003.htm
[1495] Terra, Ernani. De Nicola, José. *Português: de olho no mundo do trabalho* (Textbook), p.516.
[1496] Terra, Ernani. De Nicola, José. *Português: de olho no mundo do trabalho* (Textbook), p.517
[1497] Brazilian's literature http://www.portugueselanguageguide.com/portuguese/culture/brazil/brazilliterature.asp. Portuguese Language Guide http://www.portugueselanguageguide.com/. Visited on November 2, 2009.
[1498] http://www.bibliotecadigital.ufmg.br/dspace/bitstream/1843/BUOS-8FMH5A/1/entre_fanaticos_e_her_is___gabriel_braga.pdf
[1499] Best of Foreign http://www.rottentomatoes.com/top/bestofrt_genre.php?category=200010 at Rotten Tomatoes. Retrieved 2009-10-27
[1500] Revista de Cinema https://web.archive.org/web/20080314225548/http://www2.uol.com.br/revistadecinema/fechado/os50maisvistos/edicao24/os50maisvistos_01.html. Visited on November 8, 2009.
[1501] Ancine http://www.ancine.gov.br/media/SAM/Filmes_nacionais_mais_de_um_milhao_espectadores_1970-2007_por_publico_260308.pdf. Visited on November 8, 2009.
[1502] Filme B http://www.filmeb.com.br. Visited on November 8, 2009.
[1503] *The Guardian*, October 2, 2009, Olympics 2016: Tearful Pele and weeping Lula greet historic win for Rio https://www.theguardian.com/sport/2009/oct/02/olympics-2016-games-rio-pele
[1504] http://www.cultura.gov.br/
[1505] http://www.brazilsf.org/brazil_culture_eng.htm
[1506] http://eyesonbrazil.com
[1507] http://guides.library.illinois.edu/brazilian_culture
[1508] http://langecole.com/cultural_center/c/1-Brazil-Cultural-Center
[1509] //en.wikipedia.org/w/index.php?title=Template:Culture_of_Brazil&action=edit
[1510] apud Padre Noel Berthold, in: "Trevisan, Armindo", in *A Escultura dos Sete Povos*. Brasília: Editora Movimento / Instituto Nacional do Livro, 1978. (Portuguese)
[1511] Mariz, Vasco. *História da Música no Brasil*. Rio de Janeiro: Nova Fronteira, 2005. 6ª ed. (Portuguese)
[1512] **Castagna, Paulo.** Encarte do CD *Gabriel Fernandes da Trindade – Duetos Concertantes*. São Paulo: Paulus, 1995. (Portuguese)
[1513] http://www.rodrigolimacomposer.com/
[1514] Music http://www.fmpsd.ab.ca/schools/df/Brazil/mmusic.htm. Fmpsd.ab.ca. Retrieved on 2011-11-23.
[1515] Childhood Secrets * https://web.archive.org/web/20070709135551/http://www.bn.br/fbn/musica/enzinfa.htm. bn.br
[1516] Ernesto Nazareth – Rei do Choro http://www.chiquinhagonzaga.com/nazareth/. Chiquinhagonzaga.com. Retrieved on 2011-11-23.
[1517] A nação das cantoras http://veja.abril.com.br/110407/p_120.shtml. Veja.abril.com.br. Retrieved on 2011-11-23.
[1518] https://web.archive.org/web/20090123211659/http://trama.uol.com.br/portalv2/home/index.jsp
[1519] Funk Carioca: The Beat Goes On http://www.soundsandcolours.com/articles/brazil/funk-carioca-the-beat-goes-on/
[1520] http://www.ville-ge.ch/meg/musinfo_ph.php?what=pays=Br%E9sil&debut=0&bool=AND
[1521] http://www.bbc.co.uk/programmes/b00g3rxj
[1522] http://www.bbc.co.uk/programmes/b00hkc14

[1523] http://www.bbc.co.uk/programmes/b00hql07
[1524] http://www.bbc.co.uk/programmes/b00hgbwv
[1525] http://www.bbc.co.uk/programmes/b00gh5yw
[1526] https://web.archive.org/web/20091201050558/http://www.brazil.org.uk/culture/music.html
[1527] http://www.soundsandcolours.com/category/articles/brazil/
[1528] http://www.cas.podomatic.com/
[1529] //en.wikipedia.org/w/index.php?title=Template:Culture_of_Brazil&action=edit
[1530] //en.wikipedia.org/w/index.php?title=Template:History_of_modern_literature&action=edit
[1531] https://www.lib.utexas.edu/etd/d/2009/arcee64124/arcee64124.pdf
[1532] https://www.webcitation.org/6PeLcmCzp
[1533] //en.wikipedia.org/w/index.php?title=Template:Brazilian_cuisine&action=edit
[1534] //en.wikipedia.org/w/index.php?title=Template:Culture_of_Brazil&action=edit
[1535] One century of Japanese immigration to Brazil – News –Japanese immigrants helped a 'revolution' in Brazilian agriculture http://g1.globo.com/Sites/Especiais/Noticias/0,,MUL585682-9980,00-IMIGRANTES+JAPONESES+AJUDARAM+A+REVOLUCIONAR+AGRICULTURA+BRASILEIRA.html
[1536] One century of Japanese immigration to Brazil – News – Immigrants made a city in São Paulo in a great egg producer http://g1.globo.com/Sites/Especiais/Noticias/0,,MUL450499-9980,00-IMIGRANTES+TRANSFORMARAM+CIDADE+PAULISTA+EM+GRANDE+PRODUTORA+DE+OVOS.html
[1537] Roger, " Feijoada: The Brazilian national dish http://www.braziltravelguide.com/feijoada-the-brazilian-national-dish.html " braziltravelguide.com.
[1538] Cascudo, Luis da Câmara. História da Alimentação no Brasil. São Paulo/Belo Horizonte: Editora USP/Itatiaia, 1983.
[1539] Freyre, Gilberto. Açúcar. Uma Sociologia do Doce, com Receitas de Bolos e Doces do Nordeste do Brasil. São Paulo, Companhia das Letras, 1997.
[1540] //en.wikipedia.org/w/index.php?title=Template:Brazilian_film_list&action=edit
[1541] http://www.sensesofcinema.com/2011/great-directors/nelson-pereira-dos-santos/
[1542] http://www.iberoamericanmovies.com/brazil/top-10-movies-from-brazil/
[1543] http://www.ou.edu/worldlit/onlinemagazine/2003winter/04-Oct-Dec03-Ortolando.pdf
[1544] http://www.soundsandcolours.com/articles/brazil/the-best-brazilian-films-of-all-time/
[1545] https://web.archive.org/web/20100313082951/http://www.cinemabrasileiro.net.br/
[1546] https://web.archive.org/web/20070928104737/http://www.atlantidacinematografica.com.br/sistema2006/historia_texto.asp
[1547] http://www.ejumpcut.org/archive/onlinessays/JC21folder/BrazilStamJohnson.html
[1548] http://www.cinemabrasil.org.br
[1549] http://www.cinemateca.gov.br
[1550] http://www.adorocinemabrasileiro.com.br/filmes/a.asp
[1551] http://www.sensesofcinema.com/2006/40/brazilian-cinema/
[1552] http://www.sensesofcinema.com/2005/great-directors/rocha/
[1553] http://www.sensesofcinema.com/2003/28/mandacaru/
[1554] http://www.veracruzcinema.com.br
[1555] http://www.tupiniquim.jp
[1556] http://eyesonbrazil.com/brazilian-films-the-list
[1557] Louzada, Maria Alice & Louzada, Julio. *Os Primeiros Momentos da Arte Brasileira* http://www.juliolouzada.com.br/primeirosmomentos.asp . Júlio Louzada Artes Plásticas Brasil. Acesso 5 out 2010
[1558] Leite, José Roberto Teixeira & Lemos, Carlos A.C. *Os Primeiros Cem Anos*, in Civita, Victor. *Arte no Brasil*. São Paulo: Abril Cultural, 1979
[1559] Fernandes, Cybele Vidal Neto. *Labor e arte, registros e memórias. O fazer artístico no espaço luso-brasileiro.* IN *Actas do VII Colóquio Luso-Brasileiro de História da Arte*. Porto: Universidade do Porto/CEPESE/FCT, 2007. p. 111
[1560] Gouvêa, Fernando da Cruz. *Maurício de Nassau e o Brasil Holandês* https://books.google.com/books?id=VH_CS3ef9KgC&printsec=frontcover&hl=pt-BR#v=onepage&q=a%20corte%20nassoviana%20no%20brasil&f=false. Editora Universitária UFPE, 1998. pp. 143-149; 186-188

[1561] Costa, Maria Cristina Castilho. A imagem da mulher: um estudo de arte brasileira. Senac, 2002. pp. 55-56
[1562] Sevcenko, Nicolau. Pindorama revisitada: cultura e sociedade em tempos de virada. Série Brasil cidadão. Editora Peirópolis, 2000. pp. 39-47
[1563] //en.wikipedia.org/w/index.php?title=Template:Culture_of_Brazil&action=edit
[1564] Brazilian Football World Cup record http://www.brazilian-football.com/
[1565] http://www.therealbrazil.com/blog/2012/08/08/mma-brazils-favourite-new-sport/ MMA: Brazil's Favourite New Sport?
[1566] Torneio Touchdown http://touchdown.net/2013/05/30/bandsports-confirma-a-cobertura-do-torneio-touchdown-v
[1567] Folha de S. Paulo - Ilustrada http://www1.folha.uol.com.br/fsp/ilustrada/103496-nova-novela-das-18h-da-globo-tera-ares-de-cinema.shtml.
[1568] http://www.globoesporte.com/
[1569] http://www.lancenet.com.br/
[1570] http://www.gazetaesportiva.net/
[1571] http://esporte.uol.com.br/
[1572] http://esportes.terra.com.br/
[1573] http://br.esporteinterativo.yahoo.com/

Article Sources and Contributors

The sources listed for each article provide more detailed licensing information including the copyright status, the copyright owner, and the license conditions.

Name of Brazil *Source:* https://en.wikipedia.org/w/index.php?oldid=841898165 *License:* Creative Commons Attribution-Share Alike 3.0 *Contributors:* Acroterion, Artcyprus, BD2412, Bobrayner, Carlosguitar, Chris the speller, ClueBot NG, Cristiano Tomás, Danga, Dbachmann, Error, Felipe Menegaz, Gilliam, Happysailor, Harrisles, Hazhk, Hispalois, Hmains, Hoary, Itsmejudith, Jamesooders, Jim1138, John of Reading, Krenakarore, Krithin, Lambiam, Lordrosemount, Melcous, Mopcwiki, Natg 19, Neelix, Onel5969, Owain Knight, Quick and Dirty User Account, R'n'B, Regancy42, Rui Gabriel Correia, SchreiberBike, Slx03, SquidSK, The Utahraptor, TranquilHope, Vrenator, WadeSimMiser, Walrasiad, XPTO, 34 anonymous edits 1

History of Brazil *Source:* https://en.wikipedia.org/w/index.php?oldid=852116582 *License:* Creative Commons Attribution-Share Alike 3.0 *Contributors:* 420BlazeIt,YoloSwag69, A.amitkumar, AKS.9955, Abusque, Alumnum, Amuseclio, Aymatth2, Baxter4173, Beland, Bender235, Bequw, Bgwhite, Blue Mist 1, Bollyjeff, Braincricket, Brattbutt1234, Bringback2ndpersonverbs, CAPTAIN RAJU, Cainamarques, Callanecc, Caradamata, Chewings72, ChrisGualtieri, ClueBot NG, Color4breex79, Coltsfan, CommonsDelinker, CorbieVreccan, Coretheapple, Cyfal, DaGizza, Dawnseeker2000, Dcirovic, DemocraticLuntz, Dewritech, Diannaa, Diego barbosa silva, Dr. Kadzi, DragonflySixtyseven, Enpatrais, Eumolpo, Faisal.Aziz05bd, Favonian, Florian Blaschke, Flyer22 Reborn, Fraggle81, Gadget850, Gdheidvfgs, GeneralizationsAreBad, George8211, GeorgeBarnick, Gilliam, Giso6150, Glenncheney, Gpapazian, Grenzer22, Greyjoy, GünniX, Hello71, Highpeaks35, Hmains, Ingarix, Iridescent, IronGargoyle, JackofOz, Jdcomix, Jodosma, John of Reading, Johnhann7763, Julian Mazimpaka, K6ka, Kenereth, Knochen, Lazylaces, Lecen, LizardJr8, LuizCent, LuzoGraal, M2545, MNINC, MONGO, Marcelo roquette, Martarius, Materialscientist, MelbourneStar, Menezesfernandes, Name goes here, Natg 19, Omicroñ'R, PMLF, Paincryliedie, PhilKnight, Philip Trueman, Pifactorial, Pleiotrop3, RadiX, Rjensen, Samfreed, Sbalfour, Seahorseruler, Serols, Shellwood, Slickmoves, Stephenb, TYelliot, Tedgoertzel, Tentinator, TheCascadian, TheOtherUnknown, Thesavage1080, TyA, UY Scuti, Vinícius94, Vvven, Wiae, Widr, Wikipelli, Yoshi24517, YuriNikolai, 214 anonymous edits 7

Timeline of Brazilian history *Source:* https://en.wikipedia.org/w/index.php?oldid=853654714 *License:* Creative Commons Attribution-Share Alike 3.0 *Contributors:* Alumnum, Bgwhite, Cientific124, Cloudz679, DanielGSouza, Fixer88, Frietjes, HaeB, Highpeaks35, IVORK, Jon Kolbert, Jonesey95, Juniorpetjua, Knoterification, Kokopretzel, M2545, PMLF, Tom.Reding, Tony1, Trappist the monk, 11 anonymous edits 34

Colonial Brazil *Source:* https://en.wikipedia.org/w/index.php?oldid=847790727 *License:* Creative Commons Attribution-Share Alike 3.0 *Contributors:* Alexander Domanda, Amuseclio, AndrewV77, Anonymous from the 21st century, Antonio Basto, Aquintero82, Ariel Pontes, Arjayay, Astynax, BD2412, Bagunceiro, Bellerophon5685, Bender235, Chris the speller, Clinamental, ClueBot NG, Cnilep, Colonies Chris, CommonsDelinker, Cristiano Tomás, DIYeditor, Dewritech, Diego barbosa silva, Dogie123456789, Donner60, EamonnPKeane, Elinruby, Eyesnore, Faunas, Felipe Menegaz, GenQuest, GenuineArt, GeorgeofOrange, Gilliam, GoingBatty, Goustien, Grenzer22, GünniX, Harry Tudor, Hmains, I dream of horses, J 1982, Johanna-Hypatia, John Ericson, John of Reading, JohnCD, Joseba, Jprg1966, K6ka, Lecen, Lihaas, Look2See1, Loopy30, Loraof, LuzoGraal, MB298, Magioladitis, Manxruler, Marco polo, Marcocapelle, Mogism, Monkaap, Mouramoor, Narky Blert, Natg 19, Niceguyedc, NicoScribe, Nima1024, Nk, Omnipaedista, PMLF, PaddyViking, Patriotadoseculo, PedroPVZ, Peyre, Purpleturple, Renatokeshet, Ricky81682, Roadburns, Saqib042, Savvyjack23, Sbalfour, Shadowxfox, Shanker Pur, ShelfSkewed, Skr15081997, Smtchahal, Syrthiss, TAnthony, TRAJAN 117, The Anomebot2, The Illusive Man, The Ogre, The Photographer, Theoboyd, Tiberti, Tommy2010, Tomseattle, Tonneduroc, Tuckerresearch, Unobjectionable, WOSlinker, Waidtheduck, Winkelvi, Woohookitty, XPTO, YSSYguy, Yavorpenchev, Yintan, Zingvin, Zurkhardo, 128 anonymous edits 61

War of the Emboabas *Source:* https://en.wikipedia.org/w/index.php?oldid=848704194 *License:* Creative Commons Attribution-Share Alike 3.0 *Contributors:* Alumnum, Amuseclio, Babbage, Bagunceiro, CommonsDelinker, Erudy, Eumolpo, Flyaway1111, Giso6150, Grenzer22, I dream of horses, Infrogmation, Leandrod, Look2See1, MBaran, Macgreco, Marek69, Mschlindwein, Piccolo Modificatore Laborioso, Rsabbatini, Shadowxfox, Srnec, The Ogre, Unyoyega, Varlaam, Victor Lopes, XPTO, ネイ , 5 anonymous edits 94

Inconfidência Mineira *Source:* https://en.wikipedia.org/w/index.php?oldid=833191478 *License:* Creative Commons Attribution-Share Alike 3.0 *Contributors:* Amuseclio, Bagunceiro, Blaylockjam10, Bovineboy2008, Capmo, Carioca, Charles Essie, Closedmouth, ClueBot NG, Commander Keane, Davidnorth802, Diego barbosa silva, Edward, Everyking, Giso6150, Grenzer22, Hmains, Igordebraga, Jaraalbe, Languagehat, Loginnigol, Lord Cornwallis, Macgreco, Mateuszica, Missvain, Moagim, Mornhavon, Mouramoor, Mucky Duck, Nabla, Neodymium-142, Nnemo, Nuvolet, Piccolo Modificatore Laborioso, Picture Master, Ptbotgourou, Pularoid, Robofish, Sanya3, Ser Amantio di Nicolao, Slakr, Solar-Wind, The Photographer, Topbanana, Unbuttered Parsnip, Varlaam, Xyzzyva, 8 anonymous edits 97

United Kingdom of Portugal, Brazil and the Algarves *Source:* https://en.wikipedia.org/w/index.php?oldid=853309589 *License:* Creative Commons Attribution-Share Alike 3.0 *Contributors:* AjaxSmack, Alcacer1, Alghenius, Andrew Gwilliam, AnonMoos, Anonymous from the 21st century, Antonio Basto, Arjayay, Arthur Brum, Astynax, BBird, Bellerophon5685, Bgwhite, Buzzaz, ClueBot NG, Colonies Chris, CommonsDelinker, Completesentence, Crenelator, Crisco 1492, Cristiano Tomás, D6, DWC LR, Dbachmann, DemonicInfluence, Dewritech, Domaleixo, Domino theory, Drmies, F F 2016, Fadesga, Felipe Menegaz, Fernandoe, Gabriel Lopes Guasti, GeorgeZhao, GoingBatty, Good Olfactory, GoodDay, Grafen, Guilherme Paula, Hmains, Hume42, Iridescent, J 1982, J04n, Jaraalbe, John of Reading, Jojofunny123, Jonas Mur～enwiki, Jonesey95, Khazar, Kintetsubuffalo, LatinoLatino, Laurel Lodged, Lets Enjoy Life, Licor, Lightmouse, LilHelpa, Limongi, Look2See1, Lordbecket, M. Armando, MIKHEIL, Mackay 86, Mandarax, Martarius, Medeis, Mediran, Mel Etitis, Mimihitam, MinnesotanConfederacy, Mullet, NMaia, Nk, Odin of Trondheim, Paulista01, Piccolo Modificatore Laborioso, Pietdesomere, Pularoid, Rastrojo, RekishiEJ, Rich Farmbrough, RickMorais, Ricky81682, SchreiberBike, Shadowxfox, Sir Nasco, Skyerise, Smigs, Southern Person, Sundostund, TaBOT-zerem, TarEldamir, TelecomNut, Tercessuinotlim, The Almightey Drill, The Anomebot2, The Emperor's New Spy, Thumperward, Verbcatcher, Vinícius18, Vinícius94, Von Tamm, Vsmith, Whoop whoop pull up, William Galladryn, XPTO, Yiosie2356, Yodaki, YouNeedHelpBra101, Zeorymer, 208 anonymous edits 103

Independence of Brazil *Source:* https://en.wikipedia.org/w/index.php?oldid=844991338 *License:* Creative Commons Attribution-Share Alike 3.0 *Contributors:* 2x2leax, Ahwiv, Aidahmed1, Aisteco, Aldis90, AllyGebies, Alonso de Mendoza, American In Brazil, Anarko, Anaxial, Andrwsc, AnonMoos, Arthur Brum, Arthur Holland, Bagunceiro, Bailo26, Bgwhite, Binksternet, Brandmeister, Brianvale, Bwmcmaste, Caltas, Cambalachero, Charles Essie, Chipgc, Chrism, Cimorcus, CityOfSilver, ClueBot NG, Cwobeel, Cybercobra, Cybershore, Dcirovic, Dewritech, Dimadick, Doncram, DrKay, E. Ripley, Egsan Bacon, El rey del sol, Empmmus, Epbr123, Eugene-elgato, Excirial, Fadesga, Felipe Menegaz, Flyer22 Reborn, Francisco Seixas, Gemini1980, General Ization, GeneralizationsAreBad, Geoffrey Matthews, Good Olfactory, Gorthian, Greyjoy, Homme22, Hugo999, HugoTol, IANVS, J 1982, JMRAMOS0109, Jack Greenmaven, Jauerback, Jettionahicks, Jodosma, John of Reading, JohnRamos1988, Joseon Empire, Kappasig15, KennethSides, Klilidiplomus, Kwamikagami, LatinoLatino, Lecen, Lesgles, LilHelpa, Lolgirllol123, Meters, Mild Bill Hiccup, Minerva97, Missimack, Mogism, N5iln, Nanophosis, Orphan Wiki, Oshwah, Paulista01, Petfold, Pethr, Pleiotrop3, Queencarias, RandomAct, Rbenzecry, Rms125a@hotmail.com, Sam Diener, Sbalfour, Seyon, Shellwood, Simplexity22, Solar-Wind, Southern Person, Srnec, Sun Creator, T.R.Elven, Telecomviking, Teles, TheEsb, Tim!, Titodutta, Tonneduroc, TyA, Vegaswikian, Vinícius94, Wearsunscreen, Wikipelli, Woohookitty, Wordmoderators, XPTO, 209 anonymous edits 125

Empire of Brazil *Source:* https://en.wikipedia.org/w/index.php?oldid=854193300 *License:* Creative Commons Attribution-Share Alike 3.0 *Contributors:* Adnan bogi, Alexander Domanda, AmericanLemming, Amuseclio, Antonio Basto, Arthur Brum, Arthur Holland, Astynax, Azips, Berty688, Bill william compton, Billinghurst, Blethering Scot, Bodhisattwa, Braincricket, Calidum, Cambalachero, Candido, Charles RB, ClueBot NG, CommonsDelinker, Cristiano Tomás, Crito10, Cynko, Derekbridges, Diego barbosa silva, Donner60, EamonnPKeane, Edmundo Soares, EeuHP, Eldizzino, Elevatorrailfan, Eregli bob, FactStraight, Felipe Menegaz, Feminist, Fonadier, Gabriel Lopes Guasti, Guilherme M.R. da Fonseca, Harizotoh9, Hchc2009, Hmains, IRIS-ZOOM, Ignácio, Italia2006, J 1982, JASpencer, Jack Bufalo Head, JamesBWatson, Jasonanaggie, Juniorpetjua, Karan Kamath, KingSkyLord, Kintetsubuffalo, Knochen, Knoterification, Kristijh, Laser brain, LatinoLatino, Lecen, Limongi, LuizLSNeto, MB298, MZMcBride, Marcocapelle, Martarius, Master Uegly, Michael Barera, Mimihitam, Modest Genius, Morningstar1814, Mr rnddude, Nimetapoeg, Nitpicking polish, Nk, Noodleki, Paulista01, Pedro Aguiar, Pedro8790, Peyre, Quintus fabius, RNecross, Rafael Florentino, Ricky81682, Rui Gabriel Correia, Samsara, Shadowxfox, Simon Peter Hughes, SimonX, Srednuas Lenoroc, Srtª PiriLimPomPom, Tbhotch, Tedgoertzel, The Almightey Drill, The Anome, The Anomebot2, The Yeti, The ed17, ThecentreCZ, Thirdright, TompaDompa, Ttocserp, Vedant GAWLIKAR, Vinícius18, Vinícius94, VitorPredator, Walter Görlitz, War wizard90, Wee Curry Monster, WereSpielChequers, Xuxo, ZuluKane, باسم, ✈, 63 anonymous edits 136

First Brazilian Republic *Source:* https://en.wikipedia.org/w/index.php?oldid=851778127 *License:* Creative Commons Attribution-Share Alike 3.0 *Contributors:* -Ilhador-, 172, Abu badali, Acad Ronin, Aerolitz, Ahoerstemeier, Alarbus, AlasdairGreen27, AlbertR, AlisonW, Altenmann, Alumnum, Ardfern, Arthur Brum, Astynax, Avpop, Ben Ben, Ben Tuckett, BillMasen, Binabik80, Biruitorul, Bobblewik, CJLL Wright, Candamir, Carabinieri, Cattus, Charles Matthews, Chris the speller, ChrisGualtieri, ClueBot NG, Coltsfan, CommonsDelinker, Cuckooman4, Cybershore, D6, DO'Neil, Darthkenobi0, David.moreno72, Dcirovic, DeadEyeArrow, Diego barbosa silva, Djr13, EECavazos, EUDOXIO, Edward, Eyesnore, Felipe Menegaz, Gaius Cornelius, GoingBatty, Green Giant, Grenzer22, Ground Zero, Guilherme Paula, Guy Macon, Hemlock Martinis, Hmains, Hmainsbot1, Howcheng, Illegitimate Barrister, Ingarix, Iridescent, Iwad1, J 1982, Jack Bufalo Head, Jdcomix, John of Reading, Jonkerz, Jossi, Jpgordon, Jztinfinity, Kevin B12, Kevinsam, Knochen, Leandrod, Lightmouse, M. Armando, MCBastos, MaGioZal, Magioladitis, Malayedit, Markbassett, Megan1967, Mr Stephen, NMaia, Nabarry, NawlinWiki, Nik42, Nilmerg, Nk, Nwbeeson, Omnipaedista, PMLF, Pedro Aguiar, Pedro8790, PhnomPencil, Piccolo Modificatore Laborioso, Poli, R'n'B, Ramalha Soares, Rigadoun, Robofish, Sardanaphalus, SchreiberBike, Senjuto, Shadowxfox, Shanes, Shoeofdeath, Sincity147, Sintaku, Skavatra, Ssrose, TAnthony, Tamira C., Tcmr, Template namespace initialisation script, The Anomebot2, The Photographer, The Sage of Stamford, The ed17, ThecentreCZ, Timotheos, Travelbird, Vancouverguy, Vinícius94, Whoop whoop pull up, Wik, Woahman, Xeirxes, Xyzzyva, 181 anonymous edits 189

Vargas Era *Source:* https://en.wikipedia.org/w/index.php?oldid=854171975 *License:* Creative Commons Attribution-Share Alike 3.0 *Contributors:* Ack! Ack! Pasta bomb!, Aerolitz, AjaxSmack, Altenmann, Anonymous from the 21th century, Antonio Basto, Arthur Brum, Astynax, BD2412, Bagunceiro, Bellerophon5685, Bennymo17, BiggestSataniaFanboy89, BlueMoonlet, Bongwarrior, Chilrreh, ChrisGualtieri, ClueBot NG, CommonsDelinker, Comnenus, Cybershore, DadaNeem, Deb, Dewritech, Diamantina, Dirke, DutchDevil, Dysmorodrepanis∼enwiki, Eugene-elgato, Fasouzafreitas, Felipe Menegaz, Gabriel Yuji, Girpkmnmm, Glacialfox, Gotipe, Grenzer22, Grutness, Gustavo Szwedowski de Korwin, HADRIANVS, HangingCurve, IRIS-ZOOM, Ignácio, Illegitimate Barrister, Ingarix, J 1982, JASpencer, JHunterJ, Jggouvea, John of Reading, Jonkerz, Joseph Solis in Australia, Kelutral, Kevin9217, Kevinsam, Kku, Kleuske, Knoterification, Kweymouth, Leandrod, LilHelpa, Magioladitis, Malinaccier, Mamalujo, Marek69, Marxistfounder, Materialscientist, MinnesotanConfederacy, Mogism, MonroeDoctrine, Narky Blert, Niceguyedc, Nick Number, Nk, Nucleotide, Number 57, Numbo3, Omnipaedista, Orenburg1, Pearle, PedR, Piccolo Modificatore Laborioso, PigFlu Oink, R'n'B, Rdkamp, Rjensen, Rn.brito, Rrostrom, Rsabbatini, Saectar, Saxonthedog, Ser Amantio di Nicolao, Serial Number 54129, Shadowxfox, SigPig, Srnec, TX55, Tcmr, The Anomebot2, ThecentreCZ, Tiphareth, Topbanana, Typ932, Vanryoko, Vinícius94, WereSpielChequers, Woohookitty, Xatufan, Xyzzyva, 149 anonymous edits 204

Second Brazilian Republic *Source:* https://en.wikipedia.org/w/index.php?oldid=845698442 *License:* Creative Commons Attribution-Share Alike 3.0 *Contributors:* 172, Abc Zc, Aerolitz, AlbertR, American In Brazil, Antonio Basto, Ardfern, Arthur Brum, Astynax, Ben Tuckett, C010T3, CJLL Wright, Chronus, Cmdrjameson, Constanz, D6, Dalillama, David.moreno72, Delotrooladoo, Dewritech, Dogru144, Dr Gangrene, Everyking, Felipe Menegaz, Flarkins, Flix11, Gearsow, Geschichte, Green Giant, Ground Zero, Gssmith1, Guilherme Paula, Gurch, Hao2lian, Hemlock Martinis, Hillel, Hmains, Hmainsbot1, Illegitimate Barrister, Ingarix, J 1982, Kevinsam, Leandrod, Lights, Ling.Nut, Marcelo Reis, Mattello, Mizormice, Mucky Duck, Niceguyedc, Nk, Piccolo Modificatore Laborioso, Ricabs09, Rich Farmbrough, Rjwilmsi, Sanmartin, Sardanaphalus, Seventh Holy Scripture, Shadowxfox, Srnec, Student7, TX55, Tdowling, Template namespace initialisation script, The Anomebot2, ThecentreCZ, Vivafelis, Woohookitty, Zeeny9, 45 anonymous edits 222

Brazilian military government *Source:* https://en.wikipedia.org/w/index.php?oldid=852903866 *License:* Creative Commons Attribution-Share Alike 3.0 *Contributors:* A Great Catholic Person, Abc Zc, AdjectivesAreBad, Aerolitz, Alumnum, Anarchovegan, Aravind V R, Ardfern, Aremisasling, ArkinAardvark, Arr4, Arthur Brum, Arthur Rubin, Astynax, Ben Ben, Ben Tuckett, Bender235, Billinghurst, Bootyhunter122, Brasilialogo, C.J. Griffin, Cadiomals, Catlemur, Charles Essie, Chilrreh, ChrisGualtieri, ClaudioMB, Clerks, Cliffmark99, ClueBot NG, Colonies Chris, Coltsfan, Cowlibob, Cybercobra, DIYeditor, DadaNeem, Dalillama, Damiens.rf, DangerousPanda, Danieldasilva, Dantadd, DavidStarIsrael7, Dekimasu, Deville, Dewritech, Diego barbosa silva, Download, Drilnoth, Edsondiehl, Edward, Eladynnus, Evenfiel, Evlekis, Evolauxia, Fadesga, Felipe Menegaz, Fgnievinski, Flix11, Francisco Seixas, Gabriel Yuji, Gail, Ghirlandajo, Gimelthedog, Good Olfactory, Ground Zero, Guinsberg, Guto2003, Gyrofrog, Illegitimate Barrister, Ingarix, Ixocactus, J 1982, Jevansen, Johayek, Johnsonj1016, Katangais, Katherine.Holt, Khazar, Kikichugirl, Kintetsubuffalo, Koavf, Lecen, Lgggioia, LinguistAtLarge, Lsell@duke.edu, MBisanz, MaGioZal, Magioladitis, Mandarax, Marek69, Marlonge, Mesoderm, Mild Bill Hiccup, Missionary, Mogism, Mucky Duck, Mukkakukaku, Na voz silenciada, Niceguyedc, Ninguém, Nk, Omnipaedista, Ospalh, Pass3456, PedR, PenguinHistory, Peter G Werner, Phil Boswell, PhilipR, Piccolo Modificatore Laborioso, Pol098, Quaker Qweer, Qwertyus, RL0919, RafaelyGarabat2002, ReaperDawn, Rich Farmbrough, Rjwilmsi, Rodrigogomesonetwo, RonjaKamilla, RudolfRed, SamWinchester000, Saqib042, Sardanaphalus, Sesel, Shaded0, Shieldon, Sirshiggles, Some jerk on the Internet, Soviet Boy, Stevenmitchell, Stormwatch, Tazmaniacs, The Rambling Man, TheMuffinMan2360, ThecentreCZ, Thommy9, Tim!, Tom.Reding, Tony1, Ulric1313, Varavour, Victor Lopes, Vinícius94, Waide Piki, Whoop whoop pull up, Wuerzele, ვაჟდე ვ, 186 anonymous edits 231

History of Brazil since 1985 *Source:* https://en.wikipedia.org/w/index.php?oldid=849353250 *License:* Creative Commons Attribution-Share Alike 3.0 *Contributors:* Abc Zc, Aigma, Alumnum, Anonymous from the 21st century, Ardfern, Astynax, Betacommand, Bgwhite, Bluekelp, CJLL Wright, Cattus, Chicocvenancio, Chris the speller, ChrisGualtieri, Chrisminter, ClueBot NG, CommonsDelinker, Conscious, Constanz, DadaNeem, Dalillama, Darian Jon, Donunes, Download, DruKason, Elinruby, EoGuy, Erachi, Ettrig, Exukvera, Felipe Menegaz, Flarkins, Gabriel Lopes Guasti, Gap9551, GoodDay, Gronk Oz, Ground Zero, Guilherme Paula, GünniX, J.delanoy, JHunterJ, Jevansen, John of Reading, Joseph Solis in Australia, Josve05a, KConWiki, Kcowolf, Kelutral, Khazar, Kross, Lacarids, Lancioni, LarsHolmberg, Leandrod, LilHelpa, Luna Whistler, Macgreco, Mogism, Nk, Oliveiramatheus, OneWorld22, Piccolo Modificatore Laborioso, RadiX, Raniee09, Rodrigogomesonetwo, Rodw, Sanmartin, Sardanaphalus, Schwael, Sturm, Subsolar, THobern, Thiseye, Tim!, Tony1, Ulric1313, Vandergay, Versus22, Victor Lopes, Waide Piki, Wazcontato, Windupcanary, Woohookitty, Xandi, 126 anonymous edits . . 255

Geography of Brazil *Source:* https://en.wikipedia.org/w/index.php?oldid=850528784 *License:* Creative Commons Attribution-Share Alike 3.0 *Contributors:* 123Hedgehog456, Alan Liefting, Alansohn, Aldiazmo, Allthefoxes, AlmeidaBarros, Aymatth2, BD2412, Bazonka, Bgwhite, Biblioworm, Bobo192, Bobychass, Br100x, Bunnyhop11, CAPTAIN RAJU, Cantiorix, Catgut, Charbroil, ChrisGualtieri, ClickRick, Climaupdate, ClueBot NG, Colonies Chris, CommonsDelinker, DASHBotAV, Danielsanbebe, DantheCowMan, Darwinek, Davejcroyd, David.moreno72, DavidLeighEllis, DiscantX, Dolovis, Donner60, Dralwik, Drmies, Dthomsen8, Eastlaw, Edward, EikwaR, Epbr123, Epicgenius, Epipelagic, Ethel Aardvark, Felipe Menegaz, Fæ, Gaius Cornelius, Gatemansgc, Gikü, Gilliam, Ginsuloft, GoodGame1324, Graham87, Graphium, Grenzer22, Hamtechperson, Hentzer, Hmains, Hobbes Novakoff, HulaHippo1029, Hydrogen Iodide, IronGargoyle, JamesAM, Javierito92, Jeff3000, Jim1138, Jimp, Johnuniq, JonEastham, Joseph Solis in Australia, K6ka, Kehrbykid, Ken Gallager, Klbrain, Krys Brazil, Kwamikagami, Kwiked, Lappspira, Leafslover1234, Linan, Little Mountain 5, Logan, Lukasz Lukomski, Marek69, MarginalCost, Materialscientist, Meters, Mhockey, Missvain, Mjs1991, Mr. Ajax, Mrt3366, Musicmage4114, MusikAnimal, NMaia, Neurolysis, Oddbodz, Oganesson007, Oshwah, Owain Knight, Pablomartinez, Paste, Pepper, Peter Horn, Philip Trueman, PhnomPencil, Pinethicket, Plantsurfer, Potosino, Pseudomonas, Ramalha Soares, Renamed user Jawi1N4TzD, Sardanaphalus, Scheridon, SchreiberBike, Serols, ShelfSkewed, Shellwood, Shyshy99, Snowolf, SoCalSuperEagle, Soapthgr8, Steamroller Assault, Stickee, Svkup, TeaLover1996, The Voidwalker, Thirdright, Thricecube, Tide rolls, Tomdo08, Trusilver, Tyrol5, Una Smith, UnneededAplomb, Vitund, Vrenator, Vsmith, Waltloc, West.andrew.g, Widr, Wikipelli, Woohookitty, Yoshi24517, Zppix, زرشک, ვაჟდე ვ, 250 anonymous edits 267

Climate of Brazil *Source:* https://en.wikipedia.org/w/index.php?oldid=841613738 *License:* Creative Commons Attribution-Share Alike 3.0 *Contributors:* 42800141, Acather96, Affleck, Aidanthebossateverything, Alan Liefting, Alansohn, Albertde, Allens, Amccann421, Arjayay, Ashley2015T, Aymatth2, BD2412, Bagunceiro, Bgwhite, Brazilianlek, Brunton, Cahk, Caldhayl, CambridgeBayWeather, CasperBraske, Chris the speller, Chronus, ClueBot NG, CogitoErgoSum14, CommonsDelinker, Crystallizedcarbon, Daiyusha, Dcirovic, Dewritech, Discospinster, Edgar181, EikwaR, Epicgenius, Eteethan, Excirial, Fasouzafreitas, Fetchcomms, Florian Blaschke, Flyer22 Reborn, Fraggle81, Frietjes, G. Capo, Gilliam, Hentzer, HexaChord, Hon-3s-T, Hooman, Innotata, JamesAM, Jim1138, Jimp, Jncraton, Jojomaile, JoshuaD1991, José Henrique Campos, K6ka, Klilidiplomus, Kman543210, LeaveSleaves, Lgabriel14, Magafuzula, Markeilz, Materialscientist, Mato, Mild Bill Hiccup, Millennium bug, MrBill3, Neelix, Niceguyedc, Njardarlogar, O Seridoense, Oganesson007, Oshwah, Peter Horn, PhilKnight, Philip Trueman, Pinethicket, Pratyya Ghosh, R'n'B, Ramalha Soares, RenamedUser01302013, Ronhjones, Rrburke, SCREAM, Samohad, Sardanaphalus, Scheridon, SchreiberBike, Serols, Southrook, SteveStrummer, SuperHamster, TamCaP, TerryAlex, The Editor's Apprentice, The Thing That Should Not Be, Tide rolls, Tolly4bolly, Tslocum, TyA, Ulric1313, Victor Lopes, Vipinhari, Wbm1058, Wdfarmer, Yintan, 246 anonymous edits 287

Wildlife of Brazil *Source:* https://en.wikipedia.org/w/index.php?oldid=851031282 *License:* Creative Commons Attribution-Share Alike 3.0 *Contributors:* 5 albert square, Abracadabra1734, AdventurousSquirrel, Aeonx, Ahmadnw7, Alan Liefting, Alansohn, AlbertOfPrussia, Alexf, Ali'i, Amaury, Amorymeltzer, Andonic, Andy Dingley, Artichoker, Ben Moore, Bhadani, Blanchardb, Boktower, C . Moccasin, CRAIG JOHNSON III, Caniche, Canis-Rufus, Cannolis, Carlosguitar, Charles Matthews, Chienlit, Chris the speller, Citation bot 1, ClueBot NG, CommonsDelinker, DARIO SEVERI, DARTH SIDIOUS 2, Damiens.rf, Dcirovic, Dewritech, Donner60, Dthomsen8, Elekhh, Epbr123, Eteethan, Exlibris, Explorer256, Fish and karate, Flyer22 Reborn, Giso6150, Grolltech, Hentzer, Hike395, Hobbes Novakoff, IronGargoyle, J.delanoy, JamesBWatson, Jamirabastos, John of Reading, Joinn, João Pedro Corrêa Eboli, Jtalledo, Juliancolton, K6ka, KH-1, Kallerna, Kbog, Kingpin13, Lightmouse, Maest11, Makecat, MarnetteD, Materialscientist, Maximajorian Viridio, Mentifisto, Middgeaugh-Botteaugh, Miwuuu, MrFawwaz, NMaia, Naruo, Neelix, Nehrams2020, NeonTetraploid, Nk, Noctibus, Nondropframe, Not your average hamster, NottNott, Oliverlyc, Omicron91, Omnipaedista, Oshwah, Pinethicket, Punchi, QuadrivialMind, Qwertsar, RN1970, Racerx11, RedHillian, Rey ks, Rjwilmsi, Robyboyx50, Rrburke, Ruby Murray, Ryulong, Sardanaphalus, SchreiberBike, ScottMHoward, Serols, Sharkface217, Slazenger, Smtchahal, Snek01, Stephenb, Tassedethe, The Claw, The Emirr, Thingg, Trevor MacInnis, UnflushableTurd, Utcursch, Vsmith, Wavelength, Weirdakota, Widr, Wtmitchell, Yachtsman1, Yintan, Érico, 216 anonymous edits 305

Deforestation in Brazil *Source:* https://en.wikipedia.org/w/index.php?oldid=853685165 *License:* Creative Commons Attribution-Share Alike 3.0 *Contributors:* 1989, 7&6=thirteen, AManWithNoPlan, Alan Liefting, Aldis90, Allalone82, Amfeadan, Amorymeltzer, Anticla rutila, Arjayay, AtticusX, Aymatth2, Bakasam, BatmanArkhamOriginsV3, Bgwhite, Brittneydi, C toney, C.Fred, Capricorn42, Catlemur, Charles Matthews, ClueBot NG, Cogiati, CommonsDelinker, Daask, DadaNeem, Dan Koehl, Dcirovic, Donner60, DrDaveHPP, Draaktemmer, Dtwilliams14, Duncan.Hull, Earlgrey T, Egsan Bacon, Elinruby, Eric-Wester, Ewen, Excirial, Falcanta, Flyer22 Reborn, Fraggle81, France3470, Funandtrvl, Genetics4good, Gilliam, Graham87, Headbomb, Hugo999, I dream of horses, Inter&anthro, Iortiz786, IronGargoyle, Iuio, JJMC89, Jacob Newton, JaconaFrere, Jarble, Jiten D, Jjjjjjjjjj, JohnInDC, JonHarder, Jonathanischoice, Josh Parris, Josh3580, K6ka, Kaill3r, Kaiyr, Keith D, Khazar, Khazar2, Kinetic37, Kku, L Kensington, Lightening forks, Look2See1, Lopifalko, LukasMatt, LynxTufts, Mandarax, Marianna251, Max geek, Mr. Smart LION, MusikAnimal, Narayansg, Niceguyedc, NortyNort, Noswipingswiper, Nren4237, Optimale, Orphan Wiki, Oshwah, PigFlu Oink, Pinethicket, Primefac, Pudeo, R000t, Rathfelder, ReiceMcK, Rettetast, RhinoMind, Rileys42, Rjwilmsi, Rsrikanth05, Samwb123, Satellizer, SchreiberBike, Silvrous, Simplexity22, Skyring, Swatjester, Tbhotch, Thatotherdude, The Thing That Should Not Be, Tide rolls, Tigerjojo98, Titodutta, Tobby72, Tolly4bolly, Tom.Reding, Tpal3, Trappist the monk, Underlying lk, Utcursch, Vsmith, WOSlinker, Widr, Wikimodarator, Willking1979, ZackTheJack, 243 anonymous edits 315

Conservation in Brazil *Source:* https://en.wikipedia.org/w/index.php?oldid=839526404 *License:* Creative Commons Attribution-Share Alike 3.0 *Contributors:* Adam (Wiki Ed), Alan Liefting, Allalone82, Aymatth2, Benito103910, Chico agc, Dewritech, Elekhh, Epipelagic, Explorer256, Frietjes, Gaius Cornelius, Gd81507, Giso6150, Gorthian, Ian (Wiki Ed), Joe Roe, JonHarder, Kc1130, Kcanup1130, KylieTastic, Look2See1, Mack2, Magioladitis, Mild Bill Hiccup, RegistryKey, Rennell435, Rjwilmsi, SJ Defender, SkateTier, Southrook, TenPoundHammer, Tentinator, TheIrishWarden, Woodlot, YSSYguy, 11 anonymous edits 337

Politics of Brazil *Source:* https://en.wikipedia.org/w/index.php?oldid=851594824 *License:* Creative Commons Attribution-Share Alike 3.0 *Contributors:* Abracadabra1734, Abrahamic Faiths, Alexlange, Alumnum, Anarkitekt, Andersmusician, AnnaFrance, Arbitrarily0, Avoided, Bambam1236, Beland, Bentley4, Bgwhite, Blue-Haired Lawyer, Capricorn42, CaribDigita, Carriearchdale, Carterdriggs, Catgut, Ceranthor, Chillllls, ChrisGualtieri, Chrism, ClueBot NG, Colonies Chris, CommonsDelinker, DBigXray, DGaw, DVdm, Dalillama, Damiens.rf, Dcirovic, Ddxc, Discospinster, Dolovis, Drguillen13,

Drilnoth, EconomistBR, Elinruby, Emir of Wikipedia, Epbr123, Ericoides, Esa3000, Faradayplank, Fatal!ty, Flarkins, Folantin, FrankFlanagan, Freshbakedpie, Friginator, George The Dragon, Giraffedata, Giso6150, GlassCobra, GorillaWarfare, Graham87, HDrake, HappyInGeneral, Haunti, Hdante, Hector.C.Jorge, Hentzer, Intelligentsium, Ipatrol, Jacob Newton, JamesBWatson, Jarry1250, Jay-Sebastos, Jggouvea, Jianhui67, John Doe 1346, Kethrus, Khazar2, Koavf, KoshVorlon, Krenair, Lacrimosus, Landon1980, Lapicero, Lecen, Lightmouse, Limongi, Luizdl, Lulu Margarida, MBisanz, Manul, MasterYoshy, Masterpiece2000, Maxtremus, MayTheForce, Minimac, Missionary, Mr. Ajax, MuffledThud, Nauka, Niceguyedc, No Swan So Fine, Northamerica1000, Nuujinn, Nyttend, O.Koslowski, Observingbrazil, Ohconfucius, Open2universe, Orange Suede Sofa, PedR, Pegureiro, Porttranslate0510, Prodego, Protector of Wiki, Pufferfish101, RJFJR, Ramalha Soares, Redhill54, Renan Rabbit, Rich Farmbrough, Rodrigogomesonetwo, Seakups, Ser Amantio di Nicolao, Skullknight101, Soman, Some jerk on the Internet, Tedgoertzel, Telfordbuck, The Editor's Apprentice, The Thing That Should Not Be, The Transhumanist, Therequiembellishere, Tide rolls, Tomwood0, Tonybaloney867, Trevor MacInnis, Ulric1313, VI, Vininim, Vinícius94, Wavelength, Widr, WikiUser22222, William Avery, Woohookitty, Xyzspaniel, Yakowljew, Zap Rowsdower, زرشک, مصعب, პააჭა ბ, 235 anonymous edits 347

Federal government of Brazil *Source:* https://en.wikipedia.org/w/index.php?oldid=851595147 *License:* Creative Commons Attribution-Share Alike 3.0 *Contributors:* 0xF8E8, Alex Cohn, Anonymous from the 21st century, Anupmehra, Arthur to, ClueBot NG, Doug Weller, EdwardH, Excirial, Eyesnore, Fgnievinski, Flyer22 Reborn, Fraggle81, Giso6150, Ingarix, Isaiah1234567890, JamesBWatson, Khazar2, L235, Laberkiste, Limongi, MRD2014, Maxtremus, MayTheForce, Mdcarvalho, Mr. Ajax, MusikAnimal, NoMoreHeroes, NottNott, Optakeover, PhantomTech, Qosm jdkbkcjv, Rafael Florentino, Rsrikanth05, Rumiñawee, Simplexity22, Skyring, TerryAlex, The ed17, TwoTwoHello, Ugog Nizdast, Vinícius94, Widr, Wikipelli, William Avery, Wywin, Yintan, 84 anonymous edits 369

Elections in Brazil *Source:* https://en.wikipedia.org/w/index.php?oldid=852015848 *License:* Creative Commons Attribution-Share Alike 3.0 *Contributors:* AVM, Acntx, Akuindo, Alexanderjpoulsen, Alexius08, Android Mouse, Anir1uph, Aris Katsaris, Bgwhite, Biruitorul, Brandizzi, Candido, Carioca, Carlos enr, Carlosforonda, Checco, ClaudioFaria, ClueBot NG, DMacks, Dalillama, Dantadd, Daonguyen95, Dpark, Dtrielli, Edward, El C, Electiontechnology, Electionworld, Epbr123, Erolos, Everyking, Fabiocralves, Fabiomarques, Gaius Cornelius, Gap9551, Gerúndio, Ghost 543, Gilliam, Giraffedata, Giso6150, Gwern, Hajor, Igordebraga, JoaoBulhoesFraguas, Joseph Solis in Australia, Jra, Jvalienforce, Karina Yukie, Khazar2, Kyleess12345678, LeoO3, LilHelpa, Loginnigol, Materialscientist, Mateus RM, Maxtremus, McCorrection, Mr. Ajax, N1RK4UDSK714, Neo139, NielsenGW, Nightstallion, Number 57, Ohconfucius, Palfrey, Petrovic-Njegos, Pmerson, Preotescuandrei, Ptah, the El Daoud, Redhill54, Rodrigogomesonetwo, RolandR, Sam Blacketer, Sanmartin, Sarg, Schoen, Severino, Southrook, Tabercil, Taintain, Technical 13, Tedgoertzel, Tfine80, Vsmith, Warofdreams, Wilfried Derksen, Will Beback, 102 anonymous edits 375

Law of Brazil *Source:* https://en.wikipedia.org/w/index.php?oldid=835291259 *License:* Creative Commons Attribution-Share Alike 3.0 *Contributors:* A.R., A.Z., A3camero, Abrahamic Faiths, AlexanderGerten, Alumnum, Augusto.h, BD2412, Beegeesfan, Blue-Haired Lawyer, Briwit, Brunodn, Bryard, CavaloBranco, ClueBot NG, DavidLevinson, Eastlaw, Egsan Bacon, Elinruby, Fæ, Grafen, Hentzer, I dream of horses, Ian Pitchford, James500, JayJasper, Jeff3000, Jessicapierce, Josebarbosa, LilHelpa, Limongi, Luciano.nyc, Mais oui!, Mandarax, Maxtremus, Missionary, Mr. Ajax, Mxn, Nauka, Ottawahitech, PesquisasCMC, PhilKnight, Polocrunch, R'n'B, RodC, Shell Kinney, Shellwood, Siebren, Skoitor, Southamerica2010, Southrook, Spamhuntert, Squids and Chips, Tomer T, Warofdreams, Wayne Slam, Woohookitty, 66 anonymous edits 383

Law enforcement in Brazil *Source:* https://en.wikipedia.org/w/index.php?oldid=849440354 *License:* Creative Commons Attribution-Share Alike 3.0 *Contributors:* ABF, Andremdesouza@wikipedia.com, Anthony Appleyard, Arjayay, BD2412, Badagnani, Binningench1, Bryard, CanisRufus, Closedmouth, Dalillama, Danilodn, Degen Earthfast, Dewritech, Dpmuk, Dr Gangrene, EUDOXIO, EricEnfermero, Ernesks, Felipe Menegaz, Felisopus, Fgnievinski, Fieldday-sunday, Hentzer, Holdoffhunger, IceCreamAntisocial, Int21h, Ioeth, Jacob Newton, Jarble, Jodosma, John of Reading, KLBot2, Kalahari41, Kcpj, Kintetsubuffalo, Koavf, LilHelpa, Magioladitis, Mandarax, Missionary, Mr.choppers, Necrothesp, Ninetyone, Nurg, Officer Boscorelli, Orenburg1, Oshwah, R'n'B, RobDe68, RulapaughA, SGGH, Sdbarry1, Sparks1979, Sun Creator, Technical 13, TouristPhilosopher, UnQuébécois, Wanderer∼enwiki, Wavelength, 113 anonymous edits 391

Crime in Brazil *Source:* https://en.wikipedia.org/w/index.php?oldid=851304137 *License:* Creative Commons Attribution-Share Alike 3.0 *Contributors:* 1ForTheMoney, 72, Affleck, AndrewHowse, Arjayay, Atethnekos, AxelBoldt, BD2412, BOPEfollower, Beebee0408, Belovedfreak, Beyond My Ken, Bgwhite, Billyrohnsen, Brianbrianbrian10000, Caiaffa, Camarinha, Cantucrouch, CaribDigita, Carlosguitar, Catlemur, Chris the speller, ClueBot NG, CodeMaster123, CommonsDelinker, DVdm, Danallen46, Darwinek, DatGuy, Delirium, Delotrooladoo, Dervilo, Dlrohrer2003, Dornicke, Doug Weller, EagleFan, EconomistBR, Elockid, Eumolpo, Evan99m, Finlay McWalter, Flapski, Flarkins, FlightTime, Floor Ouwens, FourthEyeDigitalArts, Fratrep, Frze, Fsolda∼enwiki, Fyddlestix, Ginsuloft, Giso6150, Gobonobo, GoingBatty, Grafen, Grizzlebizzle, Guiletti, Hear be smirk, Hector.C.Jorge, Hentzer, Holy Goo, I dream of horses, I.am.a.qwerty, J 1982, JamesAM, Jami430, JesperEA, Jmertel23, Jncraton, John D. Croft, Jonkerz, Joobo, Karansarathy, Keith D, Kevlar67, Kingpin13, L7world, Lhil9582, Licor, Lightlowemon, Lusci, Maggiejo10, Mancunius, Mandarax, Marigold100, Maxmi91, Meters, Mhsb, Mikeblas, Missionary, Moe Epsilon, Monkey Bounce, Neelix, Niceguyedc, Nick Number, NottNott, OcarinaOfTime, Olegwiki, Orenburg1, Otolemur crassicaudatus, Ouzotech, Padenton, Palapa, Pharaoh of the Wizards, Phoxdie, Portillo, Power Society, Pro bug catcher, Prof.Vandegrift, Pularoid, Putterby, Pyronite, R'n'B, Rafa Marks, Rahlgd, Ramaksoud2000, Rd232, Revelx, Rjwilmsi, Sam Korn, Sardanaphalus, Schistocyte, Scotty no mum, ShelfSkewed, SieberNewsAt7, Skanter, Skeaggy, Southrook, Squavi, Squids and Chips, Stiaand, Stonewaters, Sue Rangell, Sunuraju, Swennsonn, SwisterTwister, Tassedethe, Tellarin, The Almightey Drill, Thecheesykid, Tide rolls, Tiger Khan, Tobby72, Uli, Ulric1313, Underlying lk, Vancouver Outlaw, Vincy06071997, Wavelength, WhatamIdoing, Winner 42, Woohookitty, XLerate, Xover, Yaboybrandon, Yodaki, 164 anonymous edits 398

Brazilian Armed Forces *Source:* https://en.wikipedia.org/w/index.php?oldid=854178900 *License:* Creative Commons Attribution-Share Alike 3.0 *Contributors:* Adamgerber80, Anotherclown, AntiVan, Antiflowvian, Antiochus the Great, Auréola, Barbara (WVS), Belovedfreak, Chris the speller, ChrisGualtieri, ClueBot NG, Colonies Chris, Coltsfan, CommonsDelinker, Crystallizedcarbon, Cyberbot II, Dolovis, Drpickem, Egs, Emirhany., Esw01407, Fahri Ahmad, Firerules7, Fox Wilson, Gabriel Lopes Guasti, Gadget850, Gaius Cornelius, Giraffedata, Giso6150, GoingBatty, Ground Zero, HIDECCHI001, Hentzer, Heroicchickens, Icarusgeek, Illegitimate Barrister, Jacobk, Jarould, Jeff3000, John of Reading, JohnRamos1988, Jon Kolbert, Jor70, Kappa 16, Khazar2, Kkm010, Klemen Kocjancic, Ktr101, Lcchueri, Lecen, Leonardo Broza, Lguipontes, Limongi, Lue2012, MB-one, Materialscientist, MelbourneStar, Michael Zeev, Millerberto, Mjuarez, Mr. Ajax, Nickin, Nikhilmn2002, Nk, Noclador, ObscureReality, Ohconfucius, Oshwah, Paladinum2, Pauli133, PleaseStand, Pratyya Ghosh, R'n'B, Renatolevanteze, Rjwilmsi, SWF88, SchreiberBike, Shaded0, ShelfSkewed, Shem1805, Sundostund, TAnthony, Tawoo, Tbhotch, Tetra quark, The Obento Musubi, The ed17, Thirdright, Tioperci, Tom.Reding, Tono Fonseca, Triangleman3, UESPArules, Valenciano, Vanamonde93, Vinícius94, VitorHeisenberg, WOSlinker, Woohookitty, YSSYguy, YUL89YYZ, Δ, Эрманарих, 木の枝, 228 anonymous edits 409

Foreign relations of Brazil *Source:* https://en.wikipedia.org/w/index.php?oldid=853923522 *License:* Creative Commons Attribution-Share Alike 3.0 *Contributors:* 08OceanBeach SD, 386-DX, Abracadabra1734, AdaCiccone, Ahmedo Semsurî, Alan Liefting, Alinor, Alumnum, Andrwsc, Andycjp, Aquintero82, Auntof6, Avala, Axeman89, Aymatth2, Bcs09, Bender235, Benjamin "Jeffrey" Powell, Biederman, Biruitorul, Boozing4u, Caio!, Calibrador, Canistabbats, Capricorn42, CaribDigita, Chicocvenancio, Chris the speller, ChrisGualtieri, Circeus, Clarkk, ClueBot NG, Cmjr, Colonies Chris, Conversion script, Damiens.rf, Dana boomer, Dewritech, Dolovis, Earthlyreason, Edward, Electionworld, Elinruby, Ellirpa, Elspamo4, Escape Orbit, Felipe Menegaz, Fellinox, Flarkins, Gaius Cornelius, Gidonb, Giraffedata, Girmitya, Giso6150, GoingBatty, Gprince007, HIDECCHI001, Hansch, Heitordp, Hentzer, Herostratus, Hmainsbot1, IANVS, ILBobby, Iaof2017, Irish12345678, Jean.artegui, Jeanjfontana, Jgsodre, John Vandenberg, John of Reading, Johnnymurda, JojoZul69, Joseph Solis in Australia, KeSSenCHu, Khairi Ahmad, Khazar, Kku, Kvng, Lihaas, Limongi, Luigi Perutti, Magioladitis, Mandarax, Marekzp, Mitsukai, Monocletophat123, MrGRA, Muffin Wizard, Mykjoseph, NTBot∼enwiki, Namiba, Narayansg, Niceoldman2, Ninguém, Nk, Nono64, Nyttend, Octane, Odie5533, Oliver Chettle, Patrick, Pichpich, Pinnecco, Pipeafcr, PlovG, Polylerus, Ptah, the El Daoud, R'n'B, RJFF, Rahlgd, RashersTierney, Rebrane, Redhill54, Rich Farmbrough, Rjwilmsi, Roaring Siren, Robin Hood 1212, Rodrigo braz, Rohilbx, Roosterfan, Russavia, Sam Barsoom, Scott Illini, Scottish12345678, SebastienPoncet, SheriffIsInTown, Sion8, Straczynski, TJH2018, The Epopt, The Wonkers, Triggerhippie4, Vargot, Vikingstad, Visesopus, WadeSimMiser, Warofdreams, Wbm1058, Welsh, Wikineek89, Woohookitty, X1\, 125 anonymous edits 439

States of Brazil *Source:* https://en.wikipedia.org/w/index.php?oldid=850951255 *License:* Creative Commons Attribution-Share Alike 3.0 *Contributors:* Aaronbrick, Affirst, Altes, Andrewpmk, Andrwsc, Antipodean Contributor, Archon 2488, Auntof6, Avrand6, Aymatth2, Bagunceiro, Bejnar, BenoniBot∼enwiki, Bobo192, Bolivian Unicyclist, BrasiliaBrasilia, Brightgalrs, BrownHairedGirl, Caerwine, Cannolis, Catfurball, Chanheigeorge, Chezi-Schlaff, ClaretAsh, ClueBot NG, Colonies Chris, CommonsDelinker, Creedence, Crosbali, Crusoe8181, Cygalder, Czarccc, Daarznieks, Dave Andrew, David Kernow, Davin, Delotrooladoo, Dewritech, Dthomsen8, Ehrenkater, Elockid, Etan Wexler, Eyesnore, Farolif, Favonian, Felipe Menegaz, Fgnievinski, Fieldday-sunday, Filemon, Fruitpunchline, Gabriel Lopes Guasti, General Ization, Giorgi13, Giraffedata, Giso6150, Green Giant, Guilherme Paula, Hazlogen, Hectorbonilia, Hede2000, HennessyC, Hongooi, Hugo999, Hvn0413, Immanuel Giel, Innv, Italodal, JaGa, Jawadreventon, Johnluisocasio, Jorunn, Joseph Solis in Australia, Juniorpetjua, Junipher2189, Kintetsubuffalo, Kutchkutch, Lastexpofan, LatinoLatino, Leoadec, LieutenantLatvia, Little Savage, Loginnigol, Loukinho, MB298, MSex, MWchat, Macgreco, Magioladitis, MeltBanana, Mikaey, MikeWazowski, Missionary, Mondolkiri1, Morningstar1814, Mosmof, Mr. Ajax, Mschiffler, Mátyás, NMaia, Nepenthes, Niceguyedc, Nnemo, Nricardo, Omnipaedista, Opinoso, Pedro Aguiar, Polylerus, Postlebury, Ppntori, R'n'B, Rafaelgr, Rafavargas, Ramalha Soares, Rarelibra, Rbka, Red Slash, Rfaquel, Rich Farmbrough, Robert1947, Roke, SJ Defender, Sagurga, Sardanaphalus, Sbalfour, Seqqis, Ser Amantio di Nicolao, Shadowxfox, Shoal.fishes, SiBr4, Southrook, T.Kimura, Teammm, The Almightey Drill, TheJJJunk, TigreTiger, Titus III, Tobias Conradi, Tomdo08, Tomtom9041, TrackTool, Treisijs, Ulises Heureaux, UrsoBR, VitorPredator, VoABot II, Vonsolms, Waggers, Waldir, Walter Holden-Belmont, Wavelength, Winner 42, Woohookitty, Worobiew, Ziz16, Parrop, 147 anonymous edits 457

Municipalities of Brazil *Source:* https://en.wikipedia.org/w/index.php?oldid=827628531 *License:* Creative Commons Attribution-Share Alike 3.0 *Contributors:* A930913, Aadavalus, Ahoerstemeier, Ahuskay, Alexsanderxm, Angelosante, Ariedartin, Avala, BenoniBot∼enwiki, Berton, Bill37212, Bolivian Unicyclist, Brokenpoem14, BrownHairedGirl, Carioca, Crusoe8181, Crzrussian, Cyberbot II, DVdm, Da Joe, Daniel Scioli, Dantadd, DerBorg, Dr. Blofeld, Earl Andrew, EorlVII, Epbr123, Explendido Rocha, Fizzerbear, Flauto Dolce, Francis-Philip Madison, Gagilia, Gcoliveira, Giso6150, Hentzer, Hmains, J.delanoy, Jaberwocky6669, Jmundo, Jnc, Joaopais, John of Reading, Johnluisocasio, K4zem, KSchutte, Kavin buchanan, KingTT, Krash, Kungfuadam, Kwsn, Lasunncty, Leannatullett, Limongi, Liz, Loukinho, MPF, Margosbot∼enwiki, Master Of Ninja, Mdiogo, Mentifisto, Mike Dillon, Mild Bill Hiccup, Morio, Mr Adequate, Mr. Ajax, Mário e Dário, NTBot∼enwiki, Nabla, Neurillon, Ninguém, Oliver Chettle, Open2universe, Pedro Fonini, Poli, Pristino, Quadell, Quuxplusone, Rarelibra, Redhill54, Redux, RexNL, Rickipedia127, Rigadoun, Rodrigogomesonetwo, Roke, Rotlink, Rsabbatini, SP-KP,

Sanmartin, Sardanaphalus, ScottDavis, Serte, ShakespeareFan00, Spaully, The Ogre, Travelbird, Txuspe, Vague Rant, Vasilcho, Victor Lopes, VoABot II, Vogensen, Warofdreams, Woohookitty, Worobiew, Xezbeth, Yamamoto Ichiro, Zazaban, Zyxw, ბააჭი ვ, 116 anonymous edits 470

Economy of Brazil *Source:* https://en.wikipedia.org/w/index.php?oldid=854169750 *License:* Creative Commons Attribution-Share Alike 3.0 *Contributors:* 123abcptd123, 42800141, A Great Catholic Person, Ab1992505, AgileMate, Alhmanic, Antandrus, Arado, Archon 2488, B777-300ER, Beland, Benniejets, BookWormFan1000, Btcbounty, Bunny2090, CLCStudent, CaribDigita, Carolina Panzarin, Celinaqi, Clpo13, ClueBot NG, Cobblet, Coltsfan, Crystallizedcarbon, Cæsey, DavisAndrew416, Dcirovic, Deranged economist, Dewritech, Dl2000, DrKay, DrunkBicyclist, Dynasty, Eimukas22, El C, Elena Tsaranova, Elinruby, Entranced98, Evarondon9, EvergreenFir, Excirial, Farolif, FoCuSandLeArN, GL19GL61, Genepangettalaga, GermanJoe, Gilliam, Giso6150, Grenzer22, GünniX, Happywriter101, Holy Goo, IagoQnsi, Iridescent, Jahangir22, Jim1138, JoeSakr1980, Just a guy from the KP, Jytdog, KGirlTrucker81, Kaltenmeyer, Kiwi128, KylieTastic, L293D, Lescandinave, Liberio, LjL, LuigiPortaro29, Luizdl, Materialscientist, MatiW97, Maxmi91, Mccapra, MishoMiqo, Mopcwiki, Narky Blert, Onel5969, Oshwah, Paulcerrito, Pcgomes, Philllgat, Redhat101, RoadTrain, Sdftyuisway, SeabassTheFish, Shearonink, Shellwood, Smd75jr, Socyology101, Southern Person, Stephiscool123, Supercell121, TAnthony, TechnicianGB, Tercessuinotlim, Tetizeraz, The Diaz, Tonneduroc, Tony1, Widr, ZiaLater, 242 anonymous edits 475

Agriculture in Brazil *Source:* https://en.wikipedia.org/w/index.php?oldid=844202237 *License:* Creative Commons Attribution-Share Alike 3.0 *Contributors:* ANNAfoxlover, AllGloryToTheHypnotoad, Animum, Arthur Rubin, BD2412, Beckdourny, Beth Holmes 1, Bexigao, Bgwhite, Billinghurst, Bluerasberry, Bongwarrior, Bücherwürmlein, Carroll Gardens, Catgut, Certes, ChrisGualtieri, ClueBot NG, Colonies Chris, Coopergado, Csa.certified, Dave Favis-Mortlock, David Kernow, Dcirovic, Denisarona, Dewritech, Discospinster, Dl2000, EconomistBR, Elockid, Flewis, Floatjon, Frietjes, Gareth Griffith-Jones, Ged UK, Gene Nygaard, Gigemag76, Giraffedata, GoShow, GoingBatty, Grenzer22, Hcs42, Hmains, I dream of horses, IcedNut, IonutBizau, J04n, JamesMoose, Jan1nad, Jarble, Jim1138, Jochen Burghardt, Joerom5883, John of Reading, Jserovicha, Julien16, Just a guy from the KP, K21 2005, K6ka, Kielbasa1, Kku, KylieTastic, Lescandinave, Lfstevens, Lightmouse, LittleWink, Luizpuodzius, MER-C, Magioladitis, Margritesmith, Materialscientist, Mboverload, McCorrection, Mogism, Mr Stephen, MuAlphaTheta, Nadya Inoubli, Nbarth, Neelix, NewEnglandYankee, Nick Number, NigerianPrince123, NortyNort, Olahus, Orenburg1, Originuc, PrestonH, Quiddity, RA0808, Razorflame, Rich Farmbrough, Richard Melo da Silva, Rjwilmsi, RobertG, Rocketrod1960, RorschachBR, RoxanneHobbs, Sam119997, Sardanaphalus, Shadowjams, SheriffIsInTown, Squids and Chips, Srednuas Lenoroc, TX55, Tchajed, The Banner, The Editor's Apprentice, Thirdright, Tide rolls, Tony1, Trappist the monk, Ugog Nizdast, Underlying lk, VSerrata, Vanisaac, Veekhr, Victor Lopes, VoABot II, Wavelength, Widr, Wiki13, Wikipelli, Willjulius, Wodrow, Woohookitty, Yamaguchi先生 , Zpeopleheart, 143 anonymous edits 492

Brazilian real *Source:* https://en.wikipedia.org/w/index.php?oldid=848692486 *License:* Creative Commons Attribution-Share Alike 3.0 *Contributors:* 6969420yolo, Aladdinlee, Alumnum, Anonymous from the 21st century, Anthony Appleyard, Arcandam, AwesomeDude13, Awmcphee, Bagunceiro, Beland, Bellerophon5685, Black Yoshi, Brunolima17, Capmo, Chris the speller, ClueBot NG, CommonsDelinker, Comp.arch, Conrado.buhrer, Dcirovic, De Boni 2007, Deflective, Divingpetrel, Dralwik, Drewmutt, EGroup, Ederson Chioli, Edward, Eladynnus, Elywagner, Emyil, Ericxpenner, Esa3000, Etp01, Flyer22 Reborn, Freddy Patel, Frietjes, GPHemsley, Gjrvarginha, Glennobrien, GoingBatty, Hairy Dude, Hammersoft, HarDNox, Heitordp, Heroeswithmetaphors, Hmainsbot1, HotdogPi, I dream of horses, Jmnbatista, Jogador 1967, John of Reading, Jonkerz, JorisvS, KConWiki, Khazar2, Kkm010, Ljgua124, Loranchet, Luiz Possamai, Luizdl, Mariordo, Markfeio, MarsInSVG, Materialscientist, Michaelm, Modest Genius, Mogism, Mortee, MrFawwaz, Natanmda, NewHikaru07, Niceguyedc, Northern Muriqui, PeRiDoTs13, Quenhitran, Quercus solaris, Quinzy, Rafael Florentino, Readro, Realvitormarques, Rodrigogomesonetwo, Rui Gabriel Correia, SchreiberBike, Secretkeeper12, ShelfSkewed, Slightsmile, Solarra, Southrook, StAnselm, TenPoundHammer, TerraHikaru, Tide rolls, Timbobel, Tmollerup, Tretraw, Ttimbul, Ugog Nizdast, Underlying lk, Varlaam, Vdfviana, Victor Lopes, Victorprosa, Vmzp85, Vítor Cassol, Waggie, Widr, ZackTheJack, ZeroUm, Սահակ, 252 anonymous edits 538

Mining in Brazil *Source:* https://en.wikipedia.org/w/index.php?oldid=824458589 *License:* Creative Commons Attribution-Share Alike 3.0 *Contributors:* Alan Liefting, Andrewman327, Apjohns54, Aymatth2, BackToThePast, Borchita1521, Bulwersator, Calliopejen1, Chiton magnificus, ClueBot NG, DrStrauss, Felipe P, Gary, Hmains, Indech, Jayjg, Kku, Mangostar, Matrixinfinity, Mccapra, Meatsgains, Nyttend, Pcgomes, Pgallert, Phil Bridger, RJFJR, Serols, Southrook, Tiddly Tom, Underlying lk, Wavelength, 9 anonymous edits 551

Industry in Brazil *Source:* https://en.wikipedia.org/w/index.php?oldid=853630616 *License:* Creative Commons Attribution-Share Alike 3.0 *Contributors:* Alansohn, Atomicrox, Augusto f. arruda fontes, Avoided, Benpopov, Bgwhite, Bogey97, Bsadowski1, Chronus, ClueBot NG, Colonies Chris, Coltsfan, CommonsDelinker, Courcelles, David Kernow, Discospinster, Dr.sarah adel, EconomistBR, Elinruby, Finetooth, Gaius Cornelius, Gilliam, Giso6150, Graeme Bartlett, Grenzer22, Guilherme Paula, HaeB, Hibernian, Hugo999, J.delanoy, Jarble, Jonkerz, Joseph Solis in Australia, Juniorpetjua, KathrynLybarger, Kuru, LW001, Lecen, Lightmouse, LlywelynII, Mentifisto, Mike Rosoft, MrFawwaz, Nick Number, R000t, Rettetast, Rich Farmbrough, Rjwilmsi, Sardanaphalus, Skizzik, Smalljim, Soumya114, Southrook, Storm Rider, Sun Creator, Trappist the monk, Tristanberkin, Underlying lk, WOSlinker, Wiki-Laurent, דויד55, 91 anonymous edits 553

Energy in Brazil *Source:* https://en.wikipedia.org/w/index.php?oldid=851918253 *License:* Creative Commons Attribution-Share Alike 3.0 *Contributors:* 42800141, Aekaplan, Arthur Rubin, Beagel, Bificus, Bunnyhop11, CesarB, Chris the speller, Chronus, ClueBot NG, CommonsDelinker, Comptrad, CybershamanX, Edward, Elinruby, Espinal86, Fexrj~enwiki, ForcaForte, Frietjes, Gbuch, Goodvac, Hentzer, Hillbillyholiday, Hlange1, Idave, Ita140188, Ixfd64, JaGa, Jbaranao, John Hill, John of Reading, Johnfos, Jonkerz, Kku, Lightmouse, Lklundin, Mbello82, Mervyn Emrys, Missionary, Mmm~enwiki, Neelix, PanchoS, Randsho, Rich Farmbrough, Ricvelozo, Rjwilmsi, Sbagstad, Shiftchange, SkateTier, Southrook, Squids and Chips, The idiot, Torchiest, Underlying lk, Utcursch, Watti Renew, Wayne Stewart, Wikieditor06, Writtenonsand, Yanguas, 42 anonymous edits 561

Tourism in Brazil *Source:* https://en.wikipedia.org/w/index.php?oldid=850007838 *License:* Creative Commons Attribution-Share Alike 3.0 *Contributors:* 42800141, ABF, Aadavalus, Adam.J.W.C., Affleck, Angenhariaus, Aymatth2, BD2412, Balthazarduju, Barticus88, Bentogoa, Bleckter, Blur82, Bqn1996, BrownHairedGirl, CardinalDan, Chronus, Cjcman, ClueBot NG, CommonsDelinker, Célio D P Jr, Darwinek, David Kernow, Deemans, Deville, Dewritech, Discospinster, Dr Gangrene, Dr. Blofeld, E43253rf4r, EuroCarGT, FSE PA, Frietjes, Funandtrvl, Gadget850, Gilliam, Glane23, HIDECCHI001, Haakonsson, Harry-, Hentzer, Hmainsbot1, Holidaytrip, Hu12, Huiva, Iohannes Animosus, J.delanoy, JaGa, JamesAM, Jeodesic, JonasGray35, Juam18, Katyinsoutham, Kman543210, KylieTastic, Lampman, LewisDaCosta98, LilHelpa, Limongi, Lucas Ciccone, LuizdeO, Macgreco, Magioladitis, Marcosalface, Mariordo, Materialscientist, Mcmatter, Mean as custard, Michael Slone, Microchip08, Moxy, Mr. Ajax, MrFawwaz, Mustafa.ccc, Niceguyedc, Onel5969, Opinoso, Oshwah, P397s362, Plastikspork, Pontificalibus, Ptb1997, Quiddity, R'n'B, RMHED, Reztiplieneht, Rich Farmbrough, Rjwilmsi, Roberticus, Ruiner247, SNUGGUMS, Sardanaphalus, SchreiberBike, Sergio Kaminski, Sfan00 IMG, ShelfSkewed, Skanter, Smalljim, Spitfire, Squids and Chips, Thiagoreis leon, Topbanana, Tpbradbury, Trevor MacInnis, Twofortnights, Tyw7, Underlying lk, WadeSimMiser, Weslleysky, Wikid77, Woohookitty, Wywin, 120 anonymous edits 571

Science and technology in Brazil *Source:* https://en.wikipedia.org/w/index.php?oldid=847463306 *License:* Creative Commons Attribution-Share Alike 3.0 *Contributors:* 1989, Adi4094, Amortias, Andersmusician, Avllr, Bearcat, Belinrahs, BenPlotke, Biginsudan, Bill william compton, CalJW, Capmo, Chris the speller, Chronus, Cloretti2, ClueBot NG, CommonsDelinker, Daniel Schitine, Danieldasilva, Deanos, Eduardoporcher, Everyking, Excelsior Deo, Fanra, Fgnievinski, Friginator, Giso6150, GoingBatty, Guilherme Paula, Hahahhahahahaahahahaha bro awesome, Hentzer, Herizora, Hmo, InglesIngles, John Cummings, John of Reading, Jonas Mur~enwiki, JoshuaD1991, Kungfuadam, Leandropls, LilHelpa, Limongi, LongDouble, Lotje, Luan, Luizdl, Macgreco, Marianocecowski, Mark Arsten, Mateuszica, Melchoir, Mhsb, Missionary, Mr Hélix, Murphyg001, Nk, Non-dropframe, Noyster, Oa01, Obiwankenobi, Oliver Chettle, Only, Open2universe, Paulogregori, Pilotax Gamer, Pontes pedro, Porventura, Pyfan, R'n'B, Rd232, Rex Imperator, Ricardo Carneiro Pires, Rjwilmsi, Rsabbatini, Sandstein, Sardanaphalus, Sion8, Sjb72, Sjö, Smalljim, StorchiBman, Susan Schneegans, TAnthony, Tomer T, Toussaint, USAnne, Unobjectionable, Wloveral, Woohookitty, Xumsimon, Yodaki, Yurit, 156 anonymous edits 589

Transport in Brazil *Source:* https://en.wikipedia.org/w/index.php?oldid=849314533 *License:* Creative Commons Attribution-Share Alike 3.0 *Contributors:* Aaron-Tripel, Againme, Agathoclea, Ahoerstemeier, Andrelot, Anthony, AntonioMartin, Antrim Kate, Barticus88, Bazza 7, Benstown, Bgwhite, BotMultichill, Bryan Derksen, CalJW, Can't sleep, clown will eat me, Chaan, ChicXulub, Chris the speller, ChrisGualtieri, ClueBot NG, Cnmaia03, Coasterlover1994, Colonies Chris, CommonsDelinker, Conversion script, Courcelles, Cultural Freedom, Curb Chain, DO'Neil, Dalillama, Darwinek, DePiep, Deleteduser2015, Dlenmn, Doug Weller, Download, Edson Rosa, Eliezersantos, Elliskev, Elockid, Epbr123, Excirial, Fasouzafreitas, Felipe Menegaz, Fellipec, Flyer22 Reborn, Fraulein451, GE1515~enwiki, Gabrieljohnson, Gilliam, GrahamTM, Gurch, Gwernol, Hack, Haus, Hentzer, Hephaestos, Hugo999, Ishnigarrab, Ita140188, JaGa, JooHater, Jturn154, Kaisershatner, Karthikndr, Kbdank71, Kdg.grigg, King Ref, Koavf, Koyaanisqatsi, Krich, Kurykh, Legobot II, Limongi, Loren36, Magioladitis, Mandarax, Mardenpb1, Maxtremus, Mendoncacruz, Michael Johnson, ModelFish, Moebiusuibeomen, Monopoly31121993, MrFawwaz, Mrwojo, N5iln, NMaia, Nick Number, Nk, Nobunaga24, P397s362, Peter Horn, Politepunk, Prolog, Puchiko, Quadell, Rich Farmbrough, Rocketrod1960, Rsabbatini, SWAdair, Sango123, Sanmartin, SchreiberBike, Ser Amantio di Nicolao, Southrook, Steel, Sting, Stroppolo, Sylx100, TAnthony, TUF-KAT, Tabletop, Tawkerbot2, The High Fin Sperm Whale, The Ogre, Thehelpfulone, Thricecube, Tom harrison, Trappist the monk, TruckCard, Ucucha, UgoEmme, Uncle Dick, Underlying lk, Valmi, Victor Lopes, VoABot II, WOSlinker, Warofdreams, Web SourceContent, WhisperToMe, Woohookitty, World8115, 121 anonymous edits 619

Health in Brazil *Source:* https://en.wikipedia.org/w/index.php?oldid=810710036 *License:* Creative Commons Attribution-Share Alike 3.0 *Contributors:* Abrahamic Faiths, Alansohn, Andonic, Archon 2488, Asderf123212321, Bagunceiro, Belovedfreak, Bepa~enwiki, Bethmills, Bgwhite, Biólogo conservacionista, Bluerasberry, Cbflagginc, Cfyang13, Chris the speller, Christiancoradini, ClueBot NG, Cureden, DisillusionedBitterAndKnackered, Diwas, Download, EEng, Felipe Menegaz, Figueirao, Freest, Gcorpart, Gobonobo, Gocbr, GoingBatty, Grafen, Hector.C.Jorge, Hellen Walker, Hentzer, Iknowyourider, Jan eissfeldt, Janzert, Joseph Solis in Australia, Kurieeto, Kwiki, Lguipontes, LincolnSt, Lucasdealmeidasm, Luiz F. Fritz, Magioladitis, MaynardClark, MelbourneStar, Mild Bill Hiccup, N5iln, Nk, OR1LEYo, Obiwankenobi, Onel5969, Ottre, Pjburland, Pnm, R'n'B, Rathfelder, Rehanna girl, Rjwilmsi, Sct72, Semmendinger, Skanter, Smalljim, SomeGuy11112, Srinaldo, Sun Creator, Sushijedi, Tabletop, Tom.Reding, Vacation9, VoABot II, WOSlinker, Welsh, Widr, Willking1979, Woohookitty, Yamaguchi先生 , 95 anonymous edits 627

Education in Brazil *Source:* https://en.wikipedia.org/w/index.php?oldid=853615100 *License:* Creative Commons Attribution-Share Alike 3.0 *Contributors:* 65HCA7, A. di M., Abrahamic Faiths, Alberto Leôncio, Alumnum, Anir1uph, Bgwhite, Billinrio, Cadito, Camarinha, CavaloBranco, Cekli829, Chill doubt, ClaudioMB, ClueBot NG, Comamir, CommonsDelinker, Compassionate727, Conifer, CrazyTerabyte, Crosbali, Crystallizedcarbon, DVdm, Darwinek, Dbfirs, Delldot, Delotrooladoo, Derek R Bullamore, Dewritech, Diannaa, Diddpql, DocWatson42, DocYako, Donner60, ERhaught, Editpage1001, Educationefficiency, Ekarajic, Elizabetsyatbu, Elockid, EoGuy, Excirial, Favonian, Felipe Menegaz, Fgnievinski, Francisco Leandro, Gadfium,

Gilliam, Ginsuloft, GoShow, Ground Zero, Hector.C.Jorge, Hentzer, Holy Santa, Ikalpo, Iohannes Animosus, Ixfd64, J 1982, J.delanoy, Jayarathina, Jomifica, Jonas Mur∼enwiki, Joseph A. Spadaro, Joshua2345, Jummai, Jummai∼enwiki, KaptainIgloo, Kbell21, Keith D, Knulclunk, Krawi, Lebossa, Lerrymoe, Licor, LilHelpa, MER-C, Macgreco, Magnus Crum, Maltls, Mangostar, Materialscientist, Maxtremus, Mboverload, Minna Sora no Shita, Missionary, Mogism, Naniwako, Napleabeau, Neils51, NelsonPretto, Nick, Nk, Northamerica1000, NotTheFakeJTP, ONUnicorn, Oa01, Onel5969, Opinoso, Otolemur crassicaudatus, Paste, Pedro Aguiar, Philip Trueman, Phulvius∼enwiki, Prof.Vandegrift, Quadpus, R'n'B, RenamedUser01302013, Renatosipe, Rhododendrites, Rickipedia127, Rjwilmsi, Sandstein, Sardanaphalus, Saturnalia0, Skanter, Sparks1979, Stesmo, Tabletop, Taesulkim, Thehelpfulone, Thomas Blomberg, ThomasAndrewNimmo, Tim!, Todor Todorov∼enwiki, Tugaworld, Unobjectionable, Victor Lopes, Vieque, Widr, Wikiphilia, William Avery, Woohookitty, Yaris678, Yodaki, 238 anonymous edits 633

Telecommunications in Brazil *Source:* https://en.wikipedia.org/w/index.php?oldid=842927857 *License:* Creative Commons Attribution-Share Alike 3.0 *Contributors:* Alumnum, AnthonyBurgess, Apolyram, Arieanna, Arthur to, Auntof6, Bonás, Btilm, CalJW, Conversion script, D6, Daniel Callegaro, Dawnseeker2000, Dewritech, Don4of4, EagleFan, Elockid, Eumolpo, Frecuentaje, Frietjes, Funandtrvl, Harryzilber, Hebrides, Hmains, Ishnigarrab, Jshdcn, KoyaanisQatsi, Lemnaminor, Magioladitis, Marc Lacoste, Martin villafuerte85, MartinVillafuerte85, MrFawwaz, Muhandes, Naddy, Neelix, Niceguyedc, Northamerica1000, O Birck, Ottawahitech, Peter Greenwell, Richietjpr, Roosterfan, SchreiberBike, Shadowjams, Slusk, Snoyes, Superzohar, Thetaylor310, Thricecube, Thue, Underlying lk, Victor Lopes, Warofdreams, Welsh, Zalunardo8, Zvx123, 31 anonymous edits 647

Demographics of Brazil *Source:* https://en.wikipedia.org/w/index.php?oldid=852437605 *License:* Creative Commons Attribution-Share Alike 3.0 *Contributors:* A bit iffy, Abrahamic Faiths, Acaciosc, Affirst, Aircorn, Airgum, Al-Andalus, Alexander Domanda, Alexlenk, Alfiuman, Altes, Ameteurdemographer, AnZhengling, Archon 2488, Azips, BD2412, Batternut, Beloki, Bender235, Bivcorp, Bleckter, Boreas74, Calmer Waters, Che829, Chronus, ClueBot NG, Cnwilliams, Cs-wolves, Ctuft, Cuchullain, Cygalder, DelftUser, Delotrooladoo, Demmo, Derek R Bullamore, Dewritech, Donner60, Download, Drpickem, Dthomsen8, Eldunayz, Elockid, EnOreg, Epicgenius, Eumolpo, Faizan, Fama Clamosa, Favonian, Firebrass11, Frank Duurvoort, Funnyhat, General Ization, Gorthian, Grenzer22, Guiresende, GünniX, Hazlogen, HilalAouam, Hmains, Huon, IXavier, In ictu oculi, Iridescent, Jasonanaggie, Juniorpetjua, Lecen, Leonina666444, LilHelpa, Linguist111, Lor, LuisEnrique10, MRD2014, Magioladitis, Mannerheimo, Mightymights, Mild Bill Hiccup, Mogism, Mr. Ajax, Mr.StateOfShock, MrFawwaz, NBAkid, Naniwako, Narky Blert, Niceguyedc, Nick Moyes, Nillurcheier, NotTheFakeJTP, ObjectivismLover, Optimus023, Otvis, PMLF, PedroNascimento2014, Pharaoh of the Wizards, Philip Trueman, PhnomPencil, Picture Master, Pratyya Ghosh, R'n'B, Rambam rashi, Ravensfire, Raymond Cruise, Rjwilmsi, Rui Gabriel Correia, SalomãoSantos, Sarcelles, Seaphoto, Seb951, Ser Amantio di Nicolao, Sileebo, Skizzik, Sole Soul, Southrook, Sspamspam711, Stumink, Swynyard, The Sage of Stamford, TheObsidianFriar, Titodutta, Tony1, Trappist the monk, Tulietto, Umbeldothel, User332572385, VC19, Velteau, WOSlinker, WereSpielChequers, Wikiaccount2015, 219 anonymous edits 653

Brazilians *Source:* https://en.wikipedia.org/w/index.php?oldid=852444239 *License:* Creative Commons Attribution-Share Alike 3.0 *Contributors:* 0xF8E8, 42800141, AManWithNoPlan, Alumnum, American In Brazil, Anaxial, Avaya1, B777-300ER, BerneCha, Bgwhite, Brunolima17, Coltsfan, Dcirovic, Dewritech, FoCuSandLeArN, Frietjes, Gilo1969, GreenC, Gusthes, Hmains, Ira Leviton, Iridescent, Iryna Harpy, Jessicapierce, JitsuFighter2, Jobas, LuK3, MB, Magioladitis, MarnetteD, Materialscientist, Mikeblas, Niceguyedc, ProKro, RA0808, Rafael Florentino, Rastrelli, Rjwilmsi, Rui Gabriel Correia, Shellwood, TAnthony, Tercessuinotlim, Theutatis, Thomas.W, Tubedogg, Vihelik, Woodlot, Xuxo, 289 anonymous edits 692

Immigration to Brazil *Source:* https://en.wikipedia.org/w/index.php?oldid=854238585 *License:* Creative Commons Attribution-Share Alike 3.0 *Contributors:* AHC300, Abrahamic Faiths, Alansohn, Alexander Domanda, Allice Hunter, Andrevruas, Andrewrp, ApprenticeFan, Axeman89, BD2412, Beland, Belovedfreak, Bender235, BokicaK, Bte99, CEBR, CambridgeBayWeather, Citation bot 1, ClueBot NG, Cyberbot II, Damsefo, Darkwind, Davshul, Delotrooladoo, Dewritech, Diego barbosa silva, Discospinster, Egmontaz, Engine Gone Loco, Fadesga, G1990, Gabriel Cypriano, Giso6150, GoingBatty, Grenzer22, Heavylove, Hentzer, Heroeswithmetaphors, Hmains, Iñaki Salazar, JaGa, Jasonli42, Jeff3000, John Cardinal, Judicial89, Kwamikagami, L3X1, Letzebuergerr, Limongi, LittleWink, Mancunius, Maokart444, Me, Myself, and I are Here, Melonkelon, Mightymights, Mrmw, Muhandes, Nick Number, Ninguém, Ohconfucius, Opinoso, PaddyM, Pdrmtt, PeterGoodbody, ProgressiveThinker, Qaphsiel, R'n'B, RVJ, Redhill54, Rejedef, Rjwilmsi, Robsavoie, Rolf h nelson, Rui Gabriel Correia, Sarcelles, Sfan00 IMG, ShelfSkewed, Sir II. Unknown, Snowolf, Super48paul, Swynyard, Tassedethe, The Interior, This is my usersame, Thrissel, Tpbradbury, UglowT, Victor Lopes, Vihelik, Viller the Great, Virtualtyper, Vitor12345, Woohookitty, Zehneh, 141 anonymous edits 714

Race and ethnicity in Brazil *Source:* https://en.wikipedia.org/w/index.php?oldid=853759605 *License:* Creative Commons Attribution-Share Alike 3.0 *Contributors:* !ComputerAlert!, AK456, Abrahamic Faiths, Ameteurdemographer, Andregoes, BD2412, Beland, Bender235, Boelex, Brandon king, CambridgeBayWeather, Candido, ClaretAsh, ClueBot NG, Com2kid, DadaNeem, Dante Alighieri, Dash9Z, Dbachmann, Derek R Bullamore, Discospinster, DoubleHammy, Doug Weller, Dthomsen8, Eduen, EricSerge, Errorsanger, Esprit15d, Fadesga, Fayenatic london, Flyte35, Funandtrvl, Furiousferret, Futurist110, Gilliam, Giso6150, Grenzer22, Guiletti, Headbomb, Hmains, Hmainsbot1, Hneto, Hoary, Husb, Ira Leviton, IronGargoyle, Jayen466, Jggouvea, John of Reading, Johnanth, Joseph Solis in Australia, Kelisi, Kou Dou, KylieTastic, LMorland, Lecen, Lenoxus, LilHelpa, MB298, Maunus, Me, Myself, and I are Here, Midas02, Mightymights, Missionary, Mr. Ajax, Mrmuk, Narayansg, Neils51, Ninguém, NuclearWizard, OccultZone, Op47, Opinoso, Orenburg1, Osnetwork, Phil Boswell, Piotrus, R'n'B, Rjwilmsi, SamEV, Sarah Canbel, Serols, Servatai, ShelfSkewed, SilkTork, Snooganssnoogans, Solar-Wind, Sun Creator, Tabletop, The Editor's Apprentice, Tony1, Umbuverde, Vanished user 1234567890, Velho, Volunteer1234, Widr, Woohookitty, Wtmitchell, X1\, Xfact, Yamaguchi先生, Yan wun, Zeiimer, Zocklandy, Δ, 106 anonymous edits 761

Religion in Brazil *Source:* https://en.wikipedia.org/w/index.php?oldid=848780204 *License:* Creative Commons Attribution-Share Alike 3.0 *Contributors:* 5823balderrama, Abrahamic Faiths, AgnosticPreachersKid, Alan Curtis (London UK), Alumnum, AmRen93, Amuseclio, Aulo BF, BD2412, Bgwhite, Bigweeboy, Blamed, Bugbeew, Burningshame, Candido, ChrisGualtieri, Christian75, ClaretAsh, Clpo13, ClueBot NG, CommonsDelinker, Crystallizedcarbon, Daniel Sant'Anna Lisbôa, Danski454, Davidcannon, Debresser, Dmm1169, Donner60, Dpcott, Drewrau, Egsan Bacon, Emanuel Santiago, Emanuelito martinez, Erp, FinalRapture, FrankCesco26, FreeKnowledgeCreator, Fsog50, FyzixFighter, Gidonb, Giso6150, Glane23, Graham87, HangingCurve, Hentzer, Herman Shurger, Highpeaks35, Hindian1947, IdreamofJeanie, Iridescent, Jakec, Jay-Sebastos, JimRenge, Jimp, Kakurokuna, Kim Batteau, Legobot II, Libertymoon, MRD2014, Mafiakkn, Magioladitis, Mahagaja, Manderper, Mangotrue, Mean as custard, Metron, Mightymights, Millermk, Molecule Extraction, Mon Vier, Monty845, North Atlanticist Usonian, Ohconfucius, Oshwah, Padresfan72, Phcgontijo, PiMaster3, Pookman7497, Porter16, Prburley, Qwyrxian, R'n'B, Rariteh, RayneVanDunem, Relógios, Rjensen, RoiVladimir, SBaker43, Shadowjams, Shellwood, SkyGazer 512, SlackerMom, Smkolins, Sodicadl, Southamerican, Stephen G. Brown, Stuart98, Tachs, Tbhotch, ThePlatypusofDoom, VQuakr, Victor Lopes, Waldir Bronsonn, Warren G82, Why Not A Duck, Wmw73, Woohookitty, Yintan, Zzuuzz, Éder Santos, 259 anonymous edits 795

Languages of Brazil *Source:* https://en.wikipedia.org/w/index.php?oldid=853648585 *License:* Creative Commons Attribution-Share Alike 3.0 *Contributors:* 72, Abrahamic Faiths, Adityavagarwal, Akellym17, Alansohn, Alexlange, Alumnum, Amortias, Anandmoorti, Andrevruas, Annieeden, Astatine-210, Av5bpvtu8, BD2412, Baerentp, Beland, Belchman, Bgwhite, Blehfu, Bmaddenwiki, Brodyargo, Byteflush, C1MM, CRGreathouse, Cerabot∼enwiki, Chris the speller, Chrisalex0207, Cjhs0056, ClaretAsh, Closedmouth, ClueBot NG, Cnilep, CommonsDelinker, Cyberbot II, D.Lazard, Damarques, Discospinster, Dl2000, Donner60, Dratman, EagerToddler39, ElCaraqueno1, Emeraldguy32, EoGuy, Erutuon, Esperant, Eteethan, Evlekis, FlavianusEP, Fluffernutter, Flyer22 Reborn, Fraggle81, Frank87, GLG GLG, GeneralizationsAreBad, Gilliam, Giuan, Gribnitz, H.Schlickmann, Hacker0520, Hans Adler, Hispace World, Hmains, Hmainsbot1, Imminent77, In ictu oculi, James Hyett, Jggouvea, Jimp, Koavf, Kusunose, Kwamikagami, KylieTastic, L'editeur, Lemccbr, Little green rosetta, Luizdl, MRD2014, Markgarret, Materialscientist, Mediavalia, Melonkelon, Moe Epsilon, Mrmw, Newtdep, Northern Muriqui, Outriggr, PMLF, Park Avenue, Pedro Aguiar, Pmlineditor, Postulatepostulate, Quebec99, R'n'B, Rhododendrites, Ricardocanedo21, Richard David Ramsey, Robert.dand, SPQRobin, Samf4u, Sarcelles, Serols, Shadowjams, Shellwood, Southern Person, StarryGrandma, Steinbach, Stephen G. Brown, Struthious Bandersnatch, Tabletop, Tassedethe, The Ogre, The Sage of Stamford, Theman213555, TicketMan, Tigercompanion25, Tony1, Vanamonde93, Vrenator, Webclient101, WhisperToMe, Widr, Wiki Wikardo, Woohookitty, Yamaguchi先生, Yupanqui, Zzuuzz, 233 anonymous edits .. 817

Culture of Brazil *Source:* https://en.wikipedia.org/w/index.php?oldid=853274545 *License:* Creative Commons Attribution-Share Alike 3.0 *Contributors:* ;aklsdhg;iajgr;, Abrahamic Faiths, Adam9007, AlexanderLevian, Altaïr, Andrevruas, Arbor Fici, Arcandam, Arjayay, AzidoAzide, BD2412, Babitaarora, BernardaAlba, Bishonen, CAPTAIN RAJU, Canibal2014, Chris the speller, ChrisGualtieri, ClaretAsh, Clarkcj12, Closedmouth, ClueBot NG, Cnwilliams, CommonsDelinker, DBigXray, DanielGSouza, DavidLeighEllis, Delotrooladoo, Dr. Ruben Stibbe, Earlgrey T, El chirri mariano, Endofskull, Esa3000, Excirial, Faizan, FlightTime, Flyer22 Reborn, Fraggle81, Frederic montanha, Fsolda∼enwiki, Fuortu, Gabbe, Gabriel Yuji, GeorgeBarnick, Gibbja, Gilliam, Gland21, GoingBatty, GoodGame1324, Graham87, Grenzer22, GünniX, Hazhk, Hmains, Howbabby, Hyperbolick, I dream of horses, InternetUser25, Iridescent, JaconaFrere, Jeff3000, Jeffro77, Jesielt, Jgsodre, Jim1138, Joaosac, John of Reading, Johnbod, Juniorpetjua, KSFT, Katleespe, Kinetic37, KylieTastic, Lamro, Let99, LilHelpa, Lugia2453, MRD2014, Magioladitis, Mandarax, Mogism, MusikAnimal, NMaia, Narsiltheblade, NewEnglandYankee, Newtdep, Niceguyedc, Nucleotide, Oddbodz, PMLF, Panther Pictures, PhnomPencil, Pppipppeeerrr, Qzd, R'n'B, Rich Farmbrough, Rn.brito, Rui Gabriel Correia, Samf4u, SchreiberBike, Shellwood, ShugSty, SimmeD, SkyWarrior, Soliloquial, Srednuas Lenoroc, Srtª PiriLimPomPom, StoneTowerSage, Stumink, Synthwave.94, TCN7JM, Tassedethe, Telfordbuck, The Transhumanist, ToBeFree, Tolly4bolly, ToonLucas22, Trappist the monk, Tutelary, UY Scuti, Ubiquity, Vieque, Vmavanti, WQUlrich, Waldir Bronsonn, Widr, Wiki Mebelin, Woohookitty, Yintan, Zloyvolsheb, 229 anonymous edits 831

Architecture of Brazil *Source:* https://en.wikipedia.org/w/index.php?oldid=788436577 *License:* Creative Commons Attribution-Share Alike 3.0 *Contributors:* Bgwhite, Closeapple, Hmains, Juniorpetjua, Wiki1011835, Yahboo, 1 anonymous edits 857

Music of Brazil *Source:* https://en.wikipedia.org/w/index.php?oldid=843053077 *License:* Creative Commons Attribution-Share Alike 3.0 *Contributors:* 23wrighs, 4meter4, Adonis Laerte Mezzano, Affleck, Alinefolle, Anonymous from the 21st century, Apparition11, Aranea Mortem, Aszlisna, AtticusX, BD2412, Beland, Bender235, Boomer Vial, Bratsche92, CanadianLinuxUser, Candido, Ccalvom, Chris the speller, ClaretAsh, ClueBot NG, ColRad85, CommonsDelinker, Cote d'Azur, Crystallizedcarbon, Cyberbot II, DanielGSouza, Darkwind, DavidJWeir, Dayvey, Der Naturfreund, Design, Dewritech, Diego barbosa silva, Download, Dr. Zombieman, Dunc0029, DutchmanInDisguise, Edgar181, Eltacotac, EoGuy, Excirial, Fixer88, Flyer22 Reborn, FreeKnowledgeCreator, GermanJoe, Gilliam, Giulianomsa, GoingBatty, Hmains, Hullaballoo Wolfowitz, Humbertoego, Hyacinth, Hyju, I dream of horses, IceBrotherhood, In ictu oculi, Jcena58, Jerome Kohl, Jiten D, Joaosac, JustAGal, KenBailey, Khazar2, Kikonio80, Kingpin13, KylieTastic, Lemurbaby, LilHelpa, Lmcasablanca, Lr1015, LucasSACastro, Lucasgiello, Macaddct1984, Magiciandude, Mannanan51, Martimsaintive, Mashaunix, Materialscientist, Maxtremus, Monty845, Moxy, Muon, Musicologa, Mutaito890, N shem22, NawlinWiki, Neelix, Neidam2016, NeilN, NewEnglandYankee, Newyorkadam, Nicolasdurazzo, Nmc233, Nono64, Oliveiramatheus, Onel5969, Opus88888, Oramfe, Oshwah, Philip Trueman, Portamento74, R'n'B,

RazaRaba, Rn.brito, Shaliya waya, Sluffs, Smokizzy, Stnwilliams, Synthwave.94, Tobby72, Tpbradbury, TracyMcClark, Vsmith, WPGA2345, WQUlrich, Walter Görlitz, Wasell, Widr, Wifsy, Wikiuser11528, Woodshed, Woohookitty, Zachlipton, ,62† 239 anonymous edits 861

Brazilian literature *Source:* https://en.wikipedia.org/w/index.php?oldid=842465783 *License:* Creative Commons Attribution-Share Alike 3.0 *Contributors:* AKeen, Ahoerstemeier, AlexanderGerten, American In Brazil, Anonymous from the 21st century, Anthrophilos, Aristophanes68, Attilios, Aude, Auréola, AxelBoldt, Babylon24, Bcat, Big iron, Brookiechass, CalJW, Calton, Candido, CanisRufus, Cerme, Chick Bowen, Chris the speller, ChrisGualtieri, ClaretAsh, Clicketyclack, Closedmouth, ClueBot NG, Cmdrjameson, CorbieVreccan, DanMS, DanielGSouza, Derek R Bullamore, Diego barbosa silva, DocWatson42, Doctor Sunshine, Download, Dwarf Kirlston, Editor br, Eladynnus, Epbr123, Epolk, F Soaj, Felipe Menegaz, Gabriel Ataide, Gaius Cornelius, Glenncheney, Guilherme Paula, Hentzer, Hmains, Hmainsbot1, Hyju, Infrogmation, Iseult, Jayjg, Jbmurray, Jim marrone, Johnsoniensis, Jonkerz, Jtkiefer, K. Annoyomous, Kallerna, Katherine.Holt, Kevyn, LilHelpa, Look2See1, Lusitanpoetry, Macgreco, Magicmonster, MakeRocketGoNow, Marcus Cyron, Mhking, Milena Popovic, Modulatum, Neelix, NickShaforostoff, Ninguém, Omassey, Only, PaddySnuffles, Parababelico, PedroPVZ, Peter Chastain, Ph7five, Philip Trueman, Psy guy, Qatter, R'n'B, Ralph Deeds, Raonisousa, Ricardo Carneiro Pires, Ricardo Frantz, Rockslave, S Marshall, Search4.0, Selecciones de la Vida, SimonP, Spesh531, Spharion, Stenzowski, The Ogre, Tom-b, Tom.Reding, Tommy amorim, Travelbird, Varlaam, Victor Lopes, Vivafeliz, WOtP, Wavelength, Wayland, Wbm1058, WhisperToMe, Woilorio, 95 anonymous edits 889

Brazilian cuisine *Source:* https://en.wikipedia.org/w/index.php?oldid=851568430 *License:* Creative Commons Attribution-Share Alike 3.0 *Contributors:* 72, AKeen, Agtx, Aguila289, Altafr, Andrevruas, Aoa8212, Aranea Mortem, Architohn, Arielslytherin, Arjayay, Avaya1, Avoided, Barek, Baron215, Ben Ben, Bender235, Bgwhite, Bigdaddydoubled, Breno, Brumchan, C3chan2014, Candido, Candleabracadabra, CarrieVS, Cekli829, Chris the speller, ClaretAsh, ClueBot NG, CommonsDelinker, Cr0, Deleteduser2015, Dewritech, Discospinster, DrDaveHPP, Dwo, Edcolins, Ejl, El Chemaniaco, Electriccatfish2, EvergreenFir, Eyesnore, Falconjh, Felipefigueiredocunha, Flyer22 Reborn, Fraggle81, Fraulein451, Gfhfgvbhhhb, Gilliam, Gilrovina, Glane23, Guslacerda, GünniX, Heroeswithmetaphors, Hewhoknows12345, HighKing, Ijon, Iridescent, IvanScrooge98, J. M., Jacira, Jack O'Neill, January2007, Jeot6, Jobas, Joseniltojr, Juniorpetjua, K6ka, KConWiki, Kphua, Lguipontes, Liance, LilHelpa, Loopy30, Lotje, LovelyEdit, Macaddct1984, Macrakis, Magioladitis, Mark Arsten, Maximajorian Viridio, Megatron Omega, Miszatomic, Morning277, MrFawwaz, Msadp06, NMaia, Nandocuca, Natesgate, NeilN, Nepenthes, Nethmi Rajapaksa, Nick Number, Nitpicking polish, Niven, Non-Lurker, Northamerica1000, Onyx321, Orduin, Oshwah, Paul "The Wall", Pitrus, Plantdrew, Psurburley, Rap17, Rwalker, SJ Defender, Sarahj2107, SashaMartin, SatanicMushroom, Serols, Sfan00 IMG, Spesh531, Stephenb, Steven Walling, Stormwaich, SupernovaExplosion, Superwolves, Tampajp, Thalgee, The Evil IP address, The Sandman, TrafficBenBoy, Victorgrigas, Vipinhari, WOSlinker, Waggers, Welsh, Wikidirectory, Willy james, Woofer215, Yamaguchi先生, ZackTheJack, ～riley, 260 anonymous edits 911

Cinema of Brazil *Source:* https://en.wikipedia.org/w/index.php?oldid=849830976 *License:* Creative Commons Attribution-Share Alike 3.0 *Contributors:* Amccaule, Andreasmperu, Andrei Rublev, Andrevruas, BernardaAlba, Bovineboy2008, Carioca, Cattus, Chronus, Clbenamou, Colonies Chris, Connor Behan, Csmrl, Danilosoares, Dayvey, Dedachan, Diannaa, Dr. Blofeld, Dualistico, El Chemaniaco, Emersoni, Emijrp, Exlibris, Extraordinary, Fages, Felipe Menegaz, GHcool, Gabriel Yuji, Gram123, Hentzer, Hmains, John of Reading, Jorge MG, Juntaria, Khazar2, Largoplazo, Lightmouse, LilHelpa, Ling.Nut, LodeRunner, Lynchkenney, MarB4, Marianocecowski, Mateuszica, Mbm233, Mhus, Mr pand, Paris1127, Rafael323, Rich Farmbrough, Rjwilmsi, Rn.brito, Rodrigogomesonetwo, Rodrigogomespaixao, Sandhillcrane, SheriffIsInTown, Singularity, Slgrandson, Spacepotato, Sparkit, Tabletop, Tassedethe, The Raincloud Kid, TheGeneralUser, Tjmayerinsf, Underlying lk, Valiantis, Wiki Raja, Will dwane, Woodlot, Xx236, Yongtchin, 90 anonymous edits 933

Brazilian painting *Source:* https://en.wikipedia.org/w/index.php?oldid=841578240 *License:* Creative Commons Attribution-Share Alike 3.0 *Contributors:* Adavidb, Benescreve85, Calliopejen1, Chris the speller, Cnilep, Dewritech, Dornicke, Gerbilo, Hebrides, Iohannes Animosus, J04n, John of Reading, LilHelpa, Milkbreath, R'n'B, Ricardo Frantz, RolandR, Rsabbatini, ScheiberBike, Shonagon, Southrook, Tetraktys, TheJJunk, WQUlrich, Woohookitty 945

Sport in Brazil *Source:* https://en.wikipedia.org/w/index.php?oldid=853027001 *License:* Creative Commons Attribution-Share Alike 3.0 *Contributors:* Andradesilva, Arielslytherin, Arthena, Ashenicio, BD2412, Bangtoliv, Baseball Watcher, BethNaught, Birdsgeek, Bmusician, Bunnyhop11, Canthusus, Cavaleiro Lusitano, Certes, Chzz, ClaretAsh, ClueBot NG, Cnwilliams, Coltsfan, CommonsDelinker, ContinueWithCaution, DaHuzyBru, Dale Arnett, Dancaumo, Daniel Callegaro, David.moreno72, Dawid2009, Dewritech, Discospinster, Djlln, Donner60, Dwanyewest, Elizium23, Epomis87, Excirial, Faizan, FalconL, Freire1, Gabriel Da Sobreira, GageTronic, Gap9551, Gilliam, Ginsuloft, Gobbleswoggler, Gulumeemee, Gz33, Harry baanerd, Hmains, I dream of horses, Iareallknowing, InedibleHulk, IronGargoyle, JHunterJ, John of Reading, Kevlar, Kn, Leano885, Leeswooaa, Leyton turner, Limongi, LittleWink, Logan, Lothar von Richthofen, LuK3, Luizengmec, MacRusgail, Marlonss1, Materialscientist, Maxtremus, Miniapolis, NaBUru38, Nikkimaria, Non-dropframe, PKT, Pegomes, PhnomPencil, Queenmomcat, R'n'B, RoseGirlXS, Rsrikanth05, SJ Defender, Sam Sailor, Samuel Valdez Bicard, Shalfour, Sean.hoyland, Sillyfolkboy, Simplexity22, Stephreef, Sun Creator, ThiagoSimoes, Truthishly, Ulric1313, Victor Lopes, Volleynet, WNYY98, Webclient101, Widr, Wikipeli, Will.I.Win, Woohookitty, Yachty4000, ZappaOMati, 299 anonymous edits 961

www.ingramcontent.com/pod-product-compliance
Lightning Source LLC
Chambersburg PA
CBHW021411300426
44114CB00010B/455